ISBN 0-675-01992-3
Published by
CHARLES E. MERRILL PUBLISHING CO.
A BELL & HOWELL COMPANY
Columbus, Ohio 43216

Examination Guide for The American Tradition

In *The American Tradition,* special attention has been given to blending content, skill development and visual presentation. The text helps students to understand the causes and effects of events in American history through a variety of elements.

p. 1	The **Prologue** introduces the text and discusses the value of studying history.
pp. 2-3, 474-475	**Unit Openers** contain a fulll-color panoramic photograph, a mini table of contents, and a time line highlighting important events covered in the unit.
pp. 4, 382, 520, 700	**Chapter Openers** contain a colorful photograph, a mini table of contents, a quotation from a contemporary source to provoke student interest, and a brief introductory paragraph that previews chapter content.
pp. 305, 529	**Chapter Organization** consists of numbered sections and two levels of subheads to provide a formal outline of content, and review questions at the end of each section to reinforce learning.
pp. 19, 223, 633	Brief **Excerpts** from primary and secondary sources enrich the chapter narrative.
pp. 282, 437, 676	Unfamiliar **Terms** and **Concepts** appear in boldface type when first introduced and are defined in context.
pp. 336, 670	**Photographs,** most in full color, include captions with a question that relates the illustration to the text.
pp. 281, 339, 462	**Maps,** all in full color, contain scales and, when appropriate, latitude/longitude indicators, with color used functionally to highlight key subject matter.
pp. 111, 128, 301, 713	Full-color **Graphics** include charts, graphs, tables, and diagrams that correspond directly to the narrative and visually reinforce or extend concepts.
pp. 360-361, 500-501	**Chapter Reviews** provide a point summary, review questions, discussion questions, an exercise on using graphics, and a skill-developing exercise.
pp. 289, 470	**Unit Reviews** provide a point summary of generalizations from the unit, cross-chapter review questions, suggested activities for individuals and groups, and suggested readings for student research and enjoyment.
pp. 299, 315 495	**People in History** features give profiles of individuals and groups. **Perspectives in History** features present issues and themes with a long-term impact on American history.
pp. 471-473, 627-629	**The Historian's Craft** presents a carefully developed sequence of in-depth skill-building activities that teach critical-thinking skills in the context of unit-related content.
p. 750	The **Epilogue** puts the text into perspective by relating it to current and future challenges faced by the nation.
pp. 758-759, 764-765	The **Appendix** includes an Atlas with full-color reference maps and a graphics section that provides data on the American population, society, political system, and economy.
p. 773	An **Annotated Constitution** provides the full text of the document along with extensive annotations to explain its meaning.
p. 791	A **Glossary** contains all the important historical and concept terms.
p. 800	A comprehensive **Index** provides a ready reference tool.

THE
American Tradition

A HISTORY OF THE UNITED STATES

TEACHER'S ANNOTATED EDITION

Robert P. Green, Jr.
Laura L. Becker
Robert E. Coviello

CHARLES E. MERRILL PUBLISHING CO.
A BELL & HOWELL COMPANY
Columbus, Ohio
Toronto London Sydney

CONTENTS

INTRODUCTION — 1

HOW TO USE THE TEACHER'S ANNOTATED EDITION — 19

INSTRUCTIONAL APPROACHES — 21

Brainstorming — 22
Audiovisual Materials — 22
Reading Guides — 22
Games and Simulations — 24
Debate — 25
Case Studies — 25

TEXT IMPLEMENTATION — 27

UNIT 1 COLONIAL AMERICA — 28
1 The Beginnings — 28
Chapter 2 The English Colonies — 31
Chapter 3 The Struggle for Independence — 35
THE HISTORIAN'S CRAFT: Interpreting Information — 41

Unit 2 FORGING A UNION — 42
Chapter 4 A New Nation — 42
Chapter 5 The Constitution — 47
Chapter 6 The Federalist Era — 51
THE HISTORIAN'S CRAFT: Distinguishing Primary and Secondary Sources — 55

Unit 3 NATIONALISM AND SECTIONALISM — 56
Chapter 7 The Jeffersonian Republicans — 56
Chapter 8 The Age of Jackson — 61
Chapter 9 Westward Expansion — 65
Chapter 10 Antebellum America — 68
THE HISTORIAN'S CRAFT: Drawing Inferences — 73

Unit 4 THE NATION DIVIDED — 74
Chapter 11 Toward Civil War — 74
Chapter 12 The Civil War — 78
Chapter 13 Reconstruction — 81
THE HISTORIAN'S CRAFT: Evaluating Secondary Sources — 85

Unit 5 THE AGE OF INDUSTRIALIZATION 86

Chapter 14 Industrial Growth _____ 86

Chapter 15 The Rise of Labor _____ 89

Chapter 16 The Last Frontier _____ 92

Chapter 17 The Gilded Age _____ 94

Chapter 18 An Urban Society _____ 98

Chapter 19 The Progressive Era _____ 101

THE HISTORIAN'S CRAFT: Evaluating Primary Sources __ 105

Unit 6 THE RISE TO WORLD POWER 107

Chapter 20 An American Empire _____ 107

Chapter 21 The United States as a World Power _____ 110

Chapter 22 World War I _____ 113

THE HISTORIAN'S CRAFT: Synthesis of Primary Sources __ 116

Unit 7 PROSPERITY AND DEPRESSION 117

Chapter 23 The Roaring 20's _____ 117

Chapter 24 The Great Depression _____ 121

Chapter 25 The New Deal _____ 124

THE HISTORIAN'S CRAFT: Analyzing Evidence in
                          Arguments _____ 127

Unit 8 THE WORLD IN CONFLICT 128

26 The Road to Global Conflict _____ 128

Chapter 27 World War II _____ 132

Chapter 28 The Cold War _____ 134

THE HISTORIAN'S CRAFT: Recognizing Schools of
                          History _____ 137

Unit 9 THE UNITED STATES IN A NEW ERA 138

29 Truman and Eisenhower _____ 138

Chapter 30 The Kennedy-Johnson Years _____ 141

Chapter 31 The Nixon-Ford Era _____ 144

Chapter 32 American Society in Transition _____ 147

Chapter 33 Carter and Reagan _____ 150

THE HISTORIAN'S CRAFT: Writing History _____ 153

Epilogue Challenges for the Future _____ 154

SUGGESTED RESOURCES 155

INTRODUCTION

PROGRAM RATIONALE

The United States was born a product of the Western European liberal tradition and the democratizing influence of a New World. At the heart of the nation's experience has been agreement over the basic principles of its society and political system: individual rights, government by consent of the governed, and equality of opportunity. The strength of these basic beliefs has rarely wavered, although the extent to which each is manifested has changed from era to era. Social and economic factors, sectional allegiances, and ideological predilections have all had an impact. Conflict and controversy have arisen. But the American tradition has been one of progress in fulfilling the promise of these basic beliefs. *The American Tradition* is a record of that progress.

PROGRAM OBJECTIVES

The American Tradition is designed to achieve the following objectives:

1. Present the causes and effects of events in American history in a clear, concise, and meaningful manner.
2. Inform students about the origins and development of this nation's government, economy, society, and culture.
3. Equip students with the critical-thinking skills that will enable them to make reasoned, objective judgments about historical interpretations and contemporary issues.
4. Help students understand the nature and significance of traditional American values.

PROGRAM COMPONENTS
STUDENT TEXT

The American Tradition is a basal high school American history text that presents a chronolog-ical, topical history of the United States for average and above-average students. The cause-and-effect approach used throughout helps students to understand *why* things happened instead of just memorizing facts. Colorful photos, graphs, charts, tables, maps, diagrams, and illustrations have been selected and designed to complement the text narrative and aid student understanding.

The text focuses on the origins and development of the government, economy, and society of the United States and on the role this nation has played in world affairs. The basic values of the American political system—individual rights, government by the consent of the governed, and equal opportunity—are discussed in depth and reinforced throughout the text.

TEACHER'S ANNOTATED EDITION

The Teacher's Annotated Edition of *The American Tradition* is designed to reduce teacher preparation time and to facilitate both teaching and learning. It includes both a teacher's guide bound into the front of the student text and teacher's annotations printed throughout the book.

The teacher's guide consists of the following major sections: Introduction, How to Use the Teacher's Annotated Edition, Instructional Approaches, Text Implementation, and Suggested Resources. The Introduction contains the program rationale, program objectives, and information on the organization of the text, including sample pages illustrating key features.

The How to Use the Teacher's Annotated Edition section familiarizes the teacher with the guide and explains how to use it effectively. The Instructional Approaches section presents basic techniques for teaching American history.

The Text Implementation section, the cornerstone of the guide, contains teaching ideas on a unit-chapter-section basis. In addition, it provides answers to the questions that appear in the text. The Suggested Resources section contains unit listings of books and audiovisual materials that can be used to supplement the text.

The annotations, appearing in blue at the top of the student text pages, are of two kinds. Content annotations offer additional or clarifying information that the teacher may wish to share with the students. Pedagogical annotations offer additional topics of discussion and other teaching suggestions.

STUDENT ACTIVITY BOOK

The Student Activity Book is organized on a unit-chapter basis with three activities per chapter and two per unit. The chapter activities vary, but focus on skill-building activities, vocabulary exercises, and understanding key concepts in history. The unit activities summarize the unit and focus on historiographical skills.

STUDENT ACTIVITY BOOK, TEACHER'S EDITION

The Teacher's Edition of the Student Activity Book contains the student material plus answers for the student activities.

EVALUATION PROGRAM

The Evaluation Program is organized on a unit-chapter basis with two one-page quizzes for each chapter and one multi-page test for each unit. Quiz A consists of matching questions and true-false questions. Quiz B consists of completion questions and true-false questions. Each unit test consists of multiple choice questions, essay questions, and a review of general social studies skills.

KEY FEATURES OF THE TEXT

CONTENT ORGANIZATION

The student text of *The American Tradition* is organized into 11 units with 33 chapters. Preceeding the first unit is a one-page Prologue,

introducing the study of history. The last unit is followed by a seven-page Epilogue, discussing challenges the nation faces in the future. In keeping with the need to emphasize more recent developments, over 60 percent of the text is devoted to post-Reconstruction history, while 20 percent is devoted to post-World War II history. In addition, the text includes an Atlas, the Declaration of Independence, the Constitution of the United States (with annotations), a detailed Glossary, and a comprehensive Index.

SKILL DEVELOPMENT

One of the most outstanding features of *The American Tradition* is its skill development exercises. The heart of these exercises is a feature called "The Historian's Craft." Placed at the end of each unit, The Historian's Craft gives the students practice in critical thinking within the context of unit-related content. Yet it is also an historiographical exercise, an exploration in the study of the nature of history. Most of the critical thinking skills that students need to practice are the very same ones used by historians when they write history. The Historian's Craft, then, is a unique combination of skills, content, and historiography.

In order to avoid the lack of continuity in most history text skills exercises, The Historian's Craft offers a carefully developed sequence of skills. Furthermore, the Using Skills exercises at the end of each chapter are specifically designed to build the skills students will need in The Historian's Craft.

In The Historian's Craft, students learn what kinds of information influence the historian, how the historian gathers facts and data, how the historian structures loosely-related data and evaluates evidence and arguments, and how the historian interprets all the material. For the culminating activity in the sequence, students are asked to write their own history. The feature stresses the very important idea that history is not cut and dried, but open to interpretation. The following sequence of skill-development activities is presented in the chapter reviews (Using Skills) and unit reviews (The Historian's Craft):

Chapter 1   Acquiring information through the senses

2	Interpreting cognitive information from pictures
3	Interpreting affective information from pictures
Unit 1	Drawing inferences from multiple pictures and seeing how selection of information can influence historical interpretation

Chapter 4	Categorizing information
5	Analyzing relationships (comparison)
6	Finding the main idea
Unit 2	Distinguishing primary and secondary sources and understanding how secondary sources are derived

Chapter 7	Analyzing relationships (cause and effect)
8	Analyzing statistical information
9	Analyzing statistical trends
10	Determining what may reasonably be inferred
Unit 3	Drawing inferences from statistical data and forming hypotheses

Chapter 11	Distinguishing statements of fact from statements of motive
12	Distinguishing statements of fact from statements of opinion
13	Recognizing biased statements
Unit 4	Analyzing frame of reference (secondary sources)

Chapter 14	Keeping an open mind
15	Putting events in chronological order
16	Analyzing frame of reference (primary sources)
17	Analyzing evidence in arguments (primary sources)
18	Determining difficulty of proof
19	Finding the main idea and supporting facts
Unit 5	Analyzing evidence in primary sources

Chapter 20	Interpreting political cartoons
21	Recognizing unstated assumptions
22	Recognizing statements that support generalizations
Unit 6	Synthesizing information from primary sources

Chapter 23	Recognizing relevance of evidence
24	Recognizing statements that support generalizations
25	Determining relative significance of questions
Unit 7	Evaluating secondary sources

Chapter 26	Recognizing unstated assumptions
27	Finding the main idea and supporting evidence
28	Recognizing unstated assumptions
Unit 8	Recognizing schools of history

Chapter 29	Analyzing arguments
30	Analyzing arguments
31	Analyzing arguments
32	Recognizing biased statements
33	Determining difficulty of proof
Unit 9	Writing history

Each of these skill-developing activities may be conducted either as individual or group exercises. Group discussion is recommended following the completion of exercises by individual students.

LEARNING AIDS

The American Tradition includes a number of additional features designed to aid both teachers and students. These features are illustrated on the following pages:

Prologue

The Prologue introduces *The American Tradition* with a discussion of the value of studying history.

PROLOGUE

To some people, history is all dates, or a dull listing of events that no longer matter. Why should you study history? Why is history important? These are fair questions. Before you begin *The American Tradition*, read the quotations below. These quotations present the views of a number of famous people about history and its uses. Some views are favorable, but others are not.

We cannot help living in history. We can only fail to be aware of it.
ROBERT C. HEILBRONER

For a people to be without history, or to be ignorant of its history, is as for a person to be without memory. . . .
HENRY S. COMMAGER

It is very difficult to trace and find out the truth of anything by history.
PLUTARCH

History never embraces more than a small part of reality.
FRANÇOIS DE LA ROCHEFOUCAULD

Peoples and governments have never learned anything from history, or acted on principles deducible from it.
GEORG WILHELM FRIEDRICH HEGEL

Those who cannot remember the past are condemned to repeat it.
GEORGE SANTAYANA

Certainly, even if history were judged incapable of other uses, its entertainment value would remain in its favor.
MARC BLOCH

History is a lie agreed upon.
NAPOLEON

The end and scope of all history is to teach us by examples of times past such wisdom as may guide our desires and actions.
SIR WALTER RALEIGH

Consider the meaning of each quotation. Which ones are saying essentially the same thing in different words? What positive reasons are given for studying history? What drawbacks are mentioned?

The American Tradition will give you first-hand knowledge of some of the positive reasons for studying history. You will increase your understanding of how this nation's government, economy, and society evolved. By learning how things were, you will better understand how things are.

At the same time, your attention will be drawn to the limits of history. It is important for you to remember that even the most detailed study of history may not provide complete answers. Some historical facts are clear, but others are difficult to determine. Interpretations of the facts can and do vary. This book stresses the interpretive nature of history and helps you to develop the skills you need to evaluate different interpretations.

1

Unit Openers

Unit title

Unit number

List of chapters in unit

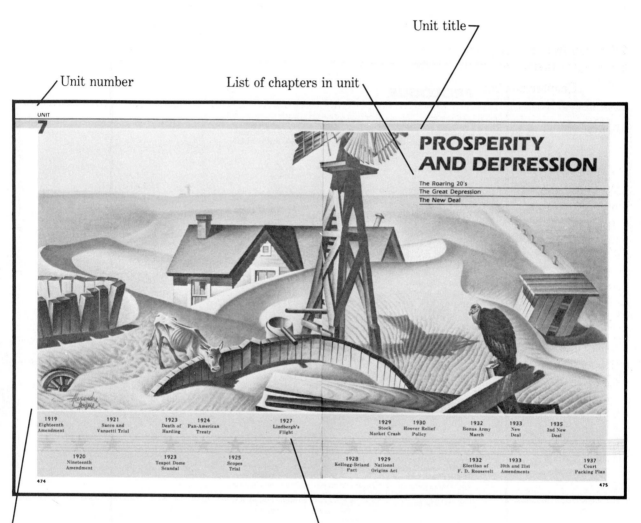

UNIT
7

PROSPERITY AND DEPRESSION

The Roaring 20's
The Great Depression
The New Deal

| 1919 Eighteenth Amendment | 1921 Sacco and Vanzetti Trial | 1923 Death of Harding | 1924 Pan-American Treaty | 1927 Lindbergh's Flight | 1929 Stock Market Crash | 1930 Hoover Relief Policy | 1932 Bonus Army March | 1933 New Deal | 1935 2nd New Deal |

| 1920 Nineteenth Amendment | 1923 Teapot Dome Scandal | 1925 Scopes Trial | 1928 Kellogg-Briand Pact | 1929 National Origins Act | 1932 Election of F. D. Roosevelt | 1933 20th and 21st Amendments | 1937 Court Packing Plan |

474

475

Full-color panoramic photograph represents main theme of unit.

Time lines highlight the chronology of major events in the unit.

Chapter Openers

Quotation from contemporary source character-izes chapter theme and creates student interest.

Chapter number

Chapter title

Full-color photograph gives visual dimension to chapter theme.

List of section titles provides overview of chapter.

Brief introductory paragraph previews chapter content.

CHAPTER
19

1	The Progressives	383
2	Progressive Goals	386
3	Theodore Roosevelt	390
4	William Howard Taft	394
5	Woodrow Wilson	397

382

THE PROGRESSIVE ERA

We have been proud of our industrial achievements, but we have not hitherto stopped thoughtfully enough to count the human cost. . . .

WOODROW WILSON

At the turn of the century the United States was prosperous, yet the gap between rich and poor was greater than ever. The demands of the Populists for reform seemed to have been forgotten. Before long, however, a new group of reformers appeared to battle the injustices that had come about as a result of industrialization and urbanization. These reformers were known as progressives. Because their ideals dominated politics during the period from 1900 to 1917, this period has been called the Progressive Era.

1 The Progressives

Although they all believed in reform, the progres-sives were a diverse lot. For one thing, progres-sivism cut across party lines. There were Republi-cans, Democrats, and even members of the defunct Populist party among their ranks. In fact, many of the stands taken by the Populists were adopted by the progressives. However, most of the Populists' support had come from farmers and workers, while progressives came from various classes in society. Some had wealthy backgrounds. Others were from the working class. Most, however, were members of the urban middle class.

The Urban Middle Class

As members of the urban middle class, the progressives were relatively comfortable economi-cally. Most of them were college-educated, and they tended to be small-business owners, professionals, or white-collar workers. Nearly all of them had been conservatives, not reformers. However, as they became more concerned about the direction of American society, they steadily moved away from conservatism.

One of their concerns was the vast power of the giant trusts. The trusts not only dominated the government, but threatened to put small companies out of business. Another concern was the growth of labor unions and other more radical signs of labor unrest. Many members of the middle class felt that the America they valued—the land of opportunity—might soon be lost in a battle between capital and labor. To preserve the life they valued, middle-class reformers wanted to reduce the power of wealthy capitalists and give more power to the working poor.

There was one difficulty, however. The philoso-phies of the day—laissez-faire and Social Darwin-ism—stood in the way of any attempt to change "natural law." Trying to close the gap between the rich and the poor was considered futile. By 1900, however, certain intellectuals had supplied the reformers with a new philosophy upon which to base their actions.

The Intellectuals

The new philosophy, known as **pragmatism**, called for a practical approach to the problems of the day. Pragmatists believed that an idea was true if it worked, even if it did not fit established theories. Therefore, people's actions should not be limited by ideas about theoretical "natural law."

The attack on natural law began with mathemati-cian Charles Peirce. He said that scientific laws stated only what was probably true, not what was absolutely true, and that ideas should be tested to see if they worked.

Peirce's ideas influenced other philosophers, notably William James and John Dewey. James rejected the idea that the universe operated accord-ing to predetermined natural laws. He believed that, if people used their minds creatively and acted courageously, they could do almost anything. Dewey

383

Narrative Organization

Chapter title appears on each page for easy reference.

Type is readable and two-column format is uncluttered.

Chapter material is enriched with frequent excerpts from primary sources.

Major section heads are numbered for easy identification.

Heading structure provides a formal outline of content.

Footnotes add important information that does not fit into the narrative flow.

Important terms are printed in boldface type and immediately defined or explained in context.

Review questions after each major section reinforce student understanding.

---

caused trouble. The rich could escape the draft by paying $300 or hiring a substitute. Resentment against this kind of unfairness led to two days of rioting in New York City.

Finally, some northerners who sympathized with the South actively tried to subvert the northern war effort. To combat their activities, Lincoln restricted civil liberties. The right of *habeus corpus* was suspended, civilians were tried by military courts, and limitations were placed on freedom of speech and press. For this, Lincoln was heavily criticized.[4]

Lincoln was sensitive to accusations of unconstitutional actions. Nevertheless, he felt that the cause of the Union justified his decisions. He said:

I felt that measures, otherwise unconstitutional, might become lawful by becoming indispensable to the preservation of the Constitution through the preservation of the nation.

Lincoln compared his actions to cutting off a limb to save a life. Whether he was right or wrong in his reasoning, his decisions certainly proved useful in saving the Union that he cherished.

South. Jefferson Davis was also an intelligent and capable leader. Like Lincoln, he was forced to make many unpopular decisions. Unlike Lincoln, however, Davis was not surrounded by capable subordinates. As a result, Davis himself became too involved in details.

Davis felt that he had a superior knowledge of military affairs. He was a West Point graduate, and had been Secretary of War at one time. But he sometimes ignored good advice from his generals, and showed poor judgment in strategic matters and the choice of commanding officers. His greatest handicap, however, was the states' rights foundation of his government. He was unable to get the broad war powers that Lincoln had. Extreme states'-righters, like governors Joseph E. Brown of Georgia and Zebulon B. Vance of North Carolina, were constantly defying the policies of the Richmond government. States' rights was simply a poor basis for modern war.

---

[4] In 1866 the Supreme Court in the case *ex parte Milligan* condemned Lincoln's use of military courts to try civilians. The individual's right to trial by jury of his peers was so fundamental, the court argued, that even war should not interfere.

Southerners were united in wanting to win the war, but they had other political conflicts. The South had passed a draft law in April of 1862, even before the North did. As in the North, there was much resentment of the fact that well-to-do men could hire substitutes. Another measure that was bitterly criticized was the Impressment Act, which allowed the Confederacy to buy goods at prices set by the government.

SECTION REVIEW

1. Identify the following: Clara Barton, Peace Democrats, Zebulon B. Vance, Impressment Act.
2. How did the North remain productive even with the loss of labor due to the war?
3. How did the North finance the war?
4. What problems did the southern economy face during the war?
5. What political groups did not agree with Lincoln's war objectives?
6. Why did Confederate governors feel they could defy the policies of President Davis?

5 Union Victory

The South's problems became more and more severe as the war continued into its third year. But, although Union armies had managed to halt the South's counter-offensive, Union momentum had also been lost. Another offensive had to be launched.

The Year of Decision

After the Battle of Antietam, Lincoln relieved McClellan to...
still had what...
McClellan, Lincoln...

*My De...
you of wh...
Are you...
that you...
constantl...
at least...
claim?*

Finally, Lincoln...
of the Army of...

Blacks also suffered economically. Slavery was gone, but a new form of dependency had developed. This was **sharecropping**. Under this system, most blacks worked small pieces of land owned by someone else—often the planter they had served. In return, they received a share of the season's crop. Tenants bought their supplies under the **crop-lien system**—promising a certain percentage of their crop as payment for goods. As a result of sharecropping and the crop-lien system, tenants always seemed to be in debt. Socially, the freedmen fared little better.

There were, however, changes coming to the South. By the 1880's southern agriculture had recovered and was producing at a rate higher than in the antebellum years. In addition, the southern economy had become more diversified, and invest-

ments had increased. Indeed, the growth of the textile and iron industries foreshadowed the appearance of a new South—a South that would be more akin to the rest of the United States.

SECTION REVIEW

1. Identify the following: Ku Klux Klan, Liberal Republicans, General Amnesty Act, Samuel J. Tilden.
2. How did Congress react to violence in the South?
3. Why did the Republicans' interest in reconstruction wane?
4. Why were the results of the election of 1876 disputed?
5. What was agreed upon in the Compromise of 1877?

CHAPTER 13　　REVIEW

SUMMARY

1. After the war there was sharp disagreement among northerners on how to handle the problem of southern reconstruction.
2. Lincoln developed a plan that was designed to restore the old relationship between North and South.
3. Congress opposed Lincoln's plan as too lenient and developed its own plan for reconstruction.
4. After Lincoln's assassination, Johnson put into effect a reconstruction program that was intended to help the common people of the South and to exclude the planter aristocracy from government.
5. Under Johnson's plan, ex-Confederates quickly regained control of the South and passed laws that severely limited the rights of blacks.

6. Alarmed by conditions in the South, Radical Republicans in Congress passed their own reconstruction acts.
7. The Radicals' reconstruction program led to control of southern states by a coalition of southern Unionists, blacks, and northerners who had moved South.
8. Johnson's opposition to the Radicals' program resulted in his impeachment.
9. Southern whites were bitterly opposed to the Radical regimes, and they sometimes resorted to violence in an effort to overthrow the Republicans.
10. By 1877 power in southern states had been restored to white leaders and the Democratic party.

VOCABULARY

reconstruction	black codes	acquittal	white supremacy
amnesty	segregation	disfranchisement	bipartisan
freedmen	vagrancy law	scalawags	sharecropping
ironclad oath	discrimination	carpetbaggers	crop-lien system
yeoman farmers	tenure of office	redemption	

Chapter Reviews

Using Graphics reinforces learning through visuals.

Using Skills gives students practice in basic critical-thinking skills.

USING MAPS

Refer to the maps on pages 351 and 355, and answer the following questions:

1. Who was the Populist candidate for President in 1892?
2. Which states showed the greatest support for the Populists in 1892?
3. Of the states that supported the Populists in 1892, which ones supported Bryan in 1896?
4. In 1896 what was McKinley's margin of victory in electoral votes?
5. Which states were most important to McKinley's victory in 1896?

USING SKILLS

The McKinley Tariff of 1890 included new duties on wheat imports. Republican William McKinley, who sponsored the tariff bill, argued in Congress that the new duties on wheat would help American farmers. Democrat Roger Mills argued the opposite case—that the duties would harm American farmers. Study each argument and then answer the questions that follow.

McKinley:

As we are the greatest wheat-producing country of the world, it is habitually asserted and believed by many that this product is safe from foreign competition. We do not appreciate that while the United States last year raised 490,000,000 bushels of wheat, France raised 316,000,000 bushels, Italy raised 103,000,000 bushels, Russia 189,000,000 bushels, and India 243,000,000 bushels. . . . Our sharpest competition [in the world market] comes from Russia and India. . . . and if we will only reflect on the difference between the cost of [producing wheat in the] United States [and in India we] will readily [see that we] have not quite [as low costs] even as our [...]

[...] ed the duty on [...] safe. We [...] ushels in wheat . imported the bushels of

What did that 1,946 bushels of wheat cost? Our wheat was at an average price of 89 cents per bushel, and the average price of the 1,946 bushels which we imported was $2.05. . . . What do you suppose that wheat was imported for? Do not all speak at once, please.

It was seed wheat, imported by the wheat-grower of the West to improve his seed. Does not every man know that? And you have made it cost him that much more to improve his agricultural product so that he can raise a better character of wheat and better compete in the markets of the world, where he has to meet all comers in free competition. . . .

The Germans, French, English, Spaniards, Austrians, and others with whom we are trading are dissatisfied with our discriminations against their products, and they have been taking steps to retaliate upon us. They have increased the duty on wheat in Germany two or three times since 1880. . . .

Why have we not the prices of 1881? Because we have cut off importation from our European customers, and they have cut off importation from us. Our surplus is increasing with our population, and we have no markets to consume it. . . .

1. What is McKinley's argument? What evidence does he present? Is his evidence pertinent to the question?
2. What is Mills' argument? What evidence does he present? Is his evidence pertinent?
3. With which argument do you agree? Give reasons for your answer.

CHAPTER 17   REVIEW

SUMMARY

1. During the Gilded Age, American government was tainted by corruption on the national, state, and local levels.
2. Leadership in government on all levels was generally undistinguished.
3. The major issues of the period were related to corruption and economic policies.
4. Farmers during this era were faced with problems caused by overproduction.
5. In an attempt to solve their problems, farmers organized groups such as the Grange and farmers' alliances.
6. Farmers joined with labor and other reform groups to form the Populist party.
7. The farmers' revolt subsided after the election of 1896, when the Populists supported the losing Democratic candidate.
8. The New South was dominated by middle-class whites who worked to industrialize the region.
9. The Populist attempt to break Democratic control of the South was unsuccessful.
10. After the Populists were defeated, southern states passed laws disfranchising blacks and separating them from whites.

VOCABULARY

conflict of interest	civil service	graduated income tax	poll tax
political bosses	face value	initiative	literacy test
political machines	bimetallism	referendum	grandfather clause
ballot stuffing	gold standard	recall	Jim Crow laws

REVIEW QUESTIONS

1. What were the effects of political corruption during the Gilded Age?
2. Why was political leadership lacking during this era?
3. How did monetary policy change during this period?
4. Why did the Populist party fail to elect a President?
5. What attempts were made to reform government in the late 1800's?
6. How was the New South different from the antebellum South?
7. Why did white southerners take steps to disfranchise blacks?
8. What was the black response to discriminatory practices in the New South?

DISCUSSION

1. Would the political climate have been different if there were strong executives during this period? Were the Presidents victims of the political times, or were they weak leaders?
2. Did civil service reform achieve the results it was intended to achieve? Why or why not?
3. If you had represented your state in Congress at this time, what would have been your position on the currency issue? Why?
4. Why did DuBois and Washington take the stands they did? With whom would you agree if you were a black living in the early 1900's? Why?

The Summary reinforces content by listing key points of the chapter in a concise, straightforward format.

The Vocabulary reviews important terms in the order of their presentation in the chapter.

Review questions stimulate learning.

Discussion questions help students gain further insight into chapter concepts through analysis, synthesis, and evaluation.

Unit Reviews

The Summary highlights major generalizations developed in the unit.

Review questions reinforce learning through questions that tie together major points presented in the unit.

UNIT **6**

SUMMARY

1. By enforcing the Monroe Doctrine, the United States established itself as one of the world's great powers.
2. By the end of the nineteenth century, the United States had acquired an overseas empire.
3. As a world power, the United States pursued an active foreign policy to promote the national interest.
4. The conflicting interests of other world powers led to World War I.
5. The United States was drawn into the global conflict and emerged from it as one of the victors.
6. As a consequence of the war, the position of the United States as a world power was greatly enhanced.

REVIEW QUESTIONS

1. By what means did the United States extend its influence in world affairs?
2. How did the role of the United States in the Western Hemisphere differ from the American role in other parts of the world?
3. What were the causes of conflict among world powers in the early 1900's?
4. How did American attitudes and objectives in the Spanish-American War compare with those in World War I?

SUGGESTED ACTIVITIES

1. Check sources such as local newspapers and municipal reports to see how people in your community reacted to (a) the Spanish-American War, (b) the building of the Panama Canal, and (c) the end of World War I.
2. Prepare a bulletin-board exhibit showing the following data from 1910 to 1920: (a) gross national product; (b) federal expenditures, (c) national debt. Can you draw any inferences from this information?
3. Suppose that the United States were at war today. Write a military draft law that specifies (a) who is eligible to be drafted into the armed forces, (b) the method of selecting people to be drafted from among those who are eligible, and (c) what to do about people who refuse to serve in the military.
4. Debate the following topic: "American activities in the Caribbean in the late 1800's and the early 1900's were necessary to safeguard the national interest."

SUGGESTED READINGS

1. Bailey, Thomas A. *Woodrow Wilson & the Lost Peace*. New York: Times Books, 1972. Paperback. Describes Wilson's attempts to bring about a just peace and the tragic failure of his efforts.
2. Lord, Walter. *A Night to Remember*. New York: Bantam Books, Inc., 1955. A fascinating account of the disaster of the *Titanic*.
3. May, Earnest R. *Imperial Democracy*. New York: Harper & Row Publishing, Inc., 1973. Paperback. Describes world reaction to America's rise
   to the status of a great power at the turn of the century.
4. Mowry, George E. *The Era of Theodore Roosevelt: 1900-1912*. New York: Harper & Row, Publishers, Inc., 1958. Paperback. An analysis of the administrations of Roosevelt and Taft.
5. Pringle, Henry F. *Theodore Roosevelt: A Biography*. New York: Harcourt Brace Jovanovich, Inc., 1956. Paperback. Anecdotes, quotes and stories about one of the nation's strongest Presidents.

470

Suggested Activities provide individual and group projects that give students the opportunity to examine unit concepts in greater depth.

Suggested Readings provide a list of works suitable for in-depth study as well as student enjoyment.

The Historian's Craft

A sophisticated sequence of in-depth skill-development activities presented at the end of each unit.

Gives students practice in high-level critical-thinking skills.

Unit-related content combined with skills and historiography.

Builds on skills introduced in earlier units and chapter exercises (for example, analyzing primary sources and interpreting cartoons).

Students are given all the source materials they need and aid in interpreting them before being asked to use The Historian's Craft.

THE HISTORIAN'S CRAFT

The historian's ultimate task is, of course, to write an account of what happened in the era he or she is studying. In order to do this, the historian usually studies what other historians have written. But the most important bases for historical writing are primary sources. The historian must synthesize or pull together the evidence and shape it into a narrative or explanation.

This activity will give you practice in synthesizing evidence from a number of different primary sources. The subject of the activity is causes of the Spanish-American War. Review the material on this subject in Chapter 20, so that you will be familiar with at least one secondary source. Then study the evidence provided on these pages. Answering the questions at the end of the activity will help you to analyze the evidence and to develop your own ideas on the causes of the war.

Write a paragraph or two based on your study of this evidence. You might begin your first paragraph by saying, "Several factors contributed to America's declaration of war with Spain in 1898."

1. From Josiah Strong, *Our Country: Its Possible Future and Its Present Crisis* (1885):

   [The Anglo-Saxon is being schooled for] the final competition of races. . . . If I read not

3. From the *New York World*, May 17, 1896:

   Blood on the roadsides, blood in the fields, blood on the doorsteps, blood, blood, blood. The old, the young, the weak, the crippled—all are butchered without mercy. . . . Is there no nation wise enough, brave enough, and strong enough to restore peace in this bloodsmitten land?

4. From a speech by Senator Redfield Proctor of Vermont to the Senate, March 17, 1898, on reconcentrado camps:

   Torn from their homes, with foul earth, foul air, foul water, and foul food or none, what wonder that one-half have died and that one-quarter of the living are so diseased that they cannot be saved? . . . Little children are still walking about with arms and chest terribly emaciated, eyes swollen, and abdomen bloated to three times the natural size. . . . I was told by one of our consuls that they have been found dead about the markets in the morning, where they had crawled, hoping to get some stray bits of food from the early hucksters.

5. The cartoon, "Cuba in the Frying Pan" (below), appeared in *Puck* (1898) with this caption: "The duty of the hour: to save her not only from Spain but from a worse fate."

471

472

and by the wanton destruction of property and devastation of the island.

Fourth, and which is of the utmost importance. The present condition of affairs in Cuba is a constant menace to our peace, and entails upon this Government an enormous expense. . . .

8. To the right is a photograph of the battleship *Maine* after the explosion in Havana harbor.

9. From Albert J. Beveridge, *Address to Middlesex of Boston* (1898):

   American factories are making more than the American people can use; American soil is producing more than they can consume. Fate has written our policy for us; the trade of the world must and shall be ours. . . . And American law, American order, American civilization, and the American flag will plant themselves on shores hitherto bloody and benighted, but by those agencies of God henceforth to be made beautiful and bright.

10. The cartoon of McKinley (below) appeared in the *New York Journal* in 1898. The caption read, "Another old woman tries to sweep back the sea."

6. The cartoon above appeared in the Hearst Press in 1898. The caption read, "Spanish 'Justice and Honor' be darned!"

7. From William McKinley, War Message to Congress, April 11, 1898:

   The grounds for such intervention may be briefly summarized as follows:

   First. In the cause of humanity and to put an end to the barbarities, bloodshed, starvation, and horrible miseries now existing there, and which the parties to the conflict are either unable or unwilling to stop or mitigate. . . .

   Second. We owe it to our citizens in Cuba to afford them that protection and indemnity for life and property which no government there can or will afford, and to that end to terminate the conditions that deprive them of legal protection.

   Third. The right to intervene may be justified by the very serious injury to commerce, trade, and business of our people,

---

473

QUESTIONS

1. What theory is reflected in the quotation from Josiah Strong?
2. What emotions toward Spain do you feel when you read the excerpts from the *New York World* and the *New York Journal?*
3. Senator Proctor was a respected, conservative politician. Would his speech, based on a personal tour of Cuba, have added to or detracted from the legitimacy of reports from the yellow press?
4. What view does the artist express in the Uncle Sam drawing? What details indicate this?
5. What new elements, not presented in the previous material, does President McKinley include in his call for war?
6. What was the reaction of the yellow press to the *Maine* incident?
7. According to Beveridge, what would be the effect of American expansionism? How might the cartoon of "Cuba in the Frying Pan" fit into Beveridge's view?
8. What does the McKinley cartoon suggest about the President's attitude toward war?

Other Special Features

Babe Didrikson

Mildred "Babe" Didrikson, born in Port Arthur, Texas in 1914, knew from the time she was a young girl that athletics was to be the focus of her life. Like her brothers and sisters, she was athletically gifted, and her parents encouraged a competitive spirit by building an outdoor gymnasium in the backyard for their active children.

Babe was a natural athlete. She easily achieved success with the high school baseball and track teams. But she was frustrated when she wanted to play basketball and the coach told her that she was too short. Determined, she practiced until she was so skilled that the coach had to accept her. By her junior year she was the high scorer for the team. This spark of determination was to be her outstanding characteristic for the rest of her life.

After high school, Babe was recruited by an insurance company for its employee athletic team. From the very beginning she was a star, and used this competitive opportunity to train for the 1932 Olympic Games. At the Olympics, she set world records in the women's 80-meter hurdles and the javelin throw.

In the 1930's Babe took up golf. Her natural coordination coupled with that spark of determination made her an excellent golfer. By 1946 she was winning most of the competitions she entered, and a year later, she won 17 consecutive tournaments.

At this point Babe, now married to wrestler George Zaharias, left the amateur ranks to become a professional. Shortly after turning professional, she was stricken with cancer. After treatment, she returned to the golf circuit and, again, achieved great success. In 1950 the Associated Press named her the outstanding woman athlete of the first half of the century. She died in 1956, after a long and courageous battle with cancer.

"People in History" focuses on individuals and groups who have contributed to the development of American society.

Full-color original illustration.

their heroes was track star Jesse Owens, who won four gold medals in Munich, Germany, at the Summer Olympics in 1936.

Entertainment

People also spent their leisure time pursuing various sources of entertainment. Radio offered adventure, drama, humor, music, and news. Adventure programs, such as *The Lone Ranger*, and comedies, such as *Amos 'n Andy*, were very popular. Daytime radio serials also drew large audiences chiefly because so many people were out of work and at home. These shows were called **soap operas** because soap companies often sponsored them. The 1930's also saw the development of the radio variety program, which included humorous skits and dialogue. As the Great Depression forced the vaudeville theaters to close, stars such as George Burns, Gracie Allen, Jack Benny, and Fred Allen, along with Edgar Bergen and his dummy Charlie McCarthy, entertained listeners.

"Perspectives in History" discusses themes and issues that have had a long-term impact on American history.

Music In Black Life

Music has always played a central role in the lives of black Americans. During slavery days, it was one of the few pleasures not forbidden to blacks, though the traditional use of drums was forbidden. Laws were passed against them out of fear that, as in Africa, drums would be used to communicate and perhaps to incite revolt.

Despite the restrictions on drumming, music helped blacks to preserve some of their African heritage. Certain general characteristics—call-and-response, improvisation, short repetitive phrases, and an emphasis on rhythm—were traits more typical of African than European music. These traits can still be heard in contemporary black musical forms, such as soul and gospel.

Music did much more than perpetuate the black heritage. Secular songs provided slaves with an outlet for feelings of resentment, love, and playfulness. Spirituals expressed their trust in God and their hopes for a better life in the world to come.

After emancipation, new kinds of music arose to express the new black experience. Blacks were technically free, yet continued to suffer serious problems. In rural areas, a form known as "the blues" took shape.

Classic blues have three line stanzas, the second line being a variation on the first. "Blue notes"—flatted thirds and sevenths—add to the distinctly mournful thrust of the lyrics. Uninhibited solo singers, often accompanied by guitar, bemoaned everything from poverty to Jim Crow laws to lost love. In the 1900's, the blues have provided a basis for many types of popular music. A choral style also evolved among rural blacks, who sang to help their work and to express their feelings.

Blues and work songs were also sung in the cities of the late 1800's. There were some distinctly urban types of black music as well. Old Testament spirituals were supplemented by gospel hymns, often set in lush harmonies sung by large church choirs.

In the creative hands of Scott Joplin and others, European classical forms were mixed with Afri-can-derived syncopations to produce ragtime. And the old black tradition of giving the deceased a big send-off into the next world, coupled with the general spread of brass bands in post-Civil War America, led to the formation of funeral bands. The freewheeling style of those in New Orleans fed directly into the most renowned form of black music, jazz.

The widespread popularity of ragtime and jazz, and the undeniable talent of performers such as trumpeter Louis Armstrong, pianist-composers Fats Waller and Duke Ellington, and singers Bessie Smith and Ma Rainey, helped to overcome white resistance to buying records and attending concerts featuring blacks. Indeed, the entertainment field was one of the earliest in which blacks could achieve national recognition and success.

Still, the racial barrier persisted. Even in the 1950's, rock-and-roll pioneer Chuck Berry could not bring about the enormous revolution in musical taste that Elvis Presley did. While Presley's distinctive voice and style are undeniable, the fact that he was white and Berry was black had a major impact on the difference in their popularity.

In the late 1950's and 1960's, however, black performers such as Johnny Mathis, the Supremes, Aretha Franklin, and Jimi Hendrix had many non-black as well as black fans. As the 1970's progressed, more and more "crossover" songs appeared—songs that were first successful on the black-oriented soul chart, then became successful on the white-oriented pop chart.

While keeping their preeminence in jazz, black performers have increasingly moved into previously white-dominated areas of the music world. Classical musicians, such as opera star Leontyne Price and pianist Andre Watts, are becoming less rare. Broadway has hosted numerous highly-acclaimed black musicals. The Afro-American contribution to American music has been great and promises to be even greater in the future.

QUESTIONS

1. What new kind of black music developed after emancipation?
2. What are "crossover" songs?

497

Each type of feature is color-coded for easy reference.

Questions reinforce learning.

Photographs and Cartoons

Numerous photographs and cartoons, most in full color, promote visual perception of ideas.

Captions identify photographs and cartoons.

Caption questions relate the visual to the narrative.

"Prairie Fire" by the Indian artist, Blackbear Bosin, depicts people and animals fleeing from one of the most dreaded of the many possible dangers on the Great Plains. What were some other hardships faced by Indians and settlers on the Great Plains?

and buffalo hunters who came to the Plains. Between 1860 and 1900 white hunters reduced the number of buffalo from 15 million to just a few hundred. The buffalo were slaughtered in order to satisfy a demand in the East for beef and leather products. Because the Indians' way of life was threatened, they responded to ... ttlements and

prompted an increasing number of easterners to eye the region as a possible place to homestead. It seemed clear that a new policy to deal with the Indians was needed.

In 1851 federal authorities met with leaders of the Plains Indians at Fort Laramie to negotiate a settlement. The treaty that resulted from this meeting defined territorial boundaries for various Indian groups, gave the government the right to build roads and military posts inside these boundaries, and gave whites **transit rights** through Indian lands. These rights allowed whites to cross Indian lands in peace. In return, the Indians received promises that the land assigned to them would remain theirs. They also received promises of **annuities**—yearly allowances of goods and money from the government.

For several reasons, the success of these agreements was short-lived. For one thing, many of the chiefs who made the agreements were elderly, and young warriors felt that the chiefs had yielded too

descended across Europe. The term became a popular metaphor for the Soviet-made barrier separating the continent into eastern and western parts. Churchill urged cooperation among the western democracies to stem the tide of Soviet expansionism.

At this time, the United States chose not to meet Churchill's plea for a western alliance. It found it difficult to devise a workable foreign policy to deal with the Soviets. American military force could not be used against them, because United States armed forces were being reduced. The United States had the atomic bomb, but the Truman administration was not willing to threaten the Soviets with it. Above all, most Americans were glad that World War II was over, and they did not want to fight either a conventional or an atomic war with the Soviets over Eastern Europe.

The alliance between the United States and the Soviet Union was terminated at the end of World War II. Americans accused the Soviets of setting up satellite governments in Eastern Europe, violating their pledge to hold free elections. How did the United States tailor its policy to respond to the Soviet threat?

Iran and Turkey. While the main area of dispute between the United States and the Soviet Union was Eastern Europe, an American-Soviet rivalry also developed in the Middle East. This region was valued by both powers for its oil. In 1946 the Soviets pressured the government of Iran for a share in that country's oil resources, which were largely controlled by the western democracies. The Soviets kept their army in northern Iran in violation of a 1942 treaty with the Allies.

Threatening the use of force to protect western interests in the region, the United States appealed to the United Nations Security Council for the withdrawal of Soviet troops from Iran. A few weeks later, the Soviet Union and Iran announced the withdrawal of Soviet troops in return for Iran's sale of oil to the Soviet Union. After the Soviet departure, the Iranian government regained control of Azerbaijan, a northern province held by Iranian Communists, and announced that it would not sell the Soviets the promised oil.

In the same year, the Soviet Union pressured Turkey for joint Turkish-Soviet administration of the Dardanelles Strait. Soviet ships passed through the Strait to the Mediterranean, and the Soviet government wanted some control over the area. It also hoped to fulfill the old Russian goal of overcoming the country's landlocked location by achieving access to warm waters. The United States, however, saw the Soviet move as an attempt to dominate Turkey, Greece, and the Middle East. When the United States sent an aircraft carrier into Turkish waters, the Soviets again backed down.

Atomic Energy. In late 1945 the United States proposed that the United Nations supervise all nuclear energy production. The following spring, United States Atomic Energy Commissioner Bernard Baruch offered a plan to ban atomic weapons. Under this plan, the United Nations would be allowed to inspect atomic facilities anywhere in the world to make sure that no country was secretly making bombs. Each country would also have to give up its veto power over United Nations decisions dealing with atomic energy. When such an international control system had been set up, the United States would destroy its stockpile of atomic weapons.

The Soviets rejected Baruch's plan. Suspicious of the strong western influence in the United Nations,

Graphics

A variety of full-color illustrations, including maps, tables, charts, graphs, and diagrams, correspond directly to the chapter narrative and visually reinforce concepts.

ISSUES CAUSING STRIKES 1881-1905

Year				Total strikes
1881	80%	7%	13%	477
1883	73%	11%	16%	506
1885	70%	10%	20%	695
1887	56%	20%	24%	1503
1889	60%	16%	24%	1111
1891	49%	19%	32%	1786
1893	57%	19%	24%	1375
1895	65%	17%	18%	1255
1897	61%	18%	21%	1110
1899	55%	26%	19%	1838
1901	47%	34%	19%	3012
1903	49%	33%	18%	3648
1905	43%	37%	20%	2186

☐ Wages/hours ☐ Right to organize ☐ Owner lockout or other issue

workers to "arm yourselves and appear in full force" at the rally site, Haymarket Square.

About 3000 people turned out. The rally was orderly, and the crowd had dwindled to a few hundred when about 200 city police arrived and ordered the crowd to break up. Suddenly, the uneasy peace was shattered. An unidentified person threw a bomb that killed 7 police officers and injured 66 others. The police then fired into the fleeing crowd. In the week that followed, the police hunted for the person who had thrown the bomb. Although that person was never found, August Spies and seven other anarchists were tried and convicted of murder.

The violence at Haymarket Square was a setback for labor. Americans were outraged by the bloodshed. Gompers said that the bomb killed not only the police officers, "it killed our eight-hour movement for a few years after." The riot tarnished the reputation of all groups with any link to recent immigrants and o...

event that finished the Knights of Labor, even though they insisted that they had no part in it.

The Homestead Steel Strike

Strikes did not cease following the tragedy at Haymarket Square. Andrew Carnegie's Homestead Steel Plant in Pennsylvania was the scene of more violence.

The 25,000-member Amalgamated Association of Iron & Steel Workers had negotiated a contract for Homestead Workers in 1889. When the union sought to renew the contract in 1892, the company refused. Most of the plant's steel workers were unskilled and not members of Amalgamated. Homestead officials contended that the union had no right to negotiate for all workers. The company refused a pay raise and countered with an 18 to 26 percent cut for all workers.

[footnote] Spies and one other of the ... commuted to life imprisonment ... committed suicide in his cell. ... in prison.

HOW A BILL BECOMES LAW

INTRODUCTION
Introduced In House

COMMITTEE ACTION
Referred to House Committee and Subcommittee May kill, amend, rewrite or approve the bill

Reported by Full Committee

FLOOR ACTION
House Debate Vote on Passage May reject, amend, or approve the bill

INTRODUCTION
Introduced In Senate

COMMITTEE ACTION
Referred to Senate Committee and Subcommittee May kill, amend, rewrite or approve the bill

Reported by Full Committee

FLOOR ACTION
Senate Debate Vote on Passage May reject, amend or approve the bill

CONFERENCE ACTION
Compromise Bill Sent Back to Both Houses

FINAL APPROVAL
House and Senate Vote on Final Passage Approved Bill Sent to President

ENACTMENT
President Signs Bill Into Law

THE WORLD AT WAR

WORLD WAR I

☐ Allied Powers ✗ Allied victory — Allied offensive
☐ Central Powers ✗ Central Powers victory — Central Powers offensive
☐ Neutral nations ✗ Indecisive battle • Major battles or campaigns

WESTERN FRONT, 1914–1918

EASTERN FRONT, 1914–1918

Epilogue

1	Foreign Policy
2	The Economy
3	Social Questions

750

The Epilogue puts into perspective the content of the preceding nine units by relating it to current and future challenges faced by the American people.

CHALLENGES FOR THE FUTURE

Let us rediscover the old strengths of the American people and apply them to the problems of a new age.

WILLIAM M. AGEE

As Americans make their way through the 1980's, they are being forced to wrestle with a large number of diplomatic, economic, and social problems. Some problems are of relatively recent origin, while others were long in the making. All defy easy solutions.

1 Foreign Policy

American foreign policy in the 1980's, as in the past, must try to balance competing political, economic, social, and strategic goals—a most difficult task. The goals themselves are not controversial. Almost all Americans would support a policy that made it possible for the United States to enhance its international trade, ensure its national security, strengthen the western alliance, and promote human freedom and well-being around the world. Unfortunately, these goals often conflict with one another.

Relations with Allies

Countries in the western alliance often have goals of their own that are incompatible with those of the United States. Many Western Europeans, for example, feel more directly threatened by the Soviet Union simply because they are closer to it. As a result, they are more likely to "go along" with the Soviets than are Americans. This has led to controversies over the deployment of nuclear weapons on European soil, which many Europeans think might provoke a Soviet attack.

Trade

Similarly improving American trade may depend on what other countries are willing to do. A case in point is Japan, whose economic growth since World War II has been called a "modern miracle."

The United States imports enormous quantities of Japanese products. However, the reverse is not true. One reason for Japan's more limited importing is that the Japanese government subsidizes Japanese manufacturers, allowing them to undercut American prices. Another reason is that the Japanese government places tight restrictions on imports. Under pressure from the United States government, Japan has finally agreed to limit some of its exports to this country. However, many Americans still feel that trade relations with Japan are unfair.

A different problem arises in dealing with countries that have natural resources vital to the United States. Many of these resources must be imported from abroad. Among them are manganese, chromium, tin, bauxite, uranium, and diamonds.

It is clearly important for the United States to maintain good relationships with countries possessing these minerals. But many of them are Third World nations with politically repressive governments. Alliances with these countries do not fit with the American desire to support democratic, or at least non-oppressive, regimes. Choosing between humanitarian goals and economic goals is a painful and controversial part of modern foreign policy.

National Security

The need for national security sometimes poses a similar dilemma, because many of the countries in areas of strategic importance to us are undemocratic. But there are many other problems connected with national security needs. For example, should the technology to wage chemical and germ warfare be expanded when accidents or uncontrolled usage could cause worldwide chaos? Evidence that the Soviets used chemicals in Southeast Asia and Afghanistan rekindled this debate in the early 1980's. Is it necessary to match the Soviet Union's nuclear

751

15

Appendix

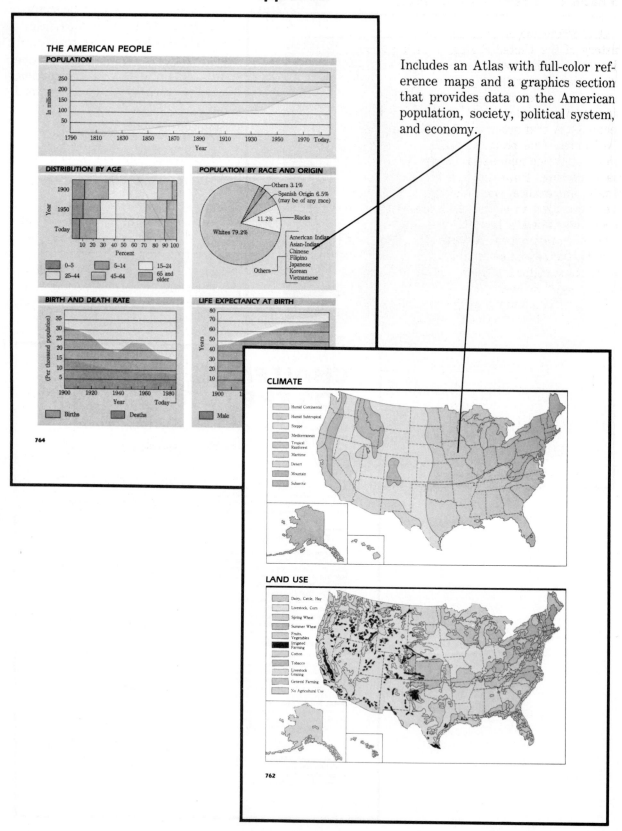

THE AMERICAN PEOPLE

POPULATION

DISTRIBUTION BY AGE

POPULATION BY RACE AND ORIGIN

Others 3.1%
Spanish Origin 6.5%
(may be of any race)
Blacks
11.2%
Whites 79.2%
American Indian
Asian-Indian
Chinese
Filipino
Japanese
Korean
Vietnamese
Others

0–5
5–14
15–24
25–44
45–64
65 and older

BIRTH AND DEATH RATE

LIFE EXPECTANCY AT BIRTH

Births   Deaths   Male

764

Includes an Atlas with full-color reference maps and a graphics section that provides data on the American population, society, political system, and economy.

CLIMATE

Humid Continental
Humid Subtropical
Steppe
Mediterranean
Tropical Rainforest
Maritime
Desert
Mountain
Subarctic

LAND USE

Dairy, Cattle, Hay
Livestock, Corn
Spring Wheat
Summer Wheat
Fruits, Vegetables
Irrigated Farming
Cotton
Tobacco
Livestock Grazing
General Farming
No Agricultural Use

762

TEXT TIMETABLE

One of the major problems in teaching the history of the United States is finding enough time to cover the material adequately. Because a school year generally ranges from 170 to 180 days, *The American Tradition* has been designed to be taught within that time. With 156 sections, the text provides a full and comprehensive course. One practical plan is to cover approximately one numbered section in each daily class meeting. However, the sections vary in length, importance, and difficulty, and teachers are encouraged to adjust their lesson plans to meet student needs. In order to allow extra time for review, testing, and activities, teachers may want to use the text selectively. It may be useful to plan courses for the entire year to assure that everything is covered.

Because of its comprehensiveness, *The American Tradition* is well suited to two-year courses.

Such courses allow enough time for the projects suggested at the end of each unit, supplemental reading, field trips, and other valuable activities. For post-Civil War courses, a brief review of early American history is suggested.

The American Tradition may also be used for short courses of one semester or less. For example, many states require that a certain amount of time be devoted to study of the Constitution. For that reason, the text has a special chapter on the document, which treats the historical background of the Constitution, the federal system, separation of powers, the legislative process, the evolution of democracy, and amending the Constitution. Used in conjunction with the annotated Constitution found in the Appendix, this chapter permits a relatively thorough study of American political development. All of this is in addition to the narrative chapter on the history of the Critical Period and the writing and ratification of the Constitution.

HOW TO USE THE TEACHER'S ANNOTATED EDITION

The Teacher's Guide in the Teacher's Annotated Edition is divided into five major sections —Introduction, How to Use the Teacher's Annotated Edition, Instructional Approaches, Text Implementation, and Suggested Resources. To help assure the most efficient use of the guide, each section is described below.

INTRODUCTION

The Introduction serves to acquaint teachers with the program rationale, objectives, and components. Because the student text is the most important component, its main features are explained and illustrated with sample pages. The Introduction also discusses text timetables.

HOW TO USE THE TEACHER'S ANNOTATED EDITION

This section, which you are now reading, explains how the guide is organized and describes each of its five sections.

INSTRUCTIONAL APPROACHES

This is a "how to" section, providing general guidelines for several strategies that are particularly effective in teaching American history. For example, it may be of value to have students debate historically significant issues. This section gives guidelines for conducting debates. In addition, the section explains how to use Reading Guides to help students who may have difficulty with comprehension.

TEXT IMPLEMENTATION

This section offers specific strategies for implementing the student text in the classroom. It begins by suggesting an introductory strategy to familiarize the students with the text. Following this, the section is organized on a unit-chapter basis to correspond with the 9 units and 33 chapters of the text. Each unit begins with a statement of unit objectives, followed by an Overview of the unit themes and a strategy for introducing the unit.

Each chapter begins with a statement of chapter objectives, followed by an Overview of the chapter themes and concepts, a Teaching Ideas section, and an Answers section.

The Teaching Ideas section is designed to make full use of the various aspects of the text. For each numbered section of the chapter, an introductory and developmental idea is suggested. In general, the introductory idea is based on the use of a visual or graphic. It "sets up" the section, directing the student's reading. The developmental idea is a more substantive exercise, allowing students to pursue a theme or concept. Following the last section, a conclusion for the chapter is suggested.

The Answers section gives answers to section questions, caption questions, chapter review questions, discussion questions, and Using Maps and Using Skills exercises at the end of each chapter. Following the last chapter of the unit, answers to the unit review questions are provided. The unit material ends with suggestions for implementing The Historian's Craft.

SUGGESTED RESOURCES

The last section of the guide contains a bibliography of resources that can be used to enrich and supplement the study of American history. Materials are listed according to the unit for which they are most appropriate.

INSTRUCTIONAL APPROACHES

The following strategies are designed to reinforce or supplement the teaching ideas provided in the Text Implementation section. They are especially suitable for enhancing more active student participation in the study of history.

BRAINSTORMING

The suggestions in the Text Implementation section of this Teacher's Guide frequently ask teachers to have students speculate over the meaning or outcome of an issue and then read to see if their speculations are correct. The teaching technique upon which this recommendation is based is brainstorming. Brainstorming involves students in a free and open exchange of ideas. Besides generating ideas about a particular topic or problem, brainstorming fosters student creativity and thinking. When brainstorming is used prior to a reading activity, it gives students ideas to look for in their reading and thus enhances reading comprehension. It is an activity in which all students can participate, regardless of academic ability.

To conduct a brainstorming session, follow these suggestions:

1. Set aside a limited amount of time and keep up the pace.
2. Allow students to say anything that comes to mind and jot it on the chalkboard.
3. Do not criticize ideas, be receptive.
4. Try to lead students to build upon other's ideas.

AUDIOVISUAL MATERIALS

Audiovisual materials include films, filmstrips, tapes, records, cassette, recordings, picture files, cartoon files and maps. Literally thousands of materials are available commercially, and many can be created by teachers and students. These materials may provide an overview of major historical eras and events as well as in-depth study of an important concept or theme. They are especially suitable for students who have difficulty reading. At the same time, they reinforce concepts and information for others.

When teachers use films and filmstrips, it is useful to keep some suggestions of audiovisual educational experts in mind:

1. Always preview the material. Look for major ideas and ways to tie in these ideas with previously-covered topics.
2. Place on the chalkboard or in a handout the major ideas or names of which you want students to be aware. Tell the students to watch for this information. Most audiovisual specialists advise students *not* to take notes during the presentation of the film or filmstrip.
3. Debrief the class using your list of names and ideas. This is the point at which students should take notes. Here the whole class can participate, with the teacher addressing questions with simple or more obvious answers to slower students. In this manner, all of the students are reinforced for paying attention.

Visual materials (tables, maps, graphs, cartoons, etc.) are also an important part of modern textbooks. They break up the print and reduce the reading level, but they also supplement the narrative. The teaching ideas in this manual frequently focus the teacher's attention on these valuable resources. Often students will be asked to *analyze* a visual. The teacher may aid the students in their analyses by directing them through the following steps:

1. Note details.
2. Look for relationships between details.
3. Draw inferences or generalizations from these relationships.
4. Make a statement summarizing these inferences or generalizations.

READING GUIDES

Although *The American Tradition* has a closely controlled reading level, some students may have difficulty with comprehension. To help these students, the teacher should use reading guides. Reading guides are designed to lead the students through the various levels of reading comprehension. Rather than assume students read and understand the material, reading guides are based on the assumption that students have difficulty comprehending written material. They serve, in effect, as an important "crutch" to readers with this difficulty.[1]

A reading guide is a series of statements each of which either accurately or inaccurately repeats an idea presented in the text. In this example, the guide fosters two levels of reading comprehension, the "literal" and the "interpretive." On the literal level of the guide, the students are asked to read a statement from the guide, then read the text to determine if the statement in the guide accurately restates what the author says in the text. On the interpretive level, the students are asked to determine whether or not a more general statement on the guide is a valid inference or generalization from the text. The example below is a two-level reading guide taken from Chapter 6, Section 2, "Hamilton's Economic Program," pages 122-126.

Literal Level. Read the following statements. Then as you read the selection, refer back to the statements in the guide and indicate those that you believe say what the authors *said* in the selection (not what you believe they *meant* by what they said). To indicate that a statement is an accurate restatement of what the author said, place the page, column, and paragraph numbers in the blank to the left of the statement. If a statement is not an accurate restatement, leave the blank empty. This facilitates future discussion.

<u>122-2-0</u> 1. Alexander Hamilton, as Secretary of the Treasury, tried to develop policies that would strengthen the national government.

<u>122-2-3</u> 2. Hamilton argued that the national debt should be funded in full.

_____ 3. Hamilton felt that a successful government depended upon the support of the common people.

<u>123-1-1</u> 4. Through his plan for assumption of the state debt, Hamilton hoped to tie the interests of wealthy state creditors to the new national government.

<u>124-1-0</u> 5. The political costs of Hamilton's policies were high: A wide breach opened within the ranks of the Federalists.

<u>124-1-3</u>
to
<u>124-2-2</u> 6. Hamilton felt that a national bank would serve a number of important functions: provide a central control over private, state-chartered banks; provide a stable national currency; further tie the interests of the wealthy to the national government; and broaden the powers of the federal government.

_____ 7. Hamilton's plan for a protective tariff was well-received, and some of his ideas were built into the Tariff of 1792.

_____ 8. Most Americans agreed that the suppression of the Whiskey Rebellion was a great victory for the government.

Interpretive Level. You have read the selection and are familiar with its content. Immediately below is a guide for responding to the selection at the interpretive level. Check each statement you believe represents what the authors meant by what they said. Refer back to the text to find bits of information which, when considered together, would form a relationship represented by the statement.

_____ 1. A conscious part of Hamilton's policies for strengthening the new national government was the identification of the welfare of the well-to-do with the success of the federal government.

_____ 2. Hamilton believed in active government to foster economic growth.

_____ 3. Jefferson and Madison felt that Hamilton's desire to strengthen the national government threatened the liberties of the people.

To develop a reading guide, first read a section and determine the most important points and generalizations. (The section review questions will help in this effort because they can be turned into statements.) Then, for the literal level, develop a list of statements that either accurately or inaccurately restate the points made in the text. For very slow readers, these statements

_____
[1] For a complete discussion of reading guides, see Harold Herber, *Teaching Reading in Content Areas* (Englewood Cliffs, New Jersey: Prentice Hall, Inc., 1970).

could be taken verbatim from the text, with gross errors included to develop inaccuracies. For better readers, wording can be turned around, synonyms used, or, for inaccuracies, statements taken out of context. To develop an interpretive level guide, list accurate and/or inaccurate generalizations.

Reading guides can be used as homework or seatwork, and students can be grouped to compare responses and arrive at consensus within the group. In this manner, group-interaction skills are fostered. Reading guides lend themselves readily to differentiation or individualization. They have proven to be a most effective tool and are highly recommended by the authors.

GAMES AND SIMULATIONS

Games and simulations are techniques which require active student participation. For this reason, advocates declare that better learning takes place. Gaming and simulation are actually separate dimensions of the same student-oriented technique. They may be combined in simulation games.[2]

Games. The most simple game is the learning game. In the case of the learning game, a student plays a game to win—there are specific rules and procedures—but needs no prior knowledge. The student learns new information by playing the game. One such game teaches students how bills become laws. A simple board game, it requires the student to advance his or her piece, representing a bill, by the roll of the die. Pitfalls abound, however, on the path from introduction to signature by the President, as the bill might be "pigeon-holed," "vetoed," or meet a similar fate. If the bill lands on a space with one of these pitfalls, the student must return to start. By playing the game, the student becomes familiar with the steps in the legislative process.

A little more sophisticated is the instructional game. This type of game combines competition and rules with drill and practice. The students must know a certain amount of information, and

the game drills them on this knowledge. Any number of popular games or sports have been adapted to the classroom for instructional gaming. The title of the old "Who, What, and Where" game suggests the suitability of these activities for history drill. In each adaptation, the class is divided into teams and that team accumulating the higher (or highest) number of correct answers wins.

Simulations. The most basic component of simulations is role-playing. In role-playing, students assume the role of another person in the reenactment of an historical event or problem. Make sure students playing roles have enough background information to accurately portray their individual's opinions. Do not let the role-play drag on. Stop it when you feel the crucial points have been covered or when students "run out of gas." Have the whole class review the major points made.

A more sophisticated form of simulation is the "social simulation." The social simulation combines role-playing with a forum for social interaction and decision-making. In designing a social simulation, the teacher should take the following steps:[3]

1. Select a problem or issue with alternative solutions.
2. Determine simulated groups, their positions, and how the class decision will be made.
3. Provide students with background information or allow them time for its development.
4. Provide some forum in which the various groups will present their cases. Have the class (or decision-making group) make its decision based upon these presentations.
5. Establish limits for behavior, time, research activities, etc.

A social simulation might be devised around an historical issue such as the Senate's consideration of the Versailles Treaty after World War I. The class could be the Senate divided into a number of positions. Two obvious positions would be isolationists and supporters of Wilson and the concept of a League of Nations. The class as a whole would vote to ratify or reject the treaty.

---

[2]For a complete discussion of these techniques, see Ron Stadsklev, *Handbook of Simulation Gaming in Social Education* (Institute of Higher Education Research and Services, The University of Alabama, 1974).

[3]Adapted from Jo Michalski, "Developing A Social Simulation, 'The Land Use Simulation'" in *Handbook of Simulation Gaming in Social Education* (Institute of Higher Education Research and Services, The University of Alabama, 1974).

Simulation Games. Simulation games combine all the features of the previously mentioned activities. As such, they are time-consuming to produce. A great number, however, are available commercially and should be considered.

DEBATE

Debating involves students in orally defending and/or attacking viewpoints on a specific topic, theory, or principle. The goal of each debater is to convince others that his or her position is either correct or the most persuasive. The process helps students gain skill in using structured oral communication to persuade others to change their positions or points of view. Debating may be a one-on-one or a group activity. Either way, the whole class can be involved because students who do not take part directly in the debate are still involved in the learning process as they listen to new information, consider the arguments, make judgments about the quality of the presentations, and come to decisions about a conclusion.

To initiate the debate, select a topic or issue about which there is a diversity of opinion. Have students indicate their positions on the issue, and then divide them into groups according to position or viewpoint. Explain that each group will have a certain amount of time in which to present its views and the justification for those views to the rest of the class. Allow each group time to analyze and solidify its position and prepare the strongest and most valid arguments

possible. This will probably require additional reading or research.

Give each group (or a spokesperson for each group) an opportunity to present its argument, allowing for rebuttal. As arguments can get heated, it is best to set a specific time frame within which all argument and discussion must be contained. After each viewpoint has been debated, survey the class to determine if the debate has led any students to change their position on the issue.

CASE STUDIES

A case study is used to supplement material in the text by focusing on a particular problem, topic, or issue for which alternative solutions or courses of action existed. Students should take the following steps:

1. Identify the problem or conflict situation.
2. Review (analyze and evaluate) alternative positions or courses of action. Here the teacher may want to use a range of materials, including primary (anthologies of documents are readily available) and secondary sources.
3. Choose a course of action or position and develop a defense of that position or course.
4. Present their positions orally or in writing.

Case studies are especially useful if teachers want their students to practice inquiry and higher-level thinking skills. This strategy may be implemented any time there is an issue or conflict to be considered.

TEXT
IMPLEMENTATION

UNIT 1 COLONIAL AMERICA

At the conclusion of this unit, the student should be able to:

1. discuss European exploration, early colonization, and Indian civilizations of the New World.
2. describe the founding and development of the original thirteen colonies.
3. discuss the events leading to the American Revolution, its major turning points, and the provisions of the Treaty of Paris.

OVERVIEW

This unit pursues American history from pre-Columbian times through the War for Independence. Chapter 1 describes the European background for the Age of Exploration, exploration and early settlement, and American Indian cultures. Chapter 2 follows the settlement and development of the English colonies, describing their British heritage and distinctive cultural and social features. Chapter 3 surveys the growing tension between England and the colonies, culminating in the American Revolution.

INTRODUCING THE UNIT

Ask students what features of American society today they are most proud of. They will probably mention such characteristics as democratic government, religious toleration, and basic civil liberties. Jot these points on the chalkboard and have students record them. As the unit is studied, have students determine how many of these features have their roots in the colonial experience.

CHAPTER 1 THE BEGINNINGS

After studying this chapter, the student should be able to:

1. describe the changes in Europe that brought about the Age of Exploration.
2. list the major figures of the Age of Exploration and their contributions to that age.
3. describe the various Indian civilizations that inhabited the Americas prior to the Europeans' arrival.

OVERVIEW

Chapter 1 provides the students with basic information concerning European exploration of the "New World," early colonization, and the Indian civilizations that existed prior to and at the time of European exploration. While introducing the different patterns of colonization, the chapter sets the stage for the series of confrontations between colonial powers that occurred over the next two centuries. Major emphasis should be placed upon the causes of the "Age of Exploration" and the patterns of Indian civilization. Important concepts in the chapter are national-ism (the rise of nation-states and international rivalry) cultural conflict (white-Indian), and cultural pluralism (Hispanic influence).

TEACHING STRATEGIES
Section 1

Introduction: When Sir Edmund Hillary was asked why he had wanted to climb Mt. Everest he reportedly said, "Because it's there." Ask the students what this statement reflects about human nature (human curiosity, challenge of the unknown) and how it relates to the desire to explore. Then, have the students read to see what the textbook describes as the causes of exploration. The Hillary quotation seems particularly related to the spirit of the Renaissance.

Development: This section affords an excellent opportunity for a review of causation. The idea of cause and effect, a chain of events, each one based upon the previous, is fundamental to historical understanding. In this section we see multiple causes for exploration: the Crusades leading to the development of trade, the relationship of trade to the development of nation-states, and the influence of the Renaissance. Have the students point out these causes and discuss how each contributed to the Age of Exploration. A graphic device like the following, written on the chalkboard, might help:

Crusades → Trade ⟶ Renaissance
⟶ Exploration
↘ Nation-States

Section 2

Introduction: Ask the students the names of any explorers they remember from earlier studies and write their names and countries on the board. The map on page 13 should provide further reminders. Have the students read the section looking for these names and others from Portugal, Spain, France, Holland, and England.

Development: An interesting aspect of the era of exploration and colonization was the differing goals and colonization patterns of the various European countries. For example, all sought wealth, but wealth came in different forms. Relationship to Indians also differed. Have the students compare and contrast the Spanish (pages 11-12) and French (page 14) patterns. As you move on to Chapter 2, these characteristics can be contrasted to English colonization.

Section 3

Introduction: During the 1970's, the campaign against pollution included a TV spot with a North American Indian riding past discarded litter, polluted rivers, and other signs of abuse of the environment. As the spot ended, the camera focused on the Indian's face—a tear rolled slowly down his cheek. Describe this spot and ask the students why the Indian made the message particularly poignant. (Indians lived close to nature.) Have the students read this section to discover the early civilizations of Central and South American Indians and how North Ameri-

can Indians adapted their lifestyles to their environments.

Development: Have students reread the quotation from Columbus on page 19. What information from the discussion of Central and South American Indians on pages 19-22 makes Columbus' description and assumptions simplistic?

After reading the material on the North American Indians, have students describe how their cultures were related to their physical environments. You might want to list these aspects on the chalkboard by geographical region.

Conclusion: Have students point out aspects of American Indian culture that would clash with European culture. Was conflict inevitable? Why do students think that the clash of cultures was tragic for the Indians but not for the Europeans?

ANSWERS
Section Review Questions
page 8
1. Vikings—Probably the first Europeans to reach the New World.
   Leif Ericson—Viking who reached northeast coast of America.
   Vespucci—First to realize that America is a continent.
   Marco Polo—First European traveler to Cathay.
   Ottoman Turks—Conquerors of much of the Middle East, northern Africa, and eastern Europe.
   Renaissance—Period in which the study of art, literature, science, medicine, and mathematics was emphasized.
2. Sponsoring the expedition was an act of national pride.
3. Europeans learned how other people lived.
4. The distances traveled and the time involved required many handlers, all of whom were paid.
5. The Church taught that everything that happened was God's will and that rewards would come in the next world.

page 19
1. Prester John—Legendary prince said to rule a great kingdom.
   Vasco da Gama—Opened route to India by sailing around southern coast of Africa.

Tordesillas—Treaty drawn to delineate claims of Portugal and Spain in the New World.

Magellan—First to circumnavigate the world; proved Indies could be reached by traveling west.

Cartier—Explored the St. Lawrence River and gave France claim to eastern Canada.

Frobisher—English traveler who explored northeastern Canada.

Raleigh—Sponsored expedition to America to start colony.

2. To bring power and trade to Portugal and to spread Christianity.
3. To find a new route to the Indies.
4. New France, Louisiana, and the land between the Mississippi and Ohio Rivers.
5. Hudson's voyages in North America.
6. Earlier they were hit by bad weather and a lack of supplies. However, no one can say why the settlers disappeared.

page 26
1. Beringia—Land bridge across the Bering Strait.

Tenochtitlán—The Aztec capital.

Inuit—Name the Eskimos have for themselves.

Basket Makers—Early Southwest Indian group.

League of the Iroquois—Union of Seneca, Cayuga, Onondaga, Oneida, and Mohawk Indians.
2. Anthropologists theorize that Asians crossed Beringia to America.
3. Mayas, Aztecs, and Incas.
4. Indians of the Northwest Coast, California, and the Southwest.

Special Feature Questions
page 21
1. Spanish Florida, which included parts of Mississippi, Alabama, and Louisiana. The Spanish Southwest included California, Utah, Nevada, Arizona, and much of New Mexico, Texas, and Colorado.
2. St. Augustine, Santa Fe, Tucson, Albuquerque, San Antonio, and San Diego.
3. Horses, pigs, sheep, and beef cattle.

Photo Questions
page 6
His discoveries helped extend Spain's power.

page 7
Promoted the growth of trade.

page 10
Proved that the world was round and that a western water route to the Orient existed.

page 11
They went on to explore and claim vast areas.

page 12
While France's claims were the largest in the north, they were smaller than those of Spain overall.

page 15
To find a route to the Orient.

page 16
England became Europe's major sea power.

page 17
He helped establish the first English colony.

page 20
They had roads, cities, suspension bridges, irrigation canals, and a welfare plan for the aged, the ill and orphans.

page 23
They adapted to their environment.

page 24
Adobe or stone houses, long houses, and teepees.

Chapter Review
page 27, Review Questions
1. To establish new trade routes to the Far East.
2. Feudalism was dying out. New foods and spices were in demand. People were more interested in worldly affairs. Nationalism was stronger. Science, mathematics, and medicine were being developed.
3. Built a school for navigators, improved the compass, astrolabe, quadrant, and ship designs, and compiled better maps and charts.
4. Spain wanted gold, silver, dye, and sugar. The French relied on the fish and fur trade.
5. Encouraged business and trade. Promoted sea power to fight enemies and capture trade.

6. Mayans developed religious art and architecture. Aztecs developed a class structure, a court system, and strong family and community codes. The Incas built roads, bridges, irrigation systems, and cities.
7. The Great Plains Indians hunted buffalo. Those from the Eastern Woodlands were deer hunters and planted crops. Eskimos hunted bear and seal. Indians of the Northwest fished for their food. Southwest Indians learned to build irrigation canals to provide water for their crops. Nomadic hunters and food gatherers were found in the Great Basin and the Plateau.
8. Europeans claimed the land, leading to clashes with the Indians.

page 27, Discussion
1. Answers may vary, but could include: that Indians were considered primitive; ethnocentrism; that military conquest and exploration were viewed as giving rights to land; that ownership of land was viewed differently.

2. Europeans felt it was a duty to spread Christianity. For some, this was a work of dedication. Others used it as an excuse to enslave and conquer.
3. Possible answers include a chance for riches and fame, an escape from restrictions of society, adventure, and spreading Christianity.
4. Possible answers include the power of Spain in South America and compatibility with the climate.

page 27, Using Maps
1. Hudson, Cabot, Cartier, Verrazano.
2. Columbus, Vespucci, Magellan, Cabral, Drake.
3. Hudson, Columbus, Cartier.
4. Hudson, Drake.
5. 50°W.

page 27, Using Skills
1. Algonquin Indians.
2. Two, four.
3. Women are working, caring for children. Men are sitting, talking.

CHAPTER 2 THE ENGLISH COLONIES

After studying this chapter, the student should be able to:

1. discuss the founding of Jamestown and the development of the Virginia colony.
2. describe the development of the New England colonies.
3. define and identify proprietary colonies.
4. identify the similarities between British and colonial governments.
5. describe the major features of the colonial economy.
6. discuss the distinctive cultural and social features of the colonies.

OVERVIEW

Chapter 2 follows the founding and development of the original thirteen colonies. There are several themes that should be developed. First, the English colonization pattern (whether the goal was commercial or religious) was quite different from the Spanish or French, and these should be contrasted. Second, the similarities between colonial and British representative government are described in the chapter. The British heritage of American political thought should be emphasized, as its significance will be apparent throughout the next few chapters.

Third, the concept of mercantilism is explained, and since much of the political history of the United States revolves around the question of the role of the central government in economic development, this concept should be understood by the students. Finally, although social classes did exist in colonial society, the chapter points out the conditions that provided much greater social mobility, religious toleration, and other freedoms for most American colonists. Other important concepts in the chapter include private ownership of property, constitutional government, balance of trade, cultural pluralism, freedom of the press, and democracy.

TEACHING IDEAS

Section 1

Introduction: One of the major differences between the English colonial pattern and that of other colonizing nations was the importance of commercial farming. Have the students look at the picture of the Indian village on page 30 and answer the question in the caption.

Development: Have the students list the various characteristics of the Virginia colony that distinguished it from the Spanish and French colonies studied in the last chapter. These might include larger numbers of settlers, commercial farming and private ownership of land bought or taken from Indians, relationships with Indians, and self-government.

Section 2

Introduction: Have the students read the quotation from John Winthrop on page 33, "We shall be as a city upon a hill. The eyes of all people are upon us." Ask them if they think that this idea of a model community has become part of the American ethos. Do we see ourselves as a model today? The theme of the model society is an important one and can be pursued throughout the study of American history.

Development: Have students describe other important attributes of American beliefs that were fostered by the New England experience. Some examples include the Puritan work ethic, Roger William's idea of the separation of church and state, and the Fundamental Orders of Connecticut as the first written constitution.

Section 3

Introduction: Have the students read the excerpt from the Toleration Act of 1649 on page 36. Ask them why this was a departure from the usual practice in those days. Why would it be an inadequate statement of religious toleration today? As they read the section, have them note other evidence of idealism in the establishment of the proprietary colonies.

Development: To pursue the theme of toleration, have students study the picture of the Quakers on page 37 and its accompanying caption. What implications would the idea of "equality in the eyes of God" have for the colony?

Section 4

Introduction: Write the following two quotations on the board, or read them to the students, and ask what they suggest about representative government in the colonies:

"You have heard my fate. I could make but 200 votes in near 700. They were the principal inhabitants but you know we are governed not by weight but by numbers." Thomas Hutchinson (Massachusetts, 1749)

"(H)alf an acre of land here makes a man as sufficient a voter, and as lawful a burgess as he that is possess'd of 10,000 acres and 100 Negroes." Alexander Spotswood (Virginia, 1736)[4]

As students read, have them look for evidence of representative government.

Development: Discuss with students the similarities between the structure of British and colonial government. The following chart might be used:

	Great Britain	Colonies
Executive		
Legislative		
Upper House		
Lower House		
Judicial		

Section 5

Introduction: When economists talk about the factors of production they emphasize the importance of land (natural resources), labor (working force), and capital equipment and buildings used for production (e.g., machines). The colonial economy was shaped by the abundance of the first, shortage of the second, and near absence of the third. Ask students to speculate about the implications of these facts (widespread land ownership, relatively high cost of labor, exportation of raw materials for finished English imports), then have students read to see if their speculations were correct.

Development: It is important that students understand the concept of mercantilism because it reflects an extreme form of government regulation of the economy. Have the students reread the section on mercantilism and cite evidence in the passage of government controls. You might point out further evidence in the nature of charters given to trade companies (monopolies granted by government). Later, mercantilism can be contrasted to laissez-faire.

---

[4]Quoted in Robert E. Brown, *Reinterpretation of the Formation of the American Constitution* (Boston: Boston University Press, 1963), p. 123.

Section 6

Introduction: Read the following quotation to the students and ask them what it might mean for the development of democracy in America: "Property is more equally distributed in the colonies, especially those to the northward of Maryland, than in any nation in Europe. In some towns you see scarce a man destitute of a competency to make him easy. . . ." (Thomas Hutchinson) Then have students read the section looking for aspects of colonial society that laid the foundation for democratic development.

Development: Have students compare colonial culture and society with English culture and society. Draw a chart similar to the following on the chalkboard and have students fill it in.

	Colonies	England
Population		
Social Charm		
Religion		
Education		
Fashion		
Architecture		
Language		

Conclusion: Have the students list aspects of colonial society that laid the foundations for democratic growth. Then, have them point out evidence of non-democratic practices (e.g., slavery). Tell the students that these latter factors will be watched for change over the course of their study of United States history.

ANSWERS

Section Review Questions

page 32

1. London Company—Joint stock company organized to colonize Virginia.
   John Smith—Leader of the Jamestown colony.
   starving time—Period of extreme hardship in the Jamestown colony.
   John Rolfe—Colonist who grew first successful tobacco crop.
   cash crop—Crop grown for export.
   House of Burgesses—First representative body in Virginia.
   Powhatan—Chief of an Indian confederation in Virginia.

   Pocohontas—Daughter of Powhatan, saved John Smith's life, married John Rolfe.
2. Finding gold and a northwest passage to the Far East.
3. Problems included lack of leadership, solved first by John Smith, later by company appointed governors and representative government; lack of food and water, solved by learning to grow food crops and digging wells.
4. Representative government was established in order to satisfy colonists' complaints.

page 35

1. Separatists—Pilgrims, Puritans who wanted to separate from Church of England.
   Great Migration—Mass movement of people from England to America in the period from 1630-1643.
   John Winthrop—Puritan leader, first governor of Massachusetts.
   Anne Hutchinson—Founded colony in Rhode Island.
   Thomas Hooker—Founded colony in Connecticut.
   King Philip—Metacomet, Indian chief who waged war against English colonists.
2. That powers of government are derived from the people.
3. To establish an ideal state based on religious principles.
4. Dissenters were banished and founded other colonies.
5. Government by consent of the governed was emphasized.

page 38

1. Lord Baltimore—George Calvert and later his son, Cecelius Calvert, founder of Maryland.
   Maryland Toleration Act—1649 act that promised religious freedom in Maryland.
   Dominion of New England—Government established by James II, combining New England colonies with New York and New Jersey.
   Edmund Andros—Governor of New York under the Dominion of New England.
   William Penn—Founder of Pennsylvania.
   James II—King of England overthrown in the Glorious Revolution.
   Ogelthorpe—Founder of Georgia.
2. The proprietary colonies were the following: Maryland, founded partly as a haven for

Catholics; New York and New Jersey, originally founded by the Dutch and taken over by the English to control trade in the New World; the Carolinas, founded for financial reasons; Pennsylvania and Delaware, founded as experiments in political and religious freedom; Georgia, founded as a haven for English debtors.

3. The colonists were unhappy with their Dutch governor and the English promised to let them keep their property and their freedom.

4. By revoking colonial charters and establishing the Dominion of New England.

page 40

1. Magna Charta—English document limiting the king's power.

   Parliament—England's legislative body.

   Glorious Revolution—Revolution that gave power to Parliament.

   town meeting—Form of local government in New England.

2. The signing of the Magna Charta and the Glorious Revolution.

3. Suffrage in the colonies was for free white adult males who met various religious and property requirements.

4. With direct representation, representatives had to live in the districts from which they were elected. With virtual representation, representatives could live elsewhere.

5. In the southern colonies the basic unit of government was the county. People were too widely scattered to attend town meetings.

page 44

1. Eliza Lucas—Colonist who grew the first successful indigo crop.

   Navigation Acts—Series of acts passed to control colonial trade.

   Staple Act—Act that required all goods imported to colonies to be shipped on English vessels.

   Hat Act—Act passed to restrict colonial manufacturing.

2. Labor was scarce because land was easily available. Solutions included child labor, cooperative efforts, and the use of indentured servants, redemptioners, and slaves.

3. The triangular trade benefited New England traders, rum manufacturers, and owners of farms and plantations who used slaves.

4. The principles of mercantilism were (a) wealth was measured by ownership of precious metals; (b) wealth could be achieved with a favorable balance of trade; (c) the purpose of the colonies was to improve England's balance of trade.

5. By restricting colonial trade and manufacturing.

page 50

1. A high birthrate and non-English immigration.

2. The Great Awakening revived religion in the colonies and contributed to the growth of religious tolerance.

3. By increasing the freedom of the press to criticize the government.

Special Feature Questions

page 48

1. It extended freedom of religion to include protection against state action.

2. No. Does not include freedom to commit immoral or criminal acts.

Photo Questions

page 30

It was a native plant and Europeans quickly picked up the habit.

page 31

Indians grew alarmed at the invasion of their land.

page 33

That governments derive their power from the people.

page 34

Hutchinson believed that truth could be revealed directly to individuals. Williams believed in separation of church and state.

page 37

To find freedom to practice their religion.

page 39

That they were free white adult males. In some cases there were religious requirements and, almost always, property requirements.

page 41

Boston, Philadelphia, New York, Newport, and New Haven in the North and Charleston in the South.

page 44

The larger towns had many different stores that sold domestic and imported goods. Smaller towns had general stores.

Zenger was found innocent.

Chapter Review

page 51, Review Questions

1. People came to the English colonies voluntarily for economic reasons and to escape religious and political persecution. They came involuntarily if they were forced by the English government (prisoners and others) or if they were kidnapped and sold as slaves (Africans).
2. Self-governing charter colonies, proprietary colonies, and royal colonies. The self-governing colonies were almost completely independent. In the royal and proprietary colonies, the governor and his council were usually appointed by the king or the proprietor.
3. All the colonies had the same English heritage. Most people were farmers and people in all the colonies faced similar difficulties in taming the wilderness and dealing with the Indians. Different forms of local government developed in New England (the town meeting) and the South (the county) and the middle colonies (mixed). Trade and manufacturing developed to a greater degree in New England and the middle colonies. Slavery was more widespread in the South.
4. Because of cultural differences and because of the colonists' invasion of Indian lands.
5. The economic relation between England and the colonies was based on mercantilism. The colonies sent raw materials to England in exchange for manufactured goods. The colonies generally prospered under the system even though their manufacturing and trade were limited.
6. An upper class, a middle class, a lower class, and slaves.
7. Slavery answered a need for labor, especially in the South, and brought profits to northern traders.
8. English heritage affected the language, customs, and forms of government of the colonies, but was modified by the different circumstances that existed in the New World and by the influence of the Indians and of non-English immigrants.

page 51, Discussion

1. Suggest the relationships among private property, representative government, religious tolerance, public education, freedom of the press, and ideas of the Enlightenment.
2. Answers may vary.
3. Answers may vary.
4. Factors contributing to social mobility included availability of land, high wages for labor, the absence of an aristocracy, and rapid growth. Social mobility was restricted by customs, advantages of land ownership and other wealth, differences in religion and education, and, of course, slavery.

page 51, Using Maps

1. New York, Charleston.
2. 900 miles or about 1500 kilometers.
3. 40°N.
4. Cadiz.
5. Naval stores, whale oil, ginger, lumber, silk, indigo, rice, and tobacco.

page 51, Using Skills

1. Six men, three women, and two children.
2. Men are reading and discussing. Women are sitting. One is reading, one is sewing, the other is playing with the children.
3. No. Women are physically separated from the document and show no interest in it.

CHAPTER 3 THE STRUGGLE FOR INDEPENDENCE

After studying this chapter, the student should be able to:

1. describe the origins and major turning points of the French and Indian War.
2. outline the changes in British policy that aggrevated relations with the colonies and describe the colonists' reactions.
3. list and explain the significance of the major American victories during the Revolutionary War.

OVERVIEW

Chapter 3 describes the French and Indian War and explains how it keyed a change in British policy toward the American colonies. The changes in policy and the American reactions to those changes—the series of events that led to the Declaration of Independence—are covered in detail. The war itself and ensuing Treaty of Paris are treated in the last two sections.

The events that led to the Revolution provide the opportunity to explore American attitudes toward government and establish some themes that can be pursued throughout the text. The concepts of balanced and limited government are especially important and are therefore treated in some detail in the following teaching strategies section. The concept of representative government is developed in this chapter, and the concepts of revolution and propaganda should also be stressed.

TEACHING IDEAS

Section 1

Introduction: Have the students read the footnote on page 53. Ask them why the French had more Indian allies. Their earlier comparisons of French and English colonizing techniques should provide the answer. Have the students read the section for information concerning the major turning points during the war.

Development: The Albany Congress was the first major attempt at intercolonial union after the short-lived Dominion of New England. Have the students reread the material on Albany. Ask them why the plan failed. What especially would the colonial governments have disliked? (They would have resented authority over westward expansion and authority to levy taxes.) Tell students to watch for these issues as the colonies/states work toward union during and after the Revolution.

Sections 2-5

These sections detail the events that led to the Declaration of Independence. Recent historical study argues that Americans were convinced that an active conspiracy against their liberties as English citizens was taking place. Give the students the following background and have them read these sections looking for what colonials would have seen as evidence of a conspiracy against liberty.

Introduction: Americans were convinced that it was the British Constitution that protected their liberties. The beauty of the Constitution was that it was *balanced*. It balanced the various forces in society, and each had a role in government: the crown was represented by the king, the nobility by the House of Lords, and the democracy (the common people) by the House of Commons. An independent judiciary served to maintain the balance. By 1765, however, colonists were becoming convinced that a conspiracy of power—the power of the executive, the king, and his followers in Parliament—was encroaching upon their rights. Between 1764 and 1776 the evidence of this conspiracy seemed to mount.

Below is a list of classical (to the colonists) examples of executive encroachment against liberty. Have the students read these sections and note those events (using the list as a guide) that would have alarmed any colonist suspecting such a conspiracy.

Threats to independent judiciary (page 40)
No right to property (page 57, "taxation without representation")
Broadly-stated search warrants (page 59, Townshend Acts)
Expanding executive control over officials (page 60, British government pays salaries)
Standing army in peacetime (page 56, Quartering Act)
Troops terrorizing civilians (page 59, Boston Massacre)

Development: After having considered these developments from the colonial perspective, have students look at the series of events from the British point of view. Ask the students to see themselves as members of Parliament who were responsible for repayment of the large war debts, debts from a war fought largely for the benefit of the colonists. Review the major pieces of legislation: the Grenville duties, Townshend Acts, Tea Act, Intolerable Acts. Were these reasonable or unreasonable from the British perspective? What else might have been done?

Section 6

Introduction: The Declaration of Independence is a statement of the "compact theory" of government. That is, governments are created to protect the rights of the people and will be obeyed only so long as they do. The compact between the people and the government is, roughly, "We'll obey you as long as you protect our rights." What rights did the colonists feel were violated in terms of "life, liberty, and the pursuit of happiness"?

Development: Ask the students to discuss the following question: "If the government exists to protect the 'life, liberty, and happiness' of the governed, should it have any power to limit those qualities? Why or why not? In what situations?" The tension between individual rights and the government's need to protect the community (maintain social stability or order) is another theme that can be pursued as American history unfolds. Ask the students to watch for ways in which Americans have come to declare their rights and liberties.

Section 7

Introduction: The American Revolutionary War was one of those wars in which all that was required for success was the maintenance of a rebel army in the field. To win the war, the British had to destroy Washington's army. Have the students keep this idea in mind as they read through the account of the war. What was the significance of the following battles in terms of that central issue—Trenton and Princeton, Saratoga, King's Mountain and the Cowpens, Yorktown?

Development: Have students list the strengths and weaknesses of the American colonies versus those of the British. What was the colonies greatest weakness? greatest strength?

Conclusion: The provisions of the Treaty of Paris would be very important to the foreign policy of the new nation. Have students review those provisions and mark carefully the boundaries of the new United States and the countries whose claims the United States abutted.

ANSWERS

Section Review Questions

page 55
1. Ohio Company—Land company organized to develop trade with the Indians in the Ohio Valley and sell land there for settlement.
   Robert Dinwiddee—Governor of Virginia who tried to prevent the French from gaining control of the Ohio Valley.
   Great Meadows—First battle of the French and Indian War.

General Edward Braddock—British general whose force was decisively defeated by the French near Fort Duquesne in July 1755.
   Louisbourg—Important fort located at the mouth of the St. Lawrence River; its capture marked the turning point of the French and Indian War.
   General James Wolfe—Commander of the British force that captured Quebec in September 1758.
   Marquis de Montcalm—Commander of the French force that unsuccessfully defended Quebec against the British in September 1758.
2. By building a series of forts between Lake Erie and the Allegheny River.
3. To unite the colonies under a single government with authority over defense, westward expansion, and Indian affairs.
4. Pitt replaced incompetent military leaders, sent reinforcements to America, encouraged colonial enlistments, and subsidized England's allies.
5. It signaled the end of the French Empire in the New World.
6. France ceded Canada and all its lands east of the Mississippi River (except New Orleans) to Great Britain; Spain ceded Florida to Great Britain and, in return, received French lands west of the Mississippi River and the port of New Orleans.

page 56
1. Pontiac—Ottawa chief who led a rebellion against the British in the spring of 1763.
   George Grenville—England's chancellor of the exchequer who, after the French and Indian War, decided that the colonies should help pay the costs of colonial administration and defense.
   Sugar Act—April 1764 act that reduced the duty on molasses but levied new and higher duties on other products; first law passed by Parliament for the purpose of raising money in the colonies.
   Currency Act—Act that prohibited the American colonies from issuing paper money as legal tender.
   Stamp Act—Act that taxed all legal documents, as well as almanacs, newspapers, playing cards, and dice; first direct tax levied on the American colonies.

Quartering Act—Act that required colonists to house British troops.

2. The disposal of western lands and the huge national debt left by the war.

3. The British issued the Proclamation of 1763, establishing the crest of the Appalachians as a boundary line between white and Indian lands. The British also sent troops to the West to enforce this decree.

4. The British reorganized the colonial customs service, enforced existing trade laws, and proposed new measures.

page 58

1. Patrick Henry—Member of the Virginia House of Burgesses who introduced the Virginia Resolutions in protest of the Stamp Act.

   Virginia Resolutions—Series of resolutions stating that the House of Burgesses, not Parliament, had the sole power to tax Virginians.

   Sons of Liberty—Organization formed in the colonies in opposition to the Stamp Act; turned to violent action.

   Samuel Adams—Ardent patriot; one of the leaders of the Sons of Liberty in Boston.

   Declaratory Act—Act passed by Parliament in conjunction with the repeal of the Stamp Act (March 1766); was a statement of Parliament's authority over the colonies.

2. It meant that Parliament had no right to tax the colonies since they were not represented in the House of Commons.

3. They influenced other colonial assemblies to pass similar measures.

4. The Stamp Act Congress, in the "Declaration of Rights and Grievances," resolved that Parliament could make laws for the colonies but could not tax them. Congress then called upon the British government to repeal the Stamp Act.

5. The Stamp Act was repealed due to pressure from British merchants hurt by colonial non-importation agreements and because the colonists refused to buy the stamps, which basically nullified the act.

page 62

1. Townshend Acts—Acts that levied duties on colonial imports of glass, lead, paper, paint, and tea; also established a Board of Customs Commissioners.

Boston Massacre—Violent conflict between colonists and British soldiers that took place in Boston on March 5, 1770.

Gaspee—British patrol ship destroyed by the colonists in June 1772 near Providence, Rhode Island.

Committee of Correspondence—Committee formed to communicate with towns in Massachusetts.

Quebec Act—Act that annexed the area west of the Appalachians and north of the Ohio River to the province of Quebec.

Joseph Galloway—Leader of the moderates in the First Continental Congress.

Declaration of Rights and Resolves—Declaration that denounced the Intolerable Acts and demanded their repeal.

2. It indicated that although the Stamp Act had been repealed, Parliament had no intention of relinquishing its authority in the colonies.

3. To save the East India Company from bankruptcy.

4. By declaring a boycott. The tea shipments were either returned to England, stored in government warehouses, or destroyed. The most famous incident of destruction occurred in Boston on December 16, 1773, when the Sons of Liberty, disguised as Indians, boarded the East India ships and dumped 342 chests of tea into the harbor.

5. The British government, angered by the Boston Tea Party, decided to make an example of Massachusetts and thereby force the colonies into submission. So, in the spring of 1774, Parliament passed the Coercive Acts (also known as the Intolerable Acts).

6. The moderates, who hoped for a reconciliation with Great Britain, supported a proposal to unify the colonies under British authority. The radicals, on the other hand, felt Parliament had no authority of any kind in the colonies and managed to defeat the moderates' proposal.

page 66

1. Lexington and Concord—Towns in Massachusetts where the opening battles of the American Revolution took place (April 1775).

   General Thomas Gage—British general and governor of Massachusetts; ordered the march on Concord.

Paul Revere—American patriot who warned the colonists of the British march on Concord.

Green Mountain Boys—Group of men from Vermont who served under Ethan Allen; instrumental in the fall of Fort Ticonderoga.

John Dickinson—Leader of the moderates in the Second Continental Congress (1775).

Olive Branch Petition—Petition that asked George III to restore harmony between England and the 13 colonies; America's final effort to negotiate with Great Britain.

General William Howe—British commander who ordered the evacuation of Boston.

2. To destroy the military supplies stored there by the colonists.
3. Because of its strategic location and its rich store of military supplies.
4. To assume the leadership of the American cause and act as the country's first central government.
5. Although the British won, the victory cost them dearly (1054 casualties out of 2400 soldiers).
6. American occupation of strategically located Dorchester Heights.

page 68
1. Thomas Paine—Author of the influential pamphlet *Common Sense*; revolutionary propagandist.

Richard Henry Lee—Representative of Virginia in the Second Continental Congress who introduced the independence resolution in June 1776.

Thomas Jefferson—Representative of Virginia in the Second Continental Congress who drafted the *Declaration of Independence*.

John Hancock—President of the Second Continental Congress; first to sign the *Declaration of Independence*.

2. *Common Sense* crystallized colonial opinion and helped commit thousands to the cause of independence.
3. Most Americans approved of the *Declaration of Independence*.
4. The philosophy upon which the *Declaration of Independence* was based is as follows: (a) all men were equal and possessed the unalien-able rights of "life, liberty, and the pursuit of happiness"; (b) to protect these rights, people formed governments; and (c) since government was based upon the "consent of the governed," the people had the "right to alter or abolish it" if it should fail to fulfill its obligations.

page 73
1. General John Burgoyne—British general who developed a three-pronged plan to crush American resistance.

George Rogers Clark—Commander of the Kentucky militia who battled the British in the West.

Lord Charles Cornwallis—Commanded British forces in the South; defeated at Yorktown.

2. Great Britain had (a) a strong army; (b) a powerful navy; (c) experienced, professional officers; (d) the support of thousands of loyalists in the colonies. However, the British had a long supply line, were fighting in a hostile land, and had difficulty facing the guerrilla tactics of the colonists. The colonists (a) were fighting in their own land; (b) were successful in obtaining valuable foreign aid; (c) had certain experienced military leaders. However, the Americans lacked a regular army, had no real navy, and had problems getting supplies.
3. Instead of pushing northward to meet Burgoyne, Howe decided to take Philadelphia. This decision left Burgoyne without reinforcement and forced his surrender at Saratoga.
4. Curbed the activities of the British and their Indian allies along the frontier, furthered America's claim to the Northwest, and played a part in the final peace negotiations.
5. The British recognized America's Independence, ceded territory east of the Mississippi River between Florida and the Great Lakes, agreed to withdraw their forces from America, and granted the United States fishing rights off Newfoundland. Spain received Florida. The Second Continental Congress agreed to recommend that the state legislatures compensate the loyalists for their losses during the war.

Photo Questions
page 54
The colonies must unite to survive.

page 55
It signaled the end of the French Empire in the New World.

page 58
The Sons of Liberty was formed, at first to voice their protests, but some members turned to violence. Mob action compelled most of the stamp distributors to resign.

page 59
It further inflamed the colonists against the British.

page 61
They seized and burned the British ship, *Gaspee*, and dumped tea into Boston harbor.

page 62
They were warned by Paul Revere.

page 65
Discovering that Washington had fortified Dorchester Heights, Howe ordered an attack. A storm prevented fulfillment of the order and Howe decided to evacuate the city.

page 66
Answers will vary, but may include rolling bandages, nursing, supplying food and water to the troops, refusing to pay taxes, withholding supplies from the British.

page 67
The people were the source of the government and had the "right to alter or abolish it."

page 70
Washington's victories at Trenton and Princeton.

page 72
The British position was safe only as long as they had control of the sea. When the French fleet in the West Indies was made available, Washington began the siege of Yorktown.

Chapter Review
page 73, Review Questions

1. The basic cause was the colonial rivalry between England and France. In North America, the struggle between these two countries stemmed from competition for land in the interior of the continent.
2. British victory in the French and Indian War signaled the end of the French empire in the New World and opened new territories to colonial settlement.
3. After the French and Indian War, England was free to turn its attention to the American colonies. In order to solve the problem of the disposal of western lands and cope with the huge postwar debt, the British government attempted to tighten its control over the colonies.
4. The colonists resented Great Britain's newly instituted policies. They objected to the boundary line which kept them from settling western lands, the presence of British troops, and the British government's attempts to raise revenue in the colonies —especially via direct taxes.
5. The colonists objected most strongly to the British government's attempt to tax them directly. At first, they responded peacefully to this change in British colonial policy (i.e., the Virginia Resolutions) but soon, some turned to violence (i.e., the Sons of Liberty) to publicize their protest. Despite the violence, colonial representatives in the Stamp Act Congress peacefully petitioned Parliament for a repeal of the Stamp Act. Finally, economic pressure (nonimportation agreements) plus the colonists' refusal to buy the stamps resulted in the repeal of the act.
6. Despite the repeal of the Stamp Act, tensions continued to increase between the colonists and Great Britain due to Parliament's determination to exercise its authority in the colonies.
7. The Coercive Acts were designed to punish Massachusetts so as to force its submission to Parliamentary authority. By making an example of Massachusetts, the British government hoped the other colonies would fall into line.
8. When the British governor of Massachusetts received instructions to take the offensive against the rebellious colonists, he ordered the destruction of colonial military supplies stored at Concord. After a brief skirmish at Lexington, during which eight Americans were killed, the British continued toward their destination. At Concord, the steadily increasing American forces attacked the British and continued to harass them on their return march to Boston. These events at Lexington and Concord opened the American Revolution.
9. The *Declaration of Independence* transformed the rebellion into a revolution and

committed the mass of patriots to separation. It also led to increased foreign aid for the rebels and prepared the way for French intervention on the American side.

10. Burgoyne's surrender at Saratoga changed the course of the war in that it led to the formation of the French Alliance.

11. Cornwallis' defeat at Yorktown plus several French victories in the West Indies ended the American Revolution.

page 74, Discussion
1. Point out that the British had financial problems, including a huge national debt (doubled during the French and Indian War).
2. Mention the various approaches used by the colonists in response to changes in British colonial policy—i.e., peaceful petitions, economic pressure, and mob action.
3. Answers may vary.
4. Answers may vary. This question has been the subject of much historical debate and provides an excellent topic for student research and reports.

page 74, Using Maps
1. Yellow.
2. The French no longer had holdings on the mainland, but were restricted to Miquelon, Guadaloupe, and Martinique.
3. All of French Canada, and the territory east of the Mississippi. The Treaty of Paris 1763.
4. Much of the territory west of the Mississippi.
5. Conflicting claims lie in the Northwest. Spain, Great Britain, and Russia.

page 74, Using Skills
1. Loading the cannon. Taking the place of the fallen man (her husband).
2. The two on horseback are calling attention to the woman. Respect.

Unit Review
page 75, Review Questions
1. At first, the Indians were friendly. However, they became hostile when their land was invaded. Europeans, in refusing to treat the Indians as equals, created further friction. Europeans learned from the Indians, but Indians lost their land and freedom.
2. At first, all art, architecture, and fashion was an imitation of England and English ways. Slowly, the colonists began developing their own ways, leading to less identification with

England and more sentiment for independence.
3. Wealth and world power through mercantilism; repayment of war debts. Rebellion.

The Historian's Craft
Use The Historian's Craft activity in the Unit Review to conclude the unit. In this activity, which may be conducted on either a group or an individual basis, students will practice interpreting visuals that depict the role of women in the Revolution. Students will also develop the understanding that history is a matter of interpretation, that interpretation is based upon available information, and that historians are influenced by the information available to them and in turn influence others by their selection and interpretation of information.

This activity is the first in a sequence of nine. As such, it lays the foundation for the development of more complex skills. Be sure students understand the interpretive nature of history, because this understanding underlies the other activities in the sequence. Stress that *all* kinds of information—pictures being only one kind —influence interpretation. Ask students what other kinds of information historians would probably examine.

Questions 1 and 2. The Using Skills activity and the end of Chapter 1 has given students practice in noting the details of a picture, and the Using Skills activities in Chapters 2 and 3 have given them practice in interpreting pictures. At this point, students should be able to tell from the photographs provided that some women actually fought in the Revolution, though this was rare; that others played a passive role, staying at home; that still others played an active role, as in nursing the wounded or as political protestors before the American Revolution. (Note the petition against the Tea Act being signed by the women in the picture on page 77, bottom.)

Question 3. Students may say that women played various roles in the Revolution. With limited information, it is not possible to generalize about *most* women. Ask students what other sources they would pursue in order to find out what *most* women did during the Revolution.

Question 4. Be sure students understand the point that much of history is biased, but that the bias is not usually deliberate or malicious. In a later activity, students will learn about factors that may produce bias (frame of reference).

UNIT 2 FORGING A UNION

At the conclusion of this unit, the student should be able to:

1. describe the nature of state and national government during the "Critical Period," and the latter's weaknesses and accomplishments.
2. discuss the major aspects of American constitutional government.
3. outline the major domestic and foreign policy developments during the Washington and Adams administrations.

OVERVIEW

Unit 2 surveys that period of American history from the conclusion of the Revolution through the election of 1800. Chapter 4 describes the United States under the Articles of Confederation and the movement for and creation of a stronger central government under the Constitution. Chapter 5 is essentially a political science chapter, designed to help teachers who are required to teach the Constitution. Chapter 6 returns to the historical narrative with a survey of the Washington and Adams administrations.

INTRODUCING THE UNIT

Ask students to react to the statement, "American Constitutional government provides a government of laws, not of men." What does this mean, and why is it important? Does it have anything to do with the survival of the Constitution as the basis of government for nearly 200 years? What do the students think the Constitution embodies? Note these ideas and have students study the unit looking for evidence to back up or broaden their conceptions.

CHAPTER 4 A NEW NATION

After studying this chapter, the student should be able to:

1. describe the major characteristics of state governments after the Revolution.
2. describe the organization, powers, and the problems with ratification of the Articles of Confederation.
3. explain why the period between 1781 and 1789 has been called the "Critical Period."
4. list the achievements of the United States under the Articles.
5. outline the major compromises required to produce the Constitution.
6. explain the differences between Federalists and Antifederalists.

OVERVIEW

This chapter surveys the new state governments, the national government under the Articles of Confederation, problems under the Articles, and the movement for and creation of a stronger central government under the Constitution. A number of significant ideas should be explored, the most important of which is the issue of the protection of liberty.

As a result of Americans' experiences with Great Britain, we see state governments with bills of rights and divisions of power and a closely circumscribed central government. However, many leading Americans felt that the new nation had decentralized too much and that one branch of government—this time state legislatures —again had too much power. Balanced government (the protector of liberty) could be restored only through a stronger central government. In the final analysis, this view won the day with the new Constitution.

Other issues and concepts may also be explored. Disagreement between states over western land policy—an issue with major ramifications through 1865—is reflected in the ratification of the Articles and its potential divisiveness hinted at in the Northwest Ordinance. The importance of compromise to republican government should be emphasized. Other important concepts are sovereignty, bill of rights, nationalism, speculation, national income, and national debt.

TEACHING IDEAS

Section 1

Introduction: We have already discussed the importance of balance in government as a protection of liberty and the colonists' conviction that the balance in the British Constitution was disturbed by the king and his Parliamentary supporters prior to the Revolution. With this background, ask the students what they might expect the structure of the new state governments to look like. (Possible answers: division of authority between branches of government, bill of rights, limited powers to executive or even absence of executive.) Have the students read the section to see if their speculation is accurate.

Development: As we shall see, many contemporaries of the Critical Period argued that during this time the balance in government required to preserve liberty was upset by the concentration of power in the elected representatives of the people, the state legislatures. Ask the students to consider the potential dangers of an unchecked legislature. You might introduce the idea of "tyranny of the majority" and ask what that means.

Section 2

Introduction: As a result of their experience with Great Britain, many Americans were also concerned with power concentrated in a central government removed from the people. As they read, ask the students to look for those aspects of the Articles that reflected this perceived threat to liberty.

Development: Review with the students the reasons for rejection of the Albany Plan of Union (Chapter 3, page 54) and compare those reasons with the difficulties over ratification of the Arti-cles. (The question of control of western lands is central to both.) Why was western land policy important? Tell the students that they will follow the western land question over the next several decades. The land question was one that helped shape many aspects of American society and politics.

Section 3

Introduction: As they read, have students complete the following chart depicting the problems faced by the government of the new nation. Students should fill in the boxes with pertinent details.

Problems of the New Nation	
Foreign	Domestic
Great Britain	Commerce
Spain	Revenue
France	Shays' Rebellion
Barbary Pirates	

Development: Shays' rebellion is often cited as an example of the Confederation's inability to "insure domestic tranquility." For some contemporaries, however, it had a much more serious implication. It again demonstrated that state legislatures were too powerful. A debtor faction could gain control—as they eventually did in Massachusetts—and pass laws favorable to their specific interests. That, of course, infringed upon the rights of the creditors. Many prominent Americans—including George Washington, James Madison, and Alexander Hamilton—felt that the power of the state legislatures had to be balanced with a stronger central government, one which could protect the rights of minorities. After explaining this aspect of the reaction to Shays' Rebellion to the students, have them watch for ways in which the Constitution constrained the powers of state legislatures (especially concerning abrogation of debts and paper money).

Section 4

Introduction: Historian John Fiske (mentioned on page 83) argued that it was the stronger central government under the Constitution that saved the United States after 1789. This is the dominant view among historians. Some historians, however, point out that such a stronger central government was not necessary to the solution of the new nation's problems. Have the students cite the evidence provided in this section that by 1787 many of the problems of the Critical Period had already been solved.

Development: The Northwest Ordinance is generally considered the greatest achievement of Congress under the Articles. Ask the students to state its two most significant aspects (policy for admission of new states and prohibition of slavery). Based on their studies so far, ask the students if this particular combination (new states/prohibition of slavery) suggests future problems for the new nation. Again, this is an area to be watched over the next several decades.

Section 5

Introduction: The subsection "The Delegates" describes a basic consensus among the delegates. Have the students point out the elements of this consensus (men of property and social standing who want economic stability, a strong national government to check irresponsible state legislatures, and a government republican in nature). How are these concerns related to the earlier discussion of Shays' Rebellion?

Development: Despite a basic consensus, compromise was necessary. Have students list the major compromises and then ask if compromise is still an important element in American government today. It is, and almost any current public issue can serve as an example.

Section 6

Introduction: Have the students read the section and list the characteristics and stands of the Federalists and Antifederalists. How does each group reflect aspects of the colonists' thinking prior to and during the Revolution? (Federalists: concern for balance in federal vs. state powers to insure liberty and rights; Antifederalists: strong central government as a threat to liberty.) We see already differing concerns and approaches —shaped by region or economic interest—to a common goal: the protection of liberty.

Development: The Antifederalists are given short shift by history, but the best evidence available indicates that roughly one-half the white voting population was opposed to the new Constitution. The major complaint of the Antifederalists was that the new central government was too strong and thus a threat to the liberty of the people. To many it seemed to put power in the hands of the rich and well-born. Write the following quotations from Antifederalists on the chalkboard and have students analyze them for their concerns. These concerns will appear again over the next few chapters (excluding Chapter 5), as the nation sets out under the Constitution.

"The vast Continent of America cannot be long subjected to a Democracy if consolidated into one government. You might as well attempt to rule Hell by a Prayer." (Thomas Wait)

"We know that private interest governs mankind generally. Power belongs originally to the people; but if rulers be not well guarded, that power will be usurped from them. People ought to be cautious in giving away power." (William Goudy)

"What have you been contending for these ten years past? Liberty! What is liberty? The power of governing yourselves. If you adopt this constitution have you this power?" (James Lincoln)

"(T)he bulk of the people can have nothing to say to it. The government is *not* a government of the people." (Samuel Chase)

"The natural Course of Power is to make the many Slaves to the few." (William Findley)

"(The new government) will fall into the hands of the few and the great. This will be a government of oppression." (Melancton Smith)

Conclusion: Have students reread Madison's defense of strong national government in *The Federalist*, No. 14 (page 95). Then ask students to restate Madison's argument in their own words. What reassurance was he offering?

ANSWERS
Section Review Questions
page 81
1. Because colonial governments were disintegrating.
2. The state legislatures.
3. The legislative branch of government.
4. Through the popular election of state legislators and other officials.

page 83
1. Each state could send as many as seven delegates to Congress but had only one vote.
2. The Confederation government was granted the powers to declare war and make peace, settle disputes between the states, coin and borrow money, establish weights and measures, regulate Indian affairs beyond state boundaries, and requisition men and money from the states.

3. The powers of Congress were limited by the fact that it could not enforce its decisions and by the number of votes needed to carry legislation.
4. Ratification was delayed by conflicts over state claims to western lands and the fact that unanimous approval was needed to put the Articles into effect.
5. The realization that a central government was necessary to win the war for independence.

page 87
1. Critical Period—The years between 1781 and 1789 when the Articles of Confederation were in effect.
   John Jay—Confederation's secretary for foreign affairs.
   Barbary Pirates—Pirates from North Africa who preyed on ships sailing the Mediterranean Sea.
   Daniel Shays—Bankrupt farmer and former captain in the Continental army who led a rebellion of debtor-farmers in western Massachusetts.
2. During the Critical Period, the British refused to evacuate the Northwest Territory and dictated the terms under which the United States could trade with the British Empire. Spain withdrew the right of deposit at the mouth of the Mississippi River, Franco-American relations deteriorated, and the Barbary Pirates attacked American ships in the Mediterranean Sea.
3. American manufacturing had developed during the war when trade with Great Britain had broken off. With the coming of peace, British goods flooded the American market, prices dropped, and American manufacturing could not compete.
4. By requisitioning money from the states, borrowing money from foreign and domestic sources, printing paper money, and selling western lands.

page 89
1. Foreign trade was expanding, domestic manufacturing had grown substantially, the national income was increasing, Congress was beginning to pay the interest on the national debt, and the states were working their way out of the financial difficulties resulting from the war.
2. Foreign affairs, finance, and war.

3. The Land Ordinance of 1785, by providing for the survey and sale of western lands, set the precedent for national land policies and speeded up settlement of the Northwest.
4. The Northwest Ordinance provided that, at first, a territory would be ruled by a governor, a secretary, and three judges. When the number of free adult males reached 5000, the voters could choose people to represent them in a general assembly. When the number of free inhabitants reached 60,000, the voters could elect delegates to a convention to frame a state constitution. Once this constitution was approved by Congress, that part of the Northwest Territory would be admitted as a state.

page 93
1. Virginia Plan—Proposal for the creation of a national government superior to the states.
   William Paterson—Delegate to the Constitutional Convention from New Jersey who proposed the New Jersey Plan.
   New Jersey Plan—Proposal for a new central government that granted additional powers to the central government but retained state sovereignty.
   Roger Sherman—Delegate to the Constitutional Convention from Connecticut who first proposed the Great Compromise.
2. To discuss commercial problems.
3. Most of the delegates at the Constitutional Convention were distinguished patriots of property and social standing who were well-educated and experienced in government.
4. The need for a new constitution that had certain constraints built into it and that set up a strong central government, republican in nature.
5. The Great Compromise provided for a bicameral legislature, consisting of a House of Representatives and a Senate. The voters in each state would elect the members of the lower house, while the members of the upper house would be chosen by the state legislatures. Each state would be represented by two Senators and would have equal power in the Senate. In the House, the number of representatives would be based on population.
6. The Three-fifths Compromise provided that for the purposes of taxation and representation, one slave would count as three-fifths of a

person, or five slaves would count as three people.

page 96
1. Federalists—Supporters of the Constitution who favored a strong central government.

   Antifederalists—Opponents of the Constitution who favored state sovereignty over a strong central government.

   George Mason—Leader of the Antifederalists in Virginia.

   George Clinton—Leader of the Antifederalists in New York.

   The Federalist—A series of essays written by Alexander Hamilton, James Madison, and John Jay, which set forth the Federalist view and played an important role in the struggle over ratification in New York.
2. Nine states had to vote in favor of ratification.
3. Small subsistence farmers tended to oppose the Constitution, while people involved in commerce tended to support it.
4. Better organization, outstanding leadership, and political guile.

Photo Captions

page 82
A guarantee that each state would retain its sovereignty and "every power not expressly delegated to Congress."

page 83
The Confederation lacked power.

page 84
Easterners gained from the treaty since all goods would have to be shipped from and to eastern ports. Transportation costs to these ports from the West were high.

page 86
It had no power to collect taxes or control the amount of money that the states printed.

page 87
It led to support for a stronger national government.

page 88
That, at first, the territory was to be ruled by a governor, a secretary, and three judges named by Congress. When the number of free male adults in an area reached 5000, the voters could choose people to represent them.

Chapter Review

page 97, Review Questions
1. Most state constitutions began with a bill of rights and went on to divide authority between a governor, a legislature, and a judiciary.
2. The states retained most of the power while the national government's powers were limited. The national government could not even enforce the powers it did have and thus could not deal effectively with the problems facing the new nation.
3. Because Congress could not make the states comply with the provisions of the Treaty of Paris (1783), the British refused to evacuate the Northwest Territory and to negotiate a commercial treaty with the United States. Spain withdrew the right of deposit at the mouth of the Mississippi River, which closed the river and deprived westerners of their major avenue of trade. The Barbary Pirates virtually drove American ships from the Mediterranean Sea because Congress was, for the most part, unable to provide adequate naval protection or pay the tribute demanded by the pirates.
4. It could not regulate commerce or impose taxes.
5. When the Massachusetts legislature refused to pass measures that would relieve the money shortage felt by the many debtor-farmers who could not pay their bills, farmers in the western part of the state rebelled. Although the revolt was put down in 1787, debtor-farmers later gained control of the Massachusetts' legislature and passed relief measures. The rebellion demonstrated to many Americans that the state legislatures had too much power, which led to demands for a stronger national government.
6. Economic recovery, the creation of a national bureaucracy, and creation of the public domain.
7. Congressional representation, the division of power between the states and the national government, and the granting of commercial powers to Congress.
8. The national government was given the power to regulate trade and levy import taxes.
9. The Constitution set up a strong central government capable of handling the problems

facing the United States, which the Federalists felt was necessary. The Antifederalists felt that a strong central government was a threat to liberty, that the new government would be too removed from the people, and that the Constitution needed a bill of rights.

page 97, Discussion
1. Shays' Rebellion was symptomatic of the chaos and conflict of the Critical Period and indicated the need for reorganizing the country. Point out that while the rebellion highlighted economic elements, it was also symptomatic of class struggle and political chaos (factional power).
2. Answers may vary. Students should identify the sources of revenue discussed in the text and recognize that various groups of people (e.g., speculators, bankers, etc.) would view the issue differently.
3. Answers may vary. Possible alternatives include: the convention would break up and government under the Articles would continue, the delegates would seek another compromise, and the convention would adopt either the Virginia or New Jersey Plan.

4. Answers may vary. Students should be able to support either position with arguments presented in the text.
5. Students should be able to analyze the quotation in relation to data in the chapter regarding foreign threats and domestic problems.
6. Answers may vary.

page 97, Using Maps
1. Parts of Alabama and Mississippi.
2. Between Mississippi River and boundaries of the states.
3. Georgia, South Carolina, North Carolina, and Virginia.
4. 23,040 acres.

page 97, Using Skills
1. South.
2. North.
3. North.
4. South.
5. North.
6. North.
7. South.
8. South.

CHAPTER 5 THE CONSTITUTION

After studying this chapter, the student should be able to:

1. describe the historical background for the development of American constitutional government.
2. explain the division of powers between federal and state governments.
3. differentiate the functions of the three branches of government and outline the system of checks and balances.
4. outline the process by which a bill becomes a law.
5. describe aspects of the evolution of democracy in the United States.
6. explain ways in which the Constitution may be changed.

OVERVIEW

Chapter 5 is designed specifically for those teachers who are required to spend a certain amount of time on the Constitution in their United States history courses. In conjunction with the annotated Constitution found on pages 773-790, a thorough study of the document can be pursued.

The first section sets the historical background for the Constitution, pulling together a number of themes considered in the earlier chapters. The remaining sections consider a number of the major aspects of American constitutional government from a political science perspective: the federal system, separation of power and checks and balances, the legislative process, the evolution of democracy, and amending the Constitution. Most of the sections afford the teacher the opportunity to consider current legislative concerns. Other important concepts are natural rights, social contracts, limited government, federalism, due process, hierarchy of laws, judicial review, and strict versus loose construction of the Constitution.

TEACHING IDEAS

Section 1

Introduction: A good deal of time has already been spent considering Americans' concern for balance in government. Have the students read the profile of James Madison on page 101 as a springboard into a review of the concept of balance, then have them read the section.

Development: American constitutional government is very much a child of Enlightenment thought. Colonial and early national experience reflected many of the ideas of Enlightenment theorists. Have the students complete the following chart:

Enlightenment Concept	American Experience	
	Colonial	Early National
Natural Rights		
Social Contract		
Limited Government		
Separation of Powers		
Hierarchy of Laws		

Section 2

Introduction: Have the students study the chart on the Bill of Rights on page 105. How does the Bill of Rights limit government? Have the students read the section looking for powers and limitations.

Development: Have the students define expressed, implied, inherent, reserved, and concurrent powers and give an example of each. For a more complete study, have the students read the pertinent sections of the annotated Constitution in the Appendix. The powers denied the federal and state governments should also be reviewed.

Section 3

Introduction: Again the theme is paramount: Remind students of balance in the British Constitution, so lauded by Montesquieu, and have them read the section looking for similarities.

Development: Have students review the idea of checks and balances, pointing out how it works in our federal government. Today, a number of observers argue that the system of checks and balances is outdated, keeping the United States from effectively treating national problems. Choose a current piece of legislation or issue over which the President and Congress are at odds and explore this criticism.

Section 4

Introduction: Literally thousands of bills are introduced into Congress during a session, but very few become law. Tell the students to record the number of places where a bill might die as they read through this section.

Development: Create a hypothetical bill based upon a student interest and trace it through the legislative process, pointing out how it might be changed or dropped along the way. For example, discuss the hypothetical fate of a bill to introduce a lower minimum wage for teenagers. Who would lobby for or against it? What stands might the major parties take (assuming union influence on Democrats and management's influence on Republicans)? If there is an actual bill of interest currently being considered, you might have students research its progress.

Section 5

Introduction: During the 1700's, many political thinkers equated democracy with mob rule (thus irresponsible and dangerous to liberty). Obviously, the United States has moved a long way from this idea. As students read this section, have them look for the ways political democracy has increased over the years.

Development: Have students speculate over the advantages and disadvantages of direct election of the President. How does the idea of direct election demonstrate this country's movement away from that earlier concept of democracy as mob rule?

Section 6

Introduction: Have the students analyze the chart "Amending the Constitution" on page 115 then read the section looking for other ways the Constitution has changed through the years.

Development: Have the students outline the section, "The Unwritten Constitution."

Conclusion: Have students read the first ten amendments to the Constitution (see Appendix, pages 784-785) and the annotations on each. Ask students to give examples of current events or issues in which these rights have been exercised or have come into question.

ANSWERS

Section Review Questions

page 101
1. Delegates were influenced by Enlightenment philosophers such as Locke and Montesquieu.
2. The people will obey the government and the government will protect the people.
3. The natural law giving the people their rights.
4. The state constitutions set up limited governments with separation of powers. Most power was vested in the legislatures.
5. The Constitution would be ratified by the states. Government power would be limited, and power would be divided between the national and state governments, with the Constitution being the highest law.

page 104
1. Congress has the right to tax, regulate commerce, raise and maintain the armed forces, coin money, and declare war. The President may make treaties, appoint officials, serve as commander-in-chief of the military, and grant pardons.
2. The "necessary and proper" clause—Article I, Sec. 8.
3. Defending the nation, gaining territory and regulating immigration.
4. The Tenth Amendment says that those powers not given to the national government or denied to the states are reserved to the states.
5. The national government cannot suspend or violate certain legal rights, including those guaranteed by the Bill of Rights. Until 1808 the national government could not interfere with the slave trade. It also cannot levy export taxes.

page 110
1. To make laws.
2. The House would be more responsive to the will of the people. The Senate would be more removed from the pressures of public opinion and could be more deliberative.

3. Chief administrator or chief diplomat and commander-in-chief of the Armed Forces. Also has the power to recommend legislation and sign veto bills.
4. Electors are pledged to vote for a specific candidate and are chosen by popular vote in state elections. Meeting in their own states, the electors cast their votes for President. The winner of the popular vote in each state receives all of that state's electoral vote. The candidate with the most electoral votes is elected to the Presidency.
5. Interpreting the laws.

page 112
1. Revenue bills.
2. Checks whether to study a bill in detail or "pigeonhole" it. May hold public hearings. May approve the bill or make changes before the bill is "reported out" for vote on the floor.
3. In the House, members may speak for no more than one hour. In the Senate, debate is unlimited unless three-fifths of the Senate votes to invoke cloture.
4. To "iron out" differences in House and Senate versions of the same bill.
5. It goes back to Congress, where a two-thirds vote of each house is needed to override the veto.

page 114
1. To help people get elected to office and provide a source of ideas on issues and policies.
2. Candidates organize campaigns to win primaries or get support from state delegates at the party's national convention. Nominations are heard and a majority vote of the delegates decides the party's candidate.
3. It allows for a President to be elected without receiving a majority of the popular vote.
4. In 1787 Senators were chosen by state legislatures. Now Senators are elected directly by voters.

page 116
1. An amendment must be proposed by a two-thirds vote of each House or the vote of a special convention called by Congress at the request of two-thirds of the states. The amendment then needs approval by three-fourths of the state legislatures or state conventions.
2. Through the process of judicial review.

3. Passed laws that fill in the vague areas of the Constitution, set up the court system, created the executive departments and passed laws to cover unforeseen problems.
4. Through executive agreements, using the military without declaration of war, and through the setting of precedents.

Special Feature Questions
page 107
1. Fear of monarchy.
2. The great respect for his military achievements and integrity influenced many to give the Presidency great power.

Photo Questions
page 102
Article 1, Section 8 gives the national government power to raise and maintain armed forces.

page 103
A power not given specifically to the national government but which it possesses simply because it is a national government.

page 106
They set up a bicameral legislature with differences between the houses in the terms of office and methods of selecting legislators.

page 108
The power to decide the constitutionality of a government's action.

page 110
They are "pigeon-holed"; in effect, killed.

page 113
In a few states they are chosen by the party; in others, the voters choose the delegates in a presidential primary election.

Chapter Review
page 119, Review Questions
1. By the limits placed on government through the federal structure, the separation and balance of powers, and the listing of specific powers granted or denied to national and state governments. Also, the Constitution was to be the supreme law of the land (hierarchy of laws) and was to be ratified by the people through state conventions (popular sovereignty).

2. By expanding the powers of the national government—providing for a strong executive, giving more powers to the legislature, and providing the basis for a national court system.
3. To provide a strong national government and at the same time to preserve state sovereignty.
4. Has allowed the powers of the national government to be greatly expanded.
5. The President can veto laws passed by Congress and appoint judges to federal courts. Congress can override the presidential veto, confirm appointments, change the number of justices in the courts, change the lower court system and impeach justices. The judiciary has the power of judicial review.
6. It indicates a concern on the part of the authors of the Constitution about an "excess of democracy" and the possibility of unwise choices by the common people.
7. The process includes the introduction of the bill into both Houses, standing committees, hearings, debate and voting on the floor, conference committees and presentation to the President for his signature or veto.
8. By organizing campaigns to present issues and the views of candidates for public office and by holding conventions to choose candidates.
9. Interpretation and the amendment process give the Constitution flexibility needed to remain a viable framework of government as the nation develops and changes.

page 117, Discussion
1. Students should identify what was said in the Declaration of Independence, the influence of Enlightenment ideas, the English tradition of government, the problems under the Articles of Confederation, problems states had regulating interstate commerce, inflation, etc.
2. Answers may vary. Teachers should point out historical shifts in power, especially the expanded powers of the President under certain executives and the expanded powers of the judiciary. Much of the shift in power is due to the vagueness of the Constitution in certain areas, allowing for interpretation.
3. Answers may vary. Students are most likely to mention criticism of the electoral college system.
4. Answers may vary.

5. Answers may vary.

page 117, Using Charts
1. True.
2. True.
3. False.

4. True.
5. False.

page 117, Using Skills
Governor, state legislatures, President, Congress.

CHAPTER **6** # THE FEDERALIST ERA

After studying this chapter, the student should be able to:

1. list the first acts of Congress and the President in launching the new government.
2. outline Hamilton's economic program.
3. describe the development of the first political parties.
4. outline the nation's early foreign policy, including problems with both Britain and France.
5. describe the relationship between foreign policy issues during the Adams' administration and domestic politics, especially with reference to the election of 1800.

OVERVIEW

This chapter surveys the events of the Washington and Adams administrations. Disagreement over Hamilton's domestic policy and differing views of the French Revolution lead to the development of political parties.

Some major themes which should be pursued include the similarities between some Antifederalist and Jeffersonian-Republican fears over the strength of the central government, the philosophy behind Hamilton's economic program, and the differing approaches of Federalists and Republicans to the same goal—the preservation of liberty. Important concepts in this chapter are compromise, protectionism, laissez-faire, neutrality, and states' rights (nullification).

Section 1

Introduction: The discussion of Chapter 4 included the importance of compromise. Write the definition of compromise on the board (to adjust or settle by mutual concessions) and have students look for continuing evidence of compromise in this section.

Development: Section 6 of Chapter 5 discussed the ways in which the Constitution has been changed over time. Review this section, then have students point out examples in the current lesson.

Section 2

Introduction: A major concern of the Antifederalists was that the new Constitution gave too much power to the central government and that government would be controlled by the few. Review these concerns—discussed at some length earlier in Chapter 4, Section 6—then have the students read this section. What might have been the reaction to Hamilton's program of those who suspected the new government?

Development: Hamilton's plan has been called neo-mercantilistic. Although it did not concern itself with the flow of specie, it did represent a great degree of government interference with the economy. Have the students outline those aspects of the plan that provided government interference to foster the nation's economic growth. Have them look especially closely at both the Bank of the United States and the tariff proposals, as both will play significant roles for years to come.

Section 3

Introduction: In the introduction to Chapter 4, Section 6, you held a discussion concerning the different approaches Federalists and Antifederalists took to the same goal, the protection of liberty. Review that discussion and have students read this section with the earlier distinctions in mind.

Development: Have the students list the similarities between the ideas of the Antifederalists and those of the new Jeffersonian-Republicans (fear of strong central government, rule by a wealthy aristocracy). Ask them to describe how the concept of laissez-faire suited this political outlook (If government does not interfere, it does not need to be strong). How did the Federalists' approach to government reflect their appreciation for the British Constitution (page 125)? Why did the Federalists so greatly fear too much democracy? Demagogues? The chart on page 128 can be used to summarize the differing views of Hamilton and Jefferson.

Section 4

Introduction: Review the reasons cited in the previous discussion for Federalists' fear of "too much liberty." Have the students read this section (especially its introduction) and explain why Federalists would be so alarmed over the French Revolution.

Development: Despite the rising political tensions, the three treaties discussed in this section proved beneficial to the young United States. Have the students list the benefits to the United States of each treaty (answers all on page 132). Review the major themes of Washington's Farewell Address, focusing on the excerpt on page 133.

Section 5

Introduction: Review the original Constitutional guidelines concerning the election of the President and Vice President, then have the students read this section for the problems with the 1796 and 1800 elections. What constitutional changes have been made since? (The Twelfth and Twenty-fifth Amendments deal with election and succession.)

Development: Have students reread the paragraph beginning at the bottom of the first column on page 120 concerning Madison's attempt to balance liberty and authority. Have the students describe how the Alien and Sedition Acts and the Virginia and Kentucky Resolutions reflect the tension in American history between

liberty and authority. Which of the above reflects concern with authority, which with liberty? In this particular debate, where did Madison stand?

Conclusion: Have students read the "Perspectives" feature, "Freedom of Expression," and answer the questions that follow. What current issues are concerned with freedom of speech and freedom of the press?

ANSWERS
Section Review Questions
page 122

1. Judiciary Act of 1789—Set up the organization of the federal courts with a Supreme Court, an Attorney General, and district and circuit courts.

   Henry Knox—Washington's Secretary of War.

   Edmund Randolph—First Attorney General.

   John Jay—First Chief Justice.
2. Instituted tariffs and tonnage duties.
3. A number of states had ratified the Constitution with the understanding that a bill of rights would be added, and Madison wanted the Federalists to keep their promise in order to gain support for the new federal government.
4. The Departments of State, War and Treasury.
5. Character and experience, political ramifications, and regional balance.

page 126

1. By issuing new certificates that promised to repay holders of the debt at par.
2. Some members of Congress opposed Hamilton's plan because they felt it was too expensive; others felt that the original holders rather than speculators should be paid.
3. Because northern states had the largest debts.
4. To control private banks, provide a stable national currency, tie the interests of the wealthy to the federal government and broaden the powers of the federal government.
5. The strict constructionists, led by Madison and Jefferson, questioned the constitutionality of the Bank.
6. He believed that a strong economy had to include industry.

7. To raise money for the government, to challenge western farmers who tended to be Antifederalists, and to gain respect for the federal government by enforcing the tax.

page 129
1. Southern planters thought Hamilton's program favored northern business, while former Antifederalists and others thought too much power was being given to the central government.
2. He trusted farmers, thought farming taught virtue, and believed there would be less need for government interference in an agrarian economy.
3. They feared the "tyranny of the majority" and thought that too much liberty would lead to instability and eventually to the loss of freedom.
4. Each party supported newspapers—The *Gazette of the United States* and the *National Gazette*—to present the party views and criticize opposition leaders.

page 133
1. Edmond Genêt—French minister to the United States who tried to get American help against the British. His actions were intolerable to Washington and strained U.S.—French relations.
   Gouverneur Morris—American ambassador to France at the time of the Genêt affair.
   Pinckney Treaty—An agreement with Spain giving Americans the right of deposit at New Orleans and navigation rights on the Mississippi and setting the northern boundary of Florida.
   Anthony Wayne—General who defeated the Indians at Fallen Timbers in the Northwest Territory.
2. To show that the United States did not intend to take sides in European wars.
3. The British continued to capture merchant ships, impressed American sailors, failed to remove their troops from the Northwest frontier, and sold weapons to the Indians.
4. To avoid war with Britain.
5. Spain was doing poorly in a war against France and feared British reactions to a separate peace with France. To combat a possible Anglo-American alliance, Spain wanted to resolve differences with the United States.
6. Warnings against political parties and entanglement in foreign affairs.

page 137
1. Aaron Burr—Republican Vice-President under Jefferson.
   Charles C. Pinckney—American ambassador to France who was ordered to leave the country by France as a protest to the Jay Treaty.
   Directory—Group that ran the government during the French Revolution.
   Talleyrand—French Foreign Minister under the Directory.
   Convention of 1800—An agreement between France and the United States to end the undeclared naval war.
2. Adams' cabinet was inherited from Washington and its members were loyal to Alexander Hamilton.
3. Public opinion in the United States turned against France.
4. The Federalists, expecting war with France, hoped to suppress the Republicans, who were pro-French.
5. By passing the Kentucky and Virginia Resolutions.

Special Feature Questions
page 135
1. Freedom of speech, the press, religion, assembly, and the right to petition.
2. Libel and conflict with public safety or national security.
3. It is not against the law to advocate certain beliefs, but it is against the law to advocate certain actions that conflict with public safety or national security.

Photo Questions
page 120
Southern planters used foreign ships for much of their trade.

page 121
To bring respect to the office of President.

page 125
He looked for people who had character and experience and tried to keep a regional and political balance.

page 126
That the government was able to act decisively in an emergency.

page 129
With the retirement of Washington, the differences between Federalists and Republicans multiplied.

page 131
He issued a Proclamation of Neutrality.

page 132
It opened more territory for settlement and reduced the danger of Indian attack.

page 134
The Federalists had raised taxes to pay for military expenses, and the people felt that the Bill of Rights had been attacked with the passing of the Alien and Sedition Acts.

Chapter Review

Page 138, Review Questions

1. The creation of a dual court system, creation of the cabinet, the way of making political appointments, the relationship between the President and the Congress, and standards of presidential etiquette.
2. In the Tariff of 1789 the issue of revenue vs. protective duties was worked out in a compromise between northern and southern states; in the Judiciary Act of 1789, maintenance of a separate state court system as well as a federal system was a compromise between supporters of strong federal government and supporters of states' rights; the decision to put the nation's capital in the South in exchange for approval of Hamilton's plan for funding and assumption was a North-South compromise.
3. He played a crucial role in passing the Tariff of 1789, in adding the Bill of Rights to the Constitution, and in creating executive departments to aid the President. He also organized the opposition to Hamilton and helped to found the Republican party.
4. Federalists believed that the educated property-holding classes should rule, while Republicans had more faith in the common people. Federalists believed in a stronger role for the federal government based on a broader interpretation of the Constitution, and Federalists were pro-British while the Republicans were pro-French.
5. The Proclamation of Neutrality, the Jay and Pinckney Treaties, the rejection of Genêt's overtures, attempts to negotiate (the XYZ Affair), and the Convention of 1800.
6. The resolutions argued that states had a right to nullify federal laws and set a precedent for future states' rights advocates.
7. The death of George Washington, controversy over the Alien and Sedition Acts, factionalism within the party, resentment of tax increases and military expansion, and the growing democratic spirit of the nation.
8. Setting up the machinery of the federal government and establishing the power and authority of the government at home and abroad.

page 138, Discussion

1. Answers may vary, but might include the need for regulating employer-employee relations and the need for safety and health standards.
2. Answers may vary.
3. Answers may vary.
4. Answers may vary.

page 138, Using Maps

1. 73.
2. North Carolina, Delaware, Pennsylvania, Rhode Island.
3. Virginia.
4. Tennessee, Delaware.

page 138, Using Skills

2. The United States should have as little political connection as possible with foreign countries.

Unit Review

page 139, Review Questions

1. Foreign problems (Great Britain, Spain, France, Barbary Pirates); domestic problems (depression, lack of revenue, Shays' Rebellion); problem of western lands. The Confederation government was unable to respond adequately to foreign threats and most domestic problems, but dealt with western lands in the Land Ordinance of 1785 and the Northwest Ordinance. The nation responded by moving toward recognizing the need for a stronger central government.
2. Issue of representation in Congress, resolved by Great Compromise and Three-fifths Compromise (also resolved taxation issue); issue of regulating commerce, solved by giving

government power to regulate commerce but no power to interfere with slave trade until 1808 or to tax exports.

3. Answers may vary.

4. Passed revenue bill (tariff of 1789), Bill of Rights, created cabinet offices, set up court system, assumed debts of states, set up national bank, passed excise tax, crushed Whiskey Rebellion, negotiated treaties (Jay, Pinckney, Greenville), carried on undeclared naval war with France, passed Alien and Sedition Acts.

The Historian's Craft

Conclude the unit with The Historian's Craft in the Unit Review. In this activity, which may be used as an individual or group exercise, students are given practice in distinguishing between primary and secondary sources that concern the relationship between Shays' Rebellion and the Constitution. Students should develop the understanding that secondary sources are derived from primary sources and/or secondary sources, and that primary sources offer the evidence to support or refute a secondary source argument.

The Using Skills activities in this unit have included categorizing information, analyzing relationships (comparison), and finding the main idea. These experiences should help the student to categorize primary and secondary resources and understand the points being made by the two readings in the activity and the relationship between the two.

The resources listed on page 40 are (1) primary, (2) secondary, (3) primary, (4) secondary. Make sure students understand that Fiske is the historian who originated the term, "Critical Period."

Questions 1-3. The editorial, appearing after the completion of the Constitution, favors the Constitution as a device that would end the rebellion of Shays and others who oppose a strong central government.

Question 4. The textbook account cites Shays' Rebellion as one of the factors that led to the Constitution (an effort to assure domestic tranquility). Note the reference to the Critical Period, which indicates that the textbook derived its account from another secondary source.

UNIT 3 NATIONALISM AND SECTIONALISM

At the conclusion of this unit, the student should be able to:

1. describe the major actions of the Jeffersonian-Republican administrations.
2. explain why the period 1828-1840 is called the "Age of Jackson."
3. describe the impact of westward expansion on American development.
4. profile antebellum American society and culture.

OVERVIEW

This unit narrates the history of the United States from the Jeffersonian Presidency through the antebellum era. The major theme is the development of contrasting nationalism and sectionalism. The unit provides more than a political narrative, however, as major social and cultural developments are surveyed. Among these we see the impact of the frontier, new industrialism, and urbanization.

INTRODUCING THE UNIT

Ask students what it means to be proud of being an American. How is this different from being proud of being a resident of a state or region? What aspects of this pride existed in the early 1800's? List student responses on the chalkboard and tell students to look for the development of these aspects in the unit.

CHAPTER 7 THE JEFFERSONIAN REPUBLICANS

After studying this chapter, the student should be able to:

1. explain how Thomas Jefferson as President was both an idealist and pragmatist.
2. describe American attempts to remain neutral during the Napoleonic wars.
3. discuss major aspects of the War of 1812.
4. contrast the growth of American nationalism to continued sectional differences.

OVERVIEW

This chapter surveys events during the administrations of Jefferson, Madison, and Monroe, "the Jeffersonians." Transition to a Republican administration—including a discussion of Jefferson's moderation—Jefferson's attempts to keep us out of war, the War of 1812, and rising nationalism and sectionalism are the major topics.

A number of themes can be developed with this chapter. First, the peaceful transition from a Federalist to Republican administration was remarkable in its time, although now commonplace. The modification of Jefferson's laissez-faire ideals is always a topic of debate. The failure of economic coercion to maintain American neutrality provides a lesson for the present. Finally, national and sectional issues will be central to the next several chapters. Important concepts in this chapter are nationalism, patronage, judicial review, neutrality, protectionism (Clay's American System), sanctity of contracts, compromise (Missouri), and states' rights.

TEACHING IDEAS

Section 1

Introduction: The peaceful transition from a Federalist to a Republican administration was remarkable because many developing nations today, recently freed from colonial status, are unable to make such changes. A major reason for our ability to make these transitions might be the fact that Americans tend to be pragmatic, or practical. Write the definition of pragmatism, "a practical approach to problems and affairs," on the board and have students give examples of how they are pragmatic in their own lives. Do they sometimes have to modify their ideals? Have them review Jefferson's ideas as presented in the chart on page 128, then read this section. As they read, have them jot down examples of Jefferson's pragmatism, then discuss them with the class.

Development: In earlier discussions of balance in government, a good deal of emphasis was placed on the role of the independent judiciary. An independent judiciary is supposed to help protect liberty. Why did Jefferson perceive the judiciary as a threat? How did *Marbury* v. *Madison* establish judicial review?

Section 2

Introduction: As the Napoleonic Wars continued, they impinged on American neutrality. Jefferson attempted to maintain neutrality through economic coercion of the belligerents—the Embargo and Non-Intercourse Acts. You might mention some recent attempts to use economic coercion in diplomacy—Carter during the Afghanistan (vs. Russia) and Iranian (freezing Iran's assets) crises, Reagan with the European natural gas pipeline—and point out their failures. Have the students read the section, looking for evidence of success or failure of Jefferson's policies. Afterward, ask the students if we should have learned something from our early history.

Development: The War of 1812 has frequently been presented as a war fought in defense of "freedom of the seas." Remind students that the region whose people were being impressed by the British was the Northeast. Have the students review the reasons New Englanders were most opposed to war, while southerners and westerners were in favor of it.

Section 3

Introduction: American naiveté upon entering the War of 1812 was incredible, both in terms of lack of preparedness and poor military strategy. The following passage from S.E. Morison's *Oxford History of the American People* sets the stage for the first part of the war:

"The administration's military strategy was as stupid as its diplomacy. The settled portions of Canada (excluding the Maritimes) may be compared to a tree, of which the St. Lawrence river was the trunk, the Great Lakes and their tributaries the branches, and the sea lanes to England the roots. Britain had conquered Canada in 1759-60 by grasping the roots and grappling the trunk. Madison had no proper navy to attempt the former; but he might well have tried to hew the trunk by a sharp stroke at Montreal or Quebec. Instead, he attempted several feeble and unsystematic loppings at the branches."[5]

Although the U.S. was never very successful on the offensive, the defensive war was another story. Have students read the section to see why this was true.

Development: It is interesting to explore the complete about-face of some New England Federalists who had been nationalists at an earlier time. Have the students describe the changes in the Federalist position as reflected in the Hartford Convention.

Section 4

Introduction: Have the students read the essay on Nationalism in the "Perspectives in History" feature on page 160, then ask them what expressions of nationalism they see today. Have them read the section looking for early examples of the phenomenon.

Development: A review of the section may be achieved by having students complete a chart similar to the one below. Have them fill in appropriate information in each column.

Nationalism			
Economic	Judicial	Foreign Affairs	Cultural

[5]Samuel Eliot Morison, *The Oxford History of the American People* (New York: Oxford University Press, 1965), pp. 383-384.

Section 5

Introduction: Ask students what they think was the most devisive sectional issue in early American history. They will probably mention slavery. Ask them why they mentioned the issues they did, then have them read the section looking for these and other issues.

Development: One of the most crucial political issues faced during the 1830's will be that of the Second Bank of the United States, chartered in 1816. It is especially important to understand the bank's function and the resentment that grew over it. Have the students review the discussion of the first BUS on page 124. The Second Bank followed that model. Why was the Bank so powerful? What happened in 1819 to cause so much resentment toward the Bank? Keep these ideas in mind for the next chapter.

Conclusion: Ask students what regions exist in the United States today. How do they differ in their economic and political interests? Is there still evidence of the sectional divisions that existed in the early 1800's?

ANSWERS

Section Review Questions

page 150

1. Albert Gallatin—Secretary of Treasury under Thomas Jefferson; developed a plan to pay national debts by reducing expenses.

   Judiciary Act of 1801—Act passed at the end of the Adams' administration; added new judgeships to which Adams appointed loyal Federalists.

   John Pickering—Federal district judge impeached as part of Jefferson's battle with the judiciary.

   Robert R. Livingston—Minister to France who helped negotiate the Louisiana Purchase.

   Tripoli—One of Barbary states which demanded tribute from the U.S., provoking Jefferson to enforce a naval blockade.

   Toussaint L'Overture—Leader of black slave revolt in Haiti.

2. Promised to pay the debt, encourage commerce and preserve the continuity of government. Left intact many Federalist programs, including the Bank.

3. Allowed the Alien and Sedition Acts to expire, freed people imprisoned under the acts, repealed the Judiciary Act of 1801 (thus eliminating the midnight appointments), reduced the size of the army and navy, and repealed the whiskey tax. Jefferson removed many Federalists from appointive offices.

4. In *Marbury* vs. *Madison* the Supreme Court established the principle of judicial review.

5. Jefferson had philosophical reservations about the constitutional right of the federal government to make the Louisiana Purchase, but he was more influenced by the benefits to the United States of controlling the Mississippi and New Orleans and by his fear of the French presence in the West.

6. Some Federalists felt the purchase of Louisiana would further weaken their voice in government. They also felt that the territory was too expensive and that the power of the national government had been stretched too far.

page 153

1. Berlin decree—Issued by Napoleon prohibiting ships that stopped in British ports from landing in any other port under French control.

   Chesapeake—Neutral U.S. ship attacked by British in 1807, causing Americans to call for war against Britain.

   Embargo Act—Prohibited American ships from trading in any foreign port.

   Tecumseh—Shawnee Indian leader who, with his brother the Prophet, organized an Indian confederation to resist white encroachment on Indian lands.

   "war hawks"—Members of Congress from the West and South who wanted war with Great Britain.

2. Both France and Great Britain issued rules limiting where Americans could trade, and seized American ships that violated their rules. Britain also seized British-born American citizens from U.S. ships and impressed them into the British navy.

3. It was ineffective against the British but hurt the American economy.

4. Napoleon promised to revoke his Berlin and Milan Decrees if the United States would restrict trade with Great Britain, causing Madison to announce that an embargo against Britain would go into effect if the Orders in

Council were not revoked. However, the French continued to attack American ships.

5. Westerners blamed Britain for cutting off their European market and for inciting Indian uprising, and wanted Canadian lands. Southerners wanted land held by Spain, Britain's ally, and blamed the British for economic hard times.

page 157

1. "Old Ironsides"—The U.S.S. *Constitution*, which got its nickname because British cannonballs bounced off its sides.

   Captain Oliver Perry—American naval officer who defeated the British on Lake Erie.

   Battle of the Thames—Battle in which the Americans under William Harrison defeated the British and their Indian allies in Canada. Battle in which Tecumseh was killed.

   Francis Scott Key—Wrote the "Star-Spangled Banner" about the American defense of Fort McHenry.

   General Andrew Jackson—Won outstanding victory over British at New Orleans.

2. Public opinion was divided, Congress had not passed war taxes, the Charter of the Bank of the United States had expired and financing was difficult, Republicans had cut back military forces, and Congress was unable to pass a draft law.

3. Napoleon had been defeated and Britain could concentrate on defeating the U.S.

4. Restored the way things were before the war and set up commissions to settle issues such as boundary disputes between the U.S. and Canada.

5. Its proposals arrived in Washington at the same time as news of Jackson's victory at New Orleans and the Treaty of Ghent. Proposals to restrict federal power were out of tune with the spirit of the times.

page 161

1. Bonus Bill of 1816—Calhoun's bill to set up fund for internal improvements. Vetoed by Madison.

   McCulloch v. *Maryland*—Supreme Court case in which Bank of the U.S. was declared constitutional on the basis of the elastic clause, and a state law taxing the Bank was found unconstitutional.

Adams-Onís Treaty—Treaty by which Spain gave up Florida and any claims to Oregon while the U.S. gave up claims to Texas as part of the Louisiana Purchase and assumed $5 million in damage claims against Spain.

Noah Webster—Wrote the *American Dictionary of the English Language*.

2. A central bank, a protective tariff and federal support for internal improvements.

3. That the Western Hemisphere was closed to colonization, that the U.S. would not interfere in European colonies or internal affairs, and that any European interference in the Western Hemisphere would be looked on as a threat to the United States.

4. The development of the Hudson Valley school, the writings of Irving, Cooper and Bryant, and the work of Webster.

page 164

1. Samuel Slater—Brought designs for spinning and weaving machines in U.S. and, with Moses Brown, set up first U.S. cotton mill.

   Eli Whitney—Invented the system of interchangeable parts and the cotton gin.

   Jesse Thomas—Senator who proposed the Missouri Compromise.

   Denmark Vesey—Ex-slave who planned slave revolt but was betrayed before it was carried out.

2. Brought out sectional differences that had been disguised by economic prosperity.

3. By attempting to restrict slavery in Missouri it brought the slavery issue to the forefront.

4. Brought in Maine and Missouri to keep the political balance between the slave and non-slave states, and set the areas in the Louisiana Purchase where slavery would or would not be allowed.

5. The South became wed to states' rights, opposed the protective tariff, internal improvements, and an active central government, and southern politicians who had been nationalists became sectionalists.

Special Feature Questions
page 160

1. Bolstered the image of American invincibility and reinforced the nation's distinctiveness from European countries.

2. It offered the opportunity to spread the American form of government and satisfy the hopes of expansionists.

Photo Questions

page 147
Allowed the Alien and Sedition Acts to expire, cut military spending, and repealed the Whiskey Act and the Judiciary Act of 1801.

page 150
Began military preparations and passed the Embargo Act.

page 152
To stop the encroachment of settlers on Indian lands.

page 156
In retaliation for the American burning of York.

page 157
March, 1931. (Answer not in text.)

page 158
The adoption of Clay's "American System," increased federal power, and Americanization of the arts.

page 161
Believed in a simple spelling of English words.

page 162
Required less skilled labor and could be put together and repaired quickly and easily.

Chapter Review

page 165, Review Questions
1. In his inaugural address, in making changes slowly and keeping some Federalist programs, and in taking actions that were sometimes against his political principles because he thought the good of the country was at stake, such as his actions against the Barbary pirates, approving the national road, and approving the Louisiana Purchase.
2. Established the doctrine of judicial review.
3. Pressures on U.S. neutrality exerted by France and Great Britain, the failure of negotiations and economic warfare (the Embargo Act), the treachery of Napoleon, anti-British sentiments in the South and West, and the influence of the war hawks in Congress.
4. Peace was restored without either country being forced to give up any territory. The Indians lost more land, and the Federalist party lost the last of its influence. The "Era of Good Feelings," a period of prosperity and increased nationalism, followed the war. American industry grew because of the years without competition from British imports. Relations with Great Britain were improved by commissions that resolved issues such as the boundary between the U.S. and Canada.
5. After 1800, Jefferson reversed some Federalist policies and used patronage to remove Federalists from office. Federalists were in conflict with mainstream opinion over such issues as the Louisiana Purchase. The Essex Junto conspiracy discredited the Federalists, and the Hartford Convention proposals made them seem ridiculous. Peace and prosperity after the War of 1812 were credited to the Republicans.
6. Federalist ideas were carried out by a new breed of nationalist Republicans. The prime example is Henry Clay's American System. The judiciary supported the old Federalist philosophy of strong central government with decisions that increased federal power.
7. The Monroe Doctrine declared the Western Hemisphere off limits to European powers, reinforced the American policy of neutrality, and became a cornerstone of American foreign policy.
8. Pride in American military power.
9. Differing economic and political interests of the North, South and West, especially the issue of whether or not new slave states should be admitted to the Union.

page 165, Discussion
1. Answers may vary. Most students will select the Louisiana Purchase and stress how it helped direct our interests westward. Some will identify the smooth transition of government under Jefferson and how it set a precedent for future Presidents.
2. Answers may vary. Point out the fact that Britain had revoked the Orders in Council. What would have happened if the news had arrived sooner? What if Madison had heeded John Quincy Adams' advice about Napoleon? How much influence did the war hawks have, and what were their motives?
3. Answers may vary. Most students will know that the compromise only postponed prob-

lems. What other solutions might have been possible?

4. Nonviolent transfers of power cannot be taken for granted in many countries —especially in countries that have undergone a revolution. Peaceful transfer showed stability of government and set a precedent.

page 165, Using Maps

1. Put-in-Bay, the Thames, Chippewa, Lake Champlain, New Orleans, Godly Wood, Ft. Bowyer; Washington, D.C., Frenchtown, Stoney Creek, Lundy's Lane, Châteaugay, La Colle Mill, Bladensburg, Lake Ponchatrain.

2. West.

3. The Chesapeake Bay and the Potomac River.

page 165, Using Skills

Answers should include the idea that foreign policy can interfere with foreign trade.

CHAPTER 8 THE AGE OF JACKSON

After studying this chapter, the student should be able to:

1. describe the elections of 1824 and 1828 and major aspects of the Adams administration.
2. explain the democratic developments during the "Era of the Common People."
3. discuss the opposing positions during the nullification controversy.
4. discuss Jackson's war against the Second Bank of the United States.
5. describe the political and economic events of the Van Buran administration and the election of 1840.

OVERVIEW

Chapter 8 surveys the history of the United States from the election of 1824 through that of 1840. Andrew Jackson emerges as a figure who overcomes sectional tensions to form a new national political party, the Democrats. Nationalists do the same, eventually forming the Whig party. Sectional issues, however, remain paramount. The issue that best defines the nature of Jacksonian Democracy—Jackson's war against the Second Bank of the United States—is treated in some detail, along with the economic policies that followed the Bank's destruction.

The central political theme of the era remains the question over government activism. Although a strong supporter of the Union, Jackson remains a Jeffersonian in principle. The great majority of Whigs, on the other hand, are proponents of governmental action to promote economic growth. This theme of limited versus active government animates most of the issues of the period. Other important concepts in the chapter are democracy, protectionism versus free trade, nullification, and soft versus hard money.

Section 1

Introduction: It is important at this stage in the students' study to review the differences between "nationalists"—those who favor active government—and "Jeffersonians"—those who favor limited government. Clay and Adams represent the former and Jackson, the latter. Have the students read this section and, with information gained from earlier reading, give evidence to show why an Adams-Clay coalition was the natural development.

Development: It is important to understand the Jacksonian coalition. Put the following chart on the chalkboard and have students fill in the information:

Jackson's Appeal	
Southerners	Jeffersonian limited government (opposition to tariffs, internal improvements, BUS)

Northerners	opposition to government-granted special privileges (monopolies, corporate charters—will be seen later in opposition to BUS)
Westerners	Jackson as westerner, Indian fighter, desire for favorable land policy

What are the implications for this coalition of heightened sectional tension?

Section 2

Introduction: Jackson was the first "self-made man" to become President. Ask the students what attributes they feel are necessary to become a "success." You might want to share the following quotation on Jackson:

". . . I have frequently seen Gen. Jackson, and such was the impression his appearance made on my mind, that I have said to myself he is a man of Iron."[6]

Development: Colonial American society was relatively democratic, yet many political thinkers of that era feared "democracy" as "mob rule." By the Jacksonian period, democracy had advanced considerably beyond the earlier periods. Have students list the changes during the Age of Jackson that increased political democracy in the United States.

Section 3

Introduction: Andrew Jackson was a Jeffersonian, but he was also a stout defender of the Union. Have the students read this section looking for evidence of both: examples of Jeffersonian limited government but firm support of the Union.

Development: The tariff was the key sectional issue of this period, but many historians feel that the major reason the South feared active government was a concern that an active government might someday interfere with slavery. Read the following excerpt from Robert J. Turnbull's *The Crisis*, and ask students to analyze it. The key question is, what does Turnbull mean when he writes, "institutions of our forefathers?"

"[Tariffs and improvement schemes were dangerous chiefly because] acquiescence in these measures, on the part of the State sovereignties, sanctions . . . the constitutional right to legislate on the local concerns of the States. . . . The question, it must be recollected, is not simply, whether we are to have a foreign commerce. It is not whether we are to have splendid national works, in which we have no interest, executed chiefly at our cost. . . . It is not whether we are to be taxed without end. . . . But the still more interesting question is, whether the institutions of our forefathers . . . are to be preserved . . . free from the rude hands of innovators and enthusiasts, and from the molestation or interference of any legislative power on earth but our own?"[7]

Section 4

Introduction: In economic terms, the most significant power of the BUS was its control over currency. Remind the students that state banks normally issued more paper than they had specie to back up that paper. This paper tended to flow toward the BUS (through collection of federal taxes, for example), which would redeem it for specie. Redemption of paper for specie checks the issue of paper. Have the students review the discussion of the Panic of 1819 to see how this power led to resentment by many (Chapter 7, pages 162-163). Then, have the students read the section to find out the reasons Jackson disliked the Bank.

Development: Have students analyze the cartoon on page 179. What is under Jackson's feet? What weapon is he holding in his hand? What does his kingly attire signify? (Recall early American fears of monarchy.)

Section 5

Introduction: This section discusses the development of the Whigs, the political party formed in opposition to Andrew Jackson. Have the students read the "People in History" feature on page 174. Calhoun, Clay, and Webster were all Whigs. Ask the students why this coalition was unlikely. What, other than opposition to Jackson, did all three have in common?

Development: To pursue the question of the nature of the Whig Party, have students indicate support for or opposition to the following measures on the part of the three Whigs listed.

---

[6]John W. Ward, *Andrew Jackson—Symbol for an Age*, (New York: Oxford University Press, 1962), p. 157.

[7]Quoted in William H. Freehling, *Prelude to Civil War; The Nullification Controversy in South Carolina* (New York: Harper & Row, Publishers, Inc., 1968), p. 127.

	Clay	Calhoun	Webster
Tariff			
Internal Improvements			
BUS			

Based upon this data, what predictions might the students make concerning the future of the Whig Party as sectional tensions increase?

Conclusion: To conclude the chapter, have students read the "Perspectives" feature on Political Campaigns, page 180, and answer the questions that follow. Ask students to give examples of campaign style from the most recent (or current) presidential election.

ANSWERS

Section Review Questions

page 169

1. William Crawford—Presidential candidate in 1824 who carried the southern states but lost the election to Adams.
   National Republicans—Supporters of Adams who favored national programs.
   Old Hickory—Jackson's nickname.
2. Slavery, the tariffs, and internal improvements.
3. Because no candidate received a majority of the electoral votes, the House of Representatives chose the President.
4. First, Adams was a nationalist during a period of growing sectionalism. He advocated economic growth directed by the national government and was opposed by those who believed in limited government. He refused to use patronage to defend himself. Finally, his personality was a drawback.
5. The campaign of 1828 focused on personalities rather than issues. There was more mudslinging than before. Voter turnout was large due to public excitement.

page 172

1. The Hermitage—Jackson's mansion.
   Martin Van Buren—Jackson's secretary of state during first term.
   Kitchen Cabinet—Informal group of advisors to Jackson.
2. Jackson was the first President who did not come from a well-established American family. He was from frontier country, was born poor, and lacked formal schooling.

3. Many states eliminated property ownership as a qualification to vote. In some states, any adult white male could vote. In addition, conventions, rather than caucuses, nominated candidates, and voters directly chose the presidential electors.
4. Used the spoils system in an attempt to reform civil service and used a more democratic approach in selecting advisors.
5. Women, Indians, and most blacks.

page 176

1. Eaton affair—A social dispute that resulted in Van Buren becoming Jackson's closest advisor.
   Indian Removal Act—Legislation that forced Indians west of the Mississippi.
   Force Bill—Part of the compromise to avoid nullification; gave President the right to enforce the tariff laws.
2. The issue of national or state sovereignty.
3. The Supreme Court.
4. Jackson believed the federal government should support only national projects. The Maysville Road was a Kentucky state project.
5. Because many Cherokee Indians died during the journey.

page 179

1. Nicholas Biddle—Head of the Second Bank of the United States.
   William Wirt—Candidate of Anti-Masonic Party.
   Specie Circular—Jackson's 1836 policy that government lands could be purchased with gold or silver only.
2. The Bank was a depository for federal funds and could use those funds without paying interest. Since the Bank issued the only national currency, it controlled the amount of money in circulation.
3. Held the first national nominating convention for a presidential election.
4. Jackson ordered federal funds removed from the National Bank of the United States and placed in state or pet banks.

page 182

1. Nationalists and states' rights advocates, northern merchants and farmers, southern bankers and planters. The Whigs were united by their opposition to Jackson.
2. An economic downturn in Europe and the lack of specie in the United States. Banks failed,

commerce was disrupted, and unemployment rose.

3. The system of subtreasuries set up by the act deprived banks of money for loans, making economic recovery difficult.
4. The Democrats were blamed for the depression. In addition, the frontier image of the Whigs' candidate, William Henry Harrison, was popular with the voters.

Special Feature Questions

page 180
1. The actual work was left to party members at local levels. Personal appearances were considered undignified.
2. It encouraged personal appearances as a way of drawing crowds and winning votes.
3. It expanded the role of advertising.

Photo Questions

page 169
Henry Clay, Andrew Jackson, and William Crawford.

page 170
He was the embodiment of the American success story: the rise from humble beginnings to the White House.

page 172
The practice of giving government jobs to political supporters.

page 173
The belief that women were incapable of taking part in government affairs is one answer. Answers may vary.

page 175
Discovery of gold.

page 177
The Bank was constitutional.

page 178
Jackson's veto of the Bank, which he thought issued too many notes (soft money), became the issue, and voters supported Jackson.

page 179
He ignored a Supreme Court decision on Indian removal, used the threat of force in internal affairs, and destroyed the Bank.

Chapter Review

page 182, Review Questions
1. Adams came from a well-established American family. He was a very reserved person. Jackson was born in poverty to immigrant parents. He was flamboyant and determined.
2. Drive and determination.
3. Opened the government to more participation by the people. The policy of appointing political supporters to positions removes many capable workers.
4. He wavered.
5. That the states could nullify an act of Congress. That states were sovereign and could therefore secede from the Union.
6. Maysville Road Bill, Indian removal, and the Bank issue.
7. To Jackson, the Bank was the epitome of special privilege, and also unconstitutional. The fight ended with the Bank destroyed and speculation out of control.
8. He was the "common man" popular enough to unite regional and sectionalist interests in 1828 and 1832. His influence helped elect Van Buren in 1836. Candidates who were in the Jackson mold—from the frontier and war heroes—appeared.
9. A national convention to select candidates and the direct selection of delegates.

page 183, Discussion
1. Answers may vary. Some students may point out that Clay's political philosophy was closer to Adams' than it was to Jackson's. It was natural then for Clay to throw his support to Adams.
2. Answers may vary.
3. Answers may vary. Jackson's prejudice towards banks because of his personal dealings should be mentioned as well as his anti-monopoly and hard money positions.
4. Answers may vary. Acceptance of different lifestyles, assimilation, and war are possibilities.
5. Because they act as a check on the national government and because the state can be more responsive in dealing with local and state problems.

page 183, Using Maps
1. Four. Two.
2. 1824: Jackson—8; Adams—6; Crawford—2; Clay—3; 1828: Jackson—14; Adams—7.

3. 1824, 26; 1828, 16.
4. Northeast. South. All areas except New England.

page 183, Using Skills
1. Popular votes.

2. 1824—3.3 percent; 1828—9.4 percent; 1832—8.9 percent; 1836—9.8 percent; 1840—14.0 percent.
3. Expansion of suffrage.
4. Yes, because the expansion of suffrage permitted more people to vote.

CHAPTER 9 WESTWARD EXPANSION

After studying this chapter, the student should be able to:

1. describe Frederick Jackson Turner's thesis concerning the significance of the frontier in American history.
2. review the Indian policy of the United States government.
3. describe American migration into the trans-Mississippi West.
4. explain the major aspects of the Mexican-American War.

OVERVIEW

Chapter 9 surveys the westward expansion of the United States through the period of the Mexican-American War. Frederick Jackson Turner's famous thesis concerning the significance of the frontier in American history is explored, as is U.S. Indian policy and migration into Texas, California, Oregon, and Utah. The final section treats the War with Mexico.

Central themes include Turner's concept of the frontier (and its implications for the development of democracy and individualism) and white perceptions that informed the debate over Indian policy. Themes developed in past chapters and continued through this chapter include nationalism versus sectionalism and the search for freedom of religious expression. Other important concepts are manifest destiny, expansionism, and cultural conflict.

TEACHING IDEAS

Section 1

Introduction: The heart of Turner's thesis concerning the frontier was that, as Americans moved west, the frontier stripped away civilization and fostered such characteristics as individualism, self-reliance, and egalitarianism. As long as there was a frontier, this process continued. Have the students read the quotation on page 185, point out the Cumberland Gap and South

Pass on a map of the United States, then have them read the section for a description of Turner's ideas.

Development: Section 1 mentions both Jefferson and Jackson as products of the frontier. A recurrent theme in American literature is the frontier hero who is unspoiled by civilization, close to nature. Ask the students for examples of other frontier heroes in fact and fiction (Daniel Boone, Davy Crockett, Cooper's "Hawkeye"). Do we still respect people today who are "close to nature"? Examples? Why?

Section 2

Introduction: Review the material on North American Indians in Chapter 1 (pages 22-26). What was the major point made in that section concerning their relationship to their environment? Have students read this section looking for the difference between Indians' and white settlers' attitudes toward the land.

Development: Have the students compare and contrast the three quotations in the "United States Indian Policy" subsection. Does there appear to be a difference between official attitude and historical fact? How did whites justify their actions? (See John Quincy Adams quotation, page 188.)

Section 3

Introduction: On a map of the United States, mark off the western boundary of the Louisiana

Purchase. Point out that the area south and west of that line is that which is about to be studied. Ask the students what states are encompassed by this territory. (See footnote 4, page 200.)

Development: We have been pursuing the themes of nationalism and sectionalism. Review the ideas, then ask how sectionalism was reflected over the annexation of Texas. How was nationalism reflected in the Oregon issue? A third major theme in American history is the development of religious toleration. How does the Mormon experience fit into this theme? Have we come further in the development of religious tolerance since that time?

Section 4

Introduction: Have the students reread the quotation from John L. O'Sullivan that opens the chapter (page 185). What is the rationale for western expansion expressed in the quotation? Have the students read the section to find out how "manifest destiny" was put into effect.

Development: As the section points out, there was a lot of opposition to the Mexican War in the United States. The following excerpt is from Charles Sumner's "Report on the War with Mexico" (1847). Have the students analyze it for Sumner's concerns. Were they justified?

The *first* [justification for the war] alleges that Mexico passed the boundary of the United States, invaded our territory, and shed American blood upon American soil. This is completely refuted by the facts . . . showing that the collision took place upon territory in dispute between the two governments, *and in the actual possession* of *Mexico*. It was the army of the United States that played the part of invaders. . . .

> "It can no longer be doubted that this is a war of conquest. . . .
>
> A war of conquest is bad; but the present war has darker shadows. It is a war for the extension of slavery over a territory which has already been purged, by Mexican authority, from this stain and curse. . . .
>
> But it is not merely proposed to open new markets for slavery: it is also designed to confirm and fortify the "Slave Power." . . .
>
> Regarding it as a war to strengthen the "Slave Power," we are conducted to a natural conclusion, that it is virtually, and in its consequences, a war against the free States of the Union. Conquest and robbery are attempted

in order to obtain a political control at home; battles are fought, less with a special view of subjugating Mexico than with the design of overcoming the power of the free States, under the Constitution. . . . [8]

Conclusion: On a map of the United States, point out the extent of the territory added to the United States by treaty, by war, and by Indian removal. Have students list all the states added to the Union from this territory.

ANSWERS
Section Review
page 187
1. The huge amount of free western land.
2. Hunters and traders, followed by ranchers and miners, and then by farmers.
3. Jefferson was the son of a pioneer whose home was the Virginia frontier. Jackson was born in the Carolina backwoods and grew up on the Tennessee frontier. His election was a political victory for frontier democracy.
4. Pioneer farmers had to provide their own shelters and all their food and clothing while on the frontier.

page 190
1. Indians did not believe in private ownership of land, and they thought of land as a resource to be used and left undamaged.
2. Whites thought that Indian claims to land were not justified because the Indians did not farm the land.
3. One of good faith and preserving peace and friendship.
4. It would free eastern Indian lands for settlement.

page 197
1. Stephen Austin—Empresario who led American colonization of Texas.
   Sam Houston—Commander of the army of Texas and the first president of the Republic of Texas.
   Webster-Ashburton Treaty—set the 49th parallel as boundary between the United States and Canada in the northeast.
   Deseret—Name given to Utah by the Mormons.

---

[8]Charles Sumner, "Report on the War with Mexico," 1847. Boston: *Old South Leaflets*, Volume 6, Number 132, pp. 147-154.

2. Gave Texans time to prepare their defenses and sign a declaration of independence. Also served as a symbol of courage for fighting forces.
3. The sea otter trade, and by the wealth and beauty of the land.
4. The reports of traders and missionaries, the favorable market and the promise of profit, the many rivers suitable for shipping and transportation, and the need for elbow room.
5. Young was a good organizer. He planned the trip west in stages so that the travel would be easier. Young also developed a cooperative economic system that proved successful.

page 200
1. John L. O'Sullivan—Editor who coined the phrase "manifest destiny.
   Nueces River—Southern boundary of Texas as proposed by Mexico.
   Zachary Taylor—Leader of the U.S. Army in Mexico.
   Stephen Kearny—Leader of the Army of the West that captured Santa Fe.
   John Sutter—Californian on whose property gold was first discovered in 1848.
   Gadsden Purchase—Land acquired from Mexico that became the southern part of Arizona and New Mexico.
2. The United States wanted a boundary between the two nations set by the Adams-Onís Treaty and a commercial treaty with Mexico. The U.S. government also insisted on payment to Americans for property damaged by Mexicans. Mexico was suspicious of American expansionism, and blamed the United States for the trouble in California.
3. Polk sent General Zachary Taylor to New Mexico to provoke the Mexicans.
4. The United States received California and the part of New Mexico north of the Gila River. The United States agreed to pay Mexico $15 million and took over $3 million in war debts Mexico owed Americans.
5. Discovery of gold lured more than 80,000 to California. In 1849 a state constitution was drafted. California was admitted to the Union a year later.

Photo Questions
page 186
Whites wearing buckskins, passing pipe, smoking meat over fire.

page 187
Vegetables for family consumption.

page 189
Some paid in beads, blankets, or whiskey. Others took land by force or trickery.

page 191
It delayed Santa Anna so that Sam Houston could raise an army. It also served as a rallying point for the Texans.

page 194
Life and property were in danger because of Mexico's inability to maintain law enforcement.

page 196
Government by leaders who are regarded as divinely guided.

Chapter Review
page 201, Review Questions
1. People were attracted to the West by fertile land, gold, opportunities in the fur and shipping trades, and, in general, by frontier spirit and a need for elbow room.
2. Since Indians had not cleared the land for farming, they were not entitled to it.
3. Indians were removed from their land by treaty and by coercion. Rebellion and warfare played a part in acquiring Texas and California. Treaties and purchases were used to acquire Oregon, New Mexico, Utah, Arizona, and other parts of the West.
4. Colonial governments tried unsuccessfully to regulate trade and purchase of Indian lands. Under the Northwest Ordinance the official policy was to preserve peace through joint treaties. Under Jackson, the policy of Indian removal was carried out.
5. Jackson favored annexing the territory, but made no effort to do so. Annexation was an unpopular issue in the North and East. Jackson also feared war with Mexico. Van Buren let the issue fade. Tyler, fearing that European powers would gain influence in Texas, sought a treaty of annexation. Texas was brought into the Union under Polk's administration.
6. Mexico cut off legal immigration from the United States and sent Santa Anna to stop American rebellion.
7. Thinking that they had no future in the United States, they finally settled outside the nation's boundaries in the Utah territory.

8. Relations with Mexico were constantly strained in the 1830's and 1840's. War broke out between the two countries in 1846. Conflict with Great Britain over Oregon stopped short of war. Claims to the territory were determined by treaty.

page 201, Discussion
1. Answers may vary. Students may point out that the theory neglects the part played by the growing economic system in fostering individualism. Others may point out that the lawlessness in parts of the frontier may have hampered the growth of democracy. Another view is that other events, such as the Revolutionary War, shared in promoting democracy and individualism.
2. Answers may vary. Students should point out that the Indians could have remained on their land had Jackson enforced the *Worcester* v. *Georgia* ruling. Attempted purchase of Indian land, assimilation, growth of an Indian nation, or Indian-settler warfare may then have resulted.
3. Answers may vary. Students may argue that warfare was the only means of redress for

Americans. Dissenters may argue against American expansionism.
4. Answers may vary. Students may speculate that colonization would have taken a longer, more peaceful route. Another possibility is that American industry and trade would have been sharply curtailed. A third theory is that the United States would not have become a world power.

page 201, Using Maps
1. 1784-1810.
2. Alabama, Mississippi, Arkansas, Oklahoma, Kansas.
3. Miami.
4. That land was settled by gradual westward movement. Indians were pushed farther west as settlers moved in.

page 201, Using Skills
1. Increase.
2. Increase. Increase.
3. Until 1850 the trends were similar. In 1850, however, the median age for males increased greatly.
4. Yes.

CHAPTER 10 ANTEBELLUM AMERICA

After studying this chapter, the student should be able to:

1. list the major aspects of the transportation and communication revolutions of the early nineteenth century.
2. describe the impact of early industrialization and urbanization on American society.
3. discuss the cultural trends of antebellum America.
4. describe and explain the reform impulse of the antebellum era, including women's rights and abolition.
5. explain the major features of the plantation-slave system.

OVERVIEW

Chapter 10 is a broad social and cultural survey of antebellum America. As such it treats the industrialization and urbanization of mid-nineteenth-century society, religious ferment, and the spirit of reform that animated much of the country. A final section is devoted to a discussion of the slave South and the continued development of sectional differences.

Themes developed earlier are studied in more depth. As noted above, continued development of sectional antagonisms is a major concern. A closer look at the American themes of individualism and democracy is provided. The Second Great Awakening allows another look at the importance of religion in American life. The impact of industrialization and urbanization has special significance for a later era. Important concepts are mass production, romanticism, transcendentalism, civil disobedience, cultural conflict, and social class.

TEACHING IDEAS

Section 1

Introduction: The impact of the transportation revolution on American economic development was truly great. For example, during the keelboat days (before steamships) 100 pounds of produce cost $5 to send downriver. By 1820 this cost was reduced to $2, and by 1840, to $.25! Share this fact with the students and have them read the section looking for other evidence of the impact of developments in transportation.

Development: Have the students study the map on page 204. Where are most of the roads and canals? Ask them what the implications of this fact might be for sectional alliances.

Section 2

Introduction: In the last chapter, the students were introduced to Frederick Jackson Turner's frontier thesis. One part of his argument was that the frontier acted as a "safety valve" for American society. That is, social unrest was avoided because there was always "free" land beckoning people, providing the opportunity for social mobility. Mention this idea to the students, then ask them if the story of the immigrants bolsters or contradicts this hypothesis (contradicts). This exercise serves as an example to students of how historians test each other's hypotheses.

Development: The growth of industry had a tremendous social impact on the American city. Have the students create *before* and *after* lists like the following to reflect that impact.

Before	After
—communities had common interests	—neighbors unrelated
—relatives lived close together	—residential patterns reflect social class-economic segregation
—all social classes in same neighborhoods	
—mutual concerns & obligations between neighbors	—religious differences increased
—economic & social leaders also political leaders	—personal relationships between employers & workers break down

Section 3

Introduction: *Webster's* defines culture as "the concepts, habits, skills, arts, instruments, institutions, etc. of a given people in a given period." Ask the students to define "culture," listing the items they think of, then give them this definition for comparison. Have them read this section for evidence of the various aspects of American culture in the antebellum years.

Development: Have students cite as much evidence as possible for the presence of the themes of individualism and democracy in American antebellum culture.

Section 4

Introduction: It is important for students to note the connection between religion and reform in antebellum America. In *Lectures on Revivals*, revivalist Charles Grandison Finney wrote that all young converts "should set out with a determination to aim at being useful in the highest degree . . ." and "if they can see an opportunity where they can do more good, they must embrace it whatever may be the sacrifice to themselves." In *Systematic Theology* he wrote that in all true Christians "their spirit is necessarily that of the reformer. To the universal reformation of the world they stand committed." Share these quotations with the students and have them read the section for information on the various reform movements.

Development: A central aspect of the antebellum reform impulse was the belief that improving individuals would improve society. Have students describe how the temperance, educational, and labor reform movements reflect this idea.

Section 5

Introduction: Ask the students why many people support an Equal Rights Amendment to the Constitution today. (Unequal treatment in employment, etc.) Have the students read the section looking for limitations on women's rights in the 1840's.

Development: Have students read the "People in History" feature on page 218. What reforms were these women involved in? Have them review the section to list successes of the women's movement in antebellum America.

Section 6

Introduction: This is a good point to reinforce the connection between religion and reform.

Have the students read the Finney quotation on page 220, then read the section.

Development: Have students list aspects of the reaction to abolitionism in both the North and South. In which area was the reaction more intense? Was there widespread support for abolitionism in the North?

Section 7

Introduction: Have students study the map on page 221. Which states had the highest concentration of slaves? How was slave ownership distributed? Have students read the section to find out why slavery was essential to the southern economy even though most southerners did not own slaves.

Development: Have the students compare and contrast West African and American slavery. Do they find differences?

Conclusion: As time passed, southerners became more defensive of their "peculiar institution." Have the students read the Calhoun quotation in the first column on page 225 and speculate about why both southern and northern views were becoming more extreme.

ANSWERS
Section Review Questions
page 205
1. Erie Canal—linked the Hudson River and the Great Lakes in 1825 to become America's longest canal.
   Robert Fulton—developed first successful steamboat in the United States.
   Donald McKay—developed clipperships that were the fastest afloat.
   Matthew Perry—negotiated trading privileges with Japan.
   Samuel F. Morse—perfected the telegraph.
   Cyrus Field—set up the first telegraph cable across the Atlantic.
2. Reduced travel time and expenses.
3. Railroads were fast and cheap and they could serve regions that did not have access to waterways.
4. The introduction of steamships and the construction of a railroad across Panama.

page 210
1. Waltham System—early factory system in which the workers, most of them girls

and women, were strictly supervised on and off the job.
   Elias Howe—introduced the sewing machine.
   Know-Nothing Party—Nativist political group that advocated stricter immigration laws.
2. The shoe, clothing, leather, rubber goods, and iron industries.
3. Corporations can accumulate capital for investments. They also provide limited liability for the owners. In addition, corporations are granted the same legal status as a person.
4. Immigration from Europe.
5. Their livelihood was threatened by mass production and improved transportation.
6. Largely unskilled, the Irish were relegated to menial work in which the pay was poor, the hours were long, and the labor was often dangerous and dirty. Having no transportation, they were forced to live in the inner city. Disease spread quickly in the Irish sections of a city because of overcrowding and poor sanitation. In addition, the Irish were victims of stereotyping because of their different culture and their poverty.

page 213
1. Walt Whitman—Leading romantic poet; author of *Leaves of Grass*.
   American Bible Society—Founded in 1816 to distribute Bibles.
   William Ellery Channing—Founder of the Unitarian Church.
2. That people could rise above reason. They thought that progress should be spiritual rather than material. They valued individualism and nonconformity.
3. Thoreau believed that a person need not depend on society to live.
4. New methods of mechanical reproduction lowered costs, allowing more people access to books, paintings, and sculpture.
5. It stressed that anyone could be saved.

page 217
1. Robert Owen—Founder of a utopian community at New Harmony, Indiana.
   Dorothea Dix—Reformer whose reports led to improved care for the insane.
   Horace Mann—Educator whose measures set standards for free public education.
   Catherine Beecher—Educator who emphasized domestic training for women.

Mary Lyon—Founded Mt. Holyoke College.

William Ladd—Founded American Peace Society.

2. To show society how an ideal community would work.

3. An attempt was made to rehabilitate prisoners through work, study, and meditations. Debtors' prisons and whipping were abolished. Child prisoners were separated from adult prisoners.

4. Public elementary schools were established. Teacher training schools were founded. Courses of study were broadened and opportunities for the education of women and blacks began to increase.

5. Unions and political associations called workingmen's parties.

page 219
1. Angelina Grimke—Antislavery reformer who fought for women's rights.

Margaret Fuller—Editor of the *Dial*; women's equality proponent.

Elizabeth Stanton—Co-organizer with Lucretia Mott of the first women's rights convention.

Elizabeth Blackwell—First woman graduate of an American medical school.

2. Women and men faced hardships together on the frontier, so a good deal of equality existed. In more settled regions, women were expected to stay at home, care for the children and the house, and serve the men.

3. Single women were considered wards of their nearest male relative. Married women were considered part of their husband's personal property. Women were not permitted to vote or own property.

4. Published magazines presenting their arguments, lobbied for women's rights legislation, and held conventions to dramatize their cause.

page 221
1. American Colonization Society—Established to free and return slaves to Africa.

David Walker—Published pamphlet in 1829 calling for slaves to revolt.

Liberty Party—Antislavery political party that sponsored presidential candidates in 1840 and 1844.

Elijah Lovejoy—Antislavery publisher who was killed trying to protect his newspaper press.

Harriet Tubman—Most famous "conductor" on the Underground Railroad.

2. Several northern states abolished slavery. Slavery was forbidden in the Northwest Territory. Emancipation societies were organized. Abolitionist publications such as Benjamin Lundy's *Genius of Universal Emancipation* were published.

3. Garrison was opposed to gradual emancipation. Instead, he demanded racial equality and immediate abolition of slavery.

4. Dropped idea of total emancipation.

5. Blacks supported abolitionist newspapers and were active in the Underground Railroad.

6. Southerners cracked down on reformers and tried to suppress abolitionist literature.

page 225
1. Middle Passage—The route for slave ships from Africa to America.

Nat Turner—Black preacher who led a slave revolt in 1831.

Cavalier—Genteel, old-fashioned southern aristocrat.

Yankee—Aggressive, money-minded northern industrialist.

2. Dominated politics and society in the South.

3. Slavery was based on race in America. In ancient societies, captives of war served as slaves.

4. Some slaves took part in violent revolts. Others worked slowly, broke tools, destroyed property, or ran away.

5. Wealth was more concentrated in the upper class. The economy depended on agriculture. Few southerners moved to cities.

Photo Questions
page 205
Social gatherings and educational programs.

page 206
Famine, land.

page 210
The stove, the reaper, plows, and mowing, threshing, and haying machines.

pages 212, 213
Longfellow, Cooper, Poe, Whitman, Emerson, Hawthorne, Melville.

page 214
Answers may vary.

page 215
The University of Iowa.

page 217
Women's rights in marriage and the home.

page 219
Genius of Universal Emancipation.

page 222
It existed in only one part of the country.

Chapter Review
page 226, Review Questions

1. Improved transportation opened new markets. New technology made the factory system feasible. Corporations were set up to acquire capital. The large labor supply required for industrialization was provided through immigration.
2. Positive results included economic growth, material progress, and greater availability of art and literature. Negative results included dehumanization of work, and poor working and living conditions.
3. Emotion, imagination, nature, the wisdom of the common people, individualism, the exotic and the supernatural.
4. Both stressed the importance of the individual and the virtues of the common people.
5. Religious revivals strengthened the reform movement. Material progress and faith in democracy led to belief in the perfectibility of society.
6. Prison conditions, education, slavery, peace, the status of women, and labor.
7. New York passed legislation that gave women some rights in controlling their own property. There were some gains in education and employment as well. The number of women's colleges was increasing. Men's colleges began opening their doors to women. Although most women were limited to domestic science, teaching, and missionary courses, some women were able to enter the fields of medicine, science, and the arts.
8. Most northerners were hostile toward abolitionists. Southerners viewed abolitionists as a threat to southern society.
9. Cotton was in great demand. It was the major American export. In addition, the South had few alternatives to a cotton economy—few factories or railroads.

10. Calhoun defended slavery by arguing that the system removed the conflict between worker and employer that can disrupt or destroy a society. He also claimed that slavery had raised blacks to a higher degree of civilization. Fitzhugh reasoned that slaves were better off than northern workers because slaves did not have to compete for jobs. He claimed that slaves were happy and well taken care of.

page 226, Discussion
1. Answers may vary. Among the possibilities are: the emphasis placed by religious leaders on good works and helping; optimism and the faith in Yankee ingenuity; and increasing awareness due to the improved transportation and communication systems.
2. Answers may vary. Some students may reason that slavery would have died on its own. Others may argue that slavery was too ingrained. Slaves would have been used in the factory and transportation industries in the South.
3. Answers may vary. Some students may theorize that, although gains were limited, these early attempts at reform laid the groundwork for future gains. Others may reason that society and the plight of women and blacks were not improved by reformers.
4. Answers may vary.

page 226, Using Maps
1. Virginia, Tennessee, North Carolina, South Carolina, Georgia, Florida, Alabama, Mississippi, Louisiana, Texas, Arkansas.
   Minnesota, Iowa, Wisconsin, Illinois, Michigan, Indiana, Ohio, Pennsylvania, New York, Vermont, New Hampshire, Maine, Massachusetts, Connecticut, Rhode Island.
2. In Iowa, Percival, Des Moines, Davenport; in Illinois, Chester, Cairo, Springfield, Chicago; Detroit, Michigan; Indianapolis and Evansville, Indiana; in Ohio, Cleveland, Toledo, Columbus, Marietta, Ironton, Sandusky; in Pennsylvania, Cumberland and Shippensville; in New York, Albany, Oswego, and New York City; Portland, Maine; Boston, Massachusetts; Providence, Rhode Island.
3. The sea route from New Bern to Boston or Portland.

page 226, Using Skills
1. b.

2. a.
3. c.

Unit Review

page 227, Review Questions

1. The forces of nationalism played a role in the era's expansion (Louisiana Purchase, Florida), in Indian removal, the war of 1812, the increase of judicial power, the Monroe Doctrine, and the developing of an American culture. Sectionalism affected the United States in the slavery question, the Mexican War and the movement towards secession.

2. The North was the richest and most populated region. Economy was based on manufacturing and shipping. Northerners generally favored a protective tariff and took an anti-war position. Lifestyle was affected by industrialization and the growth of cities. The South was agricultural, with an economy based on slavery and cotton. Most southerners were against high tariffs. Lifestyles were slower and more genteel, with more emphasis on class. The West and the South were strongholds for the war hawks. The greatest concerns of the West were transportation, land policy, and Indian affairs. Frontier lifestyles tended to be rugged and individualistic.

3. The growth of democracy influenced national pride, the various movements for reform, politics at all levels, and the economy (e.g., the Bank).

4. Answers may vary.

The Historian's Craft

Use the Historian's Craft activity on pages 228-229 to conclude the unit. In this activity, which may be conducted either as an individual or group exercise, students will practice making inferences from statistical data concerning voting patterns in Congress. They will also be given an opportunity to form a hypothesis to explain the data they are analyzing.

The "Using Skills" activities in this unit have given the students experience in analyzing cause and effect relationships, analyzing statistical information, analyzing statistical trends, and determining what may reasonably be inferred from statistical data. These skills, along with the skill of distinguishing primary and secondary sources (in The Historian's Craft for Unit 2) and the basic understanding of the interpretive nature of history (The Historian's Craft for Unit 1), should be sufficient to allow the students to complete this more complex activity.

First, ask the students if they agree with Young's definition of regions and boardinghouse groups. Note that these definitions are somewhat arbitrary. Then have students study the data and answer the questions.

Questions 1 and 2, page 228: Young's table is secondary; the *Congressional Directories* are primary.

Question 3, page 229: Parts a, b, c, and d may reasonably be inferred. Part e may not be inferred because members from New England may have been among those groups representing different regions.

Question 1, page 229: Parts a, b, and c may be reasonably inferred. The agreement of groups increased in 1809 and 1816 and decreased in 1828, showing an overall increase from 1807. The tables do not address political party membership. Therefore nothing about the influence of parties may be inferred.

Question 2, page 229: One possibility is that regional interests influenced voting patterns. Party influence is also a possibility, if regional groups tended to be members of one party. A third possibility is that the social relationships formed by boardinghouse groups influenced voting patterns. (Point out that members of Congress had their meals and spent their leisure time with others of the same boardinghouse.) Ask students how they would try to verify their hypotheses.

4 THE NATION DIVIDED

After studying this unit, the student should be able to:

1. explain the series of sectional altercations that led to civil war.
2. describe the strategy pursued by each side during the Civil War, the impact of events on those strategies, and the impact of the war on the home front.
3. define reconstruction and describe the major political, social, and economic aspects of that period in American history.

OVERVIEW

Unit 4 covers that period of sectional strife immediately preceding the Civil War, the Civil War, and Reconstruction. Chapter 11 describes how the sectional tensions, dormant since the nullification crisis of the 1830's, arise again with the Mexican War and are constantly fueled by the westward march of the nation. Chapter 12 describes the Civil War in some detail, with emphasis upon the idea of a southern war for independence. The chapter on Reconstruction places particular emphasis on the plight of the freedmen and attempts of northerners to insure that they not "lose the peace."

INTRODUCING THE UNIT

Remind students that the controversy over state's rights versus federal supremacy had existed from the beginning of the union. Review the Kentucky and Virginia Resolutions and the nullification controversy of the 1830's. Read them the following quotation from Andrew Jackson. "I consider . . . the power to annul a law of the United States, assumed by one state, *incompatible with the existence of the Union. . . .*" Ask students why they think Jackson made this statement, and explain that the issue was not settled until the Civil War.

CHAPTER 11 TOWARD CIVIL WAR

After studying this chapter, the student should be able to:

1. describe the sectional politics of the late 1840's.
2. explain the Compromise of 1850 and reaction to it.
3. evaluate the impact of the Kansas-Nebraska Act on sectional tensions.
4. describe the political events of the late 1850's that led directly to Civil War.

OVERVIEW

Chapter 11 narrates the series of sectional clashes arising out of westward expansion. These clashes, of course, led to the Civil War.

The sectional theme pursued for the last few chapters reaches its climax with the election of 1860. Compromise—successful for years—finally fails in the face of extreme sectionalism. The concepts of popular sovereignty, judicial review, states' rights, and secession are central to the chapter.

TEACHING IDEAS
Section 1

Introduction: Read aloud the quotation from David Wilmot that introduces the chapter. Reviewing the growing sensitivity of southerners described in the last chapter, ask the students to predict southern reaction to such a statement. Have them read the section.

Development: The idea of popular sovereignty was a key element of compromise during this period. Have the students review how the major parties dealt with the issue of slavery expansion in the election of 1848.

Section 2

Introduction: Review with the students the importance of compromise in American history. You might go back to the compromises in the Constitution and, of more recent vintage, the Missouri Compromise. Have the students read the section looking for evidence that compromise was becoming more and more difficult.

Development: Have the students reread the excerpt from the preface to *Uncle Tom's Cabin* quoted on page 236, and then the quotation from Calhoun on page 235. How would Calhoun have reacted to the preface—especially the last line?

Section 3

Introduction: Ask the students for the compromise that covered the question of slavery in the Louisiana Territory (Missouri Compromise) and have them review the provisions. What might be the reactions of northerners and southerners to any change in those provisions? Have the students read the selection to see if their speculations are correct.

Development: The most important effect of the Kansas-Nebraska Act and the resultant bloodshed was to speed the breakdown of national parties. Have the students list evidence of the breakdown of national parties and growth of strictly sectional political alignments (Republican party most obvious here).

Section 4

Introduction: Ask the students what American political institution has traditionally resolved issues of constitutional principle (the court system). Have them read the section to note the Supreme Court's decision concerning the issue of slavery in the territories and the political events that followed that decision.

Development: Have the students read the "People in History" feature on page 242 and review pages 241–242 on the Lincoln-Douglas debates. Have them point out the position of the Republican Party on slavery (see Lincoln quotation, page 241) and the key feature of the Freeport Doctrine. Why was the Freeport Doctrine an unacceptable compromise to southerners?

Section 5

Introduction: Have students study the map on page 245, then read the section. How did the election of 1860 reflect sectional divisions in the United States?

Development: Read the following excerpt from an editorial in the New Orleans Daily Crescent (November, 1860). How would southerners with this attitude have reacted to the election of a Republican president?

"The history of the Abolition or Black Republican Party of the North is a history of repeated injuries and usurpations, all having in direct object the establishment of absolute tyranny over the slave-holding States. And all without the smallest warrant, excuse or justification. We have appealed to their generosity, justice and patriotism, but all without avail. From the beginning, we have only asked to be let alone in the enjoyment of our plain, inalienable rights, as explicitly guaranteed in our common organic law. We have never aggressed upon the North, nor sought to aggress upon the North. Yet every appeal and expostulation has only brought upon us renewed insults and augmented injuries. . . ."[9]

Conclusion: To give the students a feeling of the level to which emotions had risen by early 1861, read them the following two excerpts:

"There is no sett of People on Gods Earth that I despise and hold in such utter contempt as I do those Southern Rebels . . . and I would rather meet them in deadly conflict than any other sett of men in [the] world, in fact I am at peace with the whole world, except them, and with them I confess, I have a deadly hatred. I have no compromise to make, short of a fulfillment of the penaltys of the violated laws."[10]

"Free society! we sicken at the name. What is it but a conglomeration of greasy mechanics, filthy operatives, small-fisted farmers, and moon-struck theorists? All the northern, and especially the New England states, are devoid of society fitted for well-bred gentlemen. The prevailing class one meets with is that of mechanics struggling to be genteel, and small

---

[9]Quoted in Kenneth M. Stampp, *The Causes of the Civil War*, (Englewood Cliffs, New Jersey: Prentice-Hall, Inc., 1965), p. 35.

[10]Franklin Livingston to A. Burnham, March 6, 1861. *Zachariah Chandler Papers*, Library of Congress.

farmers who do their own drudgery, and yet are hardly fit for association with a southern gentleman's body servant."[11]

ANSWERS

Section Review Questions

page 235

1. David Wilmot—Democratic representative from Pennsylvania who introduced a proviso barring slavery from any territory acquired from Mexico.

   "Barnburners"—Democrats led by Van Buren in 1848.

   Conscience Whigs—Nickname given to Whigs in election of 1848.

   Lewis Cass—One of the defeated candidates for election in 1848; campaigned on the platform of popular sovereignty.

   Free Soil party—Third party formed during the election of 1848.

2. Antislavery groups felt that the war was an effort by the South to extend slavery. Industrial interests did not want new agricultural states added. Westerners were upset with Polk for accepting the 49° parallel border for Oregon, and supporters of Van Buren also disliked the war.

3. Both parties avoided taking an official stand on the slavery issue. Unofficially, the Democrats endorsed popular sovereignty as a solution.

4. Against slavery in the territories and for higher tariffs and free homesteads.

page 237

1. William H. Seward—Antislavery Senator from New York who denounced the Compromise of 1850.

   Franklin Pierce—Democratic candidate who won the election of 1852.

   Winfield Scott—Whig candidate for President in 1852.

   Harriet Beecher Stowe—Northern abolitionist who wrote *Uncle Tom's Cabin*.

   Pierre Soule—American ambassador to Spain who offered $130 million for Cuba.

2. California was to be a free state; remaining Mexican lands were to be divided into territories with settlers to decide slavery ques-

tion; slave trade but not slavery was to be ended in the District of Columbia; a stronger fugitive slave law was to be enacted.

3. The new fugitive slave law could not be enforced because of the feelings of northerners.

4. Turned many northerners against slavery and made southerners more defensive.

5. It proposed the seizure of Cuba from Spain. Northerners thought that this was to gain more slave territory, the Spanish were outraged, and the Pierce administration was embarrassed.

page 239

1. John Brown—Free-stater who led a retaliatory raid on the pro-slave town of Pottowatomie, killing 5 people.

   Charles Sumner—Senator from Massachusetts who spoke out against the violence in Kansas and was beaten by Representative Brooks of South Carolina.

   John C. Frémont—The "Pathfinder" who became the Republican candidate in 1856.

2. Hoped to route a transcontinental railroad through Chicago. May have hoped to win southern support for a bid to be President.

3. Had lost the election of 1852, and Clay and Webster died. State and local elections were lost in the South when many party members went over to the conservative Democrats. In the North, some Whigs joined the Know-Nothing Party. Some southern Whigs supported the Kansas-Nebraska Act, thus further splitting the party.

4. The proslavery faction intimidated voters and cast illegal votes. When elected, they made slavery legal and passed slave codes. Antislavery settlers organized a Free State party and made slavery illegal. They elected their own governor and legislature, resulting in two governments for Kansas. Both groups committed acts of violence.

5. The Republican platform called for free territories, while the Democrats supported popular sovereignty.

page 243

1. Dred Scott—Slave who sued for his freedom and became the subject of a test case in the Supreme Court.

   Roger Taney—Chief Justice in the Dred Scott case.

---

[11]Muscogee, Georgia, *Herald*, quoted in New York *Tribune* (September 10, 1856).

Hilton Helper—White North Carolinian who published *The Impending Crisis*, arguing that slavery had enriched a few slaveholders at the expense of the non-slaveholding white majority.

Harper's Ferry—Site of federal arsenal attacked by John Brown.

2. Taney ruled that Scott was not a citizen; that residence in a free state did not make him free; that slaves were property and that southerners had a right to take their property wherever they wished.

3. Lincoln gained national attention by clearly stating the Republican position on slavery. Douglas' Freeport Doctrine proved to be a last, vain attempt to hold the Democrats together.

4. The Freeport Doctrine restated the principle of popular sovereignty, saying that people who did not want slavery in their territory could keep it out by failing to enact supporting legislation.

5. Most northerners condemned the violence; a few glorified Brown as a martyr. Southerners were horrified.

page 246

1. John C. Breckinridge—Southern Democratic nominee for President in 1860.

Constitutional Union party—Compromise party in 1860, made up mostly of former Whigs.

Jefferson Davis—Leader from Mississippi elected President of the Confederacy.

Fort Sumter—Federal fort in Charleston, S.C., where first fighting of the Civil War took place.

2. Southerners demanded a platform that called for federal protection of slavery in the territories. When this was rejected, eight southern delegations withdrew from the national party to form their own party.

3. Adopted a platform endorsing internal improvements and a protective tariff.

4. He believed the Constitution did not give the federal government the right to use force against seceding states.

5. He promised not to interfere with slavery where it already existed.

Photo Questions

page 234
Gold Rush began in 1849.

page 236
Slavery to be banned in new territories.

page 237
Banned it.

page 240
That the South's power over national affairs had gone too far.

page 243
Slave revolt.

page 244
Several states seceded.

Chapter Review

page 247, Review Questions

1. Slavery in the territories, tariffs, internal improvements, land policies, and the Mexican War.

2. The Democrats were weakened and the Whigs destroyed by sectional differences. The Republicans were basically a sectional party, supported by antislavery groups and northern and western economic interests.

3. The Kansas-Nebraska Act allowed voters in the Louisiana Territory to determine whether to allow slavery there or not. The Missouri Compromise divided the land into slave and free territories.

4. Growth of the Republican Party, "bleeding Kansas," problems over the fugitive slave law, publication of books such as *Uncle Tom's Cabin*, John Brown's raids, and the persistence of the abolitionists.

5. By narrowing its focus to slavery in the territories and by joining forces with northern and western economic interests.

6. Because the proslavery minority influenced the outcome of the popular vote. Also, the Dred Scott decision implied that popular sovereignty was unconstitutional, and southerners withdrew support for the concept in favor of the principles set forth by the Supreme Court.

7. Lincoln was not an abolitionist, but he was against slavery. He hoped to eliminate slavery by confining it and letting it die naturally.

8. Buchanan thought the federal government could not legally use force to preserve the Union. Lincoln said that secession was illegal and that the federal government would use force to defend itself.

page 247, Discussion

1. Answers may vary. Some students may argue that abolition would inevitably bring an end to the plantation system, and that westward expansion necessarily meant an end to southern political dominance. Others may argue that southerners overrated the abolitionists, who represented a minority view even in the North.

2. Point out that the Constitution did not specifically say anything about the right of secession. The question of states' rights had been argued for years (e.g., the nullification controversy).

3. Answers may vary. Point out that some abolitionists still held out for compromise plans that would end slavery gradually and provide compensation to slaveowners. However, the escalation of emotions prevented compromise.

4. Answers may vary.

page 247, Using Maps
1. Utah, New Mexico.

2. Nebraska, Utah, New Mexico, Kansas.
3. Seven.
4. 31.
5. 14 slave, 16 free.

page 247, Using Skills

Critical thinking often requires that statements of fact be distinguished from arguments that indicate purpose or motive for an action. "In order to" always indicates motive, but other phrasing may be more subtle. Sometimes it is helpful to determine whether or not the statement can be rephrased with "in order to." This exercise requires class discussion.

1. Purpose or motive ("in order to").
2. Fact.
3. Fact.
4. Purpose or motive (implies that people came to California in order to find gold).
5. Purpose or motive (in order to rescue captured slaves).
6. Purpose or motive (implies that the Pierce administration dropped the Cuba project because it was embarrassed).

CHAPTER 12 THE CIVIL WAR

After studying this chapter, the student should able to:

1. analyze the strengths of each region at the outset of the war.
2. describe the major engagements of the first one and one-half years of the war.
3. explain Lincoln's motives for the Emancipation Proclamation.
4. explain how northern strengths and southern liabilities grew during the course of the war.
5. describe the major military events of the period 1863–1865 and the eventual Union victory.

OVERVIEW

Chapter 12 tells the story of the American Civil War. The most appropriate way to conceptualize the event is as a southern war for independence. As a new nation attempting to defend its status, the Confederacy's military position was quite similar to that of the American colonies during the Revolution. Unlike England, however, the North under the leadership of Lincoln was not distracted from its purpose, and the Union was preserved. Among the important concepts in this chapter are states' rights, eco-

nomic warfare, diversified economy, war of attrition, and total war.

TEACHING IDEAS
Section 1

Introduction: Review the discussion of the American Revolution, emphasizing the idea that the colonists merely had to maintain an army in the field and garner the support of a few European powers for success. The South was in a similar position. Have the students read the section looking for the relative strengths of the two sections.

Development: Point out the Sherman quotation on page 249 concerning an agricultural versus an industrial nation. Have the students analyze the graph on page 252 to see why Sherman warned his southern friends.

Section 2

Introduction: Have the students study the maps on pages 254 and 255 to orient themselves for the section. Have them read the section looking for the major military developments.

Development: An important advantage for the North was the ability to mount joint land-water operations. Emphasize the importance of this advantage by having the students find Cairo, Illinois, on the map on page 254 (or any map of the region). Ask the students why the ability to mount joint operations from a point like Cairo would be so advantageous (note Ohio, Cumberland, and Tennessee Rivers).

Section 3

Introduction: Ask the students for the primary war aim of the North (preserve the Union). Have them read the Lincoln quotation on page 256 to reinforce this point and then read the section to see how the war was expanded into a moral crusade.

Development: Ask the students if they think a just moral cause enhances the motivation of a nation at war. Can they think of examples? (The Allies in World War II are a good example that students should recall.)

Section 4

Introduction: Have the students read the chapter introductory quotation by William T. Sherman, then read the section to find out why "War is hell" for the South.

Development: Have the students compare and contrast economic developments in the two sections during the war. The contrast will serve to highlight the growing southern liabilities during the course of the war.

Section 5

Introduction: The students may not know that as late as 1864 southern success was still possible —although dramatic military victory was extremely unlikely. Have the students read the section to find out how this was so.

Development: Have the students list the reasons why Grant, unlike earlier northern com-

manders, was eventually successful (kept pressing; fought a war of attrition; realized had to destroy southern armies, not conquer territory; had key subordinates—Sherman, Sheridan— who also understood the nature of the war).

Conclusion: Ask students why they think Grant offered generous terms to Lee at Appomattox, and what penalties, if any, the North should impose on the South. The discussion will lead naturally to the topic of the next chapter, Reconstruction.

ANSWERS
Section Review Questions
page 251

1. The goal of the South was to defend its independence, while the North wanted to save the Union.
2. The North could more easily raise an army because of its large population. It had better transportation and a better economy along with a skilled and determined leader in Abraham Lincoln. The South had a military tradition and many talented military leaders, and was conducting a defensive war.
3. The Confederacy was a new unorganized government founded on states' rights. This handicapped Davis' leadership.
4. Southern strategy was to conduct a defensive war while trying to gain recognition and aid from Europe. Northern strategy was to blockade southern ports, split the Confederacy in two by controlling the Mississippi, and capture the southern capital of Richmond.
5. Maryland was crucial because it bordered Washington, D.C. on three sides; others were slave states that would provide a buffer and a moral victory.

page 256

1. John Ericsson—Designer of the *Monitor*.
   CSS *Alabama*—Famous southern commerce raider.
   George A. McClellan—Commander of the Army of the Potomac after the battle of Bull Run.
   Braxton Bragg—Confederate general who commanded the western forces.
2. Public opinion demanded immediate action, although General Scott felt that Union troops were not ready. Under pressure, Lincoln ordered Union troops to engage the enemy.

3. The Confederacy in effect blockaded its own ports in an effort to persuade England to recognize the Confederacy. Soon the U.S. Navy became strong enough to enforce a blockade.
4. The first battle between ironclad ships. The *Monitor* kept the *Virginia* from destroying the rest of the Union fleet.
5. Forced Lee to end his invasion of the North.

page 257
1. Lincoln's objective was to save the Union. He did not want to lose support in the border states.
2. Freed slaves only in the South, not in the border states.
3. Black regiments were formed and European sympathy for the North increased.
4. To prove that they had earned their freedom.

page 262
1. Clara Barton—Nurse known as "Angel of the Battlefield"; later, president of Red Cross.
   Peace Democrats—Northern Democrats who felt that Lincoln should negotiate an end to the war.
   Zebulon B. Vance—Governor of North Carolina.
   Impressment Act—Measure that allowed the Confederacy to buy goods at prices set by the government.
2. Many women and children took over men's jobs, and labor-saving machinery was used.
3. The Morrill Act increased the tariff, internal revenue duties were increased, and a small income tax was passed. Government bonds were sold and the Union government issued "greenbacks."
4. Slavery kept the South from developing other industry. The South lacked a good transportation system and had trouble financing the war.
5. The "Radicals" felt the war should be fought to end slavery. Peace Democrats felt that peace was paramount. Some people were dissatisfied with certain laws (e.g., the draft). Finally, some northerners tried to subvert the war effort.
6. Davis' greatest handicap was the states' rights government he was trying to preserve. Confederate governors believed in states' rights.

page 268
1. Ambrose E. Burnside—Replaced McClellan as Army of the Potomac commander.
   Pickett's Charge—South's frontal attack on Union center at Battle of Gettysburg.
   Joe Johnston—Replaced Bragg as leader of Confederate forces in northern Georgia.
   David Farragut—Union admiral who captured the port of Mobile.
   John Bell Hood—Confederate general who replaced Johnston.
2. To draw the Union forces from the West and entice the British to aid the South.
3. Sherman captured Atlanta, and Sheridan swept through the Shenandoah Valley. Farragut closed the port of Mobile to Confederate ships.
4. Sherman's concept of total war included destroying property so that it could not be used by the enemy and warring against civilians in order to break the spirit of the enemy.
5. The defeated soldiers were given food and allowed to return home. Officers were allowed to keep their sidearms.

Special Feature Questions
page 259
1. Lack of knowledge of modern medicine.
2. Anesthetics, antiseptics, and discovery of germ-related diseases.
3. Increased by about 35 years.

Photo Questions
page 251
Larger population, a more varied and adaptable economy, better transportation, and a skillful leader.

page 257
Blacks could help win the war if they were free and able to enlist.

page 258
Clara Barton.

page 261
To end the war.

page 266
It involved civilians. Civilian property was destroyed.

Chapter Review
page 269, Review Questions
1. Both sides thought they had military superiority. The North knew it had the advantage

in human and material resources, while the South expected to get help from European countries.

2. By a naval blockade of southern ports and by Grant's successful siege of Vicksburg, putting the Mississippi River under Union control.

3. The border states were slave states that might have sided with the South. Maryland especially was crucial because of its proximity to Washington, D.C.

4. Lee's invasion of the North in 1862 (coupled with Bragg's attempt to take Kentucky).

5. Added the objective of freeing the slaves to the North's objective of preserving the Union. The Proclamation meant that the North could start raising black troops and made European intervention less likely.

6. Upper-class English and French tended to side with the aristocratic South, but textile workers and others favored the North (especially after the Emancipation Proclamation) because they were against slavery. British and French leaders would have liked to see the United States split into two, but were afraid to intervene unless the South seemed certain to win.

7. The Civil War was the first modern war because it affected all aspects of life, for civilians as well as military personnel.

8. Because the great and decisive battles of Vicksburg, Chancellorsville, and Gettysburg took place. The South was cut in half, leading to its ultimate defeat.

page 269, Discussion
1. Answers may vary. Students can argue that the will to win can often overcome material advantages, such as in Vietnam. Included here would be the idea of a defensive war and defending one's personal property. Those who would say there was no chance might stress the war of attrition that was waged by the North.

2. Answers may vary. Some students may argue that the only reason the South held out as long as it did was because of leaders such as Lee and Jackson. Point out that Lincoln shuffled generals regularly in an attempt to find a capable commander.

3. Answers may vary. Some students may think that a lesser man than Lincoln might have lost the war for the North. Some may think that the South was doomed no matter what its leadership.

4. Answers may vary. Some students may argue that civil rights are paramount, while others will say that winning the war is. Point out that if a country loses a war, it may have no civil liberties to defend. On the other hand, emergency powers may be abused.

page 269, Using Graphs
1. Iron production.
2. 25 percent.
3. Exports.

page 269, Using Skills
This exercise requires class discussion.
1. Opinion.
2. Fact.
3. Opinion.
4. Opinion.
5. Fact.
6. Opinion.
7. Fact.
8. Fact.

CHAPTER 13 RECONSTRUCTION

After studying this chapter, the student should be able to:

1. describe the variety of reconstruction plans offered by Lincoln, Johnson, and Congress.
2. explain why Johnson's plan alienated many northerners.
3. list the various aspects of the Radical plan and explain the Radicals' motives.
4. describe the criticisms of and achievements under the Radical regimes in the South.
5. describe the restoration of "white" government in the South.

OVERVIEW

Chapter 13 describes the period of Reconstruction after the Civil War. Major themes include the struggle between the President and Congress, the motives of the Radicals, and the plight of the freedmen. The chapter is revisionist in tone, laying the blame for much of the unfortunate nature of Reconstruction on southern intransigence rather than northern vindictiveness (although the latter was certainly in evidence). Important concepts in the chapter are checks and balances, discrimination, segregation, white supremacy, terrorism, and compromise.

TEACHING IDEAS

Section 1

Introduction: Write "reconstruct-rebuilt" on the board. After reviewing the section "War at Home" in the previous chapter—especially those parts concerning the South—ask students why the term "reconstruction" is so appropriate. Then, have them read the section.

Development: Through class discussion, have students complete a chart on the board that lists the elements of the various plans for reconstruction. Such a comparison will highlight the differences between the plans:

Lincoln	Wade-Davis	Johnson

Section 2

Introduction: This section is entitled "Restoration Under Johnson." Webster defines restoration as "a bringing back to a former position or condition" or "a reconstruction of the original form." Ask the students why the authors used that term, then have them read the section to test their hypotheses.

Development: Have the students reread the quotation from Gideon Welles on page 278. Ask them to list the evidence in the section that supports his contention. Another interesting sidelight at this point is to look at Andrew Johnson as a Jacksonian Democrat. The chapter has made references to this idea. Ask the students to point out the evidence that shows him to have been a Jacksonian. (Dislike of monied aristocracy, belief in limited government.) The purpose of this little exercise is to develop a feeling within the students for the continuity of American history.

Section 3

Introduction: Have the students read the quotation from Andrew Johnson on pages 278–279. Have them speculate as to why he might say something like this, then read the chapter to check their speculations.

Development: Have the students list the motives of the Radicals (found on pages 279–280). With the aid of the map on page 281, have them detail the Radical plan. Finally, why would the conviction of Andrew Johnson have been a bad precedent (importance of checks and balances)?

Section 4

Introduction: Have the students study the picture on page 282 and the quotation in the first column of page 283. What do these materials suggest about a number of black leaders?

Development: Have the students list the criticisms and achievements of the Radical Reconstruction regimes.

Section 5

Introduction: Have the students study the picture of sharecroppers on page 286, then read the section looking for other developments and the reasons for the end of Reconstruction.

Development: Have the students list the factors that led to waning interest on the part of northerners in Reconstruction. This would also be a good place to have students read the Perspectives In History feature on suffrage, page 277.

Conclusion: Have students read the Thirteenth, Fourteenth, and Fifteenth Amendments to the Constitution (pages 786 and 787), along with the annotations concerning these amendments.

ANSWERS

Section Review Questions

page 274
1. William H. Wadsworth—Republican Representative from Kentucky.
   Henry Winter Davis—Co-sponsor of the Wade-Davis Bill.
   John Wilkes Booth—Killed Lincoln.
2. Some believed that the southern states had never been legally outside the Union and

wanted to restore the old relationship. Others felt the South should be treated as conquered territory.

3. Wanted to avoid creating southern martyrs and hoped that leniency would help to develop the Republican party in the South.

4. Military rule in the southern states and the requirement that a majority of white males take an oath of loyalty. After repudiating secession and abolishing slavery, states could apply for readmission to the Union.

5. He was a strong Unionist, had rejected Tennessee's cession, and had attacked southern leaders.

6. Approved because he hoped it would help break down the planter aristocracy and give power to white yeoman farmers.

page 278
1. Because most southern whites were willing to follow their traditional leaders.

2. The presence of federal troops and the Freedmen's Bureau.

3. To aid refugees and freedmen with supplies, medical treatment, education, and legal advice; to help settle differences between freedmen and their employers; and to manage abandoned lands.

4. Some states repealed rather than repudiated secession, voted pensions for Confederates, refused to ratify the Thirteenth Amendment, refused to repudiate Confederate debts, and passed black codes.

5. Denied blacks the right to vote, made no educational provisions, restricted employment, passed vagrancy laws, denied blacks the right to serve on juries or to testify in court against whites, and forbade blacks to handle weapons or enter into interracial marriage.

page 282
1. Civil Rights Act of 1866—Defined citizenship and protected civil rights in states.
   Thaddeus Stevens—Republican representative from Pennsylvania.
   Command of the Army Act—restricted President's power as commander-in-chief.

2. Congress feared the Civil Rights Act would be overturned in court if not protected by a constitutional amendment.

3. By giving them more representation in Congress.

4. Set up military government in the South, required states to draw up new constitutions, ratify the Fourteenth Amendment, and guarantee black suffrage. Ex-Confederates were disqualified from voting and holding office.

5. To limit the power of the President.

6. Johnson was acquitted, but lost his influence.

page 283
1. Francis L. Cardozo—Black state treasurer in South Carolina.
   Jonathan J. Wright—Black justice on South Carolina supreme court.
   James G. Blaine—Representative from Pennsylvania who praised blacks in Congress.

2. Blacks, scalawags, and carpetbaggers.

3. For being black-dominated; for using blacks for their own gain; for fraud, graft, bribery, waste, and high taxes.

4. Tax reform, public education, reorganized judicial systems, and extended suffrage.

page 287
1. Ku Klux Klan—Secret society organized to intimidate freedmen and Unionists.
   Liberal Republicans—Group formed to oppose Grant; interested in issues other than reconstruction.
   General Amnesty Act—Restored right to most ex-Confederates to hold public office (1872).
   Samuel J. Tilden—Defeated Democratic presidential candidate in 1876.

2. Congress passed laws that gave the President the right to use force to end violence.

3. Radical leaders were disappearing from the political scene. Issues other than reconstruction interested Republicans. Many felt that southerners should take care of their own needs. Racial prejudice weakened enthusiasm for reconstruction. Northern business interests feared the impact of violence on their investments in the South.

4. Both parties claimed victory in South Carolina, Florida, and Louisiana.

5. The Democrats agreed to Hayes' election, and the Republicans had troops pulled out of the South, included southerners in the patronage system, and increased funds for internal improvements in the South.

Special Feature Questions
page 277
1. Property ownership, race, and sex.

2. People with property had a stake in society.
3. Blacks were kept from voting by both violent and nonviolent means.
4. They were not subject to the voting restrictions placed on blacks.

Photo Questions

page 272
Buildings, railroads, and schools were built.

page 273
Radicals passed laws to punish the South.

page 275
School buildings were burned. Bureau workers and teachers were attacked or ostracized.

page 279
Radicals.

page 282
Southern Unionists and northerners who had moved to the South.

page 284
That there was anarchy, misrule, and robbery and that black officeholders were pawns of unscrupulous whites.

page 286
Tenants purchased supplies from the landowner for a percentage of the crop money.

Chapter Review

page 288, Review Questions
1. Economic reconstruction and what to do about the freedmen. Also, some means of readmitting the seceded states had to be found.
2. Lincoln's plan emphasized amnesty and restoration of the old relationship between North and South, but did not push for black rights. Johnson planned to exclude the planter aristocracy from southern governments. His plan was tougher than Lincoln's in some ways (required ratification of the Thirteenth Amendment and repudiation of secession and Confederate debt), but in other ways more lenient (required fewer people to set up new government). The Radicals set stringent terms for readmitting states and took steps to bring about black suffrage.
3. The Freedmen's Bureau was set up to aid blacks in the areas of education, labor relations, legal advice and medical services. Constitutional amendments ended slavery and

gave blacks the right to vote. Federal troops were used to halt violence.
4. Moderates supported the Radicals because of anger over the black codes and other actions of southern states. Johnson drove the moderates further into the Radical camp with his intemperate attacks. Reports of race riots helped the Radicals win in the congressional elections of 1866.
5. Johnson was not as hard on the South as many members of Congress had expected him to be, and he lacked political skills. Johnson's plan resulted in control of southern states by ex-Confederates, and the Radicals strongly disapproved. Johnson vetoed bills passed by Congress to aid freedmen and tried to slow Congress' reconstruction program.
6. Blacks were part of the radical coalition, and blacks were elected to state offices and to Congress, but the Radical regimes were dominated by whites.
7. By violent means and because Republican interest in reconstruction had declined.
8. Very similar. Blacks were free after the war, but had few rights and were economically dependent.

page 288, Discussion
1. Answers may vary. Some students will say no because Lincoln had greater political skills and knew when to compromise. Others may say yes because of the strong feelings in Congress about controlling reconstruction.
2. Answers may vary. Ask students if they think any plan could have led to both freedmen and ex-Confederates taking part in reconstruction governments.
3. Answers may vary. Some students will say no because Johnson's offenses were political, not criminal. Others will say yes because he violated the law. Point out that the Tenure of Office Act was repealed in 1887.
4. Answers may vary. Point out that the Radicals gave blacks some experience in government and allowed them to get an education. However, the reaction to the Radical regimes was so strongly negative that blacks suffered from it.

page 288, Using Maps
1. South Carolina.
2. Alabama, Georgia, Florida.
3. Virginia.

4. Tennessee in 1866. Texas, Mississippi, Georgia, and Virginia in 1870.

page 288, Using Skills
1. Bias.
2. Bias.
3. Objective.
4. Bias.

Emotive words in Tillman's speech (pages 284–285): anarchy, misrule, robbery, murder, stolen, dupes, tools, dirty, vampires, robbers, preyed, prostrate, desperation.

Unit Review

page 289, Review Questions
1. Extremists on both sides had defeated all attempts at compromise. Southerners came to believe northern policies, if instituted, would destroy southern society.
2. It left the South physically and economically devastated. Slaves were freed, but ill-prepared to make their way in the world. Political fighting about reconstruction divided Americans.
3. A larger population, better system of transportation, a more productive economy, and naval superiority.
4. Blacks had their freedom, but were denied their political rights in the South. Prejudice fostered segregation in schools, housing, hospitals, and public transportation and accommodations.

The Historian's Craft

Use The Historian's Craft activity on pages 290–291 to conclude the unit. In this activity, which may be conducted as either an individual or group exercise, students will be given practice in analyzing frame of reference, using works related to Radical Reconstruction. Students should develop the understanding that every historian (and every person forming an opinion about anything) operates within the limits of his or her own experience. This fact does not necessarily invalidate the historian's point of view, but may help to explain it.

The Using Skills activities in this unit have included distinguishing statements of fact from statements of motive, distinguishing statements of fact from statements of opinion, and recognizing biased statements. These skills, along with others from previous units, such as finding the main idea and analyzing relationships, should have adequately prepared students for completing this activity.

After the students make their lists of biographical points, have them discuss how these points may have influenced the two historians. Then have the students answer the questions on page 291.

Question 1. Moore's attitude toward blacks seems to be one of little respect. They had been "pampered" and were "lame factors in the rebuilding of the South." Moore speaks of the "necessity" of segregation and the black's "place in the scheme of life."

Question 2. Moore says that Radical Reconstruction caused disfranchisement of blacks, race friction, and prejudice, but he gives no evidence for this statement. Franklin argues that violence and hostility toward blacks existed before Radical Reconstruction. As evidence, he says that the Ku Klux Klan originated before Radical Reconstruction.

Question 3. Moore says that Radical Reconstruction "caused greater discriminations against the Negroes in politics and education." He cites no evidence. Franklin says whites resisted education for blacks in order to maintain white supremacy. This resistance, he says, occurred within the first two years after the war (before Radical Reconstruction).

UNIT 5 THE AGE OF INDUSTRIALIZATION

After studying this unit, the student should be able to:

1. list and explain the factors that contributed to industrial growth.
2. discuss the growth of the labor movement in late nineteenth-century America.
3. describe the settlement of the trans-Mississippi West and the close of the frontier.
4. describe the development of urban America.
5. discuss the major domestic political issues and events of the late nineteenth and early twentieth centuries, including populism and progressivism.

OVERVIEW

Unit 5 surveys the domestic scene in the United States from the end of Reconstruction through 1917. Chapter 14 describes the factors that led to American industrial development, the philosophy of the era, and the failure of early governmental attempts to regulate business. Chapter 15 narrates the growth of the labor movement, while Chapter 16 describes the settlement of the last continental frontier. Chapters 17 and 19 describe the domestic politics of the era, from Garfield through Wilson. Chapter 18 describes the growth of urban America and sets up the discussion of progressivism that follows in Chapter 19.

INTRODUCING THE UNIT

Many observers today argue that the United States is in transition between an industrial and post-industrial economy. The former was characterized by heavy industry and a goods-oriented economy. The latter is characterized by high technology in industry and a service-oriented economy. Ask the students if this development has brought about any changes in their community. The late nineteenth century saw the transition from an agricultural to an industrial, urban America. What changes do the students think this brought to the lives of Americans?

CHAPTER 14 INDUSTRIAL GROWTH

After studying this chapter, the student should be able to:

1. list the factors that contributed to industrial growth in the United States.
2. explain the role of the railroads in the development of a national transportation network.
3. explain the importance of entrepreneurs in economic development.
4. describe laissez-faire Social Darwinism and its relationship to industrialization.
5. explain the early failure of government attempts to regulate business activities.

OVERVIEW

Chapter 14 describes the foundations for economic growth: the factors of production, the growth of national transportation and communication networks, entrepreneurship, and a philosophy that buttressed unfettered capitalism. The first attempts at governmental regulation are covered in the final section.

Of major import in this chapter is the question of government's role in the economy. Although an issue that can be traced back at least to Jefferson and Hamilton, it is one that grows in significance as the twentieth century approaches. This chapter describes the laissez-faire, Social Darwinist perspective that so permeated American thought at the end of the nineteenth century and the first moves away from that philosophy. This will become the major issue as we move into the politics of populism and progressivism. Important concepts in the chapter include mass production, free enterprise, and property rights.

TEACHING IDEAS
Section 1
Introduction: Have the students look at the picture of Bell's telephone on page 297. What other inventions can they think of that contributed to American growth? What technological advances impinge on their own lives? Have them read the section to discover other contributions to industrial development.

Development: Land, labor, and capital are the factors of production discussed in this section. It is important that students understand these economic concepts. Have them define land, labor, and capital and give examples of each.

Section 2
Introduction: Railroads played a tremendous role in the development of American industry. Not only did they require vast amounts of industrial products, they also established a national transportation network that led to mass markets. As an introduction to railroads, have the students read the feature on railroad magnates on page 299 and then read the section.

Development: Have the students study the map on page 298. Where was most of the new railroad mileage? What does this suggest? Have them review the section in order to describe those developments that fostered railroad expansion and improvement.

Section 3
Introduction: Webster's defines entrepreneur as "one who organizes, manages, and assumes the risks of a business or enterprise." Give the students this definition, then have them read the book's definition in the "Rags to Riches" subsection (page 301). Have them finish the subsection and ask them for the common characteristics of

these entrepreneurs, then have them read the rest of the section for examples.

Development: Have the students reread Rockefeller's defense of trusts on page 304 and analyze the reaction to trusts captured in the cartoon on the same page. Have the students list and define the techniques used to enhance efficiency and reduce competition (vertical integration, horizontal integration, trust, holding company, pool, interlocking directorate).

Section 4
Introduction: Before reading this section, have the students review the discussion of the financing of railroads on pages 299-300. According to this discussion, what made the greatest contribution to the development of railroad capital? (Government subsidies.) Have the students remember this point as they read the section.

Development: The philosophy of laissez-faire Social Darwinism "permeated" this era. To permeate means to spread freely through something. Using the quotations in this section, have the students defend the use of that word in the above statement. Then, have the students look closely at the Beecher quotation on page 306. Is it consistent with what we have learned about the financing of railroads?

Section 5
Introduction: "Permeation" of the era also includes influencing the nation's courts, responsible for interpretation of the law. Have the students read the section to see how the courts were influenced.

Development: Have the students list the pieces of state and federal legislation mentioned in this section and describe the fate of that legislation in the courts.

Conclusion: Have the students study the graph on page 307. What was the condition of the economy at the turn of the century? (Prosperous.) What groups did not share in that prosperity?

ANSWERS
Section Review Questions
page 297
1. William Kelly—Co-inventor of Bessemer Process.
   Christopher Sholes—Invented typewriter.

1. Alexander Graham Bell—Invented telephone.
2. Land, labor, and capital.
3. Corporations sold stock, invested part of their earnings, took loans and received grants from state, local, and national governments.
4. Rather than wait for inspiration, he set up a factory and worked on a trial-and-error basis.

page 301
1. George Westinghouse—Developed air brake.
   Grenville Dodge—Chief engineer on Union Pacific.
   Pacific Railway Act of 1862—Authorized transcontinental railroad and land grants to railroad companies.
2. More powerful locomotives and specialized cars helped increase the amounts and kinds of freight that could be carried. Railroads were expanded and consolidated. Innovations such as standard gauge tracks improved service.
3. It helped bring railroads to sparsely-populated areas and develop the West. Some areas did not really need railroads, and companies sometimes used poor building methods, which led to accidents and high maintenance costs. On the other hand, railroads were used to transport soldiers and mail.
4. Rough terrain, bad weather, and Indian attacks.

page 305
1. Horatio Alger—Wrote "rags to riches" novels.
   Philip G. Armour—Head of meat-packing company.
   John Pierpont Morgan—Banker who bought Carnegie Steel.
2. By controlling all the different levels of steel production (vertical integration).
3. Placed control of many companies in the hands of one board of trustees.
4. Because his trust had been found to be an illegal monopoly.

page 306
1. Charles Darwin—Wrote *Origin of Species*, presenting the theory of evolution.
   Herbert Spencer—English philosopher who applied theory of evolution to society.
   "The Gospel of Wealth"—Essay by Andrew Carnegie that said the rich were obligated to help the poor.

2. The idea had its roots in Enlightenment philosophy.
3. Improvement would come by eliminating the unfit.
4. Some believed that poverty was the result of moral weakness and that the poor were being punished for their sins.

page 308
1. *Munn* v. *Illinois*—Case in which the Supreme Court ruled that states could regulate certain kinds of commerce when property is "affected with a public interest."
   Sherman Antitrust Act—1890 law that made it unlawful to act in restraint of trade or commerce.
   United States v. *E.C. Knight*—Case in which the courts found that a combination of sugar-refining businesses was not in restraint of trade even though it controlled 98 percent of the business.
2. Railroads formed pools, charged high rates, charged more for short hauls than long hauls, held on to good farmland, and practiced graft.
3. By arguing that a corporation had the same right to property that a person did, and could not be deprived of property without due process.
4. To enforce the Interstate Commerce Act.

Photo Questions
page 297
Telegraph, radio, telephone.

page 300
Supplying loans and land grants.

page 302
Meat-packing, railroads, oil.

page 304
Hampers free competition.

page 306
One possible answer is that he is building a wall to hide the means by which he gained his wealth.

Chapter Review
page 309, Review Questions
1. Made natural resources more readily available and less expensive, improved capital equipment and transportation, and developed new means of communication and sources of power.

2. Expanded markets and allowed for faster and cheaper movement of resources.
3. They organized the factors of production.
4. Vertical and horizontal integration, trusts, pools, holding companies, and interlocking directorates.
5. For being against the American tradition of free enterprise, for using unfair methods, and for corruption.
6. The laissez-faire doctrine said that government should not interfere with business. Social Darwinism stated that the rise of big business was a result of natural selection and was ultimately good for society.
7. Ohio found trusts to be illegal monopolies. Other states passed laws limiting rates charged by business. Congress passed the Interstate Commerce Act and the Sherman Act.
8. They found state attempts at regulation to be unconstitutional, and generally ruled in favor of business in cases prosecuted by federal agencies.

page 309, Discussion
1. Answers may vary. Some students may point out recent entrepreneurial successes, while others may say that factors such as discrimi-

nation or government regulation make success less likely.
2. Answers may vary. Point out that the United States was better endowed than most countries.
3. Students may be aware that these ideas have enjoyed a revival in recent years, although they are not usually given these names.
4. Answers may vary.

page 309, Using Maps
1. Great Northern, Northern Pacific, Union Pacific, Central Pacific, Southern Pacific, Atchison, Topeka, and Santa Fe.
2. Southern Pacific, Atchison, Topeka, and Santa Fe. Atchison, Topeka, and Santa Fe.
3. Union Pacific, Central Pacific.
4. Chicago, Toledo, Boston.
5. Southern Pacific.

page 309, Using Skills
This is an exercise designed to demonstrate the importance of keeping an open mind. "All" and "none" answers indicate that the student has accepted an unqualified generalization. The differences between "most" and "many" and "some" are highly debatable. Any of these answers is correct.

CHAPTER 15 THE RISE OF LABOR

After studying this chapter, the student should be able to:

1. discuss the growth of the labor force during the late nineteenth century and the conditions under which laborers worked.
2. describe the major national unions of the era and the shift in philosophy that accompanied union growth.
3. list the problems the labor movement faced.
4. describe some of the major labor clashes of the era.

OVERVIEW

Chapter 15 describes the growth of the labor movement at the end of the nineteenth century. Migrants from the farm and immigrants from overseas faced many hardships in unskilled or semi-skilled occupations. Unions were their only recourse. The first unions, similar to the organizations of the 1840's, were idealistic, but success depended upon an emphasis on "nuts and bolts" issues: wages and hours.

Two themes in particular suggest themselves. The first is the transition from idealism to hardheaded collective bargaining. The second is the ideological conflict between unionization and individualism. Both are treated in the following teaching suggestions. Other important concepts in the chapter are business cycle, arbitration, capitalism, and socialism.

TEACHING IDEAS
Section 1
Introduction: Have the students study the pictures on pages 312 and 313. Here were two sources of "unskilled" labor. The caption to the picture on page 312 captures the thrust of the labor movement as a whole: poor wages led to unionization. Have the students read the section to gain insight into the background for the union movement.

Development: Have the students reread the quotations on pages 313 and 314 to get a feel for the conditions under which some people worked, then have them list common working conditions for the era.

Section 2
Introduction: Review with the students the labor movement of the antebellum period (Chapter 10, page 216). Ask them to identify the goals and techniques of that earlier era. Have them read this section to see if these change.

Development: A good example of the type of individual involved in the early phase of the labor movement was Leonora Barry. Have the students read the feature on her on page 315. What were her other interests besides labor? What was the difference between her approach and that of Samuel Gompers of the AFL?

Section 3
Introduction: Have the students study the cartoon on page 317 and read its caption. How does the statement over the entrance to the "Hall of Unionism" reflect the philosophy of the era as discussed in the last chapter? (Unions interfere with progress through individual struggle for survival.) Now have the students reread the quotation from John D. Rockefeller on page 304 (in Chapter 14). What does he have to say about individualism and corporate expansion? Can Americans accept both lines of reasoning and maintain intellectual consistency? Union organizers did not think so. Have the students read the section for a discussion of other problems faced by unions.

Development: Have the students list the tactics used by management and the courts against unions.

Section 4
Introduction: Have students study the graph on page 321 to learn the basic causes of strikes in the late 1800's. Then have them read the section for examples of some of the most prominent strikes.

Development: Have the students analyze the causes of the strikes in each case. How legitimate were worker demands?

Conclusion: Ask the students how they feel about strikes. Are they justified? If so, on what occasions? What are the costs both to individuals in the union and to the nation? What other techniques, if any, might workers in the latter part of the nineteenth century have used to improve their condition?

ANSWERS
Section Review Questions
page 314
1. The difficulty of making a living by farming.
2. On humanitarian grounds and because children were competing for jobs with adults.
3. During slack periods, workers lost their jobs or had their wages cut.
4. The emphasis put on fast, efficient production and the lack of safety regulations.

page 318
1. William Sylvis—Leader of the National Labor Union.

   Terence Powderly—Leader of the Knights of Labor.

   Leonora Barry—Labor leader.

   Chinese Exclusion Act—Limited Chinese immigration.
2. Workers' cooperatives, currency reform, the eight-hour working day, creation of a Department of Labor.
3. Because they lost several confrontations with management, because of internal conflict, and because they became associated with violence.
4. Unskilled laborers, women, and blacks.

1. A racially and ethnically mixed population, language barriers, and prejudice.
2. Companies gave workers a number of benefits, making it less tempting for them to join a union.
3. Unions were accused of "conspiracy in restraint of trade" and ordered to stop strikes.

page 324
1. August Spies—Anarchist convicted of murder in Haymarket riot.

   Henry Frick—Manager of Homestead Steel.

   George Pullman—Owner of Pullman Car factory.

   Eugene V. Debs—Leader of American Railway Union.
2. Knights were destroyed because they were blamed for the violence.
3. Locked out workers, hired strikebreakers and guards, and called for help from the National Guard.
4. Railroads cut workers' pay, lengthened hours, and discontinued the free ride policy.

Photo Questions

page 312
Equality under the law, equality in the home, and suffrage.

page 313
Unskilled labor, the recession, the availability of a large work force.

page 316
An industrial union combined all workers within an industry. Trade unions consist of workers within a trade regardless of place of employment.

page 317
One possible answer is that unions will force workers into strikes and other actions.

page 322
Attacking the barges; arbitration; hand-to-hand combat; calling in of state militia.

page 323
The control the company held over their lives and the fact that rent and other charges remained high.

Chapter Review

page 324, Review Questions
1. Dehumanized work, broke complex labor into small, repetitive parts, kept workers from seeing the results of their work, produced hazardous working conditions, and required long hours for low pay.
2. The National Labor Union organized trade unions and sought broad political reform; and tried to cooperate with other groups such as farmers and women. The Knights were open to unskilled workers, women, and blacks; also sought broad political reform. The AFL organized only skilled workers and concentrated on "bread and butter" issues.
3. Strikes, arbitration, collective bargaining, political pressure, and cooperation with other groups.
4. Americans were less class-conscious than Europeans, not sympathetic to socialism, and believed they could rise economically through individual effort. American society was also more heterogeneous.
5. By threatening job loss and by tactics such as the yellow dog contract and the lockout.
6. The courts generally supported management, issued injunctions against labor, and recognized management's right to an open shop. The government also supported management with state and federal troops when major strikes broke out.
7. The public was sometimes sympathetic to labor but was outraged by violence.
8. Some restrictions on competition from foreign labor, an eight-hour day for federal employees, and, in a few cases, managed to negotiate contracts or win minor concessions.

page 325, Discussion
1. Answers may vary. Some students may say conditions were harsh because business was exploiting workers. Others may take the position that industrialization was new and competition forced business owners to run their operations as efficiently as possible.
2. Answers may vary. Most students will suggest better organization, especially of women and blacks. Some might suggest cooperation with other political groups.
3. Answers may vary. Students will generally claim that they would be more generous to workers. Ask students what they think the results of generosity would be.

4. Answers may vary. Point out that unions are in a better legal position today, but most workers are still not unionized.

page 325, Using Charts
1. Wages/hours, right to organize, owner lockout or other issue.
2. Wages/hours.
3. 1903.

4. 20 percent.
5. Increase in the number of strikes. Right to organize became a major issue. Wages and hours, although still the number one cause of strikes, was not the overriding issue it once was.

page 325, Using Skills
1, 7, 5, 6, 3, 4, 2.

CHAPTER 16 THE LAST FRONTIER

After studying this chapter, the student should be able to:

1. describe the settlement of the trans-Mississippi West.
2. explain the problems associated with life and farming on the Plains.
3. describe the impact of white migration on the lives of the Plains Indians.

OVERVIEW

Chapter 16 describes the settlement of the trans-Mississippi West. In structure, it is quite similar to Chapter 9, pointing out the nature of settlement, the problems of the farmers, and the friction with native Americans.

Frederick Jackson Turner's description of patterns of settlement is reflected in the first section, as the mining frontier eventually becomes the farming frontier. In the second section, problems of the farmer are emphasized, laying the foundation for a later discussion of populism. The third section describes the last Indian wars and opens the topic of the Indian rights movement. Other important concepts in the chapter include internal migration, cultural conflict, and Americanization.

TEACHING IDEAS

Section 1
Introduction: Review Frederick Jackson Turner's description of the patterns of frontier settlement in Chapter 9 (page 185). To see if the pattern still holds true at the end of the century, have the students skim the title headings in the first section. Then, have the students read for details of trans-Mississippi settlement.

Development: Several ideas might be touched upon in developing this section. Have the students look at the picture of the mining town on page 328, read its caption and answer the question. Also, have the students point out the contributions mining made to American economic development. Have the students study the picture of the cattle drive on page 329 and its caption. Ask them what became of large-scale open-range ranching. Finally, have the students read the feature on the "Image of the West" on page 333 and answer its questions.

Section 2
Introduction: To orient students for this section, have them study the map on page 334 and note the farming areas. The footnote on page 331 helps by naming the states from the trans-Mississippi West. Have them read the section for details on farm life during this period.

Development: Of central importance in this section is the description of the problems faced by farmers in this region. Have the students study the picture on page 332 and the long excerpt concerning the pioneer woman on the same page. What were the problems faced by women? What other problems were faced by farmers (both natural and economic)?

Section 3
Introduction: Review the text's earlier discussion of Indian policy, found in Chapter 9 (pages 188-190). Have the students point out the key aspects of the relationship between whites and

Indians during the earlier era, then have them read the section to see if there are any changes.

Development: Have the students develop a time line showing changes in Indian policy from colonial times through the late 1800's.

Conclusion: Have the students read the quotation from Theodore Roosevelt in the Using Skill exercise on page 343 and compare it to the John Quincy Adams quotation on page 188. What do they find? (The two are similar except for element of Social Darwinism in the Roosevelt quotation.) Roosevelt recommends giving Indians a parcel of land. What was the result of the attempt at "Americanization"?

ANSWERS

Section Review Questions

page 331
1. Comstock Lode—One of biggest silver veins in the world.
   Chisholm Trail—One of standard cattle trails from Texas to Abilene.
   Joseph F. Glidden—Perfected barbed wire.
2. Fighting, rapid crowding of the towns, and lawlessness.
3. Gold was separated from the dirt by sifting it in a pan filled with water to allow the heavier gold to drift to the bottom.
4. Availability of the public domain and the arrival of the railroad in Kansas.
5. Low pay, long hours, exposure to the weather, and Indian attacks.
6. Competing for the same land. Cattle and sheep did not mix well.

page 335
1. Timber Culture Act—Gave settlers 160 acres if they would plant trees on 40.
   Desert Land Act—Gave 640 acres to people who tried to irrigate land.
   Oliver Kelley—Grange founder.
2. Opportunity to escape the scarceness of land, poverty, and political repression of their homeland.
3. Farming was made easier by windmills, dry farming, and frequent harrowing; drought-resistant strains of grains; and machines such as the self-binding reaper and steam-powered corn sheller.
4. To give farmers an opportunity to work together for reforms.

page 341
1. Red Cloud—Sioux Chief.
   Bureau of Indian Affairs—Agency responsible for managing Indian policy.
   Chief Joseph—Leader of the Nez Percé.
   Ghost Dance—Religious ritual performed to restore traditional Indian life and destroy whites.
   Helen Hunt Jackson—Wrote *A Century of Dishonor* about mistreatment of Indians.
2. They were nomadic and warlike because of their dependency on the buffalo and the horse.
3. Young warriors felt that too much had been given away by their elders. Another reason is the government did not fulfill its pledge of payments.
4. Two large reservations were set aside for northern and southern Indians. The government agreed to abandon the Bozeman Road, promised annuity payments, and provided supplies.
5. To Americanize the Indians by forcing them to give up their tradition of communal ownership and making them American citizens.

Special Feature Questions

page 333
1. That streets were paved with gold.
2. The image embodies traits that Americans admire and consider part of the national character.

Photo Questions

page 328
They were deserted and became ghost towns.

page 329
Indian attacks, cattle stampedes, and accidents.

page 330
Escape from prejudice, the independent life on the range, and adventure are answers that should be mentioned.

page 332
To cultivate the land for five years and pay a small fee. Later the requirements of irrigation and planting trees were added.

page 336
Lack of water, winter blizzards, isolation, and the threat of starvation.

Abolished the practice of treating the Indians as sovereign nations and changed Indians' status to wards of the government.

Chapter Review
page 342, Review Questions
1. It was considered unsuitable for farming because it was too dry.
2. Opportunity, open land, and a chance to become wealthy. Every miner dreamed of striking it rich. Farmers had generous governmental land policies that provided free land. Ranchers could use the vast grasslands of the Great Plains.
3. Ranchers wanted open lands for grazing and moving their cattle to shipping points. Farmers wanted to fence in the land to protect it from cattle.
4. Lack of water, weather extremes, insects, prairie fires, lack of trees, and Indian attacks.
5. Ranchers used public lands for their cattle and therefore were sensitive to the need for government permission. Farmers sought government help through laws that provided them with free land. All groups sought protection from Indians.
6. Some mining required equipment and large numbers of miners, and was therefore impossible for individual miners. Cattle raising was possible for individuals, but was taken over by large companies and cattle barons, often by illegitimate means.
7. Initially Indians went along with treaties that included resettlement. As more whites trespassed, many Indians responded with violence, but finally had to surrender. A final effort was to resort to religion (the Ghost Dances).

8. Up to the 1850's the policy was to remove Indians from the path of the whites. Later, treaties set up programs for helping the Indians, such as the Bureau of Indian Affairs, and paid annuities to compensate for lost lands. After Sand Creek the policy shifted toward "Americanization," which the Dawes Act tried to implement.

page 342, Discussion
1. Answers may vary. Warfare, treaties, and changing lifestyles should be mentioned.
2. Answers may vary.
3. Answers may vary.
4. Many were forcibly removed from land and had to adapt to a new environment. Another reason is that whites changed the nature of the land (railroads, towns, industry) and introduced Indians to a new and sometimes disruptive culture (alcohol, firearms, Christianity).

page 343, Using Maps
1. Montana, California, Colorado.
2. Southern Oregon.
3. Goodnight-Loving Trail.
4. Western Trail, Chisholm Trail, Sedalia Trail.
5. Ranching and farming.

page 343, Using Skills
1. That Indians have no right to own all the land. Compares them to whites who do not work.
2. Both inhabited land but only lived off game, did not have farms or ranches. As the hunters and trappers gave way to settlement, so should the Indians.
3. Answers may vary. Roosevelt's ancestors were wealthy landowners and business people and Roosevelt himself was a rancher and settler in the West.

CHAPTER 17 THE GILDED AGE

After studying this chapter, the student should be able to:

1. describe the major issues of the politics of the late nineteenth century.
2. list the Presidents from Garfield through Cleveland's second administration, pointing out the major aspects of each administration.
3. define populism and describe its growth.
4. discuss important features of the New South.

OVERVIEW

Chapter 17 provides an overview of the politics of the Gilded Age, touching upon aspects of political history from the Grant administration through the McKinley-Bryan election in 1896. Of special significance is the political revolt of the farmers, populism, and its impact on the nation and, especially, the New South. With regard to this last point, the chapter treats the black reaction to Jim Crow. Important concepts are corruption, conflict of interest, reform, graduated income tax, civil rights, and the separate but equal principle.

TEACHING IDEAS

Section 1

Introduction: The politics of the late nineteenth century was widely seen as "corrupt." How do students feel about politicians today? Explain the roll of lobbyists (individuals who represent to public officials the views of a certain group). Do they hear of improprieties today? Have them read the section for a description of politics in the Gilded Age.

Development: Since laissez-faire was a key concept during this era, it is important to look at governmental economic policy revolving around currency and the tariff. Ask the students to review the section and determine who benefited most from currency and tariff policy. Did the government pursue a policy of laissez-faire?

Section 2

Introduction: An historian once called the politics of this era the politics of "Tweedledee and Tweedledum." These Lewis Carol characters, it should be recalled, were mirror-like twins. What does this suggest of the party politics of the era? Have the students read the section to see if their speculations are correct.

Development: One current group of historians, using new statistical methods of research, has challenged the above view of the politics of this era. Voters, rather than seeing both parties as essentially the same, saw very significant differences. According to these historians, voters whose religious and world views were evangelical and activist in nature tended to vote Republican (except in the Solid South) and voters whose religious and world views were more passive (including Catholic, immigrant groups) tended to vote Democratic. This was because the Republican party adopted an activist approach to society and the economy while the Democrats tended to be more negative and closer to "laissez-faire" in theirs. While this distinction was especially important in local and state politics, it was also seen on the national level. Have the students review the chapter (include "Major Issues" subsection in previous section) to find evidence of this distinction (different positions on tariff, "Rum, Romanism, and Rebellion" quotation in Cleveland-Blaine campaign).

Section 3

Introduction: Explain the theory of supply and demand to students. An easy way to do this is to develop a hypothetical situation in which one student has an apple to sell. A second student offers 10¢ and a third 12¢. The first student would sell the apple to the student offering 12¢. If, however, yet another student were to offer 14¢ (this being the only spare apple around), the apple would go to this higher bidder. If supply remains constant and demand increases, prices increase. If the apple-selling student were to return to school the next day with several apples—more than enough for those who want to purchase them—the price could not be maintained, especially if someone else has extra apples to sell, also. To attract buyers, the seller would have to lower the price. In this case, supply outstrips demand, causing prices to fall. After your explanation, have the students read the section to discover the various problems (including the problem of over-supply) faced by farmers.

Development: Have the students read the excerpt from the Populist platform found on page 353. What is the attitude toward laissez-faire in that excerpt? Ask the students to speculate about what might happen to the political alignment described in the Section 2 Teaching Ideas if the Democratic party were to adopt the Populist stand. (Democrats, adopting an active-government stance, would probably lose some traditional constituents and draw less support.) Ask the students what did happen in the 1896 election. Was it as close as all the other presidential elections of the late nineteenth century? (No, McKinley landslide.) We will pick up this theme again during the Progressive Era.

Section 4

Introduction: Tell the students that this is the era in which the "Solid South" political phenomenon begins. That is, the South consistently votes Democratic. But the Democratic party in the South in the late nineteenth century is very different from that dominated by plantation owners in the antebellum period. Have the students read the section to discover the difference.

Development: It is interesting to study the application of the Fourteenth Amendment by the federal courts during the late nineteenth and early twentieth centuries. Review the Supreme Court's application of the amendment in the *Santa Clara County* v. *Southern Pacific Railroad* (1886) case (page 307). There the court accepts the argument that state regulation interferes with a corporation's (read "individual's") right to property, a right protected by the due process clause of the Fourteenth Amendment. However, the Court failed to use the amendment to protect real individuals' (blacks') rights (review the discussion on page 358). This, of course, led to a loss of rights for blacks.

Conclusion: Have the students read the feature on Washington and DuBois, page 359, to see the black response.

ANSWERS

Section Review Questions

page 349

1. "Black Friday"—Sept. 24, 1869, the day of the gold crash that caused the financial ruin of hundreds.

    Crédit Mobilier—Construction company involved in a political scandal.

    Orville Babcox—Grant's personal secretary, involved in "Whiskey Ring."

    William M. Tweed—Boss of political machine in New York City.

    Mugwumps—Reform group of Republicans.

2. The tariff, currency questions, and the problem of civil service reform.

3. Farmers and others who favored inflation wanted more greenbacks to be issued, while eastern business owners thought that issuing greenbacks had been a bad idea. The compromise position was to maintain the greenbacks in circulation but issue no more. In regard to silver, groups that favored inflation wanted the government to return to bimetallism and start coining silver again.

4. The party system was based on patronage. Officials paid off political debts by appointing supporters to office.

page 352

1. Half-Breeds—Republican group half-heartedly committed to Reconstruction.

    Stalwarts—Republicans supporting a tough Reconstruction policy.

    Pendleton Act—Set up the merit system in the civil service and created a commission to administer it.

    James G. Blaine—Leader of the Stalwarts and the Republican presidential candidate in 1884.

    Samuel D. Burchard—Member of Protestant clergy who used phrase "Rum, Romanism and Rebellion" to refer to the Democrats.

    Bland-Allison Act—Legislation requiring the Secretary of the Treasury to purchase $2–$4 million worth of silver at market price each month.

2. The parties skirted the issues. There was a great deal of mudslinging, fiery speeches, and parades.

3. Arthur came out for tariff reductions and civil service reform, and vetoed the Chinese Exclusion Act and a river and harbor improvements bill.

4. Cleveland signed the Interstate Commerce Law and helped push through the Dawes Act. He vetoed a pension bill for Civil War veterans and nullified some illegal leases of Indian lands. He also came out against the silver policy of the Bland-Allison Act.

5. Senators from the West received the support of manufacturers for the Sherman Silver Purchase Act. In return, they supported the McKinley Tariff, which increased protection on manufactured goods.

page 356

1. C. W. Macune—Leader of a local farmers' alliance in Texas and of Southern Alliance.

    Mary Ellen Lease—Populist leader who coined slogan, "Raise less corn and more hell."

Australian ballot—Secret ballot.

Tom Watson—Populist leader from Georgia.

2. A rural movement that attempted to make the government respond to the problems of the farmer.

3. Farmers had to borrow to buy land, machinery, or seed. Profits were poor because increased output caused supply to exceed demand. Shipping costs and storage fees were high. Natural disasters often destroyed crops.

4. An inflationary money policy, a graduated income tax, a sub-treasury system to make low interest loans to farmers, government ownership of railroads, telephone, and telegraph systems, the eight-hour day for workers, the secret ballot, recovery of excess lands given to railroads, direct election of U.S. Senators, and the initiative, recall, and referendum.

5. Bryan campaigned for free silver and social and economic justice. He defended unions and tried to win over urban workers. McKinley condemned inflation and felt that silver legislation was dangerous and immoral.

page 359

1. Slaughterhouse Cases—Cases in which the Supreme Court ruled that the Fourteenth Amendment applied only to certain situations and that states could decide what they would do to protect citizens' rights.

   Plessy v. *Ferguson*—Case in which the Supreme Court ruled that segregation was not illegal if separate but equal facilities were provided.

   The Souls of Black Folk—Book by DuBois recounting black history.

   Niagara Movement—Civil rights organization started by DuBois.

2. Tax exemptions and subsidies were provided for industries entering the South.

3. Farmers in the South had the same problems of debt and poverty as those elsewhere. Farmers felt that political leaders were indifferent to their plight. The leaders seemed to ignore farmers and concentrate on attracting businesses. Leaders also ignored demands to shift the tax burden to business. Government corruption was also a problem.

4. The poll tax and the literacy test.

5. The Court generally supported segregation and established the "separate but equal" principle.

Photo Questions

page 346
Revenue officers and distillers collaborated to cheat the government of taxes on distilled liquor.

page 348
He attracted attention to government corruption.

page 350
He was shot by a disappointed office-seeker.

page 353
Groups such as the Grange, Populists, and the Farmers' Alliance.

page 354
An inflationary money policy; a graduated income tax; recovery of excess public lands; government ownership of railroad, telegraph, and telephone systems; an eight-hour work day; and democratic political reforms.

page 357
Economy of the South grew slower than economy of other areas during this period. Industrialization was a slower process in the South, the region was relatively poor, and debts remained high.

Chapter Review

page 360, Review Questions

1. Scandals and corruption shook people's confidence in their leaders. Civil service reform became a major issue. The Populist party was formed to better represent the people's ideas about government.

2. The Gilded Age was materialistic and corrupt. The major parties maintained a delicate balance of power and politicians seldom took strong stands. The philosophy of laissez-faire prevailed.

3. Greenbacks printed during the Civil War had caused inflation. The inflation was diminished by a plan to leave a limited number of greenbacks in circulation, but have them redeemable by gold. Before the war, the government had used both gold and silver to back money. In 1873 the government went on the gold standard. In 1878 the Bland-Allison Act allowed limited coinage of silver. This was

increased by the Sherman Silver Purchase Act in 1890, but calls for "free silver" were rejected.

4. In 1892 the Populists could not win the support of eastern labor or the South. In 1896 they decided to support Democratic candidate Bryan rather than nominate their own candidate because the Democrats adopted the Populist idea on free silver. Bryan was unable to win labor support and better economic times blunted calls for reform, so McKinley won.

5. Attempts at reform were made by Hayes, Arthur, Cleveland, by the Liberal Republicans, the Mugwumps, the Populists, the Grange.

6. New leadership was provided by a business-oriented middle class, and the South was becoming industrialized.

7. White farmers were resentful of the way the black vote had been used against them. Democratic leaders were alarmed that some blacks had voted against them.

8. Blacks could do little in the face of violence and court support of discrimination. Washington called for patience and hard work. DuBois called for more active opposition and started the Niagara Movement, and later the NAACP was formed.

page 360, Discussion
1. Answers may vary. Discussion should include whether a strong leader could have offset the materialism and corruption of the Gilded Age.
2. Answers may vary. Civil service corrected some problems and created others.
3. Answers may vary.
4. Answers may vary.

page 361, Using Maps
1. Weaver.
2. Idaho, Nevada, Colorado, Kansas.
3. All.
4. 95.
5. Northeastern and north central states.

page 361, Using Skills
1. Increase the duty on imported wheat to keep American wheat production safe. Figures on wheat production in several countries. Point out that production figures are given, but import figures are not.
2. That raising the duty on imports to the U.S. would cause other countries to raise their duties. U.S. only imported seed wheat; Germany has raised duties; importing on both sides has decreased.
3. Answers may vary.

CHAPTER 18 AN URBAN SOCIETY

After studying this chapter, the student should be able to:

1. list the factors that contributed to urbanization.
2. describe the impact of immigration on American urban life.
3. discuss the life and culture in American urban centers.
4. describe major aspects of the urban reform movement.

OVERVIEW

The "urbanization" of American society was a major development of the late nineteenth century. This chapter studies the factors that allowed and fostered urbanization, including immigration, the cultural life of the cities, and the American reaction to urbanization and immigration. Themes include the impact of immigration, social stratification in the city, and the dual American response to immigration and urbanization: one positive, the other negative. Important concepts are cultural pluralism, assimilation, prejudice, equal opportunity, yellow journalism, realism, and reform.

TEACHING IDEAS
Section 1

Introduction: Have students study the graph on page 364 and the picture on page 365. What do these visuals tell the students about cities in the late nineteenth century? Have the students read the section to discover other details about urbanization.

Development: Have students develop a chart, based on the following format, outlining the major aspects of urban change.

Urban Changes		
Population Growth	Technological Changes	Geographic Changes
(Fill in sample cities and their growth)	(Fill in developments that allow mass population centers)	(Fill in changes in geographic patterns within cities)

Section 2

Introduction: Have the students study the graphs on page 366. What do the graphs tell the students about immigration? Have them read the section for further details.

Development: Write the definition of "assimilation" on the board: the absorption into the cultural tradition of a population or group. Using the quotation on page 368 as a springboard, ask the students to list the problems immigrants faced in the attempt to assimilate into American society. Have the students describe the American reaction to immigration.

Section 3

Introduction: Have the students read the quotations on pages 369 and 370 concerning housing. Ask them to point out the differences. Have the students read the section looking for other signs of social stratification and other aspects of life and culture in the city.

Development: Social differences in American society were, and are, real. Yet Americans are uncomfortable with this fact and have always stressed the idea of social mobility and equal opportunity. Have the students read the feature on Education ("Perspectives in History," page 371) and answer the questions to discover the role education has played in American society. On another level, stress the development of realism in American art and literature. Realism in literature plays a role in fostering recognition

of social problems, an important foundation for later progressive reform.

Section 4

Introduction: Review the quotation concerning slum housing on page 369. Have the students read the section for more problems faced by the urban poor and attempts at reform.

Development: Have the students read the feature on Addams and Wald on page 378 for a closer look at two women who were very active in one aspect of urban reform. What motivated settlement house workers?

Conclusion: Have the students read the quotation from the machine politician on page 379. What were some positive aspects of this type of machine politics?

ANSWERS
Section Review Questions
page 365

1. The influx of immigrants and the movement of Americans from rural to urban areas.
2. Provided more time for work and play because of electric lamps and increased the availability of power for transportation purposes.
3. Electric trolleys, els, subways, paved streets, and bridges.
4. Allowed the expansion of downtown areas into smaller, more specialized areas. Residents could now live farther away from their work.

page 368

1. Ellis Island—Port of entry for immigrants, where they were processed and registered.

   Jacob Riis—Danish-born writer who wrote about New York City.

   American Protective Association—Society formed by native-born Americans that sought to exclude Catholic immigrants.
2. The "old immigrants" arrived before 1880 and were usually from northern and western Europe. They were easily assimilated. The "new immigrants" came from southern and central Europe and were less easily assimilated.
3. It was difficult to leave the homeland and expensive to travel. Conditions aboard ship were filthy and crowded. The processing procedure was often lengthy and degrading.

4. Clustered around the churches and synagogues that represented the old country to
them. Gathered in coffee houses where their
native language was spoken and bought
newspapers printed in their native tongue.

page 377

1. John Dewey—American pioneer in education
who advocated that schools teac preparation for life.

James Haismith—Inventor of basketball.

John Sousa—Band leader who popularized
marches.

Ash Can School—Group of painters who portrayed grim side of life.

Louis Sullivan—Architect who designed skyscrapers; said that "form follows function."

2. Hot and cold running water, vacuum cleaners, sewing machines, canned goods, bakery
bread, and prepared packaged meat.

3. Baseball, football, basketball, bicycling, boxing, golf, tennis.

4. Yellow journalism tended to color facts with
sensationalism in order to appeal to more
people and to inspire reform. Popular magazines achieved mass circulation.

5. Realism—local-color writers and protest
writers.

page 380

1. Tenements were overcrowded, unsanitary,
and posed a fire hazard. The diet was poor;
medical care was scarce and expensive. Ignorance contributed to the problems of health
care. Crime was prevalent in the slums.

2. Educating the poor, providing day care, recreation, and counseling.

3. Stuffed ballot boxes, sold offices, and received
bribes.

4. Tried to destroy political machines through
the formation of Municipal Leagues and
through the introduction of a responsive
structure of government.

Chapter Review

page 380, Review Questions

1. Societies to protest the arrival of immigrants
were formed. Local laws were passed prohibiting immigrants from holding certain types
of jobs, and immigration was restricted by
such laws as the Chinese Exclusion Act. Politicians responded to the desperate needs of
the newcomers by trading jobs for votes.

2. Cities were lighted by electricity and transportation systems were set up. Skyscrapers
were built and communication was improved.
Streets were paved and bridges built. Cities
grew in physical size as transportation enabled people to live farther away from their
place of work.

3. Unemployment, overpopulation, discrimination, and poverty were factors that led immigrants to leave their homeland.

4. The upper and middle classes lived in residential areas with servants to wait on them. The
poor lived in tenements that were crowded
and unhealthful. Most upper-class children
had the opportunity for at least high school
education, while many of the poor did not
even make it through elementary school. In
the poorer families women and children often
had to work. The more desirable jobs were
often unavailable to the poorer workers. The
upper classes had leisure and money for shopping and sports such as golf and tennis, while
the poor had to satisfy themselves with less
expensive recreation such as cards or stickball.

5. Elementary and secondary education became
free and public. The emphasis changed from
rote learning to "learning by doing." Dewey
and Eliot brought about changes in curriculum and teaching methods. Higher learning
was expanded and graduate schools were
founded.

6. Writers such as Twain *(The Gilded Age)* and
Bellamy *(Looking Backward)* portrayed life
as it really was—often miserable and unjust.
Crane's *Maggie: A Girl of the Streets* and Riis'
How the Other Half Lives showed life in the
slums and stimulated reform. Photographers
and painters portrayed life realistically. In
architecture the idea that form should follow
function had considerable influence.

7. The realistic picture in literature of slums,
the plight of the poor, and political corruption
attracted many to reform movements.

8. Settlement houses were established and
classes were taught to immigrants in English,
hygiene, and work skills. Recreation and
counseling were available. Commissions were
formed to investigate and recommend changes in child labor, working conditions, and
housing. Municipal Leagues were formed to
fight political corruption.

Special Feature Questions

page 371

1. An informed and educated public is essential in a democratic society.
2. To provide equal opportunity, to teach patriotism and a sense of national unity, to prepare children for citizenship, and to train them for jobs and careers.
3. Wealthier communities are better able to support schools than poorer ones are.

Photo Questions

page 365

Water, sewage, police and fire protection.

page 368

People came from eastern and southern Europe in great number—many from Italy, Poland, Russia, and Hungary—and from Asia.

page 369

Churches and synagogues, coffee houses.

page 373

Stoves, irons, vacuum cleaners, sewing machines, packaged foods, ready-made clothing.

page 374

Tennis, golf, basketball.

page 376

Realism.

page 379

Education, health care, day care for children, recreational facilities, counseling.

page 381, Discussion

1. Answers may vary. Bring up the question of bilingual education. Does it prevent assimilation into mainstream American society?
2. Answers may vary. Most immigrants probably benefitted.
3. Answers may vary.
4. Answers may vary. Discussion should include suffrage, working conditions, salaries, opportunities, social activities.

page 381, Using Graphs

1. Strong increase (1 percent—11 percent—22 percent).
2. Germany.
3. 1901-1910.
4. 2,812,000.
5. Steady decrease (17 percent—12 percent—3 percent).

page 381, Using Skills

1. b
2. b
3. b
4. a
5. a

CHAPTER 19 THE PROGRESSIVE ERA

After studying this chapter, the student should be able to:

1. describe the various groups that contributed to the progressive impulse.
2. list and explain the goals of progressives.
3. discuss the contributions to the progressive movement of Presidents Theodore Roosevelt, William Howard Taft, and Woodrow Wilson.

OVERVIEW

Chapter 19 surveys the Progressive era: its philosophical foundations, goals, leaders, and accomplishments. The central theme of the chapter is the rejection of laissez-faire Social Darwinism for pragmatic government intervention. In that respect, some effort should be expanded in explaining pragmatism (covered in the first section) and the role of that individual who was the embodiment of action, Theodore Roosevelt (third section). The differences between Roosevelt's and Wilson's approach to progressivism should also be stressed, as those differences still inform debate over the role of government today. Other concepts in the chapter include reform, conservation, reserve requirement, price fixing, and trustbusting.

TEACHING IDEAS

Section 1

Introduction: Write the definition of "pragmatism" on the board: a practical approach to problems or affairs. Historian Daniel Boorstin thinks that pragmatism is one of the most important characteristics of the American people. Ask students for examples of pragmatism in their own lives, then have them read the section.

Development: A major target of progressive reformers was the monopoly, or trust. Have the students study the cartoon on page 384 and the pictures on page 385 to emphasize this point. One of the best ways to contrast progressive thought with earlier ideas is through religious spokespersons. Have the students reread the quotations from Russell Conwell and Henry Ward Beecher on page 306 (Chapter 14) and contrast them with the ideas of Rauschenbush and other practitioners of the Social Gospel, pages 384-385. Finally, this is a good place to have students complete the "Using Skills" exercise on page 401.

Section 2

Introduction: Have the students read the feature on "Fighting Bob" LaFollette on page 389 and then study the map on page 387 to see how widespread the spirit of reform was. Then, have them read the section.

Development: Have the students complete a chart similar to the following, outlining the major political and social goals of the progressive movement.

	Political	Social
local		
	commissioners city manager municipal ownership/utilities	education housing
state		
	primary initiative referendum recall women's suffrage direct election of Senators	working conditions child labor women's labor workers' compensation
national		
	trustbusting	

Section 3

Introduction: Write the quotation from Theodore Roosevelt found on page 390 on the board: "Don't fritter away your time; create, act, take a place wherever you are and be somebody; get action." Ask the students what this quotation suggests about Roosevelt. Have them read the section to see the man of action in action.

Development: Roosevelt reflects a couple of major themes in the history of this period. His pragmatic nature, leaning toward action and results and refusing to be bound by theory, can be seen in his treatment of the coal strike. Have students reread the material on the coal strike on page 392 and explain his actions in terms of pragmatism. Roosevelt was also concerned with efficiency. His concern is implicit in the "Captains of industry . . ." quotation on page 392 and in his concern over conservation.

Section 4

Introduction: Have the students study the cartoon on page 395 and then read the section to answer the question in its caption.

Development: Although Taft lost the support of progressives, it is interesting to note the progressive accomplishments under his administration. Ask the students, "Which administration saw more progressive legislation, Roosevelt's or Taft's?" Perhaps the most important idea treated in this section, however, is the contrast between Theodore Roosevelt's "New Nationalism" and Woodrow Wilson's "New Freedom." Roosevelt felt giant corporations were more efficient and therefore would merely regulate them. Wilson, on the other hand, wanted to break up the trusts, fostering greater competition. Which approach is more like federal policy today? (Roosevelt's.)

Section 5

Introduction: Ask the students if, despite the call for government action, Wilson's New Freedom was closer to the traditional Democratic view of the role of government (discussed in the Teaching Ideas of Chapter 17, section 2) than Roosevelt's New Nationalism. Help them understand that it was. Rather than leaving government in long-lasting role of overseeing business, Wilson preferred quick government strokes to break up trusts and then to leave the economy alone. Also, have the students note that Wilson's approach to the tariff was traditionally Democratic (lower it).

Development: Many historians have pointed out that, in practice, there wasn't much distinction between Wilson's New Freedom and what Roosevelt said he would have done under the New Nationalism. Have the students look for evidence in support of this contention.

Conclusion: Today, the federal government uses two major approaches in the attempt to "tune" the economy: fiscal policy and monetary policy. Fiscal policy (deficit spending or balancing the budget) is established by Congress. Monetary policy, however, is controlled by the Federal Reserve. Therefore, it is important for the students to understand how the Fed controls the money supply. This section discusses the legislation establishing the Fed and describes one way the Fed controls the money supply (loan rate to member banks). (The second major means for controlling the money supply—purchase and sale of government securities on the open market—is not discussed until Chapter 25, the New Deal's establishment of the Federal Open Market Committee as part of the Fed.) Make sure the students understand the function of the Fed described in this section.

ANSWERS
Section Review Questions
page 386
1. William James—Philosopher and pragmatist.

   Oliver Wendell Holmes, Jr.—Supreme Court justice who said that law was based on human experience.

   Ida Tarbell—Muckraker who attacked practices of Standard Oil.

   The Shame of the Cities—Book written by Lincoln Steffens about corruption in city government.

2. The growth of big business trusts, labor unrest, and corruption in government.
3. The right to make wills, to decide what to do with their wages, and equal rights to guardianship of children. In addition, some states were giving women the right to vote.
4. Municipal corruption, ruthless business practices, working conditions, food processing practices, corporate corruption.

page 390
1. Thomas L. Johnson—Reform mayor of Cleveland.

   "Wisconsin Idea"—Progressive government in Wisconsin.

   Hiram Johnson—Progressive governor of California who challenged railroad abuses in his state.

2. New forms of government: commission and city manager.
3. Direct primaries, initiatives, referendums, and recalls allowed the people to have a more direct voice in state government. Women received the right to vote in some states.
4. Workmen's compensation laws, laws limiting the number of hours women could work, minimum wages laws, and child labor laws.

page 394
1. "Square Deal"—Name given to Roosevelt's domestic program.

   Pure Food and Drug Act—Prohibited the manufacture, sale or transportation of impure or improperly labeled foods or drugs in commerce.

   Newlands Act—Law that money gained from the sale of public lands should be used for reclamation or irrigation projects.

2. Some were concerned with the public good while others were not.
3. Passed the Elkins Act and the Hepburn Act regulating activities of railroads.
4. He felt there was exploitation of natural resources. He wanted efficient use of resources and protection of wildlife and scenic areas.
5. Inelastic currency did not keep up with the demands of the economy and caused a shortage that limited credit and the lending power of banks.

page 397
1. Mann-Elkins Act—Extended the power of the ICC over communications companies.

   Joseph G. Cannon—Speaker of the House whose tactics blocked progressive legislation.

   George W. Norris—Representative from Nebraska who submitted legislation that reduced the powers of the Speaker.

   National Progressive Republican League—Group of reform-minded Republican insurgents, led by LaFollette.

2. He initiated twice as many antitrust suits as Roosevelt, supported expansion of the powers of the ICC, and increased the number of civil service workers. In addition, the Department of Labor was set up during his administration.
3. The tariff, the issue of the power of the Speaker of the House, and the Ballinger-Pinchot controversy.
4. New Nationalism wanted government to control trusts while New Freedom wanted government to eliminate trusts. The former wanted to regulate big business while the latter wanted to maintain competition.

page 400
1. Federal Trade Commission Act—Set up a commission to investigate corporate practices.
   Clayton Antitrust Act—Declared practices such as interlocking directorates and price-fixing to be unfair. Was later declared unconstitutional.
   "Wobblies"—International Workers of the World. Wanted to overthrow the capitalist system.
   Smith-Lever Act—Set up training programs for farm agents.
2. He believed that foreign competition would make American producers improve their products and lower prices.
3. It is a bankers' bank that serves as a clearinghouse for checks, makes loans to member banks, and provides flexibility in the currency.
4. He helped get the Clayton Antitrust Act passed, exempting labor from antitrust laws and injunctions, and helped improve working conditions by legislation such as the Seaman's Act, Adamson Act, and the Keating-Owen Act.

Photo Questions
page 384
Women's rights, political corruption, business reform, workers' compensation, work safety, conservation, tariffs.

page 386
Meat-packing industry.

page 388
Wyoming, Colorado, Idaho, Utah, Washington, California.

page 390
Minimum age and wage laws, laws limiting working hours, and the establishment of the Children's Bureau. The Keating-Owen Act, banning the products of child labor from interstate commerce, was later declared unconstitutional.

page 392
His investigation of the working conditions in the cigar industry. Also, he was aware of and showed concern over slum conditions during his stint as president of the New York City police commissioners.

page 393
The National Reclamation Act.

page 395
Taft had a more limited view of the Presidency. He felt that Congress should decide matters of policy.

page 399
Instituted program of agents to assist farmers. Set up a dollar-matching system to provide funds for education in agriculture.

Chapter Review
page 400, Review Questions
1. Populist support was from farmers and workers. Progressive support was more diverse and more urban and middle-class oriented. In addition, the Progressives were more successful in achieving their aims.
2. Support came from attention drawn by muckrakers. Many in the urban middle class were concerned about losing the American dream in a struggle between capitalists and labor. Middle and upper-class women had firsthand knowledge of slum activities from volunteer activities. Pragmatists provided rationale, and social gospel ministers supported reform.
3. Social gospel wanted the church to take an active role in improving society. Pragmatists supported experimenting to see what methods worked best. Pragmatism held that people had to direct the course of their lives by using reason.
4. On the local level there were changes in the forms of government (city manager and commission). State governments began adopting direct primaries, the initiative, referendum, and recall. On the national level the direct

election of Senators was provided by the Seventeenth Amendment.

5. Regulation of monopolies, public ownership of utilities, regulation of business, and trustbusting.

6. The Clayton Act, workmen's compensation laws, laws limiting child labor, and the beginnings of regulation of working hours.

7. All three wanted to restrict the unfair practices of big business. Roosevelt distinguished between good and bad trusts. Taft acted to have business comply with the letter of the law, as shown by the number of indictments issued during his administration. Wilson wanted to maximize competition and eliminate trusts and monopolies, but his practical approach was close to Roosevelt and Taft's.

8. Women got the right to vote, first in a few states, then nationally through the Nineteenth Amendment.

page 401, Discussion

1. Answers may vary. Point out that the pragmatists' emphasis on the efficacy of an action could lead to a philosophy of the ends justifying the means. On the other hand human experience is constantly changing. It could be necessary to experiment, and evaluate and adapt methods and goals.

2. Answers may vary. Women gaining the right to vote should be mentioned.

3. Answers may vary.

4. Answers may vary. Those who believe Taft did not deserve rejection should mention his role in trustbusting. Students who believe progressives were correct in rejecting him should note that Taft considered Congress the policymaker for the nation, therefore limiting the reforms a President could institute.

page 401, Using Graphs

1. 1907.
2. Rose to highest level since 1906.
3. 1905-1907.
4. Recession.
5. Six.

page 401, Using Skills

1. b.
2. Philadelphia, the purest American city, is the nation's "most hopeless," while New York City and Chicago, two cities in which immigrants from many countries live, have

instituted reform and a good system of government.

Unit Review

page 402, Review Questions

1. a, c.

2. Benefits included the creation of jobs, the newly-available material goods, and the opportunity to improve one's life. Disadvantages included the corrupt practices used in some industries, and the monotonous labor, long hours, low wages, and poor working conditions experienced by workers.

3. By 1917 government was involved in conservation, housing, and education, and the plight of the worker—issues that were not addressed by government in the mid-1800's.

4. Industrialization in the North produced new population and trade centers, and new systems of transportation were developed. Many cities experienced tremendous growth. Industrialization changed the South, but the region's economy was still based on agriculture. Industrialization in the West was slower because this region was settled later and many westerners were involved in raising cattle or farming.

The Historian's Craft

Conclude the unit by having students complete The Historian's Craft exercise on pages 403-405. In this activity, which may be conducted as an individual or group exercise, students are given practice in analyzing evidence, using eyewitness testimony concerning the Homestead Steel Strike of 1892.

The Using Skills activities in this unit have included keeping an open mind, putting events in chronological order, analyzing frame of reference, analyzing evidence in arguments, determining difficulty of proof, and finding supporting facts for the main idea. The Historian's Craft for this unit builds on these skills, as well as other chapter and unit skills, such as distinguishing statements of fact from statements of opinion and drawing inferences.

After the students read the testimony of the various witnesses, have them answer the questions on page 405:

Question 1. The witnesses seem to agree that the Pinkertons tied their barge at the landing beside the Homestead plant, that a large crowd was waiting for them on the bank, and that shots were fired on both sides. Their main point of disagreement concerns which side fired the first shots.

Question 2. Answers may vary.

Question 3. Witnesses may have been influenced by their sympathies for one side or the other as well as by their physical vantage points. Point out that biased sympathy may influence not only what a person says, but what he or she actually perceives.

Question 4. Physical evidence, such as who was wounded and from what direction, is one possibility.

Question 5. A historian who favors unions might be more persuaded by the testimony of those who claimed that the Pinkertons fired the first shot, while a historian who disapproves of unions might be influenced by testimony against the strikers.

UNIT 6 THE RISE TO WORLD POWER

After studying this unit, the student should be able to:

1. describe American expansionism at the end of the nineteenth century.
2. discuss the diplomacy of Theodore Roosevelt, William Howard Taft, and Woodrow Wilson.
3. describe the impact of World War I on American society and describe America's military contribution to the Allied victory.

OVERVIEW

Just as the last unit covered the domestic events of the late nineteenth and early twentieth centuries, this unit treats the diplomatic history of the United States during the same period. Chapter 20 follows American foreign policy from the end of the Civil War through the Spanish-American War. Chapter 21 discusses the various initiatives of Roosevelt, Taft, and Wilson. Chapter 22 treats World War I, focusing on its impact on the domestic scene.

INTRODUCING THE UNIT

Sometimes students have trouble picking up the thread of a narrative when there is a chronological break such as the one at the beginning of this unit (the return to the 1860's). Therefore, to introduce this unit, juxtapose two lines similar to the following on the board. This will help students see that the material covered in this unit was concurrent with that in the last.

1867 Alaska	1909 Taft & Dollar Diplomacy
1872 Samoan Treaty	1913 Missionary Diplomacy
1875 Hawaiian Treaty	1914 War in Europe
1890 Navy Rebuilds	1917 U.S. enters WW I
1895 Olney Corollary	1869 Grant
1898 Spanish-American War	1877 Hayes
	1881 Garfield & Arthur
1899 Open Door	1885 Cleveland
1903 Revolt in Panama	1889 Harrison
1904 Roosevelt Corollary	1893 Cleveland
	1897 McKinley
1905 Roosevelt & Russo-Japanese War	1901 Roosevelt
	1909 Taft
	1913 Wilson

CHAPTER 20 AN AMERICAN EMPIRE

After studying this chapter, the student should be able to:

1. detail American foreign policy in the years immediately following the Civil War.
2. define the new manifest destiny and describe its origins.
3. list the major engagements and outcomes of the Spanish-American War.
4. describe the nature of America's continued presence in territories won during the war.

OVERVIEW

Chapter 20 pursues American foreign policy from the end of the Civil War through the Spanish-American War. In this chapter we see the development of a new spirit of manifest destiny, one which carries expansionism beyond the continental boundaries of the United States.

Just as in the earlier discussion of a philosophy for industrial expansion, it is interesting to note the impact of Social Darwinism on geographic expansionism. The chapter does this and closes with a discussion of the Spanish-American War. Important concepts include imperialism, sphere of influence, eugenics, and yellow journalism.

TEACHING IDEAS

Section 1

Introduction: Review the provisions of the Monroe Doctrine (Chapter 7, page 159) with the students, and then have them read the section to see how these provisions were upheld after the Civil War. Have them also watch for an example of an individual who early on called for expansion beyond continental boundaries (Seward).

Development: Have the students defend the statement, "William H. Seward was ahead of his time."

Section 2

Introduction: Point out the quotation from Mahan that begins the chapter. Ask them if Seward would have agreed. Then, have them read the section to see how Americans did, in fact, follow Mahan's statement.

Development: It is interesting to note the similar justification for industrial and geographic expansionism. Have the students compare the Burgess quotation found on page 411 and the supporting material from the text to the Rockefeller quotation found on page 305 (Chapter 14) and its supporting textual material.

Section 3

Introduction: To orient the students, have them study the maps on page 420. On a world map, point out the areas on which these maps focus.

Development: After reading this section, have the students complete the "Using Skills" exercise on page 423. Next, have the students analyze the McKinley speech found on page 420 for the various attitudes toward expansion that we have seen.

Section 4

Introduction: Have the students read the quotation from William Graham Sumner in the Imperialism feature on page 414. Then, have them read this section to see how Sumner's warning was prescient.

Development: To pursue this question of liberty, ask the students what they think the reaction of Cubans seeking independence might have been to the Platt Amendment. What was the Philippine reaction to American occupation? Why?

Conclusion: Have the students read the "Imperialism" feature on page 414. How is the debate over imperialism reflected in current foreign policy issues?

ANSWERS

Section Review Questions

page 411

1. Benito Juaréz—President of Mexico.
   Seward's Icebox—Alaska.
   Danish West Indies—The Virgin Islands.
2. To recover money owed to France, use Mexico's raw materials, and check the power of the United States.
3. To establish a naval base in the northern Pacific and to serve as a link in the China trade.
4. In the Pacific and the Caribbean.

page 415

1. Rudyard Kipling—British poet.
   Naval Act of 1890—Appropriated money to build battleships.
   Sanford B. Dole—Leader of revolt in Hawaii and annexation effort.
   Richard Olney—Secretary of State under President Cleveland.
2. Applied to countries as well as to individuals.
3. Sea power would ensure the future of the United States as a great nation. In addition, colonies were needed to provide markets and raw materials and to serve as ports and refueling stations.
4. The islands were important as a link in the China trade and as a source of sugar.
5. Did not want any European country to force its control upon any American country.

page 421

1. General Valeriano Weyler—Spanish general whose harsh tactics in suppressing the revolt in Cuba earned him the nickname "Butcher."

Enrique Dupuy de Lôme—Spanish minister to the United States.

the "Rough Riders"—Volunteer cavalry unit during Spanish-American War.

Emilio Aguinaldo—Filipino rebel leader.

2. Encouraged sympathy for the rebels in Cuba.
3. Sinking of the U.S.S. *Maine*.
4. A large and modern navy.
5. Spain surrendered all rights to Cuba and assumed the Cuban debt. Puerto Rico and Guam were ceded to the United States and the U.S. purchased the Philippines.

page 422
1. Foraker Act—Ended military rule and set up a civil government in Puerto Rico.

Platt Amendment—Set requirements for withdrawal of United States from Cuba.

Jones Act—Confirmed intention of United States to withdraw from the Philippines when a stable government was established.

2. In Puerto Rico the military withdrew, and a civil government was set up with a governor and an upper house selected by the President. The people elected the lower house. In Guam administration was in the hands of the Navy Department.
3. Feared the unstable political situation would jeopardize American interests.
4. They revolted.

Special Feature Questions
page 414
1. Military advantage, religion, nationalism, economic gain.
2. Colonies revolt against outside powers; competition among imperialist powers.

Photo Questions
page 410
He believed in a strong foreign policy.

page 412
When it was revealed that the Chilean navy was stronger than the navy of the United States.

page 413
Destroyed Hawaii's advantage in the sugar trade and nearly wrecked its economy.

page 416
To increase the circulation of the newspaper.

page 418
Although the Spaniards were blamed, no proof exists. Cuban revolutionaries may have been responsible.

page 419
El Caney and San Juan Hill.

Chapter Review
page 423, Review Questions
1. Americans began to fear that they were falling behind in the race for an empire.
2. Theories of eugenics ("white man's burden") and Social Darwinism.
3. By arbitration, the threat of war, and war.
4. Treaties with Samoa and the annexation of Hawaii.
5. Disapproval of measures used by Spain to put down Cuban revolt, sensationalism in the press, the De Lôme letter, and the sinking of the *Maine*.
6. A naval force under Dewey destroyed the Spanish fleet in the Pacific. Another naval force under Sampson blockaded the rest of the Spanish navy in Santiago Harbor in Cuba. The Spanish fleet was destroyed when it tried to break the blockade.
7. The military took control. The United States withdrew when the Cubans added the Platt Amendment to their Constitution.
8. The United States emerged as a world power.

page 423, Discussion
1. Answers may vary. Supporters of an empire for the United States might mention trade, strength, and the spread of democratic ideals. Anti-imperialists should defend the rights of individuals and nations.
2. Answers may vary. The major difference is that the earlier expansion of the United States was from ocean to ocean. In the late 1800's the United States began reaching outside this area. Some students may argue that this was not an essential difference.
3. Answers may vary. Supporters of intervention should mention the mistreatment of Cubans under Spanish rule and the sinking of the *Maine*. Detractors might mention that a climate for intervention was created by the yellow press.
4. Answers may vary.

page 423, Using Maps
1. El Caney, San Juan Hill.
2. Tampa. Santiago de Cuba.
3. Philippines, Puerto Rico.
4. About 100 miles (160 kilometers).
5. From the South. To avoid bombardment.

page 423, Using Skills
1. William Randolph Hearst. Unfavorably.
2. He colors the news. Yellow press smears.
3. To illustrate childishness, ignorance.
4. b, c.
5. No.

CHAPTER 21 THE UNITED STATES AS A WORLD POWER

After studying this chapter, the student should be able to:

1. describe American foreign policy in the Far East at the turn of the century.
2. explain the American role in the creation of the Panama Canal.
3. give examples of Roosevelt's use of the "big stick" and Taft's dollar diplomacy.
4. discuss Woodrow Wilson's attempt to base foreign policy on American ideals.

OVERVIEW

Chapter 21 surveys the foreign policy of Theodore Roosevelt, William Howard Taft, and Woodrow Wilson before 1917. The scene shifts back and forth between the Caribbean and the Far East as Roosevelt pursues his "big stick" policy, Taft "dollar diplomacy," and Wilson "missionary diplomacy." While the chapter studies events in terms of their impact on American interests, the students on occasion should be asked to view actions of the United States from the perspective of other nations—particularly those of Latin America. Viewing events from such a perspective will help students to better understand United States-Latin American relations today.

TEACHING IDEAS

Section 1

Introduction: Orient the students for this section by having them study the map of Asia on page 426. From their earlier studies, they should be able to state the reason the United States was interested in China (profitable trade). Have them read the section.

Development: Ask the students to study the Theodore Roosevelt quotation on page 428. Frequently parochial attitudes cause a distorted picture of reality and endanger the national interest. Was this the case in the situation addressed by Roosevelt in this quotation?

Section 2

Introduction: At the time, the Panama Canal was an engineering feat of considerable proportions, one of which Americans were justifiably proud. In 1978, two treaties turning control of the Canal over to Panama were ratified amid much controversy. Have the students read this section to see how the United States ended up with a canal through Panama.

Development: Have the students put themselves in the shoes of the Colombians for a moment. Were the concerns which led to their failure to ratify the Hay-Herrán Treaty (page 431) legitimate? What was the role of the United States in the Panamanian revolt? How did Roosevelt explain his actions? (Review quotation, page 432.) Why might some Americans have been embarrassed by their government's behavior toward Colombia?

Section 3

Introduction: The above discussion should help students understand Latin American sensitivity to United States actions. The American attitude toward that part of the world was captured in the Olney Corollary to the Monroe Doctrine, an excerpt from which was quoted on page 414 (Chapter 20). Review that quotation and then have the students read this section to find other sources of Latin American resentment.

Development: Have the students read the excerpt from the Roosevelt Corollary on pages 434-435. If they had been Latin American, how might they have reacted? Have the students list examples of American intervention in Latin America, noting the shift in emphasis under Taft. What motives are revealed in the Taft explanation of intervention in Nicaragua (page 438)?

Section 4

Introduction: Ask the students why the diplomacy of an "idealist" like Woodrow Wilson might be labeled "missionary." Have them read the section to find out why.

Development: It appears as though American relations with Latin America remained troubled despite good intentions. Was Wilson able to maintain "missionary diplomacy" or did he also use heavy-handed techniques? What actions did Wilson pursue in Nicaragua, Haiti, the Dominican Republic, and Mexico?

Conclusion: To conclude the chapter, have students complete the "Using Skills" exercise on page 445.

ANSWERS

Section Review Questions

page 429

1. American-Asiatic Association—Business group that urged the United States to protect its economic position in the Far East.
   John Hay—Secretary of State and architect of the Open Door.
   "foreign devils"—Foreigners living in China.
   Boxers—Chinese patriotic society.
   Taft-Katsura Agreement—Recognized Japan's dominance in Korea in exchange for promise to leave Philippines under American control.
   Gentlemen's Agreement—Restricted emigration of Japanese workers to United States.
   "great white fleet"—Name given the United States Navy.
2. Trading rights of all nations would be respected, tariffs would be collected by Chinese officials, and rates and duties would not dis-

criminate against people from other countries.
3. Helped negotiate a settlement.
4. The Japanese were displeased with terms of the treaty and with reports of racial prejudice and violence against Japanese in California.
5. To uphold the Open Door in China, preserve the country's integrity, and respect territorial rights and maintain the status quo in the Pacific.

page 433

1. Clayton-Bulwer Treaty—Agreement on canal rights and canal construction with Britain.
   Ferdinand de Lesseps—Chief engineer of attempt by French company to build canal in Panama.
   Philippe Bunau-Varilla—French company engineer who helped foment revolt in Panama; Panama's first minister to U.S.
   Lieutenant-Colonel George W. Goethals—Headed Panama Canal building project.
2. Lack of money and an unhealthful environment.
3. They were unhappy with the price paid, wanted some of the money that went to France, and were afraid of losing control of Panama.
4. Financial and naval help.
5. Proud of the achievement, but many were embarrassed by the government's treatment of Colombia.

page 439

1. Cipriano Castro—Venezuelan dictator.
   Luis M. Drago—Argentina's Minister of Foreign Affairs and author of doctrine stating that no European power had the right to use force to collect debts in Latin America.
   Kaiser Wilhelm—German emperor.
   Philander C. Knox—Secretary of State under Taft.
   Henry Cabot Lodge—Senator who wrote corollary to Monroe Doctrine stating opposition to any attempt to sell strategic land located in Americas to nations or companies outside the Western Hemisphere.
2. Proposed intervention by United States under certain situations.
3. Helped reach agreement to determine status of Morocco.

4. Intervened during revolution to protect American interests.
5. A Japanese company wished to buy land in Baja, California.

page 444
1. Bryan-Chamorro Treaty—Gave the United States exclusive rights to build a canal in Nicaragua.

   General Victoriano Huerta—Reactionary leader who took over Mexican government.

   Admiral Henry T. Mayo—Naval officer whose role in Tampico incident led to confrontation with Mexico.

   ABC Powers—Argentina, Brazil, Chile; the three powers mediated the 1914 Mexico-United States dispute.
2. Pay Colombia $25 million and express regret over treatment of that country.
3. To prevent chaos and foreign intervention.
4. Was willing to recognize only governments that derived their authority from the consent of the governed.

Photo Questions
page 427
Within a region, a controlling power secured trade restrictions that eliminated other countries.

page 428
They were angered by Roosevelt's refusal to support their claims for payment for war damages.

page 432
Panama, Nicaragua, Colombia, Cuba.

page 435
Yes. Roosevelt appears strong and other nations appear eager for his help.

page 436
Overseas trade and industrial and financial expansion.

page 438
Devised "cooling-off" treaties. Ended U.S. involvement in consortium in China. Negotiated with other nations.

page 440
The foreign policy outlined by Wilson; intended to aid other countries.

page 442
Sent General Pershing into Mexico with a large force to capture Villa.

Chapter Review
page 444, Review Questions
1. European spheres of interest interfered with American business.
2. Japan was displeased with the Taft-Katsura treaty and over treatment of Japanese in California.
3. Obtaining rights to the land; conflicts with Columbia; the prevalence of malaria and yellow fever; engineering problems.
4. An interoceanic canal was essential to protect the Western Hemisphere and American possessions in the Pacific, to improve trade in the Far East, and save time and lower shipping costs.
5. His use of threat and action in Venezuela, the Dominican Republic, and Cuba. Roosevelt extended the Monroe Doctrine by threatening intervention in any nation in the Western Hemisphere.
6. By promoting American business and banking interests around the world.
7. Wilson's policy was based on moral premises —promoting peace and democracy. Roosevelt and Taft were more concerned with promoting American political and financial interests.
8. Signed "cooling off" treaties. Withdrew from consortium in China. Offered payment and apology to Columbia. Withheld recognition from Huerta government.

page 445, Discussion
1. Answers may vary. Students who believe the United States was justified may argue that the treaty was accepted and that the United States lived up to its part. On the other hand, the U.S. provided military and financial help during the revolt in Panama, thus dooming any chances Colombia had of holding on to its colony.
2. Answers may vary, but should include peace, defense, furthering of American economic interests abroad, encouraging democracy.
3. Answers may vary. Some students may suggest that moral considerations should be the only basis for a foreign policy. Others may argue that this leads to imposing ideas of one nation on another.

4. Answers may vary.

page 445, Using Maps
1. Great Britain, France, Netherlands, Germany, Russia.
2. Japan.
3. Great Britain.
4. Vladivostok, Port Arthur.

5. Japan, Russia. Russia's presence in Manchuria after the other great powers withdrew threatened economic development of Japan.

page 445, Using Skills
1. Yes (not "merely an enlarged field for our commerce and enterprise" implies assumption that Mexico *is* such a field).
2. c.

CHAPTER 22 WORLD WAR I

After studying this chapter, the student should be able to:

1. describe the outbreak of war in Europe.
2. explain the difficulty of maintaining American neutrality.
3. discuss both the impact of the war in the United States and the American military contribution to the war.
4. explain the failure of the United States Senate to ratify the Versailles Treaty.

OVERVIEW

Chapter 22 is a narrative of American involvement in World War I. Despite attempts to remain neutral, the United States, with growing economic ties to the Allied Powers and growing disenchantment with German submarine warfare, found itself sending troops to Europe. The chapter describes Wilson's attempts to maintain neutrality, the incidents leading to American involvement, the impact of the war on the home front, and the American military contribution. American isolationism is reestablished with the rejection of the Versailles Treaty. Concepts to be stressed in this chapter are propaganda, militarism, and pacifism.

TEACHING IDEAS

Section 1

Introduction: Some critics today call the United States militaristic. Have the students read the section introduction for the definition of this term. Do they agree? Have them read the section to discover the implications of militarism in the context of developments in Europe during the early twentieth century.

Development: Have the students analyze the Wilson quotation on page 448 for the position of the United States at the outset of the war.

Section 2

Introduction: The introduction of a new weapon or weapon system frequently alters the nature of rules of war. The introduction of the submarine and the airplane during World War I did exactly that. Have the students read the section to discover the impact of and problems caused by the submarine.

Development: Often the course of events requires leaders to pursue actions they earlier promised they would not. In the presidential election of 1964, Barry Goldwater was pictured by Democrats as a warmonger who would get the nation more deeply involved in overseas military ventures and Lyndon Johnson was pictured as the preserver of peace. Yet in 1965, Johnson led the United States into deeper involvement in Southeast Asia. How analagous does this situation seem to that of Woodrow Wilson in 1916-1917?

Section 3

Introduction: Ask the students to note the change in attitude of Americans between the time of the picture on page 453 and the incident described in the quotation on page 458. Have them read the section to find out how the United States geared for war and aided in the Allied victory.

Development: Review the subsection on "Government Mobilization" on page 455. These agencies are particularly important because many of the New Deal agencies were patterned after them when the United States mobilized to face a quite different crisis in the 1930's. It is interesting to note that as the country geared for war, civil liberties were restricted and propaganda techniques flourished. Is it possible that the latter helped foster the former? Have the students read the feature on propaganda on page 459.

Section 4

Introduction: Using the picture on page 466 as a springboard, tell the students that Wilson's idea for a peace treaty was "peace without victory." Other nations, however, wanted to punish Germany. Have the students read the section for details.

Development: The harshness of the Versailles Treaty and the failure of the United States to join the League of Nations are often cited as causes of World War II. The desire to return to "isolationism" among Americans, however, was strong. Have the students outline the reasons for American opposition to the Versailles Treaty.

Conclusion: Explain to the students that many historians believe that the treaty could have passed if Wilson had been willing to accept certain reservations. Wilson's wife, Edith Bolling Wilson, quoted him as saying, "Better a thousand times to go down fighting than to dip your colours to dishonorable compromise." Ask students whether they would have compromised to save the treaty.

ANSWERS

Section Review Questions

page 448

1. Triple Alliance—Germany, Austria-Hungary, and Italy.
   Triple Entente—Great Britain, France, and Russia.
   Archduke Franz Ferdinand—Heir to Austria-Hungary throne, assassinated in Sarajevo in 1914.

Gavrilo Princip—Serbian nationalist who assassinated Franz Ferdinand.
   Allied Powers—Nations that entered into war against Central Powers; Great Britain, France, Russia, Rumania, Greece, Japan, Italy.
   Central Powers—Germany and Austria-Hungary.
2. Militarism and the arms race.
3. Turned the growing tensions into war.
4. Condemned the warring nations, but saw no reason to enter the conflict.

page 453

1. Many Americans had cultural and ethnic ties with England. France had aided the American colonists during their struggle for independence. The Central Powers were viewed as the aggressors.
2. The British stopped American ships carrying goods to the Central Powers, blacklisted American companies that did not comply with their rules, and tampered with American mail.
3. He protested to German officials and said that if American ships were sunk, he would take any action necessary. After the sinking of the *Lusitania*, he demanded an apology and reparations. The Germans promised to end surprise submarine attacks after he threatened to sever diplomatic relations.
4. Wilson's opponent, Charles Evan Hughes, was considered the war candidate. Wilson was reelected because pacifist sentiment was strong.
5. An armed forces build-up was instituted. Military-training camps were set up.

page 465

1. Zimmerman Note—Intercepted German message promising Mexico territory in Texas, New Mexico, and Arizona, if the United States entered the war and Mexico joined the war on Germany's side.
   Selective Service Act—Set up draft to build military force.
   William S. Sims—American admiral who introduced convoy technique.
   John J. Pershing—Commander of the American Expeditionary Force.
   Meuse-Argonne—Site of crucial battle.
   Lost Battalion—Heroes of the battle of Meuse-Argonne.

2. The country prospered.
3. Civil liberties were adversely affected. Laws were passed punishing anyone who: aided the enemy; interfered with the draft; encouraged disloyalty; refused to serve in the armed forces; wrote, printed, published, or said anything negative about the government, the Constitution, the flag, or the uniforms of the services.
4. Used propaganda to sell America's war aims.

page 468
1. Fourteen Points—Wilson's peace plan.
   League of Nations—An international assembly of nations, proposed by Wilson to settle problems peacefully.
   Henry Cabot Lodge—Senator who led opposition to the Treaty of Versailles and the League of Nations.
   William E. Borah—Leader of the irreconcilables, a group that opposed the peace treaty in original or amended form and U.S. entry into the League of Nations.
   Treaty of Versailles—Peace treaty between Germany and Allies.
2. Made his policies a partisan issue, angering Republicans. He also alienated the press.
3. Participants were more interested in territorial gain and punishing Germany than in devising equitable boundaries and peace without victory.
4. Some argued that the treaty was too easy on the Germans, others that it was too harsh. Many feared League membership would commit the United States to a perpetual role in Europe.
5. The crowds greeted Wilson enthusiastically, but did not provide the political support he needed.

Photo Questions
page 448
They saw no reason to get involved in a conflict that they believed was based on national pride and greed.

page 451
Demanded Germany take steps to prevent a recurrence.

page 453
It helped Wilson, who campaigned on a peace platform. His opponent, Henry Cabot Lodge, was viewed as the war candidate.

page 454
It was promised that Mexico would regain areas of Texas, New Mexico, and Arizona, if Mexico would ally itself with Germany.

page 455
Some joined volunteer organizations, others worked in factories, government agencies, or took their husbands' jobs. Many joined the armed forces.

page 461
Trenches were crowded, damp, smelly, and dangerous. Poison gas settled in them and at night they were overrun by rats.

page 464
125,000 lives were lost.

page 466
There was strong opposition to it.

Special Feature Questions
page 459
1. In the United States, during the American Revolution.
2. Has become less reliant on printed propaganda, more reliant on radio and television. Also became systematic government effort in some cases.

Chapter Review
page 468, Review Questions
1. The rise of militarism, protective alliances, the arms race, and the assassination of Archduke Franz Ferdinand.
2. Germany's actions in the Atlantic and in Belgium, the Zimmerman note, to uphold a balance of power in Europe, economic considerations.
3. Selective Service Act, War Industries Board, Fuel Administration, Food Administration were instituted. Factories expanded. Propaganda was used to get the people to participate. Civil liberties were curtailed.
4. Reliance on machines and highly destructive weapons; use of trench warfare.
5. Significant naval and army support turned the tide.
6. Peace without victory, including international recognition of freedom of the seas, arms limitation, an end to secret alliances, settlement of colonial claims, self determination for all countries, and a league of nations.

7. Disarmed Germany, took some of its territory, and demanded reparations.
8. Fear that it would commit the United States to European affairs and peacekeeping missions.

page 469, Discussion
1. Answers may vary. Point out that the League was unsuccessful in dealing with militarism in the 1930's.
2. Answers may vary.
3. Answers may vary. Point out existing restrictions, such as rules for treatment of prisoners, limits on biological and chemical warfare.
4. Answers may vary. Some students may argue that arming increases the chance of war. Others will suggest that unprepared nations run the greatest risk.

page 469, Using Maps
1. Spain, Switzerland, Netherlands, Norway, Sweden, Albania, Denmark.
2. Poland, Austria-Hungary, Switzerland, France, Belgium, Netherlands, and Denmark. Poland, Czechoslovakia, Austria, Switzerland, Alsace-Lorraine, Luxembourg, Belgium, Netherlands, Denmark.
3. Austria-Hungary, Bulgaria, Turkey.
4. Germany, Austria, Bulgaria, Soviet Union.
5. Czechoslovakia, Yugoslavia, Hungary, Lithuania, Latvia, Estonia, Poland, Finland. New countries created from territory ceded by the Treaty of Versailles.

page 469, Using Skills
1. Items that support the generalization: 2, 3, 4. Items that do not support the generalization: 1, 6. Mixed, 5.

Unit Review

page 470, Review Questions
1. By enforcing the Monroe Doctrine, acquiring an overseas empire, pursuing the Open Door and an active foreign policy, building up its naval power, and helping to win World War I.
2. Greater interest and more active in the Western Hemisphere. Attempted to guarantee U.S. supremacy in hemisphere by invoking and extending the Monroe Doctrine. Intervened more readily in central and South American affairs.
3. Imperialism was one reason. Nations competed to extend their domination in order to develop sources for raw materials and to gain

land for investment, trade, and military advantage. Militarism—maintaining a strong armed force and being prepared to strike—was another cause of conflict.
4. The United States remained neutral during the world war until submarine sinkings and the Zimmerman note changed the thinking of Americans. The stated objective of the U.S. was to ensure peace in the world. In contrast, the U.S. entered into war with Spain with enthusiasm. The U.S. also exacted territory after the war.

The Historian's Craft

Use The Historian's Craft on pages 471-473 to conclude the unit. In this activity, which may be conducted as either an individual or a group exercise, students will be given practice in synthesizing evidence from several primary sources. From this evidence, they will be asked to develop conclusions and to write a paragraph based on those conclusions. (A review of paragraph structure might be useful for some students.)

In preparation for The Historian's Craft, the Using Skills exercises in this unit have included interpreting political cartoons, recognizing unstated assumptions, and recognizing statements that support generalizations. This activity also builds on the skills practiced in previous unit and chapter exercises, such as finding the main idea and supporting facts, interpreting pictures, and recognizing bias.

After the students read the material and study the cartoons, have them answer the questions on page 473:
Question 1. Social Darwinism.
Question 2. Answers will vary, but might include anger and grief.
Question 3. Added to.
Question 4. Readiness of U.S. to fight in a just cause. Facial expression, weapon in hand, woman in background.
Question 5. American citizens in Cuba and American business should be protected, and the present condition of affairs in Cuba is a menace to peace and an enormous expense.
Question 6. Outrage and calls for war.
Question 7. Improved trade and the transfer of American civilization.
Question 8. That McKinley was against the war.

UNIT 7 PROSPERITY AND DEPRESSION

After studying this unit, the student should be able to:

1. discuss the political, social, and cultural life of the 1920's.
2. describe the causes of the Great Depression and contrast Hoover's and Roosevelt's approaches to dealing with it.
3. discuss the impact of and reaction to the New Deal during the 1930's and the continued debate over its nature.

OVERVIEW

Unit 7 surveys the "prosperity and depression" decades, the 1920's and the 1930's. Chapter 23 describes the nation's attempt to "return to normalcy" during the 1920's, the political and economic policies of the Republican administrations of the decade, and the social and cultural life of the "Roaring Twenties." Chapter 24 analyzes the economy of the 1920's and the stock market crash, and describes the early years of the Great Depression and the first 100 days of Franklin D. Roosevelt. Chapter 25 is devoted to the New Deal.

INTRODUCING THE UNIT

This unit treats a number of issues that are pertinent today. Survey the students concerning their feelings about the current role of government in society. Should the government try to regulate the economy? foster employment? care for the needy? Can they cite examples of unwanted government intrusion in the lives of the people? What is their reaction to the term "bureaucrat"? Many contemporary governmental functions—and problems—can be traced directly to the nation's response to the Great Depression.

CHAPTER 23 THE ROARING 20's

After studying this chapter, the student should be able to:

1. explain the American retreat from progressivism after World War I.
2. describe the political events of the 1920's.
3. discuss the social and cultural life of the "Roaring Twenties."
4. describe the flaws in the American economy by decade's end.

OVERVIEW

Chapter 23 surveys the "Roaring Twenties." Beginning with the American retreat from progressivism after the war, the chapter describes the conservative reaction manifested in the defense of traditional values and return to "normalcy" in politics. Republican administrations dominated the decade, reestablishing the pro-business atmosphere of an earlier era. In terms of social problems, laissez-faire was the policy.

A conservative reaction after a period of rapid change is not unusual in American history. Some historians feel that Jacksonian Democracy was just such a phenomenon (attack on "monster bank" as symbol of modern economic system, Jackson as symbol of simple Jeffersonian values). Other periods of reaction include the 1950's (after the New Deal and World War II) and 1970's-1980's (after the turbulent 1960's and Vietnam). This is an interesting theme from which to analyze developments in the 1980's. Important concepts in this chapter are communism, radicalism, fundamentalism, scientific management, consumerism, sensationalism, and speculation.

TEACHING IDEAS

Section 1

Introduction: The section introduction characterizes the 1920's as an ambivalent era. Write the definition of "ambivalence" on the board: the simultaneous attraction toward the repulsion from an object, person, or action. Ask the students why the authors might have used such a word. Have students read the section.

Development: Periods of rapid change are often followed by attempts to return to a simpler age. What symbols of modernity were attacked during the 1920's? (immigrants-radicals-un-American) Both the reaction to "radicalism" and the White quotation, page 480, are typical of American thought. Ask the students which better represents the ideals upon which the nation was founded. To pursue the issue of immigration restriction, have the students study the graphs on page 482.

Section 2

Introduction: The Reagan administration is one that has called for a return to traditional values. What are some of these values? Have the students read the section for comparison.

Development: Have the students describe Prohibition and Fundamentalism as reactions to change. How has the question of the teaching of evolution appeared again? (Creationism versus evolution.) How might this be explained? (Note: Teachers should point out to students that "race riots" in the twenties were riots of whites against blacks, not black riots.)

Section 3

Introduction: The nation was in a conservative mood. Both progressivism and World War I were both most closely associated with the recent Wilson administration. What political reaction would students predict? What policies would they expect Republicans to pursue? Read the section to see if speculation is correct.

Development: To understand the reaction against business in the 1930's, it is important to understand the faith and optimism expressed by political leaders in the 1920's. Have the students review Mellon's policies (page 487), then have them study the statements of Coolidge (page 488), the Republican advertisement (page 489), and Hoover (page 489).

Section 4

Introduction: Earlier in the chapter, the ambivalent nature of the 1920's was noted. Thus far, however, students have seen only conservative aspects of the decade. For an explanation of why the era is called the "Roaring Twenties," students need to read on.

Development: Ask the students to review the technological developments that shaped the lives of Americans in the 1920's. (electricity, automobiles, media) What problems are associated with these today? Review the themes that were prevalent in the artistic lives of the "Lost Generation." Why is the Edna St. Vincent Millay poem at the beginning of the chapter so appropriate? For further information on the era, have the students read the feature on "Music in Black Life," page 497.

Section 5

Introduction: Have the students study the picture of the *Life* magazine cover on page 499. How does it treat the faith and optimism of the period? (Suggests naiveté.) Have the students read the section for problems underlying the apparently booming economy.

Development: The naive optimism of the era is also reflected in the Kellogg-Briand Pact of 1928. Ask the students why such a pact was naive. Have them list the weaknesses in the economy described on pages 499-500.

Conclusion: Read the following statement from the testimony of a witness before a House committee, and discuss the paradox of overproduction and underconsumption.

> "The farmers are being pauperized by the poverty of industrial populations, and the industrial populations are being pauperized by the poverty of the farmers. Neither has the money to buy the product of the other."[11]

ANSWERS

Section Review Questions

page 482

1. Edwin Curtis—Police Commissioner of Boston.

---

[12]Unemployment in the United States. Hearing before a subcommittee of the Committee on Labor, House of Representatives, Seventy-second Congress, First Session, on H.R. 206 (1932) p. 99.

A. Mitchell Palmer—Attorney General who started anti-radical campaign.

John L. Lewis—Leader of United Mine Workers.

National Origins Act—Set immigration quotas.

2. Because of the violence and the activities of revolutionaries in other countries.

3. To deport alien anarchists and those who believed in or advocated overthrow of the government by violence.

4. Many people believed that they were condemned for what they were (anarchists and immigrants), rather than for what they had done and that they had not received a fair trial.

5. Literacy tests and quota laws.

page 486

1. Marcus Garvey—Led movement of American blacks who wished to create an empire in Africa.

David C. Stephenson—Ku Klux Klan leader convicted of murder.

Volstead Act—Law prohibiting manufacture, sale, or transportation of intoxicating liquors.

John Scopes—Biology teacher who challenged Tennessee law by teaching theory of evolution.

Clarence Darrow—Scopes' defense lawyer.

2. To defend traditional values and resist change, and by the Klan's exclusiveness, secret rituals, passwords, and costumes.

3. Poor housing, low pay, discrimination, and violence.

4. Increased disapproval of drinking because many brewers were German; barley, used in making beer, was needed for making bread; and beer was thought to lower the fighting efficiency of the army.

5. The law could not be enforced and prohibition would mean lost revenue from liquor taxes.

6. It denied divine creation.

page 490

1. Andrew Mellon—Secretary of the Treasury under Harding.

Charles R. Forbes—Director of Veteran's Bureau involved in scandal.

World War Adjusted Compensation Act— Gave veterans bonuses.

McNary-Haugen Bill—Attempt to control farm surplus and stablilize prices; vetoed.

Alfred E. Smith—Democratic presidential candidate in 1928.

2. Powers agreed to build no capital ships for 10 years, to restrict submarine use, and outlaw poisonous gases. Also, agreement was reached to respect Pacific island possessions, return territory to China, and recognize China's independence.

3. Since the United States paid cash during the war, the Allies had a moral duty to pay their debts.

4. Corruption in several federal offices.

5. Noninvolvement in national or international affairs; favored as little government as possible at as low a cost as possible.

6. Prohibition, the role of government, aid to farmers, prosperity.

page 498

1. Frederick Winslow Taylor—Engineer and efficiency expert.

Charles A. Lindbergh—Completed first nonstop solo flight across the Atlantic.

Mary Pickford—Silent film star.

"Lost Generation"—Writers of postwar period who rejected traditional values.

Harlem Renaissance—Movement of artists and writers expressing feelings and emotions of black people.

Louis Armstrong—Jazz musician.

Paul Whiteman—Band leader known as "King of Jazz."

2. Widespread use of electric power and more efficient use of people and space.

3. Provided jobs; promoted the construction and use of highways, hotels, filling stations, and trucking; made transportation easier; and made installment buying prevalent.

4. A blending of European harmony to African rhythms.

5. Disillusion with the war and the future; the new status of women; Freud's theories; new lifestyles based on modern advertising techniques and prosperity; the motion picture, automobile, and other new technology.

page 500

1. Speculation in real estate and the stock market.

2. To ban war.

3. The smaller market after the war made prices drop; falling off of government support; the increase in the cost of freight and labor; and markets for many items were hurt or destroyed.

Special Feature Questions
page 497
1. Blues, jazz, and ragtime.
2. First successful on the black-oriented soul chart, then on the white-oriented pop chart.

Photo Questions
page 478
> The declining number of jobs, the high cost of living, disagreement over wages, and government's refusal to compensate veterans.

page 479
> Believed government was violating freedom of speech.

page 481
> Some believed they were convicted for their beliefs, not on the basis of evidence.

page 483
> Leader was convicted of murder.

page 485
> Smuggling, payoffs, and protection.

page 486
> Fundamentalist position was somewhat discredited.

page 488
> Economy was strong. Limited government deemed best.

page 491
> Created a mobile society.

page 492
> Sports journalists helped spur popularity.

page 493
> Motion pictures, music, and theater.

page 494
> That the black experience was suitable for artistic expression.

page 498
> Made people more aware of new goods, foods, and styles.

page 499
> Opportunity for riches with small investment.

Chapter Review
page 500, Review Questions
1. A strong anti-radical campaign; the Palmer raids; restriction on immigration.
2. Suppression of unions, immigrant restrictions, the Ku Klux Klan, prohibition, fundamentalism.
3. The conservative mood of the country helped elect three Republican Presidents.
4. Made society more flexible and mobile; contributed to revolution in manners and morals.
5. Despite boom times, many were unable to share in the expanding wealth; conservatism contrasted with radical change; urban and rural contrasts; prosperity and depression.
6. Blacks, farmers, some industrial workers.
7. Sports became big business; radio, movies, and records developed new stars and styles; artists and authors experimented with new themes; music and morality became less inhibited.
8. After success at the Washington Conference for Limitation of Armaments, the U.S. maintained a nonparticipation policy.

page 501, Discussion
1. Answers may vary, but might include the automobile or the changing role of women.
2. Answers may vary. Idealists should be asked to predict effects of unrestricted immigration.
3. Answers may vary.
4. Answers may vary. Those who favor government restrictions may point out that society has a stake in the health of individuals.

page 501, Using Graphs
1. More than 4 million.
2. Europe, especially northern and western Europe.
3. National Origins Act set overall quota at 150,000 immigrants per year.
4. Decreased.
5. Total decreased.

page 501, Using Skills
Relevant: 1, 2, 3, 4. Not relevant: 5, because deaths from alcohol are not necessarily reduced or increased by prohibition.

CHAPTER 24

THE GREAT DEPRESSION

After studying this chapter, the student should be able to:

1. explain the stock market fluctuations of the 1920's.
2. describe the early years of the Great Depression.
3. discuss the attempts of Hoover to deal with the depression.
4. describe the first 100 days of the Roosevelt administration.

OVERVIEW

As the last chapter pointed out, beneath the "prosperity" of the 1920's were some real economic problems. Beginning with a discussion of the stock market and its crash, Chapter 24 surveys the effects of those economic problems. It is interesting to note that, despite Hoover's commitment to laissez-faire and individualism, he moves away from a strict laissez-faire approach to the depression. His programs do not work, however, and the era of the New Deal is ushered in with the election of Franklin Delano Roosevelt. Government activism becomes a significant part of American life. Important concepts in this chapter are speculation, supply and demand, trickle down theory, and parity.

TEACHING IDEAS

Section 1

Introduction: This is a good point to explain to students how stocks are created and the stock market works. Describe a hypothetical business corporation (e.g., florist, sporting goods store) which sells stock in order to capitalize. Have it show a profit, with the profits shared among the stockholders (dividends). When dividends are high, more people want to own the stock, bidding up the value of each share. The original owners can sell their shares for whatever higher price they can get. This buying and selling of stock in major corporations is handled on the stock exchanges and reported in the newspapers in a format like that on page 505. In review, then, there are two ways to make money with stock: through dividends and through the sale of stock at a profit. Speculators are interested only in the latter way. Have the students read the section to see the impact of speculation.

Development: Two methods of fueling the Bull Market were buying on margin and stock manip-

ulation. Students might be interested in an example of each.

When a person bought on "margin," he or she purchased stock with a relatively small downpayment (the margin) and borrowed the rest of the purchase price from a broker (who in turn borrowed it from the bank). If, for example, an individual bought a $100 share of stock on 25 percent margin, he or she would pay $25 and borrow the rest. During the late 1920's, many stocks increased in value at a rapid pace. If the value of the stock increased to $300 (and between March, 1928, and September, 1929, some stocks did much better than that!) the purchaser would have gained $200 on an investment of only $25! Of course, the purchaser would have to subtract the interest on the loan, but still, a nice profit could be made.

Stock manipulation also fueled the speculative fever of the Bull Market. In one case, for example, Michael J. Meehan, a broker and investor in RCA stock, and a number of his cronies pooled their resources and traded RCA stock back and forth between themselves, each time bidding up the value. When others began to bid for RCA stock, the Meehan group sold out, having in the meantime made millions of dollars.

Section 2

Introduction: Review your discussion of the problems in the economy of the 1920's considered in the last section of Chapter 23. Have the students read this section for more discussion of these problems.

Development: Have the students list the pro-business policies of the Republican administrations during the 1920's and describe how each contributed to the depression (page 507). At issue even today is the significance of tax breaks for the wealthy. The feeling of Republican administrations during the 1920's was that the wealthy would *invest* (spend on capital goods) their extra after-tax income. This, however, was not the case, as the breakdown of the $15 billion saved in 1929 shows:

$1.5 billion bought real estate
3.2 billion invested in new industry (investment)
6.0 billion bought stocks in companies that bought stocks or bid up the value of stocks already purchased
4.3 billion bid up value of securities already purchased or bought securities in foreign countries[12].

Over two-thirds of the savings in 1929 was *not* reinvested. It did the economy no good.

Section 3

Introduction: The Republican administrations of the 1920's were committed to laissez-faire, and many people like Andrew Mellon accepted tenets of Social Darwinism. What would the students predict would be the reaction of these people to the depression? Have the students read the section to see if their speculations were correct.

Development: Have the students explain why the RFC was a move away from laissez-faire. How did it reflect the trickle down theory? Have the students reread the Frederick Lewis Allen quotation on page 512. To better understand the frustration the incident caused among those concerned with the impact of the depression, read Allen's closing statement on the affair:

"The incident was over. But it had left a bitter taste in the mouth. Bayonets drawn in Washington to rout the dispossessed—was this the best that American statesmanship could offer hungry citizens?"[13]

Section 4

Introduction: Ever since the Presidency of Franklin Roosevelt, the "first hundred days" have served as a benchmark for any new presidential administration. Have the students read the section to find out why.

[13]Figures from Thomas J. Ladenburg and Samuel Hugh Brockunier, *The Prosperity and Depression Decades* (New York: Hayden Book Co., 1971), p. 40.

[14]Frederick Lewis Allen, *Since Yesterday: The 1930's in America, September 3, 1929-September 3, 1939* (New York, Harper & Row, 1939), p. 68.

Development: Have the students describe the legislation of the "Hundred Days" in each of the following categories: banking, stocks, unemployment, utilities, agriculture, industry.

Conclusion: To conclude the chapter, have students complete the "Using Skills" activity on page 519.

ANSWERS
Section Review Questions

page 505
1. Speculation is riskier; speculators buy when prices are rising and sell when prices are high enough to make a profit. Investors, on the other hand, are interested in a safe and steady income.
2. Buying on margin.
3. Economy was getting sluggish and business was slowing down.
4. The day the stock market crashed.
5. Pooled their resources and bid up the market.

page 509
1. Share of national income increased for the rich and decreased for the poor.
2. Reduced taxes on the wealthy, cut foreign loans, increased tariffs, failed to enforce anti-trust laws.
3. Giving loans, groceries, or special bonuses.
4. Tried to keep food from entering cities until the farmers received price of production. Tried to prevent loss of property by foreclosure.

page 512
1. "trickle down" theory—Funds poured into the top would trickle down to the bottom.
   "Hoovervilles"—Shantytowns.
   Wright Patman—Member of Congress who introduced bill calling for speedup of bonus payment to veterans.
   Bonus Expeditionary Force—Unemployed and homeless veterans who marched on Washington.
2. He believed that economic depression could not be cured by legislative action but only by the producers and consumers themselves.
3. Asked industrialists not to cut pay, production, or lay off workers; asked labor leaders to discourage strikes and demands for higher pay; asked local governments to spend more on public works.

4. Signed the Hawley-Smoot Tariff, the Relief and Construction Act, and the Federal Home Loan Bank Act.

5. In support of Patman's bill to pay veterans their bonuses immediately.

page 518

1. Federal Deposit Insurance Corporation—Guaranteed individual bank deposits under $5000.

Civilian Conservation Corps—Government program to put youths to work to conserve and improve the country's natural resources.

Tennessee Valley Authority—Public body that controlled government-owned land in Tennessee used in developing hydroelectric power.

National Industrial Recovery Act—Purpose was to establish cooperation among government, business, and labor.

2. Because of the panic, people rushed to close their bank accounts.

3. Dishonest practices on Wall Street.

4. The federal development of hydroelectric power could be a standard against which private utility rates could be measured.

Photo Questions

page 505

Margin-buying, fast turnover of stock for quick profit.

page 507

Many people lost their homes.

page 510

Believed that government relief is contrary to American tradition, would destroy self-reliance and self-esteem, and halt voluntary community action.

page 511

Hoover was blamed for making these villages necessary because of his inability to end the depression quickly.

page 512

The Army was called in to disperse the marchers.

page 514

The administration acted at once and took unprecedented steps to fight the depression.

page 516

Confidence, candor, and optimism.

Chapter Review

page 518, Review Questions

1. Speculators buying on margin; stocks selling for more than they were worth; panic selling. Wiped out the fortunes of many Americans, contributed to depression.

2. Overproduction; low demand; uneven distribution of income; government policies; credit and weakness of banking system.

3. In cities, wages were cut and unemployment grew. Many people were forced to rely on breadlines or soup kitchens for food. Farmers had to develop sidelines to make a living. Drought was also a serious problem. Many farmers lost their land.

4. Reduced wages gave people less money to spend so demand remained low. Manufacturers were forced to reduce production, resulting in layoffs. The policies of the government hurt trade, cut competition, and allowed prices to remain high, further hurting demand. The collapse in investment values led to the closing of many banks.

5. Believed in laissez-faire, so he did not want the federal government involved in direct relief.

6. Roosevelt opposed the Hoover administration's laissez-faire stance and instituted government programs of relief, reform, and recovery.

7. Proclaimed a national bank holiday; stopped gold, silver, and currency export; introduced emergency banking legislation, setting up a system of reorganizing the banking system; and explained his programs and goals with the American people via radio.

8. Most people supported his program and Congress passed much of the early New Deal legislation.

page 519, Discussion

1. Answers may vary. Students may say that different government policies and laws against margin buying might have helped.

2. Answers may vary.

3. That fear paralyzes and prevents efforts needed to end the depression. Answers may vary.

4. Answers may vary. Some students may point out that increased investment should lead to more jobs. Others may point out that evidence shows little increased investment due to lowered taxes on wealthy.

page 519, Using Graphs
1. 1929.
2. Farm prices had declined.
3. 1920.

4. Received equal or higher prices until 1920, then began to receive lower prices.
5. About $180 per share.

page 519, Using Skills
Support the generalization: 3, 4.
Do not support the generalization: 1, 2, 5.

CHAPTER 25 THE NEW DEAL

After studying this chapter, the student should be able to:

1. describe the wide range of ideas that influenced the New Deal.
2. describe criticisms of the New Deal.
3. discuss the reform measures of the "Second New Deal."
4. describe the "Roosevelt Coalition" and its impact on politics.
5. discuss American culture during the 1930's.

OVERVIEW

Chapter 25 continues the discussion of the New Deal begun in the last chapter. Of particular interest in terms of the varius themes explored in the book is the eclectic, pragmatic nature of the New Deal. Of course, criticism of the New Deal abounded, and here we see it from the right and the left. Roosevelt's major efforts at relief, recovery, and reform consume the bulk of the chapter, and his court fight receives attention. The final section discusses American cultural life during the depression era. Important concepts in the chapter include national planning, deficit spending, tight and easy money policy, fascism, reform, social security, prejudice, and consumer protection.

Section 1

Introduction: Have the students read the Roosevelt quotation introducing the chapter, page 421. Ask them what American philosophy or characteristic they earlier studied is reflected in these words (pragmatism). Have the students read the section for other evidence of Roosevelt's pragmatic approach to the crisis.

Development: Have the students review the ideas of Father Coughlin. What similar themes can be found in his ideas and those of people who reacted against modernity in the 1920's? (Foreigners, Jews, radicals as scapegoats.) Based on these similarities, why do students think Cough-

lin was so popular? What was the basis for the popularity of Townshend and Long?

Section 2

Introduction: The three themes of the New Deal were relief, recovery, and reform. Have the students look for those pieces of legislation that would fit under the third theme.

Development: This is an excellent point to complete the discussion of the Fed's impact on money policy begun in section 5 of Chapter 19 (page 398). The Banking Act of 1935 established an Open Market Committee, which decides to buy or sell government securities. Have the students review the discussion on page 527. An understanding of this function is important because this is the major means by which the Fed controls the money supply today.

Section 3

Introduction: Ever since the depression, the success of a Democratic presidential nominee has depended on his ability to maintain the "Roosevelt Coalition." Have the students read this section to learn what that coalition was (and is still, perhaps).

Development: By this point, students should have a decent understanding of the use of monetary policy to maintain a healthy economy. The other major means by which government tries to maintain economic health is fiscal policy, government spending. The theorist who advocated this means was John Maynard Keynes. Noting the importance of savings and investment to a healthy economy, Keynes pointed out that these two phenomena decreased substantially during depression. To take their place, he advocated government spending. Huge deficits might arise, but that was the price the government had to pay for fueling the economy. When good times returned, the budget could again be balanced. Ask the students what, over the years, has been the problem with this use of fiscal policy (causes inflation, especially if budget not balanced during prosperous times—which it rarely has been). Should the government use fiscal policy to stimulate the economy?

Section 4

Introduction: Have the students study the picture of Count Basie and his band on page 538 and speculate upon the answer to the question in the caption. Then, have them read the section to see if their speculations were correct.

Development: Society influences the art individuals produce. Have the students defend this statement by describing the social concerns treated in works from the following areas: literature, theater, art.

Conclusion: To conclude the chapter, have students read the feature on the Role of Government on page 535. Discuss Roosevelt's statement on the preservation of democracy. Was his fear valid that unemployment and insecurity could lead to a loss of democracy? Alert students to look for this theme in the next chapter's discussion of totalitarian governments.

ANSWERS

Section Review Questions

page 524
1. Lewis W. Douglas—Director of the Budget.
   American Liberty League—Conservative critics of the New Deal.
   Father Charles E. Coughlin—critic of Roosevelt; founded National Union for Social Justice.
2. Economic concentration, they believed, was already a part of life; control was in the hands of policymakers of large companies, who had been in control at the start of the Great Depression.
3. Measures were passed that curtailed its activities.

4. Pensions for the elderly and the retired.
5. Developed a strong following; seemed likely to pull a good share of the vote on a third-party ticket.

page 529
1. National Housing Act—Insured loans made for home construction.
   Harry Hopkins—Works Progress Administration director.
   Resettlement Administration—Purpose was to resettle impoverished farmers on better land.
   Frances Perkins—Roosevelt's Secretary of Labor; first woman to serve in a presidential cabinet.
2. To provide jobs for the unemployed.
3. It defined unfair practices for employers, but not for workers.
4. By a tax on employers and workers.
5. It could adopt a tight or easy money policy, thus affecting the amount of the money supply.
6. It gave too much power to the executive branch. In addition, it was viewed as an attempt to govern intrastate commerce.

page 536
1. Congress of Industrial Organization—Industrial union movement started in 1938.
   "Little Steel"—The newer steel companies that held out against strikers in 1937.
   William Van Devanter—Supreme Court Justice.
   Farm Security Administration—Granted low-interest loans for farm tenants, sharecroppers, and agricultural workers to buy farms.
   Fair Labor Standards Act—Set wage and hour standards for industries involved in interstate commerce.
2. Recent immigrants, laborers, blacks, southerners.
3. Appoint one justice for each one that did not retire at the age of 70. Expand the number of justices from 9 to 15.
4. Helped the poor resettle; set up payments for those who restricted output and practiced conservation; granted low-interest loans; provided sanitary camps and wage and hour standards for migrants.
5. Vast areas suffered severe drought.
6. In an attempt to balance the budget, government spending was cut. However, the private

sector could not make up the difference because it had less to spend (interest rates were high and government had raised social security taxes).

page 539
1. Jesse Owens—Winner of four gold medals at 1936 Olympics.
   John Steinbeck—Writer of *Grapes of Wrath*, an account of a migrant family that leaves the Dust Bowl for California.
   Richard Wright—Wrote about racial problems in the South.
   Margaret Mitchell—Wrote *Gone With the Wind*.
2. Shorter working hours; parks and playgrounds were built or improved.
3. Criminals were no longer glorified; musicals and Disney cartoons were escape fare.
4. Offerd an escape from life's everyday problems.

Special Feature Questions
page 535
1. The Industrial Revolution, World War I, the Great Depression.
2. The government took over new areas of responsibility; created a large government bureaucracy; restored American self-confidence and faith in democracy.

Photo Questions
page 522
New Deal curtailed business activities.

page 523
Modified programs to placate critics.

page 525
Waste of money, no work was being done.

page 526
Retired persons over 65, the unemployed, handicapped, and dependent children.

page 530
Wagner Act.

page 532
Created a split in the party.

page 533
Resettlement of farmers on better land, government payments for conservation practices, low-interest loans, establishment of sanitary camps, wage and hour controls for migrants.

page 538
Offered escape from harshness of life or a way to deal with reality.

Chapter Review
page 540, Review Questions
1. Conservatives thought that free enterprise was being undermined by too much government; radicals felt that the government was not doing enough to provide for the poor and unemployed.
2. Old age pension plan, relief for the unemployed, aid to farmers.
3. Created the Resettlement Administration and the Rural Electrification Administration; instituted payments for acreage allotment and conservation programs; set up low-interest loans; set standards for migrant workers.
4. Instituted more business regulation and expanded federal antitrust efforts.
5. Instituted unemployment relief, established wage and hour standards for workers in industries involved in interstate commerce; upheld rights of workers to organize and bargain collectively; moved against employers that used unfair labor practices.
6. The major criticism was that it would give too much power to the executive branch and upset the balance of power.
7. Through its use of deficit spending and "pump priming," controlling the amount of money in circulation, regulation and reform of business and taxes, instituting public works programs and social security, and pursuing an anti-monopoly course.
8. Using themes that reflected the need to cope with, or escape from, the difficulties of living during the depression.

page 540, Discussion
1. Answers may vary. Most students will suggest that better farming methods might have helped.
2. Answers may vary, but should include social security, food and drug laws, banking reform, tax reform.
3. By using deficit spending, and instituting unemployment relief, public works programs, and banking and utility reform—all of which were, before Roosevelt took office, considered outside the jurisdiction of the federal government.

4. Answers may vary.

page 540, Using Graphs
1. Expansion.
2. Almost 20 percent.
3. Much more severe—about 4 times.
4. About 5 percent.
5. 1936-1937.

page 540, Using Skills
All the questions are meaningful.

Unit Review

page 541, Review Questions
1. Strong conservative trend in politics and traditional values brought prohibition and restricted immigration laws. Technological innovations and new consumerism brought more leisure time for sports, music and theater. The jazz age and a new morality resulted from the new status of women. The automobile and movies changed many social traditions.
2. The new consumerism and prosperity prompted speculation in the stock market and too much use of credit. As a result of overproduction, the economy was slowing down, but this fact was not realized by most speculators.
3. Provided relief for the unemployed and started the country on the road to recovery but did not completely end the depression. There was criticism of the federal government's involvement in the economy.
4. Roosevelt believed that it was the government's responsibility to assist the aged, unemployed, and handicapped. The previous Republican Presidents believed in self-reliance and laissez-faire.

The Historian's Craft

To conclude the unit, use The Historian's Craft on pages 542-543. In this activity, which may be conducted on an individual or group basis, students will be given practice in evaluating evidence in secondary sources. The exercise is designed to aid students in developing the criteria of adequacy, relevancy, and validity in analyzing conflicting points of view.

The Using Skills activities in this unit have included recognizing relevance of evidence, recognizing statements that support generalizations, and determining relative significance of questions. These skills should help students to complete The Historian's Craft. Students have received additional preparation from the activities in previous units, such as recognizing bias and analyzing frame of reference.

After the students study the two arguments, have them answer the questions on page 543:

Question 1. Robinson says that Roosevelt had damaged the Constitution. He argues that the President had become too powerful, while the court system and political parties had been weakened.

Question 2. That individual effort was weakened by Roosevelt's policies.

Question 3. Because American society had been changed in the direction of collectivism, socialism, and radicalism. (Note the emotional content of these words.)

Question 4. Because Roosevelt's policies could be traced to the 1890's. Because it was carried through so quickly and because it was in sharp contrast to the policies of the Coolidge and Hoover administrations.

Question 5. The Interstate Commerce Act of 1887, the Sherman Act of 1890, the Populists' farm relief program, Wilson's farm relief program, the Carey Act of 1894, the Reclamation Act of 1902, the Water Power Act of 1920, the grain and commodities exchange acts of the Harding and Coolidge administrations, the long history of money regulation, Bryan and Wilson's fight against Wall Street, early labor legislation, state legislation of the Progressives.

Question 6. Answers may vary, but might include Robinson's assertion that millions of Americans did not like the New Deal and his charges of socialism.

Question 7. Commager's evidence seems to be more factual, freer from bias, and easier to prove.

Question 8. Commager has more evidence.

UNIT **8** THE WORLD IN CONFLICT

After studying this unit, the student should be able to:

1. explain the rise of totalitarianism during the 1920's and 1930's and discuss American foreign policy over the same period.
2. describe the major aspects of World War II at home and abroad.
3. discuss the major aspects of the Cold War, 1947-1963.

OVERVIEW

Unit 8 again shifts the students' attention to American foreign affairs. Retracing some developments in the 1920's, the unit focuses on World War II and the periods just before and after. Chapter 26 describes America's relations with Latin America and Europe, then sets the scene for World War II. Chapter 27 is devoted to the war. Chapter 28 treats foreign affairs during the Cold War era, taking the reader up to the early 1960's.

INTRODUCING THE UNIT

World War II was a major turning point in the history of the United States, when the nation's role as a world power was established. Have the students describe their feelings about the current role of the United States in the world. How is this role different from the position of the United States from the period of the Monroe Doctrine through the early twentieth century?

CHAPTER **26** THE ROAD TO GLOBAL CONFLICT

After studying this chapter, the student should be able to:

1. describe America's relations with Latin America and Europe during the 1920's and the 1930's.
2. discuss the rise of totalitarianism.
3. list the series of aggressive moves by totalitarian nations that led to World War II.
4. describe America's transition from neutrality to involvement.

OVERVIEW

Chapter 26 describes United States foreign affairs during the period between the two world wars. While it treats American diplomatic efforts in Europe and Latin America, a good deal of the chapter is devoted to the rise of totalitarian governments and totalitarian aggression. The last sections describe the early attempts of the United States to maintain neutrality and the eventual evolution of activism and war.

It is interesting to note that a number of the nations that succumbed to totalitarianism were facing the same economic problems as the United States. While Americans, too, tended to look for scapegoats and were susceptible to demagoguery, basic democratic institutions were able to weather the storm. Important concepts are totalitarianism, collectivization, prejudice and discrimination, Naziism, sanction, appeasement, and "nonbelligerency."

TEACHING IDEAS

Section 1

Introduction: To adjust the chronological thinking of the students, review the rejection of the Versailles Treaty by the United States. Have students reread the appropriate section of Chapter 22, pages 467-468. This chapter picks up where Chapter 22 ended. Have the students read the section for information concerning United States policy during the 1920's and the 1930's.

Development: Have the students review the material on reparations payments on pages 548-550. Although the causes, of course, are different, many nations today are deeply in debt (especially some third world nations) and close to bankruptcy. Have one or two students research the process by which these nations are kept from defaulting on major international loans. What role does the International Monetary Fund play? Are there any similarities between the ways those earlier debts and those of today were and are treated?

Section 2

Introduction: It is important for students to understand that in times of poor economic conditions or social instability, people tend to look for scapegoats and are susceptible to the promises of demagogues. The quotation from Mussolini in the first paragraph on page 552 reflects this idea. Have the students read the section to see how totalitarian regimes arose.

Development: Have students briefly describe the nature of the totalitarian regimes under each of the national headings below:

Russia	Italy	Germany	Japan
Communism	Fascism	Fascism	Military dictatorship

Section 3

Introduction: That wily German of an earlier era, Otto von Bismarck, knew that one way to develop unity at home was to involve a nation in a foreign dispute. Have the students read this section to see how Italy, Japan, and Germany employed this idea.

Development: Have the students identify and explain the significance of the aggressive moves of the totalitarian regimes against the areas listed under their names:

Japan	Italy	Germany
Manchuria China	Ethiopia	Rhineland Austria Czechoslovakia Poland

Section 4

Introduction: To orient the students to the war in Europe through 1941, have them study the map on page 557. Note the extent of Axis expansion.

Development: Americans had attempted to stay neutral during other European wars (the War of 1812 and the early years of World War I). What could the student of history say about such efforts? Have the students reread the Roosevelt quotation on page 561 and explain that Roosevelt was an advocate of "collective security." This meant that the security of the United States could be maintained only through alliances with other countries who were resisting or would resist Axis expansion. Did Roosevelt react as a student of history in this case?

Sections 5 and 6

Introduction: Have the students read the excerpt on Pearl Harbor on page 570, then read the section for events that led to Pearl Harbor.

Development: Have the students describe the significance of each of the following in bringing the United States closer to war:

Europe	Asia
Neutrality Act of 1939	*Panay* incident
"non-belligerency"	British recognition of
destroyer deal of 1940	Japan's Chinese
lend-lease	conquests
extension of Monroe	Triple Alliance
Doctrine, April 1941	Indochina
Atlantic Charter	

Conclusion: Conclude the chapter by having students complete the Using Skills activity on page 571.

ANSWERS

Section Review Questions

page 550

1. Cordell Hull—Secretary of State under Roosevelt; implemented "Good Neighbor" policy.

Lima Declaration—Reaffirmed absolute sovereignty of the American states.

Charles G. Dawes—Helped establish reparations payment system for Germany.

2. Though not an official member of the League, the U.S. took part in League affairs and conferences.

3. It was, in effect, transformed into a multinational agreement.

4. In the belief that keeping out imported goods would help them rebuild their industries.

page 554

1. Paul von Hindenburg—German President before Hitler came to power.

Manchukuo—Japanese puppet state.

Joseph C. Grew—United States ambassador to Japan.

2. Isolate itself from Europe and modernize industry and agriculture.

3. Intimidated the government in Rome.

4. Jewish financiers and Marxists.

5. They viewed it as an economic pipeline and as a barrier against Russian expansion.

page 558

1. Stimson Doctrine—Warned Japan and China that the United States would not recognize any treaty that would affect the Open Door policy or the sovereignty, territory, or independence of China.

Haile Selassie—Ruler of Ethiopia.

Rome-Berlin Axis—Political and military pact between Germany and Italy.

"Artichoke Plan"—Name given to describe Hitler's plan of action: one leaf (or country) at a time until the whole plant (world) was consumed.

Neville Chamberlain—British Prime Minister who tried to appease Hitler.

Danzig—Port city in northern Poland that was demanded by Hitler.

2. Took no effective action.

3. Completed conquest and combined that country with two other Italian-held countries; became emperor of Ethiopia.

4. As a way to preserve peace.

5. The two nations signed a nonaggression pact; in the event of war, the Soviet Union would receive Finland, Estonia, Latvia, eastern Poland, and Bessarabia.

page 561

1. Gerald P. Nye—Senator who headed committee investigating munitions industry.

General Francisco Franco—Leader of Nationalists in Spanish Civil War.

Naval Expansion Act—Authorized building of a two-ocean navy.

2. That American entry into World War I was due to pressure of American financiers and munitions manufacturers.

3. Many Americans viewed it as a struggle between fascism and communism.

4. He believed the Acts would drag the United States into the war.

page 567

1. Maginot Line—Fortifications along the eastern border of France.

Siegfried Line—Fortifications along the southwestern border of Germany.

Luftwaffe—German air force.

Burke-Wadsworth bill—Selective Training and Service Act; first peacetime draft in U.S. history.

Wendell Willkie—Republican candidate for President in 1940.

America First Committee—Group of isolationists who opposed anything that might compromise the neutrality of the United States.

2. Gave President the power to prohibit arms shipments to all belligerents and to forbid Americans to travel on belligerent ships except at their own risk. In effect, the United States was becoming involved in the problems of Europe and Asia.

3. Hitler's first major defeat.

4. Strong supporters of U.S. neutrality.

5. Freedom of speech and worship and freedom from want and fear.

page 570

1. *Panay*—American gunboat sunk by Japanese bombers in 1937.

Ludlow Resolution—Made Congress' authority to declare war ineffective unless confirmed by a majority vote in a national referendum; resolution was introduced several times but never passed.

General Hideki Tojo—Prime Minister of Japan.

2. War with either nation would hurt trade.

3. Americans were less interested in conciliation because the pact was viewed as a threat to the United States.
4. Americans were taken by surprise; officials thought an attack would take place on bases in the Philippines, not Hawaii.

Photo Questions

page 549
The rate of inflation led to the government's bankruptcy and severe financial woes.

page 550
To provide security in the Western Hemisphere.

page 551
Hoped to establish trade between the countries.

page 552
Economic depression, a renewed sense of purpose, and the promise of glory.

page 553
To enforce the idea of Aryan superiority.

page 555
Raw materials and acceptance as a power in international affairs.

page 558
Appeasement.

page 559
A struggle between fascism and communism.

page 563
The United States began extending as much material aid as possible to the democracies.

page 567
Represented the end of isolation and the beginning of an era in which the United States assumed the responsibilities of a powerful nation.

page 568
The attack on Pearl Harbor.

page 569
Japanese militarism and the placing of sanctions by the United States on Japan.

Chapter Review

page 571, Review Questions
1. To establish friendship of Latin American countries essential to the security of the United States, to promote trade, and to protect the sovereign rights of Western Hemisphere nations.
2. The war produced a loss of human resources and destroyed businesses; in addition, there were shortages, inflation, and loss of trade.
3. Economic chaos, dislocation of millions of people, and lack of food, clothing, and shelter.
4. A pledge to restore the country's honor and law and order, nationalism, and subordination of the individual.
5. Many lives and material had been lost, while ideological goals had not been achieved. Many people believed it was because of bankers and munitions profiteers that there had been a war at all.
6. Reasons included: poverty, overpopulation; the need for raw materials; belief in a mission; to create more jobs; to expand colonial holdings; and build image as a world power.
7. First, isolation and noninvolvement; then a shift to offering material aid to democratic countries; finally, war.
8. Debate over neutrality and possibility of war.

page 571, Discussion
1. Answers may vary. Students may think the U.S. has too strong a tradition of democracy and individual rights.
2. Answers may vary. Some students may think that Wilson's peace plan would have allowed Germany to recover faster and thus would have removed the reasons for Hitler's rise. Others may think that if Germany had been completely broken up, the Germans could not have regained their former power.

page 571, Using Maps
1. Albania.
2. Italy, Hungary, Rumania, Bulgaria.
3. Sudetenland, Czechoslovakia, Poland, Memel Territory.
4. Where Belgium, the Netherlands, and Germany intersect.
5. Manchuria, Korea, Formosa, Haiman, French Indochina, Karafuto, Caroline Islands, Marianas, Marshall Islands, Thailand.
6. Because the territory they occupied surrounded the Philippines and the islands could be used as a base to attack Australia.

page 571, Using Skills
Statements 2 and 3.

CHAPTER 27 WORLD WAR II

After studying this chapter, the student should be able to:

1. discuss the major aspects of the war against the Axis powers, 1942-1945.
2. describe the impact of World War II on the home front, 1942-1945.

OVERVIEW

Chapter 27 tells the story of World War II from an American perspective. As such, it describes the early American setbacks and the painful march toward victory from 1943-1945. Of special interest is the impact of the war on the "home front," especially with reference to various minority groups and women. Concepts in the chapter include rationing, black market, prejudice, internal migration, genocide, and military strategy.

Section 1

Introduction: This chapter begins with the war situation in 1942. To orient the students, have them review the map on page 557 in the last chapter. Then, have them read this section for details of the American delaying actions in 1942.

Development: Have the students identify and explain the significance of the following major engagements: North Africa, Doolittle Raid, Coral Sea, Midway, Guadalcanal.

This is a good point to have the students read the feature on "Technology and War," page 578.

Section 2

Introduction: Have the students study the maps on pages 583 and 584. Orient them to a world map. Then, have them read the section for developments in 1943.

Development: Have the students describe the major strategic developments of 1943 in the following theaters of war: Pacific, Mediterranean, Eastern Europe.

Section 3

Introduction: In 1944 Franklin Roosevelt was elected to a fourth term. Have the students look up the constitutional amendment that limits the number of terms a President may serve. Have them read the section for details of Allied successes in 1944.

Development: Have the students describe the major strategic developments of 1943 in the following theaters of war: Pacific, Mediterranean, Western Europe, Eastern Europe.

Section 4

Introduction: As the war drew to a close, plans for peace were made. Have the students study the picture on page 592 and then read the section to answer the question in the caption.

Development: One of the most controversial decisions in American military history was that of Truman to drop the A-bomb. Have the students read Truman's justification on page 594, then have them do the Using Skills exercise on page 597.

Conclusion: Review the reasons for the United States' refusal to join the League of Nations (Chapter 22, pages 467-468). What had changed to make Americans willing to belong to the United Nations?

ANSWERS

Section Review Questions
page 581

1. Operation Torch—First major Allied land and water operation in the European theater.

   Douglas MacArthur—General, U.S. forces in the Pacific.

   Vannebar Bush—Head of the Office of Scientific Research.

   Donald M. Nelson—Head of the War Production Board.

   Act of Chapultepec—Regional security pact of American states to repel aggression.

   Earl Warren—California's Attorney General.

2. Allies had their hands full in western Europe and North Africa.
3. The Japanese were dominant in the Pacific.
4. First major defeat of the Japanese navy; ended Japan's naval superiority in the Pacific.
5. To make scientific and technological contributions to the war effort.
6. More people had jobs and more money to spend. However, consumer goods were scarce because of the war, so prices rose.

7. Many were bitter, but never lost loyalty to the United States. Many served in the armed forces.

page 586
1. Chester W. Nimitz—Commander in Chief of Pacific fleet.

   Cairo Declaration—Allies pledged to fight for Japan's unconditional surrender.

   Operation Husky—Ango-American invasion of Sicily.

   Cordell Hull—Secretary of State; called for a new international organization.

   Smith-Connally Anti-Strike Act—Made it illegal for unions to strike against any war industry.
2. To get within effective bombing distance of Japan.
3. Allies invaded Italy, and Mussolini and his cabinet resigned.
4. Because of the great number of people in the military.

page 591
1. Thomas E. Dewey—Republican candidate for president in 1944.

   Operation Overlord—Code name for invasion of Normandy.

   Battle of the Bulge—Late battle in which German breakthrough produced a bulge in Allied lines along Belgian border.
2. By bombing southern England.
3. Instituted an International Bank for Reconstruction and Development to aid economic development around the world and an International Monetary Fund to stabilize national currencies and promote trade.

page 596
1. V-E Day—Victory in Europe Day, May 8, 1945.

   Robert J. Oppenheimer—Director of the Manhattan Project.

   Enola Gay—B-29 bomber that released atomic bomb on Hiroshima.

   Secretariat—Body of the United Nations that handles administrative functions.
2. Mussolini was captured and shot by Italian partisans. Hitler committed suicide.
3. They were accused by critics of allowing the Soviets to dominate entire countries in return for little or no aid to the Allies in Asia.

4. Roosevelt had been warned that German scientists were developing the atomic bomb.

Special Feature Questions
page 578
1. Muskets, bayonets, cannon, Kentucky rifles.
2. Heavy artillery, grenades, flame throwers, tanks, poison gas, submarines, and wireless telegraph. Airplanes, radio, and photography were also developed and refined.
3. Is so much more devastating that it becomes an entirely different kind of warfare.

Photo Questions
page 574
The decision to launch an offensive in North Africa, starting with surprise landings in French North Africa.

page 575
With anger and renewed determination to defeat the Japanese.

page 576
Ended Japan's superiority in the Pacific.

page 577
Huge increase in government spending, high rate of inflation, and scarcity of domestic goods.

page 579
A black market and the counterfeiting of ration stamps and coupons.

page 581
Fear and prejudice.

page 582
To establish a base from which Japan could be attacked.

page 585
Women proved themselves able to do work that had traditionally been done by men.

page 588
United States regained control of the Philippines and Japan lost much of its sea power.

page 590
It stopped Germany's last offensive.

page 592
Believed the Soviet Union was given control of countries for empty promises.

page 594
Dropping atomic bomb on Hiroshima and Nagasaki.

Chapter Review

1. The defeat of Germany would leave Japan exposed to overwhelming force, but the defeat of Japan would not end the war in Europe.
2. High rate of inflation, shortage of goods, low unemployment, wage hikes.
3. North Africa, Europe, the Far East, and the Pacific.
4. It gave them the opportunity to work in occupations previously closed to them; led to migration of minorities to industrial cities.
5. In 1942 the Allies fought a defensive war; by 1943, they were on the offensive.
6. It was the largest amphibious invasion in history, and the beginning of the liberation of Europe.
7. Set up International Monetary Fund and International Bank for Reconstruction and Development. Planned postwar occupation and spheres of influence. Laid the foundation for the United Nations.
8. Because the Japanese refused to surrender, and to save the lives that would be lost were Japan invaded.

page 597, Discussion

1. Answers may vary. Most students will think that the treatment was not justified because Japanese-Americans were loyal citizens, just as were other hyphenated Americans.
2. Answers may vary. Most students will say yes, but the gains were only temporary.
3. Answers may vary. The question should be weighed against alternatives.
4. Answers may vary.

page 597, Using Maps

1. Coral Sea, Bismarck Sea, Midway, Iwo Jima, Philippine Sea, Leyte Gulf, Okinawa.
2. Manchuria, Korea, Sakhalin, French Indochina, Thailand, Burma, Malaya, and several sites on the Chinese coast.
3. Tokyo, Kawasaki, Yokohama, Nagoya, Kyoto, Osaka.
4. Casablanca, Oran, Algiers.
5. On border of Tunisia near Algeria.
6. Grasped advantage over the Mediterranean, Suez, North Africa, and the Middle East. Also, gave access to southern Europe.

page 597, Using Skills

4. Using the bomb was justified.

CHAPTER 28 THE COLD WAR

After studying this chapter, the student should be able to:

1. describe the origins of the Cold War.
2. discuss American attempts to contain communist expansion in Europe and Asia.
3. explain the "thaw" in the Cold War during the middle and late 1950's.
4. describe the foreign policy of the Kennedy and Johnson administrations as it related to Latin America.

OVERVIEW

Using the theme of "cold war" as a springboard, Chapter 28 describes United States foreign affairs from the end of World War II through the early 1960's. As such, the chapter's central theme is that of containment, the attempt to "contain" communist expansion around the world. A significant development that is noted midway through the chapter is the end of "bipolarism" and the emergence of the nonaligned and Third World nations. These new nations are especially significant in United States' foreign policy today. Additional concepts in the chapter include the arms race, the iron curtain, and peaceful coexistence.

TEACHING IDEAS
Section 1

Introduction: Ask the students to describe the difference between a "hot war" and a "cold war." Have them read the section to see how a "cold war" developed between the United States and the Soviet Union.

Development: Have the students describe the American-Soviet dispute over Soviet policies in Eastern Europe, Iran, and Turkey. What motivated the Soviet Union? What motivated the United States?

Section 2

Introduction: "Contain" means "to keep within limits." What do the students imagine this means in terms of United States policy toward the Soviet Union? Have the students read the section to see if their speculations were correct.

Development: Have the students compare the Truman Doctrine, the Vandenburg Resolution, and the North Atlantic Treaty to earlier statements of American foreign policy like the Monroe Doctrine. What are the obvious, significant differences?

Section 3

Introduction: Have the students study the picture on page 607 and read its caption. The communist takeover of China was extremely controversial. Have the students read the section for details.

Development: Have the students review the section to determine the types of foreign aid supplied to Asian nations (specifically Japan, China, Korea, Indochina, and Taiwan). Do the students see any patterns? (Generally, a tendency toward escalation of military aid, including military intervention.) Have the students read the feature on Foreign Aid on page 611.

Section 4

Introduction: Have students study the map on pages 620-621. Notice that it marks western, communist, and nonaligned nations. Tell the students that this map reflects the end of bipolarism and the beginning of a much more complicated world. Have them read the section for details.

Development: Have the students describe the new policies directed to the Third World under Kennedy. How did these differ from earlier American policies? How did Cuba's reaction to American policy (after the 1959 Castro victory) reflect the attitude of many Latin Americans toward the United States?

Conclusion: Conclude the chapter by having the students complete the "Using Skills" activity on page 625.

ANSWERS
Section Review Questions

page 602

1. Averell Harriman—United States ambassador to the Soviet Union.

   Vyacheslav Molotov—Soviet Foreign Minister.

   Dardanelles Strait—used by Russian ships to enter Mediterranean.

2. Americans were tired of war and placed hope for peace in the UN.

3. They tightened their hold over Eastern Europe by refusing to allow elections, banning freedom of religion and the press, and controlling the economy of satellite nations.

4. The Middle East was valued for its oil.

5. The Soviets would not give up their veto power to the United Nations nor allow UN inspectors into their country unless the U.S. destroyed its bombs first, which the U.S. refused to do.

page 606

1. George Kennan—State Department expert on the Soviet Union.

   COMECON—Council of Mutual Economic Assistance; the Soviet counterpart to the Marshall Plan.

   NATO—North Atlantic Treaty Organization; a mutual defense pact among the Western allies.

2. Critics felt that it was an over-extension of American influence overseas and would increase tensions with the Soviet Union.

3. To make American aid available to countries threatened by communism.

4. The United States wanted a strong united Germany with a productive economy. The Soviets preferred to keep Germany divided so it would not be a threat.

5. Because a free united Europe was essential to U.S. security.

page 613

1. Douglas MacArthur—governed Japan during occupation and headed U.N. forces in Korean War.

   Chiang Kai-Shek—Leader of Chinese Nationalists.

   Seoul—Capital of South Korea.

   John Foster Dulles—Secretary of State under Eisenhower.

SEATO—Southeast Asia Treaty Organization.
2. Adopted a political and social system that aligned it with the West.
3. Did not want to become involved in a costly, full-scale, and possibly unsuccessful Asian war.
4. Truman abandoned the idea of a unified Korea, while MacArthur publicly opposed him.

page 624
1. Nikita Khrushchev—Soviet leader after Stalin.
   Abdel Nasser—President of Egypt.
   Eisenhower Doctrine—Allowed the United States to use force in the Middle East against communist aggression.
   Peace Corps—Sent Americans to Third World countries as teachers, farmers, and technicians.
   Sputnik I—First artificial earth satellite.
   Fulgencio Batista—Ruler of Cuba.
   "hot line"—Telephone linking Washington and Moscow.
2. No specific results, but a reduction in tensions.
3. The belief that it would have started World War III.
4. By causing a serious rift in relations between the United States and its major allies.
5. Became a symbol of communist repression. Also eased tensions because it showed that Soviets were willing to accept West Berlin.
6. Called for a naval blockade of Cuba and told the Soviets that any missile launched from Cuba would meet with retaliation.

Special Feature Questions
page 611
1. In the late 1940's.
2. Critics charge that the interests of munitions manufacturers have become too powerful in determining policy, and that military aid encourages warfare.

Photo Questions
page 601
Instituted a policy of containment.

page 603
To keep nations free from communism.

page 605
Soviets recognized the failure of their blockade, and the morale of the people of West Berlin was boosted.

page 607
Did not want to involve U.S. in a costly and possibly unsuccessful Asian land war.

page 612
The United States Seventh Fleet was sent to provide a show of force.

page 613
Lessening of Cold War tensions.

page 614
Soviet forces crushed the uprising and a communist government was instituted.

page 615
The United States was blamed for not supporting its allies.

page 622
It was strengthened.

page 623
Critics felt that the United States was interfering in the internal affairs of another nation.

Chapter Review
page 625, Review Questions
1. The rivalry divided much of the world into two blocs: the Western countries, led by the U.S., and the Eastern countries, led by the Soviet Union.
2. As Cold War tensions eased, nonaligned nations began to exert their own influence and often played one superpower against the other.
3. It evolved into an arms race.
4. In many cases it tried arbitration but was not very effective.
5. The United States supported Taiwan as a means of containing communism in Asia.
6. The Soviets adopted a new policy of peaceful coexistence toward the West.
7. The United States supported Israel.
8. Concerned with stopping the spread of communism in Latin America, the United States often supported unpopular conservative or military governments.
9. Contacts were opened through diplomatic channels and summit conferences.

page 625, Discussion

1. Answers may vary. Students who take the negative position should be asked how vital American interests should be defended. Students who take the positive position should be asked to justify U.S. involvement in the affairs of other countries.
2. Answers may vary, but two aspects of the question should be discussed: Soviet intentions and Soviet ability to carry out those intentions.
3. Answers may vary. Ask students to predict the results of the policy they recommend.
4. Answers may vary.

page 625, Using Maps

1. Finland, Sweden, Spain, Switzerland, Austria, Yugoslavia.
2. Cuba, Jamaica, Guyana.
3. OAS, NATO, SEATO.
4. East Germany, Poland, Czechoslovakia, Rumania, Hungary, Bulgaria, Albania.

page 625, Using Skills
Assumptions: 1 and 3.

Unit Review

page 626, Review Questions

1. Totalitarian governments began programs of military aggression and conquest.
2. In addition to the U.S. military contribution, American war effort included research and development of more advanced weapons that became vital factors in winning the war.
3. The U.S. emerged as the most powerful nation in the world.
4. Partly successful: generally successful in Europe, Taiwan, Korea; unsuccessful in China, Africa, Cuba, Indochina; partly successful in Middle East.

The Historian's Craft

Conclude the unit by having the students complete The Historian's Craft on pages 627-629. In this activity, which may be conducted on an individual or group basis, students will be given practice in recognizing historical schools. They will develop an understanding of the way schools influence the work of individual historians and an understanding of revision and its causes.

The Using Skills activities in this unit have included recognizing unstated assumptions and finding the main idea. Previous unit and chapter skills, such as analyzing relationships and recognizing statements that support generalizations, should also be helpful in preparing students for this activity.

The historians quoted are as follows: A and D, Arthur M. Schlesinger, Jr., "Origins of the Cold War," *Foreign Affairs*, 46, October 1967, pp. 43 and 52; B, William A. Williams, "The Cold War Revisionists," *The Nation*, 205, November 13, 1967, p. 495; C, Carl Oglesby, quoted by Walter LaFeber in "War: Cold," *Cornell Alumni News*, 26, October 1968, p. 123; E and F, Samuel F. Bemis, *A Diplomatic History of the United States* (New York: Holt, Rinehart, Winston, 1965), pp. 921–922; G, Carl Oglesby, quoted in Walter LaFeber, "War: Cold," *Cornell Alumni News*, 71, October 1968, p. 12; H, Gar Alperowitz, "Why We Dropped the Bomb," *The Progressive*, 29, August 1965, p. 12; I, Joseph M. Jones, *Fifteen Weeks* (New York: Harcourt Brace Jovanovich, 1955), p. 45; J and K, Gabriel Kolko, *The Politics of War* (New York, Random House, 1968) pp. 619-620 and 622; L, John W. Spanier, *American Foreign Policy Since World War II* (New York, F.A. Praeger, 1965), p. 36.

After the students read the quotations from the various historians, have them answer the questions on page 629:

Question 1. Answers may vary, but should include the idea that the Soviet Union was the aggressor in the Cold War. That the Soviet Union acted in self-defense in the Cold War.

Question 2. A, D, E, F, I, L.

Question 3. B, C, G, H, J, K.

Question 4. Answers may vary, but should include phrases indicating which side was the aggressor. For example: A—"Russians. . . . crudely worked their will. . . ."; B—"Stalin accepted the Cold War"; D—"The Cold War could have been avoided only if the Soviet Union. . . ."; E—"Soviet Russia carried forward her revolutionary program. . . ."; F—"Stalin who called the tune."; G—"The uniformly powerful West. . . ."; H—"Soviet acquiescence to American plans. . . ."; I—"Russians had felt a sense of mission in Asia. . . ."; J—"United States . . . its specific objectives. . . ."; K—"Russians understood the American intention. . . ."; L—"a [Soviet] policy that was always pushing. . . ."

UNIT 9 THE UNITED STATES IN A NEW ERA

After studying this unit, the student should be able to:

1. discuss the major domestic and foreign policy issues during the presidential administrations of Truman through Reagan.
2. discuss the major cultural and social developments of the period 1950–1980.

OVERVIEW

Using the political history of the period as a framework, Unit 9 treats the broad range of foreign and domestic developments from the 1950's through the early 1980's. Chapter 29 treats the Truman and Eisenhower administrations, Chapter 30 the Kennedy and Johnson administrations, Chapter 31 the Nixon and Ford administrations, Chapter 32 the social and cultural developments of the 1960's and 1970's, and Chapter 33 the Carter and early Reagan administrations.

Perhaps the single most interesting theme is the continued cyclical nature of intense American involvement in social change followed by a conservative breathing spell. The 1950's can be seen as a conservative period following the New Deal and World War II, the 1970's and early 1980's as a conservative period following the activism and dynamism of the 1960's.

INTRODUCING THE UNIT

Again, this unit picks up domestic affairs during a period of time already covered in the discussion of foreign policy in the last chapter. For that reason, it is a good idea to orient the students chronologically. Using the timeline in the unit opening, plug in some of the dates with which the students are already familiar because of their study of the Cold War.

CHAPTER 29 TRUMAN AND EISENHOWER

After studying this chapter, the student should be able to:

1. describe the major domestic issues and policies during the Truman administration.
2. describe the major domestic issues and policies during the Eisenhower administration.
3. discuss the major aspects of American society and culture during the 1950's.

OVERVIEW

Chapter 29 treats domestic politics in the postwar years and the 1950's. The Truman and Eisenhower administrations provide the framework for this discussion. Themes that should be treated include the conservative mood of the nation in the late 1940's and 1950's, the overreaction to domestic communism, "modern Republicanism," and the development of cultural and leisure activities that should be familiar to everyone today. Important concepts are civil rights, integration, civil disobedience, military-industrial complex, countervailing powers, affluence, and automation.

TEACHING IDEAS
Section 1

Introduction: Have the students read the quotation from Truman on page 633. Ask them why he might have felt that way and then have them read the section to see what he did.

Development: We have previously noted the American propensity to follow a period of intense activism with a conservative reaction. The New Deal and World War II preceded the conservative era described in this chapter. To reinforce this understanding, have the students describe how developments in labor and civil rights reflected the conservative mood.

Section 2

Introduction: Have the students read the quotation from Truman on page 637 expressing the theme of the "Fair Deal." Given the conservative mood of the nation, what sort of response would the students expect to this call for continued activism? Have them read the section to see if their speculations were correct.

Development: Review the section's discussion of the American reaction to domestic communism. In retrospect, what came closer to disrupting American society (its traditional ideas and liberties), communist plots or the reaction to supposed communist plots?

Section 3

Introduction: Have the students quickly read the first two paragraphs of "Modern Republicanism" on page 640. Does this description sound like the Republican party today? Have the students read the section for details.

Development: Have the students review the discussion of the civil rights movement in this section, focusing on the Martin Luther King, Jr. quotation on pages 644–645. Ask them to explain why some students of history consider King to have been one of the great democrats of modern America. Have the students read and complete the Using Skills exercise on page 653.

Section 4

Introduction: Have students study the graph on page 648, then read the section to find the causes and corollaries of suburban growth.

Development: Ask the students to list major leisure-time activities today. Have them find similarities in the activities discussed in this section.

Conclusion: Review John Kenneth Galbraith's criticism of affluence on page 647, the criticism of television on page 649, and the observations

of Reisman and Whyte on page 651. Are any of these criticism/comments valid today?

ANSWERS
Section Review Questions

page 637

1. Employment Act of 1946—Program to create jobs.

   GI Bill of Rights—Law helping veterans with employment, housing, medical care and education.

   Robert A. Taft—Ohio Senator who cosponsored Taft-Hartley Act.

   J. Strom Thurmond—Governor of South Carolina who ran for President in 1948 on the Dixiecrat ticket.

2. Increased demand.

3. Outlawed the closed shop, required unions to make financial records public, made political contributions by unions illegal, and made 60-day cooling-off period mandatory before workers could strike.

4. Better education and jobs, which led to demand for full rights.

5. Truman was blamed for many postwar problems, and Democrats had split on choice of candidates.

page 640

1. Alger Hiss—Top-level State Department official accused of espionage.

   Millard Tydings—Head of Senate subcommittee that decided that Senator McCarthy's charges were unfounded.

   Adlai E. Stevenson—Democratic Presidential candidate in 1952.

   Checkers—Family pet that figured prominently in Vice President Nixon's effort to defend himself against charge of improperly receiving gifts.

2. Legislation covering civil rights, education, social security, housing, and labor.

3. To prevent another long-term Presidency.

4. Americans were alarmed by the Cold War and the rise of communism.

page 645

1. Saint Lawrence Seaway—U.S.-Canadian project that connected Great Lakes with Atlantic Ocean.

   Oveta Culp Hobby—Second woman to hold cabinet post.

Charles E. Bohlen—Nominee for ambassador to Soviet Union, under attack from Senator McCarthy.

Thurgood Marshall—NAACP attorney who fought segregation laws in court.

Orval Faubus—Governor of Arkansas who battled integration at a Little Rock high school.

Martin Luther King, Jr.—Black minister who became a leader in the demonstrations against racial discrimination.

2. Developed a network of highways linking major cities in the United States.
3. Cold War was viewed as less threatening, and people were turned off by McCarthy's tactics and manners.
4. To enforce school integration.
5. A business recession, unemployment, and administration scandals.

page 651

1. John K. Galbraith—Economist who criticized materialism in American life.

Edward R. Murrow—Leading television newscaster of 1950's.

Elvis Presley—First rock 'n roll idol.

James Baldwin—Novelist who wrote of the black experience.

Tennessee Williams—A leading American playwright of the 1950's.

Jackson Pollock—Painter of abstract expressionist art.

2. Impact on job market declined as many turned to homemaking duties.
3. Wealth was not fairly distributed, poverty remained high, economy geared too strongly to war production, and too many unnecessary items being produced.
4. The baby boom and a decline in death rate and immigration led to a growing, more uniform population.

Photo Questions

page 634
Job training, education, housing, and medical care.

page 636
Labor, farmers, and northern blacks.

page 638
Instituted a loyalty program and authorized FBI to investigate any government worker.

page 641
Slowed the growth of the federal government and worked to limit the role of government in social and economic affairs.

page 642
Cold War was easing. Millions witnessed McCarthy's rudeness and use of falsehood and innuendo during televised hearings.

page 644
By sending federal troops to Little Rock to enforce integration and restore order.

page 649
A sense of pride, excitement, and new opportunity.

Chapter Review

page 652, Review Questions
1. Keeping inflation down and employment high while cutting military spending.
2. Unions disapproved of the Taft-Hartley Act and of Truman's decision to seize the coal mines. However, the prosperity of the 1950's improved the workers' lot and smoothed relations with employers.
3. A growing conservative mood in the country and strong congressional opposition.
4. Creation of new government departments and agencies, including the CIA and the Department of Health, Education, and Welfare, and improving coordination among the branches of the military.
5. Institution of a loyalty program, communist leaders sent to prison, and suspected communist sympathizers removed from unions, entertainment, and education.
6. To halt growth of bureaucracy, reduce spending, balance the budget, and cut taxes.
7. Voting rights gains, school integration, and a lessening of employment discrimination.
8. Americans could afford more luxury items, more were living in suburbs and accepting suburban standards, and television became the favorite leisure activity.

page 652, Discussion
1. Eisenhower wanted to reduce the role of the federal government in business and society and did not try to be a strong, active President like Truman. In addition, Eisenhower

delegated more responsibility to his staff than Truman.

2. Answers may vary.
3. Answers may vary. Those who believe the danger exists may answer that defense spending is up or that several companies do nearly all their business with the military. Those who believe the complex is no danger may note the strong tradition of civilian government in the U.S.
4. Answers may vary.

page 652, Using Graphs
1. 1971–1980.
2. No, the percentage of growth rose in 1931–1940 compared to the previous decade.

3. The percentage of suburban population growth has continued to increase.
4. 1931–1940; 1921–1930.

page 653, Using Skills
1. That there is no legal basis for reversing previous Supreme Court decisions that separate but equal facilities are constitutional.
2. According to the Fourteenth Amendment, no person may be deprived of his or her rights. The Court interpreted the amendment in the light of current conditions.
3. The nature of education and society has changed, and greater knowledge of psychology exists today.

CHAPTER 30 THE KENNEDY-JOHNSON YEARS

After studying this chapter, the student should be able to:

1. describe the domestic policies of John F. Kennedy.
2. discuss the major features of Johnson's Great Society.
3. explain American foreign relations during the Johnson years, focusing on escalation in Vietnam.
4. describe the growing unrest in the nation during the late 1960's.

OVERVIEW

Chapter 30 covers the years of the Kennedy and Johnson administrations. Unlike recent chapters which treated either domestic or foreign affairs, this chapter and the chapters that follow treat both. Developments in civil rights and the escalation of the war in Vietnam receive the greatest attention and should be emphasized by the teacher. Other important concepts are balance of payments, gross national product, poverty level, nonviolence, de facto segregation, black nationalism, and feminism.

TEACHING IDEAS
Section 1
Introduction: Have the students read the quotation from John F. Kennedy that opens the chapter on page 655. What does Kennedy mean?

Have them read on for the story of Kennedy in office.

Development: Have the students look at the picture on page 658 of astronaut John Glenn. How did the space program reflect Kennedy's idea of a New Frontier? What other elements made up this idea?

Section 2
Introduction: A central aspect of Johnson's Great Society was civil rights. Have the students read the Johnson quotation at the bottom of page 663 to see his thinking. To what American ideals is he appealing? Have them read the section for details.

Development: It should be no surprise that many black leaders today are sensitive about the federal government's position concerning civil rights. Any back-pedaling by the federal government (such as actions during the Reagan administration) brings cries of alarm. During the 1960's, it was the federal government that spearheaded change. Have the students review this section's and the last's discussion of the civil rights movement and list the federal initiatives.

Section 3

Introduction: The Vietnam War was an extremely divisive issue in recent American history. Have the students review the discussion of early American involvement in Indochina found in Chapter 28, pages 610 and 612. Then have them read this section for further developments.

Development: Have the students describe the significance of the following dates as key points in American escalation:

May 1, 1961	April 1, 1965
February 1, 1964	January 30, 1968
August 7, 1964	March 31, 1968
February 13, 1965	

Section 4

Introduction: Have the students study the pictures on page 670, then read the section to answer the question presented in the caption.

Development: Reread the quotations from Martin Luther King, Jr. on pages 669–670. What traditional American ideals are expressed in these passages? For a view of another American minority leader, have the students read the "People in History" feature on page 672.

Conclusion: Have the students study the map on page 675. How does the voting pattern in the 1968 election reflect the deep political divisions in the country?

ANSWERS

Section Review Questions

page 661
1. Henry Cabot Lodge, Jr.—U.N. ambassador who ran for Vice President on Nixon ticket.
   Ted Sorensen—Special counsel to President Kennedy.
   Robert McNamara—Secretary of Defense in Kennedy administration.
   John Glenn—First American to orbit the earth.
   European Common Market—European nations that agreed to lower tariffs on one another's products.

James Meredith—First black to attend the University of Mississippi.
   Warren Commission—Investigated the Kennedy assassination.
2. Some Americans believed that if Kennedy, a Roman Catholic, were elected, the Pope would influence government policy.
3. To surpass Russia in exploring this newest of frontiers.
4. Establish voluntary wage and price guidelines, provide aid in form of tax credits for investment and depreciation, and enter into reciprocal trade agreements.
5. Supported civil rights, but moved slowly to avoid antagonizing Southern Democrats in Congress.

page 665
1. *Baker* v. *Carr*—Case that led to ruling to redraw legislative districts according to population.
   Operation Headstart—Provided preschool training for children of poor families.
   Barry M. Goldwater—Republican candidate for President in 1964.
   Robert Weaver—First black to serve in cabinet.
2. Evidence illegally seized could not be used, free legal council must be provided by state for those unable to pay, and a suspect must be informed of certain rights.
3. Prohibited job discrimination, strengthened equal voting rights, provided equal access to public accommodations, and empowered Attorney General to act in desegregation of schools.
4. Instituted 10 new programs, with emphasis on improving education and employment opportunities.
5. To provide medical care for the elderly.

page 669
1. Six-Day War—War between the Arab states and Israel in 1967.
   Ngo Ninh Diem—South Vietnamese leader who was overthrown and assassinated in 1963.
   Tonkin Gulf Resolution—Congressional approval to allow President to take any necessary action in Vietnam.
   William C. Westmoreland—American Commander in Vietnam.
   DMZ—Demilitarized zone; a neutral area between North and South Vietnam.

2. France pulled out of NATO, attempted to form an alliance to offset American power, and talked of developing its own nuclear arsenal.
3. To maintain Israel's military superiority in the region.
4. Said it was necessary to honor promises, to maintain world order, and to fight aggression.

page 676
1. Malcom X—A leader of the Black Muslims.
   Otto Kerner—Illinois Governor who headed commission to determine the causes of riots.
   Cesar Chavez—Mexican-American labor leader.
   Brown Berets—Organization for Chicano power.
   Dennis Banks—Cofounder of American Indian Movement.
   Betty Friedan—A leader in feminist movement.
2. Sit-ins, freedom rides, and protest marches performed in a peaceful manner.
3. Work, housing, and education.
4. Fluctuated from Americanization to helping Indians hold on to own traditions.
5. Eliminate discrimination in employment and establish day-care centers.
6. Viewed society as corrupt.

Special Feature Questions
page 664
1. Chinese Exclusion Act of 1882.
2. For humanitarian reasons, such as to help refugees from political oppression.

Photo Questions
page 656
Most analysts believe Kennedy was helped more.

page 658
To land a person on the moon within 10 years.

page 660
Blacks were appointed to high-level posts, opportunities for employment opened up, many blacks received their voting rights, and housing discrimination was reduced.

page 662
New programs under the Economic Opportunity Act included Job Corps, Upward Bound, Operation Headstart, and Vista.

page 667
An attack by the North Vietnamese on a U.S. destroyer.

page 670
Believed progress was too slow.

page 671
Frustration with inability to change their lives.

page 673
Workers organized for bargaining strength, pride in their own heritage was growing, and some discriminatory practices were ended.

page 677, Discussion
1. Answers may vary. Those who believe religion would be an issue may note that the same prejudice exists and that most candidates are members of the same few religions. Those who answer that religion would not be an issue might point out that Kennedy proved to Americans that he was an independent President.
2. Politicians represent the people and must be aware of the feelings of the people. The government cannot continue to carry out a policy that is rejected by the people.
3. Answers may vary. Students who deny the effectiveness of nonviolence may note that it provides insufficient pressure to effect change. Those who believe nonviolence works may answer that the alternative, violent action, hurts the cause and loses support.
4. Answers may vary.

Chapter Review
pages 676–677, Review Questions
1. Religion, Cuba and the Cold War, and the promise of a new direction for the United States.
2. A recession hit in the early 1960's. In the latter part of the decade, unemployment remained at a relatively low level and the gross national product grew at a consistent rate.
3. Programs devised by Kennedy administration to meet the challenges of the 1960's.
4. Programs included housing, job training, and education. In addition, programs were started to reduce poverty in slums and rural areas, and to allow the residents their say in running the programs.
5. New employment opportunities and voting rights were attained. Progress was reported

in reducing housing discrimination and segregation in the schools.
6. To resist the spread of communism and to aid the South Vietnamese after the French pulled out.
7. Some believed that the conflict was simply a civil war; others felt that the war siphoned funds that should be used for domestic programs.
8. Dissent over the war and the militant stance of minorities in fighting for equal rights.

page 677, Using Maps
1. Texas.
2. Mississippi.

3. Alabama.
4. Tennessee.
   Tennessee, Texas, Arkansas, and Florida.
5. Voting Rights Act of 1965, the outlaw of the poll tax, and the freedom marches and demonstrations of the period.

page 677, Using Skills
1. That the Roman Catholic hierarchy inevitably tries to seize political power and outlaw other religions.
2. Constitutions of Latin American countries.
3. No. Forms of government, history, and religions vary from country to country.
4. No.

CHAPTER 31 THE NIXON-FORD ERA

After studying this chapter, students should be able to:

1. describe Nixon's initiatives in foreign affairs.
2. explain Nixon's domestic policies as a reflection of the conservative mood of the nation in the late 1960's and early 1970's.
3. discuss the "Imperial Presidency" and Watergate scandal.
4. describe the continuity between Ford's and Nixon's economic and foreign policies.

OVERVIEW

Chapter 31 narrates the major events of the Nixon and Ford administrations. Beginning with Nixon's attempts to get the United States out of Vietnam, the chapter continues with his domestic policies, the series of events that led to his resignation, and the continuity of domestic and foreign policy between Nixon and Ford.

Although a good deal of time is spent on the Watergate crisis, a more interesting aspect of the Nixon administration is his attempt to exploit the conservative reaction of the period. That conservative reaction to events in the 1960's continues into the early and middle 1980's. Important concepts to be emphasized in the chapter include the silent majority, Vietnamization, détente, shuttle diplomacy, stagflation, executive privilege, deregulation, and energy crisis.

TEACHING IDEAS

Section 1

Introduction: Have the students study the picture on page 680. The 1960's was a decade of rapid change in American society. Johnson's Great Society and the rebellion of youth eventually brought about a conservative reaction. Nixon was able to tap this conservative reaction by appealing to the "silent majority." Ask the students what they think the "silent majority" was. Then have them read the section to see if their speculations were correct.

Development: Have the students list the major foreign policy developments under Nixon in the following parts of the world: Indochina, China, Soviet Union, Middle East.

Section 2

Introduction: "Stagflation" is the combination of inflation and economic stagnation or recession.

Stagflation is a phenomenon that presents a real problem to government economic advisers because the techniques used to fight one aspect of the problem contribute to the other aspect. For example, government spending to foster economic growth also contributes to inflation. Government attempts to balance the budget and control inflation slow the economy and can contribute to recession. Explain this to the students and have them read the section to see how Nixon dealt with the phenomenon.

Development: Nixon's appeal to conservatism and the "silent majority," described in the last section, was also apparent in his domestic policies. Review the section's treatment of civil rights and law and order, then have the students explain why these can be used as examples of Nixon's appeal to the conservative mood of the country.

Section 3

Introduction: Have the students view the picture on page 693 of the Ervin Senate Committee investigating Watergate. Have the students read the section for the details of the Watergate scandal and other Nixon actions that were interpreted by many as abuses of presidential power.

Development: Nixon acted in the tradition of "strong" Presidents, extending the power of his office. Soon, however, Congress reacted. Some students of government today suggest that the reaction of Congress has not yet ended. They argue that Congress' consciousness of its prerogatives has, in effect, reduced the effectiveness of the government by reducing the effectiveness of the Presidency. These critics point to the failure of many of Jimmy Carter's initiatives and the stalemates Reagan faced after 1982 as evidence. With this background, have students list and describe the attributes of the "Imperial Presidency" to which Congress reacted in the early 1970's. Was the reaction legitimate?

Section 4

Introduction: Have the students study the picture on page 695 and then read the section to answer the question in its caption.

Development: In many ways, Ford continued the policies of the Nixon administration. Using the economy and foreign policy as examples, have the students demonstrate why historians make this point.

Conclusion: Conclude the chapter by having students complete the Using Skills activity on pages 698–699.

ANSWERS
Section Review Questions
page 684
1. Henry Kissinger—National security advisor during Nixon administration.
   Nixon Doctrine—Stated United States would aid an ally, but not fight its wars.
   Lon Nol—Cambodian leader who asked for help from United States.
   SALT—Strategic Arms Limitation Talks.
2. Gradual replacing of U.S. troops with Vietnamese troops while continuing negotiations.
3. Political unrest in Cambodia. Also, the use of Cambodia by Viet Cong for sanctuary and surprise attacks.
4. He was a staunch, long-time foe of communism.
5. Produced U.S.-Soviet crisis that nearly turned into armed conflict.

page 690
1. Neil A. Armstrong—First person on the moon.
   Family Assistance Plan—Plan to guarantee a minimum income to families with no income.
   John Mitchell—Attorney General during Nixon administration.
   Warren Burger—Successor to Earl Warren as Chief Justice.
2. To shift many duties performed by federal government to state and local government.
3. Special investigations, funds for law enforcement agencies, and support for a no-knock search warrant law.
4. Children were forced to attend schools outside their neighborhoods.
5. Equal rights for women cannot be denied.
6. Increase in usage, depletion of resources, and the Arab oil embargo.

page 694
1. George McGovern—Democratic candidate for President in 1972.
   George C. Wallace—Governor of Alabama who was wounded in an assassination attempt during the 1972 presidential campaign.

H. R. Haldeman—A top aide in Nixon administration.

John Dean—President Nixon's counsel and one of witnesses in Watergate investigation.

"plumbers"—Investigating unit that used various means to stop government leaks.

"Saturday Night Massacre"—The firing of Special Prosecutor Archibald Cox and resignation of top two officials in Attorney General's office.

2. Division of the Democrats, the Eagleton Affair, withdrawal of the Wallace candidacy, and the winding down of the Vietnam War.

3. The arrest of five men, who were connected with the Committee to Reelect the President, for the Watergate break-in.

4. A taped conversation suggested that Nixon had known about the break-in and had tried to involve the CIA in the cover-up.

5. Obstruction of justice, abuse of presidential power, and defiance of the committee's subpoenas.

page 697

1. Khmer Rouge—Cambodian communists.
   Mayagüez—American ship seized by Cambodia.
   "Jackson Amendment"—Proposed that approving Soviet-U.S. trade agreement should depend on Soviet immigration policy.
   Walter Mondale—Carter's Vice President.

2. Said it was necessary to bring tranquility to the nation.

3. By relaxing government controls on business.

4. Rift grew wider and United States backed away from détente.

Photo Questions

page 680
Middle-class Americans who valued hard work, law and order, patriotism, and material progress.

page 682
The Nuclear Nonproliferation Treaty and the SALT agreements.

page 684
Programs included more moon landings and the stationing of an experimental laboratory in space.

page 689
They feared such a law would undermine family life and other traditional values.

page 690
Conservation measures were instituted, and the development of Alaskan oil and alternative energy sources was stepped up.

page 693
The scandal shook the faith of Americans in their government, but the system survived.

page 695
Pardoned former President Nixon and offered amnesty to Vietnam draft resisters.

Chapter Review
page 698, Review Questions

1. Put into effect plan to replace the U.S. soldiers with South Vietnamese. Kissinger negotiated final agreement in 1973.

2. Some trade and travel restrictions were lifted. Treaty and arms negotiations were started. Friendlier relations were begun with both the Soviet Union and China.

3. The nation was troubled by a recession and inflation for most of the early 1970's.

4. Progress in civil rights was slow, although some gains in employment and integration were made. Land was returned to Indians. Equal employment opportunities were strengthened.

5. Congress was upset with Nixon's use of executive privilege and impoundment. Some believed Nixon impinged on congressional war-making powers.

6. Administration officials were involved in the break-in and cover-up and Nixon was also implicated in the cover-up.

7. Pardon for Nixon and for draft evaders.

8. Détente early in administration, but later took a harder line.

page 698, Discussion

1. Answers may vary. Supporters of the pullout will point out that the U.S. should admit involvement was a mistake and get out. Those who believe the pullout was wrong may say that the U.S. should have committed more resources to winning.

2. Answers may vary. Supporters of détente should note that there was a lessening of tension and serious negotiations began. Oth-

ers will note that the Soviets are unreliable, and that détente was a ploy.

3. Answers may vary. Nixon supporters should mention his experience and his success in foreign affairs. McGovern supporters will mention his anti-war advocacy and his promise to aid minorities and the poor.

4. Answers may vary. Students who believe Nixon should have been prosecuted may say that no one is above the law. Others may say that resignation was punishment enough.

page 698, Using Graphs
1. About $3 billion.

2. All except 1961–1968.
3. 1969–1976.
4. 1953–1960.

page 699, Using Skills
1. That the U.S. system of government and law is nation's best protection against abuses of power.
2. Law allowed for freedom of press and an independent legislation and court system.
3. The Watergate affair might have gone undetected but for the chance discovery of Frank Wills and fact that Nixon taped his own conversations.

CHAPTER 32 AMERICAN SOCIETY IN TRANSITION

After studying this chapter, the student should be able to:

1. describe the "counterculture" of the 1960's.
2. discuss the major developments in the arts, religion, and the media during the 1960's and 1970's.
3. point out examples of social and technological change in the 1970's.

OVERVIEW

We have already seen the political implications of the conservative mood developing in the country during the 1970's, and this chapter points out the changes of the 1960's against which Americans were reacting. Beginning with a discussion of the "counterculture," the chapter describes changing themes in arts and literature, the impact of the media, and concludes with a brief discussion of sports and technology. The most appropriate way to treat this material is to contrast themes of the 1960's with those of the later 1970's. Concepts in the chapter include the generation gap, New Journalism, and pop art.

TEACHING IDEAS

Section 1

Introduction: Perhaps that one aspect of life in the 1960's against which middle-class Americans

reacted the most was the "counterculture." Have the students read the section looking for the various aspects of this phenomenon.

Development: After reading and discussing the counterculture, ask the students to name any elements of it that they still see today. This may reveal some interesting aspects of youth life today.

Section 2

Introduction: By the mid-1970's, we see a shift from the themes of the 1960's, based upon or influenced by the counterculture, to more conservative themes. Have the students look for this shift as they read.

Development: Now that students have read the material, have them contrast themes and works in literature and the movies of the 1960's with those of the 1970's. (In the 1970's more traditional themes were apparent: family, heritage, traditional values, clear-cut differences between good and bad.) Have them describe the differences by focusing on the following works:

	1960's	1970's
Books	*Catch 22*	*Roots*
	Silent Spring	
	The Feminine Mystique	
	The Autobiography of Malcom X	
Movies	*Dr. Strangelove*	*Sounder*
	Bonnie & Clyde	*Star Wars*
	Easy Rider	

Section 3

Introduction: Have the students study the picture on page 711, then read the section to answer the question in the caption.

Development: One of the most dramatic, and unfortunate, incidents of this period was the Jonestown massacre. Many Americans asked, "Why didn't the government do anything to keep this from happening?" Why did it not? This case affords an excellent opportunity to review the various aspects of the constitutional separation of church and state.

Section 4

Introduction: Quote McLuhan to the students, "the medium is the message." What do they think he meant by this statement? Have them read the section to see if their speculations were correct.

Development: Compare and contrast television programs like *Star Trek* and *All in the Family*. What are the positive features of each? What do they tell us about viewers, if anything? Ask the students to name the types of programs people watch now. Do they disagree or agree with Minnow's criticism (page 714)?

Section 5

Introduction: Have the students view the pictures on pages 716 and 717, read the captions, then read the section to find the answers. Before they begin to read, however, ask them why they think the authors chose those particular pictures —woman and black in a section on "A Changing World."

Development: This section recognizes the computer as a technological development with far-reaching ramifications. Ask the students if the computer has had any impact on their lives. Why is the computer a mixed blessing?

Conclusion: Conclude the chapter by having the students complete the Using Skills activity on page 719.

ANSWERS
Section Review Questions
page 704
1. Arlo Guthrie—A folk singer.
   Haight-Asbury—Section of San Francisco where hippies congregated.
   Diggers—Commune headed by Emmett Grogan.
2. They thought hippies were dirty, irresponsible, anti-American, and drug-ridden.
3. To express their freedom and to seek different kinds of pleasure.
4. Physical and mental damage and even death.

page 711
1. Allan Kaprow—Art historian who staged the first happening.
   Roy Lichtenstein—A leading pop artist.
   Joseph Heller—Wrote *Catch-22*.
   Alex Haley—Pulitzer Prize-winning author of *Roots*.
   Woodstock—1969 rock festival attended by 300,000 people.
2. Reflected changes taking place in the 1960's and used common objects as subject.
3. Started trend toward low-budget, more personal, and pro-youth films.
4. At first because they were trendsetters and later because of their musical ingenuity.

page 713
1. Oral Roberts—An evangelist.
   Sun Myung Moon—Head of the Unification Church.
   James Jones—Leader of the People's Temple.
2. Followed very strict rules concerning diet, smoking, drinking, drugs, and sex.
3. By the late 1970's there were more than 800 Christian and evangelical television and radio programs.
4. Claimed church practiced brainwashing.
5. Jones was convinced that the government was after him and that the United States would soon have civil war.

page 716
1. Marshall McLuhan—Canadian sociologist who analyzed effects of media on society.

Trekkies—Fans of science fiction television program *Star Trek*.

Norman Lear—Creator of innovative television show *All in the Family*.

2. That the way society receives its knowledge and news is more important than what that knowledge and news is.

3. Unbelievable, violent, and lacking in good taste.

4. Reporting that was personal, used the techniques of fiction, and used colorful language.

page 718

1. Ralph Nader—A consumer advocate.

Joe Namath—Popular football star who helped the rise of the AFL.

Wilt Chamberlain—Pro-basketball player of the 1960's.

2. Led to higher salaries and the great expansion of professional teams.

3. Made more compact and sophisticated.

4. By the 1970's used everywhere, in industry, business, home, and school.

Photo Questions

page 703

The individual, freedom, and personal commitment.

page 705

It used familiar subjects and was colorful and easy to understand.

page 709

Music using electronic effects and New Wave.

page 711

Fundamental churches gained more followers while some established churches grew more secular.

page 715

The sensationalized, unobjective approach of some news organizations led to a questioning of the power and influence of the media.

page 716

The growth of the number of professional sports and teams, the tremendous popularity, and the rapid rise in salaries.

page 717

The amount of network coverage.

page 718

Enables industries and businesses to automate. It replaces workers and creates new jobs.

Chapter Review

page 719, Review Questions

1. Their great number made them influential.

2. Less emphasis on material possessions and technology, and more emphasis on freedom and the individual.

3. Thought they were irresponsible and decadent.

4. Anti-war, environmental, feminist, and minority themes were increasingly used.

5. Music became much more diverse and sophisticated. Included folk music, acid rock.

6. Expansion of sports, rising salaries, rock, disco, and advent of athletic entrepreneurs.

7. Their use has risen greatly in homes, schools, and industry, and has threatened some jobs and created others.

page 719, Discussion

1. Answers may vary.

2. Answers may vary. Those who favor restrictions may mention their belief that cults present a danger to society. Those who reject restricting cults should note that freedom of religion is a right.

3. Answers may vary. Discussion should include the effect of the media on real-life violence, on beliefs, on fashion, on humor, and other topics.

4. Answers may vary. Discussion may include the point that automation may take away jobs from humans; in addition, some may note that technology can hinder initiative, understanding, and pride in accomplishment.

page 719, Using Charts

1. 300,000; 46.9 million.

2. A steady increase.

3. Very slight increase overall because more people are relying on other media.

4. Radio and television, if measure is the number of sets; television if measure is number of hours.

page 719, Using Skills

1. Biased.

2. Biased.

3. Objective.

4. Objective.

CHAPTER 33

CARTER AND REAGAN

After studying this chapter, the student should be able to:

1. list and explain the major domestic issues during the Carter administration.
2. describe Carter's attempt to return idealism to American foreign policy.
3. discuss the issues of the election of 1980.
4. list and explain the major features of Reagan's domestic policy.
5. describe the major shift in foreign policy under Reagan.
6. explain the significance of the mid-term elections of 1982.

OVERVIEW

Chapter 33 provides a narrative of the events of the Carter and Reagan administrations. It focuses on the political and economic aspects of domestic affairs and the contrasting approaches of the two administrations to foreign policy. With each administration, however, the conservative mood of the voters is reflected. Reagan has been the most effective politician in exploiting this mood. Concepts to be emphasized are affirmative action, supply-side economics, and nuclear freeze.

TEACHING IDEAS

SECTION 1

Introduction: The conservative mood of the American voters was reflected in the election of Carter. Have the students read the first subsection, "An Informal Presidency." Ask them to point out the traditional American values that Carter attempted to emphasize. Then, have them read the rest of the section.

Development: Political commentators have argued that the Carter administration was not a successful one, despite some achievements. Some observers maintain that, with the conflicting interests of the various power groups in the country, it is becoming harder and harder for Presidents to pursue their goals and devise middle-of-the-road policies. In the face of powerful single-interest groups and huge campaign contributions, compromise in the national interest has become more difficult. Have the students apply this argument to an analysis of Carter's programs in tax reform and energy legislation. Does the historical narrative support or contradict the argument?

Section 2

Introduction: Have the students read the quotation from President Carter that introduces this section. Carter's foreign policy reflected the most idealism since the days of Woodrow Wilson. Have the students read the section to see how Carter's idealism worked out.

Development: During the Carter years, the United States appeared to be losing ground to a more and more aggressive Soviet foreign policy. The Soviets worked through proxies (like Cuba and Vietnam) and constantly fostered communist or leftist revolution. Yet world opinion seemed more critical of the United States. Have the students place and describe the following topics in the context of the above argument:

Cuban surrogates
Asia
Crisis in Iran
Afghanistan

On the other hand, there were some foreign policy achievements during the Carter administration—the Panama Canal Treaties and the Camp David Accords. Ask students to explain how these developments would help the United States' position in the Third World.

Section 3

Introduction: The election of 1980 was, of course, won by Ronald Reagan. Have the students read and discuss the chapter's lead-in quotation from Reagan (page 721) and then read the section for details of the election.

Development: Many political analysts called the 1980 election a conservative revolution. Have the students defend that viewpoint by gathering evidence from the Republican platform, the supporters of Reagan, and the fate of congressional liberals during the election. What did those who down-played the idea of "conservative revolt" emphasize?

Section 4

Introduction: One observer of the "Reagan Revolution" argued that Reagan wanted to return the federal government to the economic policies of the 1920's. Review the economic policies of the Republicans during the 1920's, found in Chapter 23, pages 487–489 (Coolidge prosperity) and Chapter 24, page 507 (government policies contribute to economic problems during 1920's). Have the students read to see if there were any comparisons between Reagan policies and those of the 1920's.

Development: Have the students describe each of the following in the context of Reagan's attempt to reduce the role of the federal government in the lives of Americans:

Federal Regulations
Energy
Environment
New Federalism
Taxes
Government Spending

Section 5

Introduction: Reagan also seemed to want to return the United States to its position of prominence on the world scene, the position it had held in the early 1950's. Have the students read the section to see how this worked out.

Development: Reagan's policies marked a major shift from those of Carter as he pursued a much harder line against the Soviets and leftist Third World nations. However, a return to the nation's position in the 1950's seemed difficult, the world of the 1980's being a much more complicated one. To demonstrate this to the students, have them discuss the Latin American reaction to United States support for anti-Sandinista guerillas in Nicaragua and to England in the Falklands War. Then have them discuss Western European reaction to Reagan's treatment of the pipeline controversy.

Section 6

Introduction: Have the students study the graphs on page 743. What problems are evident? Have them read the section to see how the nation debated these problems in 1982.

Development: Despite the prominence of special interest groups and one-issue politics, the American system still survives on compromise and middle-of-the-road policies. Have the students demonstrate this characteristic of the American political scene with evidence from this section (tax compromises, calls for moderation).

Conclusion: Have students comment on how Reagan's economic program has fared since the 1982 elections. What is the current condition of the economy? Have students collect the latest figures on the budget deficit, unemployment, and inflation.

ANSWERS
Section Review Questions

page 725
1. Three Mile Island—Site of nuclear power plant accident.
   Proposition 13—Amendment to California constitution to reduce property taxes.
   Jack Kemp—Member of Congress who favored tax cuts and incentives to work and invest.
2. Merged agencies, formed new departments, and reformed procedures for promotion and performance in the civil service.
3. Quotas could be used in higher education, industry, and business to help minorities.
4. Government claimed that they were not political refugees.
5. To stimulate production.

page 731
1. Andrei Sakharov—A leading Soviet dissident.
   Omar Torrijos—Panamanian leader who signed agreement with President Carter.
   Anastasio Somoza—Nicaraguan President who resigned under pressure.
   Ruhollah Khomeini—Religious leader who set up an Islamic republic in Iran.
2. Entered into talks with Begin and Sadat.
3. American rule in Canal Zone continues through this century. U.S. retains right to use and defend the canal.
4. Iran was one of strongest U.S. allies in Middle East, although many people criticized its human rights record under the Shah.
5. A rescue attempt, negotiations, and political and economic pressure.

page 733

1. George Bush—Republican candidate for Vice President in 1980.

   John Anderson—Presidential candidate in 1980 as an independent.

   Moral Majority—Group that promotes Christian and conservative ideals.

2. Since President Carter's chances for reelection seemed small, many candidates entered the race.

3. Smaller government role, lower taxes, more defense spending, and opposition to abortion, busing, and ERA.

4. Coalitions that usually voted Democratic broke to support Reagan.

page 737

1. James Watt—Secretary of Interior whose policies angered environmentalists.

   John Hinckley—Tried to assassinate President Reagan.

   Thomas P. O'Neill—Speaker of the House and a Democratic leader.

2. Because it would destroy the beauty of the land.

3. They said it placed too much of a financial burden on cities and states.

4. Unemployed, elderly, poor, and disabled.

page 742

1. Alexander Haig—Secretary of State under Reagan.

   Yuri Andropov—Soviet leader who succeeded Brezhnev.

   START—Strategic Arms Reduction Talks.

   Lech Walesa—Polish labor leader.

   PLO—Palestine Liberation Organization.

   Philip Habib—U.S. representative in Middle East negotiations.

   Margaret Thatcher—British Prime Minister.

2. Placed sanctions on Poland and Soviet Union.

3. Would make allies dependent on Soviets.

4. Supported military government against rebels.

5. Grant Palestinians control in their own affairs, in association with Jordan. Called for Israel to back off on building settlements on West Bank and Gaza Strip.

6. Britain, closest ally of the United States, was violating the Monroe Doctrine.

page 744

1. Recession continued. Although rate of inflation declined, unemployment was at highest level since the depression.

2. Spending had increased and revenues had decreased.

3. Withholding taxes on interest, dividends, and tips; increased excise taxes; reduction of tax breaks.

4. A setback for Republicans although they kept control of the Senate.

Photo Questions

page 722

Promote employment and education of women and minority groups.

page 723

Raise tariffs on imported oil, eliminate price controls on domestic oil, introduce new taxes, and institute tax credits for those who practice conservation.

page 727

Some wanted to disrupt efforts, but the moderate Arab nations remained neutral.

page 728

To end bitterness over Panama Canal and assure Latin American countries of U.S. intention to treat them as equals.

page 730

End sanctions and return Iranian money frozen in U.S. banks.

page 735

Took more precautions.

page 739

Believed buildup was necessary for fruitful arms control negotiations.

page 742

Israel should stop building settlements in Gaza Strip and on West Bank and Palestinians should be allowed a greater voice in their own affairs.

Chapter Review

page 745, Review Questions

1. Instituted programs to reorganize agencies and departments, cut wasteful spending, and to reform tax system and civil service.

2. Proposed higher tariffs and taxes to encourage conservation, lifted federal controls, and called for research to develop new sources of energy.

3. Emphasis on human rights weakened ties between United States and Nicaragua and

Iran, and hindered but did not stop U.S.-Soviet talks.

4. The economy, especially unemployment and inflation, and the direction of foreign policy.
5. Reagan enjoyed a more elegant style of living, worked shorter hours, delegated more responsibility.
6. To cut taxes and cut social programs.
7. Reagan took a harder line with Soviets, but announced willingness to take part in serious arms negotiations.
8. Reagan continued to push for defense program and budget cuts, but appeared willing to compromise on certain items such as the jobs program.

page 745, Discussion
1. Answers may vary. Discussion should include: what role United States should play in affairs of other nations, whether the U.S. should risk offending its allies, and whether the human rights question should be addressed at home first.
2. Discussion should touch on conservative support for a strong defense, spending cuts, and a smaller role for the government. A description of liberal position should mention support for social programs, higher spending, and a larger role for government. Conservative-liberal view on issues such as abortion, ERA, nuclear freeze, environment, and busing should also be mentioned. Note that what is "liberal" and what is "conservative" has changed over the years.
3. Answers may vary. Possibilities include the use of force, stronger sanctions, enlarging the role of the United Nations, and playing down the crisis.
4. Answers may vary, but should include the problems of inspecting terrorist threats, and spread of nuclear power to several countries.

page 745, Using Graphs
1. 1980, although the estimated budget continues to increase.
2. 1940–1945 and 1980's.
3. late 1940's; late 1940's; end of World War II brought end to military spending.
4. Budget and debt have increased greatly since 1940.

page 745, Using Skills
1. a.
2. a.

3. b.
4. a.

Ask students to make a generalization about why some of these statements are more difficult to prove (evaluative statements more difficult than factual statements).

Unit Review

page 746, Review Questions
1. Cold War, arms race, civil rights.
2. Made them suspicious of ulterior motives, created internal conflicts (McCarthyism), led to competition for friendship of other countries, led to war (Vietnam, Korea).
3. Increased leisure time and leisure activities; increased reliance on television for entertainment and information; changed nature of jobs; led to culture predicated on use of automobile.
4. Emerged as superpower after World War II; has since had to face increasing independence of allies and increasing demands of Third World countries.

The Historian's Craft

Conclude the unit with The Historian's Craft activity on pages 747–749. This activity, which is designed for individual work, gives students practice in writing a historical essay based on their analysis of conflicting points of view. The subject of the activity is the Panama Canal treaties of 1977.

This is the culminating activity in The Historian's Craft series. All of the previous unit and chapter exercises in skill development should have prepared students for this final task.

First, have students read the pro and con arguments and discuss the main points and supporting details of each argument. The questions on page 749 may be treated as material for class discussion or as guidelines for individual students who are preparing their essays. Be sure the students understand the instructions for writing the essay (page 747, column 1, paragraph 3).

Question 1. Because Panama gains sovereignty over the canal, but gradually.

Question 2. Because it corrects an historical injustice, because it will improve U.S. relations with Latin America, and because U.S. security interests are safeguarded.

Question 3. "We bought it, we paid for it, we built it, and we are going to keep it. . . ." Ford says the U.S. never acquired full sovereignty, never "bought" the canal, but "rented" it in a "sneaky" way.

Question 4. Because the canal symbolizes American achievement and to give it up would be to accept others' criticisms of the U.S.

Question 5. Because the U.S. could adequately protect the canal.

Question 6. Feels that they should worry about American opinion, because the U.S. is the great power in the hemisphere.

Question 7. "Shenanigans" were not very serious compared to the great achievement.

EPILOGUE

After studying the epilogue, the student should be able to discuss a number of the challenges the nation faces in the last two decades of the century.

OVERVIEW

This brief epilogue suggests a number of the issues with which the nation and its people will have to deal in the 1980's. The issues are organized around the themes of foreign policy, the economy, and social questions. Most of these issues are treated daily in the nation's newspapers, and a current events discussion can reveal the present standing of each. Concepts in the epilogue are reindustrialization, mainstreaming, equivalent work, and single-parent family.

TEACHING IDEAS

Introduction: Have the students study the opening quotation from William M. Agee and discuss why it is appropriate for the epilogue.

Development: The easiest way to review concentrated material like that in the epilogue is to have students outline the major points. The following provides a model:

Challenges to the United States
I. Foreign Policy
   A. Relations with Allies
   B. Trade
   C. National Security

II. The Economy
   A. Unemployment
   B. Technology

III. Social Questions
   A. Job Training
   B. Health Care
   C. Graying of America
   D. Equal Rights
   E. The Family

Conclusion: Which of these issues are prominent in the news today? What questions/groups are involved? Are any of the positions on the issues similar to those studied throughout the course on American history?

ANSWERS
Photo Questions
page 752
Cutback in funds.

page 753
New technology has saved many lives and Americans are healthier and live longer.

page 754
The rapid growth in the number of elderly on the rolls has produced a burden that might prove too much for the system to stand.

page 755
Single-parent households are significantly poorer.

For Further Discussion
page 755
1. Discussion should include the fall of colonialism, the great population increase, the growing number of new nations, and the technological advances that have provided many nations with weapons of great power.
2. Answers may vary. The effectiveness of such a system should be discussed.
3. Answers may vary.
4. Answers may vary.
5. Answers may vary.
6. Answers may vary.

SUGGESTED RESOURCES

UNIT 1

BOOKS

Becker, Carl. *The Declaration of Independence: A Study In the History of Political Ideas.* New York: Knopf, 1942. Detailed study of the document and its sources.

Bridenbaugh, Carl. *The Colonial Craftsman.* Chicago: University of Chicago Press, 1961. Paperback. The role of the craftworker in the community gives insight into the social structure of the colonies.

Jackson, Kenneth T., ed. *Atlas of American History.* New York: Scribner, 1978. A useful source including travel and exploration routes, and military and demographic maps.

James, Edward T. and James, Janet W., eds. *Notable American Women, 1607–1950: A Biographical Dictionary.* 3 volumes. Cambridge: Harvard University Press, 1971. Provides sketches of women who made valuable contributions to American life.

Jameson, J. Franklin. *The American Revolution Considered as a Social Movement.* Boston: Beacon Press, 1963. Chronicles changes in daily life, economy, and culture resulting from the war.

Main, Jackson T. *The Social Structure of Revolutionary America.* Princeton: Princeton University Press, 1965. Paperback. Offers information on the trades and chances for advancement in 1700 America. Also, provides an interesting account of everyday life.

Miller, John C. *The Origins of the American Revolution.* Stanford, California: Stanford University Press, 1959. Paperback. A balanced view of the economic and political factors that brought about the break with England.

Peckham, Howard H. *The War for Independence: A Military History.* Chicago: University of Chicago Press, 1958. Paperback. A summary of the war effort, with emphasis on the methods used by the colonists to defeat a well-supplied, professional army.

Petry, Ann. *Tituba of Salem Village.* New York: Harper and Row, 1964. Novel that focuses on a slave who is accused of witchcraft.

Seton, Anya. *The Winthrop Woman.* New York: Fawcett, 1978. Novel based on history shows the strengths and weaknesses of some colonial leaders.

MEDIA

America's Revolution: Cause of Liberty. New York: Learning Corporation of America. 16mm film. Depicts a student of law from South Carolina who defends the American cause in England.

Boston Massacre. New York: Columbia Broadcasting System. 16mm film. Dramatic recreation of the event; from the *You Are There* series.

Colonial America: Roots of Revolution 1607–1775. Briarcliff, New York: Benchmark Films. Sound filmstrip. Examines the differences between the colonists on the issue of independence.

The Dawn of the American Revolution. Chicago: Coronet Films. 16mm film. A study of the factors that brought on the conflict.

The First People of North America. Niles, Illinois: United Learning. Sound filmstrip. A look at Indian groups and their way of life.

Game of Empire. Chicago: Denoyer Geppert. Simulation. Colonists trade under conditions set by the founding country.

Great American Trials. Bedford Hills, New York: New York Times. Sound filmstrip in six parts. Analyzes major trials in American history from the Salem witchcraft trials to the Chicago Seven.

UNIT 2

BOOKS

Beard, Charles A. *An Economic Interpretation of the Constitution of the United States.* New York: Free Press, 1965. Paperback. A classic of historical writing, this book champions the theory that economic interests shaped the Constitution.

Borden, Morton, ed. *The Antifederalist Papers.* East Lansing, Michigan: Michigan State University Press, 1967. Collection of arguments from those who supported decentralization and an agrarian-based economy during the period before the Constitution was adopted.

Borden, Morton. *Parties and Politics in the Early Republic*. Arlington Heights, Illinois: Harlan Davidson, 1967. Paperback. The development and growth of party politics is examined.

Butterfield, L.H., ed. *The Book of Abigail and John: Selected Letters of the Adams Family, 1762-1784*. Boston: Harvard University Press, 1975. Paperback. Collection of correspondence gives the reader a view of contemporary events.

Cooke, Jacob E. *Alexander Hamilton: A Biography*. New York: Scribner, 1982. Fascinating study of a statesman who helped steer U.S. foreign and domestic policy in the nation's early years.

Farrand, Max. *The Framing of the Constitution of the United States*. New Haven, Connecticut: Yale University Press, 1962. Paperback. A study of the thought processes of colonial leaders who drafted the Constitution.

Kelly, Alfred H. and Harbison, Winfred. *The American Constitution*. 5th ed. New York: Norton, 1976. A balanced treatment of the birth and evolution of the Constitution.

Meyers, Marvin, ed. *Mind of the Founder: Sources of the Political Thought of James Madison*. New York: Irvington, 1981. Paperback. Philosophy of this President, statesman, and lawmaker in his own words.

Rossiter, Clinton, ed. *The Federalist Papers*. New York, New American Library, 1961. Provides insight into the thinking of pro-Constitutionalists.

MEDIA

Democracy. New York, Western Publishing Company. Simulation. Provides an opportunity for students to learn about decision-making in a democracy.

The Fifth Amendment. Tarrytown, New York: Prentice Hall Media, Inc. Sound filmstrip. Features the evolution of the amendment and landmark cases involving its use.

The Journals of Lewis and Clark. Chicago: Encyclopedia Britannica Films. 16mm film. Follows the route of these two trailblazers through northwestern America.

Lobbying: The Fourth Branch of Government. Tarrytown, New York: Prentice Hall Media, Inc. Sound filmstrip. Shows how the actions of the government can be influenced by special interest groups.

A New Nation: The Struggle to Survive, 1789–1815. Briarcliff Manor, New York: Benchmark Films. 16mm film. Looks at the problems facing the new government and how it responded to these problems.

Our Federal Government: A Unit of Study. Niles, Illinois: United Learning. Sound filmstrip. Covers the Constitution, with emphasis on the branches of government and checks and balances.

UNIT 3

BOOKS

Bailey, Thomas. *The American Spirit: American History as seen by Contemporaries*. 2 vols. Lexington, Massachusetts: Heath, 1978. Americans from colonial times to the present express their feelings and beliefs in essays, letters, and speeches.

Cunliffe, Marcus. *The Nation Takes Shape: 1789–1837*. Chicago: University of Chicago Press, 1960. Focuses on the conflict between urban and rural interests, and examines sectionalism, conservatism, and democratic ideals.

De Voto, Bernard. *Across the Wide Missouri*. Boston: Houghton Mifflin, 1947. Detailed account of the western frontier.

Eaton, Clement. *The Civilization of the Old South*. New York: Harper and Row, 1963. Wellrounded study that includes education, industry, commerce, and the arts.

Farragher, John M. *Women and Men on the Overland Trail*. New Haven, Connecticut: Yale University Press, 1979. Paperback. Using diaries as a major source of information, Farragher details the hardships of people living under primitive conditions on the frontier.

Nye, Russel. *The Cultural Life of the New Nation: 1776–1830*. New York: Harper and Row, 1960. Chronicles movements in theology, education, literature, and the arts during the early part of our nation's history.

Peterson, Merrill D. *Thomas Jefferson and the New Nation: A Biography*. New York: Oxford University Press, 1975. Paperback. Exceptional one-volume biography of one of this nation's extraordinary individuals.

Scheiber, Harry N., et al. *American Economic History*. New York: Harper and Row, 1976. Examines the development of this nation's economy from colonial days to the present.

Taylor, George R., *The Transportation Revolution, 1815–1860*. Armonk, New York: Sharpe, 1977. Paperback. The interrelation of transportation with industry, commerce, and government in pre-Civil War days is presented.

Tocqueville, Alexis de. *Democracy in America*. New York: Washington Square Press, 1971. Impressions of a French statesman, writer, and traveler during his stay in the United States in the early 1800's.

Van Deusen, Glyndon. *The Jacksonian Era: 1828–1848*. New York: Harper and Row, 1959. Paperback. The inner workings of party politics is presented.

Wilson, Dorothy C. *Stranger and Traveler: The Story of Dorothea Dix, American Reformer*. Boston: Little, Brown, 1975. Story of the reformer who devoted her efforts to bettering the treatment of the mentally ill.

MEDIA

Economics and the American Dream. New York: Newsweek Education Division. Sound filmstrip. Study of the nation's resources and economic development.

The Industrial Revolution in America. Pleasantville, New York: Guidance Associates. Sound filmstrip. Shows the people, institutions, and forces that set industrialization in motion.

Inventions and Technology that Shaped America. New York: Learning Corporation of America. Sound filmstrip. Depicts the achievements in science and technology from colonial times to the 1970's.

The Jackson Years: The New Americans. New York: Learning Corporation of America. 16mm film. Shows the rise of Jackson and of the political power of the common people.

A Social History of the United States. New York: Learning Corporation of America. Sound filmstrip. The American way of life and the way it has changed is examined.

Tocqueville's America. National Education Television. 16mm film. The United States early in its history, as viewed by this French statesman, writer, and traveler.

UNIT 4

BOOKS

Benton, Elbert J. *The Movement for Peace Without Victory During the Civil War*. New York: Gordon Press, 1976. Examines individuals and groups that preferred compromise to war.

Catton, Bruce. *This Hallowed Ground*. New York: Washington Square Press, 1969. Paperback. Tells the story of Northern soldiers and civilians and how the war affected them.

Eaton, Clement. *A History of the Southern Confederacy*. New York: Free Press, 1954. Paperback. Focuses on the Confederacy's struggle to win the war, both on the battlefield and behind the lines.

Fuller, John F. *Grant and Lee: A Study in Personality and Generalship*. Bloomington, Indiana: Indiana University Press, 1957. Paperback. The background and military acumen of two great American generals is the focus.

Nevins, Allan. *The Emergence of Lincoln: Prologue to the Civil War, 1859–1861*. New York: Scribner, 1950. Paperback. Detailed account of

Lincoln as a member of Congress and as a presidential candidate.

Randall, James G. and Donald, David. *The Civil War and Reconstruction*. 2nd ed. Lexington, Massachusetts: Heath, 1969. Detailed one-volume history of the period.

Roland, Charles P. *The Confederacy*. Chicago: University of Chicago Press, 1960. Paperback. Part of the larger Chicago History of American Civilization series, this book concentrates on the economy, politics, and society of the Confederacy.

Stampp, Kenneth M. *And the War Came: The North and the Secession Crisis, 1860–1861*. Baton Rouge: Louisiana State University Press, 1950. Paperback. Considers the reasons compromise failed at a critical time in our history.

Williams, T. Harry. *The Union Restored, 1861–1876*. Morristown, New Jersey: Silver Burdett, 1974. Excellent account of the reconstruction process and how individuals and society were affected.

MEDIA

American Decades—The 1860's. Niles, Illinois: United Learning. Six sound filmstrips. Looks at life in the United States during the Civil War.

The Civil War: A Unit of Study. Niles, Illinois: United Learning. Eight sound filmstrips. Covers the daily life of the soldiers.

Civil War: Gettysburg to Appomattox. Culver City, California: Social Studies School Service. 10 photo aids. Depicts the important events of the war.

From These Honored Dead. Culver City, California: Social Studies School Service. Videocassette. Explores the battle at Gettysburg and the address by Lincoln.

Harriet Tubman and the Underground Railroad. BFA Educational Media. 16mm film. From the *You Are There* series, the biography of the heroic woman who led more than 300 slaves to freedom.

Lincoln and Fort Sumter. Culver City, California: Social Studies School Service. Simulation. Lincoln and advisers debate what course of action to take.

The Years of the Reconstruction. New York: McGraw Hill Films. Sound filmstrip. Examines the United States after the Civil War with emphasis on the impeachment proceedings and military occupation in the South.

UNIT 5

BOOKS

Campbell, James W. *America in Her Centennial Year, 1876*. Lanham, Maryland: University Press of America, 1980. Details the change in the United States after 100 years in existence.

Cochran, Thomas C. and Miller, William. *The Age of Enterprise: A Social History of Industrial America*. New York: Harper and Row, 1968. Paperback. Deals with the exceptional growth of the economy and industrialization in the late 1800's, and the social and political repercussions.

Dick, Everett. *The Sod-House Frontier: A Social History of the Northern Plains from the Creation of Kansas and Nebraska to the Admission of the Dakotas*. Lincoln, Nebraska: University of Nebraska Press, 1979. Paperback. Readable account of frontier homesteading, politics, religion, and customs.

Fillers, Louis, ed. *From Populism to Progressivism: Representative Selections*. Melbourne, Florida: Krieger, 1978. Paperback. Leaders of reform movements express their philosophy and programs in speeches, letters, and writings.

Franklin, John H. *From Slavery to Freedom: A History of Negro Americans*. New York: Knopf, 1980. Paperback. Chronicles the struggle of blacks to achieve equality.

Hicks, John D. *The Populist Revolt: A History of the Farmer's Alliance and the People's Party*. Lincoln, Nebraska: University of Nebraska Press, 1961. Paperback. Farmers' political organizations are extensively explored.

Katz, Jane B., ed. *Let Me Be a Free Man: A Documentary History of Indian Resistance*. Minneapolis: Lerner Publishing, 1975. Paperback. Excellent account of Indians' fight to hold on to their land and their way of life.

Leckie, William H. *The Buffalo Soldiers: A Narrative of the Negro Cavalry in the West.*

Norman, Oklahoma: University of Oklahoma Press, 1967. Paperback. Extensive study of the role of the black cavalry units.

McFeely, William J. *Grant: A Biography.* New York: Norton, 1981. Paperback. Revealing portrait of an enigmatic man whose success in the military was a sharp contrast to his career in politics.

Merk, Frederick. *History of the Westward Movement.* New York: Knopf, 1978. Paperback. Excellent sections on building new towns and on the problems faced by settlers.

Parrington, Vernon L. *Main Currents in American Thought: Beginnings of Critical Realism in America, 1860–1920.* New York: Harcourt Brace, Jovanovich, 1963. In-depth treatment of American thought and the changes it has produced.

MEDIA

America Comes of Age. Tarrytown, New York: Prentice Hall Media. Sound filmstrip. Features eyewitness accounts of important events in the United States from 1870 to the present.

The Big Push West. New York: National Broadcasting Company. 16mm film. Traces and examines the exploration and settlement of the western frontier.

The Immigrants' Experience: The Long, Long Journey. New York: Learning Corporation of America. 16mm film. Reflections of immigrants on coming to a new land.

The Innocent Years. New York: National Broadcasting Company. 16mm film. A glimpse of the social and political life during the first decade of the twentieth century.

Kitty Hawk to Paris: The Heroic Years. New York Learning Corporation of America. 16mm film. Original footage and photos shows aviation from its beginnings.

Louis L'Amour's American West. Larchmont, New York: Media Basics. Sound filmstrip. The frontier experience of a Tennessee family moving west.

Rise of the American City. Chicago: Encyclopedia Britannica. 16mm film. Urban change over the past century.

Settling the West. Chicago: Coronet Films. Six sound filmstrips. Offers a look at the forces that motivated, and the problems faced by, explorers, miners, cattle raisers, and farmers.

UNIT 6

BOOKS

Blum, John M. *Woodrow Wilson and the Politics of Morality.* Boston: Little, Brown, 1962. Paperback. Wilson is viewed as a leader whose self-righteousness was the main reason for his political downfall after World War I.

Ferrell, Robert H. *American Diplomacy.* New York: Norton, 1975. Analysis of the evolution of U.S. foreign policy.

Hofstadter, Richard. *The Age of Reform: From Bryan to FDR.* New York: Knopf, 1955. Study of the influence of Social Darwinism on reform endeavors.

Kennan, George F. *American Diplomacy, 1900–1950.* Chicago: University of Chicago Press, 1968. Paperback. Focuses on the part idealism has played in forming this nation's foreign policy.

Kennedy, David M. *Over Here: The First World War and American Society.* New York: Oxford University Press, 1982. Paperback. Good account of how people on the homefront adapted to the war effort.

Miner, Dwight C. *Fight for the Panama Route.* New York: Octagon, 1966. Details the awesome task of building the canal.

Trask, David F. *The War with Spain in 1898.* New York: Macmillan, 1981. The role of yellow journalism in rousing public opinion is ably presented.

Tuchman, Barbara. *The Guns of August.* New York: Bantam, 1976. Paperback. A masterful presentation of the first six weeks of World War I.

MEDIA

The Age of Theodore Roosevelt. Pleasantville, New York: Guidance Associates. Sound filmstrip. Study of a man who helped shape an era.

Emerging Giant. Stanford, California: Multimedia Productions. Sound filmstrip. Depicts the development of the United States into a major force in international affairs.

The Japanese Americans. Stanford, California: Multimedia Productions. Sound filmstrip. Traces the lives of Japanese-Americans who came to this country.

Portrait of Power: Woodrow Wilson. Tarrytown, New York: Prentice Hall Media. Sound filmstrip. Offers study of Wilson's attempts to end the war and gain support of the allies.

World War I. New York: Perrgamon Press, 1973. Sound filmstrip. A look at the "war to end all wars."

Wilson, Lodge, and the League of Nations. Culver City, California: Social Studies School Service. Simulation. Emphasis is placed on the issue of isolation vs. involvement.

UNIT 7

BOOKS

Baxardall, Rosalin, et al. *America's Working Women: A Documentary History, 1600 to the Present.* New York: Random, 1976. Paperback. A complete compendium of the working woman.

Coffey, Thomas. *The Long Thirst.* New York: Dell, 1976. Details the growth and victory of the prohibition movement and its effect on the nation.

Cronon, E. David. *Black Moses: The Story of Marcus Garvey and the Universal Negro Improvement Association.* Madison, Wisconsin: University of Wisconsin Press, 1969. Examines Garvey's role in the black effort to gain political and economic power.

Kirschner, Don S. *City and Country: Rural Responses to Urbanization in the 1920's.* West-port, Connecticut: Greenwood Press, 1970. Addresses the differences in culture, society, and customs between rural and urban America.

Meltzer, Milton. *In Their Own Words: A History of the American Negro.* New York: Harper and Row, 1964. 3 vols. A collection of historical documents on the efforts of blacks to attain a share of the American dream.

Schlesinger, Arthur M., Jr. *The Age of Roosevelt: The Crisis of the Old Order.* Boston: Houghton Mifflin, 1957. Paperback. Surveys the political climate of the 1920's with interesting accounts of the problems of the Democrats and the Republican alliance with business.

Wolters, Raymond. *Negroes and the Geat Depression: The Problems of Economic Recovery.* Westport, Connecticut: Greenwood Press, 1970. Reviews the role of the NAACP and its effects on the New Deal.

MEDIA

Black History: Lost, Stolen, or Strayed. BFA Educational Media. 16mm film. This film, narrated by Bill Cosby, provides a view of the problems faced by blacks throughout history.

Dust Bowl. New York: Columbia Broadcasting System. 16mm film.

Twentieth Century series film of the ravaged Midwest during the 1930's.

The Great Depression. BFA Educational Media. 16mm film. Examines the problems that gripped the nation during the 1930's.

Inherit the Wind. Larchmont, New York: Media Basics. Three sound filmstrips. Based on the Scopes Trial.

The Inheritance. New York: McGraw-Hill. 16mm film. Surveys immigration, the labor movement, and American idealism.

The Stock Market. Tarrytown, New York: Prentice-Hall Media. Sound filmstrip. Examines the history and function of Wall Street.

Women's Rights in the United States: An Informal History. New York: Altana Films. 16mm film. Documentary showing the battle for equal rights for women.

UNIT 8

BOOKS

Bullock, Alan. *Hitler: A Study in Tyranny*. New York: Harper and Row, 1964. Paperback. Portrait of Hitler with an excellent examination of the reasons for his rise to power.

Burns, James M. *Roosevelt: The Soldier of Freedom*. New York: Harcourt Brace, Jovanovich, 1970. Claims Roosevelt's main concern was seeking world freedom.

Drummond, Donald F. *The Passing of American Neutrality, 1937–1941*. Westport, Connecticut: Greenwood Press, 1968. A balanced interpretation of the events of the period.

Dulles, Foster Rhea. *America's Rise to World Power, 1898–1954*. New York: Harper and Row, 1955. A scholarly history which lends support to interventionist policy.

Galambos, Louis. *America at Middle Age: A New History of the United States in the Twentieth Century*. New York: McGraw-Hill, 1982. Brief yet interesting account, stressing social and political changes.

Goldston, Robert. *The Coming of the Cold War*. New York: Macmillan, 1970. U.S.-Soviet relations from the 1917 revolution to after World War II are examined.

Houston, Jeanne Wakatsuki and Houston, James D. *Farewell to Manzanar*. New York: Bantam, 1974. A first-hand acount of Japanese-Americans relocation and readjustment.

Lafeber, Walter. *America, Russia, and the Cold War, 1945–1980*. New York: Wiley, 1972. The policies of confrontation, brinksmanship, and détente are scrutinized.

Lord, Walter. *Day of Infamy*. New York: Bantam, 1957. Paperback. Eyewitness accounts of Pearl Harbor.

Toland, John. *Rising Sun*. New York: Bantam, 1971. World War II from the viewpoint of the Japanese.

MEDIA

The American People in World War II. New York: McGraw-Hill. 16mm film. Daily life in the United States during the war.

Developing the A-Bomb. Bedford Hills, New York: New York Times. Sound filmstrip. Traces the development of the bomb and the decision to use it.

Hitler. New York: Learning Corporation of America. 16mm film. Dramatized interview provides insight into the actions and goals of the Nazi leader.

The Making of American Foreign Policy. Culver City, California: Social Studies School Service. Filmstrip, cassette, and transparencies. A multi-media kit that can promote understanding of foreign policy decision-making.

Normandy Invasion. Washington D.C.: United States Coast Guard. 16mm film. Shows preparation for D-Day and combat footage.

The Twisted Cross. New York: McGraw-Hill. 16mm film. The rise and fall of Hitler and the Nazis are shown in this documentary.

UNIT 9

BOOKS

Aptheker, Herbert. *A Documentary History of the Negro People in the United States*. Secaucus, New Jersey: Citadel Press, 1951. An extensive collection of firsthand accounts.

Banner, Lois W. *Women in Modern America: A Brief History*. New York: Harcourt Brace, Jovanovich, 1974. Paperback. Traces the efforts of women to improve their status.

Drury, Allen. *Advise and Consent*. New York: Avon, 1972. Paperback. Novel depicting the internal struggle in Congress to maintain political balance.

Harrington, Michael. *The Other America*. New York: Macmillan, 1968. The paradox of poverty in the midst of affluence is examined.

Josephy, Alvin M., Jr. *The Indian Heritage of America*. New York: Knopf, 1968. Traces Indian culture and history to the present.

Nixon, Richard M. *RN: The Memoirs of Richard Nixon*. New York: Grosett, 1978. An inside look at the Nixon administration.

Schlesinger, Arthur M., Jr. *The Thousand Days*. New York: Fawcett, 1977. Paperback. Account of Kennedy as president.

White, Theodore H. *America in Search of Itself: The Making of the President, 1956–1980*. New York: Harper and Row, 1982. A reporter describes seven presidential campaigns he has covered.

Woodward, C. Vann. *The Strange Career of Jim Crow*. New York: Oxford University Press, 1974. Paperback. The forces that led to black segregation are explored.

MEDIA

American Decades—The 1970's. Niles, Illinois: United Learning. Sound filmstrip. A review of the political and social events of the period from Vietnam to Watergate.

Blue Collar Capitalism. Burlington, Vermont: Econ-Trek. 16mm film. Account of what occurred when the workers buy a company to keep it in business.

Hunger in America. New York: Columbia Broadcasting System. 16mm film. Documentary depicting effect of hunger and malnutrition and government attempts to solve the problem.

The Making of the President, 1972. New York: Time-Life Multimedia. 16mm film. The inside workings of a presidential campaign and election are revealed.

Martin Luther King: The Man and His Meaning. Culver City, California: Social Studies School Service. Filmstrip, cassette, study prints, and duplicating masters. Kit provides in-depth study of King's role in the civil rights movements of the 1950's and 1960's.

National Defense. Niles, Illinois: United Learning. Sound filmstrip. Depicts varying views on military preparedness.

2000 A.D. New York: Newsweek Educational Division. Sound filmstrip. Survey of the social, economic, and technological problems that this nation faces in the future.

Notes

Notes

Notes

Notes

Notes

Notes

Notes

THE American Tradition

Circle the number that corresponds most nearly to your opinion of each of the following items of *The American Tradition*. Please also star (*) three factors which most influence your evaluation or choice of a text.

Student Text	Excellent	Very Good	Satisfactory	Fair	Poor	Comments
1. Annotated Constitution	1	2	3	4	5	_____
2. Appendix Materials	1	2	3	4	5	_____
3. Approach	1	2	3	4	5	_____
4. Boldfaced Terms	1	2	3	4	5	_____
5. Chapter Openers	1	2	3	4	5	_____
6. Chapter Reviews	1	2	3	4	5	_____
7. Using Skills	1	2	3	4	5	_____
8. Comparisons	1	2	3	4	5	_____
9. Concept Development	1	2	3	4	5	_____
10. Content	1	2	3	4	5	_____
11. End-of-Section Questions	1	2	3	4	5	_____
12. Factual Accuracy	1	2	3	4	5	_____
13. People in History	1	2	3	4	5	_____
14. Graphic Illustrations	1	2	3	4	5	_____
15. The Historian's Craft	1	2	3	4	5	_____
16. Organization	1	2	3	4	5	_____
17. Photographs	1	2	3	4	5	_____
18. Perspectives in History	1	2	3	4	5	_____
19. Prologue	1	2	3	4	5	_____
20. Readability	1	2	3	4	5	_____
21. Unit Openers	1	2	3	4	5	_____
22. Unit Reviews	1	2	3	4	5	_____
23. Visual Impact	1	2	3	4	5	_____

Teacher's Annotated Edition

	Excellent	Very Good	Satisfactory	Fair	Poor	Comments
1. Teachability	1	2	3	4	5	_____
2. Introduction	1	2	3	4	5	_____
3. How to Use the Teacher's Annotated Edition	1	2	3	4	5	_____
4. Instructional Approaches	1	2	3	4	5	_____
5. Text Implementation	1	2	3	4	5	_____
6. Suggested Resources	1	2	3	4	5	_____

Supplements

	Excellent	Very Good	Satisfactory	Fair	Poor	Comments
1. Student Activity Book	1	2	3	4	5	_____
2. Student Activity Book—T.E.	1	2	3	4	5	_____
3. Evaluation Program	1	2	3	4	5	_____

Circle the appropriate information.

1. Grade level of students	9		10	11	12
2. Enrollment of that grade	1-50		51-100	101-200	200+
3. Total school enrollment	1-200		201-500	501-1000	1000+
4. Locale of school	rural		small town	suburban	large city
5. Ability level of class	below average		average		above average
6. Appropriateness of text for your class	easy		about right		difficult
7. Number of years text used	1	2	3	4	5
8. May we quote you?	Yes	No			

Name ______________________________ Position ______________________

School ____________________ City ______________ State ______________ Zip ______________

Date ____________________

Fold

NO POSTAGE NECESSARY IF MAILED IN THE UNITED STATES

BUSINESS REPLY CARD

FIRST CLASS PERMIT NO 284 COLUMBUS OHIO

Postage will be paid by:

CHARLES E. MERRILL PUBLISHING CO.
A Bell & Howell Company
Managing Editor, Elhi Social Studies
1300 Alum Creek Drive
Columbus, Ohio 43216

BELL & HOWELL

THE American Tradition

A HISTORY OF THE UNITED STATES

Robert P. Green, Jr.
Laura L. Becker
Robert E. Coviello

CHARLES E. MERRILL PUBLISHING CO.
A BELL & HOWELL COMPANY
Columbus, Ohio
Toronto London Sydney

AUTHORS

Robert P. Green, Jr. is an Assistant Professor of Education at Clemson University, Clemson, South Carolina, where he teaches social studies methods to undergraduate and graduate students and supervises student teachers. He received his B.A. in History from the University of the South and both his M.A. in History and Ed.D. in Social Studies Education from the University of Virginia. Before joining the Clemson faculty, he taught in the public schools of North Carolina and Virginia on both the middle and secondary levels. An author of numerous articles on social studies education, Dr. Green has been a consultant to both school systems and publishers. He was named in the 1976 *Outstanding Young Men of America* and in the 1982–1983 *Who's Who in the South and Southwest.* Currently he serves as editor of *The Clemson Kappan: A Journal for South Carolina Educators.*

Laura L. Becker is an Assistant Professor of History at the University of Miami in Miami, Florida, where she teaches both graduate and undergraduate courses in United States history. She received her B.A. and M.A. in History from Brown University and her Ph.D. in History from the University of Pennsylvania. Dr. Becker has published a variety of articles on American history in professional and academic journals and has written and hosted a series of public radio programs on women in America.

Robert E. Coviello is chairperson of the Social Studies Department of Walpole High School in Walpole, Massachusetts, where he teaches courses in United States history, economics, and international relations. He received his B.A. in Economics from Tufts University and his M.Ed. from Bridgewater State College. He is past president of the New England History Teachers Association and is an instructor at the Center for Economic Education at Stonehill College in North Easton, Massachusetts. Experienced in curriculum development, he acts as a consultant to school systems and has served as a consultant/contributor to educational publishers.

ISBN 0-675-1991-5
Published by
CHARLES E. MERRILL PUBLISHING CO.
A BELL & HOWELL COMPANY
Columbus, Ohio 43216

PREFACE

Words such as "equality" and "freedom" make no sense in a vacuum. They must be given a human context. History does that.

MARTHA DOERR TOPPIN

The American Tradition is a chronological, topical history of the United States. By combining a strong foundation in chronology with a thorough explanation of causes and effects, it helps students to understand not only *what* happened but also *why* it happened.

The American Tradition is designed to inform students about the origins and development of this nation's government, economy, society, and culture. The text is divided into 9 units and 33 chapters. It begins with a Prologue that tells students why they should study history and ends with an Epilogue that discusses challenges of the future.

Each unit opens with a colorful two-page photograph, a listing of the chapters in the unit, and a time line highlighting important historical events. Each chapter begins with a photograph, a list of section titles that provides an overview of the chapter, and a brief quotation from a contemporary source. The quotation serves as a thought-provoking introduction to the theme of the chapter.

Within the text, facts and concepts are presented in a readable narrative replete with high-interest excerpts from primary and secondary sources. Chapters are divided into sections and sub-sections that contribute to easier reading and understanding. Concept terms appear in boldface type and are defined or explained in context immediately after being introduced. These same terms appear in the vocabulary lists at the end of the chapter and in the glossary at the end of the book.

Two kinds of special features appear throughout the text. "People in History" presents the human side of history. "Perspectives in History" discusses the development of themes and issues over time, from the beginning of American history to the recent past.

Photographs are used extensively to reinforce or expand chapter content. Precisely executed maps, graphs, charts, and diagrams, all in full color, provide supportive data and clarify important historical, economic, political, or social relationships.

The American Tradition also contains numerous study aids. Review questions at the end of each main section serve as a check on students' understanding of important facts. Comprehensive chapter reviews include a summary of key points, a vocabulary list, questions of varying difficulty, an exercise on using graphics, and a skill-developing exercise.

Unit reviews include a list of major generalizations, analytical questions, suggested activities, and an annotated bibliography. In addition, they contain a special in-depth skill development activity, "The Historian's Craft," which teaches critical-thinking skills in a systematic way.

An Appendix at the end of the text includes a number of special items. A full-color atlas contains both general reference maps and a graphics section that provides data on the population, government, economy, and society of the United States. A copy of the Declaration of Independence and an annotated Constitution aid the student in understanding the American political system. A Glossary provides definitions of key terms, and a complete Index provides easy reference to important historical topics.

Reviewers

Linda Barone
Social Studies Teacher
Utica Free Academy
Utica, New York

Mel D. Rosen
President, California Council
for the Social Studies
Van Nuys, California

Dr. Paul R. Rivera
Supervisor of Social Studies
Baltimore County Public Schools
Towson, Maryland

Dr. Catherine C. Pickle
Curriculum Consultant
Memphis City Schools
Memphis, Tennessee

Carl H. Sears
Director of Curriculum
Elmhurst Public Schools
Elmhurst, Illinois

Irene W. Kanter
Assistant Principal
Anderson High School
Austin, Texas

Staff

Project Editor: **Mary Nye Fetters;** Editors: **Brenda Smith, Rosemarie Trenjan, Thomas Photos, Myra Immell, Robert Kohan, Jacquelyn Whitney;** Designer: **Larry Koons;** Project Artist: **Catharine Bookwalter White;** Artist: **Kip M. Frankenberry;** Graphic Artist: **David Germon;** Map Artist: **June Barnes;** Illustrator: **David M. Mankins;** Photo Editor: **Russell Lappa**

TABLE OF CONTENTS

PROLOGUE————————————————1

UNIT

1

COLONIAL AMERICA   2

CHAPTER

1 The Beginnings   4

Widening Horizons————————— 5
The Age of Exploration————————— 8
Peoples of the New World————— 19

CHAPTER

2 The English Colonies   28

The English in Virginia————————29
The New England Colonies——————32
The Proprietary Colonies——————35
Colonial Government————————38
The Colonial Economy————————40
Culture and Society————————45

CHAPTER

3 The Struggle for Independence   52

Rivalry in North America————————53
Changes in British Colonial Policy————55
Colonial Protest————————————57
The Road to Revolution————————59
From Protest to War————————62
Moving Toward Separation——————66
Winning Independence————————68
Unit Review————————————75

UNIT

2

FORGING A UNION   79

CHAPTER

4 A New Nation   80

The New State Governments——————81
The Articles of Confederation—————81
The Critical Period————————————83
Achievements Under the Articles————87
Drafting the Constitution————————89
Debate Over the Constitution——————94

CHAPTER

5 The Constitution   98

Historical Background————————99
The Federal System——————————102
Branches of Government———————105
The Legislative Process———————110
The Democratic Process———————112
The Changing Constitution——————114

CHAPTER

6 The Federalist Era   118

Launching the New Government————119
Hamilton's Economic Program—————122
Political Parties————————————127
Washington's Foreign Policy——————130
Decline of the Federalists———————133
Unit Review————————————139

UNIT

3

NATIONALISM AND SECTIONALISM 142

CHAPTER

7 The Jeffersonian Republicans 144

Jefferson in Power_____145
Trials of a Neutral Nation_____150
The War of 1812_____153
American Nationalism_____157
The Rise of Sectionalism_____161

CHAPTER

8 The Age of Jackson 166

Political Events in the 1820's_____167
The Era of the Common People_____170
States' Rights and Union_____172
The Bank War_____176
Economics and Politics After Jackson_____179

CHAPTER

9 Westward Expansion 184

Significance of the Frontier_____185
Indian Relations_____188
Moving Westward_____190
War With Mexico_____197

CHAPTER

10 Antebellum America 202

Transportation and Communication_____203
Industrialization_____205
Cultural Trends_____210
The Spirit of Reform_____213
Women's Rights_____217
The Antislavery Movement_____219
The Slave South_____222
Unit Review_____227

UNIT

4

THE NATION DIVIDED 230

CHAPTER

11 Toward Civil War 232

Sectional Politics_____233
Temporary Reprieve_____235
The Kansas Question_____237
On the Brink of War_____240
The Union Divides_____243

CHAPTER

12 The Civil War 248

North Versus South_____249
Early Stages of the War_____251
A Step Toward Freedom_____256
The Home Front_____257
Union Victory_____262

CHAPTER

13 Reconstruction 270

Presidential Reconstruction_____ 271
Restoration Under Johnson_____274
Radical Reconstruction_____278
The Radical Regimes_____282
Redemption_____284
Unit Review_____289

UNIT

5

THE AGE OF INDUSTRIALIZATION 292

CHAPTER

14 Industrial Growth 294

Foundations for Growth_____295
The Railroads_____297
The Giants of Industry_____301
Philosophy for an Era_____305
Attempts at Regulation_____306

CHAPTER

15 The Rise of Labor 310

Workers and Their Problems_____311
The Union Movement_____314
Problems of the Labor Movement_____318
Labor Clashes_____320

CHAPTER

16 The Last Frontier 326

Opening the West_____327
The Farming Frontier_____331
Conflict With the Indians_____335

CHAPTER

17 The Gilded Age 344

Postwar Politics_____345
The Presidential Procession_____349
Populism_____352
The New South_____356

CHAPTER

18 An Urban Society 362

Urbanization_____363
Impact of Immigration_____365
Urban Life and Culture_____369
Urban Reform_____377

CHAPTER

19 The Progressive Era 382

The Progressives_____383
Progressive Goals_____386
Theodore Roosevelt_____390
William Howard Taft_____394
Woodrow Wilson_____397
Unit Review_____402

UNIT

6

THE RISE TO WORLD POWER 406

CHAPTER

20 An American Empire 408

Foreign Policy After the Civil War___ 409
The New Manifest Destiny___ 411
The Spanish-American War___ 416
Aftermath of the War___ 421

CHAPTER

21 The United States as a World Power 424

The Far East___ 425
The Panama Canal___ 429
A Continuing Interest in Foreign Affairs___ 434
Woodrow Wilson's Missionary Diplomacy___ 439

CHAPTER

22 World War I 446

Europe in 1914___ 447
A Neutral America___ 448
America at War___ 453
The Aftermath___ 465
Unit Review___ 470

UNIT

7

PROSPERITY AND DEPRESSION 474

CHAPTER

23 The Roaring 20's 476

Postwar Trauma___ 477
The Defense of Traditionalism___ 483
Politics in the 1920's___ 487
Social and Cultural Life___ 490
The Dream's End___ 498

CHAPTER

24 The Great Depression 502

The Rise and Fall of the Stock Market___ 503
The Lean Years___ 505
Hoover's Reaction___ 509
A Mandate for Change___ 513

CHAPTER

25 The New Deal 520

Conflicting Ideas___ 521
The Second New Deal___ 524
The New Deal at Its Peak___ 529
American Culture During the 1930's___ 536
Unit Review___ 541

UNIT

8

THE WORLD IN CONFLICT 544

CHAPTER

26 The Road to Global Conflict 546

The Postwar Scene_____ 547
The Rise of Totalitarianism_____ 550
The Growing Crisis_____ 555
A Neutral America_____ 559
From Neutrality to Commitment____ 561
The End of the Road_____ 568

CHAPTER

27 World War II 572

On the Defensive: 1942_____ 573
Turning the Tide: 1943_____ 582
On the Offensive: 1944_____ 587
Days of Victory: 1945_____ 591

CHAPTER

28 The Cold War 598

Origins of the Cold War_____ 599
Containment in Europe_____ 602
Containment in Asia_____ 606
Cold War "Thaw"_____ 613
Unit Review_____ 626

UNIT

9

THE UNITED STATES IN A NEW ERA 630

CHAPTER

29 Truman and Eisenhower 632

Truman's First Term_____ 633
Truman's Second Term_____ 637
The Eisenhower Era_____ 640
Life in the 1950's_____ 645

CHAPTER

30 The Kennedy-Johnson Years 654

The New Frontier_____ 655
The Great Society_____ 661
Foreign Affairs Under Johnson_____ 666
Unrest in the Nation_____ 669

CHAPTER

31 The Nixon-Ford Era 678

Nixon and Foreign Affairs_____ 679
Domestic Affairs Under Nixon_____ 684
The Presidency in Crisis_____ 690
The Ford Administration_____ 694

CHAPTER

32 American Society in Transition 700

The Counterculture_____ 701
The Arts_____ 704
Religion_____ 711
The Media_____ 713
A Changing World_____ 716

CHAPTER

33 Carter and Reagan 720

Domestic Affairs Under Carter_____ 721
Carter's Foreign Policy_____ 725
The Election of 1980_____ 731
Reagan's Domestic Policy_____ 733
Reagan's Foreign Policy_____ 737
Staying the Course_____ 743
Unit Review_____ 746

EPILOGUE

Challenges for the Future   **750**

Foreign Policy_____ 751
The Economy_____ 752
Social Questions_____ 753

APPENDIX   **757**

Atlas and Historical Data_____ 758
Declaration of Independence_____ 771
Constitution of the United States____ 773
Glossary_____ 791
Index_____ 800

THE HISTORIAN'S CRAFT

Interpreting Information_____76
Distinguishing Primary and Secondary Sources_ 140
Drawing Inferences_____ 228
Evaluating Secondary Sources_____ 290
Evaluating Primary Sources_____ 403
Synthesis of Primary Sources_____ 471
Analyzing Evidence in Arguments_____ 542
Recognizing Schools of History_____ 627
Writing History_____747

PEOPLE IN HISTORY

The Spanish Missionaries_____ 9
Benjamin Franklin_____ 47
Deborah Sampson_____63
Abigail Adams_____91
James Madison_____ 101
Benjamin Banneker_____ 123
The Explorers_____ 149
John C. Calhoun, Daniel Webster, Henry Clay_ 174
The Mountain Men_____195
Elizabeth Cady Stanton, Susan B. Anthony____ 218
Stephen Douglas, Abraham Lincoln_____242
Ulysses S. Grant, Robert E. Lee_____265
Frederick Douglass_____ 285
The Railroad Magnates_____ 299
Leonora Barry_____ 315
The Indian Chiefs_____ 340

Booker T. Washington, W.E.B. Dubois_____ 359
Jane Addams, Lillian Wald_____378
Robert La Follette_____389
Joseph Pulitzer, William Randolph Hearst____417
Walter Reed, William Gorgas_____ 433
George M. Cohan_____ 456
Gutzon Borglum_____495
A. Philip Randolph_____506
Babe Didrikson_____ 537
Ernest Hemingway_____560
Eleanor Roosevelt_____ 587
Ralph Bunche_____ 616
Hiram Fong_____646
Luis Muñoz Marín_____ 672
Shirley Chisholm_____ 687
Rachel Carson_____706
Sandra Day O'Connor_____ 736

PERSPECTIVES IN HISTORY

Hispanic Influence in America_____ 21
Freedom of Religion_____ 48
The American Presidency_____ 107
Freedom of Expression_____ 135
Nationalism_____160
Political Campaigns_____ 180
Medicine_____259
Suffrage_____ 277
The Image of the West_____ 333
Education_____371
Imperialism_____414
Propaganda and War_____ 459
Music in Black Life_____ 497
The Role of Government_____535
War and Technology_____ 578
Foreign Aid_____611
Immigration_____ 664
The Environment_____ 734

CHARTS, GRAPHS, AND TABLES

The Articles of Confederation
   and the Constitution_____92
Events Leading to Ratification_____ 94
Ratification of the Constitution_____ 95
Division of Powers_____104
The Bill of Rights–1791_____105
Checks and Balances_____ 109

How a Bill Becomes Law _____ 111
Amending the Constitution _____ 115
A Comparison of Views:
    Hamilton and Jefferson _____ 128
Immigration, 1821-1860 _____ 207
American Business Cycles, 1790-1860 ____ 208
Boardinghouse Groups in Percent _____ 228
Boardinghouse Groups as Voting Blocs ___ 229
Union and Confederate Resources, 1860 __ 252
Railroad Mileage, 1900 _____ 301
American Business Cycles, 1860-1900 ____ 307
Mining Fatalities, 1870-1920 _____ 314
Union Membership in the Labor Force,
    1880-1920 _____ 318
Issues Causing Strikes, 1881-1905 _____ 321
Rural and Urban Population, 1860-1920 __ 364
Immigration, 1861-1920 _____ 366
Elementary and Secondary School
    Enrollment, 1860-1920 _____ 370
American Business Cycles, 1900-1920 ____ 391
U.S. Expansion, 1776-1917 _____ 443
Shipbuilding and Submarine Sinkings,
    1917-1918 _____ 452
The U.S. Army in World War I _____ 460
Immigration, 1921-1930 _____ 482
Automobile Sales, 1920-1929 _____ 490
Stock Prices, 1920-1932 _____ 504
Farm Prices, 1910-1940 _____ 508
Bank Failures, 1920-1934 _____ 515
Unemployment, 1920-1940 _____ 531
American Business Cycles, 1920-1940 ____ 534
Value of U.S. Exports, 1931-1940 _____ 562
Organization of the United Nations _____ 595
Marshall Plan, 1948-1952 _____ 604
Suburbanization, 1901-1980 _____ 648
Blacks Registered to Vote in the South ___ 665
U.S. Foreign Aid, 1946-1976 _____ 696
Utilization of Media, 1950-1980 _____ 713
Unemployment, 1941-1983 _____ 725
American Business Cycles, 1940-1983 ____ 737
Federal Budget, 1940-1985 _____ 743
Federal Debt, 1940-1985 _____ 743
Single-Parent Households _____ 756
Population _____ 764
Distribution by Age _____ 764
Population By Race and Origin _____ 764
Birth and Death Rate, 1900-Today _____ 764
Life Expectancy at Birth _____ 764
Education _____ 765

Health Care Expenditures _____ 765
Census of Religious Groups _____ 765
Gross National Product _____ 766
Median Income of Families _____ 766
America at Work _____ 766
Purchasing Power of the Dollar _____ 766
Consumer and Wholesale Prices _____ 766
Public Employees _____ 767
Federal Government Receipts
    and Expenditures _____ 767
Expenditures by State and Local Government _ 767
The States of the Union _____ 768
Presidents and Vice Presidents _____ 769
Third Party Movements _____ 770
Political Parties in Power _____ 770

MAPS

Spanish and French Explorations
    in the Americas _____ 13
Voyages of Exploration _____ 18
Indian Civilizations in Central
    and South America _____ 22
Indian Tribes of North America _____ 25
Colonial Settlement to 1775 _____ 38
Colonial Trade Routes _____ 43
Colonial Population: National Origin 1775 _ 45
European Land Claims in North America __ 57
The Revolution Begins _____ 64
Washington's Retreat, 1776-1777 _____ 68
Upper New York, 1777 _____ 69
The Chesapeake Campaign, 1777-1778 __ 69
The Western Campaign, 1778-1779 _____ 71
The Road to Yorktown, 1778-1781 _____ 71
The United States in 1783 _____ 85
The Northwest Territory and Land Claims,
    1787 _____ 89
Land Survey in the Northwest Territory ___ 89
Election of 1800 _____ 136
The Louisiana Purchase and
    Exploration in the West _____ 148
War of 1812 _____ 154
Missouri Compromise, 1820-1821 _____ 163
Election of 1824 _____ 168
Election of 1828 _____ 168
Indian Land Cessions and Indian Removal,
    1750-1850 _____ 190
Texas Independence, 1835-1836 _____ 192

The Mexican War, 1846-1848 — 199
Roads and Canals, 1820-1850 — 204
Slave Population and the Underground Railroad — 221
Expansion of Slavery — 238
Election of 1860 — 245
Secession of the South — 250
The War in the West, January-June 1862 — 254
The War in the East, July 1861-September 1862 — 255
The War in the East, December 1862-1863 — 263
The War in the West, July 1862-December 1863 — 264
The Final Campaigns, 1864-1865 — 267
Reconstruction in the South — 281
Mineral Resources of the United States, 1870 — 296
Railroad Lines, 1860 and 1890 — 298
Western Land Use, 1860-1890 — 334
Population of Indian Reservations, 1883 — 339
Indian Wars and Cessions, 1850-1890 — 341
Election of 1892 — 351
Election of 1896 — 355
The Progressive Movement in Government — 387
Election of 1912 — 396
Spanish-American War, 1898 — 420
Spheres of Influence in Asia — 426
Proposed Canal Routes and the Panama Canal Zone — 430
United States Acquisitions, 1858-1917 — 441
Europe in 1914 — 449
The World at War — 462
    Western Front, 1914-1918 — 462
    Eastern Front, 1914-1918 — 462
    Southern Front, 1915-1918 — 463
    Near Eastern Front, 1914-1918 — 463

Europe After Versailles — 467
Election of 1928 — 489
Election of 1932 — 513
Tennessee Valley Authority, 1933-1945 — 517
Election of 1936 — 528
Japanese Expansion, 1895-1941 — 554
Axis Expansion in Europe, 1935-1941 — 557
Destroyer Deal Bases — 565
Russian Front, 1941-1944 — 583
North African and Italian Campaigns, Oct. 1942-April 1945 — 584
Allied Offensive in Europe, June 1944-May 1945 — 589
Pacific Theater, 1941-1945 — 593
Postwar Europe — 600
Korea, 25 June-25 Nov. 1950 — 609
Korea, 26 Nov. 1950-27 July 1953 — 609
Middle East Crises, 1945-1965 — 617
Caribbean Crises, 1955-1965 — 619
The World and Western Alliances — 620
Election of 1948 — 637
Election of 1960 — 657
Blacks Registered to Vote in the South — 665
War in Vietnam — 669
Election of 1968 — 675
The Middle East, 1967-1974 — 683
Election of 1972 — 691
Election of 1980 — 732
Latin America and the Caribbean — 741
United States — 758
The World — 760
Climate — 762
Land Use — 762
Mineral Resources and Deposits — 763
Industry and Manufacturing — 763

ACKNOWLEDGMENTS

Thanks are due to the following authors and publishers for the material quoted on the pages indicated: **p. iii:** Toppin, Martha Doerr. "I Know Who's Going with Me: Reflections on the Fellowship of History." *Social Education,* October 1980, p. 460. **p. 90:** Morison, Samuel Eliot. *The Oxford History of the American People.* New York: Oxford University Press, 1965, p. 305. **p. 185:** Turner, Frederick Jackson. *The Frontier in American History.* New York: Henry Holt and Company, 1920, p. 12. **p. 223:** Du Bois, W. E. Burghardt. *Black Folk Then and Now.* New York: Holt, Rinehart and Winston, Inc., 1970, p. 144. **p. 290:** Moore, Albert B. "One Hundred Years of Reconstruction of the South." *Journal of Southern History,* May 1943, pp. 153–165. Reprinted by Permission. **p. 291:** Franklin, John Hope. *Reconstruction: After the Civil War.* Chicago: University of Chicago Press, 1961, pp. 51–52, 154–157. **p. 300–301:** Dodge, Grenville, *How We Built the Union Pacific.* Washington, D.C.: U.S. Government Printing Office, 1910, pp. 13–14. **p. 332:** Stratton, Joanna L. *Pioneer Women: Voices from the Kansas Frontier.* New York: Simon and Schuster, 1981, p. 53. **p. 352:** As quoted in Goldman, Eric F. *Rendezvous With Destiny.* New York: Alfred A. Knopf, 1952, pp. 37–38. **p. 358:** Du Bois, W. E. Burghardt. *The Souls of Black Folk.* Chicago: A. C. McClurg & Co., 1920, p. 59. **p. 364:** Le Gallienne, Richard. "Brooklyn Bridge at Dawn." As contained in *A Centenary Memoir-Anthology.* New York: Apollo Head Press, 1966, p. 54. Reprinted by Permission. **p. 370:** Gildersleeve, Virginia Crocheron. *Many A Good Crusade.* New York: The Macmillan Company, 1954, p. 23. **p. 378:** Addams, Jane. *Twenty Years at Hull House.* New York: The Macmillan Company, 1911, p. 85. **p. 464:** Berry, Henry. *Make the Kaiser Dance.* Garden City, New York: Doubleday & Company, Inc., 1978, pp. 176–178, 181–182. **p. 480:** White, William Allen. *The Emporia Gazette,* January 8, 1920. Reprinted by Permission. **p. 485:** As quoted in Kutler, Stanley (ed.). *Looking for America.* Vol. II. New York: W. W. Norton & Company, 1979, pp. 331–332. **p. 493:** Gellhorn, Martha. "God's Gift to Us Girls." *The New Republic,* August 7, 1929, pp. 310–311. Reprinted by Permission. **p. 493:** As quoted in Abels, Jules. *In the Time of Silent Cal.* New York: G. P. Putnam's Sons, 1969, p. 205. **p. 495:** Turnbull, Andrew (ed.). *The Letters of F. Scott Fitzgerald.* New York: Charles Scribner's Sons, 1963, pp. 488–489. **p. 496:** As quoted in Newell, George. "George Gershwin and Jazz." *The Outlook,* February 29, 1928, pp. 342–343, 351. **p. 498:** Chase, Stuart. "The Tragedy of Waste." *The New Republic,* August 19, 1925, pp. 342–345. Reprinted by Permission. **p. 504:** "Stocks Drop Again in Furious Trading of 5,052,790 Shares." *The New York Times,* June 13, 1928. **p. 504:** As quoted in Allen, Frederick Lewis. *Only Yesterday.* New York: Harper & Brothers, Publishers, 1957. p. 324. **p. 508:** As quoted in Ellis, Edward Robb. *A Nation in Torment: The Great American Depression 1929–1939.* New York: Coward-McCann, 1970, p. 153. **p. 512:** Allen, Frederick Lewis. *Since Yesterday: The 1930's in America September 3, 1929–September 3, 1939.* New York: Harper & Row, 1939, pp. 67–68. **p. 524:** Long, Huey P. *Every Man a King: The Autobiography of Huey P. Long.* New Orleans: National Book Co., Inc., 1933, pp. 339–340. **p. 531:** Thompson, Dorothy. Washington *Star,* February 10, 1937. Reprinted by Permission. **p. 532:** Le Sueur, Meridel. "Cows and Horses Are Hungry." *The American Mercury,* September 1934, p. 55. Reprinted by Permission. **pp. 562–563:** As quoted in Perrett, Geoffrey. *Days of Sadness, Years of Triumph: The American People 1939–1945.* New York: Coward, McCann & Geoghegan, Inc., 1973, pp. 27–28. **p. 570:** Lord, Walter. *Day of Infamy.* New York: Holt, Rinehart & Winston, Inc., 1957, pp. 73–74. **pp. 580–581:** Hosokawa, Bill. *NISEI: The Quiet Americans.* New York: William Morrow and Company, Inc., 1969, pp. 329, 333–334. **p. 586:** Wilkinson, Virginia Snow. "From Housewife to Shipfitter." *Harper's Magazine,* September 1943, pp. 328, 337. Reprinted by Permission. **pp. 588–590:** Ryan, Cornelius. *The Longest Day: June 6, 1944.* New York: Simon and Schuster, 1959, pp. 54–55. **p. 604:** Ambrose, Stephen E. *Rise to Globalism: American Foreign Policy 1938–1976.* New York: Penguin Books Ltd., 1976, p. 160. **p. 644–645:** As quoted in Commager, Henry Steele (ed.). *The American Destiny.* Vol. 17. Danbury, Connecticut: The Danbury Press, 1976, p. 61. **p. 664:** Zangwill, Israel. *The Melting Pot.* New York: The Macmillan Company, 1913, p. 199. **pp. 669–670:** King, Martin Luther. *Where Do We Go From Here: Chaos or Community.* New York: Harper & Row, Publishers, 1967, pp. 62–63. **p. 677:** As quoted in Bailey, Thomas A. *The American Spirit.* Vol. II. Lexington, Massachusetts: D.C. Heath and Company, 1978, pp. 919–920. **p. 688:** Nixon, Richard. *The Memoirs of Richard Nixon.* New York: Grossett & Dunlap, 1978, p. 443. **p. 688:** Nixon, Richard. *The Memoirs of Richard Nixon.* New York: Grossett & Dunlap, 1978, pp. 443–444. **pp. 698–699:** Sirica, John J. *To Set the Record Straight: The Break-in, the Tapes, the Conspirators, the Pardon.* New York: W. W. Norton & Company, 1979, pp. 299–302. **p. 702:** As quoted in *This Fabulous Century 1960–1970.* Vol. VII. New York: Time-Life Books, 1970, p. 59. **p. 705:** As quoted in *American Painting: 1900–1970.* New York: Time-Life Books, 1970, p. 164. **p. 709:** As quoted in Sann, Paul. *American Panorama.* New York: Crown Publishers, Inc., 1980, p. 266. **p. 712:** As quoted in Sann, Paul. *American Panorama.* New York: Crown Publishers, Inc., 1980, p. 266. **p. 712:** As quoted in Sann, Paul. *American Panorama.* New York: Crown Publishers, Inc., 1980, p. 176. **p. 719:** As quoted in *This Fabulous Century: 1900–1970.* Vol. VII. New York: Time-Life Books, 1970, p. 59. **p. 747:** "Ceding the Canal—Slowly." *Time,* August 22, 1977, p. 8. Reprinted by Permission. **pp. 747–748:** Ford, Emmett B., Jr. "Conservative Support for the Panama Treaty." *The Daily Progress* (Charlottesville, Virginia), September 18, 1977. Reprinted by Permission. **pp. 748–749:** Buechner, Northrup. "Why We Must Keep the Canal." *Washington Report,* September 19, 1977. Reprinted by Permission.

PHOTO CREDITS

Unit 6

Pages 406–407, U.S. Naval Academy; 408, The Bettmann Archive; 410, Johnny Johnson; 412, National Archives; 413, Painting by Peter Hurd, Reproduced with permission of Amfac, Inc.; 418, Library of Congress; 419, The Granger Collection; 424, West Point Museum Collections, U.S. Military Academy; 427, Library of Congress; 428, The Bettmann Archive; 432, Brown Brothers; 435, National Archives; 436, Brown Brothers; 438, The Bettmann Archive; 440, University of California at Berkeley, Bancroft Library; 442, Library of Congress; 446, Imperial War Museum; 448, Historical Pictures Service, Chicago; 451, BBC Hulton Picture Library; 453, Culver Pictures, Inc.; 455, 461, National Archives; 464, National Library of Medicine; 466, FPG; 471, The Granger Collection; 473, Navy Department, National Archives.

Unit 7

Pages 474–475, Dallas Museum of Fine Arts, Dallas Art Association Purchase; 476, New York Historical Society; 478, The Bettmann Archive; 481, Culver Pictures, Inc.; 483, UPI; 485, Jack Levine, *Gangster Funeral* (1952–53) Oil on canvas, 63 x 72 inches, Collection of Whitney Museum of American Art; 486, The Granger Collection; 488, Wide World Photos; 491, Ford Motor Company; 492 (l & r), The Bettmann Archive; 493, Kansas State Historical Society; 494, 498, File Photo; 499, 502, The Granger Collection; 505, File Photo; 507, FDR Library; 510, Louis Ribak, *Home Relief Station,* (1935–36) Oil on canvas, 28 x 36 inches, Collection of Whitney Museum of American Art; 511, Herbert Hoover Presidential Library; 512, Historical Pictures Service, Chicago; 514, UPI; 516, FDR Library; 520, Jim Aycock/Uniphoto; 523 (l), Historical Pictures Service, Chicago; 523 (r), The Granger Collection; 524, FDR Library; 525, WPA; 526, Brown Brothers; 530, 532, Library of Congress; 533, USDA, SCS; 538, The Bettmann Archive.

Unit 8

Pages 544–545, U.S. Army Photo; 546, National Archives; 549, Library of Congress; 550, File Photo; 551, Culver Pictures, Inc.; 552, File Photo; 553, BBC Hulton Picture Library; 555, FPG; 558, The Bettmann Archive; 559, Historical Pictures Service, Chicago; 563, Mauritius/Black Star; 567, FDR Library; 568, Syndication International; 569, Library of Congress; 572, U.S. Coast Guard Photo; 574, Department of The Army; 575, Wide World Photos; 576, Navy Department; 577, Department of The Army; 579, Magnum; 581, Library of Congress; 582, Department of The Army; 585, Culver Pictures, Inc.; 588, The Bettmann Archive; 590, FPG; 592, FDR Library; 594, Wide World Photos; 598, Messerschmidt/Camera Press London; 603, UPI; 605, National Archives; 607, Wide World Photos; 608, Department of The Army; 612, Werner in "The Indianapolis Star"; 613, 614, 615, Wide World Photos; 622, USAF; 623, Popperfoto.

Unit 9

Pages 630–631, NASA; 632, Harry S. Truman Library; 634, FPG; 636, Harry S. Truman Library; 638, The Bettmann Archive; 641, Wayne Miller/Magnum; 642, The Bettmann Archive; 644, Burt Glinn/Magnum; 649, Hy Peskin/FPG; 654, Arthur Rickerby/Black Star; 656, Wide World Photos; 658, NASA; 660, UPI; 662, Wide World Photos; 667, Mark Godfrey/Archive; 670 (l), Leonard Freed/Magnum; 670 (r), Ernst Haas/Magnum; 673 (l), Bob Fitch/Black Star; 673 (r), Frank Johnston/Black Star; 678, Gamma-Liaison; 680, Michael Abramson/Gamma-Liaison; 682, Bill Mauldin © 1973, Chicago Sun Times; 684, NASA; 689, Dennis Brack/Black Star; 690, Jim Moore/Gamma-Liaison; 693, Mark Godfrey/Archive; 695, David Burnett/Gamma-Liaison; 700, Jim Pazarick/Gamma-Liaison; 703, George L. Walker III/Gamma-Liaison; 705, Susan Greenwood/Gamma-Liaison; 709, Stephen McCarroll/Alpha; 711, Alpha; 715, Don Spark/Gamma-Liaison; 716, Rick Meyers/Tom Stack & Associates; 717, Michael Gaffney/Gamma-Liaison; 718, Hickson-Bender Photography; 720, David Hume Kennerly/Gamma-Liaison; 722, Gerard Photography; 723, Roschkov/Toronto Star; 727, Halstead/Gamma-Liaison; 728, Owen/Black Star; 730, Gamma-Liaison; 735, Dirck Halstead/Gamma-Liaison; 739, Gamma-Liaison; 742, Chip Hires/Gamma-Liaison; 750, Dan Connolly/Gamma-Liaison; 752, Frank Fisher/Gamma-Liaison; 753, Sheldon Moskowitz/Gamma-Liaison; 754, James N. Westwater; 755, Gerard Photography.

PROLOGUE

To some people, history is all dates, or a dull listing of events that no longer matter. Why should you study history? Why is history important? These are fair questions. Before you begin *The American Tradition*, read the quotations below. These quotations present the views of a number of famous people about history and its uses. Some views are favorable, but others are not.

We cannot help living in history. We can only fail to be aware of it.
ROBERT C. HEILBRONER

For a people to be without history, or to be ignorant of its history, is as for a person to be without memory. . . .
HENRY S. COMMAGER

It is very difficult to trace and find out the truth of anything by history.
PLUTARCH

History never embraces more than a small part of reality.
FRANÇOIS DE LA ROCHEFOUCAULD

Peoples and governments have never learned anything from history, or acted on principles deducible from it.
GEORG WILHELM FRIEDRICH HEGEL

Those who cannot remember the past are condemned to repeat it.
GEORGE SANTAYANA

Certainly, even if history were judged incapable of other uses, its entertainment value would remain in its favor.
MARC BLOCH

History is a lie agreed upon.
NAPOLEON

The end and scope of all history is to teach us by examples of times past such wisdom as may guide our desires and actions.
SIR WALTER RALEIGH

Consider the meaning of each quotation. Which ones are saying essentially the same thing in different words? What positive reasons are given for studying history? What drawbacks are mentioned?

The American Tradition will give you first-hand knowledge of some of the positive reasons for studying history. You will increase your understanding of how this nation's government, economy, and society evolved. By learning how things were, you will better understand how things are.

At the same time, your attention will be drawn to the limits of history. It is important for you to remember that even the most detailed study of history may not provide complete answers. Some historical facts are clear, but others are difficult to determine. Interpretations of the facts can and do vary. This book stresses the interpretive nature of history and helps you to develop the skills you need to evaluate different interpretations.

1492 First voyage of Columbus	**1565** Founding of St. Augustine	**1607** Founding of Jamestown

1519 Magellan circum- navigates world	**1588** Defeat of Spanish Armada	**1620** Mayflower Compact

COLONIAL AMERICA

The Beginnings

The English Colonies

The Struggle for Independence

1649	1701	1754	1770	1775	1781
Acts of Toleration	Charter of Liberties	French and Indian War	Boston Massacre	Lexington and Concord	Battle of Yorktown

	1664	1732	1765	1773	1776	1783
	English conquest of New Netherlands	Founding of Georgia	Stamp Act	Boston Tea Party	Declaration of Independence	Treaty of Paris

1	Widening Horizons	5
2	The Age of Exploration	8
3	Peoples of the New World	19

THE BEGINNINGS

*Whosoever commands the sea commands the trade and whosoever commands the trade
. . . commands the riches of the world, and consequently, the world itself.*

SIR WALTER RALEIGH

Europeans in the fifteenth century were unaware that two vast continents, already inhabited by other peoples with ancient histories, lay on the other side of the Atlantic Ocean. Europe, however, was undergoing changes that would soon lead to the discovery and exploration of what to them was a New World.

1 Widening Horizons

The first Europeans to reach the New World were probably the Vikings of Scandinavia, who founded a colony on Greenland in the late 900's. Leif Ericson, son of Eric the Red, sailed across the Atlantic Ocean from Norway in the year 1000, heading for his home in Greenland. He was blown off course and ended up on the northeast coast of America. He called the place where he landed "Vinland" because of the wild grapes growing there. Ericson was followed a few years later by a trader from Iceland named Thorfinn Karlsevni. Attempting to find Vinland, he landed instead at a place he named "Helluland," meaning "land of flat rocks."[1]

Leif Ericson's brothers, Thorvald and Thorstein, and their sister Freydis, also made exploratory trips. However, the Vikings did not set up any permanent colonies. After that, exploration was put aside until an Italian dreamer named Christopher Columbus changed the course of history.

Christopher Columbus

Three small ships—the *Niña, Pinta,* and *Santa Maria*—sailed westward from Palos, Spain, at sunrise on August 3, 1492. By October 10, the crew was ready to mutiny, throw their commander—Christopher Columbus—overboard, and set out for

---

[1] Experts disagree as to the identity of places visited by the Vikings. Vinland may have been Newfoundland, and Helluland may have been Labrador.

home. Columbus begged them to be patient for just a few more days. The large flocks of birds that had been flying overhead for the last week were a sure sign that land was near.

On October 11, weeds and driftwood floated by. A thorn branch bearing new leaves and full of red berries was fished out of the sea by a crew member. These were good signs, and the crew began to relax a little. That night, lookouts straining their eyes in the moonlight spotted a bulky shape on the horizon. At the first light of dawn on the morning of October 12, a sailor on the lead ship called out "Tierra, Tierra!" ("Land, Land!") and fired the ship's largest cannon.

Within a few hours, the three ships were anchored off a small island. Columbus had hung out all flags and dressed in his most splendid clothes. Stepping onto the sandy beach, he named the island San Salvador ("Blessed Savior"). Because he believed he had reached the East Indies off the southeast coast of Asia, he named the people who greeted him "Indians."

Columbus was an Italian sailor and mapmaker who had believed for many years that Asia could be reached by sailing directly west from Europe. Seeking financial backing, he took his plan to the Portuguese, who rejected it. Queen Isabella and King Ferdinand of Spain, however, agreed to sponsor his expedition. They had just conquered the last Moorish stronghold in Spain, making the country a consolidated Catholic nation at long last. Sponsoring the expedition was an act of national pride, undertaken for the glory of Catholic Spain.

Between 1492 and 1504, Columbus made a total of four voyages for Spain. He discovered and explored the northeastern coast of Cuba, many of the Caribbean islands, and parts of Central and South America, including the delta of the Orinoco River. On the island of Hispaniola, he founded the first European settlement in the New World.

Two years after he returned from his fourth voyage, Columbus died, still firmly convinced that he

Have students refer to map on p. 13 to identify where Columbus explored in the Caribbean. Have students read excerpts from a source that provides details of Columbus' voyages.

The age of feudalism, or the Dark Ages, began when the Roman Empire broke up in the fifth century. People were isolated on feudal estates. The Crusades helped to end that isolation.

Queen Isabella of Spain agreed to finance Columbus' explorations across the Atlantic. Columbus carried a letter of introduction from Isabella to the Khan of Cathay. Others before Columbus believed that the East was accessible by traveling westward. Columbus, however, was the first to attempt such a voyage. What did Columbus' explorations mean for Spain?

had found a western route to Asia. He never knew that his calculations, based on geographical knowledge of the time, were wrong. He had expected to find Japan and China rather than Cuba and Mexico. As a result, instead of finding the spices, silks, and pearls he sought, Columbus found wild cotton, strange plants and fruits, and a small amount of gold. Instead of finding Asia, as he had thought he would, Columbus found a New World.

However, the land Columbus discovered never bore his name. It was named for Amerigo Vespucci, another Italian who explored the eastern coast of South America for Portugal shortly after Columbus sailed for Spain. Vespucci realized that his party had "arrived at a new land which . . . we observed to be a continent." His claim led a German mapmaker to suggest in 1507 that the newly discovered world be called the "land of Americus, for Americus its discoverer."[2]

Rumblings of Change

The era in which Columbus and Vespucci lived was a complex and changing one. The age of **feudalism,** the system in which land was held by vassals in exchange for military and other services to lords, was dying out.

During the 1100's and the early 1200's, most of Western Europe was Roman Catholic. Europeans had spent much of their energy on the Crusades, religious wars dedicated to driving the Muslims out of the Middle East and stopping the spread of the Islamic religion. Europeans returned from the Middle East enlightened. They had learned about new peoples and different ways of life. The Crusades gave Europeans a taste for luxuries like silks, fine cottons, and spices, all of which were costly because they had to come from the faraway lands of Asia.

Spices especially were important. The drab diet of the Western Europeans afforded few vegetables or fruits, little sugar, and no tea, coffee, or chocolate. Because of a shortage of winter fodder with which to feed livestock, most slaughtering had to be done in the autumn and meat had to be preserved for the winter. Spices hid the rotten taste of the meat and enlivened the dull European fare. Spices were also believed to cure ills and were in demand for balms, incense, and perfumes.

Interest in the Eastern lands and their riches was heightened by overland travelers like Marco Polo, a Venetian who first traveled to Cathay, or China, in 1271. When he returned home, he told stories of precious stones, "all kinds of spicery," and "magnificent walled cities and palaces all painted in gold."

---

[2] Some historians think that the name *America* might have come from Richard Amerycke, an Englishman who was a financial backer of explorer John Cabot.

A money economy gradually replaced the barter system that was common in the age of feudalism. Ask students if a merchant class could develop without a money economy.

Compare the objectives of each social and political group at this time. Review the effects of Marco Polo's travels on trade. Use European history texts as a source for this information.

Growth of Trade

During the 1300's a strong trade grew between Europe and Asia. However, only the merchants of the Middle East knew the safe routes to the Far East. The goods traveled a long and costly road to reach Europe. Spices like nutmeg and cloves, for example, worth little in the East Indies where they grew, were first shipped to India by Malay and Hindu merchants and then brought to the Persian Gulf or the Red Sea by Arabs. Next, the spices were carried by camel to Alexandria or Beirut, where they were boarded on Venetian or Genoese ships which carried them to Italian merchants. The merchants then distributed the spices to European markets. Because each handler along the way took a profit, the prices of goods from the Far East were so high that only the very rich could afford them.

In the 1400's the Ottoman Turks took over the Middle East and Africa and put Eastern Europe in danger. When they captured Constantinople and took control of many of the land and sea routes between the Far East and Europe, trade was threatened. Thus the Europeans had reasons to look for a new route that they could control themselves.

Renaissance and Reformation

Meanwhile, commerce between Europe and the Far East had encouraged the growth of European towns as trade centers. Merchants who grew rich from trade and other people in the towns came to form a new middle class. Until this time the two major classes had been the nobles who owned the land and the peasants who worked it.

In addition, some European countries began changing from a collection of feudal estates into **nation-states,** unified in language and laws. The new nation-states were **monarchies,** headed by kings, queens, or emperors. The monarchs were powerful nobles who took steps to increase the size of their land holdings and expand their power over other nobles. In the contest for power between the monarchs and the nobles, the new middle class supported the monarchs. In return, the monarchs helped the merchants and townspeople.

At about the same time that nation-states were developing, the Renaissance began in Florence. The Renaissance was a period of rebirth in which western scholars revived their study of Greek and Roman classics, and art and culture became a source of national interest. Scholars also studied science, mathematics, and medicine. Gradually, the Renaissance movement spread from Florence to the rest of Europe, stimulating intellectual interests.

Until this time, the Catholic Church had a firm hold on most of Western Europe. The teachings of the Church fit well with feudalism. People were taught that everything that happened to them was God's will, not to be questioned. They were also taught that life

The writings of Marco Polo gave cartographers the knowledge to create more accurate maps. Polo was 17 years old when he set out for China. He reached Kubla Khan's palace after three years of travel by boat, on foot, and by camel. In what way did his exploits change relations between the East and Europe?

Portugal had a long coastline, so that many of its people lived near the sea and had an interest in seafaring.

Note that much of the knowledge Prince Henry used was obtained through Arab teachers. Henry's mother, Phillippa of Lancaster, was the prime mover in establishing Portugal as the leader in exploring West Africa for possible trade routes to the East.

after death was much more important than anything on earth, so they were not interested in learning about the world.

But the Church found it hard to adjust to the many changes taking place. Some of the new monarchs resisted the authority of the Church. Many people began to question the Church's teachings and criticize its wealth. Some people called for a **reformation**, or change in the teachings and practices of the Church. Differences of opinion about the kinds of changes that were needed led to a movement known as the Protestant Reformation and the establishment of new religions. Europe became divided between Catholicism and Protestantism, and European monarchs insisted that their subjects follow their lead in religion.

SECTION REVIEW

1. Identify the following: Vikings, Leif Ericson, Amerigo Vespucci, Marco Polo, Ottoman Turks, Renaissance.
2. Why did the Spanish king and queen sponsor Columbus' voyages?
3. How did the Crusades influence Europeans?
4. Why were goods from the Far East expensive in Europe?
5. How did the Catholic religion support feudalism?

2 The Age of Exploration

Although religion was still important, people were becoming more interested in worldly, practical affairs. The Protestant Reformation, the Renaissance, the development of nation-states, and the growth of trade all worked together to change the outlook of Western Europeans. Interest in practical matters and the world outside Europe led to advances in shipbuilding and navigation. Western Europeans were ready to strike out in new directions. Columbus' voyage was only a beginning.

The Portuguese

Portugal reacted immediately to Columbus' first voyage. By 1493 the Portuguese already had been engaged in the quest for the Orient and its riches for the better part of a century.

Prince Henry the Navigator.   The foundations for Portugal's achievements were laid in the early 1400's by Prince Henry "the Navigator," a man who neither sailed to strange lands nor discovered anything. Yet from his observatory and maritime workshop at Sagres, he kindled the fires of discovery that changed the shape of the world.

Henry wanted to break the Arab hold on Europe, bring the Portuguese more trade and power, and spread Christianity. In his mind, the key to accomplishing these goals lay in the open seas. His first step was to establish a navigational school, the first in Europe. There he brought together shipmasters, cartographers, pilots, and astronomers from all over the world. These specialists pooled their talents to advance maritime knowledge and the art of navigation. They created better charts and improved navigation instruments such as the compass, the astrolabe, and the quadrant. They compiled more detailed astronomical tables. They even improved the design of ships.

Henry hoped to have his sea captains sail around Africa and find a path to India and the Spice Islands. Such a route might lead to Prester John, the legendary Christian prince said to rule a rich, powerful kingdom south or east of Muslim territory in Africa or India. The new route also might reveal the source of the gold dust and other precious goods the Moors brought to Mediterranean ports.

Bit by bit, expedition after expedition, the Portuguese inched their way down the coast of Africa. By 1432 they had reached the Azores, 1000 miles (1600 kilometers) over the western sea. Their biggest obstacle was Cape Bajador, where geographical knowledge stopped and myth and fear took over. Said one Portuguese:

> Beyond this there is no race of men or place of inhabitants. Nor is the land less sandy than the deserts of Libya, where there is no water, no tree, no green herb. And the sea is so shallow that a whole league from land is only a fathom deep, while the currents are so terrible that no ship, having once passed the Cape, will ever be able to return.

Portuguese Explorers.   By the time Henry died in 1460, his captains had gone past Bajador, discovered the Cape Verde Islands, and reached

The Spanish Missionaries

The missionary friars who came to the New World in the service of Spain were dedicated to both their religion and their country. Their purpose in coming to America was twofold. First, they intended to convert the Indians to Christianity. Second, they intended to develop colonies for the Spanish government. To achieve these goals, they often had to undergo extreme hardships.

One of the most outstanding of these zealous missionaries was a German-born Jesuit priest and explorer, Eusebio Francisco Kino. Father Kino decided to become a missionary when he was 25 years old, after he almost died from a serious illness. He became known as the "priest on horseback" because of his extensive travels through what is now Arizona and northern Mexico. Many of his journeys took him through forbidding desert country where no white person had ever traveled.

Father Kino was an expert cartographer who mapped much of the land he explored. He established a number of missions that were later taken over by the Franciscans. One of his fellow priests praised Kino for his ascetic lifestyle as follows:

> *He neither smoked nor took snuff, nor wine, nor slept in a bed. . . . He never had more than two coarse shirts, because he gave everything as alms to the Indians. He was merciful to others, but cruel to himself.*

Another famous Spanish missionary, Franciscan priest Junipero Serra, was also willing to sacrifice his own comfort for his God and his country. Although he was lame, he made long journeys on foot to preach to Indians and build missions. In 1769 he founded the first mission in what is now California at San Diego. Before he died, Father Serra had founded eight more missions in California.

Sierra Leone. In the process, the Portuguese had found sugar in Madeira and had established a profitable trade in gold, ivory, slaves, and pepper. Portuguese trading stations and warehouse fortresses began to spring up at strategic points all along the African coast.

The Portuguese government took over where Henry left off, backing further ventures east and then south. Finally, in 1487, while sailing south along the African coast, Bartolomeu Dias was blown southward off course by a hard wind. When the wind abated 13 days later, he sailed eastward and then north to discover the tip of Africa. Dias called his discovery the Cape of Storms, but Portugal renamed it the Cape of Good Hope. Dias' voyage proved that there was an eastern route to the Orient.

Political problems at home kept the Portuguese from following up on Dias' discovery. But Columbus' journey gave them new impetus. If Columbus was right about a western route to the Orient, Portugal's own ambitions would be in peril. Four years after Columbus boasted of his findings, Vasco da Gama sailed from Lisbon with four ships, "to proclaim the Christian faith and to wrest kingdoms and new states with much riches from the hands of the barbarians."

After struggling up the east coast of Africa, da Gama went northward to the Muslim trading center of Mozambique, then on to Mombasa and Malindrix. On May 20, 1498, he landed at Calicut, where he stayed three months before returning home laden with a cargo of spices. At long last, India had been reached and the eastern sea route opened. Da Gama not only fulfilled Henry's vision, but also gave the Portuguese their first foothold in India.

The Portuguese Empire. Events moved quickly after that. Pedro Alváres Cabral, following da

Point out the technical improvements the Portuguese made in sailing, especially the development of the caravel, a very maneuverable ship compared to the Spanish galleons.

Gama's route, swung so wide around Africa that he touched Brazil. By claiming the land for his king, he gave Portugal a stake in the New World. Meanwhile, Portuguese fleets began to make annual voyages to India, returning with cargoes that made Lisbon the marketplace of Europe.

Commerce led to conquest. Before long, the Portuguese established their country's naval supremacy in the Arabian Sea and the Bay of Bengal. They also had ventured into the South China Sea and had reached the Moluccas. Eastern spices and luxury goods began to go to Europe by way of Lisbon, cutting out the Italians and the Arabs who had dominated the trade for so long. By 1524 the vast trade of Asia had become the domain of the Portuguese.

The Spaniards

The same year Columbus returned from his first voyage, the Spanish monarchs, afraid that Portugal would try to claim the lands discovered by Columbus, asked Pope Alexander VI for help. He responded by drawing a **line of demarcation,** an imaginary line running from the north pole to the south pole. The area 100 leagues (about 300 miles or 480 kilometers) west of the Azores and the Cape Verde Islands would belong to Spain. The area east of that would belong to Portugal. Portugal, however, protested the division. As a result, the Treaty of Tordesillas was drawn up in 1494. It moved the line 370 leagues (about 500 miles or 800 kilometers) to the west.

Early Exploration. Spain continued to explore new lands and to search for the gold about which Columbus had talked. Between 1508 and 1511, Puerto Rico, Jamaica, and Cuba all were claimed by Spain. In 1513, Vasco Nuñez de Balboa, crossing the Isthmus of Panama, became the first European to sight the eastern shore of the Pacific Ocean. That same year, Juan Ponce de León sailed northward from Puerto Rico and discovered Florida.

Despite these feats, the Spanish monarchs were not content. The costly expeditions they had sponsored had not brought them the great treasures they had expected. Meanwhile, rival Portugal was growing rich because it controlled the eastern route to the Indies. So, when a Portuguese explorer named Ferdinand Magellan offered to find a new westerly

Some historians consider Magellan's round-the-world exploration the greatest sailing feat of all time. According to a journal kept on board, the trip covered more than 50,000 miles. What did Magellan's voyage around the world prove?

route to the Indies for Spain, the Spanish monarchs accepted.

Magellan's Voyage. On September 20, 1519, Magellan sailed from Sanlúcar in command of a fleet of five ships. Three months later, he anchored in the Portuguese territory known today as Rio de Janeiro. From there, he headed southward in search of the strait that would lead him to what was known as the Great South Sea. The journey proved long, tortuous, and full of surprises. The sailors who caught what they called "strange geese and sea wolves" had never heard of penguins or seals.

De Vaca' s journal was a major source of information for future exploration.

By the time Magellan's fleet reached the strait, his men had almost mutinied and he had lost two ships. The strait itself, which became known as the Strait of Magellan, was stormy and took a month to navigate. When the ships left the strait and sailed into the Great South Sea, Magellan was so impressed with its sunniness and calm that he named it the Pacific.

The journey, however, was far from over. The ships moved up the coast of Chile and then headed westward. By this time, the little food and water left was thoroughly contaminated with worms, maggots, and other vermin. Soon, even that food was gone, and the crew was reduced to eating rats, sawdust, and leather. Finally, on March 5, 1521, land—the island of Guam—was sighted. The next week the ships reached the Philippine Islands. There, after making peace with a group of island chiefs, Magellan claimed the island for Christianity.

Magellan, however, did not live to make the journey home. He was killed trying to convert the hostile chief of a nearby island. The remaining crew members went on, traded for spices at the Moluccas, and were ready to head for home in December. However, while one of the ships was being repaired, the Portuguese attacked it.

On September 8, 1522, the one remaining ship, the *Victoria,* commanded by Juan Sebastián del Cano, arrived in Seville with its valuable cargo of spices. Of the 240 men who had set out on the voyage, only 18 arrived home. Those 18, however, had **circumnavigated** (circled) the globe, proving that the world was round. They had taken the measure of a world larger than anyone had ever imagined and proved that there was a western water route to the Indies.

The Conquistadores. The same year that Magellan began his journey, Hernando Cortes began his conquest of Mexico. In 1531 Francisco Pizarro began his nine-year campaign to conquer Peru. These two **conquistadores,** or conquerors, filled the coffers of Spain to overflowing with gold, silver, and other treasure.

Encouraged by these rewards, Spain went on to explore and claim vast stretches of the Americas, most of them along the Gulf of Mexico and the Atlantic coast. In 1536 Alvar Nuñez Cabeza de Vaca ended an eight-year trek from the Gulf Coast of Florida to the Gila Valley of Arizona. In 1539 Hernando de Soto began a three-year journey that took him from the Florida coast into Georgia, across the Great Smokies into Tennessee, southwest almost to the Gulf of Mexico, and across the Mississippi River as far west as Oklahoma. In 1540 Francisco Vázquez de Coronado led an army overland from Mexico deep into southwestern North America. One of Coronado's men was the first European to see the Grand Canyon.

The Spanish Empire. Thus the Spaniards who followed Columbus' lead found the lands that formed the basis for one of the greatest of the European

An Indian chief shows disgust with greedy conquistadors by casting down gold scales at their feet. How did the discovery of gold affect Spain's plans in the New World?

Besides using Indians for forced labor, the Spaniards also introduced black African slaves to the Americas.

Point out local or regional names that show the influence of early explorers or the first Europeans to live in your area.

colonial empires. Spain ruled its colonies with an iron hand, allowing no room for self-government. Each colony was administered by a **viceroy,** an official appointed by the king to rule in his name. The **audiencia,** a royal colonial council set up in 1528, kept check on the viceroys.

Most Spaniards did not want to settle permanently in America. The population of Spain's colonies was made up mostly of Indians, and Spanish colonial officials often married Indian women. The Spaniards had two chief motives for coming to the New World. One was to spread the Catholic religion by converting the Indians. The other was to become wealthy. To that end, the Indians were used as a source of cheap labor for farming, ranching, and mining gold and silver.

The sight of Spanish galleons laden with treasure brought joy to the Spanish monarchs. However, the sight brought only envy to France, Holland, and England, each of which made its own bid for the riches of the New World.

The French

While the Spaniards were busy taking gold and silver out of Mexico and Peru, logwood and dyes out of Central America, and sugar out of the Caribbean, the French found a different form of wealth—fish and furs. Knowing that the Portugese and the Spanish controlled the southern sea lanes, the French tried to find a Northwest Passage to the Far East. The French king, Francis I, made his intentions clear: "I should like to see the clause in Adam's will that cuts me out of my share in the New World."

Early Explorations.   In 1524 an Italian named Giovanni de Verrazano flew the French flag in a voyage from the Carolinas to New York harbor and on to Nova Scotia. Ten years later, a French navigator named Jacques Cartier sailed up the St. Lawrence River as far as present-day Montreal, giving the French a claim to eastern Canada. There, in an attempt to make friends with the Indians, he offered them red wine and hardtack (a hard biscuit made with flour and water). This led the Indians to believe that the strangers drank blood and ate wood. Although Cartier brought no gold back to France, he did bring tales about the abundant fish he had seen in Canada.

Lack of enthusiasm by the government, civil war, and trouble with Spain brought French exploration to a halt after Cartier's expeditions. In 1598, however, conditions changed. Fish had become a lucrative source of trade for the French because it was in great

La Salle is received in a Caddo Indian village during his exploration along the Mississippi River. La Salle's claims strengthened French hopes for a New World empire. How did French holdings in the Americas compare with Spanish holdings?

Compare the routes taken with natural features and barriers that may have aided or hindered the journeys. Note the time sequence of the explorations and compare them with events in Europe.

SPANISH AND FRENCH EXPLORATIONS IN THE AMERICAS

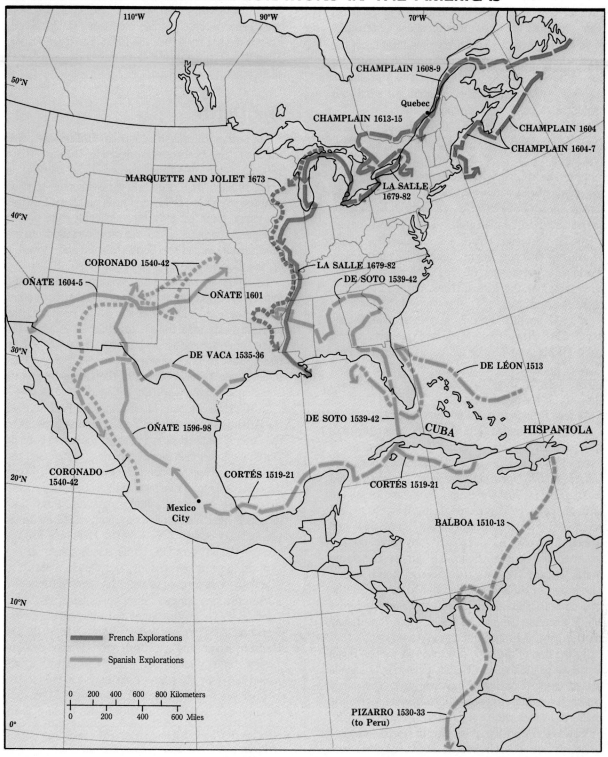

110°W 90°W 70°W

50°N

CHAMPLAIN 1608-9

Quebec

CHAMPLAIN 1613-15

CHAMPLAIN 1604

CHAMPLAIN 1604-7

MARQUETTE AND JOLIET 1673

LA SALLE 1679-82

40°N

CORONADO 1540-42

OÑATE 1604-5

OÑATE 1601

LA SALLE 1679-82

DE SOTO 1539-42

DE LÉON 1513

30°N

DE VACA 1535-36

OÑATE 1596-98

DE SOTO 1539-42

CUBA

HISPANIOLA

CORTÉS 1519-21

CORTÉS 1519-21

CORONADO 1540-42

20°N

Mexico City

BALBOA 1510-13

10°N

French Explorations

Spanish Explorations

0   200   400   600   800 Kilometers

0   200   400   600 Miles

0°

PIZARRO 1530-33
(to Peru)

Like New Spain, New France had a highly centralized government that was controlled from home. There was no popular representation.

The friendly relations of the French with the Indians were to have significance later. See the discussion of the French and Indian War in Chapter 3.

demand in Spain and other countries of Catholic Europe. French fishermen, fishing off the Canadian coast, began to set up stations on shore where they could dry their catch. This drew the attention of the Indians in the area, who began to exchange furs for fish. Gradually, the fur trade grew into a profitable business, encouraging the French to send out explorers to push more deeply inland.

Renewed Exploration. One of these explorers was cartographer Samuel de Champlain, who traveled far up the St. Lawrence River in 1603. When he returned, he brought with him a cargo of beaver skins and many stories about vast lakes. Champlain made almost a dozen trips into eastern Canada. Each time, he combined exploration and trade. In 1608 he set up a trading post and built a fort at Quebec, which became the first permanent French colony in the New World. The next year he ventured down the St. Lawrence into the lake in New York State which bears his name.

In 1604 another Frenchman, Pierre du Guast, founded Port Royal. In 1654 Médard Chouart reached Lake Michigan. With the aid of his brother-in-law, Pierre Radisson, he brought about fur-trading agreements in areas that had never before been entered by European traders.

As new French colonies in Canada began to grow, the French continued to push further west. In 1673 Quebec-born fur trader Louis Joliet and a Jesuit priest, Father Jacques Marquette, set out hoping to find the elusive Northwest Passage. They journeyed 2500 miles (4000 kilometers) by canoe westward through Lake Michigan and Lake Winnebago and southward to the junction of the Mississippi and Arkansas rivers. At this point they gave up and returned to Canada. Following almost the same route, Robert Cavelier reached the mouth of the Mississippi in 1682. There he claimed for France the land on both sides of the Mississippi and the rivers which joined it. He named the country "Louisiana" for the king of France, Louis XIV.

By the end of the 1600's, France as well as Spain had an empire in the New World, consisting of Canada (called New France), Louisiana, and the lands between the Mississippi and Ohio rivers. While the claims of France were not as large as those of Spain, France's was the largest empire in North America. Although the French built a string of forts and

missions along the borders of their empire, the French colonial population remained small. Many of the French adopted Indian lifestyles. Unlike Spain, France did not try to use the Indians as forced labor. Therefore France was able to develop a number of allies among the Indians.

The Dutch

Like other European countries, Holland was also eager to claim its share of world trade. During the late 1500's, Dutch merchants cornered the markets in grain, timber, wool, salt, and wine, making Amsterdam the greatest trading center in northern Europe. To carry their cargoes more cheaply, the Dutch designed new ships. Dutch sea captains sailed into the Mediterranean and the South Atlantic and moved in on the Portuguese empire in the East.

By 1602 so many Dutch traders were backing individual voyages and competing against one another that prices had fallen. To solve the problem, the merchants decided to join together to manage the trade. They formed a giant trading company called the Dutch East India Company and vowed that the East Indies trade "should belong to the Company and no other nation in the world should have the least part."

In 1609 the company hired Henry Hudson to cross the Atlantic and search for the Northwest Passage to the Orient. Until Hudson's voyage, there had been no Dutch exploration in North America. In his ship, the *Half Moon*, Hudson sailed along the coast of North America and into a river which he named for himself. From there, he went through a strait into a bay, both of which bear his name today, and sailed as far as present-day Albany, New York. Hudson's voyage became the basis for Dutch claims in North America.[3]

In 1621 another company, the Dutch West India Company, was formed to take charge of settlements in America and Africa. Three years later, 30 Dutch families arrived in the American colony, called New Netherland. They settled at Fort Orange on the Hudson River and on Burlington Island in New Jersey. Shortly after that, Fort Nassau was established just opposite where Philadelphia stands today.

That same year, Peter Minuit bought Manhattan Island for 60 guilders—about $24—in trading goods

---

[3] In the 1630's people from Sweden settled along the Delaware River, part of the territory claimed by the Dutch.

In 1610, Henry Hudson once again tried to find the Northwest Passage. On this voyage, which he made for England, Hudson's crew mutinied, and Hudson, his son, and several crew members were set adrift. Why did Hudson seek the Northwest Passage?

such as beads, knives, and trinkets. During the summer and autumn of that year, the settlers built 30 log cabins thatched with reed on the west side of Manhattan. The Dutch also built a stone business building and two windmills, one for sawing lumber and the other for grinding corn. Minuit then renamed the settlement New Amsterdam. Its population grew from 300 persons in 1630 to 1500 in 1664. Like Portugal, Spain, and France, Holland had found its niche in the New World.

The English

In 1485 the first Tudor king, Henry VII, took over the throne of England. The period before Henry became king had been a restless and turbulent one. Years of war with France, plague, and a struggle between two noble families for the English throne all had taken their toll. When Henry became king, he pulled the kingdom together, restored law and order, and encouraged business and trade.

Early Efforts. Columbus' voyage to the New World had piqued Henry's interest. Therefore he hired a Venetian sea captain named Giovanni Caboto—John Cabot—to find a new route to the Indies. Cabot set sail in 1497 looking for a northwestern route. He sailed to the shores of Newfoundland before returning to England. The next year he set out again. He sailed along the coast as far as Chesapeake Bay before being lost at sea. Cabot's were the first English vessels to touch the American mainland. Based on his voyages, England established its claims in the New World.

In 1509 Henry VII's son, Henry VIII, became king. Despite religious unrest, the country prospered under Henry VIII's reign. England had good land for pasture and many sheep. The English learned to process wool into a fine cloth, more attractive and less expensive than that of other countries. The demand for the English woolens brought wealth and prosperity to the country.

Between 1551 and 1558 the English did much to promote and increase trade. In Africa, Thomas Windham established a trade in sugar and fruit with the Barbary Coast and a trade in gold, pepper, and ivory with the Gold Coast. Sebastian Cabot, the son of John Cabot, became governor of a **joint stock company,** a venture in which investors pool their capital and share the risks of a business. The company was organized to seek a new route to the Orient.

Rather than look for a Northwest Passage, the company decided to look toward the northeast. An expedition under Sir Hugh Willoughby set out to find a northeast passage and open trade with China. Although Willoughby and his crew froze to death in Lapland, his chief pilot, Richard Chancellor, went on to the White Sea. He finally ended his journey in Moscow in an audience with Ivan the Terrible, the Tsar of Russia.

Chancellor's meeting with the tsar led to a commercial treaty with Russia. The tsar gave the English a **charter** (a document issued by a sovereign conferring certain rights and privileges) for the Muscovy Company, which was to manage the newly opened Russian trade. As a result of these events, there was a great deal of interest in exploration.

English merchants and nobles hungry for money and glory began to look covetously across the sea.

In 1554 Henry VIII's daughter, Elizabeth I, came to the throne. Elizabeth chartered the East India Company, which was made up of merchants who had banded together in an effort to break into the Dutch-controlled East Indies spice trade. When the company found out it could not achieve its goal, it turned instead to India, where it traded iron, lead, tin, and woolens for cottons, silks, spices, and gems.

The Sea Dogs. Elizabeth also supported the expansion of England's sea power. By this time England had become a Protestant country, and rivalry with Catholic Spain was growing. The English needed an outlet for their resentment of Spain and its riches. That outlet was provided by the forays of English **sea dogs,** sea captains turned raiders and adventurers. With Elizabeth's approval, the sea dogs plundered Spanish treasure ships.

One of the first sea dogs was Sir John Hawkins, an English admiral. Between 1562 and 1565, he led several very profitable expeditions that captured slaves on the West African coast, shipped them across the Atlantic, and against Spanish prohibition sold them in Spanish ports in the West Indies. Hawkins, by raiding Spain's Caribbean ports, deepened the animosity between Spain and England.

In 1576 another sea dog, Martin Frobisher, set out to look for the Northwest Passage. He threaded his way through Greenland's icebergs and fought through a tempest to sail into the bay that now bears his name. Frobisher returned to England with tales of "islands of ice . . . of such heighth as the clouds hanged about the tops of them" and fur-clad "little men" who shot "arrows and darts" and paddled through ice flows "in small boats made of leather." To prove he had reached Asia, he brought back one of the "little men of Cathay" and his kayak. Frobisher made three voyages in all. Although he never found the Northwest Passage, he increased English knowledge of the more remote areas of northeastern Canada and of the sea that he believed washed the northern part of Asia.

In 1578 still another of Elizabeth's sea dogs, Sir Francis Drake, sailed through the Strait of Magellan into the Pacific straight into the heart of the Spanish Empire. Along the way he raided Spanish ships and towns. Before returning home in 1580, Drake explored the coast of California, which he claimed for his queen; voyaged westward across the Pacific and picked up a cargo of cloves in the Spice Islands; and ran non-stop the 9700 miles (15,520 kilometers) from Java to Sierra Leone. He became the first explorer from England to circumnavigate the world. The English gloated over Drake's exploits, saying, "The Spaniard digged out sweete honey from the Golden Mines, and Sir Francis Drake fetched it home to be tasted in England."

The Spanish Armada, made up of 130 ships, with 8000 sailors and an army of 19,000 soldiers, was deemed invincible. Philip of Spain sent the Armada to invade and conquer England in 1588. However, the fast, maneuverable English fleet and great storms combined to destroy more than two-thirds of the Armada. What did the defeat of the Spanish Armada mean for England?

After 1550 English writers began to promote colonization with poems, dramas, and tracts.

The raids of the sea dogs kept the Spanish colonies in the West Indies in a state of turmoil and proved that English ships could handle their Spanish rivals. Finally, Phillip II of Spain became so angry about the raids that he sent an **armada,** or fleet of warships, to fight the English navy. England defeated the Spanish Armada in 1588, thus becoming Europe's major sea power.

Early Colonization. As the English became more powerful and more secure against their rivals, they became more interested in colonization. Elizabeth claimed the entire North American mainland on the basis of John Cabot's discoveries. In 1578 she gave Sir Humphrey Gilbert a charter "to search, find out, view and inhabit, such remote heathen and barbarous lands, countries, and territories not actually possessed of any Christian prince or people."

Gilbert's was not the first charter of the British Empire. But because it was the first to contain the words "to inhabit," it was the first to lead to an English colony in America. By 1583 Gilbert had made two voyages to Newfoundland, which he claimed for Elizabeth. He had not managed, however, to convince any English to settle there.

In 1584 Gilbert's half-brother, Sir Walter Raleigh, took over and sponsored an expedition to find a site for a colony. What he had in mind was a base along the South Atlantic coast from which English ships could attack Spanish treasure fleets.

Raleigh's expedition was led by Arthur Barlow and Philip Amadas. When they landed on the coast of what is now North Carolina, they claimed the land for England and named it Virginia in honor of Elizabeth, the Virgin Queen. Then they moved from the coast to Roanoke Island. Finding gardens growing there, Barlow decided to test the soil by planting English peas. He found it to be "the most plentiful, sweet, and wholesome of all the world."

The following year, Raleigh sent seven ships and 600 men under the command of Sir Richard Grenville to secure Roanoke Island as a military post. After stopping first at the West Indies to take on horses and cows to stock the colony and seeds to plant crops, Grenville arrived at Roanoke in June.

In September Grenville returned to England, leaving 300 men on the island. Before he could return, however, the men ran short of food and supplies and the island was hit by a tornado. When Sir Francis

Sir Walter Raleigh was one of the more versatile individuals of his day. He was a statesman, politician, historian, and financier. What was Raleigh's role in regard to colonization in America?

Drake arrived in June 1586 and offered to take the men home, they accepted. Shortly after, Grenville arrived with three well-provided ships. So as not to lose possession of the island, when he departed he left behind 15 men and provisions for 2 years.

In the spring of 1587, a group of more than 100 men, women, and children with tools, seeds, and household goods left England under the leadership of John White to set up the first true English colony in the Chesapeake Bay area. Although the expedition had been sponsored by Raleigh, he transferred the entire enterprise to a group of London merchants in 1589.

The plan was to stop at Roanoke to pick up Grenville's men and then go on to the Chesapeake area. But upon arriving at Roanoke, only a ruined fort and one decaying skeleton were to be found. The ship's captain, fearing stormy weather, decided to leave the settlers on Roanoke. The settlers insisted that White return with the captain to England for more supplies. Before White left, however, his daughter gave birth to a child. The baby girl, named Virginia Dare, was the first English child born in America.

White's return to Roanoke was delayed. When he finally did return in 1590, all he found was a deserted settlement and the letters CROATOAN freshly cut

VOYAGES OF EXPLORATION

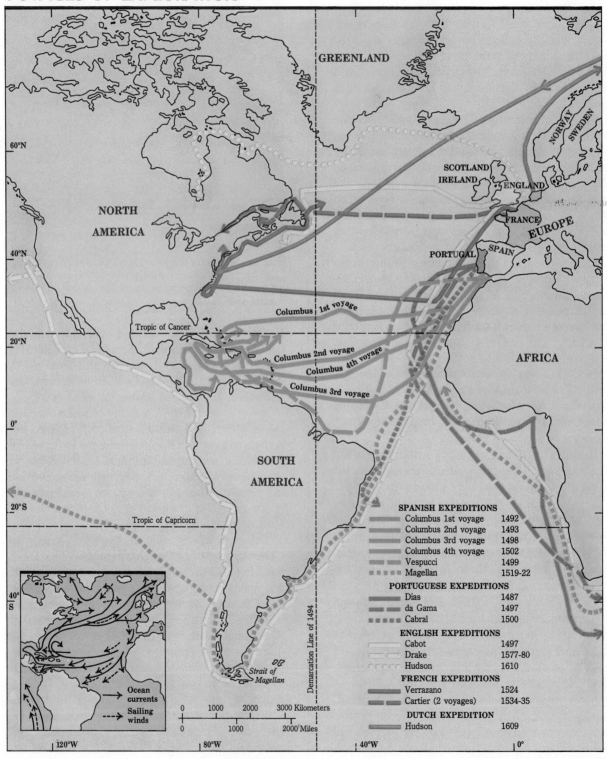

GREENLAND

60°N

SCOTLAND
IRELAND   ENGLAND

NORWAY
SWEDEN

NORTH
AMERICA

FRANCE

EUROPE

40°N

PORTUGAL   SPAIN

Columbus 1st voyage

Tropic of Cancer

20°N

Columbus 2nd voyage

AFRICA

Columbus 4th voyage

Columbus 3rd voyage

0°

SOUTH
AMERICA

20°S

Tropic of Capricorn

40°
S

Demarcation Line of 1494

Strait of
Magellan

Ocean
currents

Sailing
winds

0   1000   2000   3000 Kilometers

0   1000   2000 Miles

SPANISH EXPEDITIONS
Columbus 1st voyage   1492
Columbus 2nd voyage   1493
Columbus 3rd voyage   1498
Columbus 4th voyage   1502
Vespucci   1499
Magellan   1519-22
PORTUGUESE EXPEDITIONS
Dias   1487
da Gama   1497
Cabral   1500
ENGLISH EXPEDITIONS
Cabot   1497
Drake   1577-80
Hudson   1610
FRENCH EXPEDITIONS
Verrazano   1524
Cartier (2 voyages)   1534-35
DUTCH EXPEDITION
Hudson   1609

120°W   80°W   40°W   0°

Other theories are that the Indians originated in the Middle East or Africa and traveled to the Western Hemisphere by boat or raft. Have students check the theories in Barry Fell's *America B.C.* or Thor Hyerdahl's *Kon Tiki.*

on a post. The Croatoans were a group of nearby Indians. To this date, no one has solved the mystery of the disappearance of the settlers, and Roanoke has become the legendary "Lost Colony." Despite this misfortune, however, the English were not ready to give up their attempts to colonize America.

SECTION REVIEW

1. Identify the following: Prester John, Vasco da Gama, Treaty of Tordesillas, Ferdinand Magellan, Jacques Cartier, Martin Frobisher, Sir Walter Raleigh.
2. Why did Henry the Navigator establish a navigational school?
3. What was the purpose of Magellan's voyage?
4. Where was the French empire in the New World?
5. What was the basis of Dutch claims in North America?
6. Why did the English colony at Roanoke fail?

3 Peoples of the New World

When Columbus landed on the shores of the New World, some of the inhabitants assembled to greet him. Columbus described the Indians as follows:

All I saw were youths, none more than thirty years of age. They are very well made, with very handsome bodies, and very good countenances. Their hair is short and coarse, almost like the hairs of a horse's tail. They wear the hairs brought down to the eyebrows, except a few locks behind, which they wear long and never cut. . . . Some paint themselves white, others red, and others of what color they find. Some paint their faces, others the whole body, some only round the eyes, others only on the nose. . . . They are all of fair size, with good faces, and well made. I saw some with marks of wounds on their bodies. . . . They should be good servants and intelligent, . . . and I believe they would easily be made Christians, as it appeared to me that they had no religion. . . .

Like many Europeans after him, Columbus made assumptions based on his own prejudices. What Europeans still had to discover was that the people of

the Americas varied as much as the land and their civilization had existed for at least 200 centuries.

The Earliest Americans

For a great many years, anthropologists have debated the origins of the first Americans. Today most agree that they came from northeast Asia and entered the New World in the general area of the Bering Strait[4] during the last Ice Age. During that period, which began about 70,000 B.C. and ended about 10,000 B.C., the land was packed with glaciers, making the oceans lower and more land visible.

The theory is that during the last Ice Age, the level of the Bering Sea was lowered enough to convert the shallows of the Bering Strait into a bridge of land connecting Asia and the Americas. At its widest points, the land bridge, known today as Beringia, was about 1000 miles (1600 kilometers) across. The earliest Americans must have crossed this bridge from Siberia into Alaska as bands of hunters in pursuit of game such as giant bison and mammoths.

This crossing took place over hundreds of years. Because the people migrated in separate waves over such a long period of time, they were very different from one another in physical characteristics, skills, and talents. By the time the first Europeans came to the shores of America, the early immigrants had spread throughout the Western Hemisphere and had developed cultures in keeping with the different terrains and climates in which they had settled.

Peoples of Central and South America

A number of different peoples lived in Central and South America. Three of these—the Mayas, the Aztecs, and the Incas—developed highly sophisticated civilizations.

Mayas.   The civilization of the Mayas in southern Mexico and Central America had been brought to an

---

[4] In 1725 the tsar of Russia commissioned Danish sea captain Vitus Bering to find out if Asia was connected by land to North America. Bering and his men were the first Europeans to approach North America from the West. They traveled overland across Russia and Asia and sailed across the Bering Strait. In the following years Russian traders and hunters entered Alaska, and Russia claimed North American territory along the northwest coast.

Point out the modern nations that occupy the land where the three Indian civilizations were located. See map on p. 22. Have students report on the arts and crafts of each civilization.

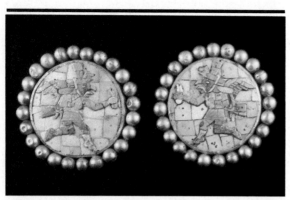

The Incas used precious metals and stones to create beautiful jewelry. Inca society was divided into classes. Only the nobility wore jewelry such as this. Why were the Incas considered to have an advanced civilization?

end several hundred years before the Spaniards arrived. At its peak, however, the Mayan civilization was one of great power, beauty, and color. Skilled artists and architects, the Mayas adorned their temple-cities with picture symbols and carvings of fanciful monsters.

Mayan life centered around religion. The people believed that the earth was surrounded by 13 separate heavens and 9 distinct hells. Each day of the week was represented by a living god whose behavior was predicted through a complex calendar system.

The importance of religion in Mayan life gave their priests great power. Priests and nobles dressed and lived in colorful splendor. Priests adorned themselves in jaguar skins, vivid red robes, iridescent bird feathers, and flower-topped headdresses. Some filed their teeth and inlaid them with semiprecious stones. Some nobles placed splintlike boards on their children's heads and wrapped them tightly with cloth to create elongated skulls, which they considered beautiful. Others hung beads from their children's foreheads to create permanently crossed eyes, a very special mark of beauty.

Aztecs.   When Cortés arrived in Mexico, he was astonished to find a city populated by about 3000 people. They had a well-regulated economy, a highly defined class structure, a system of courts, and a strong moral code that put family and community above all. These people, who had first appeared in Mexico around 1200 A.D., were the Aztecs, descendants of the Mayas. The city was the Aztec capital of Tenochtitlán, meaning "Near the Cactus," which was

settled about 1325 on an island in Lake Texcoco. Legend has it that the god of sun and war, Huitzilopochtli, told the Aztecs to build their city in the place where they found an eagle with a snake in its beak perched on a cactus.

The city of Tenochtitlán, ruled by the emperor Montezuma II, was linked to shore by causeways, had canals for streets, and maintained systems of aqueducts to carry fresh water. The city was filled with great temple-pyramids and houses of white-washed stone, stucco, and adobe. It had markets, barbershops, parks, and a zoo. Many of the inhabitants were artisans who wove cloth, made pottery, or crafted jewelry of gold, silver, and jade. Others were peasants who grew crops and raised turkeys and edible fat little dogs.

Religion was a very important part of Aztec life, and the Aztec gods required human sacrifices to assure their favor. Because the Aztecs needed an endless supply of captives for sacrifice, they were fierce warriors who were feared by neighboring Indian groups.

On the other hand, the Aztecs' religion kept them from slaughtering Cortés and his men on sight. According to Aztec legend, the god Quetzalcóatl, giver of all knowledge and good things, had sailed into the eastern sea 500 years earlier, promising to return. When Cortés arrived on the eastern sea, the Aztecs thought he was the god fulfilling his promise. Thus the way to conquest and ruin was opened. The Spaniards defeated the Aztecs, destroyed the city of Tenochtitlán, and built Mexico City in the same location.

Incas.   When Pizarro entered Peru in 1532, he too was astonished by what he found. More than 2 miles (3.2 kilometers) above sea level lay the Inca capital of Cuzco, glittering with gold. The Incas, who had come on the scene sometime after 1200, ruled an empire, the limits of which stretched for more than 2500 miles (4000 kilometers) from southern Colombia to central Chile. The emperor of the Incas was thought to be a direct descendant of the sun god.

The Incas had one of the most highly advanced and best-governed civilizations of the time. They could boast of well-built roads, cities constructed on mountains, and suspension bridges that made communication possible throughout the empire. Irrigation canals and agricultural terraces ensured a good food

Hispanic Influence in America

For many reasons, the United States is historically indebted to Spain. Christopher Columbus, sailing under Spain's sponsorship, opened the New World to European colonization. Spanish adventurers such as Cabeza de Vaca, Ponce de León, and Francisco Coronado explored the North American wilderness. Spaniards found the Mississippi River and the Grand Canyon. And by the middle of the 1500's, they had explored North America as far west as the Pacific and as far north as Oregon.

On the heels of the explorers came the Spanish missionaries. They colonized the Spanish Empire by converting Indians to the Catholic religion. The missionaries also persuaded them to follow Spanish laws and take up farming and ranching as a lifestyle.

The Spanish Empire in the New World included more than one-half the continental United States. The oldest surviving building in the United States is the Spanish fort at St. Augustine, Florida. The city of Santa Fe was founded by the Spaniards at about the same time the English Pilgrims were crossing the Atlantic on the *Mayflower*. By the time the United States won its independence from England—with help from Spain as well as France —the Spaniards had founded Tucson, Albuquerque, San Antonio and San Diego. Spanish Florida —including parts of present-day Mississippi, Alabama, and Louisiana—was acquired from Spain by treaty in 1819. The Spanish Southwest, including California, Utah, Nevada, Arizona, and much of New Mexico, Colorado and Texas, became part of the United States in 1848 as the result of a war with Mexico.

Many elements of the rich Spanish culture became part of America's heritage. Spanish art forms melded with the native Indian cultures to produce new styles in arts and crafts. Furniture, for example, was often decorated with Spanish-style flowers and curliques, applied with the bright paints made by Indians.

Perhaps the most successful blending of cultures occurred in the architecture of the Spanish missions. The mission style combined the flat-roofed adobe Indian building with the Spanish designs of open courtyards, covered arcades, rounded arches, and tiled roofs—forms that had been passed on to the Spaniards from Roman and Arab cultures. The adobe walls provided both structural support and insulation from the burning sun. At the same time, the interior courtyards provided welcome grace and privacy.

The Spanish legacy also included the introduction of horses, sheep, pigs, and beef cattle into the American Southwest. The Spanish were expert ranchers and horse breeders. The first cowboys were Spanish *vaqueros*. The American cowboy's clothing, lasso, and branding iron were all inherited from the *vaqueros*. Beautiful Spanish ballads evolved into American cowboy songs, and the Spanish rodeo became an American custom.

The most obvious element of Spanish culture in the United States is the Spanish language. Spanish is the second most widely spoken language in the country. Many Spanish terms, such as *canyon* and *fiesta*, have been incorporated into the English language. Spanish names—Los Angeles, Mesa Verde, El Paso—fill the maps of the Southwest.

Spanish-Americans are the fastest-growing minority in the United States today. Most are immigrants or descendants of immigrants from various parts of the Spanish Empire in the Americas, chiefly Mexico, Puerto Rico, and Cuba. Many Spanish-Americans have both Spanish and Indian ancestors. These Americans have a deep pride in, and commitment to, their Spanish heritage.

QUESTIONS

1. What parts of the United States were once part of the Spanish Empire?
2. What cities in the United States were founded by the Spaniards?
3. What animals were introduced into the West by the Spaniards?

Point out how the Indian inhabitants used natural resources to satisfy their needs.

INDIAN CIVILIZATIONS IN CENTRAL AND SOUTH AMERICA

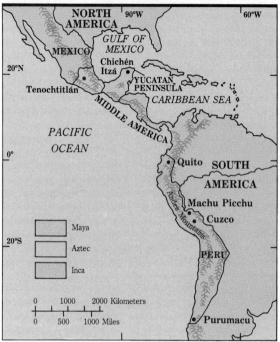

supply. The government provided for orphans, the aged, and the ill.

Most of the common people lived in small villages separated by cultivated fields in which farmers grew more than 30 different kinds of food crops. The people also raised llamas, which provided them with wool and served as the only native beast of burden. The nobles lived in large houses, had several wives and many servants, and were not expected to do any physical labor.

Peoples of North America

Compared to the 15 million or so inhabitants found by Cortés and the other conquistadores, there were only about 1 million North American Indians. Those million were greatly fragmented, with diverse physical characteristics, languages, religions, and lifestyles. Scattered across the North American continent were about 500 different groups, many of them nomadic. Because their cultures were closely related to their physical environments, they can be classified loosely by geographical area.

Arctic and Subarctic. The fur-clad "little men" described by Martin Frobisher were the Eskimos or, as they called themselves, the Inuit. Living in the cold, treeless arctic regions of North America, where the winters are sunless and the summers are brief, the Eskimos were, of necessity, excellent hunters. With spears, harpoons, kayaks, and sleds pulled by dogs, the people fished the icy waters and hunted whale, seal, walrus, and caribou.

Because few plants grew in the cold climate of the far north, the diets of the Eskimos and other inhabitants consisted mostly of meat and fish. The Aleuts, living in the Aleutian Islands 1000 miles (1600 kilometers) south of the Arctic Circle, also hunted in the sea for food. The nomadic tribes of northern Canada also lived mostly on meat and fish. Traveling by canoe and snowshoe, they hunted deer, caribou, moose, and bear.

Northwest Coast. The Northwest Coast area, which ran from the Columbia River up into Alaska, was blessed with a mild, rainy climate and an abundance of game, fish, and edible wild plants. Basically, the Indians of this region—the Tlingit, Nootkas, Haida, and Chinook—were a maritime people. They lived in villages near the ocean, hunted for sea animals, and fished the great rivers for salmon.

Because food was easy to find, the Indians of the Northwest had time to develop artistic skills. They carved wood into houses, chests, dishes, spoons, canoes, boats, and **totem poles**—posts showing a family's history and titles. They shredded bark and wove it into clothing, twined it into nets, and used it for padding.

The Northwest Indians believed in private property to a greater extent than Indians in other areas. Status depended on wealth. To show how much wealth they owned, they held ceremonies called **potlatches.** These were feasts lasting for several days, during which the host gave away valuable gifts to the guests.

California. Farther south on the western coast, the climate was mild and dry. Here lived the Chumash, Yokut, Modoc, and Pomo, groups known for their basketry arts. Most lived in brush shelters and settled in small villages. For the most part, they hunted small game and ate seeds, berries, roots, and nuts. One of their chief sources of food was the acorn,

Among most Indian groups there was little or no private ownership. Land and property were held in common.

which, after being pounded into flour and washed to remove the acid, was used to make a form of bread or mush. Sometimes the Indians of California fished or farmed. Periodically they raided other Indian tribes, carrying off women and children to keep as captives or to sell to other Indians as slaves.

Great Basin and Plateau. East of California is a dry, inhospitable region called the Great Basin. This area was the home of Indians such as the relatively primitive Shoshoni and the Paiute. They existed in almost complete isolation, hunting rabbits and other small game, and gathering wild seeds and piñon nuts. For the most part, their organization rarely rose above the family level. Survival was difficult because the land was short on water, plants, and animal life.

Farther north, in what is now Idaho and the eastern parts of Washington and Oregon, lived groups such as the Nez Percé, Palouse, and Walla Walla. They settled along rivers and lived mostly on salmon and on various roots and bulbs. After they were introduced to horses by the Spaniards, they became skillful horse breeders.

Southwest. The Southwest is a hot, dry region, partly desert and partly canyons and cliffs. Most of the Indian groups of this area were farmers. Two groups, the Pima and the Papago, were descendants of an ancient agricultural people known as the Hohokam. The Hohokam had built elaborate net-works of irrigation canals in the area of the Gila and Salt rivers to water their crops of corn and squash.

Another agricultural group, the Pueblo, built their life on that of an earlier group known as Basket Makers, who lived in the area where Utah, Arizona, and Mexico meet today. Around 100 A.D., the Pueblo withdrew to large community houses set on the ledges of canyons or cliffs. They later replaced these homes with ones built of stone or adobe. They grew cotton to weave into multi-colored patterned cloth, made pottery, and worked in shell.

By 1200 A.D. the fierce Apaches and Navahos had moved into this part of the country from Canada. They possessed Asiatic-like sinew-backed bows superior to any other weapon known in the Southwest. Traveling in bands, they hunted game and traded meat for the crops and cloth of the Pueblos. The Apaches kept moving throughout the Southwest, but the Navahos eventually settled near the Pueblos, learning from them how to farm and weave, and borrowing parts of their religion.

Great Plains. At first the Plains area was a peaceful expanse of grasslands that stretched east and southeast all the way from the Rockies to the Mississippi River. Groups like the Mandan and Arikara farmed in settlements along the rivers and hunted the huge herds of buffalo that ran free. The Commanche, Blackfoot, and Sioux also hunted the

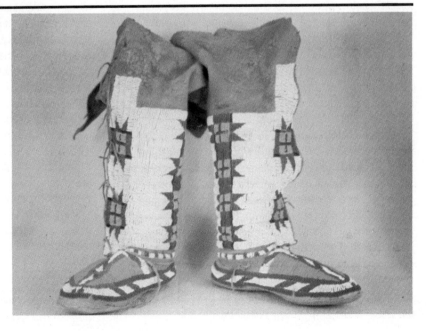

The Indians of North America had many different ways of life. The nomadic tribes of the Arctic used animal skins to make their shirts, leggings, and moccasins. Why did tribal life differ so from region to region?

Note that the Albany Plan (p. 54) was influenced by the organization of the Iroquois League.

The wigwam was home for the Algonquin Indians of the Eastern Woodlands. The wigwams varied in shape, but the covering was usually made of bark or reed fashioned into mats and laid, like shingles, on top of a frame. What types of shelter did other North American Indians build?

great beasts. They made their homes in **teepees,** movable cone-shaped dwellings covered with hides.

The introduction of the horse, however, led to a new way of life for the Plains Indians. Horses allowed the Indian hunters to move farther and faster, and horses could outrun any buffalo. As hunting became easier, the Indian had more time for feasts, ceremonies, horse raids, and war.

Eastern Woodlands. In the forests along the eastern coast lived the Indians whose names became most familiar to the English colonists—Pequot, Mohegan, Narraganset, Delaware, and Powhatan. All of these spoke varieties of the Algonquin language. The men stalked deer and rode the streams in canoes of birchbark. The women grew corn, beans, and squash. The people lived in fortified villages in homes called **wigwams,** domed or conical structures covered with bark.

These groups needed protection from the Iroquois, who over time had pushed their way north along the Appalachians and into Algonquin territory, settling there in **long houses,** long rectangular buildings made of wood poles and bark. Five tribes of the Iroquois—the Seneca, Cayuga, Onondaga, Oneida, and Mohawk—united to form the League of the Iroquois. This league, known as the Five Nations (later the Six Nations),[5] was one of the most sophisticated and powerful political organizations of the time. The Iroquois were a **matrilineal** society, tracing their descent through the maternal line. Women held a great amount of power. They chose the chiefs, called **sachems,** and decided the fate of captives brought back from raids.

Southeast. The Southeast was also a woodlands area, but with a warmer climate than the Eastern Woodlands. Here lived the Creeks, Chicasaws, and Choctaws who made up the warlike Muskhogean tribes. The 30,000 or so Creeks lived in 50 loosely

[5] In the 1700's, the Five Nations were joined by the Tuscarora Indians.

INDIAN TRIBES OF NORTH AMERICA

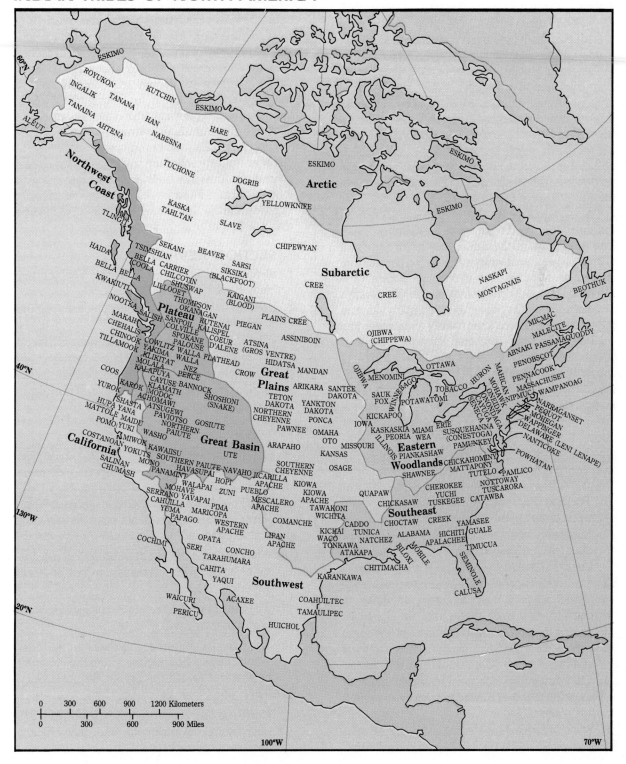

ESKIMO
ROYUKON
INGALIK TANANA KUTCHIN
TANAINA AHTENA HAN
ALEUT NABESNA ESKIMO
HARE
TUCHONE
DOGRIB ESKIMO Arctic
KASKA YELLOWKNIFE
TAHLTAN SLAVE
TLINGIT CHIPEWYAN
Northwest Coast
HAIDA SEKANI BEAVER SARSI
TSIMSHIAN CARRIER SIKSIKA
BELLA COOLA CHILCOTIN (BLACKFOOT) Subarctic NASKAPI
BELLA BELLA SHUSWAP CREE MONTAGNAIS BEOTHUK
KWAKIUTL LILLOOET KAIGANI
THOMPSON (BLOOD)
NOOTKA SALISH OKANAGAN PLAINS CREE
MAKAH Plateau SANPOIL KUTENAI PIEGAN OJIBWA MICMAC
CHEHALIS COLVILLE KALISPEL ASSINIBOIN (CHIPPEWA) MALECITE
CHINOOK COWLITZ SPOKANE COEUR ATSINA ABNAKI PASSAMAQUODDY
TILLAMOOK YAKIMA WALLA D'ALENE (GROS VENTRE) OTTAWA PENOBSCOT
KLIKITAT WALLA FLATHEAD HIDATSA OJIBWA HURON PENNACOOK
COOS MOLALA NEZ CROW Great MANDAN MENOMINI MAHICAN NIPMUC MASSACHUSET
YUROK KALAPUYA PERCE Plains ARIKARA SANTEE WINNEBAGO TOBACCO MOHAWK WAMPANOAG
KAROK CAYUSE BANNOCK TETON DAKOTA SAUK POTAWATOMI ONEIDA NARRAGANSET
SHASTA KLAMATH SHOSHONI DAKOTA YANKTON FOX CAYUGA PEQUOT
HUPA YANA MODOC (SNAKE) NORTHERN DAKOTA KICKAPOO SENECA MOHEGAN
MATTOLE MAIDU ACHOMAWI CHEYENNE PONCA IOWA ERIE WAPPINGER
POMO YUKI WASHO ATSUGEWI PAWNEE OMAHA KASKASKIA MIAMI DELAWARE (LENI LENAPE)
COSTANOAN PAVIOTSO GOSIUTE ARAPAHO OTO PEORIA WEA SUSQUEHANNA NANTICOKE
California MIWOK KAWAIISU NORTHERN Great Basin MISSOURI ILLINOIS (CONESTOGA)
SALINAN YOKUTS PAIUTE UTE KANSAS Eastern PAMUNKEY POWHATAN
CHUMASH MONO SOUTHERN PAIUTE NAVAHO SOUTHERN OSAGE Woodlands CHICKAHOMINY
PANAMINT HAVASUPAI JICARILLA CHEYENNE SHAWNEE MATTAPONY TUTELO PAMLICO
MOHAVE WALAPAI HOPI APACHE KIOWA CHEROKEE NOTTOWAY
SERRANO YAVAPAI ZUNI PUEBLO KIOWA YUCHI TUSCARORA
CAHUILLA PIMA MESCALERO APACHE CHICKASAW TUSKEGEE CATAWBA
YUMA MARICOPA APACHE QUAPAW
COCHIMI WESTERN COMANCHE TAWAKONI CADDO Southeast
PAPAGO APACHE WICHITA KICHAI TUNICA CHOCTAW CREEK YAMASEE
OPATA LIPAN WACO NATCHEZ ALABAMA HICHITI GUALE
SERI CONCHO APACHE TONKAWA MOBILE APALACHEE
TARAHUMARA ATAKAPA BILOXI TIMUCUA
CAHITA KARANKAWA CHITIMACHA SEMINOLE
YAQUI Southwest CALUSA
WAICURI COAHUILTEC
PERICU ACAXEE TAMAULIPEC
HUICHOL

60°N
40°N
130°W
20°N
100°W   70°W

0   300   600   900   1200 Kilometers
0   300   600   900 Miles

Indians had a big impact on the course of colonization. They played an important role in the fur trade. Settlers learned many things from Indians—methods of fighting in the wilderness, methods of fishing, trapping, and clearing land, and how to cultivate crops such as tobacco, corn, and potatoes.

knit farming communities in present-day Georgia and Alabama. There they grew corn, tobacco, and squash as well as other crops. The rival and warring Chickasaws, most of whom lived farther west in what is now Mississippi, farmed the river bottomlands.

Two other groups who lived in the area were the Cherokee and the Natchez. The former were progressive farmers who lived in the mountains of Georgia and the Carolinas. The latter, a powerful tribe of the Muskhogean family group, inherited from a much earlier people in the Ohio Valley the tradition of building **mounds.** These were great ceremonial earthworks made by building up piles of soil. Some of the mounds were used as burial grounds.

The Natchez were the only North American Indians whose government was a monarchy. Their king was known as the Sun. Beneath him were two distinct classes, aristocrats and common people. The aristocrats were divided into Suns, Nobles, and Honored Ones. All the common people were known as Stinkards. While Stinkards could marry anyone they pleased, aristocrats had to marry Stinkards. The children of a female aristocrat and a male Stinkard became aristocrats. Those of a male aristocrat and female Stinkard were lowered by one class. In this way, the highly structured class system was perpetuated.

End of an Era

In most cases the Indians in the various regions of the Americas were friendly when they first encountered Europeans. Columbus, for example, described the Arawaks of the Caribbean area as "a loving people, without covetousness." Sometimes the Indians were responsible for saving the lives of adventurers and colonists who came ill-prepared to deal with the hazards of a strange country.

The Europeans, however, came not only to discover, but to conquer and claim. Europeans divided the American lands among themselves with little thought for its native inhabitants. The arrival of Europeans in the New World led to a clash of cultures that resulted in tragedy for the Indians.

SECTION REVIEW

1. Identify the following: Beringia, Tenochtitlán, Inuit, Basket Makers, League of the Iroquois.
2. How did the American continents first become populated?
3. What were the three major civilizations of Central and South America?
4. Which Indian groups in North America had time to develop artistic skills or other activities not related to obtaining food?

CHAPTER 1   REVIEW

SUMMARY

1. The first Europeans to reach the New World were probably the Vikings of Scandinavia.
2. Europeans were not aware that the North and South American continents existed until after Columbus sailed to the New World in 1492.
3. The discovery of the Americas was made accidentally as a result of Europeans' desire to establish new trade routes with the Far East.
4. During the 1500's and 1600's several European nations sponsored explorations in the New World and made claims based on those explorations.
5. The Portuguese took the lead in exploration by rounding the tip of Africa and opening an eastern sea route to India.
6. Spain's conquests in Central and South America brought it riches that were envied by others.

7. The French, who had the largest empire in North America, made a profitable business of fishing and fur trading.
8. The Dutch and the Swedes established successful colonies in the northeastern part of North America.
9. The first English attempts at colonization were unsuccessful.
10. Long before Europeans arrived in the New World, Indians had migrated from the continent of Asia and spread throughout the Americas.
11. The cultures of the various Indian groups in North and South America were closely related to their natural environments and highly varied in degree of sophistication.

Read the skills section of the teacher's guide to understand how the "Using Skills" activities at the end of each chapter are related to the Historian's Craft activities at the end of each unit.

VOCABULARY

feudalism	circumnavigated	charter	wigwam
nation-state	conquistadores	sea dog	long houses
monarchy	viceroy	armada	matrilineal
reformation	audiencia	totem pole	sachem
line of demarcation	joint stock company	teepee	mound

REVIEW QUESTIONS

1. Why did Europeans want to find a new route to the Far East?
2. What changes took place in Europe that led to explorations in the New World?
3. How did Prince Henry of Portugal contribute to the Age of Exploration?
4. How did the Spanish colonies differ from the French colonies?
5. What developments under the Tudor monarchs led England to become interested in colonization?
6. In what ways were the civilizations of the Mayas, Aztecs, and Incas advanced?
7. How did the peoples of North America adapt to their various environments?
8. What interactions took place between Indians and Europeans?

DISCUSSION

1. Why do you think Europeans felt that they could claim land in the New World regardless of the fact that it was already inhabited?
2. What was the importance of religion in the exploration and colonization of the New World?
3. What do you think were the motives of those who risked their lives to explore new lands?
4. Why do you think Holland, France, and England confined their attempts at colonization to North America?

USING MAPS

Refer to the map on page 18 and answer the following questions:

1. Which explorers went to what is now the United States?
2. Which explorers went to South America?
3. Which explorers made more than one voyage?
4. Which explorer went farthest north? Which one went farthest south?
5. At approximately what longitude does the line of demarcation lie?

USING SKILLS

Study the picture on page 24, read the caption, and answer the following questions.

1. Who are the people in the picture?
2. How many of the people are women? How many are men?
3. What are the activities of the women? Of the men?

1	The English in Virginia	29
2	The New England Colonies	32
3	The Proprietary Colonies	35
4	Colonial Government	38
5	The Colonial Economy	40
6	Culture and Society	45

THE ENGLISH COLONIES

Wiser men than they, going into a wilderness to set up another strange government differing from the settled one here, might have fallen into greater errors than they have done.

THOMAS LECHFORD

Although several European nations had claims in North America, it was the English who eventually dominated the continent. By 1733, there were 13 colonies along the eastern seaboard under English control. These colonies had been founded in a variety of ways and for a variety of reasons. Regional differences had developed in their cultures and economies. All, however, had in common their English heritage.

1 The English in Virginia

Even after the failure of Roanoke, well-to-do English merchants were fascinated by tales of the riches Spain had obtained from its possessions in the New World. In the hope of acquiring similar riches, private business interests continued to finance explorations and settlements in the New World.

The Founding of Jamestown

The first permanent English colony in North America was sponsored by merchants in London, who formed a joint-stock company called the London Company. These merchants were given a charter by James I, who had succeeded Elizabeth to the English throne in 1603. The charter gave them the right to colonize land in the southern part of the region Sir Walter Raleigh had named Virginia.

The company stockholders hoped to find gold and perhaps a northwest passage to India. They hired a group of men who agreed to emigrate to Virginia to work for the company for seven years. During that period, all the gold they found and anything they produced would belong to the company. After that, they would be free to work for themselves.

Meanwhile, the company would provide the necessities such as tools, medicine, and clothing.

Shortly before Christmas 1606, three ships owned by the London Company set sail for the New World. The voyage took four months. It was marked by frequent quarrels, sicknesses, and the deaths of many passengers. Of the 144 men who started the journey, only 105 were alive when the ships reached the coast of Virginia in the spring of 1607.

Orders from the London Company called for the colonists to build their settlement upstream on a large river. Such a location would be easier to defend against an attack by sea than a site on the coast. The river would allow them to travel inland by ship, in order to trade with the natives and look for a northwest passage.

After two weeks of looking, the colonists chose a site on a small peninsula about 30 miles (49 kilometers) upstream on a river they called the James, after their king. There they built temporary shelters, and immediately began to search for gold and a passage to India.

Early Troubles

Unfortunately, the site the colonists chose was not wholesome. Nearby swamps served as breeding grounds for mosquitoes carrying malaria, and there was no fresh drinking water.

The colonists had used up most of their provisions on the long sea voyage. They planted some experimental crops such as orange trees and cotton, but not enough grain. Instead they relied on supply ships from England, while they spent most of their time looking for gold.

The things that needed to be done for survival in the wilderness were left undone. Part of the problem was that many of the colonists were gentlemen, not used to physical work or taking orders. Another problem was that the council of leaders, who had been chosen by the company, quarreled among themselves. They seemed unable to provide the leadership that was required. During the hot summer, malaria swept through the colony, and supplies dwindled. By autumn more than one-half of the colonists had died, mostly from hunger or disease.

Jamestown was without a strong leader until one of the council members, Captain John Smith, managed to take control in September of 1608. His efforts were largely responsible for saving the colony. He traded with neighboring Indians for food, and saw to it that a well was dug, houses were built, and crops were planted. He forced everyone to work, under threat of banishment to the wilderness.

A year later Smith was injured in a gunpowder explosion and returned to England. Once again the colony fell into disorder. Meanwhile, several hundred more colonists had arrived without adequate supplies. The colony now entered a period of hardship so severe that it was called the "starving time." People were reduced to eating dogs, cats, rats, and snakes. Hundreds died over the winter.

The desperate survivors had already deserted Jamestown and were sailing down the river towards the sea when they were met by a relief expedition. On board was Lord Delaware, who had been appointed governor of the colony by the London Company. After convincing the colonists to return to Jamestown, he established a strict government. During the next few years the colonists lived under a succession of company-appointed governors.

Tobacco Farming

Eventually, the colonists gave up the fruitless search for gold and a northwest passage. They made attempts at other enterprises, such as the manufacture of iron, glass, and bricks. The most successful enterprise turned out to be tobacco farming. Tobacco was a plant native to the New World. The Spanish had learned how to use it from the Indians, and Europeans had quickly taken up the habit.

In 1612, a colonist named John Rolfe, after several years of experiment, grew a variety of tobacco that was pleasing to English taste. Soon the colonists

American Indians, such as those who lived in Secota, raised tobacco long before Europeans came to the New World. Why did tobacco assume such importance for the fortunes of the Virginia colonists?

were exporting tobacco. They had finally found a **cash crop** (a crop to be exported for a profit.)

Until 1614, the colonists were still required to turn over all that they produced to the company. At that time some of the colonists were allowed to lease 3-acre (1.2-hectare) plots of land. They still had to work one month of the year for the company, and they had to contribute two and one-half barrels of grain to the common food supply. The rest of what they grew on their plots was their own. This move toward private ownership proved to be such a stimulus to tobacco farming that the governor had to order the colonists to plant food crops as well as tobacco. As one early colonist explained:

When our people were fed out of the common store, and labored jointly together, glad was he who could slip from his labor, or slumber over his task. The most honest among them would hardly take so much pains in a

Among the laws passed at the first meeting of the legislature was one that said no harm must be done to Indians. Laws were also passed against drunkenness, swearing, gambling, and idleness. Another law required attendance at church.

week, as now they will do in a day: neither cared they for the increase, presuming that howsoever the harvest prospered, the general store must maintain them.

Private ownership was greatly expanded in 1618. All the colonists who had paid their own passage to America were granted 100 acres (40 hectares) of land. In order to attract more colonists, the company gave a **headright** (a land grant) of 50 acres (20 hectares) to those who paid their own way or anyone else's. Wealthy investors could thus acquire large plantations by paying for colonists to come over and work the land.

The headright system worked so well that it was later adopted by other colonies. During the next few years, people poured into Virginia. Settlements and plantations spread out along the James River.

Representative Government

In the same year that the headright system was instituted, the London Company also adopted another important change in policy. Previously, the company had given unlimited powers to the colonial governors. Their harsh rules were often resented by the colonists. In order to remedy this problem, the company promised the settlers that they would henceforth be governed by English law and would have the same rights as English citizens.

Even more important, the colonists were given a voice in their own government. Each community or plantation was allowed to elect two representatives to an assembly. The colonial assembly, called the House of Burgesses, met with the governor and his council for the first time on July 30, 1619.

Relationship With the Indians

By this time, the colonists' relationship with the Indians in Virginia had deteriorated considerably. At first, the Indians in the area had been friendly. However, as Indians became more and more alarmed about the invasion of their land, their friendliness turned to hostility.

At one point, Indians captured John Smith. According to Smith's own story, they might have killed him except for the intervention of Pocahontas. She was the daughter of Chief Powhatan, the head of a league of Virginia Indians. In 1613, a group of colonists captured Pocahontas and brought her to Jamestown, where she married John Rolfe. For a time, the marriage eased tensions between Indians and colonists. Pocahontas was converted to Christianity and went to England, where she impressed everyone with her grace and dignity. Partly because

The marriage of the Indian princess Pocahontas to John Rolfe typified the peaceful relations that existed for a time between the Indians and the colonists. What caused the destruction of the peaceful relations?

Ask students if the problems at Jamestown could have been avoided if that colony had a contract such as the Mayflower Compact.

of her, the English decided to try to convert other Indians to Christianity.

Pocahontas died just before she and Rolfe were to return to Virginia. Soon after, her father also died. The new chief, Opechancanough, convinced his fellow chiefs that their way of life depended on driving out the English. In 1622, the Indians attacked several settlements and killed hundreds of colonists, including John Rolfe.

The Indian attack left the colony devastated. This, along with complaints from stockholders that no profits were being made, led James I to appoint a commission to investigate the affairs of the London Company. As a result, the company was charged with mismanagement and its charter was declared void. Virginia then became a **royal colony**—under the direct control of the king. The colonial assembly lost its authority along with the company, and for the next few years did not meet. But the governors appointed by the king found it difficult to rule without the cooperation of the colonists, and representative government was restored.

SECTION REVIEW

1. Identify the following: London Company, John Smith, starving time, John Rolfe, cash crop, House of Burgesses, Powhatan, Pocahontas.
2. What were the motives of the London company in colonizing Virginia?
3. What problems did the early settlers of Jamestown face? How were these problems solved?
4. What kind of government was established in Virginia? Why?

2 The New England Colonies

Virginia was colonized by a commercial company for profit. In contrast, the development of New England was shaped by people whose chief motives were related to their religious beliefs. Although profit-seeking also had a role, it was secondary.

The Plymouth Colony

In the early 1500's, Henry VIII of England broke away from the Catholic Church. The break occurred because the Pope refused Henry's request that his childless marriage to Catherine of Aragon be dissolved. Because Henry wanted to remarry, he declared that the Pope no longer had power in England. Henry established the Church of England, with himself at its head, as the **state religion** (a religion officially supported by the government). However, he made few changes in church practices. Some followers of the Protestant Reformation in England, known as Puritans, thought that reform was needed to make the Church of England less like the Catholic Church.

Most Puritans believed that the Church of England could be "purified" by changing some of the rules and rituals. One group of petitioners, for example, asked that the ring be left out of the marriage service, and that ministers be allowed more freedom to interpret church teachings. But not all Puritans agreed on exactly what changes should be made.

A minority group, called Separatists, believed that the Church of England could not be reformed from within. In 1602, they began to start their own churches. The Separatist churches were against the law, and some members were thrown into prison.

In 1608 a small group of Separatists fled to Holland, where they were allowed religious freedom. But over the next few years they became increasingly disturbed because their children were adopting the language, customs, and worldly ways of the Dutch. After much discussion, the Separatists decided to leave Holland for America. Going first to England, they obtained a land grant in Virginia from the London Company. To finance the venture, they formed a joint-stock company with some London merchants.

A small group of the Separatists, known as Pilgrims, set sail from England on the *Mayflower* in 1620. Violent storms blew their ship off course. When they finally spotted land, they were off the coast of Cape Cod, far north of the land specified in their grant. Because of this, their grant had no legal basis.

While still on board ship, therefore, they decided to draft an agreement to form a government. The agreement they signed was called the Mayflower Compact. It was a simple document which expressed their feeling that governments derived their just powers from the people who are governed.

After some exploring, the Pilgrims chose the land around Plymouth Harbor for their settlement. Unfortunately, they had arrived in December and

An Indian named Squanto was of particular help to the Pilgrims. He had been captured by one of John Smith's expeditions and had learned English before being returned to his home.

The Mayflower Compact was signed by Pilgrims on board the ship. They promised to obey the officers elected and the laws passed. All those who signed, even servants, received the right to share in the government. What idea did the Mayflower Compact express?

were not prepared for the New England winter. However, they were aided by friendly Indians, who gave them food and showed them how to grow corn. When warm weather came, the colonists planted, fished, hunted, and prepared themselves for the next winter. After harvesting their first crop, they and their Indian friends celebrated the first Thanksgiving.

By 1627, the Pilgrims were able to buy the shares of their London backers and take over ownership of the colony themselves. Later, the Plymouth Colony became part of Massachusetts.

Massachusetts

Meanwhile, the Puritans had achieved some success at reforming the Church of England. Their influence in both politics and religion increased. But in 1625 Charles I came to the throne. He was determined to end the Puritan threat to his personal power as head of the Church and the government. His persecution of the Puritans and all who dared to oppose him led many to seek religious and political freedom in the New World.

The Puritans became part of what has been called the "great migration" of English people to America. Between 1630 and 1643, about 50,000 people left England. The majority probably came to the New World for economic reasons. England was undergoing a depression, and poverty and unemployment

were widespread. Nearly one-half of those who left England during this period settled in Massachusetts.

In 1629, another joint-stock organization, called the Massachusetts Bay Company, received a charter from Charles I. Among the original investors were both Puritans and non-Puritans, and their motive was to make money from fishing and fur-trading. After persecution of the Puritans increased, however, the Puritan stockholders secretly bought out the others.

An unusual feature of their charter was the lack of a clause stating where the headquarters of the Massachusetts Bay Company should be located. Therefore, the Puritans decided to take the charter with them and have their headquarters in the New World. This allowed them to govern themselves with little interference from England.

The Puritans left for Massachusetts in 1630, led by their first governor, John Winthrop. They planned to set up a model Puritan community. Only after their ships were safely out of the harbor did Winthrop make their intentions clear. "We shall be as a city upon a hill," he said in a sermon. "The eyes of all people are upon us."

As they had planned, the Puritans set up the Massachusetts Bay colony along the lines of their religious beliefs. According to the doctrine of **predestination,** God had chosen a few people, called the **elect,** to be saved from Hell. Although no one could be sure of being saved, the elect were thought to reveal themselves through their actions.

Discuss the importance of the work ethic in American society today.

Ask students what current issues (e.g., prayer in public schools) are related to separation of church and state.

Thus, people were motivated to lead good lives, proving to themselves and others that they were among the saved.

The Puritans emphasized the virtues of hard work and thrift, and they believed that material rewards could be a sign of God's favor. The Puritan **work ethic** (belief in the value of hard work) proved to be very useful in developing a new colony, and Massachusetts was economically successful from the beginning.

By 1643 Boston and 21 other towns had been established. At first, Winthrop and a small group of stockholders made all the laws. However, other male church members demanded and got a voice in the legislature, called the General Court. Still, the church dominated the government.

When Charles I learned that Puritans were in control in Massachusetts, he tried to recall their charter. Before this could be accomplished, a civil war brought the Puritans to power in England and Charles I was executed. The Puritans held control until 1660, when Charles II returned from exile in France and the throne was restored. Meanwhile, the Massachusetts colony continued to thrive.

Branching Out

Although the Puritans had come to Massachusetts seeking religious freedom for themselves, they were intolerant of those who worshipped differently. People who had dissenting beliefs were banished from the colony if they could not be convinced to change their minds. Roger Williams and Anne Hutchinson were but two of the best known dissenters expelled by the Puritans.

Williams believed that the government should have no authority over religious matters, nor should the church have authority in the government. This idea—**separation of church and state**—eventually became widely accepted. Williams also said that the Puritans had no right to the land because they had not paid the Indians for it. The Puritans banished him in 1635. The next year he formed a separate colony in Providence, Rhode Island, on land purchased from the Narragansett Indians. Williams and his colony became known for religious tolerance.

Rhode Island soon was able to welcome another refugee from Massachusetts, Anne Hutchinson. Her belief that divine truths could be revealed directly to

Anne Hutchinson (left) and Roger Williams (right) were among the dissenters expelled from Massachusetts. Each founded colonies in Rhode Island. Hutchinson was killed in an Indian raid. Williams earned the trust of the Narragansett Indians and took part in negotiations between the tribe and the colonies. What ideas held by Hutchinson and Williams led to their banishment?

King Philip was the son of Massasoit. His older brother Alexander had died while on a journey to answer charges brought against him by the General Court. Philip blamed whites for his brother's

death and wanted revenge. Other Indians who resisted during this period were the Susquehannocks, the Tuscariras, and the Yamasees.

individuals, in contrast to the Puritan view that truth was to be found only in the Bible, had led to her banishment. She and her followers founded the town of Portsmouth in 1638.

In 1644 Rhode Island received a charter granting self-government. Under this charter all adult males had the right to vote. But the charter had been granted while the Puritans were in control of England, and it therefore became illegal when Charles II came to power. In 1664 he granted a new charter that required a man to own a certain amount of property before he could vote. This property qualification was resented, but Rhode Island still offered more freedom than other colonies.

Thomas Hooker, a minister who took about a hundred of his parishioners to settle in what today is Hartford, Connecticut, was not protesting Puritan teachings. He did, however, object to the fact that only church members could vote. He was also seeking more fertile land by moving west.

In Connecticut, Hooker joined with two other settlements in framing a **constitution** (a statement of the principles of government) called the Fundamental Orders. It provided for a representative government similar to the one in Massachusetts, except that voting for representatives and governor was not limited to church members. Government by the consent of the governed was emphasized.

In 1662, Connecticut received a charter that recognized the existing government. The charter extended the boundaries of Connecticut to include settlements at New Haven and along Long Island Sound.

People from Massachusetts also migrated to the Maine-New Hampshire region. This area was part of a 1622 grant to Sir Ferdinando Gorges and John Mason. They had started several small settlements, but the territory remained mostly undeveloped until the 1630's, when colonists from Massachusetts began moving into the area.

Massachusetts had an overlapping grant to much of the same territory as Gorges and Mason. The controversy over land claims lasted until 1677, when an English court ruled against Massachusetts regarding New Hampshire. In 1679, New Hampshire became a royal colony. Meanwhile, Massachusetts bought out the conflicting claims to Maine and held control over it until 1820.

Indian Resistance

The steady expansion of New England settlements threatened the Indian way of life. Few among the colonists were willing to treat the Indians as equals or acknowledge Indian rights to the land. In 1635 the Pequot Indians of southern New England rose up against the colonists and were defeated. Most of those who survived were sold into slavery.

In 1675 an Indian alliance led by Metacomet, called King Philip by the Puritans, was also defeated. But the Indians continued to raid frontier villages, and their bitterness against the English grew.

SECTION REVIEW

1. Identify the following: Separatists, the great migration, John Winthrop, Anne Hutchinson, Thomas Hooker, King Philip.
2. What was the underlying principle of the Mayflower Compact?
3. What was the purpose behind Puritan migration to the New World?
4. What were the results of religious dissension in Massachusetts?
5. Why were the Fundamental Orders of Connecticut significant?

3 The Proprietary Colonies

The first English colonies had been established by joint-stock companies. Another approach to colonization was the **proprietary colony.** By this method the king granted land to a person or group called proprietors, who were often friends of the king or people to whom the **Crown** (the king's administration) owed a debt. Proprietors owned the land they received and usually made any laws they wished, as long as they were consistent with English law.

Maryland

George Calvert, Lord Baltimore, acquired a proprietary grant from his friend Charles I to the territory that became known as "Mary Land," after Queen Henrietta Maria, the king's wife. Calvert died before he could start a colony there, but his proprietary rights, along with his title, were passed on to his son, Cecelius Calvert.

Pennsylvania, Rhode Island, Maryland, and New York were among the most tolerant of religious differences. Discuss how religious tolerance influenced the attractiveness of each colony.

The young Lord Baltimore knew what had happened in neighboring Virginia, and tried to learn from Virginia's mistakes. He offered land grants to attract settlers and published lists of supplies the colonists would need. He ordered that food crops be planted before anything else. Lord Baltimore's planning helped to make Maryland successful from the start. Later, tobacco became the main crop, just as it had in Virginia.

Because the Calverts were Catholics, Maryland became a haven for Catholics, although most of the settlers were Protestants. Conflicts between the two groups led to the passage of the Toleration Act in 1649:

> *No person or persons whatsoever within this province . . . professing to believe in Jesus Christ, shall from henceforth be any ways troubled, molested, or discountenanced for or in respect of his or her religion . . . nor any way compelled to the belief or exercise of any other religion against his or her consent. . . .*

The Toleration Act was an important step toward religious freedom in America. Maryland became a refuge for many different Protestant sects as well as for Catholics.

New York and New Jersey

In 1664 Charles II made a large grant to his brother James, the Duke of York. The huge grant included the land claimed by the Dutch as New Netherlands. This move on the part of the English was part of a larger struggle between England and Holland for control of world trade.

As a result of the grant to the Duke of York, Holland declared war. But the people of New Netherlands, unhappy with their Dutch governor, surrendered without a fight to the English. The terms offered by the English were generous. The Dutch were free to stay, keeping their property and their freedoms.

The Duke of York remained in England. Part of his grant, present-day New Jersey, he gave as a proprietorship to two friends, Sir George Carteret and Lord John Berkeley. He appointed a governor to rule in the northern part of his territory, which was renamed New York. The Dutch thought the English

governor's rule was fair enough. Even the Dutch governor stayed on. English settlers, however, pressed for a representative assembly. After years of struggle, the Duke finally allowed an assembly to be called in 1683.

In 1685 however, the Duke became James II, succeeding his brother to the throne. Charles II had been working on a plan to consolidate the colonies and tighten control over them. As a first step, he had revoked the Massachusetts charter. James II wanted to continue with his brother's plan. He recalled the charters of Connecticut and Rhode Island, and combined all the New England colonies with New York and New Jersey into the Dominion of New England. Sir Edmund Andros was appointed governor of the Dominion. Representative government was abolished, over the strong protests of many colonists.

The Dominion of New England did not last long, however. In 1688 the English overthrew James II in what was called the Glorious Revolution. The new king and queen, William and Mary, allowed representative government to be restored. They made Massachusetts a royal colony and gave it a new charter in 1691. New Jersey was returned to its proprietors. Connecticut and Rhode Island were allowed to reinstate their old charters.

The Carolinas

The territory between Virginia and Florida was granted by Charles II in 1663 to a group of eight proprietors. This group hoped to make money by starting settlements that would export certain kinds of agricultural products that could not be grown in England's cold climate. To attract settlers, they offered land, promises of religious freedom, and representative government.

In 1669 they introduced a new plan called the Fundamental Constitutions of Carolina. It called for a feudal system in which most of the land would be held by the proprietors and farmed by workers who would not be free to leave without permission. However, most of the provisions of the Fundamental Constitutions could not be enforced because of the resistance of the settlers.

The proprietors put most of their efforts into developing the southern part of Carolina because it

Quakers who tried to settle in other American colonies were persecuted, except in Rhode Island. Thus they developed the idea of starting a separate colony.

Quakers held religious meetings at which any member was permitted to stand up and speak. They believed that everyone was equal in the eyes of God. Why did many Quakers leave England?

had a good harbor and offered the possibility of trade with the nearby West Indies. Many of the settlers came from the West Indies. The northern part of Carolina was settled mostly by people from Virginia. North and South Carolina were officially divided in 1712. In 1729 the proprietors sold their rights back to the king, and North and South Carolina became royal colonies.

Pennsylvania and Delaware

One of the most successful English colonies was Pennsylvania. The land was granted to English Admiral William Penn in 1681, as payment for a debt owed to him by the Crown. When Penn died, the land was inherited by his son William, who had become a Quaker.

The Society of Friends, or Quakers, was a peace-loving religious sect. In England its members were persecuted by both the Church of England and the Puritans. Many Quakers, therefore, sought refuge in America.

Penn's plan was to establish a free, self-governing colony, a "Holy Experiment" in political and religious freedom. The government he established included a representative assembly and the right to vote for any

man who owned property or paid taxes. Land could be bought or rented at low prices. The advantages of Pennsylvania were advertised in pamphlets and attracted many colonists, including a large number of Germans.

Delaware, which had been settled by the Swedes, had been taken over first by the Dutch and then by the Duke of York. In 1682 the Duke gave the Delaware territory to Penn. For a while it was part of Pennsylvania. The people of Delaware requested and received the right to elect their own representative assembly in 1701.

Georgia

The last of England's 13 colonies was Georgia. Part of the original Carolina grant, it was founded by James Oglethorpe and several others in 1733, as a refuge for English debtors. Georgia's charter stated that after 21 years it would become a royal colony. The proprietors surrendered the charter early, and Georgia became a royal colony in 1752.

Oglethorpe wanted to give a new start in life to thousands of English people who had gone to jail for failing to pay their taxes. An advertising campaign raised money for this charitable project, and many

38   **THE ENGLISH COLONIES**

Ask students what changes took place in population distribution from 1650-1700.

Examples of property requirements were 59 acres of land in Georgia; an estate worth 40 shillings annually or 40 English pounds of personal property in Massachusetts; 50 acres of vacant land or 25 acres of cultivated land and a 12′ × 12′ house in Virginia. Discuss the validity of property requirements.

COLONIAL SETTLEMENT TO 1775

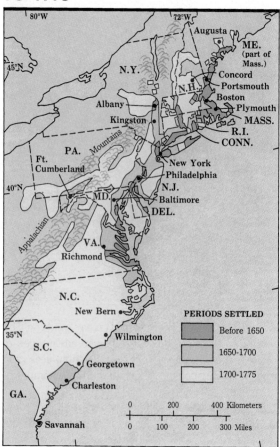

debtors did settle in Georgia. A larger number of settlers were Protestants from Scotland, Germany, and other parts of Europe. Although Georgia grew slowly, its settlement gave the English control of the Atlantic coast from Maine to Florida.

SECTION REVIEW

1. Identify the following: Lord Baltimore, Maryland Toleration Act, Dominion of New England, Edmund Andros, William Penn, James II, Oglethorpe.

2. What were the proprietary colonies? What were the reasons for their founding?

3. Why did the English takeover of New Netherlands meet with little resistance?

4. What steps did James II take to tighten control over the colonies?

4 Colonial Government

All of the English colonies, no matter how they were founded or by whom, had similar governments. Both the structure and philosophy of American government evolved out of English political thought and tradition. The concept of representative government, for example, developed in the New World in much the same way that it developed in England.

Representative Government

In England, monarchy was gradually replaced by a limited, representative government based on an **unwritten constitution.** England's constitution is said to be "unwritten" because it is taken partly from various written documents and partly from unwritten customs and laws.

One of the most important parts of the English constitution is the Magna Charta, or Great Charter, sealed by King John in 1215. This document limited the king's power in several ways. Chiefly, it took away his right to collect taxes without the nobles' consent. A few years later John's successor, Edward I, called the first meeting of Parliament, England's legislative body.

The Glorious Revolution of 1688 put power solidly into the hands of Parliament. No law could be passed, no tax collected, no army maintained without Parliament's consent. By this time, Parliament was made up of two houses. Members of the House of Lords were nobles who held their seats by right of inheritance. Members of the House of Commons were elected. Following the Glorious Revolution, the House of Commons began to assume more power than either the king or the House of Lords.

In the colonies, representative government was put into practice with the colonial assemblies. The colonists insisted that they should have the same rights as citizens in England, and they thought of their assemblies as "little Parliaments."

In both England and America, government was representative only to the extent that people had **suffrage,** or the right to vote. In both cases, only free adult white males had the privilege. Sometimes there were religious requirements, as with the Puritans of Massachusetts. Almost always there were property requirements. At that time, it was

Have students diagram the English system of government and compare it with the colonial system.

thought that only property owners, who had a stake in the community, would take a responsible interest in government.

Actually, the American government was more representative than the English. First, property ownership was more widely distributed in America than in England. Therefore a larger percentage of the American population could vote. Another reason was that colonists generally had **direct representation.** That is, representatives were elected by, and had to answer to, the voters in the towns where they lived. Members of the English Parliament did not have to live in the districts they represented, but Parliament was nevertheless supposed to represent all the people. The English called this system **virtual representation.**

Government Structure

Representative government was only one idea that the colonists brought with them from England. The organization of government was also modeled after the familiar English system.

By the 1760's, there were three types of colonies in America—**charter colonies** (self-governing), proprietary, and royal. Only two, Connecticut and Rhode Island, were still self-governing after the Dominion of New England was ended. Maryland, Pennsylvania, and Delaware were still proprietary colonies. The other eight colonies had come under royal control. In all three types, government had basically the same structure as government in England. Each colony had an executive branch, a legislative branch, and a judicial branch.

The governor was the chief executive in the colonies, as the king was in England. In the royal colonies, governors were appointed by the king, and in the proprietary colonies, by the proprietor. In the self-governing colonies, governors were elected. The powers of the governor included the right to call or dismiss the legislature, to veto laws, and to act as commander-in-chief of the militia.

As the king's power was limited by Parliament, so the governor's power was limited by the colonial legislature. Like Parliament, most colonial legislatures had two houses.[1] The upper house was the governor's council. Its members were generally

---
[1] The Pennsylvania legislature had only one house.

wealthy, prominent citizens. They were chosen by the governor except in Rhode Island, Connecticut, and Massachusetts where they were elected. The lower house was the colonial assembly. Not surprisingly, the assemblies were often at odds with the governor and the upper house. The assemblies claimed for themselves the same rights as the House of Commons had in England.

One of the most useful of the assemblies' powers was the **"power of the purse"**—that is, the control of government spending. This included even the right to hold up the salaries of governors and judges. In New Hampshire, one governor went without pay for five years because he refused to sign a bill the assembly had passed.

The judicial branch of government was patterned after England's, with several levels of courts. In the 1600's, the governor and his council acted as the supreme court in the colonies, as did the House of Lords in England. In the 1700's, the governor appointed judges to a supreme court. Lower-level judges were appointed by the governor or the Crown.

The first colonial legislature was the General Assembly of Virginia, which met in 1619. Soon each colony had instituted its own assembly and devised requirements for voting. What were some of the requirements?

The colonists' desire for an independent judiciary was one of the factors leading to the American Revolution.

At first the practice was to appoint judges for life. In the 1750's, however, the English government decreed that judges could remain in office only at the pleasure of the Crown. This meant that judges could be influenced by the threat of dismissal. The colonists protested that the judiciary should be independent. A pamphlet published in 1760 stated one colonist's argument:

> *That some men of independent circumstances, happy in the possession of virtue, have acted uprightly I will not dispute. . . . They are among mankind as a comet among the stars, rarely to be seen. But generally to look for strict impartiality . . . to expect that power should be confined within its legal limits . . . by men who are dependent is to ridicule all laws against bribery and corruption. . . .*

Local Government

Although the colonial governments had similar structures, regional differences developed in local government. In New England (Massachusetts, Connecticut, Rhode Island, and New Hampshire), local government took the form of town meetings. People gathered at the town meeting house to talk about issues. Anyone could give an opinion, although only men who met the religious and property requirements could vote. When towns became too large to permit gatherings of all their citizens, they held representative town meetings.

Another form of local government developed in the South (Maryland, Virginia, the Carolinas, and Georgia). People were too widely separated on their farms and plantations to attend town meetings. Here the basic unit of government was the county, and the chief officer was the justice of the peace. He was usually appointed by the governor and had both executive and judicial powers. Laws were enforced by the county sheriff.

The middle colonies (New York, New Jersey, Pennsylvania, and Delaware), on the other hand, practiced a mixture of town and county government. Whatever the form, local government handled everyday problems and gave people experience in self-government.

SECTION REVIEW

1. Identify the following: Magna Charta, Parliament, Glorious Revolution, town meeting.
2. What events led to the establishment of representative government in England?
3. What were the requirements for suffrage in the colonies?
4. What is the difference between direct representation and virtual representation?
5. How did local government in the southern colonies differ from that in New England?

5 The Colonial Economy

Colonial America was a land of farmers. At least 90 percent of the colonists farmed or made their livings from businesses closely related to farming, such as milling flour. Manufacturing was slow to develop. The ingredients needed for manufacturing—machines, good roads, banks, skilled workers—were lacking. Besides, England discouraged the colonies from competing with its own manufacturing industries.

Labor

Throughout the colonial period, labor was in short supply. America had plenty of cheap and fertile land, and most people preferred to have their own farms rather than work as hired hands. As Captain John Smith had put it, "This country is long on land and short on men."

The task of pushing back the wilderness required unremitting work. There were trees to be cleared, crops to be planted, and houses to be built. Farm families had to be almost completely self-sufficient, making their own butter, their own soap, and almost everything else they needed. As a result, children had to work almost as hard as their parents. Large families with ten or more children were common, and even the youngest was expected to do his or her share.

Because of the labor problem, people in farm communities often helped one another with house-raisings, corn-huskings, quilting parties, and harvests. These events combined work and play. After the day's work, people entertained themselves with activities such as foot and horse races, shooting contests, and dancing.

Indentured servants also provided a source of labor. These were people who signed an indenture, or agreement, to work for a period of four to seven years in exchange for passage to America. Most indentured servants came from England, where poverty and unemployment were widespread. Thousands of people were willing to trade a few years of work for the chance to go to the New World. Many were lured by the promise of free land after their term of service was up. Some were prisoners, orphans, or others who were not wanted in England and were forced to leave.

Indentured servants signed contracts before they sailed. Other servants, called **redemptioners,** were emigrants from Germany and other European countries who arrived in the colonies without having paid for their passage. The ship's captain would give them two weeks to find some way to "redeem" their fares. Usually this could not be done, and they would then be sold as servants.

The need for labor was a major cause of the rapid growth of slavery in America. The first black Africans had been brought to the colonies as early as 1619. A Dutch ship delivered a small group of blacks to Jamestown. Throughout much of the 1600's, blacks were legally not slaves but indentured servants. However, their indenture usually had no end date, so that they were actually slaves.

Slavery grew slowly until the beginning of the 1700's. But by 1760 there were nearly 400,000 slaves in the colonies, most of them in the South.

Most indentured servants, redemptioners, and slaves worked on farms or plantations. In the towns, labor was also scarce. As a result, wages were high. Skilled workers, such as carpenters, tailors, and blacksmiths, could earn twice as much in the colonies as they could in England. Colonial youths learned these skills by becoming **apprentices.** In exchange for several years of work, masters provided apprentices with food, clothing, shelters, and instruction.

The dominant philosophy of life in colonial America reflected the shortage of labor and the need for hard work. Sunrise to sunset was the normal working day, and idleness was considered sinful.

Regional Differences

In spite of the hard work, most farming in the New England colonies was at a **subsistence level** (the minimum needed for survival). The soil was thin and rocky, the growing season was short, and farms were small. People consumed most of what they grew. Because farming was not profitable, New Englanders looked to the ocean and the forests. Forests, fur-trading, lumbering, and shipbuilding became important sources of income.

Shipbuilding began in the colonies as early as 1631. Colonial artisans built ships for sale abroad as well as for fishing and commerce in America. Before long, the building of ships became the most important manufacturing industry in the colonies. What coastal cities, spurred by the shipbuilding industry, became trade centers?

Factors that influenced the distribution and concentration of agriculture included length of growing season, market availability, and the presence of waterways for shipping.

New England traders profited greatly from the slave trade. Newport, Boston, Salem, and New York City were centers for slave traffic.

Farms in the middle colonies were larger, and the soil and climate were better suited to farming. Some farm products, especially grain and livestock, were exported to the other colonies and to the West Indies.

On the large plantations of the South, crops were grown chiefly for export. The three cash crops were tobacco, rice, and indigo, a plant used to make blue dye. Tobacco became a major product during the early days of Virginia. Rice became important after a new type of seed was imported from Madagascar in 1694. Eliza Lucas, a South Carolina colonist, experimented with indigo and produced the first successful crop in 1744.

Large-scale production of these crops required a large labor supply. As plantations grew, southern agriculture came to depend more and more on slave labor. The economy of the South centered around slavery and the plantation system, and remained almost completely agricultural.

In the North (New England and the middle colonies), the economy turned more toward manufacturing and trade, though most people still farmed. There were small but growing industries making such products as hats from beaver furs, tools and stoves from raw iron, cloth from wool and flax, beer and ale from grain, and rum from molasses. The most important manufacturing industry was shipbuilding. Ships were in great demand for both fishing and commerce, and the colonists supplied ships for England's navy and merchant marine as well as for themselves.

The seaport cities of the North grew under the stimulus of foreign trade. By the mid-1700's, Boston, Philadelphia, New York, Newport, and New Haven all had populations in the thousands. The South remained rural, with Charleston being its only large city.

Trade

All of the colonies carried on a lively trade with England. For the most part, they exported agricultural products and raw materials in exchange for manufactured goods.

Trade with other European countries and with the West Indies was also important to the colonial economy. The West Indies were part of the **triangular trade,** so called because ships traveled a triangular route from the colonies to Africa, from Africa to the West Indies, and home again. The colonists shipped rum to Africa, where they traded it for slaves and gold. The slaves were shipped to the West Indies and traded for sugar and molasses, which was used to make rum.

The colonies traded among themselves as well as with other countries. It was by this means that those colonies without major international seaports were able to sell their products and buy goods from abroad.

The larger colonial towns had many different stores that sold both domestic and imported goods. Once or twice a week, markets were held so that farmers and townspeople could exchange goods directly. Smaller towns and rural areas had general stores, which carried a little of everything. In isolated areas where people could not easily get to a store or market, peddlers carried their wares by horsecart from house to house.

Money was always a problem. The colonies never had a single form of money that had the same value everywhere and was accepted by everyone. English currency—pounds and shillings—was supposed to be the standard, but there was never enough of it around. Some foreign coins were in circulation, but there was confusion about their value.

The colonists were forced to do a lot of their business by **barter,** or direct exchange. They also used furs, tobacco, rum, and all kinds of other goods as money. For foreign trade they sometimes used **bills of exchange**—written orders to pay someone a certain sum of money.

Eventually, each colony began issuing its own kind of paper money. Unfortunately, paper money did not always have the proper backing (something of real worth to guarantee its value). When too much paper money was printed, its value went down, causing prices to rise.

Mercantilism

The colonial economy was of great concern to England. During the 1600's and 1700's, England and other European countries followed an economic policy called **mercantilism,** in which colonies played an important role.

According to mercantilist ideas, wealth was measured by the amounts of precious metals, chiefly

COLONIAL TRADE ROUTES

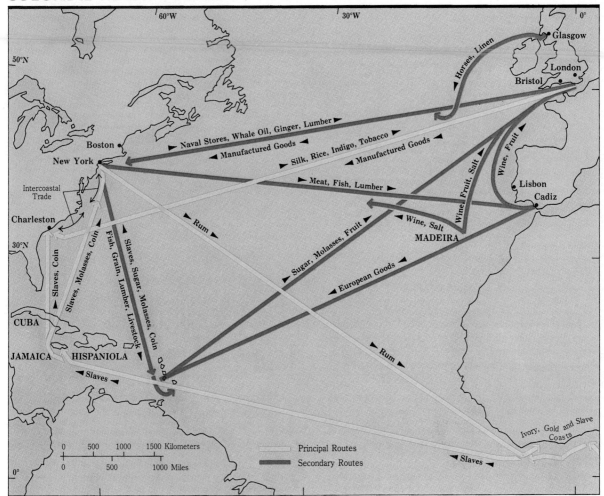

gold and silver, in the national treasury. One way of increasing wealth was by controlling world trade. The goal was to create a favorable **balance of trade**—that is, more exports than imports, with the difference paid in gold and silver.

From the English point of view, the colonies existed to improve England's balance of trade. They would provide markets for manufactured goods, thus increasing England's exports. They would also supply raw materials that otherwise would have to be bought from other nations, and might even be cut off in time of war.

Guided by mercantilist theory, England tried to tighten its control over the colonial economy. In the 1660's, Parliament passed a series of trade laws

known as the Navigation Acts. Under these laws, the colonies were restricted to shipping goods only on English or colonial ships. In addition, the ships had to have mostly English or colonial crews. This law helped the colonies by promoting the shipbuilding industry.

Parliament also made a list of products, called **enumerated commodities,** that the colonists could sell only to England. These were mostly raw materials needed by English manufacturers. At the same time, the colonists were given an exclusive right to sell enumerated commodities in the English market. **Bounties** (extra payments) were offered for the production of some special goods that England wanted.

Have students make a list of what a peddler might have carried for sale. Look for clues in the picture.

Yankee peddlers were a welcome sight to persons living far from a town or village. These peddlers carried dozens of items, among them combs, tin cups, needles, buttons, and pins, to isolated families. How did families that lived in a town or near one obtain goods?

The Staple Act of 1663 required that almost all goods imported to the colonies from other countries had to be reloaded on English ships. Various handling fees raised the prices that colonists had to pay for non-English goods.

Other laws were passed to discourage colonial manufacturing. Under the Woolens Act of 1679, woolen goods could not be exported from the colony where they were manufactured. The Hat Act of 1732 likewise prohibited the export of beaver hats from the colony where they were made. This act also limited the number of apprentices a master hatter could train. The Iron Act of 1750 allowed raw iron to be produced, but forbade the construction of new furnaces, forges, and mills that could produce finished goods.

Mercantilism was not intended to hurt the colonies. England wanted the colonies to be strong so that they could produce raw materials and buy English products. In general, both England and the colonies prospered under the mercantile laws. In some cases, however, colonists resented English interference.

When colonists found the laws to their disadvantage, they often evaded them by smuggling and by bribing customs officials. This was especially the case with the Molasses Act, passed in 1733. This law required colonists to pay stiff duties (taxes) on all imports from the French, Spanish, and Dutch West Indies. The purpose was to force the colonists to buy only from the British West Indies. The Molasses Act might have seriously disrupted the triangular trade, because the British Islands could not produce all the sugar and molasses the colonies needed. But the English followed a policy of **salutary neglect,** meaning that they did not try seriously to enforce the law. Top officials at the time believed that the economy of the empire would be better off with less interference. The colonists learned that English laws did not always have to be obeyed.

SECTION REVIEW

1. Identify the following: Eliza Lucas, Navigation Acts, Staple Act, Hat Act.
2. Why was labor scarce in the colonies? What solutions were there to the problem?
3. In what ways did the colonies benefit from the triangular trade?

Indicate which colonies were mainly of English, Scotch-Irish, or Dutch origin. What was the second largest nationality?

4. What were the principles of English mercantilism?
5. How did the English try to control the colonial economy?

6 Culture and Society

The colonies were closely tied to England by far more than trade. When English colonists first came to America, they thought of themselves as English and clung to their English cultural heritage. However, even when they tried, they could not duplicate English society in the New World. The wilderness environment forced the colonists to adapt their habits and attitudes. Colonial culture was also influenced by the Indians and by the large number of immigrants who were not English.

New Population

In the seventeenth century, most colonists came from England. By 1760, however, about two-thirds of the people living in the colonies had been born there. Many people were third- or fourth-generation Americans. The population rose rapidly, partly because of the high birthrate and partly because of a big increase in non-English immigration. Much of the new immigration was due to slavery. By the middle of the eighteenth century, black Africans and their descendants made up about one-half of the population in the South, and almost 10 percent in the North.

In the 1700's, a large number of immigrants from Western Europe came to America. They were fleeing from wars, poverty, and religious persecution, or simply hoping for a new start in life. A large percentage came as indentured servants or redemptioners. The colonies were advertised in glowing terms by proprietors, legislatures, ship captains, and others who wanted to promote colonization. High wages, cheap land, and political and religious freedom were promised. Pennsylvania, because it advertised the most, received the most immigrants.

Among those who came in large numbers were Germans, Scotch-Irish (actually lowland Scots who had settled in Ireland), Scots, French, and Welsh. Jews arrived from Spain, Portugal, and Jamaica. Each group made important contributions to the changing American culture. In a famous essay, a French writer

COLONIAL POPULATION: NATIONAL ORIGIN 1775

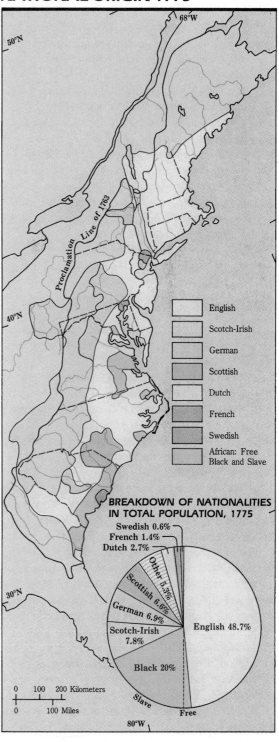

English
Scotch-Irish
German
Scottish
Dutch
French
Swedish
African: Free
Black and Slave

BREAKDOWN OF NATIONALITIES IN TOTAL POPULATION, 1775

Swedish 0.6%
French 1.4%
Dutch 2.7%
Other 5.3%
Scottish 6.6%
German 6.9%
Scotch-Irish 7.8%
English 48.7%
Black 20%
Slave
Free

0   100   200 Kilometers
0   100 Miles

Factors that influence social mobility today include education, skills, and language. Have students compare these with the 17th century.

who lived in the colonies wrote about the resulting mixture of cultures:

> *What then is the American, this new man? He is either a European, or the descendant of a European, hence that strange mixture of blood, which you will find in no other country. I could point out to you a family whose grandfather was an Englishman, whose wife was Dutch, whose son married a French woman, and whose present four sons have now four wives of different nations. He is an American, who leaving behind him all his ancient prejudices and manners, receives new ones from the new mode of life he has embraced, the new government he obeys, and the new rank he holds. . . . Here individuals of all nations are melted into a new race of men, whose labors and posterity will one day cause great changes in the world. . . .*

Social Class

One great difference between colonial and European society was that the colonists had more social mobility. Indeed, many immigrants came to America in order to improve their social position. Except for slaves, social class was not fixed. With luck, skill, and hard work, there was a chance for anyone, even a freed servant, to move up the social ladder. The ease of acquiring land, the high wages paid for skilled labor, and the rapid growth of the country made America a land of opportunity.

Nevertheless, there were class divisions based on wealth, education, and inherited status. Those who had money and power in England usually got a headstart in the New World, too. They received the largest grants of land and were offered positions with political power, as on the governor's council.

In the middle colonies, members of the upper class were wealthy landowners whose large estates were worked by **tenant farmers** (farmers who work someone else's land and pay rent). In the South, the owners of large plantations made up the elite. The fortunes of the upper class in northern cities were founded on trade. Rich merchants owned ships, warehouses, urban real estate, mills, and farms.

In all the colonies the upper class was a small, tightly-knit group that supplied most of the social,

cultural, and political leadership. Upper-class superiority and leadership was generally accepted as natural by those beneath them. This attitude is shown in the autobiography of a young middle-class colonist:

> *We were accustomed to look upon what were called gentle folk, as being of a superior order. For my part, I was quite shy of them, and kept off at a humble distance. A periwig [wig] in those days was a distinguishing badge of gentle folk—and when I saw a man riding the road, near our house, with a wig on, it would alarm my fears and I would ride off as for my life. Such ideas of the difference between gentle and simple were, I believe, universal among all of my rank and age.*

Most colonists belonged to the middle class. Members of this class were mainly small farmers, skilled workers, and small merchants. Although the men in this class had the right to vote, they rarely held important political offices.

The lower class included unskilled workers, tenant farmers, and servants. They seldom owned enough property to qualify them to vote. However, they had at least the hope of improving their lots, a hope that was denied to black slaves.

Kidnapped from their homes in Africa, the slaves were usually shipped first to the West Indies. Because of the crowded, dirty conditions on the ships, many did not survive the trip. Some killed themselves. After being "broken in" on the sugar plantations of the West Indies, they were sent to the mainland colonies. Some worked as household servants or in skilled trades, but most worked in the fields. Although many slaves were treated kindly, there was no escape from the harsh fact that they were, by law, property owned by others.

Most colonists accepted slavery. Some people, however, especially religious groups such as the Quakers and Mennonites, did protest. One of the earliest known protests against slavery was a resolution passed in 1688 by a group of Mennonites:

> *Now, though they are black, we cannot conceive there is more liberty to have them slaves, than to have other white ones. There is a saying, that we should do to all men as we will be done ourselves, making no difference of what generation, descent, or color they are.*

Benjamin Franklin

An outstanding example of the new American was a Yankee who set out at an early age to make his fortune in Philadelphia. Ben Franklin was born in Boston, the fifteenth child of English immigrants. As a youth he learned the printer's trade, but being a person of great curiosity, he dabbled in many other fields. Fascinated by science, he once flew a kite in a thunderstorm in order to learn about electricity. Later he invented the lightning rod. Many other inventions are credited to his name, including the Franklin stove and the Boston rocker.

Although his schooling ended at the age of 10, Franklin continued to read every book he could get. He became an accomplished writer and published the most successful newspaper in the colonies, *The Pennsylvania Gazette*, from 1729 to 1766.

Franklin was most well known for *Poor Richard's Almanac*, which he wrote and published every year. The almanac contained many of his famous sayings such as, "Early to bed and early to rise, makes a man healthy, wealthy, and wise," and "An ounce of prevention is worth a pound of cure." As a respected man of letters, he helped found the University of Pennsylvania. Because of his prestige, Franklin was also called on to help write the Constitution.

Recognition of Franklin's talents was worldwide. In time he served his country as postmaster general, as ambassador to France, and as a diplomatic courier to Europe. The respect he earned from Europeans translated into respect for his homeland.

And those who steal or rob men, and those who buy or purchase them, are they not all alike?

A few freed slaves lived in the colonies. But free blacks were regarded as a class apart, even by lower-class whites.

Religion and Education

Unlike religion in England and other European countries where only one church was legal, religion in the colonies was characterized by a growing tolerance. Although established churches (the Congregational Church of the Puritans in New England and the Anglican Church in the South) continued to exist, their influence weakened over time. Membership was voluntary, and other denominations were also allowed to worship. Catholics and Jews, however, were still discriminated against.

By the early 1700's, religion in the colonies had gone into a decline. Large numbers of people did not belong to any church. This period ended with a vast rekindling of religious faith known as the Great Awakening, which reached its peak around 1740. Ministers such as Jonathan Edwards of Massachusetts and George Whitefield, who came from England, swayed crowds with their vivid, emotional style of preaching.

Whitefield and other preachers appealed for an end to conflict among religious denominations. As a result of the Great Awakening, new branches of the Protestant religion were founded. But the new churches did not claim that all other churches were false. Instead, different churches were regarded as different ways of expressing the same faith. Thus the Great Awakening contributed to the growth of religious tolerance and, along with it, belief in the separation of church and state.

Freedom of Religion

In the 1600's and 1700's, most European countries had state religions. Persecution of religious dissenters was common, and many colonists who came to America sought the freedom to worship in their own way.

However, those who sought religious freedom for themselves were not always willing to grant it to others. The Puritans, for example, left their homes to escape a state religion, the Church of England. Yet one of the first things they did was to set up a government with the church elders functioning as political leaders. Even then, some colonists were dissatisfied with this state of affairs. Roger Williams was one of the first to advocate the separation of church and state.

America was a land of immigrants with many different beliefs, and religious diversity was one reason that separation of church and state gradually became an accepted idea. Americans placed a high value on freedom, and American political leaders used their influence to ensure that all citizens were free from unnecessary restraints. In 1779 Thomas Jefferson wrote a Resolution on Religious Freedom that was adopted by the Virginia state legislature. The resolution said that

no man shall be compelled to frequent or support any religious worship, place, or ministry whatsoever, nor shall be enforced, restrained, molested, or burdened in his body or goods, or shall otherwise suffer, on account of his religious opinions or beliefs; but that all men shall be free to profess, and by argument to maintain, their opinions in matters of religion, and that the same shall in no wise diminish, enlarge, or affect their civil capacities.

A few years after this resolution was adopted, the United States became an independent country, and freedom of religion was one of the principles upon which the nation was founded. The First Amendment to the Constitution stated that

Congress shall make no law respecting an establishment of religion, or prohibiting the free exercise thereof. . . .

The First Amendment protected religious freedom from invasion by the federal government. In 1868 the Fourteenth Amendment extended the guarantees regarding freedom of religion to include protection against state actions.

Over the years the meaning of these amendments has been elaborated by court decisions. In 1878 the Supreme Court decided that religious freedom did not include the right to commit immoral or criminal acts, even though the acts might be sanctioned (approved) by religious teachings.

Between 1938 and 1946, the Court heard several important cases brought to it by a religious group called the Jehovah's Witnesses. Many people resented the Jehovah's Witnesses, and some communities passed laws to restrict the activities of the Witnesses. For example, one city passed a law forbidding the distribution of literature—the Witnesses' chief means of spreading their teachings—without the consent of the city manager. In *Lovell* v. *Griffin* (1938), the Court said that this law was unconstitutional. Other towns tried to tax religious literature. In *Murdock* v. *Pennsylvania*, the Court decided that religious activities may not be taxed.

The fine points of religious freedom continue to be a matter of concern to many Americans. The Supreme Court decided in *Engel* v. *Vitale* (1962) that official school prayers are not constitutional. In recent years, however, a constitutional amendment allowing voluntary school prayer has been proposed. These and other issues demonstrate that the case on freedom of religion will never be completely closed.

QUESTIONS

1. How did the Fourteenth Amendment extend the freedom of religion?
2. Is religious freedom an absolute freedom? Why or why not?

Education was closely related to religion. The first colleges—Harvard, William and Mary, and Yale—were established mainly to train ministers. By the end of the colonial period, nine colleges had been founded, eight of them by churches. At first, the course of study generally imitated that of English colleges. Greek, Latin, Hebrew, logic, ethics, and rhetoric were taught. Later, other subjects such as history, science, French, and German were offered.

In the South, where there were few towns and people lived far apart, young children were usually educated by their parents or by tutors. In the middle colonies, schools were started by various churches. In New England, a new approach to education was taken. As early as 1647, Massachusetts established a public school system. The public schools were financed partly by tuition and partly by taxes.

In all the colonies, schools were mostly for boys. Girls sometimes learned to read and write in **"dame schools,"** which were classes taught by women in their homes. Colleges were for sons of the upper class. Lower- and middle-class boys could receive training by becoming apprentices or indentured servants.

Art and Language

The imitation of things English was common among the colonial upper class, particularly in the middle and southern colonies. London fashions dictated the wearing of wigs, breeches to the knees, high stockings, shoes with silver buckles, and lace on embroidered jackets. All of these clothing items were imported.

Houses and churches were also modeled after styles popular in England. Colonial builders followed plans drawn up from English books. After 1720 the Georgian style was in special favor, with its emphasis on external symmetry, high ceilings, spacious rooms, and lots of windows. Home furnishings such as silver serving dishes, glass goblets, linen tablecloths, and handcarved four-poster beds also came from England. "Whatever goods you send me," George Washington wrote his agent in London, "let them be fashionable."

Slowly the colonists began to develop their own ways of doing things. Building styles had to be modified to suit local conditions. Cabinetmakers began to turn out excellent furniture of their own design. Silversmiths like Paul Revere put their own designs on their products. Colonists found ways of putting beauty into things they made for practical use, such as quilts and guns.

Even the English language changed. Words were picked up from the Indians and from the non-English immigrants. People invented new words and terms, like "creek," "popcorn," and "Indian summer," to describe the new things they found in the New World.

John Peter Zenger, publisher of the New York Weekly Journal, was arrested and thrown into prison for criticizing the Governor of New York. Andrew Hamilton, Zenger's laywer, argued that the publisher had the right to speak and write the truth and to oppose arbitrary power. What was the outcome of the trial?

50   THE ENGLISH COLONIES

Discuss the importance of a free press to a democratic society.

Ideas of Freedom

By 1765 there were 22 newspapers in the colonies, publishing reports from abroad, debates of colonial assemblies, and accounts of local affairs. The first step toward the principle of freedom of the press was taken in 1735 in a case involving a printer named John Peter Zenger.

Zenger had published a criticism of New York's governor. For this he was hauled into court and charged with **libel** (publication of a false statement with intent to do harm). His lawyer, Andrew Hamilton, successfully appealed to the jury with the claim that what Zenger had printed was the truth, and therefore not libel. Afterwards, colonial newspapers had more freedom to criticize the government. Later, when the power of the press was increasingly turned on English governors and on English laws, the case of John Peter Zenger took on increasing significance in regard to freedom.

The Zenger case is an example of the way colonial Americans valued freedom of thought and action. The ideal of a free press went hand in hand with other ideals: religious tolerance, free public education, representative self-government, the blurring of class distinctions. All were elements of **democracy,** or government in which the people have supreme authority. All had their beginnings in colonial society.

SECTION REVIEW

1. Why did the population of the English colonies increase rapidly during the eighteenth century?
2. How did the Great Awakening affect religion in the colonies?
3. How did the Zenger case influence freedom of the press?

CHAPTER **2**   REVIEW

SUMMARY

1. The first permanent English settlement in the New World was Jamestown, Virginia, founded by the London Company.
2. Massachusetts was first settled by people who were fleeing religious persecution in England.
3. Religious dissension in Massachusetts led to the founding of settlements in Rhode Island and Connecticut.
4. As the colonies grew, friction mounted between the colonists and the Indians.
5. Most proprietary colonies were founded by people to whom the Crown owed debts or favors.
6. Colonial government was modeled on English government.
7. The colonial economy was mainly agricultural with some industry and commerce.
8. By the eighteenth century regional differences among the New England colonies, the middle colonies, and the southern colonies had already developed.
9. English policy in regard to the colonies was based on the philosophy of mercantilism.
10. By the mid-eighteenth century the colonies had developed a distinct cultural identity character-ized by elements of democracy.

VOCABULARY

cash crop	constitution	power of the purse	mercantilism
headright	proprietary colony	indentured servants	balance of trade
royal colony	Crown	redemptioners	enumerated commodities
state religion	unwritten constitution	apprentice	bounty
predestination	suffrage	subsistence level	salutary neglect
elect	direct representation	triangular trade	tenant farmer
work ethic	virtual representation	barter	dame schools
separation of	charter colony	bills of exchange	libel
church and state			democracy

This "Using Skills" activity is a continuation of the skill in Chapter 1 and is further developed in Chapter 3 and in the Historian's Craft.

REVIEW QUESTIONS

1. For what reasons did people come to the English colonies?
2. What were the three types of colonies founded by the English? How did they differ?
3. What were the similarities and differences among the New England, middle, and southern colonies?
4. Why did conflict develop between the Indians and the colonists?
5. What was the economic relationship between England and the colonies? How did this affect the colonial economy?
6. What were the social classes in the colonies?
7. Why did slavery become established in the English colonies?
8. In what ways did the English heritage affect colonial life?

DISCUSSION

1. What elements from colonial times helped to shape the basic principles underlying the American political system?
2. Do you think that the principles of mercantilism were reasonable or fair? Why or why not?
3. If you had lived in Puritan Massachusetts, would you have followed one of the dissenters who left? Why or why not?
4. What factors contributed to social mobility in the colonies? What factors restricted it?

USING MAPS

Refer to the map on page 43 and answer the following questions:
1. Which North American ports appear to be most active in the triangular trade?
2. How far did manufactured goods have to be shipped to reach the southern colonies?
3. What is the latitude of the northernmost colonial port on the triangular trade route?
4. What port lies at about 38° north latitude and 9° west longitude?
5. What kinds of products did the American colonies send to England?

USING SKILLS

Study the picture on page 33, read the caption, and answer the following questions:
1. How many men, how many women, and how many children are there in the picture?
2. What are the men, women, and children in the picture doing?
3. Do the women seem to be involved in the signing of the document? Why or why not?

1	Rivalry in North America	53
2	Changes in British Colonial Policy	55
3	Colonial Protest	57
4	The Road to Revolution	59
5	From Protest to War	62
6	Moving Toward Separation	66
7	Winning Independence	68

THE STRUGGLE FOR INDEPENDENCE

We cannot be happy without being free; we cannot be free without being secure in our property; we cannot be secure in our property if, without our consent, others may, as by right, take it away; taxes imposed by Parliament do thus take it away.

JOHN DICKINSON

In the seventeenth and eighteenth centuries, England and France emerged as the world's most powerful nations. Between the 1680's and 1750's the two countries engaged in a struggle for the domination of Europe and the control of an overseas empire. During the same time period, England and France fought four major wars in various parts of the globe.

The last of these wars was known in Europe as the Seven Years' War and in North America as the French and Indian War.[1] After peace was concluded, England was free to turn its attention to its North American colonies. However, changes in British colonial policy met with resistance and led, ultimately, to rebellion.

1 Rivalry in North America

The struggle between England and France in North America stemmed from competition for land in the interior of the continent. The French, basing their claims on early explorations, had established a number of footholds throughout the territory. Most importantly, the French controlled the St. Lawrence River from Montreal to Quebec. They also controlled New Orleans, and had various outposts along the Mississippi River and its branches and along the Great Lakes. As the English colonists began moving westward, they came into conflict with the French, and war broke out.

---

[1] It was known in North America as the French and Indian War because of Indian involvement in the hostilities. Though both the British and the French had Indian allies, the larger number of Indians supported the French. Note also that hostilities broke out in North America nearly two years before the Seven Years' War erupted in Europe. Some military historians view that war as the first truly world war since hostilities occurred around the world—in North America, Europe, and Asia (India).

Origins of the French and Indian War

The French and Indian War began in the Ohio Valley. By 1750 much interest in the area had been generated among English colonists. This was due, in part, to the formation of a number of land companies. One of these companies was the Ohio Company, organized in 1747. Its members hoped to develop trade with the Indians in the Ohio Valley and to sell land for settlement. In this way the company would make a profit, and England's hold on the area would be strengthened. In 1749 the British government granted the company 200,000 acres (80,000 hectares) of land along the Ohio River, and the way was prepared for an influx of settlers.

To prevent English intrusion into the Ohio Valley, the French, who also claimed the area, began to build a series of forts between Lake Erie and the Allegheny River. The British government, in retaliation, instructed colonial governors to use force if necessary to stop the French. Acting on these instructions, Governor Robert Dinwiddie of Virginia sent George Washington, then 21 years old, to warn the French against trespassing on British territory. The French, however, refused to withdraw. Washington, along with the small party that had accompanied him, returned to Virginia.

Dinwiddie responded to news of the French rebuff by sending out a small work detail to build a fort at the junction of the Monongahela and Allegheny Rivers, commonly called "the forks of the Ohio." In February 1754, Washington was sent with a larger force to occupy the post. Before Washington could arrive, however, the French seized the site and began building Fort Duquesne (Pittsburgh, Pennsylvania).

In the meantime, Washington continued moving toward his destination. On May 28, 1754, near Great Meadows (Uniontown, Pennsylvania), Washington's

The fact that the English colonies had no unified organization was a disadvantage in the war with the French. People living in eastern areas felt that people on the frontier should be responsible for their own defense.

Braddock's forces had to cut a road through the wilderness in order to move the cannon.

force surprised and defeated a small party of French. This was the first battle of the French and Indian War.

The Albany Congress

To counter the threat of the French and their Indian allies in the West, the British advised the colonies to make a treaty with the Iroquois. As a result, delegates from the New England colonies, as well as Pennsylvania, Maryland, and New York, met with representatives of the Six Nations at Albany, New York, in June 1754. Talks with the Iroquois did not, at that time, produce the desired treaty. However, the delegates did approve a plan for intercolonial union.

This Albany Plan of Union, formulated by Benjamin Franklin, was designed to unite the colonies under a single government. That government would have authority over defense, westward expansion, and Indian affairs, and would support itself by levying taxes. The individual colonies would still have a certain amount of freedom on local issues. Although approved by the Congress, the Albany Plan was rejected by most of the colonial governments.

Early Disasters for the British

While the delegates were meeting at Albany, George Washington was in western Pennsylvania,

Benjamin Franklin's "Join or Die" is considered the first American political cartoon. Appearing in the *Pennsylvania Gazette,* Franklin's own newspaper, it was used to support the Albany Plan of Union. What does the cartoon suggest?

preparing for a French counterattack. He ordered his troops to build a stockade near the site of the recent battle. On July 3, the newly constructed Fort Necessity was besieged by 500 French soldiers and 400 Indians. Washington and the troops were soon forced to surrender.

News of the French victory caused England to act. Early in 1755, although England and France were officially at peace, the British sent General Edward Braddock with two regiments of soldiers to Virginia. Accompanied by a colonial force under Washington, Braddock's troops left Virginia and marched toward Fort Duquesne. On July 9, as they were approaching the fort, the French launched an ambush. Braddock's force was surrounded and defeated. The red-coated British soldiers, unaccustomed to fighting in the wilderness, suffered over 900 casualties. Braddock, mortally wounded, murmured as he died, "We shall know better how to deal with them another time."

British Victories Under Pitt

Following Braddock's defeat, the British in North America suffered a series of reverses. England's formal declaration of war against France in May 1756 did little to alter the situation. The fortunes of war began to change, however, when William Pitt became prime minister of England in June 1757. British policy had focused on defeating the French in Europe, while carrying on a limited war in America. Pitt, however, was determined to expel the French from the New World.

Pitt replaced incompetent military leaders with talented younger officers and sent reinforcements to America. This left much of the fighting in Europe to England's allies, whom he subsidized to ensure their triumph over the French. Pitt encouraged colonial enlistments by promising to reimburse the colonies for money spent to raise and equip troops.

Pitt's strategy was successful. In July 1758, the British took Louisbourg, which guarded the entrance of the St. Lawrence River. Because of its location, Louisbourg was the most important French fortress in Canada, and its capture marked the turning point of the war. In November, the French abandoned and destroyed Fort Duquesne, which was later rebuilt as Fort Pitt by the British. In 1759, the British experienced continued success. In July, they took

Historian Francis Parkman wrote that "the fall of Quebec began the history of the United States." Have students discuss this statement.

Note that at this time the sugar-producing islands were more important to European powers than vast expanses of unsettled land.

Quebec, the capital of New France, was considered unassailable, situated as it was on a great cliff. However, in a daring maneuver engineered by General Wolfe, 4000 British troops scaled the cliff and defeated French forces in a short but bloody battle. Why was the Battle of Quebec significant?

Fort Niagara and forced the French to abandon Ticonderoga and Crown Point.

About the same time, a British army under General James Wolfe sailed up the St. Lawrence toward Quebec, located on a bluff high above the river. On September 13, under the cover of darkness, Wolfe's troops scaled the cliffs below the city. By early morning, the British had reached the Plains of Abraham west of Quebec. The French, under the Marquis de Montcalm, advanced to meet Wolfe's force. In the battle that followed the British were victorious, but both Wolfe and Montcalm were killed. A few days later, the city surrendered to the British. Although fighting continued for several years, the fall of Quebec signalled the end of the French Empire in the New World.

The Treaty of Paris, 1763

The Seven Years' War in Europe and the French and Indian War in North America ended in 1763 with the signing of the Treaty of Paris. Under the terms of this treaty, France was permitted to keep its sugar-producing islands in the West Indies, but it was forced to give up Canada and its lands east of the Mississippi River to Great Britain. Spain, which had entered the war on the side of France in 1762, gave up Florida to Great Britain. In return, Spain received French lands west of the Mississippi River as well as the port of New Orleans.

SECTION REVIEW

1. Identify the following: Ohio Company, Robert Dinwiddie, Great Meadows, General Edward Braddock, Louisbourg, General James Wolfe, Marquis de Montcalm.
2. How did the French respond to the English intrusions into the Ohio Valley?
3. Why was the Albany Plan proposed?
4. What steps did William Pitt take to ensure British victory in North America?
5. What was the significance of the fall of Quebec?
6. What were the terms of the Treaty of Paris, 1763?

2 Changes in British Policy

With the end of the French and Indian War, England turned its attention to America. Victory had brought Great Britain vast new territories but also a number of new problems. One of these was the disposal of western lands. In addition, the government had to cope with the huge debt left by the war. British attempts to solve these problems drove a

The Treaty of Paris made England the most powerful nation in the world, as both France and Spain had been defeated. The new policies in the colonies were intended to consolidate England's political empire.

wedge between England and its American colonies that eventually split the two apart.

Western Lands

British officials directed their attention first to the settlement of the West. In addition to dealing with varying colonial claims to the territory, the British government faced the problem of Indian resistance to westward expansion. The Indians had grown increasingly restive as more and more colonists moved into western lands after the fall of New France.

Things came to a head in the spring of 1763, when Pontiac, an Ottawa chief, led a rebellion against the British. Before the truce was signed, Pontiac's warriors, who were from many different Indian nations, had captured nearly every British outpost west of Fort Niagara. Hundreds of settlers were slain, and many were forced to abandon their homes.

Pontiac's Rebellion forced the British government to act. England's attempted solution was the Proclamation of 1763, which established the crest of the Appalachians as a boundary line between white and Indian lands. All whites living west of this line were required to "remove themselves." Although this was a temporary measure, the colonists resented both the line and the presence of British troops sent to enforce the new law.

Raising Revenue

The British government's attempts to raise revenue in the colonies caused even greater resentment. Faced with a debt that had doubled since 1754, George Grenville, England's chancellor of the exchequer, decided that the colonies should help pay the costs of their own administration and defense.

One of the first steps Grenville took was an investigation of the colonial customs service. This investigation revealed that England's trade laws had produced much less revenue than expected—chiefly because the colonists were evading customs duties by smuggling, bribery, or both. In fact, the colonial customs service was costing the British government four times what the officials collected.

Grenville decided to reorganize the customs service and enforce existing trade laws. He also proposed new measures. In April 1764, under his leadership, Parliament passed the Sugar Act, which reduced the 1733 duty on molasses by one-half. The British government hoped that by lowering the duty the colonists would be less likely to evade payment. The act, however, levied new and higher duties on other products.

The Sugar Act was intended not only to regulate trade but also to raise money. This was a departure from previous British policy, for earlier mercantile laws had been intended simply to control colonial trade.

Parliament also passed the Currency Act in April 1764. This act prohibited the American colonies from issuing paper money as **legal tender,** or money that is legally valid for the payment of debts. Before this bill was passed, colonial assemblies had begun to print their own money to relieve the shortage of **specie,** or money in coin. This shortage existed because the colonists imported more than they exported. When the British accepted paper currency they were losing money because the paper money was of less value than specie.

In March 1765, Parliament passed the Stamp Act, levying the first **direct tax** on the American colonies. Rather than being included in the price of goods, this type of tax is paid directly to the government. Similar to one in effect in England, the Stamp Act called for taxes on all legal documents as well as almanacs, newspapers, playing cards, and dice. All of these articles had to bear a stamp indicating that the tax had been paid.

In May 1765, as a final part of Grenville's program, Parliament passed the Quartering Act. This bill was intended to defray the cost of maintaining troops in America by requiring the colonies to **quarter,** or house, British troops.

SECTION REVIEW

1. Identify the following: Pontiac, George Grenville, Sugar Act, Currency Act, Stamp Act, Quartering Act.
2. What problems did the British face after the French and Indian War?
3. What was the British response to the conflict between Indians and settlers in the western lands?
4. What steps did the British take to make the colonies help pay the costs of colonial administration and defense?

Compare lands claimed by the French with areas traveled by French explorers. Compare this map with one on p. 13.

Have students develop time lines to follow the events leading up to war.

EUROPEAN LAND CLAIMS IN NORTH AMERICA

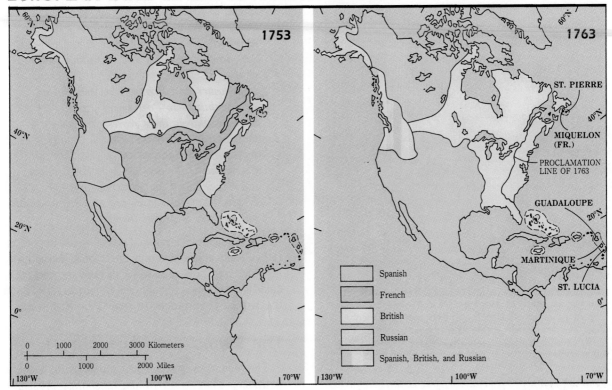

1753

1763

ST. PIERRE

MIQUELON (FR.)

PROCLAMATION LINE OF 1763

GUADALOUPE

MARTINIQUE

ST. LUCIA

- Spanish
- French
- British
- Russian
- Spanish, British, and Russian

0   1000   2000   3000 Kilometers
0   1000   2000 Miles

3 Colonial Protest

All of Grenville's measures caused resentment in the colonies. But the measure most bitterly opposed was the Stamp Act, which was scheduled to go into effect November 1, 1765. The colonists objected to this measure because Parliament, in which they had no representatives, had taxed them without their consent. In so doing, Parliament, from the colonists' view, had denied them their rights as English citizens.

The Virginia Resolutions

One of the first public protests took place in Virginia in May 1765. When the House of Burgesses met to consider the Stamp Act, Patrick Henry introduced the Virginia Resolutions, protesting Parliament's action. Henry claimed that the House of Burgesses had "the only exclusive right and power to lay taxes" upon Virginians. The Burgesses approved the principle of "no taxation without representation."

However, they rejected the more extreme of Henry's resolutions, one of which said that anyone who disagreed with them would "be deemed an enemy to his Majesty's Colony."

Influenced by newspaper accounts of Virginia's move, other colonies passed similar resolutions. In June, hoping to bring about a repeal of the Stamp Act through joint action, Massachusetts invited delegates from all the colonies to meet in New York City in October. The colonists intended to present their case to the king and Parliament, and to ask for relief.

Violence in the Colonies

Some Americans, too impatient to wait for repeal, used force to prevent the Stamp Act from taking effect. During the summer of 1765, organizations known as the Sons of Liberty were formed throughout the colonies in opposition to the Stamp Act. At first content to simply voice their protests, these organizations soon turned to violence. By the

The Virginia House of Burgesses met in May 1765 to express discontent with the Stamp Act. Inspired by Patrick Henry, the delegates denounced taxation without representation. In what other ways did colonists protest the Stamp Act?

time the Stamp Act took effect, mob action had forced most colonial stamp distributors to resign.

The Sons of Liberty were especially active in Boston, where they were led by Samuel Adams and John Hancock. In August, mobs looted the homes of Andrew Oliver, the local stamp agent, and Lieutenant Governor Thomas Hutchinson.

The Stamp Act Congress

Meanwhile, nine colonies responded to Massachusetts' invitation and sent delegates to the Stamp Act Congress in New York. In their "Declaration of Rights and Grievances," the Congress resolved that Parliament had the right to make laws for the colonies but did not have the right to tax them. This was because the colonies were not represented in the House of Commons.

The delegates rejected the idea of virtual representation. This idea was put forth by English leaders, who thought that the colonies should pay for the protection given to them by the British government. Soame Jenyns, a member of Parliament, stated England's position on the issue:

Why does not this imaginary representation extend to America, as well as over the whole island of Great Britain? If it can travel three hundred miles, why not three thousand? If it can jump over rivers and mountains, why cannot it sail over the ocean? If the towns of Manchester and Birmingham sending no representatives to Parliament, are notwithstanding there represented, why are not the cities of Albany and Boston equally represented in that assembly? Are they not Englishmen? Or are they only Englishmen when they solicit for protection, but not Englishmen when taxes are required to enable this country to protect them?

The delegates did not just reject virtual representation. They stated that only the colonial legislatures, in which the colonists were directly represented, could impose taxes. Finally, the Congress called upon the British government to repeal the Stamp Act.

The Stamp Act Repealed

The colonists were not content with peaceful petitions. They tried to use economic pressures against Parliament. Colonial merchants signed **nonimportation agreements,** which banned the importing of British goods. This hurt England's trade with the colonies, and British merchants began to pressure Parliament for repeal.

The case for repeal was made stronger by the fact that, when the act finally went into effect in November, the colonists refused to buy stamps. In March 1766, Parliament repealed the act. Amidst the general rejoicing, however, the colonists failed to notice the Declaratory Act, passed on the same day as the repeal measure. This act stated that the king and Parliament "had full power and authority to make laws and statutes of sufficient force and validity to bind the colonies and the people of America . . . in all cases whatsoever."

SECTION REVIEW

1. Identify the following: Patrick Henry, Virginia Resolutions, Sons of Liberty, Samuel Adams, Declaratory Act.
2. What did the phrase "no taxation without representation" mean?

3. What influence did the Virginia Resolutions have on the colonies?
4. What action was taken by the Stamp Act Congress?
5. Why was the Stamp Act repealed?

4 The Road to Revolution

The passage of the Declaratory Act seemed to indicate that although Parliament had repealed the Stamp Act, it did not intend to relinquish its authority in the colonies. Before long, the colonists received proof that England had not given up.

The Townshend Acts

When Charles Townshend became chancellor of the exchequer in August 1766, he faced the same financial problems that Grenville had. The size of England's debt, along with a severe depression and demands for reduced taxes at home, made Townshend determined to raise additional revenue.

In June 1767, under his leadership, Parliament passed the Townshend Acts. These acts levied duties on colonial imports of glass, lead, paper, paint, and tea, and established a Board of Customs Commissioners at Boston. The import duties were intended to raise money rather than control trade. The money collected was to be used to help pay for colonial defense and administration. The Townshend Acts also legalized the hated **writs of assistance,** or search warrants, that had been used by customs officials to look for smuggled goods.

These acts were greeted with a wave of anger in America. Merchants signed new nonimportation agreements. Colonial assemblies passed resolutions denouncing the acts and denying Parliament's right to tax the colonies. Mobs again began destroying property and giving trouble to British officials.

The worst incident of violence took place in Boston. Colonists in that city often had conflicts with British soldiers stationed there to protect customs officials. On March 5, 1770, an angry crowd attacked a small detachment of soldiers. As the crowd closed in, the soldiers fired, and five colonists were killed.

Bostonians resented the regiments of British regulars stationed in their city. Colonists often gathered to jeer and taunt the "redcoats." The bitter feelings erupted in bloodshed on March 5, 1770, when British soliders fired into a crowd, killing five. Crispus Attucks, a former slave, was one of the casualties. How did the colonists react to the Boston Massacre?

The tea trade had fallen off partly because of colonial nonimportation agreements.

They were the first to die in the conflict between England and the colonies. This incident, known as the Boston Massacre, was used mainly to inflame the people of Massachusetts against the British.[2]

Meanwhile, a movement to repeal the Townshend Acts was gaining momentum in England. British merchants, hurt by declining trade with the colonies, feared that the Townshend Acts would encourage colonial manufacturing. These merchants, backed by England's new prime minister, Lord Frederick North, pressured Parliament for repeal. Finally, in April 1770, Parliament passed a bill withdrawing all the Townshend duties except the one on tea. This duty was kept as a symbol of Parliament's power to tax the colonies. As George III declared, one tax was needed "to keep the right."

Continued Unrest

Although relations between England and the colonies improved after the repeal of the Townshend Acts, occasional outbreaks of violence testified to continued colonial unrest. In June 1772, colonists seized and burned the *Gaspee,* a British ship that had run aground near Providence, Rhode Island.

The *Gaspee* had been sent to patrol American waters in search of smugglers. Its commander and crew had antagonized colonists in the area and, when the British ship was beached, the colonists took their revenge. The British government ordered that when the guilty parties were arrested they would be tried in England rather than in the colonial courts. This order alarmed the colonists, who saw it as a threat to local self-rule. The case, however, was never tried, as the commissioners appointed to investigate the matter were unable to compile enough evidence.

About the same time as the *Gaspee* incident, the British government announced that it intended to pay the salaries of royal officials in Massachusetts. These officials had formerly been paid by the colonial assembly. The British government's action would free the officials from the assembly's control.

To discuss this latest threat to colonial freedom, Sam Adams called for a Boston town meeting, which

---

[2] Nine of the British soldiers were tried for murder by colonial authorities. The defense was undertaken by American lawyers John Adams and Josiah Quincy. Two of the soldiers were found guilty of manslaughter.

met in November 1772. At this meeting, Adams secured the appointment of a Committee of Correspondence to communicate with other towns in Massachusetts. Soon, the idea spread to other colonies. The committee system of correspondence was not new, but its revival furthered the spirit of intercolonial cooperation.

The Tea Act

While the colonies were laying the foundations for union, England was facing a serious problem regarding the East India Company. This immense trading company, so important to England's economy, was close to bankruptcy. The situation was partly the result of British trade restrictions, which required the company to sell tea, its major export, to middlemen rather than directly to the colonies. This made the cost of the product prohibitive for most people in the colonies. As a result, the company was burdened with 17,000,000 pounds (1,530,000 kilograms) of surplus tea.

To put the company back on a sound basis, Parliament passed the Tea Act in May 1773. Under the provisions of this act, the company could export tea directly to the colonies. By eliminating the middlemen's profits, the company would be able to lower its prices, and undersell even the colonial smuggler. Although the colonists would still have to pay the Townshend duty, tea would be cheaper than ever before. After the Tea Act was passed, the East India Company authorized the shipment of 500,000 pounds (225,000 kilograms) of tea to the American colonies.

Opposition to the Tea Act

The passage of the Tea Act stimulated renewed opposition to British colonial policy. Merchants in the colonies were angered at the East India Company's **monopoly,** or exclusive control of trade. They felt that the monopoly was a dangerous precedent and predicted that merchants in other trades would soon suffer the same fate. Even colonial consumers, who would benefit from the lower prices, were hostile. The colonists were still opposed to Parliamentary taxation, and payment of the tea duty would be a tacit admission of England's right to tax the colonies. The

Nonimportation agreements would be ineffective against the Tea Act because the East India Company was allowed to do its own importing.

Have students debate the moderate versus the radical position.

aroused colonists declared a **boycott,** or buyer's strike. In all the colonies except Massachusetts, the tea shipments were either returned to England or stored in government warehouses.

In Boston, however, Governor Thomas Hutchinson ordered the tea unloaded for sale. The Sons of Liberty responded immediately. On the night of December 16, 1773, a group of them disguised as Indians boarded the East India ships in the harbor and dumped 342 chests of tea into the water. This incident, known as the Boston Tea Party, was imitated in other colonies.

The Intolerable Acts

The British government viewed the Boston Tea Party as a "wanton and unprovoked insult." Determined to force the colonies into submission, British officials decided to make an example of Massachusetts. In the spring of 1774, Parliament passed the Coercive Acts, known as the Intolerable Acts in the colonies. The Boston Port Act closed the port of Boston until the colonists had paid for the tea. The Massachusetts Government Act provided that the governor's council was to be chosen by the king rather than the Massachusetts assembly. In addition, town meetings were to be held but once a year and only with the permission of the governor, who was also given the power to appoint and remove various colonial officials. The Administration of Justice Act stated that British officials who committed capital crimes in the line of duty could be tried in England. A new Quartering Act legalized the quartering of troops in private homes.

The Quebec Act, passed at the same time as the Intolerable Acts, further angered the colonists. This act set up a permanent government for Quebec and granted religious freedom to French Catholics. The most objectionable provision of this act was one that annexed to Quebec the area west of the Appalachians and north of the Ohio River. This provision ignored colonial claims to the region.

England's plan to force the colonies into submission failed. The Intolerable Acts only increased the colonists' determination to defend their liberties. Although the colonies had, in the past, found it difficult to work together, they now saw the need for united action against Great Britain.

Groups of colonists, calling themselves the Sons of Liberty, made life so miserable for British customs officials that many resigned. In what other ways did patriotic societies such as the Sons of Liberty protest British rule?

The First Continental Congress

In September 1774, the First Continental Congress met at Philadelphia. All of the colonies except Georgia sent representatives.[3] Shortly after the delegates arrived, they approved the Suffolk Resolves, drawn up by the people of Suffolk County, Massachusetts. These Resolves called upon the people to disobey the Intolerable Acts and to prepare to defend themselves in case of attack.

In Congress the **moderates** (those who favored limited change), led by Joseph Galloway of Pennsylvania, opposed this endorsement of Massachusetts' action. They felt that it might end the possibility of reconciliation with Great Britain. So, hoping to offset the Suffolk Resolves, the moderates offered a proposal to unify the colonies under British authority. This proposal, however, was defeated by the **radicals** (those who favored extreme change), led by Sam Adams. They felt Parliament had no authority of any kind in the colonies.

[3] Georgia was prevented from doing so by its royal governor.

The range of rifles at this time was not more than 70 yards. Point out the close contact between enemy lines in the picture of the Battle of Lexington.

Although the moderates and the radicals were divided over the question of Parliament's authority in the colonies, they joined together on October 14 to approve the Declaration and Resolves. This declaration denounced the Intolerable Acts, as well as other oppressive measures, and demanded their repeal. The delegates pledged to end trade with Great Britain until Parliament complied. To make sure this pledge was kept, the Continental Association was formed. On October 26, Congress adjourned. The members agreed to meet again in May 1775, if by that time American grievances had not been redressed.

SECTION REVIEW

1. Identify the following: Townshend Acts, Boston Massacre, *Gaspee,* Committee of Correspondence, Quebec Act, Joseph Galloway, Declaration of Rights and Resolves.
2. What was the significance of the Declaratory Act?
3. Why did Parliament pass the Tea Act?
4. How did the colonists respond to the passage of the Tea Act?
5. What was the British reaction to the Boston Tea Party?
6. How did the radicals and the moderates differ at the First Continental Congress?

---

5 From Protest to War

Although Congress' declaration stressed the colonies' loyalty to the king, England was in no mood for conciliatory measures. British officials, afraid that the colonies were moving toward independence, were determined to make them submit to Parliamentary authority. Meanwhile, the colonists were preparing to defend their rights. The stage was set for **revolution** (the overthrow of an established government or political system).

In this engraving, British regulars open fire on retreating militiamen at the Battle of Lexington. No one knows who fired the first shot, but the Battle of Lexington stands as the first battle of the American Revolution. How were the minutemen alerted that the British troops were approaching?

Deborah Sampson

Born in 1760 in Plympton, Massachusetts, Deborah Sampson was a direct descendant of Pilgrims John Alden and Miles Standish. But a Mayflower pedigree was no guarantee against poverty. When Sampson was still a very young child, she was "bound out" (indentured) as a servant to a farmer's family. She proved to be a diligent and conscientious worker, achieving great skill in spinning and weaving. Because of her accomplishments, she won the love and respect of her employers and was raised as a beloved sister among their ten sons.

As a teenager she watched her foster brothers and their friends go off to the Revolutionary War. Moved by a spirit of adventure, she disguised herself as a boy and attempted to enlist. She was soon discovered and sent home. Undaunted, she traveled to a town where she was a stranger and tried again. This time she was successful.

After fighting in several battles, Sampson was wounded, but by her sheer courage and determination went undiscovered and treated the wound herself. Not long after this, she became ill while on sentry duty. During her hospitalization her ruse was discovered. Both shocked and impressed by this courageous young woman, the doctor in charge returned her personally to her aunt's family in Sharon, Massachusetts.

Sampson became a respected member of the community and married a farmer, Samuel Gannett. Caught in the postwar depression, the Gannetts had to struggle to support their young family. Sampson became a lecturer, traveling around the country telling of her by-now-famous escapades. Later she was awarded a pension by the United States government.

Lexington and Concord

The revolution began in Massachusetts. In April 1775, General Thomas Gage, who had replaced Thomas Hutchinson as governor of Massachusetts, received instructions to take the offensive against the rebellious colonists. He sent 700 British soldiers under Lieutenant Colonel Francis Smith to destroy the colonists' military supplies, stored at Concord.

Word of Gage's plans spread, and before the British left Boston, Paul Revere and William Dawes were on their way to warn the countryside. When Revere reached Lexington, which was five miles (eight kilometers) from Concord, he warned John Hancock and Samuel Adams that Gage planned to arrest them. Revere's warning allowed the pair to escape.

At dawn on April 19, when the British reached Lexington, they were met by a small force of 70 **minutemen,** or militia members ready to take the field at a moment's notice. Major John Pitcairn, who led the British advance units, ordered the Americans to disperse. However, just as the Americans were beginning to break up, a shot was fired. Although the source of the shot was unknown, the British soldiers directed a volley of musketfire into the departing militia. Eight Americans were killed, and ten were wounded.

This skirmish only temporarily delayed the British, who continued their march to Concord. They entered the village without resistance and destroyed the few military supplies that the forewarned Americans had not removed. Meanwhile, more and more **Patriots,** or those colonists who supported the idea of independence, were moving into the area. Finally, late in the morning, a force of about 300 Americans attacked a small party of British at Concord's North Bridge, inflicting 14 casualties. This action was made

Arnold and his family were not well treated in England. It is said that before he died he repented and asked to be buried in American uniform.

THE REVOLUTION BEGINS

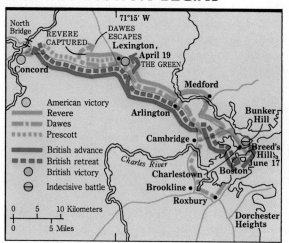

famous by Ralph Waldo Emerson in his poem entitled "Concord Hymn":

> *By the rude bridge that arched the flood,*
> *Their flag to April's breeze unfurled,*
> *Here once the embattled farmers stood,*
> *And fired the shot heard round the world.*

By the time the British began their retreat to Boston, the countryside was swarming with militia. On the return march, Americans fired at the retreating force from behind trees, rocks, and stone walls. One British soldier recorded the following in his diary:

> *They were all lined with people who kept an incessant fire upon us, as we did upon them, but not with the same advantage, for they were so concealed there was hardly any seeing them. In this way we marched between nine and ten miles, their number increasing from all parts while ours was reducing by deaths, wounds, and fatigue; and we were totally surrounded with such an incessant fire as it is impossible to conceive; our ammunition was likewise near expended.*

Despite reinforcements at Lexington, the retreat turned into a rout. After the British reached Boston, the militia closed in on the city and began a siege that was to last until March 1776. Before long, other colonies were sending troops to the colonial headquarters at Cambridge. Although it would be over a

year until independence was declared, the American Revolution had begun.

The Fall of Ticonderoga

Shortly after Lexington and Concord, Benedict Arnold, a captain in the Connecticut militia, was authorized to raise a force of 400 to seize Fort Ticonderoga on Lake Champlain. Ticonderoga was not only strategically located, but was rich in military supplies. Arnold learned that Ethan Allen was also mounting an expedition in Vermont to attack the fort. Arnold joined with Allen's force, known as the Green Mountain Boys, and together they caught the British by surprise. The garrison surrendered on May 10, 1775.[4]

The Second Continental Congress

On the same day that Fort Ticonderoga fell, the Second Continental Congress met at Philadelphia. All of the colonies sent delegates except Georgia, which was not officially represented for several months. This Congress assumed the leadership of the American cause and acted as the country's first central government.

Shortly after convening, the delegates resolved to put the colonies in a state of defense. They took responsibility for the siege on Boston, ordered the militia transformed into the Continental Army, and named George Washington its commander-in-chief.

Although the Congress was assuming the powers of an independent government, the delegates still did not intend to form an independent country. Most simply desired greater liberty within the British Empire. Only the radicals, led by Samuel and John Adams, favored complete independence at this time. The moderates, now led by John Dickinson of Pennsylvania, still hoped for reconciliation with Great Britain.

On July 5, in a last attempt to negotiate with Great Britain, Congress approved the Olive Branch Petition. This petition asked George III to prevent further

---

[4] Later, Arnold conspired to surrender the key fort of West Point to the British. He was rewarded with a commission as a brigadier general in the British army, and led British raids against the Americans in Virginia and Connecticut. After the war, he went to England.

hostile actions against the colonies and urged him to help restore harmony. The next day, in a "Declaration of the Causes and Necessities of Taking Up Arms," the delegates stated that the American people had been offered two alternatives: unconditional submission to tyranny or resistance by force. In choosing the latter, the delegates said, the colonists had wanted only to force British recognition of their rights, not to establish independence.

Even at this date, the colonists might have remained in the British Empire if Parliament had repealed the Intolerable Acts and confined its legislation to the regulation of trade. However, the king refused to receive the Olive Branch Petition and declared the colonies to be in an open state of rebellion. England prepared for full-scale war.

The Battle of Bunker Hill

While the Second Continental Congress was making a last attempt at reconciliation with England, American and British soldiers were engaged in heavy fighting around Boston. During May, both sides had increased their strength. At the end of the month, Generals Sir William Howe, Sir Henry Clinton, and John Burgoyne arrived with additional troops to assist Gage. By mid-June, there were about 6500 British and 10,000 Americans in the area.

About this time, the Americans learned that Gage intended to occupy Dorchester Heights, overlooking Boston on the south. From this position, most of the city and its harbor would be within range of British guns. The Americans decided upon an immediate countermeasure. On the night of June 16, colonial militia moved to the Charlestown peninsula and began to fortify Breed's Hill, which overlooked Boston on the north. At dawn the next day, the British discovered this maneuver, and Gage decided to attack.

In the ensuing action, mistakenly called the Battle of Bunker Hill, the colonists repelled two frontal assaults with devastating results. However, when they ran out of ammunition, the colonists were forced to retreat to Bunker Hill and then to the mainland. This left the entire Charlestown peninsula in British hands. The British had achieved victory, but at a cost of 1054 casualties. "This success," General Howe wrote afterwards, "is too dearly bought." General Clinton added that "another such would have ruined us."

The Battle of Bunker Hill, actually fought on Breed's Hill, was the first major conflict of the American Revolution. Although the British managed to drive off the American troops, the victory was costly. How did the Americans finally regain control of Boston?

Raising an army meant that the colonies had to set up means for recruiting, paying, training, supplying, and transporting personnel. The expenses strained the abilities of the colonies.

Like many other soldiers' wives, Mary Ludwig Hays had joined her husband in camp. She earned the nickname "Molly Pitcher" by carrying water to the soldiers during the Battle of Monmouth. When her husband was wounded, she took his place in battle. How could persons who were not soldiers aid in the fight for independence?

The Evacuation of Boston

Two weeks after the Battle of Bunker Hill, Washington arrived in Cambridge to take command of the colonial forces. The Americans encamped around Boston were undisciplined, and it was Washington's task to reorganize and train them. Although progress was slow and such problems as raising troops and getting supplies would plague Washington throughout the war, he managed gradually to build an army.

The new army's first venture was to drive the British out of Boston. In late January 1776, Washington's artillery commander, General Henry Knox, arrived at Cambridge with 59 cannon that had been dragged overland from Fort Ticonderoga. On the night of March 4, Washington occupied Dorchester Heights and fortified it with the cannon.

Upon discovering that the colonists held the Heights, General Howe, who had replaced Gage as the British commander, ordered an attack. However, a storm prevented the fulfillment of this order. Shortly thereafter Howe changed his mind and decided to evacuate Boston. By March 17, Howe's troops, along with some 1000 **Loyalists** (colonists who remained loyal to England), were aboard the British ships in Boston Harbor. On March 26, the fleet sailed for Halifax, Nova Scotia.

SECTION REVIEW

1. Identify the following: Lexington and Concord, General Thomas Gage, Paul Revere, Green Mountain Boys, John Dickinson, Olive Branch Petition, General William Howe.
2. Why did the British send troops to Concord?
3. Why was Fort Ticonderoga important?
4. What was the function of the Second Continental Congress?
5. What was the significance of the Battle of Bunker Hill?
6. What precipitated the British evacuation of Boston?

6 Moving Toward Separation

Although the British evacuated Boston, they had not given up their intention to subdue the rebellious colonies. Each British action toward this end lessened the colonists' attachment to England and, as time passed, more and more Americans came to favor a complete break. By mid-1776, the colonies were ready to formally declare their independence.

Paine's Common Sense was the first outspoken demand for complete independence. Paine was against all hereditary monarchies.

Rousseau's writings on the nature of man and Montesquieu's writings on the role of government influenced the thinking of colonial leaders.

Thomas Paine's *Common Sense*

Influential in swaying the colonists toward the idea of formal separation from Great Britain was Thomas Paine's *Common Sense,* which first appeared in January 1776. Paine, who had come to America from England in 1774, was a writer of revolutionary **propaganda** (ideas, facts, or rumors spread deliberately to help a cause). Stating that it was foolish to risk life and fortune simply to repeal Parliamentary laws, Paine called upon Americans to proclaim their independence. He felt that they should not only break from Great Britain, but cast off kings altogether and form a republic. A **republic** is a government in which the highest power belongs to the citizens, who choose representatives to act for them. Paine made an impassioned appeal:

> *Everything that is right or natural pleads for separation. The blood of the slain, the weeping voice of nature cries, 'TIS TIME TO PART.*

Common Sense crystallized colonial opinion. This, plus continuing evidence that Great Britain was determined to crush the rebellion, converted thousands to the cause of independence. One colony after another in the spring of 1776 instructed its delegates in the Second Continental Congress to vote for separation.

The Declaration of Independence

As a result of the growing sentiment for independence, Richard Henry Lee of Virginia introduced a resolution in the Second Continental Congress. It said that "these United Colonies are, and of right ought to be, free and independent states." On June 11, before voting on Lee's resolution, the Congress appointed a committee of five to draft a formal declaration of independence. This committee included Benjamin Franklin of Pennsylvania, John Adams of Massachusetts, Robert Livingston of New York, Roger Sherman of Connecticut, and Thomas Jefferson of Virginia. Jefferson was chosen to do the writing.

On June 28, the committee presented Jefferson's declaration to the Congress. After adopting Lee's resolution officially proclaiming America's independence, Congress turned to Jefferson's declaration.

The members of the Second Continental Congress signed the Declaration of Independence in this assembly room at Carpenter's Hall (now Constitution Hall) in Philadelphia. A committee, comprised of Thomas Jefferson, John Adams, Ben Franklin, Robert Livingston, and Roger Sherman, wrote the Declaration. How is the right of America to overthrow British rule justified in the Declaration?

On July 4, with some revision, the Declaration of Independence was adopted. John Hancock, president of the Second Continental Congress, was the first to sign it. Most Americans received the news joyously, although approval was not unanimous.

In the Declaration of Independence, Jefferson, drawing on American experience and the ideas of British philosopher John Locke, described the philosophy upon which Americans would base their new government. He stated that all men were equal and possessed of certain **unalienable rights,** or rights which cannot be taken away. These include "life, liberty, and the pursuit of happiness." To protect these rights, people formed governments which derived their authority directly from the people, or the "consent of the governed." Since the people were the source of government, they had the "right to alter or abolish it" if it should fail to fulfill its obligations. The right to abolish government was not taken lightly, however. Jefferson justified America's separation from England by charging George III with a long list of "injuries and usurpations."[5] He concluded with a statement officially establishing the colonies as an independent nation.

SECTION REVIEW

1. Identify the following: Thomas Paine, Richard Henry Lee, Thomas Jefferson, John Hancock.
2. What was the impact of *Common Sense* on colonial opinion?
3. How did Americans feel about the *Declaration of Independence?*
4. What was the philosophy upon which the *Declaration of Independence* was based?

---

7 Winning Independence

The pronouncement of independence on the part of the new United States had far-reaching effects. It transformed the rebellion into a revolution and committed the mass of Patriots to separation. Jefferson's declaration also led to increased foreign

---

[5] Though colonial grievances lay chiefly with the laws passed by Parliament, Jefferson leveled the charges against George III, the reigning monarch, who as king headed the government. Parliament and the British ministers established policy under the direction and counsel of the Crown.

WASHINGTON'S RETREAT, 1776-1777

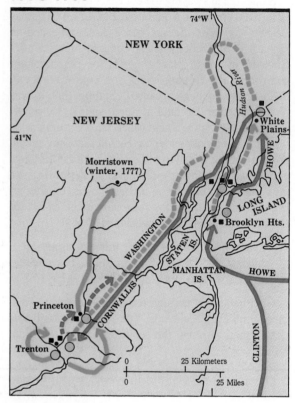

aid for the rebels and prepared the way for French intervention on the American side. In order to achieve and maintain independence, however, the new nation had to face full-scale war with Britain.

The Balance of Forces

Great Britain entered the war with certain advantages. It had a strong army and a powerful navy, both led by experienced professional officers. In addition, Great Britain could count on the support of thousands of Loyalists in the colonies. However, the British had to transport supplies from England, 3000 miles (4800 kilometers) away. They were at a disadvantage fighting in a hostile land, where the colonists employed **guerrilla warfare,** using irregular, hit-and-run tactics with deadly results.

The Americans, too, had certain advantages. They were fighting in their own land and were able to obtain

Have students discuss why anyone would volunteer to help a revolutionary group in a foreign land.

An army could travel only about 30 miles a day and was limited by its supply sources.

UPPER NEW YORK, 1777

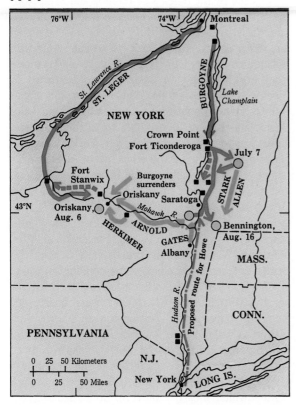

THE CHESAPEAKE CAMPAIGN, 1777-1778

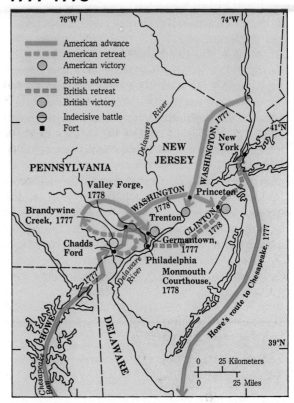

valuable foreign aid for their struggle against Great Britain. Although most American military leaders were inexperienced, some, including George Washington, turned out to be assets. In addition, many highly qualified European soldiers volunteered their services. Among them were the young Marquis de Lafayette of France, Baron Friedrich von Steuben of Prussia, and Count Casimir Pulaski of Poland.

The colonists, however, suffered serious disadvantages. They lacked a regular army and had no navy of any significant size. Americans also had problems with financing the war. Colonial legislatures did not always comply with requests for money and supplies. This lack of unity was perhaps America's greatest weakness. The Continental Congress tried printing its own paper money, but it was considered to have little value. Ultimately, the war had to be financed by loans from other countries (France, Spain, and Holland) and from private individuals.

From Dorchester Heights to Princeton

Meanwhile, after evacuating Boston, General Howe decided to seize New York City and use it as a base of operations. Anticipating Howe's movements, Washington moved his army to New York City and prepared to defend it against the British. Early in July, Howe landed on Staten Island. Shortly thereafter, his brother, Admiral Lord Richard Howe, arrived from England with the British fleet. By August, General Howe's forces numbered 32,000, about 9000 of whom were German mercenaries, or soldiers who serve for pay in the army of a foreign country. Washington, at this time, had about 23,000 troops in the New York area.

In late August, Howe landed with 20,000 troops on Long Island. On August 27, Howe's force defeated Washington's Continental Army and forced Washington to retreat to Manhattan Island. In September, the

Discuss possible reasons for desertion (homesickness, illness at home, farm work that needed to be done, low pay, hardships).

The winter of 1777-1778 was actually not severe, but the shortages of food, clothing, and blankets made it difficult for the army at Valley Forge.

British occupied New York City, and by the end of October, they had driven Washington from Manhattan Island. By late November, the Continental Army had retreated across New Jersey into Pennsylvania.

In the winter of 1776-77, the Patriot cause was near collapse. The Continental Army had dwindled to less than 6000. Soldiers deserted in large numbers or simply went home when their enlistments expired. Morale was low and received another blow when the Second Continental Congress, fearful that Howe would attack Philadelphia, fled the nation's capital. However, morale received a boost with Washington's victories at Trenton and Princeton.

On December 25 Washington crossed the ice-laden Delaware River to attack the British garrison at Trenton. Washington's surprise was complete, and the garrison surrendered almost at once. Over 900 German mercenaries were taken prisoner. Washington and his troops then moved on to Princeton, where, on January 3, 1777, they again defeated the British forces.

The courage of Continental soldiers at Valley Forge was severely tested during the winter of 1777-1778. The American army was beset by shortages of food and supplies. What events at this time helped to lift American morale?

Saratoga

Angered by the defeats at Trenton and Princeton, the British determined to end the war in 1777. To effect this, General John Burgoyne developed a plan for a three-pronged attack to crush American resistance. Colonel Barry St. Leger was to move from Fort Oswego on Lake Ontario eastward to Albany, New York, on the Hudson River. Burgoyne was to advance south from Canada along the Lake Champlain-Hudson River route to Albany. General Howe was to travel north from New York City up the Hudson River to meet the other two at Albany. This maneuver, if successful, would isolate New England and split the colonies, thereby making it easier for the British to crush the American forces.

Instead of pushing northward to meet Burgoyne, however, Howe decided to take Philadelphia. After defeating Washington at Brandywine Creek, the British entered Philadelphia on September 26, 1777. Washington launched another attack on the British at nearby Germantown, where they were quartered. Repulsed once more, Washington and his troops retired to Valley Forge[6], outside Philadelphia. Howe was in control of the capital, but his failure to meet Burgoyne would prove disastrous to the British war effort.

Meanwhile, in early August St. Leger had reached Fort Stanwix and laid siege to it. However, news of an approaching American force under Benedict Arnold caused the British to abandon the siege and return to Fort Oswego.

About the same time St. Leger was moving toward Fort Stanwix, Burgoyne and the main British force were advancing southward. On July 5, they seized Fort Ticonderoga with all its military stores. Marching south from Ticonderoga, Burgoyne was harassed on all sides by steadily increasing American forces. Short of supplies and with no reinforcements in sight, Burgoyne withdrew to Saratoga. There, the British were besieged by an American force under General Horatio Gates. Vastly outnumbered by the Americans, Burgoyne surrendered on October 17, 1777.

---

[6] Washington and his troops spent a miserable winter at Valley Forge, starving and freezing. In the spring, however, they received new provisions and were drilled into shape with the help of Baron von Steuben.

British Colonel Henry Hamilton was nicknamed "the Hair Buyer" because of reports that he was offering bounties to Indians for American scalps. The British told the Indians that the colonists intended to seize their land and destroy their homes.

After taking Georgia, the British set up a Crown-controlled legislature—the only one in America after the Declaration of Independence.

THE WESTERN CAMPAIGN, 1778-1779

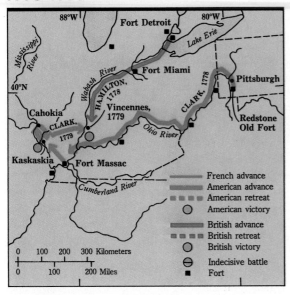

THE ROAD TO YORKTOWN, 1778-1781

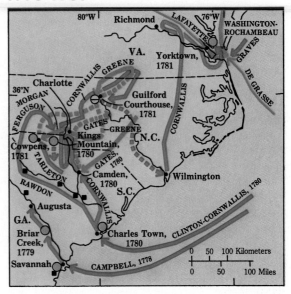

The French Alliance

Saratoga was a turning point because it brought France into the war on the American side. Although the French had been secretly aiding the United States, they wanted to be sure of success before forming an alliance that would lead to war with Britain.

The alliance was signed in February, 1778, and was to go into effect if war broke out between England and France. The purpose of the alliance was to assure the "liberty, sovereignty, and independence . . . of the United States." France renounced all claims on the North American continent east of the Mississippi River and agreed that any such territory seized in the war would go to the United States. In turn, France was to have a free hand in the British West Indies. With France's aid enlisted on the American side, Great Britain faced a two-front war.

The War in the West

While France and the United States were conducting the negotiations that were to lead ultimately to an alliance, the British and their Indian allies were raiding western settlements. In retaliation, George Rogers Clark, commander of the Kentucky militia, decided to lead an expedition against Fort Detroit, the

British headquarters in the West. In the summer of 1778, Clark's force captured the predominately French settlements of Kaskaskia, Cahokia, and Vincennes.

Although he never succeeded in taking Detroit, Clark's actions curbed the activities of the British and their Indian allies along the frontier. In addition, his conquests furthered America's claim to the Ohio basin and played a part in the final peace negotiations between the United States and Great Britain.

From Savannah to Yorktown

Meanwhile, the British, counting on extensive support from southern Loyalists, decided to wage a major offensive in the South. Late in 1778, General Clinton, who had replaced Howe as British commander, sent a force to occupy Savannah, Georgia. On December 29, the city fell, and soon the rest of Georgia was under British control. Seeking to extend their control, the British besieged Charleston, South Carolina, which fell in May. Clinton himself had directed the siege, but after the city fell, he left Lord Charles Cornwallis and about 8000 soldiers to strengthen England's hold on the South. Cornwallis did so when he defeated an American force under General Horatio Gates at Camden, South Carolina.

News of the American victory at Yorktown was received with celebrations (dancing, cheering, religious services, banquets) in America and also in Paris. The British decided to give up on the American phase of the war and concentrate on defeating France and Spain. British garrisons were evacuated and only small skirmishes were fought after Yorktown.

Surrounded by American and French forces, General Charles Cornwallis had no choice but to ask for terms of surrender. Although other skirmishes were to follow, the victory at Yorktown assured America's independence. What made Cornwallis' position at Yorktown vulnerable?

Soon, however, the tide began to turn. A British attempt to invade North Carolina failed after a defeat at King's Mountain in October. The British received another blow in January when they were defeated at Cowpens, South Carolina. Although two months later Cornwallis was victorious at Guilford Courthouse, North Carolina, his forces, weakened by losses, retreated to the coast. As a result, General Nathaniel Greene, who had replaced Gates, managed to loosen British control of the area.

While Greene was moving in on various British outposts, Cornwallis was marching northward to conquer Virginia. In August 1781, he established his headquarters at Yorktown on the tip of the peninsula between the York and James Rivers. Cornwallis' choice of Yorktown gave Washington the opportunity for which he had been waiting. The British position on the peninsula was safe only so long as the British commanded the sea. Without naval support, Cornwallis was vulnerable to attack on all sides and could thus be cut off from other British forces. When Washington received the news that the French fleet in the West Indies was available to assist in an attack on Yorktown, he marched south from his encampment in New York. On September 28, 1781, Washington's army, strengthened by French forces under the Comte de Rochambeau and Lafayette and backed by the West Indian fleet, began the siege of Yorktown. On October 18, Cornwallis surrendered. Cornwallis' defeat plus several French victories in the West Indies brought the war to a close, and the British sued for peace.

The Treaty of Paris, 1783

In the spring of 1782, informal negotiations opened in Paris between the British and Benjamin Franklin, the only American peace commissioner there at the time. Formal talks began when the other American commissioners, John Jay of New York and John Adams, arrived.

By the terms of the Treaty of Paris of 1783, England recognized America's independence and gave up all its territory between the Atlantic Coast and the Mississippi River, extending from Florida to the Great Lakes. The British agreed to withdraw

In making liberal concessions, the British were seeking the future friendship of the United States.

their forces from America and granted the United States fishing rights off Newfoundland. Spain, which had joined in the war against Great Britain in 1779, received Florida. In addition, the United States' Congress was pledged to recommend that the individual state legislatures compensate the Loyalists for their losses during the war.

Although the treaty affirmed the independence of the United States, it remained to be seen whether the new nation could survive. It was the start of a new era in which the people of the 13 states had to learn how to govern themselves as one country.

SECTION REVIEW

1. Identify the following: General John Burgoyne, George Rogers Clark, Lord Charles Cornwallis.
2. What advantages and disadvantages did the British and the Americans each have at the beginning of the war?
3. In what way did General Howe's decisions influence the Battle of Saratoga?
4. What was the importance of Clark's victories in the West?
5. What were the terms of the Treaty of Paris, 1783?

CHAPTER 3   REVIEW

SUMMARY

1. Between the 1680's and the 1750's, colonial rivalry led to a struggle for empire between Great Britain and France.
2. The final conflict in this struggle, known in North America as the French and Indian War, resulted in British domination of that continent.
3. After the French and Indian War, the British changed their policies toward the colonies.
4. These changes in policy, especially the British attempt to raise revenue through direct taxation, aroused resentment in the colonies.
5. Colonial protests and British determination to force the colonies to submit to parliamentary authority led to open warfare.

6. On July 4, 1776, the 13 colonies formally declared their independence as the United States of America.
7. Despite early American losses, the tides of battle changed when the French entered the war on the side of the United States.
8. Backed by the French, the Americans achieved ultimate victory over the British at Yorktown in 1781.
9. By the terms of the Treaty of Paris, 1783, England recognized American independence and surrendered to the United States its territories east of the Mississippi River between the Great Lakes and Florida.

VOCABULARY

legal tender	writs of assistance	revolution	republic
specie	monopoly	minutemen	unalienable rights
direct tax	boycott	Patriots	guerrilla warfare
quarter	moderates	Loyalists	mercenaries
nonimportation agreements	radicals	propaganda	

REVIEW QUESTIONS

1. What was the cause of the French and Indian War?
2. How were the colonists affected by the war?

3. How did British policy change after the war?
4. What objections did the colonists have to the changes in British policy?

5. What actions did the colonists take in response to changes in colonial policy?
6. Why did tensions continue to increase between the colonists and Great Britain after the repeal of the Stamp Act?
7. Why did the colonists regard the Coercive Acts as intolerable?

8. What events led to the outbreak of war between the colonists and Great Britain?
9. What were the effects of the Declaration of Independence?
10. What event changed the course of the war? How?
11. What ended the American Revolution?

DISCUSSION

1. Were the British justified in their policy of having the colonists help defray colonial expenses? Why or why not?
2. If you had lived in colonial times, would you have been a Patriot or a Loyalist? Why?

3. Were the colonists' actions against Great Britain a legitimate response to changes in British colonial policy?
4. Was the fundamental issue underlying the American Revolution social, economic, or political?

USING MAPS

Refer to the maps on page 57 and answer the following questions:
1. What color represents British territory in North America?
2. What changes were made in French territory in 1763?

3. What new territory was gained by Great Britain by 1763? Why?
4. What new territory was also gained by Spain by 1763?
5. Where are there conflicting claims? Which countries claimed the territory?

USING SKILLS

Study the picture on page 66, read the caption, and answer the following questions:
1. What is the woman in the picture doing? Why?

2. What are the men in the picture doing? What seems to be the attitude of the men in the picture toward the woman?

SUMMARY

1. The Europeans who explored the New World in the 15th and 16th centuries found a land rich in resources, varied in climate and inhabited by civilizations representing a wide variety of highly developed cultures.

2. Several European nations, including the countries of Spain, England, France, Holland, Portugal, and Sweden, established various colonies in the New World.

3. The English colonies carried on their national heritage but gradually developed a uniquely American culture that placed a high value on freedom.

4. Rivalry between Great Britain and France led to the French and Indian War.

5. After winning the French and Indian War, Britain made changes in colonial policy that were resented by Americans.

6. Protest against Britain's policies led to open conflict between the colonists and the Crown.

7. Americans won their Revolution and were recognized as an independent nation by Great Britain.

REVIEW QUESTIONS

1. How did the American Indians and the Europeans interact and what was their effect upon each other?

2. What developments took place in colonial culture? How did cultural developments in America influence the relationship between the American colonies and Great Britain?

3. What were the British trying to achieve with their colonial policies? What were the American responses to them?

SUGGESTED ACTIVITIES

1. Research the Indian groups who inhabited your region in precolonial times. Find out about their culture, lifestyle, governmental structure and social organization.

2. Select one of the European explorers and write a report describing his personal characteristics, his motivation for exploring America, and the details of his explorations.

3. Write a one-page newspaper article based on an interview with an English colonist who has just arrived in America. Include information based on questions you would ask about living conditions, the daily routine, why the person came to America, and any advice the person might give to someone who was thinking about going to the New World.

4. Make a physical map of your region. Identify what resources are available and where. How did the early colonists use them? How did physical features influence early development of the region?

5. Develop a questionnaire to survey people about the events that led to the American Revolution. Write a brief statement about each of the events and ask people to agree or disagree. Use the results as the basis for class discussion.

6. Study the Declaration of Independence and discuss the meaning "unalienable rights."

SUGGESTED READINGS

1. Morison, Samuel Eliot. *Christopher Columbus, Mariner.* Boston: Little, Brown & Co., 1955. Paperback by Mentor, New York, 1956. Traces the voyages of Columbus, describing Columbus' ability as a sailor and the nature of the voyages he made.

Read the teacher's guide to understand how the Historian's Craft activity is related to end-of-chapter skill activities.

2. Wright, Louis B. *The Atlantic Frontier: Colonial Civilization, 1607-1763*. Ithaca: Great Seal Books, 1963. Paperback. An account of the history of the colonies and the influences that led to the Revolution.

3. Miller, John C. *Sam Adams: Pioneer in Propaganda*. Stanford, California: Stanford University Press, 1936. Paperback. Examines the career of a propagandist who did much to stir up the colonists against the British.

4. Coakley, Robert W. and Conn, Stetson. *The War of the American Revolution*. Washington, D.C.: Center of Military History, U.S. Army, 1875. A narrative chronology of the military history of the Revolution.

5. Bristow, Gwen. *Celia Garth*. New York: Popular Library, 1974. Describes a young orphan apprenticed as a seamstress and her experiences during the British siege of Charleston during the final years of the Revolution.

6. Fast, Howard. *April Morning*. New York: Bantam Books, Inc., 1962. Relates the story of a boy who joins the colonial militia to fight the British during the Revolution.

THE HISTORIAN'S CRAFT

History is a record of what historians have been able to reconstruct of the past. Historians collect facts, sort out what is relevant, and build a framework for interpreting the past. But facts are limited and often disputed, relevance is a matter of judgment, and interpretation can never be completely without bias.

The interpretation of history is strongly influenced by the selection of materials. For this reason, historians look for as many sources of information as possible. Among the sources of information studied by historians are paintings, photographs, and other illustrations.

This activity will demonstrate how pictures may influence the perception of history. In this case, the topic is the role of women in the American Revolution.

QUESTIONS

1. Compare these three pictures with the painting of Molly Pitcher on page 66. What are the women doing in each picture?

2. Write a brief description of the role of women in the Revolution based on the picture on the left. Pretend that you have no other information. Write three other descriptions based on the picture on the right, the picture on the bottom, and the picture of Molly Pitcher. How do the descriptions differ?

3. Compare the information in the pictures to the story of Deborah Sampson on page 63. What generalizations can you make about the role of women in the Revolution?

4. If four historians had access to all of these pictures, but each chose a different one to illustrate his or her text, what would that tell you about the historians? What would it tell you about history?

1781 Articles of Confederation	1785 Land Ordinance	1786 Annapolis Convention	1787 Northwest Ordinance	1789 Judiciary Act

1781–89 Critical Period		1786 Shays' Rebellion	1787 Constitutional Convention	1789 Inauguration of George Washington

FORGING A UNION

A New Nation

The Constitution

The Federalist Era

| **1791** Bill of Rights | **1793** Jay Treaty | **1794** Whiskey Rebellion | **1795** Treaty of Greenville | **1796** Election of John Adams | **1800** Disputed Election of 1800 |

| **1791** Bank of United States | | **1794–95** Rise of Political Parties | **1795** Pinckney Treaty | | **1798** Alien and Sedition Acts |

1	The New State Governments	**81**
2	The Articles of Confederation	**81**
3	The Critical Period	**83**
4	Achievements Under the Articles	**87**
5	Drafting the Constitution	**89**
6	Debate Over the Constitution	**94**

A NEW NATION

Congress must have the same power to enact laws and compel obedience throughout the continent as the legislatures of the states have in their respective jurisdictions.

NOAH WEBSTER

When the American colonies broke their political ties with Great Britain, they were faced with the need to form independent governments at both the state and national levels. Creating a new government for the country as a whole proved to be a difficult task. Nevertheless, by the end of the Revolution, the nation's first constitution had gone into effect.

As the weaknesses of the national government under this constitution became apparent, a movement for a stronger central authority began. This movement culminated in the creation of a new constitution—one which has lasted nearly 200 years.

1 The New State Governments

Even before the colonies had formally declared their independence from Great Britain, the colonial governments had begun to disintegrate. In order to preserve law and order, the Second Continental Congress in May 1776 urged the colonies to form new state governments. South Carolina and New Hampshire had already done so. By the end of 1776, eight states had drafted constitutions. New York and Georgia followed suit in 1777, and Massachusets in 1780. Connecticut and Rhode Island retained their colonial charters as state constitutions.

In most states these constitutions were drawn up by the state legislatures. Calling upon both their British heritage and their colonial experience, the framers prepared written documents outlining the basic structure of government. Almost every state constitution also included a **bill of rights,** a statement of the fundamental rights guaranteed to the people.

Because of their experience with British tyranny, the states limited the power of their governments. Most of the new constitutions divided authority between an executive, the governor; a legislature, the state assembly; and a judiciary, the courts.

The greatest power was granted to the legislature, which represented the people. In fact, some states did not even have a governor. Yet the power of the legislature was not unlimited. In all of the states except Pennsylvania, the new assemblies were **bicameral,** or made up of two houses—each to act as a check on the other.

The Framers not only wanted to limit the power of the state governments, but wanted to keep them responsive to the people. State legislators were popularly elected, and elections were frequent. In some states, the people could elect other officials as well. This desire to keep power in the hands of the people was apparent when the new states formed a national government.

SECTION REVIEW

1. Why did the colonies form new state governments before declaring independence?
2. Who drew up the state constitutions?
3. Which of the three branches of government received the most power under the state constitutions?
4. How were the state governments made responsive to the people?

2 The Articles of Confederation

The delegates to the Second Continental Congress realized the necessity of establishing a central (or national) government for the 13 states. There was much disagreement, however, as to the nature of this union. Some delegates favored a strong national government, while most feared giving the central authority too much power.

Failing to agree, Congress finally selected a committee to draw up an acceptable plan of government. On July 12, 1776, this committee, headed by John Dickinson of Pennsylvania, presented the "Articles of Confederation and Perpetual Union" to Congress. After much debate, this plan was finally adopted on November 15, 1777. In 1781, after being ratified by the states, it went into effect.

The Articles of Confederation was the first written United States constitution.

Massachusetts, North Carolina, Georgia, New York, and Connecticut also had claims to western lands.

State seals, such as New York's, symbolized the independence of state governments under the Articles of Confederation. What powers did state governments have under the Articles?

Organization and Powers

The Articles created a **confederation,** or league of independent states. The central government of the league was to be a one-house legislature. Each state would send from two to seven delegates, selected annually by the states' legislatures. Each state delegation, however, had only one vote.

Under the Articles, the state governments, because they were closer to the people, kept most of the power. To ensure this, a clause in the Articles guaranteed that each state would retain its **sovereignty** (the right of self-government), and "every power not expressly delegated to Congress." The national government, however, did have certain specified powers. These included the right to declare war and make peace, settle disputes between the states, coin and borrow money, and establish weights and measures. The Confederation Congress was also given the power to regulate Indian affairs beyond state boundaries and to requisition troops and money from the states.

Although this was a seemingly impressive list of powers, the authority of Congress was limited. It could make decisions about a number of things but could not enforce those decisions. It could ask for money from the states, for example, but had no power to make the states comply.

The number of votes needed to carry legislation also limited congressional authority. No important matter could be settled without a positive vote of at least nine states. Changes in the Articles needed unanimous approval—that is, the approval of all 13 states. Since each state jealously guarded its own interests, agreement was often difficult to obtain.

Ratification

This difficulty was reflected in the very process of **ratification,** or approval, of the Articles by the states. Conflicts over state claims to western lands delayed ratification.

Some states, such as Virginia, had claims from "sea to sea" based on their colonial charters. States without claims to western lands, led by Maryland, urged that these lands be transferred to the national government. The land-poor states did not want the states with western claims to be able to use the money from the sale of the lands to pay war debts and other expenses. Those states could then keep their taxes low, and this would attract people from the land-poor states.

Supporting the land-poor states were the **nationalists,** who favored a strong central government. These people argued that as the western lands were being won from the British by a joint effort of all the states, the land should belong to all the states. Nationalists also hoped that national ownership of the western lands would help diminish state rivalries. In addition, the sale of these lands would provide the national government with revenue.

Speculators, or people who purchase something for the purpose of selling it later for a profit, also favored turning over the western lands to the central government. The speculators had bought land cheaply from the Indians and hoped to make money by selling it to settlers at a higher price. However, the land was located in an area claimed by Virginia, which had refused to recognize the speculators' ownership. The speculators hoped they would fare better with the national government.

Despite the problem over western lands, all of the states except Maryland had ratified the Articles by

One reason Virginia agreed to give up its claim to western lands was that some of the state's leaders thought the western territory was too large for a single republican government.

Point out that historians today are not as quick to condemn the Articles of Confederation.

1779. However, without Maryland, union was delayed because the Articles could not go into effect until all the states had ratified them.

Meanwhile, as the Revolution continued, it became more and more clear that a central government was essential for victory. Therefore, states began giving up their claims to western lands. Finally, on January 2, 1781, Virginia agreed to turn over its land to the national government under certain conditions. One condition was that Congress had to refuse to recognize earlier private purchases in the area. This provision destroyed the speculators' hopes for profits. Another condition was that future states carved from this territory were to be admitted to the Union on an equal basis with the existing states.

Despite Virginia's action, Maryland still stalled. However, threatened by the British, Maryland sought help from the French navy. When the French refused to provide this help unless Maryland ratified the Articles, the state complied. With Maryland's ratification, all 13 states had approved the Articles. On March 1, 1781, the Confederation formally became the government of the United States.

SECTION REVIEW

1. How were the states represented in Congress under the Articles of Confederation?

2. What specific powers were granted to the Confederation government?
3. How were the powers of Congress limited?
4. What problems delayed ratification of the Articles?
5. What finally brought about ratification?

3 The Critical Period

In 1888, historian John Fiske stated that the years between 1781 and 1789 were a "critical period" in the history of the early American republic. This was because the Articles of Confederation did not provide a strong enough government to handle the large number of problems facing the new United States.

Foreign Threats

As the weaknesses of the new American government became clear, the United States had problems with other countries. Trouble with Great Britain developed because of the Confederation's lack of power to enforce the Treaty of Paris.

Problems With Great Britain. The Treaty of Paris required the Confederation Congress to recommend that the state legislatures restore

After the Revolutionary War ended, British outposts remained in Niagara, Oswego, and Detroit. The British refused to abandon the lucrative fur trade they had built in the Northwest. Why were the Americans unable to remove the British from the territory?

One reason the British refused to leave the Northwest Territory was the lucrative fur trade.

Using a map of the United States (see Appendix), ask students to determine why farmers used the Mississippi River to get their products to market rather than the route overland to the Atlantic seaboard.

Loyalist property seized during the Revolution. Also, the treaty stated that no "legal impediments" were to be placed in the way of British citizens as they tried to collect prewar debts owed them by Americans. Few states, however, complied with these provisions. Using American shortcomings as an excuse, the British refused to leave their posts in the Northwest Territory as they had agreed to do. The weak Confederation government could do nothing about the presence of foreign troops on American soil.

Besides failing to evacuate the Northwest Territory, Great Britain seemed to be pursuing other policies designed to humiliate the new nation. Since the United States was no longer a part of the British Empire, the Navigation Acts excluded American ships from carrying British trade. Great Britain refused to negotiate a commercial treaty, pointing out that any of the 13 states might violate a treaty made by the Confederation government. The British knew that the United States needed their trade more than they needed American products. Furthermore, as British leader Lord Sheffield said:

> By asserting their independence the Americans have renounced the privileges, as well as the duties, of British subjects. If, in some instances, as in the loss of the carrying trade, they feel the inconvenience of their choice, they can no longer complain.

Throughout the 1780's, Great Britain dictated the terms under which the United States could trade with the British Empire. For example, in 1783, the British excluded American ships from the West Indian trade. This trade had been very important during colonial days. Adding insult to injury, Great Britain even failed to send an ambassador to the American capital at Philadelphia.

Problems With Spain. If relations with Great Britain were poor, affairs with Spain were worse. Spain, which held Florida as well as lands west of the Mississippi River, was anxious to halt American expansion to the west and south. Beginning in 1784, therefore, Spain refused to permit American ships to pass freely through the lower Mississippi River, and withdrew the Americans' **right of deposit** at New Orleans. This right had allowed westerners, who shipped their produce to the East via the Mississippi River, to unload their cargoes at New Orleans to await ocean-going ships. By withdrawing the right of deposit, Spain effectively closed the river and deprived westerners of their major avenue of trade. This presented a serious problem because moving goods overland to the East cost a great deal and was very difficult.

In May 1785, Spain sent Don Diego de Gardoqui as its minister to the United States. Congress authorized John Jay, the Confederation's secretary of

The most practical outlet for western goods was the Mississippi River, and flatboats were the principal means of transporting produce from the West. Spain's closing of the port of New Orleans dealt a serious blow to westerners who relied on the river for moving their produce to eastern markets. John Jay negotiated the treaty that regained the right of deposit at New Orleans. Why were westerners and easterners at odds over the results of the treaty?

foreign affairs, to negotiate with Gardoqui. Jay had been told not to give in on the matter of navigation rights on the Mississippi. However, the Confederation government was not strong enough to back up this demand. After a year of fruitless negotiations, Congress finally told Jay to give up United States' navigation rights on the Mississippi River for 25 years in exchange for a favorable commercial treaty with Spain.

The proposed treaty stirred up a bitter debate between westerners and eastern trading interests, who had much to gain from the commercial treaty. As a result, the treaty failed to receive the nine-state majority needed for ratification. Thus the issue was left unsettled, and the future of the West hung in the balance for some time.

Problems With France. The United States even had difficulties with its old ally, France. During the war years, France and the United States had built up a healthy trade. France hoped this would continue after the conclusion of hostilities. However, American preference for British goods soon reasserted itself, and an unfavorable balance of trade developed for France. In fact, most of America's profits from the French trade were used to buy British goods. As a result, Franco-American relations deteriorated.

The Barbary Pirates. The new nation also had troubles in other areas. During the 1780's, United States' ships were virtually driven from the Mediterranean Sea by the so-called Barbary Pirates. These pirates, from the North African states of Tunis, Morocco, Tripoli, and Algiers, raided the ships of nations that refused to pay them **tribute** (protection money). Since paying the tribute was cheaper than mounting a major naval offensive against the pirates, most European countries paid.

Before the United States declared its independence, American colonial shipping was protected by British tribute as well as by the British navy. However, after the war, American merchant vessels were on their own. As Congress was not able either to pay the tribute or provide naval protection, American shipping suffered.

Domestic Problems

The Confederation Congress had to deal with domestic problems as well as threats from other

THE UNITED STATES IN 1783

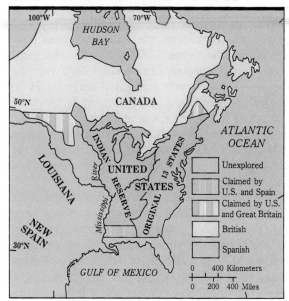

countries. Here again, the weaknesses of the new government became increasingly clear.

Regulating Commerce. One of these weaknesses was the government's inability to regulate commerce. This was never more apparent than during the postwar depression. A **depression** is a period of slow business activity, characterized by falling prices and unemployment. During the Revolution, the trade relationship between the American colonies and Great Britain had been broken off. In Great Britain, manufactured goods were being stockpiled in warehouses, while colonial manufacturing grew. With the coming of peace, however, British manufacturers flooded the American market with their goods. American demand for these goods could not keep up with British supply. Thus, prices dropped drastically.

American manufacturers were hurt because they could not compete with the low prices of the British goods. Many merchants were also hurt because they were forced to sell goods at little or no profit. In addition, because Americans bought more from Great Britain than they sold, an unfavorable balance of trade developed for the United States. This drained specie from the country, and, soon, depression set in.

Congress was unable to aid the American economy because it had no power to regulate commerce. At one point, 10 of the 13 states granted Congress the power to control trade, but lack of agreement among the states prevented any action.

While denying the central government the power to regulate commerce, the individual states took action on their own. Massachusetts and New Hampshire prohibited British ships from carrying goods from state ports and placed heavy duties on British goods coming in. These import duties raised the prices on British goods and helped keep them from underselling American products. Other states followed with similar measures. Although helpful, the measures passed by the states were not uniform, and this reduced their effectiveness.

The individual states also passed laws regulating **interstate commerce** (trade between two or more states). Each state, however, made these regulations to benefit its own citizens. New York, for example, taxed goods from Connecticut and New Jersey. Connecticut and New Jersey retaliated in kind. So it went, state against state, with the national government powerless to end domestic strife. Some years later, James Wilson of Pennsylvania was to sum up the situation:

> *No sooner were the State Governments formed than their jealousy and ambition began to display themselves. Each endeavored to cut a slice from the common loaf, to add to its*

Each state under the Confederation issued its own paper money and coin. These currencies had little value, however, since most states printed more money than they could back in gold or silver. Why could Congress not resolve this problem?

> *own morsel, till at length the confederation became frittered down to the impotent condition in which it now stands.*

Raising Revenue. The national government was not only unable to regulate trade, but it also lacked the power to tax. This made the problem of raising revenue a most serious one.

Under the Articles of Confederation, the state legislatures, not the people, elected the Confederation Congress. Therefore, since Congress did not directly represent the people, it was denied the power to tax. Only the state legislatures had this power.

The ways in which Congress could raise revenue were strictly limited. Although the states could be asked for money, they rarely met requests. Between 1781 and 1789, Congress sought $16 million from the states and received only $6 million.

Besides requisitioning money, Congress could also borrow it from both foreign and domestic sources. Although loans helped the government operate, this source also was inadequate. Another method of raising revenue was to continue to print paper money. However, by 1781, Continental currency had **depreciated,** or fallen in value, so much that it was almost worthless. People would give only one cent in gold or silver for one paper dollar.

A more lucrative source of income for Congress was the sale of the western lands transferred to the national government by the states. Revenue from the sale of these lands was slow in coming, however, because it took time to survey the area.

Attempts to remedy the government's financial situation failed. In 1782, and again in 1786, proposals allowing Congress to place a five percent tax on foreign imports were rejected by the states. As a result, monetary problems plagued Congress throughout the 1780's.

Shays' Rebellion. Another weakness of the new government was its inability to deal with internal revolt. Shays' Rebellion drew Americans' attention to this weakness and helped crystallize sentiment for a stronger government.

During the postwar depression, many debtors—especially poor, small farmers—found it more and more difficult to pay their bills. Creditors refused to accept worthless paper money in payment for debts.

Daniel Shays, a veteran of Bunker Hill, led an army of 1200 Massachusetts farmers in demanding tax relief, a moratorium on debt, and the abolishment of prison for debtors. Why was Shays' Rebellion significant?

Burdensome taxes, as well as bills, had to be paid in specie, which was increasingly scarce.

In states where debtor-farmers had enough power, laws were passed requiring individuals to accept paper money in payment for debts. In Massachusetts, however, merchants and other creditors who were against paper money controlled the upper house of the state legislature and refused to pass measures for relief of debtors. As a result, mortgages were foreclosed, property was seized to pay debts, and many people were sent to debtors' prison.

Farmers in western Massachusetts, who had been especially hard hit by the depression, were outraged. In the summer of 1786, they decided to take matters into their own hands. Led by Daniel Shays, a bankrupt farmer and former captain in the Continental Army, they took up arms. The rebels closed the courts in a number of counties, preventing the collection of debts.

In January 1787, Shays' force tried unsuccessfully to seize the federal arsenal at Springfield. By that time, merchants and other creditors in Boston had raised enough money to send a force of state militia, under General Benjamin Lincoln, against the Shaysites. Within a short time, the rebellion had been crushed.

Shays' intent had been to keep the courts from confiscating any more property or throwing anybody else into jail before the state elections in the spring. Although the revolt was put down, the debtor-farmers did gain control of the legislature with the spring elections. These events led many people to think that too much power was concentrated in the state legislatures, which were too susceptible to the will of factions. In this case, it was the debtor-farmer faction that gained control and passed laws infringing on the rights of creditors. This, plus the fear of more uprisings, increased sentiment in favor of a stronger national government that could check the power of the state legislatures.

SECTION REVIEW

1. Identify the following: Critical Period, John Jay, Barbary Pirates, Daniel Shays.
2. What foreign threats did the United States face during the Critical Period?
3. How did peace hurt American manufacturers?
4. How did the Confederation government raise revenue?

4 Achievements Under the Articles

Despite the weaknesses of the Articles, the Confederation government did not lack accomplishments. The war for independence was won, peace was secured, and there were other successes.

Economic Recovery

For one thing, by 1787, the United States was beginning to emerge from the postwar depression. Foreign trade was expanding. Although the largest part of that trade was still with the British Empire, American merchants were no longer restricted to those markets. Congress had signed commercial treaties with a number of European countries including Holland, Sweden, and Prussia. A favorable

Land companies bought much of the land from the Confederation government for a few cents an acre. This was because the government needed money to operate, and few settlers could afford to buy extensive tracts.

balance of trade was established with France, and American vessels, despite the Barbary Pirates, sailed the Mediterranean. By the end of the decade, United States commerce had become global in scope.

Even more important were signs of economic recovery at home. Farm prices and land values were rising, and domestic manufacturing had grown substantially. By 1787, the American economy was much more broadly based than ever before. Both the population and the **national income** (the total amount of money earned by all the people) were increasing. Congress was beginning to pay the interest on the **national debt** (the money owed by the national government), and many states were working their way out of their financial difficulties.

Creating a Bureaucracy

Besides economic recovery, the Critical Period saw the creation of a bureaucracy, which improved the effectiveness of the national government. A **bureaucracy** is a staff of officials divided into departments with specialized functions.

Since Congress was chiefly a policy-making body, it was given the power to create executive departments to take care of its day-to-day business. Early in 1781, Congress set up a number of departments, the most important of which were foreign affairs, finance, and war. Of the men who headed these departments, one

of the most effective was Robert Morris. As superintendent of finance, he helped shape the economic life of the new country.

Creating the Public Domain

The Confederation Congress not only laid the foundations for the administration of the national government, but provided for the systematic growth of the United States. When Congress accepted Virginia's western lands in 1784, the **public domain,** or public lands owned by the United States government, was created. Congress then went on to lay down policies for the western lands.

The Land Ordinance of 1785. To provide for the survey and sale of western lands, Congress passed the Ordinance of 1785, which set the precedent for national land policies. This law stated that the land was to be surveyed into townships six miles square (9.7 square kilometers). These townships would then be divided into 36 sections each one mile square (2.6 square kilometers). One section in each township was to be set aside for the public schools, and four were to be reserved for the United States government. The remaining 31 were to be sold for not less than one dollar an acre. This led to the sale of large amounts of land and speeded up settlement of the Northwest.

The Northwest Ordinance. Once the policy for settlement of the western lands was established,

By 1790 nearly 120,000 persons had traveled across the Appalachian Divide to new homes. The Ordinance of 1787 provided for the government of the territory northwest of the Ohio River. What provisions were established by the Northwest Ordinance?

Have students use a map of the United States (see Appendix) to determine the number of states formed from the Northwest Territory.

Have students consider why the government was concerned about the number of states to be formed from the Northwest Territory.

THE NORTHWEST TERRITORY AND LAND CLAIMS, 1787

LAND SURVEY IN THE NORTHWEST TERRITORY

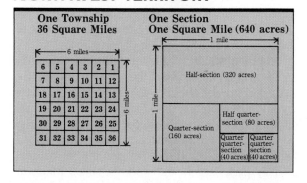

Congress turned to the problem of governing this area. In 1787, the Northwest Ordinance, perhaps the most significant achievement of Congress under the Articles, was passed.

Under this ordinance, the Northwest Territory was to be ruled at first by a governor, a secretary, and three judges named by Congress. When the number of free adult males in an area reached 5000, the voters could choose people to represent them in a general assembly. This body would share power with the governor and a legislative council appointed by the

governor and Congress. Once formed, the General Assembly could then elect a delegate to the Confederation Congress. This delegate could debate but not vote.

When the number of free inhabitants in an area reached 60,000, the voters could elect delegates to a convention which would frame a state constitution. Once this constitution was approved by Congress, that part of the Northwest Territory would be admitted to the Union on an equal basis with the existing states. At least three but no more than five states could be carved from the Territory.

Besides laying the basis for the organization of new territorial governments and setting a precedent for the method of admitting new states to the Union, the Northwest Ordinance had what might be called a bill of rights. There was even a specific provision outlawing slavery: "There shall be neither slavery nor involuntary servitude in said territory." This provision would have an important impact on the history of America in the 1800's.

SECTION REVIEW

1. What gains were made under the Articles?
2. What were the most important executive departments set up by Congress under the Articles?
3. Why was the Land Ordinance of 1785 important?
4. How did the Northwest Ordinance provide for the admission of new states?

5 Drafting the Constitution

Despite the achievements of the Confederation government, its prestige declined with its failure to solve some of the problems facing the United States. More and more Americans became convinced that the country's first experiment in government was not working and began to increase their demands for a stronger central government. These demands led to the writing of a new constitution.

Prelude to Convention

The movement for a stronger central government was given added impetus by two important interstate meetings. The first of these was held in 1785 at George Washington's Virginia home, Mount Vernon.

Maryland claimed the Potomac River was within its boundary and taxed all Virginia trade using it. Virginia, in turn, taxed all Maryland trade through the mouth of the Chesapeake Bay, which was within Virginia's boundary.

The Virginia Plan was introduced by Edmund Randolph.

There, representatives from Maryland and Virginia met to iron out problems relating to the navigation of Chesapeake Bay and the Potomac River. The two states reached an agreement on certain specific points fairly quickly, but soon realized the need for a general conference regarding commercial problems.

As a result, in January 1786, the Virginia legislature invited all the states to send delegates to a second meeting at Annapolis, Maryland. By early September, representatives of New York, New Jersey, Pennsylvania, Delaware, and Virginia had arrived at Annapolis. Their stated purpose was to "take into consideration the trade of the United States."

Although the purpose of the meeting was to discuss commercial problems, James Madison, in a letter to Thomas Jefferson, had expressed the hope that the Annapolis Convention would be the first step toward amending the Articles of Confederation. As the delegates began to discuss their concerns, they discovered that most of them agreed on the need to revise the Articles. The delegates therefore adopted a report written by Alexander Hamilton of New York. His report called upon the states to send delegates to a new convention to be held at Philadelphia in May of 1787. A copy of this report was sent to Congress, and the meeting at Annapolis adjourned. Finally, on February 21, 1787, Congress formally called upon the states to send representatives to Philadelphia "for the sole and express purpose of revising the Articles of Confederation. . . . . "

The Philadelphia Convention

The delegates who gathered in May 1787 were, for the most part, unanimous in their desire to strengthen the national government. However, once the convention got under way, the delegates realized that their task would involve more than just a revision of the Articles.

The Delegates. Over the course of the convention, 55 delegates from 12 states took part in the proceedings. Only Rhode Island refused to participate. Most of the men who came to Philadelphia had had experience in government. Many had served in the state legislatures, and 28 had served in either the Second Continental Congress or the Congress of the Confederation. Benjamin Franklin and Roger Sherman had been on the committee that

drafted the Declaration of Independence. As historian Samuel Eliot Morison wrote:

> *Practically every American who had useful ideas on political science was there except John Adams and Thomas Jefferson on foreign missions and John Jay, busy with the foreign affairs of the Confederation.*

Although certain important leaders in the struggle for independence, such as Patrick Henry and Sam Adams, refused to attend, it was largely a gathering of distinguished patriots. Washington was elected to preside at the convention. Other prominent figures were James Madison and Alexander Hamilton.

The delegates at the convention were representatives of what Washington called "the discerning part of the community." That is, they were educated men of property and social standing. As such, they were motivated by a concern for economic stability. Most felt that a strong national government was needed to check the irresponsible policies of state legislatures. However, it was agreed that the government of the United States had to be republican in nature. Therefore, it would need constraints built into its structure. Despite this basic consensus, the delegates represented different sections of the country with different interests. Some compromises had to be made in order to forge a stronger union.

The Virginia and New Jersey Plans. One of the most serious conflicts of the convention was the struggle between the large states and the small states over representation in Congress. Early in the convention, Virginia—a large state—presented a plan that was really a blueprint for a new national government rather than a revision of the Articles.

This plan, largely the work of James Madison, served as the basis for early debate at the convention. In its final form, the Virginia Plan, as it became known, called for the creation of a national government superior to the states. This government would have separate executive, judicial, and legislative branches. Little debate arose over the creation of the executive and judicial branches. However, the debate over the legislative body brought the convention to a standstill and nearly caused it to fail.

According to the Virginia Plan, the national legislature would be bicameral. The members of the lower house would be elected by the voters in each

Abigail Adams

During most of the Confederation period, Abigail Smith Adams lived in Europe with her diplomat husband John Adams, who became the first American minister to Great Britain. Abigail Smith, the daughter of a parson, grew up in Massachusetts when it was still an English colony. Eventually, as wife of the second President of the United States, she became the first First Lady to preside over the still unfinished White House.

Abigail Smith married John Adams in 1764. They had five children, one of whom was John Quincy Adams, later the sixth President of the United States. In 1774, John Adams went to Philadelphia as a delegate to the Continental Congress, while Abigail Adams remained in Massachusetts to bring up their children and manage their farm and business affairs. In letters to her husband, she called for American independence long before others thought it was a serious possibility.

Partly as a result of her frequent separations from her husband, Abigail Adams developed a notable talent as a letter writer. Letter writing, she said, was "a habit, the pleasure of which increases with practice, but becomes irksome by neglect." In one of her most well-known letters, she made the following plea to her husband and his associates in the Continental Congress:

> Remember the Ladies, and be more generous and favourable to them than your ancestors. Do not put such unlimited power into the hands of the Husbands. Remember all Men would be tyrants if they could. If particular care and attention is not paid to the Ladies we are determined to foment a Rebellion, and will not hold ourselves bound by any Laws in which we have no voice, or Representation.

Abigail Adams believed strongly in equal rights for women and blacks at a time in history when such views were not well received.

state. The members of the upper house, which was designed to be removed from the people, would be nominated by the state legislatures and elected by the lower house.

The number of representatives allotted each state in the national legislature would be proportional to the size of the state's population. The larger states, like Virginia, would thus have more representatives than the smaller states.

The main subject of the debate on the Virginia Plan was this question of representation. Delegates from the smaller states feared that the larger, more populous states, dominating the national legislature, might pass laws harmful to the smaller states' interests. Delegates from the larger states, on the other hand, argued that representation based upon population was the only fair way to set it up.

At this stage of the debate, William Paterson of New Jersey, speaking for the smaller states, presented an alternative plan. The New Jersey Plan, as it came to be called, simply revised the Articles, which was all the convention was actually empowered to do. Thus, while granting certain added powers to the central government, the plan proposed that state sovereignty be retained. As under the Articles, each state would have one vote in the national legislature.

This plan was not satisfactory either to the delegates from the larger states or to those delegates who desired a strong national government as a check on the states. The convention was at an impasse.

The Great Compromise. With the acceptance of the so-called Great Compromise, the stalemate was broken. The compromise was first offered by Roger Sherman of Connecticut and later modified. The final

Refer to the fact that Americans had had experience with representative government—unlike the French in the revolution of 1789. Americans were building on a foundation, not starting anew.

Ask students to discuss the contradiction involved in claiming slaves as property and claiming them as people for the purpose of representation.

compromise provided for a bicameral national legislature, including a House of Representatives and a Senate.

Voters in each state would elect members of the lower house, the House of Representatives. The members of the upper house, the Senate, would be chosen by the state legislatures. Each state, regardless of size, would be represented by two Senators, thereby giving each state equal power in the Senate. In the House of Representatives, however, the number of representatives from each state would be based on population.

The Three-fifths Compromise   The Great Compromise settled the question of how the states were to be represented in the national legislature. However, during the debate over representation, another issue arose that created conflict—this time between the northern and southern states.

The major question involved whether slaves should be counted in determining the number of representatives allotted each state in the lower house. The question was complicated by the fact that the convention had agreed to apportion direct taxes among the states according to population.

THE ARTICLES OF CONFEDERATION AND THE CONSTITUTION

THE ARTICLES	THE CONSTITUTION
The Legislature	
A unicameral legislature was set up with each state holding one vote regardless of population. Enacting legislation required the approval of at least nine states.	A bicameral legislature was set up with each state having equal representation in the Senate. States were represented according to population in the House. Legislation is enacted by simple majority in each house of Congress.
The Executive Branch	
No executive was provided to administer and enforce the acts of Congress. A committee of the states was chosen to serve when Congress was out of session. Congress had sole authority to empower the committee.	The chief executive is the President, who is chosen by electors. In turn, the electors are chosen by voters in their states. The President executes the laws of the land.
The Judiciary	
No national court system was provided. Congress was permitted to establish courts to hear cases involving piracy and capture on the high seas.	A national system of courts, headed by the Supreme Court, was set up. Courts hear cases involving national laws, treaties, or the Constitution; two or more states; a state and citizens of another state; citizens of different states.
In Addition:	
Admission into the Confederation was permitted with the consent of nine of the states. The Articles of Confederation could be amended only with the consent of all the states.	Congress has the power to admit new states. All states must have a republican form of government. The Constitution can be amended by proposals passed by two-thirds vote of both houses of Congress or a national convention and ratified by three-fourths of the states.

Northerners argued that if slaves were considered "property," as southerners maintained, then they should not be counted in the population for representation. Northerners did, however, want slaves counted for taxation purposes. Southerners, on the other hand, felt just the opposite. They wanted slaves counted for representation but not for taxation.

The issue was resolved by the Three-fifths Compromise—that is, a slave would count as three-fifths of a person, or five slaves would count as three free people. This Three-fifths Compromise applied to both taxation and representation.

Commercial Compromises. The different views of the North and South, apparent in the discussion of the Three-fifths Compromise, surfaced again in the debate over the commercial powers of Congress.

In the northern states, commerce was a major interest. These states favored giving the national government a generous amount of authority to regulate commerce. Southerners, however, were against giving Congress unlimited power to control trade. The prosperity of the southern states depended on exporting agricultural products. Therefore these states wanted to deny the central government the power to tax exports. Southerners felt that if Congress were given this power, buyers would have to pay higher prices for southern products, such as tabacco. These products would then be at a disadvantage in the world market, and the South's economy would suffer.

In addition to the concern over taxing exports, the southern states feared that Congress, given broad powers to regulate trade, might tax or even forbid the importation of slaves. Southerners were against any interference with the slave trade. They believed that this would strike at the South's labor supply and hurt its economy.

The continued importation of slaves was especially important to South Carolina and Georgia. In fact, Charles Pinckney of South Carolina stated that "South Carolina can never receive the plan [the Constitution] if it prohibits the slave trade." Many delegates, however, felt that the importation of slaves should be taxed or prohibited. Luther Martin of Maryland, for example, said of slavery, that it was "inconsistent with the principles of the revolution and dishonorable to the American character to have such a feature in the Constitution."

Finally, after a heated debate, compromise again was reached. The national government was given the power to regulate interstate commerce (and tax imports), but was denied the power to levy export taxes. Also, Congress was not allowed to interfere with the slave trade before 1808. It was, however, allowed to levy an import tax on slaves. This tax was not to exceed $10 per slave.

Completing the Constitution. With the resolution of these and other issues, the delegates moved slowly toward completing the Constitution. By the fall of 1787, they had shaped a document which became and still is the foundation for the government of the United States.

To achieve this end, many delegates had to make necessary compromises. Benjamin Franklin expressed the feelings of many of those present when, on September 17, he called for the unanimous endorsement of the document despite his confession "that there are several parts of this constitution which I do not at present approve."

Despite mixed feelings regarding some aspects of the Constitution, most of the delegates were hopeful about the future. As they approached to sign the document, Franklin, while looking at a rising sun painted on the back of the President's chair, was heard to observe:

> Painters had found it difficult in their art to distinguish a rising from a setting sun. I have . . . often . . . looked at that behind the President without being able to tell whether it was rising or setting: But now at length I have the happiness to know that it is a rising and not a setting sun. . . .

SECTION REVIEW

1. Identify the following: Virginia Plan, William Paterson, New Jersey Plan, Roger Sherman
2. What was the main purpose of the Annapolis Convention?
3. What characteristics did the delegates at Philadelphia have in common?
4. What issues did the delegates agree upon at the outset of the Constitutional Convention?
5. How did the Great Compromise settle the debate over representation?
6. What were the provisions of the Three-fifths Compromise?

6 Debate Over the Constitution

The delegates at Philadelphia had produced the Constitution, but its acceptance depended upon the will of the American people. In each of the 13 states, voters would elect delegates to special conventions that would decide whether to accept or reject the new plan of government. Once 9 of the 13 conventions had ratified the Constitution, it could go into effect.

Different Opinions

Ratification, however, was not assured. Many people who remembered British tyranny were still against a powerful national government. Supporters and opponents of the Constitution gathered their forces for the coming struggle.

Those who favored the Constitution called themselves "Federalists." This group was made up mostly of people who lived in cities or engaged in trade, including large landowners. The Federalists, for example, found support among merchants, land speculators, and many southern planters.

These people wanted a strong government capable of handling the problems facing the United States both at home and abroad. They felt that the new Constitution, while it protected the rights of the states, gave the central government enough power to function effectively.

Opponents of the Constitution, called Antifederalists, were supported mostly by small farmers, especially those who were in debt. Antifederalists felt that a strong central government was a threat to liberty. They were especially opposed to a clause in the new Constitution that would allow Congress to pass any laws "necessary and proper" to carry out the specifically listed powers.

The Antifederalists also felt that the new government would be too removed from the people. The President and Vice President would be chosen by individuals who were selected by the state legislatures rather than by the voters. Members of the Senate would also be chosen by the state legislatures. Only the members of the House of Representatives would be directly elected by the people. But the proposed ratio for representation (one representative for 30,000 people) seemed too high. The Antifederalists felt that the people would have a greater voice in government if the states were sovereign.

Finally, the Antifederalists objected to the Constitution's lack of a bill of rights. They feared losing the liberties they had gained during the Revolution and wanted to include a guarantee of those liberties in the Constitution.

Ratification

Federalists and Antifederalists met in state conventions to decide the fate of the Constitution. Through a combination of factors—better organization, outstanding leadership, and sometimes, political guile—the Federalists won the confrontation. One by one the states ratified the Constitution.

On December 7, 1787, Delaware became the first state to approve the Constitution, ratifying it unanimously. On December 12, Pennsylvania fell in line, but over considerable opposition. Less than a week later, New Jersey voted unanimously for ratification. On January 2, 1788, Georgia's convention also voted unanimously to approve the Constitution. Connecticut was the next to act. On January 9, its convention voted 128–40 for ratification.

EVENTS LEADING TO RATIFICATION

1765	Stamp Act Congress
1770	Committees of Correspondence are organized
1774	First Continental Congress meets
1775	Second Continental Congress meets War for Independence begins
1776	Declaration of Independence signed States begin to adopt constitutions
1781	Articles of Confederation ratified
1783	Treaty of Paris signed
1785	Mount Vernon Convention meets
1786	Annapolis Convention meets
1787	Constitutional Convention meets
1789	Constitution put into effect

John Hancock, then governor of Massachusetts, refused to take his seat as president of the convention until the Federalists promised to support him for Vice President upon ratification of the Constitution.

The authors of *The Federalist Papers* wrote under the name "Publius."

RATIFICATION OF THE CONSTITUTION

DATE	STATE	FOR	AGAINST
December 7, 1787	DELAWARE	30	0
December 12, 1787	PENNSYLVANIA	46	23
December 18, 1787	NEW JERSEY	38	0
January 2, 1788	GEORGIA	26	0
January 9, 1788	CONNECTICUT	128	40
February 6, 1788	MASSACHUSETTS	187	168
April 28, 1788	MARYLAND	63	11
May 23, 1788	SOUTH CAROLINA	149	73
June 21, 1788	NEW HAMPSHIRE	57	47
June 25, 1788	VIRGINIA	89	79
July 26, 1788	NEW YORK	30	27
November 21, 1788	NORTH CAROLINA	194	77
May 29, 1790	RHODE ISLAND	34	32

On the same day that Connecticut ratified, the Massachusetts convention met. On February 6, after a fierce struggle, the Federalists won the battle for ratification by a narrow margin. Instrumental in their victory was the support of John Hancock, who hoped for Federalist backing in seeking the Vice Presidency.

Late in April, Maryland approved the Constitution with little difficulty. South Carolina followed, voting 149–73 for ratification on May 23. About a month later, New Hampshire voted 57–47 to ratify.

Although the necessary nine states had now approved the Constitution, two of the most important states—Virginia and New York—were still in convention. A union without these states would have a doubtful future.

In Virginia, the Antifederalists were led by Patrick Henry. Another formidable Antifederalist was George Mason, who had attended the Philadelphia Convention but refused to sign the Constitution. Among the supporters of the Constitution, however, were such prominent figures as James Madison and George Washington. Finally, on June 25 after a bitter struggle, the Federalists won by a close vote of 89–79. Although Virginia ratified, however, it asked for a bill of rights as well as a number of other changes in the Constitution.

In New York, the Antifederalists were well organized and led by the state's governor, George Clinton. They held a clear majority in the convention, and victory seemed within their grasp. The Federalists, however, had Alexander Hamilton on their side. Hamilton, along with John Jay and James Madison, defended the Constitution in a series of widely read essays. Later, these essays were collected and published in a famous work, *The Federalist*—a classic in American political literature.

Many people in New York were influenced by these essays, and this helped turn the tide in favor of the Constitution. For example, in *The Federalist*, No. 14, Madison defended a strong national government:

In the first place it is to be remembered that the general government is not to be charged with the whole power of making and administering laws. Its jurisdiction is limited to certain enumerated objects, which concern all the members of the republic, but which are not to be attained by the separate provisions of any. The subordinate governments, which can extend their care to all those other subjects which can be separately provided for, will retain their due authority and activity.

New York was the scene of the fiercest debate over ratification.   Rhode Island did not even send delegates to the Philadelphia convention.

In *The Federalist,* No. 15: Hamilton condemned the Confederation government:

> *We may indeed with propriety be said, to have reached almost the last stage of national humiliation. There is scarcely anything that can wound the pride or degrade the character of an independent nation which we do not experience.* . . .

Besides writing such essays, Hamilton was active in the convention. He worked to delay the vote, hoping that news of Virginia's ratification would sway the delegates. The Antifederalists, worried that outright rejection of the Constitution might harm relations with neighboring states, went along with the delay. When the news came that Virginia had ratified the Constitution, New York followed suit.

With the ratification of the Constitution by Virginia and New York, only two states remained outside the Union. North Carolina failed to ratify the Constitution until November 1789, while Rhode Island did not enter the Union until May 1790.

However, with more than the nine votes needed for ratification, Congress, in July 1788, called for national elections to be held in January 1789. The nation's new experiment in government was about to begin.

SECTION REVIEW

1. Identify the following: Federalists, Antifederalists, George Mason, George Clinton, *The Federalist.*
2. What condition had to be met for the Constitution to be put into effect?
3. What groups of people opposed the Constitution? Supported it?
4. Why were the Federalists successful in getting the Constitution ratified?

CHAPTER 4   REVIEW

SUMMARY

1. By the end of the Revolution, most of the 13 colonies had formed new state governments with written constitutions.
2. The nation's first constitution, the Articles of Confederation, limited the authority of the central government and left most powers in the hands of the states.
3. The limitations on the power of the national government under the Articles of Confederation made it difficult to carry out effective domestic and foreign policies.
4. Despite the weaknesses of the central government, there were achievements under the Articles.
5. In order to correct the weaknesses of the national government, delegates chosen by the state legislatures met at Philadelphia in 1787 to write a revised constitution.
6. The Constitution that resulted from the Philadelphia Convention was achieved through compromises on major issues.
7. The new Constitution greatly strengthened the role of the national government.
8. Supporters and opponents of the Constitution staged an intense debate over its ratification.
9. In 1788, after 11 of the 13 states had ratified it, the Constitution became the foundation for a new national government in the United States.

VOCABULARY

bill of rights	ratification	tribute	national income
bicameral	nationalist	depression	national debt
confederation	speculator	interstate commerce	bureaucracy
sovereignty	right of deposit	depreciated	public domain

REVIEW QUESTIONS

1. What were the basic features of the state constitutions drawn up during the American Revolution?
2. What were the major weaknesses of the national government established under the Articles of Confederation?
3. How did Great Britain, Spain, and the Barbary Pirates react to the national government's weaknesses during the Critical Period?
4. Why did the national government face economic problems during the Critical Period?
5. What caused Shays' Rebellion? What effect did it have on the country?
6. What were the achievements of the Confederation government?
7. What major issues arose at the Philadelphia Convention?
8. What powers did the Constitution grant the national government that it did not have under the Articles?
9. Why did the Federalists support the Constitution? Why did the Antifederalists oppose it?

DISCUSSION

1. Why was Shays' Rebellion symptomatic of the problems of the new nation?
2. Of the sources of revenue available to the national government during the Critical Period, which was most desirable? Least desirable?
3. What might have happened if the delegates to the Constitutional Convention had not adopted the Great Compromise?
4. If you had lived during the struggle over ratification, would you have supported the Federalists or Antifederalists? Why?
5. What events during the Critical Period support Hamilton's condemnation of the Articles in *The Federalist*, No. 15?
6. How does your state's constitution compare to the Constitution of the United States?

USING MAPS

Refer to the map on page 89 and answer the following questions:

1. Where did the United States have conflicting territorial claims with other nations?
2. Where did the national government have conflicting claims with the states?
3. Which states had western land claims?
4. How many acres were in a township?

USING SKILLS

Study the following list of positions that were debated at the Constitutional Convention. Which positions were favored by delegates from southern states? Which were favored by delegates from northern states?

1. Slaves should be counted in determining the number of representatives each state should have in the House of Representatives.
2. Slaves should not be counted in determining the number of representatives each state should have in the House.
3. Slaves should be counted for taxation purposes.
4. Slaves should not be counted for taxation purposes.
5. The national government should have the power to tax or forbid the importation of slaves.
6. The national government should have broad powers to control trade.
7. The national government should not have the power to tax exports.
8. The national government should not have unlimited power to control trade.

1	Historical Background	99
2	The Federal System	102
3	Branches of Government	105
4	The Legislative Process	110
5	The Democratic Process	112
6	The Changing Constitution	114

THE CONSTITUTION

The General Government, though limited as to its objects, is supreme with respect to those objects.

JOHN MARSHALL

In 1788 the Constitution replaced the Articles of Confederation as the official plan of American government. As drafted by its Framers, the Constitution is a brief document that outlines the basic organization of the national government and sets the procedures and limitations for its operation.

Created to meet the growing needs of a changing nation, the Constitution has been the fundamental law of the United States for nearly 200 years. Of all the written national constitutions in the world, the United States Constitution is the oldest that is still operating.

1 Historical Background

When the delegates at Philadelphia framed the Constitution, they were guided by their study of the great political writers of the late 1600's and early 1700's. The writers who influenced the delegates at Philadelphia were, in general, part of a philosophic movement known as the Enlightenment. It was called the Enlightenment because the philosophers of the day saw their age as one emerging from the darkness and ignorance of earlier times. Enlightenment thinkers questioned traditional values and popularized ideas that would change concepts of government the world over.

Enlightenment Philosophy

Generally, Enlightenment thinkers believed that God had created an orderly universe governed by established laws. These laws were called **natural laws** and could be discovered by human reason. By using reason, for example, Sir Isaac Newton, the English physicist, discovered the law of gravity. Natural laws, moreover, governed not only the physical universe, but also human relations.

The idea that human relations are governed by a set of established laws laid the foundation for the philosophy of **natural rights.** This philosophy was set forth by John Locke in *Two Treatises of Government* (1690). Locke believed that people in a "state of nature," or a time before the organization of government, had certain basic rights. These were life, liberty, and property.

According to Locke, people form governments to protect their rights, and they guarantee those rights by **social contract.** This is a compact, or agreement, between the people and a government. The contract establishes the authority and responsibility of each party. The people promise to obey the government as long as that government protects their rights.

Popular Sovereignty. Locke's social contract theory was supported by the principle of **popular sovereignty**—the idea that ultimate political authority rests with the people. In other words, government is based upon the consent of the governed. If the government fails in its obligations, the people may reconsider and, as a last resort, rebel. Thus the people have the power to create, change, or even abolish government.

The principle of popular sovereignty was used by natural-rights philosophers in their attack on **absolutism,** or the idea that total power should be vested in one or more rulers. In the 1600's and 1700's, kings were absolute rulers. Their power was based on the theory of **divine right,** which held that a ruler received authority directly from God. Under these absolutist regimes, people had only those rights allowed to them by the government. They could not rightfully resist the government's authority for any reason.

Limited Government. In contrast to the idea of absolutism is the idea of **limited government.** This principle states that government may exercise only those powers given to it by the people. The idea of limited government is implicit in the principle of popular sovereignty, which states that the people are the sole source of political power.

Separation of Powers. An extension of the principle of limited government is the idea of **separation of powers,** or the division of power between the different parts of a government. This idea was also set forth by John Locke. He argued that, although government was based on the consent of the governed, other precautions had to be taken to ensure that governments did not exceed their authority.

Locke's idea of separation of powers was later refined by the French philosopher Montesquieu in *The Spirit of the Laws* (1748). Montesquieu greatly admired the British Constitution, which divided power between executive, legislative, and judicial branches. With such a division of power, no one part of the government was likely to threaten the liberties of the people.

Hierarchy of Laws. In addition to separation of powers, another aspect of popular sovereignty and limited government is the idea of a **hierarchy of laws.** That is, some laws are superior to others. The highest law is the natural law by which people have certain basic rights. Next is the contract creating a government to protect those rights. Lowest in the hierarchy are the specific laws passed by that government.

The American Experience

When Americans of the eighteenth century read the Enlightenment philosophers, the philosophers' ideas made sense in terms of the American experience. Long before the writings of Locke were published, Americans had acquired a working understanding of social contract theory.

Colonial Times. In 1620, when the Pilgrims landed at Plymouth Rock, they drew up the Mayflower Compact. This was a written contract outlining the rules by which they agreed to live. Another example of a social contract was the Fundamental Orders of Connecticut (1639). Furthermore, Americans thought of their colonial charters as contracts that guaranteed the traditional rights of English citizens.

Besides the social contract theory, colonial Americans were familiar with the idea of separation of powers. As British citizens, the colonists felt that the British Constitution was the best protector of individual rights. This constitution seemed to give an ideal balance to government. Power was divided between an executive, the king; a legislature, Parliament; and an independent judiciary. With some differences, American colonial governments reflected these same divisions.

Americans in colonial times were also familiar with the idea of a hierarchy of laws. The most important laws were those embodied in the British Constitution. Next were the laws of Parliament. Then there were the laws passed by the colonial legislatures and finally, those of towns or counties.

The Confederation Years. During the early national years, American political practice continued to reflect the ideas of the Enlightenment. Americans revolted from Great Britain because they thought their rights were being threatened. They used the theory of popular sovereignty as justification for their action. After the colonies declared their independence, they put the social contract theory into practice again.

To ensure that the governments they formed did not step beyond the powers given to them by the people, the states noted those powers in written constitutions. The powers of government were limited to those specifically stated. Thus, the state constitutions and the Articles of Confederation reflected the principles of limited government. The people further limited the powers of the new state governments by adding bills of rights to the state constitutions.

All of the state constitutions incorporated the idea of separation of powers between executive, legislative, and judicial branches. However, although the branches were separated, their powers were not balanced. Most state constitutions expressed the colonists' fear of executive authority, a fear that had grown out of their many conflicts with the crown. So, at the state level, most power remained with the legislatures.

American political practice during the Confederation years included the concept of a hierarchy of laws as well as the separation of powers. Lowest in the hierarchy was town or county law. Above that was

James Madison

Born in 1751, Madison was still a young man at the time of the Revolution, but his brilliant, incisive mind made him one of the most valuable leaders of the Patriots. After the war, he played a major role at the Constitutional Convention.

As one of the delegates from Virginia, Madison participated in the lengthy, often heated discussions that created a foundation of government. He kept meticulous notes and tried to impress upon the other delegates the need for balance. Power had to be balanced among the different levels and branches of government. Every right had to be balanced by a corresponding responsibility.

Madison became the chief architect of the Constitution, and his notes became the best record of what happened at the Convention. "Every word [of the Constitution]," he later wrote, "decides a question between power and liberty."

After the Constitution went into effect, Madison became a leader of the new national government. In developing the Bill of Rights, he once again was trying to achieve the difficult balance between the rights of the people and the power of government. In 1808 Madison became the fourth President of the United States. Throughout his career, he continued to defend the principle of balance that was built into the Constitution.

In April 1771, a young Princeton student named James Madison attended the demonstration of a marvelous machine. This European-built contraption was a working model of the then-known solar system. Madison was impressed by the way the planets made their way in perfect balance around the sun. His appreciation of the precious balance of forces was to color his thinking all his life.

---

state law, followed by the state constitution. Here the hierarchy of laws broke down. Although the national constitution was supposed to be the most important law, the Articles of Confederation provided a weak central government with greatly limited powers.

Under the Articles, the states kept control over most important government functions and dominated the national Congress. This body remained the sole organ of government, as there was neither an executive nor a judiciary. The inadequacies of the Articles, however, gave rise to a growing demand for change. This culminated in the Constitutional Convention at Philadelphia.

The delegates at Philadelphia felt the Constitution they framed took care of the problems caused by the weaknesses of the Articles. In yet another expression of the social contract theory, the new Constitution was ratified by the people through state conventions. The Constitution gave more powers to

the national government, while keeping the principles of limited government. Thus, both the national and state governments had political power. Power was also separated within the national government itself. No single part of the government could become too powerful. Finally, the new Constitution was the supreme law of the land—the highest law in the American hierarchy of laws.

SECTION REVIEW

1. What philosophers influenced the delegates to the Constitutional Convention?
2. According to Locke, what is the agreement between people and their governments?
3. What is the highest law in the hierarchy of laws?
4. How did the state constitutions express the people's fear of excessive authority?
5. How was the social contract theory applied in the Constitution?

Have students read Article I, Section 8 of the annotated Constitution in the Appendix.

The ineffectiveness of the Confederation government was partly due to its inability to tax. The power to tax gave the new national government the means to put the United States on a firm financial foundation.

2 The Federal System

The authors of the Constitution, in order to establish a strong national government and preserve state sovereignty, set up a **federal system** of government. In such a system, power is divided between a central government and a number of regional governments—in this case, the states. The system set up by the Constitution gave certain powers to the national government, reserved others to the states, and allowed some to exist on both levels.

Powers of the National Government

Although they believed in the idea of limited government, the Framers of the Constitution felt that the Confederation government had been too limited in its power. To correct this, the Constitution increased the powers of the national government. These powers fall into three different categories: expressed, implied, and inherent.

Expressed Powers. Those powers explicitly given to the national government in the Constitution are known as enumerated or **expressed powers.** Article I, Section 8, lists most of the powers given to Congress. These include the power to tax, regulate trade, raise and maintain the armed forces, coin money, and declare war. Article II, Sections 2 and 3, list most of the powers given to the President. Among these are the power to make treaties, make appointments to federal offices, act as Commander-in-Chief of the armed forces, and grant pardons.

Implied Powers. Besides the expressed powers, the national government also has **implied powers.** These are powers which may reasonably be implied from the expressed powers. For example, the power to enact draft laws is implied by the power to raise armies. The concept of implied power came from the "necessary and proper" clause in Article I, Section 8. It stated that Congress shall have the power:

> *To make all laws which shall be necessary and proper for carrying into execution the foregoing powers, and all other power vested by this Constitution in the Government of the United States, or in any department or officer thereof.*

This clause is sometimes called the **elastic clause** because it stretches the powers of Congress. The meaning of the elastic clause has been the subject of bitter disputes for much of American history. Some people have favored a **loose construction,** or broad

The national government has the power to enact draft laws. In what ways is the power to employ a draft supported by the Constitution?

The national government, through the Department of Justice, regulates the entry of citizens of other countries into the United States. The right to regulate immigration is an inherent power. What is meant by an inherent power?

interpretation, of the Constitution. This would allow the national government to use powers which could reasonably be implied as necessary and proper. Others have favored a **strict construction,** or narrow interpretation. This would allow the federal government to take only those actions absolutely necessary to carry out the expressed powers.

Inherent Powers. Along with implied powers, the national government has **inherent powers.** These are powers which are not specifically given to the federal government but which it possesses simply because it is a national government. For example, all national governments have the power to defend their countries, gain territory, and regulate immigration.

Powers of State Governments

In addition to granting certain powers to the national government, the Constitution reserved some powers to the states. These **reserved powers** include those powers not given to the national government and not denied to the states by the Constitution. The basis of the reserved powers is the Tenth Amendment, which states:

The powers not delegated to the United States by the Constitution, nor prohibited by it

to the states are reserved to the states respectively, or to the people.

This Amendment was intended to protect the states from an overextension of the national government's power and has often been used to back up strict construction arguments. One of the most important powers reserved to the states is the **police power.** This is the authority to protect the health, safety, morals, and welfare of citizens.

Concurrent Powers

Under the federal system, some powers are shared by both the national and state governments. These are called **concurrent powers,** and include those powers which the Constitution neither granted *exclusively* to the national government nor denied the states. The concurrent powers are exercised separately and simultaneously. The powers to tax, borrow money, and hold elections are examples of concurrent powers.

Limitations on Power

While the Constitution gave certain powers to the national government and reserved others to the

Have students list the powers denied to the national government under Article I, Section 9. Discuss why the government is forbidden to grant titles of nobility. What fears of the colonists does this part of the Constitution express? Has this provision made American society more democratic than countries that do have titles of nobility?

states, it also denied powers to both. The restrictions placed on government show the concern the Framers felt over the possible abuse of power.

Powers Denied the National Government. Despite support for a strong central government, most Americans in the 1700's wanted certain limitations on the power of the national government. Some of these limitations are found in Article I, Section 9, and the first ten amendments to the Constitution.

In Article I, Section 9, the national government was forbidden to take away certain legal rights. For example, it was forbidden to pass an **ex post facto law.** This is a law that prescribes punishment for an act committed before the law against it was passed. Because of the commercial concerns of some of the Framers, the national government was forbidden to levy export taxes. It was also forbidden to interfere with the slave trade until 1808.

The powers of the national government were further curtailed by the first ten amendments to the Constitution known as the Bill of Rights. These amendments gave Americans a set of guaranteed liberties. For example, the First Amendment protected freedom of religion, speech, press, and peaceful assembly. The Eighth Amendment prohibited the use of cruel and unusual punishments, and the Fifth Amendment guaranteed the right to **due process of law.** This means that the government cannot act arbitrarily against a person accused of a crime but must follow specific procedures.

Powers Denied the State Government. Just as the Constitution denied powers to the national government, so it also denied powers to the state governments. The chief purpose of this was to ensure national control over certain matters. Most restrictions on the states are found in Article I, Section 10. For example, states were forbidden to tax imports and exports or enter into treaties. Because of the Framers' concern over what they believed to be irresponsible economic legislation by the states in the 1780's, the Constitution prohibited states from coining or printing money.

SECTION REVIEW

1. What are the expressed powers the Constitution gives to Congress? To the President?

DIVISION OF POWERS

EXCLUSIVE POWERS OF THE NATIONAL GOVERNMENT	CONCURRENT POWERS	RESERVED POWERS OF THE STATE GOVERNMENTS
declare war and conduct foreign affairs coin money manage a postal system establish lower courts raise and support armed forces	levy taxes borrow money define and punish crime charter banks	maintain a system of public education create local governments provide public education direct traffic laws

POWERS DENIED TO THE NATIONAL GOVERNMENT	POWERS DENIED TO THE NATIONAL AND STATE GOVERNMENTS	POWERS DENIED TO THE STATE GOVERNMENTS
tax exports suspend writ of habeas corpus grant titles of nobility	deny due process of law pass ex post facto laws pass bills of attainder	coin money enter into treaties void contracts

Point out that different branches have at times tried to increase their powers at the expense of another branch. For example, Congress tried to limit the powers of President Johnson after the Civil War. Discuss what might happen if the balance of powers was not maintained.

Congress is bicameral partly because it was modeled after the British Parliament.

THE BILL OF RIGHTS-1791

AMENDMENT 1	Guarantees freedom of religion, of speech, and of the press, and the right to assemble peaceably and to petition the government.
AMENDMENT 2	Guarantees the right to organize state militias and to bear arms.
AMENDMENT 3	Prohibits quartering of soldiers.
AMENDMENT 4	Prohibits government searches and seizures of property without a warrant.
AMENDMENT 5	Requires a grand jury for criminal charges; prohibits military trial of civilians; prohibits forcing accused persons to testify against themselves; guarantees that no one may be deprived of life, liberty, or property without due process of law.
AMENDMENT 6	Guarantees the right to a speedy trial by jury in criminal cases; to know all charges; to question and obtain witnesses; to have counsel.
AMENDMENT 7	Guarantees a trial in most civil cases.
AMENDMENT 8	Prohibits excessive bail, fines, and punishment.
AMENDMENT 9	Gives rights not mentioned in the Constitution to the people.
AMENDMENT 10	Reserves powers not delegated to the national government for the states and the people.

2. What is the basis of the concept of implied powers?

3. What are some examples of inherent powers?

4. How does the Constitution reserve powers for the states?

5. What constitutional limitations are placed on the national government?

3 Branches of Government

The Framers not only divided power between two levels of government, but separated the executive, legislative, and judicial functions of the national government among three branches. To make certain that no single branch dominated the government, the Framers made certain provisions that allow each branch to check the operations of the others.

Congress

The first branch of government established by the Framers was the legislature. Article I, Section 1 of the Constitution states: "All legislative powers herein granted shall be vested in a Congress of the United States. . . . " The major function of the Congress is to make laws—to translate the will of the people into public policy.

As per the Great Compromise, the Constitution set up a bicameral legislature consisting of the House of Representatives and the Senate. Members of the House[1] are to be elected by the people for two-year terms. The number of representatives from each state is based on population. In the Senate, representation is equal, with each state electing two Senators. Originally, members of the Senate were to be chosen by their respective state legislatures for six-year terms.[2]

Besides variations in the terms of office and methods of selecting Senators and Representatives, there are different qualifications for each. Those who run for a seat in the House of Representatives have to be 25 years of age, a United States' citizen for 7 years, and a resident of the state in which they run. Candidates for Senate seats have to be 30 years of age, a United States' citizen for 9 years, and a resident of the state in which they run.

The differences between the House and Senate resulted from a desire on the part of the Framers to institute checks within the legislature itself. The

---

[1] The House of Representatives is commonly referred to simply as the "House."

[2] The Seventeenth Amendment to the Constitution (1913) provided for the direct election of United States' Senators by the people of their respective states.

The views of various Presidents on strict versus loose construction of the Constitution will be discussed throughout the text. Alert students to look for ways that differing views on this issue influenced presidential actions and the power of the Presidency.

In addition to making laws, Congress has among its duties the power to review the workings of the executive and judicial branches, conduct investigations, and amend the Constitution. How did the authors of the Constitution make sure that Congress would check its own powers?

authors of the Constitution wanted to make the legislature responsive to the will of the people and still provide a check on the pressures of public opinion.

Because Representatives were directly and more frequently elected, they were more responsive to the people. Senators, on the other hand, were more removed from the people. Therefore, they could be more deliberative and act as a check on public opinion.

The Presidency

After setting up the legislature, the Framers turned to the executive branch, nonexistent under the Articles of Confederation. Article II, Section 1 of the Constitution states: "The executive power shall be vested in a President of the United States of America." The executive is responsible for executing, enforcing, or administering the laws written by the legislature.

In trying to balance power among the branches of government, the Framers created a powerful chief executive. Article II outlines the powers and duties of the office. The powers to recommend and to **veto** (reject) legislation give the President an important part in forming public policy. As chief diplomat, the President is responsible for making American foreign policy. Also, the President serves as Commander-in-Chief of the armed forces.

Although this is an impressive list of powers, the fact is that many of the powers of the President were not spelled out in the Constitution. Article II has been described by some scholars as the most loosely written section of the Constitution. This has allowed room for individual interpretation of presidential powers. In general, when strong individuals have been President, the power of the office has been enhanced. On the other hand, others have not asserted the full powers of the office.

In deciding the procedure for selecting the President, the authors of the Constitution wished to avoid the possibility of unwise choices by the people. However, the Framers also knew that in a republic such as the United States, government officials must represent the people. This problem was solved with an indirect method of electing the President through the Electoral College System.

Under this system, as set forth by the Constitution, the state legislatures decide how that state's electors are to be chosen.[3] Each state has as many electors as the combined number of its Senators and Representatives in Congress. Only these electors, plus three electors from the District of Columbia, actually vote for the President. The Framers felt that

---

[3] At first, most states allowed their legislatures to choose the electors. Today, in all 50 states, they are chosen by popular election.

The American Presidency

The American Presidency is probably the most powerful elective office in the world. Not many governments allow so much real and symbolic authority to be concentrated in one person for such a long period of time, with no recall except in cases of extreme wrongdoing.

It is somewhat ironic that a people who had just rebelled to free themselves from arbitrary power should permit this kind of concentration of authority in the hands of one person. Many people still carried bitter memories of their struggles to restrain the actions of colonial governors, and most early state constitutions reduced the role and the tenure of the governor accordingly.

Members of the Constitutional Convention expressed doubts as to the wisdom of creating an office with as much power as the Presidency. According to James Madison's notes on the Convention for June 18, 1787, "As to the Executive, it seemed to be admitted that no good one could be established on Republican principles."

Why, then, did the delegates give as much power to the President as they did? One reason was a general conservative backlash in the 1780's against the Articles of Confederation, which in essence had no executive at all and were deemed unworkable by many people. Although the Framers of the Constitution did not want a king, they wanted an executive who had enough power to cope with the country's problems.

The members of the Convention debated at length how to achieve just the right balance. Some delegates wanted to have more than one executive, and some thought a President should be appointed for life. Some thought Congress should choose the President, while others favored direct popular election. But the idea that finally prevailed was that there should be a single President who would be chosen indirectly through the Electoral College. The President would have a four-year term of office and could be removed from office for serious crimes.

Another in allowing the President to have strong powers factor was the careful and effective way in which those who favored a strong executive answered the objections raised during the ratification process, such as George Clinton's protest that the President had been given "both power and time sufficient to ruin the country." Alexander Hamilton eloquently defended the decision to have a single executive, "created by a form of election which merits universal admiration."

A third reason was the reputation of George Washington. Many historians believe that he was in the back of virtually everyone's mind when the office was designed. The fact that he was the first Electoral College's *unanimous* choice for President lends credence to this idea. Americans accorded Washington great respect for his military achievements and his integrity.

At first, Washington looked upon his office as one in which he would execute the laws passed by Congress, as the Framers had intended. But experience taught him that the President sometimes had to take a stronger role.

Since Washington's time, other strong Presidents have assumed broad powers not given to the office by the Constitution. During the Civil War, Abraham Lincoln ignored the Constitution in order to save the Union. Theodore Roosevelt, when he seized Panama to build a canal for the United States, said, "I decline to adopt the view that what was imperatively necessary for the nation could not be done by the President unless he could find some specific authorization to do it." At other times, Congress or the Courts have acted to check the exercise of presidential powers. The strength of the President depends upon the person who holds the office and the circumstances of the country. The exact limit of presidential power has never been finally determined.

QUESTIONS

1. Why were members of the Constitutional Convention afraid of giving the President too much power?

2. How did the reputation of George Washington influence the Constitutional Convention?

The Constitution permits the Supreme Court to decide cases involving the Constitution, federal laws, treaties, and disputes between states. One of the most important powers of the Supreme Court, judicial review, is not mentioned in the Constitution. What is judicial review?

the electors would probably be better educated and more experienced than most people. Thus, they would be able to make wiser choices. At the time the Constitution was written, the electors had almost complete discretion, as few people could vote, and the electors were not bound in any way to the people's choice.

These electors, who as a group are called the Electoral College, meet in their own states to cast their ballots for President. At first, each elector had two votes, both cast at the same time. The candidate receiving the highest number of electoral votes (as long as that number equaled a majority of electors) became President. The candidate with the second highest number of votes became Vice President. If no candidate received enough votes to equal a majority of the electors, the House of Representatives was to elect the President from among the top five recipients of electoral votes.[4]

The authors of the Constitution were careful in setting up the qualifications for the office of President

[4] The Twelfth Amendment (1804) has since provided for electors to cast separate ballots for the office of Vice President, and changed from five to three the number of candidates from whom the House would choose in case no candidate receives a majority of the electoral vote. If no candidate receives a majority of the electoral votes for Vice President, the Senate chooses between the two leading candidates.

as well as about deciding the method of selecting a person for the office. To become President, a person has to be native-born (born in America or of American parents), 35 years of age, and a resident of the United States for 14 years.

The Judiciary

The third branch of the government set up by the authors of the Constitution was the judiciary. Article III, Section 1, provides the basis for this national court system, stating:

> *The judicial power of the United States shall be vested in one Supreme Court, and in such inferior courts as the Congress may from time to time ordain and establish.*

The major function of the judicial branch is to interpret the law. Under the Articles, laws had been interpreted by each state.

Although it was not specifically stated in the Constitution, there is little doubt that the Framers intended the Supreme Court to have the power of **judicial review**.[5] This is the power to decide the constitutionality of a government's action. In *The*

[5] Both federal and state courts exercise the power of judicial review. However, the ultimate exercise of this power lies with the Supreme Court.

Refer students to the reading on p. 40 concerning the colonists' protest over England's decree that judges should remain in office at the pleasure of the Crown. Discuss why the judiciary must be independent.

The President may be impeached for "treason, bribery, or other high crimes or misdemeanors." Discuss what should be an impeachable offense.

CHECKS AND BALANCES

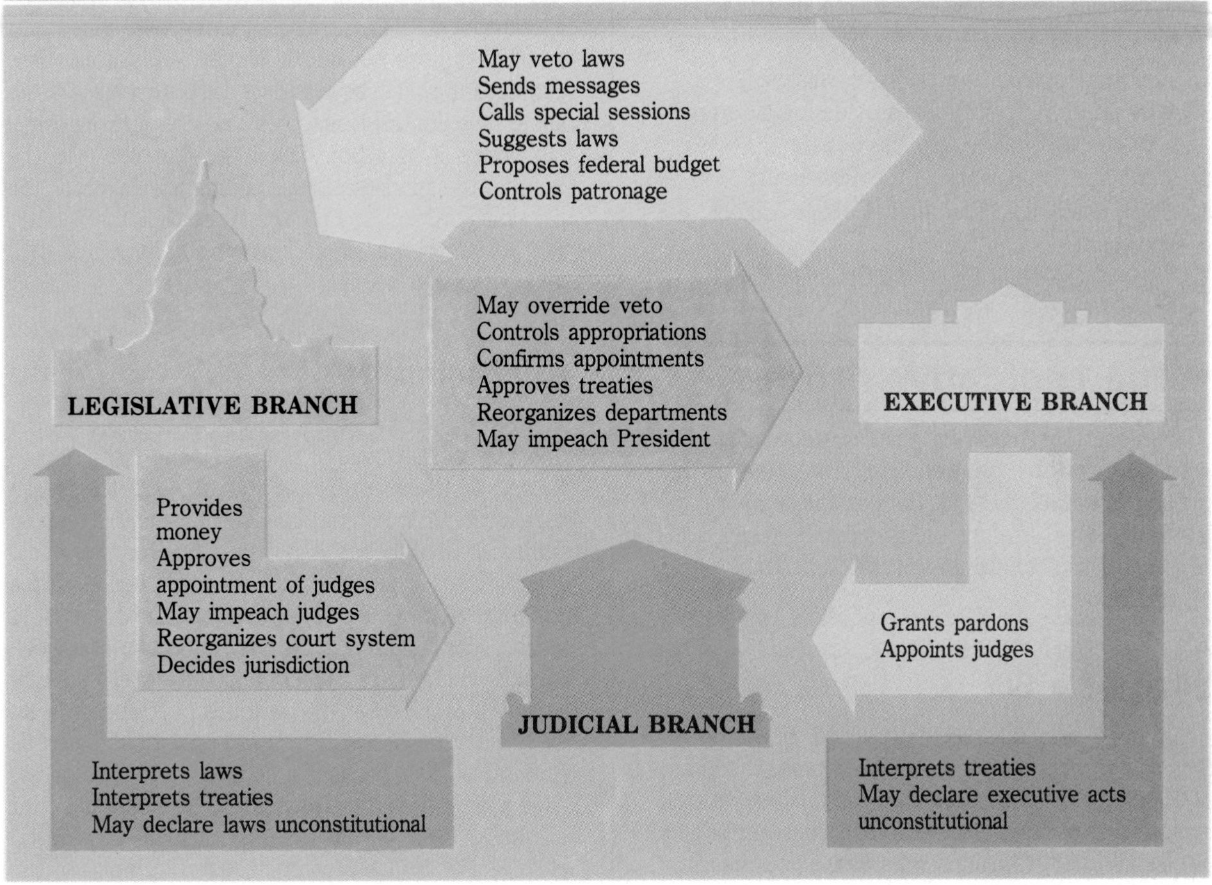

May veto laws
Sends messages
Calls special sessions
Suggests laws
Proposes federal budget
Controls patronage

LEGISLATIVE BRANCH

May override veto
Controls appropriations
Confirms appointments
Approves treaties
Reorganizes departments
May impeach President

EXECUTIVE BRANCH

Provides money
Approves appointment of judges
May impeach judges
Reorganizes court system
Decides jurisdiction

Grants pardons
Appoints judges

JUDICIAL BRANCH

Interprets laws
Interprets treaties
May declare laws unconstitutional

Interprets treaties
May declare executive acts unconstitutional

Federalist, No. 78, Alexander Hamilton wrote:

> *The interpretation of the laws is the proper and peculiar provision of the courts. A constitution is, in fact, and must be regarded by the judges as a fundamental law. It therefore belongs to them to ascertain its meaning. . . .*

To maintain the independence of the judiciary in matters of interpretation, the Constitution, in Article I, Section 1, provided that federal judges ". . . shall hold their offices during good behavior." In effect, then, they are appointed for life.

Checks and Balances

Although the Constitution established three separate branches of the national government, it did not make these branches totally independent of one another. To maintain the balance of power in government, each branch was given a number of checks on the other two. This is called the system of **checks and balances.**

The President was given a check on Congress through the use of the veto, and a check on the judiciary through the power of appointment. Congress was given the power to check the President by refusing to confirm appointments or ratify treaties, and by overriding vetoes. Congress also was given the power to **impeach** (bring charges against) the President, who could be removed from office if found guilty. Congress was given a check on the judiciary through the power to confirm appointments, change the number of justices on the Supreme Court, change the lower court system, and impeach justices. The

Nearly 1 million bills have been introduced into Congress since the process was initiated.

Have students find out the name of their Representative and which committees he or she is on.

judiciary was given a check on both Congress and the President through the power of judicial review.

SECTION REVIEW

1. What is the main function of Congress?
2. Why did the Constitution provide for differences between the House and the Senate?
3. What are the powers of the President?
4. How does the Electoral College select the President?
5. What is the main function of the judiciary?

4 The Legislative Process

The length of Article I in the Constitution, dealing with the legislature, showed the Framers' feeling that making law was the most important work of the government. Therefore the process by which a bill becomes a law is fundamental to the American system of government.

Birth of a Bill

Although bills must be introduced in Congress, they can be written by anyone. Sometimes members of Congress write bills, but they may also be written by members of the executive branch, representatives of special interest groups, or private citizens.

A bill is introduced in the House of Representatives by placing it in the hopper. The House, either as a body or in committee, considers thousands of bills every year. What happens to most of these bills?

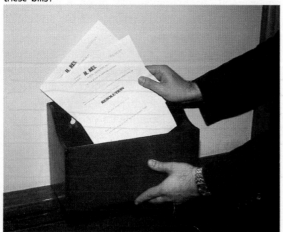

Except for revenue bills, which must originate in the House of Representatives, a bill may be introduced in either house of Congress. Since bills must pass both houses, however, legislators often arrange for a bill to be introduced in both houses at the same time. In the House, the member introducing a bill places it in a box called the "hopper." In the Senate, the sponsor of a bill addresses the chair (the presiding officer). In both the House and the Senate, the bill is given an identification number. It is then given its "first reading."

In Committee

After the first reading, the bill is referred by the Speaker of the House or the President of the Senate to one of the **standing committees.** These are regular committees that consider bills within a given subject area. Since it is not practical for the whole chamber to consider each bill, each house forms committees to facilitate lawmaking.

The standing committees are made up of legislators nominated for membership by their political party. In each house, the number of members from each party is generally proportional to the party's strength in that particular house. If the Democrats have a majority in the House of Representatives, for example, they will have a proportional majority in each of the House's committees. The head of the committee is always a member of the majority party.

The standing committee's first action is to decide whether or not to study the bill in detail. If the committee decides not to study a bill, it is "pigeon-holed," or consideration is postponed indefinitely. The bill is, in effect, "killed." This is what happens to most measures in both houses.

When a committee does decide to consider a bill, the committee members or their staffs research the merits of the bill. The committee often holds public hearings at which interested parties may testify. It is at this point that lobbyists have the greatest impact. **Lobbyists** are individuals who represent to public officials the views of a certain group.

Many bills are changed in committee. In fact, the committee may even substitute an entirely new bill. Once a bill is approved by a majority of committee members, it is "reported out" to the floor of the chamber.

HOW A BILL BECOMES LAW

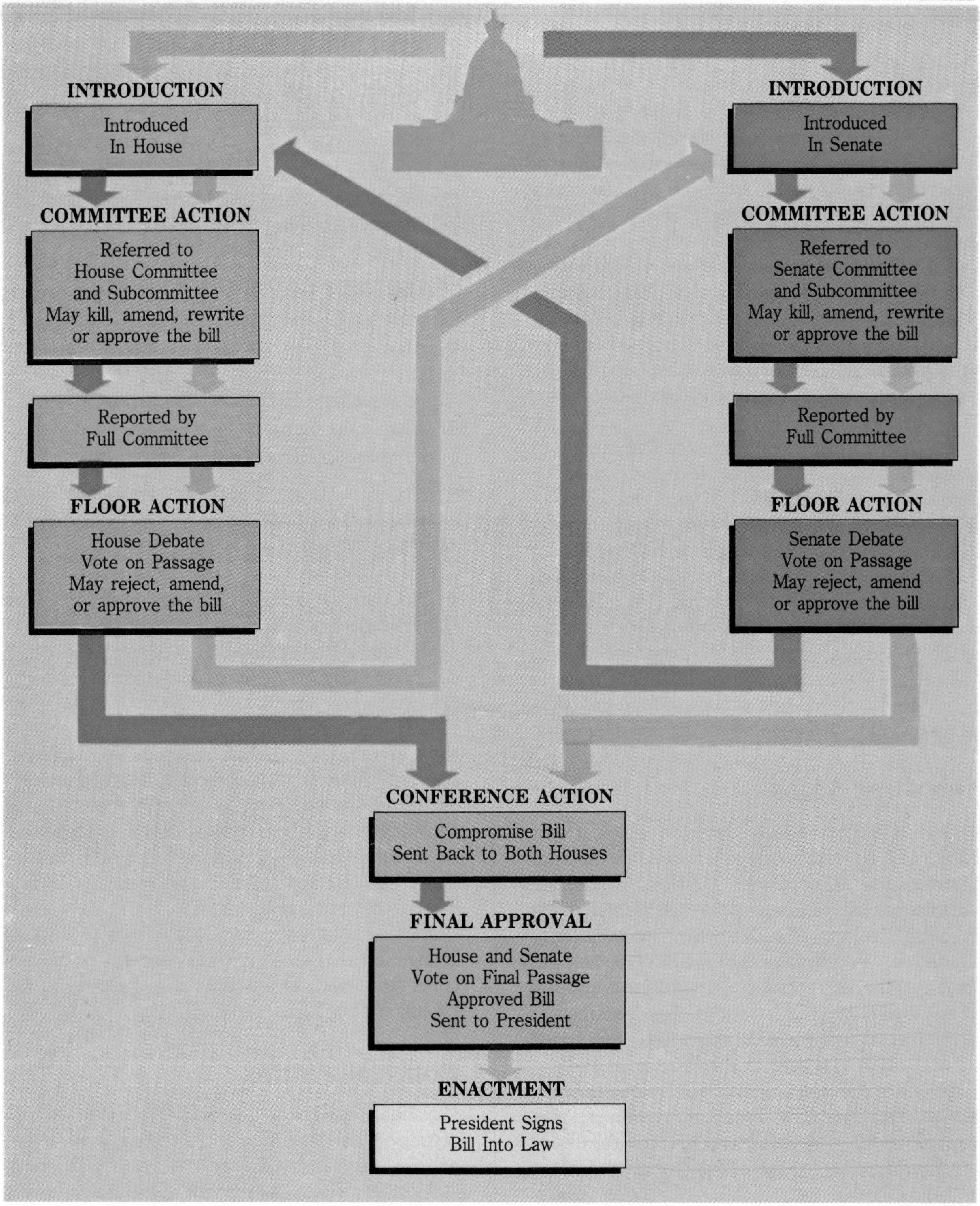

INTRODUCTION

Introduced
In House

COMMITTEE ACTION

Referred to
House Committee
and Subcommittee
May kill, amend, rewrite
or approve the bill

Reported by
Full Committee

FLOOR ACTION

House Debate
Vote on Passage
May reject, amend,
or approve the bill

INTRODUCTION

Introduced
In Senate

COMMITTEE ACTION

Referred to
Senate Committee
and Subcommittee
May kill, amend, rewrite
or approve the bill

Reported by
Full Committee

FLOOR ACTION

Senate Debate
Vote on Passage
May reject, amend
or approve the bill

CONFERENCE ACTION

Compromise Bill
Sent Back to Both Houses

FINAL APPROVAL

House and Senate
Vote on Final Passage
Approved Bill
Sent to President

ENACTMENT

President Signs
Bill Into Law

Debate and Vote

When a bill finally reaches the floor, it is given a "second reading" and placed on the calendar. This calendar indicates the order in which bills will be debated.

Different rules shape debate in the House and Senate. Because of the large size of the House of Representatives, debate must be limited. A Representative may not speak for more than one hour without the unanimous consent of the members present. In the Senate, however, debate is unlimited.

The privilege of unlimited debate has led to the development of a technique known as **filibustering.** Using this technique, Senators can hold up consideration of a bill by speaking—on any subject—for as long as they are able. They use this delaying tactic in order to gain concessions or even the withdrawal of the bill under consideration.

The only formal way to break a filibuster is to invoke **cloture,** the closing or limiting of debate in a legislative body by calling for a vote. If three-fifths of the Senate votes to invoke cloture, each Senator is limited to one hour of debate on the bill in question.

When debate has ended and the bill has been given a third and final reading, the chamber votes. The vote may be either by voice or roll call. **Voice votes,** in which the members proclaim their decision aloud in chorus, are the most common. **Roll-call votes** in which each member's vote is recorded, are taken when one-fifth of the members demand them.

The Final Steps

Once a bill passes the house in which it was introduced, it is sent to the other house. Sometimes there are differences between the House and Senate versions of a bill. However, before a bill is sent to the President, it must pass both houses in the same form. Therefore, a **conference committee** is appointed to "iron out" the differences. This committee is made up of an equal number of legislators from each house. They develop a compromise bill, which, if approved by both houses, is sent to the President.

When the President signs the bill, it becomes the law of the land. The President, however, may disapprove of the bill and veto it. In that case, the bill is returned to the house in which it originated, along with the President's objections. A two-thirds majority of each house is needed to override a veto. In any case, after receiving the bill, the President has ten days to decide whether to accept or reject it. At the end of ten days, the bill, if not vetoed, automatically becomes law. However, if Congress adjourns within that ten days, the President may kill the bill by simply ignoring it. This is called the **pocket veto.**

Since the days of the first government under the Constitution, the number of laws passed by Congress has grown significantly. Indeed, the American political system has grown far beyond what was conceived by the Framers.

SECTION REVIEW

1. What kind of bill must originate in the House?
2. What procedure does the standing committee follow on a bill?
3. How is debate limited in the House? In the Senate?
4. What is the purpose of a conference committee?
5. If the President vetoes a bill, what happens to it?

5 The Democratic Process

The American political system, established by the Constitution, has developed along with the growth of democracy in the United States. One way in which democracy has grown is through the expansion of suffrage. Over the years, property and religious restrictions were eliminated for all adult white males and **universal white male suffrage** was achieved. Next, the Fifteenth Amendment guaranteed **universal manhood suffrage,** or the right to vote for all adult males, regardless of race or color. Suffrage was extended to women through the Nineteenth Amendment. Finally, the voting age was lowered to 18 with the Twenty-sixth amendment.

Another way democracy has grown is through change in the means by which government officers come to power. This is due, in large part, to the evolution of political parties.

Political Parties

National **political parties**—groups of people organized for the purpose of directing government policies—have become a central feature in American political life. The major function of political parties is

Point out that a two-party system is more stable than a multiple-party system and more democratic than a one-party system. Note that nothing in the law requires the existence of two parties—or of any parties.

Significant third parties include the Free Soil party (1848-1852), Know-Nothing party (1856), Populist party (1892-1908), Progressive party (1912-1948), and American Independent party (1968-1972).

to get people elected to office. Political parties may also provide a base of ideas through which public issues are made known and policies shaped.

For the most part, the American political party system has been a **two-party system.** That is, two parties have dominated the political scene. Today, those two parties are the Democrats and the Republicans. Third parties, although they have at times been significant, have generally fared poorly in elections. Prominent individuals seeking office have, in general, come up through one of the major political parties.

Electing the President

A party's candidates for President and Vice President are generally chosen at a national convention, which meets every four years. To become the nominee of the party, a person must receive a majority of the votes of the delegates attending this convention. These delegates are selected in some states by party conventions or committees. In others, the voters choose the delegates in a **presidential primary** election. In a few states, delegates are chosen by the party, but are bound to support the candidate chosen by the people in a primary. In the two major parties, the number of delegates attending the convention from each state is determined by a complex formula, but is generally proportional to the population of that state.

National conventions are held in the summer of an election year. The race for nomination, however, begins two or three years earlier. At that time, presidential aspirants begin to organize compaigns to gain the support of convention delegates. The candidate must campaign in the states, meeting party officials and workers.

At the national convention, nominations of candidates are heard. Once all the nominations have been made and seconded, voting takes place. In both the Democratic and Republican parties, the nominee who receives a majority of the delegates' votes becomes

Since the 1830's, the nominating convention has been the method political parties use to choose their presidential candidates. In addition, the convention issues a platform or statement of party goals. How are delegates to nominating conventions selected?

Have students check the table of Presidents in the Appendix. How many Vice Presidents have become President?

Students may enjoy reading one of Theodore White's books on how Presidents are elected.

the party's candidate for President. The same procedure is then followed for choosing a candidate for Vice President. Generally the person who wins is someone suggested by the presidential candidate.

Once the parties select their candidates, attention focuses on the race for popular support. During the two or three months between the national conventions and the November election, the candidates travel from state to state addressing the voters. The voting public makes its decision on the Tuesday after the first Monday in November of the election year.

On election day, the voters cast their ballots. However, they do not vote directly for the candidates of their choice. Rather, they vote for slates of electors chosen by the state party and pledged to vote for their party's candidates. If a party's slate of electors wins the popular vote, those electors then vote for the party's nominee in December of the election year.

Originally, this system was designed to remove the election from the people. Today, electors simply register the voters' decision. In fact, in many states the ballot just lists the candidates' names rather than the list of electors.

The growth of democracy, then, has changed the effect of the Electoral College. Despite this fact, under the present system, it is possible for a President to be elected without receiving a majority of the popular vote. This is due to the fact that the winner of the popular vote in each state receives all of that state's electoral vote no matter what the margin of victory.

As a result, critics argue that the Electoral College should be abolished in favor of the direct election of the President. Then, the person who received the greatest number of popular votes would become President.

Electing the Congress

To become a member of Congress, a person must meet the minimal requirements outlined in the Constitution. Again, the winners of these seats have consistently been people who have come up through the state political parties. Winners are generally prominent in their states or congressional districts and have had experience in a state office or served in the state legislature.

To receive the party nomination, a candidate must win a **direct primary** (election to select candidates) or win the votes of a majority of delegates in party conventions. Once nominated, the candidate must defeat opponents in the November popular election. Once again, here is evidence that democracy has grown. Under the Constitution of 1787, although Representatives were directly elected, Senators were chosen by the state legislatures.

SECTION REVIEW

1. What are the functions of political parties?
2. By what process are party candidates nominated for the Presidency?
3. Why are some people critical of the Electoral College process?
4. How has the election of Senators changed since 1787?

6 The Changing Constitution

The authors of the Constitution understood that the framework of government they created in 1787 had to be flexible enough to adjust to changes as the country developed. The Framers provided for this in two ways. First, they set up a procedure by which an **amendment,** or formal change, could be added to the Constitution. Second, they left many areas of the Constitution vague and, as a result, open to interpretation.

The Amendment Process

According to Article V of the Constitution, amendments may be proposed by a two-thirds vote of each house of Congress or a special convention called by Congress at the request of two-thirds of the state legislatures. To be ratified, an amendment must have the approval of three-fourths of the states.

Approval is obtained through either the votes of the state legislatures or state conventions called to deal with the amendment. Congress decides which procedure the states will use. So far, 26 amendments have been added to the Constitution. All have been proposed by a two-thirds vote of each house of Congress. Only the Constitution itself and one amendment have been ratified by state conventions.

Have students report on recent decisions of the Supreme Court on constitutional questions. *The Reader's Guide to Periodical Literature* will provide sources for this information.

The Unwritten Constitution

Much of the flexibility of the Constitution is due not to the amendment process, but to vagueness in the document itself. Because of this vagueness, change has come about in several ways. One of the most important ways in which change has come about is through judicial interpretation.

Judicial Interpretation. In the years since 1787, the courts—mainly the Supreme Court—have defined and extended the meaning of the Constitution. It is judicial review that decides what is and what is not "implied" by the Constitution. Judicial review, although intended by the Framers to be a function of federal courts, was not used until the time of John Marshall, who was Chief Justice from 1801 to 1835. For example, the Supreme Court under Marshall interpreted the elastic clause in such a way as to allow a national bank to be set up.

Acts of Congress. Another way changes may be made in the Constitution is through acts of Congress. Over the years, Congress has passed laws that have filled in vague areas. Congress, for example, set up the lower federal courts and created the executive departments.

Broad interpretation of the Constitution by the federal courts has allowed Congress to pass laws in many areas and deal with unforeseen problems. Broad interpretation of the taxing and commerce powers, for example, has allowed Congress to institute social programs and regulate certain business activities.

Presidential Actions. Presidents, like Congress, have changed and extended the Constitution through the use of their powers. Strong personalities like Jackson, Lincoln, Wilson, and the Roosevelts have made the office more powerful. Recent Presidents, for example, have used executive agreements with other countries rather than seek congressional approval of treaties. Some Presidents have also used their powers as Commanders-in-Chief to engage American armed forces without declaration of war.

Custom and Tradition. Many institutions and aspects of the national government not stated in the

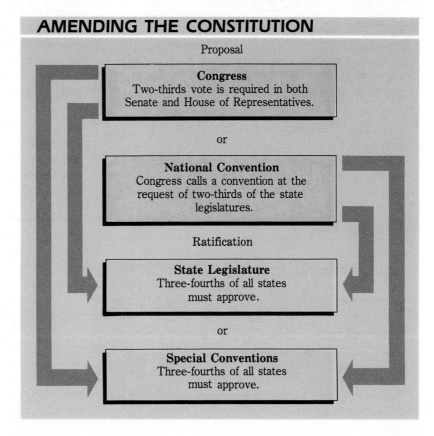

AMENDING THE CONSTITUTION

Proposal

Congress
Two-thirds vote is required in both Senate and House of Representatives.

or

National Convention
Congress calls a convention at the request of two-thirds of the state legislatures.

Ratification

State Legislature
Three-fourths of all states must approve.

or

Special Conventions
Three-fourths of all states must approve.

Constitution have come about through custom or tradition. For example, there is little doubt about the importance of committees in the legislative process and of political parties in the democratic process. Yet neither committees nor parties are part of the Constitution.

Some traditions have become parts of the written Constitution. Washington established the **precedent** (an act that serves as an example in later situations) of the two-term Presidency when he refused to run for a third term. That precedent was upheld until Franklin D. Roosevelt was elected to office four times in the 1930's and 1940's. The ratification of the Twenty-second Amendment (1951), transformed Washington's precedent into law by prohibiting a President from being elected for more than two terms.

Through different processes, then, the Constitution has maintained enough flexibility to keep up with the changing pace of life in the United States. The Framers of the country's first government, however, could not foresee the future. The Constitution was simply a plan on paper, and the challenge of making it work remained.

SECTION REVIEW

1. What is the process necessary to amend the Constitution?
2. How have the courts influenced the Constitution?
3. What contributions has Congress made to the unwritten Constitution?
4. What are some examples of ways the President has changed the Constitution?

CHAPTER 5   REVIEW

SUMMARY

1. In 1789 the Articles of Confederation were replaced by the Constitution of the United States as the basis of the American national government.
2. The Constitution set forth a political system based on ideas of the Enlightenment, British tradition, and the experience of Americans in colonial times and in the early national years.
3. A federal system was organized with powers divided between a national government and state governments.
4. The federal government was divided into three branches: the executive, the legislative, and the judicial.
5. Through a system of checks and balances, each branch of government can restrain the others to maintain a balance of power.
6. Bills go through a specific process in Congress before they are sent to the President to be signed into law.
7. Political parties have evolved as a major part of the democratic process.
8. A total of 26 amendments have been added to the Constitution.
9. The Constitution has also been modified through judicial interpretation, acts of Congress, Presidential actions, tradition, and custom.

VOCABULARY

natural laws	implied powers	veto	conference committee
natural rights	elastic clause	judicial review	pocket veto
social contract	loose construction	checks and balances	universal white male suffrage
popular sovereignty	strict construction	impeach	universal manhood suffrage
absolutism	inherent powers	standing committee	political party
divine right	reserved powers	lobbyist	two-party system
limited government	police power	filibustering	presidential primary
separation of powers	concurrent powers	cloture	direct primary
hierarchy of laws	ex post facto law	voice vote	amendment
federal system	due process of law	roll-call vote	precedent
expressed powers			

REVIEW QUESTIONS

1. How is Enlightenment theory reflected in the Constitution?
2. In what ways did the Constitution improve upon the Articles of Confederation?
3. Why did the authors of the Constitution set up a federal system of government?
4. What is the significance of the concept of implied powers?
5. How can each branch of government restrain the powers of the others?
6. Why does the Constitution provide for an indirect method of electing the President of the United States?
7. What process does a bill have to go through in Congress in order to become a law?
8. How have political parties contributed to the democratic process?
9. What is the significance of the amendment process and the fact that many parts of the Constitution are open to interpretation?

DISCUSSION

1. How was the federal system an outgrowth of American experiences?
2. Which branch of the national government is the strongest today?
3. If you had been one of the writers of the Constitution, what, if anything, would you have done differently? What would you want to change today?
4. Do you think the amendment process is too difficult? Why or why not?
5. What amendments to the Constitution are currently under consideration?

USING CHARTS

Refer to the chart on page 104 and decide if the following statements are true or false:
1. The state governments are not allowed to coin money.
2. The state governments are not allowed to manage a postal system.
3. The state governments are not allowed to borrow money.
4. The state governments are not allowed to pass bills of attainder.
5. The state governments are not allowed to charter banks.

USING SKILLS

Fill in the blanks in the following sentence with the appropriate words from below.

As the English king stands in relation to Parliament, so, in the state governments, the _____ stands in relation to the _____ and, in the United States, the _____ stands in relation to the _____ .

state legislatures, Congress, judiciary
President, governor, Supreme Court

6

1	Launching the New Government	119
2	Hamilton's Economic Program	122
3	Political Parties	127
4	Washington's Foreign Policy	130
5	Decline of the Federalists	133

THE FEDERALIST ERA

As the first of everything, in our situation, will serve to establish a precedent, it is devoutly wished on my part, that these precedents may be fixed on true principles.

GEORGE WASHINGTON

The first elections under the Constitution put the national government into the hands of the Federalists. The officials of the new government faced an enormous challenge. Nobody knew if the political system laid out by the Constitution would work, for a federal republic on such a large scale had never succeeded.

During the 1790's, the Federalists met the challenge by putting the new government into operation. They broadened the powers of the national government and, in the process, inspired opposition that led to the formation of political parties.

1 Launching the New Government

In 1788 the members of the Electoral College unanimously chose George Washington as the first President of the United States. His popularity and prestige were thought to be the best guarantee of the nation's success. The office of Vice President went to John Adams of Massachusetts, who received the second largest number of electoral votes. A majority of Federalists were elected to both houses of Congress.

When Washington took the oath of office on April 30, 1789, at the temporary capital in New York City, the new government faced what he described as "an ocean of difficulties." Rhode Island and North Carolina remained outside the Union. The machinery of government did not exist. There were no federal laws, no federal courts, and no federal law-enforcement officers. The national debt was large, and the treasury was empty. Washington and the members of Congress knew the urgency of the problems, and they were aware that their actions would set precedents, thus determining the course of government for years to come.

The First Congress

Despite the pressing problems facing the nation, the Senate spent most of its first few weeks wrangling over an appropriate title for the President. Vice President John Adams and Senator Richard Henry Lee led a faction that felt a fancy title would lend dignity to the office, especially in the eyes of foreigners.

A Senate committee appointed to choose a title, after considering suggestions such as "His Excellency" and "His Elective Majesty," settled on "His Highness the President of the United States and Protector of the Rights of the Same." The House of Representatives, however, refused to agree to a title that smacked of monarchy. Finally, over Senate objections, Congress adopted the much more republican title of "President of the United States," as given in the Constitution. Washington was addressed simply as "Mr. President." John Adams, for his pains, was given the derisive title of "His Rotundity."

The House of Representatives, under the able direction of James Madison, made more effective use of its time. Turning immediately to the most critical problem of the new nation, the House passed a bill to raise revenue.

It was agreed that tariffs (taxes on imports) and tonnage duties (taxes on the total weight of goods shipped) should be the primary source of income for the nation. Northern manufacturing interests called for a **protective tariff,** or duties high enough to protect American industry from foreign competitors. Southerners called for a lower tariff providing only revenue. Northern merchants wanted high tonnage duties on foreign ships in order to benefit American shipping, but southerners used foreign ships for much of their trade.

As a result, the tariff of 1789 was the first of many compromises. The tariff on most foreign goods was a relatively low 5 percent. However, it went as high as

Taxing goods shipped in from other ports produced the largest source of income for the new government. Why were many southerners angry over the Tariff of 1789?

50 percent on items such as ships, tobacco, and salt which might compete with American goods. Tonnage duties of 50 cents per ton were levied against foreign ships but only 6 cents per ton against American ships. Despite the compromise on the tariff, many southerners felt that the federal government was already showing favoritism to northern business interests.

The House next turned to the issue of a bill of rights for the new Constitution. A number of states had ratified the Constitution with the understanding that a bill of rights would be added. Madison was concerned that the Federalists maintain faith in the new government by upholding their end of the bargain. Some 78 amendments had been proposed by the state ratifying conventions. Madison took the lead in coordinating the state proposals and introducing them in the House. After a conference between the House and the Senate, 12 amendments were submitted to the states. Ten of these, known now as the Bill of Rights, were eventually ratified.[1]

In developing the Bill of Rights, Madison tried to establish a balance between the liberty of the people and the authority of the government. As historian John C. Miller put it, Madison's task was "to guarantee the 'unalienable' rights of men without, at the same time, impairing the necessary powers of the federal government." Madison was successful, but the balance achieved was a delicate one. Much of the constitutional history of the United States has revolved around the attempt to keep that balance.

The combination of the Bill of Rights and the tariff of 1789, which would apply to North Carolina and Rhode Island as foreign countries, brought the last 2 of the original 13 states into the Union. North Carolina ratified the Constitution in 1789, and Rhode Island followed in June 1790.

Madison also took the lead in creating executive departments to aid the President. The first Congress established three such departments—State, War, and Treasury. The office of Postmaster General was created, although the Post Office Department was not set up until 1795. Congress could have made these departments responsible to itself. Instead, it made them responsible only to the President.

Meanwhile, the Senate got down to the business of setting up a federal court system. The Judiciary Act of 1789 provided for 6 justices of the Supreme Court, an Attorney General, 13 federal district courts, and 3 circuit courts of appeal. The act was another compromise between those who favored a strong central government and those who were against it.

---

[1] One of the amendments not ratified would have provided that there be at least one representative for every 50,000 people. The other would have prevented members of Congress from raising their own salaries.

The federal courts were given a limited **original jurisdiction** (authority to hear cases the first time they go to court). Cases arising from federal laws, and certain other kinds of cases, such as those involving a foreign government, would be heard in federal courts. However, most legal questions arising under the Constitution could first be heard in the state courts, which were entrusted with enforcing federal laws. State court decisions and state actions could be appealed to the Supreme Court, but each state's own body of law was left standing. Because state and federal courts exist independently, the United States is said to have a **dual court system.**

The First President

Once the various executive and judicial positions were created, it was the President's duty to appoint people to serve in those positions. Washington was careful in making his choices. He wrote:

If injudicious or unpopular measures should be taken by the executive under the new government with regard to appointments, the government itself would be in the utmost danger of being entirely subverted by those measures.

In making appointments, Washington looked for people who had both character and experience. He also understood the political ramifications of his decisions. He tried to keep a regional balance, and, although he favored Federalists, he took pains to put some Antifederalists in lower offices.

With these considerations in mind, Washington made Thomas Jefferson Secretary of State, Alexander Hamilton Secretary of the Treasury, Henry Knox Secretary of War, and Edmund Randolph Attorney General. His Supreme Court nominations followed a strictly geographic pattern. Three were from the North and three from the South, all Federalists. Arch-Federalist John Jay was made Chief Justice.

Washington consulted his executive appointees often, especially Alexander Hamilton and Thomas Jefferson. Soon the President's advisors became known as the **cabinet** and emerged as a major government institution.

Formal receptions were held every Friday evening at the Washingtons' residence in New York. Some people criticized the gatherings as pompous. Why do you think Washington believed it was necessary to insist on such formality?

Point out that many later Presidents took a much more active role in proposing legislation.

Many of the original holders of the debt were soldiers who had been forced by economic necessity to sell their paper certificates for a small amount of cash.

When he first took office, Washington expected that he would also receive advice from the Senate. The Constitution said that the "advice and consent" of the Senate was to be obtained for appointments of high officials and for the ratification of treaties. After the President's first experience with asking the Senate for advice on a treaty in negotiation, however, he decided not to ask again. When he took a treaty with the Creek Indians to the Senators, they did not agree to it right away. Instead, they demanded time to talk about the matter privately. After that, the disgruntled Washington established the precedent of presidential negotiation of treaties. Senate approval was sought only after negotiations were over.

Washington made a conscious effort to bring respect to his office. He lived in formal style in a New York mansion. When he went out, it was in a fancy coach pulled by six cream-colored horses. He decided not to accept private social invitations. He began a system by which he delivered formal messages in person to Congress, and various ceremonies arose around the interactions between the branches of government. Although some people felt that these formalities were unrepublican, others felt they were needed to give dignity to the office.

SECTION REVIEW

1. Identify the following: Judiciary Act of 1789, Henry Knox, Edmond Randolph, John Jay.
2. What did the Congress do in order to raise money to run the federal government?
3. Why did James Madison want to add a bill of rights to the Constitution?
4. What executive offices were created by the first Congress?
5. What things did Washington consider in making appointments to executive offices?

2 Hamilton's Economic Program

In Washington's idea of what was proper behavior for the President of the United States, he did not include making proposals for laws. He felt his business was not to make laws but to administer them. As a result, others took the lead in proposing legislation. One of the most influential leaders was

Alexander Hamilton. Hamilton was an ardent nationalist. Although he supported the Constitution, he thought it left too much power to the states. As Secretary of the Treasury, he tried to form policies that would strengthen the national government.

Funding the Debt

The first problem Hamilton tackled was the national debt. In 1789 the debt totaled about $52 million. About $12 million was owed to foreign governments and the rest to American citizens.

Most of the debt had been contracted to pay for the Revolutionary War. The Continental Congress had borrowed money by selling **promissory notes**— written promises to pay a specified sum of money to the holder. The inability to pay off these debts had been one source of problems for the Confederation government, and the value of the Continental notes had depreciated dramatically. To secure the credit of the new government, some means had to be found to insure the payment of these old debts.

Hamilton, in his *Report on Public Credit,* argued that the national debt should be funded in full. That is, the new government should trade new notes (backed by its revenue-raising ability) for the face value of the old notes, plus interest.

Opposition to this plan arose immediately. Many members of Congress felt that funding the total debt was too expensive. They proposed that the foreign debt be paid in full, but that the domestic debt be discounted to some fraction of its original value. Others, led by James Madison, pointed out that Hamilton's plan failed to discriminate between the original holders of the debt and its present holders. Many of the depreciated Continental notes had been bought up by speculators. Madison proposed that the profits be divided between the original holders and later purchasers. Hamilton objected:

> *The established rules of morality and justice are applicable to nations as well as to individuals. . . . a relaxation of this kind would tend to dissolve all social obligations—to render all rights precarious, and to introduce a general dissoluteness and corruption of morals.*

The fact that Hamilton's plan did not favor the original holders of the notes was not an accident.

Benjamin Banneker

After it was decided that the capital of the United States should be moved to a new location in the South, President Washington appointed a surveying commission headed by Major Andrew Ellicott to lay out the boundaries of the District of Columbia. One of Ellicott's assistants was Benjamin Banneker, one of the nation's first black scientists, a surveyor, astronomer, mathematician, and farmer.

Banneker was born a free black in the colony of Maryland in 1731. As a child he was given the opportunity to attend a school that was open to both blacks and whites. His abilities in science and mathematics were impressive. At one point his schoolteacher introduced Banneker to someone who showed the boy a watch. With the watch and a picture of a clock as his only models, Banneker hand-carved a wooden clock that kept almost perfect time for more than 50 years.

As an adult, Banneker lived on a farm outside Baltimore, working in the morning, sleeping in the afternoon, and staying up all night to study the revolutions of the stars and planets. Fascinated by astronomy, he began in 1791 to publish an almanac that accurately predicted the movements of heavenly bodies. His work brought him to the attention of Thomas Jefferson, who recommended him for the surveying commission.

In a famous letter to Jefferson, Banneker called for an end to the cruel oppression of slavery. Banneker also became a peace advocate. It was his privilege, he said, to set aside space in his almanac for worthy causes. In his 1793 almanac, he published a proposal for a cabinet-level post of Secretary of Peace.

Hamilton knew that the speculators were generally people of wealth. He felt that a successful government depended upon the support of the prominent and wealthy members of society. By insuring the economic success of the speculators, he thought to insure the political success of the new government. Hamilton also felt that the government had to deal honestly with its creditors if it hoped for any loans in the future.

The Assumption Controversy

Hamilton's next proposal was for federal **assumption** (taking over) of $20 million in state debts that remained from the Revolution. Through this plan, Hamilton hoped to tie the interests of wealthy state creditors (those to whom the states owed money) to the national government.

Representatives from states with large debts generally supported assumption. Opposition arose from Virginia, which had already paid half of its Revolutionary debt, and from other states whose debts were small.

Proponents and opponents of Hamilton's plans for funding and assumption were evenly divided in the House. Debate raged through the spring and summer of 1790. Most of the debt was owed to citizens in the North, and the northern states had the largest debts. Southerners objected to paying the debts of the North.

The stalemate was broken through a bargain struck between Hamilton and his Virginia opponents. Hamilton agreed to a proposal that would move the nation's capital from New York to Philadelphia for ten years, then to a capital city to be built in the South. The Virginians, led by Madison and Jefferson, agreed to use their influence to change some southern votes. A few changes were made in the assumption plan to satisfy the states with small debts, and Hamilton's proposals were passed into law in August 1790.

While Hamilton's plans were successful in establishing the credit of the new nation, the political costs

The national bank remained an issue until the Federal Reserve system was established in 1913.

were high. A wide breach had opened within the ranks of the Federalists. Hamilton's one-time ally, James Madison, was frequently found in opposition to Hamilton's plans. He was joined by another prominent Virginian, Secretary of State Thomas Jefferson.

Madison, Jefferson, and others increasingly felt that Hamilton's plans benefited the North at the expense of the South, and wealthy financiers at the expense of average farmers. They saw in his plans to strengthen the national government a tendency to go beyond the bounds established by the Constitution. This tendency, which they feared as potentially threatening to the liberties of the people, was even more evident in Hamilton's plan for a national bank.

The Bank of the United States

In a report submitted to Congress in January 1791, Hamilton called for the establishment of a national bank. Chartered for 20 years, the Bank of the United States would be a joint public and private venture. Of its $10 million in stock, 20 percent would be held by the federal government and 80 percent would be sold to private investors. Just like any other bank, the national bank would accept deposits, make loans, and issue **banknotes** (promissory notes). It would also serve as the depository for federal funds and as an agent for the collection of federal taxes.

Hamilton felt that such a bank would serve a number of important functions. First, it would provide a central control over private, state-chartered banks. Although the Constitution prohibited the states from printing paper money, private banks chartered by the states could and did. Since colonial times, Americans had always been short on specie, so banknotes had become the major form of currency in the country. Issued in excess, they had led to inflation.

As a tax-collecting agency of the federal government, the national bank would, as a matter of course, receive large amounts of state banknotes. By redeeming these notes often, it would force the state banks to issue only the amount of notes they could redeem with specie. The national bank, then, would help control inflation.

A second major purpose of the bank would be to provide a stable national currency. Since banknotes put out by the national bank would be backed by large federal deposits of gold and silver, their value would

remain stable. A sound currency would be good for trade and economic growth.

The third major benefit of a national bank, in Hamilton's view, was that it would further tie the interests of the wealthy to the federal government. The private investors in the bank were likely to be creditors who would favor its control over inflation.

Finally, chartering a national bank would serve to broaden the powers of the national government. Hamilton knew that the Constitution did not specifically give the power to create a bank to the national government. By acting in such a manner, the national government would be adopting a broad interpretation of the Constitution and its implied powers.

It was over the constitutional issue that opposition to Hamilton's banking plan arose. Although the bill to charter the bank passed the Congress by a comfortable margin, the bill's opponents, led by Madison, raised doubts in President Washington's mind over its constitutionality. Washington called upon his cabinet members for advice. Randolph and Jefferson felt that the bill should be vetoed. Jefferson's opinion has become a classical defense of "strict construction" of the Constitution:

> *I consider the foundation of the Constitution as laid on this ground—that* all powers not delegated to the United States, by the Constitution, nor prohibited by it to the states, are reserved to the states, or to the people. . . . *To take a single step beyond the boundaries thus specially drawn around the powers of Congress, is to take possession of a boundless field of power, no longer susceptible of any definition. . . .*
>
> *Perhaps, indeed, bank bills may be a more* convenient *vehicle than treasury orders. But a little* difference *in the degree of convenience cannot constitute the necessity which the Constitution makes the ground for assuming any non-enumerated power.*

Hamilton, of course, argued for a "loose construction" or broad interpretation of the necessary and proper clause. Rejecting Jefferson's idea of "necessity," Hamilton argued that:

> *. . . neither the grammatical nor popular sense of the term requires [Jefferson's] construction. According to both,* necessary *often means no*

Note that the Bank quickly became one of the most effective devices for stimulating free enterprise. It also loaned the government money and aided in the management of the nation's finances.

Hamilton was suggesting that the United States follow the lead of Great Britain, France, and other powers in promoting industrialization.

During his first years in office, Washington met with the members of his cabinet individually. By 1793 he was holding about 50 meetings a year with his entire cabinet. What did Washington consider in making his cabinet appointments?

more than needful, requisite, incidental, useful, or conducive to. . . . *And it is the true one in which it is to be understood as used in the Constitution. The whole turn of the clause containing it indicates, that it was the intent of the Convention, by that clause, to give a liberal latitude to the exercise of the specified powers. . . . If the end be clearly comprehended within any of the specified powers, and if the measures have an obvious relation to that end, and is not forbidden by any particular provision of the Constitution, it may safely be deemed to come within the compass of the national authority.*

Although not totally convinced, Washington was more impressed with Hamilton's argument. The bill to establish a Bank of the United States was signed into law. A significant precedent for broad interpretation of the Constitution had been set.

Manufacturing

With the *Report on Public Credit* and the Bank of the United States, Hamilton had laid the foundation for economic growth fostered by strong central government. But his plan was not complete. Hamilton

believed that a strong economy had to include industry. Therefore, in December 1791, Hamilton submitted his *Report on Manufactures* to Congress. In this report, he said that the United States should encourage manufacturing through protective tariffs. He also said that bounties and other rewards should be offered for improvements in quality and efficiency, and that some raw materials should not be taxed.

Again, the Virginians and other southerners rose in opposition. Protective tariffs were unfair to the South, they said, and there was no constitutional ground upon which to base such economic interference. Even in the North the reception to Hamilton's plan was lukewarm. Commercial interests feared that international trade would be hurt by protective tariffs. Nevertheless, some of Hamilton's ideas were built into the Tariff of 1792. There would be no bounties, however, and the protection offered by the tariff was not great.

The Whiskey Rebellion

The expense to the government of Hamilton's programs—especially funding and assumption—was great. In 1791, to help cover that expense, Congress passed an **excise tax** (an internal tax on the manufacture or sale of a product) on whiskey.

When farmers from four western Pennsylvania counties refused to pay federal taxes, the President dispatched 15,000 militiamen to end the disturbance. What did Washington's strong response to the Whiskey Rebellion signify?

Hamilton advocated such a tax both for the revenue it would raise and the challenge it would pose to western farmers. Many western farmers had been Antifederalists, and they held the new national government in little respect. Hamilton expected these farmers to resist paying the tax, thus giving the federal government the opportunity to uphold the law through the use of force.

As Hamilton had foreseen, resistance to the whiskey tax grew. First, the tax was very high, about 25 percent of the net price per gallon. Second, whiskey was especially important to many western farmers. They were unable to ship grain down the Mississippi because the Spanish still withheld the right of deposit at New Orleans. Western trade with the East had to be overland. Farmers distilled their grain into whiskey, which was less bulky than grain, in order to transport it by wagon. Whiskey also provided a means of barter between westerners.

By the summer of 1794, a group of frontier farmers in Pennsylvania had had enough. They refused to pay the tax, terrorized the tax collectors, and disrupted federal judicial proceedings.

The opportunity for which Hamilton had been waiting had come. Here was the chance to flex federal muscle! President Washington called on the states to provide militia, and, with a force of over 12,000 men (more than he had commanded at any one time during the Revolution), he marched into Pennsylvania.[2] In the face of such numbers, the rebels quickly dispersed. Only a few of them were captured. Later, two were convicted of treason. Washington pardoned both.

Hamilton claimed a great victory for the government, declaring that it had gained "reputation and strength." Conservative easterners applauded the government's decisive action. Many people, however, questioned the need for such a show of force. Jefferson said that, "an insurrection was announced and proclaimed and armed against, but could never be found."

SECTION REVIEW

1. What was Hamilton's plan for paying the national debt?
2. Why was the funding of the war debt opposed?
3. Why did southern states oppose Hamilton's proposal that the national government assume state debts?
4. What were the chief functions of the Bank of the United States?

---

[2]Washington accompanied his forces as far as Bedford, Pennsylvania, before returning to Philadelphia and leaving them under the command of Henry Lee. This is the only time in the history of the United States, to date, that the President, acting as Commander-in-Chief, actually took to the field.

Have students decide which party they would support and present their views in a debate.

5. Why was the Bank plan opposed?
6. Why did Hamilton want the government to encourage manufacturing?
7. Why did Hamilton advocate an excise tax on whiskey?

3 Political Parties

The adoption of Hamilton's proposals established the credit of the United States at home and abroad, had a positive influence on the economy, and set precedents for a broad interpretation of the Constitution. However, the opposition aroused by Hamilton's programs laid the foundations for the development of the country's first political parties.

Republicans

The Republican party began with a split in the ranks of the Federalists. At first, Federalists had not thought of themselves as a party. Made up of northern business owners and southern planters, they had taken the name "Federalists" to show their support of the Constitution and strong central government. As Hamilton's economic program took form, however, the unity of thought among Federalists deteriorated. Southern planters began to feel that Hamilton's idea of active government would help northern business at the expense of southern agriculture.

Led by James Madison and Thomas Jefferson, the opposition gradually grew into a political party. At first they called themselves the "republican interest." By 1792 they had started to use the title "Democratic Republicans" or simply "Republicans."[3]

As the Republican party took shape, it attracted more than just the ex-Federalist southern planters. Opposition to active government also appealed to former Antifederalists, who distrusted strong central government. As a matter of fact, the ideas of the new party reflected the views of the majority of the American people at that time. Most Americans were small farmers who, remembering their experience with Great Britain, felt that a strong central

government was a threat to liberty. They also feared that Hamilton's policies would lead to the rule of a wealthy aristocracy.

Although it was Madison who first organized the anti-Hamilton forces, it was the more popular Jefferson who became the leader of the Republicans. Jefferson's opinions differed greatly from Hamilton's. According to Hamilton, the Constitution left too much power to the states. Jefferson, who never admitted to having been a Federalist, endorsed the Constitution because of the balance it created between the state and the national governments. Such a balance, he felt, would help preserve the liberty of the people.

Unlike Hamilton, who favored industrialization, Jefferson wished to see the United States remain agrarian. While Hamilton had little faith in the common people, Jefferson trusted their good sense. This trust was based on the fact that "the people" in 1790 were almost all farmers. For Jefferson, farming provided the school of "substantial and genuine virtue." He felt that industrialization in Europe had produced masses of ignorant, poverty-striken people, unsuited for republican government.

In an agrarian country, Jefferson thought, government intervention in the economy was not necessary. He became an advocate of **laissez-faire**, the concept that government should leave the economy alone. He thought that government interference led to corruption. As evidence, he could point to the recent experience with Hamilton's funding plan. A few individuals armed with inside information had rushed to buy depreciated Continental notes from people who were unaware that those notes were soon to be worth more.

Jefferson also suspected Hamilton of trying to establish a monarchy with Washington at its head. Jefferson's belief was based on Hamilton's broad interpretation of the President's constitutional powers.

Federalists

Hamilton did believe in a strong executive, but he also hoped that the experiment in republican government would be successful. Of his differences with Jefferson, Hamilton wrote in 1792:

> *One side appears to believe that there is a serious plot to overturn the state governments,*

---

[3] Not to be confused with the modern Republican party, which began as an anti-slavery party in 1854.

Note that although Washington was a Federalist, he trusted the common people, saying that "the *mass* of our citizens require no more than to understand a question than to decide it properly."

and substitute a monarchy to the present republican system. The other side firmly believes that there is a serious plot to overturn the general government and elevate the separate powers of the states upon its ruins. Both sides may be wrong. . . .

Perhaps the major difference between the Republicans and the Federalists was in their opinion of the common people. The Federalists of the 1790's came to regret what they saw as an excess of democracy, which they carefully distinguished from republicanism. To them, democracy meant that government would be subject to the whims of the ignorant masses. A republic would put restraints on the power of the people and teach respect for law and order.

Both Republicans and Federalists believed in individual rights, but they disagreed over the best means to protect those rights. While Jefferson feared monarchy, Federalists feared the tyranny of the majority. Hamilton and other Federalists believed that the real threat to liberty was the people themselves. They feared that the people would so passionately assert liberty that order and stability would be lost. **Demagogues** (leaders who gain power by claiming to be champions of the common people) would arise and turn into tyrants, and liberty would be lost altogether.

Federalists held the view that the best way to protect liberty was through the British pattern of mixed government. That pattern balanced democracy (the people as represented in the House of Commons), aristocracy (the House of Lords), and monarchy (the king, the executive). That pattern could be duplicated in a republic if the executive were

A COMPARISON OF VIEWS: HAMILTON AND JEFFERSON

Hamilton's Views	Jefferson's Views
DEMOCRACY	
The best course for the United States is government by an artistocracy.	The common people will make just and wise decisions.
THE FEDERAL GOVERNMENT	
A powerful federal government is necessary to ensure the peace and liberty of the states.	A centralized federal government infringes on the rights of the individual and leads to abuse of power.
THE ECONOMY	
Government should encourage the growth of cities, manufacturing, and shipping. Tariffs are necessary to protect American industry. The federal government should assume state debts and establish a national bank. A national debt, if not large, can aid economic growth.	The United States would be better off to remain an agricultural nation. Tariffs are harmful to the farmer and to the American economy. States should pay their own debts. A Bank of the United States is not necessary. A national debt should not be permitted.
THE PRESIDENT AND CONGRESS	
The President should serve in office for life. A lifetime senate should be recruited only from men of property.	Everyone should have an equal opportunity to serve in public office. Elections should be held regularly and often.
THE LAW	
Congress has the authority to enact any legislation that is "necessary and proper" for the security, growth, and well-being of the United States.	Congress should have the power to do only what the Constitution explicitly authorizes it to do.

Disputes between the Republicans and the Federalists gave rise to a highly partisan press. William Cobbett's pro-Republican cartoons featuring "Peter Porcupine," were typical of the period. President Washington remained aloof from party politics and attempted to bring the two sides together. Was he able to reconcile them?

strong and if the people elected their betters to office. Those of wealth and social position, those who owned what was worth owning in the country, thought the Federalists should also run the country.

Federalists realized, however, that their view was not a popular one. Their political philosophy, demanding deference to an economic and social elite, was out of date.

The Newspaper War

At first the struggle between Federalists and Republicans took place mostly within the government. In 1791, however, Hamilton and Jefferson took their differences before the public.

The *Gazette of the United States,* published by John Fenno, was the most important of the newspapers that existed at that time. Fenno's paper glorified Hamilton and praised his policies. Hamilton supported the paper with printing contracts from the Treasury Department, and sometimes with personal loans.

To counteract the pro-Hamilton news, the Republicans set up their own paper, the *National Gazette.* Its editor, a poet and journalist named Philip Freneau, was given a job as a translator in Jefferson's State Department. The post allowed Freneau plenty of free time to write. For the next two years he devoted his paper to criticizing Hamilton and praising Jefferson.

As the newspaper war heated up, the quarrel between Hamilton and Jefferson became increasingly bitter. Each took his grievances to Washington, and, at one point, each offered to resign. Washington persuaded them to put up an appearance of a truce, but could not bring about any true reconciliation. Partly because of the conflict between his two cabinet officers, Washington reluctantly agreed to a second term as President, and was reelected without opposition in 1792. He hoped to keep the conflict from becoming more serious. Instead, the differences between Federalists and Republicans were intensified by a fierce debate over foreign policy.

SECTION REVIEW

1. How did Hamilton's economic program cause trouble for the Federalists?
2. Why did Jefferson want the United States to remain agrarian?
3. In the minds of the Federalists, why did too much democracy pose a threat?
4. How was the press used to enflame the differences between the Republicans and the Federalists?

Washington's proclamation alarmed Republicans because they believed that Congress, not the President, should control foreign policy.

4 Washington's Foreign Policy

The French Revolution of 1789, in which the French people overthrew their king to establish a republic, had found most Americans sympathetic to a cause that seemed much like their own. However, as the French Revolution became more radical, American opinion divided sharply.

Shortly after Washington's second inauguration, news arrived that the French king had been beheaded, and France had declared war on Great Britain, Spain, and Holland. Hamilton and the Federalists were appalled by what was happening in France. Their worst fears about the unbridled passions of the common people were coming true. Riots, anarchy, and indiscriminate executions had brought about a "Reign of Terror" in France. Although they did not condone these extremes, Republican enthusiasm remained high. Many Republicans were eager to help the French reach their ideals of liberty and equality.

Citizen Genêt

Early in 1793, the fiery young Edmond Genêt came to America as the new French minister. His purpose was to enlist American aid in the war against Britain. Hamilton advised President Washington not to receive Genêt. Jefferson insisted that Genêt be received as the official representative of the French government.

Washington, who wanted to avoid entanglement in foreign wars, had to make a decision concerning American policy. Helping France would certainly lead to war with England, which the United States could not afford. On the other hand, failure to help France could be seen as a failure to uphold the honor of the nation. France, after all, had helped Americans win their Revolution.

Although they had different sympathies, both Jefferson and Hamilton wanted the United States to stay out of the war. After hearing their opinions, Washington decided to receive Genêt but to issue a Proclamation of Neutrality.

The proclamation, issued April 19, 1793, assured foreign governments that the United States would carry on "a conduct friendly and impartial toward the belligerent powers." Americans were warned against "aiding or abetting hostilities" against either side. Washington's Proclamation of Neutrality was the first formal statement of America's intention to remain aloof from European affairs.

Ignoring Washington's proclamation, Genêt tried to recruit Americans for French **privateers** (armed private ships) and for military expeditions against British and Spanish territories in North America. He had experienced such an enthusiastic reception by the American people that he felt Washington's position did not reflect popular opinion.

When Genêt tried to appeal to the American people over Washington's head, even Jefferson agreed that Genêt could no longer be tolerated. Washington asked for his recall by the French government and recalled the American minister to France, Gouverneur Morris.

Meanwhile, another change in power had occurred in France. The new government disavowed Genêt's actions, branded him a public enemy, and called for his arrest. Had he returned to France, he would, no doubt, have been beheaded. Genêt appealed to Washington, was given sanctuary in the United States, and lived out his days in obscurity.

The actions of Genêt pushed the Federalists even further into the British camp. President Washington drew closer to Hamilton's thinking. As a result, Jefferson, weary of his losing struggle with Hamilton, resigned his position as Secretary of State in December 1793.[4] But Federalist sympathy for Britain was about to be challenged by the British themselves.

The Jay Treaty

In June 1793, the British declared a blockade of France and ordered the Royal Navy to capture any neutral ships carrying goods to France. In early November, an Order in Council directed British sea captains to seize any neutral ships trading with the French West Indies.

Both of these actions were intended to hurt America. As a matter of fact, the British kept this last

---

[4]Washington appointed Republican John Randolph to take Jefferson's place. In 1795, Randolph was dismissed on suspicion of improper dealings with a French diplomat. This ended Washington's attempt to work with Republicans in his Cabinet.

Washington also did not like the treaty, but saw no alternative except war with Great Britain.

Leaders of the French Revolution believed the United States would aid France in its war with Britain. However, the Reign of Terror, with its use of the guillotine (right), alarmed many Americans. What did Washington decide to do in this situation?

Order in Council secret until late in 1793, thus insuring the capture of some 250 unsuspecting American merchant ships. Americans were outraged. Their outrage grew as British commanders began to **impress** (take by force to serve in the Royal Navy) American sailors whom they suspected of being British deserters.

British actions against American shipping and sailors were only part of the American grievances. The British had still failed to remove their forts and troops from American territory along the Northwest frontier. Furthermore, they had reportedly sold guns to Indians who were raiding American frontier settlements.

Congress debated various economic measures to take against Britain, but by the spring of 1794, war seemed imminent. Knowing that a war with Britain would be disastrous for the young republic, Washington sent Chief Justice John Jay to England in a last-ditch effort to negotiate a treaty.[5]

The British government was cordial to Jay and, in its eyes, conciliatory. Britain did not want war with the United States. However, Jay's bargaining position was weak because the United States lacked military strength. Furthermore, the pro-French behavior of

James Monroe, then the American minister to France, made the British suspicious of the proclaimed neutrality of the United States.

As a result, the treaty Jay negotiated was not as beneficial to the United States as many Americans had hoped. The British agreed to remove their troops from the Northwest, open some of their trade in the East and West Indies to United States ships, and negotiate conflicting monetary claims. However, Britain refused to stop seizing American ships, or to pay American slaveowners for slaves kidnapped or liberated during the American Revolution. A further provision of the treaty gave Britain **most favored nation** status, meaning that the United States would not give any other nation lower tariffs. Another clause agreed that both the British and the Americans should have the right to navigate the Mississippi River through Spanish territory.

Fearing a negative public reaction to the treaty, the Senate, in the summer of 1795, ratified it in secret. However, the terms eventually leaked to the public, and Americans—especially Republicans—were dismayed. The reaction against the treaty was "like that against a mad dog," wrote Washington. Jay was hanged in effigy, and even the President was strongly criticized. A bill to provide funds for enforcing the provisions of the treaty barely passed the House, and not until 1796.

---

[5] Before the development of a diplomatic service, prominent leaders were often appointed to negotiate treaties.

Many people concluded that Pinckney was a better diplomat than Jay because the Pinckney Treaty was so much more favorable to the United States. But the two men were dealing with different circumstances and powers.

Despite the public outcry, the Jay Treaty averted war with Britain. Furthermore, between 1795 and 1800, the value of American exports to the British Empire increased 300 percent. The treaty also had an impact on American relations with Spain.

The Pinckney Treaty

Spain, also at war with France, was doing poorly and, in 1795, decided to make a separate peace. The Spanish government was afraid, however, that such a move might bring a declaration of war by Britain. Aware of the terms of the Jay Treaty, Spain also feared an Anglo-American alliance. Spain, therefore, indicated a willingness to negotiate with the United States over the navigation of the Mississippi River, the right of deposit at New Orleans, and the boundary of Spanish Florida.

Washington sent Thomas Pinckney to negotiate and, in September 1795, the Treaty of San Lorenzo was completed. The United States was granted navigation of the Mississippi River through Spanish territory and the right of deposit at New Orleans, renewable in three years. The northern boundary of Florida was fixed at 31°, where Americans had always said it should be. Furthermore, the Spanish agreed to restrain the Indians along the Florida frontier from raiding settlements in Georgia.

The Treaty of Greenville

Indian raids from both Spanish Florida and the Northwest had vexed American settlers for years. In 1790 the Indians in the Northwest had routed an American army at the Maumee River. In November 1791, an army under General Arthur St. Clair, governor of the Northwest Territory, was also decisively defeated. Finally, in August 1794, General Anthony Wayne crushed the Indians at the Battle of Fallen Timbers. As a result, the Indians signed the Treaty of Greenville in 1795. Under this treaty the southeastern quarter of the Northwest Territory was sold to the United States for $10,000, and peace was restored on the northwestern frontier.

Washington's Farewell

As a result of the three treaties, peace was maintained for the United States, and new territories were opened for American settlement. Washington, feeling that the government had been safely launched, refused nomination for a third term. In September 1796, his Farewell Address appeared in newspapers across the country. In his Farewell Address, Washington warned the nation against political parties and entanglement in the affairs of other countries.

General Anthony Wayne's victory at the Battle of Fallen Timbers led to the treaty worked out between Wayne and Chief Little Turtle of the Miamis. What did the treaty mean to settlers moving into the Northwest?

The threat to the Union and the Constitution was Washington's chief concern. For this reason he stressed that common ideals should be found and warned against parties and factions.

Adams was highly educated. Like Hamilton, he did not believe that the common people should make complex decisions.

Let me now warn you in the most solemn manner against the baneful effects of the spirit of party generally. . . .

This spirit, unfortunately, is inseparable from our nature, having its root in the strongest passions of the human mind. . . .

So, likewise, a passionate attachment of one nation for another produces a variety of evils.

Excessive partiality for one foreign nation and excessive dislike of another cause those whom they actuate to see danger only on one side, and serve to veil and even second the arts of influence on the other.

The great rule of conduct for us in regard to foreign nations is, in extending our commercial relations, to have with them as little political connection as possible. So far as we have already formed engagements let them be fulfilled with perfect good faith. Here let us stop.

The Farewell Address charted a sensible course for the young nation. When Washington left office, however, the Federalist Party lost its only candidate with significant nationwide appeal.

SECTION REVIEW

1. Identify the following: Edmond Genêt, Gouverneur Morris, Pinckney Treaty, Anthony Wayne.
2. What was the objective of the Proclamation of Neutrality?
3. What were some of the actions of the British that antagonized Americans during the 1790's?
4. What was the major purpose of the Jay Treaty?
5. Why was Spain willing to negotiate a treaty with the United States?
6. What were the major themes of Washington's Farewell Address?

5 Decline of the Federalists

In the election of 1792, the Republicans had not attempted to defeat the popular Washington, although they had cut appreciably into the electoral vote for Vice President John Adams and had won control of the House of Representatives. In 1796, with Washington out of the running, the presidential election was fiercely contested.

The Election of 1796

The Republicans ran Thomas Jefferson for President and Aaron Burr of New York for Vice President. The Federalists nominated John Adams and Thomas Pinckney. The Constitution provided only that each elector cast two votes, and the candidate receiving the largest number (if that number was equal to a majority of the electors) would become President. Alexander Hamilton, who felt he would not have the influence with Adams that he had enjoyed with Washington, attempted to use the electoral system to make Thomas Pinckney President.

Hamilton urged the Federalist electors to leave Adams' name off their ballots. Adams' supporters retaliated by leaving off Pinckney's name. The result was that Adams won an electoral victory of only three votes, and Thomas Jefferson came in second. Thus a Federalist President was elected with a Republican Vice President.

Adams and the Cabinet

John Adams had already served the young nation with distinction. A leading advocate of independence in 1776, minister to Holland and Great Britain, and first Vice President, he was an honest, sincere, and capable man. His views, however, were distinctly Federalist at a time when most people were becoming more democratic.

When Adams took over the Presidency, he did not attempt to replace the cabinet he had inherited from Washington. He did not do so partly out of respect for Washington, and partly because good executives were hard to find. What Adams did not know was that all of his cabinet members were followers of Alexander Hamilton, who had resigned in 1795. Thus the President's closest advisors were loyal to his political rival. Factionalism within the Federalist party grew as Adams faced the biggest problem of his administration, the possibility of war with France.

The XYZ Affair

Ratification of the Jay Treaty and the election of Adams had convinced the French that the United States was firmly in the British camp. Consequently, the French government ordered the seizure of American ships and confiscation of their cargoes. The

George Logan, a Quaker, privately negotiated with Tallyrand to secure peace. Criticism of his efforts led to the Logan Act (1799), which makes such private action illegal.

American minister to France, Charles Cotesworth Pinckney, was ordered to leave the country. In March 1797, another order said that any American citizen who had been impressed into British service and later captured by the French would be hanged.

American public opinion turned distinctly anti-French. Adams, in yet another attempt to avoid war, sent Charles Cotesworth Pinckney, Elbridge Gerry, and John Marshall to France. Their mission was to try to negotiate a solution to France's grievances against the United States.

When the American delegation arrived in France, they were snubbed by the French government, called the Directory. Finally, when they were about to give up, they were approached by three agents of the French foreign minister, Talleyrand. These agents, later called X, Y, and Z by President Adams, suggested that a bribe of $250,000 to Talleyrand and the Directors would gain an audience for the Americans. The American envoys angrily declined.

In April 1798, the diplomatic correspondence of the "XYZ Affair" was published. Most Americans, including Jefferson and many Republicans, were outraged at the insult to their government. "Millions for defense but not one cent for tribute!" became the patriotic slogan of the day. The country burned with war fever. Congress appropriated money for the construction of new warships, arms and ammunition, and harbor defenses. The army was expanded, and George Washington was recalled from retirement to head it. The Franco-American treaties of 1778 were suspended.

Although American actions stopped short of a declaration of war, an undeclared naval war took place between 1798 and 1800. The United States launched three formidable frigates, the *Constitution,* the *United States,* and the *Constellation.* In the summer of 1798, Congress established the Department of the Navy. By 1800, the navy had 14 men-of-war in action, and the American ships won some impressive victories.

War fever gave new strength to the Federalist party. In the congressional elections of 1798–1799, Federalists won what was to be their last majority.

President Adams knew that his own popularity would be enhanced by a war with France. But the United States was ill-equipped for war. Also, Washington had insisted on having Hamilton as his second in command, and Adams was reluctant to give his rival a chance for military glory.

By 1799, the French government had let it be known that it was willing to negotiate. Adams nominated William Vans Murray as ambassador to France, but Hamilton's followers in the Senate refused to approve the nomination. When Adams threatened to resign, leaving the Presidency to Jefferson, the Senators agreed to compromise with a delegation of three Federalists.

The new delegation to France (Vans Murray, Chief Justice Oliver Ellsworth, and North Carolina Governor William R. Davie) was received by Napoleon Bonaparte, who by this time had overthrown the French government. In an agreement called the Convention of 1800, the undeclared naval war was ended. However, Adams' handling of the crisis had widened the split in the Federalist party.

Party Politics

With American opinion against France at its height in 1798, the Federalists saw the opportunity to strike against their political enemies. Expecting that war against France would soon be declared, the Federalists acted to suppress the supporters of France—namely, the Republicans.

Thomas Jefferson is shown on a campaign flag. Although Washington considered political parties divisive and dangerous, they continued to grow. Why did the Republicans replace the Federalists as the strongest party in the early 1800's?

Freedom of Expression

Since colonial times many Americans have known that freedom of expression is vital to democracy. An early example of American concern for this freedom occurred in 1735, when John Peter Zenger was arrested and tried for publishing pamphlets that criticized the governor of New York. The "not guilty" verdict of the jury was a landmark in the history of freedom of the press. However, the path for freedom of expression was neither clear nor straight.

The freedom of expression guaranteed by the First Amendment to the Constitution includes freedom of speech, freedom of the press, freedom of religion, the right to assemble peaceably, and the right to petition the government. Democracy could not exist without these basic rights, which allow the free, lawful, and public exchange of ideas.

However, reasonable restrictions may be placed on the freedom of expression. For example, a newspaper may be sued for libel, which involves the use of words that damage the reputation or privacy of individuals. But ideas cannot be censored by the government *before* they are expressed. Although a newspaper may be sued for what it has already published, it cannot be forbidden in advance to publish.

Expressions that conflict with public safety or national security also may be reasonably restricted. This area of law is delicate and complex. Especially in time of war, security reasons may be used as an excuse to cover political reasons for limiting freedom of speech or press. This was the case in 1798, when the Federalists used the excuse of an undeclared naval war with France to pass the Alien and Sedition Acts, which were intended to silence the Federalists' political opponents.

One of the Federalists' opponents was Matthew Lyon, a Republican member of Congress from Vermont, who criticized President John Adams. Lyons was sent to jail for "deceitfully, wickedly, and maliciously contriving to defame the Govern-

ment of the United States." Many people protested against this violation of constitutional rights. However, no one took the matter before the courts because, at this time in American history, the right of the courts to judge the constitutionality of a law had not yet been established. Republicans thought that state legislatures should have the right to decide questions of constitutionality. This view was put forth by Thomas Jefferson and James Madison in the Kentucky and Virginia Resolutions.

During World War I, national security was once again the justification for laws that limited freedom of speech. A man named Christopher Schenck was convicted of interfering with the American war effort because he distributed pamphlets that urged men to resist the draft. The Supreme Court in *Schenck* v. *United States* (1919) upheld his conviction. Justice Oliver Wendell Holmes ruled as follows:

> *Words can be weapons. . . . The question in every case is whether the words used are used in such circumstances and are of such a nature as to create a clear and present danger that they will bring about the action that Congress has a right to prevent.*

The "clear and present danger" principle was extended to "clear and probable danger" in 1951, in the case of *Dennis* v. *United States*. In this case, the Supreme Court upheld the convictions of 11 leaders of the Communist Party for advocating the violent overthrow of the United States government. Under both of these principles, it may be against the law to call for certain actions, but it is not against the law to advocate certain beliefs.

QUESTIONS

1. What freedoms of expression are guaranteed by the First Amendment?
2. What are some examples of reasonable restrictions on freedom of expression?
3. How do the principles of "clear and present danger" and "clear and possible danger" distinguish between advocating actions and advocating beliefs?

The election of 1800 showed an increase in the popular vote greater than to be expected from the increase in population. Historians attribute this increase to the appearance of political parties, with their techniques for dramatizing issues and getting out the vote.

The Alien and Sedition Acts.

Without waiting for a formal declaration of war, the Federalists pushed through Congress four measures that curbed freedom of speech and press and limited the liberties of foreigners in the United States. The Four Acts were known collectively as the "Alien and Sedition Acts." They were the Act Concerning Aliens, the Act Respecting Alien Enemies, the Naturalization Act, and the Act for the Punishment of Certain Crimes.

The first two of these acts, which gave the President certain powers to send aliens out of the country, were never enforced. The Naturalization Act raised the residence requirement for **naturalization** (the process by which immigrants become United States citizens) from 5 to 14 years. Thus the Federalists made it harder for immigrants, who often voted Republican, to become American citizens. The Act for the Punishment of Certain Crimes was known as the Sedition Act. This act allowed the arrest of citizens for **sedition,** or inciting resistance to lawful authority. Under this law, Republican political leaders and newspaper editors were prosecuted for speaking out against the President or the government of the United States. The Sedition Act was to expire at the end of Adams' term.

The Virginia and Kentucky Resolutions.

Republicans were appalled by the Federalist attack on liberties protected by the Bill of Rights. In fact, the Alien and Sedition Acts served to unite the Republicans. Jefferson and Madison anonymously wrote arguments that were adopted by the Kentucky and Virginia legislatures respectively.

In the Kentucky Resolution, Jefferson said that the Constitution was a compact between the states. When the federal government overstepped the bounds of that compact, threatening the liberties of the people, the states could **nullify,** or declare invalid, the federal government's actions. Virginia and Kentucky urged other states to adopt similar resolutions, but they received no support. Nonetheless, these statements became significant precedents for an extreme states' rights position.

The Election of 1800

The Election of 1800, following on the heels of the Alien and Sedition Acts, was again bitterly contested. The Federalists seemed to be in a solid position since they had gained peace with France. However, they had raised taxes to cover the expenses of military preparations, and the expanded army was seen by some people as a threat to American liberties. Ironically, the Federalists were hurt by the fact that war with France had been avoided. They were now accused of being warmongers. Moreover, Washington had died in 1799, and the traditional leaders of the party no longer held appeal. The youth and vigor of the country seemed to be swinging behind the Republicans.

Both parties wanted to avoid a repetition of the 1796 election, when a Federalist became President, and a Republican became Vice President. For that reason, both party **caucuses** (party members meeting privately to choose candidates) pledged equal support to their two candidates. The Federalists nominated Adams and Charles Cotesworth Pinckney of South Carolina, and the Republicans renominated Jefferson and Burr.

The Republican ticket won the electoral vote. However, because of the earlier pledge of equal support, both Jefferson and Burr received an equal number of electoral votes. In such a case, the

ELECTION OF 1800

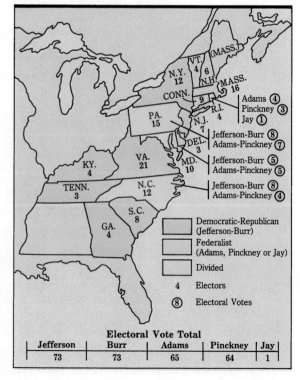

Electoral Vote Total				
Jefferson	Burr	Adams	Pinckney	Jay
73	73	65	64	1

The deadlock occurred because the Republicans did not anticipate such total party solidarity. They had expected that a few votes would be cast for someone other than Burr. Most

Federalists considered Burr unscrupulous, but many preferred him to Jefferson because Burr's political philosophy was closer to theirs.

Constitution required the House of Representatives to choose the President.[6]

In the House, the Federalists saw a chance to thwart the election of Jefferson by supporting Burr. For 35 ballots, the election remained tied. On the 36th ballot, however, Hamilton, who had no respect for Burr, threw his weight behind Jefferson. As a result, Jefferson became President, and Burr became Vice President. Because Burr had gone along with the Federalists in their attempt to make him President, he became an outcast in his own party.

The Republican victory was a sweeping one. Both the House and the Senate fell under Republican control. The Federalists had launched the new government successfully, established the power and

---

[6] To prevent the recurrence of such an electoral deadlock, the Twelfth Amendment was ratified in 1804, providing for separate electoral ballots for President and Vice President.

authority of the government at home, and achieved respect from abroad. But the Federalist political philosophy of rule by "the good, the wise, and the rich" was outdated. The growing democratic spirit of the nation found its expression in the Republican party.

SECTION REVIEW

1. Identify the following: Aaron Burr, Charles Cotesworth Pinckney, the Directory, Talleyrand, Convention of 1800.
2. What problem did President Adams have with his cabinet?
3. What was the effect of the XYZ affair on American public opinion?
4. What were the objectives of the Alien and Sedition Acts?
5. How did the Republicans respond to the Alien and Sedition Acts?

CHAPTER 6   REVIEW

SUMMARY

1. The first national government under the Constitution was put into operation by the Federalists with George Washington as President.
2. The actions taken by the first Congress and the first President set many precedents that determined the future course of how the national government would operate.
3. Alexander Hamilton's economic programs helped put the country's economy on a more stable footing.
4. Opposition to Hamilton's programs brought about the beginnings of the first national political parties, the Federalists and the Republicans.
5. The Federalists, led by Hamilton, and the Republicans, led by Madison and Jefferson,

represented different views on what the role and scope of the national government should be.
6. Conflicts over several matters of foreign policy increased the differences between Federalists and Republicans.
7. The Washington and Adams administrations successfully maintained the neutrality of the United States in spite of great pressures to become involved in European wars.
8. The powers of the national government were significantly broadened by the Federalists.
9. The election of 1800 saw a shifting of power to the Republicans as Thomas Jefferson became President of the United States, and Congress came under Republican control.

VOCABULARY

protective tariff	assumption	demagogue	naturalization
original jurisdiction	banknote	privateer	sedition
dual court system	excise tax	impress	nullify
cabinet	laissez-faire	most favored nation	caucus
promissory note			

REVIEW QUESTIONS

1. What precedents were set by the Washington administration?
2. How was compromise used to settle some of the issues during Washington's Presidency?
3. What role did James Madison play in the new government?
4. What were the major differences between the Republicans and the Federalists?
5. What diplomatic steps did the United States take to try to remain neutral under Washington and Adams?
6. What was the significance of the Kentucky and Virginia Resolutions?
7. What led to the downfall of the Federalist Party?
8. What were the major accomplishments of the Federalists during the 1790's?

DISCUSSION

1. Why might an industrial society require more government than an agrarian society?
2. Do you agree with the Federalists or the Republicans on the ability of the common people to rule wisely? Why?
3. Do you think political parties are helpful or harmful to government? Why?
4. Do you agree with Hamilton's position that it would be immoral for the United States not to pay its domestic debt in full? Why or why not?

USING MAPS

Refer to the map on page 136 and answer the following questions:

1. How many electoral votes did Jefferson receive?
2. Which states were divided in their electoral votes?
3. Which state had the largest number of electors?
4. Which state had the smallest number of electors?

USING SKILLS

Study the excerpt from Washington's Farewell Address on page 133. Which of the following is the main point being made by Washington?

1. Political parties are like foreign countries.
2. The United States should have as little political connection as possible with foreign countries.
3. The party spirit has its roots in the strongest passions of the human mind.
4. The United States should extend its commercial relations with foreign countries.
5. The United States has already formed engagements with foreign countries.

SUMMARY

1. After independence was won, the United States entered a Critical Period in which economic, political, and foreign problems had to be solved.
2. Weaknesses of the central government under the Articles of Confederation led to a movement for a stronger federal constitution.
3. Delegates to the Constitutional Convention met in Philadelphia in 1787.
4. After much debate and many compromises, a new Constitution was ratified in 1788.
5. The new Constitution greatly expanded the powers of the national government.
6. With George Washington as the first President of the United States, the Federalists successfully launched the government of the world's largest federal republic.
7. The contrasting views of Alexander Hamilton and Thomas Jefferson, particularly in regard to economic policy, led to the development of the nation's first political parties.

REVIEW QUESTIONS

1. What problems did the United States face during the Critical Period? How did the nation under the Articles of Confederation respond to these problems?
2. What issues were faced by the Constitutional Convention? How were they resolved?
3. Was the Constitutional Convention successful in creating a new government that could solve the problems caused by the weaknesses of the Confederation government? Why or why not?
4. How were the powers of government under the Constitution exercised by the Federalists?

SUGGESTED ACTIVITIES

1. Suppose the United States has just acquired a new, sparsely inhabited territory. After studying the Northwest Ordinance, organize a committee to set up a territorial government. Specify how your government would differ from that set up by Congress for the Northwest Territory.
2. Develop a visual presentation to explain implied and enumerated powers of the Constitution.
3. Taking the role of a southern planter or a northern merchant in the 1790's, write a letter to your Representative in Congress explaining your view on the national bank and the tariff.
4. Select any three current issues faced by the United States and comment on them from the viewpoints of Alexander Hamilton and Thomas Jefferson.
5. Research and report on the government of Canada, Mexico, or the Soviet Union. Compare or contrast it with the government of the United States.

SUGGESTED READINGS

1. Akers, Charles. *Abigail Adams: An American Woman.* Boston: Little, Brown, & Co., 1980. Paperback. Discusses Adams as a feminist of her time.
2. Bowen, Katherine D. *Miracle at Philadelphia.* Boston: Little, Brown, & Co., 1966. Provides insight into the personalities of the delegates to the Constitutional Convention.
3. Hale, Edward E. *Man Without A Country.* Darby, Pennsylvania, Folcroft Library Editions, 1974. A dramatic tale about a man who experiences problems associated with patriotism.
4. Padover, Saul. *Jefferson.* New York: Mentor Books, 1952. A highly readable account of Jefferson's life, using some of Jefferson's own words.

THE HISTORIAN'S CRAFT

In trying to find facts and develop interpretations, historians study materials from both primary and secondary sources. Primary sources are first-hand accounts or evidence, such as letters, diaries, photographs, and government documents. Secondary sources are second-hand. They may be derived from primary sources or from other secondary sources. When secondary sources disagree, as they often do, historians may return to primary sources for more evidence. It is important to remember that a single source, either primary or secondary, is seldom completely reliable. Even eyewitness accounts of the same event may differ.

This activity will show you how secondary sources may be derived from primary sources, and help you to distinguish between the two. The subject of the activity is the question of how Shays' Rebellion contributed to the feeling that the Articles of Confederation should be replaced with a stronger national constitution.

Study the following list of sources that provide information on this subject. Which items on the list are primary sources? Which are secondary sources?

1. A letter from Thomas Jefferson expressing his opinion about Shays' Rebellion.
2. Historian John Fiske's book, *The Critical Period of American History, 1783–1789,* published in 1893.
3. James Madison's notes on the proceedings of the Constitutional Convention.
4. What this textbook says about Shays' Rebellion on pages 86–7.

After determining which of the above are primary sources and which are secondary, read the following three sources, each of which deals with the effects of Shays' Rebellion. The first source is an excerpt from a letter written by Thomas Jefferson on January 16, 1787:

I expected [Shays' Rebellion] would have produced in Europe an unfavorable opinion of our political state. But it has not. On the contrary, the small effect of these tumults seems to have given more confidence in the firmness of our governments. The interposition of the people themselves on the side of government (remember, the militia put down the rebellion) has had a great effect on the opinion here. I am persuaded myself that the good sense of the people will always be found to be the best army. They may be led astray for a moment, but will soon correct themselves. The people are the only censors of their governors; and even their errors will tend to keep these to the true principles of their institution. To punish these errors too severely would be to suppress the only safeguard of the public liberty.

The second source is a newspaper editorial that appeared in the *Pennsylvania Gazette* on September 5, 1787:

The year 1776 is celebrated (says a correspondent) for a revolution in favor of Liberty. The year 1787, it is expected, will be celebrated with equal joy for a revolution in favor of Government. The impatience with which all classes of people (a few officers of government only excepted) wait to receive the new federal constitution can only be equaled by their zealous determination to support it.

Every state (adds our correspondent) has its Shays, who either with their pens—or tongues—or offices—are endeavoring to effect what Shays attempted in vain with his sword. In one of the states, this demagogue tries to persuade the people that it is dangerous to increase the powers of Congress. In another, he denies the authority of the Convention to redress our national grievances. In a third, he whispers distrust, saying the states will not adopt the new frame of government. In a fourth, he says the state constitutions, and the officers who act under them, are of divine right, and can be altered by no human power—and of course considers all attempts to restore order and government in the United

States as a "laughable" thing. In the fifth, he opposes a general confederacy, and urges the division of the states into three smaller confederacies, that he may the more easily place himself at the head of one of them.

The Spirit and wickedness of Shays is in each of these principles and measures. Let Americans be wise. Toryism [Loyalism] and Shaysism are nearly allied. They both lead to slavery, poverty, and misery.

We hear that the Convention proposes to adjourn next week, after laying America under such obligations to them for their long, painful, and disinterested labors to establish her liberty upon a permanent basis as no time will ever cancel.

The third source is a political science textbook published in 1972:

One of the serious responsibilities in the minds of the Founding Fathers was to form a government that would assure domestic tranquility. The decade preceding the formation of the Constitution was a turbulent one in which economic difficulties led to open violence. So widespread were the domestic disturbances that the era has been called the Critical Period.

There are many examples where internal disturbances interrupted the peaceful domestic scene. Prior to the formation of the Union, Daniel Shays led a rebellion in defiance of the State government of Massachusetts in a conflict over the question of "hard" or "soft" money. Supported by an armed band of farmers and debtors, Shays attempted to prevent county courts from sitting in debt cases and even threatened to lay siege to Boston.

QUESTIONS

1. Which of these sources are primary? Which are secondary?
2. Does Thomas Jefferson seem to think that Shays' Rebellion requires a change in government? Why or why not?
3. Is the *Philadelphia Gazette* editorial in favor of or against a new constitution?
4. How does the editorial relate Shays' Rebellion to the idea of a new constitution?
5. Did the editorial appear before or after the Constitution was completed?
6. According to the textbook, what was the relationship of Shays' Rebellion to the Constitution?
7. Does the evidence of Jefferson's letter support what the textbook says?
8. Does the evidence of the editorial support the textbook?
9. What does the reference to the "Critical Period" tell you about the origin of the textbook account?

1801	1803	1808	1815–24	1819
Inauguration of Thomas Jefferson	*Marbury* v. *Madison*	Election of James Madison	Era of Good Feelings	Acquisition of Florida

	1803	1807	1812–14	1816	1820
	Louisiana Purchase	Embargo Act	War of 1812	Second Bank of United States	Missouri Compromise

NATIONALISM AND SECTIONALISM

The Jeffersonian Republicans

The Age of Jackson

Westward Expansion

Antebellum America

1823
Monroe
Doctrine

1828
Election of
Andrew Jackson

1831
Nat Turner's
Rebellion

1840
Election of
William Henry Harrison

1824
Election of
John Quincy Adams

1830
Webster-Hayne
Debate

1836
Election of
Martin Van Buren

1846–48
Mexican
War

1	Jefferson in Power	145
2	Trials of a Neutral Nation	150
3	The War of 1812	153
4	American Nationalism	157
5	The Rise of Sectionalism	161

THE JEFFERSONIAN REPUBLICANS

In war we are one people. In making peace we are one people. In all commercial relations we are one and the same people. In many other respects the American people are one.

JOHN MARSHALL

The election of Thomas Jefferson in 1800 marked an important event in the history of the nation: the first peaceful passing of power from one political party to another. The Federalists remained active for some time, but they never again gained control of the national government. The Republicans held the Presidency for the next 24 years. During these years the United States doubled its territory and fought another war with Great Britain. Americans experienced a growing sense of national pride, while at the same time, conflicts developed among the different sections of the country.

1 Jefferson in Power

Some extreme Federalists were afraid that Jefferson's administration would bring about mob rule. They worried that the federal government would be weakened by Jefferson's narrow interpretation of the Constitution. They were concerned that Hamilton's financial system, so important to the credit and commerce of the nation, would be destroyed. Jefferson, however, was not the radical whom the Federalists feared.

Easing Federalist Fears

The new President was, in fact, a moderate and practical man. He knew that his **constituency** (the citizens he represented) included not only the members of his party but all Americans. In his inaugural address he soothed the Federalists by saying that

> *every difference of opinion is not a difference of principle. We have called by different names brethren of the same principle. We are all Republicans, we are all Federalists.*

In his speech, Jefferson praised the Republican values of agriculture, states' rights, majority rule, individual freedom, equal justice, and the supremacy of civil over military authority. To appease the Federalists, he promised to pay the public debt, encourage commerce, and preserve the continuity of government. Even Hamilton was reassured. He said that Jefferson had shown that he would not "lend himself to dangerous innovations, but in essential points tread in the steps of his predecessors."

Jefferson knew that too many sudden changes would cause confusion and alarm. For this reason he left intact some important Federalist programs. He did nothing to interfere with the Bank of the United States. The federal government went on paying the states' war debts according to Hamilton's plan. Federalist policies for encouraging American shipping were also retained.

Trimming Federalist Programs

Although Jefferson and the Republican-controlled Congress did not make radical changes in policy, they acted upon their political beliefs. They could not accept the threat to individual rights in the Alien and Sedition Acts. Therefore, the acts were allowed to expire in 1801. People who had been jailed under the acts were freed, and fines were refunded. The **residence requirement** (the requirement that people live in a place for a period of time) for naturalization was reduced from fourteen to five years.

Believing that a standing army in peacetime was dangerous to liberty, the Republicans cut the army from 4000 to 2000 men. They also sold most of the navy's ships, because they saw no need to protect overseas commerce or establish the United States as a sea power. Only a small fleet of gunboats was kept for coastal defense.

Cutting the military budget also fitted in nicely with Republicans' desire to reduce the national debt. In their opinion, the debt was of benefit only to a small group of wealthy investors. Jefferson's Secretary of Treasury, Albert Gallatin, devised a plan to pay the debt gradually by reducing expenses. A number of government offices were eliminated in order to save money.

Even though Jefferson wanted to pay the national debt as quickly as possible, he was willing to do without the hated whiskey tax. Congress repealed the whiskey tax in 1802. Revenue for the government was to come only from import duties and the sale of public lands.

Policy changes such as these diluted the Federalists' influence on government. Jefferson also used **patronage** (the power to make appointments) as a weapon against the Federalists. Pointing out that he could not act through men whose aims were to defeat his policies, he set about removing Federalists from offices and putting Republicans in their place. By the middle of 1803, only 130 of the 316 federal officers under the President's control remained in Federalist hands.

Conflict with the Judiciary

The one Federalist institution that Jefferson wanted to dismantle and could not was the judicial branch. Just before leaving office, John Adams had signed the Judiciary Act of 1801, creating a number of new federal judgeships. These judgeships and their staffs were all filled by loyal Federalists.

Jefferson was able to get the Republican Congress to repeal the Judiciary Act of 1801. This eliminated the last-minute judgeships, or **"midnight appointments,"** as Jefferson called them. He instructed his Secretary of State, James Madison, not to deliver the official letters of appointment. As a result, William Marbury, one of the men who had been appointed by Adams, sued Madison before the Supreme Court. Marbury asked the Court to issue a **writ of mandamus,** or written order, to Madison.

The result was a landmark decision. The Supreme Court ruled against Marbury on the grounds that the Judiciary Act of 1789, which gave the Court power to issue writs of mandamus, was unconstitutional. Said Chief Justice John Marshall:

It is emphatically the province and duty of the judicial department to say what the law is. Those who apply the rule to particular cases must of necessity expound and interpret that rule. If two laws conflict with each other, the courts must decide on the operation of each. . . .

If, then, the courts are to regard the Constitution, and the Constitution is superior to any ordinary act of the legislature, the Constitution, and not such ordinary act, must govern the case to which they both apply.

The Supreme Court had ruled that it did not have power in this case. Paradoxically, the Court had increased its power by establishing the principles of judicial review. By this principle the Court has the power to decide whether or not a law passed by Congress is constitutional. Jefferson and the Republicans were shocked and angered by the decision. To them it seemed that the balance of power among the three branches of government was upset.

The Republicans' only weapon against the courts was impeachment. The Constitution gave the House of Representatives the power to impeach federal judges for treason, bribery, or other high crimes. The attack began with the impeachment of Federal District Judge John Pickering for drunkenness. Pickering was convicted and removed from office.

Next the Republicans went after Supreme Court Justice Samuel Chase. Chase had been especially **partisan** (supporting of one party, in this case the Federalist Party) in enforcing the Sedition Act. But the Republicans failed to get the necessary two-thirds vote of the Senate for conviction. With this defeat, it became obvious that impeachment was not an effective way to control the courts. The failure to remove Chase from office was a victory for the independence of the judiciary.

Jefferson's Nationalism

Anti-Federalist policies such as the attack on the judiciary were seen by Jefferson and his supporters as attempts to balance the course of American government. Although Jefferson believed that the role of the federal government should be limited, he was a nationalist in many ways. He was willing to let common sense overrule political principles when the

Thomas Jefferson was a man of many interests and talents. In addition to authoring the Declaration of Independence, he served in several political posts. He founded, helped design, and supervised the building of the University of Virginia (right). He also designed his own plantation home, Monticello, where he conducted scientific experiments that led to improvements in agronomy. As President, what changes did Jefferson make in Federalist programs to conform with Republican political beliefs?

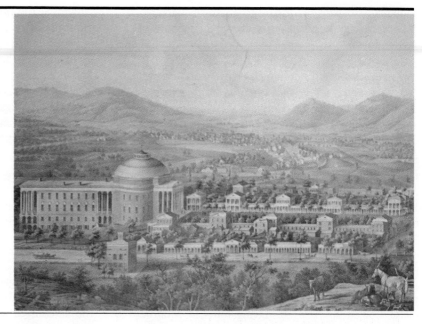

good of the country was at stake. For example, in a war with the Barbary pirates of North Africa, Jefferson acted as a Federalist might have.

For years the Muslim rulers of the Barbary states had forced the United States and European nations to pay tribute. In 1801, Tripoli increased its demands. Jefferson decided that, as President, he had a right to defend the nation even without a declaration of war by Congress. He sent the navy to enforce a blockade against Tripoli. This was a surprisingly strong action for a Republican to take. In its battles with the pirates, however, the navy was hampered by the previous reductions of its strength. In 1805 the ruler of Tripoli signed a peace treaty, agreeing to end the payment of tribute.[1] But the United States had to pay a large ransom for the release of captured Americans.

Another example of Jefferson's nationalism was his approval of a national road. After Ohio was admitted as a state in 1803, Albert Gallatin proposed that land sales be used to finance a national road to be built from the Potomac to the Ohio River. Such a road was badly needed to improve transportation and trade. Jefferson agreed, even though as a strict constructionist he was against federal financing of **internal improvements** (roads, bridges, and other construction intended to aid the national economy). In 1806 Congress voted funds for building the road.

[1] Tribute to other Barbary states was not ended until 1815.

The Louisiana Purchase

Jefferson's nationalism was also apparent in the purchase of Louisiana from France. This purchase, one of the most important acts of Jefferson's Presidency, doubled the size of the United States. As a result of the Seven Year's War (the French and Indian War), France had lost the vast, ill-defined Louisiana territory to Spain. However, in 1800, the French dictator Napoleon Bonaparte signed a treaty with Spain that gave Louisiana back to France.

By May of 1801, word of the treaty reached Jefferson. This was indeed cause for alarm. Spain was not powerful enough to interfere seriously with the American dream of expanding westward to the Pacific, but the ownership of Louisiana by France was a much greater threat. Jefferson hurriedly sent off Robert R. Livingston, the new American minister to France, with instructions to try to get the French to sell West Florida and New Orleans to the United States. Jefferson wrote to Livingston that there was

on the globe one single spot, the possessor of which is our natural and habitual enemy. It is New Orleans, through which the produce of three-eighths of our territory must pass to market. . . .

Jefferson's worry seemed to be justified when Spanish officials—at Napoleon's bidding, Jefferson

Santo Domingo was also important as a sugar-producing island. The slaves there had been inspired by the French Revolution to create a republic of their own.

Have students discuss the dilemma posed when the national interest does not coincide with strict adherence to the letter of the law.

thought—closed New Orleans to American shipping. Jefferson sent James Monroe to aid Livingston in negotiations.

Jefferson's worst fears failed to materialize, however. Napoleon's dream of a New World empire had been ended by a slave revolt in Haiti, a former French colony on the Caribbean Island of Santo Domingo. In 1791 the people of Haiti, led by Toussaint l'Overture, had won their independence. Napoleon had recognized the importance of the island as a naval base from which he could control a western empire. He had sent more than 30,000 troops to regain control. This army had been wiped out by yellow fever and the valiant fighting of the ex-slaves.

Without Santo Domingo, Napoleon had little use for Louisiana. He also needed money. By the time Monroe reached France, Napoleon had decided to give up not only West Florida and New Orleans, but all of Louisiana. Amazed, Livingston and Monroe

jumped at the offer. They arranged a treaty with a purchase price totalling roughly $15 million.

Jefferson had reservations about the constitutionality of some of the treaty's provisions. The Constitution did not explicitly give the government power to acquire territory. Finally, Jefferson overcame his reservations against loose constructionism. The benefits to the nation of owning Louisiana outweighed philosophical considerations.

Federalism in Retreat

Most Americans were delighted with the Louisiana purchase. Some New England Federalists, though, considered it a mistake. They thought that the land had cost too much and that the treaty power of the government had been stretched too far. Furthermore, New England Federalists were afraid that their voice in national affairs would be further weakened by the addition of so much western territory.

THE LOUISIANA PURCHASE AND EXPLORATION IN THE WEST

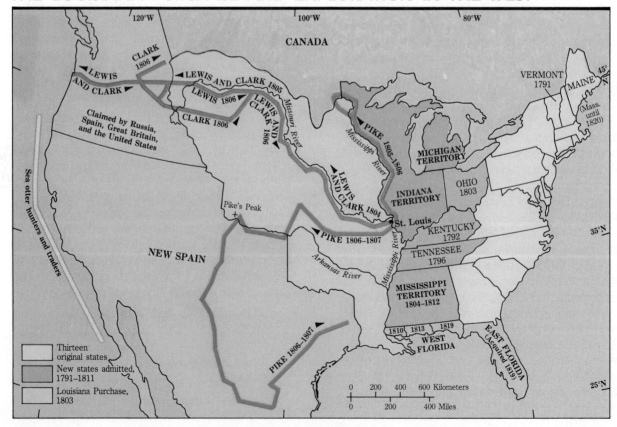

The Explorers

Even before the Louisiana Purchase was contemplated, Thomas Jefferson was interested in exploring the lands west of the United States. Meriwether Lewis, Jefferson's private secretary, shared that dream. After the Louisiana Territory became part of the United States, Jefferson authorized an army expedition to the territory. The expedition was to be led by Lewis.

William Clark was Lewis' choice as a partner. Clark had resigned from the army, but rejoined in order to go on the expedition. He was responsible for recruiting others to go on the trip. He also mapped the routes and kept records, including sketches of animals he saw in the West.

The expedition left from St. Louis in the spring of 1804 and traveled up the Missouri River. On the way they met an Indian-Canadian fur trader, Toussaint Charbonneau, and his young Indian wife, Sacajawea. Sacajawea, whose name means "Bird Woman," was a Shoshone Indian who as a child had been stolen by enemy Indians and eventually sold as a slave to Charbonneau. Sacajawea and Charbonneau accompanied Lewis and Clark on the trip westward, with Sacajawea acting as chief guide and interpreter.

On the way Sacajawea gave birth to a son. The presence of an Indian woman and a baby helped to allay the suspicions of other Indians whom the explorers encountered. On one occasion Sacajawea met her long-lost brother and other Shoshone relatives. From them she was able to obtain horses and supplies for the explorers.

The expedition went all the way to the Pacific Ocean, traveling down the Columbia River by canoe. On the return trip, Lewis and Clark took separate routes, Lewis following the Marias River and Clark, the Yellowstone. By the time they reached St. Louis in the fall of 1806, they had been given up for lost.

Other Americans also made exploratory trips westward. While Lewis and Clark were in the Northwest, Zebulon Pike was exploring the upper Mississippi River and the Southwest. Pike's Peak in the Rocky Mountains was named after him.

To some extreme Federalists the only solution seemed to be separation from the United States. A group of Federalists called the Essex Junto[2] secretly plotted **secession,** or withdrawal from the Union. The conspirators felt that if they could win elections and gain control of the state governments in New England, each state could secede from the Union. Eventually, they could combine to form a northern confederation. They even had hopes of luring New York into the deal, but their plans went astray.

In the spring of 1804, Aaron Burr was running for governor of New York as a Federalist. He had changed parties because his relationship with Jefferson had cooled considerably ever since the election of 1800. The Republicans had dropped Burr from the 1804 ticket in favor of George Clinton. The conspirators hoped that if they backed Burr in the governor's election, he might go along with their plot. In order to win their support, Burr made vague promises about what he might do if elected.

Alexander Hamilton worked actively against the election of Burr and accused Burr of plotting treason. When Burr lost, he blamed his defeat on Hamilton and challenged him to a duel. Although Hamilton was opposed to duels, he did not want to seem a coward.

The two men met in Weehawken, New Jersey, on July 11, 1804. Hamilton was fatally wounded and died

---

[2] The Essex Junto was so named because many of its leaders came from Essex County in Masschusetts. A junto is a group of persons whose purpose is to take control of a goverment.

Point out that the secession threat, usually associated with the Civil War, was in fact raised a number of times in American history.

Have students debate whether British actions were justifiable wartime measures, or simply a case of "might makes right."

the next day. Thus ended the life of one of America's most influential statesmen.[3]

With Burr's defeat, and with almost no support in the New England States, the Essex Junto conspiracy fizzled out. The results of the election of 1804 showed how thoroughly the Federalists had been discredited. Jefferson and Clinton won a sweeping victory, carrying every state except Connecticut and Delaware.

SECTION REVIEW

1. Identify the following: Albert Gallatin, Judiciary Act of 1801, John Pickering, Robert R. Livingston, Tripoli, Toussaint l'Overture.
2. How did Jefferson try to calm Federalist fears of Republican rule?
3. What steps did the Republicans take to reduce Federalist influence?
4. How did the Supreme Court expand its powers?
5. What factors influenced Jefferson's decision to purchase Louisiana?
6. Why did some of the Federalists want to secede from the United States?

2 Trials of a Neutral Nation

Most of Jefferson's second term, coinciding with war in Europe, was spent trying to maintain American neutrality. In 1803 Napoleon had set out to conquer Europe. Within a few years, only Russia and Great Britain remained undefeated. The warring nations had to depend on neutral countries for supplies. Because the United States was the neutral nation with the most active shipping industry, American trade was greatly expanded. The United States became the leading neutral carrier of trade goods. Pressures against neutrality, however, were mounting.

Freedom of the Seas

The United States was an important source of supply to both sides in the war. Each side took measures to limit what it saw as aid to the enemy and,

---

[3] Burr went on to become involved in a strange conspiracy to take control of western lands. In 1807 he was tried for treason. He was not convicted, but his political career came to an end.

THE IMPRESSMENT OF AN
American Sailor Boy

This sea chanty was distributed as an anti-British propaganda leaflet. It told of the impressment of Americans by British ships. News of the Chesapeake incident further enraged the public. What measures were taken by Jefferson to stop impressment?

in doing so, violated American freedom of the seas. In 1806 Napoleon issued the Berlin Decree, which said that no ship that stopped at a British port could land at any port under French control.

In 1807 the British passed a series of measures called the Orders in Council. These orders required neutral ships trading with the enemy to pass through British ports and pay a fee, or else be subject to capture. Napoleon replied in kind. His Milan Decree declared that any ship submitting to the British order would be seized by the French or French allies.

Although both the warring powers violated American freedom of the seas, greater friction arose between the United States and Britain. The British, being the much greater sea power, could more effectively enforce their orders. Americans also resented the British method of recruiting for their navy by impressment. The British claimed the right to seize British subjects, including naturalized Americans born on British soil. In practice, many native-born Americans were forced into the Royal Navy.

Jefferson and Americans in general found this situation intolerable. Efforts to negotiate with Britain failed, however, because the United States had no strong navy to back up its demands.

American public opinion was growing increasingly anti-British when, in June of 1807, the American frigate *Chesapeake* was stopped by the British frigate *Leopard*. The captain of the *Leopard* demanded the surrender of British deserters. The American commander refused. At that point, the *Leopard* opened fire, killing 3, wounding 18 and crippling the American ship.

The *Chesapeake* incident embarassed and outraged the American public. Many called for war to redress the nation's honor. The United States, however, was woefully unprepared for such a course.

Economic Warfare

Jefferson began military preparations, but decided first to try economic war. He asked Congress to pass an **embargo,** an order prohibiting trade. In December of 1807, Congress passed the Embargo Act. This act prohibited trade with any foreign country, but was intended primarily to affect the British. Britain, however, seemed to take the embargo in stride. In spite of smuggling by American merchants, it was the American economy that suffered. Commercial interests in New England were especially hurt, and Federalists made political gains by condemning the embargo.

After fourteen months, the embargo was replaced with the Non-Intercourse Act. This act reopened trade with all nations except Britain and France. If either of those countries would "cease to violate the neutral commerce of the United States," trade would be resumed with that country. Jefferson signed the act just before he left office in March of 1809.

James Madison inherited the problems with Britain and France when he defeated Federalist candidate Charles Cotesworth Pinkney in the election of 1808. When Madison came into office, the Non-Intercourse Act was in effect. By early 1810 it was clear that the attempt to use economic coercion against Britain and France would not work. In May Congress passed Macon's Bill Number Two, reopening trade with both. The bill stated that if either country stopped violating American rights, the United States would impose trade restrictions on the other.

Napoleon, seeing a chance to trick the United States into worse relations with Britain, sent a message saying that he would revoke his Berlin and Milan Decrees. John Quincy Adams, who was minister to Russia at that time, warned that Napoleon's move was "a trap to catch us into a war with England." Madison disregarded the warning and jumped into the trap. He announced that, in accordance with Macon's Bill, a new embargo against Britain would go into effect in three months if Britain did not revoke the Orders in Council.

Alarmed Federalists, noting the impact this would have on American trade and relations with Britain, pointed to Napoleon's treachery. French activity against American shipping actually increased after he revoked the Berlin and Milan Decrees. But, by that time, the die was cast. The congressional elections of that year placed into office a number of new men from the West and the South who were decidedly anti-British.

The War Hawks

The West and the South, oddly enough, were the most anti-British regions of the nation even though they were the least affected by Britain's policies toward American shipping. For a number of reasons, many people from these regions blamed Britain for their problems.

In 1808 the economy of the West entered a serious depression. The major cause of the depression was the poor transportation system—limited, for all practical purposes, to the Mississippi River. Westerners, however, felt that their hard times were caused by Britain's cutting them off from their European market.

Westerners also had their eyes on Canada. Western farmers, always hungry for new land, would have liked to move north into the fertile forests of southern Canada. A war with Britain might make Canadian land available.

Furthermore, Westerners blamed the British for inciting Indian uprisings. In fact, the Indians needed no encouragement from Britain. They had become increasingly bitter about losing their lands. By 1806 the Indians had been forced to give up millions of acres. Treaty after treaty had been broken by the Americans. In order to resist further encroachment on their lands, the Northwest Indians united under Tecumseh, a Shawnee Chief. Tecumseh was a bold and imaginative leader who had spoken eloquently

Note that the Indians of North America consistently allied themselves with whatever group was fighting the Americans (the French in the French and Indian War, the British in the American Revolution and the War of 1812). The fact that they were always on the losing side gave Americans a "patriotic" excuse to kill them and take more of their land.

The Shawnee chief Tecumseh was killed in the Battle of the Thames. With William Henry Harrison's victory, Tecumseh's Indian Confederacy quickly dissolved. What did Tecumseh seek to achieve by uniting the Indians into a confederacy?

against the invasion of the Indian lands by white people:

> *The way—and the only way—to check and stop this evil is for all the red men to unite in claiming a common equal right in the land, as it was at first, and should be yet. For it never was divided, but belongs to all for the use of each. . . .*
>
> *The white people have no right to take the land from the Indians, because they had it first. It is theirs. They may sell, but all must join. Any sale not made by all is not valid.*

Tecumseh was aided by his twin brother Tenskwatawa, known as the Prophet. The Prophet was a **shaman** (a priest who uses magic) who claimed to be able to control the movement of heavenly bodies. Hearing of the Prophet's supposed magical powers, Indian territorial governor William Henry Harrison issued a challenge: "If he really is a prophet, ask him to cause the sun to stand still, the moon to alter its course, the rivers to cease to flow."

Unfortunately, the challenge reached the Prophet after he had learned from the British that an eclipse of

the sun was due June 16, 1806. When the sun disappeared according to his prediction, his reputation was insured. He led a religious revival which helped to unite the Indians.

By 1810 fighting had broken out. Americans blamed the British, arguing that they supplied the Indians with guns. At the Battle of Tippecanoe on November 7, 1811, Harrison defeated an Indian attack led by the Prophet. At the time, Tecumseh was away seeking the support of other Indian nations. Although Harrison's troops suffered heavy losses, he became a popular hero. Tecumseh and the Northwest Indians thereafter fought a mainly defensive war against the United States.

Meanwhile, the South, too, was suffering from depression, and sentiment against Britain grew. Furthermore, southerners had their eyes on the fertile bottom lands of the Mississippi and territory along the Gulf of Mexico, much of which was still held by Spain. Already southern settlers had moved into West Florida. In 1810 they revolted from Spain, proclaiming the Republic of West Florida. In 1811 Madison annexed the area to the United States. However, he refused to invade East Florida. As a

Alert students to look for the role delayed communications played in the conclusion as well as the start of this war.

Debate the validity of the draft.

result, southerners began to call for war against Britain as an excuse for taking Florida from Spain, which was allied with Britain.

In November of 1811, representatives from the West and South, labeled "war hawks" because they wanted war, took control of Congress. Among them were Henry Clay and Richard M. Johnson of Kentucky, Felix Grundy of Tennessee[3], and John C. Calhoun, William Lowndes and Langdon Cheves of South Carolina. They voted Henry Clay Speaker of the House. With Clay's leadership, they pressured the President to declare war on Britain.

SECTION REVIEW

1. Identify the following: Berlin decree, the *Chesapeake*, Tecumseh, "war hawks."
2. In what ways did France and Britain violate American freedom of the seas?
3. What was the effect of the Embargo Act?
4. How did Napoleon trick Madison into worse relations with Britain?
5. Why were southerners and westerners against the British?

3 The War of 1812

Under pressure from the war hawks, Madison sent a war message to Congress on June 1, 1812. Listing grievances against Great Britain—impressment, blockades, inciting Indian uprisings, and the rejection of diplomatic efforts—Madison recommended that Congress declare war. Ironically, the British had been feeling the effects of the American embargo. They had just revoked the Orders in Council, but the news had not yet arrived in the United States. It was too late. The War of 1812 had begun.

Conflict over the War

The United States entered the war hopelessly unprepared. First of all, the American people were divided in their sentiments about the war. Most Federalists and some Republicans opposed it. This was clearly shown by the results of the 1812 election. Anti-war Republicans nominated DeWitt Clinton of

New York. Federalists also supported him. Although Madison won, Clinton carried most of the northern states, and Federalists gained seats in Congress.

Financially, the nation was also unprepared. After declaring war, Congress had adjourned without passing any war taxes.[4] The charter of the Bank of the United States had been allowed to expire in 1811, so the war had to be financed through loans handled by state banks. People opposed to the war refused to lend money to support it, and the government was forced to pay high interest to obtain the money it needed.

Furthermore, the military was not ready for war. The United States Navy was excellent, but with only 16 ships it was vastly outnumbered by the Royal Navy. The United States Army had fewer than 7000 men, including one regiment of cavalry with no horses. The states had nearly 700,000 militia, but they were poorly trained, and many were from states opposed to the war. Congress debated a draft law, but it was defeated. Federalist Daniel Webster of New Hampshire claimed that **conscription** (a draft) was unconstitutional.

> The nation is not yet in a temper to submit to conscription. The people have too fresh and strong a feeling of the blessings of civil liberty to be willing thus to surrender it. You may talk to them as much as you please, of the victory and the glory to be obtained in the enemy's provinces; they will hold those objects in light estimation if the means be a forced military service.

Because the draft law was defeated, the army had to rely on volunteers. Even in the West and the South, which favored the war, many Americans were reluctant to join. Never during the war did the army number more than 35,000 men.

Early Campaigns

Despite the nation's lack of preparation, the war hawks felt that Canada would be easy pickings. Henry Clay said that the Kentucky militia alone could take Canada. The Canadians were outnumbered and the

---

[3] Kentucky had been admitted to the Union in 1792, Tennessee in 1796.

[4] Later, Congress passed a stamp tax, a direct tax on the states, and new tariffs, but these measures brought little revenue until close to the end of the war.

WAR OF 1812

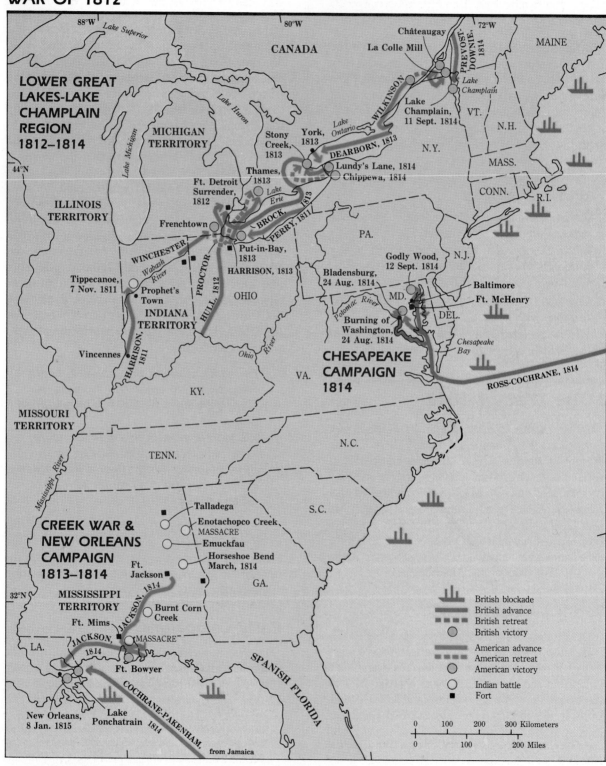

LOWER GREAT LAKES-LAKE CHAMPLAIN REGION 1812–1814

88°W   Lake Superior   80°W   CANADA   72°W   MAINE

Châteaugay
La Colle Mill
PREVOST-DOWNIE, 1814

MICHIGAN TERRITORY   Lake Huron   Stony Creek, 1813   York, 1813   Lake Ontario   WILKINSON   Lake Champlain   Lake Champlain, 11 Sept. 1814   VT.   N.H.

44°N   DEARBORN, 1813   N.Y.   MASS.

ILLINOIS TERRITORY   Lake Michigan   Thames, 1813   Ft. Detroit Surrender, 1812   Lake Erie   Lundy's Lane, 1814   Chippewa, 1814   CONN.   R.I.

Frenchtown   BROCK, 1811   PERRY, 1813   PA.   N.J.

WINCHESTER   Wabash River   PROCTOR   Put-in-Bay, 1813   HARRISON, 1813   Godly Wood, 12 Sept. 1814   N.Y.

Tippecanoe, 7 Nov. 1811   Prophet's Town   HULL, 1812   OHIO   Bladensburg, 24 Aug. 1814   MD.   Baltimore   Ft. McHenry   DEL.

INDIANA TERRITORY   Potomac River   Burning of Washington, 24 Aug. 1814

Vincennes   HARRISON, 1811   Ohio River   Chesapeake Bay

MISSOURI TERRITORY   KY.   VA.   **CHESAPEAKE CAMPAIGN 1814**   ROSS-COCHRANE, 1814

Mississippi River   TENN.   N.C.

Talladega   S.C.

CREEK WAR & NEW ORLEANS CAMPAIGN 1813–1814   Enotachopco Creek MASSACRE   Emuckfau   Horseshoe Bend March, 1814   Ft. Jackson   JACKSON, 1814   GA.

32°N   MISSISSIPPI TERRITORY   Burnt Corn Creek   Ft. Mims   JACKSON, 1814   MASSACRE   Ft. Bowyer

LA.

COCHRANE-PAKENHAM, 1814

New Orleans, 8 Jan. 1815   Lake Ponchatrain 1814   SPANISH FLORIDA

from Jamaica

British blockade
British advance
British retreat
British victory

American advance
American retreat
American victory
Indian battle
Fort

0   100   200   300 Kilometers

0   100   200 Miles

Oliver Perry was the brother of Commodore Matthew Perry, who opened Japan to world trade in the 1850's.

Point out that there has been a dispute as to whether "The Star Spangled Banner" is an appropriate national anthem. Ask students to analyze the lyrics to determine exactly what Key was celebrating in his song.

British, fully involved with Napoleon in Europe, could not support them. The Canadians did have one ally, however—Tecumseh and his Indian confederation.

Invading Canada proved to be more difficult than the war hawks expected. The American strategy was poorly planned. The first invasion was led by General William Hull, who marched into Canada from Detroit. Finding his lines of communication cut by raiding Indians, he returned to Detroit. When the British advanced on Detroit with a small army of Canadians and Indians, Hull surrendered. Another invasion across the Niagara River ended in defeat when the New York militia refused to come to the aid of the American forces. An invasion from Plattsburg also ended when the American militia refused to cross the border.

Although American armies were not doing well, sea battles usually ended in American victories. On August 19, 1812, the U.S.S. *Constitution* defeated the British ship *Guerriere*. British cannonballs bouncing off the solid planking of the *Constitution* provided the ship with its nickname, "Old Ironsides." Other American ships did equally well. However, the Royal Navy soon diverted enough ships from the war with France to blockade the American ships when they returned to port for supplies. For most of the war, American ships were stuck in port.

Although British ships dominated the ocean after the first year, American fleets were still active on the Great Lakes. At one point, Americans took temporary control of Lake Ontario. Crossing over to York (Toronto), the capital of Canada, they set fire to the public buildings. This unauthorized destruction was in response to their anger over a bomb that killed over 50 Americans.

Meanwhile William Henry Harrison, now the commander of American forces in the Northwest, decided to halt American attacks until the United States gained control of Lake Erie. During the winter of 1812–1813, Captain Oliver Hazard Perry hastily built a fleet on Lake Erie. Flying a flag that said, "Don't give up the ship," he defeated the British fleet in September of 1813. Perry sent General Harrison the message, "We have met the enemy and they are ours."

With Lake Erie in American hands, the British retreated from Detroit, which Harrison reoccupied. Harrison then pursued the British into Canada and defeated them at the Battle of the Thames. During this battle, Tecumseh was killed. With his death, the Indian confederation he created fell apart.

The British Offensive

Thus far, the British had been waging a defensive war. In 1814, however, Napoleon was defeated, leaving the British free to concentrate their forces against the United States. During the summer of 1814, about 14,000 British troops arrived in North America.

The British planned a multi-pronged attack. From Canada, armies would move south into the United States from two points: Niagara and Lake Champlain. A third army would land at New Orleans. In July, however, the Americans ended any chance of an invasion from Niagara by winning victories at Fort Erie, Chippewa, and Lundy's Lane. In August a British force of 10,000 under Sir George Prevost moved down the western shore of Lake Champlain toward the Hudson River. The Americans were in a strongly fortified position at Plattsburg, and the British advance depended on control of Lake Champlain. There, the American fleet under Captain Thomas Mcdonough defeated the British. Prevost retreated.

Meanwhile another raiding force moved up Chesapeake Bay and attacked Washington on August 24. The British entered Washington so quickly that President Madison barely escaped, leaving a meal on the table. In retaliation for the fires Americans started in York, the British burned the public buildings, including the White House. The British then proceeded toward Baltimore, where they tried to destroy Fort McHenry. The Americans were ready this time, however, and fought off the British. The British rockets inspired Francis Scott Key to write the words to the "Star Spangled Banner."

A British force under Sir Edward Pakenham attacked New Orleans on January 8, 1815. General Andrew Jackson of Tennessee had his troops dig in behind a six-foot deep canal that crossed the only firm ground before New Orleans. Jackson's force included troops from Tennessee and Kentucky, expert shots with their long rifles, and the followers of French pirate Jean Laffite. As the British approached they faced fire from American rifles and cannons. Soon the

Have students analyze why America was willing to settle for a "status quo ante bellum." Why do we claim to have won this war?

According to the treaty, the war was not to end until the document was ratified on both sides. Thus it is not true that the Battle of New Orleans was fought after the war was over.

A British fleet sailed up Chesapeake Bay and landed an army which marched against Washington. The White House, the Capitol building, and other government offices were set afire. Why did the British burn Washington?

British were forced to retreat. Over 2000 British soldiers were killed or wounded; American losses were kept to 8 killed and 13 wounded.

Results of the War

Jackson's victory at New Orleans was outstanding. However, it did not really affect the outcome of the war. Attempts to negotiate a settlement had been under way for some time. On December 24, 1814, the Treaty of Ghent had been signed, providing for a return to the **status quo ante bellum** (the way things were before the war).

Although the treaty restored peace, it did not even mention impressment or neutral rights. Neither the United States nor Britain was forced to give up any territory. Yet the war did have some important consequences. Several joint commissions were set up to settle boundary disputes between the United States and Canada. The Indians lost more territory to the United States, leaving the way open for westward expansion.[5] Another result of the war was that the Federalists were discredited.

As the war had progressed, New England Federalists had become more skeptical over the value of the Union. Ever since Jefferson's election, Federalist weight in national affairs had decreased. National policies such as the embargo and the war had been contrary to New England's interests.

In October of 1814, the Massachusetts legislature had called a convention to be held at Hartford, Connecticut. The Hartford Convention's proposals endorsed the concept of nullification found in the Virginia and Kentucky Resolutions. The proposals also included a series of constitutional amendments to

[5] Under the Treaty of Ft. Jackson (1814) the Creeks, who had taken part in a general Indian uprising known as the Creek War, were compelled to withdraw from southern and western Alabama. At almost the same time, the Northwest Indians signed the second Treaty of Greenville, restoring peace with the United States and forcing the Indians to declare war on the British.

Just as a company can change its product, parties can change their ideologies. (Republicans, once the "liberal" party of Jefferson and Lincoln, became the "conservative" party in the 20th century.)

Point out that the protective tariff has been an issue throughout American history. What industries today are calling for protective tariffs?

From a British prison ship Francis Scott Key watched the bombing of Fort McHenry. This inspired Key's writing of the "Star Spangled Banner." When did it become the national anthem?

Good Feelings." It was generally a time of peace and prosperity.

SECTION REVIEW

1. Identify the following: "Old Ironsides," Captain Oliver Hazard Perry, Battle of the Thames, Francis Scott Key, General Andrew Jackson.
2. Why was the United States unprepared for war?
3. Why did British strategy change in 1814?
4. What were the provisions of the Treaty of Ghent?
5. Why was the Hartford Convention unsuccessful?

4 American Nationalism

During the Era of Good Feelings, the spirit of nationalism took over in the United States. A national pride swept the country after the War of 1812. Although the Federalist Party died out, its philosophy of strong national government was carried on by a new breed of Republicans. Henry Clay and John C. Calhoun made a number of proposals that involved the federal governent's taking an active part in the economy—measures once advocated by Alexander Hamilton.

Economic Nationalism

The most dramatic evidence of the new nationalist spirit was the adoption of Henry Clay's "American System." There were three basic elements in the American System: a central bank, a protective tariff, and internal improvements. These were measures that once would have been rejected by Republicans.

A new central bank was needed to replace the first Bank of the United States. After its charter expired in 1811, state banks, no longer restrained by a central bank, flooded the country with paper money. Inflation was the inevitable result. The Second Bank of the United States, chartered in 1816 to remedy these ills, was modeled after Hamilton's Bank. President Madison, who had opposed Hamilton's Bank, did not veto the charter of the Second Bank.

The second part of Clay's American System was a protective tariff, intended to shield American industry from British competition. One result of the years of embargo and war had been the growth of American industry in the Northeast. Without competition from

restrict federal power. The Federalist Party, once the champion of strong national government, had now reversed its position.

A delegation was sent to Washington with these proposals. It arrived at about the same time as the news of Jackson's victory at New Orleans and the Treaty of Ghent. The end of the war had brought a wave of rejoicing and patriotic spirit. Coming at this time, the Federalist proposals seemed ridiculous. The delegates from Hartford quietly returned home. Thus the party that had successfully launched the Union died trying to unmake its own handiwork.

After the Hartford Convention destroyed the Federalist Party, the Republicans dominated national affairs without any serious competition. James Monroe, Madison's Secretary of State, succeeded Madison in 1816, easily defeating the Federalist candidate Rufus King. In 1820, Monroe ran without opposition. Due to the lack of political party strife, the period from the end of the War of 1812 through the end of Monroe's second term was called the "Era of

Madison favored federal support for internal improvements but wanted a constitutional amendment to establish the government's authority in this area.

Fourth of July celebrations in Philadelphia in 1819 point up that the Fourth had become a national tradition less than fifty years after Independence. What evidence supports a rising nationalistic spirit after the War of 1812?

the products of British factories, American manufacturing had developed rapidly. Investors, unable to put their money into commerce, had put it instead into manufacturing. The end of the War of 1812, however, had reopened trade with Britain. Congress, afraid that American industry would be hurt if goods in English warehouses were "dumped" (sold at below cost) on the American market, passed the protective tariff that Clay wanted, the Tariff of 1816.

The third part of Clay's system was federal support for internal improvements. Clay's hope was for a series of roads and canals that would tie the West to the rest of the country. With a good transportation system linking the South, Northeast, and West, each region's market would be expanded. The first National Road was already under construction, having been started in 1811. Further support for transportation came from John C. Calhoun's Bonus Bill of 1816, designed to establish a $1.5 million fund for internal improvements. Madison, however, returned to strict constructionism in this case. He vetoed the bill on the ground that the Constitution did not give the federal government power to pay for internal improvements.

Judicial Nationalism

The spirit of nationalism could also be seen in court decisions of this period. Increased federal power was supported by the Supreme Court under Chief Justice John Marshall. The Federalist Marshall, appointed by John Adams just before he left office in 1801, served until 1835.

In the case of *Marbury* v. *Madison* (1803), Marshall's court had established the principle of judicial review over acts of Congress. In later decisions, the Supreme Court established judicial review over state actions. In the case of *Fletcher* v. *Peck* (1810), the Court declared unconstitutional a Georgia act that impaired the **sanctity of contracts**—the idea that contracts are legally binding. In the case of *Martin* v. *Hunter's Lessee* (1816), the Court said that decisions of state courts could be appealed to the Supreme Court if the appeal was based on a constitutional question.

In *Dartmouth College* v. *Woodward* (1819), the court again upheld the sanctity of contracts. In this case the court found unconstitutional an attempt by the New Hampshire legislature to change the college charter. In a related decision, *Cohens* v. *Virginia* (1821), Marshall said that the Supreme Court was superior to the state courts in all questions concerning the power of the federal government.

During this same period, Marshall consolidated the power of the national government with decisions based on loose construction of the Constitution. In *McCulloch* v. *Maryland* (1819), Marshall found the charter of the Second Bank of the United States to be constitutional because of the elastic clause. Furthermore, the Court struck down as unconstitutional a Maryland law that taxed the Second Bank. Stating that "the power to tax involves the power to destroy," Marshall argued that a state's power was inferior to that of the federal government:

> *The question is, in truth, a question of supremacy; and if the rights of the states to tax the means employed by the general government be conceded, the declaration that the Constitution, and the laws made in pursuance thereof, shall be the Supreme law of the land, is empty and unmeaning declamation. . . .*

In *Gibbons* v. *Ogden* (1824), Marshall ruled that only the federal government could regulate interstate commerce. The case concerned an attempt by New York to grant a monopoly over steamboat traffic on the Hudson River. Marshall said that the monopoly was unconstitutional because a state could not regulate interstate commerce.

Nationalism in Foreign Affairs

The nationalism that had so much influence within the United States was also reflected in American diplomacy of this era. Several treaties with Great Britain, the purchase of Florida, and the Monroe Doctrine all solidified America's position among the nations of the world.

Relations with Great Britain. American relations with Great Britain improved after the Treaty of 1818 resolved a number of issues left over from the war. The boundary between the United States and Canada was set at the 49th parallel from the Lake of the Woods to the Rocky Mountains. An agreement was reached concerning American fishing in Canadian waters. The treaty also provided for joint occupation of the Oregon Territory for ten years, thus setting the stage for later American westward expansion.

Acquisition of Florida. Expansion in the Southeast was blocked because East Florida still belonged to Spain. Seminole Indians from Florida would raid American settlements. They would then return to the safety of Spanish territory. In 1818, on his own authority, General Andrew Jackson chased a band of Seminoles into Florida and captured a Spanish fort. He executed a number of Indians and two British citizens he thought were supplying the Seminoles with arms. The Spaniards were outraged, but, in fact, all they could do was protest. President Monroe, on the advice of Calhoun, considered reprimanding Jackson. Secretary of State John Quincy Adams, however, advised support of the General. Adams defended Jackson's actions and hinted that the United States might take Florida by force.

Adams convinced the Spaniards that they would be unable to hold Florida. With the Adams-Onís Treaty of 1819, Spain gave up Florida and also any claims they might have to Oregon. In return the United States assumed claims of about $5 million against Spain for damages to American shipping during the Napoleonic Wars. The United States also gave up its claim to Texas as part of the Louisiana Purchase.

The Monroe Doctrine. Meanwhile, by the early 1820's ominous sounds were coming from Europe. During the Napoleonic Wars, a number of Spain's colonies in South America had taken the opportunity to declare their independence. After the defeat of Napoleon, many European monarchs wanted to return Europe to the way it had been before the French Revolution. The United States feared that the Europeans might try to return the Latin American states to Spain. This would destroy the growing trade between North and South America. The United States was also concerned over Russian claims in the Oregon Territory.

The United States was not the only country concerned over the fate of the new Latin American republics. Great Britain had also developed a lucrative trade with these new countries. The British recommended that the Americans join them in making a statement opposing European intervention in the Western Hemisphere. John Quincy Adams, recognizing that British interests would force them to support an American statement even if it were not jointly issued, convinced President Monroe to issue such a statement alone.

In an 1823 address to Congress, the President proclaimed what has become known as the Monroe Doctrine. Written by Adams, it made four points: (1) The Western Hemisphere was closed to any further European colonization. (2) The United States would not interfere with any European colonies already established. (3) Any attempt by a European power to intervene in Western Hemisphere affairs would be interpreted as a threat to the United States. (4) The United States would not interfere in the internal affairs of any European country.

Europeans scoffed at this declaration by the United States, although they were forced to recognize it because it was backed by powerful Great Britain. Nevertheless, the Monroe Doctrine showed the world the American spirit of strength and unity. It reinforced the American policy of neutrality and independence from Europe and became a cornerstone of United States foreign policy.

Cultural Nationalism

The spirit of nationalism could be seen not only in the growing political and economic independence of

Nationalism

Historians have written scores of books trying to define the meaning of the term "nationalism." In its broadest sense, nationalism can be described as a sense of belonging to, or attachment to a country. But what is it that Americans mean when they say they are attached to their country? Clearly there is more to it than that oft-quoted trinity, "baseball, hot dogs, and apple pie." There is a feeling for the land, for the form of government and the principles on which it is based, for shared culture and history.

Why did American nationalism blossom in the late 1700's and early 1800's? Government provided the focal point. The Constitution set down the principles of a government based on a number of values that most Americans had come to share. These values included such things as a belief in representative government, trial by jury, and freedom of speech and press.

In fact, some historians think that America's lack of a collective ethnic or religious identity raised the law to a place of special prominence as a binding force in American life. Americans were convinced that their republican form of government was superior to any in the world.

By the 1820's, the country had already developed another important basis for national identity: a sense of history, a shared past. The American Revolution in particular was a source of pride. Heroes such as George Washington were made into demi-gods by early nineteenth-century biographers. Huge crowds turned out to greet Lafayette when he returned to America for a visit in 1824.

Even the War of 1812, despite its controversial beginnings and its ambivalent outcome, quickly took its place in the growing national mythology. The victories of naval commanders such as Stephen Decatur and Isaac Hull (captain of *The Constitution*) bolstered the image of American invincibility.

The War of 1812 also reinforced the concept of the nation's distinctiveness from Europe. Americans seemed convinced that their country was a unique land, rich in natural resources, blessed with good people and good government, located a fortuitous distance from the decadent Old World. These feelings are well summed up in the following verse, taken from one of the hundreds of anonymous patriotic songs written, printed, and distributed in little song books during the early 1800's.

> *The fruits of our country, our flocks and our*
> *   fleeces,*
> *What treasures immense, in our mountains*
> *   that lie,*
> *While discord is tearing Old Europe to pieces,*
> *Shall amply the wants of our people supply;*
> *New roads and canals, on their bosoms*
> *   conveying,*
> *Refinement and wealth through our forests*
> *   shall roam,*
> *And millions of freemen, with rapture survey-*
> *   ing,*
> *Shall shout out "O Liberty! this is thy home!"*

Dreams of the future as well as pride in the past fueled American nationalism. Ralph Waldo Emerson said that the United States was "a country of beginnings, of projects, of designs, of expectations." Many Americans felt that their country had a special mission. That mission was to spread its superior form of government as far as possible.

The western frontier offered enough opportunity to satisfy almost every expansionist's dream. But territorial expansion also had the potential for magnifying sectional tensions. As the country grew, so did differences that put the country's unity in danger. In the second half of the 1800's, nationalism was put to its greatest test—the Civil War. Not until that terrible conflict was settled could it be said that nationalism had triumphed over sectionalism.

QUESTIONS

1. How did the War of 1812 affect American nationalism?

2. Why was the western frontier an important element in American nationalism?

Point out that in addition to being the first Americans to use indigenous themes, these writers and painters were the first Americans whose achievements were recognized in Europe. Not until considerably later would there appear American architects and composers who gained similar recognition.

Ask students to discuss why industrialization took place largely in the North rather than in the South.

the United States but also in the development of an independent American culture. Americans were beginning to paint and write about American topics. The Hudson Valley school of landscape painting focused on scenes of the Hudson River Valley and the Adirondack and Catskill Mountains. Other artists painted typically American scenes. Currier and Ives prints are still valued today as an expression of Americana.

In literature, Washington Irving, James Fenimore Cooper, and William Cullen Bryant stand out. Washington Irving's *Sketch Book* explored the legends of New York. His stories, such as "Legend of Sleepy Hollow" and "Rip Van Winkle," are still read today. Cooper produced one of the first truly American heroes in his *Leatherstocking Tales.* His hero was an unspoiled frontier scout, honest and freedom-loving, forever in conflict with civilization. Bryant described American scenes in his poetry. His "Thanatopsis" appears in every anthology of great American poetry.

Meanwhile, Noah Webster was working on *An American Dictionary of the English Language,* which came out in 1828. He believed in a simple spelling of English words. He changed the English spelling of "theatre," for example, to "theater" in the American dictionary.

SECTION REVIEW

1. Identify the following: Bonus Bill of 1816, *McCulloch* v. *Maryland,* Adams-Onís Treaty, Noah Webster.
2. What were the basic elements of Clay's American System?
3. What were the major points of the Monroe Doctrine?
4. What were some examples of nationalism in American culture?

5 The Rise of Sectionalism

Even as the threads of economic, diplomatic and cultural nationalism bound the country together, other more divisive forces were building. **Sectionalism,** the rivalry of one region against the other, was based on economic and political interests. By the 1820's, three major sectional coalitions had de-

veloped in the country : the North, the South, and the West.

Sectional Divisions

The richest and most highly populated section was the North. It was made up of the states north and east of Maryland, including Vermont, which had joined the Union in 1791. The unity of the North was related to the development of an economy based on manufacturing. The Industrial Revolution—the change from production by hand to production by machines that began in England in the 1700's—had come early to the United States. And, this revolution had centered in the North.

In 1789 a young English mechanic named Samuel Slater had arrived in New York, bringing with him the secrets of new spinning and weaving machines built by British inventors. With the help of Moses Brown, a

The Park Theatre in New York City was evidence that an independent American culture was developing in all of the arts. Why did Noah Webster think it was necessary to write *An American Dictionary of the English Language?*

Discuss how items like guns were made before Whitney came up with his system of interchangeable parts.

Many historians feel that the cotton gin ensured the viability of the slave system in the South.

In Eli Whitney's Connecticut gun factory, manufacture of interchangeable parts was developed to meet the needs of the government for arms. Why did Whitney's system have an advantage over the skilled gunsmiths of that time?

Quaker merchant, Slater was soon operating the first cotton mill in the United States. Within a few years, cotton mills were being operated at water-power sites throughout the North.

The Industrial Revolution also spread quickly to many other kinds of manufacturing especially after Connecticut inventor Eli Whitney started the use of interchangeable parts. These were identical machine parts that could be quickly put together to make a complete product. Because all the parts were alike, they could be manufactured with less skilled labor, and they made machine repair easier.

The many years of trade restrictions before and during the War of 1812 encouraged the development of American manufacturing. In the North, manufacturing was beginning to take the place of shipping as a dominant economic force. Manufacturing interests favored a tariff to protect them from foreign competition.

The South, having little manufacturing to protect, was against a high tariff. The South was still agricultural, and tariffs only raised the prices of the goods they had to buy. The southern states were unified by their dependence on slavery and cotton, which had become a major industry after Eli Whitney invented the cotton gin in 1793. This machine, which removed the seeds from cotton, transformed the South into the "cotton kingdom." Cotton production increased from 3000 bales in 1790 to over 300,000 bales in 1820.

The West, the region west of the Appalachian Mountains, had its own particular concerns: land policy, Indian affairs, and internal improvements. Victories over the Indians during the War of 1812 had set the stage for rapid settlement of the frontier. From the old Northwest, Indiana joined the Union in 1816 and Illinois in 1818. From the Gulf Plains, Louisiana had joined in 1812, Mississippi in 1816, and Alabama in 1817. Since the West was constantly growing, its influence was increasingly felt.

The Panic of 1819

For a few years after the War of 1812, the whole country prospered. Economic prosperity temporarily disguised sectional differences. But a depression that began in 1819 brought those differences into focus.

During the good times, many people had borrowed money to invest in land or business. Many state banks had encouraged risky investments by making loans recklessly. Even the Second Bank of the United States had been guilty. The result was inflation and a shortage of specie.

In 1819 the president of the Bank of the United States resigned, and a more conservative president, Langdon Cheves, was appointed. He quickly put a brake on easy credit. Loans to state banks were called in and payment was demanded in specie. The result was a **financial panic**—a sudden, widespread fear about the value of money. State banks without enough specie in reserve were forced to call in their loans. Some had to close.

At the same time, European demand for American products had begun to decrease. An economic depression followed the panic. Cotton went from 33 cents a pound to 10 cents a pound, wheat from $2 a bushel to $1 a bushel. Factories closed, and the value of land fell. The impact of the depression was especially hard on the West. Many farmers, when their credit was cut off, faced the loss of their land. The Bank of the United States acquired huge amounts of western land. For this reason, sentiment against the "monster," as the Bank was called, ran high.

Westerners demanded relief from the federal government. They wanted federal support for internal improvements, and protective tariffs so that they could develop a market for their products in an industrialized North. They especially wanted cheaper land prices. The North and South saw western lands as a national asset that should be sold for prices as high as possible. Westerners succeeded, however, in getting Congress to pass a new land law in 1820. The new land law lowered both the price of land and the minimum amount of land that had to be bought. In 1821 Congress passed a relief act that allowed land buyers to pay off old debts at the new low price over a longer period of time.

The Slavery Issue

The depression was just getting under way when Missouri applied for statehood in 1819. A large number of the settlers in Missouri were southerners who owned slaves. Congress was considering Missouri's application when Representative James Tallmadge of New York introduced an amendment to the application. The amendment said that no more

slaves could be taken into the new state and that any slaves already there would be freed at the age of 25.

The Tallmadge Amendment was the first time the government tried to restrict slavery in the territories west of the Mississippi. The attempt touched off a nationwide debate over slavery. Northerners attacked slavery as immoral, while southerners defended it in terms of economic necessity and argued that its existence was recognized in the Constitution.

At that time, the Senate was evenly balanced between slave and free states, and a new state would upset that balance. The debate gained steam during congressional elections, as people in the North and South held mass meetings and state legislatures petitioned Congress for and against slavery.

The Tallmadge Amendment was passed by the House of Representatives, which was controlled by the North because its higher population gave it more representatives. In the Senate, however, where North and South were equally represented, the amendment was defeated.

The issue of Missouri's statehood was resolved through compromise. In February 1820, Senator Jesse Thomas of Illinois proposed the admission of Maine as a free state and Missouri as a slave state. This would keep the sectional balance in the Senate.

MISSOURI COMPROMISE, 1820–1821

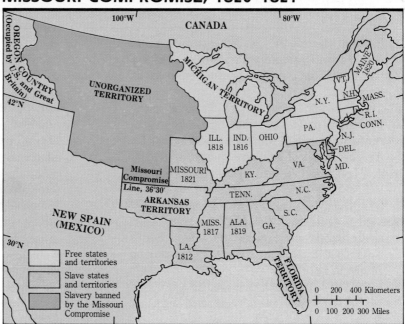

Note that in comparison to the Caribbean and Latin America, slave revolts were relatively rare in the United States. While defenders of slavery argued that this was proof that American slaves were content with their situation, historians believe that it had to do with the fact that the ratio of blacks to whites was much greater in other parts of the Western Hemisphere than in the United States. Thus, slave revolts elsewhere had a much greater chance of succeeding.

The Missouri Compromise further established a line in the Louisiana Territory at 36°30′. New states formed above that line would be free and those below the line would be slave.

As a result of the Missouri debate, the South became very sensitive about its **"peculiar institution"** of slavery. Southern sensitivity was further heightened by an abortive slave rebellion in Charleston, South Carolina. Denmark Vesey, a Charleston carpenter who had earlier purchased his freedom, was outraged by the existence of slavery. His reading of the Bible, the Declaration of Independence, and reports of the Missouri debate fueled his hatred of the institution. In 1822 he developed a brilliant plan for a slave revolt, only to be betrayed at the last moment by some of his followers. When white citizens of Charleston became aware of the conspiracy, they were terrified. They blamed northern antislavery literature.

Lines were being drawn between those who were for slavery and those who were against it. The effect on southern politics was obvious. Since any effective attack on slavery would require a strong central government, the South was wed to the concept of states' rights. Such a position meant opposition to protective tariffs and internal improvements as manifestations of active government. Southern politicians who had been nationalists, most notably John C. Calhoun, became ardent sectionalists.

As the nation grew, tension between the North and the South continued to increase. Clearly the Missouri Compromise offered only a temporary solution to the slavery issue. As John Quincy Adams wrote, "The present question is a mere preamble—a title page to a great tragic volume." From 1820 on, almost all national questions were weighed in terms of their impact on slavery.

SECTION REVIEW

1. Identify the following: Samuel Slater, Eli Whitney, Jesse Thomas, Denmark Vesey.
2. What was the effect of the Panic of 1819?
3. Why did the Tallmadge Amendment bring out sectional differences?
4. How did the Missouri Compromise temporarily resolve the slavery issue?
5. What were the effects of this issue on the South?

CHAPTER 7 REVIEW

SUMMARY

1. In 1800 control of the federal government changed hands peacefully from the Federalists to the Republicans, with Thomas Jefferson as President.
2. The Jefferson administration retained many Federalist programs, while gradually taking action in accordance with the Republican belief in the importance of individual liberty.
3. The Louisiana Purchase doubled the size of the United States.
4. After trying for several years to maintain United States neutrality in the face of war between Great Britain and France, the United States succumbed to pressures and declared war on Britain in 1812.
5. In 1814 the Treaty of Ghent brought the War of 1812 to an end, with neither side achieving major gains.
6. By the end of the War of 1812, the Federalist Party had completely lost influence in national politics.
7. During the "Era of Good Feelings" following the war, the Republican Party dominated the government without opposition and the country enjoyed peace and prosperity.
8. American nationalism was reflected in economic policy, in decisions of the Supreme Court, in foreign affairs, and in the development of an independent American culture.
9. Despite growing American nationalism, sectional divisions among the North, the South and West were revealed when economic prosperity was interrupted by the Panic of 1819.
10. Slavery in new states, the most serious sectional issue, was temporarily resolved by the Missouri Compromise.

VOCABULARY

constituency	writ of mandamus	embargo	sanctity of contracts
residence requirement	partisan	shaman	sectionalism
patronage	internal improvements	conscription	financial panic
midnight appointments	secession	status quo ante bellum	peculiar institution

REVIEW QUESTIONS

1. In what ways did Jefferson show evidence of being a moderate and practical politician, rather than the extremist feared by the Federalists?
2. What was the significance of *Marbury* v. *Madison?*
3. What were the causes of the War of 1812?
4. What were the results of the War of 1812?
5. Why did the Federalists continue to lose influence in government after 1800?
6. In what ways was the Federalist philosophy carried on after the death of the party?
7. What was the significance of the Monroe Doctrine regarding America's position in the world?
8. What accounts for the rise of nationalism after the War of 1812?
9. What were the causes of sectionalism during the Era of Good Feelings?

DISCUSSION

1. Which of Jefferson's decisions had the greatest influence on our nation's history? Why?
2. Could the War of 1812 have been avoided? Why or why not?
3. Do you think the Missouri Compromise was wise? Why or why not?
4. Why was the peaceful change of power from Federalists to Republicans important?

USING MAPS

Refer to the map on page 154 and answer the following questions:

1. Where did American victories take place? British victories?
2. In which direction did Jackson travel to reach New Orleans?
3. Where did the British come from when they attacked Washington, D.C.?

USING SKILLS

After considering the following facts, make a general statement about the relationship between the foreign policy of the United States and the value of America's foreign trade in the years before the War of 1812.

1. In 1806 the United States carried on foreign trade valued at approximately $100 million.
2. The Embargo Act was passed in December of 1807.
3. In 1808 the value of U.S. foreign trade dropped to about $20 million.
4. In 1810 the value of U.S. foreign trade was about $60 million.
5. The Non-Intercourse Act was passed in March 1809.
6. Macon's Bill Number Two was passed in May 1810.

1	Political Events in the 1820's	167
2	The Era of the Common People	170
3	States' Rights and Union	172
4	The Bank War	176
5	Economics and Politics After Jackson	179

THE AGE OF JACKSON

Whoever opposes the interests, or wishes of the public, however right in principle, or justifiable by circumstances, finds little sympathy; for, in a democracy, resisting the wishes of the many, is resisting the sovereign, in his caprices.

JAMES FENIMORE COOPER

Despite the Missouri Compromise, rivalry among the major sections of the United States continued to create conflict. Out of this conflict emerged Andrew Jackson, a man who was popular enough to unite sectional interests into a major new political party.

The years between 1828 and 1840 have been called the Age of Jackson. During those years, Andrew Jackson was the leading political figure in the United States. A self-made man, Jackson symbolized the rise of the common people in politics. During his term of office he increased the power of the presidency and thus added prestige to the national government. Some of Jackson's policies, however, led to unforeseen problems—problems with which his successors would have to deal.

1 Political Events in the 1820's

The political unity that the country enjoyed during the Era of Good Feelings was short-lived. People were divided by the issues of slavery, the tariff, and internal improvements. Politicians who took an extreme position on any issue risked alienating a large number of voters.

The Election of 1824

The election of 1824 reflected the growing sectionalism in American politics. In that election four candidates ran for President. They were John Quincy Adams of Massachusetts, Henry Clay of Kentucky, Andrew Jackson of Tennessee, and William Crawford of Georgia. All of these men called themselves Republicans.[1] However, the number of candidates

---

[1] Crawford was the official representative of the party.

testified to the fact that the party was disintegrating as a national organization.

For the most part, each of the four candidates was identified with regional interests. Because of this, the results of the popular election were largely sectional in nature. In fact, Jackson was the only candidate who showed strength outside his own region, carrying Pennsylvania and New Jersey as well as most of the South and West. Crawford carried the rest of the South; Adams, most of the Northeast; and Clay, the Northwest (Missouri, Kentucky, and Ohio).

Although Jackson won a **plurality** (the largest number but less than half) of the popular vote, he failed to receive a majority of electoral votes. Therefore, the House of Representatives had to choose the President from among the top three recipients of electoral votes. Clay, who had come in fourth, and Crawford, who was seriously ill, were both out of the running. The contest was between Adams and Jackson.

Although Clay had lost the election, he still had influence as Speaker of the House of Representatives. He decided to endorse Adams, whose principles were most akin to his. When Adams was elected with Clay's help, Jacksonians were angry. They argued that the voice of the people had been ignored because Jackson had received the largest number of popular votes.

Jackson's supporters were even angrier when, shortly after his election, Adams appointed Clay Secretary of State. They charged that a **"corrupt bargain"** had been made between Clay and Adams—that Clay had helped Adams win the election in return for a top post in Adams' administration. Jackson himself believed wholeheartedly in the charge. He resigned from the Senate and returned to Tennessee, where the state legislature nominated him for President in 1828. Thus, the next presidential race virtually began with Adams' inauguration.

167

Point out that the Adams family not only produced two Presidents, it produced several illustrious men of the late 19th century, including diplomat Charles Francis Adams and historian Henry Adams.

Have students debate whether or not it is necessary for a President to "play the politician," and why.

ELECTION OF 1824

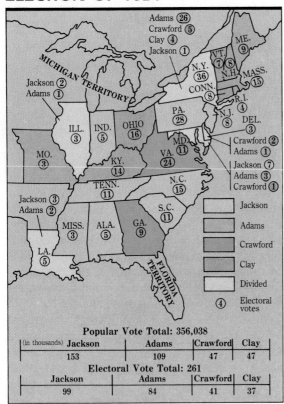

Popular Vote Total: 356,038

(in thousands) Jackson	Adams	Crawford	Clay
153	109	47	47

Electoral Vote Total: 261

Jackson	Adams	Crawford	Clay
99	84	41	37

ELECTION OF 1828

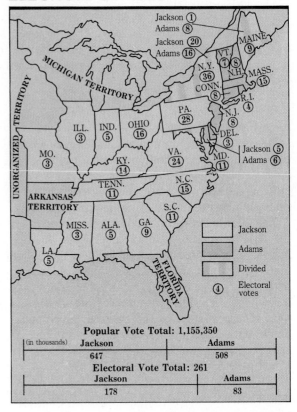

Popular Vote Total: 1,155,350

(in thousands) Jackson	Adams
647	508

Electoral Vote Total: 261

Jackson	Adams
178	83

Whether or not there was a "corrupt bargain," the alliance between Adams and Clay was not unnatural. Both men were nationalists. They favored an active government and measures such as the protective tariff and internal improvements. Jackson and Calhoun, on the other hand, believed in the Jeffersonian principle of limited government. These differences would lead to a split in the Republican party.

The Adams' Administration

By the time of his election, John Quincy Adams was already an established figure in American political life. He had served as a diplomat and as Secretary of State under Monroe. As Secretary of State, Adams had obtained Florida from Spain and formulated the Monroe Doctrine.

As President, however, Adams had several handicaps. For one thing, he was a nationalist in a time of growing sectionalism. He wanted a strong navy, called for government support for scientific expedi-

tions, and hoped to make Washington the cultural center of the country. Also, Adams was an enthusiastic champion of national economic growth and wanted the federal government to direct this growth.

Such ideas horrified those who desired a more limited role for the federal government, and Congress turned down many of his proposals. This was especially true after the congressional elections of 1826, when Adams' enemies controlled both the House and Senate.

Another of Adams' handicaps was that he refused to play the politician at a time when political organizations were becoming more and more important. He rejected the role of party leader and refused to use patronage to defend himself. Adams failed to appoint his followers to government positions, and even left in office some opponents whom he could have removed.

Adams' reserved personality, along with his other drawbacks, diminished his chance for reelection in

1828. These chances did not improve when, near the end of his term, he signed into law the Tariff of 1828. This tariff had unusually high duties and would prove a source of controversy in times to come.

The Election of 1828

In 1824 all four candidates had run as Republicans. By 1828, however, the split in the Republican party had become more clear-cut. Adams' supporters took the name National Republicans in order to emphasize the President's commitment to a national program. Jacksonians took the name Democrats in order to stress their ties to the common people.

In 1828 both the National Republicans and the Democrats campaigned on personalities rather than issues. Jackson's supporters ran their candidate on his reputation as "Old Hickory," a nickname he had picked up because of his toughness in the War of 1812. Jackson was portrayed as a man of the people whose earlier election in 1824 had been thwarted by the "corrupt bargain" between Adams and Clay. Adams was pictured as a monarchist, an enemy of the people, and a waster of public funds.

Adams' supporters, on the other hand, described Jackson as an uneducated, intemperate frontier

Early photographs produced on silver plates were named for the inventor, L. J. M. Daguerre. This daguerreotype of John Quincy Adams is the earliest photographic likeness of an American President. Who did Adams run against in the election of 1824?

brawler. The election was so bitter that slurs were made against Jackson's wife Rachel. Shortly after the campaign, Rachel died, and Jackson blamed her death on the stress caused by the campaign.

Although there was more than the usual amount of **mudslinging** (using insults, particularly against a political opponent) in the campaign of 1828, it excited Americans as no presidential election had before. The voters turned out in large numbers, and Jackson won 56 percent of the popular vote—647,286 to 508,064. The electoral vote was 178 for Jackson to 83 for the **incumbent** (present holder of an office), John Quincy Adams. John C. Calhoun, who had been Vice President under Adams, was reelected to that office.

Jackson's election was based on the efforts of the first modern American political party. The Democratic party was a loose coalition of people who believed in the Jeffersonian principle of limited government. The coalition included southern states' rights advocates, northerners who wanted the government to play a minimal role in the economy, and westerners who wanted federal lands to be sold at low prices. In Andrew Jackson, the party had found a national leader.

Jackson's Inauguration

The inauguration of Andrew Jackson was unlike that of any earlier President. People from all over the country came to Washington to witness the event. Boisterous crowds threw the inaugural reception into disarray. Jackson himself was escorted away for his safety. Washington society was aghast. To Supreme Court Justice Joseph Story, who was present, it seemed the beginning of "the reign of King Mob." For some, however, it represented the triumph of the common people.

SECTION REVIEW
1. Identify the following: William Crawford, National Republicans, "Old Hickory."
2. What were the issues in the election of 1824?
3. How was the winner determined in the election of 1824?
4. How was Adams handicapped during his time in office?
5. How did the political campaigns of 1828 differ from previous campaigns?

2 The Era of the Common People

During the Age of Jackson the United States was a nation of change, a nation on the move—socially, economically, and politically. American society was seen as a society of opportunity. People felt that, given a chance, they could make for themselves a better life. This was the era of the common people, and Andrew Jackson was one of its products.

Old Hickory

Andrew Jackson seemed to personify the hopes of his era. He was the first President who did not come from a well-established American family. On the contrary, Jackson had been born in poverty to immigrant parents in the Carolina backcountry. Although lacking in formal schooling, Jackson studied law and, in the late 1780's, became the prosecuting attorney for the western district of North Carolina (now Tennessee). By the time he was appointed a justice of the Tennessee Supreme Court at the age of 31, he had been a United States Attorney, a member of Congress, and a United States Senator.

Indeed, Jackson was the embodiment of the American success story. He rose from a log cabin to the White House. By the time he became President, Jackson owned more than 100 slaves and lived in a mansion known as The Hermitage. Yet he was closer to the people than any of his predecessors. Although he was not exactly one of the common people, Jackson thought of himself as their champion.

Jackson was best known as a military hero. He was an old Indian-fighter, having defeated the Creeks during the War of 1812. In 1815 he won national fame for the American victory over the British at New Orleans. In 1818, he was again actively engaged in fighting Indians. On this occasion, he marched into

"All Creation Going to the White House" by English cartoonist, R. Cruickshank, satirizes Andrew Jackson's inaugural reception. However, for many, Jackson's election symbolized the triumph of the common people. Why was Jackson's election viewed as such?

Florida with the Tennessee militia, captured a Spanish fort, and executed two British citizens suspected of inciting the Seminoles. His actions caused the Monroe Administration embarrassment, but people on the frontier praised his efforts. Jackson was the type of person westerners admired.

One incident that illustrates Jackson's character is his duel with Charles Dickinson on May 30, 1806. Dickinson was perhaps the most skilled pistol shot in Tennessee, while Jackson was merely an average shot. Face to face, Dickinson aimed and fired first. Jackson seemed untouched. Jackson then aimed his pistol and squeezed the trigger, but the gun misfired. Under the rules of dueling, the misfire did not count, so Jackson fired again. Dickinson was killed. Jackson walked to his carriage and was driven away. Dickinson's shot, however, had hit Jackson. The bullet, which lodged next to his heart, would menace his health for the rest of his life. Jackson's admirers said that it was his iron will that enabled Jackson to stand his ground.

The story of the Jackson-Dickinson duel was a popular one during the 1820's and 1830's. It appealed to many Americans because it showed a characteristic—determination—that helped one to succeed in a growing country. Jackson, in fact, reflected many characteristics of American society during the early 1800's. The historian John W. Ward argued that "of Jackson, people made a mirror of themselves." Perhaps that was the source of his immense popularity.

Jacksonian Democracy

Jackson became President at a time when growing numbers of people were able to take part in politics. That they were able to do so may be attributed both to an expansion of suffrage and changes in political practice.

The Growing Power of the People. The early 1800's saw the continued growth of the idea that government should be based on the will of the people—at least adult white males. By 1820 voting qualifications in many states had been lowered from the ownership of property to the payment of taxes. Some states were even more liberal. In Vermont, New Hampshire, Indiana, Illinois, and Missouri, any adult white male could vote.

In addition to expansion of suffrage, changes in certain political practices furthered the idea of democracy. One of these changes involved the method of selecting the President.

Up to the 1820's, the presidency had been removed from the people. Candidates for President and Vice President were selected by party leaders in closed caucuses. Electors picked by the state governments chose the President and Vice President from among the candidates. In 1831 a new political party, the Anti-Masonic Party, held the first national convention. This was a meeting of party delegates to decide policy and nominate a candidate for President.

The national convention was soon adopted by the major parties. Since delegates were selected either by party voters or by state or district conventions, more people had a voice in choosing presidential electors.

Democracy in Government. Soon after taking office in 1829, Jackson tried to bring about greater democracy in government by setting up a new system for appointing federal officeholders. Jackson believed that individuals who held offices too long might not be responsive to the will of the common people. He also believed that loyal party members deserved government jobs. In his view, most jobs were "so plain and simple that men of intelligence may readily qualify themselves for their performance." He therefore proposed a system of rotation in office, by which federal officeholders would be regularly replaced:

> *In a country where offices are created solely for the benefit of the people, no one man has any more intrinsic right to official station than another. . . . No individual wrong is, therefore, done by removal, since neither appointment to nor continuance in office is a matter of right. . . . It is the people, and they alone, who have a right to complain when a bad officer is substituted for a good one.*

In practice, the rotation system meant giving government jobs to political supporters. Jackson's detractors called this the **spoils system.** The term comes from the expression, "To the victors belong the spoils." Although Jackson replaced only about one-fifth of all federal officeholders, he used the system more widely than earlier Presidents. In doing so he set a precedent for a practice that was easily abused. In later years capable people were often removed from office and less capable ones appointed. However, Jackson sincerely believed that the system opened the government to participation by more citizens. Jackson also showed a willingness to listen to advice from people other than government officials.

In an attempt to maintain party solidarity, he took pains to appoint men from the different factions of the party to his Cabinet. However, other than Secretary of State Martin Van Buren of New York, there were no outstanding individuals. Jackson did not consult them formally. Instead, he counseled informally with a group that became known as the "Kitchen Cabinet." Composed of politicians, newspaper editors, and long-time supporters of Jackson, this group played an important role in the development of policies and ideas.

Although Andrew Jackson saw himself as a staunch guardian of the people's rights, some of his political enemies saw Jackson as a dispenser of public offices to loyal party members. What was the "spoils system"?

Limits on Democracy. All these changes had an impact on American politics. However, the democracy of the Age of Jackson did not extend to women, Indians, and most blacks. Some states had allowed free blacks to vote, but, during the 1820's and 1830's, a number of those states repealed that right. Slaves, of course, had no political rights at all. Although there had been progress, equal opportunity for everyone lay in the future.

SECTION REVIEW

1. Identify the following: The Hermitage, Martin Van Buren, Kitchen Cabinet.
2. How did Jackson's background compare with the background of earlier Presidents?
3. What changes took place in the 1820's and 1830's that gave people more political power?
4. How did Jackson try to bring greater democracy into government?
5. Which groups of people did not share in the growth of democracy?

3 States' Rights and Union

During his first few years in office, Jackson's position on the role of the national government was not clear. On some issues he seemed to take a states' rights position. At other times he strongly supported the authority of the Union.

The South Carolina Protest

On the issue of the tariff, Jackson wavered between the **protectionist** view (in favor of a protective tariff) and the **free trade** view (in favor of trade without tariff barriers). By the 1820's most southerners had become convinced that protective tariffs were discriminatory. Although such tariffs helped the young industries of the North, they also raised the prices of manufactured goods purchased by southern planters. People in the South felt that it was unjust for them to bear the expense for the development of another section of the country.

Angered by the Tariff of 1828, which became known as the "Tariff of Abominations" because of its high rates, South Carolina took the lead against protectionism. On December 19, 1828, the state

Note that the question of whether or not states had a right to secede would not be settled until the Civil War.

Hayne was coached by Calhoun in the debate. Webster's speech was printed and circulated throughout the country—to great acclaim except in South Carolina.

Unlike most states, New Jersey allowed women to vote in its early history. Woman's suffrage was ended, however, in 1806 due to scandal. Some women were said to vote more than once. Men dressed as women also voted more than once. Why do you think women in America during its formative years were denied the right to vote?

issued the *South Carolina Exposition and Protest.* In this document, Vice President John C. Calhoun, writing anonymously, resurrected and expanded the arguments found in the Virginia and Kentucky Resolutions of 1798.

The Constitution, Calhoun said, was a compact between the states. Therefore, the states were sovereign and had a right to decide when an act of Congress was unconstitutional. To make that decision, a state could elect delegates to a convention. If the convention decided that an act was unconstitutional, it could nullify the act (declare it not binding within the state).

Once an act had been nullified, Congress had to choose between going along with the nullification or proposing a constitutional amendment granting the desired power to the federal government. To get a law passed once a state had nullified it, three-fourths of the states would have to ratify it as a constitutional amendment.

Calhoun had raised an important issue—the supremacy of the national government versus state sovereignty. This issue had been debated since the American Revolution and had remained unresolved because the Constitution did not clearly specify the answer. With the *Exposition,* however, the states' rights' doctrine, first found in the Virginia and Kentucky Resolutions, had taken a giant step toward

the idea of secession. If states were sovereign, they had a right to secede from the Union.

The Webster-Hayne Debate

Early in 1830 Calhoun's doctrine of nullification came before the United States Senate during a debate that began over public land policy but soon involved the nature of the Union. People in the West were angry because of a bill which would limit the sale of western lands. Southerners seized the opportunity to try to win western support for nullification.

Robert Y. Hayne of South Carolina pointed out that according to the states' rights position, the western states could nullify the bill if it became law. Hayne then stated his section's grievances and appealed to the West to join the South in resisting the selfishness of the Northeast.

Replying for the nationalists, Daniel Webster of Massachusetts denied that the Constitution was just a compact between the states, to be interpreted as each state chose. On the contrary, he said, only the Supreme Court could decide whether a law was constitutional. Webster argued that the federal government was sovereign, that the Union was perpetual, and that any attempt to dismember it was nothing less than treason. Webster closed with the ringing statement, "Liberty and Union, now and forever, one and inseparable."

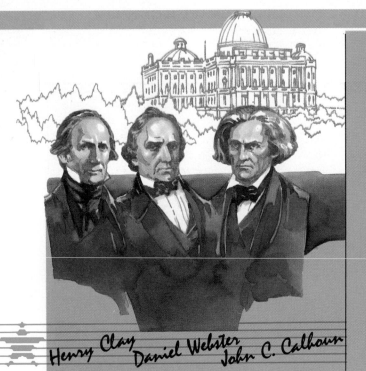

Henry Clay   Daniel Webster   John C. Calhoun

The Age of Jackson was a time of political excitement. Many people paid close attention to the daily business of Congress. Three outstanding leaders of Congress were John C. Calhoun of South Carolina, Daniel Webster of Massachusetts, and Henry Clay of Kentucky.

During their early years in Congress, Clay and Calhoun often joined in support of the young federal government. They were known as "war hawks" because of the positions they took on the War of 1812. Each argued in stirring speeches the need for a strong army and navy and for the establishment of a national bank.

After the war, however, Calhoun found that the people of South Carolina did not support a national bank or other elements of Clay's "American System." Calhoun decided that it was his duty to represent the views of the people who had elected him to office. He became an advocate of states' rights and the southern position on sectional issues. Calhoun's leadership contributed to the South's attempt to win independence in the Civil War.

Webster, by contrast, became progressively more of a nationalist in later years than he was at the beginning of his career. He opposed the War of 1812 and objected to the draft because he did not believe the national government should have that power. Later, as a supporter of northeastern business interests and a student of the Constitution, Webster changed his views and became an ardent nationalist. He was one of the most eloquent defenders of the Union when sectional strains were pulling the nation apart.

Clay was a nationalist from the beginning. His ability to find solutions to complex problems earned him the title the "Great Pacificator." He believed that compromise was the only way to save the Union. "Our system is one of compromises," he said on one occasion, and spent the rest of his life living up to that statement.

Clay was responsible for the Compromise of 1850, one of the last compromises that held the Union together before the Civil War. Webster supported Clay's compromise proposal, while Calhoun opposed it. Thus the careers of these three men reflected the conflicting forces of nationalism and sectionalism in the first half of the nineteenth century.

The Jefferson Day Dinner

At this point, no one was certain which side Jackson favored in the nullification controversy. In April 1830, the leaders of the Democratic party held a dinner in memory of Thomas Jefferson. At the dinner Calhoun and his supporters made several toasts endorsing the states' rights' argument, hoping that Jackson would join them. Jackson, however, toasted the company with the simple, yet all too clear, statement: "Our Federal Union: It must be preserved." Calhoun then rose to toast: "The Union, next to our liberty, most dear." This signalled a rift between the two highest officers in the land.

The Eaton Affair

The Jefferson Day Dinner was only one of many signs of the rift between Jackson and Calhoun. Another was the Eaton Affair. In 1829 Peggy O'Neale, the daughter of a Washington tavern keeper, had become the second wife of Secretary of War John H. Eaton. Led by Mrs. Calhoun, the wives of the Cabinet officers refused to have anything to do with Mrs. Eaton because of her background. Jackson was furious. He associated the slurs against Mrs. Eaton's character with the slurs he felt had killed his wife. He ordered his cabinet officers to make their wives accept Mrs. Eaton, but this tactic met with little success. Only Martin Van Buren, a widower, was able to follow Jackson's instructions. Van Buren was polite to Mrs. Eaton and arranged parties in her honor. As a result, Van Buren's influence with the President increased, while Calhoun's declined.

The rift between Jackson and Calhoun became complete when Jackson learned that in 1818 Calhoun, then Secretary of War, had criticized Jackson for his conduct in the Seminole campaign. In 1831 a cabinet reorganization forced Calhoun's supporters out of the administration. Thereafter, Van Buren was indisputably Jackson's closest adviser and heir to the presidency.

The Maysville Road Veto

Although Jackson did not support Calhoun's position on nullification, the President still favored a states' rights position on some issues. This fact was demonstrated by Jackson's veto of the Maysville Road Bill. Conceived as a part of the national Cumberland Road system, the Maysville Road would have connected the Kentucky towns of Maysville and Lexington.

Jackson vetoed the measure on the grounds that since the Maysville Road would be built within the state of Kentucky, it should be a state project. In other words, the federal government should support only national projects. Jackson's action pleased southerners, who opposed federal support of internal improvements. People in the West, however, were upset. The veto demonstrated that although Jackson was a strong nationalist, he also believed in a narrow interpretation of the Constitution.

Indian Removal

Another issue in which Jackson took a states' rights position was Indian removal. Many whites coveted the lands of the Indians. Because of this, some state governments forcibly removed the Indians from those lands. These states found an ally in Jackson.

The plight of the Cherokees of Georgia is a case in point. Under several treaties with the United States, the Cherokees had been recognized as a nation. They had developed a written language, adopted a constitution, and elected a legislature. In 1828, however, gold was discovered in Cherokee territory. The Georgia legislature quickly moved to extend its

The "Trail of Tears" depicts the hardship and suffering the Cherokees endured when they were forced from their lands under Jackson's Indian removal policy. In all, five tribes were forced to move from the south to lands west of the Mississippi. Some 60,000 Indians moved between 1831 and 1838. One of the main reasons for Indian removal was that whites wanted the lands of the Indians. What event in Georgia prompted the immediate seizure of Cherokee lands?

authority over the Indians and ordered the seizure of their lands. The Cherokees resisted through legal action and appealed their case to the Supreme Court.

In *Worchester* v. *Georgia* (1832), the Supreme Court, under Chief Justice John Marshall, ruled that the state of Georgia had no right to interfere with the Cherokees because they were under the protection of the federal government. President Jackson, however, refused to back the Court's decision. He is reputed to have said, "John Marshall has made his decision, now let him enforce it." During the winter of 1838–39, the Cherokees, along with some other Indian groups of the region, were forced west, leaving a quarter of their number dead along what became known as the Trail of Tears.

This process of uprooting had been going on a long time. In 1830 with Jackson's encouragement, Congress had passed the Indian Removal Act, which set up a plan for Indian resettlement west of the Mississippi River. The Removal Act gave the President the power to negotiate with the various Indian groups, and most were coerced into signing treaties. During Jackson's administration, 94 treaties were signed, and by 1840 most Indians had been forced from their lands east of the Mississippi River.

The Nullification Crisis

The Maysville Road Bill and Indian removal notwithstanding, Jackson's belief in the Union was revealed once more in the Nullification Crisis of 1832. The nullification controversy had simmered for two years until Congress passed The Tariff of 1832. This act did little to meet southern demands for lower duties.

People in South Carolina were angry. In November a popularly elected convention met and nullified the tariffs of 1828 and 1832. Furthermore, the convention warned that if the federal government tried to coerce the state, South Carolina's bonds to the Union would be dissolved.

Jackson was infuriated by South Carolina's move. He wrote:

> *The wickedness, madness, and folly of the leaders and the delusion of their followers in the attempt to destroy themselves and our Union has not its parallel in the history of the world.*

Jackson vowed to uphold the law and asked Congress for the power to use force if it was needed. However, he mixed the threat of force with conciliation. He did not want to push South Carolina into open rebellion. He supported a compromise tariff bill, proposed by Henry Clay, which would gradually lower duties. Early in March 1833, Congress passed Clay's tariff bill and the Force Bill, giving Jackson power to use the military to enforce the tariff.

In response, a South Carolina convention repealed the act nullifying the earlier tariff law. However, South Carolina also nullified the Force Bill. Although the crisis had passed and the Union had been preserved, a dangerous precedent had been set.

SECTION REVIEW

1. Identify the following: Eaton affair, Indian Removal Act, Force Bill.
2. What was the most important issue raised by the *South Carolina Exposition?*
3. According to Webster, who had the right to decide whether a law was constitutional?
4. On what did Jackson base his decision to veto the Maysville Road Bill?
5. Why was the Cherokee's westward movement called the Trail of Tears?

4 The Bank War

Before the nullification controversy had even passed, the President and Congress were engaged in a bitter dispute over the renewal of the charter of the Second Bank of the United States. The bank issue clearly demonstrated Jackson's concept of limited government.

The Second Bank of the United States

In 1816, when the charter of the first national bank expired, the Second Bank of the United States was created. It was given a 20-year charter and was designed to serve the same functions as its predecessor. The Bank had a great deal of power. The federal government deposited all of its revenues in the Bank, which could then use these monies without paying interest. It issued the only national

Note that in later controversies over hard vs. soft money, farmers often favored soft money and inflation, which gave them higher prices for their product and allowed them to pay debts in inflated currency. At this time however, farmers and workers regarded paper money as dishonest and unsafe.

NATIONALISM AND SECTIONALISM **177**

Many politicians had obtained loans from the Bank.

currency and controlled the amount of paper money in circulation by forcing state banks to maintain a certain level of specie reserves.

Theoretically, banknotes were backed by specie, but it was common for banks to issue more paper (often in the form of business loans) than they had specie, causing inflation. Also, if a large number of noteholders turned in their banknotes at one time, the bank might have to close. The restraining action of a national bank was needed to curb the excesses of state banks.

Unfortunately, the first two presidents of the Bank followed policies that made it unpopular. Some of these policies helped bring on the Panic of 1819 and the ensuing depression. Under the Bank's third president, Nicholas Biddle, however, this powerful financial institution became a more responsible and prosperous business enterprise. It followed a policy that allowed business prosperity and a gradual increase in the amount of paper money in circulation.

Criticism of the Bank

Despite its advantages, a wide variety of Americans still disliked the Bank. Many **soft money** (paper currency) advocates felt the Bank did not issue enough notes. Soft money advocates included business leaders, state bankers, and land speculators who believed that a large money supply was essential to economic growth. Farmers in the South and West, along with factory workers in the East, thought the Bank issued too many notes. They favored **hard money** (gold and silver coins).

Heads of strong state banks were jealous of the power of the Second Bank of the United States. In addition, many individuals still felt the Bank was unconstitutional, despite Chief Justice John Marshall's decision to the contrary in *McCullough* v. *Maryland* (1819).

Jackson Against the Bank

Thus, by the time Jackson became President, the Bank had incurred the hatred of many Americans. No one was more hostile to the Bank than Jackson who disliked banks in general. He had once lost a fortune in a business transaction because his banknotes turned

Under Nicholas Biddle the Second Bank of the United States was a prosperous enterprise. Still, many Americans disliked the bank and felt that it was unconstitutional. What did the Supreme Court decide about this issue in *McCullough* v. *Maryland?*

out to be worthless. Jackson was a hard-money man, an advocate of specie currency who was suspicious of paper notes and the problems that arose with their use.

To Jackson, the bank was the epitome of special privilege—a monopoly used by the rich and powerful for their own gain. Although the federal government owned one-fifth of its stock, the Bank was controlled by its directors. As a private business, the Bank was responsible not to the federal government, but to a small group of stockholders.

Jackson was against so much power being concentrated in a single corporation. He believed that such power made the Bank a corrupting influence in politics. Finally, Jackson was one of those who thought that the Bank was unconstitutional. He thought that Congress had no power, expressed or implied, to charter such a bank.

Early in his first term, Jackson made his views on the Bank known. He sent a message to Congress questioning the Bank's constitutionality. There seemed little doubt that he would veto any proposal to recharter the Bank.

When it became apparent that Jackson meant to eliminate the Bank, Nicholas Biddle began a policy of opposition. On the advice of Henry Clay, Biddle applied for a renewal of the Bank's charter in 1832, although the old charter was not due to expire until 1836. Clay thought that Jackson's certain veto of the measure would be unpopular and would cost him the upcoming election. Clay would then have a clear path to the Presidency.

In March 1832, Congress passed the recharter and, as predicted, Jackson vetoed it. In his address to the Senate, Jackson stated:

> A bank of the United States is . . . convenient and useful to the people. Entertaining this opinion, and deeply impressed with the belief that some of the powers and privileges possessed by the existing bank are unauthorized by the Constitution, subversive of the rights of the States, and dangerous to the liberties of the people, I felt it my duty . . . to call the attention of Congress to the practicability of organizing an institution combining all its advantages and obviating these objections. I sincerely regret that in the act before me I can perceive none of those modifications of the bank charter which are necessary . . . to make it compatible with justice, with sound policy, or with the Constitution of our country.

The Bank as an Election Issue

Jackson's veto made the Second Bank of the United States a central issue in the election of 1832. In this election, Jackson faced Henry Clay of the National Republican party and William Wirt of the Anti-Masonic party.

The Anti-Masonic party was basically anti-Jackson, and its strength was concentrated in rural New England and the Mid-Atlantic states. Although short-lived, it is known for holding the first national nominating convention. The Anti-Masonic Party was also the first national **third party.** In a two-party system, a third party is a significant new party that has enough support to affect an election.

Before the election, Clay campaigned against Jackson's veto of the Bank bill. Hoping to discredit Jackson, Clay even had copies of the President's Veto Message reproduced and distributed throughout the country. His strategy backfired. Jackson was re-elected with over 56 percent of the popular vote and 219 electoral votes to Clay's 49. Martin Van Buren became Vice President.

Destruction of the Bank

When the recharter of the Bank became a national issue, Jackson declared to Van Buren, "The Bank is

Business owners and land speculators felt that the Bank of the United States did not print enough banknotes. But farmers and factory workers felt that it printed too many and favored hard money instead. **How did the issue of hard and soft money affect the election of 1832?**

Biddle's retaliatory tactics included calling in loans and tightening credit. When business owners petitioned Washington for help, Jackson told them to "go to Biddle." Business people finally turned against Biddle.

After the Bank's federal charter expired, Biddle obtained a charter for a state bank in Pennsylvania.

trying to kill me, but I will kill it." Taking his victory in the election as an authorization to act against the Bank, Jackson proceeded to do just that.

Pet Banks. Soon after the election, Jackson ordered all federal monies removed from the Second Bank of the United States. He had these funds deposited in certain state banks, which his opponents called **pet banks.**

Jackson's enemies retaliated. In 1834 Clay mustered a majority in the Senate to pass a resolution **censuring** (officially disapproving) the President for removing the deposits and assuming power not granted him by the Constitution. The Senate action, however, did nothing to deter Jackson.

Before the Bank's charter expired, Biddle, in an attempt to coerce Jackson into reconsidering, followed policies that caused an economic downturn. Business began to fail, and unemployment rose. This merely hardened Jackson's resolve. The Bank lost popularity, and Jackson emerged the victor in the Bank war.

The Specie Circular. Jackson's tactics in destroying the Bank greatly increased the power of the presidency. In taking such independent actions, he set a precedent that other strong Presidents would follow. However, the immediate impact of the destruction of the Bank was unfortunate. There was no longer any institution that could control state banks. As a result, the pet banks greatly increased their note issue—often without thought to adequate specie reserves. Speculators borrowed money from these institutions to buy public lands. Government land offices deposited the money back into the pet banks, which made it available for further speculation. This upset people who favored hard money, including Jackson.

Before Jackson left office, he acted to slow down the speculative fever. In July 1836, he issued the "Specie Circular," which stated that government agents could only accept gold and silver in payment for public lands. The effects of Jackson's policy would have to be faced by his successor.

SECTION REVIEW

1. Identify the following: Nicholas Biddle, William Wirt, Specie Circular.
2. What powers did the Second Bank of the United States have?

Whig leaders denounced Andrew Jackson as a demagogue, a leader who gains power by playing on the emotions of the people. They called him "King Andrew the First," as this cartoon shows. How did Jackson increase the power of the Presidency?

3. What traditional practice was started by the Anti-Masonic Party?
4. What role did the pet banks play in Jackson's battle with the bank of the United States?

5 Economics and Politics after Jackson

At the end of his second term in office, Jackson decided to leave politics. He wanted his policies to continue, however. Therefore, he tried to ensure that Vice President Martin Van Buren followed him in office. Through Van Buren and others, Jackson's ideas would continue to influence economics and politics for many years.

Political Campaigns

Every four years the administration of the national government is subject to change by the will of the people. Because political campaigns have a strong influence on the outcome of elections, parties and candidates have almost always put a great deal of effort into campaigning. The style of campaigning, however, has evolved over the years. Changes in campaign styles have taken place because of changes in politics, technology, and the law.

Andrew Jackson was one of the first presidential candidates to use tactics such as public rallies, tree plantings, torchlight parades, and giant barbecues. The National Republicans looked down on these tactics because they seemed to attract rowdy crowds. But Jackson and his supporters realized that more and more people had obtained the right to vote. In order to win the presidency, a candidate had to find some way to reach the expanded electorate. The attention-getting parades and rallies were effective in persuading the voters.

During the 1800's presidential candidates usually left the actual work of campaigning to party members at the local level. Most candidates planned strategies at home with a campaign manager. In 1860 candidate Stephen Douglas was criticized for going on campaign tours. Personal appearances were still considered to be undignified for an aspiring President. However, the spread of railroads after the Civil War encouraged candidates to use the personal appearance campaign as a technique for drawing crowds and winning votes.

By the end of the 1800's, the "whistle stop" campaign was common. Candidates went from town to town by railroad. At each depot they found crowds waiting to hear a brief speech from the back platform of a' train. In large towns the candidate might stay long enough for a parade to the local fairgrounds or ball park. It was a feather in the cap of a town committee that could convince a presidential candidate to stay in town overnight.

The whistle-stop technique remained a major campaigning technique until the 1950's.

By the 1920's a new method of campaigning had come about. The radio brought the voices of candidates into the homes of millions of Americans. Using the radio meant that the candidate did not have to recite the same speech over and over. One nationwide presentation could reach almost all of the voters at the same time. But a nationwide audience also meant that appeals to local prejudices had to be tempered.

Franklin Delano Roosevelt was the first candidate to master the new style. During the 1930's and 1940's, he used the radio not only during campaigning but also while in office. Roosevelt's "fireside chats" were persuasive in winning support for his programs. Since that time, other Presidents, such as Ronald Reagan, have also found the media useful for that purpose.

In 1960 John F. Kennedy and Richard M. Nixon held a series of television debates. Television added another dimension to presidential campaigns. Increasingly it seemed necessary to package a public image for candidates. Advertising techniques that were successful in selling toothpaste and automobiles also proved to be effective in selling political positions and candidates.

Multi-media campaigning grew more and more expensive as it grew more effective. Until recent years, candidates depended mostly on large donations from rich individuals and organizations. In the 1970's laws were passed that limited donations and required detailed reports on contributions and expenses. These laws have forced candidates to use fund-raising methods that attract a large number of small donations—for example, direct mail campaign appeals.

QUESTIONS

1. Why did early presidential candidates not make personal appearances?
2. How did the spread of railroads affect campaign styles?
3. How did radio and television change methods of political campaigning?

Most Whigs wanted another national bank and a protective tariff. The new party appealed especially to the well-to-do.

NATIONALISM AND SECTIONALISM   **181**

The rivalry of Webster and Clay weakened the Whig party.

The Election of 1836

In May of 1836, Van Buren faced bitter opposition from the Whigs, a new political party. The crushing defeat of Clay in the 1832 election had destroyed the National Republican party. Following its demise, the Whig party, a coalition of anti-Jackson political figures, was formed.

These people thought Jackson was a tyrant. They had named themselves "Whigs" after a party in England that had fought against kings in the 1700's. Opposition to "King Andrew" made some strange bedfellows. The Whigs were composed of both nationalists, like Clay and Webster, and southern states' rights advocates who had split with Jackson over nullification.

While the Whigs agreed that they did not like Jackson, they found it hard to unite on a **platform** (statement of party principles). In general, however, although there were states' rights people in the party, the main direction of the Whigs was nationalistic. They felt that the government should act to promote economic growth.

In the North, many merchants and manufacturers became Whigs, as did teachers, reformers, and commercial farmers. In the South, many merchants, bankers, and planters became Whigs because they believed that southern prosperity was tied to the expanding commerce of the North.

In the election of 1836, the Whigs, who did not have a candidate of national appeal other than Clay, ran three separate candidates, each of whom had a following in a different part of the country. The Whig candidates were William Henry Harrison of Ohio, Daniel Webster of Massachusetts, and Hugh Lawson White of Tennessee.

By running three regional candidates, the Whigs hoped to stop Van Buren from receiving a majority in the Electoral College. However, their strategy failed. Jackson's popularity, along with the apparent prosperity of the country, allowed Van Buren to emerge the winner.

The Panic of 1837

Not long after Jackson left office, the American economy was hit by a financial panic, the Panic of 1837, and a depression. The depression had its roots in the Jackson years. As a result of the Specie Circular, land sales had dropped sharply. Few people had the gold or silver to pay for land. Banks had no specie to lend and began to call in loans. Many people could not repay their debts and lost their land to the bank. Speculators were hard hit.

People with deposits in the banks began to exchange notes for specie. Many banks, overextended in their issue of notes, faced disaster. Hundreds of banks and even some states went bankrupt. Factories closed, and unemployment climbed.

The Whigs blamed the Democrats for the Panic of 1837. They accused Van Buren of following Jackson's policies and not doing anything to end the depression.

The Independent Treasury

Insofar as Van Buren did react, he did little to improve the situation. Retaining Jackson's hard-money policy, Van Buren refused to withdraw the Specie Circular. He also rejected the idea of chartering a new national bank. In fact, Van Buren wanted to divorce the government from banking altogether.

With his support, the Independent Treasury Act was passed in 1840. Under this plan, federal money was removed from state banks and deposited in the Treasury. The Treasury consisted of government-owned vaults in various parts of the country. This system made economic recovery harder because it deprived the banks of money that could have been used for loans.

The Election of 1840

As the election of 1840 came near, the continued economic depression filled the Democrats with gloom. They renominated Van Buren without much fanfare. In contrast, the Whigs were enthusiastic. They believed their victory was ensured.

As their candidate, the Whigs chose William Henry Harrison. Having learned their lesson from the Democrats, they avoided real issues and did not even draw up a platform. Instead, they focused on Harrison's frontier image, picturing him as a simple western farmer who lived in a log cabin.[2] In fact, the campaign

---

[2] Harrison was actually descended from an aristocratic family and lived in a mansion.

Note that the modern idea that the government can fight off a depression did not exist at this time.

The Independent Treasury was abolished by the Whigs in 1841 and re-established by the Democrats in 1846, remaining in effect until the Civil War.

of 1840 was known as the "log cabin" campaign. Much was made of Harrison's victory against the Indians at the Battle of Tippecanoe in 1811.

The campaign's slogan became "Tippecanoe and Tyler Too!" when the Whigs nominated John Tyler of Virginia as Vice President. Tyler had once been a Democrat but had broken with Jackson.

The Whigs' strategy paid off. Although Harrison's popular majority was small, he won 234 electoral votes to Van Buren's 60. Hard times and party organization had put Harrison in the White House. The election of 1840 marked the emergence of a fully developed two-party system in American politics.

After 12 years of Democratic supremacy, the Whigs looked forward to pursuing a nationalistic policy under Harrison. Their plans went awry when, a month after his inauguration, Harrison died of pneumonia. John Tyler, a southern states' rights advocate, became President. In office, Tyler pursued actions so contrary to the basic Whig philosophy that his entire cabinet resigned. The Whig party became torn by factionalism and accomplished little. Without effective leadership, the government succumbed to political squabbling, and the nation became more vulnerable to sectional conflicts.

SECTION REVIEW

1. Which interest groups came together to form the Whig party?
2. What caused the Panic of 1837? What resulted?
3. How did the Independent Treasury Act affect the economy?
4. What conditions led to the Whig victory in 1840?

CHAPTER 8 REVIEW

SUMMARY

1. Sectional rivalry played a major part in the campaigns of the 1820's and 1830's.
2. The election of Andrew Jackson was viewed as a victory for the common people.
3. Expansion of suffrage and more democracy in government marked the Jackson presidency.
4. Jackson was a strong advocate of states' rights, but would not permit disunion.
5. Indians were forced to leave their lands east of the Mississippi River and move west.
6. A major issue of the Age of Jackson was the debate over supremacy of the national government versus state sovereignty.
7. Even after Jackson left office, his ideas continued to influence economics and politics for many years.

VOCABULARY

plurality	incumbent	free trade	third party	platform
corrupt bargain	spoils system	soft money	pet banks	
mudslinging	protectionist	hard money	censure	

REVIEW QUESTIONS

1. How did Adams' background and personality compare with Jackson's?
2. What characteristics did Jackson display that reflected American society?
3. In Jackson's view, what was the main purpose of the spoils system? What abuses arose from it?
4. What position did Jackson take on the issue of protective tariff legislation?

5. What was the states' rights position and its implications?
6. On what issues did Jackson support states' rights?
7. What were the causes and effects of Jackson's war with the Second Bank of the United States?
8. What roles did Jackson play in the elections of 1824 through 1836?
9. What changes in political party practices occurred during the Age of Jackson, and how did this show the growing power of the people?

DISCUSSION

1. Was the "corrupt bargain" really corrupt?
2. Do you think Jackson was truly a "man of the people"? Why or why not?
3. Do you think Jackson's opposition to the National Bank was justified? Why or why not?
4. What might have happened if Jackson had supported the court decision allowing the Cherokees to retain their land in Georgia?
5. Why are states' rights important to the American system of government?

USING MAPS

Refer to the map on page 168 and answer the following questions:

1. How many presidential candidates ran in the election of 1824? In 1828?
2. How many states went to each candidate?
3. How many electoral votes did Adams receive from New York in each election?
4. In what region did Adams receive the most support? In what region did Jackson receive the most support in 1824? In 1828?

USING SKILLS

The statistics below show the estimated population of the United States and the number of popular votes cast in the presidential elections of 1824–1840. Study the statistics and answer the questions that follow.

	Population	Percent Increase	Popular Votes	Percent Increase
1824	10,924,000	--	356,038	--
1828	12,237,000	12.0	1,155,350	224.5
1832	13,742,000	12.3	1,217,691	5.4
1836	15,423,000	12.2	1,505,278	19.1
1840	17,120,000	11.0	2,402,405	59.6

1. Which rose at a faster rate—the population of the United States or the number of popular votes cast in presidential elections?
2. What percentage of the population voted in each presidential election?
3. What accounts for the increase in popular votes during these years?
4. Does this evidence support the assertion that the Age of Jackson was a period of increasing democracy? Why or why not?

9

1	**Significance of the Frontier**	**185**
2	**Indian Relations**	**188**
3	**Moving Westward**	**190**
4	**War With Mexico**	**197**

WESTWARD EXPANSION

[It is] the right of our manifest destiny to overspread and to possess the whole of the continent which Providence has given us for the development of the great experiment in liberty and federative self-government entrusted to us.

JOHN L. O'SULLIVAN

Despite political squabbling in the years following the Age of Jackson, the nation continued to expand. Driven by a sense of destiny, Americans moved west into Texas, New Mexico, California, and the Oregon country. By 1848 the United States stretched unchallenged from sea to sea. This westward movement had an important impact on American institutions and the American character.

1 Significance of the Frontier

One of the people who recognized this impact was the American historian Frederick Jackson Turner. In 1893 he presented a paper, "The Significance of the Frontier in American History," to a meeting of the American Historical Association.

In that paper, Turner outlined his theory that the frontier had a great influence on American ideas and institutions. Although a number of Turner's points have been questioned, his basic **thesis** (theory defended by argument) is still the focal point of discussion of the frontier among historians today.

The Turner Thesis

Turner believed that the single most important element in American history was the huge amount of free land to the west. He wrote:

The existence of an area of free land, its continuous recession, and the advance of American settlement westward explain American development.

American development, first of all, involved moving toward the west. As Turner said, "From decade to decade distinct advances of the frontier occurred." When Europeans first arrived in America, the eastern seaboard was the frontier. By the time of the American Revolution, the Frontier had reached Kentucky and Tennessee as well as the upper waters of the Ohio River. By 1820 the Mississippi River marked the edge of the frontier. In the 1840's and 1850's, it advanced to California, Oregon, and Utah.

According to Turner, a certain pattern of settlement evolved as Americans conquered the frontier. The first easterners in a frontier area were the hunters and traders, followed by ranchers and miners. Later, pioneer farmers settled the frontier. Small towns and even cities sprang up. This pattern, from a hunting or trading frontier to an urban frontier, took place again and again as the frontier moved west:

Stand at Cumberland Gap and watch the procession of civilization, marching single-file—the buffalo following the trail of the salt springs, the Indian, the fur-trader and hunter, the cattle-raiser, the pioneer-farmer—and the frontier has passed by. Stand at South Pass in the Rockies a century later and see the same procession with wider intervals between.

In the process of conquering the frontier, the American character was changed. Turner believed that frontier life stripped away civilization. In order to survive in the wilderness, the pioneers often took up Indian ways. However, as time passed and the frontier became a more settled area, white civilization was rebuilt. Some elements of the rebuilt civilization were distinctly American, for the demands of frontier life brought out certain characteristics. Two of these characteristics were individualism and democracy.

The process of rebuilding civilization and the characteristics that process brought about had a great influence on American politics. For example, the lives

Ask students to analyze why the farmer has played a secondary role in stories, movies, and the general popular image of the West.

Note that the log cabin was actually an innovation of the Swedes, who settled in Delaware during the early 1600's.

of both Thomas Jefferson and Andrew Jackson reflected the democracy of the frontier. In the early and middle 1700's, Jefferson's home in Virginia was on the frontier. His father was a pioneer. In fact, Jefferson's faith in the American farmer was a direct result of his experience with the frontier farmers of his youth.

Andrew Jackson, born in the backwoods of the Carolinas, grew up in frontier Tennessee. His election as President marked the triumph of frontier democracy in national politics. As Turner noted, "The triumph of Andrew Jackson marked the end of the old era of trained statesmen for the presidency. With him began the era of the popular hero."

The Frontier Farmer

When Americans today think of heroes of the old West, they generally picture Indian warriors, gun-fighters, and law officers. However, many American historians believe that the real hero of the old West was the frontier farmer. Frontier farmers were the men and women who turned huge forests into farmland and tamed a wilderness. In a *New Guide to Immigrants to the West* (1837), John Mason Peck wrote that the frontier farmer ". . . strikes into the woods with his family, and becomes the founder of a new county, or perhaps state."

In the process of taming the wilderness, pioneer farmers had to provide themselves with shelter, food, and clothing. The first concern was the building of a cabin. While the family camped, the men and older boys cut down trees, shaped logs, rafters, joists, and flooring. When the materials were ready, neighbors joined together for a cabin raising. Logs were notched at the ends and laid alternately to form the sides and ends of the cabin. The roof was then added. Senator James Harlan of Kentucky described how his family's cabin was built when he was a boy:

The cabin was finished in about six or eight days from the date of our arrival, with no tools other than a common chopping ax, an auger, frow, and hand-saw, and without a single nail or screw, or metallic material of any description.

At trading meetings frontier settlers and Indians often shared meals around the campfire. The gatherings were also great social events. Many hunters and trappers lived among the Indians and adopted their ways. What evidence of this is found in the picture?

Eager to plant crops, the pioneers first cleared the land by girdling trees. It was believed that where many trees grew was the most fertile soil, so forest land was cleared indiscriminately. While the trees died from the girdling process, the pioneers planted their crops between the trees. Later the trees were felled for building materials, fences, and firewood. What were the first crops that pioneers planted?

Although these cabins were crude, they served their purpose. The fireplace provided both heat and light. Because there was no glass, windows were covered with oiled paper or blankets.

In addition to shelter, pioneer farmers had to be concerned with food. Families lived on wild game, pork, fruits, and a variety of vegetables. Food often was cooked in pots suspended over the fireplace. Besides providing for food and shelter, the pioneers had to make their own clothes. Pioneer wives fashioned clothes for the family out of linsey-woolsey, a coarse cloth made of wool and cotton or linen.

Work was hard for both men and women. The demands of large families took their toll of the wives, often sending them to an early grave. The historian Dan Elbert Clark wrote about pioneer women:

> *Their labors were arduous and unceasing. In addition, they suffered from the psychological hardships of frontier life—loneliness, fear of Indian attacks, longing for loved relatives and friends left behind, worry and anguish in times of sickness without the possibility of even the poor medical care of the period.*

The men's responsibilities were also arduous. Clearing the land was especially difficult. In the first year, small trees and underbrush were cleared, stacked, and burned. The ashes were used as fertilizer. Large trees were left standing but "girdled" by cutting rings through the bark and cutting off the flow of sap. Corn was planted between the girdled trees and, for the most part, left to grow without cultivation. Later the larger trees were cut down and the stumps cleared. The logs were used for fence rails and, with the coming of the sawmill, for lumber.

Some families simply could not succeed under the severe circumstances of the frontier and returned to the East. Most frontier farming families, however, stayed despite the harsh conditions. Indeed, with the coming of more settlers, they generally pushed farther west. According to Peck, frontier farmers generally stayed until they lacked "elbow room." He wrote, "Hundreds of men can be found, not over 50 years of age, who have settled for the fourth, fifth, or sixth time on a new spot." This constant westward movement brought the frontier farmer into contact with various Indian groups.

SECTION REVIEW

1. According to Turner, what was the most important element in American history?
2. What pattern of settlement developed on the frontier?
3. How did Jefferson and Jackson reflect the democracy of the frontier?
4. What were the concerns of the frontier farmer?

Ask students if they feel there was any way to reconcile Indian and white attitudes towards land use so that conflict could have been avoided.

2 Indian Relations

White settlement had serious implications for the Indians. Year after year, Indians lost more land to whites, who regarded the Indians not as the rightful owners of the land but as barriers in the way of progress. To most whites, Indian values and lifestyles were incomprehensible.

Indian Attitudes

In general, Indians did not try to change their environment in drastic ways. Instead, they adapted their lifestyles to suit the physical surroundings.

Indian attitudes toward the land were very different from European attitudes. The Indians saw the land as a resource to be used and left unchanged. The white people's concept of private property was foreign to them. The Shawnee leader Tecumseh expressed Indian attitudes when he said, "Sell a country! Why not sell the air, the clouds, and the great sea . . . ?"

White Attitudes

The white attitude toward the land was based upon entirely different values. One of these values was a belief in the importance of the farmer. During the first half of the 1800's, most Americans were members of farming families. Thomas Jefferson's idea of the noble, independent farmer as the foundation of the country had become an important part of the American self-image. In 1840 James B. Lanman of Michigan wrote in *Hunts Merchants' Magazine:*

> It can scarcely be denied that agricultural enterprise, the basis of almost every form of human pursuit, should be encouraged as the safeguard of the country, the promoter of its virtue, and the solid foundation of its permanent happiness and most lasting independence.

The more farmers, then, the better for the country. However, expanding agriculture needed more and more land. Abundant land lay to the west, but it was occupied by Indians. Most settlers felt that the Indians had no right to the land because they had not cleared it for farming. They held with John Sevier, the founder of Tennessee, that, "By the law of nations, it is agreed that no people shall be entitled to more land than they can cultivate." The Indians cultivated sparingly or not at all. Even so, they claimed vast domains. In a speech made in 1802, John Quincy Adams expressed the typical white reaction to such claims:

> The Indian right of possession itself stands, with regard to the greatest part of the country, upon a questionable foundation. Their cultivated fields; their habitations; a space of ample sufficiency for their subsistence, and whatever they had annexed to themselves by personal labor, was undoubtedly by the law of nature theirs. But what is the right of the huntsman to the forest of a thousand miles over which he has accidentally ranged in quest of prey?

By such arguments as these, white settlers rejected the claims of the Indians. The stage was set for conflict.

United States Indian Policy

Problems had existed between whites and Indians since early colonial times. Most of these problems centered on trade and white attempts to take over Indian land. The United States Indian policy grew out of colonial and early national experience.

Colonial Indian Policy. Colonial attempts to regulate trade with the Indians and the purchase of Indian lands failed. This failure was largely due to acts of unscrupulous whites. The preamble of a South Carolina Act of 1737 pointed out the difficulties with land purchases:

> The practice of purchasing lands from the Indians may prove very dangerous to the peace and safety of this Province, such purchases being generally obtained from Indians by unfair representation, fraud and circumvention, or by making them gifts or presents of little value, by which practices, great resentments and animosities have been created amongst the Indians towards the inhabitants of this Province. . . .

Have student discuss why there was such land hunger among white Americans.

To provide land for settlers, the government often sought treaty cessions from the Indians. In meeting with government officials, Indians were often forced into signing treaties that ceded many thousands of square miles of territory. The desire of whites for land pushed Indian tribes farther west almost on a continuous basis. In what other ways did white settlers obtain land from the Indians?

Governor George Thomas of Pennsylvania, in a speech to the Pennsylvania assembly of 1774, expressed a common concern of many colonial governments:

> I cannot but be apprehensive that the Indian trade as it is now carried on will involve us with some fatal quarrel with the Indians. Our Traders in defiance of the Law carry Spiritious Liquors amongst them, and take advantage of their inordinate Appetite for it to cheat them out of their skins and their wampum, which is their Money. . . . Is it to be wondered at then, if when they Recover from the Drunken fit, they should take severe revenges?

One example of such revenges was Pontiac's Rebellion. As a result of this uprising, Great Britain issued the Proclamation of 1763, setting up a boundary between white and Indian lands. This boundary, however, failed to keep settlers from moving west. Thus, in the years before the American Revolution, the situation on the frontier grew worse.

Early National Indian Policy. After the Revolution, it was most important for the new nation to maintain peace with the Indians. The United States could not handle the cost of frontier wars. Official government policy was stated in the Northwest Ordinance (1787):

> The utmost good faith shall always be observed toward the Indians . . . and laws founded in justice and humanity shall from time to time be made, for preventing wrongs being done to them, and preserving peace and friendship with them.

In its efforts to keep the peace, the United States government adopted a policy of purchasing Indian lands through treaty. Legislation was passed against people who violated such treaties. Boundary lines, across which settlers were not to pass, were established around Indian territory.

Despite such measures, whites continued to encroach on Indian lands. In fact, treaties were often renegotiated to buy the newly settled land. In such a manner, millions of acres were transferred to the United States. Still, white settlers were not satisfied. Pressure mounted to remove the Indians from the path of whites altogether.

Indian Removal. In a message to Congress near the end of his term, President Monroe offered his plan for the eastern Indians. Monroe recommended the purchase of remaining eastern Indian lands and the provision of new land for these Indians west of the Mississippi River.

This plan met with the approval of most whites, who believed that once the Indians were beyond the Mississippi River, the way would be cleared for

Explain that while the Midwest is clearly not a desert, much of it lacks the annual 20 inches of rainfall people of the time believed was necessary to sustain agriculture.

Ask students if they see any parallels between white American attitudes toward Indian land and attitudes toward Spanish or Mexican land.

INDIAN LAND CESSIONS AND INDIAN REMOVAL, 1750–1850

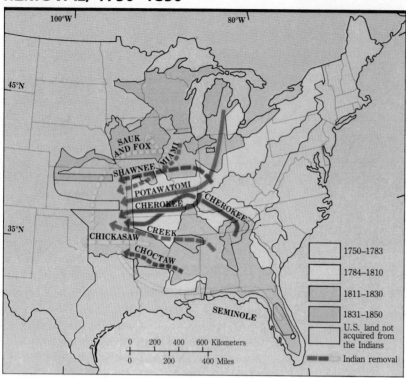

westward expansion. At this time, whites did not expect to settle the land between the Mississippi River and the Rocky Mountains. This area, known as the Great American Desert, was thought to be unsuited for agriculture.

Despite such feelings, Indian removal bills failed to pass Congress. It was not until Andrew Jackson became President that an Indian removal bill was passed. After the passage of this bill in 1830, Jackson proceeded to direct Indian removal. Removal, however, only temporarily solved the Indian problem.

SECTION REVIEW

1. What was the attitude of most Indians toward the land?
2. Why did many whites reject Indian claims to the land?
3. What was the official government policy toward Indians under the Northwest Ordinance?
4. Why was Monroe's Indian removal policy welcomed by whites?

3 Moving Westward

By the first part of the 1800's, then, the United States had developed a policy for removing the Indian barrier to westward expansion. By the 1840's the lands east of the Mississippi River were settled, and Americans were pushing into the Spanish Southwest. This area included all lands south and west of the Louisiana Purchase. These lands were claimed first by Spain and later by Mexico after it became independent in 1822. Because of American expansion into the Spanish Southwest, tension between the United States and Mexico began to build.

Texas

One area of tension between the United States and Mexico was Texas. In the early 1700's, Spaniards had settled in Texas. In the early 1800's, Americans had become interested in the area. The idea to settle Americans in Texas was conceived by Moses Austin,

Point out that tensions between the Mexican government and American settlers included cultural factors such as different religious traditions (Catholic vs. Protestant) and different political traditions (extremely limited democracy vs. extensive democracy).

a Connecticut-born pioneer, and carried out by his son Stephen.

Stephen Austin was an **empresario,** or a person who obtains grants and brings in settlers to develop an area. With a grant given his father by the Spaniards, Austin led a group of American colonizers into eastern Texas in 1821. Austin's colony grew rapidly. By 1825 the population stood at 1800. By 1832 it was over 5000.

In the early 1830's the Mexican government began to question its policy of allowing American colonization. Although most Americans in Texas cooperated with the Mexican authorities, some caused trouble. There was even one unsuccessful attempt at revolution. In addition, the Mexican government suspected that the United States had designs on Texas. This suspicion grew when Andrew Jackson became President, because Jackson was known to favor the **annexation** (attachment of a country or territory) of Texas to the United States.

In April 1830, Mexico enacted a new colonization law. This new law cut off legal immigration from the United States and provided for the military occupation of Texas. Despite the new law, immigration continued illegally. American unrest under the new Mexican restrictions grew. When the Mexican leader, General Antonio Lopez de Santa Anna, rebelled against his government, Americans in Texas sided with him. They hoped that Santa Anna's victory would give

them the opportunity to air their grievances and gain reforms. However, when Santa Anna became President of Mexico, he tried to assert even more control over the Mexican states.

Sporadic fighting between Texans and Mexicans began and, in November 1835, the Texans set up a **provisional government** (a temporary government subject to change). To put a stop to the rebellion, Santa Anna raised an army and marched into Texas.

Alarmed at the news of Santa Anna's approach, Texans prepared their defenses. To slow down Santa Anna and allow time for Texans to build an army, 187 men under William B. Travis fortified an old mission in San Antonio. This mission, known as the Alamo, lay directly in the path of the Mexican army.

Upon reaching the Alamo, Santa Anna attacked with 4000 soldiers. Although greatly outnumbered, the small Texas force, which included frontier heroes Jim Bowie and Davy Crockett, refused to surrender. On March 6, 1836, Santa Anna took the fort. All 187 of the Alamo's defenders died, but not before killing 1544 Mexican soldiers. Soon afterward, the Mexicans also defeated a Texan army at Goliad and killed 300 prisoners.

In March 1836, while Travis and his men were still fighting at the Alamo, 59 Texan delegates met and signed a declaration of independence. They also drew up a constitution for the new Republic of Texas and named Sam Houston commander of the army.

The Alamo in San Antonio was the site of the opening battle of Texas' struggle for independence. Here a force of 187 fighters held out for a time against a Mexican force of several thousand soldiers led by Santa Anna. Among the defenders were such legendary heroes as Davy Crockett and Jim Bowie. What role did the Battle of the Alamo play in Texas' War for Independence?

Point out that Bowie and Crockett were among numerous non-Texans who volunteered to help Texans win their independence.

Ask students to discuss why Texans—today renowned for their local pride and independent thinking—wanted to join the United States in the first place.

TEXAS INDEPENDENCE, 1835–1836

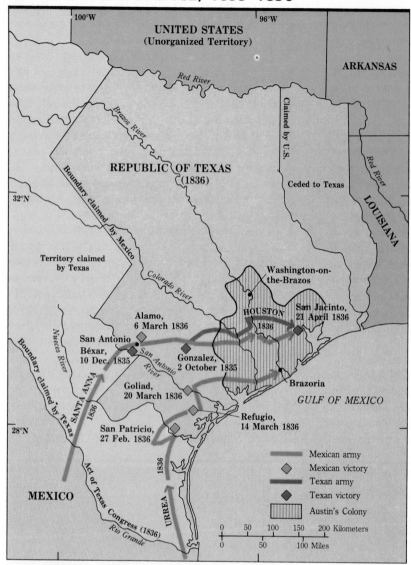

Meanwhile Santa Anna's force continued to push north, driving the Texan army before it. Although the Texan army was in retreat, Houston was shaping it into a real fighting force. On April 21, 1836, Houston was ready. At the Battle of San Jacinto, crying "Remember the Alamo!" "Remember Goliad!," the Texans attacked and routed the Mexican army. Santa Anna was captured, and the independence of Texas was the price of his release. Thus the Republic of Texas, often called the Lone Star Republic, was born. Sam Houston was chosen as its first president.

After gaining independence, the new republic applied for admission to the United States. Andrew Jackson, although privately in favor of annexation, had remained publicly neutral during the war. Afterward, he continued to follow a cautious course. He did not want war with Mexico or to stir up feelings against annexation in the North and East. These feelings stemmed from the fact that most of the settlers in Texas were from the South and owned slaves. Thus, Jackson recognized the new government in March 1837, but made no effort to annex Texas.

President Van Buren also chose not to annex Texas, and the question did not come up again until 1843. At that time, President Tyler, worried by growing ties between Texas and Europe, sought a treaty of annexation. Tyler was unsuccessful at this time. However, in 1844 the Democrats nominated James K. Polk of Tennessee for President and called for the annexation of Texas at the earliest possible time. Many people in the West favored annexation, and Polk won the election, defeating the Whig candidate, Henry Clay.

Tyler interpreted Polk's victory as a **mandate,** or authorization to act given to a representative by the people. So he asked Congress to admit Texas as a state without first being a territory. A joint resolution to that effect passed both the House and Senate and was signed by Tyler on March 1, 1845. A **joint resolution** is one passed by both houses of a legislature. It has the force of law when signed by the President or passed over a presidential veto. After assuming office, President Polk submitted Texas' state constitution to Congress, and Texas was admitted to the Union in December 1845.[1]

California

As in Texas, American interest in California brought about conflict with Mexico. Americans became interested in California in the early 1800's as a result of the sea otter trade. New England sailors hunted otter along the California coast and traded the pelts in China for a large profit. The New Englanders were impressed by the wealth and beauty of California. Other sailors, involved in whaling and the hide and tallow trade, later confirmed this opinion.

Because of the glowing descriptions of the area, the number of Americans in California began to increase. By the 1830's most of California's population was made up of American sailors and fur traders. Mexican officials soon began to worry about the presence of so many Americans. Rumors of revolution spread, and in one case, 50 Americans were convicted of taking part in a plot to overthrow the Mexican government.

Despite such actions by the Mexican government, California saw an influx of American farmers in the

1840's. Most of these traveled overland from the Mississippi Valley through the Rocky Mountains at South Pass, across the Great Basin, and over the Sierra-Nevada Mountains into California. The trip took six months, and the hardships along the way were great.

As the number of American settlers in California increased, so did the interest of the United States government. Twice during the 1830's, President Jackson tried to buy northern California from Mexico. He had no success, however. Later, President Tyler and his Secretary of State, Daniel Webster, also made plans for negotiating the **cession** (the formal surrender of territory or rights) of California. However, none of these plans had materialized when Polk took office in 1845.

While Polk pursued measures for the peaceful acquisition of California, settlers there grew impatient. They were particularly impatient with Mexico's inability to govern the province. By the 1840's California was in a chaotic state. Law enforcement had broken down, and life and property were insecure. Because of this situation, Californians felt it was time for a change. Opinion differed, however, as to the nature of that change. Some people wanted independence. Others favored annexation to the United States. Still others preferred a **protectorate** (a relationship in which one country would have authority over another) under Great Britain or France.[2] Whatever the opinion, dissatisfaction grew as the chaos continued.

Finally, in the spring of 1846, Californians decided to take matters into their own hands. American settlers in the Sacramento Valley and in Sonoma revolted. The rebels were aided by a party of United States Army surveyors led by Captain John C. Frémont,[3] who was known as "the Pathfinder" because of his explorations. On June 15 the rebels proclaimed the independence of the Republic of California. The new Republic was also known as the Bear Flag Republic because its flag bore a grizzly bear, along with a star, on a field of white cloth.

---

[1] Under the terms of the annexation, Texas could divide itself into as many as five states.

[2] The French had at one point proposed such a protectorate, and it was widely assumed by Americans that the British also had designs on the area. Actually the British were not willing to risk war with the United States over California.

[3] Whether Frémont was following secret military orders has been a matter of historical debate.

Have students study a map to see why both Great Britain and the United States wanted the territory between the 49th latitude and the Columbia River.

Note the role of pioneers' reports in determining the particular order in which the different parts of the western territory were settled.

CALIFORNIA REPUBLIC

Under the spirit of manifest destiny new lands were added to the nation. Some were gained by peaceful means. Others were taken in war. Impatient California settlers rebelled against the rule of Mexico and proclaimed the independence of the Republic of California under this flag. Why did the settlers become so impatient with the Mexican government?

By the time California declared its independence, war had broken out between Mexico and the United States. The outcome of that war would determine the fate of California.

Oregon

The United States was involved in conflicts not only with Mexico, but with other countries as well. One of these countries was Great Britain. The territory over which Great Britain and the United States quarreled was Oregon.

Oregon was originally claimed by four countries—the United States, Great Britain, Spain, and Russia. The Spanish withdrew their claims in 1819 as part of the Adams-Onís Treaty. The Russians withdrew theirs in 1824 and 1825 under treaties with the United States and Great Britain. The Americans were then left to compete with the British for control of Oregon.

Both Great Britain and the United States claimed the territory between 42° and 54°40′ north latitude. The real source of conflict, however, was the land between 49° north latitude and the Columbia River. The United States would have been satisfied with a northern boundary at 49° north latitude, and Great Britain would have been satisfied with a southern boundary at the Columbia River. Neither side pressed its claim, however, and treaties of **joint occupation** were signed in 1818 and 1827. This meant that people from both the United States and Great Britain could settle in Oregon.

Both countries knew that settlement would decide the future of Oregon. At first, settlement was sparse. Throughout the 1820's, Americans generally settled on the coast because they were interested in shipping and trading. The British, involved in the fur trade, settled the interior. During the 1830's and 1840's, however, American farmers also began to settle the interior. Soon the Americans outnumbered the British.

American settlement of Oregon was encouraged by the accounts of traders and others who had already gone west. The efforts of American missionaries also stimulated interest in the area. Intending to convert the Indians of the Northwest to Christianity, a number of American missionaries established settlements in Oregon. Reports from such people as Marcus and Narcissa Whitman attracted the nation's attention to the fertile Willamette Valley.

The reports of the missionaries and the poor economic conditions in the Mississippi Valley drew more and more farmers west. Attracted by high prices, favorable markets, rivers for transportation, and "elbow room," Americans in large numbers became infected with "Oregon fever." In 1845 alone, 300 Americans arrived in Oregon, doubling the population. Most people settled in the Willamette Valley.

Meanwhile, in 1842, the United States and Great Britain had signed the Webster-Ashburton Treaty, establishing north latitude 49° as the northeastern border between the United States and Canada. Many westerners were disappointed that the treaty did not

The Mountain Men

In the early 1800's, men of varied backgrounds sought their fortunes in the high mountains and rivers of the western wilderness. As time passed, they pushed farther and farther west. Many of these "mountain men," as they came to be known, adopted the clothing and habits of the Indians. Many of them also took Indian wives.

Several of the mountain men were colorful enough to acquire widespread reputations. James Bridger began his career as a trapper, first trading beaver skins and later buffalo skins along a route that later became the famous Oregon Trail. Bridger built a fort along the trail that served as a way station for pioneers who brought the first wagon trains west. He was probably the first white man to see the Great Salt Lake. Later, Bridger became a guide for the American Fur Company. He became famous for his tall tales of the West.

Mike Fink was a river boatman who switched to trapping for a living after steamboats replaced keelboats. Like many mountain men, Fink was a hard drinker. One day, the story goes, he accidentally killed a close friend as they took turns shooting a tin cup off each other's head. Both men had been drinking. Filled with remorse, Fink wandered from place to place telling his tale of woe. Later he was shot by a friend of the man he killed. Fink's tall tales also became part of the frontier mythology.

Jedadiah Smith was a mountain man of a different sort—a well-educated Puritan who was not interested in drinking or women. He rediscovered a lost pass in the Rockies that became the main gateway to the West along the Oregon Trail. On another trip, Smith and his companions traveled north from California to Oregon.

After the decline of the fur trade, trappers were often employed as guides for groups of pioneers moving west. The accomplishments of the mountain men helped to smooth the way for those who followed, and their stories of adventure provided inspiration and humor for generations to come.

---

deal with the boundary of Oregon. The area between 42° and 54° 40′ north latitude was still claimed by both Great Britain and the United States. However, some Americans were no longer willing to accept 49° north latitude as the country's northwestern boundary.

By 1843 expansionism in the United States had grown. **Expansionism** was sentiment in favor of expanding the land area of the United States. Reflecting the growing feeling, the Democratic party adopted the cry, "54° 40′ or fight!" as a campaign slogan during the presidential election of 1844.

Despite this seemingly warlike stance, the United States did not want war. Neither did Great Britain. The British were aware of the growing numbers of Americans in Oregon and the decline of the fur trade. Therefore, they were ready to compromise. In the spring of 1846, the British proposed that the boundary set by the Webster-Ashburton Treaty be extended. That is, 49° north latitude would serve as the boundary between the United States and Canada all the way to the Pacific Ocean. This proposal was submitted to the Senate as a draft treaty, and the Senate accepted the compromise. In August 1848, a bill establishing the Oregon Territory was passed by the United States Congress.

Utah

While some Americans pushed westward into Texas, California, and Oregon, other Americans moved into the Great Basin frontier of Utah. Unlike the farmers who traveled west seeking economic opportunity, the people who settled Utah were seeking religious freedom. They were members of

Point out that because they have a sacred text other than the Bible, Mormons generally are not considered to be Protestants. They are, however, acknowledged to be Christians.

Ask students to outline the reasons behind religious persecution, a common practice throughout world history.

Brigham Young led the Mormon people west across the Missouri River to the valley of the Great Salt Lake. Congress refused to recognize the Mormon state of Deseret and organized the area into the Territory of Utah. The Mormons established their settlement as a theocracy. What is a theocracy?

the Church of Jesus Christ of Latter-Day Saints and were called Mormons.

Joseph Smith. The Mormon church had its beginnings in New York. During the 1820's and 1830's, a religious revival known as the Second Great Awakening was occurring in western New York and adjacent areas. During this time, a number of new churches appeared. One of these was founded by Joseph Smith.

According to Smith's account, in 1823 he was led by the angel Moroni to some buried metal plates that contained the story of the lost tribes of Israel and the key to true faith in Jesus Christ. In 1827 Smith began to translate these plates, and, in 1830, the Book of Mormon was published. That same year, the Church of Jesus Christ of Latter-Day Saints was founded.

Early Wanderings. At first the church grew slowly because many people did not trust its unorthodox views. For the same reason, church members were often persecuted. In order to avoid persecution, Smith left New York in 1831 and led his followers to northeastern Ohio.

In Ohio the community thrived, and the church grew. Eventually, however, the Mormons were forced to leave because of public pressure. After a short stay in northwestern Missouri, they moved to an unsettled area of Illinois. There, Smith and his followers founded the community of Nauvoo.

For a while the Mormons lived peacefully at Nauvoo. This was largely because the Mormon vote carried a good deal of weight in state politics. Smith used this potential power to bargain with Illinois officials. He even managed to acquire a charter from Illinois establishing Nauvoo as a **theocracy,** or a government run by officials who are regarded as divinely guided. As a result of Smith's bargaining, both Nauvoo and the Mormon church prospered. By 1844 Nauvoo had a population of 15,000.

This prosperity did not last, however. People outside the Mormon community began to resent the Mormon's political clout. When Smith asked the United States Congress to make Nauvoo a federal territory free from state control, people were angered further.

Point out that the Salt Lake Valley was chosen because Young figured that its barrenness would make it unattractive to other settlers. Ironically, the Mormons' success in "making the desert bloom" did make it attractive to others.

Anti-Mormon feelings rose to a new pitch in July 1843. At that time, Smith experienced a **revelation,** or special message from God, endorsing polygamy for a few of the church leaders. Polygamy is the practice of a person having more than one spouse. In this case, it meant a husband having more than one wife. This issue divided the Mormon community. Some members even established a newspaper to present the view of Smith's opponents. Smith, however, had the presses destroyed. Word of Smith's action spread, and, soon, the countryside was alive with anti-Mormon feeling. Once again, violence seemed likely to erupt.

To keep the peace, Illinois' governor talked Smith into surrendering. He complied and was lodged at the Carthage jail for protection. Despite this precaution, a mob stormed the jail and murdered the Mormon leader.

Migration to the West. Finally persuaded that the Mormons had no future in the United States, the leaders of the church decided to move beyond the country's borders. Under the leadership of Brigham Young, the Mormons left Nauvoo to settle in an isolated area west of the Rocky Mountains. Young, who was a good organizer, planned for the trip to take place in stages. Some people were sent ahead to clear the trail, set up campsites, and plant crops. The main body of Mormons followed.

The first group of Mormons arrived in the valley of the Great Salt Lake on July 24, 1847. Upon arrival, the Mormons went to work to build a lasting settlement. Although the first two winters were very difficult, the community began to succeed. Part of this success was due to the cooperative economic system set up by Brigham Young. Under this system, land and water were given to the people according to their need. As a result of this policy, the community survived, and its members began to turn the desert into a garden.

Government. In 1848 the Mormons found that, because of the Mexican War, they were once again within the boundaries of the United States. To protect themselves, they drew up a constitution for what they called the state of Deseret in 1849. This done, they applied for statehood.

Under the new constitution, power was held by popularly elected officials, all of whom turned out to be Mormons. In effect, then, Deseret became a theocracy. Nevertheless, the government worked equally well for all. Its system of courts and law enforcement was generally fair and impartial. One traveler described the way the Mormons treated people who were passing through Deseret:

> *Appeals for protection from oppression by those passing through their midst, were not made in vain; and I know of at least one instance in which the marshal of the State was dispatched, with an adequate force, nearly two hundred miles into the western desert in pursuit of some miscreants who had stolen off with nearly the whole outfit of a party of emigrants. He pursued and brought them back to the city, and the plundered property was restored to its rightful owners.*

Despite the quality of government established by the Mormons, their application for statehood was not well-received in Congress. However, after submitting another application, Utah was given territorial status on September 9, 1850.

SECTION REVIEW

1. Identify the following: Stephen Austin, Sam Houston, Bear Flag Republic, Webster-Ashburton Treaty, Deseret.
2. What was the importance of the stand at the Alamo?
3. What drew Americans to California during the early 1800's?
4. What attracted many Americans to the Oregon Territory?
5. How did Brigham Young's leadership lead to Mormon success in Utah?

4 War With Mexico

By the time the first Mormons had arrived in Utah, war had broken out between the United States and Mexico. Although the United States had recognized Mexico's independence in 1822, relations between the two countries had been strained.

One point of dispute was the Texas boundary. Texas claimed the Rio Grande as its southern boundary. Mexico argued that the boundary was farther north, at the Nueces River. Another problem was that Mexico had stopped making payments owed to American citizens for property losses during Mexican revolutions. A third problem concerned the status of California. Mexico was becoming impatient with American expansionism and had issued orders that American settlers were to be expelled from California. The annexation of Texas simply confirmed Mexican suspicions. Also, Americans were causing trouble in California.

Manifest Destiny

Mexican concern over American expansionism was well-founded. By the 1840's many Americans were beginning to think that it was the fate of the United States to extend from ocean to ocean. In July 1845, a magazine editor, John L. O'Sullivan, coined a term that reflected this idea. O'Sullivan argued that the **"manifest destiny"** of the United States required the annexation of Texas. Later, Representative Robert C. Winthrop of Massachusetts used the term in demanding the annexation of Oregon, stating that it was "the right of our manifest destiny to spread over this whole continent."

James K. Polk, who became President of the United States in March 1845, was a firm believer in manifest destiny. Polk felt the Unites States should stretch from the Atlantic Ocean to the Pacific Ocean, from the Rio Grande to 49° north latitude. The establishment of this boundary between the United States and Canada, along with the annexation of Texas, partly fulfilled Polk's dream. However, Polk also desired California and New Mexico. This desire, along with a dispute over the boundary between Texas and Mexico, soon led to war with Mexico.

The Slidell Mission

In an effort to settle the Texas boundary dispute and gain California and New Mexico peacefully, Polk sent John Slidell to Mexico City. Convinced that California and New Mexico were destined to be part of the United States, Polk authorized Slidell to offer $30 million for the two provinces.

At that time, however, feelings against the United States were running high in Mexico. The Mexican government, which had already recalled its ambassador to the United States, refused to receive Slidell. When this happened, Slidell wrote, "Be assured that nothing is to be done with these people until they shall have been chastised."

Outbreak of War

It was clear to President Polk that war was at hand. He wanted Mexico to strike first, however. In an attempt to provoke an attack, Polk sent an army under General Zachary Taylor into the disputed territory.

From January through early May 1846, Polk awaited developments. Finally, the President received the news for which he had been waiting. On April 25 Mexican troops had crossed the Rio Grande and attacked an American patrol. Sixteen Americans had been killed or wounded. On May 5 Polk sent his war message to Congress:

> *Now, after reiterated menaces, Mexico has passed the boundaries of the United States, has invaded our territory and shed American blood upon American soil. She has proclaimed that hostilities have commenced, and that the two nations are now at war. As war exists, and, notwithstanding all our efforts to avoid it, exists by the act of Mexico herself, we are called upon by every consideration of duty and patriotism to indicate with decision the honor, the rights, and the interests of our country.*

On May 13, Congress declared war on Mexico. The war aims of the United States were to gain the Mexican provinces of New Mexico and California and to keep the war as short as possible. To achieve these aims, the United States mounted several offensives against Mexico.

Conquest of New Mexico and California. In the spring of 1846, Colonel (later General) Stephen W. Kearny marched south from Fort Leavenworth, Kansas. Advancing into New Mexico, the "Army of the West," as it was known, captured the capital of the province, Santa Fe. After winning control of the entire province, Kearny and part of his army left for California.

By the time Kearny's force arrived there, California had declared its independence from Mexico. In July a United States naval force under Commodore John D. Sloat had occupied Monterey

THE MEXICAN WAR, 1846–1848

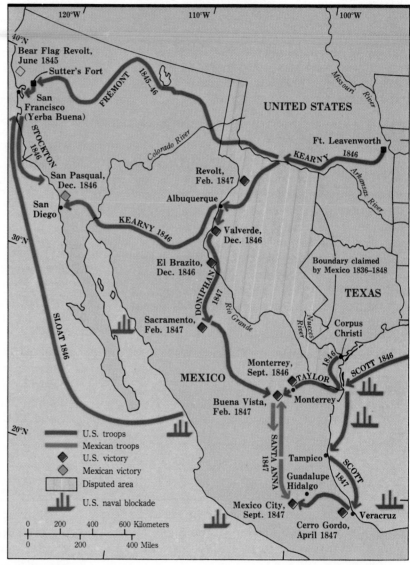

120°W   110°W   100°W

40°N
Bear Flag Revolt,
June 1845
Sutter's Fort
FRÉMONT 1845–46
San
Francisco
(Yerba Buena)
STOCKTON 1846
UNITED STATES

Missouri River

San Pasqual,
Dec. 1846
Revolt,
Feb. 1847
Albuquerque
Ft. Leavenworth
KEARNY 1846

San
Diego
KEARNY 1846
Valverde,
Dec. 1846
30°N

El Brazito,
Dec. 1846
Arkansas River

Boundary claimed
by Mexico 1836–1848
TEXAS

Colorado River

DONIPHAN 1847
Rio Grande
Sacramento,
Feb. 1847
SLOAT 1846

Nueces River
Corpus
Christi

1846
MEXICO
Monterrey,
Sept. 1846
TAYLOR
SCOTT 1846

Buena Vista,
Feb. 1847
Monterrey

20°N
SANTA ANNA 1847
Tampico
SCOTT 1847

U.S. troops
Mexican troops
U.S. victory
Mexican victory
Disputed area
U.S. naval blockade

Guadalupe
Hidalgo
Mexico City,
Sept. 1847
Cerro Gordo,
April 1847
Veracruz
SCOTT 1847

0   200   400   600 Kilometers
0   200   400 Miles

and San Francisco. In August Frémont's forces had captured Los Angeles with the help of naval commander Robert F. Stockton, who had replaced Sloat. Although there was some resistance from Mexicans living in California, Americans, including Kearny's troops, soon completed the conquest of California. Thus, in just a few months, the United States had conquered both New Mexico and California.

Invasion of Mexico. The war, however, was not yet won. General Zachary Taylor was expected to deliver the fatal blow with the seizure of Mexico City. Invading Mexico in August 1846, Taylor won victories at Monterey in September and at Buena Vista in February 1847. When the Mexicans continued fighting, Polk ordered a second drive toward Mexico City. Led by General Winfield Scott, a large American force landed near Vera Cruz in March 1847. Scott's army captured Vera Cruz after a short siege and then marched inland to Mexico City. After some fierce fighting, the Mexicans surrendered the city on September 14, 1847. The war was over.

Have students compare the size of the continental United States to other nations, and examine its borders to see if they are indeed as "natural" as proponents of Manifest Destiny claimed they were. Do most other nations have natural borders?

Treaty of Guadalupe Hidalgo. On February 2, 1848, the Treaty of Guadalupe Hidalgo was signed, formally ending the war. Under the terms of this treaty, the United States received all of California and that part of New Mexico north of the Gila River.[4] In return, the United States paid Mexico $15 million and agreed to pay over $3 million in debts that Mexicans owed to Americans.

Aftermath of the War

Between 1845 and 1848 the United States had added some 1.2 million square miles (3.1 million square kilometers) to its territory. Once the United States gained control over large areas of the West, Americans began moving into these lands in ever increasing numbers.

One event which drew people to the West was the discovery of gold in California. This discovery was made in 1848 by James Marshall on the property of John Sutter. News of Marshall's find quickly spread throughout the nation.

In 1849 over 80,000 people, known as "forty-niners," traveled west to the California gold fields.

---

[4] The territory received from Mexico included the present states of California, Nevada, Utah, Arizona, New Mexico, Texas, and part of Colorado and Wyoming.

Although many of the newcomers returned home after the uproar died down, some stayed in California. In 1849 a state constitution was drafted. In 1850, after Congress had approved this constitution, California became a state.

With the addition of California and New Mexico, the United States stretched from ocean to ocean. In 1853 President Pierce sent James Gadsden of South Carolina to negotiate a treaty with Santa Anna in order to buy land for a proposed transcontinental railroad. For $10 million, Santa Anna sold almost 30,000 square miles (77,700 square kilometers) in what is today the southern part of Arizona and New Mexico. With the acquisition of this territory, the United States reached its present continental boundaries. The nation had fulfilled its manifest destiny.

SECTION REVIEW

1. Identify the following: John L. O'Sullivan, Nueces River, Zachary Taylor, Stephen Kearny, John Sutter, Gadsden Purchase.
2. What were the grievances the United States and Mexico had against each other by the 1840's?
3. What did Polk do to provoke war with Mexico?
4. What were the terms of the Treaty of Guadalupe-Hidalgo?
5. How did the discovery of gold lead to political change in California?

CHAPTER **9**   REVIEW

SUMMARY

1. American settlers learned to rely on individualism and democracy to meet the demands of frontier life.
2. Frontier farms were responsible for taming the wilderness and opening the West for settlement.
3. Cultural differences, differing views on the use of land, and deceit practiced by some whites led to conflict between Indians and whites.
4. Removal of Indians from their tribal homes removed a barrier to the settlement of western land.
5. American expansion into Texas resulted in war with Mexico and the creation of the Lone Star Republic.

6. California declared its independence from Mexico after a revolt led by Americans.
7. The addition of the Oregon territory to the United States was accomplished through negotiations with Great Britain.
8. Utah was settled by Mormons who moved there to escape religious persecution.
9. Belief in manifest destiny made clashes with Mexico inevitable and led to war between the United States and Mexico in 1846.
10. Victory in war with Mexico, along with purchases and treaty agreements, expanded the United States from the Atlantic Ocean to the Pacific Ocean.

VOCABULARY

thesis	mandate	protectorate	theocracy
empresario	joint resolution	joint occupation	revelation
annexation	cession	expansionism	manifest destiny
provisional government			

REVIEW QUESTIONS

1. Why did Americans settle in territories outside the United States?
2. How did white Americans justify the taking of Indian land?
3. What methods did the United States use to acquire territory?
4. How did the federal government's Indian policy change from colonial times to 1850?
5. How did the administrations from Jackson to Polk address the question of Texas annexation?
6. What measures did Mexico take to halt American colonization of Texas?
7. How did the Mormons react to the persecution of their members?
8. How did the American idea of manifest destiny affect relations with other countries?

DISCUSSION

1. What criticisms can you make of Turner's theory that the demands of frontier life resulted in democracy and individualism?
2. What options were available to resolve the question of Indian removal in the 1830's?
3. If you had lived in the 1840's, would you have supported the war against Mexico?
4. What might have occurred had opponents of the manifest destiny doctrine occupied the White House?

USING MAPS

Refer to the map on page 190 and answer the following questions:

1. In which period did Indians lose the most land?
2. Which present-day states were formed from Indian land acquired between 1811 and 1830?
3. Which Indian tribe followed a route starting in northern Illinois and ending just past the Missouri-Kansas border?
4. What does this map tell about the way land was settled in the United States?

USING SKILLS

Following are statistics that show the median age of the population of the United States from 1820 to 1860:

	Total	Male	Female
1820	16.7	16.6	16.7
1830	17.2	17.1	17.3
1840	17.8	17.8	17.7
1850	18.9	19.2	18.6
1860	19.4	19.8	19.1

Study the statistics and answer the following questions:

1. What is the trend of the median age of the total population between 1820 and 1860?
2. What is the trend of the median age of males? Of females?
3. Is the trend for males changing in a different way than the trend for females?
4. Are the trends consistent?

1	Transportation and Communication	203
2	Industrialization	205
3	Cultural Trends	210
4	The Spirit of Reform	213
5	Women's Rights	217
6	The Antislavery Movement	219
7	The Slave South	222

ANTEBELLUM AMERICA

The ideas of progress and of the indefinite perfectability of the human race belong to democratic ages. Democratic nations care but little for what has been, but they are haunted by visions of what will be.

ALEXIS DE TOCQUEVILLE

America in the years before the Civil War, the antebellum years, was a nation in ferment. While the West was rapidly expanding, the North was going through major changes due to industrialization and immigration.

The antebellum period was a time of great nationalism and optimism. Americans had shown the world that a republican form of government could work, and material progress was bringing many added comforts to daily life. Although society was not yet perfect, no evil seemed impossible to remedy. Reformers attacked every kind of social injustice, including the one issue that threatened to break up the Union: slavery. Slavery was essential to the culture and economy of the South, which had changed little compared to the North and the West. In defense of their "peculiar institution," southerners became more and more determined to maintain their own way of life.

1 Transportation and Communication

Westward expansion during the years 1820 through 1860 had created an urgent need for better connections between the West and the East. Because the federal government repeatedly refused to finance internal improvements, individual states undertook the funding for such projects.

Roads and Canals

During the first half of the 1800's, much effort went into improving the old dirt roads that turned to mud in wet weather. Hard surfaces were made with wooden planks or macadam, a layer of crushed stones. Many new roads were also constructed. By 1860 more than 80,000 miles (128,000 kilometers) of roads crisscrossed the country.

Transportation was also improved by canals. A canal boom was ushered in with the completion of the Erie Canal in 1825. Although not the first canal in the United States, it was by far the longest—363 miles (581 kilometers). By linking Albany on the Hudson River with Buffalo on Lake Erie, the canal allowed goods to be shipped all the way from the Great Lakes region to New York City. Travel time and shipping expenses were cut drastically. As a result, New York City became a major commercial center. Soon other states with major seaports were scrambling to build their own canals.

The Steamboat

Another breakthrough in transportation came with the steamboat. In 1807, the *Clermont,* a steamboat designed by Robert Fulton, made the trip from Albany to New York City in five days, setting a record. In the years between 1830 and 1850, the steamboat became the most important means of transportation on major rivers. Not only were steamboats much faster than any other kind of riverboat, but their ability to travel upstream was a distinct advantage.

The Railroad

Despite the advantages of canals and steamboats, the country still needed a form of cheap, fast land transportation. This was provided by the railroad.

The first railroads were built in England, but it was in the United States that they were developed most fully. Cities without water access to the West

Explain that most railroad lines were built in the North and West rather than in the South because (1) railroads were built by private enterprise and most of the liquid capital was in the hands of northern and western businessmen; (2) denser population and a greater variety of goods produced meant that railroads were more profitable in the North and West than in the overwhelmingly rural, largely one-crop South.

ROADS AND CANALS, 1820–1850

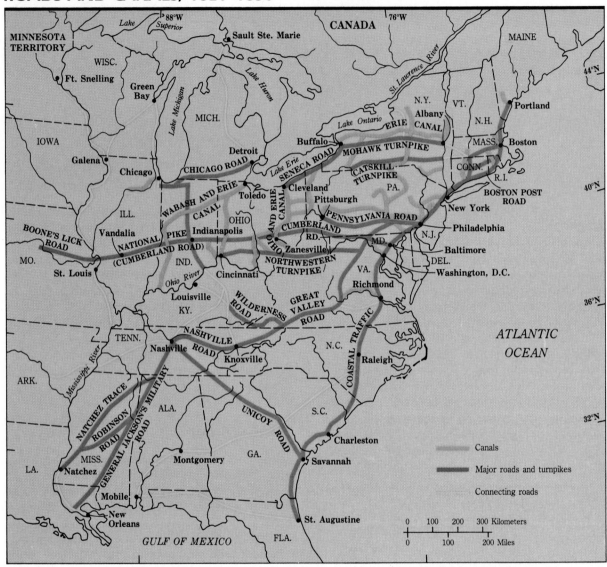

pioneered the building of American railroads. The Baltimore and Ohio Railroad was in operation by 1830. From this limited beginning, railroads spread rapidly. The first big wave of railroad building came in the 1850's.

The railroads opened new areas to settlement and stimulated trade by creating an eastern market for farmers in the West. The railroad's capability for moving raw materials into northern factories and finshed products out to ever-expanding markets also stimulated the growth of industry in the North.

Most of the railroads were built as connections between the North and the West. The South also built railroads, but to a lesser extent. Thus the South became more isolated from the rest of the country and developed fewer and smaller industries.

Overseas Transportation

Overseas trade as well as internal trade prospered during the antebellum years, which became the golden age of American shipping. Yankee clippers were the fastest sailing ships afloat. Their speed was demonstrated when shipbuilder Donald McKay produced the *Flying Cloud,* which made the trip from Boston around South America to San Francisco in only 89 days.

The clippers gave the United States a large share of world trade. Trade with China, which for years had been limited to one port by the Chinese government, was opened to Americans in the 1840's.[1] In 1853 Commodore Matthew Perry managed to negotiate limited trading privileges with Japan. Within a few years, these trading privileges were extended.

By the mid-1850's, however, British steamships were making the clippers obsolete, and Americans lost much of their overseas trade. The end of the clipper was also hastened by the construction of a railroad across Panama in 1855. This ended the need for the long trip around South America.

Communication

Commercial and industrial growth were further encouraged by improvements in communication. In 1844 Samuel F. Morse perfected the telegraph, and, soon, telegraph lines were strung throughout the country. In 1858 Cyrus Field laid the first telegraph cable across the Atlantic Ocean.

Mail delivery also slowly improved, along with transportation. At first, mail was delivered only to post offices, and people had to pick it up. Later, it was delivered to people's homes. In 1847 the Post Office Department issued the first national stamps.

SECTION REVIEW

1. Identify the following: Erie Canal, Robert Fulton, Donald McKay, Matthew Perry, Samuel F. Morse, Cyrus Field.
2. What were the advantages of canals and steamboats?
3. What benefits did railroads offer that water transportation did not?
4. What helped make clipper ships obsolete?

---

[1] Trade was opened as a result of the British victory over the Chinese in the Opium War of 1839–1842. The United States successfully negotiated for the same trading privileges won by the British.

2 Industrialization

Improved transportation and communication increased the importance of northern cities as centers of trade. As city merchants grew wealthier, they sought investments that would further increase their business. Much of their **capital,** or investment money, went into new manufacturing industries.

Early Factories

In 1820 most manufacturing was done in homes or small shops. After 1820, however, the **factory system** began to take over. In factories, the total process of manufacturing took place at one location. The need for a single location was due chiefly to the use of new sources of power—water and steam. The first factories used water power and were built in rural areas along rivers and streams.

The Boston Manufacturing Company at Waltham, Massachusetts, was the first factory to combine all

---

In early textile factories, women published their own periodicals. The *Lowell Offering* was "a repository of original articles written exclusively by females" employed in the Lowell mills. What other activities were available under the Waltham System?

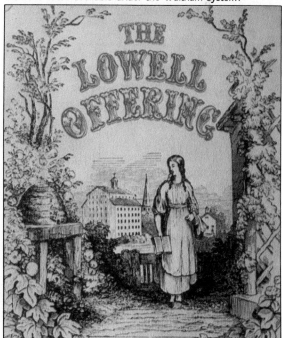

Note that factory work was not considered to be inherently unfeminine in the early years of industrialization. However, when inexpensive male labor became available, it was preferred by factory owners. Ask students to explain why.

the operations for making cotton cloth under one management. The "Waltham System" included an attempt to provide decent working and living conditions for workers. Labor was still scarce, as it had been since colonial times. Women and girls were recruited from New England farms to work in the Waltham factory. The factories were clean and pleasant. The women lived under strict supervision in company-owned boarding houses. In the evenings they attended social gatherings and educational programs sponsored by the company.

The Waltham System was tried on a larger scale in Lowell, Massachusetts. Other factories employed whole families. The system began to break down, however, as competition increased, factories grew in size, and new forms of technology changed the way products were made.

New Technology

Advances in technology took place first in the textile industry. In 1814 Frances Lowell and Paul Moody perfected the power loom for weaving cloth. In 1846 Elias Howe introduced the sewing machine which revolutionized the shoe, clothing, and leather industries. During the 1850's hundreds of factories were producing ready-made shoes and clothes. Textile manufacturing became the core of the New England economy.

In 1844 Charles Goodyear discovered vulcanization, a chemical treatment of natural rubber that made it resist heat and cold. The rubber-goods industry was soon turning out hundreds of products. Improvements in methods of iron production allowed the iron industry to expand to meet the needs of railroads and makers of machinery. Eli Whitney's system of interchangeable parts, together with steam power and the new types of machinery, made **mass production** (production in large quantities) a reality.

The Corporation

Along with these developments came a new instrument by which business owners could acquire capital for large investments—the corporation. A **corporation** is a group of people with the same legal status as one person, distinct from the people who make up the group. A corporation can own property, make contracts, sue and be sued.

The biggest advantage of the corporation is the limited liability (financial responsibility) of its owners. The owners are people who buy shares of **stock** (certificates of ownership) sold to the public. Money from the sale of shares becomes capital for running the business. But owners cannot lose more money than they have invested in their stock. If a corporation goes bankrupt, the owners do not have to pay its debts with their personal property.

These German villagers bid farewell to their friends and families as they prepare to emigrate to America. Harsh rule led to numerous uprisings in several of the German states. Many Germans looked to the United States as a haven for the oppressed. For what other reasons did immigrants come to America?

Note that America attracted—and continues to attract—immigrants because it has always been perceived as a land of economic opportunity and political freedom. Even low wages seemed good to many who came from Europe.

Ask students to calculate the overall increase in immigration between 1821 and 1860. (Note that 1820 was the first year that immigration statistics were kept.)

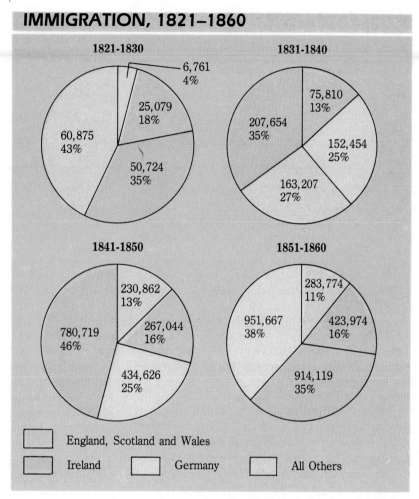

IMMIGRATION, 1821–1860

1821-1830

6,761 — 4%
25,079 18%
60,875 43%
50,724 35%

1831-1840

75,810 13%
207,654 35%
152,454 25%
163,207 27%

1841-1850

230,862 13%
780,719 46%
267,044 16%
434,626 25%

1851-1860

283,774 11%
951,667 38%
423,974 16%
914,119 35%

England, Scotland and Wales
Ireland   Germany   All Others

Immigration

At the same time as the corporation and new technology were changing the nature of industry, a new source of labor appeared. During the 1830's and 1840's, economic and political upheavals in Europe brought a massive wave of immigration to the United States. In Ireland, the potato crop failed several years in a row, causing famine and flight to America. In 1848 a series of revolutions in Europe failed. Political refugees, in particular large numbers of Germans, flocked to the United States.

While many of the immigrants were farmers or professionals, most were unskilled peasants. Without money to move west, they stayed in the northern port cities where they first arrived. There they became a huge unskilled labor force.

Industrial Change

Unskilled immigrants could be hired at low wages. Under the system of mass production, less skill was required from the workers. The making of a product was divided into small, repetitive tasks. The products were not so well-made as those produced by skilled artisans, but the loss of quality was thought to be less important than the gain in quantity. Working conditions deteriorated as workers became less valuable, more easily replaced.

The coincidence of cheap labor with technological and legal developments had a tremendous impact on industry. Whereas early factories were located in rural areas, newer factories were built in the cities. There, labor was supplied by immigrants and power by steam. A woman who had worked in the early

Have students speculate about the psychological effects industrialization had on artisans and other skilled workers. Are there similar threats in modern America?

Point out that one reason the largely rural Irish immigrants settled in eastern coastal cities is that lack of money forced them to remain wherever their ship landed. Have students discuss why immigrants, especially the Irish, were perceived as "a threat to the American way of life."

AMERICAN BUSINESS CYCLES, 1790-1860

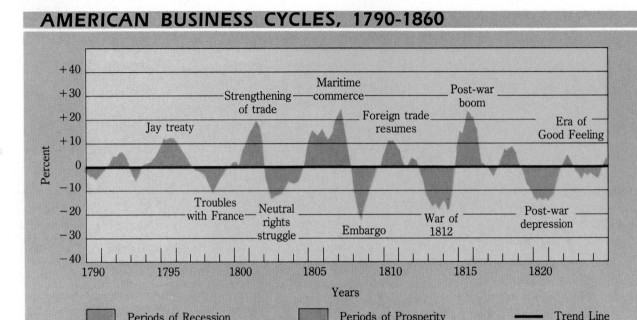

Lowell factories described the difference between the old factories and the new.

> *Once they were light, well ventilated, and moderately heated. Each factory building stood detached, with pleasant sunlit windows, cheerful views, and fresh air from all points of the compass. But these buildings are now made into a solid mass by connecting "annexes" and often form a hollow square, so that at least one half of the operatives can have no outlook except upon brick walls, and no fresh air but that which circulates within this confined space.*

Social Conflict

The changes in industry were hard on workers, both the old artisans and the new immigrants. The position of artisans and mechanics in the community was threatened. Once they had been able to corner local markets. But now the factory system could produce more goods for less money, and improved transportation systems allowed mass-produced goods to be sold anywhere in the country. As the value of their skills decreased, the artisans and

mechanics had to work longer hours for less pay. Much of their resentment and frustration was directed toward the new labor force, especially the Irish immigrants.

The plight of the Irish immigrants, however, was not to be envied. Uprooted from the peasant world they had known in Ireland, they found themselves in an unfamilar environment. With no skills to peddle, they became the working poor of the industrial cities, performing the most menial tasks. Wages were low, hours were long, and the work was often dirty and dangerous.

Living conditions were even worse. Since the immigrant workers could not afford transportation, they lived close to their jobs in the inner city. There, large families doubled up—or even tripled up—in single rooms. Sanitation was very poor. As a result, the Irish section of town was a breeding place for disease. Smallpox, cholera, and tuberculosis were common. Of 700 people who died in Boston from a cholera epidemic in 1849, more than 500 were Irish.

Because of their poverty and their cultural differences, the Irish became victims of unfortunate stereotypes. Furthermore, their Catholic religion led to hostility on the part of some Protestant Americans. On occasion, hostility bred violence. **Nativist,** or

Note that some leading Americans, including Thomas Jefferson and Henry David Thoreau, perceived city life as artificial and corrupting because it was out of touch with nature. Novels of English urban life, such as those by Charles Dickens, reinforced this negative image of the city.

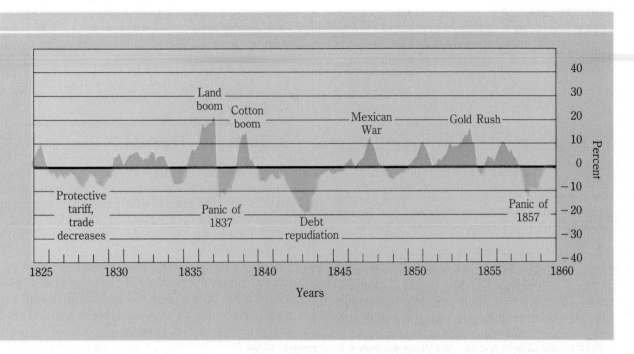

anti-foreign, sentiment even led to the development of the "Know-Nothing" party in the 1850's. When asked about the party, members said, "I know nothing." The Know-Nothings saw the immigrants as a threat to the American way of life. They urged Protestants to unite against the Catholic "menace," and called for stricter immigration laws.

Growth of Cities

Immigration and the growth of factories greatly increased the number of people in northern cities. While the total American population increased from 17 million in 1840 to 31 million in 1860, the urban population more than tripled, from under 2 million to over 6 million. By 1860 over 40 percent of the labor force worked at nonfarm jobs.

Rapid growth of the cities created new problems. Before industrialization, members of most urban communities were closely tied to each other. People had common interests to hold them together. Relatives often lived close to one another. People of all classes lived in the same neighborhoods. Relationships among neighbors were marked by mutual concern and obligations. The economic and social leaders were commonly the political leaders as well.

As more and more people moved into the cities, many of these older ties were broken. Fewer neighbors were related to one another. Residential patterns changed as rich families moved to exclusive neighborhoods, and middle-class families moved away from the inner city. Religious differences also increased as Protestant churches splintered, and the Roman Catholic Church—the church of the Irish— grew. Finally, the old personal relationships between employers and workers broke down in the face of the factory system.

Material Progress

Although industrial growth caused problems, economic progress also made life easier in many ways. Improved transportation and mass production meant that more goods were available to more people. American living standards were surpassing those of European countries.

In the cities, people were beginning to enjoy new comforts and conveniences such as gas streetlights and better sewer systems. Some homes had piped-in water and central heating with hot-air furnaces. Better designs made stoves more efficient for heating and cooking.

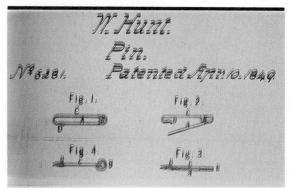

The safety pin, made by W. Hunt, was one of the many patents granted in the 1800's. What were other inventions of the time that gave Americans a reputation for "Yankee ingenuity"?

On the farms, work became somewhat easier with the invention of the cast-iron plow and, later, the steel plow. In 1831 Cyrus Hall McCormick invented a mechanical reaper that soon came into widespread use. Mowing, threshing, and haying machines also made the work easier and increased production.

Partly because of the chronic labor shortage in the United States, Americans had always been open to new methods or machinery that would increase efficiency. As early as 1790 the federal government had passed patent laws to encourage inventions. **Patents** gave inventors exclusive rights to the profits from their ideas for a certain number of years. During the years before the Civil War, inventions were made at such a pace that Americans became known in Europe for their "Yankee ingenuity."

Americans came to believe that they were living in an age of progress. Optimistically, they expected that Yankee ingenuity, along with America's abundant resources and democratic ways, would eventually lead to an ideal society, an example for other countries of the world. English author Harriet Martineau, who visited in the United States, said that Americans were "in possession of the glorious certainty that time and exertion will infallibly secure all wisely desired objects."

SECTION REVIEW

1. Identify the following: Waltham System, Elias Howe, Know-Nothing Party.
2. What industries were revolutionized by improved technology in the 1840's and 50's?
3. What are the features of a corporation?
4. What new source of labor appeared in the 1830's and 1840's?
5. How did industrial changes affect artisans and mechanics?
6. What disadvantages did the Irish immigrants face?

3 Cultural Trends

The optimism of the antebellum years was well-suited to a cultural movement called **romanticism,** which took place in both Europe and America during the first half of the 1800's. Romanticism was a revolt against the logic, order, and reason of the Enlightenment.

Romanticism valued emotion and imagination over reason, nature over civilization, and the wisdom of the common people over the sophistication of the upper classes. Romantics were interested in folklore and legend; in exotic, faraway places; and in the supernatural. The romantic hero was an individualist who rebelled against unjust rules. This stress on individualism and the virtues of the common people fitted the democratic spirit of the Age of Jackson.

Transcendentalism

The romantic view was best expressed in the United States by a philosophy called **transcendentalism.** The word came from the optimistic idea that human beings could transcend or rise above reason. Transcendentalism was not an organized movement, but rather a loose body of ideas developed by a group of people in Massachusetts. They disapproved of the scramble for wealth that they saw going on around them. Progress, they thought, should be spiritual.

The leading transcendentalist was Ralph Waldo Emerson, a poet, essayist, and lecturer. He believed in a universal soul of which everything was a part. Individualism was a basic part of Emerson's philosophy. "Whoso would be a man must be a nonconformist," he wrote. In this view he was joined by another member of the group, Henry David Thoreau. "If a man does not keep pace with his companion," Thoreau wrote, "perhaps it is because he hears a different drummer." In 1845 Thoreau built a cabin beside Walden Pond, on some land owned by

Emerson, and lived there alone for two years. Thoreau's purpose was to show that a person need not depend on society to live. His book *Walden* told the story of his experiment.

Thoreau was also a political nonconformist. To protest the Mexican War, he refused to pay his taxes. For this he was jailed briefly, until an aunt paid the tax for him. Thoreau then published an essay in favor of **civil disobedience,** or refusing to obey unjust laws in order to call attention to their injustice.

Literature and Art

The various themes of romanticism were taken up in different ways by writers of poetry and fiction. James Fenimore Cooper's hero, Natty Bumppo, was an early expression of a romantic theme. Natty Bumppo was a natural man, an innocent in the wilderness, continually in conflict with civilization. In the mid-1800's this theme was taken up by other writers. Nathaniel Hawthorne's *The Scarlet Letter* explored the tension between a natural woman and the rules of Puritan society. Herman Melville's heroes moved from innocence through bitterness in *Moby Dick* (1851) to new hope in *Billy Budd* (unfinished until 1891).

Edgar Allen Poe was a romantic writer who had a gloomy imagination and a fascination with the supernatural. His poem "The Raven" brought him his first fame. He was one of the writers who invented the modern detective story. He was also a master of horror tales such as "The Pit and the Pendulum" and "The Tell Tale Heart."

One of the best known of the romantic poets was Walt Whitman. He was deeply influenced by the writings of Emerson, who felt strongly that American literature should have a distinct cultural identity. Whitman's book, *Leaves of Grass,* was written in free verse. That is, the poems did not have a regular rhythm. His nonconformist poetry revealed his optimism, patriotism, and love of nature.

Another of the romantic poets was Henry Wadsworth Longfellow. He is most famous for his long poems on themes of American history, such as *The Song of Hiawatha* and *The Courtship of Miles Standish.*

American artists of this period also expressed the romantics' appreciation of nature. Thomas Cole painted wilderness scenes. John James Audubon painted American wildlife in rich detail.

Composers took the themes of art and literature and set them to music. Anthony Phillip Hendrich wrote orchestral pieces on the Indians and scenes of nature. George F. Bristow was the first American to compose an opera on an American theme, *Rip Van Winkle.*

Popular Culture

The technology of the early industrial period made art and literature available to more people than ever before. Sculptures and paintings could be mechanically reproduced and sold at low prices. Improved methods of printing lowered costs and brought novels and magazines into American homes. The first penny newspaper, the New York *Sun,* was published in 1833. Full of gossip and crime stories as well as political news, the *Sun* set an example that was copied by other newspapers.

The American people were hungry for knowledge and culture. Self-improvement books were widely read. People flocked to debates, lectures, and stage shows. They formed organizations called **lyceums,** which held discussions and lectures, put together libraries, and called for better schools.

Religion

The desire for self-improvement was closely connected to a renewed interest in religion. By 1800 revivals were beginning on college campuses, and revivalism soon spread throughout the country. Almost every religious denomination formed missionary societies for home and abroad. The American Bible Society was founded in 1816 to distribute Bibles. Groups called "tract societies" put out religious pamphlets.

By the 1830's the Second Great Awakening, the second great period of religious revival in America, was in full swing. It had the greatest impact on the frontier, where the most successful preachers were Baptists and Methodists.

Thousands of people were converted at camp meeting revivals. The camp meeting was especially important to isolated frontier families, who had few chances to get together socially. In the West people

Ask students to examine the role of emotion in religious belief and practice.

Point out that the U.S. has by far the greatest variety of Christian denominations in the world. Most countries have only a few, with one predominating. The constant splitting of groups and the founding of new ones in this country is another example of American tendencies toward individualism and perfectionism.

"Dream of Arcadia" (above) by Thomas Cole is a landscape with a definite American style. Stephen Foster's "plantation melodies" (p. 213, left) are rooted in American folk tradition. John J. Audubon painted birds of the United States (p. 213, right). American romanticism was reflected in the art, music, and literature of the time. Who were some authors who developed a distinctly American style?

turned out in large numbers to hear traveling preachers. One preacher, James Finley, described a camp meeting as follows:

> The noise was like the roar of Niagara. . . . Some of the people were singing, others praying, some crying for mercy in the most piteous accents, while others were shouting most vociferously. . . . At one time I saw at least five hundred swept down in a moment, as if a battery of a thousand guns had been opened upon them, and then immediately followed shrieks and shouts that rent the very heavens.

Religion had always been part of the American experience. Over the years, however, the nature of religion had changed. In colonial times the Puritan Church had been most influential, but Puritan influence had weakened with the growth of religious tolerance. Partly as a result of the first Great Awakening in the early 1700's, a number of new churches had been formed, giving people more choice in matters of religion.

The ideas of the Enlightenment had also led to the rejection of Puritan beliefs. For a group called the deists, which included Thomas Jefferson, Benjamin Franklin, and Thomas Paine, religion meant the use of reason to understand God's natural law. Although they accepted Christian ethics, they did not believe that Jesus Christ was divine. Some of the ideas of the deists were taken up by the Unitarians. They saw Christ not as divine but as a good man and a model for moral behavior. Unitarians did not believe in the Puritan idea of predestination. They thought that a person could choose to be good. William Ellery Channing, who founded the Unitarian Church, said, "The adoration of goodness—this is religion." Similar to Unitarianism was Universalism, which preached universal salvation and denied the existence of hell.

Thus the idea of predestination gave way to a belief in the importance of individual choice. This idea was found to an even greater extent in the Second Great Awakening, which had the optimistic, democratic, individualistic nature of antebellum America. Everyone was seen as equal before God. Anyone could be saved. Furthermore, if enough people could be

Note that prior to the 20th century, government efforts to reform society were limited to the occasional passage of protective legislation. Most organizations and institutions designed to help people were private.

Robert Owen was a British factory owner whose ideas ultimately became too radical for his followers.

perfected through religion, society, too, could be perfected. Charles G. Finney and other revival leaders urged their followers to practice good works.

SECTION REVIEW

1. Identify the following: Walt Whitman, John James Audubon, American Bible Society, William Ellery Channing.
2. What did the transcendentalists believe?
3. Why did Thoreau live alone at Walden Pond?
4. How did the new technology help spread culture?
5. In what way was the Second Great Awakening optimistic?

4 The Spirit of Reform

During the first half of the 1800's, many Americans were interested in perfecting their society. The result was an age of social reform, which was strengthened by the religious revivals of the Second Great Awakening. Reformers banded together in voluntary organizations to work for their goals. Voluntary organizations provided social ties that were missing in a rapidly changing industrial society.

Utopias

Some of the most interesting voluntary organizations were the **utopias,** or communities seeking to achieve perfection. People who were discouraged by the effects of industrialization and religious groups who wished to pursue their own ideas formed their own societies. The utopias were intended to show the world in general how an ideal community would work. Robert Owen established New Harmony in Indiana to show how a perfect division of labor would lead to harmony in society. The purpose of Brook Farm, near Boston, was much the same. Labor was divided so that there was time for intellectual pursuits. As its founder George Ripley explained, it aimed to

prepare a society of liberal, intelligent, and cultivated persons, whose relations with each other would permit a more wholesome and simple life than can be led amidst the pressure of our competitive institutions.

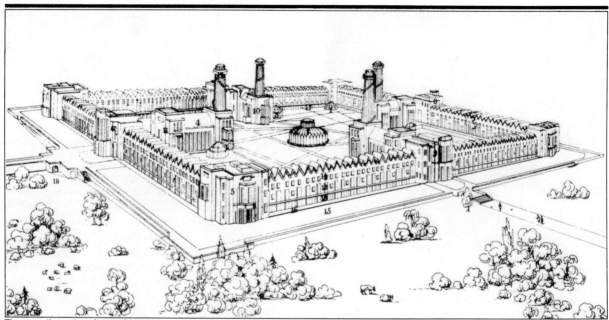

The grandiose plans for the New Harmony utopia never came to fruition. As Emerson wrote, "... utopia was sought less as a refuge against religious oppression and more as an asylum for those unhappy with the aggressive materialistic aspects of society." Do you think such a "utopia" would work today?

The Oneida community, founded by John Humphrey Noyes in western New York, was an example of a radical religious community. The people of the Oneida group did not believe in private property or in traditional marriage and family arrangements. Another radical religious group was the Shakers, founded by preacher Ann Lee in 1774. Although she died in 1784, by the 1830's her followers had established several successful communities in New England. The Shakers, who were so named because they danced and shouted as they worshipped, later became famous for their furniture designs.

Although dozens of utopias were founded in these years, most lasted for only a short time. Money troubles, internal dissent, and natural disasters contributed to their downfall.

Prison Reform

Some reformers were more practical than the utopians. Rather than remake society as a whole, they tried to correct specific problems.

One of the evils attacked by the practical reformers was the treatment of criminals. Prison conditions in the early 1800's were wretched. Reformers in New York and Pennsylvania set up new prison systems in the 1820's. New York's Auburn System tried to rehabilitate prisoners by dividing their time into work, Bible study, and meditation. Prisoners were not allowed to talk to each other and had little contact with the outside world. The Pennsylvania System provided total solitary confinement and solitary labor. Although this system was intended to help, it drove some prisoners mad.

Imprisonment for debt was gradually abolished, state by state, in the first half of the 1800's. The death penalty for many crimes was eliminated, and whipping of prisoners was outlawed. In many states child offenders were separated from adults and given special schooling.

Mental Hospitals

Another problem tackled by practical reformers was treatment of the insane. Although a few mental hospitals had been established by the mid-1800's, most people thought to be insane were kept in jails, poorhouses, or private homes. The person who had the most influence on changing this treatment was Dorothea Dix. As a Sunday school teacher at the

House of Correction near Boston, she was appalled to find that the mentally ill were kept in unheated cells, separate from other prisoners.

Dix spent the following months visiting all the jails and poorhouses in Massachusetts. She took notes on what she saw and made a report to the Massachusetts legislature. People were shocked by her vivid description of sick persons "in cages, closets, cellars, stalls, pens, chained naked, beaten with rods and lashed into obedience." The Massachusetts lawmakers agreed to spend the money for better care of the mentally ill.

Dix then carried her campaign beyond Massachusetts. As a result of her efforts, many states established mental hospitals.

Temperance

Concern for prisoners and the insane was closely related to another reform movement—**temperance,** or the control of drinking habits. Many people, including leaders of the Second Great Awakening, believed that drinking was the cause of poverty, crime, and a host of other social evils.

By the 1820's the temperance movement had attracted over a million followers. Some advised only that people limit their drinking. Others said that people should not drink at all, not even beer or wine. Eventually some states passed laws prohibiting the sale of alcoholic drinks. These laws were so unpopular, however, that they were soon repealed.

Educational Reform

Education was seen by some reformers as a means to control social problems such as drinking, poverty, and crime. Although New England had free public elementary schools, support for education had declined. In other parts of the country, educational opportunities were worse, except for those who could attend private schools or have private tutors.

The leader of educational reform was Horace Mann, a lawyer who became Massachusetts' first superintendent of education in 1837. During his term, state money for schools was increased, teacher-training schools were established, and teachers' salaries were raised.

Mann felt that free public education was the only means by which democracy could be preserved. He said that education was the "great equalizer" and the "balance wheel of the social machinery." Educated people, Mann believed, would never remain

A daguerreotype of a class at the Emerson School in Boston in 1850. Every prominent American put education high on the list of priorities to attain a successful and powerful United States. It was not considered necessary to educate girls beyond some reading, writing and "reckoning," so that they could keep household accounts. Which state university was the first to admit women?

permanently poor. He also argued that educated workers could better serve the needs of industry.

By the mid-1800's public elementary schools were being established in many northern states. Public high schools were also growing in number, though more slowly. College education was expanded and reformed. Large numbers of small religious colleges were founded, and by the 1850's, 16 states had set up state universities. Courses were expanded to include literature, history, science, and other subjects.

Education for Women. Education for women was still restricted. Although many private schools accepted women, they were taught mostly domestic and social skills and religion. As the century progressed, pioneers in women's education began to move away from this limited course of study. Although early pioneers like Catherine Beecher and Emma Hart Willard felt that women should be educated for their traditional roles in life, they did think that women could be capable teachers.

Beecher, who felt women could be trained as "missionary teachers," emphasized domestic science and physical fitness. Her pamphlet, *Essay on the Education of the Female Teacher,* was considered a classic. The Milwaukee College for Women set up courses based on her ideas, "to train women to be healthful, intelligent, and successful wives, mothers, and housekeepers." Emma Hart Willard's Troy Female Seminary, which opened in 1821, however, taught mathematics, history, geography, and physics, as well as the usual homemaking subjects.

The best known of the early female educators was Mary Lyon, founder of Mount Holyoke College in Massachusetts. She, too, wanted to train women as teachers and missionaries. Mount Holyoke opened in 1837 with entrance requirements and instruction on the same level as men's colleges.

Further advances were made as women were accepted at previously all-male institutions. In 1837 Oberlin in Ohio became the first private college to admit women. The University of Iowa, in 1856, was the first state-supported school to do so.

Education for Blacks. Education for blacks was also extremely limited. In the South, education of slaves was generally forbidden. In the North, if public schooling was provided, it was usually separate and inferior. In cases where blacks and whites attended the same schools, blacks had to sit in special seats and were subjected to other mistreatment. As a result, blacks in the North began to operate their own schools. Usually the schools were run by black churches or charities. Funds were often obtained from antislavery groups.

On the college level, some private schools began to admit blacks in the 1820's. Two all-black colleges were opened in the 1850's. Presbyterians founded the Ashmun Institute in Pennsylvania, later known as Lincoln University, to train black missionaries for Africa. In 1855 the African Methodist Episcopal Church founded Wilberforce College in Ohio.

Labor Reform

Labor reformers called for many of the same changes as reformers in other fields. They wanted free public schools, an end to imprisonment for debt, limits to child labor, and universal free white manhood suffrage. Unions were formed by the workers to deal with their problems. In the early days, usually only skilled white male workers were involved.

What the workers wanted most of all was a 10-hour day—that is, 12 hours with 2 hours off for meals. Strikes, or work stoppages, were attempted in order to achieve this goal. However, the courts usually ruled that strikes were illegal. Employers could force workers back to the job through court action, or simply hire nonunion labor.

Beginning in the 1820's, workers also began to join workingmen's parties. These were political associations that campaigned for workers' goals. The unions and workingmen's parties were severely weakened by the Panic of 1837, which led to high levels of unemployment. Nevertheless some of labor's goals were reached. Universal white manhood suffrage, free public education, and an end to debtor imprisonment came about through other reform movements. In 1842 Massachusetts recognized the right to strike in *Commonwealth* v. *Hunt.* In some cities the 10-hour day was established. In 1840 President Van Buren declared a 10-hour day for work done for the federal government. Some states also limited child labor.

The Peace Movement

One of the most idealistic reform movements was the peace movement. Many reformers agreed that war was the greatest evil of all. After the War of 1812, peace societies were formed in various parts of the United States. In 1828 these groups were combined by William Ladd into the American Peace Society.

Most members of the peace movement were against the Mexican War of 1846–1848. Some people approved of defensive wars. Others insisted that killing even in self-defense was not morally justified.

SECTION REVIEW

1. Identify the following: Robert Owen, Dorothea Dix, Horace Mann, Catherine Beecher, Mary Lyon, William Ladd.
2. Why were utopian communities established?
3. What prison reforms were tried in the early 1800's?
4. How was education improved?
5. What associations did workers form to help them deal with their problems?

5 Women's Rights

Many women were active in various reform movements. In working for the rights of others, they were often made aware of their own lack of rights. For example, they were forbidden by custom from speaking in front of mixed groups. When antislavery reformers Sarah and Angelina Grimke tried to speak to mixed groups, they found themselves booed by the men. In 1840 the World Antislavery Convention in London refused to seat women delegates. Experiences such as these propelled women into a fight for their own cause. Angelina Grimke wrote:

> We are placed very unexpectedly in a very trying situation, in the forefront of an entirely new contest—a contest for the rights of woman as a moral, intelligent and responsible being.

On the frontier, where men and women faced hardship and loneliness together, a good deal of equality existed between the sexes. In the more settled portions of the country, however, women were supposed to be "ladies." They were expected to be pure, delicate, and dependent on men. Woman's place was in the home. They were expected to take care of children, do household duties, and act as servants to men.

A single woman was legally the ward of her nearest male relative. A married woman was part of her husband's personal property. A husband was responsible for crimes committed by his wife in his presence or with his consent. Wife beating "with a reasonable instrument" was legal in almost every state. Women had no right to vote or to own property. They could not keep their own earnings or file a lawsuit. In case of divorce, they often were not allowed to keep their children. Many careers, such as medicine, law, and the ministry, were closed to women.

One of the first American statements of women's rights was made in 1845 by Margaret Fuller, editor of the transcendentalist magazine, the *Dial*. She published a book, *Women in the Nineteenth Century,* in which she argued women's basic equality to man.

The first of a series of women's rights conventions was organized by Lucretia Mott and Elizabeth Cady

Elizabeth Blackwell was the first woman physician in the United States. She helped break down prejudice against women in the professions. On what area was most of the early women's rights movement centered?

EQUAL RIGHTS FOR WOMEN

WOMEN'S RIGHTS

Elizabeth Cady Stanton
Susan B. Anthony

Two of the most prominent leaders of the women's rights movement were Elizabeth Cady Stanton and Susan B. Anthony. Elizabeth Cady, born in 1815, rebelled early in life against the view that women were inferior to men. In 1820 her only brother died. When she tried to comfort her father, he said, "Ah, my daughter, I wish you were a boy." She resolved to prove that a daughter was as good as a son.

Cady studied Greek, Latin, and other subjects that were considered masculine, and in 1832 graduated from the Troy Female Seminary. As a result of her work for the temperance and antislavery causes, she met and married abolitionist Henry Stanton. Soon she became involved in the controversy over the seating of women delegates at the World Antislavery Convention in London.

Along with Lucretia Mott, Stanton organized the first women's rights convention in the United States. At this convention she drafted the Declaration of Rights and Sentiments and made the first public demand for women's right to vote.

In 1851 Stanton met Susan B. Anthony. Anthony, born in 1820, was the daughter of a Quaker and had been taught the Quaker belief that men and women are equal before God. Stanton and Anthony began a collaboration that lasted 50 years. Their talents were complementary. Anthony was a skilled and tireless organizer who enjoyed traveling and campaigning. Stanton was a talented speaker and writer, but with seven children she could not do much traveling.

Stanton and Anthony fought for black rights as well as women's rights. During the Civil War they organized the Women's Loyal National League, which presented to Congress a petition with 300,000 signatures, calling for an immediate end to slavery. After the war, however, Stanton and Anthony were afraid that giving black males the right to vote would add weight to the forces against women's suffrage. They opposed black suffrage unless women also received the right to vote.

In 1869 Stanton and Anthony formed a women's suffrage organization. Other women who opposed their stand formed a rival organization. About 20 years later, the two united as the National American Woman Suffrage Association. Stanton was president of the group for two years, and Anthony for eight years. But neither lived to see the passage of the Nineteenth Amendment, giving women the right to vote in 1920.

Stanton and held in Seneca Falls, New York, in 1848. This convention adopted a Declaration of Sentiments. Modeled after the Declaration of Independence, it began by saying, "We hold these truths to be self-evident: that all men and women are created equal. . . ." The women listed 18 grievances. They passed nine resolutions, including demands for less discrimination in education and employment, and one in favor of women's suffrage.

Most of the concern of the early women's movement centered on women's rights in marriage and the home. After much effort, Mott and Stanton succeeded in getting New York to pass the Married Women's Property Act of 1848. It gave women certain limited rights to control their own property.

Another leader of the women's movement was Susan B. Anthony. After attending her first women's rights convention in 1852, she devoted her exceptional organizational and political skills to the cause.

Against tremendous odds, many women struggled against what Stanton called their "degraded and inferior position." Elizabeth Blackwell was the first female graduate of an American medical school. She had been admitted only because the school thought her application was a joke. Maria Mitchell taught herself astronomy and made a name for herself by discovering a comet in 1847. Other women were successful authors and artists. One prominent example was Louisa May Alcott, author of *Little Women* and many other well-known books.

SECTION REVIEW

1. Identify the following: Angelina Grimke, Margaret Fuller, Elizabeth Stanton, Elizabeth Blackwell.

2. Why did the treatment of women differ from region to region?

3. What were some of the rights denied to women?

4. What actions did women take in the fight for equality?

6 The Antislavery Movement

Of all the reform movements that took place in the early 1800's, the one with most far-reaching consequences was the antislavery movement. The movement for **abolition** (putting an end to slavery) had begun even before the American Revolution. The first antislavery society was formed by Quakers in 1775. It was not until the 1830's, however, that abolition became a major cause.

Early Efforts

By 1800 several states in the north had abolished slavery, although the rights of free blacks were far from equal. Slavery had also been prohibited in the Northwest Territory. Antislavery reformers were active in the South as well. Of 143 **emancipation** (freedom) societies that existed in 1826, 103 were in the South.

The American Colonization Society was established in 1817 with the purpose of freeing the slaves and returning them to Africa. Some of those in favor of colonization wanted to protect blacks from American racism and show how well blacks could do on their own. Others wanted only to get rid of blacks. Most black leaders were opposed to colonization. In

spite of the leaders' opposition, several thousand slaves were taken to Liberia, a nation established especially for free blacks. The number was small, however, compared to the millions still in bondage.

Of the several abolitionist newspapers that existed in the early 1800's, the most important was the *Genius of Universal Emancipation*. Its publisher, Benjamin Lundy, called for the federal government to abolish slavery in the territories, allow no more new slave states in to the Union, put an end to the slave trade, and repeal the three-fifths Compromise. Recognizing that the South depended economically on

The American Anti-Slavery Almanac carried the message of emancipation throughout the United States. The journal stressed slavery's denial of human rights. Which was the most important of the abolitionist newspapers that existed in the early 1800's?

NORTHERN HOSPITALITY—NEW YORK NINE MONTHS' LAW.
The slave steps out of the slave-state, and his chains fall. A free state, with another chain, stands ready to re-enslave him.

Thus saith the Lord, Deliver him that is spoiled out of the hands of the oppressor.

NEW YORK:
PUBLISHED BY THE AMERICAN ANTI-SLAVERY SOCIETY,
NO. 143 NASSAU STREET.

the slaves, Lundy and other moderates called for gradual emancipation.

Radical Abolition

By 1830 it was clear that the antislavery reformers were not reaching their goals. At this point William Lloyd Garrison appeared with a much more radical approach. He was against gradual emancipation and colonization. Through his newspaper, the *Liberator,* founded in 1831, Garrison demanded slavery's immediate and total abolition. In the first issue, Garrison made his position clear. He wrote:

> *On this subject, I do not wish to think, or speak, or write, with moderation. . . . . I am in earnest. I will not equivocate—I will not excuse—I will not retreat a single inch—AND I WILL BE HEARD.*

Garrison's forceful words were matched by other writers, most notably ex-slave David Walker. In 1829 he published *Walker's Appeal in Four Articles,* a pamphlet which called for black revolt.

The abolition movement grew because of the work of people like Garrison and Walker. The emancipation of slaves throughout the British Empire in 1833 encouraged American reformers. Even more important was the influence of the Second Great Awakening. Charles G. Finney called on all Christians to end slavery:

> *Let Christians of all denominations meekly but firmly come forth, and pronounce their verdict, let them clear their communions, and wash their hands of this thing, let them give forth and write on the head and front of this great abomination, SIN! and in three years a public sentiment would be formed that would carry all before it, and there would not be a shackled slave in this land. . . .*

In December 1833, the American Antislavery Society was formed. By 1838 there were 1350 local societies in the national organization, with a total membership of about 250,000. Within the society, however, there were disagreements over tactics. Garrison supported women's rights and other reform movements. He also opposed political action as a way to end slavery, because politics meant compromise.

Another group, led by Arthur and Lewis Tappan, broke with Garrison over these issues and formed their own society. In 1839 the Tappans and James Birney, an ex-slaveholder, formed the Liberty Party. In 1840 and 1844 Birney ran for President on the Liberty Party ticket. In order to broaden the party's appeal, its members dropped their commitment to total abolition. They changed to a position that called for limiting slavery to states where it already existed.

Black Support

Free blacks supported abolition wholeheartedly. They made up most of the subscribers to abolitionist newspapers such as the *Liberator.* They also printed their own papers, such as *Freedom's Journal* and *The Colored American.* They formed their own organizations as well as joining those formed by whites. Well-known black leaders of the movement included Frederick Douglass, Samuel Ward, Lunsford Lane, and Sojourner Truth.

Blacks were active in the famous "Underground Railroad," a series of escape routes to the North for runaway slaves. Over the years, more than 50,000 slaves were aided in their escapes. The most famous "conductor" on this "railroad" was Harriet Tubman. A fugitive slave herself, her repeated trips to the South helped over 300 slaves to escape, earning her the title, "Moses of her people."

Reaction

To most white Americans in the North, the abolitionist movement held little appeal. Efforts of the abolitionists to end discrimination against free blacks aroused hostility. Angry mobs in the North, upset by what they felt to be the extreme positions of some abolitionists, broke up rallies and destroyed abolitionist presses. In 1835 Garrison was attacked by a Boston mob and barely escaped being hanged. In 1837 Illinois antislavery editor Elijah Lovejoy was killed when he tried to protect his newspaper press from a mob.

The impact of abolition was far greater in the South. When some abolitionists spoke of all slaveholders as cruel and evil, southerners became defensive. They grew to hate and fear the abolitionists. The South cracked down on reformers—not

Have students discuss the legal and intellectual implications of the South Carolina reward.

Point out that despite the fact that the large majority of white southerners owned no slaves at all, most defended the institution as an integral part of regional life, and as an appropriate condition for blacks.

SLAVE POPULATION AND THE UNDERGROUND RAILROAD

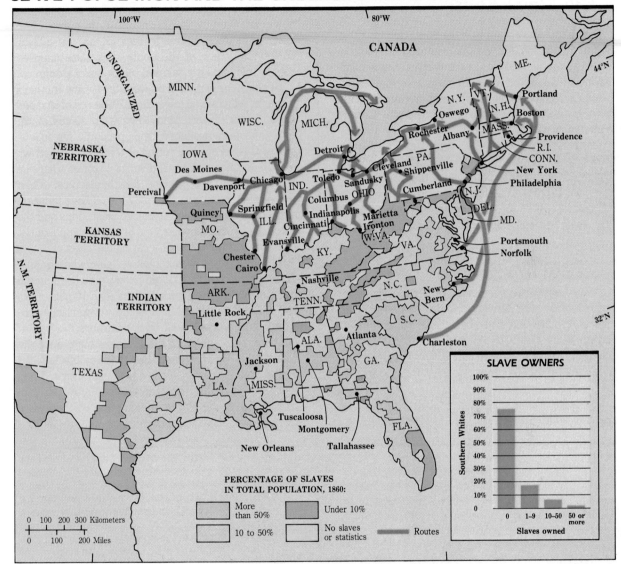

PERCENTAGE OF SLAVES IN TOTAL POPULATION, 1860:

More than 50%　　10 to 50%　　Under 10%　　No slaves or statistics　　Routes

0　100　200　300 Kilometers
0　100　200 Miles

SLAVE OWNERS

Southern Whites / Slaves owned

only abolitionists, but all kinds. People who sympathized with the cause of abolition no longer dared to speak out. In South Carolina, for example, a $1500 reward was offered for the conviction of anyone distributing the *Liberator*. Southerners had begun to feel that their entire culture was under attack.

SECTION REVIEW

1. Identify the following: American Colonization Society, David Walker, Liberty Party, Elijah Lovejoy, Harriet Tubman.

2. What attempts were made to abolish slavery prior to 1830?

3. How did Garrison's position on slavery differ form that of earlier reformers?

4. In what way did the Liberty Party finally differ from Garrison's position?

5. In what ways did blacks support the abolitionist movement?

6. How did southerners react to the abolitionist movement?

Note the differences in northern and southern class structure. While the North had large farmers, few lived as opulently as the wealthy southern planters. In the North, political and social leadership was largely in the hands of bankers, merchants, and manufacturers, not farmers. The North also had far more middle- and lower-class people engaged in non-agricultural pursuits than did the South. And the "underclass" of blacks in the North was much smaller, and free.

7 The Slave South

The culture and economy of the South depended on cotton production for export. Demand for cotton soared as textile factories in the northern states and Europe found faster, cheaper ways to make cloth.

Southern planters rushed to meet the demand with the help of slave labor and the cotton gin. Cotton production went from 200,000 bales a year in 1800 to 2 million bales by the 1830's and 3 million by the 1850's. In the 30 years before the Civil War, cotton accounted for more than one-half of the total value of American exports. The increase was due mainly to the spread of the plantation system into new areas. The plantation was the basis of southern society.

Southern Society

Society and politics in most of the South were dominated by the large plantation owners. The census of 1860 showed that there were 46,274 planters in the South who owned 20 or more slaves. However, fewer than 3000 planters owned over 100 slaves. About 10,000 planters owned from 50 to 100 slaves.

The large plantation owners, however, set the tone for southern society. An imposing mansion, complete with veranda and columns, was an indication of wealth and prestige. Many well-to-do planters, however, lived in plain farmhouses. In either case, they were the natural leaders of an agricultural society. In much of the South, this class supplied county and state officials and members of Congress.

Beneath the planter class were the typical southern farmers, who owned fewer than 200 acres of land and 10 or fewer slaves. Many owned no slaves at all. These farmers produced crops primarily for subsistence. Cash crops like cotton or tobacco were grown to sell for necessities and small luxuries that the farmers could not produce for themselves. Their standard of living was generally low. These families, along with the overseers of large plantations and the mechanics, professionals, and business people of the cities, made up the southern middle class.

The lower class was known as "poor white trash." They were poverty-stricken people who lived on the poorest lands. They made up less than 10 percent of the white population. Also in the lower class were white farm workers and tenant farmers.

Lower than whites on the southern scale were the free blacks. By 1860 about 250,000 free blacks lived in the South, mostly in the towns and cities. They were severely discriminated against, more so than free blacks in the North. In some places they were even forbidden to learn to read or write.

After the Missouri Compromise and the nullification controversy, many Southerners became active in explaining their way of life. In general, they believed that the plantation and slave system on which it was based, were indispensable to the South's prosperity. Every aspect of southern life was dependent upon the crops. The production of cotton, tobacco, and sugar cane were well-suited to unskilled labor, and the numbers necessary for the crops' cultivation gave rise to the South's "peculiar institution." Why was slavery in the South called the "peculiar institution"?

Point out that the slave trade—the importing of slaves from Africa—was the most notorious aspect of slavery, and the first to be outlawed (in 1808). However, smuggling continued long afterwards, and the "domestic slave trade"—the breeding and selling of slaves within the United States—increased. In older parts of the South, where the soil had been depleted (such as the tobacco regions of Virginia, Maryland and eastern North Carolina), planters turned to slave breeding as a profitable alternative or supplement to farming.

At the very bottom of southern society were the slaves. Although most southern whites did not own slaves, it was the presence of slavery, the "peculiar institution," that made the South so different from the rest of the nation.

The Peculiar Institution

Slavery was called "peculiar" because it existed in only one part of the country. Actually, slavery had existed in many different cultures throughout history. But slavery in America was different from the slavery of ancient Egypt or Rome. In those societies, almost anyone might become a slave if taken as a captive in war. In America, slavery was based on race.

The Europeans had tried to make slaves of the Indians, but they either became sick and died or escaped. Attempts to enslave poor whites were also unsuccessful, because whites could escape and blend into the general population. Black slaves also died, but they seemed to be stronger than the Indians. And if they escaped, they found themselves in an unknown country where their dark skins made them obvious.

Roots. The slaves with which western European nations populated their American colonies were from the Guinea Coast of West Africa. This area encompassed the West African coast from the Seneca and Gambia Rivers to Angola. The tribes and kingdoms of the Guinea Coast had largely agricultural economies. Political institutions ranged from extended-family groups to village states, kingdoms, and empires with armies, courts, and tax collectors. Religion, art and music were important parts of African culture.

Although slavery existed in West African society, slaves had certain rights. The various tribes or kingdoms followed somewhat different customs, but generally slaves could own property, marry free people, or purchase their freedom. They frequently gained freedom through adoption into the families of their captors.

The Slave Trade. The first European country to trade in slaves was Portugal. During the first half of the 1700's, the French, English, and Dutch began to challenge the Portuguese monopoly. By the 1780's, the British and the American colonists controlled roughly one half of the European slave traffic. The British colonial merchants who most profited from the slave trade were those from Massachusetts and Rhode Island.

European and American slave traders rarely took part in the raids to capture slaves. They usually traded with African rulers or merchants who sold their war captives. Among those captured were priests, princes, warriors, and merchants. Because of the slave trade, raiding for slaves became the primary cause of war among West African kingdoms. Many Africans, however, refused to take part in the slave trade.

Once sold to a slave trader, the new slaves were branded with red-hot irons and chained. They were then packed into ships for what was called the "Middle Passage"—the voyage across the Atlantic, which lasted from 40 to 60 days. The slaves were forced to lie between decks which were less than four feet apart. Unable to move, suffering from a lack of fresh air, many suffocated or died from epidemics of smallpox and other diseases. The dead were thrown overboard. William E. B. DuBois, historian and early leader of the civil rights movement, described the slave trade eloquently:

> *For four hundred years, the dark captives wound to the sea amid the bleaching bones of the dead; for four hundred years the sharks followed the scurrying ships; for four hundred years America was strewn with the living and dying millions of a transported race. . . .*

Of the hundreds of thousands who survived the trip, the greatest number were taken to the West Indies or Brazil. Many of those who went first to the West Indies were later shipped to the North American colonies. Others were taken directly to North American ports, where they were sold from the ships or shown in markets and taverns.

The Life of a Slave. Most slaves in the North American colonies worked in the cotton fields. Other slaves were house servants, artisans, or factory hands.

All of the Southern states had **slave codes**—laws which defined slaves as property, with few if any legal rights. Slaves could not sue, testify against whites in court, make contracts, buy or sell goods, or—with minor exceptions—own property. The marriages of slaves had no legal standing. Husbands, wives, and children could be sold separately. Slaves were

Note that a major area of interest to contemporary historians is the psychological effect of slavery on the slaves. The debate centers on how much personal freedom slaves had. Ask students to speculate about ways slaves were free to run their own lives, then note that field hands often lived in slave quarters away from whites, so they were able to maintain some semblance of family life, to evolve their own style of speech, music, storytelling, and to some extent religion. Resistance, subtle or open, also provided an important outlet for frustration.

Throughout the South, the plantation system was geared to producing one cash crop. Although cotton was "King," some plantations grew such cash crops as sugar cane or tobacco. Why did the plantation owners rely so heavily on a one crop system?

encouraged to have as many children as possible, because the children of slaves belonged to the slaveowners. Some slaveowners actually bred slaves for sale. In spite of this treatment, family life was highly important to most slaves.

Field hands usually lived in crudely-built, one-room cabins with little furniture. The slave's diet was mostly hominy and fatback, with some cornmeal and saltpork. Some planters allowed their slaves to have their own gardens.

Discipline was often severe. The most common punishment was whipping. A slave's crime might be oversleeping or using a less than humble tone of voice. Masters also did their best to convince slaves that they were truly inferior beings who deserved to be slaves.

Slave Resistance. Many slaves rebelled against their masters in any way they could. One of the major slave revolts was Nat Turner's rebellion in Virginia in 1831. Turner, a black preacher, felt divinely inspired to lead his people to freedom. He and his followers killed about 60 whites before they were caught.

Violence such as this was a source of great fear to southern whites. The slave codes forbade slaves to leave their plantations or to gather in large groups, so that the organization of a widespread revolt was impossible.

Slaves also rebelled in more subtle ways such as working as slowly as possible or breaking tools on purpose. Another method of revenge was setting fire to barns, houses, and crops.

Perhaps the most effective form of slave resistance was running away. Although most runaways were caught and punished, some made it to the northern states or to Canada. Ex-slaves spoke at abolitionist meetings and had a great influence on the opinions of northern whites.

Cavalier and Yankee

From the 1820's through the 1860's, the differences between northern and southern societies grew. The industrial North was symbolized by the aggressive, money-minded "Yankee." In contrast,

NATIONALISM AND SECTIONALISM   **225**

Have students discuss the trade-off between freedom and social order.

the more agrarian South was symbolized by the old-fashioned aristocrat, the "Cavalier."

In fact, the North and the South had much in common. Both had experienced the political upheavals of the age of Jackson. Both had experienced the Second Great Awakening. Yet there were also great differences. The spirit of democracy had less impact in the South. Wealth remained more concentrated in the upper class. The economy of the South remained agricultural, with fewer than 8 percent of people in the South living in cities with populations over 4000. But the existence of slavery was the most striking difference of all.

As attacks against slavery increased, many southerners began to see it as the basis for their different—and they felt, superior—society. They saw slavery as good for both the slave and the South. John C. Calhoun argued that slavery improved the slave "so much so, that it had attained a degree of civilization never before attained by the black race in any age or country." In a speech to Congress in 1838, Calhoun spoke of the South's changing views on slavery:

Many in the South once believed that it was a moral and political evil; that folly and delusion are gone; we see it now in its true light, and regard it as the most safe and stable basis for free institutions in the world. It is impossible

with us that the conflict can take place between labor and capital, which make it so difficult to establish and maintain free institutions in all wealthy and highly civilized nations where such institutions as ours do not exist.

George Fitzhugh, in his *Sociology for the South* (1854), argued that slaves were better off than the free workers of the North because slaves did not have to compete for jobs. Fitzhugh wrote, "The slaves are all well fed, well clad, have plenty of food and are happy."

These attempts of southerners to justify slavery hardened the views of abolitionists. By the mid-1800's the slavery issue was approaching a crisis. Tension was reaching a peak that threatened to split the nation in two. These tensions were increasingly apparent in national politics.

SECTION REVIEW

1. Identify the following: Middle Passage, Nat Turner, Cavalier, Yankee.
2. What influence did plantation owners have on southern society?
3. How did slavery in America differ from slavery in other societies?
4. How did blacks rebel against slavery?
5. In what ways did southern society differ from northern society?

CHAPTER 10   REVIEW

SUMMARY

1. Improved communication and transportation systems contributed to major economic and social changes in the United States.
2. The factory system, stimulated by new technology and the development of the corporation, began to take over the process of manufacturing.
3. A wave of immigration from Europe provided a new labor force for the factories.
4. Rapid industrialization and growth of the cities created new social problems.
5. In spite of problems, many Americans came to believe that they were living in an age of progress that would eventually result in an ideal society.

6. A cultural movement called romanticism was reflected in American literature, arts, and philosophy.
7. A widespread religious revival provided support for various reform movements.
8. Women began a concerted effort to gain equality in all fields of endeavor.
9. The antislavery movement gained force, but abolitionists aroused hostility in the North as well as the South.
10. Southerners began a more vigorous defense of slavery to combat the arguments of radical abolitionists.

VOCABULARY

capital	stock	romanticism	lyceum	abolition
factory system	nativist	transcendentalism	utopias	emancipation
mass production	patent	civil disobedience	temperance	slave codes
corporation				

REVIEW QUESTIONS

1. What improvements and developments advanced industrialization in the early 1800's?
2. What were the positive and negative results of industrialization?
3. What were some of the values of romanticism?
4. What elements did romanticism share with democratic thought?
5. What ideas and events contributed to the spirit of reform?
6. What were the major targets for reform during the antebellum years?
7. What rights did women obtain during this period?
8. How did northerners and southerners react to abolitionists?
9. Why did the South remain tied to an economy based on cotton?
10. What arguments were used to defend the institution of slavery?

DISCUSSION

1. Why was there a surge of reform movements at this time?
2. What would the future of slavery have been if the South had undergone industrialization?
3. Did the reform movements result in any lasting achievements?
4. Did the benefits of industrialization outweigh the problems caused by it?

USING MAPS

Refer to the map on page 221 and answer the following questions:

1. Which states had areas in which slaves made up 50 percent or more of the population? Which states had no slaves?
2. What northern cities were located on routes of the Underground Railroad?
3. Which route on the Underground Railroad would a runaway slave from the coastal area of North Carolina be likely to take?

USING SKILLS

Refer to the graph on page 221 and determine which of the following a) is true based on the graph, b) may or may not be true but proof is not in the graph, or c) is not true based on the graph.

1. Most slaveowners were white.
2. Most free southerners in 1860 did not own slaves.
3. About 50 percent of free southerners owned 10–50 slaves.

SUMMARY

1. The spirit of nationalism was a potent force in life and politics of the early 1800's.
2. By the 1850's political party realignments had brought about two newly dominant parties, the Democrats and the Whigs.
3. By 1853 the United States had grown to its present continental boundaries by acquiring territory through wars and peaceful treaties.
4. Although politics became more democratic, women, Indians, and blacks benefited little from the change.
5. The United States entered an Industrial Revolution that led to profound social and economic changes.
6. A dynamic American society experienced social conflict, reform movements, religious ferment, and cultural growth.
7. By the middle of the nineteenth century, sectional issues dominated American politics.
8. The agrarian South, dependent on slavery for its culture and economy, became increasingly isolated from the industrial North.

REVIEW QUESTIONS

1. How did the forces of nationalism and sectionalism affect the United States during the first half of the 1800's?
2. How did the North, South, and West differ in lifestyles and political outlook?
3. In what ways was democracy an influential factor in the early 1800's in America?
4. Which President had the most influence on the future of the United States—Jefferson, Jackson, or Polk? Why?

SUGGESTED ACTIVITIES

1. Make a chart showing our nation's territorial growth from 1800 to 1850. List the year, prior owner, method of acquisition and states that have been formed from each area.
2. Write an editorial on the Bank of the United States issue, basing your position on the philosophy of Hamilton or Jefferson.
3. Identify and locate those states that were admitted to the Union from 1800 to 1850. Which ones were slave states? Which ones were free states? Which ones were formed from the Northwest Territory? From the Louisiana Purchase of 1803? From the original territory of 1783?
4. Assume that you are an easterner who wants to join the westward movement in the 1830's. Decide where you want to go, the route you will take, and what you will have to bring with you on the journey.
5. Research one of the reform movements of the antebellum period. Who were some of the leaders? What techniques were used to try to achieve reform? What were the results?
6. Write a newspaper editorial on the subject of Jackson's vetoing of the Maysville Road Bill. Write from the viewpoint of a member of the Kentucky state legislature, a New England shipowner, or an immigrant newly arrived in Philadelphia.

SUGGESTED READINGS

1. Bontemps, Arna. *Black Thunder*. Boston: Beacon Press, 1968. Paperback. Story of a slave who attempts to lead an uprising in Richmond in 1800.
2. Bontemps, Arna. *Great Slave Narratives*. Boston: Beacon Press, 1969. Three classics are presented in the stories of Gustavus Vassa, James Pennington and William and Ellen Craft.
3. DeVoto, Bernard. *Across the Wide Missouri*. Boston: Houghton Mifflin, 1947. A description of mountain men, Indians, and the fur trade.

4. Guthrie, Alfred B., Jr. *The Big Sky*. Boston: Houghton Mifflin, 1947. The story of a young man and his Indian wife in the West during the 1830's and 1840's.

5. Lerner, Gerda. *The Grimke Sisters from South Carolina: Rebels Against Slavery*. New York: Schocken Books, Inc., 1971. Paperback. Story of two sisters of southern origin and their life-long dedication to the abolitionist movement.

6. James, Marquis. *The Raven: A Biography of Sam Houston*. Marietta, Georgia: Larlin Corp., 1970. A solid biography of a man whose life is also the story of early Texas.

7. Pessen, Edward. *Jacksonian America: Society, Personality and Politics*. Homewood, Illinois: Dorsey Press, 1978. Paperback. A very readable book that presents a different view of Jackson and the times.

THE HISTORIAN'S CRAFT

When historians examine primary sources for information, the information is not always spelled out in exactly the form it is wanted. Instead, information must be inferred from details given in the source. An *inference* is a meaning or interpretation that is not stated directly. Making inferences is a skill that enables historians to know things that they have not been told.

This activity will give you practice in drawing inferences—in this case, from data presented in tables. The subject is voting patterns in Congress between 1807 and 1829.

Political scientist James S. Young pointed out that, in the early 1800's, Washington, D.C. was a brand new city. The homes and families of members of Congress were in their home states. During legislative sessions, they came to Washington and lived in boardinghouses.

Young studied the *Congressional Directories* for 1807, 1809, 1816, 1822, and 1828 to find out where members of Congress in those years lived. From this information he prepared the table to the right.

Young defined the categories as follows: **A**, groups representing one state; **B**, groups representing one region; **C**, groups representing different regions; and **D**, those living alone. In addition, he defined the regions as follows:

New England: Massachusetts, Connecticut, Rhode Island, Vermont, New Hampshire, and Maine.

Middle Atlantic: New York, New Jersey, Pennsylvania, Delaware, and Maryland.

South: Virginia, North Carolina, South Carolina, Georgia, Florida, Alabama, Mississippi, and Louisiana.

West: Tennessee, Kentucky, Ohio, Illinois, Indiana, Missouri, Arkansas, and Michigan.

A boardinghouse group was defined as representing a single region if all the members of the group came from the same region except one, and that one came from a state bordering one or more of the states in the region.

BOARDINGHOUSE GROUPS IN PERCENT

	1807	1809	1816	1822	1828
A	11.3	13.4	17.7	11.4	4.0
B	72.4	69.4	74.2	66.8	68.9
C	13.2	14.7	15.0	15.5	18.5
D	3.1	2.5	3.1	6.3	9.6
	100.0	100.0	100.0	100.0	100.0

QUESTIONS

1. Is Young's table a primary source or a secondary source?

2. Are the *Congressional Directories* a primary source or a secondary source?

3. Which of the following can reasonably be inferred from the information in the table?
   a. Between 1807 and 1828, most members of Congress lived in boardinghouses.
   b. Between 1807 and 1828, most Senators lived in boardinghouses.
   c. Most boardinghouses in Washington were composed of members of Congress from one region.
   d. Most members of Congress lived in boardinghouses with other members of Congress from the same state or region.
   e. Most members of Congress from New England lived in the same boardinghouse.

Young also studied 116 roll call votes in the House of Representatives in order to determine the voting patterns of boardinghouse groups. He prepared the table below to show the results of his analysis.

BOARDINGHOUSE GROUPS AS VOTING BLOCS

	1807	1809	1816	1828	1829	ALL CONGRESSES Number	Percent
Number of roll calls	32	15	28	19	20	116	
Number of groups	17	21	23	28	29		
Number of cases	544	357	644	532	580	2657	
Cases of unanimity	44.7%	70.9%	38.5%	47.4%	42.4%	1243	46.8
Cases of more than one dissent in the group	26.3%	20.2%	28.9%	25.8%	33.1%	729	27.4
Totals: Cases of group agreement	71.0%	91.1%	67.4%	73.2%	75.5%	1972	74.2
Cases in which two-thirds or more of group members agreed	87.0%	98.0%	90.5%	89.2%	83.3%	365	89.0

QUESTIONS

1. Which of the following statements can reasonably be inferred from the combined data in the two tables?
   a. In the roll call votes that were studied, boardinghouse groups usually voted the same way.
   b. The agreement of boardinghouse groups increased between 1807 and 1828.
   c. In the cases studied, regional groups usually voted the same way.
   d. Regional groups were more important than political party membership in determining the votes of members of Congress.
2. What reason can you suggest to explain why members of boardinghouse groups would vote as blocs?

1850	1854	1858	1860	1862
Compromise of 1850	Kansas-Nebraska Act	Lincoln-Douglas Debates	Election of Abraham Lincoln	*Monitor* and *Virginia*

1851	1857	1859	1861
Uncle Tom's Cabin	*Dred Scott v. Sandford*	John Brown's Raid	Firing on Fort Sumter

THE NATION DIVIDED

Toward Civil War

The Civil War

Reconstruction

1863
Emancipation
Proclamation

1865
Lincoln's Assassination
Appomattox

1868
Fourteenth
Amendment

1870
Fifteenth
Amendment

1863
Battle of
Gettysburg

1865
Thirteenth
Amendment

1868
Impeachment of
Andrew Johnson

1877
Compromise
of 1877

1	Sectional Politics	233
2	Temporary Reprieve	235
3	The Kansas Question	237
4	On the Brink of War	240
5	The Union Divides	243

TOWARD CIVIL WAR

The issue now presented is not whether slavery shall exist unmolested where it now is, but whether it shall be carried to new and distant regions, now free, where the footprint of a slave cannot be found.

DAVID WILMOT

Ever since the Missouri Compromise of 1820, politicians had avoided the slavery issue. After the Mexican War added a huge territory to the United States, however, the issue could no longer be suppressed or evaded. The major question was whether or not slavery should be allowed in the new territory.

Sectional pressures increased until the national political parties could no longer hold together under the strain. New parties based on sectional interests were formed. By 1860, extremists on both sides of the question had defeated all attempts at compromise, and the country plunged into civil war.

1 Sectional Politics

In the middle of the 1800's, the issues dividing the nation seemed to be increasingly sectional in nature. The North and West opposed the South on the protective tariff, cheap land policies, and federal spending for internal improvements. More than anything else, however, it was the Mexican War that inflamed sectional feelings.

The Wilmot Proviso

President Polk had hoped that the war would unite the country. The West and the South generally supported the war. However, many people in the North felt that the war was largely a southern attempt to extend slavery. Besides, northern industrial interests did not want new agricultural states added to the Union. Some people in the West resented Polk for having agreed to an Oregon border at 49° after campaigning on a promise of "54° 40′ or fight!" Supporters of former President Van Buren were also against the war.

Antiwar and antislavery feelings were expressed in Congress by Democratic Representative David Wilmot of Pennsylvania. In August 1846, Congress was debating measures for funding the war. Wilmot introduced a **proviso** (a clause that imposes a condition) that slavery be barred in any territories won from Mexico. Northerners praised the Wilmot Proviso, while southerners—both Whigs and Democrats—denounced it. The measure passed the House, where northern states held a majority. In the Senate, where northern and southern states were represented equally, the measure failed.

Although the Wilmot Proviso was defeated, it opened a new round of debate on slavery. Northerners argued that Congress should bar slavery in the western territories. Southerners said that the federal government had no right to restrict the movement of slaveholders. Moderates of both regions offered compromises. President Polk suggested that the Missouri Compromise line be extended westward. But passions were too high. Extremists defeated all such proposals.

The Election of 1848

It was in this heated atmosphere that the election of 1848 took place. Both major parties had groups who favored the Wilmot Proviso. The Democrats, led by Van Buren, were called the "Barnburners." The Whigs were called "Conscience Whigs."

Both mainline Democrats and mainline Whigs, however, in order to maintain party unity, looked for ways around the slavery issue. The Whigs did not even mention slavery in their platform. They nominated war hero Zachary Taylor for President. As a Louisiana slaveholder, he was expected to reassure southern Whigs. Millard Fillmore of New York was nominated for Vice President.

The willingness of the Free Soil party to separate abolitionism from the issue of slavery in the territories was due to the desire to strengthen the northern majority in Congress and avoid competition from slave labor.

After Polk announced that he would not run again, the Democrats, after much party in-fighting, nominated Senator Lewis Cass of Michigan for President. Cass, along with Stephen Douglas of Illinois, had been one of the people who developed the idea of **popular sovereignty.** According to this concept, the slavery question should be left up to the settlers of individual states and territories. The idea was also called "squatter sovereignty," after the name given to settlers who had no title to their land.

The only party that really came to grips with the slavery issue was a third party, the Free Soil Party. It was made up of Barnburners, Conscience Whigs, and abolitionists from the old Liberty Party. Meeting in Buffalo, they nominated Van Buren and adopted a platform that endorsed the Wilmot Proviso. They also called for a higher tariff and free **homesteads** (tracts of land acquired from public lands by living on and farming the tract). Thus the Free Soilers combined the antislavery cause with an economic position that appealed to northerners and westerners. The party's slogan was "Free soil, free speech, free labor, and free men." However, some supporters of the Wilmot Proviso wanted to keep all blacks, not just slaves, out of the territories. Significantly, the Free Soil platform said nothing about ending slavery in the southern states, or about the rights of free blacks in the North.

Thus the issue of slavery in the territories became separated from the broader demands of abolitionists.

The Free Soil Party received 10 percent of the popular vote but no electoral votes. Taylor, supported by the South, won the election by a small margin. However, the antislavery position had gained strength by focusing on the narrow issue of slavery in the territories.

Debate Over California

By the time Taylor took office in March 1849, events had moved rapidly. Congress had adjourned without deciding what to do about territorial governments in the lands acquired from Mexico. Meanwhile, the **gold rush** (the westward movement spurred by the discovery of gold) had raised the population in California to over 100,000. With so many people coming into the area, a civil government was urgently needed to provide law and order. President Taylor advised the people of California and New Mexico to apply for admission as states. As states, they could do whatever they wanted about slavery. Taylor reasoned that this move would bypass the issue of slavery in the territories.

Taking Taylor's advice, Californians drew up a constitution and applied for admission as a free state.

The discovery of gold in California quickly led to an influx of thousands seeking to strike it rich. Some traveled west by ship around Cape Horn. Others crossed the Isthmus of Panama. Most, however, made the dangerous transcontinental crossing by wagon train. Why were these people called the "Forty-niners"?

Mississippi called for a convention of southern states to meet in June 1850, thereby adding to the atmosphere of crisis.

The Senate debate on the Compromise of 1850 was the last meeting of the triumvirate of Calhoun, Clay, and Webster. Calhoun died in March. Clay and Webster followed him two years later.

When Congress met again in 1849, Taylor surprised his southern supporters by urging that California's application be accepted.

Southerners strongly rejected the proposal. Three new free states (Michigan in 1836, Iowa in 1846, and Wisconsin in 1848) had been admitted to the Union. They were balanced by three new slave states (Arkansas in 1831, Florida and Texas in 1845). If California came in as a free state, the sectional balance in the Senate would be lost. In the bitter debates that followed California's application, members of Congress actually armed themselves. Southern leaders threatened to leave the Union if California was admitted as a free state.

SECTION REVIEW

1. Identify the following: David Wilmot, "Barnburners," Conscience Whigs, Lewis Cass, Free Soil Party.
2. What groups opposed United States entry into the Mexican War and what were their reasons?
3. How did the major parties try to maintain party unity during the election of 1848?
4. What was the platform of the Free Soil Party?

2 Temporary Reprieve

California's statehood was only one of the issues being debated. Something had to be decided about the other Mexican territories as well. Northerners were demanding that slavery be abolished in the District of Columbia. Southerners were demanding a stronger fugitive slave law that would stop northerners from aiding runaway slaves.[1] Moderates on both sides knew that these issues had to be settled to save the Union.

The Compromise of 1850

A set of resolutions, known as the "Great Compromise," was designed by Henry Clay. His proposals were as follows:

(1) California was to be admitted as a free state.

(2) The remaining Mexican lands were to be divided into the territories of New Mexico and Utah, leaving the slavery question to the settlers.

(3) The slave trade, but not slavery itself, would be ended in the District of Columbia.

(4) A stronger fugitive slave law would be enacted.

Clay's proposals met strong resistance. John C. Calhoun protested that compromise was no longer possible.

The Union cannot . . . be saved by eulogies on the Union, however splendid or numerous. The cry of "Union, Union, the glorious Union" can no more prevent disunion than the cry of "Health, health, glorious health!" on the part of the physician, can save a patient lying dangerously ill. . . .

Nothing could save the Union, said Calhoun, but a complete end to the antislavery movement. If the North could not agree to that, the South would have to part from the Union.

Antislavery Senator William H. Seward of New York also denounced the compromise. He spoke of a "higher law than the Constitution" that would eventually bring an end to slavery. Most northern Whigs were strongly against the compromise. An exception was Daniel Webster, who made one of the greatest speeches of his career:

I wish to speak today, not as a Massachusetts man, but as an American, and a member of the Senate of the United States. . . . I speak today for the preservation of the Union.

Webster appealed to the people of the North to accept the compromise. Gradually, opinions in Congress began to turn in favor of Clay's plan. At first the bill did not pass, partly because Clay presented the several proposals as one package. Another reason was that President Taylor was against the compromise. In July, however, he died suddenly. Millard Fillmore, who agreed with Clay's plan, became President.

Finally, Stephen Douglas maneuvered the measures through Congress as separate pieces of legislation, and the Compromise of 1850 became law. Compromise leaders conducted a massive propaganda campaign to win public acceptance. Although neither the North nor the South was pleased, both

---

[1] According to the Fugitive Slave Law of 1793, owners of runaway slaves were entitled to recover their property, but northerners often hindered recovery efforts.

Point out the fact that some northerners, who were generally indifferent to slavery in the South, felt compelled to take a stand when they were forced to become a part of the system by returning runaways.

Ask students to discuss why a single fictional treatment of slavery had a much greater impact on northern opinion than hundreds of abolitionist pamphlets on the subject.

Animosity over the "free soil" issue reached such heights that it led to physical quarrels between members of Congress, such as that between Representatives Grow of Pennsylvania and Keitt of South Carolina. What did the Wilmot Proviso propose?

sides were relieved. Economic good times had returned, and people were glad to turn away from slavery toward more productive interests.

For a while the compromise seemed to be working. In the congressional elections that followed, candidates who favored the compromise won. In the presidential election of 1852, both major parties supported the compromise.

In choosing a candidate for President, the Democrats turned down party leaders in favor of a **dark horse** (a candidate who is unknown or whose chances are not good). Their choice was Franklin Pierce of New Hampshire. The Whigs, divided into northern and southern factions, turned to another war hero, General Winfield Scott of Virginia. His views on the compromise were unknown, but the party platform accepted it.

Scott was suspect in the South because of his friendship with antislavery Senator Seward.

Strengthened by the return of the Barnburners, the Democratic Party and Pierce won the election. The Free Soil Party, which had nominated John Hale of New Hampshire, was the only party that rejected the compromise. It received only about half as many votes as it had in 1848. Pierce promised in his inaugural address to enforce the compromise.

Breakdown of the Compromise

Soon it became clear, however, that one part of the compromise, the new fugitive slave law, could not be enforced. In some parts of the North, public feeling was simply too much against it. In several cases, people used force to rescue captured slaves. Some states passed **personal liberty laws,** which thwarted the fugitive slave law by forbidding state and local courts and police to assist in returning runaway slaves.

Uncle Tom's Cabin. Abolitionists continued to publish antislavery pamphlets and newspapers. The single most effective piece of antislavery propaganda was a novel about slave life called *Uncle Tom's Cabin,* by Harriet Beecher Stowe. It appeared first as a newspaper serial in 1851. The next year it was printed in book form and became an instant success. The preface to the book explained Stowe's beliefs:

The scenes of this story . . . lie among a race hitherto ignored by the association of polite and refined society; an exotic race, whose ancestors, born beneath a tropic sun, brought with them, and perpetuated to their descendants, a character so essentially unlike the hard and dominant Anglo-Saxon race, as for many years to have won from it only misunderstanding and contempt. But, another and better day is dawning. . . .

Uncle Tom's Cabin was one of the first books to portray slaves as human beings with feelings. It soon became a bestseller in the North and turned many people against slavery. In the South, the book was banned.

Southerners were becoming more alarmed as the abolitionists' attack on slavery became more intense. Not only slavery, but the entire southern culture was condemned. Southerners were angered by the personal liberty laws and the continued attacks of

Until the Mexican War, United States policy had been to keep Great Britain and France from gaining control of Cuba.

Buchanan's participation in the Ostend affair gained him the notice of southern Democrats and led to his nomination for President in 1856.

abolitionists. Talk of secession, or leaving the Union, once again was heard in the South.

The Ostend Manifesto. The Compromise of 1850 was further weakened by the foreign policy of the Pierce administration. Because President Pierce was a believer in manifest destiny, people in the North were afraid that he meant to seize foreign territories suitable for slavery. The South had coveted Cuba for some time. Central and South America offered other possibilities, and there was even talk of annexing Hawaii.

In 1854 the American minister to Spain, Pierre Soulé, offered to buy Cuba from Spain for $130 million. When the offer was refused, Soulé met with the minister to England, James Buchanan, and the minister to France, John Y. Mason. The three met at Ostend, Belgium, and later at a town in Germany. They drew up a report which came to be known as the Ostend Manifesto. (A **manifesto** is a public declaration of intentions or views.) This report argued that if Cuba could not be bought, it should be seized. The

report went on to suggest that a current black revolt in Cuba, if it were successful, might be a threat to slavery in the United States.

When the contents of the Ostend Manifesto were published in the spring of 1855, northerners were outraged. It seemed to them that the Pierce administration was trying to add a new slave state to the Union. Spain also was indignant. The embarrassed administration quickly dropped the Cuba project.

SECTION REVIEW

1. Identify the following: William H. Seward, Franklin Pierce, Winfield Scott, Harriet Beecher Stowe, Pierre Soulé.
2. What were the provisions of the Compromise of 1850?
3. What was the weakest part of the Compromise of 1850? Why?
4. How did *Uncle Tom's Cabin* influence feelings on the slavery issue?
5. Why was the Ostend Manifesto so controversial?

Sectional conflict over the slavery issue was intensified by the abolitionists' use of the printed word. One of the most effective publications was *Uncle Tom's Cabin* by Harriet Beecher Stowe. How did southerners react to this book?

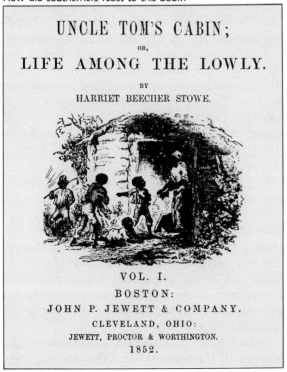

UNCLE TOM'S CABIN;

OR,

LIFE AMONG THE LOWLY.

BY

HARRIET BEECHER STOWE.

VOL. I.

BOSTON:

JOHN P. JEWETT & COMPANY.

CLEVELAND, OHIO:

JEWETT, PROCTOR & WORTHINGTON.

1852.

3 The Kansas Question

By the time the Ostend Manifesto was published, the truce produced by the Compromise of 1850 had been shattered by another event. In January of 1854, Senator Stephen Douglas of Illinois set off a new round of conflict with the Kansas-Nebraska bill.

The Kansas-Nebraska Act

The Kansas-Nebraska bill called for dividing the unorganized part of the Louisiana Territory into two parts, Kansas and Nebraska. The people of each territory were to decide the slavery issue when they applied for statehood. In effect, the Kansas-Nebraska bill was a repeal of the Missouri Compromise, which divided the Louisiana Territory at 36° 30′. According to the Missouri Compromise, both Kansas and Nebraska would be free.

Certainly Douglas did not intend to increase sectional tensions. His chief motive in presenting the bill was probably his desire for a transcontinental railroad. Such a project had been discussed for years, but there was disagreement about the route. The city

The South wanted New Orleans to be the eastern terminus of the transcontinental railroad. While Douglas was preparing the bill, Secretary of War Jefferson Davis was completing the Gadsden Purchase, which was essential to southern plans.

The Republican party was considered the most successful third party in American history because it became one of the major parties.

EXPANSION OF SLAVERY

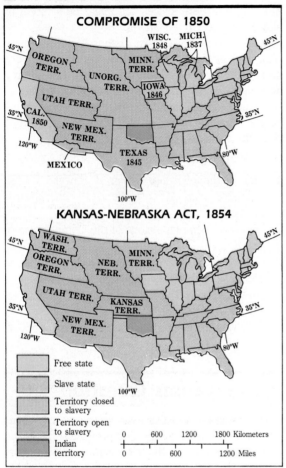

COMPROMISE OF 1850

KANSAS-NEBRASKA ACT, 1854

Free state
Slave state
Territory closed to slavery
Territory open to slavery
Indian territory

and region on the eastern end of the route stood to gain tremendous economic benefits. Douglas wanted to win this prize for his own city and section—Chicago and the Old Northwest. One objection to Chicago was that a route from that city would have to go through unsettled Indian country. If the Kansas-Nebraska territory was organized and settled, this objection could be overcome.

It may also be that Douglas hoped to win southern support for a try at the Democratic nomination for President. Privately, he thought that both Kansas and Nebraska would become free states anyway. Their climate and soil were not suited to cotton. Besides, the North had a larger and more mobile population, so the territories were likely to be settled by northerners. But the idea of popular sovereignty appeared on the surface to be a concession to the South. And

the South did support the bill. After three months of debate, it was passed by a coalition of Democrats and southern Whigs. In its final form, it included a specific repeal of the Missouri Compromise.

To northerners, the repeal of the Missouri Compromise seemed a violation of a sacred pledge. Northern anger at Douglas was so great that he himself remarked that he could travel from Boston to Chicago by the light of his burning effigies.

New Political Alliances

The Kansas-Nebraska Act had an extremely divisive effect on the nation. The national political parties, which in the past had served to resolve sectional differences, were no longer able to do so.

The Whigs had already been stunned by the loss of the 1852 election. In the same year, the deaths of Whig leaders Henry Clay and Daniel Webster had demoralized the party. More losses in state and local elections followed. Many southerners who had joined the Whigs in the 1830's deserted to return to the more conservative Democrats. Some northern Whigs joined the American or "Know-Nothing" party. But it was the Kansas-Nebraska Act that sealed the fate of the Whigs. After southern Whigs crossed party lines to support the bill, the split between northern and southern Whigs was almost complete.

The Democrats seemed to be more unified, but they, too, were showing signs of stress. For years the party had been divided into northern and southern factions. The return of the southern Whigs upset the balance. Northern Democrats became increasingly uneasy over the domination of the party by the South. The Kansas-Nebraska Act finally led many northern Democrats to rebel.

The Kansas-Nebraska Act sparked protest meetings all over the North. Within a short time, the various protest groups had united to form a new party, the Republicans. Their alliance was based on a single principle—opposition to the spread of slavery. The new party soon became the home of northern Whigs and former free soilers. A large number of Democrats who opposed the Kansas-Nebraska Act and some northerners from the American party also joined the Republicans.

In the North, the Republicans quickly showed their strength. In the election of 1854 they won control of

Have students explain what could have been done to prevent the escalation of violence in Kansas.

THE NATION DIVIDED   **239**

Note that while political parties had served to unify America by appealing to people across sectional lines, this function broke down under the impact of the slavery crisis.

the House of Representatives and of several state governments. In the South, the Republicans had almost no support. They were strictly a sectional party. During the next two years, they gained even more northern support because of events in Kansas.

Bleeding Kansas

The Kansas-Nebraska Act had turned Kansas into a battleground between pro- and antislavery forces. The fertile soil drew settlers from the old Northwest, from Missouri and other states of the upper South, and from New England. Most of the settlers came to make homes. Some, however, came determined to make Kansas a free state. Others were just as determined to make it a slave state.

In the spring of 1855, elections were held in Kansas for a territorial legislature. To assure that the outcome was proslavery, some 5000 **"border ruffians"** crossed over from Missouri on election day. They took over the polls, bullied voters, and cast illegal votes. Over 4000 votes were counted, although there were only about 1500 registered voters.

Although the election was clearly a fraud, neither the governor of Kansas nor President Pierce took any action. The new legislature made slavery legal and passed a severe slave code. It included the death penalty for anyone aiding an escaped slave.

Antislavery settlers countered by organizing a free-state party. They drew up a constitution that made slavery illegal. However, many free-staters were not abolitionists. Some were people who did not want to have competition from any black labor, slave or free. The free-state constitution also prohibited free blacks from entering the territory.

In January of 1856, the free-state settlers elected their own governor and legislature. Kansas now had two governments. President Pierce declared the antislavery government illegal, and roving bands of border ruffians terrorized free-state settlers in the name of "law and order." The proslavery leaders tried to have the antislavery leaders arrested. In the spring of 1856, a proslavery mob attacked the free-state town of Lawrence. The mob sacked the town, burned down a hotel, and broke up the printing press. One man was killed.

In retaliation, a militant abolitionist named John Brown led a midnight attack on the proslavery town of Pottowatomie. Five people were killed by Brown and his followers. In the summer of violence that followed, over 200 people died, and property losses reached nearly $2 million.

The violence in Kansas was paralleled by violence in Congress. Charles Sumner, Senator from Massachusetts, was an outspoken critic of slavery. On May 19, 1856, he delivered an inflammatory two-day speech on "The Crime of Kansas." His speech included several unkind remarks about the moderate Senator Butler of South Carolina. Three days later, South Carolina Representative Preston Brooks, a distant relative of Butler, upheld "Southern honor" by attacking Sumner in the Senate. Brooks beat Sumner senseless with a cane, becoming an instant hero in the South. Sumner became a northern martyr.

The Election of 1856

Bleeding Kansas was the chief issue in the presidential election of 1856. By this time the Republicans were strong enough to nominate a presidential candidate. They chose John C. Frémont, "the Pathfinder" of western fame. The party platform called for free territories, and its campaign slogan became "Free soil, free speech, and Frémont."

The Democratic nominee for President was James Buchanan of Pennsylvania. Like Pierce, he was a **"doughface"**—a northerner with southern sympathies. He had been one of the diplomats who wrote the Ostend Manifesto. In the campaign, he supported popular sovereignty.

The election of 1856 showed that the Democrats were finally losing their national appeal. Buchanan won, but with a bare electoral majority based largely on a solid South. Frémont carried 11 out of 16 northern states. The American party candidate, ex-President Millard Filmore, carried only one state.

SECTION REVIEW

1. Identify the following: John Brown, Charles Sumner, John C. Frémont.
2. Why did Douglas want the Kansas-Nebraska Act?
3. Why did the Whig Party decline in the 1850's?
4. What steps did the pro- and antislavery groups take to gain control of Kansas?
5. What were the differences between the Republicans and Democrats in the election of 1856?

Point out that Supreme Court justices come from particular backgrounds and have certain political bents. They are also influenced by the Presidents who appoint them.

In Illinois, slavery had been prohibited by the Northwest Ordinance (1787) and in the territories, by the Missouri Compromise.

4 On the Brink of War

President Buchanan began his administration with optimism. He hoped to settle the question of slavery in the territories. Before his inauguration, he urged the Supreme Court to rule on the issue. The Court agreed and, only two days after Buchanan took office, handed down its decision. Although Buchanan approved the decision, its effect was not what he had hoped.

The Dred Scott Decision

The case before the Supreme Court involved the freedom of Dred Scott. Scott was the slave of army surgeon John Emerson. A resident of Missouri, Dr. Emerson was, in the course of his service, stationed briefly in the free state of Illinois and later in the unorganized territory of Minnesota. He took Scott with him on both occasions.

Dred Scott's freedom was the subject of *Scott v. Sanford.* In that case, the Supreme Court held that Congress could not outlaw slavery in the territories. How did northerners view this decision?

Some years later, Dr. Emerson died and left Scott to his wife. Having no wish to retain Scott, but by Missouri law unable to free him, Mrs. Emerson arranged for Scott to sue for his freedom in the Missouri courts. On earlier occasions, the Missouri courts had awarded freedom to slaves based on the claim that residence in a free state automatically made a slave free. In this case, however, the Missouri Supreme Court reversed earlier decisions.

In the meantime, Mrs. Emerson's property, including the slaves, came under the control of her brother, John F. A. Sanford of New York.[2] Because two states were now involved, the family was able to get Scott's case considered in the federal courts. Another unfavorable ruling was appealed to the United States Supreme Court. Scott's case was a **test case,** or a case whose outcome is likely to serve as a precedent. Both sides to the dispute were eager for a Supreme Court decision on the status of slavery in the territories.

Once again the verdict was against Scott. According to Chief Justice Roger Taney, Scott had no right to sue in the federal courts because, as a slave, he was not a citizen. Furthermore, Taney argued, residence in a free state did not make Scott free.[3] Slaves were property, and southerners' rights to take their property wherever they wanted were protected by the Fifth Amendment to the Constitution.

> *Now . . . the right of property in a slave is distinctly and expressly affirmed in the Constitution. The right to traffic in it, like an ordinary article of merchandise and property, was guaranteed to the citizens of the United States, in every State that might desire it, for twenty years. And the Government in express terms is pledged to protect it in all future time, if the slave escapes from his owner. . . . And no word can be found in the Constitution which gives Congress a greater power over slave property, or which entitles property of that kind to less protection than property of any*

---

[2] Sanford, whose name was misspelled as "Sandford" in official court records, became executor of his sister's estate according to Missouri law, because she had remarried (to abolitionist C. C. Chafee).

[3] Ten weeks after the Supreme Court decision, Scott was freed on the death of his owner.

The Dred Scott decision denied Congress the right to exclude slavery in the territories and therefore cast doubt on the territorial legislature's rights in this matter. The people of a territory, it seemed, could do nothing about slavery until they drew up a

constitution prior to admission as a state. Many northerners believed that slavery would then be too entrenched. Emphasize that state governments controlled slavery.

other description. The only power conferred is the power coupled with the duty of guarding and protecting the owner of his rights.

The Missouri Compromise, which had prohibited slavery in the Louisiana Territory north of 36° 30′, was thus found to be unconstitutional. The Supreme Court decision also implied that popular sovereignty was unconstitutional. If the Constitution protected slaveowners when they entered a United States territory, then slavery could not be legally banned from the territory.

Reaction to the Court's decision was intense. People in the South were jubilant because their reasoning had been endorsed by the highest court in the land. In the North, however, the decision was widely denounced.

The Dred Scott decision had a strong impact on both the Republican and Democratic parties. On the surface, the more serious blow seemed to have been delivered to the Republicans. Their chief goal, to check the spread of slavery, had been declared unconstitutional. However, the Dred Scott case finally convinced thousands of northerners that the South's power over national affairs had gone too far. The anti-South backlash strengthened the Republican party.

The impact on the Democrats, though less immediately visible, was disastrous. Popular sovereignty—the one position around which the party's national unity had been maintained—was no longer viable. Southern Democrats rejected it in favor of the Dred Scott decision. Northern Democrats were torn between their dislike of the Scott decision and their desire to maintain party unity. Their one hope was that leader Stephen Douglas would devise yet another compromise.

The Lincoln-Douglas Debates

An opportunity for Douglas to preserve party unity soon arose. In 1858 he was challenged for his Senate seat by Republican Abraham Lincoln. A self-educated and self-made man, Lincoln was a lawyer who had had mixed success in politics. His down-home humor and ready wit, combined with a conviction that slavery was morally wrong, made him a serious threat to Douglas. In accepting the Republican nomination for the Senate, Lincoln stated his belief that the

Union could not survive under compromises such as popular sovereignty.

I believe this government cannot endure, permanently half slave and half free. I do not expect the Union to be dissolved; I do not expect the house to fall; but I do expect it will cease to be divided. It will become all one thing, or all the other.

In a series of dramatic debates, Lincoln and Douglas sparred over the issues of the day. Lincoln ably outlined the position of the Republican party:

The sentiment that contemplates the institution of slavery in this country as a wrong is the sentiment of the Republican party. They insist that it should, as far as may be, be treated as a wrong; and one of the methods of treating it as a wrong is to make provision that it shall grow no larger. . . .

Lincoln knew that there was no easy way to eliminate slavery where it already existed. His hope was to confine the institution and let it die a slow, natural death.

In a debate at Freeport, Illinois, Lincoln asked Douglas, "Can the people of a United States territory in any lawful way exclude slavery from its limits prior to the formation of a state constitution?" Douglas was in a tight position. With his eye on the Democratic presidential nomination in 1860, he did not want to say anything that would upset southerners. On the other hand, in a close Senate race with Lincoln, he had to please the Illinois voters.

In his reply, known as the Freeport Doctrine, Douglas argued that slavery could not survive without laws that supported it. If the voters of a territory were against slavery, they could simply fail to pass the slave codes that were needed for its existence. Douglas' Freeport Doctrine was really another way of stating the idea of popular sovereignty, but without going against the Court's rule in the Dred Scott case.

The Freeport Doctrine only further split the Democratic party. Popular sovereignty was no longer an acceptable middle ground. Southern Democrats violently rejected Douglas' idea. They felt he had flouted the Constitution.

Northern Democrats, too, had become less comfortable with popular sovereignty. The principle

Stephen Douglas   Abraham Lincoln

Stephen Douglas of Illinois was one of the most respected orators in Congress. A short, stocky man with a big head, the "Little Giant," as he was known, was elected to the House of Representatives in 1843 and to the Senate in 1847.

As chairman of the Senate committee on territories, he struggled to deal with the problem of slavery. He did not own slaves himself, but he was not opposed to slavery. His chief concern was saving the Union. He became convinced that compromise was the only way to do this.

Therefore he believed in the principle of popular sovereignty and backed the Kansas-Nebraska Act of 1854.

This stand was challenged by Abraham Lincoln, a lawyer who, like Douglas, had a talent for making speeches. Lincoln had been a member of the House of Representatives from 1846 to 1849, but by 1850 he thought his career in politics was over.

The Kansas-Nebraska Act changed Lincoln's mind. He joined the new Republican party and in 1858 faced Douglas in a contest for the Senate seat.

The debates between Lincoln and Douglas attracted a great deal of interest from the whole country. Up to 12,000 people turned out to hear each debate.

Douglas stuck by the principle of popular sovereignty. He saw no reason why the Union should not continue "forever divided into free and slave states, as our fathers made it." Lincoln said that the Union could survive only by becoming all one thing or all the other. Both men loved the Union above all.

Douglas won the election, but the debates made Lincoln a national figure and helped him to gain the Republican nomination for President in 1860. When the Civil War broke out, Douglas backed Lincoln's stand. At Lincoln's request, Douglas began a tour of the border states to win support for the Union cause. Shortly after he began this tour, however, he died of typhoid.

had failed in Kansas. There, the southern minority had pushed through a proslavery constitution and applied for admission to the Union as a slave state. Even Douglas had opposed the proslavery constitution as a fraud, and it was ultimately rejected.[4]

Rising Hostilities

Although Douglas won the Senate race in Illinois, the Democrats did poorly in other congressional

---

[4] The proslavery constitution was known as the Lecompton constitution because it was drawn up in that town. Congress offered the people of Kansas a compromise that allowed them to postpone a decision on slavery and remain a territory. In 1858, the people voted to accept this compromise. In 1859, they ratified a free-state constitution, and in 1861, Kansas entered the Union as a free state.

elections that year. The Democrats were becoming hopelessly divided. The national party was no longer able to act as a check on sectional feelings.

An economic depression beginning in 1857 added to resentment against the South. By 1859 the North and West had still not recovered. Northerners and westerners blamed the South for blocking a protective tariff, a cheap land policy, and internal improvements—all measures that would have helped the North and West. Southern planters recovered more quickly from the depression because of a high demand for cotton exports. Southerners thought this proved that their way of life was superior.

Nevertheless, southerners remained anxious. Their anxiety was intensified by the 1857 publication of a book by Hinton Helper, a white North Carolinian who was against slavery. Helper's book, *The*

Ask students to explore the logic of Helper's argument by trying to envision the economy of the antebellum South without slavery.

Brown obtained money from abolitionists in New England and New York. Note that he was tried and hanged by the state of Virginia, not by the federal government.

Impending Crisis of the South, argued that slavery had made a few planters rich at the expense of the non-slaveholding white majority.

This attack on slavery by a southerner seemed highly dangerous. Southern postmasters kept the book from being delivered in the South. What worried southern leaders was the possibility that Republicans would win control of the national government. If that happened, the Republicans could see to it that Helper's book and other attacks on slavery were circulated in the South.

Southerners worried that if northern propaganda reached the slaves, it might lead to a slave revolt. There was nothing that the South feared more. Thus their reaction was extreme when they learned of a plot by John Brown, the violent abolitionist from Kansas. In October of 1859, Brown led a raid on the federal arsenal at Harper's Ferry, Virginia. Apparently he intended to obtain guns and arm slaves. Brown and his men were quickly defeated by local citizens and federal troops. Brown was tried for treason and hanged.

Even though Brown had failed southerners were horrified. Most northerners condemned Brown, but southern newspapers quoted only those few northerners who praised Brown as a hero and a martyr.

SECTION REVIEW

1. Identify the following: Dred Scott, Roger Taney, Hinton Helper, Harper's Ferry.
2. What principles determined the court's ruling in the Dred Scott case?
3. Why was the Senate race in Illinois important?
4. What was the basic principle of the Freeport Doctrine?
5. What was the North's reaction to Brown's raid on Harper's Ferry? The South's reaction?

5 The Union Divides

Many people in the South were sure that the Republicans were behind John Brown's raid. For the Republicans to win the Presidency was more than

Although John Brown was an outlaw, he received sympathy and support from many people. Some who helped Brown did not know that he was planning a raid on the federal arsenal at Harper's Ferry. What did southerners fear most about Brown's attack?

southerners could stand. They threatened to leave the Union if the Republicans won the election of 1860. But northerners had heard talk of secession for years and did not take the threat seriously. This time, however, the South was not bluffing.

The Election of 1860

The Democratic nominating convention met in Charleston, South Carolina, in April 1860. Jefferson Davis of Mississippi demanded a platform calling for federal protection of slavery in the territories. When radical southern demands were turned down, eight southern states withdrew from the convention.

The Democrats had finally become two separate parties. The northern Democrats met in Baltimore, where they nominated Stephen Douglas for President. The Southerners held their own convention and nominated John C. Breckinridge of Kentucky. They adopted the radical platform the Charleston convention had turned down.

The Republican party had high hopes for 1860. It had broadened its appeal by adopting a platform endorsing internal improvements and a protective tariff. To please westerners, the party promised to give settlers a free quarter-section of public land. The platform opposed the extension of slavery but promised not to interfere with it in states where it already existed. John Brown's raid was condemned. The Republicans nominated Abraham Lincoln for President.

A fourth party, the Constitutional Union party, nominated John Bell of Tennessee. The Constitutional Union party, made up mostly of former Whigs, was created for this election as a compromise party. Calling for no more than the Constitution, the Union, and law enforcement, Bell appealed to those people who felt that a middle-of-the-road course was still possible.

In the election, Lincoln carried every free state—including Minnesota and Oregon, admitted in 1858 and 1859, respectively—and received a large majority in the electoral college. Although he had more popular votes than any other candidate, he did not have a majority. Douglas was close behind Lincoln in the popular vote but won only Missouri. Breckenridge carried the deep South along with North Carolina, Delaware, and Maryland. Bell carried the border states of Virginia, Kentucky, and Tennessee. Thus the vote was generally sectional.

Abraham Lincoln was chosen by the Republicans as their presidential candidate at the party's national convention held in Chicago in May of 1860. His position on the spread of slavery in the territories was well known from statements made during the 1858 Lincoln-Douglas debates. Many southerners, however, feared Lincoln would seek to end slavery throughout the nation. How did they react to his election?

The constitutional issue in secession was whether or not the Constitution was a social contract or a compact among the states. See p. 99 on social contracts and p. 136 on the argument over the Virginia and Kentucky Resolutions.

At this time, many people in the Upper South believed that southern grievances could be settled without secession.

ELECTION OF 1860

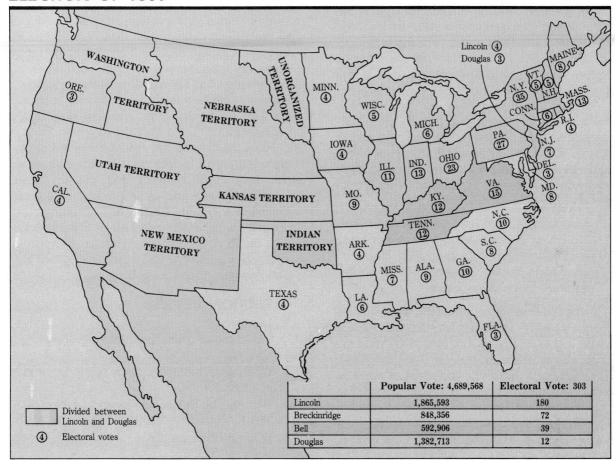

	Popular Vote: 4,689,568	Electoral Vote: 303
Lincoln	1,865,593	180
Breckinridge	848,356	72
Bell	592,906	39
Douglas	1,382,713	12

Divided between Lincoln and Douglas
④ Electoral votes

Secession

Southern radicals had argued that if a "Black Republican" were elected to the Presidency, then the South would have no other recourse than to leave the Union. More moderate leaders pointed out that the Republicans did not control either Congress or the Supreme Court. They wanted to wait and see what Lincoln would do. But the radicals were better organized, and secession seemed to offer an end to existing tensions. Believers in states' rights, southerners thought they had a legal right to leave the Union, and they hoped to do so peacefully.

South Carolina led the way. On December 20, 1860, a state convention meeting in Charleston declared "that the union now subsisting between South Carolina and other states, under the name of 'The United States of America' is hereby dissolved."

Within six weeks South Carolina was followed by Mississippi, Florida, Georgia, Alabama, Louisiana, and Texas.

The seven seceding states met in Montgomery, Alabama, in February 1861 and formed the Confederate States of America. Jefferson Davis was chosen as President and Alexander Stephens of Georgia as Vice President. The constitution of the Confederate States was similar to that of the United States, except the power of the central government was much more limited. Slavery was explicitly protected.

Lincoln's Position

In the four months between the election and Lincoln's inauguration, President Buchanan stood meekly by as the Union fell apart. Although he

In December 1860, Senator John J. Crittenden of Kentucky introduced a resolution calling for the recognition of slavery south of the Missouri Compromise line. This was unacceptable to Lincoln.

Have students discuss what possible advantages Lincoln gained by forcing the South to make the first move in the war.

deplored secession, he believed that the Constitution did not give the federal government the right to use force against the seceding states. In his 1860 message to Congress, he said, "The fact is that our Union rests upon public opinion, and can never be cemented by the blood of its citizens shed in civil war."

All eyes turned to Lincoln, but he gave little indication of his plans other than to reject any compromise that allowed the further expansion of slavery. Therefore his inaugural address in March 1861 drew rapt attention. In this address, Lincoln eloquently called for the preservation of the Union:

> *The mystic chords of memory, stretching from every battlefield and every patriot grave to every living heart and hearthstone all over this broad land, will yet swell the chorus of the Union, when again touched, as surely they will be, by the better angels of our nature.*

To the South he was both conciliatory and firm. He promised that he would not interfere with slavery where it already existed. But he also said that the Union was perpetual and that secession was illegal. Any violent acts against the United States would be considered "insurrectionary or revolutionary." The Union would "constitutionally defend and maintain itself" and, although the federal government would not be the first to use force, it would "hold, occupy, and possess" its forts and other property in the southern states. It would also continue to collect import duties at southern ports.

Fort Sumter

After Lincoln's inauguration, attention was drawn to the federal forts in the South, especially Fort Sumter in Charleston harbor. Fort Sumter was lightly garrisoned and had provisions for only six weeks. As supplies dwindled, Lincoln informed the Confederate authorities that he was sending a ship with supplies to the fort. He promised he would not send troops without notice.

The Confederates had thousands of troops encamped around Charleston and batteries placed so that they could bombard Fort Sumter. When Lincoln's message arrived, Jefferson Davis ordered Confederate General Pierre G. T. Beauregard to demand the fort's surrender. Major Robert Anderson, the fort's commander, refused. On April 12, 1861, the Confederate shore batteries opened fire. The American Civil War had begun.

SECTION REVIEW

1. Identify the following: John C. Breckinridge, Constitutional Union Party, Jefferson Davis, Fort Sumter.
2. What caused the Democrats to split in the election of 1860?
3. How did the Republicans expand their appeal in 1860?
4. Why did Buchanan choose not to act against the seceding states?
5. How did Lincoln try to satisfy the South before the opening of hostilities?

CHAPTER 11   **REVIEW**

SUMMARY

1. Sectional differences strained traditional political alliances during the 1840's and 1850's.
2. By mid-century the dominant political issue was the spread of slavery into the western territories.
3. The Compromise of 1850 brought about a temporary reprieve on the slavery issue.
4. The truce produced by the Compromise of 1850 broke down under the continued strains of sectional conflict. _____
5. The Republican Party was formed as an alliance opposed to the spread of slavery.
6. The Supreme Court's decision in the case of Dred Scott led to an antislavery backlash that strengthened the Republicans.
7. Abraham Lincoln gained national prominence as a result of a Senate race with Stephen Douglas.
8. The election of Lincoln as a Republican President in 1860 resulted in the secession of seven southern states in February 1861.
9. The attack on Fort Sumter at Charleston, South Carolina signaled the start of the American Civil War.

VOCABULARY

| proviso | homesteads | dark horse | manifesto | doughface |
| popular sovereignty | gold rush | personal liberty laws | border ruffians | test case |

REVIEW QUESTIONS

1. What issues reflected sectional differences?
2. How did sectional conflict affect the major political parties?
3. How did the Missouri Compromise and the Kansas-Nebraska Act compare on the issue of slavery?
4. What events of the 1850's drove the South to believe that compromise could not work?
5. How did the antislavery position gain political support?
6. Why did the principle of popular sovereignty prove to be unworkable?
7. What was Lincoln's position on the question of slavery?
8. How did Lincoln's position on secession differ from Buchanan's?

DISCUSSION

1. Do you think that the events of the 1850's were really a threat to the southern way of life? Why or why not?
2. According to the Constitution, did the South have a right to secede?
3. Before the southern states seceded, was any compromise that would save the Union still possible?
4. What would have happened to the South if Lincoln had made no effort to prevent it from seceding?

USING MAPS

Refer to the maps on page 238 and answer the following questions:

1. Which territories were open to slavery under the Compromise of 1850?
2. Which territories were open to slavery under the Kansas-Nebraska Act?
3. How many organized territories were in the United States in 1854?
4. How many states were in the United States in 1854?
5. How many were slave states, and how many were free?

USING SKILLS

Study the statements below and decide which is a statement of fact and which is a statement indicating purpose or motive. (Do not try to decide if the statements are true or false.)

1. Both Democrats and Whigs, in order to maintain party unity, looked for ways around the slavery issue.
2. Some supporters of the Wilmot Proviso wanted to keep blacks out of the territories.
3. Southern leaders threatened to leave the Union if California was admitted as a free state.
4. The gold rush raised the population in California to over 100,000.
5. Northerners sometimes used force to rescue captured slaves.
6. After the Ostend Manifesto was published, the embarrassed Pierce administration quickly dropped the Cuba project.

1	North Versus South	249
2	Early Stages of the War	251
3	A Step Toward Freedom	256
4	The Home Front	257
5	Union Victory	262

THE CIVIL WAR

It is only those who have neither fired a shot nor heard the shrieks and groans of the wounded who cry aloud for more blood, more vengeance, more desolation. War is Hell.

WILLIAM T. SHERMAN

After the firing on Fort Sumter, President Lincoln called on the states to supply 75,000 militia to put down the rebellion. The South, regarding this as a declaration of war, also called for volunteers to fight. At this point, four more slave states—Virginia,[1] Arkansas, Tennessee, and North Carolina—left the Union and joined the Confederacy.

In the spring of 1861, each side expected a brief war and an early victory. Few people foresaw that four years of bloody struggle lay ahead. The Union would survive, and the slavery issue would be settled, but at great cost.

1 North Versus South

The war aims of both sides were simple. The goal of the South was to defend its independence. The goal of the North was to restore the Union by force. Although neither side was prepared for war, each was confident of its military superiority.

Regional Strengths

The confidence of the North was bolstered by knowledge of its advantages in human and material resources. One advantage of the North was its much larger population, fed throughout the war by immigration. This meant that the North could more easily raise armies. At first this advantage was minor, but it became significant by the end of the war.

A most important advantage for the North was its economy. About 80 percent of the nation's factories were located in the North. William T. Sherman, who was to become a general for the North, warned his friends in the South that "no nation of mere agriculturists ever made successful war on a nation of

mechanics." And, though the South was agricultural, its main crop was cotton. Most of the nation's food crops were produced in Union states. Southerners managed with difficulty to produce enough food. By the end of the war, however, they were suffering from hunger due to their inability to move supplies where they were needed. The southern states were haphazardly connected by only 9000 miles (15,300 kilometers) of railroads, while the North had more than 21,000 miles (33,600 kilometers). The North also had better roads and better water transportation.

Another of the North's great assets was that it had a determined and skillful leader in Abraham Lincoln. The Confederacy was a new, unorganized government. Furthermore, it was a government founded on the philosophy of states' rights. The leadership of Jefferson Davis was handicapped by this philosophy. The individual Confederate states often resisted his authority in matters such as raising armies and financing the war.

However, the South did have some advantages. It had a stronger military tradition, and many of the nation's outstanding military leaders were southerners. More importantly, the South planned to fight a defensive war. The southern states had declared themselves an independent nation, and it was up to the North to prove differently. Even a stalemate would be a victory for the South. Southerners could fight on familiar home ground, and, therefore, their lines of communication and supply would be shorter.

Another advantage of the South was that it had the sympathy of many Europeans. A number of British people, for example, saw no difference between the South's struggle for independence and that of the original 13 colonies. Many upper-class British and French felt closer to the aristocratic society of the South and wanted to see the republican government of the United States discredited. Furthermore, British and French leaders saw the United States as a growing threat to their interests. This threat would be easier to contain if the nation was split in two.

---

[1] In western Virginia, 46 counties refused to secede. They broke away from Virginia and joined the Union in June of 1863 as the state of West Virginia.

Have students discuss the advantages and disadvantages of the
Confederacy's decision to conduct the war on its own territory.

SECESSION OF THE SOUTH

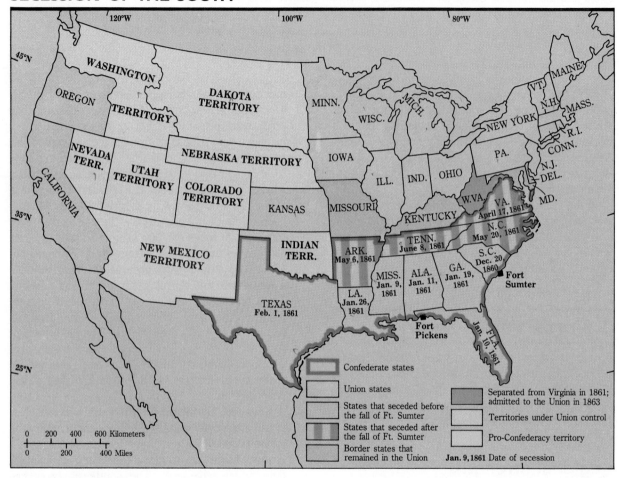

War Strategies

The South counted heavily on support from
Europe, especially from Britain and France. Southerners figured that these countries could not do
without southern cotton. Therefore **"cotton diplomacy"** (using cotton as a basis for negotiation with
other countries) became a major element of southern strategy. One of the South's major goals was to
gain **recognition** (acknowledgement of independence) and perhaps even active intervention from
Europe.

The basic strategy of the South, however, was to
conduct a defensive war, holding on to as much
territory as possible. Southerners believed that if
they showed their determination to be independent,
northerners would tire of the war. The only exception

to this defensive strategy was a plan to attack
Washington, D.C.

The North's war plan came from General Winfield
Scott, hero of the Mexican War, now 75 years old.
Knowing that the North would have to subdue the
South completely, he advised that the Union should
blockade southern ports, then split the Confederacy
in two by taking control of the Mississippi River. Thus
the heart of the Confederacy would be cut off from
both Europe and the Southwest. Scott's plan was
called the "Anaconda Plan," after the snake that
squeezes its prey to death. Another objective of the
North was to capture the Confederate capital at
Richmond, Virginia.[2]

---

[2] The first Confederate capital was at Montgomery, Alabama.
The government moved to Richmond in June of 1861.

Discuss the reasons why the border states were pivotal. Note that they were important to military victory because they provided easy communications around the edge of the Confederacy. Control of these states exposed Tennessee to Union penetration. Maryland was very close to the Union capital.

The border states' decisions affected the balance of forces, the availability of supplies, and military strategy. Also discuss the violation of individual constitutional rights with the suspension of habeas corpus. Ask if such measures are justified in wartime.

The Border States

After Lincoln's call to arms, every state had to choose whether to secede or stay with the Union. The decisions of the **border states**—slave states on the border between the North and the South—were pivotal. The state legislature of Delaware voted unanimously to defend the Union. But the other three border states—Maryland, Kentucky, and Missouri—were slow to decide. People in these states were divided, and there were strong feelings on both sides.

Maryland was crucial because it bordered Washington, D.C., on three sides. Lincoln acted swiftly to secure the nation's capital by imposing **martial law** (government by military forces). He also suspended the right to a **writ of habeas corpus,** a court order to bring a person who has been arrested before the court and show cause for the imprisonment. After leading Confederate sympathizers were arrested, the Maryland legislature voted to stay in the Union.

Kentucky at first tried to remain neutral. Lincoln wisely recognized its neutrality and worked quietly with Unionist leaders to prevent secession. In September of 1861, after a Confederate invasion of the state, Kentucky sided with the North.

Missouri was the most seriously divided state. Several battles were fought between Union and Confederate sympathizers. Finally, in March of 1862, the Union won control of the state.

SECTION REVIEW

1. What were the major war aims of the North and the South?
2. What advantages did each side have at the start of the war?
3. How did political conditions influence the ability of the South to wage war?
4. How did the strategy of the South compare with that of the North?
5. Why were the border states crucial?

2 Early Stages of the War

Even before the choosing of sides was completed, northerners and southerners alike were calling for battle. Many people, including Lincoln, hoped that the war could be ended quickly.

Union volunteers poured into Washington. Not far away near Manassas, Virginia, a Confederate army was also gathering. In the early months of the war, most of the volunteers of both sides were state militia. They were not trained for large-scale army movements. Their officers were elected, and usually knew no more about military tactics than their men. General Scott figured it would take a year to train the Union volunteers, but public opinion demanded immediate action.

After the Confederate bombardment of Fort Sumter, Lincoln realized that the preservation of the Union could only be settled by war. In the first flush of war fever patriotism ran high, and Lincoln's request for volunteers brought thousands to enlist in the Army. Recruiting posters of the time helped capture this patriotic fervor. What advantages bolstered the Union's confidence of winning the war?

UNION AND CONFEDERATE RESOURCES, 1860

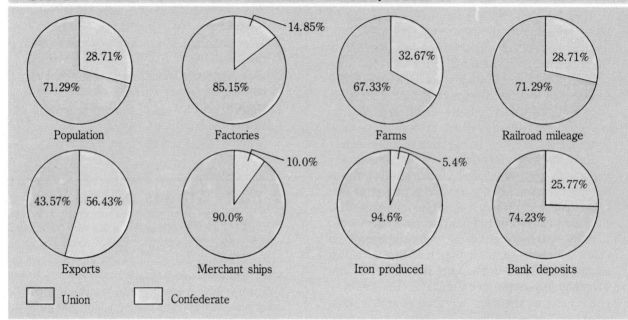

Population — 71.29% / 28.71%
Factories — 85.15% / 14.85%
Farms — 67.33% / 32.67%
Railroad mileage — 71.29% / 28.71%
Exports — 43.57% / 56.43%
Merchant ships — 90.0% / 10.0%
Iron produced — 94.6% / 5.4%
Bank deposits — 74.23% / 25.77%

□ Union   □ Confederate

The First Battle of Bull Run

Pressured by public opinion, Lincoln ordered Union troops under General Irvin McDowell to advance. On July 21, 1861, near a stream called Bull Run, they attacked the Confederate army under General Pierre Beauregard.

At first, the Union seemed to be winning. But with the help of reinforcements brought in by railroad and the bravery of General Thomas J. "Stonewall" Jackson, the Confederates were able to turn defeat around. When the Union lines began to break, McDowell ordered a retreat. Civilians from Washington, who had packed picnic lunches and followed the army to watch the show, blocked the army's path. The orderly retreat turned into a rout.

The Confederates might have won the war right then if they had marched into Washington. But they were as raw and disorganized as the northerners. From this first important battle of the Civil War, both sides learned that there would be no quick victory.

Naval Warfare

Even before the first Battle of Bull Run, Lincoln had declared a blockade of southern ports. This move was part of General Scott's Anaconda Plan. In 1861, however, because of the small size of the United States Navy, the blockade could not be enforced. It was merely a "paper blockade."

Lincoln's declaration might have been meaningless except that the Confederacy had placed an embargo on cotton exports to England. The hope was that, deprived of southern cotton, Britain would be forced to recognize the Confederacy. In one of the major blunders of the war, the Confederacy in effect blockaded its own ports until the United States Navy was able to do so. And the Navy did not take long. Millions of dollars were poured into new warships.

The Monitor and the Merrimac. The South did not let the blockade go unchallenged. On April 20, 1861, the Confederates seized the Union naval shipyard in Norfolk, Virginia. Along with other invaluable war equipment, the Confederates captured the great steam frigate *Merrimac*. Although the Union had scuttled the ship, Confederate engineers were able to raise the hulk. They then transformed the wooden frigate into a new kind of ship. Removing most of the parts above the waterline, the Confederates built an **ironclad**—a floating fort with slanted sides covered with 2 inches (50 millimeters) of iron plate. On the front of the ship they fixed an iron ram.

Note that in wartime, innovations can play a vital psychological as well as military role, giving one side a boost in confidence not only in the ultimate outcome of the conflict, but also in their own sense of superiority. Cite later examples, such as the submarine, the V-2 rocket, the atom bomb.

	UNION	CONFEDERACY
Population	21,833,275	8,792,726
Factories	119,579	20,854
Farms	1,362,680	681,320
Railroad Mileage	21,500	8,500
Exports	$175 million	$226 million
Merchant ships	152,847	16,984
Iron produced (in thousands of long tons)	2721	155
Bank deposits	$110.5 million	$38.4 million

On March 8, 1862, the Confederates unleashed the *Merrimac,* renamed *Virginia,* on the Union fleet in Norfolk Harbor. This fleet, composed entirely of wooden ships, had nothing that could compete with the *Virginia.* The *Virginia* destroyed two Union warships, and it ran another Union warship aground before steaming back into the harbor for the night.

Officials in Washington had known for some time about the Confederate attempt to build an ironclad. In response to the threat, they had contracted to build their own ironclad. The task fell to John Ericsson, a Swedish-American inventor. Ericsson's design was as unorthodox as that of the *Virginia,* though very different. The deck of his ship also barely rose above the waterline. In the middle of the deck was a revolving iron turret designed for two large guns. This design gave the effect of a cheesebox on a raft. Ericsson rushed to complete his ship, the *Monitor,* in time to meet the threat of the *Virginia.* The *Monitor* arrived on March 8 just as the *Virginia* was leaving for the night.

The next day, March 9, the *Virginia* steamed out to finish its work of the day before. However, the *Monitor* was waiting. The battle that followed was the first ever between ironclad warships. Neither ship was able to inflict much damage on the other, but the *Monitor* did keep the *Virginia* from destroying the rest of the Union fleet.

Both the North and the South used their ships as models for the production of still more ships. The two ironclad ships had helped bring about a revolution in naval warfare.

Blockade Runners. Although effective, most Confederate ironclads were useful chiefly for defense. A much more active role was taken by blockade runners. **Blockade runners** were privately owned, shallow-draft speedsters that dodged the Union blockade. They formed the Confederacy's only link to the outside world. These ships, filled with cotton, would dash to the Bahamas and there trade for English goods that were dearly needed in the South.

Commerce Raiders. The Confederacy also had **commerce raiders.** These were large, fast warships—some built in England—designed for use against United States commerce on the high seas. The most famous of these was the CSS *Alabama.* It sank or captured many United States merchant ships until it was caught and defeated by the USS *Kearsarge* in 1864.

The War in the West

The great imbalance between the naval forces of the North and South was simply too much for the Confederacy to overcome. The Union's naval superiority was demonstrated time and again through the ability to mount joint land-sea operations against Confederate forts and cities.

In the West, the North used its Navy in a "river war" that supported land operations. The springboard for northern efforts in the West was Cairo, Illinois. The city was strategically located at the junction of the Ohio and Mississippi Rivers and only a short distance from the Cumberland and Tennessee Rivers. The Union commander at Cairo was General Ulysses S. Grant.

Early in 1862, Grant was ordered to move against Confederate forces under General Albert Sidney Johnston in Kentucky and Tennessee. On February 6, with the aid of a fleet of newly-made ironclad gunboats under Andrew Foote, Grant captured Fort Henry on the Tennessee. Ten days later he attacked

THE WAR IN THE WEST, JANUARY–JUNE 1862

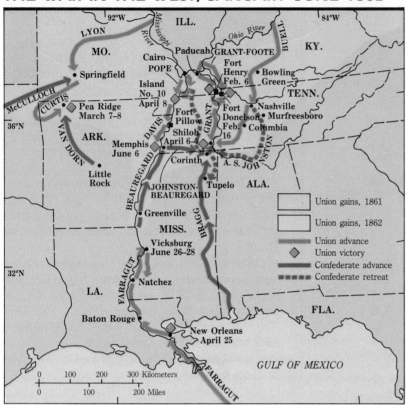

Fort Donelson on the Cumberland. When the Confederate commander at Fort Donelson realized he was trapped, he asked Grant for his terms. Grant's reply was, "No terms except unconditional and immediate surrender can be accepted." "Unconditional Surrender" Grant became the North's new hero.

Grant's successes, combined with a Union victory at Pea Ridge in northwestern Arkansas, gave the Union control of Missouri, Kentucky, and western Tennessee. Johnston's Confederate army in the West was forced to withdraw. Grant gave chase, but on April 6, Johnston attacked Grant's camp at Shiloh Church near Pittsburgh Landing, Tennessee. Caught by surprise, the Union army was pushed back, but the arrival of reinforcements allowed Grant to recapture lost ground.

The Battle of Shiloh was the bloodiest battle that had ever taken place on American soil. The North lost 13,000 men and the South lost 10,000, including General Johnston. Militarily, the battle was a

standoff. The result, however, was that Union control of western Tennessee was strengthened.

The War in the East

Union advances in the West continued as both Memphis and New Orleans fell to Union forces. These victories, however, were not matched in the East.

After McDowell's defeat at Bull Run, Lincoln gave command of the Army of the Potomac to General George B. McClellan. The young McClellan, who had been successful in chasing southern troops from western Virginia, seemed ideal for the job. He restored the confidence of the Army of the Potomac and built it into a solid fighting force. His one fault, however, was his cautious nature. He consistently overestimated the strength of his Confederate opponents.

As pressure for action mounted, McClellan responded with a plan for the invasion of Richmond. He proposed to sail his army of 100,000 down the Chesapeake Bay to the Virginia Peninsula, disembark near Yorktown, and attack Richmond from the South. McClellan's caution cost him throughout the campaign. He was stalled at Yorktown by a much smaller Confederate force. When he finally reached the outskirts of Richmond in May of 1862, the Confederates had built up an army of 85,000. At that point the campaign became a stalemate.

Meanwhile, "Stonewall" Jackson was defeating Union forces in the Shenandoah Valley in Virginia. His successes there led the North to believe that the capital at Washington was in danger. As a result, troops that were to have been sent to McClellan stayed near Washington. Jackson then slipped away to join the Confederate army in Richmond.

At Richmond, McClellan was still waiting for reinforcements. The Confederates, however, now under the command of General Robert E. Lee, took the initiative. With 65,000 men, Lee savagely attacked the Union positions. The series of engagements which followed, known as the Battle of Seven Days, forced the Army of the Potomac back to the James River. Another northern invasion of Richmond had been turned back.

The South's Best Chance

While Lee held his forces in defense of Richmond and McClellan remained on the James, the North raised another large army around Washington. Lincoln gave the command to Major General John Pope. Northern strategy called for Pope to move south and McClellan to move north, catching Lee in a vise. Lee, however, was too quick.

Knowing McClellan's excessive caution, Lee broke all military rules and divided his army. He sent "Stonewall" Jackson north with 25,000 men to take on Pope's force of 50,000. Jackson met Pope at the Second Battle of Bull Run on August 29, 1862 and was able to hold out. As expected, McClellan failed to attack Lee, allowing Lee to slip away and join Jackson on August 30. Together they crushed Pope. Lincoln, disgusted with McClellan, ordered him to return to Washington to defend the capital. Richmond was no longer threatened.

The victory at Second Battle of Bull Run gave Lee the opportunity to take the war to the North. If he could march northwest and then circle back to cut off Washington from the rest of the Union, the South could win the war. With that in mind, Lee disappeared into the mountains of Maryland, with McClellan in pursuit.

Meanwhile, the huge Union army in the West—one that no southern force could have beaten—had been broken up. General Henry W. Halleck, believing his job was to occupy southern territory, divided his forces into several parts. Taking advantage of this opportunity, southern troops in the West began to move. Confederate General Braxton Bragg marched north from Chattanooga, Tennessee, with 30,000 men. Bragg planned to retake western Tennessee and Kentucky by joining another force of 20,000

THE WAR IN THE EAST, JULY 1861–SEPTEMBER 1862

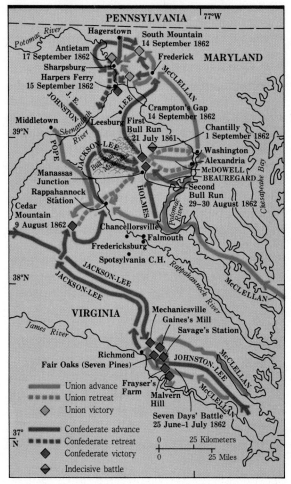

Confederates from Knoxville. The Confederates were also able to scrape together an army of about 20,000 men in northern Mississippi. This army was to keep Grant occupied, then try to slip north to join the other two in Kentucky.

By the middle of September, with Bragg's plan close to completion and Lee loose in Maryland, the Union's position was precarious. However, a series of events, beginning with a stroke of good luck for McClellan, ended the South's best chance for military victory.

To protect his line of communications, Lee had split his army into several smaller pieces. Through incredible luck, McClellan's men found a lost Confederate dispatch detailing Lee's plan. If McClellan moved fast enough, he could destroy the Confederate Army of Northern Virginia one piece at a time. But once again McClellan was overly cautious. On September 17, when he finally hit Lee at Antietam Creek, near Sharpsburg, Maryland, most of Lee's forces had reunited, and the rest appeared during the battle.

Nevertheless, the Battle of Antietam was an important strategic victory for the Union. In the bloodiest day's fighting of the war (McClellan lost over 12,000 men and Lee almost as many), McClellan fought Lee to a draw. The next day, Lee returned to Virginia. His invasion had been stopped.

In the West, the Confederate effort was no more successful. In September Bragg had pushed through Kentucky, but on October 8 a Union force caught up with him at Perryville. Although the battle was a draw, Bragg decided his invasion was a failure and returned to Tennessee. The Confederate forces in Mississippi were defeated about the same time. Thus, by the middle of October, Lee had retreated into Virginia, and Bragg was back in Tennessee.

SECTION REVIEW

1. Identify the following: John Ericsson, CSS *Alabama*, George B. McClellan, Braxton Bragg.
2. How did public opinion influence military decisions in the early days of the war?
3. What developments allowed the blockade of southern ports to succeed?
4. Why was the battle between the *Monitor* and the *Virginia* significant?
5. Why was the battle of Antietam important?

3 A Step Toward Freedom

The Union victory at Antietam gave Lincoln an opportunity to expand the meaning of the war. He had already made up his mind to free the slaves, and had only been waiting for a northern victory to make the announcement.

Abolitionists had long wanted to make **emancipation** (freeing the slaves) a war objective. Many northerners, however, preferred to save the Union first and worry about slavery later. Lincoln himself had proposed a program of gradual emancipation, with compensation paid to slaveowners. He explained his views in a letter to newspaper editor Horace Greeley:

> *My paramount object in this struggle is to save the Union, and it is not either to save or to destroy slavery. If I could save the Union without freeing any slave I would do it; and if I could save it by freeing all the slaves I would do it; and if I could save it by freeing some and leaving others alone I would also do that. . . . I have stated my purpose according to my view of official duty; and I intend no modification of my oft-expressed personal wish that all men everywhere could be free.*

In the first part of the war, Lincoln had been afraid that freeing the slaves would cause the Union to lose support in the border states. As the war dragged on, however, northern opinion shifted toward the abolitionist view. One reason was that northerners were beginning to see that blacks could help win the war by serving in the army.

Noting the shift in opinion, Lincoln decided that he would use his war powers to free the slaves. On September 22, 1862, he issued the Emancipation Proclamation. As of January 1, 1863, he declared, all slaves held in states that were still in rebellion would be "forever free." Slaves in the border states would not be affected.

The Proclamation was of doubtful legality because Lincoln had broadly interpreted the constitutional war powers of the President. The Proclamation was also limited in scope, freeing slaves only in areas over which the Union had no control. Nevertheless, an important step toward emancipation had been taken.

Throughout the North and the border states, free blacks rushed to join the Union army. One of the most famous units was the Fifty-fourth Massachusetts Regiment, shown here attacking Confederates at Fort Wagner, South Carolina. During the course of the war, blacks made up 161 Union regiments and took part in almost 500 different military engagements. Some 29,000 blacks also fought for the Union as members of the United States Navy. How did the enlistment of blacks speed up Lincoln's decision to make his Emancipation Proclamation?

Eventually, as Union troops swept through the South, more and more slaves were set free. Lincoln also advised the border states to start working on plans for emancipation. It was not until 1865, however, that the Thirteenth Amendment, ending slavery in the entire nation, became part of the Constitution.

The Proclamation had two effects that were beneficial to the Union's war effort. First, the North was able to start raising black regiments. Many of these became combat units and fought extremely well. This was true even though they were given inferior arms and supplies. Blacks were more than willing to fight. As black leader Frederick Douglass said, once the black man was called in to fight, "no power on earth . . . can deny that he has earned the right to citizenship." By the end of the war, almost 190,000 blacks had served the Union cause.

The second way in which the Proclamation was beneficial to the North was its effect on diplomacy. Although the South had the initial advantage with England and France, neither of these countries was willing to intervene and risk war with the North until the South seemed certain to win. This never happened. Southern efforts at "cotton diplomacy" also failed. England and France found enough other sources of cotton to keep their textile mills from shutting down completely. Furthermore, textile workers generally supported the North because they favored free labor over slavery. Slavery was almost universally despised. After the Emancipation Proclamation was issued, European sympathy for the North increased, and the possibility of European aid to the South became more remote. Ultimately, the European countries remained neutral.

SECTION REVIEW

1. Why had Lincoln hesitated to free the slaves at the beginning of the war?
2. What was the scope of Lincoln's Emancipation Proclamation?
3. What effects of the Emancipation Proclamation were beneficial to the Union?
4. Why were blacks willing to fight on the Union side?

4 The Home Front

The reaction of northerners to emancipation was, like that of Europeans, generally favorable. The sacrifices demanded of the people at home seemed to have a more noble purpose.

The sacrifices had been heavy on both sides. The Civil War was the first "modern" war, requiring the total commitment of society's resources. Such a war has an impact on every part of life. However, the impact on the North was less devastating than the impact on the South.

Life at Home

Almost everyone who stayed home was touched in some way by the war. But, while everyday life in the North suffered little disruption, life in the South was dramatically changed.

North. For the most part, northerners saw the war from a distance, since most of the battles took place in the South. The constant absence of friends and kin kept the war in peoples' minds, but life went on much the same as it had before. This was true in both rural and urban areas. Farming still meant hard work and few amusements: church socials, barn dances, religious revivals, county fairs, and, on occasion, a traveling circus. Urban life had always offered more variety, and it continued to do so during the war. Dinners and parties, roller and ice skating, lyceums, shows, dance halls, beer gardens, museums, and sports were common amusements.

For the most part, northerners took the war in stride. One area in which considerable change did take place, however, was in the role of women. Many women joined the workforce when men were called away from farms and factories. Although women had always done their share of farm work, they now took on a larger part of the burden. One observer wrote of Iowa in 1863, "I met more women driving teams on the road and saw more at work in the fields than men."

Other women joined relief societies, worked as nurses, and played important roles in the United States Sanitary Commission (providing aid to soldiers) and other charities. Clara Barton, for example, who later became the first president of the American Red Cross, became known as the "Angel of the Battlefield" for her nursing activities.

South. In the embattled South, the antebellum world was lost forever. The fighting and the ever-tightening blockade totally disrupted everyday life. Those who lived in the paths of marching armies lost crops and homes. Thousands became refugees,

On the homefront, patriotism ran high among the relatives of those fighting the war, both North and South. The progress of the war was closely followed in newspaper reports, and many women were engaged in some form of war work. The unprecedented casualties suffered by both sides created problems of hospitalization and treatment of the sick and wounded, so many women worked as nurses. Who was the "Angel of the Battlefield"?

Medicine

Medicine in America took its beginnings from Europe. In colonial times through the 1800's, the best doctors were trained in European medical schools. The first American medical school opened in Philadelphia in 1765, and several more were in existence by the early 1800's. However, doctors who went to American medical schools generally went to Europe for their clinical training. Many doctors did not go to medical school at all, but learned their skills as apprentices to older doctors. Others took up the practice of medicine with no training at all.

Early medicine depended a great deal on superstition and folklore. Sometimes this kind of medicine worked. Old Indian remedies often turned out to be as good as anything from the apothecary shop (the drugstore). For example, moldy bread was used as a cure for infections. Not until 1928 was it discovered that penicillin, present in the mold, was the real agent of cure.

At other times, medical practices did more harm than good. George Washington might not have died of a throat infection if he had not been so weakened by bleeding. Doctors thought that this practice of drawing blood from patients helped to purify the body.

At the time of the Civil War, medicine was still relatively primitive. More than 600,000 men died in the war. Of these, by far the largest number—at least 500,000—died from wounds or diseases that could have been cured with modern medical care. Medical science had not yet discovered that antiseptics could prevent infections. No one knew that germs caused disease. Poor diet and poor sanitation contributed to the spread of illness among the soldiers. No doubt the death rate would have been even higher had it not been for thousands of women who volunteered to serve as nurses.

Medical research had begun as far back as the 1600's, when English doctor William Harvey experimented to learn how blood circulates and dissected bodies to find out how they were put together. But progress was slow. In the same century, Dutch scientist Anton van Leeuwenhoek used a microscope to study bacteria. However, he did not understand that bacteria could cause disease.

An important advance was made in the 1840's, when two Americans (Crawford Long and William Morton) found that ether would put patients to sleep during surgery. With ether as an anesthetic, doctors could perform operations that had never been possible before. Anesthetics also made things a lot more comfortable for patients.

In the late 1800's, English doctor Joseph Lister discovered how to use antiseptics to keep wounds from becoming infected. Later, doctors learned how to do antiseptic surgery. Also in the late 1800's, German doctor Robert Koch and French chemist Louis Pasteur proved that some diseases are caused by germs. By the end of the century, scientists had discovered the organisms that cause pneumonia, cholera, and many other diseases.

By the time of World War I, medicine had progressed to the point where disease no longer took more soldiers' lives than bullets. So many advances were made in the 1900's, that medicine was said to be going through a revolution. American medical schools were greatly improved. The discovery of vitamins helped to cure diseases such as scurvy and rickets. Vaccines helped to control the spread of infectious diseases. Doctors could cure many illnesses with drugs such as penicillin and sulfa.

Modern medicine has brought Americans wonders such as heart transplants and laser surgery. Life expectancies have increased from about 40 years in George Washington's time to about 75 years today. In the twentieth century American medicine has moved into a position of world leadership.

QUESTIONS

1. Why did so many soldiers die in the Civil War?
2. What were some medical advances made in the late 1800's?
3. How has life expectancy changed since George Washington's time?

Have students discuss the oft-cited statement that "war is good for the economy."

and even those who lived outside the war zones suffered. As one observer noted, the South had depended upon the outside world "for everything from a hairpin to a toothpick, and from a cradle to a coffin." As the war dragged on, shortages became commonplace.

The South ran out of almost everything. Shortages in feed for animals and salt for curing meant that little meat was available. Fish and fowl disappeared from meals as tackle and ammunition were used up. In the absence of other meat, people ate rats. Jefferson Davis was quoted by a resident of Richmond as approving the practice because rats were "as good as squirrels." Shortages in food were matched by shortages in clothing, medicine, and even shelter. Deprivation at home, combined with losses on the battlefield, sapped the energy of the South.

As in the North, women played a significant role in the war effort of the South. When the men left the plantations and farms, the women stepped in. "Measuring corn, weighing shucks, and soaking wheat is a new business for me," wrote one North Carolina woman. Such work was taxing. One Georgia woman wrote in 1862, "I am so tired for I never get any rest night or day, and I don't think I will last much longer." As the casualties and shortages of the war mounted, even the strong-willed began to lose spirit.

Economics and Finance

The suffering of the South was largely due to the nature of its economy. Winning a modern war depended upon the ability to convert resources into military striking power. The North had this ability to a far greater degree than the South.

North. The northern economy was **diversified** (based on many different kinds of production). It had a sound agricultural base and, in the Northeast, expanding industry. Even with the loss of labor, both farm and factory were able to maintain and even increase production. The growing use of machinery solved many problems.

On the farm, widespread use of mowers and reapers, along with the development of new harrows, cultivators, threshers, and other farm machinery, allowed women and children to do the jobs that only years before had needed the greater physical strength of men. In 1862, the Cincinnati *Gazette* observed:

> *A hundred thousand agricultural laborers are gone; how are we to meet the deficiency? We have met it chiefly by labor-saving machinery.*

Labor-saving machinery allowed the cultivation of more land, especially in the West. Farming in the West was also increased by the Homestead Act of 1862, which virtually gave away land to settlers. As a result, the North produced so much grain that huge quantities were sold to England, balancing that country's dependence on southern cotton. Livestock output also went up.

Factory production grew as manufacturers responded to the demands of the war effort. The army needed countless items, from guns and ammunition to shoes and uniforms. Greater use of machinery and the standardization of parts made it possible for the North to produce what it needed.

Of course, all the items that the northern armies needed cost money, and several measures were pursued to finance the war. The Morrill Tariff Act of 1862 increased the tariff, protecting industry and raising revenues at the same time. A wide range of internal revenue duties were also established or increased. The first income tax—a very small one—was passed in 1861.

One of the best means of raising money was through the sale of government bonds. The establishment in 1863 of a National Banking System aided in those sales and provided a national currency. Finally, the federal government issued some $450 million in paper money, called **"greenbacks."** This money was not backed by specie. It changed in value with the rise and fall of battlefield fortunes.

For many parts of the economy the war brought economic boom. The foundations for the fortunes of many business magnates—John D. Rockefeller, Andrew Carnegie, J. P. Morgan, and George M. Pullman—were laid during the Civil War. But prosperity was uneven. Inflation hurt wage earners whose incomes did not keep up with rising prices. Unskilled workers were especially hurt, and in some industries wages actually fell while prices rose.

The economy of the North was quite capable of sustaining modern war. Such was not the case in the South.

Have students speculate as to why, in the face of what seemed to be obvious major economic and numerical disadvantages, the South showed so little hesitancy about seceding.

South. The way of life that the South was trying to save, the plantation-slave system, was its greatest liability in the war. Slaves provided agricultural labor while white males were off fighting. In every other respect, the "peculiar institution" was a handicap. The plantation-slave system had kept the South from developing its own factories and skilled workers.

Another problem was that the South had concentrated its efforts on the sale of cotton overseas. As a result, it had failed to build a good system of internal transportation. Without factories to produce new parts, the South was unable to maintain even the poor transportation system it had. When northern armies marched across the South, they tore up railroads along the way. Because goods could not be moved, southerners had to live through the irony of an agricultural region starving to death.

The South also had trouble financing the war. Expected revenues from cotton never materialized because of the naval blockade. The sale of bonds and levying of taxes failed to produce enough revenue. The Confederacy turned to "printing press money"—paper money not backed by specie—which led to staggering inflation.

Southerners made valiant attempts to remedy the shortcomings of their economy. But starting from scratch in so many areas proved too great a disadvantage. As time went on, the disadvantage grew.

Government and Politics

Just as the economies of the two sections had an effect on the outcome of the war, so did the political systems and the men who ran them. The two Presidents, Abraham Lincoln and Jefferson Davis, were the key figures. Both had to pursue extraordinary measures to support the war.

North. Lincoln, an astute politician, was able to maintain the war effort despite conflict in the North over war aims. Most northerners were fighting to save the Union. However, a number of influential Republicans, known as "Radicals," had close ties with the antebellum abolition movement. Men like Secretary of War Edwin M. Stanton, Senator Charles Sumner of Massachusetts, and Representative Thaddeus Stevens of Pennsylvania felt that the war should be fought to end slavery. This conflict was not settled until the Emancipation Proclamation was made.

As the war progressed, opposition to Lincoln's policies came from many other quarters. Some northern Democrats felt that peace was paramount. These "Peace Democrats," (called "Copperheads" by their enemies) felt that Lincoln should negotiate an end to the war. When Union armies did poorly, support for these Democrats increased.

Some people disliked specific policies. By 1863 reaction to the first draft law in the United States had

Many northern Democrats opposed Lincoln's war policies. Some even favored letting the South secede. Lincoln's supporters called them "Copperheads." This cartoon pictures the Copperheads as snakes that would strike the Union without warning. What was the primary aim of the "Copperheads"?

caused trouble. The rich could escape the draft by paying $300 or hiring a substitute. Resentment against this kind of unfairness led to two days of rioting in New York City.

Finally, some northerners who sympathized with the South actively tried to subvert the northern war effort. To combat their activities, Lincoln restricted civil liberties. The right of *habeus corpus* was suspended, civilians were tried by military courts, and limitations were placed on freedom of speech and press. For this, Lincoln was heavily criticized.[4]

Lincoln was sensitive to accusations of unconstitutional actions. Nevertheless, he felt that the cause of the Union justified his decisions. He said:

> *I felt that measures, otherwise unconstitutional, might become lawful by becoming indispensable to the preservation of the Constitution through the preservation of the nation.*

Lincoln compared his actions to cutting off a limb to save a life. Whether he was right or wrong in his reasoning, his decisions certainly proved useful in saving the Union that he cherished.

South. Jefferson Davis was also an intelligent and capable leader. Like Lincoln, he was forced to make many unpopular decisions. Unlike Lincoln, however, Davis was not surrounded by capable subordinates. As a result, Davis himself became too involved in details.

Davis felt that he had a superior knowledge of military affairs. He was a West Point graduate, and had been Secretary of War at one time. But he sometimes ignored good advice from his generals, and showed poor judgment in strategic matters and the choice of commanding officers. His greatest handicap, however, was the states' rights foundation of his government. He was unable to get the broad war powers that Lincoln had. Extreme states'-righters, like governors Joseph E. Brown of Georgia and Zebulon B. Vance of North Carolina, were constantly defying the policies of the Richmond government. States' rights was simply a poor basis for modern war.

Southerners were united in wanting to win the war, but they had other political conflicts. The South had passed a draft law in April of 1862, even before the North did. As in the North, there was much resentment of the fact that well-to-do men could hire substitutes. Another measure that was bitterly criticized was the Impressment Act, which allowed the Confederacy to buy goods at prices set by the government.

SECTION REVIEW

1. Identify the following: Clara Barton, Peace Democrats, Zebulon B. Vance, Impressment Act.
2. How did the North remain productive even with the loss of labor due to the war?
3. How did the North finance the war?
4. What problems did the southern economy face during the war?
5. What political groups did not agree with Lincoln's war objectives?
6. Why did Confederate governors feel they could defy the policies of President Davis?

5 Union Victory

The South's problems became more and more severe as the war continued into its third year. But, although Union armies had managed to halt the South's counter-offensive, Union momentum had also been lost. Another offensive had to be launched.

The Year of Decision

After the Battle of Antietam, Lincoln had urged McClellan to advance on Richmond. But McClellan still had what Lincoln called "the slows." In a letter to McClellan, Lincoln expressed his displeasure:

> *My Dear Sir: You remember my speaking to you of what I called your overcautiousness. Are you not overcautious when you assume that you cannot do what the enemy is constantly doing? Should you not claim to be at least equal in prowess, and act upon the claim?*

Finally, Lincoln removed McClellan from command of the Army of the Potomac, replacing him with Major

---

[4] In 1866 the Supreme Court in the case *ex parte Milligan* condemned Lincoln's use of military courts to try civilians. The individual's right to trial by jury of his peers was so fundamental, the court argued, that even war should not interfere.

General Ambrose E. Burnside. Burnside was to advance on Richmond, this time by way of Fredericksburg. At the same time, the Union forces in central Tennessee were to push from Nashville toward Chattanooga. The forces in western Tennessee, under Grant, were to take Vicksburg. This was the last Confederate stronghold on the Mississippi.

By early 1863 all three of these drives had stalled. In December 1862 Lee smashed the Army of the Potomac at the Battle of Fredericksburg. Lee's Army of Northern Virginia was entrenched on high ground west of the city. Confederate fire massacred the Union brigades, approaching across an open plain.

In central Tennessee, Union troops attacked the Confederates under General Bragg at Stone's Creek, near Murfreesboro. Bragg was forced to withdraw farther south, but the Union army had suffered such losses that it was unable to move for six months. In the West, Grant's operations in Mississippi came to a halt north of Vicksburg. The end of January found him in a position from which the city could not be approached.

Chancellorsville. In April 1863 Lee's Army of Northern Virginia was still at Fredericksburg when the Army of the Potomac, now under General Joe Hooker, began yet another offensive toward Richmond. Lee slipped away from Fredericksburg and, before Hooker could find out where he was, attacked the Union camp at Chancellorsville. Taken totally by surprise, the Army of the Potomac was knocked back. In several days fighting around Chancellorsville and Fredericksburg, the Union lost 17,000 men to an army half its size.

Lee's victory could not have been more complete, but it was costly. Among the Confederate dead was "Stonewall" Jackson, mortally wounded by his own troops during the confused fighting. But the victory once again opened the door for an invasion of the North. This would prove to be the South's last chance for military victory.

Gettysburg. Lee's invasion of the North was based on the hope that a victorious battle there would draw Union forces from the West. This would relieve the pressure on Vicksburg, and perhaps Britain would finally come to the South's aid. It was a gamble, but it was the only chance the South had. In early June Lee moved his army toward the Shenandoah Valley, then up through Maryland and into Pennsylvania.

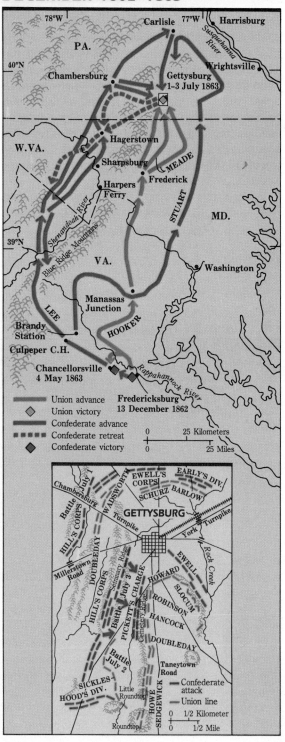

THE WAR IN THE EAST, DECEMBER 1862–1863

The location of the Battle of Gettysburg was a matter of chance. Commanding officers did not decide on it, but some detached units happened to clash on the northern side of the town, and then Meade quickly concentrated his army there.

General Hooker had resigned, and the Army of the Potomac was now commanded by General George G. Meade and positioned on high ground around Gettysburg, Pennsylvania. It was Lee's job to dislodge them. The fighting began on July 1, and on that day and the next, the Confederates had the better of it. But they could never quite get far enough to break the Union position. On July 3 Lee ordered a direct attack on the strongest part of the Union center. Southern forces advanced over a lengthy open space, under a barrage of enemy fire. This attack, known as Pickett's Charge after the leader of one of the Confederate divisions, also failed. Lee was forced to withdraw.

In the greatest battle of the war, the North had 23,000 **casualties** (losses) and the South, 28,000. The South would never again be able to put an army together like the one that had marched into Pennsylvania.

Vicksburg. The Battle of Gettysburg was a terrible blow to Southern hopes, and in the West another great loss occurred. Grant and his Army of the Tennessee were still on the western side of the Mississippi, from which Vicksburg could not be attacked. Finally, Grant came up with a plan that was as daring as Lee's invasion of Pennsylvania. Grant's men marched down the Mississippi River on the swampy, Louisiana side. Meanwhile, the navy ran transports past Confederate batteries in the dead of night. Then the troops were ferried across the river on the navy transports.

Once on the eastern side of the river, Grant struck out for Jackson, the capital of Mississippi. After capturing Jackson, he then marched back toward Vicksburg. General John C. Pemberton, the Confederate commander at Vicksburg, tried to stop Grant's advance, but was beaten back. Unable to take Vicksburg by storm, Grant settled down for a siege. Finally, on July 4, 1863, Pemberton surrendered. The Mississippi River was in Union hands. The South was cut in half, and the second part of the Anaconda Plan had been accomplished.

THE WAR IN THE WEST, JULY 1862–DECEMBER 1863

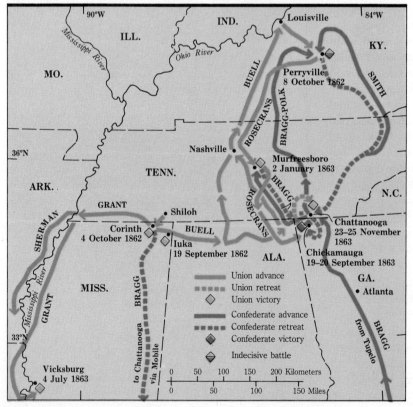

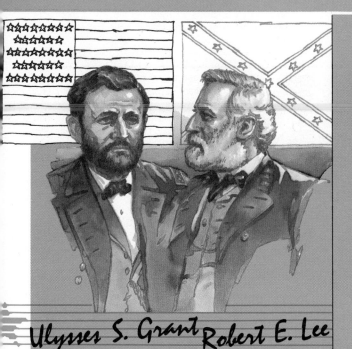

Ulysses S. Grant Robert E. Lee

Mexican War, he proved his skill and daring as a soldier.

When the Civil War broke out, Lincoln asked Lee to take command of the Union forces. Lee was torn, for he did not believe in slavery or secession. But when Virginia seceded, he felt that his loyalty had to lie with his home state. Instead of fighting for the Union, he became the South's most brilliant strategist.

When Lee surrendered at Appomattox, he yielded to a general who was almost his complete opposite. Grant was born in 1822, the son of a farmer and a tanner. Although he went to West Point, he was only an average student. He distinguished himself in the Mexican War, but later resigned from the army. During the next few years he failed repeatedly in farming and in business.

When the Civil War started, Grant volunteered his services. At first he had trouble being accepted into the Union army. Once accepted, however, he impressed Lincoln with his ability. In 1864 Grant was given command of the Union armies. His abilities to plan and make decisions, backed by the North's superior resources, gave Grant his victory.

After the war, Grant went on to become the President of the United States. Lee became a private citizen and spent his last years as head of Washington's College in Lexington, Virginia.

The two outstanding generals of the Civil War, Robert E. Lee and Ulysses S. Grant, were both excellent officers. But only one could emerge the victor. At the beginning of the war, most people would have guessed that Lee would be the winner.

Lee was born in 1807 to one of the prominent landed families of Virginia. In 1828 he graduated from West Point at the top of his class. During the

---

After the momentous fights at Gettysburg and Vicksburg, attention focused on central Tennessee, where the Confederate army of Braxton Bragg remained undefeated. In September of 1863 Bragg's army defeated Union forces at Chicamauga Creek in northern Georgia. The northern army then retreated to Chattanooga, Tennessee, and was there besieged by Bragg. Late in October Grant arrived with fresh supplies and reinforcements. By this time Lincoln had made Grant supreme commander in the West. By the end of November, the Union forces had driven Bragg back into Georgia. Tennessee was in Union hands.

Grant in Command

In March 1864 Lincoln made Ulysses S. Grant, the North's most successful general, commander of all the Union armies. The President had finally found a military genius to match Lee. Grant understood the

nature of the war. He knew that the way to defeat the Confederacy was to destroy Confederate armies. He would relentlessly apply the North's overwhelming advantage in men and resources to that task. His tactic was to wage a war of **attrition** (a gradual wearing down) against the South.

Grant's aim was to destroy the two main Confederate armies still in the field, Lee's Army of Northern Virginia and the army in northern Georgia, where Bragg had been replaced by General Joe Johnston. General William Tecumseh Sherman was sent against Johnston. Grant himself went to tackle Lee, moving with Meade's Army of the Potomac. Each of the Confederate armies had around 60,000 men, while Sherman had 100,000 and Grant nearly 120,000. The offensive began in May.

From the Wilderness to Petersburg. Never one to await developments, Lee attacked Grant's army before it got into position. In the Battle of the

Have students try to devise a negotiated settlement that might have been viable in early 1864. What were the grounds for compromise?

The destruction of railroads and property by Union forces during Sherman's march from Atlanta to the sea added heavily to the devastation suffered by the South. Sherman's campaign was one of total war, with no allowance given to civilian property or civilian life. Why is the Civil War called a "modern war"?

Wilderness, Grant suffered 17,000 casualties. Rather than retreat and regroup, as other Union generals had in the past, Grant pushed on.

Through May and June the two armies were engaged almost constantly. At Spotsylvania Courthouse and Cold Harbor, Grant lost thousands of men. Slowly he pushed toward Richmond, finally circling to the east of the capital and down toward Petersburg. There, Lee occupied strong defenses. Grant was again forced into a siege. The siege wore down Lee's army, and Lee was prevented from dashing away in some bold counterstroke. But the cost of the siege to the Union was tremendous—nearly 60,000 casualties. As the summer approached, northern spirit for such a war began to diminish. Richmond seemed no closer to falling, and the situation in Georgia was no better.

Sherman in Georgia. Sherman had pushed from Chattanooga toward Atlanta, hoping to bring Johnston to a major battle. Johnston, however, realized that his army was more important than territory. He carefully avoided a pitched battle in which Sherman could take advantage of his greater numbers. Consequently, by the middle of July, Sherman was outside Atlanta but had failed to take the city, and Johnston's army was stronger than ever.

Union Victories. To the war-weary North, the events of the first half of 1864 looked like yet another stalled offensive. Grant was stuck outside Richmond and Petersburg, and Sherman was stuck outside Atlanta. Sentiment for a negotiated peace grew. As the 1864 election drew nearer, Lincoln actually feared that he would be beaten. However, news began to arrive of northern triumphs.

In August, Admiral David Farragut led a Union fleet into Mobile Bay, braving the Confederate defenses with the cry, "Damn the torpedoes, full speed ahead!" His victory closed that port, and his cry rallied sentiment in the North.

In September, Sherman marched into Atlanta. Jefferson Davis, disgusted with Johnston's strategy of avoiding battle, had replaced him with John Bell Hood. Hood attacked Sherman boldly, but without success. After Sherman took control of Atlanta's only railroad, Hood was forced to withdraw from the city. Sherman captured Atlanta and, before he left, ordered it

For decades, southerners regarded General Sherman as one of the great villains of all time. Ask students how they feel about his tactics. Were they justified?

destroyed. First, however, he ordered the people of Atlanta to evacuate. When Atlanta city officials appealed his evacuation order, he replied as follows:

> *You might as well appeal against the thunderstorm as against these terrible hardships of war. They are inevitable, and the only way the people of Atlanta can hope once more to live in peace and quiet at home, is to stop the war, which can only be done by admitting that it began in error and is perpetuated in pride.*

Sherman's words demonstrated his belief in the necessity of total war. **Total war** meant war against civilians as well as armies. Sherman's armies took whatever they needed for supplies, living off the countryside. What they could not use themselves, they destroyed so that the Confederates could not use it. This kind of warfare was intended to break the enemy's spirit, destroying psychological resources as well as material ones.

Not long after the burning of Atlanta, a Union army under General Philip Sheridan marched down the Shenandoah Valley of Virginia, pushing back the Confederate army. These victories helped Lincoln to victory at the polls. With Lincoln reelected, it was only a matter of time before the South had to surrender.

The Final Months

Despite the victories in the fall of 1864, Grant had not achieved the destruction of the two major Confederate armies. As long as they survived, so would the Confederacy.

After retreating from Atlanta, the Confederate army under Hood marched back up into Tennessee. Although greatly outnumbered, Hood engaged another Union army under General George Thomas. On December 15 and 16, the Union forces crushed Hood's army outside Nashville. The great Confederate Army of Tennessee was no more.

Sherman's March to the Sea. In the meantime, Sherman took the concept of total war from Atlanta to the sea. In late December of 1864, he reached Savannah, Georgia. The following February he struck north for the Carolinas. The South had nothing to match his army. He marched through the Carolinas with ease, leaving behind him a charred landscape 60 miles (96 kilometers) wide. In Virginia, however, Lee was still holding out.

THE FINAL CAMPAIGNS, 1864–1865

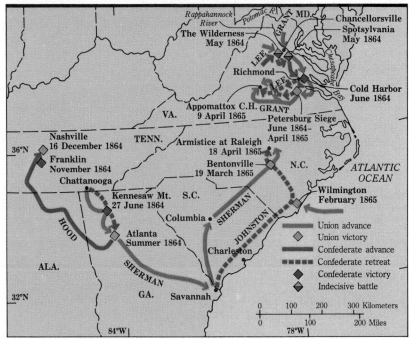

Ask students to speculate as to why Grant offered Lee such generous terms at Appomattox, and as to what would have been the effect of harsher terms.

Appomattox. Throughout the fall and winter of 1864–65, Grant and Lee faced each other in a long line that stretched from Richmond south to Petersburg and then west. Lee's lines were terribly thin, and Grant stretched them even further by constantly moving to Lee's right. On April 2 Grant was finally able to pierce Lee's defenses. Lee evacuated Richmond and Petersburg, pushing west to get past Grant and into North Carolina. But the once-proud Army of Northern Virginia was a shambles.

When Lee's men camped at Appomattox Courthouse on the evening of April 8, they could see by the reflection of campfires against the clouds that they were blocked on three sides by Union forces. Lee surrendered to Grant at Appomattox on April 9, 1865. Grant's terms were generous, with officers being allowed to keep their side arms and rations issued to the defeated army. All of Lee's soldiers were allowed to go home.

Within a few weeks, the remaining southern armies also capitulated. Johnston surrendered to Sherman on April 18. Jefferson Davis was captured on May 10. The last important Confederate force, under General Edmond Kirby-Smith, laid down its arms at New Orleans on May 26. The war was over.

SECTION REVIEW

1. Identify the following: Ambrose E. Burnside, Pickett's Charge, Joe Johnston, David Farragut, John Bell Hood.
2. What was Lee's objective for the invasion of the North?
3. What military events contributed to Lincoln's political victory in 1864?
4. Why did Sherman burn Atlanta?
5. What were Grant's terms of surrender at Appomattox?

CHAPTER **12**   REVIEW

SUMMARY

1. The North, with its larger population, better transportation system, and more productive economy, had advantages that outweighed the South's superior military leadership during the war.
2. The South's strategy was to fight a defensive war, whereas the North, on the other hand, had to invade Confederate territory and subdue the South completely.
3. The Union's naval superiority was a significant factor contributing to the defeat of Confederate forces.
4. In the early stages of the war, the Union forces were successful in the West, but the Confederate forces held out against Union attacks in the East.

5. Confederate General Robert E. Lee's first invasion of the North was repulsed at the strategic battle of Antietam in September 1862.
6. The Emancipation Proclamation freed the slaves in the rebellious states.
7. The Civil War was a "modern" war that had impact on everyday life, especially in the South.
8. The Union victory at Gettysburg in July of 1863 ended the South's last chance for military victory.
9. Under General Ulysses S. Grant, the Union armies used tactics of attrition and total war to deplete Confederate forces.
10. After Lee's surrender to Grant at Appomattox on April 9, 1865, the remaining Confederate armies soon surrendered.

VOCABULARY

cotton diplomacy	martial law	blockade runners	diversified	attrition
recognition	writ of habeus corpus	commerce raiders	greenbacks	total war
border state	ironclad	emancipation	casualty	

REVIEW QUESTIONS

1. Why did both sides in the Civil War feel confident of victory?
2. How was the Anaconda Plan accomplished?
3. Why were the border states important in determining the outcome of the war?
4. What was the South's best chance for military victory?
5. How did the Emancipation Proclamation affect the war?
6. What attitudes did the British and the French have about the American Civil War?
7. Why was the Civil War considered the first modern war?
8. Why was 1863 called "The Year of Decision"?

DISCUSSION

1. Was it realistic for the South to think that it could win a war against the North? Why or why not?
2. How did the North's military leadership compare with the South's?
3. Do you think it would have made a difference if either side had changed executive leadership during the war?
4. Is the suppression of civil liberties in wartime justified? Why or why not?

USING GRAPHS

Refer to the graphs on pages 252–53 and answer the following questions:

1. In which resource did the North have the greatest edge?
2. Approximately what percentage of the country's wealth was owned by the South?
3. In what resources did the South have an advantage?

USING SKILLS

Study the statements below and decide which are statements of fact and which are statements of opinion or interpretation. (Do not try to decide if the statements are true or false.)

1. The North's economy helped it to win the war.
2. When the war started, about 80 percent of the nation's factories were located in the North.
3. Abraham Lincoln was a better leader than Jefferson Davis.
4. The South made a mistake when it placed an embargo on cotton exports to England.
5. The South had European sympathizers.
6. The Battle of Antietam was an important strategic victory for the North.
7. Blacks were willing to fight on the side of the North.
8. After the Emancipation Proclamation, the North was able to start raising black regiments.

1	Presidential Reconstruction	271
2	Restoration Under Johnson	274
3	Radical Reconstruction	278
4	The Radical Regimes	282
5	Redemption	284

RECONSTRUCTION

All should unite in honest efforts to obliterate the effects of war, and to restore the blessings of peace.

ROBERT E. LEE

The United States faced a grave situation after Appomattox. The war for southern independence had failed, and the cost had been great. Politically, some means had to be devised to readmit the seceded states to the Union. Economically, the South had to be put back upon its feet. Socially, the question of the freed slaves had to be faced. Although the problems were clear, the methods used to deal with them remain controversial to this day.

1 Presidential Reconstruction

Northern opinion varied over the best way to deal with a defeated South. Some northerners, who believed that the war had been fought to preserve the Union, argued that the task before the country was to restore the old relationship between the North and South. President Lincoln was the leading proponent of this point of view.

There were others, however, who felt that the South should be punished. Some, like Radical Republicans Charles Sumner of Massachusetts in the Senate and Thaddeus Stevens of Pennsylvania in the House of Representatives, wanted to be certain that the South would never again think of rebelling.

Because of their strong beliefs, the Radicals wanted to control **reconstruction,** or the process of readmitting the southern states to the Union. But Lincoln saw reconstruction as chiefly a presidential task.

Lincoln's Plan

Lincoln had begun to consider the question of reconstruction long before the end of the war. After the North's victory seemed assured, Lincoln began thinking of ways to return the seceded states to the Union. By December 1863, he had developed a plan.

Lincoln made his plan public on December 8, 1863, when he issued his *Proclamation of Amnesty and Reconstruction.* In this proclamation, Lincoln offered **amnesty** (a general pardon) to former Confederates. In return, the Confederates would take an oath to support "the Constitution of the United States and the Union of the states thereunder." Although military and government leaders were excepted from this amnesty process, they could still apply for a special pardon.

Lincoln's plan also offered recognition to state governments formed by those who had taken the oath to support the Constitution and the Union if their number was equal to 10 percent of the votes cast in the presidential election of 1860. Although these new state governments had to recognize the freedom of blacks, Lincoln did not push for further changes. He did not think the time was right.

The Ten Percent Plan revealed Lincoln's practicality as a politician. First of all, he wanted to avoid creating martyrs to the Confederate cause. Therefore he made his plan lenient. Secondly, he wanted to develop a strong Republican party in the South. Lincoln, who at one time had been a Whig, saw that many southerners who had been Whigs were now without a party to represent them. He felt that the Republican party, with its position on tariffs, internal improvements, and a national banking system, was the Whig's logical heir. Lincoln hoped that ex-Whigs in the South would gravitate toward the Republican party.

Finally, although recognition of the abolition of slavery was implicit in the Ten Percent Plan, no direct mention of the subject was made. The plight of the **freedmen,** or freed slaves, was not addressed. Lincoln, who for a long time had favored colonization of blacks, was not sure of the future of free blacks in the United States. He recognized the general distrust of blacks in the North and seemingly decided to let the South handle the issue.

In Congress, opposition to Lincoln's plan surfaced at once. The Radical Republicans, of course, were against Lincoln's Ten Percent Plan. They felt that it was too lenient, and they were strongly opposed to the President controlling reconstruction. This was

Have students look up presidential and congressional powers in the Constitution and debate who had the right to shape Reconstruction.

Remind students that there were hardly any southern representatives in Congress at this time to soften the hard line taken by the Radicals.

apparent in the words of Representative William H. Wadsworth of Kentucky:

> *Where does sovereignty rest? In Congress and not in the President and his army. Conquests made by this country, foreign or domestic . . . are to be appropriated and settled and enjoyed and governed according to the laws of Congress, and by Congress admitted to the equal fellowship of the states.*

The debate over Lincoln's plan raged on through the winter and spring of 1864. By July Congress had developed its own plan of reconstruction. The Wade-Davis Bill, sponsored by Benjamin F. Wade of Ohio and Henry Winter Davis of Maryland, offered a plan much harsher than Lincoln's. The bill provided that each Confederate state be ruled by a military governor who was to take a census of all white male citizens. After a majority of these citizens took an oath of loyalty to the United States, the governor could call an election for a state constitutional convention to form a new government.

The new constitution had to abolish slavery and repudiate (reject as not binding) secession and the Confederate debt. Then, if Congress approved, the state could return to the Union. However, only those who took an **ironclad oath** that they had never willingly aided or fought for the Confederacy could vote or serve as delegates to the state conventions.

There can be no doubt that the Wade-Davis Bill was designed to be harsh and to place control of reconstruction in Congress' hands. Henry Winter Davis argued that it deserved the backing of anyone who thought that the rebellion "has placed citizens of rebel states beyond the protection of the Constitution, and that Congress has supreme power over them as conquered enemies."

Davis' feelings underlined another point of contention between the President and Congress. Lincoln felt that the southern states had never been legally outside the Union and thus had all the rights of any other state. The Radicals, on the other hand, thought that the South had left the Union and therefore should be treated as a conquered territory.

The Wade-Davis Bill was passed in July of 1864, on the last day of the congressional session. This allowed Lincoln to kill the bill by using the pocket veto. A stalemate ensued. Arkansas, Tennessee, and Louisiana were ready to return to the Union under Lincoln's plan, but Congress refused to seat their Representatives and Senators. The practical Lincoln realized that he would have to compromise with the Radicals, and

Devastation of the South was widespread, as much of the fighting during the Civil War had taken place there. Factories, railroads, and whole sections of cities were destroyed. Farms were laid waste, and animals killed. What measures were taken by Congress to reconstruct the devastated South?

Note the role that chance circumstance (in this case Lincoln's assassination) plays in history.

Many Vice Presidents, especially those serving under strong Presidents, have been given little to do. As a result, people often do not know what to expect of them if they are called upon to assume the Presidency.

President Abraham Lincoln was shot and killed while attending a play at Ford's Theater. After lying in state at the Capitol, his body began a 1700-mile journey to Springfield, Illinois, for burial in Oak Ridge Cemetery. The train paused in many cities for services by the shocked and grieving nation. After his death, what happened to his plans for postwar Reconstruction?

he began to hold conferences with congressional leaders.

There the matter stood when, on April 14, 1865, Lincoln was assassinated by John Wilkes Booth,[1] an actor who was under the delusion that he was helping the Confederate cause. The task of presidential reconstruction then fell to Lincoln's Vice President, Andrew Johnson.

Johnson's Plan

The Radicals in Congress expected that they would be able to work with Andrew Johnson. Because of his record, the Radicals thought that Johnson would adopt a firm policy toward the South.

Although a Democrat, Johnson was a strong Unionist. When Johnson's state (Tennessee) seceded in 1861, Johnson rejected its action and remained in his Senate seat. Later, as areas of Tennessee fell to federal forces, Johnson was made military governor of the state. In 1864 he was chosen as Lincoln's

---

[1] Booth escaped, but 12 days later was trapped in a barn. After he refused to surrender, the barn was fired upon, and Booth apparently shot himself. Of 9 other people tried for conspiracy in the assassination, 4 were hanged, 4 were imprisoned, and 1 went free.

running mate to broaden the ticket's appeal. As Lincoln's running mate, Johnson had sharply attacked southern leaders. He once said:

Treason is a crime and crime must be punished. Treason must be made infamous and traitors must be impoverished.

The Radicals were well-pleased with Johnson's statements and expected him to be harsher than Lincoln toward the South.

In fact, Johnson and the Radicals had little in common. Johnson was a Jacksonian Democrat. As such, his attitude toward southern leaders grew out of his concern for the common people in the South and his dislike of the planter aristocracy. For Johnson, the common people were the white **yeoman farmers** (small farmers who cultivate their own lands), not the freedmen. A one-time slaveholder himself, Johnson accepted emancipation only when he saw that slavery was going to be a casualty of the war. Later, he began to see the destruction of slavery as a positive good. However, this was largely because he believed that emancipation of the slaves would break down the planter aristocracy.

Johnson differed from the Radicals in other ways. As a Jacksonian Democrat, he was against protective tariffs, a national banking system, and other measures favored by the Republicans.

The potential for conflict between Congress and the President was made greater by Johnson's personality. He did not have Lincoln's political astuteness and tact. Having once made up his mind on any subject, Johnson was not likely to compromise.

Johnson presented his program for reconstruction soon after he took office. Under his plan, most southerners would be granted amnesty once they had taken a loyalty oath. The exceptions were Confederate leaders and people who owned property worth $20,000 or more. This provision was Johnson's attack on the wealthy leaders who he felt had tricked the common people of the South into seceding.

Johnson went on to outline the steps for the formation of new state governments. Once the loyalty oaths had been taken, the President would choose provisional governors. The governors would call state conventions and supervise the election of delegates to these conventions. Only people who had been eligible voters in 1860 and had taken the loyalty oath would be allowed to vote or run for election. When the state conventions met, they would determine the qualifications for voting and holding office in the reconstructed governments.

In addition to setting up these qualifications, the conventions had to repudiate secession and the Confederate debt. The conventions also had to ratify the Thirteenth Amendment. This amendment, which abolished slavery and "involuntary servitude" except as punishment for a crime, had been approved by Congress in January 1865.

Once the new state constitutions had been written and new state governments formed, the President would revoke martial law. The state would then be readmitted to the Union.

By December 1865, all the southern states but Texas had followed Johnson's plan and were ready to return to the Union. But Johnson's plan was very unpopular among the Radicals. They thought that his plan was too soft. In some ways it was even more lenient than Lincoln's. A case in point was Johnson's provision for the readmission of a state to the Union after "that portion of the people . . . who are loyal" had written a constitution and set up a government. "That portion" could have been far less than Lincoln's Ten Percent Plan had required. It would certainly be less than the majority of white male citizens required by the Wade-Davis Bill.

In addition, although Johnson excepted more people from amnesty than Lincoln, those excepted could apply for special pardons. These pardons, Johnson promised, would be as "liberally extended as may be consistent with the facts of the case and the peace and dignity of the United States."

SECTION REVIEW

1. Identify: William H. Wadsworth, Henry Winter Davis, John Wilkes Booth.
2. What points of view were held by northerners regarding the treatment of the defeated South?
3. Why did Lincoln want to be lenient with the southern states?
4. What were the terms set forth in the Wade-Davis Bill?
5. Why did the Radicals view Johnson as more reasonable than Lincoln?
6. What was Johnson's view of emancipation?

2 Restoration Under Johnson

As Johnson's plan took shape, the Radicals became more and more alarmed. They were especially worried because Congress had adjourned and would not meet again until December 1865. During this time, the leniency of Johnson's plan allowed for the restoration of traditional southern leadership.

Ex-Confederates in Control

Johnson hoped that his policies would lead to the political rise of the southern yeoman farmers. Unfortunately for Johnson's plan, most southern whites were satisfied with the leadership of the planter class. The yeoman farmers had followed the planters' lead regarding secession and now looked to them to set up the new state governments.

The Civil War seemed to have changed southern politics very little. Union officer John W. Deforest described the role of the large planter as follows:

Every community has its great man . . .
around whom his fellow citizens gather when
they want information and to whose

Note that the selection of ex-Confederate military and political leaders indicates that southerners had neither changed their ideas in the face of military defeat nor blamed their leaders for that defeat.

This Freedman's Bureau schoolroom in Richmond, Virginia, was one of many built throughout the South. The Bureau also provided housing, clothing, food, medicine, and work for many ex-slaves. What was the reaction of many southerners toward the Freedman's Bureau?

monologues they listen with respect akin to humility. . . . [Everywhere] that I went . . . I found the chivalrous Southerner still under the domination of his ancient leaders.

Thus, in one election after another, the planters and ex-Confederate leaders captured the reconstruction governments. James L. Orr, governor of South Carolina, had been a member of the Confederate senate. Benjamin G. Humphreys, governor of Mississippi, had been a brigadier general in the Confederate army. Even Alexander H. Stephens, Vice President of the Confederacy, was elected to the United States Senate.

Johnson realized that his plan was not working the way he had hoped. However, instead of rejecting the new governments because traditional southern leaders were in control, Johnson granted the leaders special pardons. He argued that the officials of the new governments, although former Confederates, were completely loyal to the United States. Johnson also stated that these men were reestablishing their governments in good faith and that their treatment of the freedmen was fair.

More and more members of Congress, however, began to voice doubts that this was the case. Alarmed at the course of reconstruction under Johnson, the Radicals began to gather forces to move against him.

Southern Attitudes

While Republicans were preparing to move against Johnson, southerners were reacting to their defeat. Although they realized that further resistance was useless, many were bitter.

For one thing, they disliked having federal troops in the South—especially when those troops included blacks. Although northern troops were rapidly being demobilized, or disbanded, southerners complained loudly. The Alabama legislature, for example, described the troops as a "constant source of irritation to the people."

Another irritation to southerners was the Bureau of Refugees, Freedmen, and Abandoned Lands,[2] or the Freedmen's Bureau. This agency was set up by

---

[2] "Abandoned" lands were lands whose owners were dead or missing and lands confiscated from Confederate leaders.

Have students discuss the validity of the plan to give land to blacks and the significance of the Bureau's general failure to do so.

The vagrancy laws were written with an eye to ensuring a cheap labor supply to planters, whose livelihood would have suffered had blacks sought work elsewhere.

Congress in March of 1865 to aid refugees (people who had fled their homes) and freedmen. It handed out food, clothing, and medical supplies, set up schools, drew up contracts between freedmen and their employers, and tried to settle some blacks on abandoned lands.

The Freedmen's Bureau was especially active in the fields of education and labor relations. By 1870 it had spent over $5 million on education, and there were about 250,000 blacks in 4300 schools. In labor relations, the Bureau tried to protect the freedmen's rights to choose the jobs they wanted and to be paid fairly for their work. Courts and boards were set up to settle differences between employers and workers.[3] Such interference upset many whites in the South.

Southerners also felt the Bureau caused trouble by leading the freedmen to believe that abandoned lands would be distributed to them. Actually, Johnson's plan allowed for land to be returned to pardoned rebels. The hopes of blacks were raised, but only a small amount of land was given to freedmen.

Southerners sometimes showed their dislike for the Freedmen's Bureau by burning black schools and attacking northern white teachers or Bureau agents. Accounts of violence soon reached the North. Such accounts supported the Radicals' argument that the South remained "unreconstructed." Other evidence also backed up this view. Several of the state constitutional conventions repealed, rather than repudiated, secession. The Arkansas legislature voted pensions for Confederate veterans. Mississippi refused to ratify the Thirteenth Amendment, and South Carolina refused to repudiate the Confederate debt. Most alarming to northerners, however, were the laws passed by the new southern legislatures to deal with the freedmen.

Black Codes

The series of laws passed after the Civil War to deal with the freedmen were known as the **black codes.** These laws severely limited the rights of blacks.

One reason that the southern states were able to pass such laws was that President Johnson felt that federal jurisdiction ended with the order to abolish

---

[3] This was the first time in United States history that the federal government took a direct part in bargaining between employers and workers.

slavery. Any other questions regarding the freedmen were left up to individual states.

The states did everything they could to ensure black subordination and **segregation,** or separation. For one thing, no state extended to the freedmen the franchise, or the right to vote. Blacks were denied the right to vote even if they were educated. In fact, a state Democratic convention in Louisiana passed a resolution on the subject:

> We hold this to be a Government of White People, made and to be perpetuated for the exclusive political benefit of the White Race, and . . . the people of African descent cannot be considered as citizens of the United States.

The state governments also made no provision for black schools. This was not surprising, given the southern antipathy for black education. Indeed, northerners often heard southerners state that black education would be the ruin of the South.

The southerners' attitude toward the freedmen's economic role was little better. Most southerners saw blacks as nothing more than unskilled workers. Some of the most extreme measures of the black codes involved the freedmen's place in the South's economy. For example, in South Carolina freedmen had to get a special license to enter any employment other than that of agricultural worker. Mississippi would not allow blacks to buy or rent farm land and authorized "any person" to arrest blacks who quit before the end of their labor contracts.

Many states enacted **vagrancy laws.** These laws were designed to limit the number of vagrants, or people who had no established home nor visible means of support. Because of these vagrancy laws, any freedman who was unemployed was arrested and then hired out to anyone who would pay his or her fine.

There were still other restrictions on blacks in the postwar South. They could not testify against whites in court, serve on juries, or handle weapons of any kind. In one Louisiana town, blacks were even forbidden to come inside the town limits without the permission of their employers. Many towns had curfews for freedmen. They were also prohibited from entering into interracial marriages. The lives of the freedmen in the postwar South, then, were not much different from the lives of slaves in the

Suffrage

Suffrage, or the right to vote, lies at the heart of the American system of government. The right to vote is the basis for political equality. Since a democratic government is supposed to derive its power from the people, suffrage is a measure of democracy.

Yet even in the United States, a country that prides itself on its democratic traditions, the right to vote has never been open to everyone. Today, voting rights are restricted to people over the age of 18, and most states deny suffrage to people who are mentally ill or severely retarded, or who have been convicted of certain crimes. Many states also require a person to have lived in the state for a certain amount of time before voting. Most people consider these restrictions reasonable. In the past, however, restrictions were much more widespread.

Early restrictions on voting rights were based chiefly on property ownership, race, and sex. Property requirements were common until the mid-1800's. Theoretically, only people who owned property had a stake in society. Property owners were thought more likely to be concerned and informed citizens. Furthermore, owning property was seen as a sign of ability. Property owners, it was argued, were more deserving of the right to vote.

In the 1800's property requirements were gradually abolished. On the frontier, conditions of life encouraged a spirit of equality. Many of the new western states that joined the Union gave the right to vote to all adult males—or at least to those who paid taxes, which was a much looser requirement than property ownership. Older states, not wanting to lose too much of their population to the West, also began to lower property requirements. By 1860 almost all adult white males had the right to vote.

Racial restrictions were the next to fall. After the Civil War, Radical Republicans insisted that blacks be given the right to vote before the former

Confederate States could be readmitted to the Union. At this time, many states in other parts of the country also restricted black suffrage, and no one could argue that what was fair for the South was not fair for the country as a whole. The movement for national black suffrage led to the passage in 1870 of the Fifteenth Amendment to the Constitution. This amendment said that states could not deny the right to vote to any citizen because of race or color.

The victory for blacks was only technical, however. Although blacks voted during the reconstruction period, by the 1880's they had again lost their right to vote. The Fifteenth Amendment was still in effect, but various states found ways to get around the spirit of the law. Blacks were kept from voting by means both violent and nonviolent. Most blacks stayed away from the polls until the federal government began taking action to protect them. Not until the 1960's did Congress make a real effort to see that blacks were allowed to use their right to vote.

After the Fifteenth Amendment was passed, women were angry because they had not been included, and the drive for women's suffrage grew stronger. In 1890 Wyoming became the first state to allow women to vote. By 1920 a total of 15 states, most of them in the West, had given this right to women, but most states did not allow women to vote until 1920, when the Nineteenth Amendment was passed. Although suffrage came much later for women than it did for blacks, women were able to exercise their right to vote much earlier. They were not subject to the various kinds of voting restrictions that were placed on blacks.

QUESTIONS

1. What were three main categories of restrictions on voting rights in the United States?
2. Why was property ownership considered an important qualification for voting?
3. Despite the passage of the Fifteenth Amendment, why did many blacks fail to vote?
4. Why were women often able to exercise their right to vote before blacks?

antebellum South. In short, freedmen were being returned to near slavery.

Northerners were outraged by the black codes. An editorial in the Chicago *Tribune* warned Mississippi that the North would convert that state "into a frog pond" rather than allow the reestablishment of slavery. Even those who supported Johnson's plan were alarmed by the actions of the southern states. Gideon Welles, Johnson's Secretary of the Navy, expressed the fears of many:

> *The tone of sentiment and action of people of the South is injudicious and indiscreet in many respects. . . The entire South seem to be stupid and vindictive, know not their friends, and are pursuing just the course which their opponents, the Radicals, desire. I fear a terrible ordeal awaits them in the future.*

These fears were well-founded. Accounts of what was happening in the South led more and more northerners to back the position of the Radicals in Congress.

SECTION REVIEW

1. Why was Johnson's plan unsuccessful?
2. What were the major complaints of white southerners about reconstruction?
3. What were the functions of the Freedmen's Bureau?
4. What evidence was there that the South had not been reconstructed?
5. How did black codes limit the rights of blacks?

3 Radical Reconstruction

When Congress met in December 1865, the Radicals moved to put their plan for reconstruction into effect. At first, they had difficulty because the balance of power in Congress was held by moderate Republicans who, for the most part, were not interested in the troubles of freedmen. However, reports from the South seemed to support the Radicals' argument that Johnson's plan of reconstruction was robbing the North of its hard-won victory. Anger with the South finally united the moderates with the Radicals.

Radical Progress

In December 1865, Republicans in Congress refused to seat the Representatives and Senators from the "reconstructed" southern states. About the same time, Congress set up a Joint Committee on Reconstruction to study problems in the South. On December 18, 1865, the Thirteenth Amendment, having been ratified by 27 states, went into effect. Slavery was formally ended.

To help the freedmen, Congress acted in February 1866 to extend the life of the Freedmen's Bureau. The New Freedmen's Bureau bill gave the bureau power to try in a military court persons who were accused of depriving freedmen of their civil rights. Congress also passed the Civil Rights Act of 1866. The most important part of this act stated that citizens are

> *persons born in the United States and not subjected to any foreign power . . . of every race and color, without regard to any previous condition of slavery or involuntary servitude.*

This act was the first federal law to define citizenship and to protect civil rights in the states. In effect, the act was a law against **discrimination** (different treatment) based on race or color.

Fearing that the Civil Rights Act might be overturned in court, Congress in June 1866 passed the Fourteenth Amendment to the Constitution. This amendment defined citizenship to include blacks. It also said that no state could take away a citizens' life, liberty, or property without due process of law, and that every citizen was entitled to equal protection of the laws. States that prevented any adult male citizen from voting could lose part of their representation in Congress. Anyone who had sworn to uphold the Constitution and then taken part in a rebellion against the United States could not hold public office. Finally, the amendment declared Confederate debts illegal.

The progress made by the Republicans was inadvertently aided by Johnson, whose behavior drove moderate Republicans farther into the Radical camp. In a speech on Washington's birthday, he attacked the Joint Committee on Reconstruction:

> *I fought traitors and treason in the South . . . now, when I turn around and at the other end of the line find men—I care not by what name*

During the congressional election of 1866, President Johnson went on a speaking tour to encourage needed support for his Reconstruction policy. Many members of Congress felt that Reconstruction was not a matter for the executive branch of government. A struggle between the executive and the legislative branches of government began. Who won the struggle for control of Reconstruction?

you call them—who will stand opposed to the restoration of the Union of these States, I am free to say to you that I am still in the field.

When asked to name northern "traitors," Johnson responded, "I say Thaddeus Stevens of Pennsylvania is one; I say Mr. Sumner of the Senate is another; and Wendell Phillips is another."

The split between the Congress and the President was widened by Johnson's vetoes of the new Freedmen's Bureau bill and the Civil Rights Act of 1866. Johnson vetoed the first on the grounds that it had been passed by a Congress in which 11 states were not represented, and that the provision for military trials violated the Fifth Amendment. He vetoed the second on the ground that it violated states' rights. Both bills were passed by Congress over Johnson's vetoes.

In the summer of 1866, Johnson attacked the Fourteenth Amendment and urged southern states not to ratify it.[4] As the summer passed, it became

clear that the upcoming congressional elections would serve as a test of Johnson's reconstruction policies. In these elections, bitter charges were leveled by each side. Johnson's position, however, was weakened by reports of race riots in Memphis and New Orleans. These reports, as well as the skill of the Radicals' campaign, brought an overwhelming victory for the Radicals.

Motives of the Radicals

With this victory in hand, the Radicals began to put together their plan for reconstruction. The motives of the Radicals have been the subject of lengthy debate. Modern scholars have identified four basic aims of the Radicals' plan.

First, the Radicals felt that the South should be punished. Therefore they wanted to return the seceded states to the Union under tougher terms than those set by Lincoln or Johnson. The reason behind this policy was revealed by Representative Thaddeus Stevens when he described the war as one "waged with fiendish cruelty against the best government on earth."

---

[4]Of the 11 southern states, only Tennessee ratified the Fourteenth Amendment. Because ratification was a condition of restoration to the Union, Tennessee became the first seceded state to return to the Union.

Note the way in which political decisions are based partly on practical concerns.

Second, the Radicals wanted to keep the Republican party in power. They were afraid that the Democratic party could make a comeback. The agrarian South and the agrarian West might join to oppose measures such as the protective tariff. The Democrats also might be aided by the abolition of slavery, because blacks would now be counted as full citizens in determining the South's representation in the House.

To counter the Democratic threat, the Radicals moved to make the Republican party stronger by giving freedmen the right to vote. Blacks were expected to vote for the Republicans, the party of emancipation. Thaddeus Stevens stated the Radicals' position on black suffrage:

> *If impartial [black] suffrage is excluded in the rebel states, then every one of them is sure to send a solid rebel representative delegation to Congress, and cast a solid rebel electoral vote. They, with their kindred Copperheads of the North, would always elect the President and control Congress. . . For, these, among other reasons, I am for negro suffrage in every rebel state. If it be just, it should not be denied; if it be necessary, it should be adopted; if it be a punishment to traitors, they deserve it.*

Third, the Radicals had an economic motive. The Republican party was linked with northern business interests. Although northern business people were not always politically unified, most wanted the government to promote economic growth. They favored a protective tariff and a national debt. A Democratic comeback would be a threat to such policies.

Finally, Radicals honestly cared about the plight of the freedmen. Many Radicals had been abolitionists. They had pushed Lincoln into making the Civil War a war to end slavery as well as a war to save the Union. They believed that every person had an equal right to justice. As Thaddeus Stevens put it, "Such is the law of God and ought to be the law of man."

The Radical Plan

With these motives in mind, the Radicals began to take stock of their new power. The elections of 1866 had given the Radicals and their allies an overwhelming majority in Congress. Congress could therefore pass any legislation over the President's veto. The Radicals lost little time in wielding this new power over the executive branch.

The basic plan of the Radicals was outlined in March 1867. Ten of the former Confederate states were to be divided into five military districts: (1) Virginia; (2) North and South Carolina; (3) Georgia, Alabama, and Florida; (4) Mississippi and Arkansas; and (5) Texas and Louisiana. Each of these districts was to be headed by a military governor backed by federal soldiers.

The southern states had to call constitutional conventions, the delegates to which would be elected by universal manhood suffrage. These conventions had to ratify the Fourteenth Amendment and draw up new state constitutions that guaranteed black suffrage. Once a state constitution had been approved by Congress and the Fourteenth Amendment had become part of the United States' Constitution, the state could return to the Union.

Ex-Confederates who were disqualified under the Fourteenth Amendment could not vote or hold office. Thus freedmen were given the vote at the same time that traditional southern leaders lost that right.

Besides its political value to the Republican party, giving the vote to the freedmen was an attempt to give southern blacks the ability to defend their new position. Black suffrage was ensured with the Fifteenth Amendment to the Constitution, passed by Congress in 1869 and ratified in March 1870. This amendment said that the right to vote "shall not be denied . . . on account of race, color or previous condition of servitude." The southern states that had not completed political reconstruction by 1870[5] had to ratify the Fifteenth Amendment as a further condition for readmission to the Union.

Attack on the Presidency

Not all of Congress' legislative might was directed toward the South. Some was directed toward curbing the power of the President. In March 1867, the Command of the Army Act restricted the President's powers as Commander-in-Chief. The Tenure of Office Act said that the President had to have Senate

---

[5] Virginia, Georgia, Mississippi, and Texas.

RECONSTRUCTION IN THE SOUTH

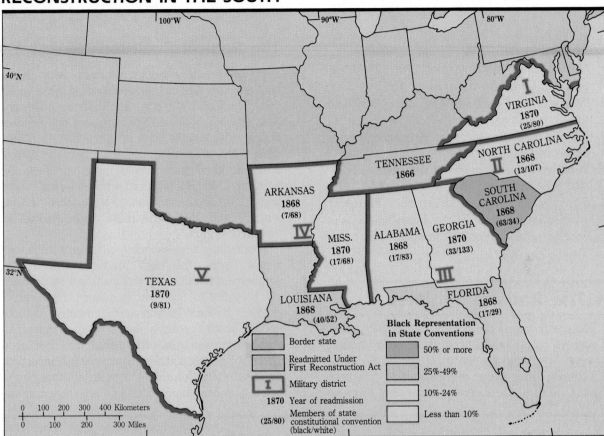

approval to remove officials who had been appointed by and with the Senate's consent. **Tenure of office** is the length of time a person can stay in office.

Although these acts restricted the President's power, many Radicals were not satisfied. In fact, many wanted to impeach Johnson. From January through June 1867, the House Judiciary Committee investigated various charges against the President. Finally, the Committee voted 5-4 against impeachment.

Johnson, however, failed to understand the message in these actions. Throughout the summer and fall of 1867, he tried to impede the Radicals' plan for reconstruction. In June he gave orders restricting the powers of the commander of the five military districts. Later he removed commanders who seemed to sympathize with the new reconstruction plan. Finally, in August 1867, Johnson dismissed Secretary of War Edwin M. Stanton from office

without Senate approval. This was in direct violation of the Tenure of Office Act. In early March 1868, the House adopted 11 articles of impeachment against Johnson.

The President's trial began shortly thereafter, with Chief Justice Salmon P. Chase presiding. Advocates of the House's position argued that the charges against Johnson fell within the constitutional requirement that a President be impeached only for "high crimes and misdemeanors." However, the House advocates failed to convince enough Senators of this. The vote was 35 for conviction and 19 for **acquittal,** or a verdict of not guilty. This was just one vote short of the number needed to convict Johnson.[6]

---

[6] Of the 19 who voted for acquittal, 7 were Republican and 12 were Democrats. Many scholars believe that this failure to remove the President for what were essentially political rather than criminal reasons preserved the system of checks and balances provided by the Constitution.

The term "scalawag" was a slang expression for a runty cow, while the term "carpetbagger" was derived from a common type of suitcase—the carpetbag. The latter term was used to refer to northerners who came to the south with an empty bag, planning to fill it up with goods that rightfully belonged to southerners.

After his acquittal, Johnson served out the rest of his term. However, any influence he might have had was lost.

SECTION REVIEW

1. Identify: Civil Rights Act of 1866, Thaddeus Stevens, Command of the Army Act.
2. Why was the Fourteenth Amendment added to the Constitution?
3. Why did the Radicals fear that abolition of slavery might aid the Democrats?
4. What were the provisions of the Radical reconstruction plan?
5. What was the purpose of the Tenure of Office Act?
6. What was the result of the impeachment proceedings against President Johnson?

4 The Radical Regimes

Despite Johnson's attempts before his trial to slow Congress' plan for reconstruction, new Radical governments were formed in the South. Although short-lived, they were unpopular with southern whites. In fact, the Radical governments were so intensely disliked that bitterness in the South has only lately begun to subside.

The Radical Coalition

By 1870 each of the ten southern states falling under military rule had been readmitted to the Union under the Radicals' terms. The **disfranchisement** (loss of the right to vote) of many ex-Confederates, plus a widespread boycott of the polls by southern whites, left government in the hands of the Radical coalition. This coalition was made up of blacks, southern Unionists, and northerners who had moved South. The southern Unionists were called **"scalawags,"** and the northerners were known as **"carpetbaggers."**

Southerners were especially bitter over the former slaves having the right to vote. One reason southerners felt this way was that most blacks were not prepared to take part in politics. However, a number of black leaders were educated, capable people. South Carolina's state treasurer, Francis L. Cardozo, for example, had received his schooling in Great Britain and had been a minister in Connecticut before the war. Jonathan J. Wright, a justice on the South Carolina supreme court, had studied at the

Seven blacks served in the United States Congress during Reconstruction. Senator H. R. Revels of Mississippi, seated at the left, was the nation's first black senator. During Reconstruction many black office holders were well educated, having attended school in the North. Who, besides blacks, made up the Radical coalition in the Reconstruction governments?

Much of the bitter reaction towards the Radical governments was due to the fact that they were different from traditional southern governments in both personnel and policies. However, southern whites also resented the fact that these governments had been imposed on them.

University of Pennsylvania and had been a member of the Pennsylvania bar. Some blacks went to the Congress of the United States, where their conduct led Representative James G. Blaine of Pennsylvania to praise them:

> *The colored men who took their seats in both Senate and House did not appear ignorant or helpless. They were as a rule studious, earnest, ambitious men, whose public conduct . . . would be honorable to any race.*

Even though some black officials were able and intelligent, they never really directed reconstruction in the postwar South. In fact, the closest blacks came to controlling a state government was in South Carolina. Until 1874, they were a majority in the lower house of that state's legislature.

Despite southern white claims to the contrary, the Radical regimes were not dominated by blacks, but by scalawags and carpetbaggers. The southern view was that scalawags and carpetbaggers were unscrupulous people who used the black vote for their own gain. There is little doubt that there were many people of this kind. Scalawags and carpetbaggers, however, were a diverse lot.

Scalawags were described by their fellow southerners as the lowest element in society. But many scalawags were people who had had doubts about secession and felt that the South should accept defeat and begin to rebuild itself. Carpetbaggers, too, in many cases, were people who came to the South for legitimate reasons. A large number saw business opportunities there. Many were veterans of the Union Army who were attracted by the South's potential. Others were teachers, members of the clergy, or agents of northern benevolent societies who came south to aid the freedmen. Whoever they were and whatever their motives, Radicals were bitterly attacked by southern whites.

Criticisms of the Radicals

The Radical governments were often guilty of fraud, graft, and waste. Governor Henry C. Warmouth of Louisiana, for example, was said to have pocketed $100,000 during his first year in office. Another governor admitted accepting bribes of over $40,000.

Bribery seemed to be the accepted practice in many of the legislatures. Corruption was widespread in the granting of charters, negotiation of contracts, and collection of taxes. Also, state debts grew enormously. A Charleston, South Carolina, newspaper reflected the feelings of many southern whites when it described a recently adjourned session of the state legislature:

> *In life it has been unlovely, and in death it has not belied its record. As it lived, it has died—an uncouth, malformed and abortive monstrosity, its birth a blunder, its life a crime, and its death a blessing.*

Achievements of the Radicals

There is little doubt that there was corruption in the Radical governments, but such corruption was by no means limited to the South during the latter half of the 1800's. There is also little doubt that the Radical governments were wasteful. However, much of the increase in state debts was due to necessary spending. For example, public buildings had to be repaired or rebuilt. Furthermore, many of the actions of the Radical governments resulted in long overdue reforms.

Because many of the Radical reforms were costly, opposition to them grew. Tax reforms placed a heavier load on wealthy whites, who complained loudly. Setting up public schools was also costly, especially so because schools for black children had not existed before the Civil War.

Under the Radicals, states expanded railroads and other public services. Many states reorganized their judicial systems, changed their penal codes, and passed civil rights legislation. Finally, the Radical governments—the most democratic the South had ever seen—gave voting rights both to the freedmen and to previously disfranchised whites.

SECTION REVIEW

1. Identify: Francis L. Cardozo, Jonathan J. Wright, James G. Blaine.
2. What groups made up the Radical coalition?
3. Why were the Radical governments often publicly criticized?
4. What reforms were introduced by the Radical regimes?

Have students analyze and critique Tillman's position.

5 Redemption

Despite such achievements, southerners were determined to rid the South of the Radicals. Indeed, political opposition to the Radical regimes began as soon as they were formed. Between 1871 and 1876, most of the southern governments came under the control of white southern leaders. Many of these leaders were ex-Whigs, but they now operated as Democrats and called themselves "Redeemers." **"Redemption"** meant the restoration of white leadership. Whites were encouraged to vote Democratic in order to restore **white supremacy,** or the power of whites over blacks.

Violence

Violence was one of the most effective ways of overthrowing the Radical governments. Secret societies such as the Ku Klux Klan and the Knights of the White Camelia tried to destroy the Radicals in the postwar South. Members of the Klan, which was founded in Tennessee in 1866, dressed in white sheets and rode through the night intimidating freedmen and Unionists. The Klan used threats, beatings, and murder to keep freedmen and other Republicans from voting. Although many southern whites disapproved of these methods, others felt justified in using violence. Years later, Benjamin R. Tillman of South Carolina defended their actions in a speech to the Senate:

> It was in 1876, thirty years ago, and the people of South Carolina had been living under Negro rule for eight years. There was a condition bordering on anarchy. Misrule, robbery, and murder were holding high carnival. The people's substance was being stolen, and there was no incentive to labor. Our legislature was composed of a majority of negroes, most of whom could neither read nor write. They were the easy dupes and tools of as dirty a band of vampires and robbers as ever

Many southern whites opposed voting by blacks. Some formed associations to scare them away from the polls and out of politics. The Ku Klux Klan was one such organization. It used force and violence to intimidate freedmen and prevent them from voting. Members of the Klan hid their identities behind masks and sheets. Blacks who protested against being denied their right to vote, or who were "disrespectful" to whites, were the main victims of this terrorism. How did members of the Ku Klux Klan try to justify their actions?

Frederick Douglass

Frederick Bailey was born a slave in Maryland in 1817. He escaped at the age of 21 and fled to New York. To avoid capture, he changed his name to Douglass. Later he moved to Massachusetts, where he became a lecturer at antislavery rallies.

In 1845 Douglass published his autobiography, *Narrative of the Life of Frederick Douglass*. Fearing that he would be discovered as a fugitive slave because of his book, he went to England. There he continued his fight against slavery and raised money to buy his freedom.

In 1847 he returned to the United States and began to publish an antislavery newspaper, the *North Star*. When the Civil War broke out, he helped to recruit black soldiers for the Union army.

After the Union victory, Douglass once again took up the battle for black rights. He was instrumental in the passage of the Thirteenth, Fourteenth, and Fifteenth Amendments.

Douglass was naturally disappointed at the restoration of white supremacy in the South during the 1870's. He said:

> Peace with the old master class has been war to the Negro. As the one has risen, the other has fallen.

However, Douglass tried to analyze these troubling events from a broad historical view. He believed that eventually blacks would obtain their full rights in American society.

---

preyed upon a prostrate people. . . . Life ceased to be worth having on the terms under which we were living, and in desperation we determined to take the government away from the negroes.

Word of the Klan's atrocities reached the North, causing a public outcry. Congress passed a series of laws that gave the President power to use troops to halt violence. By 1872, the Klan had lost a good deal of power. The decline of the Klan, however, did not mark the end of violence in the South.

Waning Interest

Although there was violence, some blacks made it to the polls. In fact, in the presidential elections of 1868 and 1872, the black vote helped elect Ulysses S. Grant. Despite this fact, Republican interest in reconstruction began to wane.

This lack of enthusiasm came about for a number of reasons. First, the old Radical leaders began to disappear from the political scene. Thaddeus Stevens

died in 1868, and others retired or lost elections. Younger supporters of the Radicals grew disenchanted with the Grant administration. In fact, they had formed a Liberal Republican party to oppose him.

The Liberal Republicans had become interested in issues other than reconstruction and began to feel that southern problems should be handled by the South. One of the first steps toward that goal was the passage of the General Amnesty Act in May 1872. This act restored the right to hold public office to most ex-Confederates who had been disqualified by the Fourteenth Amendment.

A second factor that weakened enthusiasm for reconstruction was racial prejudice in the North. This prejudice was exploited by opponents of reconstruction. They argued that only southerners really knew how to deal with blacks and that the fate of the freedmen should be left to the South.

A third factor that influenced Republican attitudes was the party's association with northern business interests. Northern businesses with investments in the South were concerned about the impact of

Following the Civil War, the plantation system was replaced by sharecropping. Under the sharecropping system, landless whites and freedmen planted land that was not their own. All financial return obtained from cash crop production had to be shared with the landowners. Sharecroppers also planted small vegetable gardens for their own use. What was a crop-lien?

violence on those investments. Restoration of the southern white leadership seemed to be the answer to the problem.

The Compromise of 1877

The final blow to Radical reconstruction came as a result of the election of 1876. The Democratic party had grown stronger in the north, and in the South all but three of the Radical governments (South Carolina, Florida, and Louisiana) had been overthrown. Once again, the Democrats were ready to challenge the Republicans for the Presidency.

The Republicans nominated Governor Rutherford B. Hayes of Ohio. The Democrats chose Governor Samuel J. Tilden of New York. Tilden received a margin of 250,000 in the popular vote, but there was a dispute over the electoral vote. Both Republicans and Democrats claimed victory in South Carolina, Florida, and Louisiana. In Oregon, there was one vote in question. Tilden needed only one of the disputed votes for election, while Hayes needed all of them.

As passions rose over the disputed votes, Congress created a **bipartisan** (involving members of two parties) commission to settle the matter. Its members were chosen from the House, and Supreme Court. There were 15 members of this commission—8 Republicans and 7 Democrats. The vote, when it came, followed party lines. Thus, all of the disputed electoral votes went to Hayes.

The Democrats were up in arms. However, in a series of meetings between leaders of both parties, a compromise was reached. As a result of this compromise, the Democrats agreed to the election of Hayes. In return, the Republicans promised to remove all federal troops from the South, include southerners in the distribution of patronage, and legislate money for internal improvements in the South. As soon as federal troops were withdrawn, the last three of the South's Republican governments fell. With the Compromise of 1877, reconstruction in the South was ended.

Aftermath

In many ways the South after Reconstruction was similar to the South before the Civil War. By 1877 the southern states were back under the control of southern whites. With the Southern Democrats again in power, blacks suffered a loss of their political rights.

Blacks also suffered economically. Slavery was gone, but a new form of dependency had developed. This was **sharecropping.** Under this system, most blacks worked small pieces of land owned by someone else—often the planter they had served. In return, they received a share of the season's crop. Tenants bought their supplies under the **crop-lien system**—promising a certain percentage of their crop as payment for goods. As a result of sharecropping and the crop-lien system, tenants always seemed to be in debt. Socially, the freedmen fared little better.

There were, however, changes coming to the South. By the 1880's southern agriculture had recovered and was producing at a rate higher than in the antebellum years. In addition, the southern economy had become more diversified, and invest-ments had increased. Indeed, the growth of the textile and iron industries foreshadowed the appearance of a new South—a South that would be more akin to the rest of the United States.

SECTION REVIEW

1. Identify the following: Ku Klux Klan, Liberal Republicans, General Amnesty Act, Samuel J. Tilden.
2. How did Congress react to violence in the South?
3. Why did the Republicans' interest in reconstruction wane?
4. Why were the results of the election of 1876 disputed?
5. What was agreed upon in the Compromise of 1877?

CHAPTER 13   REVIEW

SUMMARY

1. After the war there was sharp disagreement among northerners on how to handle the problem of southern reconstruction.
2. Lincoln developed a plan that was designed to restore the old relationship between North and South.
3. Congress opposed Lincoln's plan as too lenient and developed its own plan for reconstruction.
4. After Lincoln's assassination, Johnson put into effect a reconstruction program that was intended to help the common people of the South and to exclude the planter aristocracy from government.
5. Under Johnson's plan, ex-Confederates quickly regained control of the South and passed laws that severely limited the rights of blacks.
6. Alarmed by conditions in the South, Radical Republicans in Congress passed their own reconstruction acts.
7. The Radicals' reconstruction program led to control of southern states by a coalition of southern Unionists, blacks, and northerners who had moved South.
8. Johnson's opposition to the Radicals' program resulted in his impeachment.
9. Southern whites were bitterly opposed to the Radical regimes, and they sometimes resorted to violence in an effort to overthrow the Republicans.
10. By 1877 power in southern states had been restored to white leaders and the Democratic party.

VOCABULARY

reconstruction	black codes	acquittal	white supremacy
amnesty	segregation	disfranchisement	bipartisan
freedmen	vagrancy law	scalawags	sharecropping
ironclad oath	discrimination	carpetbaggers	crop-lien system
yeoman farmers	tenure of office	redemption	

REVIEW QUESTIONS

1. What problems faced the South after the Civil War?
2. How did the reconstruction plans of Lincoln, Johnson and the Radicals compare?
3. What attempts were made to help the freedmen during the Reconstruction?
4. How did the Radicals gain enough political power to put through their reconstruction program?

5. Why did conflict arise between President Johnson and Congress?
6. What role did blacks play in the Radical regimes?
7. How was the South able to overthrow the Radical regimes?
8. How did the South after reconstruction compare to the South before the Civil War?

DISCUSSION

1. Do you think Lincoln would have suffered the same fate as Johnson had he lived?
2. What could have been done differently that would have made the postwar reconstruction more satisfactory to everyone?

3. If you had been in the Senate, would you have voted for or against conviction of President Johnson?
4. Were the Radical regimes helpful or harmful to the interests of freedmen?

USING MAPS

Refer to the map on page 281 and answer the following questions:

1. Which states had 50 percent or more black representation in state conventions?

2. Which states were in military district III?
3. Which state was in a military district by itself?
4. Which was the first state to be readmitted to the Union? The last?

USING SKILLS

Study the following statements and decide which ones show evidence of emotional bias and which ones show an attempt to be objective. Then refer to the excerpt on pages 284–5 and make a list of words that carry an emotional content.

1. "I understand traitors. I have been fighting them at the south end of the line." (Andrew Johnson)
2. "The real human tragedy is the upward striving of downtrodden men, the groping for light among people born in darkness . . ." (W. E. B. Dubois on reconstruction.)

3. "If the question was, Is Andrew Johnson a fit person for President? I should answer, no; but it is not a party question, nor upon Andrew Johnson's deeds and acts, except so far as they are made to appear in the record, that I am to decide." (Senator Lyman Trumbell of Illinois on Johnson's impeachment.)
4. "It seems strange to us that he should have condescended to submit to an election at all." (A southern newspaper's comments on Lincoln's election in 1864.)

SUMMARY

1. After the Mexican War, the question of slavery in the territories dominated politics in the United States.

2. All attempts at compromise on the slavery issue broke down, and the country was divided by civil war.

3. The Civil War resulted in the defeat of the South and the emancipation of the slaves.

4. The war left the South physically and economically devastated.

5. During the reconstruction period, the southern states that had seceded were brought back into the Union.

6. Reconstruction of the South left many problems unsolved, including the place of blacks in American society.

REVIEW QUESTIONS

1. Why were northerners and southerners unable to resolve their differences peaceably?

2. What effects did the Civil War have on the nation?

3. Why did the North win the war?

4. How did life change for blacks after the end of the Civil War?

SUGGESTED ACTIVITIES

1. Role-play a congressional committee meeting in 1859, with some members of the committee from the North, some from the South, and some from the West. Develop a compromise proposal to resolve sectional issues and avoid war.

2. Draw a cartoon showing the objectives of the Civil War from the northern, southern, or British viewpoint.

3. Write a one-week diary of (a) a Confederate soldier with Lee's army in 1864, (b) a black freed by the Emancipation Proclamation, or (c) the brother or sister of a Union soldier.

4. Research and prepare a report on (a) Civil War songs, (b) military weapons in the Civil War, or (c) Civil War prisons.

5. Make a chart of the reconstruction plans of Lincoln, Johnson and the Radical Republicans. Show the basic proposals for each plan, the objectives of the proposals, and the results of the proposals.

SUGGESTED READINGS

1. Bishop, Jim. *The Day Lincoln Was Shot.* New York: Harper & Row Publishers, Inc., 1964. Paperback. A readable book offering a journalistic view of the last day of Lincoln's life.

2. Commanger, Henry Steele, ed. *The Blue & the Gray: The Story of the Civil War as Told by Participants.* New York: Mentor Books, 1973. 2 vols. Paperback. Uses reports, letters, and other documents to provide a good view of the war as seen by those who experienced it.

3. Crane, Stephen. *The Red Badge of Courage.* New York: Bantam Books, Inc., 1959. A well-written story of a youth facing the realities of life and war.

4. Eaton, Clement. *Jefferson Davis.* New York: Free Press, 1977. Paperback. A sympathetic work giving the reader insight into the social conservatism of the South and the character of the man who led the Confederacy.

5. Kantor, MacKinley. *Andersonville.* New York: Signet Books, 1971. Paperback. A dramatic novel about life at a Confederate prisoner-of-war camp.

6. Sandburg, Carl. *Abraham Lincoln: The Prairie Years & the War Years.* New York: Dell Publishing Co., Inc., 1959. 3 vols. Paperback. An abridged version of Sandburg's epic biography of Abraham Lincoln.

THE HISTORIAN'S CRAFT

When historians study the work of another historian, they are studying a secondary source that is written from a particular point of view. Point of view influences a historian's interpretation of history. Point of view, in turn, may be influenced by many things.

This activity will show you how historians' viewpoints may differ and how their viewpoints may have been influenced. The subject of the activity is reconstruction. On this subject historians have held widely different views. One view is that reconstruction was a tragedy for white southerners because the Radical governments were hypocritical and corrupt. Another view is that the Radicals were honestly concerned about blacks, and that reconstruction was a tragedy only because it failed to guarantee black rights.

Following are brief biographies of two historians and excerpts from their work on reconstruction. Read the biographies and excerpts. Then list the biographical points that you think may have influenced what each historian wrote.

Albert Burton Moore

Moore, a white American, was born in Belk, Alabama, in 1887. He went to college at Alabama Polytechnic Institute. In 1921 he received his doctorate in history from the University of Chicago. For over 30 years, Dr. Moore was a professor of history at the University of Alabama. He died in 1967. Possible formative influences: During his childhood and youth, relations between the races in the South hit their low point. Segregation became official policy. In 1947 Moore published the following account of reconstruction:

The political enfranchisement of four million Negroes, from whose necks the yoke of slavery had just been lifted, is the most startling fact about Reconstruction, and a fact of tremendous impact in southern history. There is nothing in the history of democracy comparable to it. To give the Negroes the ballot and office—ranging from constable to governor—and the right to sit in state legislatures and in Congress, while depriving their former masters of their political rights

and the South of its trained leadership, is one of the most outstanding facts in the history of reconstruction after war. It was a stroke of fanatical vengeance and design. . . .

Negro voting laid the basis for the Carpetbag regime. For eight years Radical northern leaders, backed by the Washington authorities and the army and aided by some native whites, pillaged and plundered and finished wrecking the South. . . .

Radical Reconstruction corrupted southern politics, and the prejudice aroused against Negro participation in politics led ultimately to the disfranchisement of most of the Negroes. Political habits formed in counteracting Carpetbag machinations and the presence of Negro voters continued to influence politics. Fraudulent methods were employed to control the Negro votes and when factions appeared among the whites they employed against each other the chicanery and frauds which they had used against the Radicals. . . .

Race friction and prejudice were engendered by Reconstruction, which was an unfortunate thing for both races and especially for the Negroes. It caused greater discriminations against the Negroes in politics and education, and in other ways. The Negroes had been so pampered and led as to arouse false notions and hopes among them and to make them for many years lame factors in the rebuilding of the South. The Negro after Reconstruction, and in large degree because of it, continued and continues to be a source of division between the North and South. The North either could not or would not understand the necessity of race segregation, and the idea that the Negro must have a definite place in the scheme of life was obnoxious. Disfranchisement of the Negro, occasional race riots, and the sporadic mobbing of Negroes accused of heinous crimes gave rise to continued charges of "Southern outrages." Criticisms from the North, generally based upon a lack of understanding of the problem, seemed more a matter of censure than of true interest in the Negro. Thus, those who expected to see sectional strife over the status of the Negro disappear with the emancipation of the slaves were disillusioned. . . .

John Hope Franklin

Franklin, a black American, was born in Rentiesville, Oklahoma, in 1915. He attended college at Fisk University and received his doctorate in history from Harvard University in 1941. Dr. Franklin is a professor of history at the University of Chicago. Possible formative influences: The 1950's and 1960's were decades of substantial improvement in the civil rights of black Americans. In 1961 Franklin published this account of reconstruction:

The violence directed against the Negro on almost every hand indicated how determined the former Confederates were to maintain . . . white supremacy. . . .

The hostility to the education of Negroes was a part of the scheme to keep the whites superior. Within the first two years after the war Southerners themselves not only did little to educate the Negro but they also resisted the efforts of others. . . . White teachers from the North were ostracised and occasionally run out of the community. Negro schools were often burned or razed. In dozens of other ways Negroes were discouraged from seeking education. While many whites insisted that they were not opposed to the education of the freedmen, they did little or nothing to make it possible. . . .

Long before Negroes became a political factor and while the governments of the Southern states were still in the hands of the former Confederates, the Klan organization was being perfected and was spreading to many parts of the South. . . .

It would be historical fallacy to assert that the Ku Klux Klan and its compatriots were organized to combat the Union League and to overthrow Radical Reconstruction. They came on the scene much too early to support such a view and they were, indeed, too much a reflection of the general character of Southern life to require the unique conditions of Radical

Reconstruction to spawn them. Radical Reconstruction was, however, a powerful stimulus for such endeavors, and the struggle against it gave the Klan respectability and a dignity that it had not anticipated. . . . Within a matter of months it was being claimed that the "instinct of self-protection" prompted the organization of the Klan. . . .

Acting "purely in self-defense" assumed curious forms. It involved the murder of respectable Negroes by roving gangs of terrorists, the murder of Negro renters of land, the looting of stores whose owners were sometimes killed, and the murder of peaceable white citizens. . . . It was reported that in North Carolina the Klan was responsible for 260 outrages, including 7 murders and the whipping of 72 whites and 141 Negroes. In one county in South Carolina 6 men were murdered and more than 300 were whipped during the first six months of 1870. Meanwhile, the personal indignities inflicted upon individual whites and Negroes were so varied and so numerous as to defy classification or enumeration. There were the public whippings, the maimings, the mutilations, and other almost inconceivable forms of intimidation.

The fact that different points of view led to different descriptions of events does not relieve the student of history from critically comparing those descriptions. It cannot be assumed that, since all accounts are influenced by points of view, all accounts are equally reliable. The following questions will help you to decide which of the two accounts seems more reliable to you.

QUESTIONS

1. What appears to be Moore's attitude toward blacks? What is Franklin's attitude toward blacks? (Give examples to back up what you say.)
2. According to Moore, what caused the disfranchisement of blacks, race friction, and prejudice? What evidence does he give for his position? Does Franklin agree? What evidence does Franklin give?
3. How does each historian explain the reason for the poor education of blacks? What evidence does each give?

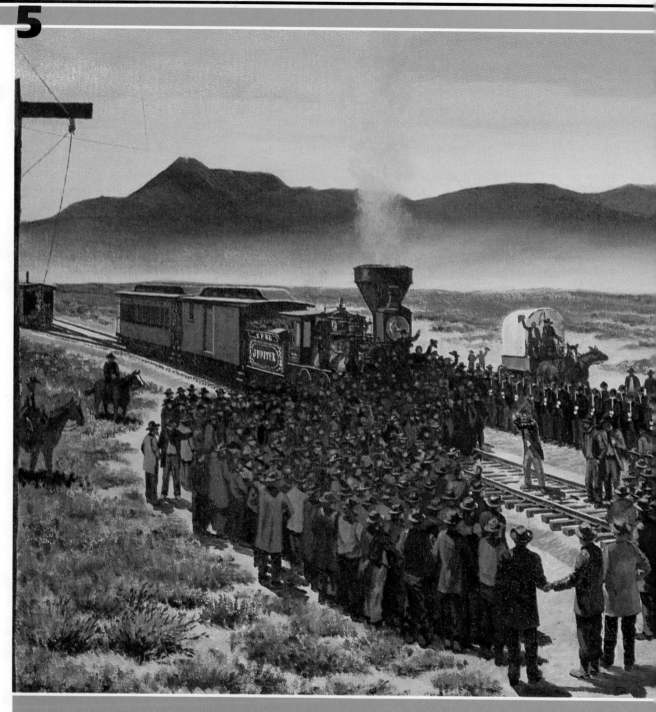

1862 Morrill Act	1867 Founding of Grange	1872 Crédit Mobilier Scandal	1882 Chinese Exclusion Act	1886 Founding of AFL	1887 Dawes Act

1862 Homestead Act	1869 Founding of Knights of Labor	1876 Battle of the Little Big Horn	1883 Pendleton Act	1887 Interstate Commerce Act

THE AGE OF INDUSTRIALIZATION

Industrial Growth

The Rise of Labor

The Last Frontier

The Gilded Age

An Urban Society

The Progressive Era

1890
Sherman
Antitrust Act

1896
Plessy v.
Ferguson

1906
Pure Food
and Drug Act

1913
16th and 17th Amendments
Federal Reserve Act

1892
Birth of
Populist Party

1901
Assassination of
William McKinley

1912
Bullmoose
Party

1914
Clayton
Antitrust Act

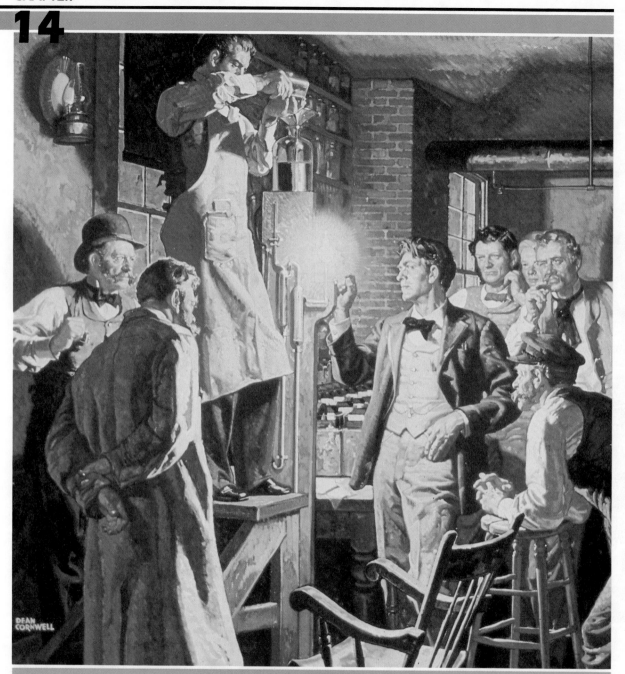

1	Foundations for Growth	295
2	The Railroads	297
3	The Giants of Industry	301
4	Philosophy for an Era	305
5	Attempts at Regulation	306

INDUSTRIAL GROWTH

So far as we can see ahead there is every reason for even rash optimism in regard to the material or economic welfare of mankind.

William Graham Summer

The period from the end of the Civil War to 1900 was an era of unmatched economic growth in the United States. Although agriculture was important, the key to this growth was industrialization. In 1889 income from manufactured goods exceeded that from farm goods for the first time. By 1894 the United States had taken the place of Great Britain as the leading manufacturing nation in the world.

New methods in technology and business allowed the country to tap its rich supply of natural resources, increase its production, and raise the money needed for growth. The growing transportation system made it easier for merchants to reach distant markets.

American business leaders played a vital role in organizing the growth of industry. Their efforts were generally backed by the public, the government, and the courts.

1 Foundations For Growth

The change from a predominantly agricultural society to an industrial one was possible because the United States had the basic resources needed for a growing economy. Among those resources were what economists call the **factors of production:** land, labor, and capital.

The Factors of Production

The first factor of production, land, means not just the land itself but all natural resources. The United States owned an abundance and variety of natural resources that were useful for industrial production.

Coal, so important as fuel for steam-powered factories, was mined in Pennsylvania, West Virginia, Kentucky, and Ohio. The first oil well was drilled in Pennsylvania in 1859, and oil refining (changing the crude oil from the ground into useable products) soon became big business. Oil was used as a lubricant for machines and as a fuel for lamps.

Huge amounts of iron ore, the raw material of the steel industry, were discovered in Michigan, Wisconsin, and Minnesota. Sizeable deposits were also mined in Pennsylvania, New Jersey, and Alabama. The country also had large supplies of copper, lead, zinc, magnesium, gypsum, salt, sulphur, and other minerals. America's forests contained a variety of products essential to building. Although not completely self-sufficient, the United States had many resources from which it could draw.

The second production factor, labor, was especially important in the early stages of industrialization. Large numbers of workers were needed to turn raw materials into goods. This need was met by the rapid growth of population, due largely to immigration. Between 1860 and 1900 the population of the country more than doubled, from 31 million to nearly 75 million. Millions of immigrants entered America each year, providing a pool of labor for factories and mines. Most of the immigrants settled in the industrial cities of the Northeast, where they were joined by migrants from American farms. The growing need for workers in these industrial cities set a wheel into motion. The United States was changing from a rural society to an urban society.

The third production factor, capital, is the equipment—buildings, machinery, and tools—used in production. Land and labor are needed to produce capital goods, which in turn are essential for the production of consumer goods.

The term "capital" is also used to mean money for investment. Huge amounts of money were needed to finance industrial growth. One source of money was the selling of stock by corporations. Another was corporate saving, or businesses investing a portion of their earnings in better equipment. Other sources of money were loans from banks and life insurance

Have students determine what energy resources are available in their region. To what extent are these resources being currently exploited?

By 1900 the United States had passed England as the world's chief producer of steel.

MINERAL RESOURCES OF THE UNITED STATES, 1870

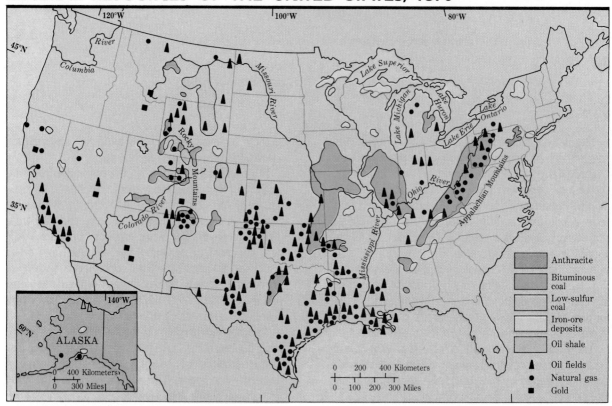

companies, and government **subsidies** (grants to aid an enterprise considered to be good for the public).

New Technology

Business leaders invested billions of dollars in new forms of technology. The late 1800's was a period of invention and innovation. The number of patents filed in the United States increased from about 2000 per year in the 1850's to over 20,000 per year in the 1880's and 1890's.

Two discoveries revolutionized the iron and steel industries. The first was the use of coke (soft coal with the impurities removed). Coke was found to be an excellent fuel for iron-smelting blast furnaces. The second was the Bessemer Process, discovered independently by William Kelly and Henry Bessemer. The process used blasts of cold air to burn off impurities from heated iron. Because steel could now be made cheaply, steel production soared. Cheap,

durable steel then became the basis for other industrial advances. Train rails made of steel lasted up to ten times longer than iron rails. Steel beams supported bigger, heavier bridges and buildings. Steel was used for making new machinery and a host of other products.

Inventions of all sorts changed old industries and created new ones. The refrigerator car, introduced in 1857, created an industry in fresh-meat shipping. New machines that could cut off corn kernels, shell peas, and make cans were the basis for the canning industry. Another invention that created an industry was the typewriter, invented by Christopher Sholes in 1867.

One advance that stood out in this age of invention was the harnessing of electric power. Electric arc light proved a sensation at the 1876 Centennial Exposition in Philadelphia. Soon many cities were lighting their streets with arc lights. Inventor Thomas Alva Edison boasted that he could devise a better system, and he made good his boast.

Edison developed a new approach to invention. Rather than wait for a flash of inspiration, he set up an invention "factory"—a laboratory where several people worked on a trial-and-error basis. The method was effective. Out of Edison's laboratory came many inventions and improvements that were helpful to American industry. Edison patented his incandescent light bulb in 1880. In 1882 he set up the first permanent central power station.

Within a few years, George Westinghouse and other inventors had found ways of using electric motors in factories. However, the full impact of electricity as a source of power did not come until after 1900.

Improvements in communication also allowed businesses to expand their operations. By 1886 Western Union was providing telegraph service for more than 14,000 towns in America. Transcontinental and overseas telegraph lines delivered news in minutes that had previously taken weeks.

The outstanding invention in communications was the telephone. It was developed by Alexander Graham Bell, a young teacher of the deaf, who filed for a patent in 1876. A few years later, the American Bell Telephone Company was established. The American Telephone and Telegraph Company was organized in 1885 to handle long distance lines and, in

1900, combined with American Bell to form the Bell Telephone System. This new form of communicating proved to be extremely successful. By 1902 the United States had 1.3 million telephones in operation.

Experiments were beginning in radio communication as well. In 1895 Italian inventor Guglielmo Marconi transmitted the first messages, and, by 1902, radio messages were being sent as far as 2000 miles.

SECTION REVIEW

1. Identify the following: William Kelly, Christopher Sholes, Alexander Graham Bell.
2. What are the factors of production?
3. What sources did businesses use to raise money for investment?
4. How were Thomas Edison's methods different from those of other inventors?

2 The Railroads

Communication and transportation systems were fundamental to industrial growth. The railroads especially played a major role in supporting industrialization. Because of the railroads, isolated communities were vanishing. The merchants' goods and farmers' products could be shipped almost anywhere. By 1890 railroad freight had reached 691 million tons (621.9 metric tons). In that same year railroads carried 520 million passengers, nearly three times the number carried in 1877.

Expansion and Improvement

Inventions and improvements helped the railroads meet the growing demand for their services. More powerful locomotives were developed to pull heavier trains. Specialized cars, among them refrigerator, tank, and coal cars, carried goods across the nation.

Traveling was easier and more relaxing. A traveler in 1884 could enjoy the larger, more comfortable passenger cars or, if drowsy, turn in for the night. The Pullman Company had put its first sleeping cars on the tracks in 1865.

Trains were also safer than they had been. In 1887 the automatic coupler, a device used to connect railroad cars, was introduced. The coupler replaced

After the Civil War, good means of communication in an expanding United States became increasingly necessary. Alexander Graham Bell helped to provide one means through his invention of the telephone. What other communication systems came into use?

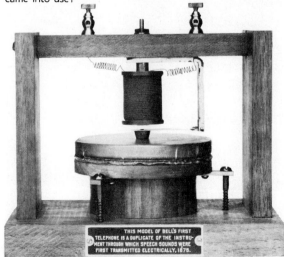

THIS MODEL OF BELL'S FIRST TELEPHONE IS A DUPLICATE OF THE INSTRUMENT THROUGH WHICH SPEECH SOUNDS WERE FIRST TRANSMITTED ELECTRICALLY, 1875.

Standardization of parts was aided by competition for government contracts.

After the Civil War, the federal government became a major supporter of improvements in transportation. Recall the long-standing debates over federal support of internal improvements.

the unsafe "link and pin" device. That same year, the air brake, developed by George Westinghouse, was put into use. Furthermore, trains were faster than ever before. On May 10, 1893, a New York Central engine set a new speed record of 112 miles (179.2 kilometers) per hour.

Increased use made it necessary for the railroads to expand and unify their system. In 1866, there were 37,000 miles (59,200 kilometers) of tracks in the United States. By 1890, the railroads had increased their network to 166,703 miles (266,735 kilometers). Dozens of short lines were consolidated into a few major systems that were able to offer continuous connections between major cities.

Travel from one city to another was confusing because each city had a different sun time (time based on the position of the sun). Railroads adopted their own time systems because time on a moving train could not easily be adjusted to local times. To remedy this situation, William F. Allen suggested a **standard time** system that was adopted by the United States and Canada in 1883. Under this system, the country is divided into time zones. Each zone uses the sun time of its central meridian.

Standard time improved railroad service, but other problems remained. Until the Civil War, track widths varied in size in different parts of the country. By 1886 the railways, with few exceptions, had adopted the standard gauge track width of four feet, eight and one-half inches (1.35 meters). Standard gauge allowed faster shipment of goods at a reduced cost. No longer was it necessary to load and unload goods from one train to another. One train could make the entire journey.

The biggest project of all in the postwar era was the building of the transcontinental lines. The last spike joining the Union Pacific and Central Pacific Railroads at Promontory Point, Utah, was hammered into place May 10, 1869. The last spike—a golden spike struck with a silver hammer—marked the completion of the first transcontinental railroad. For the first time East and West were connected by a transportation link. By 1900 five transcontinental lines were operating in the United States.

RAILROAD LINES, 1860 AND 1890

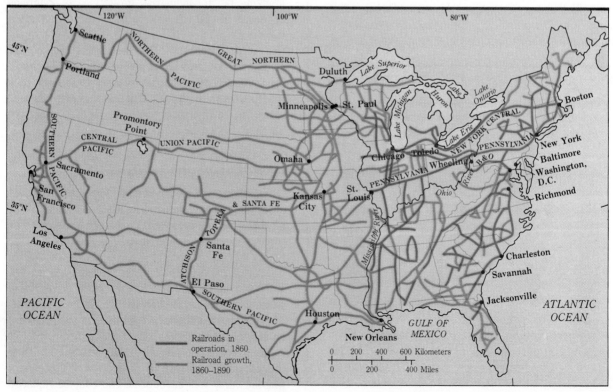

The Railroad Magnates

The first American companies to qualify as "Big Business" were the railroads. The entrepreneurs who planned, built, financed and controlled the railroads were some of the country's first business tycoons.

One of the railroad tycoons was James J. Hill, the "Empire Builder." At the age of 18, he moved to the trading post of St. Paul in the Minnesota Territory from Ontario, where he had been born in 1838. As a trader and shipping agent, he saved money until he had piled up a small fortune.

Hill could see how quickly the frontier around him was developing, and he knew that transporta-

tion would be needed. When a small railroad in the Minnesota Territory went bankrupt in the 1870's, he convinced a few of his friends to go in with him on what seemed to be a risky investment.

Hill and his friends bought the railroad for a fraction of its real value. The first few years were rough, but Hill had a business philosophy that called for helping his whole region to grow and prosper. He wrote to a partner:

> *It is our best interest to give low rates and do all we can to develop the country and create business.*

Hill's philosophy was successful. Soon his railroad was making a good profit hauling the bumper crops grown by Norwegian and Swedish immigrants in Minnesota. Later, Hill was reponsible for the first transcontinental railroad built without help from the federal government—the Great Northern Railway. This railroad, completed in 1893, ran from Lake Superior to Puget Sound.

Another railroad tycoon was Cornelius ("Commodore") Vanderbilt, who made a fortune first as an owner of steamship lines and later as an owner of railroads. A third tycoon was Leland Stanford, one of the organizers of the Central Pacific Railroad. These railroad magnates were aggressive and competitive men. They lived in an age when few laws had been passed to regulate business, and some of their methods were highly questionable. Nevertheless, the railroad magnates played an important part in building the nation's transportation system.

Financing the Railroads

Huge sums of money were required to finance the building of a transcontinental railway system. The promise of quick profits made the railroad an attractive investment for shrewd business leaders. Millions of dollars were raised through the sale of stock to private investors, both American and European. Because a railroad promised growth and prosperity for those along its path, state and local governments offered loans and land grants in order to obtain railroad connections.

Nothing contributed more to the rapid growth of the railroad than the subsidies offered by the federal

government. In 1862 Congress passed the Pacific Railway Act, authorizing the construction of the transcontinental railroad and granting parcels of land to the Central Pacific and Union Pacific companies. In 1864 a second Pacific Railway Act expanded the land grant program to include other railroad companies.

Each company received a 400-foot (120-meter) right-of-way and the free use of timber and building materials from government lands. Additional land on both sides of the track was granted for each mile of railroad that was built. The railroads could sell this property to raise money. The 1864 act also provided loans ranging from $16,000 to $48,000 a mile, depending upon the nature of the land. Before the

Many of the Union Pacific workers were Irish immigrants. Scarcity of labor was a problem for the railroad companies.

land grant program expired in 1871, the federal government gave away more than 175 million acres (70 million hectares) of public land to 29 railroads.

The government's land policy was controversial. Critics argued that the land giveaway led railroads to lay tracks in sparsely-populated territories that did not need transportation. In the scramble to build quickly and get more land, the companies sometimes used poor building methods. This led to high operating and maintenance costs—costs that the consumer paid—and sometimes to accidents.

Railroad companies also came under heavy criticism for **graft** (illegal gain) and corruption. It was not unusual for companies to hire construction firms owned by financial promoters of the railroad. The contracted price was set much higher than the actual building cost. Company officials then pocketed the illegally-earned money.

Defenders of the land grants pointed out that the railroads were required by law to carry government troops and mail free or at reduced rates. The railroads also did a great deal to stimulate settlement of the West.

Laying the Tracks

Work on the railroads was plentiful, and Americans from all parts of the nation flocked to help modernize old tracks and construct new lines. Building the transcontinental lines was the most monumental task the nation had ever undertaken, requiring great engineering skill and six years of backbreaking toil. Union Pacific workers, starting at Omaha, Nebraska and moving westward, had to battle difficult terrain and, at times, Indian attacks. Grenville Dodge, chief engineer for the Union Pacific, described how the work was done:

> *All the supplies for this work had to be hauled from the end of the track, and the wagon transportation was enormous. At one time we were using at least ten thousand animals, and most of the time from eight to ten thousand*

Equally as important as the development of communication systems was the development of transportation networks. In the post Civil War period railroads were one of the first industries to experience great expansion. How did the Pacific Railway Acts help railroads develop?

Management is often considered to be the fourth factor of production.

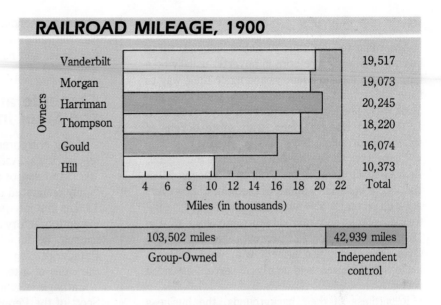

RAILROAD MILEAGE, 1900

Owners	Total
Vanderbilt	19,517
Morgan	19,073
Harriman	20,245
Thompson	18,220
Gould	16,074
Hill	10,373

Miles (in thousands)

103,502 miles	42,939 miles
Group-Owned	Independent control

laborers. *The bridge gangs always worked from five to twenty miles ahead of the track, and it was seldom that the track waited for a bridge. To supply one mile of track with material and supplies required about forty cars, as on the plains everything—rails, ties, bridging, fastenings, all railway supplies, fuel for locomotives and trains, and supplies for men and animals on the entire work—had to be transported from the Missouri River. Therefore as we moved westward, every hundred miles added vastly to our transportation. Yet the work was so systematically planned and executed that I do not remember an instance in all the construction of the line of the work being delayed a single week for want of material.*

The task facing Central Pacific crews, laying tracks eastward out of San Francisco to Promontory Point, was even harsher. The land was rockier, the hills steeper, the winters more severe. Snowdrifts, some piled as high as 50 feet, blocked their path.

Immigrants from China made up most of the Central Pacific crews. They had first begun coming to the United States in the 1840's, leaving behind a China crippled by famine and war. The Chinese found opportunity for work on the railroads. Company officials welcomed their steady work habits and their willingness to accept low wages. By 1882 nearly

375,000 Chinese had come to America, most of them settling in California, particularly in San Francisco.

SECTION REVIEW

1. Identify the following: George Westinghouse, Grenville Dodge, Pacific Railway Act of 1862.
2. How did railroads meet the growing demand for their services?
3. What were the pros and cons of the government's land grant policy?
4. What difficulties were faced by crews building the transcontinental railroads?

3 The Giants of Industry

The expansion of the railroads, along with other improvements in transportation and communication, created the mass market. No longer were manufacturers limited to local or regional sales. The mass market made mass production practical. Mass production—production of large quantities of goods at low cost—was the heart of the new industrial system.

Because of the general trend toward large-scale operations, the late 1800's has been called the Age of Big Business. The heroes of big business were the **entrepreneurs.** They were the business leaders who organized land, labor, and capital, raised money, adopted new technology, and made huge profits.

Rags to Riches

According to the "rags to riches" legend, these business leaders were born in poverty, usually on a farm or in a foreign country, and made their way to fame and fortune through hard work, good luck, and quick wits. The legend was promoted by novels such as those by Horatio Alger, who wrote dozens of stories about young boys who got rich.

There were some whose lives matched the legend, such as Philip Armour and Andrew Carnegie. Most successful business leaders of the period, however, grew up in comfortable surroundings. A survey of the textile, steel, and railroad entrepreneurs of the 1870's shows that only 25 percent came from farms. Over 50 percent had fathers who were business leaders themselves, and nearly 37 percent attended college.

Regardless of their backgrounds, the business entrepreneurs played a vital role in the changing American economy. They were the individuals who had the ability and the vision to organize people, machines, and natural resources productively.

Carnegie and the Steel Industry

If any entrepreneur embodied the rags to riches legend, it was Andrew Carnegie. Born in Scotland in 1835, the son of a poor weaver, Carnegie and his family emigrated to the United States when he was 13. His first job was as a bobbin boy, winding threads in a cotton factory for $1.20 a week. Looking to better himself, he found work as a messenger boy in a Pittsburgh telegraph office. Not long after, he learned the skills of a telegraph operator.

Carnegie left the telegraph office when Thomas A. Scott of the Pennsylvania Railroad hired him as his personal secretary and telegrapher. Intelligent,

The stimulus toward industrialization began gathering momentum before the Civil War. It was not until after the War, however, that heavy industry expanded rapidly. Shown here is the Carnegie Steel Company in Homestead, Pennsylvania, one of many steel plants built in the late 1800's. What other industries developed during that time?

Other major entrepreneuers of this period were Gail Borden, who patented condensed milk; Henry John Heinz, who dominated the canning industry; and George Eastman, inventor of the Kodak camera.

All of these entrepreneurs used technology and management to develop their companies. Have students identify examples of each.

hard-working, and ambitious, Carnegie was eager to rise higher in the business world. He was named superintendent of the Pittsburgh division of the Pennsylvania Railroad when he was 24. In this post, he helped develop the Pullman Car.

Certain that steel would be important in the changing American economy, Carnegie purchased stock in several steel companies. He formed his own Keystone Bridge Company in 1865. In the 1870's he decided to concentrate all his efforts on steel.

For nearly 20 years Carnegie attempted to make his new company, Carnegie Steel, self-sufficient. He wanted to control every part of steel-making from start to finish. His company owned coal and iron ore mines, facilities for making coke, and plants that produced finished products. Carnegie steel was transported on Carnegie-owned railroads and ships. This ownership of all levels of production is called **vertical integration.** Carnegie described the process of steel production as follows:

> *Two pounds of ironstone mined upon Lake Superior and transported nine hundred miles to Pittsburgh; one pound and one half of coal, mined and manufactured into coke, and transported to Pittsburgh; a small amount of manganese ore mined in Virginia and brought to Pittsburgh—and these four pounds of materials manufactured into one pound of steel, for which the consumer pays one cent.*

By 1900 Carnegie's company was making a quarter of the nation's steel and serving a world market. When Carnegie retired he sold the company to banker John Pierpont Morgan for $447 million. The sale was the beginning of a shift from **industrial capitalism,** in which corporations were controlled by industrial owners, to **finance capitalism,** in which corporations are controlled by bankers. Morgan and his associates combined Carnegie Steel with other steel companies to form United States Steel in 1901, the first billion-dollar corporation in American history.

Armour and the Meat-Packing Industry

Philip Armour was born in 1832 in Madison County, New York and grew up on his family's farm. At 20, he

left for California where he worked as a miner and a box-builder. He saved several thousand dollars from his labor and returned to Madison County in 1856. Dissatisfied with the life of a farmer, he moved to Milwaukee and entered the wholesale grocery and trading business. During the Civil War, he formed a company that dealt in grain and meats and made about $2 million speculating in pork prices.

With these profits, Armour built a meatpacking plant in Chicago. Like Carnegie, he strived to make his company self-sufficient through vertical integration. Armour revolutionized the meat-packing industry by combining slaughtering and packing under one company. Rather than pay shipping costs, he purchased and used refrigerator cars. Armour and Company devised a use for every part of the cattle. Horn and hooves were made into buttons, hide was made into leather, and cattle hair was made into brushes.

Due to its efficiency and innovation in the meat-packing industry, Armour and Company was extremely successful . Armour's own net worth was estimated at $50 million when he died in 1901.

Rockefeller and the Oil Industry

John D. Rockefeller was born in western New York in 1839, when Armour was a farm youth and Carnegie lived in Scotland. When Rockefeller was 14, his family moved to Cleveland, Ohio. There he completed high school and, for a short time, studied at a commercial college.

Rockefeller's first job was with a trading company at a salary of $15 a week. He then decided to go into the trading business for himself. In 1859 he and a partner formed a company that traded in grain, hay, and meats. In 1863 he and his partner began investing in the oil refining industry. Rockefeller reasoned that industrialization would change America's economy. He believed that oil would be in constant demand, so he sold his half of the business to devote his energy to oil.

Rockefeller's first goal was to corner the Cleveland oil refining industry. By 1872 he controlled 21 of the city's 26 refineries. This expanded ownership in one area of production is called **horizontal integration.** Next, he expanded his company, Standard Oil, into

Have students debate whether or not business consolidation was an inevitable movement.

other cities, including Pittsburgh, Philadelphia, and New York.

Rockefeller's next goal was self-sufficiency. All the processes of oil production were combined under Standard Oil, thus combining vertical and horizontal integration. The company produced and used its own sulfuric acid, tank cars, and even it own barrels, made from forests owned by Standard Oil. Rockefeller controlled the pipelines he used to ship his oil, and distributed and sold his product through licensed dealerships.

Business Consolidation

To consolidate his investments in mining, lumber, and transportation, Rockefeller created the Standard Oil Trust. A **trust** was a combination of corporations that agreed to turn over their stock to a central board of trustees in return for trust certificates. These certificates paid dividends, like any other stock. Control of the companies was in the hands of the trustees. Central control meant that competition among the companies in the trust was eliminated. Thus Standard Oil became a monopoly.

Other businesses followed Rockefeller's example. Trusts were formed in steel, sugar, and other major industries. Rockefeller defended trusts as inevitable:

> This movement was the origin of the whole system of modern economic administration. . . . It had to come, though all we saw at the moment was the need to save ourselves from wasteful conditions. . . . The day of the combination is here to stay. Individualism is gone, never to return.

Trusts were criticized by many workers, consumers, and owners of smaller businesses. They said that trusts went against the democratic tradition of **free enterprise,** the economic system in which individuals have the right to compete freely. One of Rockefeller's competitors, George Rice, made the following complaint:

> I have been driven from pillar to post, from one railway line to another, for twenty years, in the absolutely vain endeavor to get equal and just freight rates with the Standard Oil Trust, so as to be able to run my refinery at

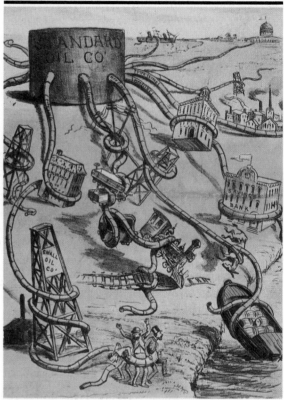

This cartoon reflects the growing concern many Americans had about the power of big business—especially that of monopolies. The Standard Oil Company controlled all processes of oil production. Why would people object to such consolidation?

> anything approaching a profit, but which I have been utterly unable to do. I have had consequently to shut down, with my business absolutely ruined, and my refinery idle.

In 1892 the Ohio Supreme Court declared the Standard Oil Trust to be illegal under Ohio's anti-monopoly laws. Rockefeller therefore devised the holding company as another way to retain his control of the oil industry. A **holding company** was a company that bought controlling shares in other corporations. New Jersey state law permitted a corporation to own the stock of other companies. Rockefeller's holding company, Standard Oil of New Jersey, controlled the production and prices of 20 different oil companies.

Other forms of business consolidation included the pool and the interlocking directorate. The **pool** was an agreement by competing companies to eliminate

Matthew Josephson's book, *The Robber Barons,* popularized the term in the 1930's.

According to social Darwinism, natural law doomed all attempts by labor to organize and all attempts by government to regulate the economy.

competition by dividing their business. The **interlocking directorate** was an arrangement in which some or all of the directors of one company were directors for other companies as well. Business leaders also sometimes made secret agreements in order to create a monopoly.

SECTION REVIEW

1. Identify the following: Horatio Alger, Philip G. Armour, John Pierpont Morgan.
2. How did Carnegie try to make his steel company self-sufficient?
3. How did trusts control competition?
4. Why did Rockefeller set up a holding company?

4 Philosophy for an Era

Rockefeller, Armour, Carnegie and other entrepreneurs were often condemned as **"robber barons"** because of their ruthless business methods. Rockefeller, for example, did not hesitate to use any means to defeat his competitors. If they refused his offer to buy their companies, he cut his prices below their level, selling at a loss until they were forced out of business. Then, with no competition, he could raise his prices even higher than before. Rockefeller also hired industrial spies, bribed legislators, and forced railroads to give Standard Oil **rebates** (money back) on shipping costs.

Entrepreneurs justified their methods by citing the American tradition of individual freedom along with the idea of progress. They believed that people should be free to acquire as much property as they were able, without interference from the government. Most Americans accepted these ideas. They believed that they had the same opportunity to succeed that Rockefeller had.

Laissez-Faire

The American tradition of respect for individual rights was a strong one. The nation's founders had argued that all persons had certain "inalienable" rights. The Constitution was amended, through the Bill of Rights, to protect several of these rights. The founders had been influenced by John Locke's argument that individuals had natural rights to life, liberty, and property. By the late 1800's, liberty, for many, meant primarily economic liberty.

Economic liberty was protected by the idea of laissez-faire, that is, the economy should be run without government interference. This idea had its roots in the Enlightenment. Jefferson advocated a laissez-faire philosophy for the United States because he believed that a strong government threatened freedom. In the late 1800's, laissez-faire, turned into a defense of economic freedom, seemed to be supported by a new scientific theory.

Social Darwinism

In the *Origin of Species* (1859), Charles Darwin presented the theory of **evolution.** Darwin said that human life on earth developed from lower forms of life through a process of natural selection. Theoretically, this process tends to result in the survival of those species that can best adapt to their environments.

Some thought that Darwin's ideas could also be applied to society. Herbert Spencer, an English philosopher, defined **Social Darwinism** as the belief that social progress was based upon the struggle for survival among all people. In their struggle, only the strongest, or fittest, survive. "Survival of the fittest" led to a better society as the unfit were eliminated.

Social Darwinism was perfect for explaining the rise of Rockefeller, Carnegie, and other entrepreneurs. "Millionaires are a product of natural selection," wrote the American social scientist William Graham Summer. Cut-throat competition was also excused. According to Rockefeller, the growth of large business was an example of survival of the fittest:

> *The American Beauty rose can be produced in the splendor and fragrance which bring cheer to its beholder only by sacrificing the early buds which grow up around it. This is not an evil tendency in business. It is merely the working-out of a law of nature and a law of God.*

Defense of Social Darwinism. To those who defended Social Darwinism, its beauty lay in the idea that improvement through competition and survival of the fittest was natural, and, thus, society improved automatically. Since everything was working out for the best, there was no need for government to act. The role of government, they said, was to keep the peace and protect property.

Although few ministers accepted Darwin's theory of evolution, many religious leaders supported a pro-business philosophy. Social Darwinism was consistent with the traditional Puritan work ethic. Most churches, especially the Protestant, encouraged personal ambition. For example, Baptist preacher Russell H. Conwell had a sermon called "Acres of Diamonds" that he delivered about six thousand times:

> *I say that you ought to get rich, and it is your duty to get rich. How many of my pious brethren say to me, "Do you, a Christian minister, spend your time going up and down the country advising young people to get rich, to get money?" "Yes, of course I do." They say, "Isn't that awful! Why don't you preach the gospel instead of preaching about man's making money?" "Because to make money honestly is to preach the gospel."*

Conwell believed that poverty was the result of moral weakness. The poor, he said, were being punished for their sins. He and other ministers agreed that the government should not provide help for the poor. The Reverend Henry Ward Beecher, perhaps the best-known preacher of the post-war period, stated this belief in one of his sermons:

> *The American doctrine is that it is the duty of the Government merely to protect the people while they are taking care of themselves— nothing more than that. "Hands off," we say to the Government: "See to it that we are protected in our rights and our individuality. No more than that." God has intended the great to be great and the little to be little.*

The Gospel of Wealth.   Andrew Carnegie had a somewhat more humane view of how the poor should be treated. He gave millions of dollars to causes such as public libraries, education, and medical research. In an 1889 essay called "The Gospel of Wealth," he said that the rich had a duty to help the poor. The rich should offer their "superior wisdom, experience and ability" to those less fortunate than

BUILDING A VERY SOLID TEMPLE OF FAME

After Carnegie sold his business interests and retired, he donated over $35 million to education and scientific research. What do you think is the cartoonist's position about "captains of industry" who turned to philanthropy?

themselves. However, the "main consideration should be to help those who help themselves." Furthermore, the efforts of the rich to help the poor had to be voluntary. The government was not to interfere.

SECTION REVIEW

1. Identify the following: Charles Darwin, Herbert Spencer, "The Gospel of Wealth."
2. What was the historical basis for the idea of laissez-faire?
3. How was "survival of the fittest" supposed to benefit society?
4. Why did some religious leaders think that the government should not help the poor?

5 Attempts at Regulation

Not all Americans were ready to accept the twin philosophies of laissez-faire and Social Darwinism. Some people questioned the fairness of an economy based on such principles. Farmers and workers began pushing for laws placing restrictions on big business. Farmers were especially concerned about the way railroad companies abused their power.

In areas where competition was high, railroad pools divided the region's business and fixed rates. In one-railroad towns, the company often charged extremely high rates. Some railroads charged more for short hauls than for long hauls. Railroad companies often held onto good farm land in the hope of higher land values in the future. Furthermore, occurrences of graft and corruption in the railroad industry were commonplace.

State Regulation

As a result of pressure by farmers, several midwestern states passed regulations aimed at the railroads and other big businesses. In Illinois, the legislature passed a measure that limited the amount grain elevator companies could charge for grain storage.

Company owners challenged the law's constitutionality before the Supreme Court in the case of *Munn* v. *Illinois* (1877). The owners argued on two points. First, they said, the law deprived a corpora-

tion of its rights under the Fourteenth Amendment. According to the Fourteenth Amendment, no state can deprive a person of his or her rights without due process of law. The owners argued that corporations were considered persons, with legal right to life, liberty, and property. For the government to limit rates was to take away their property. Second, the owners said, the State of Illinois was interfering with **interstate commerce** (trade between two or more states), the special province of Congress.

The Supreme Court rejected the owners' claim. Regulation of private property was constitutional, the Court found, when the public interest was at stake. The argument that the grain elevators were operating in interstate commerce was also rejected.

Soon, however, the Court reversed itself. In the case of *Wabash, St. Louis and Pacific Railway* v. *Illinois* (1886), the Court said that states did not have the right to fix the rates of businesses involved in interstate commerce. In *Santa Clara County* v. *Southern Pacific Railroad* (1886), the Court accepted the argument that the Fourteenth Amendment protected corporations from state regulation. The Supreme Court adopted the philosophy of laissez-faire and applied it in a way that reduced state powers to regulate business.

AMERICAN BUSINESS CYCLES, 1860-1900

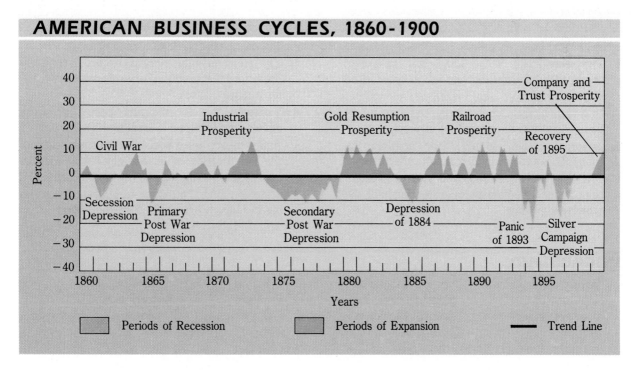

Many early members of the ICC were from railroad backgrounds and were considered to be sympathetic to the railroads.

Federal Regulation

Because state regulation was not working, the federal government tried to fill the gap. The Interstate Commerce Act was passed by Congress in 1887. In this act, 24 sections applied to railroads. The law required publication of railroad rates and stated that all rates should be "reasonable and just." The act also outlawed pools; discrimination between persons, places or kinds of traffic; and charging more for short hauls than for long hauls. Most importantly, the law set up an Interstate Commerce Commission to enforce the law. Over the next few years, however, the Supreme Court made the Interstate Commerce Commission almost powerless. Of the first 16 cases that the ICC brought against the railroads, the Court decided 15 against the Commission.

Other attempts at regulation met the same fate. In 1890, Congress passed the Sherman Antitrust Act. This act said that any "contract, conspiracy or combination" in restraint of trade or commerce was against the law. However, the government rarely prosecuted under the Sherman Act. When it did prosecute, the courts usually favored business.

In *United States* v. *E. C. Knight* (1895), the Supreme Court found that a combination of sugar refineries that controlled 98 percent of the nation's refining business was not a violation of the Sherman Act. The refineries, said the Court, were involved in manufacture, not in trade or commerce, so they could not be prosecuted.

By the 1890's both the individual's and the corporation's "right to property" had been endorsed by the courts. The victory for laissez-faire forces seemed to be total. Despite state and federal legislation, big business at the turn of the century was bigger than ever and still growing.

SECTION REVIEW

1. Identify the following: *Munn* v. *Illinois,* Sherman Antitrust Act, *United States* v. *E. C. Knight.*
2. Why did farmers feel that the railroads abused their power?
3. How did business corporations use the Fourteenth Amendment to defend themselves against regulation?
4. What was the purpose of the Interstate Commerce Commission?

CHAPTER **14**   REVIEW

SUMMARY

1. The second half of the 1800's was an era of unprecedented economic growth in the United States.
2. New technology in steel, energy, and communications supported the growth of industry.
3. Government land grants made possible the completion of transcontinental railroad systems.
4. The expanded and improved railroad system helped meet the transportation demands of the growing economy.
5. The trend in industry was toward large-scale operations that produced large quantities of goods for a mass market.
6. Various tactics for reducing competition were developed by business leaders.
7. A new theory called Social Darwinism, along with the old doctrine of laissez-faire, was used to explain and justify the rise of big business.
8. State and federal attempts to put restrictions on big business were blocked by the courts.

VOCABULARY

factors of production	vertical integration	free enterprise	rebates
subsidies	industrial capitalism	holding company	evolution
standard time	financial capitalism	pool	Social Darwinism
graft	horizontal integration	interlocking directorate	interstate commerce
entrepreneur	trust	robber barons	

REVIEW QUESTIONS

1. How did technology help to develop the resources of production?
2. What impact did railroads have on the economy at this time?
3. What was the importance of entrepreneurs to economic growth?
4. What organizational techniques were used to try to make businesses more efficient?

5. What criticisms were made of big business?
6. How did the doctrine of laissez-faire and the theory of Social Darwinism support the development of big business?
7. What attempts were made to regulate railroads and big businesses?
8. How did the courts protect business from state and federal regulation?

DISCUSSION

1. Do you think that it is still possible today to go from "rags to riches"?
2. Why do you think the United States developed economically at a faster rate than other countries in the world?

3. Do the doctrines of laissez-faire and Social Darwinism have any following today?
4. Would you consider the entrepreneurs of this period "robber barons" or "captains of industry" who built up the economy? Why?

USING MAPS

Refer to the map on page 298 and answer the following questions:

1. What principal railroads were built between 1860 and 1890?
2. What railroads went through El Paso, Texas? Through Kansas City?

3. What major railroads went from Omaha, Nebraska to San Francisco, California?
4. What major cities were connected by the New York Central?
5. What railroad would a person take in 1890 to get from New Orleans to Houston?

USING SKILLS

In your opinion, which of the first five words in each of the following statements makes the statement true?

1. All, Most, Many, Some, None of the resources needed for industrial production were available in the United States.
2. All, Most, Many, Some, None of the most important inventions made in the 1800's were made by Americans.

3. All, Most, Many, Some, None of the railroad companies were guilty of using corrupt business practices.
4. All, Most, Many, Some, None of the small businesses in the United States could successfully compete with the giant trusts.
5. All, Most, Many, Some, None of the efforts to control big business were effective.

1	Workers and Their Problems	311
2	The Union Movement	314
3	Problems of the Labor Movement	318
4	Labor Clashes	320

THE RISE OF LABOR

Respect industry in the person of every intelligent worker.

Uriah Stephens

As industrialization spawned large cities and huge corporations, it also created a growing work force. The men, women, and children whose labor transformed the American economy found their own lives changed as well.

Working conditions in industry were poor. Hours were long, wages were low, and the work itself was often dangerous. When little was done to improve their lot, workers in growing numbers accepted the idea of forming unions. The union movement was stymied by the resistance of big corporations, which were supported by the government. Nevertheless, union efforts during the late 1800's did succeed in laying the groundwork for future labor gains.

1 Workers and Their Problems

In the new industrial centers like Pittsburgh and Chicago, there was work available for millions. Since colonial times, labor had been in short supply in America. In the latter half of the 1800's, however, the labor force expanded greatly.

Growth of the Labor Force

One reason for the rapid growth of the work force was a general migration from farms to cities. In 1870, 53 percent of all American workers were farmers. By 1910 the proportion had dropped to 37 percent.

The difficulty of earning a steady living from farming made industrial wages attractive to many rural Americans, who made up the bulk of the new urban workers. Farmers, many of them from the South, abandoned their farms to work in factories and mines. Agriculture in the post-Civil War South was undergoing a difficult period. The price of cotton declined drastically, most deeply affecting the sharecroppers who relied on cotton for their livelihood. Most of them eventually settled in industrial cities in the North. Others took jobs in industries that were beginning to develop in the South—textile mills, coal mines, and steel plants.

Another reason for the growth of the labor force was increased immigration from Europe. Between 1870 and 1900, 13 million people came to the United States from overseas. By 1890, over one-quarter of all American workers were foreign-born. The proportion in some sectors of the economy, like the garment industry, was much higher.

Women also entered the work force in growing numbers. The accepted role for middle and upper-class women was to stay at home, devoting their time to their families and doing volunteer work for worthy causes. But few lower-class women had such options. Many helped to fill the need for clerks and secretaries—positions that had been filled by men until the introduction of the typewriter in the 1880's. Other women became teachers, social workers, and switchboard operators. The largest number were employed in manufacturing, especially in textile mills, tobacco factories, and the garment industry. By 1900, 5.3 million women had jobs outside the home. Working women made up over 12 percent of the labor force.

The labor force also included 1.75 million children under the age of 15. Nearly 20 percent of all children between the ages of 10 and 15 had jobs. Children had to work either because their families could not survive without extra income, or because their parents expected them to help pay their own way. Employers were eager to hire children because they could perform tasks for which small size and dexterity were assets. Furthermore, children could be paid less than adults.

States began restricting child labor as early as the 1860's, partly for humanitarian reasons and partly because adults objected to losing jobs to children. But the laws were not always enforced. When challenged

Note that children had always worked on farms. Therefore it was not considered wrong for them to work in factories. Discuss current child labor laws in your state.

Astoria, New York (Steinway and Sons) and Hopewell, Massachusetts (Draper Corporation) were examples of company towns.

In the 1800's American women began to assert their independence in a variety of ways. A number of women went to work in offices, doing work that had previously been done by men. But as women were paid only one-third as much as men for the same work, some formed the Women's Trade Union League to fight for equal pay. In what other areas did women seek equality?

in the courts, child labor laws were often overturned on the ground that they infringed on free enterprise.

Working Conditions

People in the industrial labor force faced profound changes in their lives. Many workers were forced to make a painful transition from skilled to semi-skilled or unskilled labor. Semi-skilled and unskilled jobs could be learned by almost anyone. Thus they had lower status and lower pay.

As previously complex jobs were broken down into smaller parts, workers had to concentrate on highly specific, repetitive tasks. Work became monotonous, and workers had little chance to see or take pride in the results of their labor.

At the same time, factories grew larger. More and more people worked for fewer and fewer employers. These changes were made in order to increase the efficiency of production. But the workers began to feel like "cogs in a wheel"—part of a big, impersonal machine.

Although the general dehumanization of work was unpleasant, wages and hours presented more tangi-

ble problems for workers. **Real wages**—wages with the inflation factor taken out—rose more than 10 percent during the last 30 years of the 1800's. But a large number of people did not earn enough to supply their families with adequate food, clothing, and shelter, let alone niceties. And there was widespread resentment over the fact that increases in wages never kept pace with increases in corporate profits.

In some industries, especially mining, workers were obliged to live in **"company towns."** These were towns built and run by companies to provide housing for their workers. The houses were often shabby and small. Employees had to pay rent, taxes, and other fees. The only store in town was the company store, which usually charged higher prices than stores in other towns. Many workers were continually in debt to the company store.

Workers also faced frequent pay cuts, unemployment, and **underemployment** (less than full-time work). Workers were very vulnerable to the **business cycle**—the recurring sequence of changes in business activity. Beginning with a period of prosperity, the business cycle declines into a recession, or worse, a depression, followed by a

One of the main reasons that workers supported a shorter work week was that they hoped it would result in less unemployment.

Workers who suffered in industrial accidents received no compensation for their injuries.

recovery. In the late 1800's, business went through many such ups and downs. During slack periods, employers kept their costs down by reducing wages or laying off workers. Millions of people lost their jobs or had their wages slashed during depressions in 1873, 1882, and 1893. Even during good years, workers suffered periodic layoffs.

Long hours were another burden to workers. During the late 1800's, 65 and 70-hour work weeks were common. By 1900, the average work week was still 59 hours long. One of the most popular labor songs from this era called for "eight hours for work, eight hours for rest, eight hours for what we will." But the 8-hour day was still a dream.

Industrial work was as dangerous as it was long. Heavy machines were bunched together on shop or mill floors for the sake of efficiency. There were few safety devices or regulations. The injury rate was appallingly high. One reason was that people had to work at an inhuman pace. Following is the account of a young woman employed in New York City's garment industry, in which the bulk of the workers were Jewish immigrants from eastern Europe:

At seven o'clock we all sit down to our machines and the boss brings to each one the pile of work that he or she is to finish during the day. . . . This pile is put down beside the machine and as soon as a skirt is done it is laid on the other side of the machine. . . . The machines go like mad all day, because the faster you work the more money you get. Sometimes in my haste I get my finger caught and the needle goes right through it. . . . We all have accidents like that. . . . Sometimes a finger has to come off. . . . All the time we are working the boss walks about examining the finished garments and making us do them over again if they are not just right. So we have to be careful as well as swift. . . .

Accidents were also common, and more often fatal, in the mining industry, where most workers were Welsh, Scottish, or English immigrants. Some mines were open pits above ground. But more often, miners spent long hours with picks and shovels in shafts and tunnels below the ground. Working in these mines was compared to working in an open grave that might close at any time.

In addition to accidents, workers were exposed to conditions that slowly but certainly undermined health. Miners breathed coal dust all day. Workers in other factories breathed sawdust, stone dust, cotton dust, or toxic fumes. Postures were bent by long

After the Civil War, many blacks moved to cities throughout the South. There they found work in industry as unskilled laborers. In the tobacco industry they soon constituted a majority of the work force. Many worked thirteen hours a day for a wage of 78¢ to $1.20. Women and children, shown here stripping stems from the tobacco leaves, were paid the lowest wages. What factors in industry made wages so low?

Have students prepare a photo essay on working conditions in the late 1800's.

hours in twisted positions. Children as well as adults suffered from unhealthful conditions, as the following description shows:

> *In a little room in this big, block shed—a room not twenty feet square—forty boys are picking their lives away. The floor of this room is an inclined plane, and a stream of coal pours constantly in. They work here, in this little black hole, all day and every day . . . picking away among the black coals, bending over till their little spines are curved. . . . Not three boys in this roomful could read or write. Shut in from everything that is pleasant, with no chance to learn, with no knowledge of what is going on about them. . . . They know nothing but the difference between slate and coal.*

Children were often employed in **sweatshops**—small, makeshift factories in which workers were hired on a piecework basis. Sweatshops were usually dimly lighted and poorly ventilated. Children working under such conditions suffered more than just physically. They were deprived of opportunity for either school or play—deprived, in short, of their childhood.

SECTION REVIEW

1. Why did many American farmers migrate to cities in the late 1800's?
2. What objections were made to the use of child labor?
3. How were workers affected by the business cycle?
4. What were the causes of industrial accidents?

2 The Union Movement

Individual workers were powerless against hazardous working conditions, low pay, and long hours. Following the old saying that "in union there is strength," they formed or expanded a large number of unions during the late 1800's.

The National Labor Union

Most of the unions were craft or **trade unions**—organizations of skilled workers in one line of work. There were also some regional organizations whose chief goal was the 8-hour day. There were even a few so-called "national" unions, or federations of local

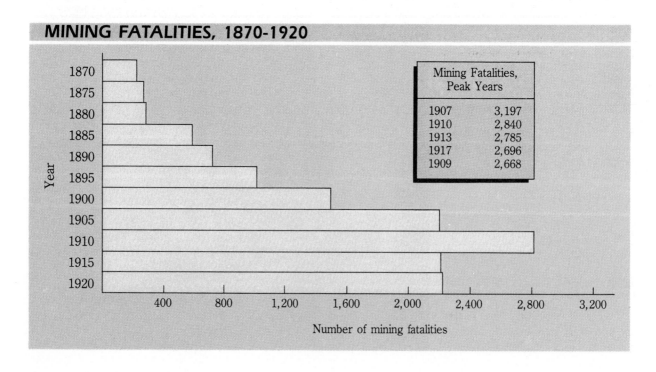

MINING FATALITIES, 1870-1920

Mining Fatalities, Peak Years	
1907	3,197
1910	2,840
1913	2,785
1917	2,696
1909	2,668

Number of mining fatalities

Leonora Barry

Labor organizer Leonora Barry was born in Ireland in 1849. In 1852 she emigrated with her family to the United States and settled in New York, where she became a teacher. In 1881 her husband died, and she was left with two young children to support.

Barry found work in a hosiery mill in Amsterdam, New York, but she rebelled against the low pay—65 cents a week. She was appalled that other women who worked at the mill did nothing to improve their lot. After studying the problem, she realized that acceptance of whatever was offered to them was a trait that society expected of women. She decided that someone had to arouse women to the need for organization.

In the Knights of Labor she found a parent organization for her efforts and quickly rose to a position of leadership. First she became president of her local assembly. Later she became a general investigator, paid to gather statistics on women's work. She was also a traveling organizer, lecturer, and troubleshooter. She organized several cooperatives and was largely responsible for the passage of the first Pennsylvania factory inspection act. But she was always disappointed in the failure of women to organize more thoroughly.

Barry was not a radical and believed that women should not work outside the home unless forced to do so by economic circumstances. Therefore she retired as a labor organizer when she remarried. Later she took an active part in the temperance and women's suffrage movements.

---

trade unions. But these were generally weak and ineffective.

The first major union that was able to build a wide base was the National Labor Union (NLU) founded in 1866. The first part of the NLU constitution read as follows:

> *Heretofore, the highest form labor associations have taken is the national union of some of the trades. Between these organizations, however, there was no sympathy or systematic connection, no cooperative effort, no working for the attainment of a common end, the want of which has been experienced for years. . . .*

The NLU tried to unite a large number of local trade unions with other groups, such as farmers' societies and women's suffrage organizations. Under the leadership of William Sylvis, the NLU worked for broad political reform. One major goal was developing workers' **cooperatives,** in which workers managed their own production and sold their own goods. Another goal was currency reform. The union wanted more paper money to be printed. More paper money in circulation would mean that the real value of money was lower, and workers hoped this would mean that wages would go up and debts would be easier to pay.

In 1872 the NLU became the National Labor Reform Party. The party convention nominated Judge David Davis of Illinois for President. When Davis withdrew from the race, and other party candidates were badly defeated, the party faded away. However, union efforts led Congress to adopt an 8-hour day for federal employees. The NLU also set up a permanent lobby in Washington to press for the creation of a Department of Labor.

Among the strikes won by the Knights was one against the Southwest Railway, owned by financial giant Jay Gould.

The Knights of Labor under Terence Powderly (left center) worked to improve conditions for industrial workers. As factory goods became commonplace, trade unions began to make endorsements (right) as a means of obtaining recognition and acceptance. How do industrial and trade unions differ?

The Knights of Labor

The next major union to appear was the Knights of Labor. Founded in Philadelphia in 1869, it was led first by tailor Uriah Stephens, then by railroad worker Terence Powderly. Like the NLU, the Knights promoted political causes such as temperance and currency reform, as well as workers' causes such as the 8-hour day, an end to child labor, safety inspections for factories, and cooperatives.

The Knights became the largest union America had ever seen. Unlike most other labor organizations, this one was open to unskilled workers. The Knights believed that all workers had common interests and should cooperate. Women and blacks were also allowed in the union, although this policy caused trouble among many members of the white male majority. In most cases, both women and blacks were

organized in separate locals, and they did not enjoy the full privileges of white male members. Nevertheless, some blacks, such as Frank Farrell, and some women, such as Leonora Barry, rose to positions of prominence in the Knights.

In conflicts with employers, the Knights thought of strikes as a last resort. They preferred to use the boycott. Another method favored by the Knights was **arbitration.** This is an arrangement whereby two parties to a dispute agree to allow an impartial third party to settle the matter. While trying to avoid strikes, however, the Knights found them to be the best weapon in some cases. Strikes helped the union to win several minor victories against management in the 1880's.

The Knights also used political pressure to reach their goals. The union was instrumental in getting

Anti-Chinese sentiment was strongest in California, where race riots occurred. The Workingmen's party of California was organized to oppose Chinese immigrants.

Cartoons were an effective means of communicating to people who could not read.

Congress to take measures that would keep foreign workers from competing for jobs in the United States. In 1882 Congress passed the Chinese Exclusion Act, which severely limited the immigration of Chinese laborers. In 1885 the Contract Labor Law was repealed. Under this law, employers had been able to sign contracts with workers in Europe for temporary work in the United States.

After reaching a peak of about 700,000 members, the Knights declined in the 1890's. The decline was due partly to the fact that the union had failed to win a number of confrontations with management. Another reason was the union's association in the public mind with violence. A third reason for the Knights' decline was the conflict among groups within the union.

The American Federation of Labor

The only union to endure into the 1900's was the American Federation of Labor, or AFL. It was founded in 1886 by an immigrant cigar-maker named Samuel Gompers.

Cigar-making was one of those industries in which skilled workers were rapidly being replaced by machines. It was natural for Gompers to tailor the union to the needs of skilled workers. The AFL was chiefly a federation of trade unions. However, some **industrial unions**—organizations of all the work-

ers, skilled or unskilled, in one industry—were also included.

Instead of broad political reform, Gompers concentrated on "bread and butter" issues. These were issues that had a direct effect on workers, such as shorter hours, better pay, job security, and injury benefits. Gompers was a practical man. He wanted no part of what were, in his view, the misguided and futile programs of the Knights of Labor. He took a no-nonsense, matter-of-fact approach to unions.

There is nothing in the labor movement that employers who have had unorganized laborers dread so much as organization; but organization alone will not do much unless the organization provides itself with a good fund, so that the operatives may be in a position, in the event of a struggle with their employers, to hold out. . . .

Gompers favored down-to-earth tactics such as **collective bargaining,** a process in which union leaders negotiated with employers. To make sure that this process led to good results for labor, Gompers encouraged professionalism in the union. "Each side ought to have an equal chance to propose and insist again upon what it considers a fair agreement," Gompers said.

Unlike the NLU and the Knights, the AFL favored the use of strikes if collective bargaining failed. But strikes were called only when the union had enough

The American press sometimes aroused antagonism toward labor by accusing unions of violence and unrealistic goals. At the same time the press was against the exploitation of the labor force. This cartoon shows a worker caught between the wolf of "hunger" and the captivity of "union tyranny." Above the entrance to the hall of unionism is written, "All Independence Abandon, Ye Who Enter Here." What do you think the cartoonist is trying to say?

Have students report on current labor union membership and
current labor-related issues.

UNION MEMBERSHIP IN THE LABOR FORCE 1880–1920

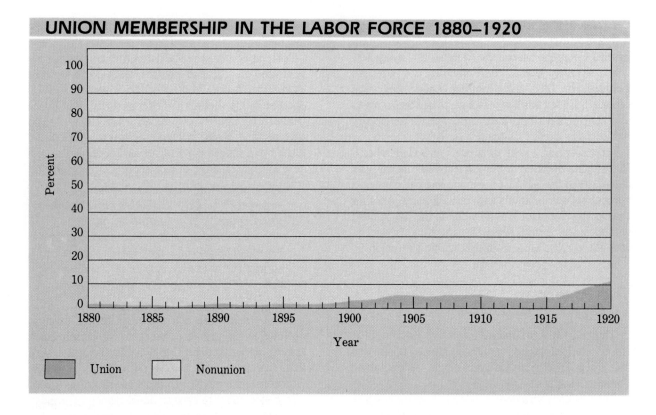

Union   Nonunion

---

money to help strikers. Many strikes backed by the
AFL achieved at least some success.

The AFL appealed to many workers. By 1900 it
had 500,000 members. However, the union was
weakened by its failure to organize unskilled workers,
women, and blacks. In the North, most black workers
were unskilled, and were, therefore, excluded by the
AFL's policy of organizing only skilled workers. In the
South, many blacks were skilled workers. But the
national AFL, although officially against discrimination, allowed local unions to decide whether or not to
admit blacks as members.

SECTION REVIEW

1. Identify the following: William Sylvis, Terence
Powderly, Leonora Barry, Chinese Exclusion
Act.
2. What were the major goals of the National Labor
Union?
3. Why did the Knights of Labor decline in the
1890's?
4. What labor groups were not organized by the
American Federation of Labor?

3 Problems of the Labor Movement

Taken as a whole, the union movement of the late
1800's was not very successful. While membership
grew as the years passed, it never kept pace with the
growth of the labor force as a whole. No more than 10
percent of all workers ever belonged to a union during
this era. In Europe, the proportion was much higher.

American workers were hard to organize. For one
thing, joining a union was a sacrifice for individual
workers. Even when union dues were low, they took
money out of the pockets of people who were already
hard-pressed. More importantly, joining a union could
cost a person his or her job. The reluctance of
workers to join unions was also related to some
uniquely American social patterns.

American Attitudes

The population of the United States was far more
heterogeneous (ethnically and racially mixed) than

Employers formed the National Association of Manufacturers to defend their interests.

UNION MEMBERSHIP

Year	Total	Year	Total
1897	447	1909	2006
1898	501	1910	2140
1899	611	1911	2343
1900	808	1912	2452
1901	1125	1913	2716
1902	1376	1914	2687
1903	1914	1915	2583
1904	2073	1916	2773
1905	2022	1917	3061
1906	1907	1918	3467
1907	2080	1919	4125
1908	2131	1920	5048

(in thousands)

any country in Europe. Language barriers and prejudices against ethnic groups, blacks, and women divided workers, making it hard for them to see themselves as one group. Furthermore, skilled workers did not like being associated with unskilled workers. These divisions and conflicts made union organization difficult.

Another special problem for unions was that American workers did not generally have a deep sense of class consciousness. The entire union movement rested on at least a vague idea that the working class had interests different from those of other classes. In some European countries, this class consciousness was much stronger and more explicit. Many workers supported **socialism,** a political and economic system in which the government controls the means of production.

Some American workers, especially those raised in Europe, had socialist sympathies. But most Americans believed in **capitalism,** the economic system based on private property and free enterprise. American optimism gave workers hope that they could rise to middle-class status through their own

efforts. A deeply-rooted tradition of individualism also added to the belief that people should make it on their own.

Most Americans did not believe that radical changes in the economy or the government were needed. Workers, whether or not they belonged to unions, were free to take part in the established democratic process. They could work for public policies that helped labor causes and vote for political candidates who were sympathetic to workers.

Opposition from Management

Whether unions worked through the political process or confronted employers more directly, strength seemed to be on the side of management. Employers had several ways of weakening the union movement.

One tactic used by employers was the threat of job loss. Owners could even **"blacklist"** (pass around the names of) union sympathizers so that no one would hire them. Another management device was the **"yellow dog contract."** This was an agreement workers had to sign before taking a job. They had to swear that they were not and would not become union members while holding that job.

Employers sometimes used a system known as "welfare capitalism" to weaken the appeal of unions. Under this system, the company gave workers a number of benefits, including, in some cases, a company-sponsored union. Workers were then less likely to join an outside organization. Management could buy off potential union leaders with promotions and raises. If that was not possible, companies could use their influence to smear the reputations of union leaders. Managers could also play upon ethnic or racial prejudices to keep workers from uniting.

When workers did organize, employers sometimes hired private detectives to infiltrate union ranks. When strikes broke out, management had other weapons. One was the **lockout,** in which employers closed factory doors to keep workers out. "Scabs" or "strikebreakers" could be hired to take the place of strikers. Employers also instigated acts of violence, which were then blamed on workers.

The courts generally supported management tactics. The Sherman Antitrust Act of 1890, passed to regulate big business, was turned against the unions.

Unions were accused of "conspiracy in restraint of trade." On these grounds, the courts issued **injunctions** (court orders) to stop strikes.

The courts also recognized the factory owners' right to **"open shops,"** in which the owners could hire anyone they wished. This stand gave owners the right to refuse union demands for a **"closed shop,"** in which only union members were employed. Open shops became, in effect, closed non-union shops.

SECTION REVIEW

1. Why did American workers find it difficult to see themselves as a group and work together?
2. How did "welfare capitalism" weaken the appeal of unions?
3. How was the Sherman Antitrust Act used against unions?

4   Labor Clashes

The major weapon of workers against management was the strike. Legally or illegally, this weapon was used with increasing frequency and passion. Massachusetts, for example, experienced more strikes between 1881 and 1886 than it had for the 50 previous years. The country as a whole averaged more than 1000 strikes a year during the 1890's. Many strikes were local, but several were large-scale, violent clashes.

The Railway Strike of 1877

One of the worst strikes occurred among railroad workers. After years of prosperity, railroad companies were hit hard by a financial panic in 1873. They turned to drastic measures to cut their losses. Some railways cut workers' pay as much as 35 percent. Workdays were lengthened up to 15 and sometimes even 18 hours. Companies discontinued the "free ride" policy that had allowed workers to travel free to and from their jobs. These measures made railway workers bitter and angry.

In 1877 wages were cut another 10 percent by the Pennsylvania Railroad and then by the Baltimore and Ohio (B & O) line. Workers threatened to walk off the job if nothing was done. Management refused to budge, certain that replacements for the strikers

could be found. On July 16 about 40 B & O workers held a work stoppage. The trains rolled anyway, but down the line at Martinsburg, West Virginia, the firemen abandoned the trains. Strikers soon took over the town. The governor of West Virginia, at the urging of a B & O vice president, sent two companies of state militia to Martinsburg. But it took federal troops to regain control of the town.

The scene at Martinsburg was only the beginning. Troops and workers clashed in the streets of Pittsburgh, Buffalo, San Francisco, and Toledo. In late July, 20 persons were killed in Philadelphia, and, in another Pennsylvania city, Reading, 11 were killed. Railway traffic was halted for two weeks on 50,000 miles (80,000 kilometers) of track—nearly two-thirds of the nation's system.

However, little was gained from the strikes and the violence. A few companies postponed wage cuts to calm rioting workers. Most companies managed to hire replacements by early August. The strike, disorganized from the start, collapsed under the pressure of state and federal force.

Public opinion and some newspapers had been sympathetic with the workers' grievances. However, the violence and the transportation tie-up caused a shift in feeling. In editorials and on street corners, workers were blamed for the trouble.

The Haymarket Riot

Chicago was the center of violence relating to another strike, a long-standing dispute between workers and management of the McCormick Harvester Company. Strikebreakers had been hired to replace workers locked out by McCormick officials. On May 3, 1886, a demonstration was organized outside the doors of the plant to protest the company's action. When the strikebreakers left the plant, they were attacked by a group of about 200 striking workers, armed with sticks and stones. Police waded in to break up the melee. Some turned their guns on the strikers, killing four.

A rally was organized the next day to condemn the action of the police. Among the rally leaders were several immigrant anarchists. An **anarchist** is a person who advocates the overthrow of all government and complete freedom for individuals. One anarchist, August Spies, issued a vehement appeal to

One of the executed Haymarket speakers, Albert Parsons, was a member of the Knights.

The safety record at the Homestead Plant was also an issue adding to the friction between workers and management.

ISSUES CAUSING STRIKES 1881-1905

Year	Wages/hours	Right to organize	Owner lockout or other issue	Total strikes
1881	80%	7%	13%	477
1883	73%	11%	16%	506
1885	70%	10%	20%	695
1887	56%	20%	24%	1503
1889	60%	16%	24%	1111
1891	49%	19%	32%	1786
1893	57%	19%	24%	1375
1895	65%	17%	18%	1255
1897	61%	18%	21%	1110
1899	55%	26%	19%	1838
1901	47%	34%	19%	3012
1903	49%	33%	18%	3648
1905	43%	37%	20%	2186

workers to "arm yourselves and appear in full force" at the rally site, Haymarket Square.

About 3000 people turned out. The rally was orderly, and the crowd had dwindled to a few hundred when about 200 city police arrived and ordered the crowd to break up. Suddenly, the uneasy peace was shattered. An unidentified person threw a bomb that killed 7 police officers and injured 66 others. The police then fired into the fleeing crowd. In the week that followed, the police hunted for the person who had thrown the bomb. Although that person was never found, August Spies and seven other anarchists were tried and convicted of murder.[1]

The violence at Haymarket Square was a setback for labor. Americans were outraged by the bloodshed. Gompers said that the bomb killed not only the police officers, "it killed our eight-hour movement for a few years after." The riot tarnished the reputation of all groups with any link to the anarchists, including recent immigrants and organized labor. It was this

---

[1] Spies and one other of the convicted men had their sentences commuted to life imprisonment. Four men were executed, one committed suicide in his cell, and one was sentenced to 15 years in prison.

event that finished the Knights of Labor, even though they insisted that they had no part in it.

The Homestead Steel Strike

Strikes did not cease following the tragedy at Haymarket Square. Andrew Carnegie's Homestead Steel Plant in Pennsylvania was the scene of more violence.

The 25,000-member Amalgamated Association of Iron & Steel Workers had negotiated a contract for Homestead Workers in 1889. When the union sought to renew the contract in 1892, the company refused. Most of the plant's steel workers were unskilled and not members of Amalgamated. Homestead officials contended that the union had no right to negotiate for all workers. The company refused a pay raise and countered with an 18 to 26 percent cut for all workers.

As a result, Homestead's 3000 unskilled workers joined the plant's 800 union members in a strike. The company manager, Henry Frick, ordered a lockout and called in strikebreakers. The strikers formed picket lines around the plant, which they disparagingly referred to as "Fort Frick."

The Homestead strike is the subject of the Historian's Craft activity at the end of this unit.

Labor's mounting grievances against the power of great monopolies led to a series of strikes throughout the nation, such as the Homestead Strike of 1892. These drawings depict some of the things that took place. What kind of tactics were employed?

The company hired the Pinkerton Private Detective Agency to insure the safety of the strikebreakers. When 300 Pinkerton guards arrived on the morning of July 6, they were met by armed strikers ready for battle. The Pinkertons were forced to surrender and were returned to Pittsburgh. Three guards and seven strikers were killed.

"The strikers are in control," wrote the sheriff of Homestead to Robert Pattison, the governor of Pennsylvania. "Only a large military force . . . will restore order." Pattison responded by sending the Pennsylvania National Guard to protect the plant and the strikebreakers. By July 26 the *New York Times* could report that "the Homestead Strike or lockout has had its back broken." The company took legal action against some of the strike leaders for murder and conspiracy. Amalgamated, once the most powerful trade union in the AFL, was crushed.

Troubles in Pullman

A bigger strike was coming and from an unexpected source. George Pullman had built Pullman, Illinois, as a model company town for the workers at his Pullman car factory. Situated near Chicago, the town featured the most modern lighting, water, and drainage systems. The company provided a library and free schools. Attractive new houses were set in a landscaped environment with a lake, paved streets, parks, and bright flower beds. At first glance, Pullman appeared to be an ideal community.

However, Pullman workers resented the control the company held over their lives. City laws reflected George Pullman's personal views. As an example, alcohol was forbidden. Company officials kept a close watch on all aspects of workers' lives. Furthermore, workers who lived in Pullman had to do business with company stores and banks. Rent, taxes, and dues for services were deducted from the worker's salary. Although Pullman workers were not forced to live in the company town, those who lived elsewhere were the first workers to be laid off and the last workers to be rehired.

Economic hardship strengthened the bitterness of the workers. During the Depression of 1893, the company laid off nearly 6000 workers, about one-half of those on the payroll. The remaining workers' pay was cut by one fourth. Rents and other charges, however, were not reduced. In 1894 another pay cut was implemented, forcing many workers to live on a few dollars a week. One employee received, after deductions, a check for two cents. He had the check framed.

A committee of workers met with Pullman in May of 1895. They asked that rents and taxes be reduced. Pullman refused and, despite a company promise not to punish any organizers, three committee members were laid off. At noon the following day, 10,000 Pullman workers walked off the job.

The American Railway Union, led by Eugene V. Debs, requested that the dispute be settled by arbitration. Pullman refused this offer, saying "There is nothing to arbitrate." The strike spread when ARU members refused to handle any Pullman cars. By June 30, most of the nation's major rail centers were tied up.

On July 4 President Grover Cleveland ordered federal troops into Chicago on the pretext that the

An economic depression gripped the country in the 1890's. Lay-offs and pay cuts made workers desperate. In the company town of Pullman, Illinois, shown here, a strike began that ultimately led to a tie-up of the nation's railroad system. What other conditions in Pullman did the workers resent?

AFL membership increased every year between 1886 and 1892, survived a major depression in the mid 1890's, and increased again after 1897. By 1904 it had 1.7 million members.

strikers were interfering with the federal mail service. Cleveland reportedly said:

If it takes every dollar in the Treasury and every soldier in the United States to deliver a postal card in Chicago, that postal card should be delivered.

In spite of the army, the strike kept spreading, and violence increased. Finally, the railroads persuaded the courts to issue an injunction based on the Sherman Antitrust Act. As a result, union leaders were prohibited from interfering with interstate commerce and from urging railroad workers to stay off the job.

Debs asked Gompers for help in organizing a general strike—a sympathy strike of workers in other industries. But Gompers refused to risk the AFL for a losing cause. Debs then offered to call off the strike if the Pullman Company would reinstate all its workers. But the company saw no need to compromise. Soon

Debs and other strike leaders were jailed for violating the injunction. The strike was broken.

Once again, workers had been defeated and their union destroyed. Labor was unevenly matched against the combined powers of big business and government. By 1900 working conditions, wages, and hours were little improved, and only about three percent of all workers belonged to unions. However, the AFL survived and continued to organize in various industries. Labor's fight remained to be carried into the next century.

SECTION REVIEW

1. Identify the following: August Spies, Henry Frick, George Pullman, Eugene V. Debs.
2. What was the longterm effect of the Haymarket affair?
3. What was management's response to the Homestead Steel strike?
4. What caused the Railway Strike of 1877?

CHAPTER 15 REVIEW

SUMMARY

1. In the second half of the 1800's the industrial labor force grew rapidly.
2. Growth of the labor force was due to immigration from rural areas, immigration from Europe, and the entry of women and children into the labor market.
3. Hazardous working environments, long hours, and low pay were greatly resented by workers.
4. In order to combat these conditions workers formed and expanded a large number of unions.

5. The three biggest unions were the National Labor Union, the Knights of Labor, and the American Federation of Labor.
6. The unions faced strong opposition from management and court support of management tactics.
7. There were a large number of strikes in the late 1800's, but most strikes failed to win significant gains for workers.
8. As a whole, the labor movement of this period was unsuccessful.

VOCABULARY

real wages	sweatshop	industrial union	blacklist	open shop
company town	trade union	collective bargaining	yellow dog contract	closed shop
underemployment	cooperatives	socialism	lockout	anarchist
business cycle	arbitration	capitalism	injunction	

REVIEW QUESTIONS

1. How did industrialization affect the lives of workers?

2. How did the three major unions differ from one another?

3. In general, how did the unions try to achieve their goals?

4. What problems did labor unions have that were unique to the United States?

5. What tactics did management use to deal with labor unions?

6. How did the government respond to labor-management conflicts?

7. What was the attitude of the public toward organized labor?

8. What gains were made by labor during the late 1800's?

DISCUSSION

1. Why do you think working conditions in the late 1800's were so harsh?

2. What, if anything, could American workers have done differently to improve their situation?

3. If you had been a business owner whose workers went on strike, what would you have done?

4. Are American unions stronger today than they were in the 1800's? Why or why not?

USING CHARTS

Refer to the chart on page 321 and answer the following questions:

1. What were three classifications of issues causing strikes between 1881 and 1905?

2. Which issue was the chief cause of strikes?

3. In which year did the most strikes take place?

4. In 1885, what percentage of strikes was caused by lockouts?

5. What is the trend in the number of strikes between 1881 and 1905?

USING SKILLS

Put the following events in chronological order:

1. The McCormick Harvester company hired strike-breakers.

2. An unidentified person threw a bomb into the crowd.

3. About 3000 people turned up at a rally in Haymarket Square.

4. City police arrived and ordered the crowd at Haymarket Square to break up.

5. The police killed four strikers outside the McCormick plant.

6. A rally was organized to condemn the action of the police.

7. Strikebreakers were attacked by striking workers.

1	Opening the West	327
2	The Farming Frontier	331
3	Conflict with the Indians	335

THE LAST FRONTIER

I thought if we killed all the white men we saw, no more would come. We killed all we could, but they came more and more. . . .

MODOC INDIAN CHIEF

In 1865 there remained one last frontier for Americans to conquer—the Trans-Mississippi West. This area lay between the Mississippi River and the Sierra-Nevada Mountains and included the Great Plains, the Rocky Mountains, and the Great Basin.

Before the Civil War, Americans had settled in various parts of the territories that were added to the United States in the 1840's. However, few had settled in the Trans-Mississippi West. When the war was over, large numbers of people from eastern states begain to move into this region. Their coming led to a long series of conflicts with the Indian inhabitants.

1 Opening the West

White Americans had begun moving into the West in the early 1800's. They came in overlapping waves of settlers, each with its own distinct goals, lifestyles, and problems.

Western Mining

The first Americans in the West were the fur traders. By the time of the Civil War, however, mineral discoveries had drawn another type of pioneer to the West—the miner. Soon the whole region was a mining frontier.

Miners were lured first to California when gold was discovered there in 1848. In the 1850's and 1860's, they moved on to exploit new discoveries elsewhere. In 1859 gold was found at Pike's Peak in Colorado. That same year, one of the biggest silver veins in the world was discovered in Nevada. This silver vein came to be known as the Comstock Lode. During the next 20 years, precious metals, along with less valuable minerals such as copper, were unearthed throughout the West.

Mining Towns. The discovery of precious metals brought thousands of miners into a single area, giving rise first to makeshift camps and later to formal towns. People of all backgrounds mingled in these places. A census of one camp revealed that it held 73 white Americans, 8 black Americans, 37 Chinese, 35 Britons, 29 Mexicans, and 24 people from other countries. Non-miners, including a substantial number of women, set up businesses to serve the miners.

Despite differences in background, all of the miners had one thing in common: a single-minded desire to find that lucky strike that would make them rich. After they exhausted the minerals in an area, miners would leave town, and a once bustling community could become a deserted **ghost town** almost overnight. While the wealth lasted, however, mining communities could be lively places, as shown by the following description of Virginia City, Montana:

> This human hive, numbering at least 10,000 people, was the product of 90 days. Into it were crowded all the elements of a rough and active civilization. Nearly every third cabin in the town was a saloon where vile whiskey was peddled out for 50 cents a drink in gold dust. Many of these places were filled with gambling tables and gamblers, and the miner who was bold enough to enter one of them with his day's earnings in his pocket seldom left until thoroughly fleeced. Hurdy-gurdy dance houses were numerous, and there were plenty of camp beauties to patronize them. . . . Not a day or night passed which did not yield its full fruition of fights, quarrels, wounds or murders. . . . Street fights were frequent, and as no one knew when or where they would occur, everyone was on his guard against a random shot.

Because the mining towns were far from the seat of governmental authority, residents often took the law

A placer is a deposit of earth that contains a valuable mineral.

Another effect of mining was to magnify the currency issue in politics.

The discovery of gold in Colorado and silver in Nevada started another rush to the West. Thousands flocked into "boom towns" like Creede, Colorado, to strike it rich. What happened to many mining towns when the precious metals started to run out?

into their own hands. This system of private individuals maintaining order was known as **vigilantism.** A vigilante committee in Leadville, Colorado, actually posted a list of undesirables and wrote these words at the bottom:

> *These and a great many others well known to us, have twenty-four hours to get out of the Leadville mining district. Do not fail to go.*

Methods of Mining. The excitement of the mining towns did not deter the miners from their major purpose of finding gold and silver. The earliest form of mining was the **placer method,** in which a pick, shovel, and pan were used to separate gold from common dirt by sifting the dirt in water. The heavy gold stayed in the pan, while the lighter dirt washed away. This method was used to mine small veins close to the surface. Such veins were generally worked by individuals, who staked out claims giving them exclusive rights to mine in that area.

A different method was used to mine the larger veins of precious metals. While some gold and silver lay close to the surface, most of it was imbedded in other material such as quartz, and much of it lay underground. It took machines as well as many laborers to exploit these veins, and the job was beyond the capacity of individual prospectors. Out of such conditions arose large mining companies, often backed by eastern **capitalists** (people who invest money in businesses). These mining companies relegated the miners to the status of paid laborers.

Benefits of Mining. Mining had a significant impact on American development. It added a huge amount of wealth to the nation's economy, enabling the United States to increase its trade with Europe and rebuild the war-torn South. In addition, mining encouraged the building of railroads and paved the way for further settlement of the West. A number of important cities, including Denver, Colorado, and Helena, Montana, got their start as mining towns.

The Cattle Kingdom

Although gold strikes grew rarer as the years passed, the West yielded a new source of wealth—cattle ranching. The Great Plains, with its vast open grasslands, was particularly well-suited to raising cattle. Faced with such an opportunity, ranchers moved rapidly into the last frontier.

The rise of the cattle business was related to the rise of industry. People in the growing cities created a huge new market for meat and other products.

Cowboys needed hats, boots, saddles, saddle bags, vests, lassos, rifles, pistols, chaps, and other supplies. Catalog companies such as Montgomery Ward were major suppliers of this equipment.

Open-range cattle raising had its heyday between 1865 and 1885. During this time ranchers allowed cattle to roam freely over the **open range** (unclaimed public grasslands) after having been branded for identification.

The leading cattle-raising center was Texas. By 1865 there were over 4 million longhorn cattle in that state, descendants of the cattle brought to North America by Spaniards in the 1500's. Longhorns were hardy animals, able to withstand blizzards, drought, and disease. Thus they were better suited to the Great Plains than were eastern stock. Although longhorns did not produce the highest quality beef, their market value remained fairly high. In order to realize that value, cattle raisers had to get their herds to market.

In the 1850's Texas cattle raisers drove their herds to the Gulf Coast for shipment to the East by water. This method of transporting cattle was slow and costly. However, by the 1860's the railroad had reached Abilene, Kansas. Joseph McCoy, an Illinois cattle dealer, made an agreement with the Kansas Pacific Railroad to transport cattle from Abilene to eastern stockyards at certain rates. By 1870 the number of cattle shipped from Abilene had reached 300,000.

The Long Drive. In order to take advantage of the quick, cheap transportation provided by the railroads, cattle raisers had to bring their cattle to the railroad terminal. The journey from Texas to Abilene was called the **long drive.** The long drive generally followed one of several standard cattle trails northward, the most famous of which was the Chisholm Trail. Sometimes the cattle were driven farther north into the lush grasslands of Colorado and Wyoming to be fattened for market.

The men responsible for driving the cattle on the long drive were the cowhands or cowboys. Most of them were young men, who had the physical stamina for life on the trail. The majority of cowboys were white, but there were also a large number of Mexicans, blacks, and Indians among them.

Although the life of the cowboy has been idealized, the reality often bore little resemblance to the image. To begin with, the pay was poor. In addition, cowboys had to endure long hours in the saddle, dust, boredom, stampedes, and sometimes attacks by Indians or cattle rustlers. At night, cowboys slept in the open on the ground, exposed to snakes, insects, and bad weather.

Despite such hardships, the life of the cowboy had a certain appeal. For many, it offered freedom,

The raising of cattle and the long drive to bring meat to eastern markets helped to shape another kind of lifestyle—that of the American cowboy. Their work was hard, often boring, and sometimes dangerous. The hot dry summers and winter blizzards created very difficult conditions under which cowboys had to work. What other dangers did they face?

Cattle ranchers formed associations to function as a kind of government that made rules about matters such as land and water rights, registering of brands, and punishment of rustlers.

Even before the severe winters of 1885 and 1886, overstocking of cattle on the range had lowered cattle prices.

independence, and an escape from the confinement of town living. Although many cowboys were drifters, some were highly skilled men, good with a horse and a rope, handy with a gun, and able to cope with danger. In fact, they seemed to embody the rugged individualism Americans associated with themselves in general and the West in particular.

Big Business and Cattle Raising. As with mining operations, cattle raising soon became big business. A few large companies, generally owned by eastern and English investors, and **cattle barons** (cattle ranchers with vast holdings) dominated life on the Great Plains. They took advantage of the vast public domain to give their cattle a huge grazing area. By buying up a small amount of land adjacent to rivers and creeks, they cornered the water supply and made it difficult for anyone else to share the surrounding land. One cattle baron in Colorado controlled an estate the size of Connecticut and Rhode Island combined, although he owned only 15,000 acres (6000 hectares) along a river. Even some of this was acquired in a shady manner. Because the government would grant only a limited amount of land to one person, the owner had his hired hands file for plots and sell them to him.

Range Wars. Despite such monopolies, cattle barons did face competition for the open range. They came into conflict with each other, with small ranchers, and with sheep raisers.

After the Civil War sheep raising began to compete with cattle raising in the Plains area. As time passed, the number of sheep raisers increased. In fact, by 1900 there were more sheep than cattle on the Great Plains.

The conflict between cattle raisers and sheep raisers stemmed from the fact that cattle and sheep did not mix well. Sheep damaged the grass by cropping it low and cutting the roots with their hoofs, and cattle would not graze after sheep. In addition, cattle shied away from waterholes used by sheep because of the smell left on the water by the sheep. Fierce **range wars** ensued between people engaged in these two seemingly incompatible businesses. Both men and animals were killed in these conflicts.

The cattle raisers' major conflict, however, was with frontier farmers. Farmers threatened the cattle industry by fencing and cultivating land that had been used for grazing. The introduction of barbed wire, perfected by Joseph F. Glidden in 1874, was a blessing to farmers. Previously, farmers had made do with earth embankments and hedges to keep cattle out of their crops. Most cattle raisers were opposed to barbed wire because it was a device that aided the farmers. The clashes between cattle raisers and farmers involved fence cutting, crop trampling, cattle shooting, and **"necktie parties"** (lynchings).

Eventually, some cattle raisers began to use barbed wire themselves, to confine their cattle to a manageable area and keep out sheep. But this approach failed to prevent disaster in the cattle industry. In the severe winters of 1885 and 1886, about four-fifths of the cattle on the Great Plains starved to death. This staggering loss ruined a number of big cattle companies. As a result, the cattle business was reorganized into smaller, more carefully controlled units. The era of large-scale open-range ranching was over.

After the Civil War, a large number of blacks moved to the frontier. Some worked as cattle drovers on cattle ranches. Many of the best known cowboys were black. Why would this life appeal to freedmen?

Have students develop a time line tracing land and Indian policies.

SECTION REVIEW

1. Identify the following: Comstock Lode, Chisholm Trail, Joseph F. Glidden.
2. What problems did mining towns experience?
3. How did the placer method work?
4. What factors helped the cattle industry to grow at this time?
5. What problems did cowboys encounter on the long drive?
6. Why did cattle raisers come into conflict with sheep raisers?

2 The Farming Frontier

In the end, farmers won the battle with the cattle raisers for control of the West. With government encouragement, new agricultural techniques, and determination, farmers completed the conquest of the last frontier.

Government Land Policy

To encourage settlement in the last frontier, Congress passed the Homestead Act in 1862. This act offered 160 acres of land (64 hectares) to anyone who would cultivate it for five years and pay a small fee. However, 160 acres was not enough land for farmers trying to make a living in dryer parts of the West. Therefore, in 1873 Congress passed the Timber Culture Act, which allowed settlers an additional 160 acres if they would plant trees on at least 40 acres. In 1877 Congress passed the Desert Land Act. Its purpose was to encourage irrigation in the Southwest by allotting 640 acres to farmers who made an effort to irrigate their claims.

All of these acts were subject to abuse, due chiefly to the lack of enforcement procedures. People who were supposed to farm, plant trees, or irrigate their homesteads might do so in a minimal way, obeying the letter of the law while actually doing little to improve their land. Furthermore, just as cattle barons bought more than their allotted share of land through others, land speculators also acquired large holdings.

Millions of acres that could have gone to farmers were granted instead to big railroad companies. The land grants to the railroad companies accomplished their intended purpose, which was to encourage the extension of railroad lines across the country. As a result, in the 1870's and 1880's, railroads moved ahead of the frontier, drawing many Americans west. Although a great deal of land was granted to the railroads, much of it was ultimately sold to individuals, and thousands of pioneers managed to find a place to settle in the West.

Patterns of Migration

The majority of the frontier farmers were whites from the states bordering the Mississippi River. Blacks also pioneered the West, lured by the desire to escape racism in the reconstructed South.

Life in the Trans-Mississippi West appealed to Europeans as well as Americans. Germans and Scandinavians, faced with land scarcity, poverty, and political repression at home, were attracted by promotional literature. This literature, prepared by American railroad agents and territorial governments, often exaggerated the benefits of the West. Nevertheless, many immigrants established successful farms throughout the region. People from southern and eastern Europe also came to the United States, but in smaller numbers. They formed farming communities on the Plains and helped populate the growing cities of the West.

As a result of all this migration, 13 states from the Trans-Mississippi West entered the Union between 1860 and 1912.[1] More land was occupied and improved in the closing years of the nineteenth century than had been occupied and improved during the first 250 years of American history.

Life on the Plains

The immigrants soon discovered that life on the Plains was far from easy. Those who chose to homestead faced a difficult task. The lack of trees made it hard to build homes and fences or to keep a fire going for warmth and cooking. To provide themselves shelter, settlers often resorted to building sod houses, made from blocks of hardened soil. Where there were hills, houses were sometimes

---

[1] Kansas, Nevada, Nebraska, Colorado, North Dakota, South Dakota, Montana, Washington, Wyoming, Idaho, Utah, New Mexico, and Arizona.

A good source for the role of women on the frontier is Dee Brown's *The Gentle Tamers: Women of the Old Wild West* (Lincoln, Nebraska: University of Nebraska Press, 1981).

A large number of farmers moved to the Plains during the late 1870's and 1880's—years when rainfall was well above average.

built right into the earth. These **"dugouts"** looked very much like caves. For fuel in this woodless environment, settlers used cow dung and old grain.

Life was primitive and lonely, as one pioneer woman discovered when she arrived in Kansas to join her husband:

> She had never seen a "Dugout" or even a picture of one. She was taken into one underground room about fourteen feet square, dug in the side of a bank. The roof was supported by a ridgepole, the ends of which rested in the crotches of two upright poles, and these formed the gables of the roof. . . .
>
> Across [the rafters] were willows and straw, and on top of all were sod and dirt. It made a roof overhead, weatherproof but not snakeproof!
>
> When daylight came and she had time to view the landscape o'er, she discovered two other dugouts less than a mile away which were the homes of her only neighbors. . . . "Bleak and lonely" was her only comment, but she soon fell into line and was using all her energies in making a home and providing for her family.

In providing for her family, the pioneer woman performed many tasks. She used buffalo skins, bits of cloth, quilts, boxes, and anything else she could find to make rugs, curtains, wallpaper, and other comforts of home. She collected cow chips for fuel, drew water for bathing and cooking, made and laundered the family's clothing, prepared meals, tended the children, and helped her husband with the family's main task—farming.

Farming on the Plains

Farming on the Great Plains was especially difficult for the homesteader. For one thing, the climate was one of extremes, with freezing winters and scorching summers. For another thing, although the flatness of the land made plowing easier, the soil was very hard.

The main problem facing the Plains farmer was lack of water. There were few rivers in this region, and annual rainfall was often below the 20 inches (50 centimeters) generally needed to sustain agriculture. There was water underground, but it was usually inaccessible, either too deep or trapped beneath impenetrable rock.

The picture was not wholly bleak, however. The obstacles facing the farmer were overcome in a number of different ways. By the 1880's windmills and better well-drilling equipment tapped water far below the surface. In addition, homesteaders used a technique known as **dry farming**. This involved plowing deep furrows in the soil to bring subsurface water to the plant roots. Frequent harrowing

The lack of trees on the Great Plains forced homesteaders to build homes from materials other than wood. One of the most common was sod cut from the grassy turf. Only the ability to adapt to the hardships of the prairie made it possible to meet the requirements of homesteading. What were these requirements?

The Image of the West

The West has always had a special mystique. Henry David Thoreau wrote, "Westward is heaven, or rather heavenward is the West." The West seemed to be a place where natural resources were bountiful and life was exceptionally healthy and free. Where did this picture come from, and just how accurate was it?

Glowing images of the West were in the minds of human beings long before anyone reached the New World. Ancient Greeks thought that there might be a paradise in this direction. Generations of Christians believed that the Ten Lost Tribes might be found there. The Spaniard Ponce de León hoped to find the Fountain of Youth in the Western Hemisphere. Early explorers believed that gold would be found in abundance.

Gold and silver *were* found in the New World. However, the amounts were smaller than expected, and the opportunities for quick wealth were more limited than many colonists had hoped. Yet throughout the 1800's, gold strikes in the West sustained the dream. Even in the early 1900's, a large number of immigrants arriving on the East Coast admitted that they came because they had heard that the streets were paved with gold.

Another of the West's most celebrated offerings was land. Colonial settlers praised the good, fertile soil. Because land was easy to obtain, people could increase their wealth and status far more readily than in Europe.

As settlement got thicker, new areas opened up, each portrayed as a new natural paradise. Daniel Boone's Kentucky was described as a virtual Garden of Eden. Less accurately, boosters of settlement in the Midwest promised good land, abundant rainfall, and moderate climates. Immigrants lured to Michigan, Wisconsin, Minnesota, and North Dakota found a much harsher environment, as did those who tried to wrest a living from homesteads elsewhere on the prairie.

But hardships made people strong, it was claimed. The lonely, dangerous lives of the "mountain men" were perhaps the best examples of the kind of freedom and individualism that the West meant to Americans. But all pioneers seemed heroic. Presidential candidates Andrew Jackson, William Henry Harrison, and Zachary Taylor made much of their images as strong, capable men who helped to conquer the West. Many descendants of pioneers look with pride on their hearty ancestors and continue to favor government policies that encourage independence and self-reliance.

Today when people think of the West, they think of the area from the Great Plains to the Rockies. The plains were the last frontier, the final link in America's manifest destiny.

Americans have shown great nostalgia for the Old West. They have tried to resurrect the nearly extinct buffalo, and bemoaned the loss of the "safety valve," where land was still available to those wanting to escape the overcrowded (or "overcivilized") East. Above all, Americans have kept alive the romantic image of the cowboy. Even in the 1980's, urban cowboys dress in western-style clothing and go to "western" night clubs.

First portrayed in "dime novels" of the late 1800's, the cowboy was characterized as a kind of rustic cavalier in turn-of-the-century novels such as Owen Wister's *The Virginian* and the works of Zane Grey. The image has been enhanced by western movies, radio dramas, and country-western songs. The myth is also carried on by a recent resurgence in western art.

According to the myth, the cowboy was strong, handsome, and independent. He was basically a loner, but he knew how to have a good time. This image embodies many of the traits Americans admire most and like to think of as part of their national character. The reality of cowboy life is overlooked. The myth satisfies a national need for heroes. Even in the computer age, the West will undoubtedly continue to supply such images for some time to come.

QUESTIONS

1. What images did many Europeans have of the Western Hemisphere in the 1800's?
2. Why do Americans value the idea of the cowboy?

Farmers had to have some capital to invest in labor-saving machinery. Therefore the West was not a "safety valve" for the restless urban poor. Most of the people who settled in the West were farmers from the Midwest, the East, or Europe.

WESTERN LAND USE, 1860–1890

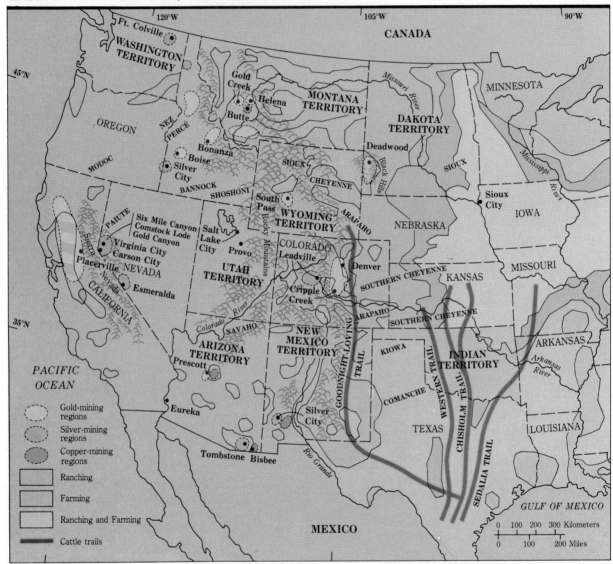

(breaking up clods of earth) also aided in moisture retention. In addition, the development of drought-resistant strains of corn, wheat, barley, and rye led to increased production, as did planting a large number of acres.

Farming a larger area was an option made possible by the development of labor-saving machinery. The self-binding reaper cut, gathered, and bound sheaves of wheat in record time. Thus the farmer was able to harvest many acres of grain and to do it quickly when weather or market conditions called for it. The

steam-powered threshing machine further aided efficient wheat production. Farmers who raised other crops besides wheat also benefited from the new machines. A bushel of corn that took 100 minutes to shell by hand took only one and a half minutes with a steam-powered corn sheller. Tooth harrows, grain drills, fertilizer spreaders, and many other devices also became available in the latter half of the 1800's.

Productivity was also increased by specialization, or concentration on one or two cash crops. Along with increased productivity came the expansion of the

Compare problems of Plains farmers to problems of farmers today.

market area. Improved transportation made it possible for western farmers to sell their crops not only in the East, but in other countries as well. Wheat exports rose from 35 million bushels to 200 million bushels between 1860 and 1900. Pork and cotton showed like increases. The total output of wheat, corn, cotton, beef, and other major crops increased over 130 percent.

Despite this progress, the farmer faced serious problems. People who had pinned their hopes on western land were often unable to overcome the harsh conditions. Homesteaders in Lane County, Kansas, sang with bitter humor about "Starving to Death on a Government Claim":

> *Hurrah for Lane county, the land of the free,*
> *The home of the grasshopper, bedbug, and flea,*
> *I'll holler its praises and sing of its fame,*
> *While starving to death on a government claim.*

The grasshoppers referred to in the song came in 1874, devouring their way from Texas to the Dakota Territory. Blizzards, drought, and prairie fires were also part of life on the Plains. Starvation was a real possibility for some families.

Added to these hardships were unfavorable prices for grain, the high cost of machinery, heavy transportation charges, and high interest rates. These problems left farmers angry and bewildered. Many gave up and moved to the cities. Others, determined to improve their lot, resorted to a variety of reform efforts.

These efforts began with the Patrons of Husbandry, popularly called the Grange, founded by Oliver Kelley in 1867. The Grange grew slowly at first, but by 1874, it had about 1.5 million members. Although at first the Grange served chiefly as a social club, its members were intent on furthering farmers' interests. They established a number of cooperative enterprises, such as grain elevators, warehouses, and farm equipment factories. Most of these projects failed, and in time the Grangers turned to politics.

SECTION REVIEW

1. Identify the following: Timber Culture Act, Desert Land Act, Oliver Kelley.
2. What attracted European immigrants to the West?
3. What new techniques were developed to make farming the Plains easier?
4. Why was the Grange founded?

3 Conflicts With the Indians

Of all the problems the farmer had, perhaps the most immediate was conflict with the Indians. In 1860 about 240,000 Indians lived in the Trans-Mississippi West, and nearly two-thirds of these lived on the Great Plains. It was on the Plains that the major post-Civil War confrontation between whites and Indians took place.

The Plains Indians

The Indian groups who inhabited the Plains region in the second half of the 1800's were nomadic and warlike. Both of these characteristics were the result of their dependence on the buffalo and the horse. The buffalo was central to the life of the Plains Indians, providing them with food, clothing, and shelter. The horse, which had been brought to America by Spaniards in the 1500's, had transformed the life of the Plains Indians by increasing their mobility. On horseback, Indians could hunt buffalo more effectively and could cover greater distances in pursuit of the herd.

Most Indians lived a fairly precarious existence on the Plains, sometimes going hungry between successful buffalo hunts. Competition for buffalo led to competition between Indian groups and the development of warlike attitudes. Indeed, the glorification of warfare was an important part of Plains Indians' culture. Nevertheless, warfare among the Indians generally involved less bloodshed than European warfare. For example, the highest status in some Indian groups was reserved for **"counting coup"**—touching a living enemy brave and escaping unharmed. Such practices as "counting coup" kept warlike skills sharp without spilling blood. The Indians avoided bloodshed partly because most groups were small and therefore vulnerable to annihilation. When Indians did fight to kill, it was often to avenge the death of a group member.

Some of the practices of the Plains Indians, such as scalping, earned them a reputation for cruelty. It should be pointed out, however, that whites also scalped Indians. In fact, the Indians may have learned this practice from Europeans.

Although rival groups of Indians fought each other, their greatest hostility was toward the white settlers

Excursions were arranged for easterners to shoot buffalo for sport.

"Prairie Fire" by the Indian artist, Blackbear Bosin, depicts people and animals fleeing from one of the most dreaded of the many possible dangers on the Great Plains. What were some other hardships faced by Indians and settlers on the Great Plains?

and buffalo hunters who came to the Plains. Between 1860 and 1900 white hunters reduced the number of buffalo from 15 million to just a few hundred. The buffalo were slaughtered in order to satisfy a demand in the East for beef and leather products. Because the Indians' way of life was threatened, they responded to white intrusions by attacking white settlements and wagon trains.

Early Indian Policy

Many of the Plains Indians lived in that region because they had been driven there by pressure from white settlers. Prior to 1850 American policy was based on the idea that the Indians should be moved out of the reach of white settlement. The Great Plains was perceived as a Great American Desert, unsuitable for farming. But as more and more wagon trains rolled across this territory, land scarcity back home

prompted an increasing number of easterners to eye the region as a possible place to homestead. It seemed clear that a new policy to deal with the Indians was needed.

In 1851 federal authorities met with leaders of the Plains Indians at Fort Laramie to negotiate a settlement. The treaty that resulted from this meeting defined territorial boundaries for various Indian groups, gave the government the right to build roads and military posts inside these boundaries, and gave whites **transit rights** through Indian lands. These rights allowed whites to cross Indian lands in peace. In return, the Indians received promises that the land assigned to them would remain theirs. They also received promises of **annuities**—yearly allowances of goods and money from the government.

For several reasons, the success of these agreements was short-lived. For one thing, many of the chiefs who made the agreements were elderly, and young warriors felt that the chiefs had yielded too

Although the Indians were able fighters, technology gave the army the advantage. Whites had the Colt repeating rifle, railroads to transport troops, and the telegraph for quick communication.

much. These young warriors and their followers refused to stay on the reservation or let whites cross their land in peace.

Another reason that the treaties failed was that the American government did not fulfill its pledge of payments. In addition, some of the supplies sent to the Indians included spoiled beef and germ-filled blankets. Meanwhile, white settlers continued to kill buffalo and move on to lands set aside exclusively for the Indians.

The United States government did not have the means to carry out its intended policy. The administration of Indian policy was divided between the United States Army and the Bureau of Indian Affairs, an agency set up in 1849 as part of the Department of the Interior. The Bureau could dispose of Indian lands, disburse annuities, and distribute supplies. But many of its agents were incompetent, and some were outright dishonest.

The army was called in only when there was trouble. Its function was to punish the Indians, and its methods were often harsh. One of the most tragic examples of the army's methods occurred in Colorado in 1864. The Cheyenne and the Arapaho had been assigned to the Sand Creek reservation, described by one official as "the most dry and desolate region" in the Colorado territory. Finding it impossible to survive when the buffalo herds moved elsewhere, many Indians left the reservation, and some staged raids against white settlements.

The governor of the territory asked all friendly Indians to report to certain army posts. Chief Black Kettle led several hundred Indians back to Fort Lyons at Sand Creek, where they expected to be safe. Instead, most of them were slaughtered in a surprise attack by the First Colorado Volunteer Regiment under Colonel John Chivington, who ignored the Indians' white flag. This event became known as the Sand Creek Massacre.

Indian Resistance

The failure of American Indian policy led to almost constant warfare in the West. During and after the Civil War, three main groups involved in conflicts were the Navaho, the Apache, and the Sioux.

Navaho and Apache. In the Southwest, the Navaho offered fierce resistance until 1864, when an army under Colonel Kit Carson forced them onto a military reservation known as Bosque Redondo. There they were expected to raise their own food even though the soil was poor, and they had little experience as farmers. Heat, crowded conditions, and disease added to the Indians' problems. Nearly one-quarter of the Navaho population died within five years. The remaining Navahos were later moved to a larger and slightly less barren reservation. After the defeat of the Navaho, the Apache under the leadership of Cochise continued to war against whites.

Sioux. While the Navaho and Apache were fighting in the Southwest, the Sioux were resisting white intrusion on the Plains. They were enraged that white miners were trespassing on their land to reach Montana gold mines and further angered by the fact that the government was planning to build a road to the mining centers. The Bozeman Road was planned to go from Fort Laramie, Wyoming, straight through the heart of the Sioux hunting ground.

Led by Chief Red Cloud, the Sioux staged a series of attacks from 1865 to 1867. This was the First Sioux War, or Red Cloud's War. The bloodiest incident of the First Sioux War was the ambush and killing of 82 American soldiers in December 1866. This incident was known as the Fetterman Massacre, after the group's commanding officer, Captain William J. Fetterman.

Changes in Policy

Shocked by continued hostilities in the West, Congress appointed a committee to carry out an investigation. In 1866, after studying the committee's report, Congress created a peace commission to recommend a new Indian policy.

The Peace Commission. The peace commission, made up of both soldiers and civilians, called southern Indian groups to a meeting at Medicine Lodge Creek in 1867. At Medicine Lodge, the Arapaho and Cheyenne accepted lands in the Indian Territory (Oklahoma). The area in which the Arapaho and Cheyenne would have their reservation had been confiscated from the Five Civilized Tribes (Cherokee, Choctaw, Chickasaw, Creek, and Seminole) because some of them had supported the South during the Civil War.

Debate the merits of Americanizing the Indians. Have some students take the Indian point of view and others take the government point of view.

The intrusion of white ways often disrupted the Indians' way of life. Cultural stress can be seen in this photograph of attempted "Americanization." What was Congress' first step to assimilate Indians into American society?

In 1868 the peace commission met with northern Indian groups at Fort Laramie. At this meeting the Sioux accepted lands in the Dakotas with hunting rights as far as the Big Horn Mountains in Wyoming. The government agreed to abandon constructing the Bozeman Road through the heart of Sioux territory and promised the Indians annuity payments and supplies.

"Americanization." After 1870 a new policy began to take shape. With the Indians now concentrated on two large **reservations** (areas set aside or reserved), the Board of Indian Commissioners proposed that the government begin thinking about assimilating Indians into white culture, or **"Americanizing"** them. As a first step, Congress in 1871 abolished the practice of treating Indian groups as sovereign nations. From this point, they were to be treated as **wards,** or people under the protection of the government.

The Last Indian Wars

The efforts of the peace commission were not successful for long. In 1874 gold was discovered in the Black Hills of South Dakota, and once again, miners began trespassing on Sioux lands. At first the government tried to keep the prospectors out of the Dakotas in order to prevent bloodshed. Surrendering to the inevitable, however, the government opened the Black Hills to settlement in 1875.

The Second Sioux War. In protest, many Sioux left the reservation and gathered for war under their leaders Sitting Bull and Crazy Horse. The government ordered the Indians to return to their reservation. When the Sioux refused, the government sent an army into the Dakotas to force the Sioux to comply.

The United States Army finally managed to defeat the Indians, although not before Lieutenant Colonel George Armstrong Custer and the 264 men of the Seventh Calvary were annihilated at the Battle of the Little Big Horn on June 25, 1876. Indian resistance was gradually worn down, and, by the end of the 1870's, most Sioux were on reservations.

Nez Percé. The 1870's saw the defeat of other Indian groups besides the Sioux. One of these was the Nez Percé of eastern Oregon. In 1877 the government ordered the Nez Percé to move to a smaller reservation in Idaho. When they were given the order to move, some young braves staged a series of raids. Fearing reprisals, the Nez Percé attempted to escape to Canada, led by Chief Joseph. This group of 800 Indians evaded capture for 75 days before surrendering to United States troops just 40 miles (64 kilometers) from the Canadian border. In advising his people to give up, Chief Joseph made a moving speech:

I am tired of fighting. Our chiefs are killed. . . . The old men are all dead. It is the young men who say yes or no. He who led the young men is dead. It is cold and we have no blankets. The little children are freezing to death. My people, some of them, have run away to the hills, and have no blankets, no food. No one knows where they are—perhaps freezing to death. I want to have time to look for my children and see how many of them I can find. Hear me, my chiefs. I am tired. My

Have students write a first-person account of a day in the life on an Indian reservation in the late 1800's or a day in the life on an Indian reservation today.

What is the Indian Territory (see map) today?

heart is sick and sad. From where the sun now stands, I will fight no more forever.

To punish the Nez Percé for their resistance, the government forced them onto a barren Oklahoma reservation instead of resettling them in their native Northwest. Unused to the climate and terrain, many of them died.

Apache. One of the last Indian groups to be defeated was the Apache, who held out far longer than the Navaho in the Southwest. Excellent riders and hunters, the Apache were comfortable hiding in the hills. Their swift surprise attacks took many lives. They were not subdued until 1886, when the Apache leader Geronimo, with only a few dozen men, surrendered to federal troops.

Wounded Knee. One final episode of Indian resistance took place in the Dakota Territory. In the late 1880's a religious revival known as the Ghost Dance Movement began among the Paiutes of Nevada and spread to many of the Plains Indians, including the Sioux. The Ghost Dance was performed

POPULATION OF INDIAN RESERVATIONS, 1883

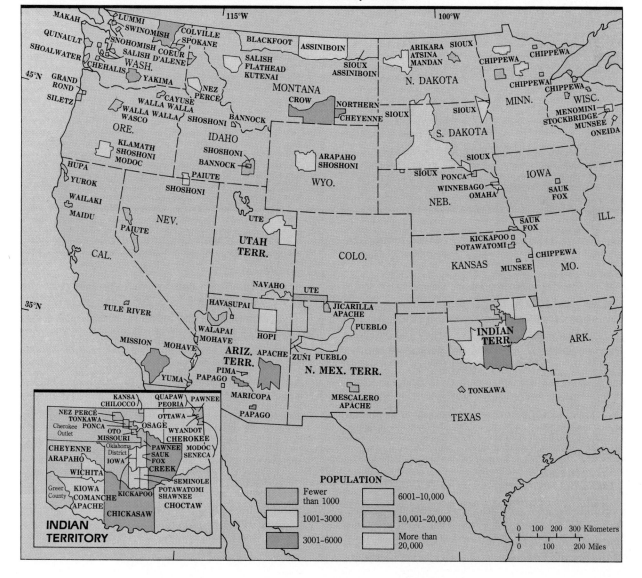

SIOUX WAR '76-'77

The Indian Chiefs

The Indians had many great leaders who rose to meet the challenge of the whites. One of the most famous was Tatanka Iyotake, or Sitting Bull, a Shaman and leader of the Hunkpapa Sioux Indians. As a boy he was known as Hunkesni, meaning Slow. But, after counting his first coup at the age of 14, he received the name Sitting Bull for showing bravery in battle.

In 1875 he had a vision telling him that all his enemies would be defeated. He encouraged the Sioux to change their way of fighting. They should fight to kill, he said, instead of counting coup. The result of his vision and his leadership was the Indians' defeat of Custer at Little Big Horn in 1876.

After Custer's defeat, Sitting Bull led a group of 2000 Sioux to escape in Canada. In 1881, however, the threat of starvation forced them to surrender. Sitting Bull died in 1890, shot while being arrested at a Ghost Dance. He had never stopped hating white people.

Another great Indian leader was Cochise, an Apache Chief. He and his tribe, the Chiricahua Apache, were peaceful until Cochise was falsely accused of kidnapping a white child. To avenge his personal honor, Cochise waged 11 years of war against the whites.

Other notable Indian chiefs included Red Cloud, who defeated the United States in the First Sioux War; Geronimo, who led a band of Apache raiders; and Chief Joseph, the beloved leader of the Nez Percé. Even in defeat, they won the respect of their enemies for their courage and determination.

as a ritual that the Indians believed would destroy the whites, bring back the buffalo, and restore the Indian way of life.

The Ghost Dance movement alarmed the white settlers, and federal troops were sent to prevent outbreaks of violence. In December 1890, United States soldiers tried to disarm a large band of Ghost Dancers gathered at Wounded Knee Creek on the Pine Ridge Reservation in South Dakota. The result was a massacre in which more than 150 Indians, many of them women and children, were killed. In addition, 25 soldiers lost their lives. The incident at Wounded Knee marked the end of armed conflict between the United States government and the Indians.

The Indian Rights Movement

During the 1880's the plight of the Indians led to an Indian rights movement in the East. Sentiment for humanitarian reform grew with the publication in 1881 of Helen Hunt Jackson's book, *A Century of Dishonor*. This book highlighted the broken treaties and general mistreatment of Indians by the government and by private citizens.

Most reformers believed that the answer to the Indians' problems was assimilation into white culture. The culmination of the Indian rights movement was the passage in 1887 of the Dawes Act. This act, sponsored by Senator Henry L. Dawes of Massachusetts, dissolved the Indian tribes as legal entities and provided for tribal lands to be divided among individual Indians. The act was intended to force Indians to give up their traditional collective ownership of the land.

The chief effect of the Dawes Act was to further deprive Indians of their land. After individual Indians received their plots, about 75 million acres (30 million hectares) of remaining Indian lands were released to white settlement. The attempt to Americanize the Indians was generally unsuccessful. Although separated from their traditional ways, most Indians remained outside the mainstream of American life.

With the settling of the frontier, huge amounts of land were brought under cultivation. This led to an increase in the supply of farm products that outstripped the increase in population and affected farm prices adversely. This in turn created political unrest among farmers. (See Chapter 17.)

Although there was no longer a frontier, there was still plenty of land. Between 1890 and 1930 the government gave away almost four times as much land as it had before 1890.

With Indian resistance at an end, nothing remained to stop white settlers. In 1890 the census report stated that the Trans-Mississippi West was so broken up by acres of settlement that a frontier line could no longer be identified. The last frontier, and with it the Old West, had disappeared.

SECTION REVIEW

1. Identify the following: Red Cloud, Bureau of Indian Affairs, Chief Joseph, Ghost Dance, Helen Hunt Jackson.

2. What characteristics of the life of the Plains Indians brought them into conflict with white settlers?

3. Why were the treaties signed at Fort Laramie unsuccessful?

4. What settlements were made by the Peace Commission?

5. What was the purpose of the Dawes Act passed in 1887?

INDIAN WARS AND CESSIONS, 1850–1890

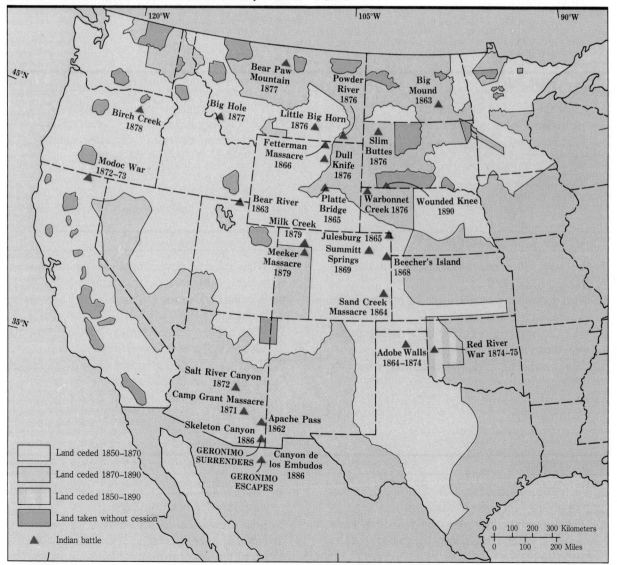

SUMMARY

1. After the Civil War, Americans began moving into the last frontier in the continental United States, the Trans-Mississippi West.
2. Discoveries of gold, silver, and other minerals attracted many people and led to the growth of mining towns.
3. Another source of wealth that attracted people to the West was the cattle business.
4. Cattle raisers came into conflict with sheep raisers and farmers.
5. Beginning in 1862, government land policies encouraged farmers to settle in the Great Plains.
6. New technology helped pioneers to overcome the harsh realities of farming on the Plains.
7. The movement of white settlers into the West was forcefully resisted by the Western Indians.
8. The Indians were ultimately defeated and forced onto two large reservations.
9. After 1870, a new government policy called for assimilating Indians into white culture.

VOCABULARY

ghost town	open range	range war	dry farming	amuities
vigilantism	long drive	necktie party	counting coup	reservation
placer method	cattle baron	dugout	transit rights	Americanizing
capitalist				ward

REVIEW QUESTIONS

1. Why was the Trans-Mississippi West the last frontier to be settled?
2. What appeal did the West have for miners, cattle raisers, and farmers?
3. How did the objectives of the cattle raisers conflict with those of the farmer?
4. What conditions made Plains farming especially difficult?
5. What role did government play in the lives of miners, cattle raisers, and farmers in the West?
6. Why did both mining and cattle raising become big business?
7. What actions did the Indians take to resist the advances of the white settlers?
8. How did government policy toward the Indians change between 1850 and 1890?

DISCUSSION

1. What alternatives did the Plains Indians have to try to stem the intrusion of white settlers?
2. Which frontier lifestyles do you find most appealing—that of the miner, the cowboy, or the farmer?
3. What would have been a fair way for white Americans to deal with Indians?
4. Why were the Indians unable to retain the lifestyles that had characterized their culture for centuries?

USING MAPS

Refer to the map on page 334 and answer the following questions:

1. In which states were major gold-mining regions located?
2. Where did the Modoc Indians live?
3. Which of the cattle trails passed closest to Denver, Colorado?
4. Which cattle trails went through the Indian Territory?
5. What were the chief uses of land in Iowa?

USING SKILLS

The following words were written by Theodore Roosevelt in 1885. After you read what Roosevelt has to say about Indians, go to the library and read about Roosevelt's life. Then answer the questions that follow the reading.

When my cattle came to the Little Missouri the region was only inhabited by a score or so of white hunters; their title to it was quite as good as that of most Indian tribes to the lands they claim; yet nobody dreamed of saying that these hunters owned the country. Each could eventually have kept his own claim of 160 acres, and no more.

The Indians should be treated in just the same way that we treat the white settlers. Give

each his little claim; if, as would generally happen, he declined this, why then let him share the fate of the thousands of white hunters and trappers who have lived on the game that the settlement of the country has exterminated, and let him, like those whites, who will not work, perish from the face of the earth from which he comes.

1. What is Roosevelt's attitude toward the Indians and their rights of ownership to land? How does he justify his attitude?
2. How does Roosevelt compare Indians to hunters and trappers?
3. What in Roosevelt's background may have influenced his point of view?

1	Postwar Politics	345
2	The Presidential Procession	349
3	Populism	352
4	The New South	356

THE GILDED AGE

Corruption dominates the ballot-box, the legislatures, the Congress, and touches even the ermine of the bench. The people are demoralized.

IGNATIUS DONNELLY

In the years after the Civil War, the quality of American government left much to be desired. Few public officials exhibited real leadership, and corruption was widespread. At first, the corruption was not apparent. Industrialization and material progress had produced a society that appeared to be bright and attractive. But society and government were not what they appeared to be on the surface. Because of this, Mark Twain called the late 1800's the Gilded Age.

As time passed, many people became aware of problems beneath the surface and began to call for reforms. One vehicle for reform was a new political party—one that had a decided impact on the whole country and a particularly unfortunate impact on the South.

1 Postwar Politics

In the late 1800's, there were scandals at all levels of government. In the eyes of many critics, politics reached a low point. Although that low point was not maintained, it dealt a lasting blow to the image of politicians.

Corruption

During the Gilded Age a general moral laxity seemed to prevail. In the scramble to make money in America's rapidly growing postwar economy, some people used unscrupulous tactics to get ahead. The success of such tactics often depended upon the cooperation of government figures. Scandals arose at every level of government.

Scandals in the National Government.
Although Ulysses S. Grant had been a brilliant general and was honest and well-meaning, he was not a success as President. This was, in part, because he had little experience in politics. However, the main reason for Grant's ineffectiveness was his poor judgment of people. He often placed his trust in those

who were not worthy of it. His poor judgment was evident early in his first term, when a major scandal took place.

In September 1869, stock speculators Jay Gould and Jim Fisk tried to corner the gold supply in order to control prices in the gold market. To keep the price high, Gould and Fisk needed the help of the government. They tried to persuade President Grant not to sell government gold because any increase in the supply would drive prices down. Grant, however, refused to do as they asked.

Although Grant had refused, a rumor that he had agreed to withhold the sale of government gold caused prices to climb. Gould and Fisk were able to sell their gold at inflated prices until Grant realized what was happening and ordered the United States Treasury to release $4 million in gold for sale.

As a result of the government's action, the price of gold dropped sharply. On September 24, 1869—a day which came to be known as "Black Friday"—hundreds of people were ruined when the price of gold plunged. Although it was the manipulations of Gould and Fisk that caused the crash, most people blamed the federal government and President Grant.

In addition to "Black Friday," two other major scandals took place during Grant's term in office. One of these concerned the Crédit Mobilier. The Crédit Mobilier was a construction company formed by the promoters of the Union Pacific Railroad. The company had received favorable treatment from Congress and had made huge profits.

In 1872 the New York *Sun* discovered that certain members of Congress, as well as Vice President Schuyler Colfax, had received gifts of stock in the company. Suspicion about the nature of these dealings increased when Congress tried to block any investigation of the *Sun's* charge. In the end, two members of Congress were censured (officially reprimanded).

The other scandal of Grant's administration involved Grant's private secretary Orville Babcox and several other government officials, some of whom were Grant appointees. These people were part of the so-called "Whiskey Ring"—a conspiracy of revenue (tax) officers and distillers formed to cheat the government out of taxes on distilled liquor. By the time the plot was discovered, the government had lost millions of dollars.

Although Grant had had nothing to do with these two scandals, they damaged his reputation and that of his administration. More and more people came to think that all politicians were corrupt.

Much of the corruption in Congress was due to the large number of lobbyists in Washington, D.C. Lobbyists used a number of techniques to influence legislation, ranging from honest argument to outright

This cartoon shows Grant as a strong support for corrupt members of his administration. Such cartoons helped to arouse public opinion against political corruption. What was the "Whiskey Ring" conspiracy?

bribery. Furthermore, some members of Congress commonly accepted favors from business people and held financial interests in businesses that were affected by congressional legislation. These members of Congress had what is called a **conflict of interest**—that is, a difference between their personal interest and the public interest for which they were supposed to be responsible.

Scandals in State Government.   Scandals in state government, like those in the national government, generally involved the purchase of favors from legislators by business people. For example, when financiers Jay Gould, Daniel Drew, and Jim Fisk fought Commodore Vanderbilt for control of the Erie Railroad, both sides bribed members of the New York legislature.

Scandals in Local Government.   Some of the worst examples of corruption showed up in city government. Frequently **political bosses** dominated **political machines** (party organizations that act automatically, like a machine).

The greatest strength of the political machines came from immigrant groups. Political bosses would help immigrants find work and help them when they were in trouble. In return, these people would vote for the machine politicians. This method of getting votes was legitimate, because the politicians were performing valuable services for the people. But some other practices of political bosses, such as **ballot stuffing** (filling ballot boxes with extra or illegal votes), were not legitimate.

The most well-known political machine was that of "Boss" William M. Tweed. In the 1860's and the early 1870's, Tweed's organization controlled New York City politics. The corrupt practices of the "Tweed Ring," as it was called, cost New York City over $100 million.

Reaction to Corruption.   In reaction to such corruption, the Liberal Republican party was formed. The Liberal Republicans promised to reform **civil service** (the rules that cover government jobs). They wanted jobs to be given on the basis of merit rather than as a reward for political services. This reform, it was hoped, would break up political machines and help bring an end to corruption in government.

Civil service reform became an important political issue during the late 1800's. In 1872 the Liberal Republicans nominated newspaper editor Horace

Greeley received over 40 percent of the popular vote, but died shortly after the election and did not get any electoral votes.

THE AGE OF INDUSTRIALIZATION   **347**

Have students discuss who benefits and who is hurt by inflation.

Greeley for President, and the Democrats also endorsed Greeley. After Greeley was defeated by Grant, the Liberal Republicans disbanded, but individuals from the group remained influential.

Lack of Leadership

Government in the late 1800's was affected not only by corruption but by a marked lack of leadership. Neither Congress nor the President provided the direction the country needed.

Members of Congress were often petty partisans, and Presidents were not activists. That is, they were unable or unwilling to take a direct, active approach to government. Moisei Ostrogorski, a Russian who visited the United States in the 1880's and 1890's, echoed the thoughts of others when he wrote, "Ideas, convictions, character, disqualify a man from public life."

One reason for the lack of distinction among political leaders was the delicate balance of power between the Republicans and the Democrats. Neither party had enough power to dominate politics. None of the Presidents who served during the Gilded Age ever received a real mandate (an authorization to act that comes from a widespread show of support).

Another reason for the political leaders' lack of distinction was the limited view of government in American life. In most matters, laissez-faire, or noninterference, was the accepted role of government. For example, the government was not expected to do anything to lessen the impact of depressions that took place in the late 1800's.

Many people felt that the President had become a mere figurehead. There were several reasons for this state of affairs. One was the dominance of Congress during Reconstruction. Another was the impeachment of Andrew Johnson. A third was the traditional Republican belief—inherited from the Whigs—that the chief executive should not take part in legislative matters.

Those who served as President in the late 1800's were not without ability. A number of them had outstanding records of service in the Civil War. Others were well-known lawyers, reformers, or individuals noted for their integrity. However, their shortcomings outweighed their merits.

Major Issues

The major political issues of the Gilded Age arose from corruption and Civil War economic policies. In order to raise the huge sums needed to win the war, the federal government had raised tariffs and other taxes, borrowed heavily, and printed paper money.

After the war many people expected the government to change these policies. The government did cut its borrowing and eliminate many of the special taxes. The tariff and currency questions, however, were not resolved so easily.

The Tariff. Despite expectations, tariffs were not lowered after the war. One reason that taxes on imports remained high was that politicians wanted to protect the economic interests of their constituents. Members of Congress often demanded high tariffs on imports that would compete with businesses in their districts. In order to get tariff bills passed, the politicians compromised by supporting each other's demands. These compromise bills, then, often meant higher duties all around.

Opinions on the subject of tariffs differed. In general, Republicans favored high tariffs, while Democrats were against them. The chief support for protection came from industrialists who wanted foreign competition priced as high as possible. Many workers also favored high tariffs because they felt the tariffs protected jobs and supported high wages. Opposition to high tariffs came from advocates of free trade as well as groups that opposed active government.

Currency. The currency question also gave rise to debate during the Gilded Age. During the Civil War, the federal government had printed some $450 million in greenbacks (paper money not backed by specie). Adding this currency to the money supply caused inflation. As a result, public feeling after the war was largely in favor of removing the greenbacks from circulation.

However, as depression set in and farm prices dropped, farmers began to favor inflation. They wanted an increase in greenbacks so that they would be paid more for their crops and have more money to pay their debts. At the same time, eastern business interests became even more certain that issuing greenbacks had been a bad idea. In fact, they stood against any manipulation of the money supply that

Those who had government bonds from the Civil War used their influence to keep inflation down. Remind students of Hamilton's idea that the interests of those who lend money to the government should be protected.

Americans in the last half of the nineteenth century were entertained by Thomas Nast's political cartoons. Nast popularized the political symbols of the Democratic donkey and the Republican elephant. What role did Nast play in the politics of the period?

might lead to inflation. They wanted greenbacks to be removed from circulation entirely.

There were those, however, who took a middle position that the number of greenbacks in circulation should not be either increased or decreased. In 1875 Congress adopted a modified version of this plan. About $300 million in greenbacks would be left in circulation, but as of January 1, 1879, greenbacks could be exchanged for gold. At that point greenbacks would be worth their **face value** (value printed on the face of the money) in gold. This policy counteracted the inflationary impact of the greenbacks.

In the late 1800's, those who favored inflation turned their attention to silver. In 1834 Congress had passed a law setting up **bimetallism**—a policy of using two metals, gold and silver, to back paper money. Gold was valued at a ratio of 16 to 1 to silver. That is, the government would pay the same price for 16 ounces of silver as for one ounce of gold.

Because silver was scarce at the time, it was really worth more in relation to gold, and, therefore, people hoarded silver or sold it to private buyers for more than the government would pay. As a result, the government stopped coining silver in 1873 and went on the **gold standard.** Only gold was used to back paper money.

The discovery of new deposits of silver in the West, however, changed the situation. As the supply of silver increased, its value declined. By 1874, 16 ounces of silver was worth less than an ounce of gold. Silver producers now would have been glad to sell

their silver to the government. When they discovered that Congress had taken silver dollars off the coin list, they were furious and demanded that the government start coining silver again. Others who benefited from inflation, including farmers, supported the demand for silver dollars.

Civil Service Reform. The question of civil service reform also proved to be difficult. By the late 1800's, the spoils system could no longer meet the needs of a growing and increasingly specialized bureaucracy. Furthermore, the civil service system was very corrupt. Government jobs could often be bought, and sometimes government employees had to donate part of their salaries to a political party in order to keep their jobs.

One strong movement for reform came from within the Republican party itself. Reform-minded Republicans were called "Mugwumps," an Indian term meaning "big chief." Most of them had been members of the short-lived Liberal Republican party.

To reduce corruption in government, the Mugwumps called for a federal civil service based on merit. Civil service reform, however, was not popular because the whole party system was based on patronage. Elected officials paid political debts by appointing supporters to office.

The reaction of other Republicans to the Mugwumps was anything but positive. James G. Blaine, the leader of one group of Republicans, said that the Mugwumps were "upstarts, conceited, foolish, vain. . . ." Roscoe Conkling, the leader of the other

Have students develop a time line to follow the events of the various administrations.

THE AGE OF INDUSTRIALIZATION **349**

Garfield's assassin was a Stalwart who wanted Arthur to be President.

major group in the Republican party, called them "dilettanti" whose "stock in trade is rancid, canting, self-righteousness."

SECTION REVIEW

1. Identify the following: "Black Friday," Crédit Mobilier, Orville Babcox, William M. Tweed, Mugwumps.
2. What were the major political issues of the Gilded Age?
3. What were the different viewpoints on the currency question?
4. Why was civil service reform not a very popular issue?

2 The Presidential Procession

Subjects such as civil service reform were not often addressed in the political campaigns of the day. Instead, campaigns were based largely on appeals to party loyalty and charges of corruption against the other party. National elections were spectacles with fiery speeches and torchlight parades. Although these elections turned out more voters than ever before, the enthusiasm of the campaigns rarely led to significant activity on the part of those elected to office.

Hayes

Rutherford B. Hayes, who followed Grant as President, came into office as part of a deal between the Democrats and Republicans (the "Compromise of 1877"). Hayes received some disputed electoral votes in return for concessions to the Democrats, including a promise to withdraw federal troops from the South. Hayes was a man of principle, but he failed to accomplish much as President. He made some effort toward civil service reform by trying to use merit as a basis for appointments.

As part of his reform campaign, he removed two Republicans, Chester A. Arthur and Alonzo B. Cornell, from their jobs as customs collectors in New York because the two men had been involved in some questionable activities. The two were part of Roscoe Conkling's group, and Conkling fought back. He used his influence to keep the Senate from confirming the appointments Hayes made to replace Arthur and Cornell. But Hayes kept submitting new appoint-

ments until the Senate finally ratified his choices.

Hayes won this battle. However, any effectiveness he had as President was lost when he announced early in his term that he would not run again.

Garfield and Arthur

In 1880, when President Hayes refused to run for a second term, the Republicans nominated James A. Garfield of Ohio. The Democrats ran Winfield Scott Hancock of Pennsylvania. A third party, the Greenback party, which arose out of the controversy over greenbacks, nominated James B. Weaver of Iowa as its candidate.

With the two major parties skirting the real issues, the candidates indulged in mudslinging. Each side accused the other of corruption. Garfield won the electoral vote with 214 to Hancock's 155. Garfield also won the popular vote, but by a narrow margin of only a few thousand votes.

Garfield, who had been a Union general in the Civil War and then governor of Ohio, was faced with questions of patronage as soon as he took office. As a "dark horse" nominee, Garfield had tried to steer a middle course between the two major factions in the Republican party—Blaine's "Half-Breeds" and Conkling's "Stalwarts." These groups had been formed during Reconstruction. The Half-Breeds were given that name because of their half-hearted commitment to Reconstruction, while the Stalwarts had received theirs because they supported a tough Reconstruction policy.

Once Garfield was in office, each of these groups urged him to reward their loyal followers with political positions. These efforts ended suddenly on July 2, 1881, when President Garfield was shot by a disappointed office-seeker. On September 19, Garfield died and Vice President Chester A. Arthur of New York became President.

Arthur was a lawyer whose only political experience had been as customs collector of the port of New York. He had been nominated as Vice President to please Conkling's Stalwarts. But despite his inauspicious credentials, Arthur was not a weak President. Surprisingly, he developed a certain measure of independence and even became something of a reformer. For example, although most Republicans favored high tariffs, Arthur favored reductions.

At first only about 14 percent of federal jobs came under the merit system of the Pendleton Act. But the act provided that future Presidents might enlarge the number of jobs subject to civil service. By the 1940's most people working for the government were under civil service.

Arthur further disappointed his Stalwart friends by supporting civil service reform. In fact, it was during his term of office that a reform bill was finally passed. The Pendleton Act of 1883 set up the merit system in the civil service and created the Civil Service Commission to run it. The new rules required that certain government jobs be given only to people who had passed a competitive examination.

Arthur showed further independence by vetoing two bills—one that limited Chinese immigration and one that appropriated $18 million for river and harbor improvements. Arthur's actions spoiled his chances for renomination. Instead, the Republicans named James G. Blaine of Maine as their candidate.

Blaine was one of the most influential politicians of his time. He had been Speaker of the House of Representatives for a number of years, had served in the Senate, and had been Secretary of State under Garfield. Because Blaine was a political boss, tainted with corruption, the Mugwumps backed the Democratic nominee, Grover Cleveland.

On July 2, 1881, President Garfield was shot by a disappointed office seeker. To escape Washington's heat, the wounded President was removed to the seashore at Elberon, New Jersey, where he died. Why was the "spoils system" blamed for his death?

Cleveland

At that time, Cleveland was governor of New York, which was to prove a key state in the election of 1884. The Tammany machine of "Boss" Tweed opposed the reform-minded Cleveland, and Cleveland might have lost New York to Blaine. However, Blaine lost some of his appeal in an incident that occurred shortly before the election. When a delegation of Protestant clergy called on Blaine, the leader of the group, Reverend Samuel D. Burchard, referred to the Democrats as the party of "Rum, Romanism, and Rebellion." This was a slur against the Irish Catholics, who were a large part of the Democratic constituency in New York. The fact that Blaine did not disavow the remark or rebuke Burchard cost him many Irish votes. Cleveland won New York by a narrow margin, and New York's electoral votes gave him the Presidency.

Once in office, Cleveland took stands on a number of important issues. He signed the Interstate Commerce Act into law in an attempt to regulate big business and railroads. After the Haymarket Riot in Chicago, he suggested that Congress develop some means for voluntary arbitration of strikes. His interest in the plight of the Indians led to the passage of the Dawes Act—a law that was well-intended, though its wisdom has since been questioned.

Many of Cleveland's stands were politically risky. For one thing, he vetoed a large number of private pension bills for Civil War veterans. This caused dismay among many who had served in the Union Army. He nullified certain illegal leases of Indian lands, causing loud protests from the cattle ranchers who held them. He urged Congress to lower the tariff, although he had been warned that this was a dangerous move.

Cleveland also opposed the silver policy established under the Bland-Allison Act of 1878. Richard P. Bland of Missouri had proposed in 1877 a bill that called for "free and unlimited" coinage of silver at a ratio of 16 to 1. Adding so much silver to the currency would have been inflationary, but the bill was amended by Senator William B. Allison of Missouri.

In its final form, the act required the Secretary of the Treasury to buy and convert into coins from $2 to $4 million of silver each month. Because the Treasury bought only the minimum amount of silver required by the law, the Bland-Allison Act was not too inflation-

ELECTION OF 1892

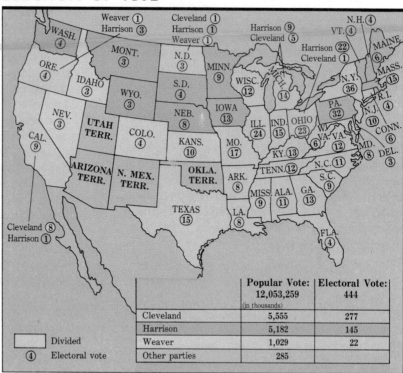

	Popular Vote: 12,053,259 (in thousands)	Electoral Vote: 444
Cleveland	5,555	277
Harrison	5,182	145
Weaver	1,029	22
Other parties	285	

Divided

④ Electoral vote

ary. In opposing the act, however, Cleveland alienated not only silver producers but also groups that favored inflation.

Stands such as these made Cleveland a number of enemies. He made further problems for himself over the question of patronage. Because Cleveland was the first Democrat to be elected President since 1856, party members expected him to appoint Democrats to government offices. Cleveland's Mugwump supporters, however, hoped that he would reject the idea of the spoils system. By trying to steer a middle course, Cleveland upset both Democrats and Mugwumps. As a result, he was not in a strong position for reelection in 1888.

Harrison

The Democrats renominated Cleveland with a marked lack of enthusiasm. The Republicans chose Benjamin Harrison of Indiana, grandson of William Henry Harrison, as their candidate. Although Cleveland won the popular vote by a margin of almost 100,000, Harrison won the electoral vote, and with it the Presidency.

Benjamin Harrison was not a particularly effective President. His administration was dominated by special-interest groups. The House was controlled by gold-standard easterners, while western silver interests controlled the Senate. Special-interest politics produced the McKinley Tariff of 1890, which was backed by eastern manufacturers. This act raised the duties on manufactured goods. In return for help in passing that measure, western silver interests were able to push through the Sherman Silver Purchase Act of 1890, whch substantially increased the coinage of silver.[1]

The public was not pleased by such special-interest politics. In 1890 the people voted many Republicans out of office. The stage was set for the presidential campaign of 1892.

---

[1] The increased coinage of silver contributed to a decline in the value of silver. As many people tried to exchange their silver for gold, the government's gold reserves shrank. In 1893 Cleveland called a special session of Congress to repeal the Sherman Silver Purchase Act. Gold reserves continued to shrink, however, because of the amount of silver still in circulation. In 1895 a group of bankers led by J. P. Morgan lent gold to the government to solve the crisis.

Cleveland Again

In the presidential election of 1892, Harrison again faced Cleveland. This time, however, Cleveland won by more than 350,000 popular votes and an electoral majority of 277 to 145. Thus Cleveland became the only President in American history to serve two non-consecutive terms.

Of greater significance than Cleveland's margin of victory was the support given to a third party candidate, James B. Weaver. Weaver, who had been the candidate for the Greenback party in 1880, ran in 1892 under the banner of the new People's party, better known as the Populist party. By this time a large part of the American electorate was already responding to the Populist philosophy.

SECTION REVIEW

1. Identify the following: Half-Breeds, Stalwarts, Pendleton Act, James G. Blaine, Samuel D. Burchard, Bland-Allison Act.
2. What were the characteristics of political campaigns during the Gilded Age?
3. How did President Arthur show his independence while in office?
4. What stands did Cleveland take while in office?
5. How did special-interest groups influence the government's policy on silver?

3 Populism

Populism had its roots in the Granger era and reached its peak in the election of 1896. It was largely a rural movement—an attempt to make the government respond to the problems of the farmer.

Before the Civil War, farm products represented about one-half of the country's total wealth. By the 1900's, the value of farm products had declined to about one-fifth of total wealth. These figures indicate the extent of the farmers' problems.

Problems of Farmers

The agricultural revolution (the introduction of new techniques and machines that increased productivity) caused many changes in the life of the American farmer. With the resulting shift from subsistence to commercial farming, farmers often found themselves in a cycle of debt. Having borrowed to buy land, machinery, or seed, farmers had to use most of their profits to pay their debts. However, profits were often poor at best. Prices for farm products remained low because the output of American farmers increased faster than the ability of people to buy. In fact, sometimes the market was so poor that farmers did not even try to sell their crops.

Farmers faced a difficult situation. To produce more would contribute to lower prices by adding to the supply. To produce less would result in less income and insufficient funds to pay their debts.

Other factors also affected the farmers' profits. One of these was the high cost of shipping and storing produce. Another was high interest rates. During the Civil War, when farm prices were high and money was cheap, many farmers borrowed to increase production. Their debts often came due at a time when prices were low, and money was dear. Natural disasters also took their toll of the farmers' profits. Drought, floods, and insects often destroyed their crops.

The farmers' plight often gave rise to bitter feelings. Historian Vernon Louis Parrington recalled his boyhood on a Kansas farm as follows:

> Many a time have I warmed myself by the kitchen stove in which ears [of corn] were burning briskly, popping and crackling in the jolliest fashion. And if while we sat around such a fire watching the year's crop go up the chimney, the talk sometimes became bitter . . . who will wonder?

The bitterness Parrington described was not undirected. Aware of their economic position, farmers blamed their troubles on the so-called "monied interests." These included railroads, manufacturers, bankers, speculators, and those who shaped the monetary policy of the United States government.

Farmers' Organizations

Early attempts to remedy the farmers' situation were made by the Grange. Turning to politics to gain reforms, the Grange succeeded in getting sympathetic legislation passed in a number of midwestern states. In these states, Granger laws, as they were called, regulated the rates and practices of railroads,

On the Great Plains, farming had its agonies. Bumper crops brought low prices, and drought brought no crops. "A Prayer for Rain" by A.B. Frost shows the anguish of a Kansas farmer. Who promoted settlement of the Great Plains?

warehouses, and grain elevators.[2] On the whole, however, the Grange directed its attention to running cooperative business and educational enterprises. In the 1870's, when a number of these ventures failed, the group began to decline.

As the Grange declined, other organizations appeared to take its place. In the 1880's and 1890's, reform was carried on by farmers' alliances, which were first formed at the local level. One especially important local group was started in Texas in the mid-1870's. This group, guided by Dr. C. W. Macune, soon joined with similar groups in Louisiana and Arkansas to form a national alliance. It was called the National Farmers' Alliance and Industrial Union and was referred to as the Southern Alliance.

By the early 1890's, the Southern Alliance was the largest farm organization in the United States. Like the Grange, it set up cooperatives, but soon turned to politics. To achieve its goals, the Southern Alliance worked with the National Colored Farmers' Alliance.

---

[2] Between 1870 and 1874, Illinois, Iowa, Minnesota, and Wisconsin passed Granger laws.

Meanwhile a similar process was taking place in the North. In the 1880's the National Farmers' Alliance of the Northwest, or the Northern Alliance, was formed. When its membership neared 2 million, talk of a merger between the Northern and Southern Alliances grew. However, the northerners had a grander scheme. They wanted to form a third national political party.

A National Party

The first signs of the farmers' strength at the national level showed in the elections of 1890. In the West independent or people's parties were formed and backed by the Alliance. In Kansas the independents elected six members to Congress and gained control of the lower house of the state legislature. In Nebraska the independents elected one member to Congress and a majority of state legislators. In the South the Alliance gained control of eight legislatures, and Alliance-backed candidates won four races for governor and 44 congressional seats.

Pleased with such successes, farmers joined with representatives of labor and other reform movements to form the Populist party in 1892. Populist leader Mary Ellen Lease coined the party's slogan, "Raise less corn and more hell." The party's song was "The Farmer is the Man":

When the banker says he's broke,
And the merchant's up in smoke,
They forget that it's the farmer feeds them all.
It would put them to the test
If the farmer took a rest,
Then they'd know that it's the farmer feeds
  them all.

In July 1892, the Populists met in Omaha, Nebraska, to draw up a party platform and choose candidates for national office. The party platform drawn up at this meeting asked for economic and social reform and rejected the prevailing belief in laissez-faire:

We believe that the powers of government should be expanded . . . as rapidly and as far as the good sense of an intelligent people and the teachings of experience shall justify, to the end that oppression, injustice, and poverty shall eventually cease in the land.

The Populists wanted to join forces with labor, but the labor movement at this time was practically nonexistent. The Knights were on the way out, and the AFL was still a small organization.

Certain specific reforms were set down in the Populist platform. For one thing, the Populists called for an inflationary money policy. They also proposed a **graduated income tax**—a tax system in which people with higher incomes pay higher taxes. In addition, the platform called for a sub-treasury system. Under this system, the government would make low-interest loans to farmers, using their crops as security. This would allow farmers to keep produce off the market until prices rose.

Several other points were mentioned in the Populist platform. One was the recovery of excess public lands granted to the railroads and other corporations. Another was government ownership of railroad, telephone and telegraph systems. In a show of support for labor, the platform called for an eight-hour work day. Finally, a call was made for certain democratic political reforms. Among them were the secret (Australian) ballot, the direct election of United States Senators, the initiative, referendum, and recall. The **initiative** was a method by which citizens could propose new laws at any time. The **referendum** was a method that allowed citizens to vote on any bill brought up by the legislature. The **recall** was a way for citizens to vote on removing elected officials from public office.

Mary Ellen Lease was a leader and supporter of the Populist party. The party advocated one of the most advanced social programs to that time. What did the party platform call for?

Tom Watson, a Populist leader from Georgia, captured the essence of the new party when he declared that the Populists' chief target was "monopoly—not monopoly in the narrow sense of the word—but monopoly of power, of place, of privilege, of wealth, of progress." Presidential candidate James B. Weaver put it another way: "Equal rights for all and special privileges for none."

The huge appeal of this philosophy was seen in the 1892 election results. Weaver carried 6 states and received over a million popular votes. In addition, he received 22 electoral votes. This was the first time since 1865 that a third party had received electoral votes. Nevertheless, the election results also revealed certain weaknesses in the Populist party. Most of Weaver's votes came from the Midwest and the West. The hoped-for support from eastern workers did not materialize. Even more important was the Populists' failure to win the agrarian South, where farm issues were paramount.

Despite these weaknesses, the Populists commanded significant support. The party won further victories in the congressional elections of 1894, and its members looked forward to the presidential election of 1896.

The Election of 1896

As the Democrat and Republican parties held conventions to select their candidates for the 1896 election, it became clear that certain elements in both parties agreed with some of the Populists' goals. This was not surprising. In the history of American politics, when a third party has shown considerable strength, one or the other of the major parties has incorporated some of its ideas. One Populist goal that became popular was unlimited coinage of silver at a ratio of 16 to 1. This issue was raised at the conventions of both parties.

At the Republican convention, some members of the party hoped to add a free-silver plank to the platform. However, the front-runner, William McKinley of Ohio, opposed that plank, and the free-silver faction walked out of the convention. This left the party in the hands of the conservatives, who nominated McKinley.

At the Democratic convention, a large faction favored free silver. One reason why a large number of

ELECTION OF 1896

	Popular Vote: 13,910,203 (in thousands)	Electoral Vote: 447
McKinley	7,102	271
Bryan	6,493	176
Others	315	

Divided between McKinley and Bryan
④ Electoral vote

Democrats supported this position was their dissatisfaction with Cleveland's handling of the depression that began in 1893. Cleveland's approach, based on a tight money policy, was repudiated by western and southern Democrats. This farm wing maneuvered to gain control of the convention and throw the party behind free silver. Conservatives still had a strong following, however, and it was not clear that the party would adopt the free silver position. At that point, William Jennings Bryan gave a stirring speech:

> *Having behind us the producing masses of this nation and the world, supported by the commercial interests, the laboring interests, and the toilers everywhere, we will answer their demand for a gold standard by saying to them: You shall not press down upon the brow of labor this crown of thorns, you shall not crucify mankind upon a cross of gold.*

Bryan's speech won the needed backing for the silver plank and secured him the nomination for President. But the fact that the Democrats had added a free-silver plank to their platform presented the Populists with a dilemma. Since a major party had adopted one of their ideas, the Populists had to decide whether to name their own candidate or to support Bryan.

Those who favored naming their own candidate pointed out that free silver was just one of the reforms the party wanted. In fact, many Populists felt that concentrating on free silver alone might destroy the party. In the end, the Populists decided that the practical course was to support Bryan and the Democratic platform.[3]

For the first time in many years, American voters were faced with a distinct choice in a presidential election. Bryan campaigned with enthusiasm. He pushed the idea that the Democratic program would bring about social and economic justice. Trying to broaden his appeal to include urban workers, he defended unions and announced that he intended to have labor leader Samuel Gompers in his cabinet.

McKinley also appealed to the workers, arguing that the last thing workers needed was inflation. He said that free silver would be dangerous and

---

[3] Although the Populists supported Bryan, they nominated Tom Watson as their own candidate for Vice President. The Democratic candidate was Arthur Sewell of Maine.

After 1896 farmers began working with existing parties. Within the next 20 years, many of their proposals were enacted into law. See Chapter 19.

Note that much southern industry consisted of supplying raw materials to producers in other areas.

immoral—that it threatened "the very structure of law and order on which society rested."

In November, McKinley won a decisive victory. Bryan had not been able to win labor's support. Better times also helped McKinley. By the fall of 1896, the country had begun to come out of the depression, and people's enthusiasm for more radical measures had lessened.

McKinley's election signaled the end of the farmers' revolt. Despite its positive aspects, the Populist movement had unfortunate results in one part of the country—the South.

SECTION REVIEW

1. Identify the following: C. W. Macune, Mary Ellen Lease, Australian ballot, Tom Watson.
2. What was populism?
3. What elements contributed to the farmers' cycle of debt?
4. What reforms did the Populists favor?
5. What were the differences between the candidates for President in 1896?

4 The New South

The New South—the post-Civil War South—was different from the antebellum South. Chiefly, its leadership had changed. The old planter class had lost its position to a new, business-oriented middle class. The new leaders shared many beliefs with northern business interests and faced similar challenges. However, the question of race relations made politics in the South more complex.

Bringing Industry to the South

The new leaders of the South were members of the Democratic party of redemption, which had close ties to the antebellum Whig party. These people were middle-class capitalists. Recognizing the region's potential, they worked hard to industrialize the postwar South.

Like their counterparts in the North, the political leaders of the New South were generally in favor of laissez-faire. However, they also wanted government help to promote industrialization. At the urging of these leaders, several state legislatures and many cities passed tax exemptions and other subsidies for businesses.

Such measures brought much-needed capital into the New South. The textile industry boomed, and there was also substantial growth in the tobacco, iron, coal, and lumber industries. The result was a more balanced economy, not so dependent on agriculture as the prewar South. However, the economy of the South was not growing as fast as the economy of the nation as a whole. Most southerners still made their living from the land. The region was still relatively poor, and the debts of southern states remained high.

The Farmers' Revolt

Generally, those who shouldered the tax burden for the state debts were those who could least afford it—farmers and small landowners. Most small farmers of both races were in poor shape. As in other parts of the country, profits were low and poverty high. The debt cycle drove farmers into tenancy, where the crop-lien system kept them.

The political leaders of the New South seemed indifferent to the farmers' plight. Because the leaders' attention was chiefly directed towards attracting capital, they ignored the farmers' charges that they were favoring business. The leaders also ignored demands to shift the tax burden to business.

Unable to convince the Democratic leaders of their needs, the farmers turned to the ballot box. In so doing, however, they discovered another grievance—machine politics. Like their counterparts in the North, the leaders of the New South were not above manipulating votes to stay in power. Furthermore, other scandals in state government took place in the late 1870's. Indeed, the treasurers of no fewer than seven southern states—Democrats who had condemned the corrupt Radical regimes—were discovered to be involved in various kinds of fraud.

Political revolt, however, was slow to develop. Racial differences kept poor farmers from uniting. Poor whites, who felt challenged by freedmen, were susceptible to arguments for white solidarity. When the question of race arose, they voted almost automatically for the Democrats.

The first signs of the farmers' revolt came in the late 1870's, when farmers called for repudiation (refusal to acknowledge or pay) of state debts. The small gains

Emphasize that these attempts to disfranchise blacks were intended to get around the Fifteenth Amendment, which forbade states to deny the right to vote on the basis of race.

The leaders of the new South believed that industrialization could enrich the South. Cotton mills were built, lumbering was expanded, and coal and copper mines were opened. The manufacture of iron such as that at Rockwood, Tennessee, helped to provide part of the new system. What made industrialization of the South more difficult than the North?

made by the farmers were lost when they were accused of political collusion (secret agreement or cooperation) with the Republicans. Later, as economic conditions worsened, the farmers' alliances grew in power. Finally, in the 1890's, the Populist party tried to break the Democrats' hold on the South.

The Populist revolt had a strong impact. For the first time white farm leaders appealed directly to black voters on the grounds of common economic interest. Populist Tom Watson addressed both races:

> *You are made to hate each other because upon that hatred is rested the keystone of the arch of financial despotism which enslaves you both. You are deceived and blinded that you may not see how this race antagonism perpetuates a monetary system which beggars you both. . . . The colored tenant . . . is in the same boat with the white tenant, the colored laborer with the white laborer. . . .*

Ultimately, however, Populism failed in the South, in large part, because the Democrats once again exploited the whites' old fear of domination by blacks. The Democrats said that the Populists, in trying to appeal to blacks, were threatening white supremacy. The Populist platform was simply not attractive enough to overcome this fear. In addition, the Democrats, by using corrupt methods, were often able to use the black vote against the Populists. For

example, blacks who cooperated with the Democrats were given offices in state and local governments.

A Loss of Rights for Blacks

For a time, then, both Democrats and Populists appealed to the black vote. After the Populist revolt failed, however, white farmers were resentful of the way the black vote had been used against them. Democratic leaders were also alarmed that some blacks had voted with the Populists. In the 1890's, white farmers and Democrats joined in an effort to disfranchise blacks. Thus, although white farmers were not able to reap the benefits of reform, the worst losers of the Populist revolt were blacks.

To deprive blacks of their voting rights, southern whites used two methods. One was the **poll tax,** a head tax to be paid at election time. Most blacks did not have the money to pay the tax and were therefore ineligible to vote. Another means used to deny blacks their political rights was the **literacy test.** This was a test given to potential voters to prove that they could read and explain any part of the state constitution. Many blacks did not have enough schooling to pass the test. Even if they did, local officials, who were almost always white, had the power to decide whether someone passed or failed.

One problem with these methods of disfranchising blacks was that both the poll tax and the literacy test

The National Urban League was another interracial organization formed in 1910. It concentrated on the problems of blacks in cities. Among its leaders were George Edmund Haynes and Eugene Kinckle Jones.

could keep many poor whites from voting. To remedy this problem, many southern states wrote **"grandfather clauses"** into their constitutions. People who could not pay the poll tax or pass the literacy test could still vote if they, their fathers, or their grandfathers had been eligible to vote on January 1, 1867. That date was before Radical Reconstruction, and thus only whites could benefit from the "grandfather clauses."

Besides limiting the political rights of blacks, southern states passed laws to segregate blacks from whites in daily life. The first of these so-called **"Jim Crow" laws** segregated railroads. Later, the practice of segregation spread. By the early 1900's, Jim Crow laws were widely adopted in the South. Blacks and whites were separated everywhere—from hospitals and schools to theaters and sporting events. Even restrooms and water fountains were segregated.

Some people looked to the Supreme Court to stop segregation. However, during this period, Court rulings favored states' rights. In the Slaughterhouse cases (1873), the Court ruled that, although the Fourteenth Amendment guaranteed equal protection and due process to all citizens, it applied only in certain limited cases. The majority of Supreme Court Justices felt that the federal government did not have the power to decide what a state could or could not do to protect the rights of its citizens.

In 1883 the Supreme Court ruled that the Fourteenth Amendment could not be used to prevent segregation in private business. The Court said that the amendment protected a person's rights only against actions of state governments, not against actions of private individuals or companies. Only state laws could do that.

In 1896 a Supreme Court ruling in the case of *Plessy* v. *Ferguson* added support to "Jim Crow" legislation. Louisiana passed a law requiring railroads to have separate cars for blacks and whites. Homer Plessy, a black, was arrested when he refused to vacate a car for whites. The Court ruled that segregation in itself did not violate the Fourteenth Amendment. In upholding the Louisiana law as constitutional, the Court put forth the idea that all that was necessary to make any form of segregation legal was the provision of equal facilities. This idea was known as the "separate but equal" doctrine.

In 1898 the Court in *Mississippi* v. *Williams* said that "grandfather clauses" were illegal. In the same case, however, the Court upheld the literacy test as a basis for voting rights. In 1899 the Court extended the "separate but equal" principle to schools in *Cumming* v. *County Board of Education*.

The Black Response

In the face of this legislative onslaught, blacks had little defense. Furthermore, violence against blacks enforced the color line. A major attempt to maintain black dignity was voiced by Booker T. Washington. A conservative ex-slave, Washington was the founder of the Tuskegee Institute in Alabama, where he preached the virtues of hard work and economic advancement.

Washington's philosophy was best captured in a speech given in 1895 at the Cotton States International Exposition in Atlanta, Georgia. In this address, which became known as the "Atlanta Compromise," Washington said that black participation in politics had been a mistake. He felt blacks should work for economic security before seeking equal rights:

> *No race can prosper till it learns that there is as much dignity in tilling a field as in writing a poem. It is at the bottom of life we must begin, and not at the top. Nor should we permit our grievances to overshadow our opportunities.*

Washington's position was well-suited to the political and social realities of his day. White leaders in both the North and South praised his words, and his influence grew rapidly. Some blacks, however, felt Washington was giving up too much. The major representative of that group was W. E. B. DuBois of Massachusetts—the first black to receive a Ph.D. from Harvard University.

In 1903 DuBois published *The Souls of Black Folk*, an account of black history. In that work, DuBois recognized Washington's contributions, but criticized his ideas:

> *So far as Mr. Washington apologizes for injustice, North or South, does not rightly value the privilege and duty of voting, belittles the emasculating effects of caste distinctions, and opposes the higher training and ambition*

Booker T. Washington   W. E. B. DuBois

In the late 1800's and early 1900's, two of the most important black leaders were Booker T. Washington and William E. B. DuBois. Both men had the same goals, but they took different approaches to reaching those goals.

Washington was born a slave in 1856. After slaves were freed in 1865, he attended an industrial school for blacks and later became a teacher at the same school. As a teacher, he developed his own theories about education, which led him to found the Tuskegee Institute.

Washington became an influential leader who advised Presidents and governors on political appointments for blacks, raised large amounts of money to help black organizations, and owned or controlled many black newspapers. Whites approved of him because he was willing—temporarily—to compromise on political rights for blacks. In return he wanted support for black schools, economic gains for blacks, and an end to violence against blacks.

Washington's influence began to decline as DuBois and other black leaders began new, more aggressive movements for black rights. DuBois, born in 1868 in the small town of Great Barrington, Massachusetts, experienced little of the racial hatred that was directed at most blacks. When he was orphaned at an early age, the people of his home town sent him to college on a scholarship. He became a well-known historian and sociologist.

However, as a teacher of history and economics at Atlanta University, DuBois was painfully aware of the sufferings of his people. He decided that Washington's conciliatory approach to race relations was not working.

DuBois became the editor of the NAACP magazine, *The Crisis*. In fiery editorials he called upon blacks to fight openly against discrimination. His work influenced Washington, who began to change his mind. Just before Washington died in 1915, he wrote a magazine article that was an open attack on segregation.

In the 1930's, DuBois developed a deep interest in the plight of black Africans. He believed in Pan-Africanism, the idea that all people of African descent should work together. In his later years he was so dissatisfied with the progress of race relations in America that he moved to Africa. He lived in Ghana, where he carried on his fight against inequality until his death in 1963.

of our brighter minds—so far as he, the South, or the Nation, does this—we must unceasingly and firmly oppose them.

In 1905 DuBois and other blacks started the Niagara Movement. They pledged themselves to work for political and civil rights. In 1910 the Niagara Movement joined forces with whites who were concerned about the rights of black Americans, forming the National Association for the Advancement of Colored People (NAACP). It would be another 50 years, however, before blacks would be able to make any real gains in the area of civil rights.

SECTION REVIEW

1. Identify the following: Slaughterhouse cases, *Plessy* v. *Ferguson*, *The Souls of Black Folk*, Niagara Movement.
2. How did government help in the industrialization of the South?
3. What brought about the farmers' revolt in the New South?
4. What methods did southern whites use to disfranchise blacks?
5. What was the Supreme Court's reaction to southern efforts to limit black rights?

CHAPTER **17**

SUMMARY

1. During the Gilded Age, American government was tainted by corruption on the national, state, and local levels.
2. Leadership in government on all levels was generally undistinguished.
3. The major issues of the period were related to corruption and economic policies.
4. Farmers during this era were faced with problems caused by overproduction.
5. In an attempt to solve their problems, farmers organized groups such as the Grange and farmers' alliances.
6. Farmers joined with labor and other reform groups to form the Populist party.
7. The farmers' revolt subsided after the election of 1896, when the Populists supported the losing Democratic candidate.
8. The New South was dominated by middle-class whites who worked to industrialize the region.
9. The Populist attempt to break Democratic control of the South was unsuccessful.
10. After the Populists were defeated, southern states passed laws disfranchising blacks and separating them from whites.

VOCABULARY

conflict of interest	civil service	graduated income tax	poll tax
political bosses	face value	initiative	literacy test
political machines	bimetallism	referendum	grandfather clause
ballot stuffing	gold standard	recall	Jim Crow laws

REVIEW QUESTIONS

1. What were the effects of political corruption during the Gilded Age?
2. Why was political leadership lacking during this era?
3. How did monetary policy change during this period?
4. Why did the Populist party fail to elect a President?
5. What attempts were made to reform government in the late 1800's?
6. How was the New South different from the antebellum South?
7. Why did white southerners take steps to disfranchise blacks?
8. What was the black response to discriminatory practices in the New South?

DISCUSSION

1. Would the political climate have been different if there were strong executives during this period? Were the Presidents victims of the political times, or were they weak leaders?
2. Did civil service reform achieve the results it was intended to achieve? Why or why not?
3. If you had represented your state in Congress at this time, what would have been your position on the currency issue? Why?
4. Why did DuBois and Washington take the stands they did? With whom would you agree if you were a black living in the early 1900's? Why?

USING MAPS

Refer to the maps on pages 351 and 355, and answer the following questions:

1. Who was the Populist candidate for President in 1892?
2. Which states showed the greatest support for the Populists in 1892?
3. Of the states that supported the Populists in 1892, which ones supported Bryan in 1896?
4. In 1896 what was McKinley's margin of victory in electoral votes?
5. Which states were most important to McKinley's victory in 1896?

USING SKILLS

The McKinley Tariff of 1890 included new duties on wheat imports. Republican William McKinley, who sponsored the tariff bill, argued in Congress that the new duties on wheat would help American farmers. Democrat Roger Mills argued the opposite case—that the duties would harm American farmers. Study each argument and then answer the questions that follow.

McKinley:

As we are the greatest wheat-producing country of the world, it is habitually asserted and believed by many that this product is safe from foreign competition. We do not appreciate that while the United States last year raised 490,000,000 bushels of wheat, France raised 316,000,000 bushels, Italy raised 103,000,000 bushels, Russia 189,000,000 bushels, and India 243,000,000 bushels. . . . Our sharpest competition [in the world market] comes from Russia and India. . . . and if we will only reflect on the difference between the cost of labor in producing wheat in the United States and in competing countries, we will readily perceive how near we are, if we have not quite reached, the danger line so far even as our own markets are concerned. . . .

Mills:

[The Republicans] have increased the duty on wheat and that great produce is safe. We exported last year 90,000,000 bushels in wheat and flour . . . and last year . . . imported the inconsiderable amount of 1,946 bushels of wheat.

What did that 1,946 bushels of wheat cost? Our wheat was at an average price of 89 cents per bushel, and the average price of the 1,946 bushels which we imported was $2.05. . . . What do you suppose that wheat was imported for? Do not all speak at once, please.

It was seed wheat, imported by the wheat-grower of the West to improve his seed. Does not every man know that? And you have made it cost him that much more to improve his agricultural product so that he can raise a better character of wheat and better compete in the markets of the world, where he has to meet all comers in free competition. . . .

The Germans, French, English, Spaniards, Austrians, and others with whom we are trading are dissatisfied with our discriminations against their products, and they have been taking steps to retaliate upon us. They have increased the duty on wheat in Germany two or three times since 1880. . . .

Why have we not the prices of 1881? Because we have cut off importation from our European customers, and they have cut off importation from us. Our surplus is increasing with our population, and we have no markets to consume it. . . .

1. What is McKinley's argument? What evidence does he present? Is his evidence pertinent to the question?
2. What is Mills' argument? What evidence does he present? Is his evidence pertinent?
3. With which argument do you agree? Give reasons for your answer.

1	Urbanization	363
2	Impact of Immigration	365
3	Urban Life and Culture	369
4	Urban Reform	377

AN URBAN SOCIETY

We find the wealth and luxury of our cities mingled with poverty and wretchedness and unremunerative toil.

GROVER CLEVELAND

A new America—a changing America—emerged during the late 1800's. This new America was shaped by an urban environment that replaced an older agrarian setting. People from rural areas of America, as well as immigrants from other countries, flocked to expanding urban centers. As cities grew, American society took on an increasingly urban character. This development brought with it not only new opportunities, but also new problems calling for new solutions.

1 Urbanization

Between 1870 and 1900, great cities became an important part of the national scene. Cities were vital centers of physical, social, and cultural change during this period. One of the most obvious changes was sheer growth.

Changes in Population

Urban growth was not new. Most American cities had been growing steadily since colonial times, and New York City already had over 1 million people by 1860. But the rate of growth rose significantly in the late 1800's. By 1900 New York's population had more than tripled. During the same span of years, Chicago's population rose from 440,000 to about 1.7 million. Philadelphia grew from 565,529 to approximately 1.3 million, while both Boston and Baltimore increased from about 200,000 to more than 500,000.

The greatest growth occurred in the industrial cities of the Northeast, but cities in all regions experienced rapid growth. Nashville went from just under 17,000 people to over 80,000, Minneapolis from 2500 to over 200,000, and Los Angeles from 4400 to over 100,000.

The growing population was due to the influx of immigrants from other countries and Americans from rural areas. For these people, the industrial city seemed to be the gateway to opportunity. Immigrants, who came to America to better their lot, were grateful for the chance to fill the demand for urban workers caused by industrialization. On farms, fewer workers were needed because of advances in technology. Rural Americans, especially the young, traveled to cities in search of jobs. Business people, in turn, were attracted by the opportunity to serve these new urban workers.

Not only was there a growth in city population, but the entire nation was undergoing **urbanization.** That is, there was a rise in the proportion of the total population living in urban, as opposed to rural, settings. In 1860 less than 21 percent of the population of the United States lived in towns and cities with populations of 2500 or more. By 1900 that figure had reached about 40 percent, with much of the growth occurring in the larger cities. By 1920 a majority of Americans would be city dwellers.

Technological Changes

As cities grew, city land became more valuable, especially land in the central business district, or downtown area, where business owners found it profitable to locate their stores and offices. Soaring land values led architects to look for ways to build up rather than out.

Before 1890 buildings of more than five stories were rare. Beginning in the 1880's, however, architects began designing skyscrapers, some of which were over 25 stories high. The problem of making such a tall structure steady was solved by using a steel frame. The problem of getting people to the upper floors of these buildings was solved by the use of electric elevators. As symbols of technological progress, skyscrapers were sources of great civic pride.

Progress was made in other areas as well. The electric arc lamp and the electric light bulb increased the number of hours available for work and play. Electricity was also a great boon to communication. One of the major advances in communication was Alexander Graham Bell's invention of the telephone in 1876. Soon almost all major population centers were linked by telephone lines.

The late 1800's also saw technological improvements in transportation. One of these was the paving of streets. During most of the 1800's, city streets remained poorly paved. For example, although the rapid growth of Cleveland's population in these years made that city an important urban center, nine-tenths of its streets were nothing more than sand and gravel. Other cities used wood blocks, brick, or cobblestone, all of which were bumpy, noisy, and hard to repair. The coming of asphalt in the 1890's made city streets noticeably smoother and quieter.

Another improvement was the electric trolley, which drew its power first from overhead wires and later from underground lines. These trolleys could move more people faster, cheaper, and more comfortably than older vehicles, such as horsecars.

Electric trolleys, however, did not do enough to take care of the congestion that plagued nineteenth-century American cities. Therefore the cities turned to more expensive but out-of-the-way modes of transportation. These included elevated electric railways, known as els, and subways.

Bridge construction provided yet another improvement in urban transportation. Most of America's large cities were either surrounded or intersected by water. The lack of an efficient means of crossing rivers and bays kept outlying areas from growing. To take care of this problem, a number of bridges were built throughout the country during the 1880's and 1890's. The most famous of these was the Brooklyn Bridge, which was completed in 1888. Over one mile (1.6 kilometers) in length, it was the world's longest suspension bridge (a bridge hanging from cables attached to towers). A technological feat and an artistic triumph, the Brooklyn Bridge captured the imaginations of people around the world. One English poet wrote of the bridge:

Frail as a gossamer, a thing of air,
A bow of shadow o'er the river flung,
Its sleepy masts and lonely lapping flood;
Who, seeing thus the bridge a-slumber there,
Would dream such softness, like a picture hung,
Is wrought of human thunder, iron and blood?

Geographical Changes

Improvements in transportation stimulated certain new trends in urban geography. In the first half of the 1800's, most cities had a single downtown area where nearly all factories, stores, and other businesses were located. The development of transportation allowed the downtown area to expand, dividing into a network of smaller, more specialized regions. For example, factories were concentrated in one area,

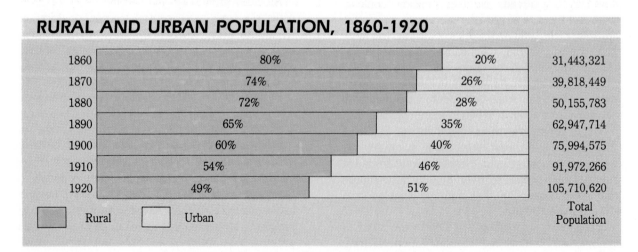

RURAL AND URBAN POPULATION, 1860-1920

Year	Rural	Urban	Total Population
1860	80%	20%	31,443,321
1870	74%	26%	39,818,449
1880	72%	28%	50,155,783
1890	65%	35%	62,947,714
1900	60%	40%	75,994,575
1910	54%	46%	91,972,266
1920	49%	51%	105,710,620

As the United States became a nation of cities, public services expanded to serve the public. Paved roads, electric streetlights, and streetcars improved inner-city transportation. What other services did cities provide?

shops in another, and banks in yet a third. Although no longer adjacent, the different areas were connected through the new transportation and communication systems.

Another geographical trend was the expansion of the city itself. Up to this point, those people who had worked in the downtown area also had lived there. The development of new means of transportation allowed the middle and upper classes to move away from their place of work. New residential areas were built away from downtown. The lower classes, however, found it too costly to move and had to remain in the heart of the city.

SECTION REVIEW

1. What caused city populations to grow at this time?
2. How did the use of electricity change life in the city?
3. What significant improvements were made in urban transportation?
4. How did transportation affect urban geography?

2 Impact of Immigration

Among the lower classes who lived in the increasingly crowded urban cores were large numbers of immigrants. During the four decades before 1880, the number of immigrants coming to America totaled about 9.5 million. Between 1880 and 1920, more than 25.5 million arrived. The fact that many of them clustered in the cities heightened their impact on urban life and made them particularly visible.

The New Immigrants

The people who came to the United States in the late 1800's were different from those who had come earlier. Before the 1880's, a large majority of immigrants to the United States were what became known as **"old" immigrants.** They were from northern and western Europe—from places such as Great Britain, Holland, Germany, and Scandinavia.

Many European immigrants also went to Canada, Australia, South America, or to neighboring countries in Europe, but the United States received the most immigrants.

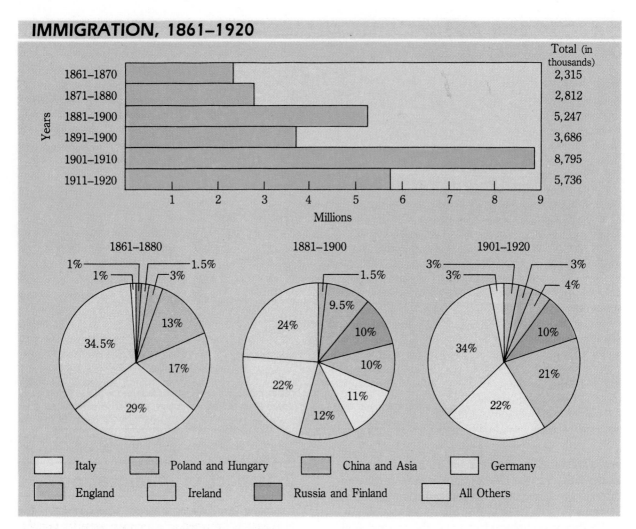

IMMIGRATION, 1861–1920

Most of these immigrants were white Anglo-Saxon Protestants.[1] Their customs and appearance were similar to those of native-born Americans.

Beginning in the 1880's, an increasing percentage of so-called **"new" immigrants** came to the United States. By the 1890's they made up more than one half of total immigration. Some of the "new" immigrants were from Asia, but most were from southern and eastern Europe—from Italy, Poland, Russia, and Hungary. The newcomers were generally Catholic, Jewish, or Eastern Orthodox. They

had different languages and customs from the "old" immigrants. The "new" immigrants even looked different.

One of the largest groups of "new" immigrants were the Italians, most of whom came from Sicily and the southern part of Italy. People in this region faced economic disaster. Unemployment and overpopulation, coupled with backward agricultural techniques, made existence precarious. As a result, millions of Italian Catholics chose to go to America. Many of them were young men who came over just to earn money, intending to return to their families who had remained behind. Such immigrants were known as "sojourners," or "birds of passage." Many did return to their homeland, but many more made a permanent home in the United States.

[1] The Irish are also classified as "old" immigrants. Although they were neither Anglo-Saxon nor Protestant, they did speak English. They faced initial hostility when they began to arrive in large numbers before the Civil War, but gradually they became assimilated into American society.

After about 1870, most immigrants came by steamship. The journey took approximately 10 days.

Immigrants tended to cluster in provincial rather than in national groups.

Another large group of "new" immigrants was eastern European Jews. Although scattered throughout many countries, the Jews of eastern Europe faced common problems wherever they lived. For one thing, they were frequently the victims of religious discrimination. Jews were often forbidden to own land, engage in certain trades, or move out of areas that had been set aside for them.[2]

These restrictions on Jews created widespread poverty. Furthermore, eastern European Jews were subject to a series of **pogroms,** or organized massacres. Jewish immigrants, seeking personal safety, religious freedom, and economic opportunity, tended to see America as a permanent home.

Slavs from eastern Europe made up a third large group of "new" immigrants. "Slavs" is a broad ethnic label given to a people, generally from eastern Europe, who have similar languages and customs. In the late 1800's, large numbers of Slavs left areas in Russia, Poland, Bohemia (Czechoslovakia), and other countries.

Most of the Slavs came to the United States to escape economic hardship. In rural areas of eastern Europe, the long-standing custom of dividing land among sons had resulted in smaller and smaller farms. By the late 1800's, most of these plots could barely support a family. At the same time, careers in the crafts were suffering from the competition of a more industrialized western Europe. Many Slavs also came to the United States in search of political freedom. Of those who came, some planned to return to eastern Europe. Others, however, intended to make a new life in America.

The Journey

The journey to America was not an easy one. Leaving one's homeland was traumatic in itself, but the difficulties of travel made the trip an experience few forgot. Over and above the cost were the conditions of the ships that took the immigrants to the United States. Most of the immigrants booked passage in **steerage.** This was a section of the ship set aside for those people paying the lowest fares. Accommodations in steerage were generally crowded and dirty. These conditions bred illness that sometimes resulted in death.

Having reached the United States, the immigrants had to go through yet another ordeal. At the port of entry, the immigrants had to be processed. That is, they had to be registered and checked for disease and criminal records. In addition, women and children traveling alone were checked to make sure they had sponsors who would take responsibility for them in America. For many immigrants, processing was a trying experience.

The largest and most famous processing center was Ellis Island in New York Harbor. Ellis Island was next to the Statue of Liberty, a gift to the United States from the French government. The statue stood as a symbol of hope for a better life in the new country.

Immigrant Communities

Once they had been allowed to enter the United States, immigrants had to adjust to life in a new land. Although some settled on farms, the majority of the "new" immigrants settled in cities. Often they stayed in the city that had been their port of entry. They generally moved into communities made up of people from the same area of origin. Jacob Riis, a Danish-born writer, described the patterns of settlement in New York City at the turn of the century:

> *A map of the city, colored to designate nationalities, would show more stripes than the skin of a zebra, and more colors than any rainbow.*

The clustering of immigrants was to a large extent voluntary. Homesick for the familiar, they sought to recreate some of the life they had left behind. The communities they established revolved around a number of traditional institutions. First and foremost were the churches and synagogues, where worship was conducted, and holidays were celebrated as they had been in the old country. Priests and rabbis often acted as community leaders. Coffee houses, which were common in Europe, opened up to enable area residents to get together and speak their native languages in a friendly atmosphere. Ethnic newspapers provided further exposure to familiar ways.

---

[2] The term "ghetto" originated as a label for the Jewish section of Venice, Italy, and came to mean any section of a city to which members of a particular group are restricted.

One of the worst problems for immigrants was being separated from their families, since lack of money often made it impossible for the whole family to come to America at the same time.

The new wave of immigrants that flooded the United States in the late 1800's was not welcomed by some Americans. A demand for a selective immigration policy was supported by unions that saw immigrants as a threat to American labor. However, even those who were not native-born Americans had anti-immigrant feelings. In his cartoon, Joseph Keppler mocked successful Americans who had forgotten their own origins. What peoples made up the "new" immigrants?

All of these things helped the immigrants cope with the new environment. However, the continuing focus on the old ways of life also slowed assimilation into American society. One Polish immigrant wrote:

I am a polish man. I want to be an american citizen. . . . But my friends are polish people—I must live with them—I work in the shoe-shop with polish people—I stay all the time with them—at home—in the shop—anywhere.

I want to live with american people, but I do not know anybody of american. . . . In this way I can live in your country many years—like my friends—and never speak—write well English—and never be good american citizen. . . .

Reaction to Immigrants

Assimilation was also slowed by the attitudes of many native-born Americans, who reacted to the "new" immigrants with hostility. The immigrants spoke languages that were diverse and unfamiliar. They were, for the most part, Catholics and Jews in a country of Protestants. Their customs and appearance seemed strange to Americans with a northern and western European heritage.

Native-born Americans also objected to the immigrants from an economic standpoint. The newcomers needed jobs badly and were willing to work for low pay. Because they were willing to settle

for less, they posed a real threat to American-born workers.

As "new" immigrants continued to enter the country, hostility increased. Some Americans formed groups to counter the immigrant threat. One of these groups, the American Protective Association, was founded in 1887 to protest the large number of Catholic immigrants. In some parts of the country, local laws were passed that prohibited immigrants from holding certain kinds of jobs and denied them other rights. Jewish immigrants, for example, were denied admission to some universities. In addition, the immigrants faced actual physical attacks. Calls for restrictions on immigration mounted.

In response to these calls, Congress passed the first law aimed at controlling immigration. This was the Chinese Exclusion Act of 1882, which prohibited Chinese workers from entering the United States for ten years. Congress then passed an act that restricted immigration in general. It stated that criminals, the mentally ill, poor people, and certain others could not enter the country.

SECTION REVIEW

1. Identify the following: Ellis Island, Jacob Riis, American Protective Association.
2. How did immigrants in the late 1800's differ from previous immigrants?
3. What problems did immigrants experience during their journey to America?
4. How did the immigrants try to adjust to life?

Have students develop a photo essay showing different kinds of housing in cities of the late 1800's and different kinds of housing today.

3 Urban Life and Culture

The immigrants were part of a new way of life evolving in urban America—a style of life unique to the cities. Within the cities, however, not everyone lived in the same manner. The lives of the urban poor and those of the middle and upper classes differed dramatically in a number of ways.

Housing

The urban poor, including most of the "new" immigrants, could not afford transportation and therefore could not take advantage of lower land prices in the suburbs.

The poor remained in the central city, where they lived in old houses or commercial buildings that were divided or converted into apartments. These buildings, called **tenements,** were often substandard. Areas in which a large amount of substandard housing was concentrated were called **slums.** An investiga-

tion of the New York Charities Aid Association described one of the tenements:

A basement was unfurnished except with a stove, a keg of stale beer, and boxes used for seats. Around the former were huddled four men and three women, four others being in the room. . . . The proprietor of this room, (which is $14\frac{1}{2}$ by 10 feet in extent) takes from eight to twelve lodgers a night. . . . Another room, the darkest in the house, is occupied by two Italian men and three women. . . . In this house are 14 rooms, occupied by 72 persons.

Housing for the middle and upper classes differed sharply from that of the urban poor. By the late 1800's, exclusive residential areas separated one class from another. Although some of the most expensive neighborhoods were still located near the downtown area, many middle- and upper-class homes were in the suburbs. Life in these neighborhoods bore little resemblance to life in the slums. One New

In the late nineteenth century "new" immigrants poured into the cities of the United States and moved into crowded tenement districts. As shown here, the streets became the center of daily activity. Peddlers with carts, neighbors meeting, and children playing were all part of tenement life. Each ethnic group moved into a separate, well-defined area, and that area often became a ghetto from which there were few opportunities to escape. Around what traditional institutions did ethnic groups gather?

Yorker, Virginia Gildersleeve, recalled her home during the late 1800's:

> West Forty-eighth Street, just off Fifth Avenue, where we lived, was a quiet and respectable street in those days. Our house was brick with brownstone trim, but practically all the other houses on both sides of the street were orthodox brownstone complete, four stories and a basement, high stoop in front. They were inhabited by solid American families. A few of them were more wealthy and more socially prominent than we were. My mother used to remark that we of course were not "in society" exactly, we were professional people. . . . But I suppose most of the families in the block lived about on the same standard that we did. They had two maids,—a cook and a chambermaid-waitress—and they had someone come in by the day to do the washing.

The upper classes lived in palatial homes staffed by scores of servants. In addition to their urban residences, the rich often had country homes. The middle classes generally lived in a less splendid but comfortable fashion. For example, in 1870 about one of every eight households had at least one servant.

Education

The lives of the various urban classes also differed regarding education. American education was changing in the late 1800's. Before the Civil War, the idea of public, tax-supported schools had been accepted but not implemented. After the war, American education in time became free, public, and almost universal. In fact, by 1900 most states had compulsory attendance laws. These laws required that children attend school for a certain part of each year.

As a result, enrollment increased. In 1870, 57 percent of all children between the ages of 5 and 17 were enrolled in elementary and secondary schools. By 1900 the figure was over 72 percent. The number of public high schools increased from 160 in 1870 to 6000 in 1900. The greatest increases took place in the Northeast and the Midwest.

However, the benefits of a public school education were not shared by everyone. Most pupils were middle and upper-class children who chose to go to a public school rather than to be educated by a private tutor or in a private school. Slum children rarely went to high school. Forced to work at an early age in the factories of the urban centers, they sometimes did not even finish elementary school.

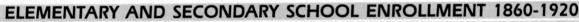

ELEMENTARY AND SECONDARY SCHOOL ENROLLMENT 1860-1920

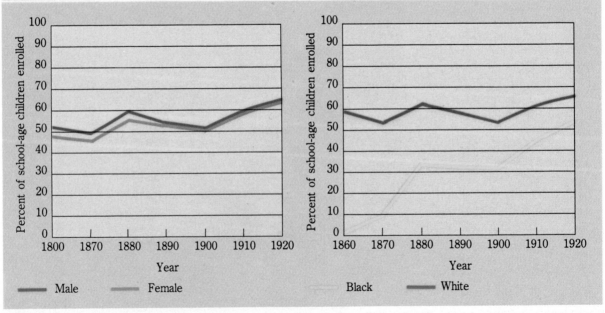

Education

Throughout American history education has been recognized as vital to a democratic society. Thomas Jefferson wrote:

If a nation expects to be ignorant and free in a state of civilization, it expects what never was and never will be. There is no safe deposit for the functions of government but with the people themselves nor can they be safe without information.

In George Washington's Farewell Address, he urged the promotion of "institutions for the general diffusion of knowledge." He said, "It is essential that public opinion be enlightened."

Thus, from the beginning, America had a commitment to education. Even in colonial times, the Puritans of Massachusetts passed a compulsory education law, and New England led the way in providing tax support for schools.

Some people objected to public schools on the grounds that they would injure private schools. Others said that it was unfair to tax the middle and upper classes to educate children of the poor and unfair to tax people without children. But the democratic spirit of the Age of Jackson increased support for free, tax-supported public schools. Advocates of public schools argued that education was the right of all individuals in a democracy. One by one, the states of the nation passed laws to provide tax support for public schools.

Public schools have been given many functions and responsibilities. Besides teaching intellectual skills, they are to teach patriotism and give Americans a sense of national unity. Schools are supposed to prepare children to be good citizens and to train the nation's youth for jobs and careers.

With the great increase in immigration in the late 1800's, another function was thrust upon the schools—the job of assimilating newcomers into American culture. The schools taught English to the immigrants and stressed American values.

Public schools have also been given the responsibility for one of America's highest ideals: equal opportunity. Americans believe in the importance of family life. However, children brought up in different families learn different skills and values, and some receive more opportunities than others. As a result, family life comes into conflict with other American ideals, such as social mobility and fair competition.

Some societies, in attempting to achieve fairness and equality, have tried to do away with families or with economic competition. But Americans have taken a different approach. That approach is to use education as a means to minimize the differences that result from different backgrounds. It is to schools that the nation has entrusted the goals of mediating social change and realizing a fuller democracy.

The task of providing equal opportunity for everyone is an enormous one. In 1954 the Supreme Court decided that segregation of whites and blacks in public schools denied equal opportunity to black children. Court-ordered busing to end segregation, which began in the 1970's, shows the extent of the nation's commitment to equal opportunity. Other examples of this commitment are the attempts to guarantee equal education for children with handicaps and to provide bilingual education for children who do not speak English.

Currently, one of the biggest controversies in education concerns financing. This issue is related to equal opportunity. Because schools are financed chiefly by local property taxes, wealthy communities are able to have better schools than poor communities. Many people think that, in the interest of equality, some way should be found to equalize school financing.

Americans are also concerned about other issues in education. Among the areas of concern are the subject matter and values taught in schools, the question of how much control local communities should have over schools, and the quality of American education as compared to that in other countries.

QUESTIONS

1. Why is education important in a democracy?
2. What are the functions of public schools?
3. Why is school financing a controversial issue?

Note that historically, culture has always depended upon the patronage of the wealthy. The age of industrialization produced wealth in the United States, and education received the benefit of this wealth.

Another change in education involved teaching methods. Until the 1880's, the traditional "three R's"—reading, writing, and arithmetic—dominated the curriculum (course of study) in the public schools. The emphasis was on rote learning, or memorizing and reciting facts.

Under the influence of new educational ideas from European and American thinkers, notably John Dewey of the University of Chicago, some schools began to place less emphasis on rote learning and more on "learning by doing." According to Dewey, schools should not just provide students with useless knowledge, but prepare them for life. In order to accomplish this purpose, courses of study were broadened, and teaching methods were tailored to suit the needs of children. More emphasis was put on teaching students to solve problems and be creative. All of these techniques were considered to be part of a progressive trend in education.

Higher education also changed and expanded. Colleges and universities added courses in modern languages and the social sciences. The introduction of the elective system allowed students to choose some of their courses. As president of Harvard University, Charles Eliot pioneered a number of these progressive changes.

During the late 1800's, the number of colleges and universities increased and enrollment climbed. This was made possible partly by the Morrill Act of 1862. Under this act, the Federal government gave huge land grants to states. Money from the sale or rental of this land was to be used for colleges that emphasized agriculture and engineering. Many states established **"land-grant" colleges** as a result of the Morrill Act. In addition, many business leaders donated large sums of money to colleges and universities.

After the Civil War, graduate education became available for the first time. Harvard and Yale Universities began to grant advanced degrees, and in 1876 the Johns Hopkins University was founded solely as a center for graduate study. In 1875 there were 399 graduate students in the United States. By 1900 there were over 5000.

In the late 1800's, higher education was almost exclusively the province of the middle and upper classes. It was also largely a man's province. Although girls were admitted to most elementary and secondary schools before the Civil War, most colleges would not accept women. After the war more schools became coeducational, and more women's colleges were founded. Some women's schools, such as Vassar, Mount Holyoke, Smith, and Bryn Mawr, dedicated themselves to providing an education equal to that offered by top men's institutions.

Although certain strides were made by women at the college level, very little progress was made at the graduate level. For a long time, American graduate schools were open only to men. Women who were interested in advanced degrees generally had to go abroad. By 1900 several graduate and professional schools were admitting women. However, before long admission again began to be restricted.

Blacks were also denied the full benefits of higher education. In the South and most of the North, black children continued to be segregated in elementary and secondary schools. In addition, blacks were still barred from attending most white colleges. They had to enroll at one of the few institutions of higher learning established exclusively for blacks alone, such as Howard University in Washington, D.C.

Work and Leisure

Class differences also appeared in the area of work. The urban poor—women and children included—provided the unskilled labor for meat-packing factories, steel plants, garment factories, and other urban industries. Although opportunities to better themselves did exist, most of the urban poor remained on the lower rungs of the economic ladder, and the income gap between rich and poor was widening.

Work was different for the upper and middle classes. Instead of jobs in factories, men of these classes had careers in public, professional, or business life. Such careers offered status and power as well as a high standard of living.

Women of the middle and upper classes, especially if they were married, generally did not work outside the home. Although an unmarried woman could be an office worker, a teacher, or even a doctor, her proper role after marriage was to make a home for her husband and children. Married women and wealthy single women often found a socially acceptable use for their time and talents in volunteer activities.

Note that many upper-class women had domestic servants—usually immigrants.

Discuss the importance of retail distribution of goods to an industrial society. What would happen to the economy if nobody had time to shop?

Technology in the late 1800's helped free people to pursue new interests. New department stores with escalators (left) made shopping quicker and easier. Many people, such as Nellie Bly, a journalist (right), became active in social reform. What other technological innovations gave people more free time?

For middle- and upper-class women, time for such activities was increasing. Before the Civil War, running a house had been a difficult and time-consuming task. By the late 1800's, it was less so. Most middle-class homes had hot and cold running water, which eliminated trips to street pumps and made washing much easier. Vacuum cleaners made it easier to keep the home clean, while sewing machines and ready-made clothing freed women from much of the burden of sewing. The availability of items such as canned goods, bakery bread, and pre-packaged meat allowed women to spend less time cooking or overseeing the kitchen help.

Even shopping became less difficult. Catalogs offered by companies such as Montgomery Ward and Sears Roebuck had more impact in rural areas than in cities, but urban women were more affected by a new kind of store, the department store. John Wana-

maker's in Philadelphia, R. H. Macy's in New York, and Marshall Field's in Chicago were examples of the new department stores. Founded after the Civil War, these establishments offered customers a wide variety of goods at a lower cost. The cost was low because the retailers bought in volume. Shopping at department stores was exciting, as well as efficient, and became a regular pastime for some women.

Shopping was a recreational activity mostly for the upper and middle classes. The poorer classes worked such long hours that they had little time or energy for recreation. Besides, incomes from factory jobs were so inadequate that there was no money for anything but necessities. Stickball, card games, and street fairs served as sources of relaxation for the urban poor. The middle and upper classes, however, had varied uses for their growing leisure time.

In the late 1800's, Americans of all walks of life developed an ardent interest in spectator sports such as football and baseball (left). Bicycling in city parks became the most popular of the participatory sports. In what other sports did Americans participate?

Sports

A favorite leisure-time activity for many people was watching sports events. Baseball, invented in 1839 by Abner Doubleday of New York, became the most popular spectator sport in America. The first professional team, the Cincinnati Red Stockings, was formed in 1869. By the turn of the century, both the National and American Leagues had been founded—each comprised of teams from major cities. Their games drew large crowds of enthusiastic fans, and in 1903 the first World Series was held.

Another popular spectator sport was football, which developed from the English game of rugby. The game had first been played as an intramural sport (a sport played between teams of students from the same school). In 1869 the first intercollegiate game took place between Princeton and Rutgers. By the 1890's, college games were drawing huge crowds. The first professional game was played in 1895.

Basketball, invented by Dr. James Naismith in Springfield, Massachusetts, also became popular. Naismith had developed the game in the 1890's as an indoor winter sport for the boys in his YMCA physical education classes. Considered the only major sport that is completely American in origin, basketball soon spread to other countries. Boxing also became a respectable sport in the late 1800's.

Americans not only watched but participated in sports. Tennis and golf were enjoyed by the wealthy, usually in exclusive private clubs. Bicycling became a fad after the "safety" bicycle had been developed. Older bicycles had metal-rimmed wheels—a large one in front and a small one in back—while the new ones had two air-filled rubber tires of the same size. Because of such advances, bicycling became so popular that by 1900 about 10 million Americans were riding.

Much of this bicycling took place in parks that had been created to beautify the cities and provide recreation areas for urban residents. Many city parks were designed by Frederick Law Olmstead, whose greatest achievement was Central Park in New York City.

Theater

The theater was another popular pastime. Before the Civil War, theater circuits had begun to take shape. Troupes of actors traveled these circuits, performing in different places around the country. The business was so successful that certain stars, such as Edwin Booth, were able to earn over $120,000 in one season. After the war there were even greater successes along these lines, as more and more Americans developed a very definite taste for the theater.

The types of plays varied. They ranged from works by William Shakespeare and other great writers to popular melodramas (plays built around exaggerated emotionalism). The former tended to be patronized by the upper classes, while the latter was generally preferred by the middle classes. Vaudeville—stage shows with a variety of unrelated acts—also attracted large audiences.

Music

Americans also enjoyed musical theater. Grand opera remained the favorite of the upper classes, while the operetta (comic light opera) appealed to a wider audience. Many operettas were the works of European composers or American immigrants from Europe. Two of the most popular were Victor Herbert's "Babes in Toyland" and Sigmund Romberg's "Student Prince."

In addition, the middle and upper classes attended the symphony, where the works of Europeans also

dominated. Many of the great American symphony orchestras were founded during the late 1800's. For example, between 1862 and 1900, New York, Chicago, Pittsburgh, and Philadelphia established orchestras.

More distinctively American kinds of music were also becoming popular. John Philip Sousa and his band thrilled thousands with marches such as "The Stars and Stripes Forever." Ragtime caught on in the late 1890's with Scott Joplin's "Maple Leaf Rag." It was a while, however, before ragtime was accepted as a serious form of music.

Middle- and upper-class city dwellers were interested in music not only as patrons, but as performers. In the late 1800's, a number of amateur music groups—from choral societies to string quartets—were formed. The parlor piano became a standard feature in middle-class homes, and the sale of sheet music, featuring popular melodies, became big business.

Sculpture and Painting

Art as well as music and theater flourished in the late 1800's. Between 1865 and 1900, American art reflected a European influence. Indeed, most American artists of the time had studied in Europe. Some artists, such as James McNeill Whistler and John Singer Sargent, chose to remain abroad, while others returned to the United States.

Some of those who returned began to develop a uniquely American style of art. One such artist was August Saint-Gaudens, one of the greatest American sculptors of the era. His most outstanding work was the Adams Monument in Washington, D.C. Another talented sculptor was Daniel Chester French, whose most important work was the statue of Lincoln at the Lincoln Memorial in Washington, D.C.

The most notable trend in painting was **realism,** or the attempt to show the world as it really is. One of the leading realist painters was Thomas Eakins. He painted subjects such as surgeons at work and boxing matches. But the realistic way he painted the human body offended many people, and he was neglected during his lifetime. Another example of realism was a group of painters known as "The Ash Can School." These artists, one of the most famous of whom was Robert Henri, earned this name because of their

Louis Sullivan pioneered the skyscraper. Many people did not appreciate his style—Gothic and Romanesque styles were still in favor—but his influence was carried on through Wright.

In the late nineteenth century Americans developed new trends in the arts. In music, John Philip Sousa (left) gained fame for his march compositions. Mark Twain (right) created a unique American literary style. What trends characterized American paintings of the late 1800's?

portrayal of the various and often grim sides of urban life.

Photographers also captured the real world with their art. After the Civil War, a growing number of artists used the camera instead of the canvas to picture the city. Among them were Alfred Steiglitz, who was one of the first to insist that photographs were works of art, and Jacob Riis, famed for his pictures of lower-class life.

In architecture, Americans were developing their own unique style. Louis Sullivan, who designed skyscrapers, said that "form follows function." By this he meant that a building's design should be realistic, reflecting its use and purpose. For example, an office building with an iron frame should not look like a Renaissance palace. Instead it should have straight lines and be free of decoration. Sullivan and his most famous student, Frank Lloyd Wright, had a strong impact on American architecture.

Literature

The literature of the late 1800's also reflected the idea of realism. One group, the so-called "local-color writers," described their own locales with as much detail as possible. In *The Country of the Pointed Firs* (1896), Sarah Orne Jewett described declining settlements in New England. George Washington Cable, in *Old Creole Days* (1879), told of life in Louisiana. Another famous southern writer, Joel Chandler Harris, portrayed the life of blacks in Georgia in *Uncle Remus, His Songs and Sayings* (1880). Edward Eggleston wrote of the Midwest— specifically, of Indiana—in *The Hoosier Schoolmaster* (1871). Bret Harte painted a realistic picture of the far West in *The Luck of Roaring Camp* (1870), which described California mining camps.

The most famous of the local-color writers was Samuel L. Clemens, better known as Mark Twain. His *Roughing It* (1872) also portrayed life in the

Have students look for examples of yellow journalism in current newspapers.

western mining camps. In *The Adventures of Tom Sawyer* (1876) and *The Adventures of Huckleberry Finn* (1885) Twain described life in rural Missouri. His fame as a novelist rests chiefly upon these two works.

Not all Twain's works were local-color stories. One of his more well-known novels was *The Gilded Age* (1873), which he wrote with Charles Dudley Warner. In this work, Twain criticized society in the industrial age. Indeed, the title of the book gave a name to the post-Civil War era. *The Gilded Age* was one of the works that could collectively be called the "literature of protest." This literature drew attention to certain problems in urban society and pointed the way to reform.

Among the protest works, a number stand out. Edward Bellamy's *Looking Backward* (1888) contrasted the urban America of 1887 with an ideal America in the year 2000. In this utopian society, wealth was shared by all. Henry George's *Progress and Poverty* (1879) called for a single tax on all those who owned land in order to narrow the gap between rich and poor. Stephen Crane's *Maggie: A Girl of the Streets* (1893) painted a realistic picture of slum conditions. Such conditions were also described in *How the Other Half Lives* (1890) by Jacob Riis. This work included some very realistic photographs taken in the slums of New York City. *Wealth Against Commonwealth* by Henry Demarest Lloyd denounced monopolies in general and the Standard Oil Trust in particular.

Realism was also important in the works of William Dean Howells, who was among the best novelists of his age. *The Rise of Silas Lapham* (1885) was a study of the nouveau riche, or the newly rich. In other novels, such as *A Hazard of New Fortunes* (1890), Howells dealt with social injustices in nineteenth-century American society. All such works stimulated reform.

Newspapers and Magazines

Newspapers and magazines were more widely read than books. Magazines such as *Collier's, McClure's,* and the *Saturday Evening Post* achieved mass circulation. These magazines were published using the techniques of mass production and supported financially by heavy advertising.

For news of everyday life, Americans turned to newspapers. Joseph Pulitzer of the New York *World* and William Randolph Hearst of the New York *Morning Journal* founded what was called **"yellow journalism"** by their critics. This type of journalism emphasized attention-grabbing subjects such as murder and scandal. Despite the sensationalism, these newspapers reported facts and paved the way for reform by reporting political corruption.

SECTION REVIEW

1. Identify the following: John Dewey, James Naismith, John Sousa, Ash Can School, Louis Sullivan.
2. What developments made housekeeping easier for the upper and middle classes?
3. What sports became popular during this period?
4. What changes took place in newspapers and magazines?
5. What trends characterized the literature of this period?

4 Urban Reform

The need for reform was very apparent in the cities. Reform-minded men and women, generally from the middle and upper classes, set out to deal with a wide range of urban problems. Among their chief concerns were improving the living conditions of the poor, Americanizing the new immigrants, and putting an end to political corruption.

Settlement Houses

The living conditions of the urban poor left a great deal to be desired. Life in the crowded tenements was hazardous at best. Fires were an ever-present threat. In the late 1800's, the amount of damage from urban fires was on the rise. Much of Chicago's downtown burned in 1871, and two years later Boston experienced a devastating fire.

Another threat facing slum dwellers was illness. There were several reasons for the high incidence of disease in slum areas. One was poor diet. The daily fare of the slum dwellers was lacking in both quality and quantity. Another reason was unsanitary conditions. Most tenement houses had neither indoor plumbing nor good ventilation. Garbage filled the

20 YEARS AT HULL HOUSE
JANE ADDAMS

Jane Addams Lillian Wald

Many of the most prominent leaders of the urban reform movement were women of the upper and middle classes. Two outstanding examples of these leaders were Jane Addams and Lillian Wald.

Addams, born in 1860, decided as a young girl that she wanted to spend her life helping others. She wanted to become a doctor, but poor health forced her to give up her medical studies. For several years after that, she was restless and troubled. She traveled in Europe, did charity work, and studied philosophy in an attempt to find a purpose in life.

After seeing the human misery produced by industrialization and urbanization in both Europe and the United States, she wanted more than ever to help the poor. In her book, *Twenty Years at Hull House,* she wrote:

> I gradually became convinced that it would be a good thing to rent a house in a part of the city where many primitive and actual needs are found, in which young women who have been given over too exclusively to study . . . might try out some of the things they have been taught. . . .

Addams and her friend Ellen Starr then visited a settlement house in London. Impressed with what they saw, they returned to Chicago and opened Hull House. At first Addams paid all the expenses from her own income, until the activities at Hull House grew beyond her means. She then turned to the public to raise funds.

Settlement houses such as Hull House became centers for reform movements of all kinds, where a number of influential women began their careers. Addams went on to become a leader in the women's suffrage and world peace movements, and in 1931 was awarded the Nobel Peace Prize.

Another leader who founded a settlement house was Lillian Wald. Born in 1867 to a wealthy Cincinnati family, Wald was not content with the life of luxury available to upper-class women. Feeling the need for "serious, definite work," she went to New York City and trained as a nurse. In 1895, she organized the Henry Street Settlement.

Wald was also a pioneer in the field of public health nursing. Under her supervision, 92 nurses in the Henry Street Visiting Nurses Service provided home care for the urban poor. In addition, Wald founded the first public school nursing program in the United States.

streets because cities were growing too fast for government to provide adequate services. A third reason was poor medical care. People were ignorant about the causes and treatment of illness and could not afford to pay for proper health care.

Slum dwellers were also plagued by crime. Prostitution was common, and gang wars occurred frequently. Gang warfare was a particular problem among young people.

One step reformers took to correct such problems was the establishment of **settlement houses**—neighborhood centers that offered a wide range of services to slum dwellers. Working out of these centers, reformers helped to educate the urban poor, especially the immigrants. Settlement-house workers taught classes on subjects ranging from English to hygiene to stenography. They also provided the urban poor with day care, recreational facilities, and counseling. By 1900 more than 50 settlement houses had been established in American cities. The most famous of these was Chicago's Hull House, founded by Jane Addams in 1889.

Although settlement houses and other private efforts accomplished a great deal, they were not enough to solve the immense problems of America's cities. Reformers urged government to act. As a result, public commissions were formed to investigate and recommend changes in such areas as child labor, working conditions, and housing.

Attack on Political Corruption

Reformers also turned their attention to urban political machines. Machine politicians used a number of tactics to stay in power. For one thing, they responded to people in a personal way in order to gain support. George Washington Plunkitt, one of the bosses in New York's Tammany Hall machine, described his techniques:

What tells in holdin' your grip on your district is to go right down among the poor families and help them. . . . I've got a regular

system for this. If there's a fire in Ninth, Tenth, or Eleventh Avenue, for example, any hour of the day or night, I'm usually there with some of my election district captains as soon as the fire engines. If a family is burned out I don't refer them to the Charity Organization Society, which would investigate their case in a month or two and decide if they were worthy of help about the time they are dead from starvation. I just . . . fix them up till they get things runnin' again. It's philanthropy, but it's politics too—mighty good politics. Who can tell how many votes one of these fires brings me? . . .

Plunkitt summed up by stating "I don't trouble them with political arguments. I just study human nature and act accordingly. . . ." Machine politicians also resorted to various forms of political corruption. They stuffed ballot boxes, sold offices, received bribes, and even stole city funds. Such corruption spread to all parts of

In city tenements, poverty and overcrowding brought on numerous social problems. To help overcome some of the problems, settlement houses were established, which offered a variety of services to the poor. Shown here is a settlement house nurse taking a shortcut over rooftops to make a call on the sick. What other services were offered by settlement houses?

One of the most prominent reform organizations was the National Civil Service Reform League, whose main goal was to institute the merit system for city employees.

the machine—even to the police force. Some police officers, for example, collected **protection money.** This was money paid to the police by the owners of illegal businesses. In return, the police allowed the businesses to remain in existence.

To make urban government more honest and efficient, reformers set out to destroy the political machines. One way in which they tried to do this was through the formation of Municipal Leagues. At first, the Leagues battled politicians. Before long, however, reformers realized that they would have to change the system itself. Their efforts were part of an overall spirit of reform that was sweeping the country in the early 1900's.

SECTION REVIEW

1. Why were urban living conditions hazardous for the poor?
2. What kinds of services did settlement houses offer?
3. What illegal methods were used by political machines?
4. How did reformers try to make government more honest and efficient?

CHAPTER **18**   REVIEW

SUMMARY

1. America in the late 1800's was becoming an increasingly urban society.
2. The growth of city populations was due chiefly to influx of immigrants from Europe and American migrants from rural areas.
3. Immigration in the late 1800's was predominantly from southern and eastern Europe.
4. Immigrants provided unskilled labor for urban industries.
5. Immigrants attempted to adjust to life in the United States by living in ethnic communities and by centering their activities on traditional ethnic institutions.
6. Urban life and culture reflected a growing income gap between rich and poor.
7. Education was expanded and improved during the late 1800's.
8. The urban middle and upper classes experienced increased leisure time, which was used to pursue a variety of recreational and cultural activities.
9. The plight of the urban poor, the problems of immigrants, and corruption in city government became the targets of reform efforts.

VOCABULARY

urbanization	pogroms	slums	yellow journalism
"old" immigrants	steerage	land grant colleges	settlement houses
"new" immigrants	tenements	realism	protection money

REVIEW QUESTIONS

1. What was the effect of immigration on cities?
2. What technological changes took place in cities after the Civil War?
3. What factors led immigrants to come to the United States during this period?
4. How did the lives of the urban poor differ from those of the upper and middle classes?
5. How did education change during the nineteenth century?
6. How did literature and the arts reflect the trend toward realism?
7. How did literature stimulate reform in the cities?
8. What new solutions were proposed for urban problems?

DISCUSSION

1. Should immigrants to the United States try to maintain their own cultures or try to become assimilated into the mainstream culture? Why?
2. What effect did machine politics have on the lives of immigrants?
3. Do you think that the cities of the late 1800's were desirable places to live? Why or why not?
4. How different do you think the role of women is today from the role of women in the late 1800's?

USING GRAPHS

Refer to the graph on page 366 and answer the following questions:

1. What was the trend in immigration from Italy between 1861 and 1920?
2. Which country was the source of the greatest immigration between 1881 and 1900?
3. What were the peak years of immigration to the United States?
4. How many people came to the United States between 1871 and 1880?
5. What was the trend in immigration from Ireland between 1861 and 1920?

USING SKILLS

Study the following sets of statements and determine which one of each pair would be the *more* difficult to prove:

1. (a) Most "new" immigrants lived in slums.
   (b) Poor housing was the most difficult problem faced by "new" immigrants.
2. (a) New York City's population more than tripled between 1860 and 1900.
   (b) The increase in New York City's population was due chiefly to immigration.
3. (a) Mark Twain was the author of *The Gilded Age*.
   (b) Mark Twain was the best American novelist of the late 1800's.
4. (a) Machine politics was harmful to cities.
   (b) Machine politicians sometimes used corrupt methods.
5. (a) Settlement houses significantly improved the lives of the urban poor.
   (b) Settlement houses offered many services to the urban poor.

1	The Progressives	**383**
2	Progressive Goals	**386**
3	Theodore Roosevelt	**390**
4	William Howard Taft	**394**
5	Woodrow Wilson	**397**

THE PROGRESSIVE ERA

We have been proud of our industrial achievements, but we have not hitherto stopped thoughtfully enough to count the human cost. . . .

WOODROW WILSON

At the turn of the century the United States was prosperous, yet the gap between rich and poor was greater than ever. The demands of the Populists for reform seemed to have been forgotten. Before long, however, a new group of reformers appeared to battle the injustices that had come about as a result of industrialization and urbanization. These reformers were known as progressives. Because their ideals dominated politics during the period from 1900 to 1917, this period has been called the Progressive Era.

1 The Progressives

Although they all believed in reform, the progressives were a diverse lot. For one thing, progressivism cut across party lines. There were Republicans, Democrats, and even members of the defunct Populist party among their ranks. In fact, many of the stands taken by the Populists were adopted by the progressives. However, most of the Populists' support had come from farmers and workers, while progressives came from various classes in society. Some had wealthy backgrounds. Others were from the working class. Most, however, were members of the urban middle class.

The Urban Middle Class

As members of the urban middle class, the progressives were relatively comfortable economically. Most of them were college-educated, and they tended to be small-business owners, professionals, or white-collar workers. Nearly all of them had been conservatives, not reformers. However, as they became more concerned about the direction of American society, they steadily moved away from conservatism.

One of their concerns was the vast power of the giant trusts. The trusts not only dominated the government, but threatened to put small companies out of business. Another concern was the growth of labor unions and other more radical signs of labor unrest. Many members of the middle class felt that the America they valued—the land of opportunity—might soon be lost in a battle between capital and labor. To preserve the life they valued, middle-class reformers wanted to reduce the power of wealthy capitalists and give more power to the working poor.

There was one difficulty, however. The philosophies of the day—laissez-faire and Social Darwinism—stood in the way of any attempt to change "natural law." Trying to close the gap between the rich and the poor was considered futile. By 1900, however, certain intellectuals had supplied the reformers with a new philosophy upon which to base their actions.

The Intellectuals

The new philosophy, known as **pragmatism,** called for a practical approach to the problems of the day. Pragmatists believed that an idea was true if it worked, even if it did not fit established theories. Therefore, people's actions should not be limited by ideas about theoretical "natural law."

The attack on natural law began with mathematician Charles Peirce. He said that scientific laws stated only what was probably true, not what was absolutely true, and that ideas should be tested to see if they worked.

Peirce's ideas influenced other philosophers, notably William James and John Dewey. James rejected the idea that the universe operated according to predetermined natural laws. He believed that, if people used their minds creatively and acted courageously, they could do almost anything. Dewey

Under the leadership of Holmes, the courts increasingly looked toward the social influence of laws and put less emphasis on property rights. In 1908 Justice Louis D. Brandeis used sociological and statistical arguments in the case of *Muller* v. *Oregon,* in which the Supreme Court upheld an Oregon law limiting women's working hours. This kind of argument became a model for future cases.

At the beginning of the twentieth century, progressive reformers attacked many of the injustices that industrialization had brought about. Most progressives blamed big business for the social ills they saw. Their belief is reflected in this cartoon that shows monopolies, trusts, and franchises as parts of a single monster devouring the country. With what other issues were progressives involved?

applied the philosophy of pragmatism to government. He said that the role of government should be determined experimentally. In short, if actions taken by the government worked for the good, they should be pursued.

Another influential intellectual was Oliver Wendell Holmes, Jr., the chief advocate of pragmatism in the law. Holmes, who had become a member of the Supreme Court in 1902, said that law was not based on unchanging principles, but on human experience. According to Holmes, the law evolved from people's moral, political, and economic ideas, and even their prejudices. As people's experiences changed—as society changed—so should the law. Holmes' ideas began to influence Supreme Court decisions in the early 1900's, just as earlier philosophies had influenced Court decisions in the late 1800's.

The ideas of the pragmatists soon became even more widespread. Progressive writers such as Walter Lippman helped in the process of spreading the new ideas. Lippman, in *Drift and Mastery* (1914), said that people had to direct the course of their lives by using scientific knowledge and reason. An educated, informed public, he said, could correct many of the problems in American society.

Religious Reformers

Religious reformers, as well as intellectuals, formed a major part of the progressive movement. During the early 1900's, new religious leaders began to question some of the old accepted ideas in religion.

In the 1800's ministers such as Russell Conwell and Henry Ward Beecher had defended the acquisition of wealth and the resulting gap between rich and poor. The ideas of such men were typical, especially among Protestant ministers. One critic of the Protestant church even called its ministers "spiritual Pinkertons," whose main job was that of "guarding the loot of the unrighteous rich." However, the new religious leaders—ministers such as Josiah Strong, Washington Gladden, and Walter Rauschenbush—were concerned about social problems. Rauschenbusch spoke out for the new point of view in these words:

Our business is to make over an antiquated and immoral economic system. . . . Our inherited Christian faith dealt with individuals; our present task deals with society.

Rauschenbusch and other leaders developed the **"social gospel"**—the view that the church should take an active part in changing society for the better. Followers of the social gospel wanted to bring the church into the factory, the street, and the marketplace. They supported reforms aimed at eliminating poverty and injustice.

Women and Reform

Women also became a driving force for progressive reform. The fact that women figured so largely in the progressive movement was an indication that their status had improved.

By 1900 women's colleges in the North and East had been turning out well-trained graduates for two generations. These women were aware of and interested in the various issues of the day. National women's clubs devoted to the study of such issues were common. In fact, by 1910 these clubs had nearly 1 million members.

Furthermore, the rights of women had been expanded. By 1900 every state recognized the right of women to make a will. Most states recognized their right to dispose of their own wages, and some states had given them the right to equal guardianship of children. Most importantly, five states had given women the right to vote.[1]

The professions remained a male domain, and women were mostly confined to educational or charitable work. This limitation served them well in one respect, however. In volunteering their time to settlement houses, child-welfare centers, and consumers' groups, middle-class women acquired first-hand knowledge of the conditions that needed to be reformed.

The Muckrakers

Certain American writers played a major part in exposing social problems. Because of the critical nature of their works, Theodore Roosevelt compared them to a character in John Bunyan's book, *The Pilgrim's Progress,* "who could look no way but downward with the muckrake in his hands." The character was so intent on raking filth that he would not look up when offered a crown. After Roosevelt's comment, these writers who described social ills were called "muckrakers."

The muckrakers were important because they were able to gain widespread attention for social problems. They addressed a variety of subjects and, backed with alarming facts, tried to describe to the public what was wrong with society.

One of the leading muckrakers was Lincoln Steffens. In 1902 Steffens wrote an article entitled "Tweed Days in St. Louis," which appeared in *McClure's Magazine.* The article described municipal corruption in St. Louis, Missouri. Later this article became part of a book by Steffens on corruption in city government. Steffens' book, *The Shame of the Cities* (1904), was widely read.

Another muckraker was Ida M. Tarbell, whose *History of the Standard Oil Company* attacked John D. Rockefeller's ruthless business practices. The first installment of this highly critical work appeared in the November 1903 issue of *McClure's. McClure's* sales rocketed, and soon other popular magazines were featuring **exposés** (articles that expose or reveal scandal).

Other writers joined Steffens and Tarbell. The muckrakers included Charles E. Russell, whose *The Greatest Trust in the World* (1905) was an exposé of the beef trust; David Graham Phillips, who wrote *The Treason of the Senate* (1906); and Ray Stannard Baker, whose article, "The Railroads on Trial," appeared in *McClure's* in 1906.

Another muckraker was novelist Upton Sinclair, whose book *The Jungle* (1906), told of conditions in the Chicago stockyards and in the meat-packing industry. Sinclair described diseased cattle covered with boils:

> *It was a nasty job of killing these, for when you plunged your knife into them they would burst and splash foul-smelling stuff into your face. . . . It was stuff such as this that made the "embalmed beef" that had killed several times as many United States soldiers as all the bullets of the Spanish. . . .*[2]

Americans were appalled by such descriptions and the influence of the muckrackers on the public was enormous. S. S. McClure's editorial in the January

---

[1] Wyoming, Colorado, Idaho, Utah, and Montana.

[2] This statement referred to the Spanish-American War in 1898.

Tarbell's father was an oil producer who was destroyed by Rockefeller. This motivated her to write about Rockefeller's ruthless methods.

Many long-sought reforms were realized by progressives as a result of exposes in newspapers and books by muckrakers. Upton Sinclair (left) and Ida Minerva Tarbell (right) were two social critics of the Progressive Era. What industry did Sinclair attack in his book, *The Jungle?*

1903 issue of *McClure's* struck a responsive chord in the hearts of many Americans:

> *Capitalists, workingmen, politicians, citizens—all breaking the law, or letting it be broken. Who is left to uphold it? The lawyers? Some of the best lawyers . . . advise corporations and business firms how they can get around the law without too great a risk of punishment. The judges? Too many of them so respect the laws that for some "error" or quibble they restore to office and liberty men convicted on evidence overwhelmingly convincing to common sense. The churches? We know of one, an ancient and wealthy establishment, which had to be compelled . . . to put its tenements in sanitary condition. . . .*
>
> *There is no one left: none but all of us. . . . We have to pay in the end, everyone of us. And in the end the sum total of the debt will be our liberty.*

As greater numbers of Americans were made aware of the problems existing in society, demands for reform increased. In the early 1900's, progressives began to make proposals for specific reforms.

SECTION REVIEW

1. Identify the following: William James, Oliver Wendell Holmes, Jr., Ida Tarbell, *The Shame of the Cities*.
2. What was occurring in American society that caused the progressives to be concerned?
3. What kinds of legal gains were made by women at this time?
4. What were some of the abuses that the muckrakers described?

2 Progressive Goals

Progressives had faith in the wisdom of the American people and believed that the people would support social and economic reforms. First, however, government had to be made more responsive to the people's will. Therefore the first item in the progressives' agenda was political reform.

THE AGE OF INDUSTRIALIZATION   **387**

Have students analyze map to see where progressive reforms were most successful.

Political Reform

On the local level, progressives turned their attention to corruption. To eliminate corruption, progressives called for new forms of city government that would take power away from politicians and give it to business and management experts. One of these new forms was **commission government,** under which the citizens chose a number of commissioners to administer city business. Each commissioner was in charge of one area of business, instead of one person —the mayor—being responsible for all areas. Commission government was first set up at Galveston, Texas, in 1901. Before long about 400 cities had commission governments.

Another reform was **city-manager government,** in which a professional manager was hired to handle city administration. The first government of this type was set up at Staunton, Virginia, in 1908. In a short time, over 40 cities had city-manager governments.

Certain reform mayors also made headway in the fight against political machines. For example, Hazen S. Pingree of Detroit, Samuel M. ("Golden Rule") Jones of Toledo, and Tom M. Johnson of Cleveland all gained national reputations as reformers.

Progressives were active on the state level as well. They instituted a number of reforms that allowed the people to have a more direct role in government. One of these reforms was the direct primary, which allowed voters to choose candidates for government offices. This method of choosing candidates took the place of the caucus and convention methods, in which machine politicians had considerable influence. Thus the direct primary reduced the power of political machines.

Two other reforms—the initiative and referendum—were intended to give voters more power to make laws. Another reform, the recall election, allowed voters to remove a public official from office before the end of his or her term.

The state that provided the best example of the progressive spirit was Wisconsin. The man who was largely responsible for Wisconsin's record was Robert M. La Follette, governor from 1900 to 1906. His program of progressive reform, known as the "Wisconsin Idea," was imitated in many other states. Wisconsin under La Follette was later called "the laboratory of democracy" by Theodore Roosevelt.

Progressives also worked to achieve women's suffrage, partly because it was generally believed that

THE PROGRESSIVE MOVEMENT IN GOVERNMENT

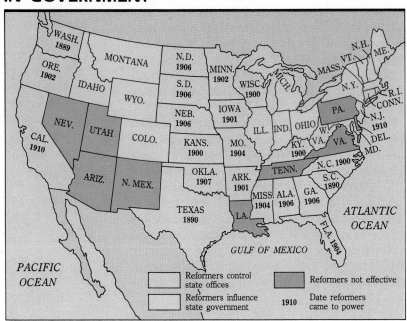

In the early 1900's, the women's suffrage movement gained strength, attracting not only women but also men who wanted to democratize voting. Carrie Chapman Catt and Alice Paul were two of the most prominent leaders of the women's movement at this time.

Note that the methods of the progressives showed their faith in the democratic system.

Three thousand women marched in New York to demonstrate their desire for suffrage. They maintained that their votes could strike a blow at political machines and big business. What states had granted full suffrage to women by 1911?

when women could vote they would help push through other reforms. By 1911, six states[3] had granted full suffrage to women. Many other states had given them the right to vote in specific elections. **Suffragists** (people who believed in extending the right to vote, especially to women) hoped eventually to obtain a constitutional amendment giving women the right to vote.

At the national level, the progressives called for direct election of Senators. By 1900 the Senate was viewed as a "millionaires club" because so many Senators were wealthy. Critics felt the chamber had little understanding of the needs of the people.

Up to this time, Senators had been chosen by the state legislatures. Although some states allowed voters to indicate their choices, state legislatures were rarely guided by the results. Progressives felt that, if people could vote directly for Senators, the Senators would have to be more responsive to the people's will. Choosing Senators in this way would also reduce the power of the state machines.

Economic Reform

Another goal of the progressives was economic reform. Many people feared that monopolies were destroying the free enterprise system. Progressives worked for the regulation of business by all three levels of government—local, state, and national.

At the local level, reformers often called for "gas and water socialism," or public ownership of utilities. In most American cities, utilities were owned by private companies. The companies operated under long-term franchises (contracts to handle goods and services in certain territories) from city governments. Since the profit from these franchises was so large, some companies bribed government officials in order to get contracts. Public ownership of the utilities was intended to put a stop to this corruption in government as well as to provide more efficient services to the public. But the call for public ownership had only limited success. A number of cities took over municipal waterworks, and a few took over other utilities such as gas, electricity, and public transportation.

At the state level, a number of reform governors actively pushed for the regulation of business. For example, Wisconsin under La Follette set up a commission to regulate railroads operating inside the state. In addition, the legislature passed laws setting up a more effective system of taxation for railroads and other corporations. Hiram Johnson of California and Woodrow Wilson of New Jersey challenged railroad interests in their states. In New York, Governor Charles Evans Hughes exposed corruption in the life insurance business.

At the national level, demands grew for **trust-busting** (the breaking up of giant trusts). Progressives attacked giant trusts like United States Steel. These giant trusts had tremendous economic power, and progressives were determined to break their stranglehold on the American economy.

Social Reform

Progressives were active in seeking reforms in education, housing, and working conditions. One of

---

[3]Wyoming, Colorado, Utah, Idaho, Washington, and California.

Robert La Follette

Robert La Follette was one of the most popular and respected politicians of the Progressive Era. He was known as "Fighting Bob" because he was not afraid to fight political machines and other powerful institutions. One of the reasons for his success was that he was a great orator. Another was that he truly cared about people. "Go back to the first principles of democracy," he said. "Go back to the people."

Born in 1855, La Follette was a Wisconsin lawyer who was elected to Congress in 1885, but was defeated for reelection in 1890. He then returned to his law practice in Madison and became the leader of a group of progressive Republicans.

In 1898 he lost a hard-fought convention battle to become the Republican candidate for governor of Wisconsin. But he was not a man to give up easily. After the convention was over, he took the night train home to his family. His words to a friend as he got off the train were characteristic of his attitude:

Well, Albert, we lost the day. But we made a fight that was worth the making. There is another day coming and I shall expect to see you again.

In 1900 La Follette ran successfully for governor. Under his leadership, Wisconsin became the most progressive state in the nation. Two chief goals of his reform program were the direct primary and a tax on railroads. In fighting for these causes, he drove himself to the point of exhaustion and serious illness.

After achieving his first two goals, he went on to fight for railroad regulation. He carried on with this issue when he became a United States Senator in 1906. He also supported trustbusting, conservation, consumer protection, and other reform programs.

In 1924 La Follette broke with the Republicans and ran for President as the candidate of a new Progressive party. Although he received 5 million popular votes, he carried only his home state. Weakened by the rigors of campaigning, he died in 1925 at the age of 70.

their chief concerns was the problem of child labor. Most states adopted laws barring the employment of children under 14 years of age in certain industries. Some also passed laws fixing a minimum wage for children.

Progressives also wanted to protect women in the labor force. Laws that limited the number of hours women could work per day were passed in some states. Oregon adopted the first such law in 1903. Minimum-wage laws for women were passed by a number of states.

Another important reform was the passage of **workmen's compensation** laws. These laws granted payment to workers hurt in industrial accidents. In certain dangerous occupations, an employer was held liable for all injuries that employees suffered at work. Formerly, workers had to prove an employer's carelessness in order to receive compensation for injuries. The first state workmen's compensation law was passed by Maryland in 1902. Other states soon followed Maryland's lead.

Have students discuss the importance of effective leadership in political movements. Ask if they think progressivism would have happened without Roosevelt.

One of the most needed social reforms of the late 1800's and early 1900's was the regulation of child labor. Businesses hired young children, many of whom were under 10 years of age, to work at very low wages. They often worked in mines or with dangerous machines in factories, toiling for long hours six days a week. Shown here are children in a Delaware canning company busily working under adult supervision. What child labor laws were enacted during the Progressive Era?

SECTION REVIEW

1. Identify the following: Thomas L. Johnson, "Wisconsin Idea," Hiram Johnson.
2. What changes did the progressives advocate for city government?
3. In what ways did states allow people a more direct role in government?
4. What kinds of social legislation were the progressives able to get passed?

3 Theodore Roosevelt

By 1900 the progressive movement was gaining momentum. The only element needed to launch it nationally was a charismatic leader. The progressives acquired that leader when Theodore Roosevelt became President of the United States.

Roosevelt's Background

Theodore Roosevelt—the man who was to make progressivism a national creed—was a unique individual, with broad experience in life and in politics. Roosevelt—often called TR—was intelligent and energetic. Above all, he was a man of action. He told others, "Don't fritter away your time; create, act, take a place wherever you are and be somebody; get action."

Roosevelt certainly led the strenuous life that he advocated. Sickly as a child, he built himself up physically by boxing in college and later by ranching in the West. Besides being an active man, TR was an aggressive leader. This showed up clearly in his political career.

Roosevelt was born into a well-to-do New York family and educated at Harvard University. Shortly after graduation, he began his political career as a representative in the New York state legislature.

As a member of a committee investigating sweatshops in the New York City cigar industry, Roosevelt was exposed to the horrible conditions under which many of the poor lived and worked. He supported bills to abolish cigar sweatshops, limit the working hours of women and children, and improve industrial safety.

In 1886 Roosevelt ran unsuccessfully for mayor of New York City. This defeat was followed by his appointment to the United States Civil Service Commission a few years later. After serving on the commission for six years, Roosevelt returned to New York City in 1895. There, as president of the board of police commissioners, he continued to show concern over slum conditions.

Roosevelt entered national politics again when he was appointed Assistant Secretary of the Navy during William McKinley's first term as President. He resigned his post in 1898, however, to serve in the Spanish-American War.

Returning a hero as head of the famed "Rough Riders," Roosevelt was elected governor of New York. As a reform governor, he constantly angered the conservative Republican party machine. To rid themselves of Roosevelt, the conservatives supported his nomination for Vice President in 1900.

In the election of 1900, McKinley won the Presidency, once more defeating William Jennings Bryan. However, on September 6, 1901, President McKinley was shot by an anarchist, Leon Czolgosz, and died shortly thereafter. With McKinley's assassination, Roosevelt became President.

Roosevelt as President

To the surprise of conservative members of his party, Theodore Roosevelt moved cautiously during his first term as President. Although he initiated some reforms during these years, he moved slowly until he was elected President in his own right in 1904, when he defeated conservative Democrat Judge Alton B. Parker. In his campaign for that election, Roosevelt promised the people a "square deal."

Trustbusting. One part of Roosevelt's square deal program involved the trusts. He made his first move against the trusts in February 1902. At that time, he ordered the Attorney General to file suit under the Sherman Antitrust Act against the Northern Securities Company. Since 1895, when the Supreme Court had ruled in *United States* v. *E. C. Knight* that a huge sugar trust was not in violation of the Sherman Act, the act had been ineffective. Roosevelt hoped to put some life into it.

Northern Securities was a holding company that had been organized by James J. Hill and J. P. Morgan. Through this company, a merger of three major railroads in the Northwest had been put into effect. As a result of the merger, a major part of the

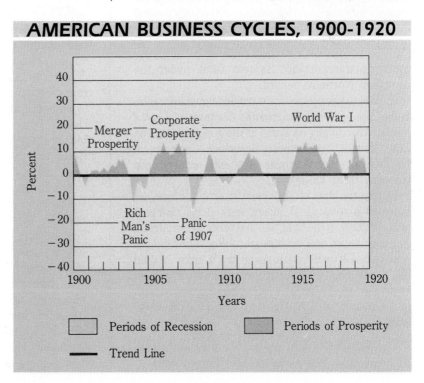

AMERICAN BUSINESS CYCLES, 1900-1920

J. P. Morgan tried and failed to have his lawyer negotiate a settlement with the Attorney General. Roosevelt's successful attack on the Northern Securities Company symbolized a transfer of power from business to government.

Visiting workers on the job was one way Theodore Roosevelt showed his interest in people's problems. He was very aware of the need for labor reforms. What experiences prior to his Presidency helped form Roosevelt's concern for the worker?

country's transportation system came under the control of Northern Securities.

In 1904 the Supreme Court handed down a decision in the case of *Northern Securities Company* v. *United States.* Abandoning its stand in the *Knight* case, the Court found the Northern Securities Company in violation of the Sherman Act and ordered the company to be broken up.

During the rest of Roosevelt's term in office, he obtained a total of 25 indictments (legal charges) against trusts in the beef, oil, and tobacco industries. Although hailed as a "trustbuster," Roosevelt did not want to break up all trusts. As he saw it, trusts should be regulated, not destroyed. He distinguished between "good trusts," which were concerned with public welfare, and "bad trusts," which were not. He said:

> *Captains of industry . . . have on the whole done great good to our people. Without them*

the material development of which we are so justly proud could never have taken place.

In 1901 Roosevelt had asked for a new Department of Commerce and Labor with a Bureau of Corporations to be added to the cabinet. This was done in 1903. The Bureau was to collect information about big business and make the information public. This, Roosevelt hoped, would pressure big business into following the law, so that prosecution would not be needed.

Labor. Another part of Roosevelt's program had to do with labor. Knowing that many employers exploited workers, Roosevelt approved of unions— as long as they were nonviolent. Although Roosevelt was not always against trusts, he did move against them when he felt they acted irresponsibly toward workers.

One such occasion took place in 1902. In Pennsylvania the anthracite coal miners struck for shorter hours, higher wages, and recognition of their union. Mine owners refused to negotiate with the workers. As winter approached, coal supplies dwindled. Because of the widespread suffering such a shortage would cause, public opinion began to turn against the owners.

At first Roosevelt did not act because his advisors told him that he did not have constitutional power to do so. Finally, as public pressure mounted, he decided to act in spite of this advice. He invited representatives of the workers and the mine owners to a meeting at the White House. At the meeting, the United Mine Workers of America, under John Mitchell, agreed to submit the dispute to arbitration. However, the owners, led by George F. Baer, remained inflexible. They demanded that TR send in troops to break the strike.

Roosevelt was outraged at the owners. A few days later he threatened to send federal troops into Pennsylvania to take over the mines from the owners and produce the coal. Under this threat, the owners finally agreed to arbitration.

In March 1903 a commission appointed by Roosevelt announced that mine workers would get a 10 percent increase and hours would be cut, but their union would not be recognized. It was the first time a President had negotiated a settlement between management and labor.

Congress was generally hostile to Roosevelt's conservation program and ignored many of his recommendations. But Roosevelt succeeded in bringing the cause of conservation to public attention.

Railroad Regulation. A third part of Roosevelt's program dealt with the regulation of railroads. Despite earlier reforms, many of the railroad abuses that had so angered the Populists were still going on. Roosevelt took steps to remedy the situation.

In 1903, with Roosevelt's backing, Congress passed the Elkins Act, which forbade railroads to depart from their set rates. The act also made it illegal for customers of the railroad to accept rebates, or refunds. (The Interstate Commerce Act had already made it illegal for railroads to give rebates.) To show he meant business, Roosevelt fined the American Sugar Refining Company $300,000 for accepting a rebate.

Although the Elkins Act forbade rebates, the railroads could still set exorbitant rates. Roosevelt therefore backed a law that gave more powers to the Interstate Commerce Commission. The Hepburn Act, passed in 1906, gave the Commission power to set maximum rates and establish uniform methods of bookkeeping. The act also extended the jurisdiction of the ICC to include carriers besides the railroads, such as ferries and oil pipelines.

Food and Drugs. Roosevelt understood how the public felt about the meat-packing industry. He had read Sinclair's novel, *The Jungle,* and asked for legislation to correct some of the worst abuses. As a result, Congress passed the Meat Inspection Act in 1906. This act gave government the right to inspect meats that were to be sold in interstate commerce as well as the right to enforce cleaner conditions in meat-packing plants.

Evidence of abuses in the food and drug industries led to the Pure Food and Drug Act of 1906. This act prohibited the manufacture, sale, or transportation of impure or falsely labeled food and drugs that were sold in interstate commerce.

Conservation. Conservation, or saving the country's natural resources, was another part of Roosevelt's program. He abhorred the way the country's natural resources were being exploited. For example, trees were chopped down and not replaced, irreplaceable resources such as natural gas were wasted, and fires and floods, caused by poor management of land and water services, were common. Roosevelt wanted not only to protect wildlife and scenic areas, but also to ensure efficient use of soil, minerals, and forests.

The first major conservation law passed under Roosevelt was the National Reclamation Act, or Newlands Act of 1902. The Newlands Act provided for **reclamation** (reclaiming or replacing natural resources) by setting up a Reclamation Service in the Department of the Interior. The act also provided that nearly all the money from public land sales was to be used for irrigation projects in the West.

Roosevelt increased the size of the national forests from 43 to 194 million acres (17.2 to 77.6 million hectares). He worked to preserve other valuable lands as well. At his direction, for example, the Secretary of the Interior set aside 80 million acres (32 million hectares) of coal lands.

The Panic of 1907. Some people felt that conservation, trustbusting, and other parts of Roosevelt's program were harmful to business and cut into profits. Business leaders were quick to blame Roosevelt and the progressives for the Panic of 1907.

Theodore Roosevelt was an avid supporter of the conservation movement. Here he is enjoying the scenery at Yosemite National Park with John Muir (right), a noted naturalist. What was Roosevelt's first major conservation law?

By the end of his second term, Roosevelt had come to favor reforms that he had found too radical a few years earlier. He called for federal regulation of all interstate business, compulsory

investigation of labor disputes, federal regulation of the stock market, income and inheritance taxes, and other measures.

However, the real reason for the panic was chiefly the fact that currency in the United States was relatively **inelastic.** Currency is inelastic when a change in demand causes very little change in supply. In a word, the federal government was not able to increase the money supply in an emergency. If an emergency arose, people began to hoard money, and a shortage resulted. Credit was also inelastic because it was limited by the lending power of a few leading New York banks. Because these bankers had the power to keep the country's business moving by giving or withholding credit, they were known as the "money trust."

The panic began with a run on the Knickerbocker Trust Company and other New York City banks. Business leaders told Roosevelt that unless he allowed the United States Steel Corporation to take over shares of Tennessee Coal and Iron Company that were owned by Knickerbocker Trust, the bank would fail. Roosevelt agreed not to prosecute United States Steel for violation of the antitrust laws. United States Steel was thus able to take over a competing company and, as a result, competition in the iron and steel industry was weakened. However, the bank was saved. The federal government also deposited $25 million in certain New York banks to prevent them from failing.

After the panic was over, Congress moved to correct some of the faults of the money and credit systems. The Aldrich-Vreeland Act, passed in 1908, said that banks could issue more currency in times of financial difficulty. The act also set up the National Monetary Commission to report on various currency and credit systems and make recommendations for reform.

Other Issues. There were some progressive issues that Roosevelt did not address. One of these was the tariff. He did nothing about the Dingley Tariff of 1897, which provided higher rates than ever before. Instead of working to lower rates, Roosevelt used the threat of tariff reform to ensure that protectionist members of Congress would support his other programs.

Another issue that Roosevelt for the most part ignored during his years in office was minority rights. Although some progressives wanted to help minorities, little was done during the Progressive Era. In fact, the plight of blacks actually worsened. Any

attempt to help blacks drew the anger of white southerners. For example, white southerners were outraged when Roosevelt invited Booker T. Washington to dine at the White House.

SECTION REVIEW

1. Identify the following: "square deal," Pure Food and Drug Act, Newlands Act.
2. What did Roosevelt think was the difference between "good" trusts and "bad" trusts?
3. How did Congress implement Roosevelt's program for regulating railroads?
4. Why did Roosevelt stress the conservation of the nation's natural resources?
5. What caused the Panic of 1907?

4 William Howard Taft

Although Roosevelt failed to address certain important issues, he was viewed by the public as an effective progressive leader. When he left office, he passed the mantle of leadership to his chosen heir, William Howard Taft.

The Election of 1908

In the election of 1908, Roosevelt's heir, William Howard Taft of Ohio, faced Democrat William Jennings Bryan. There was little difference between the two candidates. Both ran as progressives, which indicated that most Americans favored more reforms. In fact, it was simply a question of who could better carry out progressive policies. The people chose Taft.

Roosevelt had supported Taft partly because of his experience in government—as a judge, as the first civil governor of the Philippine Islands, and as Secretary of War. Another reason was that Taft had promised to carry on Roosevelt's policies.

Taft in Office

Taft, however, did not live up to Roosevelt's expectations. Compared to Roosevelt, Taft had a more limited view of the Presidency. He felt that Congress, rather than the President, should decide matters of policy. Furthermore, Taft had inherited the leadership of the Republican party at a time of tremendous tension between the conservative "Old Guard" and the progressive "Insurgents." Although Taft came to be associated with the conservative faction of his party, he continued reforms in a number of areas.

Progressive Actions. Roosevelt had been labeled the trustbuster, but Taft initiated twice as many antitrust suits as his predecessor. As President, Taft broke up such giants as the Standard Oil Company and the American Tobacco Company.

Taft pursued other progressive actions as well. He supported the Mann-Elkins Act of 1910, which gave the ICC power to regulate telephone and other communications companies. This act also gave the ICC power to suspend rates until a court decided whether or not they were fair.

Under Taft, the Department of Commerce and Labor was split, and a Children's Bureau was set up within the Department of Labor. The function of this bureau was to investigate the health, education, and working conditions of children.

Taft had a hand in getting measures passed that ensured safety in mines and gave accident insurance to workers hired on government contracts. Taft added to the number of civil service jobs under the merit system and backed the cause of conservation.

Finally, two progressive amendments to the Constitution were passed by Congress during Taft's term of office. The Sixteenth Amendment set up the federal income tax.[5] The Seventeenth Amendment provided for the direct election of United States Senators.

Political Problems. Despite this record, Taft's handling of certain issues led the progressives to break with him. One of these issues was the tariff. Lowering the tariff was important to progressives. They were against high duties because high taxes on imports meant high prices for consumers.

Taft had promised to work for tariff reductions in his campaign speeches. Shortly after taking office, he called a special session of Congress to carry out this reform.

Representative Sereno Payne of New York sponsored a bill that lowered the tariff. The bill passed

In 1908 the Republicans nominated Roosevelt's choice, William Howard Taft, on the first ballot. This cartoon shows Roosevelt presenting his baby, Taft, to the people. How did Taft's view of the Presidency compare with the views of Roosevelt?

the House, but ran into trouble in the Senate. Senator Nelson Aldrich of Rhode Island added 847 amendments to the bill, raising the duties on all kinds of products. The progressives were furious and wanted Taft to fight openly for a lower tariff. Instead, Taft worked privately to gain concessions from Aldrich and the Old Guard. Finally, a compromise bill—the Payne-Aldrich Tariff—was passed by Congress and signed by Taft. The progressives felt betrayed.

The progressives were further displeased when Taft failed to back their attempt to curb the power of the Speaker of the House, Joseph G. Cannon of Illinois. Cannon was an Old Guard conservative who repeatedly blocked progressive legislation. In March 1910 Representative George W. Norris of Nebraska presented an amendment to the House rules that

---

[5] Although there had been a temporary income tax during the Civil War, the Supreme Court had later found the tax unconstitutional.

Have students compare the map on this page with the one on page 387. Did states in which reformers had influence vote for reform candidates in 1912?

would remove the Speaker's power to appoint the rules committee and instead allow the committee to be elected by the House as a whole. The progressives won their point, but they won it without the President's help.

The Ballinger-Pinchot controversy also drove a wedge between Taft and the progressives. The trouble occurred when Gifford Pinchot, chief of the United States Forestry Service, made charges against the conservative policy of Secretary of the Interior Richard A. Ballinger. Ballinger had reopened for sale certain lands in Wyoming and Montana that had been withdrawn under Roosevelt. Pinchot criticized Ballinger's move and accused him of hurting the conservation program in order to aid big business. Taft defended Ballinger and, angry at the attack on his administration, dismissed Pinchot. There was such an outcry from the public, however, that Ballinger was forced to resign.

The Ballinger-Pinchot controversy became a major issue that widened the split between Taft and the progressives. The issue also contributed to Taft's

break with Roosevelt. By 1912 many progressive Republicans were calling for a return of their hero.

The Election of 1912

After Taft's inauguration in 1909, Roosevelt had gone on a hunting trip to Africa. On his way home, he was met in Italy by his friend Pinchot, who told of the progressives' disenchantment with Taft. Roosevelt began to turn against Taft.

In the congressional elections of 1910, Roosevelt campaigned for the progressive wing of the party, while Taft backed the conservatives. Because of the growing split in the Republican party, the Democrats made important gains. They won control of the House by a large majority and made significant gains in the Senate. In the Senate, the Republican margin was so slim that a small number of Insurgents held the balance of power. They often voted with the Democrats against the Old Guard Republicans.

The progressives had been trying for some time to gain control of the Republican party. A major step was

ELECTION OF 1912

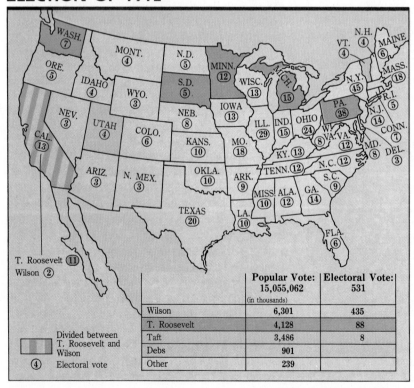

	Popular Vote: 15,055,062	Electoral Vote: 531
	(in thousands)	
Wilson	6,301	435
T. Roosevelt	4,128	88
Taft	3,486	8
Debs	901	
Other	239	

T. Roosevelt ⑪
Wilson ②

Divided between T. Roosevelt and Wilson
④ Electoral vote

The platform of the Bull Moose party also called for women's suffrage.

Note that divisions in one political party or movement tend to give the opposition an advantage.

taken in January 1911 when a group of them founded the National Progressive Republican League. Under the leadership of Robert M. La Follette, they drew up a comprehensive program for reform.

The progressives had hoped to run La Follette for President in the upcoming election, but when his health failed they called on Theodore Roosevelt. In February 1912 Roosevelt agreed to seek the Republican nomination.

The Bull Moose Party. During the nominating campaign, Roosevelt swept the states in which voters could indicate their choices. Taft, however, won in states where the convention system was still in force. In June, at the Republican convention in Chicago, Taft received the nomination because he controlled the party machine.

When the outcome became apparent, the progressives left the convention and formed the Progressive party. Because the party took the bull moose as its symbol, it was often referred to as the Bull Moose party. Meeting separately in Chicago, it chose Theodore Roosevelt as its standard-bearer and adopted the New Nationalism as its platform.

The New Nationalism. The New Nationalism was Roosevelt's program for progressive action. It set forth the idea that government should use Hamiltonian means to achieve Jeffersonian ends. That is, a strong central government should use its power to "promote the general welfare."

Roosevelt called for an active government that would regulate big business, protect labor, advance social welfare, and increase political democracy. He wanted workers' compensation laws, a minimum wage, the direct primary, and the right to vote for women.

Wilson and the New Freedom. Opposing Roosevelt and the New Nationalism was Democrat Woodrow Wilson and the New Freedom. Born in the South, Wilson was trained as a political scientist and historian. As president of Princeton University, he gained a reputation as a leader in progressive education. He left this post in 1911 to become the Democratic governor of New Jersey.

As governor, Wilson carried out a number of progressive reforms. The New Freedom—Wilson's program for reform—was similar in many ways to the New Nationalism. There were certain differences, however. One of the chief differences had to do with

trusts. While Roosevelt wanted simply to control trusts, Wilson wanted to destroy them. He felt that business concentration was bad because it interfered with the free enterprise system. Wilson thought the government's role should be to maintain competition, not just regulate big business.

The Socialists. Wilson, Roosevelt, and Taft were not the only candidates running for President in 1912. Another was Eugene V. Debs of the Socialist party. The Socialist party had been founded in 1900, and Debs had played a principal role in the process. Debs and the more radical members of his party favored government ownership of industry. Debs, therefore, differed from both Roosevelt and Wilson, although all three saw the need for some kind of change.

By 1912 Debs had been a presidential candidate three times—in 1900, 1904, and 1908. In 1908 he had received over 400,000 votes. In 1912, therefore, the Socialists for the first time posed what seemed to be a real threat to the major parties.

A Four-Way Race. With the Republicans divided, Wilson's chances to be the first Democratic President since Cleveland looked good. Although he received only 42 percent of the popular vote, Wilson won a landslide in the electoral college with 435 votes to Roosevelt's 88 and Taft's 8. Together the three reform candidates—Wilson, Roosevelt, and Debs—received 73 percent of the popular vote indicating that the spirit of reform was still a strong force.

SECTION REVIEW

1. Identify the following: Mann-Elkins Act, Joseph G. Cannon, George W. Norris, National Progressive Republican League.
2. What actions did Taft take that could be considered progressive?
3. What issues caused a split between Taft and the progressives?
4. How did New Nationalism and New Freedom differ?

5 Woodrow Wilson

Reform was to dominate politics for the next four years. Upon taking office, Wilson began at once to institute his New Freedom, which called for sweeping changes in a number of areas.

The Tariff

Wilson first directed his efforts toward the tariff. In a nearly unprecedented move, the President appeared before Congress to ask for rates to be lowered. Wilson believed that the pressure of foreign competition would lead American manufacturers to improve their products and lower their prices. Since both houses of Congress were in Democratic hands as a result of the 1912 election, Wilson was able to push through lower rates.

In October 1913 the President signed the Underwood-Simmons Act, which set duties 8 percent lower than the Payne-Aldrich tariff. This measure also enlarged the **free list,** or list of items exempt from duties. To make up for lost revenues, a graduated income tax—a tax system under which people with higher incomes pay higher tax—was included in the bill.[6] Several years after the passage of the Underwood-Simmons Act, a tariff commission was established to make recommendations concerning rate changes.

Banking and Currency

Wilson next sought reforms in the field of banking and currency. As a result of the Panic of 1907, many Americans felt that government should act to ensure a reliable supply of currency and credit. Wilson himself believed in this type of public control of the money supply.

In 1912 the National Monetary Commission, set up under the Aldrich-Vreeland Act (1908), gave its report on banking and currency. The Commission recommended a central banking system run by bankers. However, many Americans felt that the "money trust" already had too much power and that the public should have some control over banking and currency. Under Wilson's leadership, Congress passed a compromise bill—the Federal Reserve Act of 1913.

The Federal Reserve Act divided the United States into 12 banking districts, each with a Federal Reserve bank. This system is still in effect. All national banks have to join. State banks may also join. Each member

---

[6]This provision was made possible by the ratification of the Sixteenth Amendment in 1913.

bank has to deposit a certain amount of money in the district Federal Reserve bank. This **reserve requirement** helps protect people's deposits.

Federal Reserve banks do not do business with individuals, but are bankers' banks. They serve as clearinghouses for checks, make loans to member banks, and provide a more flexible currency—Federal Reserve notes. The number of notes in circulation may be changed if necessary. This helps to solve the problem of an inelastic currency and gives the Federal Reserve System (the Fed) some control over the money supply.

The entire system is directed by a Federal Reserve Board from Washington, D.C. The board is made up of seven members who are appointed by the President for 14-year terms and confirmed by the Senate.

The Federal Reserve Board has the power to set interest rates on loans made by the district banks to member banks. This power gives the Fed control over the credit supply. If the Fed lowers rates, it makes loans easier to obtain. This increases the money supply and stimulates the economy. If the Fed raises rates, it tightens the supply and slows economic growth.

The Trusts

After the Federal Reserve System was established, Wilson turned his attention to trusts. Although in theory Wilson's policy was different from Roosevelt's, in practice they were much alike. In 1914, with Wilson's backing, Congress passed two important measures regulating trusts. The first was the Federal Trade Commission Act, which set up a five-member commission to investigate corporate practices. This commission had the power to issue "cease and desist orders" whenever unfair practices were discovered. These orders directed an offending corporation to stop an unfair practice at once.

The second measure was the Clayton Antitrust Act, which made certain business practices against the law. One of these was the interlocking directorate, in which the same persons could serve on the boards of several companies. Another was **price-fixing,** or secret agreements made by companies in the same industry to charge the same or similar prices.

Point out that many of the reforms sought by the labor and farm movements (see Chapters 15 and 17) were realized with the support of the middle-class progressives.

The Clayton Act also said that labor and farm organizations could not be prosecuted as trusts and limited the use of injunctions against unions. These provisions made the act an important victory for labor. In fact Samuel Gompers called the act "Labor's Magna Carta."

Wilson took other actions helpful to labor. He appointed William B. Wilson, a union man, as Secretary of Labor and backed laws regulating working conditions. One of these was the La Follette Seaman's Act (1915), which set safety standards for maritime workers. Another was the Adamson Act (1916), which established the eight-hour day for workers on interstate railroads.

Under Wilson, the government also tried to regulate child labor. In 1916 Congress passed the Keating-Owen Act, which banned the products of child labor from interstate commerce. This law, however, was later declared unconstitutional by the Supreme Court.

Although these measures pleased many workers, the more radical among them were still dissatisfied. The Industrial Workers of the World (IWW), a union of skilled and unskilled workers founded in 1905, wanted more revolutionary changes. The "Wobblies," as they were known, wanted to overthrow the capitalist system. Although they won some strikes in the early 1900's, their power declined because they acquired a reputation for violence and were prosecuted by the government. Many IWW leaders were sent to jail.

Farmers

During Wilson's term of office, the government took steps to help farmers as well as workers. In 1914 Congress passed the Smith-Lever Act, setting up a system of trained agents to assist farmers. This system was funded by **dollar-matching.** That is, every dollar contributed by a state was matched by the federal government. In 1917 the government once again used dollar-matching in the Smith-Hughes Act. This act provided federal money for education in agriculture and the trades.

Congress also passed the Federal Farm Loan Act (1916), which set up a banking system much like the Federal Reserve. In this case, 12 Federal Farm Loan banks made long-term loans to farmers at low rates.

Other Issues

On other issues, Wilson's progressivism was not so evident. Wilson had promised "absolute fair dealing" to black Americans in his campaign speeches. However, once in office, his actions disappointed blacks. They were especially angered by the fact that he allowed segregation in government offices. Wilson also opposed women's suffrage at first. Later, however, he modified his position. During his second term, the Nineteenth Amendment gave women the right to vote.

The Election of 1916

Still, Wilson had a strong progressive record. Therefore, it was not surprising that he was

Woodrow Wilson wanted to give new chances to small businesses and small farmers. Under his leadership, Congress passed laws to regulate big business and to provide for agricultural education. How did the Smith-Lever Act help small farmers?

renominated at the end of his first term. Recognizing the country's continued desire for reform, the Republicans chose Charles Evans Hughes to oppose the President. In the election of 1916, Wilson won a close popular and electoral victory. Wilson's victory gave him a mandate to continue his domestic program. However, by 1917, Americans were turning their attention from domestic to foreign affairs.

SECTION REVIEW

1. Identify the following: Federal Trade Commission Act, Clayton Antitrust Act, "Wobblies," Smith-Lever Act.
2. Why did Wilson want to reduce the tariff rates?
3. What are the functions of the Federal Reserve system?
4. How did Wilson try to help labor?

CHAPTER 19   REVIEW

SUMMARY

1. Beginning in 1900, the United States went through a period known as the Progressive Era, when reformers dominated politics.
2. The progressives were concerned with fighting some of the inequities in American society that had come about as a result of industrialization and urbanization.
3. Although many of the progressives' goals were similar to the goals of the Populists, the progressives were more successful in achieving reforms.
4. A new philosophy, which was known as pragmatism, provided the rationale for the progressive movement.
5. Writers who drew public attention to society's problems played a major part in the reform movement.

6. Progressives called for political, economic, and social reforms on all levels of government.
7. In 1901 Republican Theodore Roosevelt inherited the Presidency when William McKinley was assassinated.
8. Roosevelt brought leadership to the progressive cause and backed a reform program called the "square deal."
9. William Taft, Roosevelt's successor, carried out further progressive reforms.
10. In spite of Taft's progressive record, Roosevelt and other progressives became disenchanted with him, and a split in the Republican party resulted.
11. In 1912, Democrat Woodrow Wilson won the Presidency and continued to seek progressive reforms.

VOCABULARY

pragmatism	city-manager	workmen's compensation	reserve requirement
social gospel	government	reclamation	price-fixing
exposé	suffragists	inelastic currency	dollar-matching
commission government	trustbusting	free list	

REVIEW QUESTIONS

1. How did the progressive movement compare to the populist movement?
2. Why did the progressive movement gain widespread support?

3. How did pragmatism and the social gospel support the progressive movement?
4. What kinds of political reforms were instituted by the progressives?

5. What kinds of economic reforms were sought by the progressives?

6. In what ways did labor benefit from progressive reforms?

7. How did Roosevelt, Taft, and Wilson compare in their approach to trusts?

8. How did blacks and women benefit from the progressive movement?

DISCUSSION

1. Do you agree with the philosophy of the pragmatists? Why or why not?

2. Of the political reforms of the era, which were the most important? Which have lasted the longest?

3. Which President—Roosevelt, Taft, or Wilson— was the most progressive? Why?

4. Did Taft deserve to be rejected by Roosevelt and the progressives? Why or why not?

USING GRAPHS

Refer to the graph on page 391 and answer the following questions:

1. When between 1900 and 1920 did the American economy reach its lowest point?

2. How did World War I affect the American economy?

3. How long was the period of "corporate prosperity" in the early 1900's?

4. In 1920, was the economy in a period of expansion or in a period of recession?

5. How many periods of prosperity did the United States enjoy between 1900 and 1920?

USING SKILLS

The following paragraph comes from the introduction to *The Shame of the Cities*. Lincoln Steffens discussed the widely held idea that foreigners and immigrants were responsible for corruption in city government. After you read the paragraph, answer the questions that follow.

When I set out on my travels, an honest New Yorker told me honestly that I would find that the Irish, the Catholic Irish, were at the bottom of it all everywhere. The first city I went to was St. Louis, a German city. The next was Minneapolis, a Scandinavian city, with a leadership of New Englanders. Then came Pittsburg, Scotch Presbyterian, and that was what my New York friend was. "Ah, but they are all foreign populations," I heard. The next city was Philadelphia, the purest

American community of all, and the most hopeless. And after that came Chicago and New York, both mongrel-bred, but the one a triumph of reform, the other the best example of good government that I had seen. The "foreign element" excuse is one of the hypocritical lies that save us from the clear sight of ourselves.

1. What is the main idea of the paragraph?
   (a) Cities with the lowest foreign populations have the most corruption.
   (b) Blaming corruption on foreigners is not justified.
   (c) All city governments are corrupt, no matter what kind of population they have.

2. What evidence in the paragraph supports the main idea?

SUMMARY

1. The rise of industry after the Civil War brought unparalled growth to the American economy.
2. Workers organized unions in an attempt to gain a larger share of the nation's economic prosperity.
3. Industrialization contributed to the settlement of the last frontier in the West by American farmers.
4. Industrialization and immigration resulted in the urbanization of the nation.
5. Politics in the age of industrialization was tainted by corruption.
6. The revolt of farmers against big business in the late 1800's was generally unsuccessful.
7. In the early 1900's, a new reform movement made some progress in solving the problems caused by industrialization and urbanization of the United States.

REVIEW QUESTIONS

1. In the late 1800's, which of these groups made social progress: (a) farmers, (b) Indians, (c) women, (d) blacks?
2. How did the benefits of industrialization compare to the problems?
3. How did the role of government change between 1860 and 1917?
4. How did the effects of industrialization vary in the different regions of the United States—North, South, and West?

SUGGESTED ACTIVITIES

1. Research the economic development of your region following the Civil War. What were the major economic activities? How were they influenced by the war? What were the influences of geography, technology, and politics? How does the economy today compare with that of 100 years ago?
2. Prepare a bulletin board display showing major and minor inventions of the late 1800's.
3. Prepare a report on one of the following topics: (a) the current efforts of American Indians to regain some of their land through court action; (b) the Ku Klux Klan in the late 1800's compared to the Ku Klux Klan in the 1980's; or (c) current anti-trust legislation being carried on by the United States.
4. Develop a time line showing the events that occurred with the opening of western lands to white settlement. Include major white-Indian conflicts, major mining strikes, federal laws to help settlers on the frontier, and the completion of major railroads.

SUGGESTED READINGS

1. O'Neill, William. *The Progressive Years.* New York, Dodd, Mead & Company 1975. A good overview of the reform movements of this era.
2. Berger, Thomas. *Little Big Man.* New York, Crest Books, 1978. Paperback. The tales of a man who claims to be the only white survivor of Custer's Last Stand. Brings to life Wild Bill Hickok, Calamity Jane, and Wyatt Earp.
3. Cochran, Thomas C. and Miller, William. *The Age of Enterprise: A Social History of Industrial America.* New York, Harper & Row, Publishers, 1968. Paperback. Focuses on the social and political consequences of industrial growth.
4. Dobie, J. Frank. *Longhorns.* New York, Universal Library, 1957. History of the Texas longhorns from the early Spanish settlers to the cattle barons of the 1800's.
5. Hofstadter, Richard. *Social Darwinism in American Thought.* Boston, Beacon Press, 1955.

Paperback. Provides an in-depth understanding of the philosophy that influenced business and political leaders of the late 1800's.

6. Livesay, Harold. *Samuel Gompers & Organized Labor in America.* Boston, Little, Brown, & Company, 1978. Paperback. Traces the career of one of the most important union leaders in America.

7. Portis, Charles. *True Grit.* New York, New American Library, 1969. Paperback. Story of a 14-year-old girl searching for her father's killer in Indian territory.

THE HISTORIAN'S CRAFT

Good historians make every attempt to be objective. They weigh evidence carefully and try to neutralize their own biases. Objectivity can be difficult, however, because of the very nature of historical evidence.

This activity will give you practice in evaluating evidence for reliability. The subject of the activity is the Homestead Steel Strike of 1892.

Henry Frick, the manager of the Homestead plant, planned to hire non-union workers to take the place of strikers. He arranged for Pinkerton guards to protect the strikebreakers. Striking workers were picketing the plant and allowing nobody to enter. Frick had the Pinkertons brought to the plant by barge at night. As dawn was breaking on July 6, two barges full of Pinkertons approached the landing at the Homestead plant.

Later, Congress appointed a committee to investigate the events surrounding the Pinkertons' attempt to land. As you read the testimony, keep in mind how bias might affect a witness's point of view.

Testimony of William B. Rodgers, owner of a boat pulling the barges:

Everything was quiet at the lock, and nothing occurred of an unusual character until we were within about 2 miles of Homestead, when we heard many whistles blowing, which impressed us with the idea we were expected. . . . When within 1 mile of Homestead and until we reached the landing they were firing into us, the balls striking the pilot house and chimneys, but hurting no one up to that time. We proceeded to land, just above the railroad bridge, on the property of the Carnegie Steel Company, which was fenced in. We went right on against the shore and were there met by an armed mob, I think

about 50 to 100, whose numbers were being reenforced by the crowd on the river bank following the boat, until there were probably a thousand there within five minutes after we made the landing.

The first crowd attacked and tried to stop our tying up and putting out a stage plank. As they came it was something like a charge over the river bank, with the evident intent to get on barges. They got on the stage and were met by the Pinkerton men. One young man threw himself flat on the stage, when Capt. Hines, of the Pinkerton corps, went forward to push him off. His lying there looked like a piece of bravado, and the others were trying to crowd in over and pass him. While another Pinkerton man was endeavoring to keep the crowd back with an oar, the man lying on the landing stage fired the first shot at the captain—I mean the first shot that did any damage—wounding him in the thigh.

Immediately the crowd began firing from the bank, as well as on the river's edge near the barge. . . . All this occurred before the Pinkerton men fired. . . .

Testimony of Hugh O'Donnell, union leader:

I could not say the exact hour, but I think the alarm came up about 2 o'clock or 3 that two barges loaded with Pinkertons were coming up the river. . . . I, with others, got out of bed and with Capt. Coon, who was a near neighbor of mine, we both went down to the river bank and there had already assembled a very large crowd of people—men, women, and children. There were a lot of half-grown boys and there were Slavs, Hungarians, and others who were firing pistols in the air. They must

403

have been firing in the air. . . . We were going along with the crowd, following the crowd, and there had been a few random shots, but whether they were fired at the boat or not I could not say.

. . . Capt. Coon and I and another friend who accompanied us went down close to the beach, and there was quite an excited crowd standing around there and they were hallooing to the captain to pull back and not to land. I do not know how it came about, but there was some scuffle around the gang plank; I stood with my back to the beach about 40 feet, as I showed you yesterday, and there was some firing. I did not see any rifles in the congregation on the river bank and I saw no one, but I think I heard a rifle shot and then a regular volley at that. I was still addressing the crowd. One ball crossed my thumb (holding up same)—it is nearly well now—and struck another man in the head and I crawled up the bank and got behind a sewer trap until the firing ceased, which I should say was about five minutes duration.

Q. Do you know what direction the ball came from which struck your finger? A. Certainly: I was standing with my back to the barges.

Q. Did it come from there or from the front? A. It came from the barges.

Testimony of Joseph H. Gray, deputy sheriff who accompanied the Pinkertons:

When we came in sight of Homestead, whistles began to blow there, some miles away, and [from] some steamboat lying at the wharf, and all through the town, and there was a firing on the wharf, a promiscuous firing of small arms, pistols, etc. We ran on up past the crowd, and there was some fog on the river, and we were going pretty rapidly. When we got up pretty well and as we were nearing the shore I commenced to hear balls rattle against the boat fired by small arms, but before we passed into the Carnegie place—there is a fence running down to the river dividing it from the line—there was a ball came through the pilot-house. I examined the glass,

and I concluded that there was a rifle ball. Another struck the whistle and another struck the smoke stack, and we had a good deal of firing of that kind. . . . I could see the crowd coming, and when we reached the landing they came down through the mill property in a large number. When we came to the bank the captain asked Mr. Potter to send a couple of men out to assist them in tying the boat, which he did. Capt. Rodgers came and Mr. Potter and he sent some person out to protect him when he was tying the boat, and immediately upon his going to tie his boat they commenced coming down over the embankment and to the water's edge, and very soon thereafter commenced firing.

Q. Who commenced firing? A. The mob on the bank.

Testimony of Charles Mansfield, real estate clerk, ex-journalist, and resident of Homestead:

Q. I am not asking you what particular persons did, but do you know which way the firing was? A. Yes, sir: the first firing was done outside of the mill probably, and from where I was standing I could see the flashes in the air. They were fired generally most in the air. I did not see any firing done in the direction of the boat.

Q. The firing was from the bank? A. Yes, sir: into the air.

Q. You went along with the crowd up to where the boat landed? A. Yes, sir: I did not go up with the first rush.

Q. When you got there did you see the men on the boat attempt to land? A. Yes, sir: after the crowd run up I went up behind them and stood at the corner of the pump house to be out of range. I did not want to get hurt at all, and I stood there and saw the firing.

Q. Who commenced the firing? A. The firing was off the boat first. From where I stood the boat was tied above the pump house, and I stood at the corner of the brick pump house, the new one the machinery is not in yet, and from that corner I saw them fire off the corner of the boat. The fire was from the boat first, and a man fell.

Q. Did a man on shore fall? A. Yes, sir: I did not know who he was at the time, but I learned afterwards.

Testimony of John Kennedy, barge watchman:

Q. You tied up to the bank? A. We tied up to the bank; yes, sir.

Q. What else occurred? A. They came down, that is the strikers came down to the end of the gangway plank and said that we should not come off, that we should not tie up, but we were tied up at that time. We got tied up before they came there; that is, a good many of them. They then commenced shooting down the bank at the barges and . . .

Q. Did you see the first shot? A. That is where I saw the first shot at the barges, at the men. They shot at the men on the barges and I was standing at the lower end of the barges; I was on the inside barge next to the shore, and I could see everything that was going on.

Q. When did the men on the barges fire? A. Not until after there were several shots fired from the Homestead people, and I think there were one or two crippled before there was a shot fired from our men; I think so.

Testimony of A. J. Taylor, owner of grocery store in Homestead:

The boat by this time had got tied and I could see the barges plain, and they were saying something; I could not understand what they were saying. Those men were all excited and you could not tell much about what was

said there. Then some man went down to the plank and this man started off—

Q. The gangplank, you mean? A. Yes, sir; that was launched for the Pinkertons to come off, and I saw a man throw his hand up that way and fall and then I saw another man who was on the shore—no more than that much difference between them (snapping his thumb)—throw up his arms.

Q. Did you see any firing? A. I saw firing on both sides after that.

Q. After that both from the boat and from the shore? A. They opened fire on the men on the shore, I suppose.

Q. Which side fired first? A. The first man I saw fall was one of the strikers; one man who had hold of the plank.

Q. You heard a report and saw the flash of guns? A. Yes, sir; I saw the flash.

QUESTIONS

1. On what points do the witnesses agree? On what points do they disagree?
2. Can you come to a conclusion about what happened at Homestead on the morning of July 6, 1892, on the basis of this evidence? If so, what is your conclusion?
3. What factors might have influenced the testimony of each of the above witnesses?
4. What other pieces of information might help you in reconstructing the events of the morning?
5. Might a historian's view of unions influence his or her selection of evidence in this case? If so, in what way?

1850
Clayton-Bulwer
Treaty

1898
Spanish-American
War

1867
Purchase
of Alaska

1898
Hawaii
Annexed

1899
Open Door
Policy

THE RISE TO WORLD POWER

An American Empire

The United States as a World Power

World War I

1901	1904	1912	1914	1917	1919
Hay-Pauncefote Treaty	Roosevelt Corollary	Election of Woodrow Wilson	Tampico Incident	U.S. Enters World War I	Treaty of Versailles

1901	1903	1906	1914–18	1917
Platt Amendment	Panama Canal Treaty	Algeciras Conference	World War I	Purchase of Virgin Islands

1	Foreign Policy After the Civil War	409
2	The New Manifest Destiny	411
3	The Spanish-American War	416
4	Aftermath of the War	421

AN AMERICAN EMPIRE

Whether they will or no, Americans must now begin to look outward.

ALFRED THAYER MAHAN

For many years Americans were absorbed in the dream of expanding their territory from ocean to ocean. They had little interest in foreign affairs except when other countries threatened that dream. In 1823, however, the Monroe Doctrine had declared that American interests extended to the entire Western Hemisphere. In the second half of the 1800's, the ability of the United States to uphold the Monroe Doctrine was tested on more than one occasion. Furthermore, in the late 1800's Americans began to be interested in expansion overseas. Before long, the United States had established an empire.

1 Foreign Policy After the Civil War

One goal of American foreign policy in the years after the Civil War was territorial expansion. Another, more important objective was upholding the Monroe Doctrine, which had warned European countries not to interfere with countries in the Western Hemisphere. In the 1860's events in Mexico threatened the Monroe Doctrine.

The Maximilian Affair

Since its independence from Spain in 1821, Mexico had been in a state of constant political turmoil. In 40 years the country had no fewer than 73 presidents. The latest president, Benito Juaréz, had taken office in January 1861. In July of that year, Juaréz stopped making payments on Mexico's foreign debt. This action prompted the country's creditors—France, Spain, and Great Britain—to mount a joint expedition against Mexico to recover the money owed them. By May 1862, Great Britain and Spain had withdrawn, leaving the field to France.

Emperor Napoleon III of France proceeded to set up a **puppet regime** (a government controlled by an outside power) in Mexico. The French ruler plotted with Mexicans who opposed President Juaréz to offer the throne of Mexico to Archduke Maximilian, brother of Francis Joseph I of Austria. Maximilian, backed by French troops, was made Emperor of Mexico in 1863. Napoleon had several reasons for setting up a puppet government in Mexico. First of all, he wanted to check the power of the United States. He also saw Mexico as a source of markets, raw materials, and soldiers for his European armies.

William H. Seward, Secretary of State under Lincoln and Johnson, protested France's violation of the Monroe Doctrine and called for withdrawal of the French troops. However, the Civil War kept the United States from acting immediately. As soon as the fighting was over, the United States moved to get the French out of Mexico.

In 1865 Seward warned Napoleon III that the United States was becoming impatient with the French presence in Mexico. Seward's warning was backed by some 40,000 United States' troops stationed along the Rio Grande. Unable to get help from other European powers, Napoleon III withdrew his army from Mexico. Maximilian, however, decided to remain. In 1867 he was captured and executed by his former subjects. For the United States, the most important aspect of the Maximilian affair was the fact that the Monroe Doctrine had been upheld.

Alaska

As Secretary of State, Seward believed in a strong foreign policy, which he felt would unify the country during the Civil War. He insisted on upholding the Monroe Doctrine. In addition, he was interested in acquiring new territory for the United States. At his instigation, the United States acquired Alaska.

For some years, Alaska had belonged to Russia. Indeed, for most of Alaska's history, it had been known as Russian America. Russia had made a

Many Alaskan proper names show the influence of Alaska's Russian beginnings—e.g., Pribilof, Sitka, Bering.

Alaska's Mount McKinley is the tallest peak in North America at a height of 20,320 feet (6096 meters). The wealth of resources found in this scenic state proved Alaska's worth, even though its purchase was originally called Seward's Folly. Why did Seward want territories beyond the United States?

number of attempts to colonize the area, with very little success. By the 1860's, money problems forced Russia to consider selling its North American possession. Seward wanted to buy Alaska because he thought the United States should have a naval base in the northern Pacific to protect shipping. In addition, an American Alaska would serve as a vital link in the China trade.

Despite the criticism of the eastern press, which referred to Alaska as "Seward's Icebox" and "Seward's Folly," the Secretary of State remained undaunted. Consequently, when the Russian minister to the United States received orders to sell the vast territory, Seward acted immediately. On March 30, 1867, the United States Senate approved the purchase of Alaska from Russia for $7.2 million—just a few cents per acre.

Island Ventures

As an expansionist, Seward also tried to obtain territory for the United States overseas. In this respect, he was ahead of his time. It was under his guidance that the foundations of the American empire were laid.

In the Pacific, Seward secured the Pacific island of Midway for the United States in 1869. He had hopes of annexing the Hawaiian Islands, but these hopes were not realized during his lifetime.

In the Caribbean, Seward sought the purchase of the Danish West Indies.[1] The Danes were willing to sell, and Seward negotiated a treaty with them, but the Senate failed to ratify it. The Senate also refused

[1] Today, the Danish West Indies are known as the Virgin Islands. They were purchased from Denmark in August 1916.

After Seward's time, the philosophy of continentalism prevailed for about 20 years. This was the idea that the U.S. should not expand beyond its continental limits—should not absorb peoples from different cultures, should not spend money on a navy, and should not govern without consent of the governed.

THE RISE TO WORLD POWER   **411**

to ratify a treaty annexing the Dominican Republic. Few Americans were willing to back Seward's schemes.

SECTION REVIEW

1. Identify the following: Benito Jauréz, Seward's Icebox, Danish West Indies.
2. Why did Napoleon III want to influence affairs in Mexico?
3. Why was Secretary of State Seward interested in purchasing Alaska?
4. In what other parts of the world besides Alaska did Secretary of State Seward support American expansion?

2 The New Manifest Destiny

Although most Americans did not support Seward when he was in office, by the end of the 1800's they began to think in terms of a broader manifest destiny. The original concept was transformed to include overseas as well as westward expansion. The idea that it was the fate of the United States to extend its boundaries beyond the seas has been called the **new manifest destiny.**

Origins of the New Manifest Destiny

Capturing the American imagination, the spirit of the new manifest destiny spread throughout the land. The change in attitude toward foreign affairs was due to certain ideas and developments that occurred in the late 1800's.

Imperialism.   One such development was **imperialism,** the policy of extending the domination of one country over another. In the late 1800's many European countries were trying to establish new empires around the globe, especially in Africa and the Far East. These areas were important sources of raw materials and provided new avenues of investment for European capital.

European countries tried to exert political and military control over areas in which they had investments. Sometimes, protectorates or colonies were established. At other times, control was exercised indirectly, often through special trading rights. Areas which were under the indirect control of an outside power were called **spheres of influence.**

The example of European countries influenced Americans, who began to fear that they were falling behind in the race for an empire. The United States had traditionally followed a policy of **isolationism**—that is, of avoiding involvements with other countries. American foreign policy had been focused on conquering the American continental domain. By the late 1800's, however, the United States had reached its continental limits, and expansionists were ready to look elsewhere.

Social Darwinism.   A philosophy that provided a rationale for imperialism was Social Darwinism, the idea that only the fittest people in society could or should survive. In the late 1800's, Social Darwinism was applied to countries as well as to individuals. The countries of Europe used this theory to justify their actions in Africa and the Far East.

Along with Social Darwinism went the idea that whites were superior to people of other races. This idea was supported by the theory of **eugenics,** which held that certain racial and ethnic groups were superior to others because of inherited characteristics. Two of the superior groups were supposed to be the Anglo-Saxons and the Teutons, who were of Germanic origin. John W. Burgess, a historian who believed this theory, wrote of his feelings on the subject:

> *Indifference on the part of Teutonic states to the political situation of the rest of the world is . . . not only mistaken policy, but disregard of duty.*

Like Burgess, many people who believed in white superiority felt that it was their duty to "civilize" less fortunate peoples. The British poet, Rudyard Kipling, called this duty the "white man's burden."

By the end of the 1800's, this idea of the "white man's burden" had taken hold in the United States. Americans had always felt that their democratic ways were superior. Many came to believe that American institutions could serve as a model for the rest of the world. In America a new sense of mission arose.

Mahan and the Navy.   More justification for imperialism was provided by Captain Alfred Thayer Mahan of the Naval War College at Newport, Rhode

By 1900 the United States Navy had moved up from twelfth to third place in the world. Note that a bigger navy also strengthened the arguments for a canal across Central America.

At Captain Alfred Mahan's urging to build up the Navy, Congress finally allocated money to build ships. By 1895 a great fleet was under construction. What incident convinced Americans that a strong navy was important?

Island. In *The Influence of Sea Power Upon History, 1660–1783* (1890), he supplied an argument for both the improvement of the United States Navy and overseas expansion.

Mahan believed that sea power was what made a country great and that the United States should build a strong navy to ensure its future. He also stressed that foreign trade was important. He said that the country needed colonies to provide markets and raw materials and to serve as ports and coaling stations for ships.

The United States Navy had made some strides earlier in the century. One of these was the development of ironclad ships during the Civil War. However, after the war America had allowed its navy to deteriorate, while other countries were modernizing theirs. Although the 20 years after 1865 saw revolutionary developments in naval warfare, the United States' Navy still depended mostly on a few wooden sailing ships.

Most Americans—their attention on domestic matters—did not see the need to enlarge or modernize the navy. Thus, Congress appropriated (set aside) very little money for that purpose.

As time passed, the weakness of the navy became more apparent. In 1881, during the course of a disturbance in Latin America,[2] it was discovered that Chile had a stronger navy than the United States. It was then that Americans began to realize that having a strong navy was important. Early in 1883 Congress authorized the building of three steel battleships.

Mahan's book, however, provided a real impetus to change. Influenced by this work, Congress passed the Naval Act of 1890, which appropriated additional money for battleships. By 1900 the United States had the naval power it needed to back up an expanded role in foreign affairs.

Expansion of the United States

During the last half of the 1800's, the United States began to acquire an empire. The country's first expansion into overseas areas took place in the islands of the Pacific.

The Samoan Islands.   The United States had been interested in the Samoan Islands in the South Pacific since before the Civil War. Early in 1872 the United States negotiated a treaty with Samoa's local rulers. Under the terms of this treaty, Samoa granted the United States the right to establish a naval base at Pago Pago. The Senate, however, refused to ratify the treaty. President Grant then sent a special agent to the islands, hoping to extend American influence there. This was accomplished when the agent became prime minister of Samoa. In January 1878 the United States and Samoa's local rulers again signed a treaty which gave the United States the right to build a naval base at Pago Pago. This time the treaty was approved.

The United States was not the only country that was interested in Samoa. Great Britain had claims there, and in the 1880's, the islands became the target of German expansionism. Therefore, in June 1889 the United States, Great Britain, and Germany met at Berlin to discuss the future of Samoa. The agreement gave the Samoan Islands **autonomy,** or the right to self-government, under a tripartite (three-power) protectorate.

This arrangement lasted until 1899, when continuing differences among the three powers led to a new agreement. The new agreement divided the islands between the United States and Germany. Great

---

[2] This was the War of the Pacific begun by Chile against Bolivia and Peru.

Britain gave up its claims in return for other considerations, such as rights in Africa.

The Hawaiian Islands. The United States was also interested in the Hawaiian Islands. Discovered by British Captain James Cook in 1788, these islands were important to the China trade. American ships stopped there for supplies on the long voyage to the Orient. Further ties with the Hawaiian Islands were established when Americans began settling there in the early 1800's. Some of the settlers were Christian missionaries, whose purpose was to convert the natives. Others came for adventure or profit. One source of profit for many settlers was the sugar trade.

By the 1870's sugar planters had established a lucrative trade with the United States. An 1875 treaty allowed Hawaiian sugar into the United States duty-free, which helped the economy of the islands. A second provision of the treaty stated that no other powers could be given territorial rights in the islands. Thus the treaty made Hawaii a virtual colony of the United States. Relations were further solidified when a treaty of 1884 gave the United States Navy the exclusive use of Pearl Harbor as a naval base.

A series of events in the 1890's changed the state of affairs in the Hawaiian Islands. The McKinley Tariff of 1890 removed the duties on imported sugar, which had been applied to other countries since 1875. This destroyed Hawaii's advantage in the sugar trade. Since 1875, only Hawaiian sugar had entered the United States duty-free. Other countries had had to pay a tariff. Therefore, their sugar was higher priced than that of Hawaii.

The tariff also awarded a bounty of 2 cents per pound to domestic sugar producers. This made the price of American-grown sugar lower than that of imported sugar. As a result, Hawaiian sugar planters had to drop their prices drastically in order to sell any sugar. The McKinley Tariff nearly ruined the Hawaiian economy.

American sugar planters in Hawaii wanted the United States to annex the islands because, once the islands were a part of the United States, Hawaii would be eligible for the bounty. In 1887 these planters managed to take control of the Hawaiian legislature and drew up a liberal constitution.

However, in 1891 Queen Liliuokalani came to the throne. The queen was strongly anti-American. In January 1893 she took steps to return control of the government to Hawaiians. One of her first acts was to proclaim a new constitution, which gave her autocratic (absolute) powers.

At this point, the Americans, led by Sanford B. Dole, overthrew the monarchy. They did so with the backing of the American minister to Hawaii, John L. Stevens, who even called out the marines to assist them. Stevens, acting on his own, proclaimed Hawaii a protectorate of the United States on February 1.

Having gained power, the new Hawaiian government, with Sanford Dole at its head, drew up a treaty of annexation to be submitted to the United States Senate. At that time, Benjamin Harrison, who

The first large sugar plantations in Hawaii were owned by Americans. Under their control, sugar cane became one of the largest and most profitable crops in the islands. Sugar planters shipped most of their crop to the United States. How did the McKinley Tariff affect the sugar industry in Hawaii?

Imperialism

The drive to create empires is as old as civilization itself. The history of the world includes the rise and fall of vast empires—for example, the Egyptian empire, the Persian empire, and the Roman empire. The European nations of the 1500's and 1600's were practicing imperialism when they established empires in the New World.

Imperialism has many motives. One motive is military advantage. Countries often feel the need to control territories near their borders in order to protect themselves from attack. More distant territories may be seen as desirable because they are important to military strategy.

Religion is another motive that sometimes contributes to imperialism. The Arabs of the seventh century conquered a huge empire in order to spread the religion of Islam. The European nations that colonized the New World wanted to spread Christianity.

A third motive for imperialism is nationalism. In the late 1800's, nationalism was a strong force in Europe. During this period, which is sometimes called the Age of Imperialism, several European nations established empires in Africa and in the Far East. The United States joined the ranks of imperialist powers when it won territory from Spain in the Spanish-American War.

One of the most important motives for early twentieth-century imperialism was economic gain. By this time the United States and Europe had become industrialized. Industrial nations needed new markets, new sources of raw materials, and new outlets of investments. Albert J. Beveridge, who shortly after making the following speech was elected Senator, called for the United States to acquire overseas territories:

But today we are raising more than we can consume. Today we are making more than we can use. Today our industrial society is congested; there are more workers than there is work; there is more capital than there is investment. We do not need more money—we need more circulation, more employment. Therefore we must find new markets for our produce, new occupation for our capital, new work for our labor.

Imperialism was not without its critics. Many Americans asked if the ideals of democracy were compatible with competition for empire. Yale Professor William G. Sumner wrote:

Now, the great reason why all these enterprises which began by saying to somebody else, "We know what is good for you better than you know yourself and we are going to make you do it," are false and wrong is that they violate liberty; or, to turn the same statement into other words, the reason why liberty, of which Americans talk so much, is a good thing is that it means leaving people to live out their lives in their own way, while we do the same.

Imperialism has been responsible for many conflicts among the nations of the world. Competition among European powers led to World War I. The imperialistic designs of Germany and Japan led to World War II. Throughout history, subjugated people all over the world have rebelled against the rule of outside powers. As William Jennings Bryan said in 1901, "Hatred of an alien government is a natural thing and a thing to be expected everywhere."

Today, many former colonies have won their independence. However, the world powers still exercise considerable influence—some for good and some for ill—in various parts of the globe.

Americans still debate what role the United States should take in the world. Some would like to see their country return to isolationism. Others insist that the United States still has a responsibility to promote its national interests, to encourage democracy and economic development in other countries, and to fight communist aggression.

QUESTIONS

1. What are some of the motives of imperialism?
2. How has imperialism led to conflicts?

favored annexation, was President. However, the Senate did not act quickly enough. It failed to ratify the treaty before Harrison left office.

The new President, Grover Cleveland, was a decided anti-imperialist. He took steps to stop annexation by withdrawing the treaty before it could be ratified. He then ordered an investigation of what had been happening in Hawaii. As a result, Cleveland discovered the part played by Stevens and the American planters. He also learned that most Hawaiians did not favor annexation. Nevertheless, Cleveland reluctantly recognized the Republic of Hawaii shortly after it was proclaimed on July 4, 1894 with Sanford Dole as its first and only president. In July 1898, under President McKinley, the islands were finally annexed by the United States.

The Venezuelan Dispute. In addition to acquiring territory in the Pacific, the United States also became involved in Latin America. In the 1880's gold was discovered along the border of Venezuela and British Guiana. Venezuela and Great Britain had had a dispute over this border for some time. With the discovery of gold, the situation got out of hand.

Venezuela broke off relations with Great Britain in 1887. Then, with the threat of war in the air, Venezuela asked the United States to arbitrate. In 1887 and again in 1894, the United States offered to step in. Both times, the British refused. These refusals angered Americans. Secretary of State Richard Olney objected to the British stand largely on the grounds that it jeopardized the Monroe Doctrine.

Influenced by public opinion, President Cleveland ordered Olney to send a message to the British government. That message, sent in July 1895, made it clear that the United States would not allow any European power to subjugate (force control upon) an American country. Olney emphasized the supremacy of the United States in the Western Hemisphere:

Today the United States is practically sovereign on this continent. . . . Why? It is not because of the pure friendship or good will felt for it. It is not simply by reason of its high character as a civilized state, nor because wisdom and justice and equity are the invariable characteristics of the dealings of the United States. It is because, in addition to all other grounds, its infinite resources combined with its isolated position render it master of the

situation and practically invulnerable as against any or all other powers.

This statement was a **corollary** (a proposition that follows from one that has already been established), which became known as the Olney Corollary to the Monroe Doctrine. Lord Salisbury, Great Britain's foreign secretary and prime minister, replied to Olney's message. In his reply, Lord Salisbury said that the British did not recognize the Monroe Doctrine as international law:

The United States have a right, like any other nation, to interpose in any controversy by which their own interests are affected; and they are the judge whether those interests are touched, and in what measure they should be sustained. But their rights are in no way strengthened or extended by the fact that the controversy affects some territory which is called American.

Cleveland responded almost at once. He asked Congress to appropriate money for a commission to determine the Venezuelan boundary. Further, Cleveland stated that America would use "every means in its power" to guard that boundary.

The British, who were beginning to have problems in other parts of the world, decided that it would be to their advantage to remain on friendly terms with the United States. In February 1897 they agreed to arbitration. The Venezuelan boundary commission had already been appointed, and the matter was settled when the commission set a boundary in 1899.

The settlement marked the end of a successful venture for the United States. The Monroe Doctrine had been upheld. Also, the country's active intervention in Venezuela was a sign of the coming trend toward a more aggressive foreign policy.

SECTION REVIEW

1. Identify the following: Rudyard Kipling, Naval Act of 1890, Sanford B. Dole, Richard Olney.
2. How was the theory of Social Darwinism expanded in the late 1800's?
3. Why did Alfred Thayer Mahan believe that the United States should build a strong navy?
4. Why were Americans interested in Hawaii?
5. Why was the United States concerned with the dispute between Venezuela and Great Britain?

Have students discuss the obligation of the press to report news accurately.

3 The Spanish-American War

The United States not only intervened in Venezuela, but it also intervened in Cuba. This time, intervention led to war with Spain. The war lasted only three months. However, by the end of the war, the United States had acquired possessions in the Caribbean and in the Pacific, and it had gained the status of a world power.

Revolution in Cuba

Cuba had remained loyal to Spain throughout a period of Latin American revolutions in the early 1800's. However, in 1868 the Cubans had rebelled against Spanish rule. After ten years of fighting, the rebels were defeated. During the years of peace that followed, Cuba enjoyed some prosperity due to its active sugar trade with the United States. After the McKinley Tariff of 1890, Cuban sugar could enter the United States duty-free. However, in 1894 Congress passed the Wilson-Gorman Tariff, which once more placed a tax on imported sugar. The Cuban economy suffered, and the hard times led to a new revolt in 1895.

The 1895 Revolt. The Cubans, determined to win this revolution, followed a **scorched-earth policy.** That is, they pursued a policy of widespread destruction, burning a large number of sugar plantations and mills, many of which were owned by Americans. The revolutionaries hoped that the United States would intervene to save its investments. At first, however, the rebels received little support from the United States. Both the Cleveland and McKinley administrations disapproved of the Cubans' tactics.

American opinion began to change when the Spaniards employed even harsher tactics to put down the revolt. Spain gave the task of suppressing the revolt to General Valeriano Weyler. To make his job easier, Weyler, known as the "Butcher," set up **reconcentrado camps,** or detention camps. Conditions in the camps were squalid, and the prisoners were brutally treated. A Senate report described the lives of the prisoners:

> Their huts are about 10 by 15 feet in size, and for want of space are usually crowded together very closely. They have no floor but the ground, no furniture, and, after a year's wear, but little clothing, except such stray substitutes as they can extemporize, and with large families, or more than one, in this little space, the commonest sanitary provisions are impossible. Conditions are unmentionable in this respect. Torn from their homes, with foul earth, foul air, foul water, and foul food or none, what wonder that one half have died and that one quarter of the living are so diseased that they cannot be saved?

Nearly 200,000 Cubans died in the camps. Americans were shocked by these conditions, and American sympathy for the Cuban revolutionaries grew.

This cartoon shows William Randolph Hearst as the "Yellow Kid of Journalism." It accuses him of an alliance with Tammany Hall's "Boss" Richard Croker and of bringing on war with Spain. Why do you think Hearst resorted to yellow journalism?

Joseph Pulitzer   William Randolph Hearst

Pulitzer was a Hungarian immigrant who came to the United States after being hired to fight for the Union in the Civil War. After the war, he became an American citizen.

He started his newspaper career as a reporter for a German-language paper in St. Louis. Later, he bought two small papers, combined them into one, and made a fortune. He bought the New York *World* in 1883. Under his direction, the paper soon acquired the largest circulation of any paper in the country.

Pulitzer died a rich man in 1911. His will provided for a number of large bequests to support journalism and the arts. He left money to Columbia University for a school of journalism, and said that the school should award yearly prizes to people who made outstanding contributions in journalism, literature, music, drama, and public service. Pulitzer prizes are still considered a high honor.

Hearst was born in 1863 to a wealthy San Francisco family. After he was expelled from Harvard for playing practical jokes on his professors, his father gave him the *San Francisco Examiner.*

Hearst bought the New York *Journal* in 1895, and became Pulitzer's chief competitor. Later, he bought a large number of other newspapers and magazines, and founded the International News Service.

When the Cubans rebelled against Spain in 1895, newspaper publishers Joseph Pulitzer and William Randolph Hearst both sent teams of artists and writers to cover the conflict. Both of their papers played up the misdeeds of the Spaniards and called for American intervention.

Neither paper was scrupulous about the facts. Hearst is reported to have told an artist, "You furnish the pictures, and I'll furnish the war."

Yellow Journalism

Sympathy for the Cubans continued to grow as William Randolph Hearst's New York *Journal* and Joseph Pulitzer's *New York World* competed with each other in reporting stories of Spanish atrocities. Although some of the stories were true, many were exaggerated, and some were more fiction than fact. Both papers used the techniques of yellow journalism to appeal to readers. An editorial in Pulitzer's *World* is a case in point:

> How long are the Spaniards to drench Cuba with the blood and tears of her people?
> . . . How long shall old men and women and children be murdered by the score, the innocent victims of Spanish rage against the patriot armies they cannot conquer?

> . . . How long shall American citizens, arbitrarily arrested while on peaceful and legitimate errands, be immured in foul Spanish prisons without trial?
> . . . How long shall the United States sit idle and indifferent . . . ?

This sensationalism was criticized by more conservative journalists. One critic was E. L. Godkin, editor of *The Nation.* He wrote, "Nothing so disgraceful as the behavior of these two newspapers . . . has ever been known in the history of journalism." Despite such criticism, yellow journalism had an enormous impact on public opinion in the United States.

The De Lôme Letter.   Anti-Spanish feeling increased with the publication of the so-called De Lôme Letter. This letter had been written by the

The term "jingo" came from a jingle printed by the Detroit *News* during a fisheries dispute between Canada and Great Britain. "We do not want to fight/ But, by jingo, if we do / We'll scoop in all the fishing grounds/ And the whole dominion too."

Spanish minister to the United States, Enrique Dupuy de Lôme, to a friend. It fell into the hands of Cuban rebels and ended up on the pages of the *Morning Journal*. Unfortunately for De Lôme, the letter criticized President McKinley:

> [*McKinley is*] *weak and a bidder for the admiration of the crowd, besides being a would-be politician (politicastro) who tries to leave a door open behind himself while keeping on good terms with the jingoes of his party.*

The **jingoes** De Lôme referred to—people who believed in a warlike foreign policy—saw the letter as another cause for war. Although De Lôme resigned at once, pressure for war began to mount.

The Maine. What finally brought about the Spanish-American War, however, was the sinking of the U.S.S. *Maine*. The *Maine* had been ordered to Havana, Cuba, in January 1898 to protect Americans in that city. On February 15, while at anchor in the Havana harbor, the ship exploded, killing 260.

Joseph Pulitzer's *The World* front page coverage of the sinking of the U.S.S. *Maine* shows the type of newspaper reporting that helped bring on war with Spain. Who was responsible for the sinking of the *Maine*?

Americans blamed the Spaniards for the explosion, although there was no proof of their guilt. In fact, it was more likely that the *Maine* was blown up by Cuban revolutionaries, who were desperate for United States intervention. Nevertheless, Americans all over the country called for war with Spain. The cry "Remember the Maine!" was heard everywhere.

A Short War

On April 11, 1898, McKinley sent a war message to Congress. On April 20, despite Spanish agreement to earlier demands made by the United States, Congress passed a joint resolution against Spain. The resolution recognized Cuban independence, called for Spain's withdrawal from the island, and gave the President power to use military force against Spain. Added to the resolution was the Teller Amendment, which denied that the United States intended to take control of Cuba after Spain withdrew. The amendment said that once peace had been restored in Cuba, the United States would turn over control of the island to its people. McKinley signed the resolution, and on April 25 the United States formally declared war on Spain.

Preparations for War. The opening of the Spanish-American War found the United States ill-prepared to fight. In 1898 the U.S. Army had only 28,000 soldiers. Furthermore, its forces were widely scattered. To correct the situation Congress approved the addition of over 30,000 soldiers to the regular army, and authorized a volunteer force of 200,000.[3] Among the volunteers was a cavalry unit called the "Rough Riders," led by Colonel Leonard Wood and his second in command, Lieutenant Colonel Theodore Roosevelt. Even with the additional soldiers, however, the army had problems due to inadequate supplies and a lack of trained leaders.

The Spaniards were not much better prepared. While they had a large, well-equipped army in Cuba, it had few real leaders. Because Cuba was such a long way from home, Spain had trouble supplying its soldiers. The Spanish navy was also weak. Although on paper it was larger than that of the United States,

---

[3] The regular army is the permanent or standing army. The volunteer forces served only for the duration of the Spanish-American War.

Americans suffered over 5000 deaths in the Spanish-American War—most of them the result of diseases such as malaria, typhoid, and yellow fever. Fewer than 400 died from wounds received in combat.

There were many blacks among the 200,000 volunteers who joined the armed forces during the Spanish-American War. The 9th and 10th Colored Cavalry are shown here fighting with the Rough Riders at the Battle of Quasimas in Cuba. These forces surrounded and overcame the Spaniards guarding the fortifications that protected Santiago. What other victories put the Americans in a position to take Santiago and win the war in Cuba?

its ships were outdated and its sailors were poorly trained. On the other hand, the United States Navy, due to the recent improvements, had modern ships and well-trained sailors and officers.

The Pacific Theater.   The advantage enjoyed by the United States Navy was first seen in the Pacific theater. In late February Assistant Secretary of the Navy Theodore Roosevelt[4] ordered the United States fleet in the Pacific, under Commodore George Dewey, to stand by for action. If war was declared, Dewey was to sail from Hong Kong, where he was based, to Manila, the capital of the Philippine Islands. These islands belonged to Spain and served as a base for part of the Spanish fleet. Dewey was to keep the fleet from raiding the West Coast of the United States.

On May 1, 1898, shortly after war was declared, Dewey sailed into Manila Bay. With his command, "You may fire when ready, Mr. Gridley," the onslaught began. When the firing was over, the Spanish fleet was destroyed. Not a single American vessel was lost.

At the time, Dewey did not have the support needed for a land attack. He therefore decided to blockade Manila until help arrived. In July, support troops under General Wesley Merritt arrived in the

---

[4] Shortly after this, Roosevelt resigned his position to join the Rough Riders.

Philippines. American forces, backed by Filipino rebels under General Emilio Aguinaldo, captured Manila on August 13, 1898.

The Caribbean Theater.   Meanwhile, in the Caribbean, the rest of the Spanish fleet under Admiral Pascual Cervera y Topete was blockaded in Santiago Harbor by a naval force under Admiral William T. Sampson. Sampson's task was to **neutralize** (destroy the effectiveness of) Cervera's fleet.

Meanwhile, an American land force under General William Shafter was ordered to take the city of Santiago. By the end of June, Shafter's force, including the "Rough Riders," had landed in Cuba and was pushing toward Santiago. Shafter's troops met resistance at El Caney, but after fierce fighting, took the village on July 1. Next, San Juan Hill was taken by the "Rough Riders." Theodore Roosevelt led the charge up San Juan Hill. These two victories put the Americans in a position to take Santiago and bombard the Spanish ships.

In order to avoid such bombardment, Cervera tried to slip through Sampson's blockade. The attempt failed, and in a four-hour battle the Spanish fleet was destroyed. Shortly thereafter, Santiago fell to the Americans.

About the same time, an American force under General Nelson A. Miles took the Spanish colony of Puerto Rico with little difficulty. Further resistance

Have students debate the validity of McKinley's reasons for taking the Philippines.

seemed pointless to the Spaniards. On August 12 an **armistice** (truce) was signed between the United States and Spain.

The Treaty of Paris

In October 1898 representatives from Spain and the United States met in Paris to discuss peace. Under the terms of the treaty, which was signed in December, Spain surrendered all rights to Cuba and assumed the Cuban debt. Puerto Rico and the Pacific island of Guam were ceded to the United States. Spain agreed to sell the Philippines to the United States for $20 million.

Spain had been very reluctant to sell, but McKinley had been firm. Later, he spoke of his reasons:

> When . . . I realized that the Philippines had dropped into our laps, I confess I did not know what to do with them. I sought counsel from all sides—Democrats as well as Republicans—but got little help. I thought first we would take only Manila; then Luzon; then other islands, perhaps, also.
>
> I walked the floor of the White House night after night. . . . And one night late it came to me this way—I don't know how it was, but it came:
>
> (1) That we could not give them back to Spain—that would be cowardly and dishonorable;
>
> (2) That we could not turn them over to France or Germany, our commercial rivals in the Orient—that would be bad business and discreditable;
>
> (3) That we could not leave them to themselves—they were unfit for self-government, and they would soon have anarchy and misrule worse than Spain's was; and
>
> (4) That there was nothing left for us to do but to take them all, and to educate the Filipinos, and uplift and civilize and Christianize them. . . .

SPANISH–AMERICAN WAR, 1898

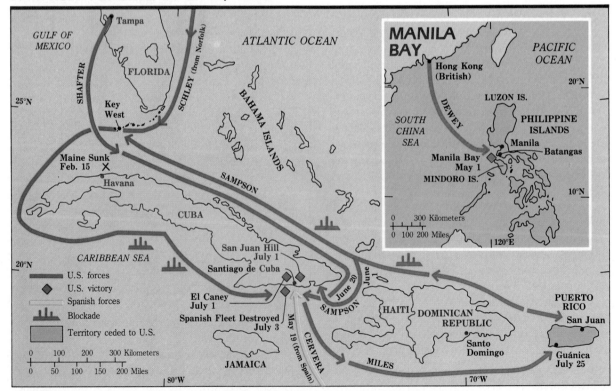

Some anti-imperialists predicted that war with Japan would result from United States expansion in the Pacific.

A rider is a provision that is unlikely to pass on its own merits. Opponents of the rider are forced to accept it if they want the major bill to become law. Some governors have item veto power, but the President does not.

And then I went to bed . . . and the next morning I sent for the chief engineer of the War Department . . . and I told him to put the Philippines on the map of the United States . . . and there they are, and there they will stay while I am President!

The acquisition of the Philippines made the treaty subject to debate in the Senate and throughout the country. Many people objected on moral grounds to annexing a people who wanted to be free. There were still some isolationists who thought the United States should avoid foreign entanglements. Imperialists argued that the United States should keep the islands so that no other power could take them. Finally, in February 1899, the treaty was narrowly ratified.

SECTION REVIEW

1. Identify the following: General Valeriano Weyler, Enrique Dupuy de Lôme, the "Rough Riders," Emilio Aguinaldo.
2. How did the press influence American attitudes toward the Cuban revolution?
3. What single event had the most influence on the United States' decision to declare war on Spain?
4. What advantages did the United States have in the war with Spain?
5. What were the terms of the peace treaty?

4 Aftermath of the War

As a result of the war, the United States emerged as a world power. The possessions acquired from Spain enhanced its new position. However, along with empire came certain responsibilities.

Puerto Rico and Guam

The transition from Spanish to American rule was fairly smooth in Puerto Rico. An American force under General Miles met little resistance from the people when it occupied the island in July 1898. In October the Spanish governor-general left, and the military took control of the government.

In April 1900, Congress passed the Foraker Act, which ended military rule and set up a civil government in Puerto Rico. The act provided that the President of the United States choose a governor and an executive council of 11 members, 5 of whom were to be Puerto Ricans. This council would serve as the upper house of the legislature. The lower house was to be chosen by the people.

In 1917 the United States made Puerto Rico a territory and granted its people citizenship. Later, in 1950, Puerto Rico became a **commonwealth.** This meant that, although voluntarily associated with the United States, the island was autonomous.

The transfer of power in Guam was also smooth. Not long after the Treaty of Paris, President McKinley placed the administration of Guam in the hands of the Navy Department. The islands' people played no important role in government until Guam became a territory some years later.

Cuba

There were greater difficulties in Cuba. In the Teller Amendment, the United States had denied any desire to control Cuba. When the war ended, however, it decided not to withdraw from the island, fearing that leaving might undermine the political stability of Cuba and jeopardize American interests there. Therefore, the military took control.

The military government, headed by General Wood, built roads, hospitals, and schools, and introduced reforms in health and sanitation on the island. Cuba also made strides politically. In November 1900 General Wood authorized the calling of a constitutional convention. By 1901 the Cubans had written a constitution based upon that of the United States and were ready to begin governing themselves. At this point, Wood told the Cubans that American withdrawal depended on their accepting the Platt Amendment, which had been added as a **rider** (an unrelated amendment) to another bill in Congress. This amendment stated:

1. Cuba could not enter into any treaty that might impair its independence.
2. Cuba's debt must not exceed its revenues.
3. The United States could intervene in Cuba to keep order.
4. The United States could establish naval bases on the island.

The Cubans added the Platt Amendment to their Constitution in June 1901, and in May 1902 the United States withdrew.

Have students report on the current status of the Philippines.

The Philippines

Greater problems existed in the Philippines. The Filipinos had helped to defeat Spain because they hoped to win their own independence. When they learned that the United States had taken control of the islands, the Filipinos revolted against their new rulers. It took 70,000 United States soldiers to put down the uprising, but toward the close of 1899, organized resistance came to an end. Guerrilla warfare, however, continued for some time.

Meanwhile, President McKinley had appointed a commission to look into the Philippine situation. After studying the matter, the commission recommended that the islands be given their independence following a period of United States control. In 1900, therefore, McKinley appointed another commission to set up a civil government in the Philippines. This was done July 4, 1901, and William Howard Taft, president of the commission, became the first civil governor of the Philippines.

In July 1902 the islands gained partial self-government under the Philippine Government Act. This act provided that the lower house of the legislature be elected by the people. Taft's commission was to serve as the upper house.

The Jones Act of 1916 confirmed that the United States intended to withdraw from the islands and to recognize the Filipinos' independence once they had established a stable government. The act also increased self-government by making the upper house of the legislature elective. Therefore, the Philippines were virtually autonomous. In 1946 they gained full independence. Meanwhile, the United States' presence in the Philippines extended American interests in the Far East. Eventually, those interests would come into conflict with those of other world powers.

SECTION REVIEW

1. Identify the following: Foraker Act, Platt Amendment, Jones Act.
2. How was the transition from Spanish to American rule accomplished in Puerto Rico and Guam?
3. Why was the United States reluctant to withdraw its forces from Cuba?
4. How did the Filipinos react to United States control?

CHAPTER **20**   REVIEW

SUMMARY

1. The ability of the United States to uphold the Monroe Doctrine was tested during the Civil War, when France tried to intervene in Mexican affairs.
2. The United States purchased Alaska from Russia in 1867.
3. In the second half of the 1800's, American foreign policy expanded to include a new interest in overseas expansion.
4. The United States extended its influence to the Samoan and Hawaiian Islands in the South Pacific.
5. In the 1890's the Monroe Doctrine was once again upheld when Venezuela became involved in a dispute with Great Britain.
6. In 1898 American intervention in a Cuban revolution led to the Spanish-American War.
7. With the defeat of Spain, the United States emerged as a world power.
8. As a result of the war, the United States acquired an empire that included Puerto Rico, Guam, and the Philippines.

VOCABULARY

puppet regime	isolationism	scorched-earth policy	armistice
new manifest destiny	eugenics	reconcentrado camps	commonwealth
imperialism	autonomy	jingoes	rider
spheres of influence	corollary	neutralize	

REVIEW QUESTIONS

1. How did European expansionism influence American expansionism?
2. How did Americans and Europeans justify their expansionism?
3. By what means did the United States uphold the Monroe Doctrine during the second half of the 1800's?
4. By what means did the United States extend its influence in the Samoan and Hawaiian Islands?
5. What were the causes of the Spanish-American War?
6. What was the role of the United States Navy in the war?
7. What was the relationship between Cuba and the United States after the Spanish-American War?
8. How did the war expand the role of the United States in world affairs?

DISCUSSION

1. Is it desirable for the United States to have an empire? Why or why not?
2. Was American expansionism in the late 1800's essentially different from earlier expansionism? Why or why not?
3. Was the United States right to intervene in the Cuban revolution? Why or why not?
4. If you were a Cuban, Filipino, or Hawaiian in 1900, how would you feel about the United States? Why would you feel this way?

USING MAPS

Refer to the map on page 420 and answer the following questions:

1. What American victories occurred on July 1, 1898?
2. From what point did General Shafter's army sail? Where did it land?
3. What Spanish territory was acquired by the United States?
4. Approximately how far is Key West from the city of Havana?
5. How did Cervera approach the harbor at Santiago? Why?

USING SKILLS

Refer to the cartoon on page 416 and answer the following questions:

1. Who is portrayed in the cartoon? Is he portrayed favorably or unfavorably?
2. What do the paintbrush and can of paint in the cartoon symbolize?
3. Why are words misspelled and letters printed backwards in the cartoon?
4. Which of the following ideas can be interpreted from the cartoon?
   a. The news in the *Journal* is unbiased.
   b. The *Journal* favors war with Spain.
   c. The *Journal* has connections with machine politics.
5. Does the artist who drew the cartoon approve of the *Journal*?

1	The Far East	425
2	The Panama Canal	429
3	A Continuing Interest in Foreign Affairs	434
4	Woodrow Wilson's Missionary Diplomacy	439

THE UNITED STATES AS A WORLD POWER

There is a homely adage which runs, "Speak softly and carry a big stick; you will go far."

THEODORE ROOSEVELT

As a world power, the United States became increasingly involved in foreign affairs. The country's handling of these affairs varied according to the situation and the views of the President in office. In general, however, the United States pursued an active foreign policy. This was seen in the Far East, Latin America, and elsewhere.

1 The Far East

The acquisition of the Philippines furthered American interests in the Far East. However, the United States came into conflict with other powers that had claims in that area. As time passed, conflicts occurred more frequently.

The Open Door

While America was fighting the Spanish-American War, important changes were taking place in certain areas of the Far East. One of these areas was China. The country had emerged from a war with Japan[1] in a weakened state and was therefore vulnerable to other powers. Great Britain, France, Germany, Russia, and Japan took advantage of China's position, and divided the country into spheres of influence.

Great Britain leased the port of Kowloon opposite Hong Kong, which it already held. France took control of Kwangchow Bay in southern China. Germany leased Kiaochow Bay and its port of Tsingtao on the Shantung Peninsula. Russia obtained a lease on the southern Liaotung Peninsula, including Port Arthur, and acquired rights to build railroads in Manchuria. Japan secured rights in Fukien province across from Formosa.

The establishment of these spheres of influence threatened American business interests in China. If the country were divided, American trade would suffer. Within a certain sphere, the controlling power could set up trade restrictions that would keep out other countries, including the United States.

Trade between the United States and China, which had been growing steadily since 1844, had reached sizeable proportions by 1900. In fact, American businesses such as the Standard Oil Company had invested heavily in China by that time. Business groups such as the American-Asiatic Association urged the United States to protect the country's economic position in the Far East.

To preserve equal economic opportunity in China, Secretary of State John Hay, in September 1899, sent notes to Great Britain, Germany, and Russia, and later to Japan, France, and Italy. To each of these great powers he proposed what he called the Open Door. According to his proposal, within each sphere of influence (1) the trading rights of all nations would be respected; (2) existing tariffs would be collected by Chinese officials rather than by foreigners; and (3) railroad rates and harbor duties would not discriminate against people from other countries. Although Great Britain responded to Hay's proposal favorably, all of the other powers responded with caution. Nevertheless, on March 20, 1900, he announced that the Open Door was in effect.

The Boxer Rebellion

In May 1900 a Chinese patriotic society known as the Boxers staged a revolt that threatened the Open Door. Foreigners living in China were the Boxers' major target. Determined to rid their country of these "foreign devils," the Boxers killed over 200 foreigners and laid siege to the embassies of the great powers at Peking.

Secretary of State Hay feared that the great powers would use the Boxer Rebellion as an excuse to divide China further. To prevent such an

---

[1]This was the Sino-Japanese War of 1894–95.

occurrence, he sent another Open Door note in July 1900. In this note he clarified United States policy:

> The policy of the government of the United States is to seek a solution which may bring about permanent safety and peace to China, preserve Chinese territorial and administrative entity, protect all rights guaranteed to friendly powers by treaty and international law, and safeguard for the world the principle of equal and impartial trade with all parts of the Chinese Empire.

After the second Open Door note, the great powers joined together to put down the Boxer Rebellion. In August an international force including American troops rescued the diplomats at Peking, and resistance came to an end. Just over a year later,

at Hay's urging, Great Britain, France, Germany, Russia, and Japan signed the Boxer Protocol, in which they agreed to accept money rather than territory from China. Although it had to pay $332 million, China was not dismembered.

The Russo-Japanese War

After the suppression of the Boxer Rebellion, most of the great powers withdrew from China. Russia, however, remained in Manchuria. Its presence threatened Japan's economic development, as Japan had begun to industrialize and needed Manchuria's natural resources to continue the process.

Therefore, the Japanese decided to drive the Russians from the area. To prepare for this move, Japan signed a treaty of alliance with Great Britain in

SPHERES OF INFLUENCE IN ASIA

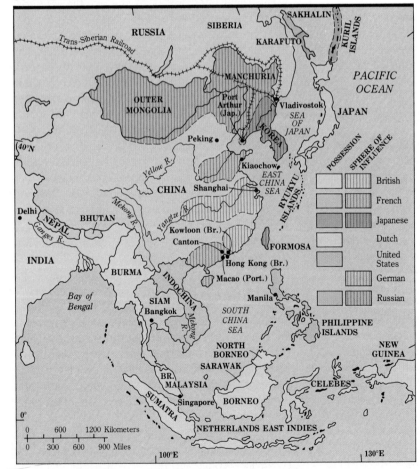

Have students observe the location of Manchuria (see map on page 426) in relation to Russia and Japan.

After winning the war with Russia, Japan repaired many of the Russian ships and built many new ones.

As the Chinese imperial government lost control over the trading practices of foreign powers in China, these powers carved out "spheres of influence." Foreign interference with ancient traditions led to an uprising by a group of Chinese known as Boxers who wanted to drive all foreigners from China. The Boxers laid seige to the residences of the representatives of the foreign powers in Peking. A multinational force was assembled to end the Boxers' seige. That force quickly smashed the Boxer Rebellion. What is a "sphere of influence"?

1902. Under its terms, Great Britain had to come to Japan's aid in the event of war. Once this alliance was concluded, Japan was free to move against Russia in Manchuria.

Tension between Russia and Japan mounted. Finally, in February 1904, the Japanese attacked the Russian fleet at Port Arthur, winning a decisive victory. This victory was followed by a successful attack on Russia's Baltic fleet. More successes followed for Japan.

Early in the war, the United States had favored Japan due to the fact that Russia's actions in Manchuria had threatened the Open Door. In time, however, the American attitude changed. As Japanese victories mounted, Americans became concerned that Japan would not free Manchuria from foreign control, but simply take Russia's place there.

In reality, both Russia and Japan had jeopardized the Open Door. In February 1904, therefore, the United States asked Japan and Russia to respect the "neutrality" and "administrative entity" of China. At the time, however, neither of the warring countries was willing to cooperate.

Later, in April 1905, the Japanese indicated their willingness to cooperate by informing the United

States that they would maintain the Open Door in Manchuria and restore the area to China. This change in attitude was due to the fact that although Japan was winning, its resources were becoming exhausted.

Finally, a month later, after its victory over the Russians at Tsushima Strait, Japan asked President Roosevelt to help negotiate a settlement of the war. Russia accepted the idea, and on June 8 the President invited Russia and Japan to a peace conference.

In August 1905 representatives of the two countries met with Roosevelt at Portsmouth, New Hampshire. Under the terms of the Treaty of Portsmouth, signed on September 5, Japan was awarded the Southern Manchurian Railroad and the southern half of Sakhalin island as well as Russia's lease on the Liaotung Peninsula. Further, Japan secured recognition of its control over Korea.[2] In return, the Japanese had to give up demands for an **indemnity,** or payment for war damages. Both Russia and Japan promised to maintain the Open Door in China.

---

[2] During the war, Japanese troops had moved through Korea to attack Manchuria. After the war, Japanese troops remained in Korea. Japan formally annexed Korea in 1910 and continued to rule until 1945.

Roosevelt saw the Philippines as an Achilles heel because the American fleet would have difficulty trying to fight over such long distances.

President Theodore Roosevelt met with representatives of Russia and Japan at Portsmouth to negotiate a peace treaty and put an end to the Russo-Japanese War. How did the results of the Conference affect United States-Japanese relations?

Thus, the Russo-Japanese War came to an end. For his efforts to bring about a peaceful settlement of the conflict, Roosevelt was awarded the Nobel Peace Prize in 1906. Roosevelt's efforts at Portsmouth, however, did not win him the friendship of Japan. The Japanese were angered by his refusal to support their demands for an indemnity.

Relations with Japan

Relations between Japan and the United States had been under a strain for some time. However, Roosevelt had taken steps to improve the situation between the two countries before the peace conference ever took place.

The Taft-Katsura Agreement. In July 1905 Roosevelt sent Secretary of War William Howard Taft to Tokyo. There, Taft negotiated an **executive agreement** (an agreement reached by the President with foreign powers that does not require the approval of the United States Senate) with Japan's foreign minister, Taro Katsura. In this agreement, the United States recognized Japan's dominance over Korea in return for Japan's promise to leave the Philippines under American control.

Thus, there would be no Open Door in Korea. Roosevelt agreed to this because he thought it was unlikely that the United States could stop the Japanese in Korea without going to war. In addition, he saw the Philippines as the next target for Japanese expansionism, and desired to protect American interests there.

Despite the improvement in relations that resulted from the Taft-Katsura Agreement, affairs between the United States and Japan worsened after the Treaty of Portsmouth. The Japanese were not only displeased with terms of the treaty, but also angered by events taking place in California.

Events in California. Although the total number of Japanese immigrants in America was relatively small, most had settled on the West Coast, especially in California. These immigrants aroused considerable resentment there. Some people objected to the newcomers because they took jobs from American workers. Others disliked the Japanese because they were of a different race.

A prime example of racial prejudice occurred in October 1906, when the San Francisco school board ordered all Oriental children to attend a separate school. The school board stated that it had ordered segregation so that white children would not be "affected by association with pupils of the Mongolian race." Japanese officials, angered by the order, lodged a protest with the United States government.

Roosevelt then stepped in to find a solution. He deplored the school board's action, mainly because it insulted Japan at a time when that country was rising to a position of world power. He feared that the Japanese would retaliate and that war would result.

Earlier, the President had stated his views on California's treatment of the Japanese in a letter to a friend:

I have no doubt that some Japanese . . . will behave badly to foreigners. They cannot behave worse than the State of California, through its legislature, is now behaving toward the Japanese. . . . These Pacific Coast people wish grossly to insult the Japanese and to keep out the Japanese immigrants on the ground that they are an immoral, degraded, and worthless race; and at the same time that they desire to do this for the Japanese . . . they expect to be given advantages in Oriental markets; and

The "great white fleet" included 16 battleships, 10 of them brand new. The fleet had never sailed as a unit before, and the cruise served as training for the navy.

with besotted folly are indifferent to building up the navy while provoking this formidable new power—a power jealous, sensitive, and warlike, and which if irritated could at once take both the Philippines and Hawaii from us if she obtained the upper hand on the seas.

In an attempt to solve the crisis, Roosevelt invited the San Francisco school board to attend a conference in Washington, D.C. In March 1907, as a result of this conference, the board withdrew its order. In return, the federal government agreed to take the immigration question under consideration. Roosevelt then issued an executive order that allowed the President to exclude immigrants with passports to another country if their presence in the United States would be detrimental to American workers.

The Gentlemen's Agreement. Further action on Japanese immigration was taken when the United States and Japan concluded the so-called Gentlemen's Agreement. In this agreement, Japan promised to restrict the emigration of Japanese workers to the continental United States by refusing to issue them passports. The United States could then apply Roosevelt's executive order to Japan. In other words, the United States could refuse to allow Japanese to enter the country unless their passports had been specifically issued for the United States.

After the Gentlemen's Agreement was made, Roosevelt wanted to impress Japan and other nations with the might of the United States. Therefore, he ordered the United States Navy's "great white fleet" to take a world cruise. During this cruise, which lasted from December 1907 to February 1909, the fleet stopped at Tokyo. The Japanese received the Americans cordially, and relations between the two countries began to improve.

The Root-Takahira Agreement. One evidence of improved relations between Japan and the United States was the agreement concluded by Secretary of State Elihu Root and Japanese Ambassador Baron Kogoro Takahira in November 1908. In the Root-Takahira Agreement, each nation pledged to (1) uphold the Open Door in China; (2) preserve that country's integrity by peaceful means; (3) respect the other's territorial rights in the Pacific; and (4) maintain the status quo in the Pacific. Thus, the agreement contributed toward stability in the Far East.

SECTION REVIEW

1. Identify the following: American-Asiatic Association, John Hay, "foreign devils," Boxers, Taft-Katsura Agreement, Gentlemen's Agreement, "great white fleet."
2. What were the main points of the Open Door proposal?
3. What role did President Roosevelt play in the Russo-Japanese War?
4. How did United States immigration policy affect relations with Japan?
5. What were the terms of the Root-Takahira Agreement?

2 The Panama Canal

There were other areas of the world more important to the United States than the Far East. In Latin America, the United States was particularly interested in Panama. Americans began directing their attention toward building a canal there. Indeed, one of the most important legacies of the Roosevelt administration was the Panama Canal.

Americans had been interested in building a canal across Central America since the mid-1800's. Such a canal would eliminate the trip around South America and shorten the voyage from New York to San Francisco by thousands of miles. The shorter trip would lower the cost of shipping and avoid altogether the cost of maintaining separate fleets on the Atlantic and Pacific. An interoceanic canal would have strategic as well as economic value. In the event of war, ships could move quickly between the two oceans, which would aid in the defense of the Western Hemisphere.

Canal Negotiations. As early as 1850, the United States and Great Britain signed the Clayton-Bulwer Treaty.[3] In this treaty, they agreed never to seek exclusive rights to build a canal through Panama or Nicaragua. Both agreed that the neutrality of any future canal would be maintained, that it would remain unfortified, and that there would be no attempt to control surrounding territory.

---

[3] The treaty was negotiated by Secretary of State John M. Clayton and the British minister to the United States, Sir Henry Lytton Bulwer.

Have students compare the proposed routes for the canal. Note that the presence of volcanoes in Nicaragua seemed a threat to the safety of the canal.

PROPOSED CANAL ROUTES AND THE PANAMA CANAL ZONE

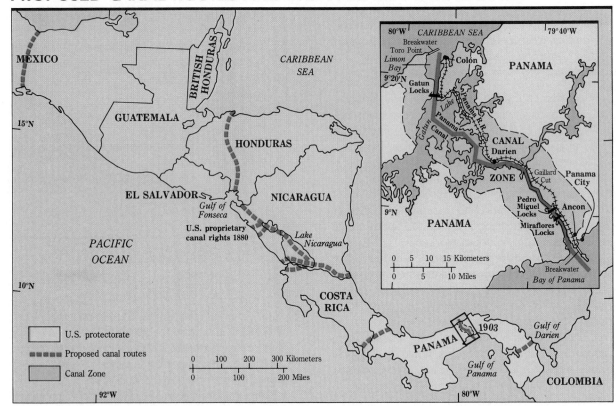

Although an agreement was reached, neither Great Britain nor the United States undertook to build a canal at that time. It was not until the late 1800's that the United States was motivated to begin such a project. During the Spanish-American War, Americans realized just how vital an interoceanic canal was to the defense of the United States. At that time, the U.S.S. *Oregon,* stationed on the West Coast, had to travel more than 14,000 miles (22,400 kilometers) to reach Cuba, and barely made it in time for the fighting. America's acquisitions in the Pacific, as well as the growth of its trade in the Far East, made it even more essential that ships be able to move quickly from one ocean to another.

Once the United States decided to build a canal, it sought to change the Clayton-Bulwer Treaty in order to make the project an entirely American venture. At the direction of President Roosevelt, who saw the canal as "one of the future highways of civilization," Secretary of State John Hay negotiated a new treaty with Great Britain.

Under the terms of the Hay-Pauncefote Treaty (1901), the British surrendered their rights under the Clayton-Bulwer Treaty. They did so because of the desire to maintain good relations with an increasingly powerful United States, and because of the need to deploy British troops elsewhere in the Caribbean.

Next, the United States had to choose a site for a canal and obtain the right to build it from the Central American country that owned the land. The choice lay between Panama, which was a province of Colombia, and Nicaragua. In November 1901 a commission set up by President McKinley to look into the matter recommended that the canal be built through Nicaragua. The commission chose Nicaragua mainly because a French company had received rights from Colombia to the land in Panama, which provided the shortest route.

In 1881 the French company, under the direction of its chief engineer, Ferdinand de Lesseps, started to build a canal across Panama. However, handicapped by lack of money and the unhealthful environment in

Roosevelt was prepared to seize the canal on the basis of an 1846 treaty with Colombia that guaranteed free transit across the Isthmus of Panama. The revolution in Panama made this action unnecessary.

Panama, the French discontinued work on the project in 1889.

By the time the United States was ready to select a site, the land rights in Panama had been acquired by a second French company, which was willing to sell those rights for $109 million. Rejecting this price as too high, the House of Representatives decided to support the Nicaraguan route, as the commission had suggested. However, the French company, anxious for the sale to go through because its rights to the land were due to expire, lowered its price to $40 million. Shortly thereafter, the commission recommended the Panamanian route. Congress agreed, and in June 1902 authorized Roosevelt to purchase the land rights owned by the French company, as well as to purchase from Colombia other land needed for the project.

At first, Colombia appeared somewhat reluctant to sell. However, when Secretary of State John Hay threatened to choose the Nicaraguan route, Colombia told its minister to the United States, Tomás Herrán, to go ahead with negotiations. An agreement was signed in January 1903.

This agreement, the Hay-Herrán Treaty, stated that the United States would receive a 99-year lease, with renewal privileges, on a strip of land 6 miles wide (9.6 kilometers) in Panama. Within this area, the United States would have control. In return, the United States was to pay Colombia $10 million, plus an annual sum of $250,000, beginning in 1912. In addition, Colombia was not to receive any part of the $40 million that was to go to the French company.

The United States Senate ratified the treaty in March 1903. Colombian leaders, however, raised objections. For one thing, they were not satisfied with the monetary provisions, claiming that the rights to an international waterway were worth far more than $10 million. In addition, they objected to Colombia's not receiving any part of the sum the United States had offered the French. If action were delayed, Colombia could collect the entire $40 million, since French rights in Panama were about to expire. Colombia's leaders also feared that by giving up land along the canal route, Colombia might lose control of Panama altogether.

Roosevelt had little patience with Colombia's objections and refused to allow any changes in the treaty. He sharply criticized Colombian leaders, saying, "Those contemptible little creatures in Bogotá ought to understand how much they are jeopardizing and imperiling their own future."

With Roosevelt's approval, Hay wrote to the American minister in Colombia on June 9. The message stated that if Colombia delayed or rejected the treaty, it could jeopardize "the friendly understanding between the two countries [and] action might be taken by Congress next winter which every friend of Colombia would regret." Despite this threat, the Colombian Senate rejected the Hay-Herrán Treaty in August.

A Revolt in Panama

Colombia's action infuriated Roosevelt. For a time, he thought of seizing Panama by force. However, a revolt occurred that made his plan unnecessary.

Panama had never been an easy area for Colombia to control. Geographically separated from the capital at Bogotá, the people of Panama felt that they were looked down upon by Colombians and had rebelled a number of times in the more than 50 years of Colombian rule.

On November 3, 1903, Panama again rebelled and declared its independence from Colombia. Much of the credit for starting the revolt in Panama was attributed to French company officials, especially Philippe Bunau-Varilla and William Nelson Cromwell. Bunau-Varilla was chief engineer for the company, while Cromwell, an American lawyer, handled its legal affairs.

The United States played a role in the revolt as well. In fact, the revolt was secretly planned and financed in New York City. Roosevelt, among others, provided moral support. Although not stated publicly, his views on the subject of Panama were well known. In a private letter of October 1903, the President wrote:

I freely say to you that I should be delighted if Panama were an independent state, or if it made itself so at this moment; . . . but for me to say so publicly would amount to an instigation of revolt, and therefore I cannot say it.

Even before the revolt broke out, Roosevelt had provided indirect military support by ordering the

Note the significance of Bunau-Varilla's negotiating for Panama. He was French, not Panamanian.

The canal cost about $375,000,000 to build.

U.S.S. *Nashville* to Panama. This action prevented Colombian troops from landing there and suppressing the revolt.

On November 6, the United States recognized the Republic of Panama. A week later, Philippe Bunau-Varilla became the country's first minister to the United States. Shortly thereafter, the Hay-Bunau-Varilla Treaty was concluded between the two countries.

The treaty gave the United States control over a canal zone 10 miles wide (16 kilometers), including the right to fortify the area. As outlined in the Hay-Pauncefote Treaty, the neutrality of the Canal Zone was to be maintained. The United States agreed to pay Panama $10 million, along with $250,000 a year, beginning 9 years after ratification of the treaty. In February 1904, the United States Senate ratified the treaty.

Roosevelt was very pleased with the arrangement. He spoke of his role in the revolt:

> *I did not lift my finger to incite the revolutionaries. . . . I simply ceased to stamp out the different revolutionary fuses that were already burning. . . . I deeply regretted . . . that the Columbian government rendered it imperative for me to take the action I took: but I had no alternative, consistent with the full*

performance of my duty to my own people, and to the nations of mankind.

Building the Canal

Having secured a site, the United States turned to the difficult task of building the canal. Digging began in 1904. A year later, however, work was virtually halted because of the large number of deaths in the Canal Zone. The high death rate was due, for the most part, to the prevalence of malaria and yellow fever, both of which were transmitted by certain types of mosquitoes. To combat the problem, Colonel William C. Gorgas of the United States Army Medical Department was appointed to establish a sanitation program.

Gorgas' program succeeded, and in 1907, under Lieutenant-Colonel George W. Goethals of the United States Army Corps of Engineers, work on the canal resumed. Goethals used over 40,000 workers to dig the "big ditch," as it was called.

The Panama Canal was regarded as one of the great engineering feats of the time. One remarkable feature was a set of five locks designed to raise and lower ships as they passed from one ocean to another. The project, which cost more than $365 million, took seven years to complete. The first trip through the Panama Canal was made in 1914. Many

Under the Roosevelt Corollary, the United States assumed the right to intervene in Latin America to protect American lives and property during periods of upheaval. During the next few years, United States marine and naval forces became a familiar sight in Latin America. In which Latin American countries did the United States become involved?

PANAMA

Walter Reed William Gorgas

For years people had dreamed of a great canal that would connect the Atlantic and Pacific Oceans. The French had failed largely because of the presence of three insidious diseases in the Canal Zone. Plague, yellow fever and malaria struck at most of the workers who were brought into the area. Even those who recovered were left so weak that they either had to be sent home or could work for no more than a few hours a day.

When Americans took over the canal-building project in 1904, they based their hopes on the work of two dedicated doctors, Walter Reed and William Gorgas. Both were part of a team of army doctors that had helped eradicate yellow fever in Cuba.

Walter Reed was born in Virginia in 1851. He joined the army in 1875 and spent many years teaching bacteriology in the army medical school.

After the outbreak of the Spanish-American War, he was called to Cuba, where he studied the causes of typhoid fever. In 1900 he became the head of a commission that studied an epidemic of yellow fever among American soldiers in Cuba.

Reed became aware of a theory held by a Cuban doctor, Carlos Finlay, who thought that the disease was carried by the bite of a certain species of mosquito. Working with several colleagues, Reed established that the carrier was indeed a mosquito. Several doctors and soldiers volunteered to be infected by the disease so that it could be studied.

At this point, Doctor William Gorgas was summoned to Cuba and put in charge of a mosquito-control program. Gorgas worked tirelessly to eliminate the stagnant water areas in which the mosquitoes bred.

Gorgas had been born in Alabama in 1854. As a young man he had survived an attack of yellow fever. After working with Reed in Cuba, he was considered an expert on control of the disease. In 1904 he was appointed chief sanitary officer of the Panama Canal Commission. His task was to bring yellow fever and malaria under control in the Canal Zone.

As he had done in Cuba, Gorgas concentrated on sanitary measures—draining swamps, installing sewers, and screening buildings. Soon the dangerous mosquitoes had no place to lay their eggs and no way to penetrate the houses of their potential victims. By 1906 yellow fever was under control. The incidence of malaria, which is also carried by mosquitoes, was reduced.

By waging a war against fleas and rats, Gorgas also helped to eliminate the plague. The conquest of these diseases removed one of the most serious obstacles to the success of the Panama Canal.

Americans were proud of their country's achievement in building the canal. Others, however, were embarrassed by their government's behavior toward Colombia.

SECTION REVIEW

1. Identify the following: Clayton-Bulwer Treaty, Ferdinand de Lesseps, Philippe Bunau-Varilla, Lieutenant-Colonel George W. Goethals.

2. Why did the French fail to build a canal across Panama?

3. Why did Colombia object to the terms of the Hay-Herrán Treaty?

4. What role did the United States play in Panama's revolt?

5. How did Americans feel about the building of the Panama Canal?

Have students develop a time line showing Roosevelt's policies in
Latin America and in the Far East.

3 A Continuing Interest in Foreign Affairs

Panama was but one of a number of areas that interested Roosevelt and his successor, William Howard Taft. Under their leadership, the United States demonstrated a continued interest in Latin America, the Far East, and, to a lesser degree, Europe. Although the two approached foreign affairs differently, both assumed an active role.

Roosevelt's Foreign Policy

Roosevelt believed that the United States had an obligation to promote democracy and economic growth throughout the world. He was also concerned with protecting the nation's interests in the Western Hemisphere. At times, he was willing to use force or the threat of it to gain certain ends. As a result of his fondness for quoting the African proverb, "Speak softly and carry a big stick," his policy at such times came to be known as the **"big stick policy."**

Venezuela. The "big stick" policy was implemented in Venezuela in 1902. Venezuela, under the rule of dictator Cipriano Castro, was deeply in debt to Germany, Great Britain, and Italy. Venezuela's failure to repay its debts caused the European nations to consider using force to obtain payment. However, in light of the Monroe Doctrine, they felt the need to clear the proposed action with the United States. In December 1901, a message was sent to Washington, denying that the powers involved had any intention of seizing territory in Venezuela.

Roosevelt, however, did not interpret the planned intervention as a violation of the Monroe Doctrine. He said:

> The United States does not guarantee any state against punishment if it misconducts itself, provided that punishment does not take the form of acquisition of territory by any non-American power.

Having tried and failed to get Castro to submit the dispute to arbitration, the European powers blockaded the Venezuelan coast. During the course of the blockade, some settlements were bombarded. As a result, Castro changed his mind and asked Roosevelt to propose arbitration.

By this time, Roosevelt had become alarmed that the European powers did have territorial ambitions in Venezuela. Thus, he readily agreed to Castro's requests, and submitted the proposal for arbitration to the Europeans on December 12, 1902. Roosevelt warned that the United States would not hesitate to use force to stop any European power from acquiring territory in Latin America. The proposal was accepted, and the question of Venezuelan debts ultimately was settled by the Permanent Court of Arbitration, which had been established at The Hague in the Netherlands.

One result of the Venezuelan incident was the Drago Doctrine, formulated in 1902 by Argentina's minister of foreign affairs, Luis M. Drago. This doctrine stated that no European power had the right to use force to collect debts in Latin America. Thus, the meaning of the Monroe Doctrine was extended to include debt collection as well as territorial acquisition. A modified version of the Drago Doctrine was adopted at a conference on world peace held in 1907 at The Hague.

The Dominican Republic. The Drago Doctrine was reinforced by Roosevelt's use of the "big stick" in the Dominican Republic in 1903. Like Venezuela, the Dominican Republic was heavily in debt to foreign powers, including the United States. Customs duties were its main source of revenue. These were provided chiefly through the customhouse in the port of Santo Domingo. In order to meet its financial obligations, the country often promised these duties to different creditors in advance, with the understanding that if the government were to **default** (fail to pay its debts), those creditors could take over the administration of customs.

In 1903 the Dominican government was on the verge of defaulting. About this time, a revolt put a new government into power. It was willing to allow the United States to control customs. The situation became critical in 1904 when American creditors were given preference over others. The Europeans protested, and armed intervention threatened.

Roosevelt took the opportunity to extend the Monroe Doctrine further. Having claimed that he had "about the same desire to annex [the Dominican Republic] as a gorged boa constrictor might have to swallow a porcupine wrong-end to," he announced what became known as the Roosevelt Corollary:

Have students identify the assumptions underlying the Roosevelt Corollary—e.g., that the U.S. government has the right and ability to judge what is "chronic wrongdoing" and what would be harmful to the "entire body of American nations."

All that this country desires is to see the neighboring countries stable, orderly, and prosperous. . . . If a nation shows that it knows how to act with reasonable efficiency and decency in social and political matters, if it keeps order and pays its obligations, it need fear no interference from the United States. Chronic wrongdoing, or an impotence which results in a general loosening of the ties of civilized society, may in America, as elsewhere, ultimately require intervention by some civilized nation, and in the Western Hemisphere the adherence of the United States to the Monroe Doctrine may force the United States . . . to the exercise of an international police power. . . .

We would interfere with them only if it becomes evident that their inability or unwillingness to do justice at home or abroad had violated the rights of the United States or had invited foreign aggression to the detriment of the entire body of American nations.

Thus, the emphasis of the Monroe Doctrine shifted from opposing intervention by European nations to proposing intervention by the United States. Roosevelt's announcement brought the crisis in the Dominican Republic to an end.

In 1905, acting on the Roosevelt Corollary, the United States signed an agreement with the Dominican Republic. This agreement gave the United States the right to administer Dominican customs and manage the debt. A **receivership** (an arrangement in which one party administers the property of another) was established. From this point on, 45 percent of the revenues from customs was given to the Dominican

This cartoon shows Theodore Roosevelt in the role of the world's policeman. Roosevelt was given the title because of his "big stick" diplomacy and his intervention in several international quarrels. Does the cartoonist agree with Roosevelt acting as an international policeman? Why or why not?

Have students speculate about what would have happened if the United States had annexed Cuba.

Have students locate Morocco on a world map (see Appendix).

government, and the rest was paid to foreign creditors.

Although the Senate at first withheld its approval of this agreement, Roosevelt carried it out by executive order. In 1907 the United States Senate ratified a treaty containing these provisions. Shortly thereafter, the United States withdrew from the Dominican Republic.

Cuba. In the meantime, the United States had intervened in Cuba, where widespread rioting had erupted following a national election in 1906. To put an end to this, Roosevelt sent troops to Havana and made Secretary of War Taft responsible for restoring order on the island. Once this was accomplished, the President set up a provisional government, which ruled until elections were held again in 1908.

After the newly elected government had taken over, American troops and officials returned to the United States. However, a naval base, which had been established at Guantanamo in accordance with the Platt Amendment of 1901, was maintained. Roosevelt's actions in Cuba pleased neither American imperialists, who favored annexation, nor anti-imperialists, who believed that the United States should not become involved in Cuban affairs.

The Algeciras Conference. Roosevelt also intervened in European affairs when he took part in the Moroccan crisis of 1905. The French had been trying to set up a protectorate in the North African country of Morocco since the turn of the century. To this end, France had made agreements with Great Britain, Italy, and Spain, that those powers would give up their interests in Morocco in return for French recognition of their rights elsewhere in North Africa.

French interests in Morocco, however, still conflicted with those of Germany. An earlier treaty had established the Open Door in Morocco, and the Germans wanted equal economic opportunity preserved there. An independent Morocco would

Dollar diplomacy encouraged overseas investment by American businesses. The United Fruit Company's establishment of plantations in Central America was one such endeavor. Besides providing employment, American companies helped improve living conditions. What benefits did the United States gain?

Taft made little effort to maintain a balance of power in Europe or Asia, as had Roosevelt.

Have students locate Nicaragua on a world map (see Appendix).

facilitate this goal. The situation grew worse when the German emperor, Kaiser Wilhelm, in a speech made at Tangiers on March 31, 1905, publicly supported Moroccan independence.

As tension heightened, the Kaiser asked Roosevelt to arrange an international conference to determine the status of Morocco. Although reluctant to depart from the traditional American policy of non-intervention in European affairs, Roosevelt agreed in order to prevent war. He persuaded France and Great Britain to attend a conference at Algeciras, Spain, in January 1906. The United States also sent delegates to the conference. Because of a deep distrust of Germany, the American delegates generally supported France and Great Britain at the conference table. As a result, Germany was isolated, and the settlement—embodied in the Act of Algeciras (1906)—reflected French desires.

In December 1906, the United States Senate ratified the Act of Algeciras. However the Senate pointed out that ratification did not in any way change American policy "which forbids participation by the United States in political questions which are entirely European in their scope." Thus, once the Moroccan crisis was over, the United States returned to its traditional policy of non-intervention in Europe.

Taft's Foreign Policy

William Howard Taft, who succeeded Roosevelt, upheld this policy. He believed that affairs in Europe were of no real concern to the United States. Taft did, however, play an active role in the Far East and Latin America, where he substituted "dollars for bullets" to further United States' interests. As a result, his foreign policy came to be called **"dollar diplomacy."**

The Far East. In the Far East, dollar diplomacy generally had little impact. After Taft's inauguration, a **consortium** (international business association) of French, British, and German bankers took steps to provide money for building railroads in southern and central China. About that time, an American banking group was formed for a similar purpose. The Americans asked for admission to the consortium, but were refused. In July 1909 Taft appealed directly to the Chinese, and the Americans ultimately were allowed to join. In May 1911 a four-power agreement

was signed between France, Great Britain, Germany, and the United States. A year later Japan and Russia joined the consortium.

Meanwhile Taft backed a proposal made by his Secretary of State, Philander C. Knox, for a consortium that would lend China enough money to purchase all foreign-held railroads within its borders, including those in Manchuria that were owned by Russia and Japan.[4] For the most part, the European powers were unenthusiastic. Japan and Russia, however, reacted strongly to the threat to their interests.

In July 1911 the two powers signed a treaty that deliberately violated the Open Door by staking out spheres of influence in Manchuria, with Russia getting the north and Japan the south. Thus, the loan to China fell through. Furthermore, as a result of the treaty signed by Japan and Russia, the United States lost prestige in the Far East.

Latin America. Although dollar diplomacy had little impact on the Far East, it played a larger role in Latin America. Under Taft, the United States intervened in Nicaragua, which was important to the United States because of the possibility that a foreign power might build a canal there.

In 1909 a revolt occurred in which José Zelaya, Nicaragua's dictator, was overthrown. Adolfo Díaz, who was a friend of the United States, took over the government. Secretary of State Knox was therefore able to negotiate the Knox-Castrillo Treaty in June 1911. This treaty established a receivership under which the United States administered Nicaraguan customs and managed its debt.

Before the Senate had a chance to act on the treaty, the Nicaraguan government defaulted on a British loan, and Knox persuaded American bankers to carry out the provisions of the treaty even though it had not yet been ratified. American bankers loaned Nicaragua $1.5 million in return for control of the country's finances as set forth in the Knox-Castrillo Treaty. In the end, the Senate rejected the treaty. Nevertheless, the financial arrangement continued.

Despite American aid, the situation in Nicaragua did not improve. The majority of people in the country still supported Zelaya, and staged a revolt against Díaz in 1912. At this point, the United States

---

[4] Russia owned the Chinese Eastern Railroad and Japan, the Southern Manchurian Railroad.

Have students speculate about the reaction of Latin Americans to Taft's policies. (The policies were resented.)

One purpose behind Wilson's missionary diplomacy in Latin America, the Caribbean, and the Pacific was to encourage economic stability. As seen by this American-built school in the Philippines, education was one way Wilson hoped to achieve this ideal. What other means were used by the United States?

intervened, sending a large force of Marines to Nicaragua to protect American interests there. In December, Taft outlined his reasons for intervention:

> *The national benefit to the United States is two-fold. First, it is obvious that the Monroe Doctrine is more vital in the neighborhood of the Panama Canal and the zone of the Caribbean than anywhere else. . . . Hence, the United States has been glad to encourage and support American bankers who were willing to lend a helping hand to the financial rehabilitation of such countries because this financial rehabilitation and the protection of their custom-houses from being the prey of would-be dictators would remove at one stroke the menace of foreign creditors and the menace of revolutionary disorder.*
>
> *The second advantage of the United States is that . . . the Republics of Central America and the Caribbean possess great natural wealth. They need only a measure of stability and the means of financial regeneration to enter upon an era of peace and prosperity, bringing profit and happiness to themselves and at the same time creating conditions sure to*

> *lead to a flourishing interchange of trade with this country. . . .*

Once the revolt was suppressed, Secretary of State Knox negotiated a treaty granting the United States exclusive rights to build a canal in that country, to establish a naval base on the Pacific Coast, and to lease two of Nicaragua's Caribbean Islands. For these rights, plus other considerations, the United States would pay Nicaragua $3 million. The Senate, however, again failed to ratify the treaty. Marines remained in Nicaragua for several years to see that the agreement made with the American bankers was carried out.

Taft and the Monroe Doctrine. In another crisis that took place during the Taft administration, the Monroe Doctrine was once more extended. In 1911 a Japanese company tried to buy land in Lower California (Baja). The United States opposed this purchase for strategic reasons, because it did not want a strong power on its southern border. Therefore, the American government registered its disapproval. As a result, the Japanese backed off, and the crisis came to an end. Senator Henry Cabot Lodge used the land purchase crisis to establish a broad policy:

The cooling-off treaties were suggested to Wilson by Bryan.

During the crisis Wilson ordered the navy not to take any action that might be misinterpreted by Japan. Contrast Wilson's approach with Roosevelt's.

When any harbor or other place in the American continents is so situated that the occupation thereof for naval or military purposes might threaten the communications or the safety of the United States, the Government of the United States could not see without grave concern the actual or potential possession of such harbor or other place by any Government, not American, as to give that Government practical power of control for naval or military purposes.

Thus, any attempt to sell strategic land located in the Americas to a nation or company outside the Western Hemisphere would be opposed by the United States. This Lodge Corollary to the Monroe Doctrine, as it became known, was approved by the Senate in 1912.

SECTION REVIEW

1. Identify the following: Cipriano Castro, Luis M. Drago, Kaiser Wilhelm, Philander C. Knox, Henry Cabot Lodge.
2. What principle was established by the Roosevelt Corollary?
3. What role did the United States play in the Moroccan crisis?
4. How did the United States become involved in Nicaragua?
5. What developments led to the Lodge Corollary?

4 Woodrow Wilson's Missionary Diplomacy

The election of Woodrow Wilson in November 1912 promised a significant change in American foreign policy. In his campaign speeches, Wilson pledged to dispense with the approaches followed by Roosevelt and Taft. Instead, he wanted to promote democracy and further the cause of world peace. This new policy was called **"missionary diplomacy"** because its purpose was to help other countries.

One example of missionary diplomacy was the **"cooling-off" treaties.** Under the terms of such treaties, international disputes were referred to a commission that would investigate and make a report. This usually took about a year. During this year—the

"cooling-off" period—the parties involved promised to refrain from war. Shortly after he became Wilson's Secretary of State, William Jennings Bryan negotiated treaties with 30 countries and secured 21 ratifications.

The Far East

Wilson moved to implement missionary diplomacy in certain specific areas. One of these was the Far East, where he took steps to repudiate dollar diplomacy. In 1913 he ended American participation in the consortium formed to finance the building of railroads in China. He did so on the grounds that it endangered China's independence. American bankers, who had never been enthusiastic, withdrew, and the final agreement was signed without the United States in April 1913.

Relations with Japan presented greater difficulties for Wilson's policy. California had never given up its efforts to restrict Japanese immigration. In May 1913 the state passed an alien land law, which prohibited the purchase of land by persons "ineligible for citizenship." Orientals were considered "ineligible for citizenship" because the naturalization laws of the time stated that only whites and blacks could be citizens. Once the act was passed, therefore, Japanese could not buy or inherit land in California.

Japan was angered by California's treatment of its immigrants. Wilson did nothing at first to remedy the situation. However, after he realized that war between the United States and Japan might break out over this question, he acted. He appealed directly to California, and sent Secretary of State Bryan to that state to persuade the legislature to modify its stand.

Nevertheless, the law was passed. On the same day, the Japanese government sent an official protest to Washington. Among other things, it stated that in allowing California's action, the American government had failed to uphold the terms of an earlier treaty in which the United States had promised to treat Japanese immigrants fairly.

After this, relations with Japan grew worse. American military leaders begged Wilson to send battleships to the Far East to forestall any attack on the Philippines. Instead, the President chose to use diplomatic means to handle the crisis. Such means were not completely effective, and relations between

Ask students if they think Latin Americans could tell the difference among the policies of Roosevelt, Taft, and Wilson.

William Jennings Bryan (center), as Wilson's Secretary of State, believed in arbitration of differences between countries. Bryan worked out arbitration treaties with over thirty nations for settlement of disputes. These treaties were part of Wilson's missionary diplomacy. What was missionary diplomacy?

the United States and Japan continued on an uneasy course.

Latin America

Wilson used missionary diplomacy in Latin America as well as the Far East. In 1914 he proposed a treaty in which the United States expressed regret over its treatment of Colombia during the Panama Canal crisis, and agreed to pay the country $25 million. The treaty was defeated in the Senate, where supporters of Roosevelt had a majority.

In Nicaragua, however, the Wilson administration did not practice missionary diplomacy. Instead it followed the policies of its predecessors. Wilson had inherited the still-unratified treaty that Knox had negotiated with Nicaragua, giving America the right to build a canal there. Secretary of State Bryan wanted to add a provision that would allow the United States to intervene militarily in times of crisis. He negotiated a new agreement in August 1914.

The terms of the new agreement, the Bryan-Chamorro Treaty, were about the same as those outlined in the earlier one. Nicaragua received $3 million in return for granting the United States exclusive rights to build a canal, to establish a naval base on the Pacific Coast, and to lease two of Nicaragua's Caribbean

islands. In addition, however, the United States was given the right of intervention as proposed by Bryan. After some delay, the Senate ratified the treaty without Bryan's provision, in February 1916.

The Wilson administration also intervened in Haiti. The country was in debt to many foreign powers, including the United States. France and Germany were considering the use of direct measures to straighten out Haiti's finances. Before they could act, a revolt in Haiti brought Vibrun Guillaume Sam to power. At the time, the debt stood at about $24 million, and Wilson proposed that the United States take over Haitian customs.

In the summer of 1915, President Sam was assassinated. To prevent further chaos, as well as European intervention, Wilson ordered the Marines to Haiti. The revolt was put down, and a new president signed a treaty with the United States. Under its terms, Haiti had to get American approval before it could increase the size of its debt or lower its tariffs. Marines remained in the country until 1934, and some financial control was maintained until 1941.

The situation in the Dominican Republic was similar to that in Haiti. Even after years of American control over customs, the country's finances remained in a chaotic state. Because the debt had increased, the United States in 1914 appointed an official to check

Have students use the map to make a list of U.S. acquisitions.

government spending. However, the Dominican government was reluctant to give the United States any further control. After a revolt occurred, Wilson sent troops to occupy the country. They remained for eight years.

Wilson's ideas were challenged severely in Mexico. Dictator Porfirio Díaz had controlled the country for many years, during which time American companies had invested more than $1 billion in Mexican resources. However, in November 1910, a revolt broke out under the leadership of Francesco

Madero, who in May 1911 replaced Díaz and set up a liberal government. President Taft recognized the Madero government, but other than placing an embargo on the shipment of arms to Madero's opponents, did not intervene.

Madero was not in power long. In February 1912 he was assassinated, and the **reactionary** (extreme conservative) General Victoriano Huerta took over the government. Although the European powers recognized the Huerto government, Taft refused to do so. He left the problem for Wilson to solve.

UNITED STATES ACQUISITIONS 1858–1917

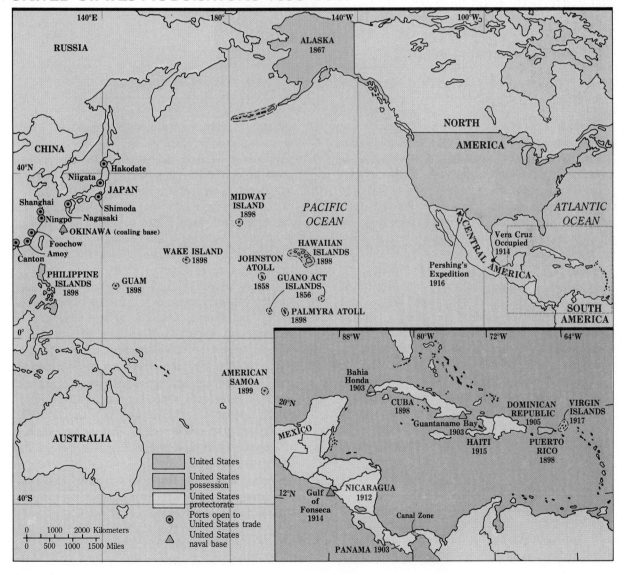

Ask students to evaluate to what extent it is possible for the United States to increase democracy in other countries.

Pancho Villa (center) sought to overthrow the Carranza government. In fighting against that government, Villa's guerrillas came into conflict with the United States when they shot some American engineers working in northern Mexico. Later Villa and his followers crossed the United States border and raided the town of Columbus, New Mexico. What action did President Wilson take when told of these attacks on American citizens?

The situation was difficult for Wilson. After he was elected, business groups urged him to recognize the Huerta government because they felt that American investments were safer under more stable dictatorships. The new President, however, was willing to recognize only governments that derived their authority from the consent of the governed. He withheld recognition, hoping that this action would further democracy in Mexico.

In March 1913 Wilson showed further disapproval of Huerta by limiting American investments in Mexico. As opposition to Huerta grew, Wilson tried another tactic. He offered to reinstate dollar diplomacy by promoting American loans to Mexico if free elections were held in which Huerta was not a candidate. Huerta, however, refused the offer.

Therefore, Wilson continued to withhold recognition, and instituted an arms embargo against all parties. He was not willing to go further than that until he saw how events progressed in Mexico. The United States' policy toward that country would be one of "watchful waiting."

In October 1913 Huerta formally proclaimed a military dictatorship in Mexico. Shortly thereafter, Wilson made a speech at Mobile, Alabama, in which he stated that the United States "will never again seek one additional foot of territory by conquest." The statement became known as the Mobile Doctrine

and was a prime example of the President's basic views on foreign policy.

However, Wilson did attempt to put further pressure on the Huerta government. He requested that Huerta resign, and made it clear that the United States would force him from office if necessary. To this end, the United States began selling arms to Venustiano Carranza, Huerta's principal opponent. In addition, Wilson sent ships to prevent the delivery of European arms to Huerta.

Tension between Mexico and the United States was increased by an incident that took place in April 1914. At that time, sailors from an American ship anchored off Tampico, Mexico, went ashore for supplies. When they inadvertently entered a restricted area of the city, they were arrested by Huerta's troops. The Mexican officer in charge apologized, and released the sailors almost at once. Nonetheless, Admiral Henry T. Mayo was not satisfied. He demanded, among other things, that the commander at Tampico raise the American flag over the city and fire a 21-gun salute.

When this was not done, Wilson asked Congress for permission to use force to uphold the rights of the United States:

The [Tampico] incident cannot be regarded as a trivial one. . . . But had it stood by itself, it might have been attributed to the ignorance or arrogance of a single officer. Unfortunately, it was not an isolated case. A series of incidents have recently occurred which cannot but create the impression that the representatives of General Huerta were willing to go out of their way to show disregard for the dignity and the rights of this government, and felt perfectly safe in doing what they pleased. . . .

The manifest danger of such a situation was that such offenses might grow from bad to worse until something happened of so gross and intolerable a sort as to lead directly and inevitably to armed conflict. It was necessary that the apologies of General Huerta and his representatives . . . be such as to attract the attention of the whole population to their significance, and such as to impress upon General Huerta himself the necessity of seeing to it that no further occasions for explanation and expressed regrets should arise. . . .

Before Congress could act, Wilson made his move. Having learned that a German ship was on its way to Vera Cruz with arms for Huerta, Wilson ordered Mayo to proceed to that port and prevent the cargo from being unloaded. On April 21, 1914, American forces took the city. In the process, 19 Americans were killed, and 71 were wounded. The Mexicans suffered greater losses, with 126 killed and 195 wounded.

As a result of American action at Vera Cruz, Huerta broke off diplomatic relations with the United States. War became a real possibility. Wilson managed to avoid this, however, by accepting the offer of Argentina, Brazil, and Chile—the so-called ABC Powers—to mediate the dispute.

In mid-1914 representatives of the United States, Mexico, and the ABC Powers met at Niagara Falls, Ontario. There, the mediators proposed that Huerta step down and a provisional government be formed to run the country. On its part, the United States was to receive no indemnity for costs incurred at Vera Cruz. Although Mexico rejected the plan, Huerta resigned in July, and Carranza became the new president. In October 1915, the United States recognized the Carranza government.

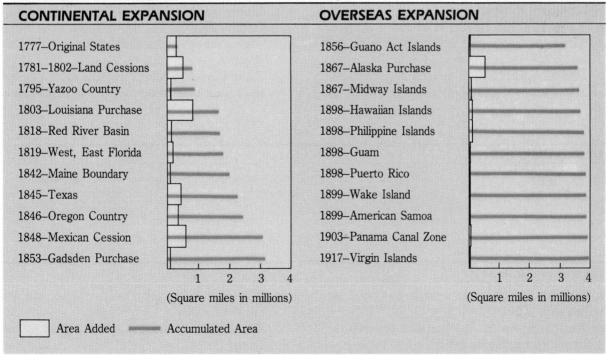

Wilson and Bryan at first favored Villa because he represented himself as a reformer. Wilson had wanted Huerta to resign, but did not approve of Carranza either.

Huerta's resignation had not ended civil war in Mexico. In the north, Carranza was opposed by Francisco (Pancho) Villa, who led a revolt against the new government. Villa hoped to discredit Carranza by forcing the United States to intervene in Mexico. In January 1916 Villa and his band stopped a Mexican train at Santa Ysabel and shot 18 American engineers who were in Mexico at the invitation of Carranza. Shortly thereafter, 17 more Americans were killed when Villa staged a raid on Columbus, New Mexico.

In response, Wilson sent General John J. Pershing across the border with a large force to capture Villa. Pershing pursued Villa deep into Mexico with no success. The pursuit penetrated farther south than expected, arousing the antagonism of Carranza—who had agreed to the expedition—and of the Mexican people. A joint commission was formed to work out the problems between the two countries. Finally, events in Europe drew America's attention away from troubles in Mexico. Early in 1917, when war with Germany became imminent, Wilson withdrew Pershing's force.

SECTION REVIEW

1. Identify the following: Bryan-Chamorro Treaty, General Victoriano Huerta, Admiral Henry T. Mayo, ABC Powers.
2. What did Wilson propose to do about relations with Colombia?
3. Why did the United States intervene in Haiti?
4. Why did Wilson refuse to recognize the Huerta government?

CHAPTER 21   REVIEW

SUMMARY

1. During the early 1900's, the United States became increasingly involved in foreign affairs.
2. In China, the United States sought to establish an Open Door policy.
3. The United States made efforts to improve uneasy relations with Japan.
4. The United States acquired exclusive rights to build a canal across the Isthmus of Panama, and completed the project in 1914.
5. Under President Theodore Roosevelt, the United States followed an aggressive foreign policy that included the threat of force to promote American interests.
6. Under President Taft, foreign policy concentrated on promoting American business and banking interests around the world.
7. During the Roosevelt and Taft administrations, the Monroe Doctrine was extended to allow the United States to take a more active role in Latin America.
8. Under President Wilson, foreign policy emphasized the causes of democracy and world peace.

VOCABULARY

indemnity	default	dollar diplomacy	missionary diplomacy
executive agreement	receivership	consortium	cooling-off treaty
big stick policy			reactionary

REVIEW QUESTIONS

1. Why did the United States pursue an Open Door policy in China?
2. What were the causes of tension between the United States and Japan?
3. What problems were involved in building the Panama Canal?
4. Why was the Panama Canal important to the United States?

5. How did Roosevelt uphold and extend the Monroe Doctrine?
6. How did Taft attempt to implement dollar diplomacy?

7. How did Wilson's foreign policy conflict with that of Roosevelt and Taft?
8. How did Wilson put his ideas on foreign policy into practice?

DISCUSSION

1. Do you think the United States was justified in the actions it took to secure rights to build the Panama Canal?
2. What should be the chief objectives of American foreign policy?

3. Are moral considerations such as Wilson's a sound basis for American foreign policy? Why or why not?
4. How does current foreign policy compare to that of the early 1900's?

USING MAPS

Refer to the map on page 426 and answer the following questions:

1. Which European powers had spheres of influence in Asia?
2. What power controlled Formosa?

3. What power controlled Kowloon?
4. What cities were connected by the Trans-Siberian Railroad?
5. What powers had conflicting interests in Manchuria? Why?

USING SKILLS

In August 1913, after General Huerta came to power in Mexico, President Wilson sent a special message to Congress. Read the excerpt from that message and answer the questions that follow:

The peace, prosperity and contentment of Mexico mean more, much more, to us than merely an enlarged field for our commerce and enterprise. They mean an enlargement of the field of self-government and the realization of the hopes and rights of a nation with whose best aspirations, so long suppressed and disappointed, we deeply sympathize. We shall yet prove to the Mexican people that we know how to serve them without first thinking how we serve ourselves. . . .

1. Does Wilson think that American economic interests are at stake in Mexico?
2. Does Wilson think that American interest in Mexico is (a) entirely selfish, (b) entirely unselfish, or (c) partly selfish and partly unselfish?

1	Europe in 1914	447
2	A Neutral America	448
3	America at War	453
4	The Aftermath	465

WORLD WAR I

You have laid upon me this double obligation: "We are relying upon you, Mr. President, to keep us out of war, but we are relying upon you, Mr. President, to keep the honor of the nation unstained."

WOODROW WILSON

In 1914 the United States found itself in the midst of a European crisis. A war had broken out in Europe that over the next few years engulfed 28 countries including the United States. Although the principal campaigns were fought in Europe, armies also fought in the Middle East, Africa, and China, and navies clashed on all the oceans.

The people of the time called the conflict the World War, or the Great War, because they believed that never again would there be another like it. Although the United States tried to remain neutral, it was drawn into the conflict. The war had a profound effect on the nation, touching on all aspects of life. When the fighting was over, the United States emerged as one of the greatest powers in the world.

1 Europe in 1914

During the early 1900's **militarism,** the policy of maintaining strong armed forces and being ready and willing to use them, was on the rise in Europe. Rival countries had been in an arms race for many years, and some had begun forming protective alliances. Because of the way the alliances were set up, an attack on one nation by another was all that was needed to trigger a war involving many countries.

The Alliance System

Two major alliances were established. One was the Triple Alliance, which was made up of Germany, Austria-Hungary, and Italy. The other was the Triple Entente, which was made up of Great Britain, France, and Russia. In addition, various smaller nations were associated loosely or informally with each alliance. In each case, member nations signed treaties in which they agreed to go to each other's aid in time of crisis.

On June 28, 1914, Archduke Franz Ferdinand, heir to the throne of Austria-Hungary, visited Sarajevo, the capital of the Balkan kingdom of Bosnia. While there, he was shot and killed by Gavrilo Princip, a 19-year-old Bosnian student who was a member of a Serbian nationalist group. At the time, Serbia was a small Balkan country whose people were Slavs. Princip's group resented Austria-Hungary's rule over the Slavs who lived in the Balkans and wanted the Slavs to unite and form independent states.

The assassination of the Archduke was the spark that turned existing tensions into war. The Austrians, who were afraid of the Serbian influence on their Slavic minority, blamed the Serbian government for the assassination and mobilized for war against Serbia. The Russians, declaring themselves protectors of the Slavs, mobilized to counter the Austrian threat by coming to the aid of Serbia. This brought Germany to the side of its ally, Austria. Germany then turned on France, demanding to know where that country stood. When France gave Germany a defiant answer, it declared war on the French.

On August 3, 1914, the Germans struck at France through the neutral country of Belgium. In doing so, they ignored a treaty signed in 1839 by Germany, Great Britain, France, and Russia. That treaty had guaranteed Belgium's neutrality and borders. As a result, the next day Great Britain declared war on Germany and Austria.

Other nations began to join in. Italy, because it had territorial grievances against Austria, switched its allegiance to the Triple Entente, which became known as the Allied Powers. Rumania, Greece, and Japan also joined the Allied side. Germany and Austria-Hungary, left alone, became known as the Central Powers. Later they were supported by Bulgaria and Turkey.

The American Response

The swift chain of events that took place in Europe stunned most Americans. They condemned the nations taking part in the growing conflict and saw no

Contrast American attitudes toward World War I with attitudes toward the Spanish-American War. Note that events in Europe received little media coverage in the U.S. until combat actually

began. Most Americans thought of the war as just another squabble that would be over quickly. Events in Mexico (Huerta vs. Carranza) received more attention.

SECTION REVIEW

1. Identify the following: Triple Alliance, Triple Entente, Archduke Franz Ferdinand, Gavrilo Princip, Allied Powers, Central Powers.
2. What led to the formation of alliances in Europe during the 1900's?
3. What effect did the assassination of Archduke Franz Ferdinand have on the rest of Europe?
4. What was the American reaction to events in Europe?

2 A Neutral America

Despite Wilson's plea to remain neutral and their own condemnation of the war, Americans soon began to take sides. Many Americans felt deep social and cultural ties to England. In addition, the United States had not forgotten the aid France had given the American colonists during the Revolutionary War. Furthermore, the Central Powers seemed to be the chief aggressors. They had refused outside arbitration after Archduke Franz Ferdinand was killed, had ignored Belgium's right as a neutral nation, and were conducting the war chiefly on Allied soil.

Other Americans, however, viewed things differently. Many of the 8 million or so Americans of German and Austrian extraction tended to side with the Central Powers. So did many Americans of Russian and Irish extraction. Many Russian-Americans could not forget or forgive the indignities they had suffered under Russia's tsarist regime. Many Irish-Americans hated England for its long-standing domination of Ireland.

The Role of Propaganda

American sentiment about the war was heightened by the huge amount of propaganda put forth by both sides. The British had proclaimed a blockade of all ports under German control, and they used their naval might to enforce it. The Germans called it "the hunger blockade," pointing out that it was against international law, and used it for propaganda purposes. They launched a massive campaign to convince Americans that by blockading German ports, the British were starving innocent women and children.

The assassination of Archduke Franz Ferdinand and his wife proved to be a fateful event. Within a month the continent of Europe was ablaze with war. What was the immediate reaction of most Americans to these events?

reason for the United States to get involved in a conflict that they believed was based on national pride and greed.

Aware of these sentiments, President Wilson moved quickly to set forth a detached role for the United States. On August 20, 1914, he told the American people:

The effect of the war upon the United States will depend upon what American citizens say and do. Every man who really loves America will act and speak in the true spirit of neutrality, which is the spirit of impartiality and friendliness to all concerned. . . . Divisions among us would be fatal to our peace of mind and might seriously stand in the way of the proper performance of our duty as the one great nation at peace, the one people holding itself ready to play a part of impartial mediation.

The British, on the other hand, focused on German actions in Belgium. The Germans had not expected any resistance when they overran Belgium. When the Belgians fought back, the Germans retaliated by destroying libraries and churches and shooting civilian hostages. They went so far as to execute Edith Cavell, an English nurse who helped many convalescent Allied soldiers to escape. The German Chief of Staff himself admitted that "our advance in Belgium is certainly brutal." But he excused the brutality on the ground that "we are fighting for our lives and all who get in the way must take the consequences." The British played up the brutality, accused the Germans of committing all kinds of atrocities, and argued that the war was one between civilization and barbarism.

Economic Considerations

Economic considerations also played a part in American sentiment. The United States had had extensive trade dealings with Europe for years. It wanted to maintain those dealings and at the same time capitalize on the growing wartime demand for American goods.

There was, however, a great deal of difference in the amounts of trade the United States had with each of the powers. In 1914, for example, nearly $825 million in trade was with the Allies, while less than $170 million was with the Central Powers. The war made the gap even greater, largely because of the British blockade of the North Sea.

By 1916, although the Central Powers made an effort to trade more with the United States, trade with Germany and Austria was reduced to $2 million. At the same time, trade with the Allies rose to more than $3 billion. Knowing that Americans would resent the loss of trade with the Central Powers, the Allies made a conscious effort to buy extra amounts of goods such as cotton, which in the past had a large German market. This effort served to keep America from suffering economically and to further increase America's dealings with the Allies.

Problems with Great Britain

Although American sentiment in general tended to favor the Allies, some Allied practices irritated Americans. One such practice had to do with shipping rights. Shortly before the war broke out, the major world powers had tried to draw up a code defining the rights of neutrals in time of crisis. Out of this effort came some guidelines about goods and equipment being shipped from one country to another during wartime.

All **war materiel** (weapons and equipment) was considered **contraband**, or prohibited goods. As such, it could be seized by a declared enemy of the nation to which it was being sent. Non-military goods that could be used as military supplies could also be seized under certain circumstances. Food, raw materials, and finished goods for civilian use were the exception. They could not be seized under any conditions.

The problem arose because the British stopped American ships carrying non-military goods to the Central Powers. When the United States protested, Great Britain argued that the goods could end up being used by German soldiers. The British reasoned

EUROPE IN 1914

Americans were also outraged at the news that Germany had used poison gas against the Allies.

that almost anything that helped the Central Powers was detrimental to the Allied cause, and therefore should be treated as contraband.

In addition to seizing American ships carrying goods for the Central Powers, the British also blacklisted American companies that did not comply with their rules, and tampered with American mail to Germany and Austria. While these acts made Americans angry and brought a storm of official protests from the White House, the situation was allowed to go on. There were several reasons for this. For one, Allied trade had increased so sharply that the British actions did not seriously damage America's overall volume of trade. For another, the British blockade was so thorough that about the only way to oppose it was to declare war on Great Britain, which the Americans were not willing to do. And, more importantly, the problems with the British seemed minor in comparison to those with Germany.

Problems with Germany

Upset by the British blockade and the fact that America's policy of non-involvement had led to a growing trade with the Allies and a diminishing one with the Central Powers, the Germans were determined to disrupt Allied shipping. To do this, they introduced into sea warfare a potent new weapon—the **submarine,** or U-boat, a ship capable of operating under water. The effectiveness of the submarine became clear for the first time in September 1914, when two German submarines sank four British ships in the North Sea. Americans were enraged. They argued that the submarines flouted international law and the rules of "civilized war."

On February 14, 1915, Germany announced that submarines would sink without warning any Allied ships found in the waters around the British Isles. They further warned that since submarines might not be able to tell the difference between Allied and neutral vessels, neutral countries should keep their ships out of the area. The announcement further angered Americans because, according to international law, a ship had to warn a non-military target before attacking it so that the passengers and crew could be evacuated.

The submarine, however, did not fit into the existing rules of warfare. In order to give such a

warning, it would have to surface. This would make it vulnerable even to the light guns often carried on merchant ships. Therefore, the Germans chose to ignore the law and fire on Allied vessels without warning.

The Germans also warned that, because British ships often flew the flags of neutral nations rather than their own, all vessels headed for Allied ports would be attacked. A furious President Wilson, however, refused to stop American ships from sailing into the blockade zone. He viewed the German action as a threat to American lives, trade, and rights as a neutral nation. He warned Germany that if an American were killed or an American ship sunk, the United States would consider it "an indefensible violation of neutral rights," would hold the German government strictly accountable, and would take any steps necessary.

The *Lusitania*. In the spring of 1915, the Germans attacked the British passenger liner *Falaba*, killing an American passenger. On May 1 an American ship, the *Gulflight*, was torpedoed but not sunk. In the panic that followed, however, three Americans died.

On the same day the British luxury liner *Lusitania* sailed from New York with 1257 passengers, many of them prominent Americans. The German embassy had placed warnings in New York newspapers telling people not to sail on the *Lusitania* because it was sailing into a war zone. The British, aware of the problem, warned the ship's captain to steer a zigzag course as protection against submarines. Both the German and the British advice went unheeded.

On May 7 German submarines torpedoed the liner off the Irish coast. The torpedo struck the ship's starboard bow and blew up a boiler. Within a half hour, the ship sank. The death toll of 1198 passengers and crew included 128 Americans.

While the sinking of the *Lusitania* brought forth an enormous public outcry, most Americans still did not want to take an active part in the war. President Wilson said:

> There is such a thing as a man being too proud to fight. There is such a thing as a nation being so right that it does not need to convince others by force that it is right.

The week after the *Lusitania* went down, the American government delivered a carefully worded note to German officials. The note stated that the

Wilson's stand for neutrality without abridgement of the rights of American citizens was put to the test when the *Lusitania* was sunk by a German submarine. Americans had died, and the distinction between "combatants" and "civilians" seemed to disappear. What steps did Wilson take in this crisis?

United States expected the German government to "make reparation so far as reparation is possible for injuries which are without measure" and take "immediate steps to prevent the recurrence of anything so obviously subversive of the principles of warfare."

Germany responded 18 days later. It justified the sinking on the grounds that the passengers had been warned not to sail on the ship and that the ship was carrying munitions and had orders to sink submarines on sight. The Germans suggested that the United States investigate these matters.

Secretary of State William Jennings Bryan wanted President Wilson to press for arbitration and to warn Americans not to sail on belligerent vessels in the war zone. He also wanted the President to send a note to the British protesting their violations of neutral rights. This, he felt, would show the world that America was truly committed to neutrality. President Wilson, however, listened to other advisers and refused to do as Bryan asked. As as result, Bryan resigned.

The next day, President Wilson sent another note to Germany, repeating the earlier demands. The Germans replied, but in an inconclusive way. At the same time, however, they secretly ordered submarine commanders not to attack passenger-carrying vessels. When the attacks stopped, Wilson was appeased, believing that the Germans were "modifying their methods."

The Sussex Pledge. In August 1915 the attacks began again, and the British passenger liner *Arabic* was sunk. President Wilson protested, and submarine activity again came to a stop.

Then, on March 24, 1916, German submarines torpedoed the French steamer *Sussex* in the English Channel. Although the ship did not sink, several American passengers were killed. At first President Wilson tried to get the Allies to stop arming their merchant ships so that the U-boats would feel safe to

Ask students what might have happened if Roosevelt had been President at this time.

SHIPBUILDING AND SUBMARINE SINKINGS, 1917–1918

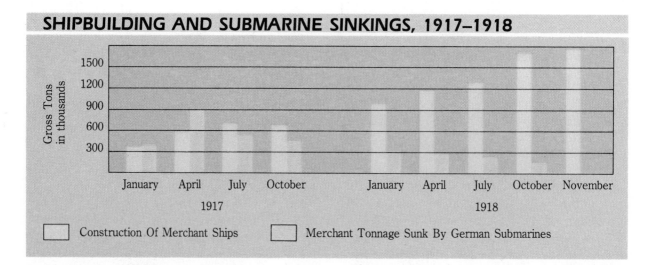

surface and give warning before attacking. The British, however, refused to do this, saying that it would leave their ships vulnerable to German attack.

The British refusal led President Wilson to reassert his earlier policy holding Germany fully accountable for any American lives lost in submarine attacks. He also went before Congress to declare that unless Germany stopped attacking passenger and freight vessels, the United States would sever diplomatic relations with that country. The result of this threat was the Sussex Pledge, an agreement in which the German government said it would suspend surprise submarine attacks.

On the Home Front

President Wilson hoped that the threat of American entry into the war would be enough to moderate German actions and keep America at peace. At the same time, he knew that before America could enter any war, it would have to build up its small armed forces and limited supply of weapons.

Preparedness and Pacifism. Some Americans had been arguing for **preparedness,** military readiness for war, since the early days of the war in Europe. The foremost champion of preparedness was Theodore Roosevelt at whose urging summer military-training camps were set up for business and professional men at Plattsburg, New York in 1915.

There were other Americans, however, whose strong feelings about American involvement led them to become **pacifists**—people opposed to war or

violence as a means of settling a dispute. Their views were expressed in a song which became popular in 1915—"I Didn't Raise My Boy to Be a Soldier." The cover for the sheet music for the song showed a gray-haired woman protecting her son from the shells bursting around him.

One ardent pacifist was auto magnate Henry Ford. In December 1915 he set sail with a group of pacifists in his "peace ship," the *Oscar II*. The group traveled to the neutral Scandinavian countries, hoping to persuade them to use their influence against the war.

That same month, President Wilson went before Congress with a preparedness program. Congress, however, did not pass it until mid-1916, at which time it ordered a build-up of the armed forces. This, Congress felt, would make America more prepared, but would not compromise the country's assertion that this was Europe's war.

Election of 1916. In 1916 Wilson ran for reelection on a peace ticket, under the slogan, "He kept us out of war." Although Wilson never used the slogan himself, he emphasized that he had kept "peace with honor." His Republican opponent, Supreme Court Justice Charles Evans Hughes, took a moderate stand on the issue of military preparedness, but he was backed by Theodore Roosevelt and others who favored American intervention in the war. This led many to think of Hughes as the war candidate.

On the eve of the election, the Wilson Business Men's National League published the following full-page advertisement in all the leading newspapers:

The Germans knew that the return to unrestricted submarine warfare would bring the U.S. into the war, but they hoped that this move would help them to defeat France and Britain before the U.S. could move effectively.

You Are Working—*Not Fighting!*
Alive and Happy;—*Not Cannon Fodder!*
Wilson and Peace with Honor?
or
Hughes with Roosevelt and War?

Wilson won the election. After re-election, he stepped up the efforts he had begun in 1914 to end the crisis through mediation.

On December 18 Wilson sent a note to all combatants asking them to tell him in confidence their conditions for peace. The Allies answered in full and precise statements, but the German response was vague. To gain greater German cooperation, Wilson delivered a speech on January 22, 1917, calling for a settlement of all international issues, limitation of arms, and the opening of the seas to all nations. He promised that the United States would join other nations in guaranteeing peace if it were a "peace without victory."

The combatants, however, were not interested in that kind of peace. The Allies were firm in their belief that Germany must be defeated and humiliated before there could be a lasting peace. The Germans wanted territory, colonial gains, and reparations. To make clear that their goal was total victory, the Germans announced on January 31, 1917 that they were launching unrestricted submarine warfare.

SECTION REVIEW

1. What factors led Americans to take sides in the war despite the U.S. stand on neutrality?
2. What problems did the United States have with Great Britain?
3. How did President Wilson attempt to deal with the problem of submarine warfare?
4. What effect did the war have on the U.S. presidential election of 1916?
5. What did the United States do to prepare for war?

3 America at War

For several weeks after the Germans announced that they were launching unrestricted submarine warfare, President Wilson tried to convince them to back down. The only concession the German government would make, however, was to grant one American ship a week the right to travel through the war zone. In addition, the ship had to be painted with red and white stripes and could not carry contraband. Most Americans took this as an insult. Many American ships refused to sail at all, and goods piled up on the docks. Wilson, believing he had to carry out the threat he had made during the Sussex crisis, broke off diplomatic relations with Germany.

At the outbreak of the war, most Americans wanted nonparticipation in European affairs. Parades for peace showed that the feeling was widespread. It seemed to Americans that the war was just one more episode in the struggle for power in Europe. How did the peace movement affect the election of 1916?

The Russian Revolution, setting up a constitutional monarchy, lasted only until November, when Lenin and the Communists came to power.

The Zimmerman Note

While Americans were still smarting over the German announcement, the British handed over a translation of a coded message they had intercepted from the German foreign minister, Arthur Zimmerman, to the German minister in Mexico City. It proposed that if America entered the war, Mexico should ally itself with Germany as follows:

> *That we shall make war together and together make peace. We shall give general financial support, and it is understood that Mexico is to reconquer the lost territory in Texas, New Mexico, and Arizona.*

The message, known as the Zimmerman note, arrived at the White House the last week in February. At almost the same time, the White House received the news that a German U-boat had sunk the British passenger liner *Laconia*, and that three Americans were among the dead.

As a result of these events, Wilson asked Congress to allow American merchant ships to arm themselves to fight submarines. He also asked that he be given broad authority to "respond to Germany's challenge." When Congress hesitated, he used an executive order to authorize the arming of merchant ships.

Publication of the Zimmerman note in the United States created immediate reaction. In the Southwest, where war issues had aroused little interest, there was complete outrage. Why would people of the Southwest be particularly angry?

Declaring War

In March 1917, within a few days time, the Germans attacked and sank four American ships— the *Algonquin*, the *City of Memphis*, the *Illinois*, and the *Vigilancia*. Thirty-six lives were lost.

That same month, the tsarist regime of Russia was overthrown by an internal revolution. The revolution seemed to make invalid the argument of some Americans that Russia was not a suitable ally for a democratic country like the United States. These events did much to push Wilson and the American public into a pro-war mentality.

Wilson continued to struggle with his conscience. He was convinced that war would destroy much of the optimism and sensitivity to human needs that had allowed America to make the social progress it had. His cabinet, on the other hand, strongly favored war. One government official later explained:

> *If we had stayed out of the war, and Germany had won, there would no longer have been a balance of power in Europe, or a British fleet to support the Monroe Doctrine and to protect America.*

Finally, on April 2, 1917, Wilson went before a joint session of Congress to ask for a declaration of war. In his speech, he talked about the broad ideals America had to defend in order to keep its integrity and its place in the world. He also made it clear that the United States had "no selfish ends to serve," desired "no conquest, no dominion," and "no indemnities."

The speech was in line with Wilson's inclination to define issues and situations in moral terms. He thought that if the United States were to enter the war, it should do so to serve the needs of humanity and to ensure a new and peaceful world. He had made his view of America's relation to other countries clear in 1914 with the following statement:

> *America will come into the full light of day when all shall know that she puts human rights above all other rights and that her flag is the flag not only of America but of humanity.*

Congress did not agree at once to a formal resolution of war. Some members of Congress agreed with Senator George Norris of Nebraska. He

Note that, with the U.S. as a neutral, American businesses were making enormous profits from war trade.

Because of the wartime emergency, the federal government acquired sweeping powers over the economy.

held that America's involvement in the war was the fault of American financiers and arms manufacturers who were determined to profit from the war no matter what it cost the rest of the country. Norris and his supporters believed that America should keep to itself, perfect its own institutions, and have as little as possible to do with the rest of the world.

In the end, however, most members of Congress agreed that if America wished to remain a great world power it must defend its rights. As a result, on April 6, 1917, by a vote of 373–50 in the House and 82–6 in the Senate, the United States declared war on Germany.

Training the Nation

President Wilson proved to be right when he stated in May 1917 that "It is not an army that we must train for war, it is a nation." At the time, the United States was poorly prepared for war. It had no **selective service,** or draft; few military training camps; very few arms; and virtually no tanks or airplanes. The regular army numbered only about 200,000, many of whom were recent enlistments in early stages of training. The United States Navy was the third largest in the world, but more than 60 percent of its ships needed some kind of repairs, and only about 10 percent had enough people to run them.

As a start the government decided that the army needed draftees as well as volunteers. On May 18, 1917, Congress passed the Selective Service Act. It authorized the President to increase the size of the regular army, take the National Guard and the National Guard Reserve into federal service, and raise an additional military force by selective draft.

All men between the ages of 21 and 30 were required to register for military service. Fifteen months later, the act was amended to make eligible all men between the ages of 18 and 45. In 1917 and 1918, more than 24 million registered. Of these, 4.8 million had volunteered or been drafted by the war's end.

Government Mobilization. The war effort took in almost every segment of American society and had a profound effect on the American economic system. The American military had to be equipped and sent to France. Once there, it had to be supplied and maintained. At the same time, the Allies had to be sent an on-going supply of food and munitions.

During the war women became an important part of the nation's labor force. These women delivering ice supplied a daily need in pre-refrigerator households. In what other jobs did women replace men fighting overseas?

To achieve these goals, Congress gave President Wilson broad wartime powers to regulate the economy. Wilson expressed these powers by setting up different boards to mobilize America's resources. In July 1917 he formed a War Industries Board to coordinate the manufacture and purchase of all supplies needed in the war effort. In March 1918 the board was reorganized and given greater powers. Headed by Bernard M. Baruch, a well-to-do stock speculator, it had the cooperation of major industrialists. Baruch and the others succeeded in getting the economy to produce huge amounts of supplies for both the American and the Allied armies.

In August 1917 the Fuel Administration was formed to increase production and reduce consumption of fuels. Most important was coal, which was essential to the operation of American factories and the transportation of war materiel. Among other

George M. Cohan

"Ladies and gentlemen, my father thanks you, my mother thanks you, my sister thanks you and I thank you!"

George M. Cohan was born in Providence, Rhode Island on July 3, 1878 to a theatrical family who traveled throughout the country on vaudeville tour. As he later proudly claimed, he grew up in dressing rooms. He and his sister performed with their parents in an act called "The Four Cohans." It was not long before young George became the star and chief writer for the act.

Success came quickly. By the age of 27, he had written a hit play, *Little Johnny Jones,* in which he starred and for which he had written a catchy song that appealed greatly to patriotic Americans. This song, "I'm a Yankee Doodle Dandy," made Cohan a leading figure in American musical theater.

In company with other great producers, particularly his long-time associate, Sam Harris, Cohan produced delightful new plays for nearly half a century. Such all-American songs as "You're a Grand Old Flag," and "Give My Regards to Broadway" are still popular today.

In 1941 President Franklin D. Roosevelt presented Cohan with a special medal struck by congressional order to honor him for his song, "Over There." This patriotic song had inspired Americans during World War I and kept up their spirits during that conflict.

In his later years, Cohan tried writing serious drama and won recognition as an actor. He starred in Eugene O'Neill's play, *Ah, Wilderness,* and played Franklin D. Roosevelt in *I'd Rather Be Right.* But it is as a writer of musical comedy, America's contribution to the world of theater, that he is best remembered. To Americans and to admirers of things American, Cohan was a "Yankee Doodle Boy."

things, the Fuel Administration put into effect Benjamin Franklin's idea of daylight savings time to help conserve energy.

At the same time, the Food Administration was set up to encourage farmers to produce more and to persuade the public to eat less. Under Herbert Hoover, the American engineer who had organized the feeding of the Belgians after the German invasion, the Food Administration campaigned to get Americans to set voluntary limits on the amount of vital commodities they consumed. It urged the people to pledge themselves to "meatless and wheatless" days and to add to their store of food by planting "victory gardens."

In December 1917 the United States Railroad Administration was formed. Under the Secretary of the Treasury, William G. McAdoo, it began to coordinate and strengthen the vital network of American railroads. The following June, the War Labor Policies Board was formed to deal with labor disputes. This board could regulate wages and hours in war-related industries.

The problem of financing the war was also solved. In October 1917 Congress passed the War Revenue Act, which raised corporate and individual taxes and made the income tax a major source of revenue during the war. The government also held bond drives to sell interest-bearing Liberty or Victory bonds. Stage and motion picture stars entertained at the bond drive rallies and urged each American to "do your bit for your country." Americans did as they were asked, and the government took in more than $21 billion through bond drives—almost double the amount raised through taxes.

After the war, an official count estimated that the war had cost the United States more than $1 million

President Gompers of the AFL promised no strikes in return for recognition of unions and wage increases. The prestige of organized labor was enhanced by its cooperation in the war effort.

Compare the restrictions on civil liberties with the Alien and Sedition Acts of 1798 and Lincoln's suspension of rights during the Civil War.

an hour for two years. The count also estimated that the total cost of the war—$31.5 billion—was equal to the amount needed to operate the government from 1791 to 1914.

The Economy. Despite the expense of the war, the nation actually prospered. Corporate profits increased sharply as demand for finished and unfinished goods soared. Bankers capitalized on the great demand for loans. Prices rose, but wages rose even faster. Farmers found an increased market for their produce, sending three times as much food to Europe as before.

The war created new job opportunities as well. Factories expanded, and the armed forces provided ready-made jobs for millions. Minorities especially were affected. The shortage of white male workers created new job opportunities in factories that in the past had hired only white workers. Over 500,000 blacks left their rural homes in the South to seek jobs and settle in the great urban areas of the North.

Many Hispanics took advantage of the new opportunities as well, leaving low-paying jobs on farms for better-paying ones in factories. Women, too, took on new roles. Some joined vital volunteer organizations such as the Red Cross, the Y.M.C.A., the Knights of Columbus, the Jewish National Welfare Board, and the Salvation Army, all of which sent groups to Europe to serve. Some women found jobs in factories or government agencies. Others stayed in their homes and took over the responsibilities their husbands, fathers, or brothers had always shouldered. About 11,000 women became "Yeomanettes" in the Navy, while another 300 or so became "Marinettes" in the Marines.

Children also contributed. Boy Scouts made a special project of planting, tending, and harvesting their own vegetable gardens. Girl Scouts rolled bandages, assembled first-aid kits, and knitted socks, mufflers, and sweaters. Many boys took part in early morning military drills before classes at school. Boys and girls in school bands marched in parades to help promote Liberty Loan drives.

Civil Liberties. While the war enhanced democracy in the job market, it did just the opposite in the area of civil liberties. In the interest of national security and to make sure that the war effort abroad would not be hurt by incidents at home, Congress passed the Espionage Act of 1917. The act provided a heavy fine and up to 20 years in prison for anyone who aided the enemy, interfered with the draft, encouraged disloyalty, or refused to serve in the armed forces.

The Sedition Act, passed the following year, set the same penalty as the Espionage Act. It made it a crime to write, print, publish, or say anything negative about the government, the Constitution, the flag, or the uniforms of the services. The act was so broadly interpreted that a film on the American Revolution was condemned as anti-British, and Eugene V. Debs, the leader of the Socialist Party in America, was jailed for making critical statements about the war in a political speech. Under these two laws, more than 1500 people were arrested and sent to jail. Also jailed were 450 **conscientious objectors** (persons who refuse to bear arms or serve in the military because of their religious or moral principles) who would not accept alternative service.

Propaganda. At the same time, propaganda was used to get the people to participate. On April 14, 1917, President Wilson set up the Committee on Public Information. Under Missouri journalist George Creel, the Committee's domestic goal was to "sell" the rest of the world on America and on Wilson's war aims. It called for, and generally received, voluntary censorship of the press. It hired writers, lecturers, artists, photographers, and filmmakers to develop material favorable to the war. The war was promoted as a crusade against oppression and militarism, and the enemy was shown in the most negative light possible.

The Germans, for example, were a prime target. They were linked to the barbarian Huns who had attacked Europe during the Dark Ages. Anything German was discouraged. The music of Bach, Beethoven, and Brahms was no longer heard in concert; paintings by German artists were removed from museums; courses on the German language were suspended; and sauerkraut was renamed "liberty cabbage."

Although President Wilson had been careful in his war message to state that most Americans of German descent were "true and loyal citizens," the anti-German propaganda often caused them suffering. All **hyphenated Americans**, Americans tied by birth or ancestry to another country, were under special pressure to demonstrate their loyalty. Almost any immigrant was suspected, as in the following

The British provided about 70 percent of the escorting ships for the convoys. The United States supplied about 27 percent and the French about 3 percent.

incident described by Secretary of War Newton Baker:

> *In Cleveland a few days ago a foreign-looking man got into a street car and taking a seat noticed pasted in the window next to him a Liberty Loan poster, which he immediately tore down, tore into small bits, and stamped under his feet. The people in the car surged around him with the demand that he be lynched, when a secret service man showed his badge and placed him under arrest, taking him in a car to the police station, where he was searched and found to have two Liberty Bonds in his pocket and to be a non-English speaking Pole. When an interpreter was procured it was discovered that the circular which he had destroyed had had on it a picture of the German Emperor, which had so infuriated the fellow that he destroyed the circular to show his vehement hatred of the common enemy. As he was unable to speak a single word of English, he would undoubtedly have been hanged but for the intervention and entirely accidental presence of the secret service agent.*

This incident demonstrated the impact of propaganda in the United States. Creel's Committee on Public Information also made effective use of propaganda in other parts of the world. To publicize America's war aims, efforts, and way of life, it offered free English lessons in Mexico, set up window displays in American businesses in other countries, and handed out educational pamphlets in China. It also began a government-run newspaper wire service, which supplied stories to foreign subscribers free of charge. Creel proved that America could be "advertised" through the mass media, and his efforts had lasting effects on America's position in international communications.

The American Military Contribution

America's first military contribution came at sea. At the time, Great Britain did not have enough warships to protect its merchant ships from German submarine attacks. The British were losing ships and vital supplies at an alarming rate.

In 1917 American Admiral William S. Sims was sent to London to discuss with British officers how to deal with the submarine campaign. While there, he introduced a system that helped cut Allied losses greatly. The system, known as the **convoy technique,** consisted of having a large number of merchant ships travel in a pack surrounded by a small number of armed vessels capable of keeping marauding U-boats at bay.

Sims cabled the American government to send to England right away whatever destroyers the British needed. The first trial convoy of merchant ships sailed from Gibraltar in May 1917. Escorted by destroyers and submarine chasers, it arrived safely in London on May 20. Soon afterward, the system was used for almost all ships crossing the Atlantic. By the close of the war, 90 percent of Allied shipping was sailing in convoys, and less than 1 percent of the protected ships were lost to the enemy.

At about the same time the Admiral was discussing the convoy technique with the British, General John J. Pershing arrived in Washington to lay out plans and select a staff. Pershing had been appointed commander of the American Expeditionary Force—American soldiers serving abroad. At the end of May he and his party went to England and then to France for a round of war talks.

The following month, an American division of about 14,000 men embarked for France in an effort to bolster Allied morale. They paraded through the streets of Paris, stopping at the tomb of Lafayette. There, an American colonel declared, "Lafayette, we are here," implying that the Americans had come to repay their debt to the Revolutionary War hero. One Frenchman, upon seeing the ill-equipped and out-of-step soldiers, commented, "If this is what we may expect from America, the war is lost. These men are not soldiers; they are a uniformed rabble."

Pershing was well aware of the problems that faced him. He set up headquarters not far from Paris and began building an American army in France. Because he wanted to make sure that no Americans were sent into combat without the training they needed, he refused to place his soldiers directly under Allied command. But he did promise to have 1 million Americans in Europe by the end of 1918. This, however, did not satisfy the British and French generals, who were desperate for new soldiers.

Propaganda and War

Nations cannot successfully wage war without the cooperation of their people. Because people contribute to a war effort more readily when they believe in the cause, propaganda has been important in every American war since the Revolution.

Propaganda takes many forms. Prior to the 1930's, the printed word was the main outlet for propaganda. American patriots, seeking to encourage opposition to British rule, wrote and published more than 1500 political pamphlets before and during the Revolution. Pamphlets, such as those turned out by the Loyal Publications Societies, were a factor during the Civil War as well.

Another form of printed propaganda used in both the 1700's and 1800's was the broadside. These were single sheets of paper, printed on one side, which were sold on street corners or nailed to trees. They had eye-catching headings designed to get people to read the propaganda that followed. Broadsides were also a favorite means of publicizing the call for volunteer soldiers.

Then, of course, there were the newspapers. Before the early 1900's, newspapers made little pretext of being objective. Editors used their presses to promote their own particular viewpoints. Propaganda in newspapers reached its peak in the Spanish-American War, which some historians say would not have occurred had it not been for the stories of the yellow press.

Political cartoons also became an important newspaper feature during the late 1800's. But pictorial forms of propaganda were used before and after this time as well. Paul Revere made a widely distributed engraving of British soldiers in an orderly line, firing cold-bloodedly on an unarmed crowd of colonists. This did much to promote the idea that the confrontation in Boston on March 5, 1770, deserved to be called the "Boston Massacre." Similarly, World War II posters showed the enemy as vicious and brutish.

Songs, too, served to encourage the fighting spirit. The War of 1812 saw the publication of hundreds of patriotic songs, though few proved lasting except "The Star Spangled Banner." During the Civil War, such tunes as "Battle Hymn of the Republic" and "Dixie" stirred soldiers and civilians. George M. Cohan's rousing "Over There" gave courage to Americans during World War I.

While Cohan wrote under his own inspiration, World War I as a whole saw the first systematic government effort to use the media for propaganda purposes. The Wilson administration's Committee on Public Information was an organized effort to sell the war to Americans through as many means as possible, including pamphlets, posters, newsreels, and newspaper censorship.

World War II also had its organized government propaganda. This time the government had a major new medium to exploit: radio. President Franklin Roosevelt, a gifted orator, used "fireside chats" to inform the public of the perils abroad during the 1930's. He also made sure that his addresses to Congress were broadcast live. Thus he was able to reach millions of people at once. Perhaps his greatest impact came when he called the day of the attack on Pearl Harbor (December 7, 1941) "a day which will live in infamy." The radio also allowed Americans everywhere to keep up-to-date with the war and to feel involved in the effort.

With the coming of television in the 1950's, the government faced both new advantages and new disadvantages in its propaganda efforts. By adding sight to sound, television heightened the impact an inspiring presidential speech could make on the public. Yet it also brought home the realities of war: the human carnage, the devastation of land, the discouragement of battle-weary soldiers.

Many observers feel that the anti-war sentiment of the 1960's and 1970's, which helped to undermine the struggle in Vietnam, derived much of its strength from the nightly presentation of the horrors of war on the evening news. As the mass media continues to grow, generating war fervor may become increasingly difficult.

QUESTIONS

1. When was war propaganda first used?
2. How has propaganda differed over time?

THE U.S. ARMY IN WORLD WAR I

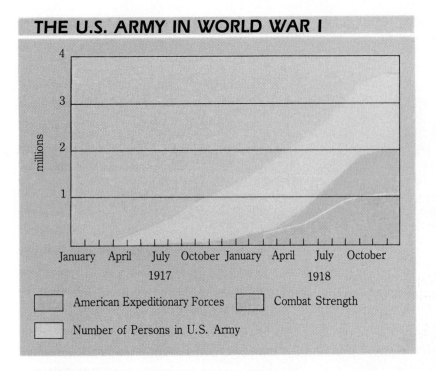

millions

4
3
2
1

January April July October January April July October
          1917   1918

American Expeditionary Forces   Combat Strength

Number of Persons in U.S. Army

A Different Kind of War. This war was different from any before, with machines and weapons taking over the direction of battle from human beings. Further, the weapons were making war much more destructive. For the first time, the airplane, flame-thrower, machine gun, submarine, armored tank, and chlorine, or "poison" gas, were used effectively as war weapons.

Also used for the first time there was **trench warfare.** Under this system, soldiers settled in ditches that were about 6 feet (1.82 meters) deep and 4 feet (1.21 meters) wide. From these ditches they fired at each other across "No Man's Land," the area that separated the friendly lines from the enemy lines. Soldiers advanced from one position to another by charging "over the top" of one line of trenches and running to another.

Not only were many lives lost during the advances, but the trenches themselves were dangerous, smelly places. Poison gas settled in them, and the smell of stagnant mud and rotting corpses of men and horses hung over them. At night, they were overrun by rats that came to feed on the corpses. The cold, the damp, and the crowding also took a toll. Hundreds of thousands of soldiers were killed trying to capture relatively small pieces of territory. Many of the

soldiers who had thought war would be a wonderful, exciting, and romantic experience lost their illusions—and their lives—in the trenches.

By 1917 the Germans controlled most of Belgium and Poland as well as a large part of northern France. With the Austrians, they also occupied Serbia and Rumania. At sea, their submarine campaign was inflicting huge losses on Allied shipping. The Germans hoped to win a victory before the Americans came in number and tipped the balance against them.

German efforts were aided by a change in Russia's role. Until 1917 the Germans had been fighting a war on two fronts—the Western front in France and the Eastern front in Russia. So long as the Russians had kept the Germans busy in the east, Germany had fewer soldiers to use against the British and French in the west. But the political revolution inside Russia in 1917 led it to pull out of the conflict,[1] leaving Germany free to concentrate on the Western front. By May

---

[1] On December 8, 1917, the new Russian government began peace talks with Germany. In February 1918 the peace talks broke down, and Germany resumed warfare. As a result, on May 3 Russia signed the Treaty of Brest-Litovsk, giving up Poland, Finland, the Baltic States, and other territory. Finland and the Baltic States (Lithuania, Estonia, and Latvia) became independent countries.

Europeans had doubts about Americans' combat ability and did not like the idea of their operating as a separate unit. Instead, the Europeans wanted to use American troops as reinforcements for their own lines. But, by the time the Russians withdrew, the Allies were so desperate that they had to trust the Americans.

1918 the Germans had been so successful that General Pershing had to allow several American divisions to be placed under Marshal Ferdinand Foch, the supreme commander of all Allied forces in Europe.

Americans in Combat. While the British and the French, nearing the point of exhaustion, remained on the defensive waiting for the Americans to arrive, the Germans decided to launch an offensive. The goal was to smash the British and French armies before the Americans could fully mass their strength. As a result, by the time the Americans were assigned their first divisional area north of Paris at Cantigny in May 1918, the Germans were about 50 miles (80 kilometers) from Paris.

At Cantigny, about 4000 soldiers of the First Division made the first American offensive action of the war. After a bitter battle in which they suf-

fered more than 1000 casualties, these troops won the first victory ever by Americans fighting in Europe. The battle proved to the Allies that Americans could fight.

In June American divisions were ordered to the Marne River to try probing the enemy line to see if it could be pushed back. The objective was to recapture Belleau Wood, a kidney-shaped area less than a mile (1.6 kilometers) wide and two miles (3.2 kilometers) deep. For 24 hours a day for the next two weeks, United States Marines fought their way through the forest, which was a solid wall of German machine guns. The Americans finally took the wood—but at a cost of more than 4000 casualties.

The Germans launched a massive offensive at Chateau-Thierry along the Marne in July. Together the Americans and the French fought back the Germans, breaking their offensive strength, and for

Much of World War I was fought from trenches where soldiers spent days, or even weeks, in mud and unsanitary conditions. These conditions gave rise to sickness and disease from which many thousands died. What were the distinguishing characteristics of trench warfare?

Using the maps on pp. 462 and 463, have students list the countries in which most of the fighting took place.

THE WORLD AT WAR

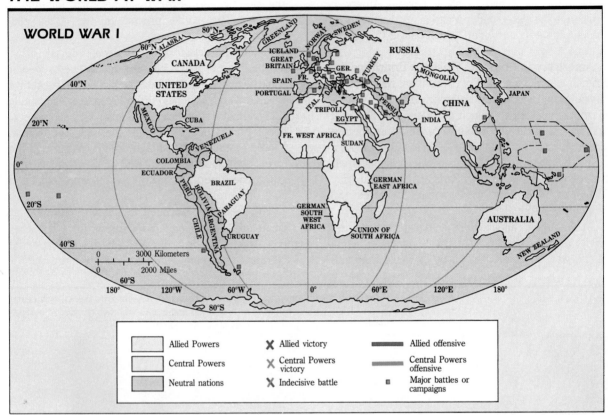

WORLD WAR I

Legend:
- Allied Powers
- Central Powers
- Neutral nations
- ✕ Allied victory
- ✕ Central Powers victory
- ✕ Indecisive battle
- ▬ Allied offensive
- ▬ Central Powers offensive
- ▪ Major battles or campaigns

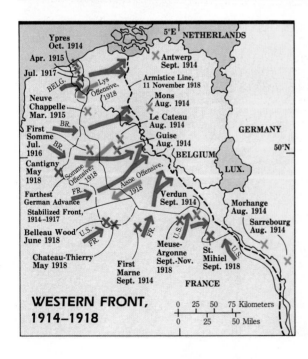

WESTERN FRONT, 1914–1918

Ypres Oct. 1914
Apr. 1915
Jul. 1917
Antwerp Sept. 1914
Armistice Line, 11 November 1918
Mons Aug. 1914
Lys Offensive, 1918
Neuve Chappelle Mar. 1915
Le Cateau Aug. 1914
Guise Aug. 1914
First Somme Jul. 1916
Cantigny May 1918
Somme Offensive 1918
Aisne Offensive, 1918
Verdun Sept. 1914
Morhange Aug. 1914
Farthest German Advance
Stabilized Front, 1914–1917
Sarrebourg Aug. 1914
Belleau Wood June 1918
Meuse-Argonne Sept.-Nov. 1918
St. Mihiel Sept. 1918
Chateau-Thierry May 1918
First Marne Sept. 1914
NETHERLANDS
GERMANY
BELGIUM
LUX.
FRANCE
5°E
50°N

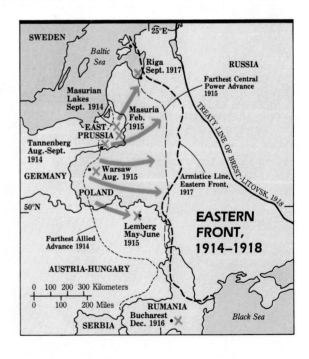

EASTERN FRONT, 1914–1918

SWEDEN
Baltic Sea
Riga Sept. 1917
RUSSIA
Farthest Central Power Advance 1915
Masurian Lakes Sept. 1914
Masuria Feb. 1915
EAST PRUSSIA
Tannenberg Aug.-Sept. 1914
Warsaw Aug. 1915
GERMANY
POLAND
TREATY LINE OF BREST-LITOVSK, 1918
Armistice Line, Eastern Front, 1917
Farthest Allied Advance 1914
Lemberg May-June 1915
AUSTRIA-HUNGARY
SERBIA
RUMANIA
Bucharest Dec. 1916
Black Sea
25°E
50°N

Note that American forces supplied the margin of victory, although their total contribution in defeating Germany was less than that of the British or the French.

the first time, the initiative on the Western front passed to the Allies.

In September 550,000 American troops, the largest single American force yet assembled, routed the Germans from Saint-Mihiel. It was the largest single campaign of the war and the first battle in which United States infantry and fliers fought as a completely independent service under an American commander-in-chief.

In October came the battle of Meuse-Argonne. The campaign got its name because to the right, or east, of the attacking American First Army lay the Meuse River and to its left, or west, lay the Argonne Forest. Across the region between the two, the Germans had built defensive positions a dozen miles (19.2 kilometers) deep with barbed wire, machine-gun nests, concrete artillery emplacements, and deep lines of permanent trenches.

Between October 2 and 7, the "Lost Battalion" made its legendary stand in the forest. The battalion, made up of about 550 men from different regiments, was ordered to take the Argonne Forest by a frontal assault. Without the Americans knowing it, the Germans had worked their way up behind them,

stringing barbed wire and machine guns and cutting the battalion off from the rest of the troops. The battalion commander, Lieutenant Colonel Charles Whittlesey, was determined to hold his ground even though he had Germans both in front and in back of him. Each messenger sent out to contact the other Americans was killed. Even the carrier pigeons sent out were shot down. Still, the men held their ground. By the time troops arrived on October 7 to relieve them, the men of the battalion had been reduced to eating tree leaves and roots.

The Allies won the battle of Meuse-Argonne. The Americans, in conjunction with the British and the French, caused the enemy's lines to crumble. On November 6, 1918, the Germans asked President Wilson for an armistice. They had approached Wilson because they knew of his views on peace, and thought they could negotiate more lenient terms with him than with the other Allied heads of government. Wilson, however, could not convince the other leaders to accept his terms and had to tell the Germans there could be no peace negotiations, only "surrender." On November 11, 1918, an armistice based on Allied demands was signed by both sides.

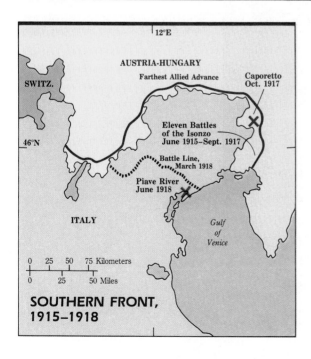

SOUTHERN FRONT, 1915–1918

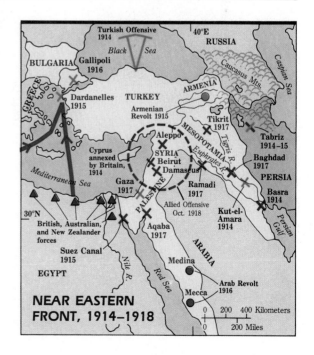

NEAR EASTERN FRONT, 1914–1918

More than 125,000 American lives were lost during the brief period the United States was engaged militarily in the war. This loss was small, however, when compared to the 900,000 British, 1,385,000 French, and 1,700,000 Russian lives lost in battle. In all, nearly 9 million soldiers and more than 13 million civilians died within a span of 4 years. An American soldier who survived the war had this to say about it many years later:

You must realize that when we actually did go to war, very few people in this country knew what it was all about. Really, no one had any idea what the actual fighting was like. I had a great many friends in old Troop B, and all I knew was they were going and I wanted to go. I felt that if I didn't go, the world would come to an end. . . . Our job was to be a mobile machine gun battalion. We had these converted Ford ambulances. Whenever any area would get hot, they were supposed to rush us in as support. . . . When the Saint Mihiel . . . drive came, we had to march 18 kilometers at night. The gun and the tripod weighed a total of 110 pounds; then we had all that ammunition. . . .

Then there was Chateau-Thierry—to me that was our toughest fight! . . .

Well, the trucks dropped us off near the front. . . . The first thing we knew, the shells were flying so fast we could only move forward on our bellies . . . trying to find a place to set up our guns. The Germans were letting loose with rapid fire. . . . A fellow named Hezekiah Porter was over on my right. I could see him out of the corner of my eye. Then this shell landed, and he completely disappeared. Can you imagine that—seeing a buddy one minute, then a minute later he's gone? I still have nightmares over that one! . . . Shortly after that we moved into the Meuse-Argonne campaign down near Verdun. . . .

Well, as I was saying, we were down near Verdun, trying to push the Germans back. . . .

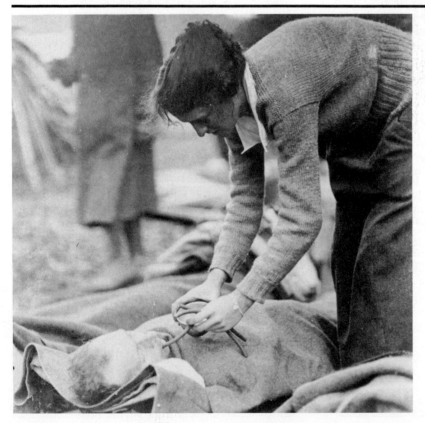

During World War I, women's work was not restricted to the home front. Following in the footsteps of Clara Barton, ambulance drivers and nurses of the American Red Cross worked on the front lines to heal the sick and treat the wounded. Without the care of nurses, many more Americans might have died. What were American losses during World War I?

The "Big Four" leaders were David Lloyd George, Prime Minister of Great Britain; Vittorio E. Orlando, Premier of Italy; Georges Clemenceau, Premier of France; and President Wilson.

Then, early in the morning of November 11, I was sitting in this dugout . . . when this Doughboy [soldier] came running by yelling, "There's going to be an armistice! There's going to be an armistice!" At that exact time a German shell landed close enough to make us hit the ground. . . .

About an hour later an officer came by and told us it was on the level; the whole thing would be over at 11:00 A.M. You can bet we stayed down in that dugout until we heard them blow the whistle. I wasn't going to be the last guy to catch it. The funny thing is that when it was over, there was no cheering or waving, or anything like that—just an exhausted silence.

SECTION REVIEW

1. Identify the following: Zimmerman note, Selective Service Act, William S. Sims, John J. Pershing, Meuse-Argonne, Lost Battalion.
2. How did the war affect the American economy?
3. How did the war affect American civil liberties?
4. What did the Committee on Public Information do?

4 The Aftermath

Long before the war was over, Wilson had begun to think about what would happen when the fighting stopped. He wanted a peace without victory, one which would "rest upon the rights of people, not the rights of governments."

After the armistice was signed, the President explained to Congress his Fourteen Points. This was a peace plan whose terms included international recognition of freedom of the seas and of trade, limitation of arms, an end to secret alliances, a just settlement of colonial claims, the right of self-determination for all countries, and the establishment of a "general assembly of nations" to settle future problems peacefully. Wilson's speech was relayed simultaneously by radio transmitter to Europe, the Far East, and Latin America, making him the first international figure to address the world.

Wilson faced many obstacles in his effort to win American support for his program. Some of the problems were of his own making. Because he was angry with conservative Republicans who called his peace plan "soft," he made his policies a partisan issue. He called on everyone to vote Democratic in the 1918 elections, and appointed no Republicans or Senators to the peace conference that was to take place in Paris in January 1919. Therefore when the Republicans won control of the Senate that year, Wilson faced strong opposition.

Wilson also alienated the press. Already a little resentful over the censorship it had to exercise during the war, the press became even further irritated when Wilson agreed to European demands that the treaty negotiations be conducted in secret.

The Paris Peace Conference

Wilson arrived in Europe in late December 1918. He settled down in Paris to thrash out a peace treaty. It did not take him long to discover that he would have difficulty in getting his peace program accepted by other countries.

The representatives of the other 27 countries[2] that took part in the conference did not really trust one another. In addition, no one knew what to expect from Russia now that it was controlled by a communist government.

The greatest obstacle, however, was that most of the countries were interested chiefly in gaining territory and inflicting harsh punishment on Germany. These views were in direct conflict with Wilson's proposals for equitable national boundaries and peace without victory.

Wilson had believed all along that his plan for an international assembly of nations was the most important of his proposals. In order to get the delegates to agree to it, he had to yield on many other points. In the end, however, he got his way, and in February 1919, a Covenant of the League of Nations was drawn up. The Covenant was to be part of the broader treaty which was still under discussion.

When Wilson returned home later that month, he found that Senator Henry Cabot Lodge had circulated a resolution against the League of Nations, and more than one-third of the Senate had signed it. The Senators wanted Wilson to get the other countries to

---

[2] Although 27 countries took part in the conference, most of the decisions were made by the "Big Four"—the United States, Great Britain, France, and Italy.

Wilson hoped that the League of Nations would later be able to correct some of the compromises he was forced to make.

The harsh terms forced on the Germans led some liberals in the United States to predict that the treaty would eventually lead to another war. Have students discuss this prediction.

At the Paris peace conference Wilson's idealism was generally not shared by his colleagues. Nevertheless the President was able to get some of his ideas incorporated into the treaty, the most important being the Covenant of the League of Nations. How was the Covenant received by Congress?

agree to certain amendments. The amendments safeguarded the Monroe Doctrine, confirmed each country's rights to set tariffs and immigration quotas, and allowed a country to withdraw from the League of Nations.

Wilson returned to Paris, where, to get the changes the Senators wanted, he had to compromise further. Premier Georges Clemenceau of France reportedly remarked, "God gave us his Ten Commandments, and we broke them. Wilson gave us his Fourteen Points—we shall see." In the end, only four of President Wilson's Fourteen Points and nine supplementary principles emerged intact in the overall treaty, known as the Treaty of Versailles.[3] The treaty, which was signed by the Germans on June 28, 1919, disarmed Germany, forced it to admit its guilt in the war, stripped it of some of its territory, and exacted reparations that were later fixed at $56 billion.

[3] The Allies signed separate peace treaties with Austria, Bulgaria, Hungary, and Turkey. The five treaties together were known as the Peace of Paris. Three new countries (Austria, Czechoslovakia, and Hungary) were created from the old Austria-Hungary. Poland was created out of Russian, German, and Austrian territory. Yugoslavia was created from Serbia and parts of Austria-Hungary, Bulgaria, and Montenegro. Rumania, Greece, and Italy received additional territory.

Have students debate the merits of the treaty.

American Opposition to the Treaty of Versailles

Once again, President Wilson returned home, this time to present the Treaty of Versailles to the Senate. But the treaty was badly received.

Many German-Americans argued that the measures taken against Germany were too strong. Italian-Americans claimed that Italy should have been awarded the vital Adriatic port of Fiume. Irish-Americans thought that Wilson should have come out openly for self-determination for Ireland, which was still under British rule. Most Americans based their objections to the treaty on the fear that membership in the League of Nations would commit the United States to a continuing role in the affairs of Europe and to peacekeeping tasks around the globe.

Senator Henry Cabot Lodge also opposed the treaty, mostly on the basis of the Covenant. He knew, however, that the American public wanted acceptance of peace. Since the Covenant of the League of Nations was an integral part of the treaty, turning it down meant turning down the treaty as a whole. For this reason, Lodge decided that it would be wiser to amend the proposals out of existence. To do this, he and a group of supporters proposed a number of reservations, 12 of which were passed by the Senate, to limit America's obligations under the treaty. One reservation, for example, stated that the League would have no say about situations arising out of the Monroe Doctrine. Another stated that the United States had to have Congress' approval before it could agree to help another country.

Neither the **reservationists,** those in favor of the treaty as amended by Lodge, nor those who favored the original treaty had enough votes to pass their version of the treaty. Both were checked by the **irreconcilables,** a group of one Democrat and 14 Republican Senators. They were sure that joining the League would be bad for the United States. They believed that it would put dangerous limits on the country's sovereignty and on its ability to stay out of international problems. Their leader, Senator William E. Borah of Idaho, stood his ground. He said:

We are told that this treaty means peace. Even so, I would not pay the price. Would you purchase peace at the cost of any part of our independence?

The End of the Debate

President Wilson, a long-time and bitter antagonist of Senator Lodge, refused to allow the Democrats to make the compromises that would bring the reservationists to their side. Instead, he decided to take his case to the people, who he believed were strongly behind his proposals. When his wife and doctor protested that his health was not good enough for travel, he replied:

If the treaty is not ratified by the Senate, the war will have been fought in vain, and the world will be thrown into chaos. I promised our soldiers, when I asked them to take up arms, that it was a war to end wars. . . . I must go.

Throughout the month of September 1919, President Wilson delivered some 40 speeches to

EUROPE AFTER VERSAILLES

enthusiastic crowds all across the United States. The speeches, however, did not get the political results he needed. They served instead to anger the Republicans even more while leaving the Democrats in Washington without presidential guidance. The trip also ruined Wilson's health. On September 26, he was rushed back to the capital. On October 2, he suffered a stroke that left him weak, partially paralyzed, and generally unable to give the country the leadership it needed.

Debate over the treaty continued, but neither side was willing to yield. When the vote was taken on November 19, 1919, the treaty was defeated. A second vote taken in March 1920 produced the same result. In the end the United States did not officially make peace with Germany until 1921, at which time it signed a separate peace treaty with that nation.

Although the League of Nations was formed, the United States never joined it. The League became an ineffective organization that bore little resemblance to the one conceived by Woodrow Wilson.

SECTION REVIEW

1. Identify the following: Fourteen Points, League of Nations, Henry Cabot Lodge, William E. Borah, Treaty of Versailles.
2. What obstacles did Wilson create in his efforts to win acceptance for his peace plan?
3. What was the greatest obstacle Wilson faced at the Paris Peace Conference?
4. What objections did the Senate and the American public raise to the Versailles treaty?
5. What were the results of Wilson's decision to take his case to the people?

CHAPTER 22 REVIEW

SUMMARY

1. In 1914 World War I broke out in Europe with the Allied Powers of Great Britain, France, and Russia facing the Central Powers of Germany and Austria-Hungary.
2. The United States remained neutral for almost three years but finally declared war on Germany in April 1917.
3. Mobilization for war involved almost every part of American society and boosted the American economy.
4. The United States made a significant contribution to an Allied victory in 1918.
5. President Wilson presented a peace program that included a proposal for a League of Nations to settle future disputes without war.
6. At a peace conference in Paris, 27 countries took part in drawing up the Treaty of Versailles which imposed harsh measures against Germany and included an agreement to form a League of Nations.
7. The United States failed to ratify the Treaty of Versailles and did not join the League.
8. The United States signed a separate peace treaty with Germany in 1921.

VOCABULARY

militarism	preparedness	conscientious objector	trench warfare
war materiel	pacifist	hyphenated Americans	reservationists
contraband	selective service	convoy technique	irreconcilables
submarine			

REVIEW QUESTIONS

1. What were the causes of World War I?
2. Why did the United States enter the war on the side of the Allied Powers?
3. How did the American nation mobilize for war?
4. What made this war different from others before it?

5. What was America's role in the Allied victory?
6. What was the nature of President Wilson's peace program?

7. What were the terms of the Treaty of Versailles?
8. Why did the United States fail to join the League of Nations?

DISCUSSION

1. If the League of Nations had existed before 1914, do you think World War I could have been avoided?
2. Does a state of war justify the suspension of civil liberties?

3. How is war technology related to the ethics of war? Can there be, or should there be, rules of warfare?
4. Should the United States and other countries arm themselves to prepare for war? Why or why not?

USING MAPS

Refer to the maps on pages 449 and 467 and answer the following questions:

1. Which European nations were neutral in 1914?
2. What countries bordered Germany in 1914? In 1920?

3. Which European nations were allied with Germany in the war?
4. Which nations ceded territory after the war?
5. What countries existed in 1920 that did not exist in 1914? Why?

USING SKILLS

Consider the following statement: *Americans at home supported the war effort during World War I.* Which of the following support that statement? Which do not?

1. The photograph on page 453.
2. The fact that the War Revenue Act was passed.
3. The fact that the war was financed chiefly by Liberty Bonds.

4. The fact that many people planted "victory gardens."
5. The fact that the vote on the war resolution was 373–50 in the House and 82–6 in the Senate.
6. The fact that Eugene Debs, who was against the war, received almost 1 million votes in the election of 1920.

SUMMARY

1. By enforcing the Monroe Doctrine, the United States established itself as one of the world's great powers.
2. By the end of the nineteenth century, the United States had acquired an overseas empire.
3. As a world power, the United States pursued an active foreign policy to promote the national interest.
4. The conflicting interests of other world powers led to World War I.
5. The United States was drawn into the global conflict and emerged from it as one of the victors.
6. As a consequence of the war, the position of the United States as a world power was greatly enhanced.

REVIEW QUESTIONS

1. By what means did the United States extend its influence in world affairs?
2. How did the role of the United States in the Western Hemisphere differ from the American role in other parts of the world?
3. What were the causes of conflict among world powers in the early 1900's?
4. How did American attitudes and objectives in the Spanish-American War compare with those in World War I?

SUGGESTED ACTIVITIES

1. Check sources such as local newspapers and municipal reports to see how people in your community reacted to (a) the Spanish-American War, (b) the building of the Panama Canal, and (c) the end of World War I.
2. Prepare a bulletin-board exhibit showing the following data from 1910 to 1920: (a) gross national product; (b) federal expenditures, (c) national debt. Can you draw any inferences from this information?
3. Suppose that the United States were at war today. Write a military draft law that specifies (a) who is eligible to be drafted into the armed forces, (b) the method of selecting people to be drafted from among those who are eligible, and (c) what to do about people who refuse to serve in the military.
4. Debate the following topic: "American activities in the Caribbean in the late 1800's and the early 1900's were necessary to safeguard the national interest."

SUGGESTED READINGS

1. Bailey, Thomas A. *Woodrow Wilson & the Lost Peace*. New York: Times Books, 1972. Paperback. Describes Wilson's attempts to bring about a just peace and the tragic failure of his efforts.
2. Lord, Walter. *A Night to Remember*. New York: Bantam Books, Inc., 1955. A fascinating account of the disaster of the *Titanic*.
3. May, Earnest R. *Imperial Democracy*. New York: Harper & Row Publishing, Inc., 1973. Paperback. Describes world reaction to America's rise to the status of a great power at the turn of the century.
4. Mowry, George E. *The Era of Theodore Roosevelt: 1900-1912*. New York: Harper & Row, Publishers, Inc., 1958. Paperback. An analysis of the administrations of Roosevelt and Taft.
5. Pringle, Henry F. *Theodore Roosevelt: A Biography*. New York: Harcourt Brace Jovanovich, Inc., 1956. Paperback. Anecdotes, quotes and stories about one of the nation's strongest Presidents.

THE HISTORIAN'S CRAFT

The historian's ultimate task is, of course, to write an account of what happened in the era he or she is studying. In order to do this, the historian usually studies what other historians have written. But the most important bases for historical writing are primary sources. The historian must synthesize or pull together the evidence and shape it into a narrative or explanation.

This activity will give you practice in synthesizing evidence from a number of different primary sources. The subject of the activity is causes of the Spanish-American War. Review the material on this subject in Chapter 20, so that you will be familiar with at least one secondary source. Then study the evidence provided on these pages. Answering the questions at the end of the activity will help you to analyze the evidence and to develop your own ideas on the causes of the war.

Write a paragraph or two based on your study of this evidence. You might begin your first paragraph by saying, "Several factors contributed to America's declaration of war with Spain in 1898."

1. From Josiah Strong, *Our Country: Its Possible Future and Its Present Crisis* (1885):

   [The Anglo-Saxon was being schooled for] the final competition of races. . . . If I read not amiss, this powerful race will move down upon Mexico, down upon Central and South America, out upon the islands of the sea, over upon Africa and beyond. And can any one doubt that the result of this competition of races will be the "survival of the fittest?"

2. From the New York *Journal*, February 23, 1896:

   It is not only Weyler the soldier . . . but Weyler the outrager of women. . . . Pitiless, cold, an exterminator of men. . . . There is nothing to prevent his carnal, animal brain from running riot with itself in inventing tortures and infamies of bloody debauchery.

3. From the New York *World*, May 17, 1896:

   Blood on the roadsides, blood in the fields, blood on the doorsteps, blood, blood, blood. The old, the young, the weak, the crippled—all are butchered without mercy. . . . Is there no nation wise enough, brave enough, and strong enough to restore peace in this bloodsmitten land?

4. From a speech by Senator Redfield Proctor of Vermont to the Senate, March 17, 1898, on reconcentrado camps:

   Torn from their homes, with foul earth, foul air, foul water, and foul food or none, what wonder that one-half have died and that one-quarter of the living are so diseased that they cannot be saved? . . . Little children are still walking about with arms and chest terribly emaciated, eyes swollen, and abdomen bloated to three times the natural size. . . . I was told by one of our consuls that they have been found dead about the markets in the morning, where they had crawled, hoping to get some stray bits of food from the early hucksters. . . .

5. The cartoon, "Cuba in the Frying Pan" (below), appeared in *Puck* (1898) with this caption: "The duty of the hour: to save her not only from Spain but from a worse fate."

6. The cartoon above appeared in the Hearst Press in 1898. The caption read, "Spanish 'Justice and Honor' be darned!"

7. From William McKinley, War Message to Congress, April 11, 1898:

The grounds for such intervention may be briefly summarized as follows:
    First. In the cause of humanity and to put an end to the barbarities, bloodshed, starvation, and horrible miseries now existing there, and which the parties to the conflict are either unable or unwilling to stop or mitigate. . . .
    Second. We owe it to our citizens in Cuba to afford them that protection and indemnity for life and property which no government there can or will afford, and to that end to terminate the conditions that deprive them of legal protection.
    Third. The right to intervene may be justified by the very serious injury to commerce, trade, and business of our people,
and by the wanton destruction of property and devastation of the island.
    Fourth, and which is of the utmost importance. The present condition of affairs in Cuba is a constant menace to our peace, and entails upon this Government an enormous expense. . . .

8. To the right is a photograph of the battleship *Maine* after the explosion in Havana harbor.

9. From Albert J. Beveridge, *Address to Middlesex of Boston* (1898):

American factories are making more than the American people can use; American soil is producing more than they can consume. Fate has written our policy for us; the trade of the world must and shall be ours. . . . And American law, American order, American civilization, and the American flag will plant themselves on shores hitherto bloody and benighted, but by those agencies of God henceforth to be made beautiful and bright.

10. The cartoon of McKinley (below) appeared in the *New York Journal* in 1898. The caption read, "Another old woman tries to sweep back the sea."

QUESTIONS

1. What theory is reflected in the quotation from Josiah Strong?

2. What emotions toward Spain do you feel when you read the excerpts from the *New York World* and the *New York Journal?*

3. Senator Proctor was a respected, conservative politician. Would his speech, based on a personal tour of Cuba, have added to or detracted from the legitimacy of reports from the yellow press?

4. What view does the artist express in the Uncle Sam drawing? What details indicate this?

5. What new elements, not presented in the previous material, does President McKinley include in his call for war?

6. What was the reaction of the yellow press to the *Maine* incident?

7. According to Beveridge, what would be the effect of American expansionism? How might the cartoon of "Cuba in the Frying Pan" fit into Beveridge's view?

8. What does the McKinley cartoon suggest about the President's attitude toward war?

1919	1921	1923	1924	1927
Eighteenth Amendment	Sacco and Vanzetti Trial	Death of Harding	Pan-American Treaty	Lindbergh's Flight

1920	1923	1925
Nineteenth Amendment	Teapot Dome Scandal	Scopes Trial

PROSPERITY AND DEPRESSION

The Roaring 20's

The Great Depression

The New Deal

1929	1930	1932	1933	1935
Stock Market Crash	Hoover Relief Policy	Bonus Army March	New Deal	2nd New Deal

1928	1929	1932	1933	1937
Kellogg-Briand Pact	National Origins Act	Election of F. D. Roosevelt	20th and 21st Amendments	Court Packing Plan

1	Postwar Trauma	**477**
2	The Defense of Traditionalism	**483**
3	Politics in the 1920's	**487**
4	Social and Cultural Life	**490**
5	The Dream's End	**498**

THE ROARING 20's

My candle burns at both ends;
It will not last the night;
But ah, my foes, and oh, my friends—
It gives a lovely light.

EDNA ST. VINCENT MILLAY

In America the decade immediately following World War I is often described as "The Return to Normalcy." Tired of war and world responsibilities, Americans were eager to return to normal life. They turned their backs on Europe and concentrated on building a free and prosperous society. In the words of President Calvin Coolidge, "The business of America is business."

The 1920's was a time of mixed reactions, conflict, and strange contradictions. There was a tremendous ambivalence—between conservatism and liberalism, between urban and rural lifestyles, and, ultimately, between prosperity and depression.

1 Postwar Trauma

By the time World War I ended, America had one of the most industrialized economies in the world. At the same time, however, it had one of the weakest labor movements. Although labor unrest was nothing new in the United States, labor and management had put aside their differences during the war years. A sense of patriotism, high wages, and wartime laws helped keep conflict to a minimum.

Labor-Management Conflicts

Once the war was over, however, conflict flared anew. The system of government arbitration came to an end, and wage and price controls were allowed to die out. The war-stimulated economy cooled down, and veterans found they had to compete for a declining number of jobs. Frustration was further heightened by the government's refusal to give veterans bonuses to compensate them for the time they had spent in the armed services. The veterans argued that they needed the bonuses to help them cope with the inflated prices and high cost of living brought on by the war.

Workers in general wanted to preserve and, if possible, augment the high wages paid during the war. When management refused to cooperate, many workers resorted to their chief bargaining tool—the strike. Although strikes had been in use in America since the 1870's, those which took place after World War I were especially numerous and violent. In 1919 alone, there were close to 3000 strikes, involving nearly 4 million workers.

The Shipyard Workers Strike. One major strike of 1919 involved shipyard workers in Seattle, Washington. They were one of the few groups of workers almost completely unionized.

In February the workers walked off their jobs to protest management's refusal to give them a 10 percent raise in pay. The Seattle Central Labor Council stepped in and urged workers in other fields to back those in the shipyards by calling a general strike. Many workers in other trades complied with the council's request.

The effort failed, however, because of the actions of Mayor Ole Hanson of Seattle. He labelled the strike organizers as dangerous radicals, called in the state militia, and broke the strike. The shipyard workers did not get their pay increase. Further, many of the shipyards' orders were cancelled, and the yards were forced to cut back or shut down entirely.

The Boston Police Force Strike. In Massachusetts, members of the Boston police force worked a 12-hour day for which they earned between $1100 and $1600 a year. Out of this money, they were expected to buy their uniforms. The police officers felt that they would stand a better chance of getting a pay raise if they belonged to a union.

Police unions were not unusual, as police forces of several other cities were already members of the American Federation of Labor (AFL). However, Police Commissioner Edwin Curtis believed that police officers who belonged to a labor union could not perform their sworn duty. He told the Boston police

Ask students if they concur with Coolidge's statement: "There is no right to strike against the public safety."

officers that they could not unionize and threatened to suspend union organizers from their jobs.

At this point, Mayor Andrew Peters stepped in and appointed a 34-member citizens' group to look into the matter. After careful study, the group suggested that the dispute be arbitrated, that the punishment of the police officers be put off indefinitely, and that the Boston Policemen's Union be recognized, so long as it had no formal links with the AFL.

When Curtis refused to go along with the suggestions of the citizens' group and suspended 19 officers, the police went on strike. Soon hoodlums and looters took to the streets, smashing windows and looting stores. Since neither the governor nor Curtis would act, Mayor Peters called in the Boston contingent of the state guard to maintain order. He also recruited volunteers to help. Within a few days, six people had been killed in clashes with the guard and the inexperienced volunteers.

Finally, Governor Calvin Coolidge called out the entire state guard. He also issued an executive order taking over the police department and reinstated Curtis, whom Mayor Peters had removed from office. When the head of the AFL protested, Coolidge answered, "There is no right to strike against the public safety by anybody, anywhere, anytime."

Coolidge received national recognition for his stand on the strike issue. The striking police officers received nothing. In fact, they all lost their jobs, and a whole new police force was recruited to take their place.

The Steelworkers Strike. In September 1919, more than 350,000 steelworkers went on strike. The strike spread across ten states, bringing 50 towns and cities to a standstill. The cause of the strike was the steel companies' refusal to agree to workers' demands for better wages, an 8-rather than a 12-hour day, and the right to have a union.

Two-thirds of the workers were foreign-born, while most of the supervisors and office workers, who refused to join the strike, were American-born. The steel companies played up this fact, handing out antistrike circulars with messages such as the following:

WAKE UP AMERICANS!! Italian laborers, organized under the American Federation of Labor are going to strike Monday and are threatening workmen who want to continue working. These foreigners have been told by labor agitators that if they would join the union they would get Americans' jobs.

Nearly 3,000 strikes involving 4 million workers swept the nation in 1919. Perhaps no strike raised as much interest and debate as the strike by members of the Boston Police Department. State troops were ordered to the city by Governor Calvin Coolidge to keep order. Why were labor-management conflicts so frequent after World War I?

Ask students to explain the relationship between advocacy of workers' rights and left-wing ideology.

Note that throughout American history, belief in a "conspiracy" as an explanation for problems has been common.

Violence broke out when the steel companies brought in strikebreakers protected by federal and state troops. In January 1920, the strike was called off. Meanwhile, more than a dozen lives and $112 million in wages were lost, and the strikers gained nothing at all.

The Coalminers Strike. A few weeks after the steelworkers went on strike, the coalminers did the same. At the time, coal was America's chief source of energy. The coalminers, who formed the backbone of the United Mine Workers, resented the profits mine owners were making at their expense. Overworked and underpaid, the miners demanded a 60 percent increase in base pay, a 6-hour day, and a 5-day week. When the demands were not met, almost 450,000 coalminers refused to report to work.

The mining companies appealed to United States Attorney General A. Mitchell Palmer for help. He responded with a court injunction declaring the strike illegal. Union leader John L. Lewis told the miners, "We cannot fight the government," and urged them to return to work. All but about 50,000 miners took Lewis' advice. Ultimately, the miners won a partial victory in the form of a 31 percent increase in base pay. This gave them a minimum of $7.50 a day, the highest base wage in the industry.

The Red Scare

Most Americans believed there was a strong tie between union activism and radicalism. This belief helped fuel a movement to curtail radicalism in the United States.

Known as the Red Scare, the movement began with a general concern with communism. **Communism** is a theory that advocates the elimination of private property. It is also a totalitarian system of government in which a single political party controls state-owned means of production. Communist doctrine is based on the theories of German philosopher Karl Marx, who believed that history is a series of conflicts between workers and the ruling class, and that eventually a workers' revolution would produce a classless society. When revolutionaries called Bolsheviks took over the Russian government in 1917, many Americans felt that the Russian people now had a chance to enter the ranks of democratic countries. But the Bolsheviks, led by Lenin, were guided by

A 1919 cartoon makes the point that anarchists, Communists, and other radicals might be lurking anywhere. Government agents seized thousands of political and labor agitators for questioning. Nearly 250 people were deported. Why did some Americans object to the government's action against protestors?

Marxist ideas. As the nature of the new government's Communist leadership and programs became clear, American opinion about what had taken place in Russia changed.

One of the Communists' chief aims was to bring about worldwide revolution in order to overthrow capitalism anywhere it existed. When several European countries were shaken by revolutions, Americans realized that a small group of activists could overthrow a long-established government. Thus, when a Workers' party was formed in the United States in 1919, millions of Americans began to fear that there would be a revolution in America. Rumors began to circulate about a huge radical conspiracy against the American government and institutions. This served to deepen people's fears.

Fuel was added to the fire when 36 bombs were mailed to such important Americans as Seattle Mayor Ole Hanson, Georgia Senator Thomas R. Hardwick, financier J. P. Morgan, and Supreme Court Justice Oliver Wendell Holmes, Jr.[1] The bombs were not

---

[1] All the bombs but one were intercepted by the Post Office. The bomb mailed to Senator Hardwick reached its destination and injured his maid.

planted by Communists, but by anarchists. The American public, however, paid little attention to this fact. In their eyes, anarchists, like labor agitators and Communists, were radicals, and radicals of any kind posed a threat to the United States.

The Palmer Raids. A short time later, there was another series of bomb explosions. This time one damaged the front of the Washington, D. C. home of Attorney General A. Mitchell Palmer and killed an innocent passerby. The incident angered Palmer. He went before Congress to ask for money to pay for an anti-radical campaign. With the funds he received, he set up a new division in the Justice Department.

From November 1919 to May 1920, Palmer staged a series of raids on political and labor agitators all over the country. The wartime Sedition Act gave him the right to deport any aliens who were anarchists. It also gave him the right to deport those who believed in or advocated the overthrow of the government by violence or were members of any group that so believed or advocated.

More than 6000 people were arrested during the raids, most without warrants. Those arrested were held without bail. However, very few aliens were actually deported, due to a lack of evidence.

Before long, some Americans became disgusted with Palmer's tactics and spoke out against them. One such person was William Allen White, a prominent midwestern newspaper editor, who wrote:

> *The Attorney General seems to be seeing red. He is rounding up every manner of radical in the country; every man who hopes for a better world is in danger of deportation by the Attorney General. The whole business is un-American. There are certain fundamental rules which should govern in the treason cases.*
>
> *First, it should be agreed that a man should believe what he chooses.*
>
> *Second, it should be agreed that when he preaches violence he is disturbing the peace and should be put in jail. . . .*
>
> *Third, he should be allowed to say what he pleases so long as he advocates legal constitutional methods of procedure. Just because a man does not believe this government is good is no reason why he should be deported.*

Sacco and Vanzetti. While some Americans did not like Palmer's methods, many agreed with him about the danger presented by radicals. In the minds of many Americans, the terms "radical" and "foreigner" became synonymous. This led to an antagonism toward and a general distrust of all immigrants.

The matter came to a head on May 5, 1920 when two Italian immigrants, Nicola Sacco and Bartolomeo Vanzetti, were arrested. They were charged with taking part in a payroll robbery in South Braintree, Massachusetts, in which a paymaster and a guard had been killed.

Sacco and Vanzetti were brought to trial in July 1921. Although many people thought that the evidence presented during the trial was far from clear-cut, both men were convicted and sentenced to death.

Defense committees managed to secure a stay of execution. This, however, did not satisfy the many people who believed that Sacco and Vanzetti had been condemned more for what they were than for the crimes of which they had been accused. Neither Sacco nor Vanzetti spoke English well. Both were anarchists who had fled to Mexico during World War I to avoid the draft.

Demonstrations were held in the United States, Latin America, and Europe to protest that Sacco and Vanzetti had not received a fair trial. Italian-Americans rallied to help the convicted men. Anarchists and Communists agitated in their behalf. More than 15,000 sympathizers gathered together in New York to demonstrate for the unconditional freedom of Sacco and Vanzetti.

As a result of the protests, Governor Alvan T. Fuller of Massachusetts appointed a commission of prominent Americans to examine the evidence and conduct of the trial. The committee came out in favor of the original verdict, and on August 23, 1927, Nicola Sacco and Bartolomeo Vanzetti were put to death in the electric chair.

Immigrant Restriction

American feelings about foreigners could also be seen in the attitude toward immigration. World War I had dramatically slowed the huge flow of immigration that had begun in the 1880's. After the war ended,

Explain that theories of the time tended to see social and cultural traits as inherent rather than acquired.

Lack of opportunity was the major reason why the majority of the population was illiterate in southern and eastern Europe.

Nicola Sacco and Bartolomeo Vanzetti are escorted under heavy guard to the courthouse in Dedham, Massachusetts, during their trial. The two immigrants were tried and convicted of the 1920 payroll robbery and murder of a paymaster and his guard. Although thousands rallied to their defense, Sacco and Vanzetti were ultimately executed in 1927. Why did this case create so much controversy?

however, heavy immigration resumed. Many Americans saw this as a threat and voiced the fear that some of the newcomers would not blend in and become "good Americans."

American opposition to immigration was not something new. It had been going on since the late 1800's, when southern and eastern Europeans had begun to enter the United States in large numbers. In the 1920's, the opposition was based on several different factors, including ethnic background, language, customs, and religion. In the view of some Americans, any one of these factors could be a barrier to assimilation as well as a sign of intellectual or spiritual inferiority.

Each of the various interest groups in the country had its own reasons for not liking the influx of foreigners. Conservatives viewed the newcomers

as radicals. Politicians believed that immigrant voting blocks were a threat to American political traditions. Reformers felt that any more immigrants would add to the many problems of the cities. And labor leaders insisted that most immigrants were unskilled workers, with which the labor market already was flooded.

Before the war, those against unrestricted immigration persuaded Congress to pass a bill that said all immigrants had to pass a literacy test before they could enter the United States. President Wilson, however, vetoed the bill. He said that education was one of the opportunities immigrants were seeking in this country. But when the matter was raised again during the war, the literacy bill was passed.

After the war, Congress went one step further and voted for a strong quota system to restrict immigra-

From 1900 to 1920, more than 700,000 immigrants came to the United States each year. In the decade following the 1929 legislation, the number dropped to around 50,000 annually.

ton. A 1921 quota law limited immigration in any year to three percent of the number of each nationality living in America in 1910. In 1924 Congress passed a new quota law that dropped the percentage to two percent and based it on the census of 1890. In 1929 the National Origins Act set the overall quota at 150,000 immigrants per year, and changed the base for the calculation of percentages from 1890 to 1920. The main purpose of these laws was to reduce the number of immigrants from southern and eastern Europe.

SECTION REVIEW

1. Identify the following: Edwin Curtis, A. Mitchell Palmer, John L. Lewis, National Origins Act.
2. Why did Americans equate union activities with radicalism?
3. What was the purpose of the Palmer raids?
4. Why was there public sympathy for Sacco and Vanzetti?
5. What changes took place in immigration laws following World War I?

IMMIGRATION, 1921–1930

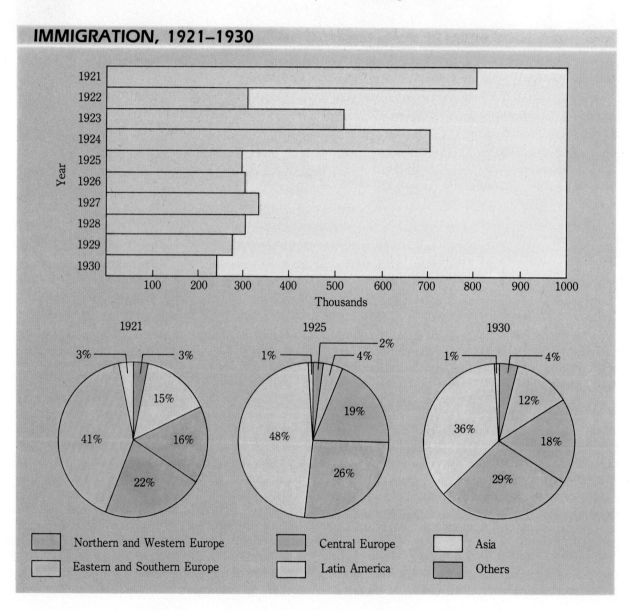

Northern and Western Europe

Eastern and Southern Europe

Central Europe

Latin America

Asia

Others

Point out the fact that the regions in which the Klan was strongest were not necessarily the regions in which the groups they despised were most numerous. Catholics and Jews were rare in the rural South, and Catholics, Jews, and blacks were rare in the rural Midwest.

Ku Klux Klan parades, such as this one in Washington, D.C., were common in the mid-1920's. The Klan, nearly powerless since Reconstruction, was reorganized in 1916. Membership passed 4 million in 1924. By the end of the decade, however, the movement had collapsed and its influence had vanished. Why?

2 The Defense of Traditionalism

Immigration restriction was only one example of a strong conservative trend in politics during the 1920's. Many Americans felt the need to defend traditional values in the face of the many changes that were taking place. The effort to resist change took many different turns. One such case was the revival of the Ku Klux Klan.

The Ku Klux Klan

The original Ku Klux Klan had died out during the Reconstruction era, but in 1915 a new Klan emerged in Atlanta, Georgia. It started with 16 men. By 1922 it had more than 100,000 members. Despite its reputation for violence, the Klan kept growing, until by 1924 it had a membership of more than 4 million. It invaded almost every part of the country and in some areas wielded great political power.

The Klan drew people for a number of different reasons. Some were attracted by its claim to be a private and exclusive "club" open only to white, American-born, Protestant men.[2] Others were attracted by its secret rites and passwords, the colorful names it gave to its officers, the special costumes members wore, and its symbolic flaming cross. Most, however, saw in the Klan a means to express their opposition to change.

The Klan lashed out against minorities—Catholics, Jews, immigrants, and blacks. At the time, most Catholics and Jews lived in the cities and were not American-born. Their customs and values seemed very alien to the rural southerners and midwesterners who made up the greatest part of the Klan membership. Catholics were viewed as a threat because of their allegiance to the Pope and their opposition to **prohibition,** the ban on the manufacture and sale of alcoholic beverages.

The Plight of Black Americans. The chief target of the Klan, however, was blacks. Between 1915 and 1922, more than 430 blacks were lynched. Most of the lynchings took place in the South. However, the North, where a great many blacks had migrated during the war, also experienced race problems.

---

[2] Although women were not allowed to be members of the Ku Klux Klan, they did take part in Klan activities.

Note that other efforts to help blacks return to Africa were sponsored by white people.

Have students discuss the validity of the statement: "You can't legislate changes in attitude."

Urban blacks, especially those in the North, were angered by their social and economic status. They suffered from poor housing, low pay, and job discrimination. The National Association for the Advancement of Colored People (NAACP) and the Commission on Interracial Cooperation fought for federal anti-lynching legislation and for civil rights. Their efforts, however, met with little success.

In 1919 race riots occurred in more than two dozen American cities. Often these riots were started by nothing more than the presence of a black in a place where whites did not want a black to be. The riots resulted in a great deal of property damage and the loss of hundreds of lives.

A great many blacks, especially those living in urban ghettoes, turned to an organization called the Universal Negro Improvement Association. Its leader, a West Indian black named Marcus Garvey, believed in black superiority and wanted blacks to return to Africa to create a black empire. Garvey's movement was the first mass movement of American blacks. However, Garvey's plans ran aground financially, and only a few people actually left the country. In 1925 Garvey was sent to prison for using the mails to defraud, but black nationalism persisted.

The Decline of the Klan. The Klan reached its peak in the mid-1920's. To millions of Americans it was a thing of terror. Exposés of its violent and illegal activities seemed to have no effect on its power.

Finally, in November of 1925, the Klan's Grand Dragon, David C. Stephenson, was convicted on a charge of murder. This became a turning point for the Klan. By the following year, its membership was on the decline. By 1930 it had only about 9000 members.

Prohibition

Another sign of the conservative mood of the times was the drive for prohibition. Groups such as the Women's Christian Temperance Union and the Anti-Saloon League had been campaigning against alcohol for years. During World War I disapproval of drinking alcohol increased for three major reasons. First, many brewers were German or of German descent, and Germany was the enemy. Second, brewing used up barley that was needed to make bread for soldiers. Third, alcohol could hurt the fighting efficiency of the nation. By 1917 prohibition

had been established in 19 states. This, however, did not satisfy the Anti-Saloon League, which pressed for a national prohibition amendment.

The Eighteenth Amendment and the Volstead Act. In December 1917 Congress adopted and submitted to the states the Eighteenth Amendment, known as the Prohibition Amendment, which prohibited the "manufacture, sale, or transportation of intoxicating liquors." Ratified by the states in January 1919, it was to go into effect on January 20, 1920.

The amendment, however, did not outlaw buying or drinking liquor. Nor did it define the term "intoxicating liquors" or offer any means of enforcement. For these reasons, on October 28, 1919, Congress passed the National Prohibition Enforcement Act, or Volstead Act. This act, which was to go into effect on the same day as the Eighteenth Amendment, stated that any beverage containing more than one-half of one percent alcohol was to be considered intoxicating liquor. It also gave the Bureau of Internal Revenue power to enforce the law.

The Enforcement and Effects of Prohibition. Enforcement was difficult, because drinking was a habit thoroughly ingrained in the fabric of American social life. The saloon had grown out of the frontier and had matched the pace of industrialization and urbanization each step of the way. Therefore, by the 1920's, it was almost impossible to do away with drinking, especially in the cities. Before long, law enforcement officials found that they were battling not individual abusers, but gangsters such as Al Capone, king of the Chicago underworld, who saw the illegal rum-running business as a way of making a lot of money.

The rise of organized crime was due partly to prohibition. **Bootleggers,** those who dealt in the illegal traffic of alcohol, made millions of dollars selling liquor to the public. Most of the liquor was made at illegal stills in the United States. Much of the rest was smuggled in from Canada and the islands of the Caribbean.

By the early 1930's more than 200,000 **speakeasies,** illegal saloons hidden from the public eye by a legitimate store or store front, had sprung up. Some were run by owner-hostesses such as Texas Guinan, Belle Livingston, and Helen Morgan.

Prohibition was more than a protest against "Demon Rum." It also was a defense of the old rural

Ask students to discuss alternatives to prohibition.

Fundamentalists were religious conservatives who were generally Protestant.

An unwanted result of Prohibition was the stimulus it gave to organized crime. Rival gangs fought one another to control the profit derived from the production and sale of illegal alcohol. Jack Levine's painting, ''Gangster Funeral,'' is symbolic of the times. During the 1920's nearly 500 gang-related murders were committed in Chicago alone. In what other illegal activities did organized crime take part?

America against the threat of urbanization and social change. As such, it was a legal triumph for the conservatives in American society. Supporters of prohibition argued that the ban was a good one and enforcement simply had to be strengthened. One Iowa social worker explained:

> *With the passing of the saloon in our neighborhood, families who had no furniture began to collect a few pieces. Bedsteads and mattresses were seen where before there had been heaps of rags. Children who stayed away from school for lack of suitable clothing became more regular in attendance. . . . Men who had never been seen publicly with their wives and children escorted them occasionally to Roadside [settlement house] parties.*

Critics of prohibition, on the other hand, argued that there were more bad effects than good ones. Many citizens simply paid no attention to the law. Many officials, who felt that it could not be enforced, did not even try to make it work. This kind of thinking led to a blasé attitude toward law in general. Further, prohibition was bad for the country economically. In

the past, federal, state, and local governments supplemented their revenues by taxing liquor sales. Now the money went to smugglers, bootleggers, gangsters, corrupt police officers, and crooked politicians and judges who accepted payoffs for looking the other way.

Eventually, the critics of prohibition won out. In 1933 the Eighteenth Amendment was repealed by the Twenty-First Amendment.[3]

The Fundamentalist Crusade

Among those who came out strongly in support of prohibition were the **fundamentalists,** people who believe in the letter of the Bible and refuse to accept any teaching that seems to conflict with it. Another issue even more important to the fundamentalists was the teaching of evolution in public schools. The fundamentalists felt that Darwin's theory was a denial of divine creation as revealed in the Book of Genesis of the Bible.

---

[3] The Twenty-First Amendment repealed national prohibition, but not prohibition by states. Transportation of liquor into states that had prohibition laws also remained a federal crime.

Early in the 1920's, the fundamentalists launched a campaign to ban the teaching of Darwinism. Although they failed in Kentucky, they succeeded in Tennessee. In 1924 Tennessee passed the Butler Act, which made it illegal for any public school teacher "to teach any theory that denies the story of the Divine Creation of man as taught in the Bible and to teach instead that man has descended from a lower order or animals."

The next year, several university science instructors were dismissed for disobeying the new law. Shortly after, John Thomas Scopes, a high school biology teacher in Dayton, Tennessee, was dismissed for the same reason. On the advice of some friends, Scopes decided to take his case to court. The trial, which took place in July 1925, attracted national attention. The newspapers made it front page news and dubbed it the "Monkey Trial."

Scopes was supported by the American Civil Liberties Union (ACLU) and defended by Clarence Darrow, a well-known trial lawyer with liberal views. The state was represented by William Jennings Bryan, a prominent politician and fundamentalist leader. The ACLU maintained that the firing of Scopes was an infringement on the right of free speech. Bryan maintained that the theory taught by Scopes represented a direct threat to religion because it encouraged children to repudiate their faith.

Scopes admitted that he had taught his students the theory of evolution, and the case quickly moved beyond the question of whether or not Scopes had broken the law. Instead, it turned into a debate between evolutionary theory and fundamentalist beliefs—between science and religion. The trial took on a circus-like atmosphere. Food vendors set up stalls along the streets, and reporters and photographers arrived by the hundreds. Western Union telegraph operators sat ready to pass on every word spoken at the trial.

The climax came on July 20 when Bryan agreed to take the stand as an expert witness on the Bible. Darrow was relentless in his questioning of Bryan. As the day grew longer and hotter, tempers flared. Darrow announced that he was examining Bryan "to prevent bigots and ignoramuses from controlling the educational system of the United States." A furious Bryan retorted that his intent was "to protect the

In 1925 nationwide attention was focused on the small town of Dayton, Tennessee, site of the "monkey" trial. Clarence Darrow (left) defended John Scopes, who was indicted for teaching evolution. William Jennings Bryan (right) led the prosecution. What is significant about the outcome of this trial?

word of God against the greatest atheist and agnostic in the United States."

In the end, Scopes was found guilty and fined $100. Later, the state supreme court freed Scopes on a technicality. At the same time, however, it upheld the anti-evolution law. In theory, the fundamentalists had won. But reporters at the trial, most of whom were from the big city papers and sympathetic to Darrow from the start, wrote stories that showed Bryan as ignorant of science. As a result, the fundamentalist point of view was somewhat discredited and came to be regarded by many as an attempt to stifle intellectual freedom.

SECTION REVIEW

1. Identify the following: Marcus Garvey, David C. Stephenson, Volstead Act, John Scopes, Clarence Darrow.
2. Why were some people attracted to the Ku Klux Klan?
3. What kinds of problems did the blacks face in the 1920's?
4. How did World War I contribute to the prohibition movement?
5. What were the arguments against prohibition?
6. Why were fundamentalists opposed to Darwin's theories?

Ask students to explain what was meant by the statement that Harding "had risen to the Senate by serving Ohio's political machine."

Have students discuss why, after refusing to join the League of Nations, the United States involved itself in a series of international treaties.

3 Politics in the 1920's

The conservative mood of the country worked to the disadvantage of Wilson and the Democrats. By 1920 the Democrats had been in power for nearly eight years. During that time a great deal of resentment had been built up towards some of their policies. With Wilson lying ill in the White House, most Democrats knew that their party had little hope of winning the upcoming presidential election.

The Republicans, on the other hand, were very optimistic about their chances for success. By the middle of 1920, the prosperity of the war years had just about come to an end. People were running out of money, the economy was slowing down, and unemployment was on the rise. Most Americans were tired of President Wilson's sermons on duty, obligation, and national mission, and wanted a change. The Republicans were thus confident that their time had come.

The Harding Administration

In 1920 the Republicans nominated Warren Gamaliel Harding for President and Calvin Coolidge, the hero of the Boston police strike, as Vice President. Harding was a small-town newspaper publisher who had risen to the Senate by serving Ohio's political machine.

Against Harding and Coolidge, the Democrats nominated James M. Cox, a former progressive governor of Ohio, for President and Assistant Secretary of the Navy Franklin D. Roosevelt for Vice President. Cox and Roosevelt campaigned vigorously, but the people cast their votes overwhelmingly for the conservative Republicans.

Harding, who wanted to be liked more than he wanted to be a strong President, believed that the country's present need was "not heroics but healing; not nostrums but normalcy; not revolution but restoration; . . . not surgery but serenity." He later explained what he meant by normalcy:

I don't mean the old order but a regular steady order of things. I mean normal procedure, the natural way, without excess. I don't believe the old order can or should come back, but we must have normal order or, as I have said, normalcy.

Harding promised the people to form an administration made up of the "most experienced minds" in the country. Among these was industrial tycoon Andrew Mellon, whom Harding named Secretary of the Treasury. A favorite of the American business community, Mellon got Congress to raise tariffs on imports and reduce taxes on the wealthy. He also cut the federal deficit and strongly opposed bonuses for veterans. Mellon stayed on to serve as Secretary under the next two Presidents.

The Washington Conference and War Debts. One of the outstanding achievements of the Harding administration was the Washington Conference for the Limitation of Armaments, which began on November 12, 1921. From this conference came several important treaties. The United States, Japan, France, Italy, and Great Britain agreed to build no capital ships for the next ten years, to restrict the use of submarines in war, and to outlaw the use of poisonous gases. The United States, Great Britain, France, and Japan agreed to respect one another's island possessions in the Pacific and to settle disagreements that occurred in that area by conciliatory negotiations. Japan agreed to return certain territory to China and confirmed America's cable rights on Yap Island. All nine powers[4] present at the conference agreed to guarantee China's independence and territorial integrity. They also agreed to respect the Open Door in China.

The agreements reached at the Washington Conference were a major accomplishment for the United States in view of its strained relations with the Allies over the issue of war debts. During the war the United States loaned the Allies huge sums of money. After the armistice it loaned even more for relief purposes and as advances for the payment of surplus war goods left in Europe.

The Allies still owed the United States $10 billion, and the Americans made it clear that they expected the debts to be paid. Government officials pointed out that during the war they had to pay for everything the United States got from the Allies—$100 for every American soldier carried to Europe on a British ship, cash on the spot for every item from cabbages to ammunition provided by the French. The Allies had not suggested then as they were doing now that all

---

[4] The United States, Great Britain, Japan, France, Italy, China, Portugal, Belgium, and the Netherlands.

resources be pooled. Americans felt that the Allies had a moral duty to pay their debts.

Administrative Scandals. Less than a year and a half after Harding took office, his administration was racked by scandal. It was discovered that Charles R. Forbes, the Director of the Veteran's Bureau and a close friend of Harding, had made illegal deals that had netted him hundreds of thousands of dollars in commissions. When this fact became public, the attorney for the Bureau, who was also involved, shot himself. His suicide was closely followed by that of Jesse Smith, a close friend of Attorney General Harry M. Daugherty, who himself was later accused of corruption while in office. Before Smith shot himself, he took care to burn many of his and Daugherty's private papers. This led to rumors about murder and the Attorney General.

These scandals greatly affected President Harding. Complaining of insomnia and depression, he set out in June 1923 on a cross-country tour and a trip to Alaska. On his return trip from Alaska, he fell ill and died on August 2, 1923.

After Harding's death, the Teapot Dome Affair, the greatest scandal of all, broke loose. This episode involved Secretary of the Interior Albert B. Fall and the oil reserves set aside for the Navy at Teapot Dome, Wyoming, and Elk Hills, California. Fall requested that control over these reserves be transferred to his department. Then, without allowing competitive bidding, he granted secret leases on the land to private oil companies. In return, the oil companies gave him huge sums of money. When the deal was exposed, Fall was tried and sent to prison for taking bribes. He became the first member of a presidential cabinet to go to jail.

The Coolidge Administration

After President Harding's death, Vice President Calvin Coolidge became President. In 1924 he was elected President in his own right under the slogans "Keep Cool with Coolidge" and "Coolidge or Chaos."

Coolidge continued to support programs favorable to economic growth, saying that "this is a business country; it wants a business government" and that "the man who builds a factory builds a temple. . . . The man who works there worships there."

On the whole, the Coolidge administration practiced non-involvement. The American people seemed

After the Harding scandals, Americans seemed relieved that the reins of government fell to Calvin Coolidge (left) shown here with Secretary of Commerce Herbert Hoover. Why were most Americans satisfied with Coolidge's brand of leadership?

to want as little government as possible at as low a cost as possible, and the administration was willing to oblige. It avoided intervention in international affairs and stepped in only when it absolutely had to. It did, however, collect some war debts and pass the World War Adjusted Compensation Act. The act gave veterans the bonuses they had fought so hard to get.

In domestic affairs, the administration was just as cautious, exerting itself only to maintain the status quo for the benefit of business. Much to the distress of the farmers, however, the administration refused to pass the McNary-Haugen bill. This bill sought to deal with agricultural problems by controlling farm surplus and stabilizing prices. Coolidge vetoed the bill twice on the grounds that it involved price-fixing and benefited only certain groups. Coolidge believed that by limiting the role of government in the economy and by lifting the tax burdens of the rich, he was helping the whole country.

The Election of 1928

Since Coolidge decided not to run again for President in 1928, the Republicans chose Herbert Hoover as their candidate. Hoover was the son of a midwestern farmer. He was the very model of the self-made man admired by so many Americans. He was well-liked by the American people and well-known for his honesty, efficiency, and humanitarianism.

The Republicans based their hopes for winning the election on "Coolidge Prosperity." They ran the following advertisement in newspapers from coast to coast:

> *The Republican Party isn't a "poor man's party." Republican prosperity has erased that degrading phrase from our political vocabulary. Republican efficiency has filled the working-man's dinner pail—and his gas tank besides—made the telephone, radio and sanitary plumbing standard household equipment. And placed a whole nation in the silk stocking class. Republican prosperity has reduced hours and increased earning capacity, silenced discontent, put the proverbial "chicken in every pot" and a car in every backyard to boot.*

Hoover, upon accepting his party's nomination proclaimed:

> *We in America today are nearer to the final triumph over poverty than ever before in the history of the land. . . . We have not yet reached the goal, but, given a chance to go forward with the policies of the last eight years, we shall soon, with the help of God, be in sight of the day when poverty will be banished from this nation.*

The Democrats, who felt they had little chance against Republican prosperity, chose a far different kind of candidate—New York governor Alfred E. Smith. Like Hoover, Smith was well-known for his honesty and efficiency, but the similarities ended there. Smith was an easterner associated with Tammany Hall. He was the son of immigrants. More importantly, he was a Catholic, the first ever to be nominated for President or Vice President by either the Democratic or Republican party.

Smith openly opposed prohibition and favored temperance instead. Further, he favored programs to enhance public health and recreation facilities, government ownership of utilities, and government aid to farmers. As a result, many people agreed with the journalist who stated, "The whole Puritan

ELECTION OF 1928

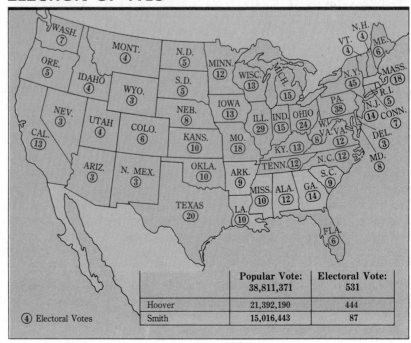

	Popular Vote: 38,811,371	Electoral Vote: 531
Hoover	21,392,190	444
Smith	15,016,443	87

④ Electoral Votes

Given the repetitive nature of many factory jobs, saving a fraction of a second in each operation could add up to a substantial increase in production over time.

civilization which has built a sturdy, orderly nation is threatened by Smith."

Smith and the Democratic party worked in vain to convince the American people that their concerns about him were unfounded. Hoover won the election, taking 58 percent of the popular vote and carrying all but 8 states. Hoover even carried Smith's home state of New York.

SECTION REVIEW

1. Identify the following: Andrew Mellon, Charles R. Forbes, World War Adjusted Compensation Act, McNary-Haugen bill, Alfred E. Smith.
2. What important agreements were reached at the Washington Conference for the Limitation of Armaments?
3. Why did America demand repayment of war debts?
4. What problems did Harding's administration experience?
5. What was Coolidge's belief about the role of government?
6. What were the main issues in the election of 1928?

4 Social and Cultural Life

With the end of World War I and the start of the 1920's came another industrial revolution. One cause of the new wave of technological innovation and increased productivity was the widespread use of electrical power. In 1912 only 16 percent of the American people lived in electrically lighted homes. By 1927 the number had risen to 63 percent. Americans developed a voracious appetite for energy. In less than ten years, the sale of electricity doubled. Consumption of fuel oil more than doubled, while that of gas quadrupled.

Another cause of the revolution was the newly introduced idea of **scientific management,** the efficient use of people and space. The pioneer of scientific management was engineer Frederick Winslow Taylor, who did time-motion studies of workers in factories in order to see how goods could be produced more quickly. Many industries also set up research laboratories to develop new tools and products.

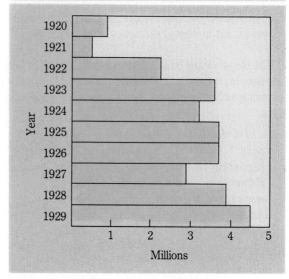

AUTOMOBILE SALES, 1920–29

The New Consumerism

As energy poured into industry, goods poured out. As productivity increased, private ownership gave way to corporate ownership. In time, huge corporations merged and grew even larger. The result of all this was twofold. People found they now had a wide array of new products that they could buy. Many of the products not only were fun but also made life easier. Thus Americans also found they had more leisure time in which to enjoy themselves.

Among the products that gained popularity in the 1920's were telephones, vacuum cleaners, refrigerators, and canned goods. While these items and others like them made it possible for Americans to spend less time on household chores and more time on recreation, another product had an even greater impact. The product was the automobile.

In 1908 Henry Ford had introduced the Model T automobile—a plain, black, no-frills car that sold for about $950. The car, which had only 20 horsepower, could go at the most only 45 miles (72 kilometers) an hour. Called the "Tin Lizzie," it was "designed for everyday wear and tear" and became the first reliable car within easy reach of most wage earners. Farmers especially prized it. With a pickup truck attachment, it could take crops to market. By jacking up the wheels and attaching a pulley, it could be a churn in the dairy or a cider press in the orchard. It could also saw wood, fill a silo, and bale hay in the fields.

In 1914 Ford started the first electrically powered assembly line, which made production more efficient and allowed him to drop the price of the car considerably. As a result, by 1929 the automobile industry was turning out 4,750,000 cars a year. Between 1920 and 1929, the number of registered cars jumped from 8 million to 23 million, and about 20 percent of all Americans now owned a car.

The automobile industry revolutionized American society. The industry used so much steel, glass, wood, gasoline, and rubber that it provided jobs for 5 million people. It transformed American buying habits, making installment buying a way of life for most Americans. It promoted highway construction and travel, which in turn produced hotels and restaurants in what had once been considered out-of-the-way places.

The first modern filling station opened in 1913. By 1929 there were more than 120,000 of them. Trucking services also grew, as did taxi and bus services. Parking lots, garages, and automatic traffic lights made their appearance in most cities and towns.

The automobile made Americans mobile. Housewives could go out during the day to shop, lunch in tearooms, and enjoy one another's company. Families could go away from home on vacations. The young and old could take Sunday drives. Teenagers could go places unchaperoned for the first time. In short, Americans could escape, even if it was only for a few hours at a time. Humorist Will Rogers' salute to Henry Ford summed up the situation perfectly:

It will take us a hundred years to tell whether you have helped us or hurt us, but you certainly didn't leave us like you found us.

Pleasures and Pastimes

Recreation became the order of the day in the 1920's. It was a time of heroes and fads. Glossy new magazines and paperbacks were everywhere. Crossword puzzles, word games, and the Chinese game of Mah Jong became national obsessions. Evangelist Aimée Semple McPherson drew thousands with her Four-Square Gospel. Emile Coué, a retired French pharmacist, became the rage with his formula for curing ills. He had people repeating over

The finishing touches are put on a Model "A" at a Ford plant in Dearborn, Michigan. The auto quickly became the 1920's most popular form of diversion. In 1920 there were 7 million autos in the United States. By the end of the decade, 24 million passenger cars were in use. How did the auto change the way Americans lived?

and over again, "Day by day, in every way, I am getting better and better."

Sports. One recreational activity that occupied the minds—and often the bodies—of most Americans was sports. College sports soared in popularity as did professional sporting events. Football especially became a major attraction. It became easier for a college to raise money to build a football stadium than to raise a professor's salary. Football brought in enough money to support other minor college sports and provided hundreds of students with jobs as ticket takers and ushers.

Sports in general became big business as large crowds turned out to watch—and often to bet. Baseball became a national pastime, and the number of golfers, tennis players, bowlers, and amateur baseball players increased greatly. Thanks in great part to the efforts of sports journalists, athletes became larger-than-life heroes. In baseball, there was "Babe" Ruth and Ty Cobb; in boxing, Jack Dempsey and Gene Tunney; in football, Red Grange and Knute Rockne; in tennis, Bill Tilden and Helen Wills; in golf, Bobby Jones and Walter Hagen. These

athletes provided entertainment for millions of fun-seeking Americans.

Sound and Sensationalism. Another source of entertainment was the media. In 1920 the first commercial radio broadcast, which carried the Harding-Cox election returns, was transmitted by station KDKA in Pittsburgh. In 1922 New York station WBAY opened, offering to provide its services to anyone who would pay for them. Thus began commercial radio. By the end of that same year, there were 22 radio stations on the air, and home radio receivers were common. The people could stay at home and enjoy music, sportscasts, comedy skits, and special programs such as political conventions.

The radio itself started out as a crystal set with headphones. In 1926 most radios were large, with lots of dials, a horn loudspeaker, and a long outside aerial. Two sets of batteries were required—a storage battery that had to be replaced every two weeks and a set of dry cell batteries that had to be replaced every three weeks or so. By 1927, however, radio sets could get their power from an

The 1920's was a sports-minded decade. Fans thrilled to the accomplishments of baseball's Babe Ruth, Notre Dame's "Four Horsemen" on the gridiron, Gertrude Ederle in swimming, tennis player Helen Wills Moody (left), and golfer Bobby Jones (right). What accounts for the popularity of these athletes?

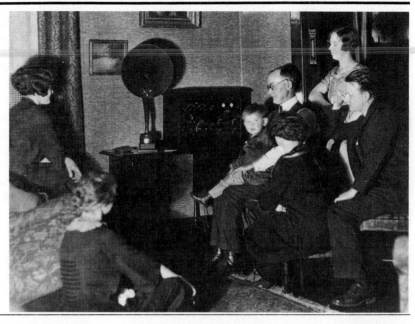

The 1920's ushered in the Golden Age of Broadcasting. By the end of the decade nearly half the homes in the United States had radios. Millions of households tuned in regularly to hear their favorite comedy, drama, music, and news broadcasts. What other forms of entertainment were popular during this period?

ordinary electric socket in the home. But even then, the radio had to be shut off frequently because moisture in the air kept causing static.

Radio created many popular personalities, one of the most famous of whom was singer Rudy Vallee. Vallee became the "dream man" of a generation of women. As one reporter explained:

> *It would seem that American women want a beau. Their husbands are busy earning the money that sends the ladies to the movies and buys them their radios. The poor men cannot be expected to come home from work, hurry through a shower, gussy up in white linens and start singing in a languid, cajoling way "I Kiss Your Hand, Madame." Rudy fits the bill. And that is that.*

Newspapers, too, came into their own. Newspaper publisher Joseph Pulitzer once told a *New York World* editor that a newspaper should contain "what is new, what is original, distinctive, dramatic, romantic, thrilling, unique, curious, quaint, humorous, odd, apt to be talked about without shocking good taste . . ." This credo of the yellow press was carried to new extremes during the 1920's.

A new kind of paper came into being. Called a **tabloid,** it was in business to peddle thrills. Usually it was one-half the size of an ordinary newspaper, and it

specialized in sensational pictures and short news stories. The *New York Daily News,* which was the leading tabloid of the time, justified this policy in an editorial in which it stated:

> *Newspapers print the news. That's why they're called newspapers. That part of the news happens to be scandalous is the result of the people who make it, not the fault of the papers.*

Newspapers catered to the public's desire for excitement, with pictures and headlines about crime, scandal, and the sensational. The Leopold-Loeb trial, for example, dominated the front pages for weeks.

The Leopold-Loeb trial took place in 1924. In May of that year, two wealthy Chicago teenagers, Nathan Leopold, Jr. and Richard Loeb, were charged with kidnapping and killing a 14-year-old boy and then demanding ransom from his father. At first, Leopold and Loeb denied the charges. Then they confessed, saying they had done what they did chiefly to experience the thrill of committing a perfect crime. For more than a month, their attorney, Clarence Darrow, fought to save them from the death sentence. In the end, he won, and the boys were sentenced to jail for life.

The journals also reported adventurous exploits like that of Captain Charles A. Lindbergh. On May 20, 1927, Lindbergh took off alone from New York in a

In the movie industry, many of the silent film stars were rendered "obsolete" by the advent of talking pictures because they had heavy foreign accents or unattractive voices.

single-engine monoplane, the *Spirit of St Louis.* More than 33 hours later, he landed in Paris, France. Lindbergh had completed the first nonstop solo flight across the Atlantic.

The Lively Arts. Still another form of recreation that prospered in the 1920's was the theater. Vaudeville shows drew large crowds. On a larger and more costly scale were extravaganzas like the Ziegfield Follies, which featured huge musical production numbers with scores of beautiful chorus girls in glamorous costumes.

Above all, there was the motion picture, rivaled in popularity only by the automobile. The first full-length feature film, *Birth of a Nation,* had appeared in 1915. The next innovation, a "talking picture," came 12 years later. Called *The Jazz Singer,* it featured Al Jolson in the starring role.

By the time *The Jazz Singer* appeared, the movie industry had become the fourth largest industry in the United States. More than 20,000 movie theaters were serving the millions of Americans who flocked to see their favorite motion pictures. The largest and newest movie palace of the day was the Roxy Theater, located in New York City a few blocks from Times Square. The theater, which cost $12 million to build, could seat more than 6000 persons and boasted 125 ushers, all elegantly uniformed. Called the Cathedral of the Motion Pictures, its huge marble lobby was filled with statues and paintings. From the ceiling hung a huge chandelier, and on the floor lay a flaming red rug that weighed 2 tons (1.8 metric tons) and cost $100,000.

The movies produced heroes for the masses. Stars such as Rudolph Valentino, Douglas Fairbanks, Mary Pickford, and Clara Bow were the romantic ideals for many people. The movies also afforded adventure and the humor of such comedians as Charlie Chaplin, Buster Keaton, Harold Lloyd, and Stan Laurel and Oliver Hardy.

The Palette and the Pen. Like the theater and the movies, art and literature were enjoyed by many in the 1920's. Some Americans were pleased, while others were shocked, as painters broke away from the traditions of the past to explore new ways of portraying the world. Joseph Stella portrayed evocative images of huge new bridges and ships, while Stuart Davis caught the rhythm of simple, everyday objects. Georgia O'Keefe used a unique combination of abstract design and realistic detail in her paintings of the American Southwest. But traditional realism remained an important trend as well. Edward Hopper came out with spare, muted paintings that featured city streets with lonely, anonymous people. Grant Wood painted country scenes that captured the harshness as well as the majesty of rural America.

A general rejection of the past was seen in literature. Poets, playwrights, and novelists expressed a great disillusionment with the postwar era. These writers, who came to be known as the Lost Generation, rejected traditional values. They felt alienated from everybody and everything. Many left America and went to Paris.

From this Lost Generation came some of the most creative and memorable writers of the century. Playwright Eugene O'Neill filled his plays with depression, disappointment, and torment. Sinclair Lewis wrote about the materialism and prejudice of the American small town and the cultural poverty of the middle class. H. L. Mencken, whom some thought "the most powerful personal influence on this

Painter Aaron Douglas used geometric designs to give his work its uniqueness. Douglas was one of a group of black artists, writers, and musicians whose works came to be part of the Harlem Renaissance. What philosophy did this group share?

Gutzon Borglum

One of the outstanding artists of the 1920's was sculptor Gutzon Borglum. Born in the frontier country of Idaho in 1871, he was encouraged by his Danish-born parents to paint. He especially enjoyed painting horses and Indians. Later Borglum studied art both in San Francisco and in Paris.

While in Europe, Borglum created a statue of a horse standing over a dead Indian. This work won him an award and the attention of the European art community.

In 1901 Borglum returned to the United States. As a monument to Confederate heroes of the Civil War, he designed a mammoth sculpture to be cut into the side of Stone Mountain in Georgia. The sculpture was never finished because of a quarrel between Borglum and his sponsors.

Meanwhile Borglum had begun plans for another giant sculpture—the heads of Washington, Jefferson, Lincoln, and Theodore Roosevelt. He began cutting the heads of the Presidents into Mount Rushmore in 1927. He died 14 years later with the work not yet done. However, he had trained his son, Lincoln Borglum, to take over. Less than a year later, the Mount Rushmore Memorial was completed.

whole generation of educated people," spoke out against the conventional. He enjoyed shocking everyone with his impudent wit. William Faulkner exposed the contradictions between the myths and realities of life in the South. Ernest Hemingway critiqued war, dramatizing violent death and life's cruelty and stupidity. F. Scott Fitzgerald captured the emptiness and lack of meaning in the "good life" led by many rich young Americans in their endless search for excitement and pleasure.

In a letter written in Paris in 1925, Fitzgerald explained how those of the Lost Generation felt:

> *America's greatest promise is that something is going to happen, and after awhile you get tired of waiting because nothing happens to people except that they grow old. . . . The young people in America are brilliant with second-hand sophistication inherited from their betters of the war generation who to some extent worked things out for themselves. They are brave, shallow, cynical, impatient, turbulent and empty. I like them not.*

Other artists, poets, authors, and playwrights, such as Claude McKay, Langston Hughes, James Weldon Johnson, Walter White, and Alain Locke, also became well known during the 1920's. These creative people, however, were not members of the Lost Generation. They were, instead, products of the Harlem Renaissance, a general flowering of artistic endeavor among blacks, centered in the Harlem district of New York City. In Harlem, black artists and writers began to explore their existence and to express what it meant to be black in a white America.

The use of the black experience as a theme for novels, poems, paintings, and sculpture was new in a society that until now had recognized a few black artists. It was a sign of the times that Harlem was looked upon with interest and admiration by many white Americans.

The Revolution in Music and Morals

Change was the keynote of the era. And without doubt, one of the biggest changes was in music and dancing. The waltz gave way to the Charleston with its suddenly shifting rhythms and breathtaking pace. The Charleston and other "modern dances" shocked the older generation. In the words of one cleric, the dances "put the bodies of men and women in unusual relations to each other."

The Jazz Age. During the 1920's, people danced to the beat of a new kind of music called **jazz,** an indigenous musical form developed by black Americans. First played by funeral bands and honky-tonk pianists in New Orleans, jazz was a blending of European harmony and instrumentation and African-derived rhythms and scales. One of its major characteristics was **syncopation,** a shifting of the usual musical accent. Jazz attracted a great many Americans and it captured the spirit of the era so well that the 1920's is often referred to as "The Jazz Age."

Although black musicians such as Louis Armstrong and Duke Ellington made the new music popular and had white as well as black fans, many white Americans remained generally uncomfortable about black culture. As a result, jazz was brought to many by white musicians such as Leon "Bix" Beiderbecke and Red Nichols. These musicians picked up elements of the black style and smoothed them out to make the music sound more "white."

Band leader Paul Whiteman became known as the "King of Jazz." He gained many fans with his big, lush, watered-down jazz sound. Whiteman also helped to establish jazz as "serious music." In 1924 he arranged and conducted a jazz concert at New York City's Aeolian Hall, which had traditionally been the home of classical music and musicians. The concert, one of the most famous cultural events of the time, featured composer George Gershwin performing his "Rhapsody in Blue." One conductor later commented:

> *Various composers have been walking around jazz like a cat around a plate of hot soup, waiting for it to cool off so they might lift it to the level of music respectability. George Gershwin seems to have accomplished that miracle.*

The New Morality. Along with the new music, there was a new morality that became a basic part of the life of many Americans during the 1920's. At its root was pleasure-seeking.

Other people in other times in the past had brought about changes in morality, but never quite like in the 1920's. During this time, several factors came together to produce changes. One factor was the disillusionment brought on by World War I. The war had destroyed many Americans' innocent optimism about the future of the human race. For many, it was hard to believe that something that had cost so much could solve so little. Convinced that there was no guarantee that good would triumph over evil or that the world would be made safe for democracy, some people became cynical. They decided not to worry about tomorrow and to live instead for the moment.

A second factor in the changing morality was the new status of women. During the war, women had shown that they could be as capable as men. After the war, they were neither content nor willing to return to their earlier subservient roles. More than 20 percent of the total work force was women—women who now had the vote. For the first time, women had the status of full citizens. They were more secure and confident and felt they should have full social equality as well as the vote.

As a result, many women began to assert themselves more within society and to rid themselves of the symbols associated with their sex before the war. They cut their hair, raised their hemlines from below the ankle to above the knee, donned one-piece bathing suits, smoked and drank, and went to night spots without male escorts. Many women became known as **"flappers,"** unconventional females who wore short skirts, used makeup, and behaved boldly.

Some women gained national recognition for their activities. Margaret Sanger, a nurse in New York's tenement districts, battled well-entrenched laws by opening clinics to promote the use of birth control and prevent unwanted pregnancies. Gertrude Ederle challenged men in sports. In 1926 she became the first woman to swim the English Channel, beating the male mark by more than two hours.

A third factor that produced change was the influence of a German physician and neurologist named Sigmund Freud. Freud's theory that sexuality was an essential part of being human interested both men and women during the 1920's. Traditionally, married women had been looked upon chiefly as mothers. Now married women were seen more as wives and companions, and unhappy marriages were less tolerated. Divorce, which had been greatly frowned upon, became more acceptable. Between 1912 and 1920 the number of divorces doubled.

A fourth factor that contributed to the new morality was the combination of prosperity, technology, and

Music In Black Life

Music has always played a central role in the lives of black Americans. During slavery days, it was one of the few pleasures not forbidden to blacks, though the traditional use of drums was forbidden. Laws were passed against them out of fear that, as in Africa, drums would be used to communicate and perhaps to incite revolt.

Despite the restrictions on drumming, music helped blacks to preserve some of their African heritage. Certain general characteristics—call-and-response, improvisation, short repetitive phrases, and an emphasis on rhythm—were traits more typical of African than European music. These traits can still be heard in contemporary black musical forms, such as soul and gospel.

Music did much more than perpetuate the black heritage. Secular songs provided slaves with an outlet for feelings of resentment, love, and playfulness. Spirituals expressed their trust in God and their hopes for a better life in the world to come.

After emancipation, new kinds of music arose to express the new black experience. Blacks were technically free, yet continued to suffer serious problems. In rural areas, a form known as "the blues" took shape.

Classic blues have three line stanzas, the second line being a variation on the first. "Blue notes"—flatted thirds and sevenths—add to the distinctly mournful thrust of the lyrics. Uninhibited solo singers, often accompanied by guitar, bemoaned everything from poverty to Jim Crow laws to lost love. In the 1900's, the blues have provided a basis for many types of popular music. A choral style also evolved among rural blacks, who sang to help their work and to express their feelings.

Blues and work songs were also sung in the cities of the late 1800's. There were some distinctly urban types of black music as well. Old Testament spirituals were supplemented by gospel hymns, often set in lush harmonies sung by large church choirs.

In the creative hands of Scott Joplin and others, European classical forms were mixed with Afri-can-derived syncopations to produce ragtime. And the old black tradition of giving the deceased a big send-off into the next world, coupled with the general spread of brass bands in post-Civil War America, led to the formation of funeral bands. The freewheeling style of those in New Orleans fed directly into the most renowned form of black music, jazz.

The widespread popularity of ragtime and jazz, and the undeniable talent of performers such as trumpeter Louis Armstrong, pianist-composers Fats Waller and Duke Ellington, and singers Bessie Smith and Ma Rainey, helped to overcome white resistance to buying records and attending concerts featuring blacks. Indeed, the entertainment field was one of the earliest in which blacks could achieve national recognition and success.

Still, the racial barrier persisted. Even in the 1950's, rock-and-roll pioneer Chuck Berry could not bring about the enormous revolution in musical taste that Elvis Presley did. While Presley's distinctive voice and style are undeniable, the fact that he was white and Berry was black had a major impact on the difference in their popularity.

In the late 1950's and 1960's, however, black performers such as Johnny Mathis, the Supremes, Aretha Franklin, and Jimi Hendrix had many non-black as well as black fans. As the 1970's progressed, more and more "crossover" songs appeared—songs that were first successful on the black-oriented soul chart, then became successful on the white-oriented pop chart.

While keeping their preeminence in jazz, black performers have increasingly moved into previously white-dominated areas of the music world. Classical musicians, such as opera star Leontyne Price and pianist Andre Watts, are becoming less rare. Broadway has hosted numerous highly-acclaimed black musicals. The Afro-American contribution to American music has been great and promises to be even greater in the future.

QUESTIONS

1. What new kind of black music developed after emancipation?
2. What are "crossover" songs?

advertising. Prosperity was sufficiently widespread to provide many Americans with extra spending money. Technology made it possible for industry to turn out the products on which people could spend that extra money. And advertising gave people the reasons to do so.

Advertising aimed at the emotions rather than at the mind, selling a way of life centered on the happy home and the healthy family. Photographs were skillfully contrived to make people believe they were denying themselves unnecessarily if they did not share the joy others derived from owning, eating, or using a certain product. Advertising copywriters played on the desire for prestige. In the words of one author of the time:

> When all is said and done, this much can be said in behalf of advertising, that it gives a

certain illusion, a certain sense of escape in the machine age. It creates a dream world.

Still another factor was the motion picture, which did more than just entertain. It gave Americans who lived in small towns a glimpse of a glamorous lifestyle far different from the conservative one they and their neighbors knew. The revealing dresses, elaborate makeup, fancy hair styles, risqué dance steps, passionate speeches, and lingering kisses seen in movies were exciting things many wanted to experience for themselves.

These and other factors led many Americans, especially those of the urban middle and upper classes, to turn the 1920's into one big party. For these people, the automobile was a means of escape and prohibition was a special challenge. They made the speakeasy a national institution and the flapper the symbol of the times. The fact that the police often raided the speakeasies and that the liquor generally was supplied by bootleggers only added to the excitement.

SECTION REVIEW

1. Identify the following: Frederick Winslow Taylor, Charles A. Lindbergh, Mary Pickford, "Lost Generation," Harlem Renaissance, Louis Armstrong, Paul Whiteman.
2. What were the causes of increased productivity in the 1920's?
3. How did the automobile change American society?
4. What was the origin of jazz?
5. What brought about the new morality of the 1920's?

5 The Dream's End

The new morality, then, was to a large extent supported by the nation's prosperity in the 1920's. Indeed, at the time Herbert Hoover won the 1928 presidential election, the American economy seemed to be booming.

The Grand Illusion

Hoover shared the faith of most Americans that a conservative, business-oriented government could continue to preside indefinitely over boom without

Advertising became big business in the 1920's. The growth of newspapers and magazines, the rise of radio, and the introduction of installment buying made national advertising campaigns possible. How did advertising affect the way Americans lived?

During the 1920's, as in the Populist era, farmers found their livelihood affected by economic and social circumstances that were difficult for them to anticipate and virtually impossible for them to control.

bust. There was little reason to suspect that anything was wrong. Mass production was well-entrenched. People were flocking to buy new goods. Savings bank deposits and life insurance policies had doubled in amount since 1920. Credit was plentiful.

In addition, general prosperity had encouraged the search for new and better ways to make money. One way was real estate speculation. Miami and other settlements along the Florida coast lured investors who had visions of hotels and resorts on what was then a swampy wilderness. Another way to make money was the stock market. In the past, the market had been an occupation for the rich and the professional. But by 1924 the average wage earner began to plunge in on a large scale. People who managed to put aside a bit of cash often used it to buy a piece of a big corporation. This allowed them to share in the profits being made by business under sympathetic Republican administrations.

Faith in the future was further supported by the Kellogg-Briand Multilateral Treaty for the Renunciation of War. The idea behind the treaty was the banning of war as an instrument of national policy. It was proposed to the United States by Aristide Briand, the French Minister, on April 6, 1927, the tenth anniversary of America's entry into World War I. Briand intended it to be a treaty only between France and the United States. However, Secretary of State Frank B. Kellogg amended it to include other countries as well. In 1928 the treaty was signed by 60 nations. In January 1929 it was ratified by the United States Senate. Kellogg won the Nobel Peace Prize for his efforts in bringing about the treaty.

The Grim Reality

Despite all the signs of prosperity and the mood of optimism, all was not as it seemed. There were ominous cracks beneath the surface. Many people did not share in the country's expanding wealth. There were people in urban ghettos and in rural areas who were easily overlooked as they struggled to make ends meet. There were industrial workers whose pay did not increase as rapidly as prices, and who knew they would be laid off from time to time.

American farmers had an especially difficult time. During the war, many had cultivated increasingly more land to meet the great demand for food. But in

Life poked fun at speculators who sometime purchased Florida beachfront property sight unseen. Nothing could stop the flow of speculators to the state. Why was the Florida land boom so attractive to investors?

1920 the government stopped supporting the farmers, and Europe began to produce its own food. The market shrank, and prices dropped. Most of the farmers who had bought extra land, stocks and bonds, and prize livestock had done so on credit.

The farmers figured they could earn a decent living and keep from going under by selling large quantities. Therefore they increased production still further, but the costs of increased production were steep. Freight rates had risen, and farm labor cost more. The change from horses to automobiles destroyed the market for hay and oats, while the need for good roads raised taxes. People needed less food for energy because of electric machines and shorter work hours. In addition, a new rage for slim figures meant that people were eating less. There was less demand for cotton and wool because of a change in fashions and the development of synthetic fibers such as rayon. On top of everything else, prohibition had done away with

Note that purchasing goods on credit reflects an optimism concerning one's future financial well-being.

nearly one-half of the market for barley and much of the market for grapes.

Farmers, however, were not the only ones feeling the pinch. Other businesses were not doing so well as they had earlier. The construction boom that had taken hold in 1922 began to slump, and, by early 1929, construction was at a standstill. Automobile manufacturers found themselves facing a glutted market, as most families who could afford a car already owned one. By August 1929, automobile factories had begun laying off thousands of workers each week.

Other ventures, such as Florida real estate, also suffered setbacks. In 1926 Florida was seriously shaken by hurricanes, and many people lost interest in real estate speculation as a result. In addition, most of the many worldly goods acquired by Americans had been bought on the installment plan. At first, credit had been used only for large and permanent purchases, such as homes and cars. But by 1928, 85 percent of all furniture and 75 percent of all washing machines and refrigerators were being purchased on time. Only the stock market seemed stable. Between 1928 and 1929 many stocks doubled and tripled. As a result, when the stock market crashed in 1929, many of the American people crashed with it.

SECTION REVIEW

1. What ways did people use to make quick money in the 1920's?
2. What was the purpose of the Kellogg-Briand Treaty?
3. What added to the problems of farmers in the 1920's?

CHAPTER 23 REVIEW

SUMMARY

1. After World War I, Americans turned away from involvement in foreign affairs.
2. Fear of communism fueled a public reaction against organized labor, a strong anti-radical campaign, and restrictions on immigration.
3. Racial tension existed both in the North and in the South, and the Ku Klux Klan experienced a revival.
4. The Eighteenth Amendment to the Constitution prohibited the sale of intoxicating liquor, but illegal drinking continued and contributed to the rise of organized crime.
5. The politically conservative mood of the country led to the election of three business-oriented Republican Presidents—Harding, Coolidge, and Hoover.
6. A new industrial revolution led to increased productivity and general prosperity for the nation.
7. American lifestyles underwent profound changes as a result of the availability of new products such as the automobile and the motion picture.
8. Old social traditions were abandoned in favor of a new consumerism and uninhibited behavioral standards.

VOCABULARY

communism	bootleggers	fundamentalists	tabloid	syncopation
prohibition	speakeasies	scientific management	jazz	flappers

REVIEW QUESTIONS

1. What was government's reaction to labor unrest in the postwar period?
2. What trends showed a resistance to change in the 1920's?
3. How did the major political parties fare during the decade?
4. What changes did transportation and communications technology bring about in American social life?
5. Why were the 1920's called a decade of contradictions?
6. Who failed to share in the prosperity of the 1920's?

7. What new cultural developments occurred in this decade?

8. What role did the United States play in international affairs during this period?

DISCUSSION

1. Of the events and developments of the 1920's, which one was the most important? Which had the most lasting influence?

2. Should immigration to the United States be restricted? On what basis?

3. Do you agree or disagree with William Allen White's statement that Attorney General Palmer's tactics were "un-American"? Why?

4. Should the government enforce laws against alcohol and drugs? Why or why not?

USING GRAPHS

Refer to the graph on page 482 and answer the following questions:

1. Approximately how many immigrants came to the United States in the period between 1921 and 1930?

2. What was the chief source of immigration during this time?

3. Why did the number of immigrants drop in 1930?

4. Did the 1924 immigration law increase or decrease the quota for immigrants from southern and eastern Europe?

5. What was the effect of the National Origins Act on total immigration?

USING SKILLS

If you were trying to decide whether the effects of prohibition were good or bad, which of the following kinds of evidence would be relevant in reaching a conclusion?

1. Statistics on the number of arrests for public drunkenness before and after prohibition went into effect.

2. Statistics on the number of people arrested for breaking the prohibition law.

3. Statistics on the cost of enforcing prohibition laws.

4. Statistics on tax revenues from liquor sales before prohibition.

5. Statistics on the number of deaths caused by alcohol-related diseases.

1	The Rise and Fall of the Stock Market	503
2	The Lean Years	505
3	Hoover's Reaction	509
4	A Mandate for Change	513

THE GREAT DEPRESSION

Sooner or later, a crash is coming, and it may be terrific . . . factories will be shut down . . . men will be thrown out of work . . . the vicious circle will get in full swing and the result will be a serious business depression.

ROGER W. BABSON

In the fall of 1929, the stock market crashed, wiping out the fortunes of many Americans. The crash ushered in the Great Depression of the 1930's—the worst economic decline in the history of the United States. It was a time when millions of Americans could not find work, thousands were turned out of their homes, and many roamed the land in freight cars. Banks failed, and people lost their life's savings.

The Great Depression changed the American way of thinking. The government took on a more active role in the peacetime economy than ever before. For the first time, it assumed responsibility for relief. And, most importantly, out of the depths of the Great Depression came the modern presidency and the welfare state.

1 The Rise and Fall of the Stock Market

If one looked at the stock market, the 1920's seemed to be a period of prosperity. The values of common stock had been increasing steadily throughout the decade. In 1926, 451 million shares of stock were traded on the New York Stock Exchange. In 1927 that number rose to 577 million. In addition, between January and December of that same year, **brokers' loans,** (money borrowed from banks by stock brokers) increased from a little over $3 billion to $4.5 billion. Bankers accepted stocks as **collateral,** or property pledged to guarantee these loans. Bankers, however, could see a trend developing, and those who were conservative feared that stock prices might inflate too much. This, they said, could lead to disaster, and they urged caution.

In January 1928 it looked as if the bankers had been right and that the market might break. But President Coolidge and Treasury officials assured everyone that the volume of brokers' loans was not too great and that the country had never been in better shape. In early March, therefore, a group of the largest operators on the New York Stock Exchange launched a huge buying campaign of General Motors and Radio Corporation of America stock. The price of these and other stocks took off on a journey upward that became known as the big bull market. A **bull market** is one in which stock values are rising.

The Impact of Speculation

The big bull market of the 1920's was not the normal market. Under normal circumstances, two kinds of people are involved in the stock market. Those who buy in anticipation of rising prices are called **bulls,** while those who sell in expectation of falling prices are called **bears.** In the 1920's the market belonged to the bulls.

There was another difference in the 1920's. Generally, as a corporation's profits increase, more people want to own its stock. As the demand for ownership grows and more people buy the stock, its price increases. In the 1920's, however, much of the increase was due to speculation. Instead of buying stock to hold indefinitely, people bought it when prices were rising and held it only long enough for its price to increase to the point where they could make a profit by selling it.

Speculation is risky. It can cause stock prices to rise even though a corporation is not making a profit or paying good dividends. Price no longer means value. The speculator is concerned with a quick profit and is willing to risk the money he or she has invested to get it. The investor, on the other hand, is concerned with a steady income and the safety of the money he or she has invested.

New capital issues totaled $3.2 billion in 1923 and $10 billion in 1927.

By 1927 speculators dominated the stock market. To add to the problem, many of the speculators were **buying on margin.** In other words, they were using their own money to make a relatively small down payment on the stock and borrowing the rest of the purchase price from a stock broker. The broker, in turn, borrowed the money lent to the speculator from a bank. The brokers' loans were **call loans,** loans that can be terminated (called in) at any time by the borrower or lender. Most call loans were intended to remain in force only a few weeks or months.

Speculators believed they could make a quick profit in the market. Bankers knew they could make money by lending to brokers. Brokers knew they could come out ahead by lending to customers. Everyone, it seemed, was trying to get rich quickly. The nation's leaders, confident of the general prosperity, encouraged this, urging ordinary people to play the stock market and make their fortunes.

Boom and Bust

The first phase of speculation lasted until June 12, 1928. On that date, according to the *New York Times:*

> *Wall Street's bull market collapsed with a detonation heard around the world. . . . Individual losses were staggering. Hundreds of small traders were wiped out.*

Within two weeks, however, the market stabilized. Stock values began to climb again. For more than a year, they fell and rose, only to fall and rise again and again. Each time the market recovered, share prices rose to new heights.

Some analysts pointed out that the economy was getting sluggish, that business was slowing down, and that many stocks were not paying attractive dividends. The financial editor of the *New York Times* predicted that in 1929 the market would crash and the bull market would end for all time. But not many people paid attention. Most kept on speculating.

By the middle of 1929, the boom was out of control. Some stocks had risen in price as much as 100, 200, and even 500 percent. Many were selling for much more than they were actually worth. On September 3 the big bull market reached its peak. In general, the wave of prosperity and speculation reached its highest point, and the future looked bright.

But during the summer, the London Stock Exchange crashed, and British banks began selling off large holdings of American stock. On September 26, the Bank of England raised its **rediscount rate,** the interest rate for banks, to stop the outward flow of gold and protect British currency in international exchange. This led to the withdrawal of several hundred million dollars from New York to London.

Stock prices began to fall. They rallied for a few weeks, and then they began to fall again. Major spokespersons for the financial community, however, assured the public that there was no need to worry. Charles E. Mitchell, chairman of the National City Bank of New York, stated:

> *Although in some cases speculation has gone too far in the United States, the markets generally are now in a healthy condition. The last six weeks have done an immense amount of good by shaking down prices. . . . The market values have a sound basis in the general prosperity of our country.*

When prices kept falling despite such assurances, people began to panic. Brokers received order after order to sell. Total panic finally took hold on October 24, "Black Thursday." That day, nearly 13 million shares of stock changed hands. Prices fell so rapidly that the ticker tape machines could not keep up. The panic let up, however, when J. P. Morgan & Company and several other large banks pooled their

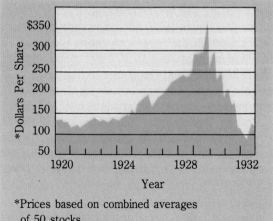

STOCK PRICES, 1920–1932

*Dollars Per Share

Year

*Prices based on combined averages of 50 stocks.

Ask students to analyze the relationship between the stock market crash and the Depression.

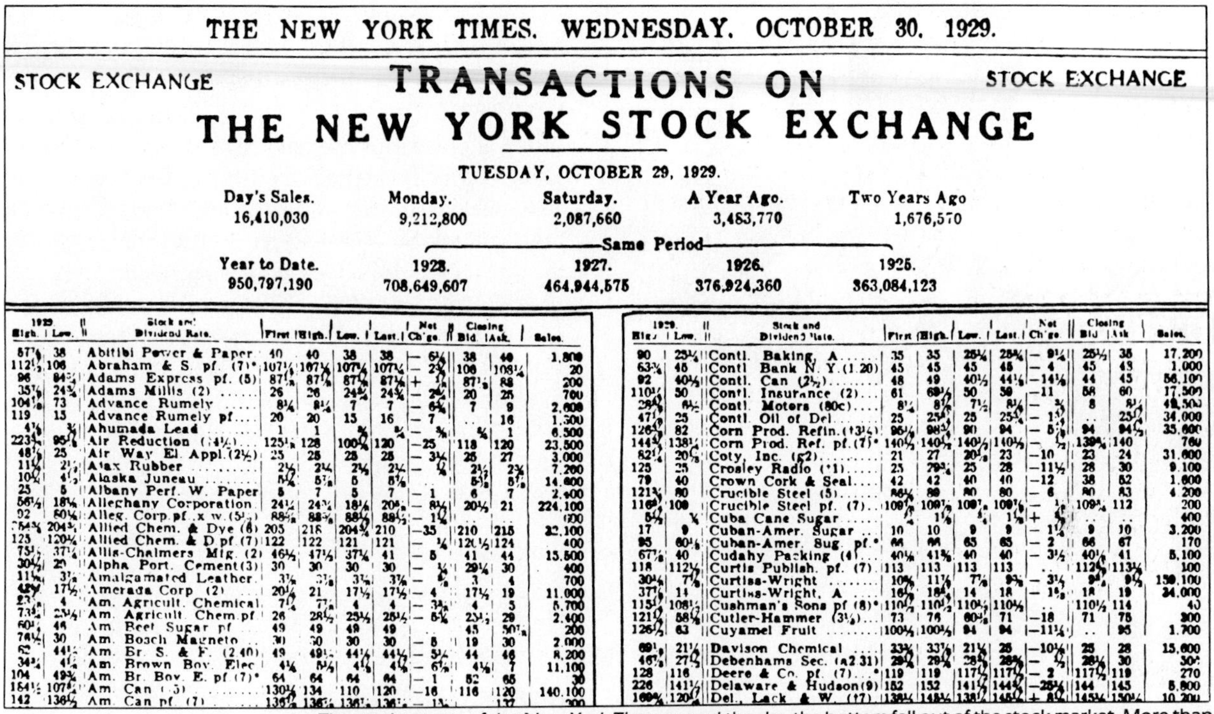

THE NEW YORK TIMES. WEDNESDAY. OCTOBER 30. 1929.

STOCK EXCHANGE TRANSACTIONS ON STOCK EXCHANGE

THE NEW YORK STOCK EXCHANGE

TUESDAY, OCTOBER 29, 1929.

Day's Sales.	Monday.	Saturday.	A Year Ago.	Two Years Ago
16,410,030	9,212,800	2,087,660	3,483,770	1,676,570

Year to Date.	1928.	1927.	1926.	1925.
	Same Period			
950,797,190	708,649,607	464,944,575	376,924,360	363,084,123

1929 High.	1929 Low.	Stock and Dividend Rate.	First	High.	Low.	Last.	Net Ch'ge.	Closing Bid.	Closing Ask.	Sales.
57⅞	38	Abitibi Power & Paper	40	40	38	38	−6⅝	38	40	1,800
112½	106	Abraham & S. pf. (7)*	107¼	107¼	107¼	107¼	−2¾	106	108¼	20
96	84½	Adams Express pf. (5)	87⅛	87⅛	87⅛	87⅛	+⅛	87⅛	88	200
35⅞	24¾	Adams Millis (2)	26	26	24¾	24¾	−2¼	20	25	700
104⅞	73	Advance Rumely	8¼	8¼	7	7	−6¾	7	9	2,600
119	15	Advance Rumely pf	20	20	15	16	−7	..	16	1,300
4⅞	⅜	Ahumada Lead	1	1	⅝	¾	−⅜	⅝	1	6,500
223¾	95⅛	Air Reduction (†4½)	125⅛	128	100¾	120	−25	118	120	23,500
48⅞	25	Air Way El. Appl. (2½)	25	28	28	28	−3¼	28	27	3,000
11½	2½	Ajax Rubber	2½	2¼	2½	2¼	−½	2½	2¾	7,200
10¾	4½	Alaska Juneau	5¾	5⅞	5	5⅞	..	5⅜	5⅞	14,800
25	5	Albany Perf. W. Paper	5	7	5	7	−1	6	7	2,400
56½	18⅝	Alleghany Corporation	24½	24¾	18⅛	20⅝	−8½	20½	21	224,100
92	80¼	Alleg. Corp. pf. x w. (5½)	88⅝	88⅝	88½	88½	−1½	..	..	600
354⅜	204¾	Allied Chem. & Dye (6)	205	218	204¾	210	−35	210	215	22,100
125	120¼	Allied Chem. & D. pf. (7)	122	122	121	121	−¼	120½	124	400
75½	37¼	Allis-Chalmers Mfg. (2)	46½	47½	37¼	41	−5	41	44	15,500
30½	29	Alpha Port. Cement (3)	30	30	30	30	−½	29¼	30	400
11⅝	3⅞	Amalgamated Leather	3⅞	3⅞	3⅞	3⅞	−⅝	3	4	700
42⅞	17½	Amerada Corp (2)	20½	21	17½	17½	−4	17½	19	11,000
23⅞	4	Am. Agricult. Chemical	7¼	7⅞	4	4	−3⅞	4	5	5,700
73¾	25½	Am. Agricult. Chem. pf	26	28½	25½	25½	−5¾	25½	29	2,400
60½	48	Am. Beet Sugar pf	49	49	49	49	..	45	50⅞	200
78½	30	Am. Bosch Magneto	30	30	30	30	−5	19	30	2,000
62	44½	Am. Br. S. & F. (2.40)	49	49½	44½	44½	−5½	44	46	8,200
34¾	4⅛	Am. Brown Bov. Elec	4⅛	5½	4⅛	4½	−6⅞	4⅛	7	11,100
104	49¾	Am. Br. Bov. E. pf. (7)*	64	64	64	64	−1	52	65	30
184½	107¼	Am. Can (5)	130½	134	110	120	−16	116	120	140,100
142	136½	Am. Can pf. (7)	136⅞	136⅞	136⅞	136⅞	−1½	..	137	300

1929 High.	1929 Low.	Stock and Dividend Rate.	First	High.	Low.	Last.	Net Ch'ge.	Closing Bid.	Closing Ask.	Sales.
90	25¼	Contl. Baking, A	35	35	25¼	25¾	−9¼	25½	35	17,200
63¾	45	Contl. Bank N. Y. (1.20)	45	45	45	45	−4	45	48	1,000
92	40½	Contl. Can (2½)	48	49	40½	44⅛	−14⅛	44	45	56,100
110¼	50	Contl. Insurance (2)	61	69½	50	59	−11	58	60	17,500
29½	6½	Contl. Motors (80c)	8¼	8½	7½	8¼	−⅜	8	8¼	48,500
47⅞	25	Contl. Oil of Del	25	25¾	25	25¾	−1½	..	25½	34,000
126½	82	Corn Prod. Refin. (†3½)	95½	98¾	90	94	−5⅞	94	94½	35,600
144¾	138½	Corn Prod. Ref. pf. (7)*	140½	140½	140½	140½	−½	139¾	140	760
82¼	20⅝	Coty, Inc. (g2)	21	27	20⅛	23	−10	23	24	31,600
125	25	Crosley Radio (*1)	25	29¾	25	28	−11½	28	30	9,100
79	40	Crown Cork & Seal	42	42	40	40	−12	38	52	1,600
121½	80	Crucible Steel (5)	86½	80	80	80	−6	80	83	4,200
116¾	100	Crucible Steel pf. (7)	109⅞	109⅞	109⅞	109⅞	−½	109¾	112	200
5½	⅜	Cuba Cane Sugar	¾	1⅛	¾	1⅛	+⅜	..	..	400
17	9	Cuban-Amer. Sugar	10	10	9	9	−1¼	9	10	3,200
95	60½	Cuban-Amer. Sug. pf.*	66	66	65	65	−2	66	67	170
67⅞	40	Cudahy Packing (4)	40⅛	41⅜	40	40	−3½	40½	41	5,100
118	112½	Curtis Publish. pf. (7)	113	113	113	113	..	112½	113½	100
30¼	7⅞	Curtiss-Wright	10⅝	11½	7⅞	9⅜	−3½	9¼	9½	150,100
37½	14	Curtiss-Wright, A	16½	18¼	14	18	−1⅞	18	19	34,000
115½	108½	Cushman's Sons pf (8)*	110½	110½	110½	110½	..	110½	114	40
121½	58⅞	Cutler-Hammer (3½)	73	76	60⅞	71	−18	71	75	300
126½	63	Cuyamel Fruit	100½	100½	94	94	−11¼	..	95	1,700
69⅞	21½	Davison Chemical	33½	33½	21½	25	−10½	25	28	15,600
46⅞	27½	Debenhams Sec. (a2.31)	29½	29½	28½	28½	−½	28½	30	300
128	116	Deere & Co. pf. (7)*	119	119	117½	117½	−2	117½	119	270
226	141½	Delaware & Hudson (9)	152	152	141½	144½	−25½	144	145	5,800
169¾	120½	Del., Lack. & W. (†7)	138½	148½	138½	145½	+8½	145½	150½	10,200

The stock reports of the *New York Times* record the day the bottom fell out of the stock market. More than 16 million shares were unloaded during the selling spree. Thousands of stockholders were forced into bankruptcy. What speculative practices led to the collapse of the stock market?

resources and heavily bid up the market, thus saving it from collapse. Even so, the market closed that day with an average loss of $30 per share.

The next day President Hoover assured the American people that "the fundamental business of the country, that is, production and distribution of commodities, is on a sound and prosperous basis." As a result, prices remained stable that day and the next. But on Tuesday, October 29, the bottom fell out of the market again. This time the bankers did nothing to save the situation. In one day's time, a record of 16.4 million shares of stock changed hands at unbelievably low prices. The average price of 50 leading stocks declined drastically. For all intents and purposes, the stock market had crashed.

SECTION REVIEW

1. What is the difference between speculating and investing?
2. How were speculators able to make quick profits?
3. Why did some financial analysts think that the stock market was going to crash?
4. What was "Black Thursday"?
5. How did the banks try to save the stock market from collapse?

2 The Lean Years

While the stock market crash came as a shock, many upper- and middle-income Americans were hardly aware that a depression was taking shape. For these people, the Great Depression was just something they read about, and life in 1930 was much like life in 1929.

By 1932, however, the situation had changed. All of America not only knew about the Great Depression but had been affected in some way by it. Between 1929 and 1933, national income fell from $87.8 billion to $40.2 billion. Stock dividends decreased 56.6 percent, salaries 40 percent, and manufacturing wages 60 percent. Close to 14 million Americans were out of work.

BROTHERHOOD
OF
SLEEPING CAR
PORTERS

A. Philip Randolph

A leading figure in the labor movement of the 1920's was Asa Philip Randolph, born in Crescent City, Florida in 1889. As a young man he moved to the Harlem district of New York City and went to college at night. He quickly became aware of the discrimination blacks faced in employment and tried to organize black workers. When the United States entered World War I, Randolph and his friend Chandler Owen founded a magazine called *The Messenger* (later called *Black Worker*) that called for more jobs for blacks in war industry and in the armed forces.

In 1925 Randolph organized the Brotherhood of Sleeping Car Porters and built the first successful black trade union. For a while Randolph's union was in the AFL, but he withdrew in protest over the AFL's failure to fight discrimination. Later he took his union into the new rival of the AFL, the Congress of Industrial Organizations (CIO).

Randolph's power was such that when he called for a march on Washington in 1941 to protest discrimination in factories having federal contracts, President Roosevelt issued an executive order setting up the Fair Employment Practices Committee. Later, Randolph influenced President Truman to ban segregation in the armed forces.

In 1955, when the AFL merged with the CIO, Randolph became a vice president of the organization. He continued to fight against discrimination in the labor movement.

In 1963, at the height of the struggle for civil rights, Randolph joined the leader of the new black protest movement, Dr. Martin Luther King, to call for a modern-day march on Washington. People of all races and from all walks of life were invited to join. On August 28, 1963, about 200,000 Americans gathered at the Lincoln Memorial to hear King's stirring call to action. Following the speeches, Randolph was among those who met with President John F. Kennedy to talk about the future of the movement.

In 1965 Randolph founded an institute to study the causes of poverty. He retired as head of the porters' union in 1965 and died in 1979.

The State of the Economy

After the stock market crashed in 1929, stock prices kept falling. They did not stop until November 13, when they finally reached their bottom for the year. The losses suffered in the market hurt the American economy, but the crash alone did not cause the Great Depression. The economy was faltering long before the bottom fell out of the market. Agriculture and the construction, textile, and automobile industries had all overproduced. Farm income, in fact, was at an all-time low.

One problem was that America's wealth was not distributed evenly during the 1920's. Throughout the decade, the share of national income that went to the very rich had increased, while the share that went to the poorer segment of the population had decreased. Productivity was high, so a lot of goods were available. But wages were low, and therefore **demand,** the willingness and ability to buy, was down. Henry Ford summed up the situation perfectly when he announced that "American production has come to equal and surpass, not our people's power to consume, but their power to purchase."

Because people did not buy, business was slow. After the crash, it became even slower because even the rich began to economize. Businesses that catered to the rich now began to feel the pinch. With business slow, employees were laid off, and expansion plans

PROSPERITY AND DEPRESSION   **507**

Remind students that the crash took place at a time when the
economies of European nations were already in bad shape.

set aside. Domestic workers who had always been able to find jobs as servants in the homes of the rich suddenly found it harder, if not impossible, to find work. Even those who eventually did find new jobs ended up working for lower wages than they had before.

Government policies also contributed to the onset of the Great Depression. The government reduced taxes on the wealthy, expecting the money saved in taxes to build new plants and hire more workers. But the wealthy did not use the money for business investments. Instead, most of it went into speculation on **securities,** or documents giving a right to some form of property, such as stocks, bonds, or mortgages. In addition, the government began to cut back on the loans it had been making to foreign countries, which made it impossible for some of them to keep buying American products. Then, in trying to protect American businesses, the government raised the tariffs on imported goods. This not only hurt trade with other countries but also cut down on competition, which in turn allowed prices at home to stay high. Further, by not doing much to enforce antitrust laws, the government made it easier for trade associations and monopolies to keep prices high even after demand fell off.

Credit and the weakness of the American banking system were two other important factors. The collapse in investment values hurt the country's credit system in several different areas. Loans, mortgages, and corporate structures were all endangered. When the American stock market crashed, most brokers' loans were called in. Many of the borrowers simply could not pay. When they did not pay the brokers, the brokers could not pay the banks, and the banks were caught short with nothing but the almost worthless stock they had taken as collateral. Banks all over the country, which had invested heavily in stocks, bonds, and mortgages, began to collapse. When England went off the gold standard in September 1931, American banks, which were already weak, were hit even harder as the value of their foreign bonds dropped. In that month alone, more than 300 American banks closed. The next month, another 522 banks followed suit. At the time, since bank deposits were not yet insured, many people lost their entire life savings when the banks went under.

The Plight of the American People

On May 1, 1930, President Hoover announced that "we have passed the worst and with continued unity of effort we shall rapidly recover." The President, however, was wrong. The worst was yet to come.

In the City. Shortly after the stock market crash, major American business leaders promised Hoover that they would not cut workers' wages. Until the last quarter of 1930, most kept their word, although some companies resorted to cutting down on work hours in order to maintain the wage rate.

In October 1931 the situation changed. United States Steel, which set the pattern for thousands of other employers, cut salaries and wages by ten percent. It did not take long for other employers to follow suit. As a result, 2 million workers—three times the number in the steel industry—saw their wages drop.

The unemployed stood in breadlines that stretched for blocks to get something to eat. The depression was at its worst in 1933 when one worker in four was out of work. In what other ways were Americans affected by the depression?

Before long, lay-offs replaced wage cuts. At first, some of the bigger companies tried to help the workers they laid off by giving them loans, groceries, or special bonuses. A very few, like Eastman Kodak and General Electric, even had their own unemployment insurance plans. But after a year or two, the money ran out, and the unemployed were left to fend for themselves.

In New York, **breadlines,** or lines of persons waiting to be given free food, grew. The breadlines provided cheese sandwiches and coffee; beans, bread, and coffee; stew and bread; or oatmeal and milk. In other cities, there were **soup kitchens,** or places where food was offered for free or at low cost to the needy. But in many cities, there was nothing.

All over the country, families not able to pay their rent or mortgages were evicted from their homes. Some ended up in communities of makeshift shacks on the outskirts of cities. Desperate men could be found grubbing food from garbage cans outside restaurants and sleeping in doorways or on park benches. One man who spent a night in a shelter on the New York docks later remembered it as the most terrifying experience of his life. He described it in this way:

I had been in the trenches in World War I, but the cold dock was worse. It was damp and bitterly cold. There was one thin blanket to a man on a rough spring. Outside, you could hear the tugs. Inside, you could hear the guys coughing their lungs out. . . . About midnight I couldn't stand it. I got out of bed to find half the place was up, sitting around wrapped in their blankets. . . . I'll never forget the man who sat next to me. He gave me a drag from his butt. Later he told me he was a graduate of Wisconsin.

At the height of the Great Depression, whole families lived on stale bread and a single can of soup for days at a time. In Pennsylvania the families of unemployed miners lived three or four to a one-room shack, barely surviving on dandelions and weed roots.

Some people resorted to selling apples on street corners. But even that was not what it seemed. The International Apple Shippers Association wanted to get rid of the apple surpluses building up in the Pacific Northwest. So it allowed an unemployed person to take a crate of 100-to-120 apples on a credit of $1.75 and sell the apples at 5 cents each. As demand for the crates of apples grew, the Association raised the price to $2.25 a crate. As a result, apple vendors who sold half a crate or less made nothing.

About 1 million people, including 200,000 children, became drifters. Many would do anything for a job. In Connecticut young girls considered themselves lucky if they could be hired by a company willing to pay them 60 cents for a 55-hour week.

On the Farm. Farmers fared no better than city people. By 1930 wheat, cotton, and corn prices had all collapsed. In order to make a living, most farm families had to develop some kind of sideline. Some opened roadside stands. Others sent their children to

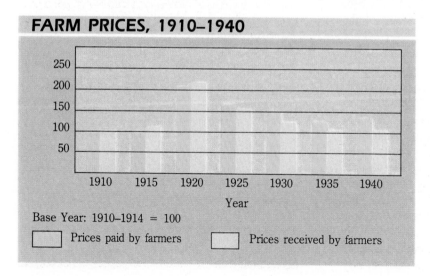

FARM PRICES, 1910–1940

Base Year: 1910–1914 = 100

☐ Prices paid by farmers   ☐ Prices received by farmers

In 1932 wheat, which was $2.16 a bushel in 1919 and $1.03 in 1929, sold for $.38.

work in the factories or mills. Still others sold off most of their property.

The collapse of farm prices was compounded by a lack of rain. Farmers all over the country counted on the spring rains to water their crops. But in 1930 the rains never came. Instead, farmers faced one of the worst droughts in American history. It covered most of Kentucky and Arkansas and much of Illinois, Missouri, Virginia, Ohio, Tennessee, Mississippi, and Louisiana. The drought lasted more than a year and affected between 6 and 7 million people.

Before long, many farmers, realizing there was no relief in sight, began to act. Some banded together outside Sioux City, Iowa, to keep food from entering the city for 30 days or "until the cost of production has been obtained." They blockaded highways, stopping milk trucks and dumping their contents on the ground. In other parts of the country, farmers joined forces to make sure that no one in the area lost property through mortgage foreclosure. They appeared at foreclosure sales, chased away serious buyers, and bid pennies for the animals and goods being sold off. The next day they returned their purchases to their former owner.

SECTION REVIEW

1. How had the distribution of wealth in America changed during the 1920's?
2. How did governmental policies contribute to economic conditions?
3. During the Great Depression, how did companies try to reduce problems for their employees?
4. How did farmers try to resolve problems?

3 Hoover's Reaction

As the dimensions of the Great Depression grew, private charities and local and state governments ran out of money to provide relief to the needy. Not knowing where else to turn, the American people began to look to the federal government for help. It did not take them long, however, to realize that the government did not intend to intervene directly.

Direct Relief

The Hoover administration firmly believed that the policies the federal government had pursued during the 1920's were the basis for the prosperity of that decade. The administration also believed that the economy in the 1930's was still fundamentally sound and saw no need to tamper with it.

Both Hoover and his advisers put their trust in laissez-faire. Secretary of the Treasury Andrew Mellon, for example, argued that the course of the depression had to be run, even if economic activity hit rock bottom. In his view, the Great Depression was a good thing because "people will work harder, live a more moral life. Values will be adjusted, and enterprising people will pick up the wrecks from less competent people."

Throughout 1930 Hoover kept reassuring the people that the economic downturn would play itself out, that business and industry had turned the corner, and that prosperity was "just around the corner." He flatly refused to involve the federal government in direct relief. He told the American public:

Economic depression cannot be cured by legislative action or executive pronouncement. Economic wounds must be healed by the action of the cells of the economic body—the producers and consumers themselves.

In Hoover's view, relief should be administered locally to deal with local problems. Relief was not the responsibility of the federal government but of the individual, the family, the boss, the landlord, and, at times, the local community. Direct relief by the federal government, he felt, would destroy American self-reliance and self-esteem. It also would put a halt to voluntary community action and many democratic institutions. Hoover did go so far, however, as to set up the President's Committee on Unemployment Relief. Formed in 1930, its aim was to promote and coordinate local relief efforts. Under its guidance, 3000 local relief offices were opened.

A Limited Program

Despite his sentiments about direct relief, Hoover did take some steps to try to help the economy. In the months after the stock market crashed, he called together leaders of finance, industry, trade, and state and local government and assured them that he would keep the federal budget balanced and hold the line against inflation. In return, he asked something of

During the Hoover administration the burden of public relief was left for state and local government and private charity to shoulder. Why was Hoover reluctant to provide a federal relief program?

each of them. He asked the leading industrialists not to cut pay, production, lay off workers, or lower wages. He asked labor leaders to discourage demands for strikes and higher pay. He asked governors and mayors to spend more on public works to create jobs. He asked the heads of the public utilities to invest $1.8 billion in new construction and repairs in 1930. After he got almost all the leaders to agree to what he had asked, he set up a committee to check on them to make sure they kept their word.

For a while, it looked as if Hoover's program of cooperation was going to carry the nation through the storm. But in May and June of 1930, employers slowly began to reduce production. This, in turn, led to more unemployment. By October about 4 million workers were out of jobs.

The economy continued to tumble, and Hoover began to move away from his strict laissez-faire stand. In June 1930 he had signed the Hawley-Smoot Tariff, which increased protection and reduced imports. Tariff rates had badly hurt weak European economies, which needed to sell their goods in the United States. Now, afraid that America's financial difficulties were the result in part of the instability in Europe, he tried to get tariffs revised downward. When this failed, he proposd a moratorium on World War I reparation payments. His actions, however, came too late. Several major European banks had already failed, as had a great many American ones.

Next, Hoover acted to try to save as many American banks and businesses as he could. In his annual message to Congress on December 8, 1931, he urged passage of a bill establishing a Reconstruction Finance Corporation (RFC), a giant government credit agency designed to make loans to banks, insurance companies, farm mortgage associations, building and loan associations, and other businesses. Hoover, who saw the RFC as an emergency measure to be used moderately and for no longer than two years, thought that its existence would "strengthen confidence." On January 22, 1932, he signed the bill creating the RFC and told the following to the press:

It brings into being a powerful organization with adequate resources . . . to permit business and industry to carry on normal activities free from the fear of unexpected shocks and retarding influences. . . .

Its purpose is to stop deflation in agriculture and industry and thus to increase employment by the restoration of men to their normal jobs. It is not created for the aid of big business or big institutions. . . . It is created for the support of the smaller banks and financial institutions. . . . It should give opportunity to mobilize the gigantic strength of our country for recovery.

Although the RFC made many loans, many Americans were not satisfied with it. While some of the loans went to small institutions, most of the money went to big ones. Banks and railroads used RFC loans to pay back debts and to keep their credit standing rather than to create new jobs. In addition, while RFC money kept salaries for executives and dividends for stockholders high, it did not find its way into the pay envelopes of average workers. In the view of many Americans, the RFC typified Hoover's "trickle down" or "percolation" theory of relief. That is, if enough funds are poured in at the top, some of them may trickle down or seep through to the bottom of society.

On July 21, 1932, Hoover reluctantly signed the Relief and Construction Act. It boosted the resources of the RFC to $3.5 billion, allowed the RFC to make big loans for construction of public works and unemployment, created Agricultural Credit Banks, and allowed the RFC to lend money to states and cities. For the first time, the federal government had committed itself to helping the unemployed. By the end of 1932, it had lent $30 million for relief.

Also in July of 1932, Hoover signed the Federal Home Loan Bank Act, designed to stimulate home building, increase employment, and increase home ownership. To do this, the act set up 12 regional banks with a fund of $125 million to discount home loans.

The Bonus Army

Meanwhile, the American people were suffering. The Great Depression was getting worse, a fact for which Hoover was blamed. His image dropped as low as the economy. Shantytowns became known as "Hoovervilles," and discarded newspapers people wrapped around their bodies to keep out the cold were tagged "Hoover blankets."

In July 1932, while the House and the Senate were in the process of approving the Relief and Construction Act, a group of World War I veterans were making their particular grievances known. The veterans had been promised bonuses for their services during the war. The bonuses, however, were in the form of 20-year endowment policies that matured at death or in the year 1945. There was a part-payment provision of the bonus bill, but the payments generally took at least two years to come through. Many veterans felt they could not wait that long. They convinced Representative Wright Patman of Texas to introduce legislation that would authorize full payment before 1945.

In May and June of 1932, a Bonus Expeditionary Force made up of over 12,000 unemployed and homeless veterans from all over the country marched to Washington, D.C., to voice their support of

Many families lost their homes during the Great Depression because they were unable to meet mortgage payments or pay rent. Some of the homeless found living quarters in shacks constructed of tin and old crates. Villages of these makeshift shacks sprouted up throughout the United States. Why were these villages called "Hoovervilles"?

Veterans of World War I converged on Washington, D.C. in 1932. They hoped to persuade Congress to grant them immediate payment of a bonus, not due until 1945. How did the federal government react to the bonus marchers?

Patman's bill. They built a shantytown on Anacostia Flats outside the capital and said they would stay there until the bonus bill was passed.

To pay the bonus would have cost $2.3 billion, 25 percent of the 1932 federal budget. Hoover felt that the veterans were already receiving many benefits that others were not. He refused to inflate the economy on such a large scale for them. The Senate concurred and refused to approve the bill.

Congress appropriated funds to provide transportation home for the marchers. About 5000 or 6000 veterans, many with wives and children, refused to leave. They stayed on until late July, when the Washington police were ordered to clear them from some of the old buildings they inhabited. Conflict broke out, and two veterans were killed and several police officers injured.

Hoover responded by calling on the army to control the situation. He sent specific orders to Major

General Douglas MacArthur, the Army Chief of Staff. No soldier was to be armed. The bonus marchers were to be cleared from the downtown area and escorted to their camps. Those who resisted were to be arrested and turned over to the police. As the army first approached, veterans and bystanders cheered. What happened next is described below by historian Frederick Lewis Allen:

> *Then suddenly there was chaos: Cavalrymen were riding into the crowd, infantrymen were throwing tear-gas bombs, women and children were being trampled and were choking from the gas; a crowd of three thousand or more spectators who had gathered in a vacant lot across the way were being pursued by the cavalry and were running wildly, pell-mell, across the uneven ground, screaming as they stumbled and fell.*
>
> *The troops moved slowly on, scattering before them veterans and homegoing government clerks alike. When they reached the other end of the Anacostia bridge and met a crowd of spectators who booed them and were slow to "move on," they threw more gas bombs. They began burning the shacks of the Anacostia camp—a task which the veterans themselves helped them to accomplish. That evening the Washington sky glowed with fire. Even after midnight the troops were still on their way with bayonets and tear-gas bombs, driving people ahead of them into the streets of Anacostia.*
>
> *The Bonus Expeditionary Force had been dispersed. . . . The incident was over. But it left a bitter taste in the mouth.*

SECTION REVIEW

1. Identify the following: "trickle down" theory, "Hoovervilles," Wright Patman, Bonus Expeditionary Force.
2. Why did Hoover feel there was no need for direct government intervention in the economy?
3. How did Hoover try to use business, labor and local government to try to help improve the economy?
4. What steps did Hoover take to move away from his laissez-faire stand?
5. Why did the veterans march on Washington?

Point out that Americans had endured depressions before and ask students to explain why there was a call for stronger government intervention at this time.

Al Smith tried unsuccessfully to wrest the nomination from Roosevelt.

4 A Mandate for Change

By 1932 the American people were demanding action. They were tired of abstract ideals like "self-reliance" and "rugged individualism" and talk about prosperity being just around the corner. Farmers in debt, workers without jobs, and bankrupt business people wanted bolder federal action than Hoover was willing to approve. Even those who still had jobs and could manage to buy food and other goods were afraid that tomorrow might be their turn to be laid off. Many people thought the time had come for a change in government.

The Election of 1932

In June 1932 the Republicans met in Chicago and again nominated Herbert Hoover as their candidate for President. They knew that to do anything else would have meant admitting that Republican policies had failed. Hoover's popularity, however, was at its lowest, and throughout the campaign he was forced to defend his actions in dealing with the Great Depression. Still, he remained firm in his faith in

rugged individualism and predicted there would be dire consequences if government began to tamper with the economy. "Any change in policies," he warned, "will bring disaster to every fireside in America."

The Democrats also met in Chicago in June to nominate their candidate. They chose Franklin Delano Roosevelt, a distant cousin of Theodore Roosevelt. The son of a well-known and wealthy New York family, Roosevelt had attended Harvard University and Columbia Law School. He had served as Assistant Secretary of the Navy under Woodrow Wilson and had received the Democratic nomination for Vice President in 1920. In 1932 he was serving his second term as governor of New York. His attempts to deal with the Great Depression in New York had been attracting national attention. He was the first governor to push for direct relief by the states, and he was also one of the first to speak out in favor of unemployment insurance.

Roosevelt conducted a campaign that was aggressive, yet relaxed. He set the tone when, breaking with tradition, he flew to Chicago to accept his nomination in person. He had been stricken with polio

ELECTION OF 1932

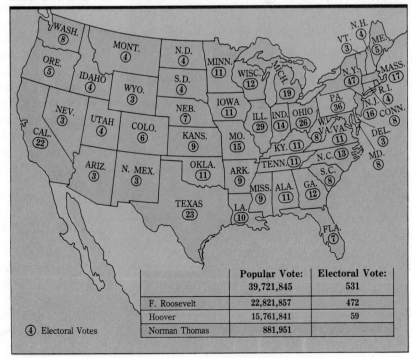

	Popular Vote:	Electoral Vote:
	39,721,845	531
F. Roosevelt	22,821,857	472
Hoover	15,761,841	59
Norman Thomas	881,951	

④ Electoral Votes

Roosevelt's program reflected ideas reformers had proposed in the 1920's.

The American people responded enthusiastically at the polls to Franklin Roosevelt's call for action to rescue the nation from the Great Depression. What is the significance of the First Hundred Days of the Roosevelt administration?

in 1921 and wanted to prove that his disability would not affect his performance as President. So he set out on a grueling cross-country campaign trip, during which he blamed the Republicans for the Great Depression. He summed up the history of the Hoover administration in four sentences:

> *First, it encouraged speculation and overproduction through its false economic policies. Second, it attempted to minimize the crash and misled the people as to its gravity. Third, it erroneously charged the cause to other nations of the world. And finally, it refused to recognize and correct the evils at home which it had brought forth; it delayed reform, it forgot reform.*

Roosevelt then promised to help the victims of the Great Depression. He called for financial reforms, lower tariffs, federal power projects, controls on crop surpluses, old age and unemployment insurance, and federal relief.

Hoover, meanwhile, was trying hard to prove to the American people that the present administration did care and was acting. In July he told the public that he was taking a 20 percent pay cut. He was also quick to point out that things were getting better. The RFC had slowed up the rate of bank failures, and the stock market was beginning to show an upturn. Gold no longer was leaving the country, and the financial tension in Europe was easing.

Hoover's efforts were not enough, however, to convince the American people, who were charmed by Roosevelt's confidence, personal magnetism, and promise of action. On November 8 they went to the polls and chose Roosevelt as their next President. He won the election by a landslide victory, taking 57.3 percent of the popular vote and 472 of 531 electoral votes.

The First Hundred Days

In his nomination speech, Roosevelt had declared, "I pledge myself to a new deal for the American people." In his inaugural speech on March 4, 1933, he informed a waiting nation that he intended to address them "with a candor and a decision which the present situation of our nation impels." He went on to drive home his point, saying:

From 1930 until Roosevelt's inauguration, over 5000 banks closed their doors. Their deposits totalled nearly $3.5 million.

In the two weeks after Roosevelt's actions, stock prices climbed 15 percent.

This is preeminently the time to speak the truth, the whole truth, frankly and boldly. Nor need we shrink from honestly facing conditions in our country today. This great nation will endure as it has endured, will revive and will prosper. So first of all, let me assert my firm belief that the only thing we have to fear is fear itself—nameless, unreasoning, unjustified terror which paralyzes needed efforts to convert retreat into advance.

Roosevelt set to work at once. He attacked the Great Depression and pushed through an unprecedented number of new government programs. Known as the New Deal, his programs aimed to restore the shattered economy, give a new sense of purpose to the federal government, and restore the faith of the American people.

Roosevelt called Congress into a special session that lasted from March 9 to June 16. During this first "Hundred Days" of the New Deal, the federal government tried to do something for everyone. In all, Roosevelt sent 15 separate proposals to Congress and Congress adopted every one of them.

The Banking System and Wall Street. The month before Roosevelt's inauguration, the governor of Michigan, in an attempt to save the state's largest banks, had declared a bank holiday and had closed all the banks in the state. The closing saved the banks, but at the same time it triggered nationwide panic. People rushed to close out their bank accounts, withdrawing nearly $1.75 billion in little over a month's time. Before long, banks in several other states had been given a holiday, and this was only the beginning.

By March 3, over 20 states had declared bank holidays. In Wall Street and in Chicago's Loop, frightened depositors stormed banks, screaming for their savings. New York's Bowery Savings Bank, the largest private savings bank in the world, shut its doors in the face of a frenzied mob. By the time Roosevelt took the oath of office, almost every commercial bank in the United States was shut, and the American banking system was paralyzed.

To add to the problem, many people had withdrawn their money in gold, which they then hoarded or used to buy European securities. Because of this, between February 1 and March 4, nearly $300 million in gold was exported or set aside for foreign depositors, who

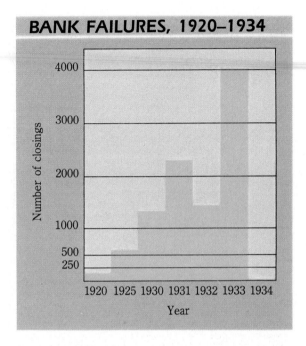

BANK FAILURES, 1920–1934

were expected to withdraw their funds from American banks.

Roosevelt dealt with the banking problem on his first day in office. He proclaimed a national bank holiday starting March 6 and ending March 9. At the same time, he stopped the export of gold, silver, and currency. On March 9 Congress passed the Emergency Banking Relief Act. The act proposed a wide range of presidential powers over banking and set up a system by which banks would open again or be reorganized.

The next day, Roosevelt asked Congress for an Economy Act, which was designed to balance the budget. To do this, the act cut the salaries of government employees and the pensions and other allowances of veterans. It also reorganized government agencies so they could function more economically. Roosevelt declared that these steps were necessary to avoid a billion dollar deficit. Ten days later, Congress passed the act.[1]

On March 12 President Roosevelt gave his first radio "fireside chat," or talk to the American people, in which he discussed the banking problem and assured the American people that it was now safe to entrust their savings to the banks. In the words of

---

[1] Under pressure from veterans, Congress later rescinded the pension cuts over Roosevelt's veto.

Note that the dole was common in Europe.

From the first days of his administration, Roosevelt used the radio to present informal reports to the American people. Millions tuned in weekly to hear these "fireside chats." What made Roosevelt effective in his use of the radio?

humorist Will Rogers, Roosevelt "made everybody understand it, even the bankers." When the banks in the 12 Federal Reserve cities opened their doors the next morning, a great many more deposits than withdrawals were made. Within two weeks, more than 75 percent of all banks, with well over 90 percent of the country's banking assets, were operating.

On April 19 Roosevelt announced that the United States was going off the gold standard and would no longer redeem currency in gold. While waiting to see how Congress and the people would react, he turned his attention to Wall Street, where, according to a Senate investigation, dishonest practices were resulting in financial gains for insiders and losses for small investors. To put an end to this, the Federal Securities Act was passed. It gave the Federal Trade Commission the power to police all new stock and bond issues and required that new stock be accompanied by a statement of certain financial information. The act also made company officials civilly and criminally liable for misrepresentation.

On June 5 Congress came out in favor of Roosevelt's action in taking the country off the gold standard. On June 16 Congress passed the Banking Act of 1933, also known as the Glass-Steagall Act. Among other things, it removed banks from the investment business and placed restrictions on the use of banking funds for speculation. It also established the Federal Deposit Insurance Corporation (FDIC), which guaranteed individual bank deposits under $5000.

The Unemployed. At the same time he was working on the banking problem, Roosevelt was asking Congress for legislation to help the unemployed. He wanted legislation that would involve government in direct relief, provide money for public works projects, and set up a program to put youths without jobs to work.

Congress responded on March 31 by passing a bill to form a Civilian Conservation Corps (CCC) which would help conserve or improve the country's natural resources. By early summer about 1300 CCC camps had been set up. The camps provided work for young men between 18 and 25 in reforestation, prevention of soil erosion, flood control, fire prevention, road building, and park and recreational area development. By the time the CCC was closed down in the 1940's, it had given work to 2.5 million young Americans.

On May 12 Congress passed the Federal Emergency Relief Act. It set up the Federal Emergency Relief Administration (FERA). FERA was authorized to distribute $500 million through grants to state and local agencies for relief. Neither Congress nor the people, however, really liked the idea of Americans being on the dole. As a result, on November 8, Congress passed legislation forming the Civil Works Administration (CWA) to create public jobs to help the unemployed through the winter of 1933–34. By January 1934 about 4 million Americans, most of them relatively unskilled men, were on the CWA's payroll.

The Tennessee Valley Authority. In April Roosevelt asked Congress to create the Tennessee Valley Authority (TVA). The TVA was to be an independent public body that, under the direction of a three-member board, would have control of government-owned property at Muscle Shoals, Tennessee.

The idea of a bill calling for further development of this area of the Tennessee Valley region was not new. Progressives in Congress, under the leadership of George Norris of Nebraska, had been trying to get such a bill passed for years. Norris and his followers believed that the dam and munitions plant built at Muscle Shoals during World War I could be used as the basis for federal development of hydroelectric power. Others saw in the site the potential for flood control and the production of fertilizer. Norris and the others, however, could not get such a bill passed. They had pushed bills through Congress twice, only to have them vetoed by Republican Presidents who believed that such bills went against the American tradition of free enterprise.

Roosevelt, however, did not view the matter in the same way as his predecessors. He had thought of using federal development of hydroelectric power as a "yardstick" against which private utility rates could be measured. Because of this, he pushed the bill through. It made the TVA responsible for flood and erosion control, the development of navigation, the generation and sale of electric power, and the manufacture and distribution of fertilizer. It also gave the TVA the power to build recreation areas, help with reforestation, and build and run additional dams, reservoirs, and power plants. The activities of the TVA covered seven states and affected the lives of 7 million people.

Agriculture and Industry. Nor did Roosevelt forget agriculture or industry. On May 12 Congress passed the Agricultural Adjustment Act (AAA) to deal with the problem of low farm prices. The act gave the

Department of Agriculture the power to pay a subsidy to farmers who agreed to produce less rice, wheat, cotton, tobacco, dairy products, and hogs. The subsidy was to be based on **parity,** a formula intended to bring the farmer's purchasing power back to what it had been before World War I. To raise money for the subsidies, the act also placed a tax on the processors of farm goods.

Although the AAA did increase national farm income from $5.6 billion in 1932 to $8.7 billion in 1935, it had some unfortunate side effects. At the time the act was passed, some farmers had already begun the production process for cotton and hogs. In order to meet the requirements of the AAA program, they had to plow under some 10 million acres of cotton and slaughter 6 million young pigs. Even though 100 million pounds of the slaughtered pork went to families on relief, many people remained critical of the slaughter.

On June 16 Congress passed the Farm Credit Act. It halted mortgage foreclosures by helping farmers with loans for production and marketing and by providing for the refinancing of farm mortgages at favorable terms.

TENNESSEE VALLEY AUTHORITY, 1933–45

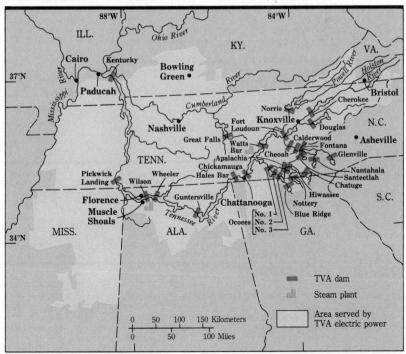

On the same day the Farm Credit Act became law, Congress passed the National Industrial Recovery Act (NIRA). This act tried to establish a cooperative relationship between government, business, and labor. One section of the act set codes of fair practice for working conditions, wages, and business practices. The codes were to be enforced by the National Recovery Administration (NRA). Another section of the act guaranteed labor the right to organize and bargain collectively through representatives of their own choosing. Still another section formed the Public Works Administration (PWA). Its goal was to stimulate the economy through the building of huge public works projects that needed large numbers of workers. The projects included the building of dams, port facilities, sewage plants, bridges, roads, airports, and hospitals.

Before long, the blue eagle symbol of the NRA appeared all over the country. It was the people's way of showing their faith in Roosevelt and his New Deal.

SECTION REVIEW

1. Identify the following: Federal Deposit Insurance Corporation, Civilian Conservation Corps, Tennessee Valley Authority, National Industrial Recovery Act.
2. Why was the banking system in trouble?
3. What problems led to the passage of the Federal Securities Act?
4. Why did Roosevelt favor the TVA?

CHAPTER 24 REVIEW

SUMMARY

1. The prosperity of the 1920's encouraged increasing speculation in the stock market, causing stock prices to rise much higher than they had ever been.
2. Meanwhile, the American economy was slowing down as a result of overproduction, reduced purchasing power, and government policies on taxes and tariffs.
3. The weakened economy could not sustain the stock market boom, and the market crashed in the fall of 1929.
4. The stock market crash was the beginning of the Great Depression, the worst economic decline in American history.
5. Unemployment, low wages, and the collapse of farm prices resulted in hard times for millions of Americans.
6. President Hoover, following his personal and political beliefs concerning the role of government, took limited steps to improve the nation's economy.
7. In 1932 the American people elected a new President, Democrat Franklin D. Roosevelt, who promised action to help victims of the Great Depression.
8. In his first 100 days in office, Roosevelt presented an unprecedented number of new programs designed to restore the economy.

VOCABULARY

brokers' loans	bull market	buying on margin	demand	soup kitchens
collateral	bulls	call loans	securities	parity
	bears	rediscount rate	breadlines	

REVIEW QUESTIONS

1. What were the causes and effects of the stock market crash?
2. What were the underlying problems that contributed to the Great Depression?
3. How did the problems of urban people compare with those in agricultural areas?
4. How did various elements of the economy interact to worsen the Great Depression?

5. How did Hoover's actions reflect his political philosophy?
6. How did Roosevelt's approach to solving the problems of the Great Depression differ from Hoover's?

7. What did Roosevelt do to remedy the problems of the financial system?
8. What was the initial response of the Congress and the American people to President Roosevelt's New Deal?

DISCUSSION

1. Could the Great Depression have been avoided? If so, how? If not, why?
2. Do you agree with Treasury Secretary Mellon's view on the benefits that would come out of an economic decline? Why or why not?

3. What did Roosevelt mean when he said that "the only thing we have to fear is fear itself"? Do you agree or disagree with this idea?
4. Is the "trickle down" theory effective? Why or why not?

USING GRAPHS

Refer to the graphs on pages 504 and 508 and answer the following questions:

1. In what year did stock prices reach their all time peak?
2. When stock prices were at their peak, what was the percentage of unemployment?

3. What was the best year for farmers between 1910 and 1940?
4. How did farmers' incomes compare to manufacturing workers' incomes for this period?
5. How much did the GNP decline between 1929 and 1932?

USING SKILLS

Consider the following general statement: *The New Deal was a revolutionary change in the role of government in the United States.* Which of the statements below support the generalization, and which do not?

1. The TVA produced and sold electricity in rural areas.
2. Roosevelt's Economy Act was designed to balance the budget.

3. On April 19, 1932, President Roosevelt announced that the United States was going off the gold standard.
4. Under the New Deal, the federal government became involved in direct public relief for the first time.
5. Hoover's Reconstruction Finance Corporation made loans available for the construction of public works.

1	Conflicting Ideas	521
2	The Second New Deal	524
3	The New Deal at Its Peak	529
4	American Culture During the 1930's	536

THE NEW DEAL

It is common sense to take a method and try it. If it fails, admit it frankly and try another, but above all, try something.

FRANKLIN D. ROOSEVELT

During the first "Hundred Days," President Roosevelt supplied the action needed to keep the American economy from collapsing. He provided relief for the unemployed and started the country on its road to economic recovery. However, the situation was still grave. Roosevelt, therefore, continued with his programs of relief and reform. As the crisis receded, criticism of the New Deal mounted and affected its progress. Nonetheless, the New Deal had a lasting impact on American life.

1 Conflicting Ideas

Although Roosevelt had no specific plan of action when he took office, he had a vast store of ideas upon which to draw. Some ideas were supplied by his advisors, whose views often conflicted. In fact, Roosevelt's method of government has been called **broker-state government**—a type of government in which the President acts as a broker (intermediary) between different groups. Because different groups held influence at different times, no one was ever completely satisfied.

Roosevelt's Advisors

Roosevelt tolerated a wide range of opinion among his advisors, many of whom had very definite views on such subjects as **national planning** (economic planning by the federal government), inflation, and **deficit spending** (the practice of spending funds not yet collected). Roosevelt's **"brain trust"** (a group of experts drawn from the academic world) held ideas similar to Theodore Roosevelt's New Nationalism. That is, they favored national planning over laissez-faire.

Furthermore, these advisors believed that economic concentration was already a part of American life. As evidence of this, they pointed out that **free markets** based on supply and demand had largely been replaced by **administered markets,** in which control was exercised by policymakers who ran large companies. These policymakers were the same people who had been in control of the American economy at the beginning of the Great Depression. Members of the brain trust, therefore, called for government control of the economy. They helped Roosevelt formulate policy during the early years of the New Deal.

Other advisors, such as Professor Felix Frankfurter of Harvard University and Supreme Court Justice Louis D. Brandeis, rejected the idea of national planning. They did not believe that economic concentration was a fixed part of American life. Their main object was to preserve free enterprise, and they proposed policies designed to foster competition in the market. Generally, this meant curbing big business. The views of these advisors were closer to Woodrow Wilson's New Freedom than to the New Nationalism.

Roosevelt's advisors disagreed on other subjects as well. Some, like Director of the Budget Lewis W. Douglas, were committed to the gold standard and advocated a balanced federal budget. Others, who favored inflation, advocated deficit spending. Deficit spending tends to cause inflation because the Federal Reserve may increase the money supply when the government borrows money to cover the deficit.

At times such disagreements led to contradictions in policy, and after awhile some of Roosevelt's advisors became disenchanted with the New Deal. This first group to do so was the one with the closest ties to business. As measures were passed that curtailed its activities, big business became more and more critical of the New Deal.

One of the measures with which the business community was not pleased was the Securities Exchange Act, passed by Congress on June 6, 1934. This act set up the Securities and Exchange Commission (SEC) and gave it the power to regulate trading in securities and to license **securities exchanges**—places where stocks and bonds were bought and sold.

Have students speculate as to why, even in hard times, fascism and communism made less headway in America than in Europe.

Probably no President since Lincoln has been so admired or criticized as Franklin Roosevelt. Some people believed that FDR's "one-man super-government" would lead to the nation's ruin. Why did big business turn against Roosevelt?

In addition, the Securities and Exchange Act gave the Federal Reserve Board power to regulate the money supply used to finance trading in securities. This was accomplished by controlling the **margin requirement,** or the amount of money an investor must put up when making a purchase. If the Fed (the Federal Reserve Board) raises the margin requirement, the investor must then either put up more money or sell some stock. Thus, raising the requirement would curb speculation, because investors would not be able to make as many purchases.

Regulation of big business continued with the passage of the Communications Act on June 19, 1934. This act set up the Federal Communications Commission (FCC). Its function was to regulate radio, telegraph, and cable communications—both interstate and foreign.

Critics of the New Deal

As time passed, the ranks of New Deal critics swelled. Some conservatives felt that the government was interfering too much in American life. One such group was the American Liberty League, founded in 1934. Made up largely of conservative Democrats, it included among its members many people associated with big business interests. They opposed the New Deal on the ground that it undermined free enterprise by restricting business through taxes and regulations. They saw the government's expansion of power as a threat to individual liberty and attacked the New Deal as unconstitutional. These conservatives wanted government to let business alone and play a less active role in the economy.

Radicals criticized the New Deal from a different standpoint. They wanted a more active government, and they were not worried about the possible threat to individual liberty.

One radical group on the far right was the fascists. **Fascism** is a political philosophy that holds the individual second to nation and race and advocates government by dictatorship. In a fascist regime, there is private ownership of land and capital. However, most economic activity is controlled by the state.

The American fascist movement got its ideas from fascist governments that were evolving in Europe in the 1930's. Although the movement never attracted many Americans, it drew enough attention to make it dangerous. Its aim was to subvert democracy and set up a fascist government in the United States. During these years of economic crisis, fascists blamed Jews, Communists, and liberals for the country's troubles.

On the far left, Communists presented another threat to democracy. The American Communist party was openly hostile to the Roosevelt administration. Communists had reached the conclusion that the Great Depression signalled the end of capitalism in the West. Therefore they were against any democratic leader who could offer hope of recovery. Although the Communists gained some converts, they made little impression on most Americans.

More threatening to Roosevelt was Father Charles E. Coughlin of Royal Oak, Michigan. Coughlin had set up a radio station in 1926—called "the Shrine of the

The National Union for Social Justice appealed to Populist types in the Midwest and Irish Catholics in large cities.

Long's ideas were so appealing that many people were willing to excuse his tactics, which included fixing elections and harassing opponents. When accused of violating the Louisiana constitution, Long replied, "I'm the Constitution around here now!"

Little Flower." Known as the "radio priest," he supported Roosevelt in 1932, urging listeners to choose "Roosevelt or ruin." Before long, however, Coughlin became unhappy with the New Deal, chiefly because he felt that the government should take stronger action to curb the monied interests. Finally, in 1934, Coughlin broke with Roosevelt, accusing him of selling out to bankers and Jews.

That same year Coughlin founded the National Union for Social Justice. This organization advocated social reform and supported silver inflation. Father Coughlin saw inflation as a cure for America's ills. Coughlin used his radio station to promote his policies and to attack bankers, Jews, Communists, labor, and the New Deal. His speeches appealed to people all over the country. In fact, by 1934, he had developed an audience of 10 million people and was receiving $500,000 a year in contributions.

Dr. Francis E. Townsend, a retired California physician, also had a large following. Dr. Townsend proposed the Old Age Revolving Pension Plan as his solution to the nation's problems. The Townsend Plan called upon the federal government to provide a monthly pension of $200 to people 60 years of age and over who had retired. Those who received money would agree to spend it in the United States within a month after they had received payment. This was meant to stimulate the economy. Funds to carry out the plan were to be obtained from a tax on commercial transactions. Townsend's ideas caught on quickly. By the end of 1934, about 1200 Townsend Clubs had been organized throughout the country.

Of greatest concern to Roosevelt, however, was Senator Huey P. Long of Louisiana, known as the "Kingfish." This critic of the New Deal was a Democrat who had worked his way through state politics to become governor of Louisiana in 1928. Despite a record of social reform, Long ruled as a virtual dictator, and corruption in the state was widespread. Two years after becoming governor, he moved into national politics with his election to the United States Senate.

Although most critics of the New Deal were conservatives, the administration was also attacked by those who believed radical measures were needed to combat the Great Depression. A political movement headed by Dr. Francis Townsend (left) and Huey Long (right) gained support as the Great Depression lingered. How did Roosevelt indicate that he took these movements seriously?

Long promised every family a house, a car, and a radio.   The administration increased its majority in both the House and Senate. All but seven states had Democrats as governors.

In 1932 Long supported Roosevelt, but within a year, the two had split. One of Long's major complaints against the President was that he had not taken steps to redistribute wealth in the United States. By 1934 Long had developed his own plan for doing so. His Share Our Wealth Plan called for the federal government to guarantee every family in America a minimum annual income of $5000. To finance this plan, Long proposed that the government tax the property, inheritance, and income of the wealthy. In a speech given in 1933, he summed up the plan:

> The foregoing program means all taxes paid by fortune holders at the top and none by the people at the bottom; the spreading of wealth among all the people and the breaking up of a system of Lords and Slaves in our economic life. . . .
> Then . . . the food of the land will feed, the raiment clothe, and the houses shelter all the people. . . .
> Then . . . EVERY MAN A KING.

Such ideas attracted millions. By early 1935 Long claimed about 27,000 Share Our Wealth clubs and a mailing list of 7.5 million people. As his appeal spread, he became a threat to Roosevelt. Polls indicated that he might receive as many as 4 million votes on a third-party ticket in 1936. But Long was assassinated in September 1935.

Following the assassination, the Reverend Gerald L. K. Smith became leader of the Share Our Wealth movement. Within a short time, Smith formed an alliance with Townsend and Coughlin. The strength of this alliance influenced Roosevelt to incorporate some of its ideas into his own programs.

SECTION REVIEW

1. Identify the following: Lewis W. Douglas, American Liberty League, Father Charles E. Coughlin.
2. Why did some of Roosevelt's advisors recommend government control of the economy?
3. Why did big business become alienated from the New Deal?
4. What plan was recommended by Dr. Francis E. Townsend?
5. Why did Huey P. Long become a threat to Roosevelt?

2 The Second New Deal

Despite mounting criticism, the New Deal continued in 1934. For example, the National Housing Act, passed on June 28, stimulated home building by setting up an agency that insured loans made for construction. Roosevelt received a sweeping endorsement of his programs in the mid-term elections of 1934. In January 1935, in his annual message to Congress, Roosevelt introduced his second New Deal, a broad program of social reform to help farmers, workers, the poor, and the unemployed.

Relief for the Unemployed

By the end of 1934, the government had spent over $2 billion on relief. The President, however, wanted to get people off the dole. He wrote:

> What I am seeking is the abolition of relief altogether. I cannot say so out loud yet but I hope to be able to substitute work for relief.

Ask students to respond to the accusation that, in sponsoring jobs, the government competed with the private sector.

Have students list the kinds of work projects they feel would be legitimate rather than "make work."

Many work programs for the unemployed were started during the Roosevelt administration. CCC enlistees (left) helped to reforest the land. The WPA (above) was responsible for the building or rebuilding of bridges, highways, and the like. What were the criticisms of these programs?

Shortly thereafter, Roosevelt asked Congress for about $5 billion for a large-scale public works program. On April 8, 1935, the Emergency Relief Appropriation Act was passed. The main agency created by the act was the Works Progress Administration (WPA). Its director was Harry Hopkins, former head of the Federal Emergency Relief Administration (FERA) and the Civil Works Administration (CWA).

Hopkins began at once to provide jobs for the unemployed. Between May 1935 and June 1943, the WPA spent about $11 billion on nearly 1.5 million separate projects. WPA workers built or improved 5900 schools, 1000 airfields, more than 2500 hospitals, and almost 13,000 playgrounds. The WPA provided jobs in the arts as well as in construction. Actors, writers, and artists were hired for individual projects that allowed them to carry on their own work. By the time the WPA was terminated, it had employed a total of more than 8.5 million workers.

The WPA was highly controversial. The major objection raised was that many of the projects created were "make-work" assignments. That is, they were based on the need to give people jobs rather than on the validity of the project. The WPA, for example, spent $78,000 repairing a ditch in Denver, Colorado, and $12,000 replacing street signs in Montgomery, Alabama. In defending "make-work," Roosevelt argued, "If we can boondoggle ourselves out of this Depression, that word is going to be enshrined in the hearts of people for many years to come." Thereafter, critics used the term **"boondoggle"** in referring to any project that, in their eyes, had little merit or value.

There were other agencies besides the WPA that participated in the public works program. One of these was the National Youth Administration (NYA), established on June 26, 1935. The NYA provided employment to young people between the ages of 16 and 25 who were no longer in school. In addition, it gave part-time jobs to high school, college, and graduate students, allowing them to stay in school and earn money as well. By 1936 the NYA had employed some 600,000 youth.

Ask students to explain why so few farms had electricity prior to the 1930's.

Note that, when Social Security began, there were more than 30 workers for every retiree, so the tax on employers and workers was relatively small.

Help for Farmers

Roosevelt also provided more help for American farmers. On May 1, 1935, he created the Resettlement Administration (RA) by executive order. Its purpose was to resettle impoverished farm families on better land. In addition, the RA was given the power to loan small farmers, tenants, sharecroppers, and agricultural workers money to buy land and equipment.

Next, Roosevelt moved to provide electricity to rural areas. Until the 1930's, only about 10 percent of American farms had electricity. On May 11 Roosevelt set up the Rural Electrification Administration (REA). The task of this agency was to see that electricity went to rural areas that were not served by private utilities. To carry out this task, the REA made low-interest loans for the construction of light and power lines in these areas. By 1941, 40 percent of American farms had electricity.

Support for Labor

The New Deal helped the cause of labor as well. The National Labor Relations Act, or Wagner Act, was passed by Congress and signed by Roosevelt on July 5, 1935. The Wagner Act upheld the right of workers to organize and bargain collectively.[1] It set up the National Labor Relations Board (NLRB) to certify the unions formed and to supervise elections in which workers chose their bargaining agents. The NLRB was also given power to act against employers who used unfair labor practices, such as firing workers known to have joined a union. The business community opposed the Wagner Act and complained that it had defined unfair practices for employers, but not for workers.

Social Security

Roosevelt was particularly concerned with providing security for the unemployed, the aged, and the handicapped. He appointed a committee to look into the problem and develop a program to meet the needs of these people. The committee was headed by

---

[1] This provision replaced one in the NIRA, struck down by the Supreme Court in May 1935.

Secretary of Labor Frances Perkins was the first woman to serve in the Cabinet. Her efforts were essential in shaping and passing the Social Security Act of 1935. Who were to be the recipients of social security?

Secretary of Labor Frances Perkins, the first woman cabinet member. The ideas that resulted were embodied in the Social Security Act of August 14, 1935.

This act established a national system of old age and survivors' insurance, giving a pension to retired persons 65 years of age and over. The pension was to be financed by a tax on employers and workers. The size of the pension was determined by the number of years a person had worked. In addition, the act set up a joint federal-state system of unemployment compensation. The funds for this were to come from a tax on the payrolls of employers. The act also authorized grants to the states for various social services, including aid to the handicapped and dependent children. The Social Security Board was set up to administer the different parts of the program.

Banking Reform

Further reforms were also made in banking. The Banking Act, passed on August 23, 1935, increased the membership of the Federal Reserve Board, now

May 27, 1935, was referred to as "Black Monday" by New Dealers. In addition to declaring the NIRA unconstitutional, the Court also ruled against a farm-mortgage relief act.

called the Board of Governors. Another part of the act involved **open market operations,** or the buying and selling of government securities in the bond market. An Open Market Committee, made up of the Board of Governors and five regional reserve bank presidents, made decisions to buy or to sell bonds in order to raise or lower the amount of money in circulation.

In times of inflation, the Fed could adopt a **tight money policy** to slow the growth of the money supply. That is, it could sell bonds to take money out of circulation. If the Fed sold bonds to an investor, the investor would purchase those bonds with a check. This would reduce the size of the investor's bank account. The investor's bank would then have less on deposit, and could, therefore, lend less money. As a result, the money supply would contract.

On the other hand, if the nation were going through a recession, the Fed could use an **easy money policy** to make money more readily available and stimulate the economy. In that case, the Fed would buy bonds. If the Fed bought bonds from an investor, it would pay for the purchase with a check drawn on itself. This check would be deposited by the investor, increasing the size of his or her account. The bank would then send the check to the Fed, which would pay it by increasing the member bank's reserves. With more reserves, the bank could make more loans. Thus, the money supply would expand.

Utilities Reform

Roosevelt also took action to regulate the utilities. The President, like many other Americans, disliked monopolies. Therefore he sought to break up the giant utility holding companies, which controlled the distribution of gas and electricity in various parts of the country. Because these companies had no competition, they could set rates as high as they pleased.

To remedy the situation, Congress passed the Public Utilities Holding Company Act on August 28, 1935. It forbade holding companies from controlling more than a "single integrated public utility system" in a given area of the country. In a "death sentence" clause, the act set a term of five years, at the end of which the government could dissolve any utility company that could not prove that it was local in

character and giving efficient service. The act succeeded in breaking up most of the great utility empires.

Tax Reform

The last major measure passed in 1935 changed the tax system. Roosevelt saw the need for reform in this area, and asked Congress for a tax measure that would redistribute wealth. In his message to Congress on tax reform, he stated:

> *Our revenue laws have operated in many ways to the unfair advantage of the few, and they have done little to prevent an unjust concentration of wealth and power.*

Acting on Roosevelt's recommendation, Congress passed the Wealth Tax Act on August 30. This act increased taxes on incomes over $50,000—both corporate and personal. There were also increases in estate and gift taxes. Taxes on small corporations, however, were lowered. Conservatives attacked the act as a scheme to "soak the rich."

The Supreme Court Attack on the New Deal

Just as Roosevelt had most of his important programs in place, the Supreme Court began to find some New Deal measures unconstitutional. On May 27, 1935, the Court struck down the National Industrial Recovery Act (NIRA) in *Schechter* v. *The United States.* This so-called "sick chicken" case centered on some New York poultry dealers who had been convicted of violating an NRA (National Recovery Administration) code. After hearing the case, the Court unanimously declared the NIRA unconstitutional.

The decision was based upon two grounds. One was that the NIRA had given too much power to the executive branch of government. Another was that the NRA code governed **intrastate commerce,** or commerce that took place within a given state. Congress was only allowed to regulate interstate commerce. When Roosevelt learned of the Court's action, he said, "We have been relegated to a horse-and-buggy definition of interstate commerce."

On January 6, 1936, the Supreme Court struck down the Agricultural Adjustment Act (AAA). In *United States* v. *Butler,* the court ruled that the AAA's processing tax, levied on middlemen to finance subsidies for farmers who agreed to cut back on production, was unconstitutional. Justice Owen Roberts wrote that this tax was nothing but "the expropriation of money from one group for the benefit of another." Later in the same year, the Court found other New Deal measures unconstitutional. It seemed likely that there would be further attacks.

The Election of 1936

Despite the actions of the Court, the Democrats felt confident that Roosevelt would be re-elected in 1936. The assassination of Huey Long had removed one threat to Roosevelt. The Smith-Townsend-Coughlin group emerged as a third party movement and backed Representative William M. Lemke of North Dakota for President, but the new party had little impact.

On June 11, at Cleveland, Ohio, the Republicans nominated Governor Alfred M. Landon of Kansas to run against Roosevelt. At first Landon showed little desire to end the New Deal. As time passed, however, Landon's campaign became more conservative. It tended to focus on the charge that the New Deal was undermining traditional American initiative and self-reliance. In fact, the theme of the campaign became "Save the American Way of Life." Big business and the wealthy, attracted by these ideas and angered by some of Roosevelt's measures, backed the Republicans.

The campaign was a bitter one. Attacks on the New Deal increasingly became personal attacks on Roosevelt and his family. Roosevelt, in turn, lashed out at these "economic royalists." After his nomination at Philadelphia on June 23, Roosevelt said that the forces of "organized money" were "unanimous in their hate" for him and that he welcomed this hatred:

I should like to have it said of my first Administration that in it the forces of selfishness and of lust for power met their match. . . . I should like to have it said . . . of my second Administration that in it these forces met their master.

ELECTION OF 1936

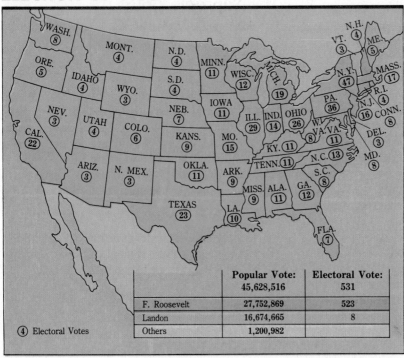

	Popular Vote: 45,628,516	Electoral Vote: 531
F. Roosevelt	27,752,869	523
Landon	16,674,665	8
Others	1,200,982	

④ Electoral Votes

During the campaign about 80 percent of the press opposed Roosevelt.

PROSPERITY AND DEPRESSION **529**

Ask students to explain how a sit-down strike differed from a traditional strike.

Liberals from both parties joined Roosevelt in his fight against these forces. Indeed, the campaign became a crusade against conservatism. In the end, the liberals won out. Roosevelt received 60.7 percent of the popular vote and 523 out of 531 electoral votes. It was one of the biggest landslides in American political history.

SECTION REVIEW

1. Identify the following: National Housing Act, Harry Hopkins, Resettlement Administration, Frances Perkins.
2. What was the purpose of the Works Progress Administration?
3. Why did the business community oppose the Wagner Act?
4. Under the Social Security Act, how were pensions for retired people to be financed?
5. How did the Banking Act give powers to the Federal Reserve to influence the country's money supply?
6. On what grounds did the Supreme Court strike down the National Industrial Recovery Act?

3 The New Deal at Its Peak

Roosevelt's victory at the polls was based upon a new coalition. The strength of that coalition and the obvious popular support for the New Deal led the President to move against the Supreme Court and continue his reforms.

The New Roosevelt Coalition

The new coalition responsible for Roosevelt's victory in 1936 included recent immigrants, labor, and a growing number of blacks. The "Solid South," where a dislike for Republicans had lingered since the Civil War, also remained in the Democratic fold, although many conservative Democrats had split from the party.

Recent Immigrants. The new immigrants—mostly from southern and eastern Europe—supported Roosevelt in great numbers. They were influenced by the manipulations of city machines, which continued to deliver votes to the Democratic party. New Deal policies had helped the immigrants, who

were generally members of the working class. In addition, most of the newcomers were Catholic, and members of the Catholic Church had generally supported the Democrats. In 1936, 104 of 106 American cities with populations over 100,000 went for Roosevelt.

Labor. Labor had made huge gains under the New Deal. Union leaders took advantage of the NIRA and, when that was declared unconstitutional, the Wagner Act to organize further.

Some leaders of the AFL, such as John L. Lewis, wanted the organization, which was made up mostly of skilled workers in craft unions, to include unskilled workers in the mass production industries. As the head of the United Mine Workers, one of the few industrial unions in the AFL, Lewis was sympathetic to the cause of unskilled workers. He also saw that by organizing along industrial lines, the AFL could bring thousands of workers into the labor movement.

At the AFL convention in 1935, Lewis presented a plan to organize along industry rather than craft lines. Although his plan was turned down, Lewis continued working for the industrial union movement. Eventually, Lewis and his followers were thrown out of the AFL. In 1938 they set up the Congress of Industrial Organizations. Competition between the AFL and the CIO brought more workers into unions during Roosevelt's second term of office.

As a result, labor made further gains against big business. This was first apparent in the automobile industry. In 1937 workers in several General Motors plants used a new device to great effect. This was the **sit-down strike**—a strike in which workers stopped production and sat down next to their machines until employers gave in to their demands. In reaction to the strike, General Motors called in the National Guard. Incidents of violence occurred, but the union remained firm. In the end, the company recognized the United Automobile Workers.

To avoid a similar situation, United States Steel signed an agreement with steel workers in March 1937. Other steel companies refused to follow that example, however. The newer steel companies, known collectively as "Little Steel," held out against strikes in the late spring and summer of 1937. After a good deal of bloodshed, the NLRB intervened, forcing the steel companies to negotiate with the union.

The NRA had provided the union movement with an impetus to mass organization—the first since World War I.

Despite federal instructions directing that blacks be considered for public jobs, local officials often continued to discriminate against them. In Mississippi blacks made up more than 30 percent of the population but were given only 1.7 percent of CCC jobs.

John L. Lewis later attacked the steel companies for their actions:

> These groups are encouraging a systematic organization of vigilante groups to fight unionization. . . . They equip these vigilantes with tin hats, wooden clubs, gas masks, and lethal weapons, and train them in the arts of brutality and oppression. . . .
>
> Fascist organizations have been launched and financed under the shabby pretext that the C.I.O. movement is Communistic. The real breeders of discontent and alien doctrines of government . . . are such as these who take the law into their own hands. No tin-hat brigade of goose-stepping vigilantes or bibble-babbling mob of blackguarding and corporation-paid scoundrels will prevent the onward march of labor, or divert its purpose to play its natural and rational part in the development of the economic, political, and social life of our nation. . . .

Union membership, which had been less than 3 million in 1933, reached 9 million by 1939. The growth of organized labor, which was fostered by the New Deal, in turn aided the growth of the Democratic party. Labor provided both votes and a major source of campaign funds. In 1936 labor swung a number of midwestern states behind Roosevelt, and the United Mine Workers' contribution was the largest the party received.

Blacks. Blacks also joined forces with Roosevelt. In 1932 black Americans had shown their traditional allegiance to the Republican party—"the party of Lincoln"—and voted for Hoover. Many NAACP leaders were critical of the early stages of the New Deal. This was because blacks continued to be the victims of racial discrimination. In industry, they were usually the last to be hired and the first to be fired. If they had jobs, they were generally paid less than whites. In agriculture, AAA policies actually drove black tenants and sharecroppers from the land. In addition, the government failed to enact any civil rights measures during the New Deal.

Nevertheless, life for black Americans improved somewhat under Roosevelt. Roosevelt's measures helped unemployed blacks, and an effort was made to administer programs such as the WPA and the NYA without regard to race. In addition, Roosevelt appointed blacks to office, and both Eleanor Roosevelt and Secretary of the Interior Harold Ickes had close ties to black leaders. By 1936 blacks were switching to the Democratic party in great numbers. In fact, a *Fortune* magazine poll taken in 1938

Workers from 17 General Motors plants went on strike in 1937 in an attempt to gain management's recognition of the United Auto Workers Union. Instead of picketing, the strikers occupied the factories in a sit-down strike. What New Deal legislation made it easier for unions to bargain with management?

By the end of its 1936 term, the Supreme Court had found New
Deal legislation unconstitutional in seven out of nine cases.

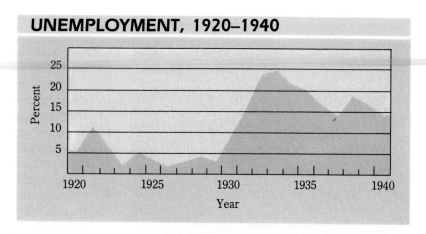

UNEMPLOYMENT, 1920–1940

revealed that 84.7 percent of the black respondents
favored Roosevelt.

Roosevelt Versus the Supreme Court

The overwhelming vote of confidence Roosevelt
received in 1936 moved him to take action against the
Supreme Court to prevent futher disruption of the
New Deal, which seemed likely given the makeup of
the Court. Although four justices usually voted for
New Deal measures, they were offset by four
conservative justices. The ninth justice, Owen
Roberts, often voted with the conservatives.

On February 5, 1937, Roosevelt submitted to
Congress a plan for reorganizing the federal judiciary.
Arguing that the nine men were too old to keep up
with the heavy judicial workload, Roosevelt asked
that Congress pass a law that would allow him to
appoint one additional justice for each one who failed
to retire at the age of 70. In addition, the number of
justices was to be increased from 9 to 15.

The plan aroused bitter opposition not only from
anti-New Dealers, but from Roosevelt's supporters.
The President's action was viewed as an attempt to
"pack" the Supreme Court with pro-New Deal
justices, which would destroy the independence of
the judiciary and gain more power for the executive.
This could destroy constitutional government in the
United States. One columnist stated this point of
view:

*If the American people accept this last
audacity of the President without letting out a*

*yell to high heaven, they have ceased to be
jealous of their liberties and are ripe for ruin.*

*This is the beginning of pure personal
government. Do you want it? Do you like it?
Look around about the world . . . and make
up your mind.*

*The Executive is already powerful . . . and
will be strengthened even more if the
reorganization plan for the administration,
presented some weeks ago, is adopted. We
have, to all intents and purposes, a one-party
Congress, dominated by the President. . . .
And now the Supreme Court is to have a
majority determined by the President and by a
Senate which he dominates.*

*When that happens we will have a one-man
Government. . . .*

Despite such opposition, Roosevelt refused to
accept defeat. Although he continued to press for
action, the bill failed to pass the Senate for a number
of reasons. One was that conservative Justice William
Van Devanter announced his retirement, giving
Roosevelt a chance to replace him with a liberal
without the planned reorganization of the Court.
Another reason was that on March 21, Chief Justice
Charles Evans Hughes took issue with Roosevelt's
argument that the Court was too old to keep up with
its job, stating that the Court was up-to-date on its
caseload. Even more important was the fact that the
Supreme Court softened its position on the New
Deal. In the period from March 29 to May 24, the
Court upheld certain pieces of New Deal legislation,
such as the Wagner Act and the Social Security Act.

Note that soil erosion in the Dust Bowl was worsened by the fact that many farmers had abandoned their land, and thus large areas lacked crops to help hold the soil.

President Roosevelt's proposal to add six justices to the Supreme Court aroused strong opposition. Critics labeled the plan a court-packing scheme. What effect did the President's plan have within the Democratic Party?

Finally, Senator Joseph T. Robinson of Arkansas, who had championed Roosevelt's plan in the Senate, died.

Roosevelt claimed that he had "lost the battle but won the war." In 1937 he appointed the liberal Senator Hugo Black of Alabama as Van Devanter's replacement and in the next four years made six more appointments. The Court fight, however, cost Roosevelt a great deal of support and triggered a split in the Democratic party. Conservative Democrats deserted the President in large numbers and joined with Republicans to block other New Deal measures.

Continued Reform

After the Court fight, the progress of the New Deal slowed considerably as Roosevelt turned his attention toward foreign affairs. There were, however, a few attempts to broaden the scope of the New Deal.

Agriculture. In agriculture, the New Deal focused on the plight of tenants, sharecroppers, and migrant workers. Early New Deal farm policy had not helped these people. The AAA forced many tenants to move when landowners reduced the number of acres planted in order to cut surpluses and receive payments from the government. With no land to work, the tenants generally became migrants. This meant more competition for jobs among migrant workers. The Resettlement Administration, set up in

1935, had tried to resettle the poor on better land. A shortage of money, however, hampered the effectiveness of the program. As a result, the RA resettled only about 4000 families.

Tenants and sharecroppers were helped by a new measure meant to replace the AAA. The Soil Conservation and Domestic Allotment Act, passed by Congress on February 29, 1936, allowed the government to restrict agricultural output and further conservation at the same time. Landowners who wanted to take part in the program agreed not to plant soil-depleting crops and to practice conservation on the land withdrawn from use. In return, they received payments. Part of these payments went to tenants and sharecroppers.

From 1932 to 1936, the farmers' plight increased as vast areas of the Great Plains suffered a severe drought. The worst hit areas became known as the "Dust Bowl."[2] The soil—exhausted by poor farming methods—turned into dust, and dust storms were created by the wind. A September 1934 magazine article described conditions in the Dust Bowl:

> *On Decoration day the wind started again, blowing hot as a blast from hell and the young corn withered as if under machine gun fire, the trees in two hours looked as if they had been beaten. The day after Decoration day it was so hot you couldn't sit around. . . . We got in the car and drove slowly through the sizzling countryside.*
>
> *Not a soul was in sight. It was like a funeral. The houses were closed up tight, the blinds drawn, the windows and doors closed. There seemed to be a menace in the air made visible. It was frightening. You could hear the fields crack and dry, and the only movement in the down-driving heat was the dead withering of the dry blighted leaves on the twigs. . . .*
>
> *There was something terrifying about this visible sign of disaster. It went into your nostrils so you couldn't breathe: the smell of hunger. It made you count your own ribs with terror. You don't starve in America. Everything looks good. There is something around the*

[2] Parts of Texas, Oklahoma, Colorado, New Mexico, Texas, and Kansas.

More than 800,000 families had received loans by 1940.

PROSPERITY AND DEPRESSION   **533**

The Agricultural Adjustment Act of 1938 also set up the Federal Crop Insurance Corporation (FCIC) to insure wheat crops.

corner. Everyone has a chance. That's all over now. The whole country cracks and rumbles and cries out in its terrible leanness, stripped with exploitation and terror—and as sign and symbol, bones—bones showing naked and spiritless, showing decay and crisis and a terrible warning, bare and lean. . . .

Because of such conditions, many people left the Dust Bowl to seek work in the fields and orchards of California, Oregon, and Washington. But the refugees, known as "Okies" and "Arkies," were often unable to find work even after they reached their destination.

To combat the decline in farm ownership, Congress passed the Bankhead-Jones Farm Tenant Act on July 22, 1937. The act established the Farm Security Administration (FSA), which granted low-interest loans for farm tenants, sharecroppers, and agricultural workers to buy farms. The FSA also tried to help migrants. It developed a program for regulating the supply, as well as the wages and hours, of migrant workers. In addition, sanitary camps were set up and medical services were provided.

Before long, the government had to turn its attention back to the problem of overproduction on farms. The Soil Conservation and Domestic Allotment Act of 1936 had not been able to check surpluses or stop prices from dropping.

Therefore, on February 16, 1938, Congress passed the second Agricultural Adjustment Act, a modified version of the 1933 act. Under this act, marketing quotas—limits on export commodities—could be set. Crop production was limited by setting **acreage allotments,** the amount of land each farmer was allowed to plant.

In addition, the act set up the "ever-normal granary." Under this plan the federal government stored surplus crops and loaned money to farmers. If a poor harvest occurred, farmers could pay back the loans and sell the stored crops on the open market. This process helped to stabilize agricultural prices. The money to finance this program would come from the federal government rather than from the processing tax that had caused the first AAA to be struck down by the Supreme Court.

Housing.   In his second inaugural address, Roosevelt had stated that one third of the nation was still "ill-housed, ill-clad, and ill-nourished." On September 1, 1937, Congress moved to help the "ill-housed" by passing another National Housing Act, known as the Wagner-Steagall Act. This act, intended to provide improved housing for low-income families, set up the United States Housing Authority (USHA) under the Department of the Interior.

The USHA gave long-term, low-interest loans to local public agencies that met ten percent of the cost

Years of high winds and drought in the Great Plains left once-productive land unfarmable. Hardest hit were the Oklahoma panhandle, northern Texas, eastern Colorado and New Mexico, and western Kansas. Many farmers in the Dust Bowl region headed west to start over. What was done to lessen the problems of these farmers and migrants?

Point out that, prior to the establishment of TNEC, President Roosevelt had sent recommendations for curbing monopolies to Congress.

Note that farm laborers and domestic servants were not covered under the Fair Labor Standards Act.

of building low-income housing. The USHA could also award subsidies to local agencies to keep rents in such projects at a lower level. To receive such subsidies, local agencies had to put up 25 percent of the amount granted by the government. By 1941 over 500 low-rent public housing projects were in process.

Business. In the early New Deal, Roosevelt had accepted the idea of an administered market. To keep the economy in balance, he had followed a policy of business regulation in the tradition of Theodore Roosevelt. Later, the government became more Wilsonian in tone. It stressed the ideal of the free market and stepped up its attacks on monopolies.

The anti-monopoly thrust of the later New Deal was reflected in the establishment of the Temporary National Economic Committee (TNEC) on June 16, 1938. The committee held hearings to study the effects of monopoly on profits, prices, wages, and other aspects of the economy. In the end, its report substantiated the view that federal antitrust procedures should be expanded.

The President's campaign against monopolies was helped by Thurman Arnold, who served as head of the Antitrust Division of the Department of Justice during the later New Deal. He instituted nearly 100 antitrust suits while in office.

Consumers. To protect consumers, Congress passed the Food, Drug, and Cosmetic Act on June 24, 1938. More stringent than the Pure Food and Drug Act of 1906, this act required manufacturers of food, drugs, and cosmetics to label the ingredients used in their products. It forbade the mislabeling of products as well as the use of false or misleading advertising. The law was to be enforced by the Food and Drug Administration and the Federal Trade Commission.

Labor. On June 25, 1938, Congress passed the Fair Labor Standards Act. It set up basic standards for industries involved in interstate commerce. These included a minimum wage of 40 cents an hour, a maximum work week of 40 hours, and a ban against child labor.

Recession

With the New Deal largely in place and the economy apparently well on its way to recovery, a

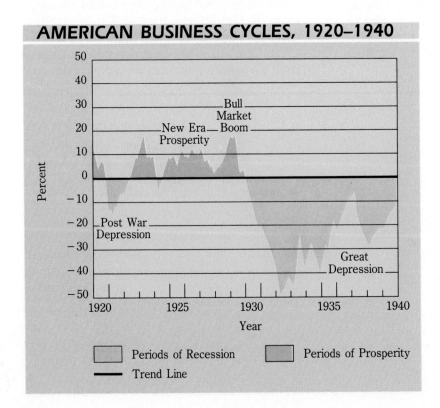

AMERICAN BUSINESS CYCLES, 1920–1940

The Role of Government

Ever since the Revolution, Americans have debated about the role of the national government. When the Confederation government was found to be too weak, it was replaced by a stronger one under the Constitution. But the argument about the role of government went on. Thomas Jefferson, a believer in laissez-faire, said, "Government that governs least, governs best." Alexander Hamilton argued for a bigger, stronger government. Their different views were seen in the struggle over the national bank.

Still, the role of government in the economy was small by today's standards. For years it did little but set tariffs and excise taxes and issue currency. The first income tax was not passed until the Civil War. Until that time, federal funding for internal improvements was resisted. After the war, however, the government began to finance internal improvements on a grand new scale.

The Industrial Revolution led to demands for regulation of the railroads and other big businesses. The Interstate Commerce Act of 1887 was a turning point in the history of relations between the federal government and the economy. In the late 1800's, however, when the government intervened, it was usually to take the side of business against organized labor.

Not until Theodore Roosevelt and Woodrow Wilson debated the New Nationalism versus the New Freedom was there any well-defined review of government's role. Roosevelt called for intervention in the economy in the interests of the people—"to make this country economically as well as politically a genuine democracy." Wilson called for even more intervention. He wanted to break up all trusts in favor of free competition. During World War I, Wilson headed an administration that took a more active role in the economy than ever before. The wartime emergency led most people to accept government controls to which they otherwise might have objected.

The Great Depression was another emergency that led many people to reject laissez-faire government. Under Franklin Roosevelt, the government took over new areas of responsibility. His programs served the needs of the nation during the 1930's, and a number of New Deal reforms benefited American society. There were shortcomings, however. The New Deal never truly defeated the Great Depression. Although business improved, unemployment remained high. And, the creation of a great government bureaucracy—with a bureaucracy's tendency to associate its own well-being with the public welfare—would plague Americans in the future.

The greatest effect of the New Deal was that it restored American self-confidence and faith in democracy. The idea that the government is responsible for the welfare of its people became much more generally accepted. Roosevelt said that the preservation of democracy depended on the government's social and economic programs:

> Democracy has disappeared in several other great nations, not because the people of those nations disliked democracy, but because they had grown tired of unemployment and insecurity. . . . We in America know that our democratic institutions can be . . . made to work. But in order to preserve them we need . . . to prove that the practical operation of democratic government is equal to the task of protecting the security of the people. . . .

The government's responsibilities continued to expand after the New Deal. But by the late 1960's, a new conservative viewpoint began to emerge. Conservatives said that people had come to expect too much of their government. Under Presidents Nixon and Reagan, the government began to retrench. But critics of the conservative view called for more government action. It is an argument that is likely to become even more intense.

QUESTIONS

1. What major events led to increases in the role of the national government?
2. What were the effects of the New Deal?

Keynes justified this view in his *General Theory of Employment* (1936).

Bridge, pinball, and monopoly were popular indoor games.

number of Roosevelt's advisors argued that it was time to balance the budget and give business a "breathing spell." Roosevelt agreed and cut government spending in a number of areas.

Roosevelt and his advisors hoped that the private sector would make up the difference, but this was not the case. The Fed had acted to raise interest rates, which made less money available to business and caused cutbacks. In addition, the government had raised social security taxes for employers and employees, with the result that both business and consumers had less money to spend. Thus, with less spending by government, business, and consumers, a new recession took place in late 1937 and early 1938.

To stimulate the economy, Roosevelt decided to return to his earlier policy of deficit spending. On April 14, 1938, he sent Congress a number of recommendations reversing the government's current spending policy. His plan called for the expansion of WPA rolls from 1.5 to 3 million, a $3 billion recovery and relief program, **"pump priming"** (pumping government money into the economy to stimulate the flow of money) through RFC loans, and an easy money policy to be authorized by the Fed. On June 21, Congress passed another huge spending bill.

The return to the policy of deficit spending marked the victory of advisors led by Marriner Eccles of the Federal Reserve Board. Eccles believed that the government was obligated to counteract depression with increased spending. Eccles said:

> *The Government must be the compensatory agent in this economy; it must unbalance its budget during inflation and create surpluses in periods of great business activity.*

Eccles and others like him were influenced by the English economist John Maynard Keynes. In Keynes' view, the Great Depression was caused by a lack of spending in the economy, especially by business. If the private sector was unable to spend enough to keep the economy going, the government should increase its own spending and take other steps to encourage spending by business and consumers.

SECTION REVIEW

1. Identify the following: Congress of Industrial Organizations, "Little Steel," William Van Devanter, Farm Security Administration, Fair Labor Standards Act.

2. What groups made up the new Roosevelt coalition?

3. What was Roosevelt's plan of attack on the Supreme Court?

4. How did the New Deal attempt to help tenant farmers, sharecroppers, and migratory workers?

5. Why did many farmers leave the Great Plains and travel to the Pacific coast?

6. Why did a new recession occur in late 1937?

4 American Culture During the 1930's

The Great Depression and the New Deal had a strong influence on almost every part of American life. The Depression had undermined Americans' confidence in themselves and their future. Cultural trends reflected the need to cope with—or the desire to escape from—the harsh realities of life in the 1930's.

Recreation

Americans spent more and more time at recreation. More leisure time was available, partly because working hours were reduced. During the 1930's the 40-hour week became standard. It had been established during the Great Depression in order to spread the work or reduce it to match wages. With the growth of unions, NRA codes, and finally, the Fair Labor Standards Act, the shorter work week remained.

At the same time, more parks and playground areas were being built or improved. In these new facilities, people took part in various activities. Softball was a rage. By 1938 there were an estimated 500,000 teams and 5 million players. Bicycling and roller skating also attracted many to the new parks and playgrounds. As public golf courses were built, golf became a game for more than just the wealthy. Snow skiing grew in popularity, stimulated by the 1932 Winter Olympic Games held at Lake Placid, New York.

Americans also enjoyed spectator sports. College football and basketball as well as professional baseball remained the preeminent attractions, but people were also interested in sports such as track. One of

Babe Didrikson

Mildred "Babe" Didrikson, born in Port Arthur, Texas in 1914, knew from the time she was a young girl that athletics was to be the focus of her life. Like her brothers and sisters, she was athletically gifted, and her parents encouraged a competitive spirit by building an outdoor gymnasium in the backyard for their active children.

Babe was a natural athlete. She easily achieved success with the high school baseball and track teams. But she was frustrated when she wanted to play basketball and the coach told her that she was too short. Determined, she practiced until she was so skilled that the coach had to accept her. By her junior year she was the high scorer for the team. This spark of determination was to be her outstanding characteristic for the rest of her life.

After high school, Babe was recruited by an insurance company for its employee athletic team. From the very beginning she was a star, and used this competitive opportunity to train for the 1932 Olympic Games. At the Olympics, she set world records in the women's 80-meter hurdles and the javelin throw.

In the 1930's Babe took up golf. Her natural coordination coupled with that spark of determination made her an excellent golfer. By 1946 she was winning most of the competitions she entered, and a year later, she won 17 consecutive tournaments.

At this point Babe, now married to wrestler George Zaharias, left the amateur ranks to become a professional. Shortly after turning professional, she was stricken with cancer. After treatment, she returned to the golf circuit and, again, achieved great success. In 1950 the Associated Press named her the outstanding woman athlete of the first half of the century. She died in 1956, after a long and courageous battle with cancer.

their heroes was track star Jesse Owens, who won four gold medals in Munich, Germany, at the Summer Olympics in 1936.

Entertainment

People also spent their leisure time pursuing various sources of entertainment. Radio offered adventure, drama, humor, music, and news. Adventure programs, such as *The Lone Ranger*, and comedies, such as *Amos 'n Andy,* were very popular. Daytime radio serials also drew large audiences chiefly because so many people were out of work and at home. These shows were called **soap operas** because soap companies often sponsored them. The 1930's also saw the development of the radio variety program, which included humorous skits and dialogue. As the Great Depression forced the vaudeville theaters to close, stars such as George Burns, Gracie Allen, Jack Benny, and Fred Allen, along with Edgar Bergen and his dummy Charlie McCarthy, entertained listeners.

Light music was also a part of the radio variety program. Rudy Vallee and Bing Crosby were two of the popular singers favored by audiences. Dance music was featured as well. The big bands, with such artists as Benny Goodman, Glenn Miller, Tommy Dorsey, Artie Shaw, "Count" Basie, and Louis Armstrong, played a new kind of dance music over the airwaves. It was known as **swing**—a kind of jazz in which a steady beat, simple harmony, and basic melody are coupled with some improvisation.

The decade of the 1930's was also a golden era for movies. By 1939 more than 80 million people went to the movies each week. In the 1920's, many movies had questioned the value of traditional virtues in a chaotic world. Indeed, gangsters were frequently movie heroes. Even comedies, such as the Marx Brothers' *Duck Soup,* dealt with the problem of social disorder.

With the coming of the New Deal, the emphasis shifted. Hollywood producers and directors tried to restore the faith of the American people in the social order. The movie heroes of the 1930's were federal agents rather than criminals. Other heroes were developed by such directors as Frank Capra in *Meet John Doe* and *Mr. Smith Goes to Washington.* Capra's populist-type characters struggled against society and achieved what they set out to do.

In addition, more musicals—with stars such as Fred Astaire and Ginger Rogers—and film versions of the classics of literature provided audiences with a brief escape from reality. So did Walt Disney's cartoons.

Magazines also provided entertainment for the American people during the 1930's. *The Saturday Evening Post,* a conservative magazine, enjoyed a wide circulation. The *New Republic,* the *Nation,* and *Harper's*—more liberal in tone—also had a considerable following, chiefly among the intellectuals. Magazines such as *Life* and *Look* used the techniques of **photojournalism,** in which articles are developed through the use of photographs. *Reader's Digest,* which condensed articles from other journals, became increasingly popular. *Time* and *Newsweek* were read for their reports of current events.

In the 1920's, American writers, who scorned the present, criticized the past. In the 1930's, despite the desperate condition of the country, American writers had a more positive view of the past.

Literature and the Arts

Literature and the arts reflected the different approaches Americans used to cope with life in the 1930's. Some writers and artists tried to deal directly with issues raised by changes occurring in society. They developed a heightened sense of social consciousness. Others chose escapism.

In literature, Erskine Caldwell's *Tobacco Road* (1932) studied the life of an impoverished tenant family in the South. James T. Farrell's *Studs Lonigan* (1935) portrayed the life of a lower-middle-class Catholic boy in Chicago, and told of his futile struggle against his environment. In *It Can't Happen Here,* Sinclair Lewis described how easily fascists could take over the United States. John Dos Passos spoke out against the materialism of American life in *U.S.A.* (1937). One of the most well-known novels of the New Deal years was John Steinbeck's *Grapes of Wrath* (1939), an account of an Oklahoma family who travel from their home in the Dust Bowl to become migrant workers in California.

Black writers also shared the spirit of the times. Richard Wright in *Uncle Tom's Children* (1938) talked about racial problems in the South. In *Native Son* (1940), his most famous novel, he painted a bleak picture of black life in the slums of Chicago during the Great Depression. He attempted to deal with the hidden factors that led the main characters into a life of crime—factors inherent in society.

The 1930's were times of experimenting in the arts. Swing music, featuring informal arrangements, lively rhythm, and improvised solos, were popular. Among the leading practitioners of swing were Count Basie and his band. Why was entertainment so popular during the Depression years?

Many left-wing writers favored **proletarian literature**—a literature that focused on the plight of the workers and glorified their fight against capitalism. These writers were attracted by Communism and the apparent prosperity and stability of the Soviet Union during the Great Depression. Proletarian authors included Albert Maltz, Meyer Levin, and Gran Grace Lumpkin.

Certain novelists wrote for those who wanted to escape from the problems of everyday life. One was Pearl Buck, whose best-seller, *The Good Earth* (1931), described life in China. Another was Margaret Mitchell. Her *Gone With the Wind* (1936) transported readers to the Civil War South.

In the theater, social themes were evident. Maxwell Anderson explored the tragedy of social injustice in *Winterset*. *Tobacco Road,* based on the novel by Erskine Caldwell, soon became the longest running New York play. *Pins and Needles,* a musical review put on by a company of garment workers, furthered the cause of labor. It also set a record for longevity. In addition, the Federal Theater Project dealt with current politics in *Triple A Plowed Under* and *One Third of a Nation.*

In art, the works of William Gropper, Peter Blume, and Jack Levine reflected social concerns. So, too, did the works of Reginald Marsh, which portrayed different aspects of life in the New York City slums. Thomas Hart Benton and Grant Wood, on the other hand, reflected a new interest in the regional character of American life.

There was no doubt as to the impact of the Great Depression and New Deal on American culture. However, as the 1930's drew to a close, Americans turned their attention from domestic to foreign affairs. As a result of events taking place in Europe and Asia, the world was once again moving toward war.

SECTION REVIEW

1. Identify the following: Jesse Owens, John Steinbeck, Richard Wright, Margaret Mitchell.
2. Why was there more leisure time in the 1930's?
3. How did movies change during the New Deal?
4. Why was escapist literature popular?

CHAPTER 25   REVIEW

SUMMARY

1. President Roosevelt had no plans for dealing with the Great Depression when he took office, but drew upon the ideas of a team of advisors.
2. The New Deal was opposed by conservative critics, who thought that free enterprise was being undermined by taxes and regulations, and by radicals, who wanted the government to take a more active role.
3. Despite criticism, Roosevelt was supported by a large majority of the voters.
4. In 1934 and 1935 the New Deal continued with new programs to aid farmers, the unemployed, the aged, and the poor, and with reforms in a number of areas.
5. The Supreme Court found several New Deal measures unconstitutional.
6. In 1936 Roosevelt was reelected by a landslide.
7. After the election, Roosevelt tried but failed to subvert the independence of the Supreme Court.
8. Reforms continued during Roosevelt's second term.
9. The Depression and New Deal had a strong influence on American life and culture.

VOCABULARY

broker-state government	securities exchanges	tight money policy	pump priming
national planning	margin requirement	easy money policy	soap operas
deficit spending	fascism	intrastate commerce	swing
brain trust	boondoggle	sit-down strike	photojournalism
free markets	open market operations	acreage allotments	proletarian literature
administered markets			

REVIEW QUESTIONS

1. What criticisms were made of the New Deal?
2. Which of his critics' ideas did Roosevelt later develop into New Deal programs?
3. What did the New Deal do to help the problems of farmers?
4. What was the effect of the New Deal on big business?
5. How did the New Deal further the cause of labor?
6. Why did Roosevelt fail to win support for his attack on the Supreme Court?
7. How did the New Deal increase the role of government in the economy?
8. How did American culture reflect the social concern of the 1930's?

DISCUSSION

1. Could the problems of the Dust Bowl have been prevented? If so, how? If not, why?
2. What New Deal programs are still in effect today? What long-run effects have these programs had?
3. How did Roosevelt increase the power of the presidency?
4. Should the government supply jobs for the unemployed during a depression? Why or why not?

USING GRAPHS

Refer to the graph on page 534 and answer the following questions:

1. At the beginning of 1929, was the American economy in a period of expansion or in a period of recession?
2. What was the GNP at the peak of prosperity between 1920 and 1940?
3. How did the severity of the Great Depression compare to that of the depression that followed World War I?
4. What was the GNP in the best year of the Great Depression?
5. What was the largest period of expansion during the Great Depression?

USING SKILLS

If you were trying to decide whether or not the Works Progress Administration was effective, which of the following questions would you want to have answered? That is, which questions would provide meaningful answers, and which would not?

1. How many people were employed by the Works Progress Administration (WPA)?
2. How many WPA workers were members of minority groups?
3. How many of the people employed by the WPA would have been able to find other jobs if the WPA had not existed?
4. Was the work done by the WPA useful or necessary?
5. How much did the government spend on the WPA?
6. Could private businesses have done the same jobs at a lower cost?

SUMMARY

1. The 1920's was a decade of rapid social change and political conservatism.
2. Although many Americans enjoyed prosperity during the 1920's, the nation's economic base was weakening.
3. During the 1930's, the United States suffered an unprecedented economic decline.
4. Under President Franklin D. Roosevelt, the federal government instituted a number of new programs designed to restore the nation's economy.
5. As a result of Roosevelt's programs, the responsibilities of the federal government for economic and social welfare increased to a new level.

REVIEW QUESTIONS

1. What factors contributed to changes in American lifestyles during the 1920's?
2. How did the philosophies and lifestyles of the 1920's contribute to the Great Depression?
3. How successful was the New Deal?
4. What was Roosevelt's philosophy of government? How did it differ from that of his Republican predecessors?

SUGGESTED ACTIVITIES

1. Write a report on one of the following topics: (a) the effects of women's suffrage, (b) advertising techniques of the 1920's, (c) the rise of organized crime, or (d) a comparison of life among blacks in the South and in the North during the period of the 1920's.
2. Read aloud poems by Langston Hughes, Carl Sandburg, Edna St. Vincent Millay, or other poets of the period.
3. Write a series of newspaper headlines tracing the events of the 1920's. Experiment with styles that might have been used by the yellow press as well as by more conservative newspapers.
4. Research the effects of the New Deal on your community. Find out if the federal government sponsored any local projects in conservation, construction, or the arts.
5. Draw a political cartoon on one of the following topics: (a) a comparison of the philosophies of Presidents Hoover and Roosevelt, (b) a return to "normalcy," or (c) the problems of farmers in the 1920's.

SUGGESTED READINGS

1. Allen, Frederick Lewis. *Only Yesterday*. New York: Harper & Row Publishers, Inc., 1964. Paperback. A contemporary description that lets the reader sense the frustrated hopes, disillusions, scandals, and harshness of the 1920's.
2. Arnow, Harriet. *The Dollmaker.* New York: Avon Books, 1972. Paperback. Describes the problems of alienation and urban living experienced by a southern family in the industrial North.
3. Galbraith, John K. *The Great Crash, Nineteen Twenty-Nine.* Boston: Houghton Mifflin Co., 1979. Paperback. Causes and effects of this complex event as seen by one of the nation's leading economists.
4. Handlin, Oscar. *Al Smith & His America*. Boston: Little, Brown & Co., 1958. Paperback. Describes Smith's attempts as a Catholic to gain acceptance as a presidential candidate in Protestant America.
5. Steinbeck, John. *The Grapes of Wrath*. New York: Penguin Books, Inc., 1976. Paperback. A classic novel about a family who move from Oklahoma to California and the hardships they endure during the depression years.
6. Wilson, Joan Huff. *Herbert Hoover, The Forgotten Progressive*. Boston: Little, Brown & Co., 1975. Paperback. A sympathetic insight into the man and his accomplishments.

THE HISTORIAN'S CRAFT

In studying secondary sources, the historian must be able to analyze the evidence that other historians offer to support their different points of view. A thesis or an interpretation is convincing only if it is backed by solid evidence.

This activity will give you practice in evaluating conflicting points of view on the basis of evidence. The subject of the activity is the New Deal. Some historians argue that the New Deal represented a revolutionary change in American government. Others argue that Roosevelt's activism was the result of an evolutionary change. Historians who hold the second point of view say that the trend toward increasing government activism can be traced to earlier periods—the Populist and Progressive eras in particular.

Read the following excerpts from two historians who argue over the nature of the New Deal and evaluate the evidence each historian uses. The questions at the end of the activity will help you make your evaluation. It should be noted, however, that excerpts cannot represent a historian's total thinking. For a truly fair comparison, you would have to make a more thorough study of the original works.

Edgar E. Robinson

In truth, the office of President had been altered beyond recognition as Mr. Roosevelt exercised the powers of a dictator. The Constitution had been given deep wounds by his procedures. The courts had been brought from a position of wide acceptance to the necessity for self-defense. Party responsibility had been all but destroyed by the personal power exercised frequently to accomplish quick results. . . .

The individual citizen had been raised in his own estimation, and particularly in his own physical welfare. But the basis of individual effort had been weakened at a time when adaptability to the world of change made it imperative that individual willpower be retained and exercised as never before. Contemporary democracy was adrift in a sea of uncertainty, because for a dozen years the issues had been

blurred and the basis for definite and positive judgment weakened. . . .

Mr. Roosevelt had frequently maintained that he was helping the people resume a familiar direction and reassert their traditional attitude. He assured them that he was doing what they, as conservators of old ways, and not radicals of a new dispensation, wished to do.

But in time it became clear that he had in fact, changed not only the direction but the fabric of American society and had done much to alter the American spirit of self-reliance and faith. Millions of Americans did not like the results. They found themselves committed to attributes of a collectivist state, and certainly to the central point of view of a Socialist philosophy. However much this continued to appeal to the radicals, of whom there were many, it did not satisfy those who had for the most part dominated in American society and government and who had done much to make the democracy identified with the "American way."

Henry Steele Commager

We can see now that the "Roosevelt revolution" was no revolution, but rather the culmination of half a century of historical development, and that Roosevelt himself, though indubitably a leader, was an instrument of the popular will rather than a creator of, or a dictator to, that will. Indeed, the two major issues of the Roosevelt administration—the domestic issue of the extension of government control for democratic purposes, and the international issue of the role of America as a world power—emerged in the 1890's, and a longer perspective will see the half-century from the 1890's to the present as an historical unit. . . .

What was really but a new deal of the old cards looked, to startled and dismayed contemporaries, like a revolution for two reasons: because it was carried through with such breathless rapidity, and because in spirit at least it contrasted so sharply with what immediately preceded. But had the comparison been made not with the Coolidge-Hoover era, but with the Wilson, the Theodore Roosevelt, even the Bryan era the contrast would have been less striking than the similarities. Actually, precedent for the major part of New Deal legislation was to be found in these earlier periods. Regulation of railroads and of business dated back to the Interstate Commerce Act of 1887 and the Sherman Act of 1890, and was continuous from that time forward. The farm relief program of the Populists, and of Wilson, anticipated much that the Roosevelt administrations enacted. The beginnings of conservation can be traced to the Carey Act of 1894 and the Reclamation Act of 1902, and the first Roosevelt did as much as the second to dramatize—though less to solve—the program of conserving natural resources.

Power regulation began with the Water Power Act of 1920; supervision over securities exchanges with grain and commodities exchange acts of the Harding and Coolidge administrations; while regulation of money is as old as the Union, and the fight which Bryan and Wilson waged against the "Money Power" and Wall Street was more bitter than anything that came during the New Deal. . . . Labor legislation had its beginnings in such states as Massachusetts and New York over half a century ago, while much of the program of social security was worked out in Wisconsin

and other states during the second and the third decades of the new century.

There is nothing remarkable about this, nor does it detract in any way from the significance of President Roosevelt's achievements and contributions. The pendulum of American history swings gently from right to left, but there are no sharp breaks in the rhythm of our historical development; and it is to the credit of Roosevelt that he worked within the framework of American history and tradition.

QUESTIONS

1. What, according to Professor Robinson, was the impact of Roosevelt's actions on the Constitution? List his arguments concerning the Presidency, the courts, and political parties.
2. What does Robinson say about individual effort?
3. Why does Robinson say that the New Deal was dissatisfying to those "who had done much to make the democracy identified with the 'American Way'"?
4. Why, according to Professor Commager, was the "Roosevelt revolution" not a revolution? Why did it appear to be a revolution to contemporaries?
5. What precedents does Commager cite for various types of New Deal legislation?
6. Does either historian present arguments or evidence that appear to you to be irrelevant?
7. Does either historian present arguments or evidence that appear to you to be more valid? That is, which evidence seems to be more factual, freer from bias, or more easily ascertained?
8. Which historian has more evidence?

1922		1933		1938		1941		1944	1945
Italian		Rise of		Spanish		Atlantic		D-Day	Atomic
Fascism		Third Reich		Civil War		Charter			Bomb

	1931			1938	1939–45	1941			1945
	Japanese in			Munich	World	Pearl			United
	Manchuria			Pact	War II	Harbor			Nations

THE WORLD IN CONFLICT

The Road to Global Conflict

World War II

The Cold War

1947	1949		1955	1956	1959
Marshall	NATO		Spirit of	Suez	Rise of
Plan	Alliance		Geneva	Crisis	Castro

1947	1948	1950–53	1956	1958	1962
Truman	Berlin	Korean	Revolt in	Eisenhower	Cuban
Doctrine	Blockade	War	Hungary	Doctrine	Missile Crisis

1	The Postwar Scene	**547**
2	The Rise of Totalitarianism	**550**
3	The Growing Crisis	**555**
4	A Neutral America	**559**
5	From Neutrality to Commitment	**561**
6	The End of the Road	**568**

THE ROAD TO GLOBAL CONFLICT

But our personal preferences count for little in the great movements of history, and when the destiny of nations is revealed to them, there is no choice but to accept that destiny and to make ready in order to be equal to it.

WALTER LIPPMANN

While the United States was enjoying the prosperity of the 1920's and trying to pull out of the depression of the 1930's, nations in Europe and Asia were trying to recover from World War I. In their effort to do this, several countries turned to undemocratic forms of government. Some of the new governments built their programs for change around militaristic schemes aimed at gaining new territory. Before long, conflict broke out, and much of Europe and Asia became engulfed in war. At first the United States managed to avoid direct involvement. But by 1941 Americans once again found themselves fighting in a world war.

1 The Postwar Scene

Even though the United States had not officially joined the League of Nations after World War I, it took part in League affairs. By 1931 more than 200 Americans had been officially appointed to represent their country in League conferences, and five Americans were stationed in Geneva to represent American interests in the League. Many Americans, however, still had isolationist sentiments, so American foreign policy was based on diplomacy rather than on armed intervention and direct involvement.

The Good Neighbor Policy and Latin America

In his 1933 inaugural speech, President Franklin D. Roosevelt dedicated the United States to the policy of the "Good Neighbor" in foreign affairs. He pledged to respect the sovereign rights of all nations in the Western Hemisphere. A few weeks later, on Pan-American Day, he applied the phrase "Good Neighbor" specifically to the United States' Latin American policy.

At the time, United States trade with Latin America was at a low. Much of Latin America was suffering from poor economic conditions and internal problems. In addition, there were disputes between several different Latin American countries. The United States sought to ease the situation and to put relations between itself and its Latin American neighbors on a cordial basis by applying the Good Neighbor policy. The American government believed that the friendship of Latin America was essential to the security of the United States. It also believed that only a policy of nonintervention would win that friendship.

In May 1933 the United States appointed an American to a League of Nations committee working to settle a border dispute between Peru and Colombia. In the same year the United States concluded an agreement with Haiti to withdraw American marines from that country by 1934. Then, when a revolution broke out in Cuba, the United States stood by patiently and did not take sides. For those still not sure of American policy, Secretary of State Cordell Hull spelled it out at the December 1933 Inter-American conference in Montevideo, Uruguay. He announced that the United States stood ready to renounce any right it had once claimed to intervene in the affairs of neighboring states. Shortly after, Roosevelt reinforced Hull's pledge, declaring, "The definite policy of the United States from now on is one opposed to armed intervention."

The result of the Good Neighbor policy was a new spirit of friendship between the United States and Latin America. This, in turn, resulted in a number of important inter-American treaties. On May 29, 1934, the United States and Cuba signed a treaty formally annulling the Platt Amendment and ending special American rights in Cuba. The only right retained was the one to maintain a United States naval base at Guantanamo. The United States also reduced the

In one year prices increased more than one trillion percent in Germany.

tariff on Cuban sugar, which led to a 100 percent increase in trade with Cuba by the next year.

In 1936 the United States gave up its control over Haiti's financial affairs and put an end to the American right to interfere in the affairs of Panama. That same year, at a special conference held in Buenos Aires at the request of the United States, Roosevelt called for hemispheric cooperation in case of outside attack. The delegates responded by adopting a pact pledging consultation whenever war threatened. This, in effect, transformed the Monroe Doctrine into a multi-national agreement. It also helped to lay the basis for future inter-American unity.

That unity was further strengthened in December 1938 at the Lima Conference. Out of this conference came the Lima Declaration, which reaffirmed the absolute sovereignty of the American states. It also expressed the determination of those states to resist "all foreign intervention or activities that may threaten them" and provided for consultation when any state's "peace, security, or territorial integrity" might be threatened.

The Situation in Europe

The United States' relationship with European countries during the 1920's and early 1930's was not on as firm a footing as Americans had hoped. The Washington Treaties of 1922 and the Kellogg-Briand Pact of 1928 were not enough to make up for the economic, physical, and psychological problems brought on by World War I. The Allied Powers had expected to come away from Versailles with more territory and large financial gains, but had ended up with neither. In addition, the war had brought about a loss of human resources and had destroyed many businesses. Other nations, such as the United States and Japan, had taken over markets once monopolized by Western European countries.

The Allies had increased their problems by ignoring President Wilson's pleas for low trade barriers. Believing that keeping out imported goods would help them rebuild their industries, they set high tariffs on imports. This led to greater shortages and a higher rate of inflation.

Conditions were even worse in the countries that had made up the Central Powers. On top of everything else, they had to face the punishments forced on them at Versailles. The Austro-Hungarian Empire no longer existed. Its territory was distributed among several countries, including the newly formed Czechoslovakia and Yugoslavia. Germany had to give up its colonies and suffer the humiliations of admitting its war guilt and of disarming. In addition, it was saddled with $32 billion in reparation payments, the total Belgian war debt, and the costs of **occupation** (control by foreign military forces). In an effort to meet these obligations, Germany began to export heavily. This, however, upset the European balance of trade, created shortages in Germany, and brought about a sharp rise in inflation.

Reparation Payments and War Debts

By 1923 Germany had defaulted twice on its reparation payments. This angered the French who, along with Belgian troops, responded by invading the Ruhr valley, the heart of German industry and coal-mining. The German government, angered at being subjected to occupation, ordered passive resistance in the Ruhr. Workers walked off their jobs; and mines, factories, and offices shut down. To provide financial support for the striking workers, the German government began printing more and more German currency. This led to such a high rate of inflation that it bankrupted the government and sent the economy to the brink of total ruin.

The Dawes Plan. Fearing the effect all of this would have on the rest of Europe, the United States, as Germany's chief creditor, stepped in. An international committee was formed to set up a workable plan of reparation payments. In April 1924, under the leadership of Chicago banker Charles G. Dawes, the committee submitted the Dawes Plan. The plan cut Germany's annual installments for the next few years and recommended large loans from foreign banks to help the Germans recover economically. Most of the loans were to come from American bankers. Thus, the Dawes Plan helped to establish a system of intergovernmental debt and reparations payments that would work only so long as Germany kept getting loans.

The Dawes Plan allowed Germany to stabilize its currency, but it did not stop the financial situation in Europe from worsening. By 1925 the United States

The United States collected about $3 billion in debt payments from its allies.

This cartoon suggests that Germany, despite its ability to pay, was making little effort to make payments owed to the United States and its allies. Germany owed the United States $11 billion when it stopped making payments in 1931. Why was it difficult for Germany to continue paying reparations?

was forced to reduce the principal and interest rates on war debts owed by Italy. The following year, it did the same on the debts owed by France. The United States, however, was not prepared to cancel the debts entirely. Its insistence on at least partial payments contributed to anti-American feelings among Europeans, who felt that their economic situation was bad enough without the burden of war debts.

The Young Plan. These feelings were intensified in July 1929 by the Young Plan, named for American banker Owen D. Young. It stated that Germany was to pay $9 billion instead of the original $32 billion, and that the payments were to end in 1988. The Germans were not pleased with the fact that they would be indebted to other powers for so many years. Nor were the other powers pleased that the Germans were getting off so easily.

Financial Crisis and Default. In 1931 the *Kreditansalt* of Vienna, the largest bank in Austria, failed. The failure led to heavy withdrawals of gold from Germany. By June 1931 Germany no longer could meet its obligations, and its president appealed personally for help to President Hoover.

Hoover was afraid that if the Germans were forced to pay, Germany would become bankrupt and the entire international economy would collapse. Therefore, on June 21, he proposed a one-year **moratorium** (an official period of delay) on all intergovernmental and reparation payments. But the moratorium eased the strain only for a short while. Then actions taken by French bankers led the British to go off the gold standard. During the spring and summer of 1931, the crisis worsened, just about destroying the existing system of international exchange and trade and setting off a sharp depression in Western Europe.

Germany's reparation payments totalled about $4.5 billion.

Stalin did not play a major role in the communist takeover in Russia. However, in the history of the revolution written under his direction, Stalin emerges as top assistant to Lenin.

Relations between the United States and Latin America were strengthened during the 1930's. Cordell Hull, Secretary of State under Roosevelt, helped form and implement the "Good Neighbor" policy. What was the goal of this policy?

By 1932 Germany simply could not pay its reparations. When it stopped paying the Allies, they stopped paying the United States. If they had paid their debts, they might have gone bankrupt. In June of that year, representatives of the western and central European powers met in Lausanne, Switzerland to resolve the problem. Their solution was once again to reduce Germany's reparations. By 1934 all of America's debtors except Finland had stopped making their war debt payments.

SECTION REVIEW

1. Identify the following: Cordell Hull, Lima Declaration, Charles G. Dawes.
2. What was the United States involvement with the League of Nations?
3. How was the Monroe Doctrine changed?
4. Why did many European countries set high tariffs?

2 The Rise of Totalitarianism

World War I had done more than leave Europe in a state of economic chaos. The damage and destruction wrought by the war had dislocated millions of people and left them struggling to survive. Many people, bitter and disillusioned, blamed their country's leaders and institutions for the lack of food, clothing, shelter, and safety. When an individual or group of individuals came along pledging to restore law and order, redeem the country's honor, and lead it back to glory, the people responded warmly.

The result was the rise to power in several countries of regimes that were **totalitarian,** or controlled by one individual or group that suppresses all opposition and takes charge of most aspects of people's lives. The extreme nationalism of the regimes only added to their appeal. People were willing to overlook the fact that the individual was subordinate to the state.

The Soviet Union

After the death of Lenin in 1924, there was a struggle over who would take his place. In 1928 Joseph Stalin, whose name meant "man of steel," took control. Several years before, Stalin had persuaded the Communist party to give up its plan to allow Russia to be a federation of autonomous republics. Instead, he convinced the party to turn the federation into a Union of Soviet Socialist Republics under the centralized control of Moscow. Lenin wrote of Stalin, "He has concentrated enormous power in his hands, and I am not sure he always knows how to use that power with sufficient caution."

Under Stalin, individual freedoms became more restricted. Stalin decided that the Soviet Union had to turn inward, isolate itself from Europe, and modernize on its own. He began a plan of forced industrialization and **collectivization** of agriculture (organization as one unit for operation under government control). He pushed ruthlessly ahead, not allowing anything to keep him from achieving his goal.

Stalin's authority was as absolute and brutal as any tsar's had ever been. People who got in his way were exiled or executed. For more than a decade, he

One reason for Mussolini's rise was the dissatisfaction he expressed with the territorial changes that took place after World War I. Many Italians agreed with Mussolini that their postwar leaders had failed to get Italy's share of land.

pushed the Soviet people to their limit. The result was one of the greatest long-term economic efforts ever made by a single country.

In the early 1930's Stalin was afraid that the Japanese would attack the Maritime Territory, an area of the Soviet Union bordering on the Sea of Japan. Should a war arise with Japan, he wanted to be able to buy supplies on credit in the United States. Therefore he pressed for American friendship. He also sought official diplomatic recognition, which, until now, the United States had refused to give to the Soviet Union for various reasons, including the fact that it would not assume the debt owed to the United States by the tsars.

Stalin was successful in his efforts, and in November 1933, the United States recognized the Soviet regime. In return, the Soviets promised to refrain from propaganda activity in the United States, to guarantee religious freedom and fair trials to

Americans on Soviet soil, and to negotiate a settlement of the debt owed by the tsars.

The United States hoped to establish trade with the Soviets. In February 1934, an Export-Import Bank was established to promote full economic activity between the two countries. Although trade never reached American expectations, the Soviet Union came out of its self-imposed isolation. In 1935 it became a member of the League of Nations.

Italy

In Italy, too, a totalitarian regime came to power. In 1919 Benito Mussolini, an ex-Socialist and newspaper editor, formed a group to fight "against the forces dissolving victory and the nation." The first meeting he held was attended mostly by dissatisfied veterans of the Italian army. He told them of his plan to organize a *fascio di combattimento,* or combat group. The group was to have three goals—upholding "the material and moral claims" of veterans, opposing "the imperialism of any countries damaging to Italy," and fighting "the candidates that were milk-and-water Italians." The small number of men who signed the pledge to support this program adopted the black uniforms of the *Arditi,* the shock troops of the Italian army. From this small beginning emerged Mussolini's particular brand of fascism, which in a few years completely enveloped Italy.

By 1921 Mussolini's movement had more than 2000 local *fasci,*[1] or political groups, and 320,000 enrolled members. That same year, 35 members of his Fascist party won seats in Italy's Chamber of Deputies. Still, things were not moving fast enough for Mussolini. On October 24 of the following year, he threatened, "Either the government will be given to us or we will seize it by marching on Rome!"

Mussolini's threat scared the government in Rome and prompted the prime minister to offer him a post in the Italian cabinet. The king, however, went one step further and invited him to form a government. Mussolini responded by taking office as premier, making him at age 39 the youngest premier in the history of the country.

Joseph Stalin gained control of the Soviet government following Lenin's death. To solidify his power, Stalin instituted a series of purges in the 1930's. This, plus Stalin's criticism of the American system, strained United States-Soviet relations. Why did the Soviet Union then seek to normalize relations with the United States?

---

[1] The *fasci* took their name from the word "fasces," which is a bundle of rods bound around an ax. This was a symbol of authority in the Roman Empire, and became a symbol of Italian fascism.

Hitler labelled his party socialist but did little to institute socialistic policies, such as redistributing wealth.

Benito Mussolini of Italy and Adolph Hitler of Germany visit the Heroes' Temple in Munich. At first, few regarded either of these two leaders as a threat to peace. What events and movements made the rise of Hitler and Mussolini possible?

Mussolini did not wait long to make his next move. In 1924 he obtained a huge majority in the Chamber of Deputies, using intimidation and violence to make sure the elections went his way. On January 23, 1925, he announced that he would rule as a dictator. He made his intentions clear, stating, "Italy wants peace and quiet, work and calm. I will give these things with love if possible, with force if necessary."

Mussolini slowly and carefully consolidated his authority. Known as *Il Duce,* or chief, he became the government of Italy. Civil liberties and the free press ceased to exist. Black-shirted Fascists monopolized political activity. Boys and girls of all ages were enrolled in military organizations that taught them total loyalty to the regime.

The Italian people in general supported Mussolini and made him the object of national adoration. His fascism was aimed at enhancing Italy's strength and image through military means, and he brought a new discipline and sense of purpose to Italian life.

Germany

The same year Mussolini set out to form his *fascio di combattimento* in Italy, a 30-year-old Austrian ex-soldier of the German army named Adolph Hitler attended a meeting of the German Workers party. The party was no more than a tiny group of subversives, but it gave Hitler what he was seeking. The next year, he changed the name of the group to the National Socialist German Workers Party—Nazi, for short—and gave it an emblem—the **swastika,** an ancient cosmic symbol. At the same time, he issued a manifesto that demanded the Versailles Treaty be abrogated, that Jews be denied German citizenship, and that war profits be confiscated. He also called for pensions to be increased and profit-sharing to be imposed in industry.

By 1921 Hitler had totally reorganized the party and increased its membership. The word *Heil,* which in old German meant whole or healthy, became the obligatory greeting between party members. The members, dressed in brown shirts and dark trousers and boots, were known as storm troopers.

In 1923, when the bottom fell out of the German economy, a new government took over and declared a state of emergency. Hitler saw his chance for fame, and on November 3 attempted a Nazi *putsch,* or takeover of the government. The attempted takeover failed, and Hitler was arrested, tried for treason, and sent to prison.[2] The publicity surrounding the incident, however, made Hitler known throughout Germany.

---

[2] While in prison, Hitler wrote *Mein Kampf,* "My Struggle," which became the bible for Nazism.

The Nazi Party was outlawed in Germany after the putsch failed, but the government soon agreed to let the party reorganize.

Hitler left prison in 1924 with two goals. One was to strengthen his party. The other was to achieve power by legal means. He told his supporters, "If outvoting them [his opponents] takes longer than shooting them, at least the result will be guaranteed by their constitution. Sooner or later we will have a majority—and after that Germany."

By 1929 Hitler had gained the support of the masses. An accomplished orator, he told each segment of the German people what they wanted to hear. He promised the economically depressed to get even with "Jew financiers" whom, along with the Marxists, he held responsible for the German defeat in World War I. He promised the workers security. He promised the bankers and industrialists to control trade unionism and to contain communism. In return, they gave him the financial support he needed.

In 1930 the Nazis won 107 seats in the Reichstag, Germany's National Assembly, making them second only to the Social Democrats, the leading political party. Two years later, Hitler ran for president. Although he lost to the popular war hero Paul von Hindenburg, the Nazis won enough seats to become the largest party in the Reichstag. This led Hindenburg to offer Hitler a post in the cabinet.

On January 30, 1933, Hitler became Chancellor of Germany. He demanded—and got—the Reichstag to pass an act that would allow him to rule by decree for four years without limitation of powers. By that summer, Hitler had outlawed all political parties except the Nazis, and had jailed, exiled, or placed in concentration camps most of his political opponents.

By early summer of 1934, Hitler decided to clean house. He ordered a purge of the storm troops, which the army disliked and feared and which Hitler felt no longer fit the image of a ruling government party. The purge was carried out by the SS, Hitler's newer and smaller black-clad elite guard. Its members had been carefully selected for their "nordic" qualities and physical fitness and had been trained to obey without question.

Five weeks later, President Hindenburg died, and the chancellorship and presidency were united in the person of Hitler. Now known as the Führer, or leader, he focused on rebuilding the country's shattered economy and the people's shattered pride. He convinced the Germans that they were a master race, true Aryans, racially and culturally superior to everyone else. He said that certain people, particularly Jews, contaminated society. Under Hitler, Jews were systematically deprived of citizenship, confined to ghettos, and eventually forced into slave-labor camps.

A man is forced to walk through streets bearing a sign that reads "I am a Jew but I won't complain about the Nazis." Hitler attacked the Jews violently, calling them an inferior race and blaming them for Germany's economic woes. Why did Hitler make a scapegoat of the Jews?

Japan had a history of militarism. The samurai warriors and their code of unswerving loyalty and obedience were revered.

Japan

Europe was not the only area of the world that fell prey to totalitarian movements. In the Far East, Japan also succumbed. In 1930 the small island nation suffered from poverty, overpopulation, and the need for raw materials. Many Japanese viewed their country as the most advanced in the East and thought that they, not the nations of the West, should have the riches of Asia. They firmly believed that Japan had a divine mission to lead Asia into a new era of economic expansion and prosperity.

In 1905, when Japan won the Russo-Japanese war, it became recognized as a world power. The Chinese had allied themselves with Russia during the war. After Russia's defeat, the Japanese had taken over the southern half of Manchuria, a region in China rich in resources. By the 1920's Manchuria had become a colony of Japan, viewed as an economic lifeline and a barrier against Russian expansion.

In 1929 Soviet armies invaded northern Manchuria and forced the Chinese to allow them joint control of the Chinese Eastern Railway, which ran from Siberia to Vladivostock. Then the Russians began building huge air and naval bases at Vladivostock. The return of Russian power to the Far East worried the Japanese and led them to reinforce their half of Manchuria in the hope of halting Soviet expansion. The Chinese, meanwhile, were making an attempt to regain control of Manchuria.

These events, combined with the worldwide depression of the 1930's which ruined Japan's silk trade, inflamed the more militarist and nationalist elements in Japan. Many people blamed their country's problems on corrupt officials and thought that the government's foreign policy was not sufficiently aggressive.

In March 1931 some Japanese army officers came up with a plan for the army to take over the government. First, a mob would blow up the buildings that housed the government. Then, in the midst of the confusion, the army would step in and proclaim a military dictatorship. At the last minute, however, the plan was called off.

Six months later, the army saw another chance to achieve its goal. Japanese army units stationed in Manchuria provoked an incident that they used as an excuse to overrun Manchuria. The action took place without the knowledge or the approval of the

JAPANESE EXPANSION, 1895–1941

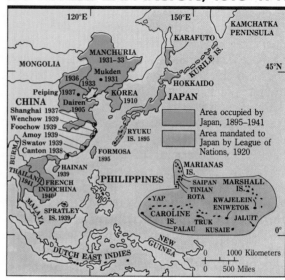

Japanese government. However, in 1932 it gave its stamp of approval to the action by detaching Manchuria from China and setting it up as the puppet state of Manchukuo.

The takeover, the first important assault on the post-World War I peace structure, had several important effects. For one, it gave Japan a major overseas source of raw materials. For another, it led to the widespread acceptance of the army as the true guardian of Japanese national welfare. And lastly, it led some young officers and superpatriots to initiate four days of terror, during which they killed any politician who had resisted the Manchurian adventure. Afterward, any politicians who stood in the way of the army's plans lived in fear for their lives.

Gradually, the military extended its control over the government. The United States ambassador to Japan, Joseph C. Grew, summed up the situation by declaring, "One thing is certain and that is that the military are distinctly running the government and that no step can be taken without their approval."

SECTION REVIEW

1. Identify the following: Paul von Hindenburg, Manchukuo, Joseph C. Grew.
2. What were Stalin's goals for the Soviet Union?
3. How did Mussolini obtain power in Italy?
4. Who did Hitler blame for Germany's defeat?
5. Why were the Japanese interested in Manchuria?

The League of Nations had no police force to back its resolutions. Discuss whether such a force could have changed the policies of Germany, Japan, and Italy.

More than one-half of the disarmament treaties of the 1920's were broken before the mid-1930's.

3 The Growing Crisis

During the 1930's tensions grew and deepened as Japan, Italy, and Germany set out on programs of military conquest. The international situation was rapidly reaching the point at which it presented a clear danger to world peace. In the Far East, the Japanese were pushing forward into northern China. In Europe, Hitler was rearming Germany in defiance of the Versailles Treaty, and Mussolini was casting his eyes in the direction of Africa.

The Japanese Advance on China

The Japanese aggression in Manchuria violated not only the Covenant of the League of Nations but several peace treaties as well. Yet no outside country took any effective action to halt the aggression, even when China appealed to the League of Nations for protection.

In January 1932 the United States finally acted by issuing the Stimson Doctrine. It warned Japan and China that the United States would not recognize "any treaty or agreement . . . which may impair the sovereignty, the independence, or the territorial and administrative integrity of the Republic of China . . . or the Open Door Policy. . . ." Later that month, the Japanese attacked the port city of Shanghai in order to break an unofficial boycott of Japanese goods by the part of the city that was under Chinese control. During the attack, thousands of civilians were killed.

On March 11, 1932, the League of Nations adopted a resolution that incorporated almost to the word Stimson's doctrine of non-recognition. Shortly after, the League named Japan as the aggressor and called on it to return Manchuria to China. Japan responded by withdrawing from the League. For the next five years, Japan engaged in the gradual economic and political penetration of northern China.

Mussolini and Ethiopia

While Japan was fighting with China, Mussolini was looking toward Africa. He wanted to expand Italy's colonial holdings and build up its image as a world power.

In the late 1800's, Italy had signed a treaty of friendship and cooperation with the ruler of Ethiopia, a country in northeast Africa. Italy, however, claimed

Soldiers of the Japanese Kwantung Army march through Mukden, Manchuria, on their way to the front. The Japanese had first moved into Manchuria in 1931. They established the puppet state of Manchukuo a year later. What benefit did Japan hope to derive from its holdings in Manchuria?

Nearly 3.5 million Sudeten Germans resided within Czechoslovakia.

that the treaty had given it a protectorate over Ethiopia. When the Ethiopian ruler denied this claim, conflict broke out. Italy lost the battle, signed a new treaty, and recognized Ethiopia's independence.

In 1930 Haile Selassie became the new ruler of Ethiopia. Very shortly after, he faced threats from Mussolini, who saw a chance to establish an Italian empire and, at the same time, avenge the earlier Italian defeat. In December 1934 Ethiopian and Italian troops clashed on the border of southeastern Ethiopia.

Mussolini turned down all offers of conciliation and mediation. On October 5, 1935, he marched his army into Ethiopia. Two days later, under strong pressure from the British, the League condemned the action and named Italy as the aggressor. Four days after that, it voted to impose economic sanctions on Italy. **Sanctions** are measures designed to inflict losses, adopted to force compliance on a nation violating international law. But the sanctions were ineffective. They did not, for example, include restrictions on oil or coal, both of which Italy needed to make war.

Great Britain moved its main fleet to the Mediterranean, but neither the British nor the French really wanted a showdown with Italy. The French were afraid that if they pushed Mussolini too far, he would turn to Germany for help. Further, both the French and the British were sure that if a war broke out with Italy, they would get no help from the United States. As a result, in May 1936 Mussolini completed his conquest of Ethiopia. The following month, the king of Italy became the new emperor of Ethiopia, which was combined with two other Italian-held countries (Eritrea and Italian Somaliland) to form Italian East Africa.

Hitler on the March

By this time, Hitler had promised to build a new German empire that would last a thousand years. He called the new empire the Third Reich.[3] In order to create more jobs and prepare for war, he expanded the armaments industry, made the armed forces larger, and sponsored large-scale public works. In October 1933 he withdrew from the Geneva Disarmament Conference and the League of Nations.

The Rhineland. On March 7, 1936, at the height of the Ethiopian crisis, Hitler's armies marched into the Rhineland, a demilitarized area in western Germany along the Rhine River. Although this violated the Versailles Treaty and the Locarno Pact of 1925,[4] Hitler was not concerned. On October 25, he signed the Rome-Berlin Axis, a political and military accord with Mussolini. The following month, he signed the Anti-Comintern Pact, an alliance between Germany, Japan, and Italy against communism.

The Soviets, afraid that these new alliances posed a threat to their security, asked the democracies of the West to unite to contain fascism. But the Western powers, as afraid of communism as they were of fascism, were not willing to risk war.

Austria. In March 1938 Hitler annexed Austria, insisting that he was only promoting political stability by uniting German-speaking peoples. Only the Soviets expressed alarm, arguing that Hitler would not be content to stop with Austria. The Soviets were right. Austria was just the beginning of Hitler's "Artichoke Plan"—one leaf (or one country) at a time until the entire plant (or world) was consumed.

Czechoslovakia. Next on Hitler's agenda was the Sudetenland, a border region of Czechoslovakia that was home to about 8 million Germans. When Hitler demanded autonomy for the Germans of the Sudetenland, the Czech government refused. Such autonomy, it said, would be contrary to Czechoslovakia's national interests.

On September 15, 1938, British Prime Minister Neville Chamberlain met with Hitler to discuss the problem of the Sudetenland. When Hitler insisted that he would accept nothing less than the outright cession of the area, Chamberlain and French Premier Edouard Daladier agreed that the Czech government must give in to his demands. When Hitler did not like the arrangements Chamberlain made for the transfer of the land, Chamberlain suggested a meeting to discuss the matter.

On September 29, 1938, Chamberlain, Hitler, Mussolini, and their aides met in Munich. There, they

---

[3] The Third Reich was intended to be the successor to two previous empires in Germany, the Holy Roman and the German Empire from 1870 to 1918.

[4] The Locarno Pact included a treaty that guaranteed the Franco-German and Belgo-German frontiers. The treaty was signed by Germany, France, Belgium and by Great Britain and Italy as guarantors.

The Treaty of Versailles limited Germany to an armed force of 100,000. By 1935 Germany had 600,000 soldiers.

signed the Munich Pact, in which they agreed to give Germany sovereignty over the Sudetenland and all vital Czech fortresses. In return, Hitler promised not to try to acquire any more territory in Europe, to respect Czech sovereignty, and to settle any future disputes by peaceful negotiation.

The agreement was initially welcomed by Europeans as a means of preserving peace. But, when accepting Hitler's word proved to be a mistake, the Munich Pact became a symbol of **appeasement** (giving in to potential enemies to keep the peace). Furthermore, the Soviets objected to the pact because they believed that the British and French were using it to turn Hitler away from their countries and eastward toward the Soviet Union.

Poland. On March 15, 1939, Hitler broke his word and sent his armies into Prague, taking control of what remained of Czechoslovakia. This act

AXIS EXPANSION IN EUROPE, 1935–1941

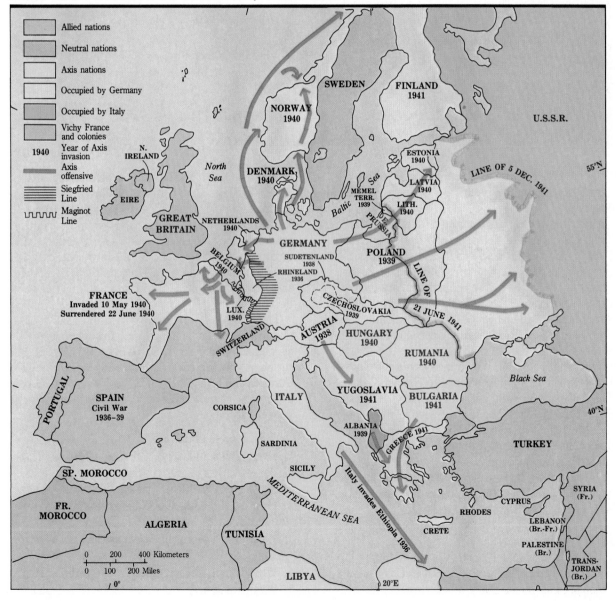

Leaders of the major European powers—Chamberlain of Great Britain, Daladier of France, Hitler of Germany, and Mussolini (with Count Ciano) of Italy—met in Munich in an attempt to settle the Sudetenland question. Chamberlain promised the Munich Pact would bring "peace in our time." What did Munich come to symbolize?

stripped away all illusion that his aggression was merely an attempt to unify the German-speaking peoples.

Hitler, however, was far from finished. On March 23, 1939, he made demands of Poland regarding Danzig, a port city in northern Poland, and the Polish Corridor, a strip of territory separating East Prussia from the rest of Germany. Eight days later, Great Britain and France pledged to help Poland if Hitler threatened its independence. The next month, they promised to help Rumania and Greece defend their borders should the need arise.

Next, Great Britain and France asked the Soviet Union to join them in an alliance to contain Nazism. The Soviets, however, had not forgotten the Munich Pact or the fact that they had not been invited to join the Munich Conference. They told the Western democracies that they were willing to become their ally only under certain conditions. For one, the West had to guarantee the security of all of Eastern Europe and the Baltic states. For another, the West had to acknowledge the Soviet right, under certain circumstances, to occupy a broad zone stretching from Finland to Bulgaria.

Great Britain and France refused to grant the Soviet conditions. Therefore the Soviet Union signed a nonaggression pact and other agreements with Hitler. The pact, signed in Moscow on August 23, 1939, provided that neither the Soviet Union nor Germany would attack one another and that each would remain neutral if the other were attacked by someone else. It also provided that in the event of a territorial rearrangement in Eastern Europe, the Soviet Union should have Finland, Estonia, Latvia, eastern Poland, and the Rumanian province of Bessarabia.

The pact freed Hitler from the possibility of a two-front war and left him secure enough to increase his demands on Poland. On September 1, 1939, he cut short the negotiations on Danzig and the Polish Corridor and invaded Poland. Two days later, Great Britain and France declared war on Germany. World War II had begun.

SECTION REVIEW

1. Identify the following: Stimson Doctrine, Haile Selassie, Rome-Berlin Axis, "Artichoke Plan," Neville Chamberlain, Danzig.
2. How did the League of Nations react to Japanese aggression in China?
3. What was the result of Mussolini's invasion of Ethiopia?
4. Why did the British agree to the Munich Pact?
5. What agreement did Hitler make with Stalin?

Isolationist forces mounted a strong drive to allow Congress the right to declare war only in the event of invasion of the United States.

Congress passed an arms embargo applying to both sides in the Spanish Civil War. Only one dissenting vote was cast.

4 A Neutral America

As Europe headed for war, the United States did all it could to avoid involvement. This time around, most Americans preferred to let Europe settle its own affairs. They felt that the United States should never have gotten involved in World War I. They pointed to the fact that a great many lives and a lot of material had been lost, but American ideological goals had not been achieved. If anything, they said, democracy was in retreat.

The Nye Hearings

American isolationist feelings were strengthened by the findings of the Senate Munitions Investigating Committee. This committee was formed in 1934 to investigate the manufacture and traffic in arms in the United States. Its chairman was Senator Gerald P. Nye, an isolationist Republican from North Dakota. From 1934 to 1936, the committee held public hearings, from which it concluded that America's entry into World War I had been due to covert pressure exerted by American financiers and armament makers. The bankers, it said, had favored American intervention because they wanted to make sure that Great Britain and France remained strong enough to pay back their loans. The munitions industry wanted to profit from the increased demand for weapons.

The Nye committee's activities set the domestic background for the passage of neutrality legislation. The committee's findings heightened the resolve of those who thought war in general was wrong—a rich person's game played with poor people's lives. The findings also influenced those who believed that taking sides would compromise basic American interests, especially in its foreign trade. In a poll taken in April 1937, two-thirds of the people questioned said that American participation in World War I had been a mistake, one which they did not care to repeat.

The Neutrality Acts

Both Congress and President Roosevelt knew how most of the American people felt. For this reason, most of their early actions were designed to keep the United States out of the problems of Europe and Asia.

When Mussolini attacked Ethiopia, the Neutrality Act of 1935 was passed. This act said that when a state of war existed, the President had the power to prohibit arms shipments to all belligerents. He could also forbid Americans from traveling on belligerent ships except at their own risk. In 1936 a second Neutrality act was passed. It extended the 1935 act and forbade loans or credit for belligerents.

The following year, two more acts were passed. The first, passed in January 1937, came into being because of a civil war that broke out in Spain in July 1936. That year, Spanish army chiefs in Spanish Morocco, long discontented with the policies of

The Spanish rebels, led by General Francisco Franco, were aided by Hitler and Mussolini in their attempt to overthrow Spain's Republican government. Although the United States remained neutral, many Americans fought on the side of the Republicans, also known as the Loyalists. What did the struggle in Spain represent to most Americans?

Ernest Hemingway

One of America's most influential writers, Ernest Hemingway, rose to fame during the period between World War I and World War II. As a member of the "Lost Generation" of the 1920's, he was disillusioned by war. This feeling is strongly reflected in one of his most famous novels, *The Sun Also Rises* (1926).

Born in Oak Park, Illinois in 1899, Hemingway had a happy childhood, with summers spent hunting and fishing in northern Michigan. His love of the outdoors influenced his writing throughout his life. By the time he finished high school, he had already started gathering material for his stories.

After graduation, he worked for a short time as a reporter on the *Kansas City Star*. His experience in journalism is considered to be a strong influence on his work.

During World War I Hemingway volunteered to drive an ambulance in Italy and later served in the Italian army. In 1918 he was seriously wounded. Hemingway's wartime experiences provided the basis for his novel, *A Farewell to Arms*, which was set in Italy.

After the war, he returned to the United States. Later, he joined other American writers in Paris. He continued to write short stories as well as nonfiction, such as *Death in the Afternoon* (1932), the subject of which is bullfighting.

During the Spanish Civil War, Hemingway worked as a war correspondent. His experiences in Spain served as the setting for another of his best novels, *For Whom the Bell Tolls*.

Throughout his writing career, Hemingway often used himself as the hero of his stories. He admired tough, unemotional behavior in the face of danger, and this attitude was evident in both his writing and his life-style, which included adventures such as big-game hunting in Africa.

Despite frequent illnesses and an accident-prone nature, he continued to travel and to write. In 1953 he received the Pulitzer prize for his novel, *The Old Man and the Sea* (1952), and in 1954 he received the Nobel prize for literature. In his later years, however, he suffered increasingly from physical and mental illnesses, and in 1961 he took his own life.

Spain's Republican government, began a revolt. General Francisco Franco took formal command of the Army of Africa, which already had a firm grip on Spanish Morocco, and headed with his troops to Madrid. The war lasted for three years. During that time, Franco's Nationalists received the support of the army, monarchists, landowners, and the Roman Catholic Church. They also received planes, troops, munitions, and the like from Mussolini and Hitler. The Republicans, or Loyalists, received a great deal of support from Stalin. In addition, individual sympathizers from many different countries formed international brigades to fight on the Loyalist side. Included

were 3000 Americans who made up the Abraham Lincoln Brigade.

To many Americans, the Spanish Civil War was a struggle between fascism and communism, and they wanted no part of it. Since the Neutrality Acts of 1935 and 1936 applied only to wars between nations, a resolution was passed forbidding the export of munitions "for the use of either of the opposing forces in Spain."

In May 1937 another act was adopted. It authorized the President to list commodities other than munitions to be paid for on delivery and made travel on belligerent ships unlawful.

One reason that isolationism lost support was the great improvement in airplanes and ships. The United States could no longer rely on its traditional ocean barriers for protection.

Discuss why American opinion was more united before World War II than it had been before World War I.

The Push for Change

The restrictions of the Neutrality Acts did not please Roosevelt, who believed they would "drag us into war instead of keeping us out." He had wanted legislation that would allow him more discretion—for example, to embargo supplies to one side but not to the other. On October 5, 1937, he warned the American people that war was contagious:

> Innocent peoples are being cruelly sacrificed to a greed for power and supremacy. . . . Let no one imagine that America will escape. . . . There is no escape through mere isolation or neutrality. . . . War is contagion, whether it be declared or not. It seems unfortunately true that the epidemic of lawlessness is spreading. When an epidemic of physical disease starts to spread, the community . . . joins in a quarantine of the patients in order to protect the health of the community against the spread of the disease.

The speech, however, did not have the effect Roosevelt wanted. Most Americans remained opposed to any moves which would draw the United States into war.

On April 7, 1938, Mussolini invaded Albania. This led Roosevelt to ask Hitler and Mussolini for assurances against attack on 31 different European and Near Eastern countries. Hitler replied but gave no such assurances. The next month, he and Mussolini concluded a military pact between their countries.

The United States responded with the Naval Expansion Act of 1938, also known as the Vinson Naval Act. It authorized the spending of $1 billion over the next ten years to create a two-ocean navy strong enough to deal with the combined fleets of Japan, Germany, and Italy. The fact that the bill was passed was a sign that American opinion was starting to change. Although most Americans still wanted no part of the war, they now were willing to admit that they needed strong defenses against any threats that might arise to the security of the Western Hemisphere.

In 1939, after Hitler's invasion of Czechoslovakia, Roosevelt asked Congress to repeal the arms embargo. The isolationists, however, made sure the proposal was defeated. One of their leaders, Senator William Borah, dismissed the President's fears. He told Secretary of State Hull, "I have my own sources of information in Europe that I regard as more reliable than those of the State Department and I can say to you that there is not going to be any war."

When Hitler invaded Poland that year, he proved Borah wrong. Roosevelt went on the air to declare that the United States would remain neutral. Then he added, "I cannot ask that every American remain neutral in thought as well. Even a neutral cannot be asked to close his mind or his conscience." Two days later, he issued an official proclamation of neutrality and forbade the export of arms and munitions to belligerents.

SECTION REVIEW

1. Identify the following: Gerald P. Nye, General Francisco Franco, Naval Expansion Act.
2. What were the conclusions of the Nye committee?
3. How did Americans regard the Spanish Civil War?
4. Why did Roosevelt disapprove of the Neutrality Acts?

5 From Neutrality to Commitment

By the fall of 1939, polls showed that five out of every six Americans sympathized with Great Britain and France, while only one in 50 favored Germany and Italy. Roosevelt believed that the only way Great Britain and France could defeat Germany was by obtaining the arms and munitions they needed from the United States.

The Neutrality Act of 1939 and the Phony War

On September 21, 1939, Roosevelt called a special session of Congress to plead for the repeal of the Neutrality Acts. He argued that the United States could provide Great Britain and France with weapons and still remain neutral by applying a **cash-and-carry** principle. In other words, such goods could be sold only if they were paid for in full and transported by the country that bought them. That way, no American ships would have to enter European war zones.

"Cash and carry" was one way to avoid the war debts that had troubled economies and foreign relations.

Roosevelt's request brought mixed reactions. Senator Borah warned that lifting the arms embargo would mean taking sides in a war in which American interests were not involved. Pacifists argued that weapons were instruments of destruction and that having nothing to do with them was the only way to prevent war. Communists argued that Great Britain and France should not be helped because they were not fighting for survival but to save imperialistic capitalism.

There were others, however, who favored the President. This group included a powerful new combination of southern and eastern Democrats in Congress, Republicans who favored preparedness, business interests, big-city newspapers, and intellectuals.

On November 4 Congress passed the Neutrality Act of 1939. It officially lifted arms embargo and authorized cash-and-carry exports of arms and munitions to belligerents. The tide had turned in the President's favor.

The winter of 1939–1940 was quiet. The French sat braced along the Maginot Line, a line of fortifications along their eastern border. They faced the Siegfried Line, built by the Germans along their southwestern border. The French waited for a German attack that did not come. This period, called the "phony war," led optimistic Americans to think that Hitler was too weak to attack.

During the "phony war," Americans reacted most strongly to Stalin's invasion of Finland, a move intended to protect Russia's northern flank from possible German attack. Americans instantly showed sympathy for the small country, but they were still not willing to go to war. Roosevelt, therefore, felt he could do nothing more than verbally denounce the Soviet Union's action. The State and Treasury departments, however, instituted a moral embargo—one based on persuasion rather than law—on the export of war supplies to the Soviets.

The Blitzkrieg

American optimism was shattered in 1940, when Hitler's armies waged a **blitzkrieg,** or lightning war, against Western Europe. On April 9 the Germans invaded Denmark and Norway by sea and air. On May 10 they invaded Luxembourg, the Netherlands, and Belgium. In a May 16 address, Roosevelt warned the American people that they must "recast their thinking about national production." He emphasized that the developments of the past few weeks should have "made it clear to all of our citizens that the possibility of attack on vital American zones ought to make it essential that we have the physical, the ready ability to meet these attacks."

Most Americans felt defenseless and confused. One writer explained the atmosphere in this way:

Someday the survivors of this generation will tell their grandchildren what it meant to live through a critical week in the world's history.

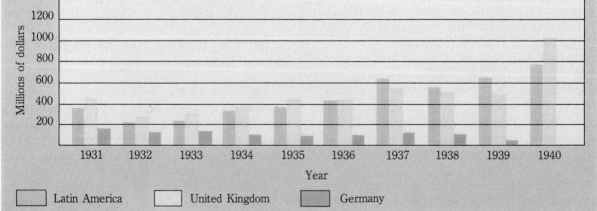

VALUE OF U.S. EXPORTS, 1931–1940

Millions of dollars (vertical axis: 200, 400, 600, 800, 1000, 1200)

Year (horizontal axis: 1931, 1932, 1933, 1934, 1935, 1936, 1937, 1938, 1939, 1940)

Legend: Latin America — United Kingdom — Germany

Discuss the advantages and disadvantages in warfare resulting from Germany's geographical position.

German soldiers marched through Paris in June, 1940, after conquering Denmark, Norway, Belgium, and Holland. Americans were stunned by the swiftness of France's fall, since the French army was considered by many military experts to be the finest in the world. How did the United States alter its foreign policy after the fall of France?

They will tell of the newspapers bought, edition after edition, each with its record of new disasters. About the perfect May weather . . . the shudder as an airplane passed overhead. . . . About turning the radio knob for news, and instead getting sales plugs and dance music—till a new voice broke in to announce that Antwerp had fallen, or St. Quentin, so that the war seemed to be fought in one's living room. . . . But worst of all, they will say, was the feeling of helplessness.

Roosevelt called for the production of more planes and large new expenditures for the armed forces. A few weeks later, he asked for $1 billion more for defense and for the authority to call the National Guard and reserve personnel into active service.

Then he ordered the War and Navy departments to turn over to private firms all available guns and ammunition for resale to the British.

On June 5 the Germans crossed the Somme River, and the Battle of France was underway. Five days later, Mussolini declared war on both France and Great Britain, and Italian forces penetrated southern France. Mussolini's actions prompted Roosevelt to declare, "On this the tenth day of June, 1940, the hand that held the dagger has struck it into the back of its neighbor." That same day, in an address at the University of Virginia, he announced the end of American isolation and the beginning of a new phase of **"nonbelligerency."** That is, although the United States would not enter the war, neither would it remain neutral. Instead it would extend as much material aid as possible to the democracies.

Compare the advantages and disadvantages to the victor of a puppet government and direct occupation.

The Battle of Britain

By the end of May 1940, the British had been driven to the sea at Dunkirk, a port in northern France. More than 300,000 British troops, cut off from retreat on land, were evacuated by vessels of all types, including private pleasure craft. This extraordinary rescue operation became a symbol of heroism.

On June 14 German troops entered Paris. With the fall of France,[5] only the remnants of the British army that had been rescued from Dunkirk remained to oppose the Germans. In August the Battle of Britain began. For months the *Luftwaffe,* the German air force, bombed Britain day and night in preparation for a major invasion. However, the Royal Air Force held off the Germans, forcing Hitler to abandon his plan for an invasion of the British Isles. The new British prime minister, Winston Churchill, speaking of British fighter pilots, said, "Never in the field of human conflict was so much owed by so many to so few." The Battle of Britain was Hitler's first major defeat. He had made a serious mistake in underestimating the British.

At the same time the Battle of Britain was being fought in Europe, the Burke-Wadsworth bill was approved in the United States. Better known as the Selective Training and Service Act, it constituted the first peacetime program of compulsory military service in the United States. Although polls showed that two-thirds of the American people were in favor of the draft, the bill had been strongly opposed by anti-conscription groups. Yet, when the draft went into effect on October 16, National Registration Day, only 36 men refused to register. By this time, German troops had occupied Rumania. Shortly after that, Italy invaded Greece.

The Election of 1940

In the midst of the crisis in Europe, it was time for the presidential election in the United States. The Democrats broke with the traditional two-term limit on the Presidency and nominated Roosevelt for a third term. The Republicans chose as their candidate a former Democrat—businessman Wendell L. Willkie

---

[5] The Germans occupied the northern part of France. In the unoccupied southern part, known as Vichy France, they set up a puppet government under French Marshal Henri-Philippe Pétain.

of Indiana. Willkie approved almost all of Roosevelt's New Deal reforms and generally agreed with his foreign policy.

While Willkie campaigned extensively, Roosevelt did not campaign at all for several months. For him, the campaign had to take a back seat to events in Europe and to what he felt were threats to American security. The fear that the Nazis might try to take the French islands of Guadeloupe and Martinique in the Caribbean led Roosevelt to arrange for a conference of the 21 member-countries of the Pan-American Union.

The Pan-American representatives met on July 21, 1940 in Havana, Cuba, and issued the Act of Havana. It provided that in the interest of common defense, the American republics collectively or singly could take over and administer any European possession in the New World in danger of aggression. In this way, they hoped to prevent any of the European colonies in the Western Hemisphere from being transferred to the Nazis.

Willkie, meanwhile, realized that if he hoped to win the election, he would have to listen to some of the old-time professional politicians, who begged him "to abandon this nonsense about a bipartisan foreign policy—to attack Roosevelt as a warmonger—to scare the American people with warnings that votes for Roosevelt meant 'wooden crosses for their sons and brothers and sweethearts.'" Willkie reluctantly took this advice and accused Roosevelt of making secret agreements with Great Britain—agreements that would lead the United States into war with Germany. Roosevelt flatly denied Willkie's charges. He told Americans, "I have said this before, but I shall say it again and again and again. Your boys are not going to be sent into any foreign wars." Even so, the charges added fuel to the debate already in progress over the question of American neutrality and aid to the French and British.

The Committee to Defend America. One group very much involved in the debate was the Committee to Defend America by Aiding the Allies (CDA). Back in 1939, when Hitler took over Czechoslovakia, a small but influential group of Americans decided that if Nazism ever enveloped Europe, the United States would be in danger of the same fate. Under the leadership of newspaper editor William Allen White, these Americans formed the Non-Partisan Commit-

Discuss whether there is any significance to the fact that the CDA was strongest in the East, while the America First movement was strongest in the Midwest.

tee for Peace through the Revision of the Neutrality Law. By the end of 1939, the committee had branches in 30 states. Its propaganda helped swing public opinion in favor of repealing the arms embargo.

During the phony war, the committee had quietly died out. In 1940, however, it reorganized in New York as the CDA. Within a few months, it had more than 600 branches. It worked feverishly to stimulate public support for Roosevelt's policy of all aid short of war. The CDA argued that the war in Europe would decide "the future of western civilization," and that America was no safer than any other country.

DESTROYER DEAL BASES

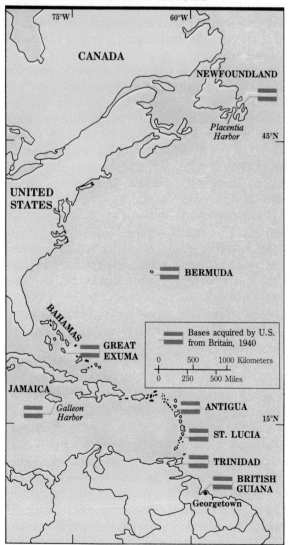

The America First Committee. Another group involved in the campaign debate was the America First Committee, which had its headquarters in Chicago. The committee, incorporated in September 1940, had as its leaders Alice Roosevelt Longworth, the daughter of Teddy Roosevelt; Eddie Rickenbacker, the World War I hero; Charles Lindbergh, the famous pilot; and General Robert E. Wood, Chairman of the Board of Sears, Roebuck and Company.

The America First movement included thousands of patriotic Americans who sincerely believed that the only way for America to remain safe was for it not to intervene in Europe's affairs and to concentrate instead on the defense of the Western Hemisphere. For this reason, committee members opposed anything that compromised American neutrality. In their view, neither Great Britain nor Germany could conquer the other. The only thing that kept the British from accepting Hitler's offers of a negotiated peace was the belief that they could convince America to enter the war on their side. Therefore, if the United States refused to get involved, the war would come to an abrupt end.

Election Results. The debate over neutrality continued throughout the election campaign. Most people who favored Roosevelt's program for aiding the Allies voted for him, while those who opposed aid and feared intervention voted for Willkie, even though the Republican platform approved aid to "all peoples fighting for liberty." Roosevelt was reelected for a third term, winning 449 electoral votes and 54 percent of the popular vote.

Aid to the British

In May 1940 Churchill cabled President Roosevelt that there was a good chance of Hitler conquering Europe. To prevent this, he asked the United States to lend Great Britain 40 or 50 old destroyers and supply aircraft and ammunition.

Roosevelt responded by releasing to Great Britain millions of dollars worth of surplus or outdated stocks of arms, munitions, and aircraft. In exchange, the United States received 99-year leases on eight military bases within the British empire. Most Americans favored the aid, even though it meant the end of formal neutrality and the beginning of limited American participation in the war.

Ask students to define what President Roosevelt meant by "arsenal of democracy."

The Four Freedoms and Lend-Lease. In December 1940 Churchill indicated that America's cash-and-carry policy no longer would work for the British. Not only were they short of cash, but German submarines were making it almost impossible to transport the goods they bought. Roosevelt responded on December 29 in one of his fireside chats. After explaining to the American people that Great Britain and the British fleet stood between the Western Hemisphere and Nazi aggression, he stated that "we must be the great arsenal of democracy."

Roosevelt followed this up in his January 6, 1941 message to Congress. In this message, he offered the following set of aims:

> *Freedom of speech and expression—everywhere in the world. . . . Freedom of every person to worship God in his own way—everywhere in the world. . . . Freedom from want— everywhere in the world. . . . Freedom from fear—everywhere in the world.*

Roosevelt then went on to propose a **lend-lease plan,** in which he would have the authority to lend war equipment to countries "whose defense the President deems vital to the defense of the United States." This plan avoided direct loans, which were forbidden by the Neutrality Act of 1939.

Isolationists strongly criticized the lend-lease plan. If enacted, it would allow the President to take anything he wished and use it for any purpose he felt was important to the nation's security. He could completely ignore any existing legislation that did not fit in with his desires. The America First Committee campaigned long and hard against the policy, calling it the "War Dictator Bill."

The night before Congress voted on Lend-Lease, Winston Churchill made a worldwide broadcast in which he stated his country's needs and prospects. Emphasizing that Great Britain wanted American arms and food, not America's young men, he stated, "Give us the tools, and we will finish the job." On March 11 Congress passed the Lend-Lease Act. It formally committed the United States to the policy Roosevelt had been following since May, pouring out all resources to help the British defeat Hitler.

Crisis in the Atlantic. The same month that the Lend-Lease Act was passed, Hitler extended the German war zone to include Iceland and the Denmark Strait between Greenland and Iceland. Because Iceland and Greenland commanded the American sea lanes to Great Britain, this worried both the Americans and the British.

In April 1941 Roosevelt extended the protection of the Monroe Doctrine to Greenland, and American naval ships began to patrol far out into the Atlantic. When they came across a German submarine, they reported it to the British.

On May 10 the British claimed Iceland. Less than a week and a half later, a German submarine sank the American merchant vessel *Robin Moor* off the coast of Brazil. When the Germans announced that this would not be the last of such sinkings, Roosevelt closed down all the German and Italian consulates in the United States. He also froze all assets owned by Germany and Italy and the countries they occupied. At the same time, he declared a state of unlimited national emergency.

In June attention was diverted briefly from the Atlantic as Hitler ignored his pact with Stalin and attacked the Soviet Union. Military historians consider that invading the Soviet Union before defeating Great Britain was a great blunder on Hitler's part. Roosevelt responded by promising American aid to the Soviets. Within a few months time, the United States granted the Soviets $1 billion worth of Lend-Lease credits.

In July attention shifted back to the Atlantic as the Icelandic government agreed to allow the United States to land forces in Iceland. The American forces were to keep Germany from occupying Iceland and using it as a naval or air base against the Western Hemisphere. At the same time, the United States Navy escorted American and Icelandic ships between the Atlantic Coast and Iceland.

In August Roosevelt and Churchill finally met face-to-face off the coast of Newfoundland to discuss the Nazi threat. Out of this meeting came an eight-point program known as the Atlantic Charter. In it, the United States and Great Britain declared that they had no territorial ambitions. Instead, what they sought was a world in which there was free trade, freedom of the seas, freedom for people to choose their own government, an end to the use of armed force, and "the final destruction of Nazi tyranny."

Most people did not consider the charter itself as important as the face-to-face meeting of Roosevelt and Churchill. In fact, the charter was thought by

Americans viewed the Nazis as a greater threat when Hitler extended submarine attacks halfway across the Atlantic.

At a meeting aboard the Prince of Wales off the Newfoundland coast, Roosevelt and Churchill set out a declaration of joint aims. The Atlantic Charter, as it came to be called, emphasized the rights of people to choose their own form of government. Why was the Atlantic meeting between these two leaders significant?

some to be "an uninspired plagiarism of Wilson's Fourteen Points." According to the *New York Times,* however, it represented "the end of isolation" and "the beginning of a new era in which the United States assumes the responsibilities which fall naturally to a great power."

Next Roosevelt decided to allow British and Allied ships to join American convoys between the United States and Iceland. While the President was trying to decide how to break this news to the American people, the *USS Greer,* an American destroyer that was tailing a German submarine so it could report its position to the British, was torpedoed south of Iceland.

Seven days later, on September 11, President Roosevelt declared that the attack had been part of a Nazi plan to control the Atlantic and attack the Western Hemisphere. He announced that the time had come for an active defense. Therefore, a "shoot-on-sight" order had been given to United States naval forces in the area between the United States and Iceland. Thus Roosevelt declared an unofficial naval war against Germany.

On October 9, 1941, Roosevelt asked Congress to revise the Neutrality Act of 1939, allow American merchant ships to arm, and permit American ships to enter war zones and belligerent ports. While Congress was deliberating the request, a German submarine torpedoed the *USS Kearny,* an American destroyer that had been helping a British convoy under attack by German submarines. The incident resulted in the loss of 11 American lives. Less than two weeks later, a German submarine sank the *USS Reuben James,* an American destroyer on convoy duty in waters off Iceland. This time, 115 American lives were lost. As a result, on November 13, Congress granted Roosevelt's request.

By the end of November 1941, there were very few Americans still preaching or thinking isolation. Most felt they had a job to do—to make sure Great Britain and the Soviet Union were delivered supplies. Some 15,000 Americans were already in the war overseas. Most were in the uniform of the British or Canadian armed forces.

SECTION REVIEW

1. Identify the following: Maginot Line, Siegfried Line, *Luftwaffe,* Burke-Wadsworth bill, Wendell Willkie, America First Committee.
2. How did the Neutrality Act of 1939 change American foreign policy?
3. What was the significance of the Battle of Britain?
4. What was the Committee to Defend America?
5. What were Roosevelt's Four Freedoms?

Ask students to discuss the merits and the drawbacks of the Ludlow Resolution.

The placing of American-Japanese trade on a day-to-day basis pressured the Japanese to change their policies and was less likely to produce a hostile reaction, such as an ultimatum might have done.

6 The End of the Road

While Hitler and Mussolini were waging war in Europe, the Japanese were making military conquests in the Far East. In 1937 Japan invaded China. When the Chinese resisted, the result was a full-scale, though undeclared war. America did not want conflict with Japan any more than it did with Germany or Italy. The Japanese bought a great deal of raw materials from the United States, and a war with Japan would hurt trade. On the other hand, China also traded with the United States, and the Chinese were in desperate need of help. The best course, reasoned most Americans, was not to take sides.

The *Panay* Incident

In December 1937 Japanese bombers sank the American gunboat *Panay* and three Standard Oil tankers in the Yangtze River near Nanking. Two Americans were killed and 30 wounded. The *Panay* had been flying American flags and was transporting civilians. The United States government demanded that the Japanese apologize, make reparations, and guarantee that there would be no more such incidents. The Japanese quickly did as they were asked, saying that the bombing had been a mistake and offering to pay $2 million in damages.

Most Americans, eager not to repeat the rash anger that had led them into World War I, were willing to forget the incident. In a poll taken a month later, 70 percent of those interviewed said they would like to see American withdrawal from the Far East.

In Congress, some members tried to reintroduce the Ludlow Resolution. This resolution, first introduced in 1935, had failed to pass several times. It called for a constitutional amendment making Congress' authority to declare war ineffective until it was confirmed by a majority vote in a nationwide referendum. The only exception would be those instances in which the United States or its territorial possessions were actually invaded. Once again the resolution did not get approved. In Roosevelt's view, it "would cripple any president in his conduct of our foreign policy, and it would encourage other nations to believe that they could violate American rights with impunity."

Relations between the United States and Japan steadily worsened during the 1930's. Despite cutting its export trade to Japan, the United States still hoped to avert a full break in relations. What event made conciliation impossible?

Increasing Tensions

In 1938 and 1939 relations between the United States and Japan continued to deteriorate. The Japanese military pressed their government to ally itself with Germany in order to offset the power of the United States and the Soviet Union.

At the same time, the Japanese army moved against Soviet forces along the Manchurian border, and the Japanese government worked through diplomatic channels to force the British to recognize Japanese conquests in China. When the British finally gave that recognition in July 1939, Americans changed their stance, determining to play a stronger role in the Far East.

On January 26, 1940, the commercial treaty affirmed in 1911 by Japan and the United States ran out. The United States informed the Japanese that from this date on, trade between Japan and America would rest on a day-to-day basis. Two months later, a Japanese-dominated government was established in China at Nanking.

In July there was a change in government in Japan, and the new, more militaristic cabinet announced a plan to achieve a "new Order in Greater East Asia." Its first move was to demand the right to build

The Japanese camouflaged their attack by sending their fleet across the less-traveled North Pacific and by avoiding the use of radio transmissions and lights.

airfields and station troops in northern French Indochina. Its second move, on September 27, 1941, was to formally ally Japan with Germany and Italy under the Tripartite Agreement, or Triple Alliance. Japan, Germany, and Italy now made up the Axis Powers, each pledging mutual assistance in the event of war with a country not yet a belligerent.

There was no doubt in anyone's mind that the pact was meant to threaten the United States. Most Americans suddenly became less interested in conciliation. The State Department ordered Americans in the Far East to return home, and Roosevelt proclaimed an embargo on exports of scrap iron and steel to all countries outside the Western Hemisphere except Great Britain.

On July 24, 1941, Japan occupied southern Indochina. To prevent further Japanese conquest and increased Japanese-American hostility, Roosevelt told the Japanese that if they would withdraw from Indochina, he would help them find access to the raw materials they so desperately needed. When the Japanese turned him down, he froze all Japanese assets in the United States. This brought Japanese-American trade to an abrupt halt. Two days later, after Japan had ordered the freezing of all American funds, Roosevelt called the Philippine militia into active service and closed the Panama Canal to Japanese shipping. At the same time, he warned that any further attempts to extend Japanese control in the Far East would force the United States to take steps to protect American interests and rights.

Pearl Harbor

On October 18, 1941, the Japanese prime minister, Prince Fumimaro Konoye, resigned. Konoye had been willing to negotiate with the United States because he did not believe Japan could defeat America in a war. The new prime minister, General Hideki Tojo, did not share Konoye's views. Nonetheless, on November 20, negotiations were opened in Washington between Secretary of State Hull, Japanese ambassador Admiral Kichisaburo Nomura, and special envoy Saburo Kurusu.

At the same time the negotiations were going on, Japan made military preparations in Asia and the Pacific. The Japanese had decided that if the negotiations did not come to a satisfactory conclusion

by early December, they would attack. On November 29, Tojo stated flatly that American and British influence must be eliminated from Asia. By this time American officials expected an attack. But they thought that the target would be the Philippines or one of the other American bases in the Far East. While the Japanese were planning assaults on these bases, they also planned a more major blow—one they hoped would stop the United States from interfering with their plans for expansion.

On December 6 Roosevelt appealed directly to Japanese Emperor Hirohito to use his influence to have Japanese troops withdrawn from Indochina and to preserve the peace. That same afternoon, the Japanese notified the United States government by wire that negotiations were terminated. By the time the message was decoded and given to Roosevelt on Sunday morning, December 7, the Japanese had attacked the naval base of Pearl Harbor in Hawaii.

The American installations at Pearl Harbor could not have been more vulnerable to attack. Ships were anchored in a neat row and airplanes were grouped together on the airfield, easy targets for a Japanese

The day after Pearl Harbor, newspapers carried little else but news about the sneak attack. Nearly 2300 Americans were killed, and the Pacific fleet suffered staggering losses on the "Day of Infamy." What events led to the Japanese attack?

The Japanese attack force lost about 30 planes and 100 men.

air attack. As the following excerpt shows, the Americans at Pearl Harbor were taken completely by surprise:

> *In the Navy housing areas around Pearl Harbor, people couldn't imagine what was wrecking Sunday morning. Captain Reynolds Hayden, enjoying breakfast at his home on Hospital Point, thought it was construction blasting. . . . Lieutenant C. E. Boudreau, drying down after a shower, thought an oil tank had blown up near his quarters . . . until a Japanese plane almost grazed the bathroom window. Chief Petty Officer Albert Molter, puttering around his Ford Island flat, thought a drill was going on until his wife Esther called, "Al, there's a battleship tipping over."*

Within less than two hours time, 19 ships were sunk or disabled; 188 airplanes were destroyed; about 2400 soldiers, sailors, and civilians were killed;

and more than 1100 people were wounded. The attack on Pearl Harbor sent shock waves throughout America. On December 8 Roosevelt went before Congress. Calling December 7 "a day which will live in infamy," he asked for a declaration of war on Japan. Within an hour, Congress responded in favor of the declaration.

On December 11 Germany and Italy officially joined their ally Japan and declared war on the United States. That same afternoon, the United States responded in kind, without a single opposing vote.

SECTION REVIEW

1. Identify the following: *Panay,* Ludlow Resolution, General Hideki Tojo.
2. Why did the United States want to avoid taking sides in the conflict between China and Japan?
3. What was the effect of the Tripartite Agreement on American attitudes toward Japan?
4. Why was the Japanese attack on Pearl Harbor successful?

CHAPTER 26 REVIEW

SUMMARY

1. After World War I, American foreign policy was based on non-involvement, including non-interference in Latin America.
2. Postwar economic problems in Europe led to a reduction of Germany's reparation payments and of European war debts to the United States.
3. During the 1930's totalitarian governments in Japan, Italy, and Germany began programs of military conquest.
4. In 1936 Germany and Italy became allies.
5. World War II began in September 1939, when Great Britain and France, in response to extensive German aggression, declared war on Germany.

6. Most Americans were opposed to becoming involved in the war.
7. After the fall of France in 1940, the United States began to give material help to Great Britain.
8. President Roosevelt was reelected to a third term in 1940.
9. When Germany attacked the Soviet Union, the United States began giving material aid to the Soviets.
10. In 1941 Japan allied itself with Germany and Italy.
11. On December 7, 1941, the Japanese attacked the United States naval base at Pearl Harbor, precipitating America's full-scale involvement in the war.

VOCABULARY

occupation	collectivization	appeasement	nonbelligerency
moratorium	swastika	cash and carry	lend-lease plan
totalitarian	sanction	blitzkrieg	

REVIEW QUESTIONS

1. What was the purpose of the Good Neighbor policy?
2. Why did European countries fail to pay their war debts to the United States?
3. What conditions contributed to the rise of totalitarianism?
4. What elements did the various totalitarian governments have in common?
5. Why was isolationist sentiment so strong in the United States after World War I?
6. Why did Germany, Italy, and Japan set out to conquer other countries?
7. How did American attitudes toward the war evolve between 1939 and 1941?
8. What were the major issues in the election of 1940?

DISCUSSION

1. Could the United States ever succumb to a totalitarian government? Why or why not?
2. Could Hitler's rise to power have been avoided if Germany had been punished either more severely or less severely for its actions in World War I?
3. Should the United States have intervened earlier in World War II? Why or why not?
4. If world conditions today were similar to conditions in 1940, what role would you want the United States to take? Why?

USING MAPS

Refer to the maps on pages 554 and 557 and answer the following questions:

1. What country in Europe was occupied by Italy?
2. What countries were allied with Germany?
3. What countries were invaded by the Axis in 1941?
4. How far north did the Siegfried line extend?
5. What areas were under Japanese control by 1941?
6. Why would American military experts think that the first Japanese attack against the United States would be in the Philippines?

USING SKILLS

Some historians think that America's entry into World War II was avoidable. This position involves making certain assumptions. Which of the following ideas are assumptions that must be made in order to believe that war was avoidable?

1. President Roosevelt deliberately misled the American people by telling them he wanted peace when he really wanted war.
2. Germany presented no direct threat to the United States.
3. Japan would not have attacked Pearl Harbor if Japanese differences with the United States could have been resolved without having to go to war.
4. Roosevelt knew that his policies toward Japan would lead to war.

1	On the Defensive: 1942	**573**
2	Turning the Tide: 1943	**582**
3	On the Offensive: 1944	**587**
4	Days of Victory: 1945	**591**

WORLD WAR II

The war came as a great relief, like a reverse earthquake, that in one terrible jerk shook everything disjointed, distorted, askew. Japanese bombs had finally brought national unity to the U.S.

TIME, DECEMBER 15, 1941

Less than 30 years after World War I, the United States found itself at war again. This war, however, was different from World War I. It was a fight for survival, and, before it was over, it involved almost every country in the world. By the end of 1941, 29 countries had already declared their support for the Allies—Great Britain, France, the United States, and the Soviet Union. The Axis Powers—Germany, Italy, and Japan—were supported by 7 other countries. By 1945 only 5 European countries—Ireland, Sweden, Switzerland, Spain, and Portugal—remained neutral.

By the time the United States entered the war, the fighting had already been going on for more than two years, and it was to drag on for almost four more. The war years had a profound effect on Americans and on the country as a whole. Out of the war came new technology, a new prosperity, and a new sense of power and strength.

1 On the Defensive: 1942

By 1942 the war was being fought on several fronts. In Eastern Europe, the Soviet Union stood alone against Germany. In Italy and in North Africa, the Allies battled the Italians and Germans. In Western Europe, the Allies tried to protect England and to push back German advances in France, the Low Countries, and Scandinavia. In the Far East, the Allies were pitted against the Japanese. The question of which front was to be given priority was a major dilemma for Allied planners.

As soon as the United States joined the war, it began to take a leadership role among the Allies. For example, the United States took the initiative in drafting the United Nations Declaration, setting forth the aims of the Atlantic Charter. On January 1, 1942, the document was signed by the United States and 25 other countries at an international conference held in Washington, D.C.

Early Decisions

The United States, along with Great Britain, also took a leadership role in military planning. When American strategists had begun to discuss war plans several months before Pearl Harbor, they had decided to take on the Germans before the Japanese. But when Japan attacked Pearl Harbor, key leaders such as General Douglas MacArthur argued for a firm offensive against the Japanese.

After serious consideration, military strategists decided to stay with the original plan and concentrate first on the defeat of Germany. One reason was that most American officials agreed with Churchill that "the defeat of Germany . . . will leave Japan exposed to overwhelming force, whereas the defeat of Japan would by no means bring the World War to an end." A second reason was that the United States had much closer ties with the countries under siege by Germany than with those under siege by Japan. A third reason was the belief that, ultimately, Germany rather than Japan posed the most direct threat to the Western Hemisphere. Not only would a German takeover of Western Europe greatly affect control of the Atlantic Ocean and European trade, but the Nazi sympathies of some Latin American countries could create problems close to home.

A fourth reason was that the Germans, who were known for their innovative technology, might develop new and powerful weapons to use against the Allies. A fifth reason was the belief that in time the Germans would force the Soviet Union out of the war, which would deprive the Allies of their two-front advantage.

The War in Europe and the Mediterranean

Until late in 1942, the Axis held the upper hand in Eastern and Western Europe and in North Africa. On June 28 the Germans began their summer offensive against the Soviet Union. Throughout the summer

Using a map of the world, discuss the different terrain on which soldiers fought in the Far East, Europe, and North Africa.

Have students consider why the British, with the world's strongest navy, were unable to repel attacks on Singapore and Malaya by the Japanese.

Field General Erwin Rommel, examining a campaign map, was one of Germany's most able military leaders. His Afrika Korps nearly drove the British out of Africa in 1941–1942. What strategy helped turn the tide in Africa for the Allies?

and early fall, they took one Soviet city after another, from Sevastopol to Kostov to Stalingrad, but were finally checked at Leningrad and Moscow. A concerned and angry Stalin wanted to know why the Soviets were fighting alone in Eastern Europe.

At the Moscow Conference held in August, Churchill told Stalin that the Allies had no plans to open a second front in Europe that year. They had their hands full in Western Europe and in North Africa. In Western Europe, Allied raids on France and Germany had not kept the Germans from advancing. And in North Africa, due in great part to the strategies of Field Marshal Erwin Rommel—the "Desert Fox"—the Axis held firm control. Rommel's forces had advanced as far as El Alamein, 70 miles (112 kilometers) west of Alexandria, before being checked by the British.

American leaders wanted to cross the English Channel and launch a major attack on continental Europe, forcing the Germans to defend the heart of their own empire. Churchill, however, argued that, given the German military might in the area, such an assault would be too difficult. Setbacks suffered throughout the winter and spring of 1942 led the Americans to conclude that Churchill was right. Thus they made plans to invade North Africa instead.

On November 8 an Anglo-American force commanded by General Dwight D. Eisenhower and Admiral Sir Andrew Cunningham staged Operation Torch, the first major Allied **amphibious** (land and water) operation in the European theater. The British and Americans made surprise landings in French North Africa at Casablanca, Oran, and Algiers and quickly gained control of the northwestern part of Africa. Meanwhile, the British surprised Rommel at El Alamein and forced him to make a full retreat.

The War in the Pacific and the Far East

At the same time the Allies were trying to defeat Italy and Germany in Europe and the Mediterranean, the British and the Americans were trying to contain the Japanese in the Far East and the Pacific. During the six months following the attack on Pearl Harbor, the Japanese had pushed the British out of Malaya, Singapore, and Rangoon and had occupied Burma and the Dutch East Indies (Indonesia).

By this time the Japanese had achieved such complete domination in the Pacific that one naval historian referred to the area as "practically a Japanese lake." Within a few weeks after Pearl Harbor, the Japanese had taken the American protectorates of Guam and Wake Island and had laid siege to the Philippines, which were under the command of General MacArthur. When the major city of Manila fell to the Japanese, MacArthur's forces, following a prearranged plan, retreated to Bataan, a small peninsula that extended into a bay opposite Manila. MacArthur then set up headquarters at Corregidor, an island fortress located at the entrance to Manila Bay.

The fighting in the Philippines was fierce and unlike any known by American soldiers. In the following letters, one young Army lieutenant tells his parents what the conditions were like:

January 5, 1942
Almost a month of war now. Still going strong and in perfect health. I've developed a slight case of jitters, but that's only natural, I

One reason for the harsh treatment of prisoners by Japanese soldiers was their belief that surrender is shameful.

guess, with so many bombs dropping every day. . . .

There have been airplanes overhead constantly for four hours now, and the ground is always shaking from some bombing or another. Planes are so common they are not even scouted any more. We know whose they are. We just yell "cover" and jump into our foxholes. There are holes of all sizes all around. Some we have dug, and some others have dug before us. They get deeper every time we are bombed.

February 12, 1942

I am as well as can be and in good spirits. We have been through some very rugged times in these past weeks with very little sleep, if any, and it becomes rather tiresome being on the constant alert dodging shells, bombs, and machine gun fire. . . .

I wonder if God is not only caring for ours but for the thousands of young Japanese left lying in the jungles of Luzon. We have taken a toll of lives many times what we have lost. I have seen what deadly effect my own firing has had among the ranks of the attackers in places where we have retaken the ground. They do not bury their dead except as an afterthought. . . .

I suppose this awful war has really just begun, but nine weeks has seemed an eternity. I'm so tired of killed men littering the jungle paths, of the stench of dead bodies being always in the air.

Will you please tell all the boys and girls I know that it's O.K. so far. Tomorrow isn't in our vocabulary.

Bataan and Corregidor. In March, shortly after Japanese troops landed at New Guinea, MacArthur secretly left for Australia to take command of the Allied forces in the Southwest Pacific. The Americans and Filipinos remaining on Bataan under the command of General Jonathan M. Wainwright held out until early April. When Bataan fell to the Japanese, the surrender marked the largest capitulation in history by an American military command.

The Americans withdrew to Corregidor, but they held it only for about a month. The 13,000 Filipinos and Americans taken prisoner at Corregidor did not get any food for a week. Then, to celebrate the Japanese victory, they were hauled ashore in freighters and driven through the streets of Manila like animals before being shipped by train to a prison camp.

The approximately 50,000 American and Filipino survivors of Bataan fared even worse. Most of them already were sick and starving, and the Japanese did

After surrendering at Bataan and Corregidor, 50,000 American and Filipino soldiers were forced to make what has since been called the Bataan "Death March." Thousands of prisoners died on the way to Pampanga Province. Thousands more died from malnutrition and harsh treatment in Japanese prison camps. How did Americans react to these events?

Australia served as the Allies' major base in the Atlantic. Its loss would have doomed Allied military operations in the region, according to some historians.

Three aircraft carriers—the *Hornet*, the *Yorktown*, and the *Enterprise*—were part of the Pacific Fleet that defeated a Japanese task force at the Battle of Midway. Earlier, in the battle of the Coral Sea, Navy aircraft turned back Japanese battleships bound for New Guinea. Why were these naval battles significant?

not have enough food, water, or medicine for them all. The prisoners were to go to a camp 65 miles (104 kilometers) north. Because there were not enough trucks or trains to take them, they were forced to walk. During the six-day "Death March," at least 7000 died. At the camp, more than 400 Americans and Filipinos died each day of malaria, dysentery, malnutrition, or brutality.

Allied Resistance. By the middle of April, the Allies began to stiffen their resistance and take the offensive in both the Far East and the Pacific. On April 18, 1942, Major General James H. Doolittle stunned the Japanese with the first offensive against Japan. Doolittle's forces raided Tokyo in carrier-based B-25 bombers. Although the raids caused little damage, they brought the war home to Japan and boosted American morale.

On May 7 and 8 several American carriers intercepted a Japanese fleet in the Coral Sea between Australia and the Solomon Islands. For the first time in the history of sea warfare, the ships in combat did not fire on each other. The entire Battle of the Coral Sea was fought in the air by carrier-based planes. The damage done to the Japanese stopped them from taking Port Moresby in southern New Guinea and cutting the Australian supply line. This, in turn, foiled Japan's plan to invade Australia.

In June the Japanese tried to take the Midway Islands, a coral atoll in the Central Pacific about 1200 miles (1920 kilometers) northwest of Hawaii. The naval and air Battle of Midway that ensued was a great victory for the Allies, resulting in the first major defeat of the Japanese navy. It slowed the Japanese advance across the Central Pacific, brought an end to the threat to Hawaii, and ended Japanese naval superiority in the Pacific.

Guadalcanal. The Japanese, however, were still well-entrenched in the South Pacific, with bases on the Solomons that posed a threat to the entire area. In addition, they had bombed two cities in Alaska and occupied the islands of Attu and Kiska in the Aleutians.

On August 7, to counteract Japanese advances in the Solomons, the United States Marines launched the first major Allied offensive in the Pacific at Guadalcanal. The Japanese had occupied this island in the Solomons the month before and had started to build an air base there—a base that would be within striking range of islands still in Allied hands. If those islands fell, the Japanese would be in a good position to hit at the chief shipping routes from the United States to Australia.

The American attack took the Japanese by surprise, and the marines were able to seize the

Guadalcanal was one of several Japanese bases being developed for air raids against American supply routes to Australia.

Of the 15 million people who entered the service after Pearl Harbor, 5 million were volunteers.

little difficulty the airfield and the other installations the Japanese were building. Holding on to them, however, was not quite so easy. Two days after the attack, the naval Battle of Savo Island broke out north of Guadalcanal. The Japanese won the battle, and as a result, they were temporarily able to deprive the American forces on Guadalcanal of their air and naval support.

The Americans, however, were not ready to give up. For the next six months, one battle followed another. In November the United States Navy won a decisive victory in the Battle of Guadalcanal. The victory kept the Japanese from landing reinforcements and helped the American forces to complete their conquest of the island. By February 9, 1943, there were no Japanese forces left on Guadalcanal, which the Japanese had come to call the "Island of Death."

In a Japanese report written during the battle and found after the Japanese had evacuated the island, the importance of the battle was summed up as follows:

> *It must be said that success or failure in recapturing Guadalcanal, and the results of the final naval battle related to it, is the fork in the road that leads to victory for them or for us.*

The Home Front

American entry into the war brought many changes to the home front. After Pearl Harbor, millions of Americans rushed to enlist in the armed forces. Of the more than 15 million who volunteered or were drafted, more than two-thirds served in the army.

Those who remained at home had to provide food, shelter, training, equipment, transportation, and medical care for all those in uniform. In order to accelerate military production as rapidly as possible, Roosevelt created dozens of new boards, offices, and agencies.

The Office of Scientific Research. Of all the agencies created in 1941 and 1942, one of the most important was the Office of Scientific Research and Development (OSRD). The OSRD, established in 1941 and headed by mathematician Vannebar Bush, commanded the services of some 30,000 physicists, chemists, doctors, lawyers, business managers, generals, laborers, and civil servants. As a group, these people made a great number of scientific and technological contributions to the war effort. One area in which their achievements went beyond expectations was that of war weapons.

At the beginning of the war, Germany had been much more advanced than the United States in the

The United States was beginning to gear up for a wartime economy before Pearl Harbor. After the attack, production of war materiel and development of new weapons, such as the bazooka rocket launcher, were greatly stepped up. Factories built nearly 300,000 planes, 100,000 tanks, and about 3 million machine guns in five years. How was the economy changed by the emphasis on military production?

War and Technology

When the minutemen mustered on Lexington Green in 1775, they formed neat rows and readied their muskets to do battle with the British. During the American Revolution, both sides relied chiefly on muskets (heavy shoulder guns with a range of about 100 yards, or 90 meters), bayonets (long blades attached to the guns), and cannon. Some Americans were fortunate enough to carry Kentucky rifles, which had been invented by German gunsmiths in Pennsylvania. The lighter weight and increased accuracy of these rifles made them much more practical for use on the frontier.

The soldiers who fought in the American Revolution could not have imagined the changes that technology would produce in warfare over the next 200 years. When they fought, they could see and hear the enemy. By the time World War II was over, thousands of people who were too far away to be seen could be killed by a single bomb dropped from the air.

The American Civil War has been called the first conflict of the technological age. Both sides carried Springfield rifles, which had a range of about 250 yards (229 meters). These were still relatively primitive muzzle-loading, one-shot guns. Battles were often won by the soldiers who could load and fire more quickly than the enemy. However, more advanced breech-loading rifles (loaded at the rear of the bore, so that the rifle did not have to be turned around) were used by Union cavalry. The first machine gun, the Gatling, was also introduced during the Civil War. In addition, both sides made use of railroads for moving troops and supplies, telegraph cables for field communications, ironclad warships, and observation balloons.

The deadlier weapons of the Civil War proved that mass charges were doomed. By the time of World War I, trench warfare had become standard. Trench warfare involved the use of heavy artillery, grenades, flame throwers, tanks, missiles, and poison gas. Other major developments of the war included the submarine and the wireless telegraph.

World War I also saw the beginning of an entirely new kind of battle—the battle in the air. At the beginning of the war, airplanes were used for reconnaissance. Until radios were fitted, pilots had to land to deliver their reports, or else drop messages on headquarters. Along with the use of airplanes for reconnaissance went the development of aerial photography, which made the art of camouflage very important.

Meanwhile, with both sides flying over enemy territory, the pilots soon started their own war. At first they shot at each other with rifles or handguns. Later the planes were mounted with machine guns.

During World War II, science was organized more systematically than ever before in the interests of war. Many new developments were made in both offensive and defensive technology. But one weapon—the atomic bomb—was so much more devastating than any previous weapon that the difference became one of kind rather than degree. As Albert Einstein said:

> *The unleashed power of the atom has changed everything save our modes of thinking, and thus we drift toward unparalleled catastrophes.*

Since the last world war, much more sophisticated nuclear weapons have been developed. The bomb dropped on Hiroshima had a destructive power equal to about 20 kilotons (thousands of tons) of dynamite. Today's bombs are measured in megatons (millions of tons), and can be delivered not only by long-range bombers but also by missiles fired from submarines or underground silos. Nuclear weapons are possessed by several different countries, and several others await the opportunity to join the ranks of nuclear powers. The world now lives in fear that a nuclear war might mean the extinction of human life.

QUESTIONS

1. What weapons were used during the Revolution?
2. What technology developed in World War I?
3. Why is nuclear warfare different from earlier forms of warfare?

development of such weapons as high-speed missiles and short-range rockets. Because of the efforts of the OSRD, Allied scientists began to catch up by the end of 1942. They developed the bazooka rocket launcher, which allowed two soldiers to destroy a tank, and the proximity fuse, which allowed a shell to be exploded when it came within a certain distance of its target. They also developed **radar,** radio detecting and ranging equipment that used high-frequency radio waves to detect and determine the position, velocity, and other characteristics of airplanes and ships. Another development was **sonar,** a sound navigation ranging apparatus that used transmitted and reflected soundwaves to detect and locate underwater objects such as submarines.

The War Production Board. Another important agency was the War Production Board (WPB), created in January 1942 to maximize the production of war materials. Roosevelt decided to form the WPB for two reasons. One was a nationwide call for a single director of the war effort with enough power to do whatever was necessary. The other was a Senate investigating committee report that called the war production effort "an unholy mess."

Roosevelt chose Donald M. Nelson of Missouri as the head of the WPB. As head of the WPB, Nelson had more authority than any other American except the President himself. He could commandeer materials and assign priorities for their use. He could also order plants to be converted and expanded for war use and bar the manufacture of goods he did not feel were essential to the war effort.

Within a few weeks after the WPB was created, the manufacture of more than 300 products was curtailed or banned as nonessential. Included were such items as refrigerators, bicycles, beer cans, toothpaste tubes, and metal caskets. Their manufacturers were told to make do with substitute materials or start manufacturing essential items instead.

Under the new demand, some industries underwent major transformations. The automobile industry, for example, was told to stop making cars and trucks and use its assembly lines to produce tanks and other war matériel instead. In addition, new industries sprang up overnight. The synthetic rubber industry, for example, became of major importance when America's rubber supply from the Dutch East Indies and Malaya was cut off by the war.

By the end of 1942, 33 percent of the economy—15 percent more than the year before—was devoted to the production of military goods. Further, America's production of vital war goods matched the total output of Germany, Italy, and Japan combined.

The Economy. America's war effort required a huge increase in government spending. To get the funds it needed, the government levied taxes and borrowed money. War bonds were sold in denominations ranging from $25 to $10,000.

The economy, however, was out of kilter. Because more people had jobs than before, most Americans had more money to spend. But so much industry was devoted to the production of military goods that consumer goods became relatively scarce. As a result, prices of consumer goods soared.

Early in 1942, Congress passed the Emergency Price Control Act, which established the Office of Price Administration (OPA). Its job was to control inflation. At first the agency tried to do this by setting price ceilings on all commodities except farm products and by controlling rents in defense areas. But with farm products exempted, prices kept rising. This led workers to demand higher wages, which compounded the problem.

Next, the OPA instituted nationwide **rationing,** a system of distributing scarce goods, in an effort to keep a lid on inflation and see that everyone got a fair share of goods that were in short supply. The first

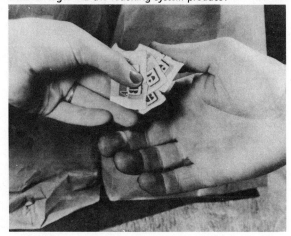

Ration stamps were used during World War II in an attempt to distribute essential goods fairly. Meat, butter, sugar, and gasoline were among the items that were rationed. What abuses and disadvantages did the rationing system produce?

Have students discuss why action was taken against the Japanese although they were fewer in number than German and Italian immigrants.

thing to be rationed under this program was sugar. Next came coffee, then gasoline, and then fuel oil. By the end of the war, 20 different items had been rationed, including meat, fats and oils, butter, cheese, processed foods, and shoes. Ration books containing stamps or coupons were given to each family. The coupons were required as part of the purchase of rationed items.

Before long, however, a **black market** (an illegal market) began to grow in meat, gasoline, and other rationed items. Organized crime also got involved. Despite the government's efforts to outwit them, black marketeers still managed to print and sell counterfeit ration stamps.

Another government agency, the National War Labor Board (NWLB), tried to help the OPA keep down inflation. Its main purpose, however, was to settle labor disputes by mediation and arbitration and thus to prevent strikes. In July the NWLB came out with the "Little Steel" formula. This formula tied wage increases to the rise in the cost of living since January 1941.

Despite all these efforts, prices still rose—but not at the rate or to the level they otherwise could have. In addition, rationing acted as a daily reminder that the United States was at war and made the people feel that the inconveniences, shortages, and sacrifices they had to endure were their contributions to the war effort.

Defense and National Security. The attack on Pearl Harbor made Americans think about national security and defense. The Roosevelt administration turned to Latin America, promoting a united front and hemispheric solidarity. Starting in January 1942 with the Rio de Janeiro Conference, representatives from the United States and Latin America met again and again in friendship.

From these meetings came the pledge of all Latin American countries, except Chile and Argentina, to sever relations with the Axis. Another result was the Act of Chapultepec, a regional security pact stating that aggression on one American state would be viewed as aggression against all, and that armed force could be used to "prevent or repel aggression."

The Roosevelt administration also set up an Office of Civilian Defense (OCD). The job of the OCD was to protect citizens in the event of an air attack and to enroll them in war-related community activities. The

OCD urged families to make themselves into "a fighting unit on the home front," to conserve food, to salvage essential materials, to buy war bonds regularly, and not to "spread rumors designed to divide our Nation."

During this period, suspicion rose concerning the 900,000 **"enemy aliens"**—people of Japanese, German, or Italian birth who lived in the United States but who were not American citizens. The greatest amount of suspicion was focused on the Japanese, who had been regarded with hostility even before the war. Those living in California, Oregon, Washington, and Arizona were especially affected, because many Americans in those areas believed that with the Pacific Fleet crippled, they were vulnerable at any moment to a Japanese invasion.

In California, in particular, many Americans allowed this fear to prejudice their thinking about anyone and everyone of Japanese heritage. California Attorney General Earl Warren went so far as to urge that, in the interest of national security, all Californians of Japanese descent be sent to relocation centers away from the coast where they could be under army supervision.

As the pressure mounted for action against Japanese-Americans, Roosevelt felt he had to act. On February 19 he signed an executive order authorizing the Secretary of War to prescribe certain "military areas" from which "any or all" persons could be kept. Although the Japanese-Americans were not actually named, everyone knew that the order was aimed at them.

Under this order, 112,000 Japanese-Americans, more than one-half of whom were American citizens, were sent to special assembly centers. From there they were eventually taken to permanent camps in isolated areas, where most of them had to stay for the next three years or so. The evacuation order had come swiftly, and many of them had as little as 48 hours to sell their homes, businesses, and farms. Because of this, they ended up disposing of their property at a loss or abandoning it completely. One author described their plight:

> *One day these Japanese-Americans were free citizens and residents of communities, law-abiding, productive, proud. The next, they were inmates of cramped, crowded American-style concentration camps, under*

Relocation was one of several ways Japanese-Americans were deprived of rights. They were dismissed from civil service jobs. Many doctors and lawyers had their licenses revoked. In some California communities, Japanese-Americans were banned from all jobs and were unable to shop for groceries, cash checks, or be insured.

armed guard, fed like prisoners in mess hall lines, deprived of privacy and dignity, shorn of all their rights. . . .

Rain made the camp areas a quagmire through which the evacuees had to wade to get to the central toilets and mess halls. Summer's heat turned the shacks into bake ovens. . . . The partitions between units in most cases did not go up to the ceiling; a child wailing at one end of a 100-foot long barracks disturbed everyone.

In the camps, the Japanese-Americans were put to work, generally at menial, low-paying jobs. They also found that they had to help run the camps in order to prevent total chaos. One evacuee explained why and how he helped:

I was quite bitter when I went into the Santa Anita Assembly Center and had decided to simply sit out the war and not lift a finger. . . . After the first week, seeing the chaos and confusion, I couldn't sit back any longer. I took it upon myself to talk to a number of friends and got their support to suggest a self-government program to help the Caucasian administrators. We divided the camp into eighteen districts and held open elections for district representatives. I was elected representative in my district, and then elected chairman of the council. . . . One day the military guards ordered a crackdown on "weapons," and went from family to family picking up anything they considered dangerous—kitchen knives, scissors, even crochet and knitting needles and hotplates mothers were using to warm milk for their babies. We not only were able to get the confiscation order tempered, but we persuaded the administration to set up milk stations instead of each family trying to handle its own.

Almost all of the Japanese-Americans cooperated with the evacuation order and never lost their loyalty to the United States. Ironically, those who were American citizens were subject to the draft. More than 8000 Nisei (second-generation Japanese-Americans) were drafted and more than 9000 others volunteered to serve in the armed forces. The 442nd

During World War II, persons of Japanese descent were sent to relocation camps in Arkansas, Utah, Colorado, and other inland states. More than 71,000 were Nisei, or American-born. Why was there little public reaction against this practice?

Regimental Combat Team, made up almost entirely of Nisei, was the most decorated combat force in the army during the war.

Attempts to have the evacuation declared unconstitutional were not successful. In December 1944 the Supreme Court in *Korematsu* v. *the United States* upheld the government's right to act as it did on the ground of military security. At the same time, however, the Court ruled that a person whose loyalty had been proved could not be held.

SECTION REVIEW

1. Identify the following: Operation Torch, Douglas MacArthur, Vannebar Bush, Donald M. Nelson, Act of Chapultepec, Earl Warren.
2. Why were the Soviets fighting alone on Europe's eastern front?
3. Why was the Pacific Ocean in 1942 called a "Japanese lake"?
4. What was the significance of the Battle of Midway?
5. What was the function of the OSRD?
6. What caused inflation in the United States?
7. How did most Japanese-Americans react to their forced evacuation?

2 Turning the Tide: 1943

By 1943 Americans were beginning to see changes taking place in both the Pacific and European theaters of war. In mid-January Roosevelt and Churchill met with other Allied leaders in French Morocco at the Casablanca Conference. Stalin had been invited but could not attend. During the conference, it was decided that the Allies would keep fighting until the enemy surrendered unconditionally. A decision was also made to open a second front and to name General Dwight D. Eisenhower Supreme Commander of the North African theater.

Inroads in the Pacific and the Far East

In the Pacific the battle raged on, but now it was the Allies who were scoring victories and advancing. In March 1943 the Battle of the Bismarck Sea took place when Australian and American planes attacked a huge Japanese naval force carrying troops and supplies to the east coast of New Guinea. The Japanese lost 12 troop ships and 10 warships. At about the same time, they also lost one of their most important leaders—Admiral Isoroku Yamamoto, Commander-in-Chief of the combined fleet—when the plane in which he was traveling was shot down.

Three months later American forces began their offensive in the South Pacific, where by October they gained control of the waters adjacent to the Solomons. On November 1 marines landed at Bougainville, the largest island in the Solomons. At the naval Battle of Empress Augusta Bay, which took place the next day, the Japanese again were defeated. The defeat allowed the Allies to cut Japanese supply lines, isolate the enemy forces left in the Solomons, and secure the American flank for an advance toward the Philippines.

The American strategy was to get within effective bombing distance of Japan. While ground troops crept forward under MacArthur's command, naval forces advanced under Admiral Chester W. Nimitz, Commander in Chief of the Pacific fleet. Nimitz's plan was to capture islands in the Central Pacific—the Solomons, Gilberts, Marshalls, Marianas, and Bonin Islands. On November 21 landings were made on

In the Far East, control of the 700-mile Burma Road, used to transport supplies to China, was tactically important. At stake in the Burma-India theater was the fate of China and control of the natural resources of the area. What was the main Allied strategy in the Pacific and Far East?

Makin and Tarawa, two heavily fortified Japanese outposts in the Gilberts. Although the Americans secured the islands within a few days, the cost was high—more than 900 marines killed and missing and over 2000 wounded.

That same month, Roosevelt, Churchill, Chinese leader Generalissimo Chiang Kai-shek, and Madam Chiang Kai-shek met in Cairo to discuss the war in the Far East. Out of this conference came the Cairo Declaration, in which they all pledged to fight for Japan's unconditional surrender. They also agreed that Japan would be deprived of all the territory it had acquired since 1914, that the territory originally belonging to China would be returned, and that in time Korea would become free and independent.

Progress in the Mediterranean and Europe

The Allies were also active in the Mediterranean and Europe. In North Africa, American and British forces, working first separately and then together, pushed Rommel and his Afrika Korps into Tunisia. Under the command first of Major General Lloyd R. Fredendall and then of Major General George S. Patton, American forces checked Rommel's drive at Kasserine Pass and took El Guettar and Bizerte. Under General Bernard L. Montgomery, the British took Tripoli and Tunis. By May Rommel had fled,

close to 250,000 Axis troops had surrendered, and the campaign in North Africa was over.

The Axis also suffered severe defeat in Eastern Europe. In January the Soviets freed Leningrad from its 17-month siege. The following month, they forced the German army at Stalingrad, exhausted by months of heavy fighting and by the severe winter, to surrender. From March through December the Soviets pushed forward, retaking city after city. On December 29 they broke the enemy lines west of Kiev, and five days later they entered Poland.

The Invasion of Sicily and Italy. At the Casablanca Conference in January 1943, the Allies

RUSSIAN FRONT, 1941–1944

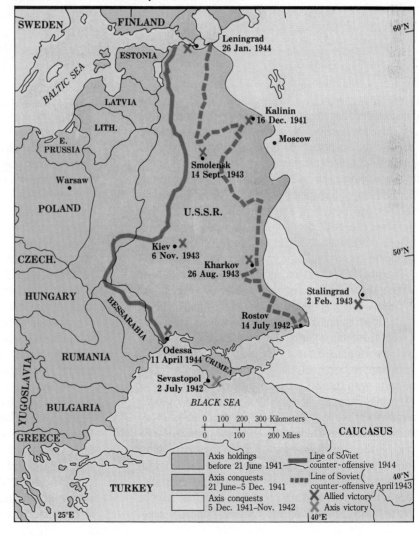

Its willingness to help organize an international organization indicates that the United States rejected isolationism and would assume a strong role in world affairs.

NORTH AFRICAN AND ITALIAN CAMPAIGNS, OCT. 1942–APRIL 1945

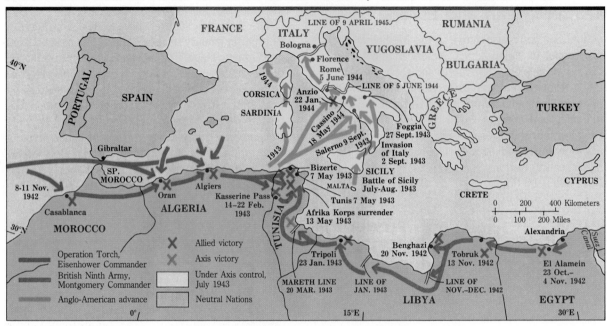

had decided that they could secure the Mediterranean by invading Sicily and Italy. That July, Operation Husky, the Anglo-American invasion of Sicily by sea and air, got underway.

A week after the invasion began, Victor Emmanuel II, the King of Italy, announced that Mussolini and his cabinet had resigned, and that Pietro Badoglio had become the new head of the Italian government. Three days later Badoglio ordered that the Fascist party be dissolved.

Meanwhile, American and British forces had been advancing in Sicily. By the middle of August, its conquest was completed. The taking of Sicily meant that Allied shipping in the Mediterranean would be safer. More importantly, it meant that the Allies now had a springboard for an attack on Italy.

In September 1943, the Allies began their invasion of Italy, with the British coming across the Straits of Messina from Sicily, and the Americans making amphibious landings at Salerno. On September 8 Italy surrendered unconditionally. However, on September 10 the Germans seized Rome. Two days later they helped engineer the escape of Mussolini, who had been interned earlier by the Italian government. The Allies, temporarily stymied by this action, formed an Allied Control Commission for Italy.

Then they kept pushing forward toward the city of Rome.

Plans for the Future. At the same time the fighting was going on, the Allies were meeting to make plans for the future. In May, at the Anglo-American Conference in Washington, D.C., Roosevelt, Churchill, and various British and American military officials discussed the opening of a second front in Europe. They decided that they would invade Normandy, a region of northwest France on the English Channel, in the spring of 1944.

In August 1943 the Allied leaders met again, this time in Quebec. There, they reaffirmed the date for the invasion of Normandy. They also decided to step up military operations in the Far East and formed a Southeast Asia Command with Lord Louis Mountbatten at its head.

Two months later, the first three-power meeting of the war took place in Moscow. There, Secretary of State Cordell Hull, British Foreign Minister Anthony Eden, Soviet Foreign Minister Vyacheslav Molotov, and various military officials established a European Advisory Commission to decide how to deal with Germany after the war ended. They also issued a joint declaration calling for the establishment of "a general international organization, based on the principle of

One reason for black migration to the North was economic. The average salary for blacks in southern cities was $632 a year. A job at a northern war plant could double that figure.

the sovereign equality of all peace-loving states, and open to membership by all such states, large and small, for the maintenance of international peace and security.[1]

Still another meeting, the Teheran Conference, took place in November in Iran. For the first time, Stalin took a personal part in the proceedings. During the four-day conference, several topics were discussed, the major one being the Anglo-American invasion of Western Europe and the timing of it with the Soviet offensive against Germany.

Life at Home

By 1943 the war and all that it entailed had become an accepted fact of life for most Americans. By mid-year, farm prices had been rolled back and wages were generally holding. As a result, the rate of inflation also held fairly steady. This did not mean, however, that there were no problems. The war had brought about some domestic changes that not all Americans were willing to accept.

Minority Migration. The need for increased production and the entry into the military of so many workers had opened up many jobs. This was especially the case in the cities of the North, where industry was concentrated. The lure of jobs brought many blacks to the North, especially after Roosevelt issued an order that nondiscrimination clauses must be incorporated in all war contracts.

This migration, however, ultimately led to racial conflict. The conflict was heightened by the presence in the cities of many southern whites who had also come looking for jobs. Some of these southerners, who had brought with them preconceived notions about the place of blacks, resented black competition in the job market. The southerners fanned the fires of antagonism many northern whites already felt toward blacks. The result was race riots in several cities. The worst riot took place in Detroit late in June 1943. It got so bad that federal troops were called in to restore order. By the time the rioting was brought to an end 36 hours later, 9 whites and 25 blacks had been killed.

[1] After World War II broke out and before Pearl Harbor, Secretary Hull had proposed such a new international organization. Roosevelt, determined to avoid Wilson's mistakes with the League of Nations, encouraged Hull to include prominent Republicans in the planning. In March 1943 a bipartisan Senate group introduced a resolution calling for United States leadership in forming an international organization.

A parallel situation existed in California, where many Mexican-Americans from rural areas of Texas, New Mexico, and Arizona had migrated in search of work. In early June 1943, matters came to a head in Los Angeles. White sailors on leave clashed with *pachucos,* teenage Mexican-Americans, wearing "zoot suits"—full-legged, tight-cuffed trousers and a long coat with heavily padded shoulders and wide lapels. When a rumor spread that a gang of *pachucos* had beaten up a sailor, more than 2000 soldiers and sailors gathered and began beating some 100 young Mexican-Americans, ripping off their zoot suits. The "Zoot Suit Riots" went on until military authorities placed Los Angeles off limits to members of the armed services.

At the time, much of the press and the public blamed the incident on unruly Mexican-American street gangs. Later investigations, however, suggested that the sailors had provoked the incident.

The Role of Women. As the war progressed, women found their roles changing. An act had been passed in 1942 enlisting women for noncombat duties in various branches of the military. More than 250,000 volunteered to serve in the Women's Auxiliary Army Corps (WAAC) and the Women

Women working at formerly all-male jobs were a common sight in plants during World War II. Over 2 million women were working in war industries by 1943. How did the role of women change during the war effort?

Women served as pilots delivering planes and cargo. However, women in the military did not receive the benefits given to male veterans after the war.

Appointed for Voluntary Emergency Service (WAVES).

Even more women, however, entered the civilian labor force. In the work world, women were more in demand than ever before. They were encouraged, and at times even badgered, to enter new spheres of work, many of which had been viewed in the past as unfeminine. The government itself encouraged women to work in the construction industry or on assembly lines turning out tanks and airplanes. The call for women to enter war work was repeated again and again on the radio. Before long, "Rosie the Riveter," a woman dressed in overalls depicted in Lockheed Aircraft's posters, became a national symbol of women's vital role in the war effort.

In a 1943 magazine article, one woman told about her experiences as a new defense worker:

> When I reached the shipyards . . . I was borne along by the crowd and permitted to enter through the guarded gate when I had shown my temporary pass. I stood in a long line to receive papers; I stood in another line to receive tool checks. . . . At last some sixty of us women were herded to a personnel building, where a young man addressed us on safety precautions, the woman counselor for the day shift advised us about our clothing, and then, after a tour of the yards, we were divided into the trades for which we had been employed. The names of the welders were called. . . . The burners were selected, the flangers, the chippers, the checkers. Only a sparse group remained to be grouped as shipfitters' helpers—six women besides myself, white and Negro. Again we started out en masse: this time to a little cottage which was labeled "Master Shipfitter." The man upon whom the cottage door opened was small and harrassed. . . .
>
> "What have you got there?" the shipfitter asked.
>
> "Just a few shipfitter helpers, Mr. Jepson."
>
> "Oh, my God! Women shipfitters. Why do they treat me like this? Women shipfitters. . . ."
>
> I had promised myself two months in which to find myself here in the shipyards but my probation was not to last so long. It seemed

> that we, the women, were being assimilated gradually, if slowly. . . . The great need was for experienced workmen, men or women; and time on the job . . . adds up finally to experience. I was given more and more to do. . . . Six weeks from the date of my arrival at the yard I was given a unit to handle by myself.

This new encouragement of women to enter the work force, especially in what had been nontraditional jobs for females, led many men and women to change their perception of women's role in society. Although the majority probably viewed the war as a unique crisis calling for short-term changes only, some women began to question the notion that they were inherently suited only to be homemakers.

Labor and the Economy. Early in 1943, in an effort to maintain production with a shortage of workers, Roosevelt ordered all American war plants to require a minimum work week of 48 hours. Workers, however, were to be paid time-and-a-half for the extra 8 hours.

Shortly afterward, about 500,000 coal miners demanding higher wages went on strike despite the no-strike pledge labor leaders had taken shortly after Pearl Harbor. When the miners would not come to terms, Roosevelt ordered Secretary of the Interior Harold L. Ickes to take over the coal mines. He then threatened to use soldiers to operate the mines.

About a week later, Roosevelt issued a "hold-the-line" order, freezing prices, wages, and salaries. At the same time, the War Manpower Commission (WMC), which had been created in 1942, adopted regulations to "freeze" 27 million workers in defense jobs.

On May 2 the miners' strike was called off, with the miners receiving a small wage increase. The following month, the Smith-Connally Anti-Strike Act was passed. This act made it illegal for a union to strike against any war industry.

SECTION REVIEW

1. Identify the following: Chester W. Nimitz, Cairo Declaration, Operation Husky, Cordell Hull, Smith-Connally Anti-Strike Act.
2. What was the American strategy in the Pacific?
3. What events led to the surrender of Italy?
4. Why did a labor shortage exist during the war?

UNIVERSAL
DECLARATION
OF
HUMAN
RIGHTS

Eleanor Roosevelt

Anna Eleanor Roosevelt, born in 1884, was the niece of President Theodore Roosevelt. In 1905 she married a distant cousin, Franklin Delano Roosevelt, and embarked on a career that made her famous around the world.

Franklin Roosevelt was already deeply involved in politics when he was stricken with polio in 1921.

Despite the best of care, it was soon evident that he would never walk again. Eleanor Roosevelt began political work in his behalf. She also campaigned vigorously for causes she personally favored, such as the rights of women in labor unions.

When her husband became President, she served as his advisor, traveling throughout the country on fact-finding missions. During World War II, her travels took her to Europe, Latin America, and various other parts of the world. She became a strong advocate of rights for minorities and other humanitarian concerns and began holding her own press conferences, to which only women reporters were invited. She also had her own radio program and her own syndicated newspaper column. She was one of the most greatly admired first ladies in American history.

After her husband's death in 1945, Eleanor Roosevelt offered President Truman her help. Truman accepted her offer and appointed her as delegate to the newly created United Nations. In 1946, she was elected chairperson of the UN's Human Rights Commission. In this position she helped to write the Universal Declaration of Human Rights. She continued to work with the UN until her death in 1962.

3 On the Offensive: 1944

In the United States, the year 1944 brought another presidential election. Roosevelt ran for a fourth term of office. Because he was visibly aging, the Democrats were especially concerned about choosing a candidate for Vice President. Different factions of the party pushed their favorites. Out of this party in-fighting came Roosevelt's suggestion for a compromise candidate, Senator Harry S Truman of Missouri.

Roosevelt faced strong criticism from both conservatives and liberals. Conservatives felt that his New Deal policies were destroying the very fibre of the nation, while liberals resented his lukewarm support of labor and civil rights. In addition, there

were many who felt that 12 years was more than enough for any one man to lead the nation.

The Republican candidate was New York Governor Thomas E. Dewey. His moderate views were balanced by those of his conservative running mate, Governor John W. Bricker of Ohio.

Although the campaign was spirited, it failed to generate much controversy, and Roosevelt once again proved that he had not lost his appeal. Many people voted for him because of his experienced war leadership. He won the election with 25.6 million popular votes and 432 electoral votes, compared to Dewey's 22 million popular votes and 99 electoral votes.

The election notwithstanding, the war remained the major issue on everyone's mind. Almost every

One reason for the success in the Pacific was the use of a tactic called "leapfrogging," which included evacuating territory and attacking in what appeared to be random fashion.

General Douglas MacArthur wades ashore at Leyte Island, in the Philippines, fulfilling his pledge to return. Accompanying MacArthur were 600 ships and 250,000 troops. The Japanese keyed their defense of the Philippines by attacking transports and supply ships. Why was the Battle of Leyte Island an important confrontation?

American had a relative or a friend fighting somewhere overseas. In 1944, however, the news was good for the most part. At long last the Allies were definitely on the offensive.

Action In the Pacific

In January 1944, the Allies intensified their efforts in the Pacific, invading and taking one island after another. By June the Americans had started an air offensive against the Japanese home islands. That same month, MacArthur and Nimitz began their Philippines campaign, and the naval and air battle of the Philippine Sea took place. As in the Coral Sea, all the fighting was done in the air by carrier-based planes. Japanese costs were high, as carriers and planes were lost, and battleships and cruisers were crippled. Shortly afterward, Japanese Premier Tojo and the entire Japanese cabinet resigned.

On October 20 MacArthur, keeping a promise made to the Filipinos when he left in 1942, returned to invade the central Philippine island of Leyte. Three days later, the naval Battle of Leyte Gulf began. The last and greatest naval engagement of the war, it cost the Japanese most of their remaining sea power. Even more importantly, the Americans now controlled the Philippine waters once again.

Toward Victory in Europe

January 1944 was a busy month on the western front as the Allies began their air offensive from the British Isles and General Eisenhower arrived in Great Britain to set up SHAEF, the Supreme Headquarters of the Allied Expeditionary Forces. All of this was in preparation for Operation Overlord, the invasion of Normandy decided upon at the 1943 Anglo-American Conference. Because it was to be the largest amphibious invasion of the war—and of history— great care had been taken to prepare for it. In his work *The Longest Day,* author Cornelius Ryan described the preparations in this way:

The build-up was enormous. Even before the plan reached its final form an unprecedented flow of men and supplies began pouring into England. Soon there were so many Americans in the small towns and villages that the British who lived there were often hopelessly out-numbered. . . .

By May southern England looked like a huge arsenal. Hidden in the forests were mountainous piles of ammunition. Stretching across the moors, bumper to bumper, were tanks, half-tracks, armored cars, trucks, jeeps,

D-Day was postponed from the beginning of May until early June in order to produce the landing crafts.

and ambulances. . . . In the fields were long lines of howitzers and antiaircraft guns, great quantities of prefabricated materials . . . , and huge stocks of earth-moving equipment. . . . At central depots there were immense quantities of food, clothing, and medical supplies. . . . But the most staggering sight of all were the valleys filled with long lines of railroad rolling stock. . . .

There were also strange new devices of war. There were tanks that could swim, others that

carried great rolls of lath to be used in antitank ditches or as stepping stones over walls, and yet others equipped with great chain flails that beat the ground in front of them to explode mines. There were flat, block-long ships, each carrying a forest of pipes for the launching of warfare's newest weapon, rockets. Perhaps strangest of all were two man-made harbors that were to be towed across to the Normandy beaches. They were engineering miracles and one of the big Overlord secrets;

ALLIED OFFENSIVE IN EUROPE, JUNE 1944–MAY 1945

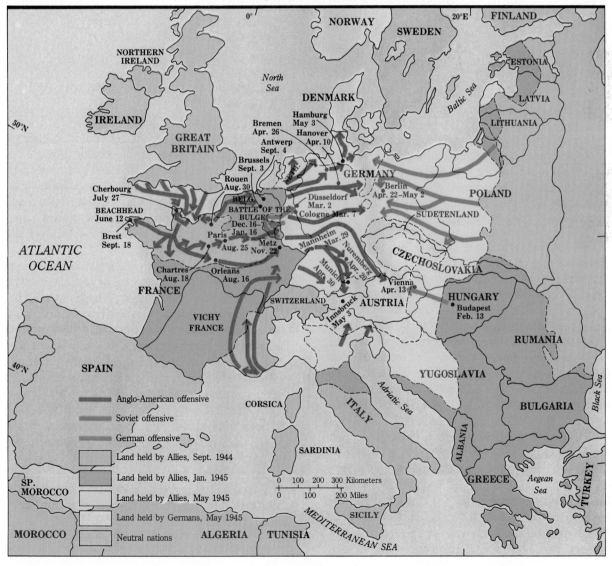

Hitler thought at first that the invasion would come at Normandy, but was persuaded to change his mind.

France also had collaborationists, those who cooperated or sympathized with the Nazis.

A sentry checks the identification papers of a driver during the Battle of the Bulge, one of the harshest battles of the war. The Allies sought to withstand a German blitz in the Ardennes Forest, but were gradually pushed back. Finally, the Allies stopped the last German offensive of the war, and ultimately regained the territory they had lost. Why was the Battle of the Bulge significant?

they assured the constant flow of men and supplies into the beachhead during the first critical weeks until a port could be captured. . . . In position off the invasion beaches of Normandy, each harbor would be the size of the port of Dover.

The invasion took place on June 6, 1944—D-Day—along a 60-mile (96-kilometer) line of the Normandy coast, extending from the mouth of the Orne River to beaches near Ste.-Mère-Église on the Cotentin Peninsula. Although the Germans knew the attack was coming, they could not figure out where. Thus they were taken by surprise when the Anglo-American forces landed. To retaliate, the Germans began bombing southern England with V-1's, jet-propelled guided missiles carrying a ton of explosives and traveling at 350 miles (560 kilometers) an hour. The rockets were launched from special sites in France and Belgium. Their chief target was London.

The bombings, however, did not deter the Allies. By early July more than 1 million Allied troops had landed on the continent, and northern France had become the channel for a massive infusion of fresh forces and supplies. For nearly six weeks, the Allied advance was slowed by a combination of German

resistance, bad weather, and rough terrain.[2] But on July 18, the Americans finally broke through the German lines at St. Lo, which linked Normandy with Brittany, a French province on a peninsula extending into the Atlantic between the English Channel and Bay of Biscay. By early August they had taken Brittany. Operation Overlord was over, and the Battle of France began.

On August 25, 1944, the Allies marched into Paris and liberated it from four years of German occupation. Eisenhower had planned to bypass Paris, but changed his mind when the French **underground** (secret organization formed to resist the Germans) led a popular uprising in Paris. In early September, Allied forces, now numbering over 2 million, liberated the cities of Brussels and Antwerp and the countries of Belgium and Luxembourg. By then, the Germans had started bombing London with their first V-2's— missiles with almost ten times the speed of the V-1's—and, Hitler had survived an assassination plot by some of his generals.

In early September, the Allies undertook an assault on Germany itself, pressing forward all through the fall. In October they took Aachen, their first large

---

[2] Thick hedgerows stalled Allied vehicles until cutting blades were installed on the front ends of tanks.

Note the efforts to prevent a repeat of the economic chaos that followed World War I.

German city. In December, however, the Germans launched a counteroffensive in the Ardennes, a forested plateau in northeastern France, southeastern Belgium, and Luxembourg. There, inexperienced and overstrained American troops were trying to hold the Belgian border area. The battle that ensued was known as the Battle of the Bulge because the Germans broke through the Allied lines, causing a dangerous "bulge" in them. The German drive was eventually checked, largely because of the Allied defense of Bastogne. There, the Allies stood firm and refused to surrender, suffering a major setback because of heavy losses.

At the same time the Allies were fighting in France, they also were advancing in Italy and in Eastern Europe. In late January 1944, months before D-Day, Anglo-American forces landed at Anzio, a port town about 30 miles (48 kilometers) south of Rome, in an effort to outflank the German defenses in southern Italy. By early June, they had liberated Rome. By August Florence had also been taken.

Meanwhile, the Soviets cleared the Germans from the Moscow-Leningrad area and retook several Soviet cities. On December 29, 1944, they entered Budapest. The war in Europe was drawing to a close.

Postwar Plans

While the battle against the Axis raged, Allied leaders held a series of conferences to discuss strategies and prepare for peace. The first of these, the Bretton Woods Conference, was held in July 1944 at Bretton Woods, New Hampshire, and was attended by 44 countries. There, an International Monetary Fund was set up to help stabilize national currencies and promote world trade. At the same time, an International Bank for Reconstruction and Development was established to aid economic development around the world.

The next month, the Dumbarton Oaks Conference began just outside Washington, D.C. At this conference, representatives of the United States, Great Britain, the Soviet Union, and China laid the groundwork for the Charter of the United Nations, a permanent international organization that would maintain peace and security after the war.

In September a second Quebec Conference was held at which Roosevelt and Churchill discussed plans for the final defeat of Germany and Japan and the conduct of the postwar occupation. The next month, the final conference of the year was held in Moscow. There, Churchill and Stalin divided the Balkans into British and Soviet spheres. Since Roosevelt did not attend the meetings, however, he refused to be bound by what had been decided at them.

SECTION REVIEW

1. Identify the following: Thomas E. Dewey, Operation Overlord, Battle of the Bulge.
2. How did the Germans react to the invasion of Normandy?
3. What was accomplished at the Bretton Woods Conference?

4 Days of Victory: 1945

In February 1945, American troops penetrated the Ruhr Valley. The next month, they crossed the Rhine River and took Mannheim and Frankford am Main. As they went, they liberated the concentration camps at which the Nazis had murdered about 12 million civilians, including 6 million Jews. The mass murder of European Jews became known as the Holocaust. The Nazis had carried out a policy of **genocide,** or racial destruction, against the Jews.

On April 11 the Allies reached the Elbe River. Two weeks later they met with Soviet troops at Torgeau on the Elbe.[3] Germany had finally been crushed.

May 8, 1945 was V-E Day—Victory in Europe Day, when the war in Europe came formally to an end, and the celebrations could be heard worldwide. By then, Mussolini had been captured while trying to escape to Switzerland and had been shot by Italian partisans in Dongo, an Italian town on Lake Como. In Berlin, Hitler had committed suicide in a **bunker,** a fortified chamber below the ground. Berlin had fallen, and, in the Allied headquarters at Rheims, France, Germany signed a formal unconditional surrender.

The war in the Pacific, however, was not yet over. The Japanese still had 5 million dedicated soldiers willing to fight and die for their country.

---

[3] The Allies could have moved farther eastward and reached Berlin and Prague before the Russians, which would have given the West a political advantage in Europe after the war, but would have cost lives.

One reason for the division of Germany was to make it impossible for another militarist leader to gain power.

Discuss with students why Americans found the kamilkaze method so unthinkable.

The Yalta Conference

In February 1945 Roosevelt, Churchill, Stalin, and their chief advisors met at Yalta, a port in the southern Crimea on the Black Sea. Their purpose was to discuss the problems that would confront them in the postwar world.

Out of this meeting came the Yalta Agreement, in which Stalin agreed to enter the war against Japan within three month's of Germany's surrender in return for varying degrees of control over Outer Mongolia, Manchuria, Korea, and several Japanese-held islands off the Soviet coast. In return for the eastern half of Poland, Stalin also agreed to hold free elections in occupied Eastern Europe. In addition, it was agreed that Germany was to be divided into four zones of occupation—American, British, French, and Soviet. Germany's former capital of Berlin, located in the Soviet zone, was likewise to be divided into four zones. Also, it was decided to ask China and France to join in sponsoring a conference to found the United Nations. The conference was to be convened in San Francisco on April 25, 1945.

The Yalta Agreement became one of the most controversial aspects of Roosevelt's Presidency. Critics accused Roosevelt of selling out to the Soviets, allowing them to dominate whole countries in return for little and unnecessary aid in defeating Japan

and empty promises of free elections. Roosevelt's supporters, however, point out that at the time of the conference, Soviet aid in Asia seemed very important. Further, because the Soviets already occupied most of the Asian and Eastern European territory allowed them, America and Great Britain had few means short of war to regain the areas.

The Japanese Holdout

Between January and early August 1945, one battle followed another in the struggle for the Pacific. Two of the most bitter battles were fought on the islands of Iwo Jima and Okinawa. The purpose of taking these islands was to bring the Allies' medium bombers within range of the Japanese homeland.

In trying to take the islands, however, the Allied forces faced more than just the usual dangers of landing on open beaches where they were vulnerable to enemy fire. They also were confronted with the **kamikazes,** specially trained Japanese pilots willing to sacrifice their lives to cause damage to the enemy. They did this by deliberately crashing their airplanes into Allied ships and land positions.

The battle for Iwo Jima lasted from February 19 to March 17. The one for Okinawa went on from April 1 until June 21. Although the Americans won both

Allied leaders Winston Churchill, Franklin Roosevelt, and Joseph Stalin met at Yalta on the southern coast of the Crimean Peninsula to discuss Soviet entry in the war against Japan, occupation of Germany, and creation of an international peace organization. Several agreements were reached. Why were some observers critical of these agreements?

The emigration to the West by scientists such as Albert Einstein, Enrico Fermi, and Lise Meitner helped develop Allied science and technology.

PACIFIC THEATER, 1941–1945

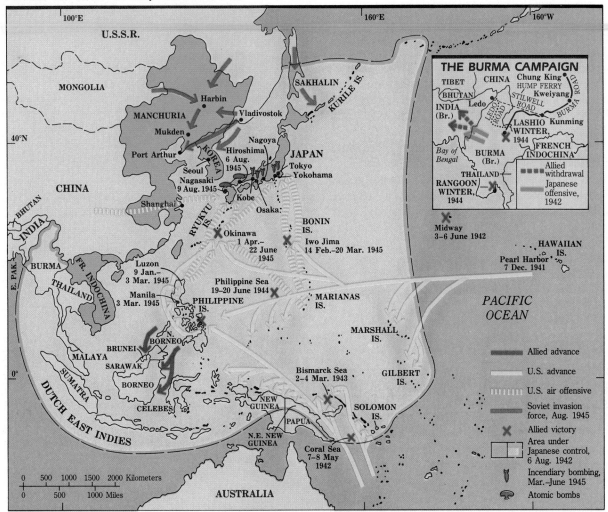

battles, the cost was high—more than 15,000 dead and nearly 40,000 wounded. These victories, however, made it possible for the Allies to step up their direct assaults on Japan itself.

The assaults, which had begun in May, were the greatest in the Pacific and Far East war. Still, when the United States, Great Britain, and China demanded late in July that Japan surrender unconditionally, the Japanese refused.

The Atomic Bomb

When the Japanese refused to surrender, the Americans, reluctant to engage in still another costly

and bloody assault,[4] turned to a powerful new weapon. The new weapon was the **atomic bomb,** a bomb whose destructive force is caused by the release of energy resulting from the splitting of atoms. American scientists had been working on the bomb since 1942. In 1939 physicist Albert Einstein had warned Roosevelt that German scientists had split the atom, the first crucial step in the development of a potentially awesome new weapon. Einstein urged that the United States develop a bomb first. Roosevelt took his advice and authorized the spending of $2 billion for the project.

---

[4] Military experts estimated that an invasion of Japan would result in 500,000 to 1,000,000 American casualties.

Under the code name of Manhattan Project, an all-out effort was launched to build the bomb. In 1945, under the direction of physicist J. Robert Oppenheimer, the first bomb was built at the Los Alamos Atomic Laboratories, a top-secret plant located in an isolated area not far from Santa Fe, New Mexico.

On July 16, 1945, the bomb was tested atop a steel tower in a lonely desert track at Alamogordo, New Mexico called *Jorada del Muerto,* Journey of Death. The results exceeded everyone's expectations.

President Truman, who had taken office after President Roosevelt's death on April 12, received word of the test results in Potsdam, Germany where he was in conference with Churchill, Stalin, and their top advisors.[5] Truman had not been informed about the Manhattan Project or the bomb until after he had become President. Roosevelt had told Churchill about it, but Stalin still did not know. When Stalin heard about the new weapon, he told Truman that he hoped the United States would "make good use of it against the Japanese."

Surrender of Japan

The United States had warned the Japanese that if they did not surrender, Japan would face "utter destruction." They, however, refused to heed the warning. By this time, then, Truman believed that he had no choice but to use the atomic bomb.

As a result, a special B-29 bomber called *Enola Gay* released the atomic bomb over the city of Hiroshima, a center of the Japanese munitions industry, on August 6, 1945. The bomb destroyed three-quarters of the city and killed or injured more than 160,000 persons.

The Japanese, however, would still not surrender. Therefore, a second bomb was dropped on August 9—this time on the city and naval base of Nagasaki. That same day, in a radio address to the American people, Truman justified his decision:

> I realize the tragic significance of the atomic bomb.

[5] The purpose of the Potsdam Conference was to make concrete plans for the occupation and control of Germany and to settle outstanding territorial questions. Provision was also made for the trial of war criminals. Under this provision, an international court at Nürenburg, Germany, tried Nazi leaders and sentenced a number of them to prison or to death.

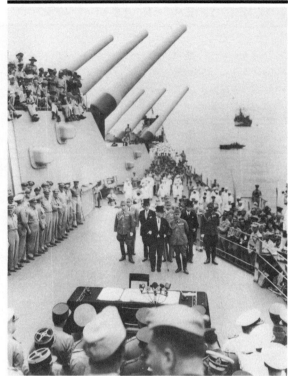

The Japanese delegation, led by Foreign Minister Mamoru Shigemitsu, boards the U.S.S. *Missouri* to sign the declaration of surrender. The ceremonies on September 2, 1945 brought a formal end to World War II. What forced Japan to surrender?

> *Its production and its use were not lightly undertaken by this Government. But we knew that our enemies were on the search for it. We know now how close they were to finding it. And we knew the disaster which would come to this Nation, and to all peace-loving nations, to all civilizations, if they had found it first.*
>
> *That is why we felt compelled to undertake the long and uncertain and costly labor of discovery and production. . . .*
>
> *Having found the bomb we have used it. We have used it against those who attacked us without warning at Pearl Harbor, against those who have starved and beaten and executed American prisoners of war, against those who have abandoned all pretense of obeying international laws of warfare. We have used it in order to shorten the agony of war, in order to save the lives of thousands and thousands of young Americans.*

Fewer soldiers died of disease or bleeding in this war than in World War I because of the availability of blood plasma and penicillin.

Five days after the bombing of Nagasaki, the Japanese government agreed to unconditional surrender. On August 27, American forces began occupying Japan. A week later, the Japanese premier and military leaders signed the formal surrender on board Admiral Nimitz' flagship, the USS *Missouri*, in Tokyo Bay.

The war was finally over, but the cost was even higher than it had been for World War I. Almost 300,000 Americans were dead, and another 700,000 had been wounded. These losses were light, however, compared to those of other combatants. The Soviet Union, for example, saw more than 20 million of its soldiers and civilians die as a result of the war. In financial terms, the United States government had spent more than $320 billion, twice as much as the total amount of money spent during its entire previous existence.

The United Nations

As planned at Yalta, a conference was convened in San Francisco on April 25, 1945, to draft the Charter of the United Nations. The 50 nations represented all took part in formulating the Charter, the organization's governing treaty.

In early June the Charter was completed. It provided for six major bodies, which are still in existence today. The first, a policymaking body called the General Assembly, is made up of all member nations, each of which has a vote. The second is an 11-member Security Council that decides diplomatic,

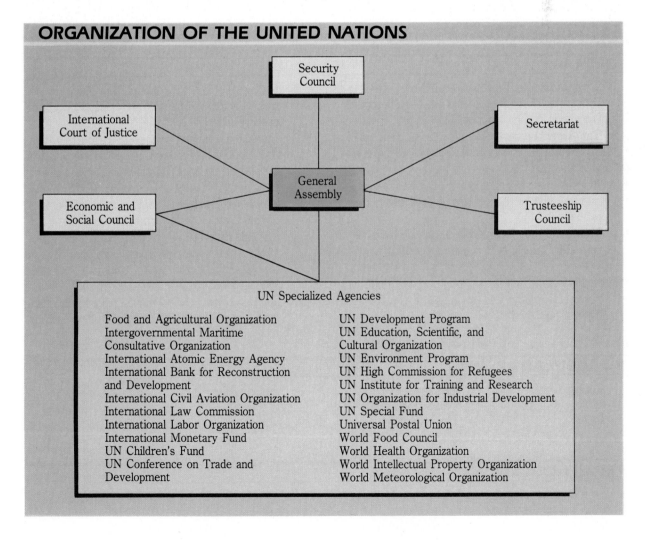

ORGANIZATION OF THE UNITED NATIONS

Security Council

International Court of Justice

Secretariat

General Assembly

Economic and Social Council

Trusteeship Council

UN Specialized Agencies

Food and Agricultural Organization
Intergovernmental Maritime Consultative Organization
International Atomic Energy Agency
International Bank for Reconstruction and Development
International Civil Aviation Organization
International Law Commission
International Labor Organization
International Monetary Fund
UN Children's Fund
UN Conference on Trade and Development

UN Development Program
UN Education, Scientific, and Cultural Organization
UN Environment Program
UN High Commission for Refugees
UN Institute for Training and Research
UN Organization for Industrial Development
UN Special Fund
Universal Postal Union
World Food Council
World Health Organization
World Intellectual Property Organization
World Meteorological Organization

political, and military disputes. The United States, Great Britain, the Soviet Union, France, and China all have permanent seats on the Security Council,[6] while six other members serve two-year terms.

Third is an 18-member Economic and Social Council, which deals with human welfare and fundamental rights and freedoms. Fourth is a 15-judge International Court of Justice that deals with international legal disputes. Fifth is a Trusteeship Council, which is intended to promote the welfare of people in colonial territories and help them toward self-government. Sixth is a Secretariat, headed by a

---

[6] Each of the five permanent members has veto power. This provision removed one of the main American objections to the League of Nations, but also made the Security Council powerless to settle disputes among the permanent members.

Secretary-General, which takes care of the organization's day-to-day administrative work.

On June 26, 1945, all 50 nations signed the United Nations Charter. On July 28, it was ratified by the United States Senate. Optimistically, the American people looked forward to a future in which peace would be preserved through international cooperation. But they were soon to be disillusioned.

SECTION REVIEW

1. Identify the following: V-E Day, Robert J. Oppenheimer, *Enola Gay*, Secretariat.
2. What were the fates of Mussolini and Hitler?
3. What criticism was made of Roosevelt's and Churchill's agreement with Stalin at Yalta?
4. Why was the Manhattan Project undertaken?

CHAPTER 27   REVIEW

SUMMARY

1. When the United States entered World War II in December 1941, it decided to make the defeat of Germany its first priority.
2. The American war effort included a major push for the development of more advanced types of weapons.
3. American society underwent major transformations as the economy was converted to war production.
4. Thousands of Japanese-Americans were interned in special camps for the duration of the war.
5. In 1942 American forces fought in North Africa against Germany and Italy and in the Pacific against Japan.
6. In 1943 the Axis Powers suffered major defeats in the Pacific, in Africa, in Italy, and on Europe's eastern front.
7. Franklin Roosevelt, reelected to a fourth term as President in 1944, died in April 1945 and was succeeded by Vice President Harry Truman.
8. In May 1945 the Germans were finally crushed between Allied forces coming from the west and Soviet forces coming from the east.
9. The Japanese refused to surrender until August 1945, after a new weapon developed by the United States, the atomic bomb, was used against them.
10. Just before the war ended, 50 nations, including the United States, formed the United Nations.

VOCABULARY

amphibious	rationing	underground	kamikaze
radar	black market	genocide	atomic bomb
sonar	enemy aliens	bunker	

REVIEW QUESTIONS

1. Why did military strategists decide to give priority to defeating Germany?
2. How was the American economy affected by the war?

3. What were the major regions in which World War II was fought?

4. How did the war affect women and minority groups?

5. How did the status of the war change between 1942 and 1943?

6. What was the significance of the Allied invasion of Normandy?

7. What postwar plans were made by the Allies, including China and the Soviet Union?

8. Why was the atomic bomb finally used against Japan?

DISCUSSION

1. Was the treatment of Japanese-Americans during World War II justified by the need for national security? Why or why not?

2. Was the position of women in American society improved by the war? Why or why not?

3. Was the decision to use the atomic bomb justified? Why or why not?

4. Does the United Nations promote the national interests of the United States? If so, how? If not, why not?

USING MAPS

Refer to the maps on pages 584 and 593 and answer the following questions:

1. What were the sites of Allied victories in the Pacific?

2. What parts of mainland Asia were under Japanese control as of August 6, 1942?

3. What were the sites of incendiary bombing in Japan?

4. Where did the Allies land during Operation Torch?

5. Where is the Kasserine Pass located?

6. What was the strategic importance of Allied victories in Africa?

USING SKILLS

Refer to President Truman's speech about the atomic bomb on page 594. Which of the following statements best expresses the main idea of Truman's speech? What evidence does he give to support the main idea?

1. The atomic bomb is a tragedy.

2. Developing the bomb was difficult and costly.

3. The Japanese deserved to be bombed.

4. Using the bomb was justified.

5. Our enemies were also trying to make an atomic bomb.

1	Origins of the Cold War	599
2	Containment in Europe	602
3	Containment in Asia	606
4	Cold War "Thaw"	613

THE COLD WAR

Let every nation know, whether it wishes us well or ill, that we shall pay any price, bear any burden, meet any hardship, support any friend, oppose any foes, in order to assure the survival and success of liberty. This much we pledge—and more.

JOHN F. KENNEDY

At the end of World War II, the United States emerged as the most powerful nation in the world. However, it soon faced a growing challenge from its wartime ally, the Soviet Union. Differences in ideology and policy pulled the two countries apart and eventually led to a struggle between them known as the *Cold War*.[1] Each nation sought world influence by means short of total war, such as the threat of force, the use of propaganda, and the sending of military and economic aid to weaker nations.

1 Origins of the Cold War

The Cold War became the focus of United States foreign policy during the late 1940's and early 1950's. This period is often called the era of **bipolarism,** or the dominance of world affairs by two superpowers. The superpower rivalry divided much of the world into two blocs: the free world (or western) countries, led by the United States, and the communist (or eastern) countries led by the Soviet Union.

During the bipolar era, relations between the superpowers were very tense. The United States and its allies feared the threat of communist expansion and tried to control world events in the West's favor. At the same time, the Soviet Union and its allies looked for opportunities to advance their own influence at the West's expense. Both superpowers saw all international developments as part of the Cold War. Solutions to world problems became difficult, because each side refused to compromise. The United States and the Soviet Union also engaged in an

---

[1] The term "cold war" was first used during the 1930's to describe Nazi Germany's use of threats and terror against small nations. American financier Bernard Baruch employed the term in its present meaning in an April 1946 speech. American political commentators adopted "cold war" shortly thereafter as the standard description of the struggle between the United States and the Soviet Union.

arms race, or a competition to strengthen their armed forces and weapons systems. Fears soon developed that any regional conflict could lead to a superpower crisis that would spark World War III.

The Soviet Challenge

In 1945 the United States looked forward to an era of tranquility in foreign affairs. As a World War II victor, it had unequalled military strength and a productive industrial economy. It also was the only nation in the world to have the atomic bomb. Most Americans, however, were tired of war and did not want to assume the burden of world leadership. In response to public opinion, the United States government began to demobilize. It placed its hopes for world peace in the new United Nations. American diplomats and political leaders also expected that friendly relations with the Soviet Union would continue in the postwar period. However, this optimism about American-Soviet ties soon faded as a result of Soviet actions in Eastern Europe.

Soviet troops had captured much of Eastern Europe from the Nazis during the closing months of World War II. At the Yalta and Potsdam conferences, the Allies recognized the region as a Soviet "sphere of influence." Stalin claimed that the Soviet Union needed a friendly Eastern Europe as protection against any future western attack, especially from Germany. Roosevelt and Churchill were willing to grant his request, but they expected Stalin to fulfill the Yalta promise to allow political freedom for such nations as Bulgaria, Poland, Hungary, and Rumania. Stalin, however, feared the emergence of anti-Soviet governments in Eastern Europe. He did not want the West to control the region, and therefore he refused to accept the western interpretation of the Yalta agreements.

Beginning in the spring of 1945, the Soviets tightened their hold over Eastern Europe. They refused to allow free elections and eliminated

Discuss with students how a satellite differs from a colony.

POSTWAR EUROPE

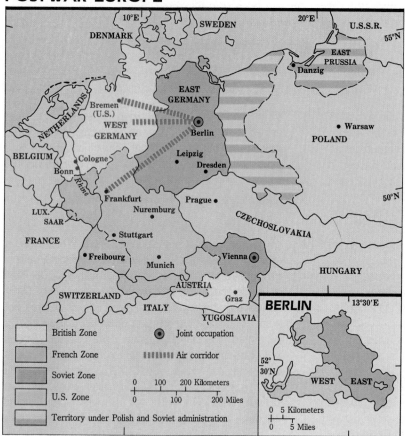

freedom of speech, religion, and the press in Bulgaria and Poland. In the next few years, the same tactics were used in other countries of Eastern Europe. Communist-led governments came to power, and contacts between the West and Eastern Europe were gradually curtailed. By 1947 most of the nations of the region had become Soviet **satellites,** with their governments and economies controlled by the Soviet Union.

The American Response

President Roosevelt had believed that postwar cooperation with the Soviets was possible. But a few weeks before his death in April 1945, he realized that Soviet policies in Eastern Europe were undermining the spirit of the wartime alliance. Roosevelt's successor, Harry Truman, began to take a hard line toward the Soviets. Inexperienced in foreign policy, Truman relied for advice on Averell Harriman, the American ambassador to the Soviet Union.

Harriman told Truman that the Soviets were not likely to break with the United States because they needed American funds to reconstruct their war-damaged economy, but that they were breaking all their promises about Eastern Europe. Truman bluntly told Soviet Foreign Minister Vyacheslav Molotov that the Soviet Union had to keep its promises. Molotov is reported to have told Truman, "I have never been talked to like that in my life." Truman is said to have replied, "Carry out your agreements and you won't get talked to like that!"

Throughout 1945 and 1946, suspicions mounted, and positions hardened on both sides. Winston Churchill, in a speech given in Fulton, Missouri, in March 1946, said that an **"iron curtain"** had

Soviet failures in Iran and Turkey suggest a degree of weakness that might have been exploited. Discuss possible reasons why the United States did not challenge the Russians more.

descended across Europe. The term became a popular metaphor for the Soviet-made barrier separating the continent into eastern and western parts. Churchill urged cooperation among the western democracies to stem the tide of Soviet expansionism.

At this time, the United States chose not to meet Churchill's plea for a western alliance. It found it difficult to devise a workable foreign policy to deal with the Soviets. American military force could not be used against them, because United States armed forces were being reduced. The United States had the atomic bomb, but the Truman administration was not willing to threaten the Soviets with it. Above all, most Americans were glad that World War II was over, and they did not want to fight either a conventional or an atomic war with the Soviets over Eastern Europe.

The alliance between the United States and the Soviet Union was terminated at the end of World War II. Americans accused the Soviets of setting up satellite governments in Eastern Europe, violating their pledge to hold free elections. How did the United States tailor its policy to respond to the Soviet threat?

Iran and Turkey. While the main area of dispute between the United States and the Soviet Union was Eastern Europe, an American-Soviet rivalry also developed in the Middle East. This region was valued by both powers for its oil. In 1946 the Soviets pressured the government of Iran for a share in that country's oil resources, which were largely controlled by the western democracies. The Soviets kept their army in northern Iran in violation of a 1942 treaty with the Allies.

Threatening the use of force to protect western interests in the region, the United States appealed to the United Nations Security Council for the withdrawal of Soviet troops from Iran. A few weeks later, the Soviet Union and Iran announced the withdrawal of Soviet troops in return for Iran's sale of oil to the Soviet Union. After the Soviet departure, the Iranian government regained control of Azerbaijan, a northern province held by Iranian Communists, and announced that it would not sell the Soviets the promised oil.

In the same year, the Soviet Union pressured Turkey for joint Turkish-Soviet administration of the Dardenelles Strait. Soviet ships passed through the Strait to the Mediterranean, and the Soviet government wanted some control over the area. It also hoped to fulfill the old Russian goal of overcoming the country's landlocked location by achieving access to warm waters. The United States, however, saw the Soviet move as an attempt to dominate Turkey, Greece, and the Middle East. When the United States sent an aircraft carrier into Turkish waters, the Soviets again backed down.

Atomic Energy. In late 1945 the United States proposed that the United Nations supervise all nuclear energy production. The following spring, United States Atomic Energy Commissioner Bernard Baruch offered a plan to ban atomic weapons. Under this plan, the United Nations would be allowed to inspect atomic facilities anywhere in the world to make sure that no country was secretly making bombs. Each country would also have to give up its veto power over United Nations decisions dealing with atomic energy. When such an international control system had been set up, the United States would destroy its stockpile of atomic weapons.

The Soviets rejected Baruch's plan. Suspicious of the strong western influence in the United Nations, they stated they would not allow UN inspectors into the Soviet Union nor would they give up their veto power. Instead, they demanded that the United States destroy its bombs at once. Unwilling to trust the Russians, the United States refused to agree. In 1949 the Soviets successfully exploded their first atomic bomb. A nuclear arms race between the two powers soon increased international tensions.

SECTION REVIEW

1. Identify the following: Averell Harriman, Vyacheslav Molotov, Dardenelles Strait.
2. What was the American attitude toward involvement in foreign affairs after World War II?
3. How did the Soviet Union increase its power in Eastern Europe?
4. Why did American-Soviet rivalry develop in the Middle East?
5. Why did the United Nations plan to ban atomic weapons fail?

2 Containment in Europe

During 1947 the Truman administration developed a new foreign policy to deal with the Soviet Union and other communist countries. This policy was known as **containment** because its purpose was to contain, or hold back, the spread of communism. Through a display of firmness, Truman hoped to keep communism inside its existing borders and to encourage its leaders to compromise with the West. He planned to carry out the containment policy by increasing American military strength, sending military aid to countries threatened by communist takeover, and giving economic aid to needy areas overseas. Before applying the policy, however, Truman had to convince the American people that the Soviet threat was real and that steps had to be taken to confront it.

The Kennan Article

The idea of containment was first presented in early 1947 by George Kennan, a State Department expert on the Soviet Union. In an article in the *Journal of Foreign Affairs,* Kennan said the Soviets believed that communism would triumph over capitalism all over the world. In their desire to reach this goal, the

Soviets would seek to expand their territory at the West's expense. However, Kennan thought that the Soviets did not want a war with the West and were willing to take their time in pursuing world conquest. Therefore, he proposed that the United States pursue a "policy of firm containment, designed to confront the [Soviets] with unalterable counterforce at every point where they show signs of encroaching upon the interests" of the West.

In the long run, Kennan hoped that containment would lead to the collapse of the Soviet system or at least weaken Soviet belief in the ultimate triumph of communism. His ideas were accepted by the Truman administration and became the basis of United States foreign policy for the next thirty years.

The Truman Doctrine

In the spring of 1947, Truman applied the containment policy for the first time in the eastern Mediterranean. In Greece, Communists were fighting a guerrilla war against the pro-western monarchy. They received aid from the Eastern European communist nations of Yugoslavia, Bulgaria, and Albania. Britain had been aiding the Greek monarchy but could no longer bear the burden of this expense. In February 1947 Britain informed Truman of this fact and asked the United States to assume British responsibilities in the area.

Truman feared that the fall of Greece to the Communists would endanger western influence in an area near the oil-rich Middle East. In March he asked Congress for a $400 million aid program for Greece and Turkey. In asking Congress for support of the program, Truman made a new statement of foreign policy that became known as the Truman Doctrine. He stated:

> I believe that it must be the policy of the United States to support free peoples who are resisting attempted subjugation by armed minorities or by outside pressures. . . . The free people of the world look to us for support in maintaining their freedom. . . . If we falter in our leadership, we may endanger the peace of the world—and we shall surely endanger the welfare of our own nation.

The Truman Doctrine made American military aid available to countries threatened by communism. It

Greek army officers and an American observer (far right) watch a gun crew in action during the 1947 spring offensive against communist rebels in the Goina Mountains. President Truman justified military aid to Greece and Turkey in the Truman Doctrine, a pledge to support nations against outside aggression. Why did President Truman believe such a policy was important?

explained aid to Greece and Turkey as an important part of a "world-wide crusade for freedom."

Congress approved Truman's aid request. His proposal, however, sparked much controversy. The majority of Americans supported the Truman Doctrine, but some criticized it as an overextension of American power and influence overseas. Former Vice President Henry Wallace said that the Truman Doctrine would only increase tensions between Moscow and Washington. Others said that too much emphasis was being placed on the role of communist ideology in Soviet actions. They claimed that Soviet expansion also expressed old Russian ambitions that existed long before the rise of the Soviets. In spite of these criticisms, the Truman Doctrine became an important part of United States foreign policy for the next two decades.

The Marshall Plan

Later in 1947 Truman applied the containment policy to Western Europe. As a result of the destruction of World War II, Europe's economy and social structure were in bad shape. United States leaders feared that a European economic collapse would open the area to communism. They believed that the military and economic security of the United States required a strong and free Europe. Only with a healthy economy and society could Europe trade with

the United States and support troops to resist the Soviet army.

Therefore, the United States government devised a new approach to provide aid to the Europeans. Speaking at Harvard University on June 5, Secretary of State George Marshall proposed a European aid program that became known as the Marshall Plan. Its purpose, he said, was to restore "the confidence of European people in the economic future of their own countries." In order for the plan to work, Marshall urged a united European effort to determine where Europe's economic needs lay and how the United States could help:

> The initiative, I think, must come from Europe. The role of this country should consist of friendly aid in the drafting of a European program and of later support of such a program so far as it may be practical for us to do so. The program should be a joint one, agreed to by a number, if not all, European nations.

The Plan's Participants. The United States even invited the Soviet Union and its satellites to participate in the plan. The Soviets, however, would have to open their economic records to American inspection in order to receive aid. Also, Eastern European economies would be more closely linked with those of Western Europe. The Soviet Union

Using the chart, discuss with students what basis was used to determine the amounts for each country.

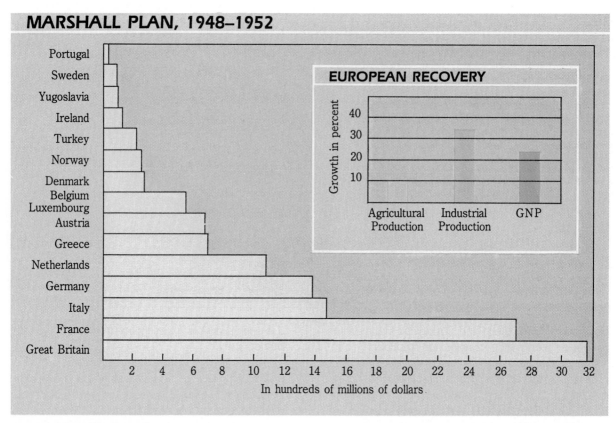

MARSHALL PLAN, 1948–1952

In hundreds of millions of dollars

EUROPEAN RECOVERY

Growth in percent

Agricultural Production   Industrial Production   GNP

rejected the invitation and prevented Poland and Czechoslovakia from joining.

Western European countries, on the other hand, responded enthusiastically to the Marshall Plan. In the summer of 1947, representatives of 16 nations met in Paris and set up a Committee for European Economic Cooperation. They worked out plans calling for nearly $23 billion in American aid and agreed to work together to boost productivity, reduce trade barriers, and use resources efficiently.

The Plan's Presentation. In December 1947 Truman submitted the European Recovery Program to Congress. He asked for about $17 billion to spend in Europe during the next four years. Some members of Congress feared that the Marshall Plan would strain the United States treasury. Others called it an "international WPA" and a "socialist blueprint." However, Congress finally gave its support on the assurance that economic recovery would reduce the communist threat in Western Europe. Also, the plan appealed to a wide group of Americans for different reasons. As historian Stephen F. Ambrose stated:

Those who feared a slump in exports and a resulting depression within the United States could envision a continued vigorous export trade; those who thought communist expansion would result from economic chaos saw salvation in an integrated, healthy European economy; those who thought the real threat was the Red [Soviet] Army fairly drooled at the thought of reviving Germany and then rebuilding the Wehrmacht [German Army]. For the humanitarian, the Plan offered long-term aid to war-torn Europe.

The Plan's Effects. The Marshall Plan became the economic arm of the containment policy. It proved to be a brilliant success. By 1951 Western European economies were prospering, and the influence of communism in these nations had declined. The Marshall Plan extended American influence in Western Europe and united the region into a single economic bloc to counter the Soviets. In reaction to the Marshall Plan, the Soviet Union set up a rival known as the Council of Mutual Economic Assistance, or COMECON, in 1949. Eastern Europe was thus formed into a single economic bloc under the leadership of the Soviet Union.

Germany

Another aspect of containment in Europe was the West's resolve to defend its interests in Germany. After World War II, the United States and the Soviet Union were divided in their policies toward Germany. The United States wanted a strong united Germany that would be independent and have a productive economy. The Soviet Union, however, wanted to keep Germany weak and divided so that it would never again threaten the peace. As a result of this disagreement, a peace treaty that would determine Germany's future could not be signed.

The Berlin Blockade. In 1948 the United States, Britain, and France decided to act without the Soviet Union and create out of their zones a united West German state. As a first step toward this goal, they introduced a new currency into western Germany to bolster the region's economy.

The Soviets did not want the formation of a German state closely allied to the West and disliked the existence of West Berlin (the American, French, and British zones of Berlin) in the heart of their territory. On June 23, 1948, Stalin placed a total blockade on all western ground and water traffic passing through the Soviet zone of Germany to West Berlin. As a result,

Nearly 2.5 million people lived in West Berlin, more than in Detroit, Cleveland, or Los Angeles. The airlift hauled about one ton of food, medicine, fuel, and supplies for every person in the city.

West Berlin became isolated and was dependent on the West for its very survival.

Truman and other western leaders were determined to remain in West Berlin. American military leaders suggested that the President use military force to open the traffic routes to West Berlin. Truman, however, decided to use an **airlift**—air transportation for supplies. The airlift brought in up to 13,000 tons (11,700 metric tons) of goods per day to the people of West Berlin and boosted the morale of the city. As a result, the Soviets recognized the failure of their effort and lifted the blockade on May 12, 1949.

West Germany. Following the Berlin blockade, the western powers carried out their plans for the formation of an independent West German state. In May 1949 a constitution was approved that set up a federal system of 11 states. In the fall of that year, the Federal Republic of Germany, or West Germany, was proclaimed, with its capital in Bonn. The Soviets then set up the German Democratic Republic, or East Germany. Thus Germany was divided into two different countries.

Defense of the West

The policy of containment required the swift buildup of United States military forces. In May 1948 Senator Arthur H. Vandenburg of Michigan, Chairman of the Senate Foreign Relations Committee,

After the East Germans blockaded the corridor to Berlin, supplies were airlifted in by the American and British air forces. As many as seven tons of supplies were flown into Templehoff Airport each day for nine months. What effect did the Berlin airlift have?

The North Atlantic Treaty Organization moved beyond its original western orientation to include any European nation willing to join in an anticommunist alliance.

introduced a resolution stating the "determination" of the United States "to exercise the right of individual or collective self-defense . . . should any armed attack occur affecting its national security." The fact that Congress passed the resolution signified the official end of isolationism in American foreign policy and prepared the way for the United States to enter into a military alliance with Western Europe.

The North Atlantic Treaty. In February 1948, when Czechoslovakia was taken over by Communists, Western Europeans became concerned about their military defense. Political and military leaders recognized the need to rearm and to unite their fighting forces. In March 1948 Britain, France, Belgium, the Netherlands, and Luxembourg met in Brussels, Belgium, where they signed a five-year alliance in which they pledged to defend each other against outside attack.

The United States soon announced that it would play a direct role in safeguarding Western European security. It began immediate negotiations with the other western powers. In April 1949 the North Atlantic Treaty was signed in Washington, D.C., creating the North Atlantic Treaty Organization (NATO). As members of NATO, the United States, Britain, France, Italy, Belgium, the Netherlands, Iceland, and Canada agreed "that an armed attack against one or more of them in Europe or North America shall be considered an attack against them all."[2]

The North Atlantic Treaty was a break with the traditional policy of the United States in avoiding "entangling alliances." As a result, it caused a considerable stir among Americans. Some "internationalists" considered the treaty a retreat from support for the United Nations. Isolationists, such as Senator Robert Taft of Ohio, feared that it would cause an arms buildup, place a drain on the economy, and lead to war. They wanted the United States to provide only for its own defense and to leave Europe to the Europeans. The Truman administration reassured NATO opponents that a free united Europe was essential to United States security and that such security could only be maintained with

American military support. The treaty was finally approved by the Senate in July 1949.

NATO. The North Atlantic Treaty set up the structure of NATO. Congress approved $1.5 billion to arm the alliance. In 1950 Supreme Headquarters, Allied Powers, Europe (SHAPE) was established outside of Paris. In late 1951 General Dwight D. Eisenhower became the supreme commander of all NATO forces, which included four American divisions. Although NATO forces were never as large as the Soviet and Eastern European armies, American nuclear power made NATO a formidable counterforce to the Soviet presence in Eastern Europe.

SECTION REVIEW

1. Identify the following: George Kennan, COMECON, NATO.
2. Why was the Truman Doctrine controversial?
3. What was the purpose of the Marshall Plan?
4. What conflict did the United States and the Soviet Union have over Germany?
5. Why did the United States sign an alliance with Western European nations?

3 Containment in Asia

Events in the Far East after 1945 made that area a center of the Cold War. Japan, once the strongest Asian power, was defeated and lay in ruins. The vacuum left by the defeat of Japan heightened political turmoil in the area and allowed communist power to increase in many Asian lands.

As a result of its interest in containing the Soviets in Europe, the United States had no clear and definite policy toward the Far East. In addition, it lacked strong and steadfast allies in the region.

Japan

President Truman did not want the Soviets to introduce communism into Japan. After the war, a four-power council was set up, but Japan was actually governed by the United States Army under General Douglas MacArthur.

Under MacArthur, Japan adopted a new political and social system that aligned it with the West. The Japanese monarchy was maintained as a symbol of

---

[2] In 1952 Greece and Turkey also joined the alliance. In 1954 West Germany was admitted. In response to NATO, the Soviet Union and its Eastern European allies signed a military alliance in 1955 known as the Warsaw Pact.

The United States needed a strong ally in the Far East to act as a bulwark against Communist China. With this in mind, the United States halted Japanese reparations in 1949, helped revive Japan's industry, and opened the way for rearmament.

national unity, but it lost all of its power. The role of the military in Japanese life was reduced, and a number of reforms were carried through that established universal suffrage, democratic government, and greater social equality. In addition, the economy was strengthened.

In 1951 the United States and Japan signed a peace treaty that ended the American occupation but allowed the United States to maintain military bases and to station troops in Japan. After 1951 Japan emerged as a strong ally of the United States in the Far East.

China

Following World War II, the United States hoped for a strong, friendly China to maintain a balance of power in the Far East. China, however, was too exhausted by internal upheaval to fulfill this role. For years the country had been embroiled in a civil war between the Nationalists, led by Chiang Kai-shek, and the Chinese Communists. Truman tried to work out a compromise between the two forces, recognizing that the cooperation of both was necessary for the creation of a strong government. In 1945 he sent General George Marshall to China to arrange a settlement of the civil war. But, as neither side was willing to make concessions, negotiations broke down, and fighting resumed in China.

United States China Policy. Fearing a victory of the Chinese Communists, Truman decided to aid Chiang Kai-shek. But the Nationalist government suffered from corruption and lack of popular support. Truman sent General Albert Wedemeyer to China to investigate the situation. Upon his return, Wedemeyer claimed that Chiang had little chance of winning unless he received massive American military support, including American troops. Since Truman did not want to involve the United States in a costly and possibly unsuccessful Asian land war, he gave only limited military aid to the Chiang government.

The China Debate. By late 1949 Chiang Kai-shek had been defeated. The Nationalist government and army fled to the offshore island of Formosa, or Taiwan, while mainland China was left in the control of the Communists under Mao Tse-Tung.

The loss of China to communism deeply divided the United States and caused a national debate. Critics charged that Truman had failed to realize the strength

Communist Chinese celebrate the liberation of Canton in 1949. The United States was criticized for failing to support the Nationalists. How did Truman defend this position?

of the Chinese Communists and had not given enough support to the Nationalists. In an official government report, Secretary of State Dean Acheson defended the administration's China policy:

> *A realistic appraisal of conditions in China leads to the conclusion that the only alternative open to the United States was full-scale intervention on behalf of a government which had lost the confidence of its . . . people. Such intervention would have required the expenditure of even greater sums than have been fruitlessly spent thus far, the command of Nationalist armies by American officers, and the . . . participation of American armed forces. . . . Intervention of such scope and magnitude would have been resented by . . . the Chinese people . . . and would have been condemned by the American people. . . .*

Korea

Not long after the rise of Communist China, the United States faced problems in Korea. At the end of World War II, the Allies took Korea from Japan. In August 1945 Soviet troops occupied the northern half

The Korean conflict marked the first time a President entered into war without consulting Congress. Discuss this in relation to the idea of balance of powers.

Soldiers of the United States 24th Infantry Division search for a communist position about ten miles north of Seoul. The Korean War was officially a police action, not a declared war. Why was the United States reluctant to declare war in Korea?

of the country as far south as the 38th parallel. The United States wanted to check Soviet expansion into areas that had been ruled by Japan. A month later, therefore, American troops occupied the southern half of Korea.

The occupying powers could not agree on how to unify Korea. Soon there were two Korean governments: the Democratic People's Republic of Korea, or North Korea, a communist government backed by the Soviet Union; and the Republic of Korea, or South Korea, supported by the United States and the United Nations. In 1948 the United Nations supervised free elections in South Korea, but North Korea refused to allow the United Nations to conduct elections.

By 1950 both the Soviets and the Americans had withdrawn their troops from Korea. The Soviets continued to support a strong and well-trained North Korean army, but the United States decided not to include Korea in its defense plans.

The Korean War. On June 25, 1950, North Korean troops invaded South Korea in an effort to unify the country by force. This surprise action began the Korean War, which lasted from 1950–1953. Truman acted quickly to defend South Korea, reversing his earlier policy of withdrawal. On June 27 he ordered naval and air forces to the Korean

peninsula and, fearing further communist aggression, sent the Seventh Fleet to Taiwan to protect the Nationalist Chinese government. A few days later, he ordered American planes and troops sent to Korea.

In the Korean conflict, the United States for the first time was directly fighting a communist country. Congress, however, was not asked to declare war against North Korea, because Truman did not want to enlarge the local conflict into a war between the western and communist blocks.

The United States received the support of the United Nations Security Council, which voted to send UN forces to help the South Koreans.[3] The UN army, led by General Douglas MacArthur, was made up of troops from 17 countries. More than 90 percent of the army, however, was American and South Korean. General MacArthur was under the authority of President Truman rather than the United Nations.

At the beginning of the war, the North Koreans rapidly pushed the UN army back to the southern end

---

[3] At this time, the Soviets were boycotting the Security Council because the UN had refused to give China's seat on the Security Council to the Chinese Communists. As a result, the Soviet Union did not veto the UN action to help South Korea. The Korean War was the first conflict in which troops of a world organization fought a nation accused of aggression.

Note that North Korea borders on Communist China. This helps explain why China was unwilling to allow an invasion of North Korea.

of the Korean peninsula. An impressive buildup of American troops soon turned the tide and developed a front around the port of Pusan. Then, MacArthur carried out a daring landing from the sea behind enemy lines at Inchon, a port city far up the east coast of the peninsula. This bold move proved to be a brilliant success. United Nations forces soon captured Seoul, the South Korean capital, and isolated the bulk of North Korean forces surrounding Pusan. The remaining North Koreans fled northward, losing thousands of men and much equipment.

Chinese Intervention. In October 1950 MacArthur's troops moved north of the 38th parallel with the approval of President Truman and the United Nations. They captured all of North Korea up to the Yalu River, the boundary between Korea and China. Communist China warned that it would not accept an American invasion of North Korea. On October 14 Truman and MacArthur met at Wake Island in the Pacific, where Truman asked what were the chances of Chinese or Soviet interference. MacArthur answered, "Very little." But he had miscalculated.

On November 26, 1950, 250,000 Chinese troops broke through the center of MacArthur's line. In a short time, the "bottomless well of Chinese manpower," as MacArthur described the Chinese forces, forced the UN army into a southward retreat to the 38th parallel and below.

KOREA, 25 JUNE–25 NOV. 1950

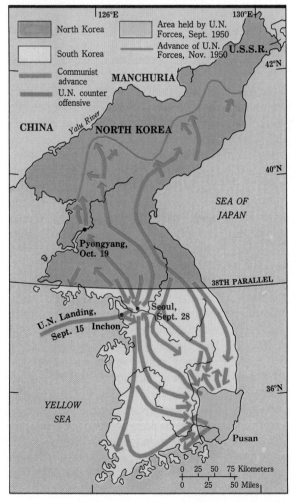

KOREA, 26 NOV. 1950–27 JULY 1953

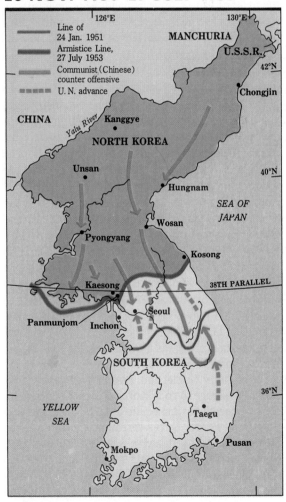

Truman versus MacArthur. In the middle of this setback, a rift developed between Truman and MacArthur. Truman decided to abandon the unification of Korea as a war aim and to settle for dividing the country at the 38th parallel. MacArthur opposed him and asked for permission to bomb Chinese bases and installations north of the Yalu. He also supported a naval blockade of China's coast and the use of Chiang Kai-shek's army in Korea. Truman turned down MacArthur's proposals, stating that they would bring the Soviets into the war and cause a world conflict.

MacArthur publicly declared his opposition to Truman's policy and went to Congress and the people for support. When he refused to stop his activities, Truman dismissed him as commander and replaced him with General Matthew Ridgway. Truman justified his action on the ground that civilian control over the military had to be maintained. Most military and congressional leaders backed the President and his policy of limited force in Korea.

Truce Negotiations. By 1951 the war had become a stalemate along the 38th parallel. In June of that year, the United Nations and the North Koreans began negotiations for an armistice. For two years, while the fighting continued, the talks dragged on. A major deadlock developed over **repatriation,** or the return of prisoners of war to their homelands. The Americans wanted the prisoners to decide where they wanted to go. But since close to 45,000 North Koreans did not want to return to their country, the North Korean government insisted on forced repatriation of all prisoners.

A break in the Korean conflict finally occurred in 1953, when Stalin died. He was replaced by a group of Soviet leaders who wanted a lessening of world tensions in order to handle domestic problems. The year before, Republican Dwight D. Eisenhower had been elected President of the United States, and the new administration was anxious to bring the Korean War to an end.

Shortly after his election, Eisenhower carried out a campaign pledge to go to Korea. When Eisenhower's trip produced no immediate results, Secretary of State John Foster Dulles threatened to remove the Seventh Fleet from Taiwan's waters, "unleashing" Chiang to invade the Chinese mainland. He also threatened to bomb bases in Manchuria. In July 1953 the North Koreans accepted voluntary repatriation

under a neutral international authority, and both sides finally agreed to an armistice.

Results. After the war, Korea remained divided at about the 38th parallel, with a demilitarized zone 2.5 miles (4 kilometers) wide between North and South Korea. As a result of the fighting, many of Korea's people were homeless and poor, relying on outside aid. The United States suffered over 135,000 casualties, and over 33,000 American soldiers were killed. Although costly, the Korean War was viewed as a success for the containment policy in Asia. It also introduced to the Cold War the practice of **limited warfare,** in which each side, to avoid an expansion of fighting, sets limits in attacking territory and using weapons.

Indochina

After the Korean War, new difficulties developed for the United States in French-ruled Indochina. In 1945 three kingdoms—Vietnam, Laos, and Cambodia—were established in the region. However, France continued to control the area. A year later, Vietnamese forces led by Communist leader Ho Chi Minh began fighting the French for the independence of Vietnam. Ho's soldiers, known as the Viet Minh, received military supplies from Communist China.

Although not in favor of French rule, the Truman administration saw Ho Chi Minh as the agent of China and the Soviet Union. Consequently, it backed its French ally. As part of its effort to contain communism in Asia, the United States in 1950 began supplying economic and military aid to French forces in Indochina.

The Eisenhower administration expanded aid to the French. In justifying this step, it introduced the **"domino theory,"** that if one country in Southeast Asia fell to communism, others would fall, one after another. By 1954 the United States was paying nearly 75 percent of war expenses in Indochina, and American aircraft were carrying French troops into battle.

In spite of American help, the French soon faced defeat. In 1954 the Viet Minh trapped the best of the French army in the remote fortress of Dien Bien Phu in northern Vietnam. Faced with the loss of 20,000 troops, France asked the Eisenhower administration to use American air power against Ho's forces.

Foreign Aid

Foreign aid has become a major aspect of American foreign policy. Yet it is a surprisingly recent phenomenon. American foreign aid was left almost entirely to private organizations until the post-World War II era.

After the war, the government launched an enormous foreign aid program. In the late 1940's, most foreign aid was directed at rebuilding war-torn free Europe. By the mid-1950's, aid to the Near and Far East took precedence, these being areas that seemed to be most threatened by communism. Aid to Latin American and African countries became important in the 1960's.

Some people object to foreign aid because it involves the distribution of American resources abroad. Thus objections were raised to America's financing the reconstruction of Europe. But aid to the Third World has been far more controversial. In the first place, aid to Europe had very specific goals, while aid to other parts of the world has tended to be less clear-cut in aim. Secondly, aid to Europe generally turned out to be a short-term project. But helping Third World countries has been far more difficult, with no end in sight.

Finally, the American alliance with Western Europe is long-standing and firm, whereas the relationships with many other countries receiving American aid have been quite uneven. Indeed, many of them view themselves as nonaligned.

Some people argue that the United States should concentrate its aid on countries that are located in strategic areas or that permit United States military bases on their territory. But others feel the United States should use economic aid to strengthen all non-communist governments. Much aid to Asian, African, and Latin American nations has been based upon their willingness to remain independent of Moscow. The fact that many of these same countries have been guilty of gross violations of human rights, however, complicates matters. In the late 1970's, President Jimmy Carter tried to link foreign aid to human rights. His effort was widely criticized as impractical, but still appeals to freedom-loving Americans.

Another major area of debate is the role American business interests should play in determining which countries should receive aid. Much aid takes the form of surplus food or goods produced in the United States, or credits to buy American-made materials. Most people praise this policy because it helps both the United States and the country receiving the aid.

On the other hand, foreign aid encourages high-pressure lobbying from economic interest groups. Further, foreign aid can cause unanticipated problems abroad. For example, people in some Third World countries have developed a taste for food products they cannot possibly produce themselves. Thus, the aid program sometimes helps to make people dependent rather than self-sufficient.

Conflicts also arise with regard to military aid. Such aid is in keeping with the desire to help countries defend themselves against a communist threat, and it also helps American arms manufacturers to tap a wider market. But many critics charge that the interests of the munitions industry have become too powerful in determining policy. Others say that military aid encourages warfare.

Many other problems can be noted. For example, loans may seem wiser than outright grants. But high interest rates and a sluggish world economy can bring borrowers to the brink of default, putting the international banking system in danger. Recent evidence also suggests that much aid to Third World nations does not reach the people for whom it is intended. Instead, it ends up in the hands of corrupt officials or thieves.

Finally, there is the question of "how much aid?" This issue is particularly difficult when times are hard in America. If the United States hopes to remain a world leader, it cannot turn its back on other countries. But the nature and extent of its obligations will be debated for years to come.

QUESTIONS

1. When did American foreign aid begin?
2. Why is military aid controversial?

The division of Vietnam left 60 percent of the land under communist control.

The French appeal prompted a debate among high officials of the United States government. Some argued for the use of both American troops and air power against the Viet Minh. Military advisors and Secretary of State John Foster Dulles believed that Communist China would eventually enter the fighting in Indochina. To prevent this, they urged the President to threaten the Chinese with **massive retaliation,** or an all-out nuclear attack. Eisenhower rejected this idea and added that American troops and planes would be sent to Indochina only if Britain, France's other major ally, participated. Congress, aware that public opinion would oppose the use of American troops, dismissed the proposal. As a result, the United States remained out of the struggle.

In May 1954 the French soldiers at Dien Bien Phu surrendered, ending French rule in Indochina. In July the United States, France, Britain, the Soviet Union, and Communist China met in Geneva to decide the future of Indochina. The United States withdrew when it became known that Ho Chi Minh would receive part of Vietnam. The other powers signed the Geneva Accords, which established the independence of Vietnam, Laos, and Cambodia. Vietnam was divided along the 17th parallel. The northern part became the Democratic Republic of Vietnam under Ho Chi Minh, while the south remained in the hands of pro-French Indochinese emperor Bao Dai.

Following the Geneva settlement, the United States sought allies in Southeast Asia to check the further spread of communism. In September 1954 the Southeast Asia Treaty Organization (SEATO) was established at Manila by Britain, France, Australia, New Zealand, and the United States. Only three Asian nations—the Philippines, Thailand, and Pakistan—joined the alliance. The SEATO agreement pledged joint action against aggression upon any member of the alliance, and also extended protection to South Vietnam, Cambodia, and Laos.

SEATO, however, lacked the military power and organization to carry out a containment policy. Many Asian nations, such as Burma, Ceylon (now Sri Lanka), India, and Malaya (now Malaysia) viewed it as a western attempt to interfere in Asian affairs. The alliance was further weakened because it was based on the expectation that future communist problems would come from outside attack. Thus SEATO was powerless to check the growth of communism.

The United States signed a treaty in 1954 promising to protect Taiwan (Formosa). A crisis arose when Communist China began shelling the offshore islands. How was this crisis resolved?

Taiwan

During the mid-1950's, tensions arose between Communist China and the Chiang Kai-shek government in Taiwan. In January 1953 the United States allowed Chiang to use American-built planes to bomb shipping and ports on the Chinese mainland. In September 1954 the Communist Chinese began air and artillery attacks on the Nationalist-held islands of Queymoy and Matsu. Three months later, the United States signed a treaty with Chiang that guaranteed the security of Taiwan. In return, Chiang pledged not to attack the mainland or to reinforce troops on Quemoy and Matsu without American consent. In January 1955 Congress allowed the Eisenhower administration to use American armed force, if necessary, to protect Quemoy and Matsu.

Both sides soon backed down, and the crisis ended. Eisenhower refused to challenge the Communist Chinese directly over the two tiny islands. At the same time, the American determination to defend Taiwan caused the Communist Chinese to reduce their pressure.

Three years later, the Communist Chinese resumed the shelling of Quemoy and Matsu. Eisenhower responded by sending the Seventh Fleet to Taiwan. This show of force ended the crisis. By 1960 the United States had established a complete line of containment around Communist China.

SECTION REVIEW

1. Identify the following: Douglas MacArthur, Chiang Kai-shek, Seoul, John Foster Dulles, SEATO.
2. What happened in Japan after World War II?
3. Why did the United States fail to give military support to the Chinese Nationalists?
4. What was Truman's conflict with MacArthur?
5. How did the United States become involved in Indochina?

4 Cold War "Thaw"

By the mid 1950's both the United States and the Soviet Union had developed hydrogen bombs, nuclear weapons that were many times more powerful than atomic bombs. The terrible threat of nuclear war led leaders of both countries to seek ways of relaxing Cold War tensions. The superpowers gradually opened contacts with each other through diplomatic channels and **summit conferences,** or high level meetings of political leaders.

The Spirit of Geneva

When Stalin died in 1953, Nikita S. Khrushchev became the new Soviet leader. Under Khrushchev the Soviets adopted a new Soviet policy toward the West known as **peaceful coexistence.** This meant that they would compete with the West but would avoid war.

The first sign of a thaw appeared in May 1955. In that month, the western powers and the Soviet Union signed a peace treaty with Austria, ending the post World War II occupation of the country. All western and Soviet troops left the country, allowing Austria to become an independent neutral nation.

The Eisenhower administration also agreed to a diplomatic summit meeting with the Soviets, the first between top western and Soviet leaders in a decade. In July 1955, Eisenhower, British Prime Minister Anthony Eden, and French Premier Edgar Faure met at Geneva with Khrushchev and his colleague, Nikolai Bulganin, to discuss disarmament and German reunification. The Soviets submitted a proposal for limiting the size of their armed forces and abolishing nuclear weapons. Eisenhower proposed an "open skies" agreement between the United States and the Soviet Union, allowing air inspection of each other's military bases and installations. Such an agreement would prevent either side from launching a surprise attack against the other.

Delegates from the Big Four powers—the United States, France, Britain, and the Soviet Union—meet at the opening session of the summit conference held in Geneva during the summer of 1955. The Geneva summit was the first big-power meeting since Potsdam ten years earlier. What effect did the talks at Geneva produce?

Many nonaligned nations sympathized with either the United States or the Soviet Union, but they were not formally allied with either.

Under communism it is not uncommon for history to be officially rewritten. Stalin came under such total attack that images of him virtually disappeared from public places. Communist China recently did the same with Mao Tse-Tung.

Soviet tanks in strife-torn Budapest block a street leading to the Danube Bridge. The Hungarian Revolt began in the fall of 1956 when students and workers demonstrated for reform. How did the Soviets respond to the rebellion?

Although the meeting produced no specific results, observers noted a reduction of tensions that was promptly called the "Spirit of Geneva."[4] The summit conference placed the Cold War on a different basis. The superpowers admitted that a nuclear stalemate had developed and that the current balance of power in Europe and Asia had to be accepted. Following Geneva, the rivalry between East and West increasingly shifted to the **Third World,** or the developing nations in Asia, Africa, and Latin America. There, the superpowers sought economic and political influence.

As tensions eased, individual countries within the two power blocs acted independently of American and Soviet policies in certain areas. At the same time, newly independent countries in Asia and Africa declared themselves **nonaligned** (neutral) in the Cold War and began to exert their own influence on world affairs.

By the early 1960's, the bipolar world had been replaced by a more diverse one of regional groups. Both superpowers continued to play leading roles in world affairs, but they no longer could control events to their liking. The United States, in particular, had difficulty checking communist expansion and influencing the foreign policies of other nations.

---

[4] Secretary of State Dulles still distrusted the Soviets in spite of their new emphasis on "peaceful coexistence." In January 1956 he stated that the United States must be willing to go to the brink of war to defend its commitments. "If you are scared to go to the brink, you are lost," Dulles warned. As a result, the term "brinkmanship" was used to describe the Dulles brand of American foreign policy.

Unrest in Eastern Europe

In February 1956 Khrushchev began a campaign of **de-Stalinization,** or removal of the rigid policies of Joseph Stalin. This new attitude encouraged the people of Eastern Europe to expect more freedom.

In June riots and strikes broke out in Poland for better pay, improved working conditions, and more consumer goods. The Poles also demanded greater political freedoms and a more liberal government. The Stalinist government collapsed, and Vladyslaw Gomulka, an independent communist, came to power. Soviet leaders, alarmed at first, accepted the Gomulka government when it pledged to keep Poland communist and a member of the Warsaw Pact.

The Polish crisis led to a more serious uprising in neighboring Hungary. In October 1956 students and workers demonstrated in the Hungarian capital of Budapest for changes in the government. Strikes, riots, and demonstrations soon spread throughout the country. A new government came to power and demanded the withdrawal of all Soviet troops from Hungary. The Soviets accepted this demand and began pulling out their forces. The Hungarian government then declared Hungary's neutrality and its withdrawal from the Warsaw Pact. Free elections and an end to the communist dictatorship were promised. The Soviets, however, would not permit Hungary to endanger Soviet control of Eastern Europe. Early in November, Soviet forces returned to Hungary, crushed the uprising, and set up a communist government loyal to Moscow.

President Eisenhower ordered that 21,500 Hungarian refugees be admitted to the United States.

The Suez Canal was built and owned by a private company whose major stockholders were British and French.

Although Secretary of State Dulles had promised a "rollback" of communist control in Eastern Europe, the United States did not help the Hungarians. The Eisenhower administration believed that such an action would have caused a third world war. As a result of the Hungarian crisis, the United States dropped its call for the liberation of Eastern Europe and recognized that the region was under Soviet control.

Middle East

The mid-1950's saw the spread of the Cold War to the Middle East. The United States wanted to restrain Soviet influence in the area and to preserve western access to the rich oil fields of Iran, Iraq, Kuwait, and Saudi Arabia. Further, the United States wanted to protect the Jewish state of Israel, which had been established in the British-controlled area of Palestine in 1948. Many European Jews had fled to the Palestine area as a result of Nazi persecution before and during World War II.

Israel. The Truman administration immediately recognized Israel. But the surrounding Arab countries bitterly resented the presence of a Jewish state in their midst, and soon they attacked Israel. Although the better-trained Israelis quickly drove them off, the conflict did not end. United Nations mediator Ralph Bunche negotiated an Arab-Israeli armistice in 1949, but tensions continued. As a result

of the Arab-Israeli conflict, nearly a million Palestinian Arabs were left homeless, creating a critical refugee problem in neighboring countries. American support for Israel and failure to show sympathy for Palestinian grievances increased Arab hostility toward the United States.

Suez. The most important Arab state was Egypt, ruled by President Abdel Gamal Nasser. Both the Soviets and the Americans sought Egypt's support by offering economic aid. Nasser accepted help from both sides, but he refused to join any power bloc. His primary goals were to maintain Egypt's prestige in the Arab world and to destroy the state of Israel.

As a result of Egypt's anti-Israeli policy, the United States refused to sell Nasser arms. Nasser obtained weapons from communist countries and began to adopt a more pro-Soviet foreign policy. In response, the United States cancelled its offer to help build the Aswan High Dam, an important part of an Egyptian irrigation project designed to increase agricultural production.

A week later, Nasser retaliated by seizing the Suez Canal, saying he would use its profits to build the dam. The canal, although located in Egypt, was owned by an international company that allowed equal access to ships of all nations. Britain and France, outraged by the seizure of their traditional water route to Asia, moved to take back the canal by force. Israel, angered by repeated Arab attacks along its borders, agreed to help by invading Egypt.

Warfare in the Middle East was close at hand after Egyptian President Nasser seized the Suez Canal. The Israelis, British, and French responded with a show of force. Refusing to take sides, the United States urged a peaceful settlement. How did the Suez crisis affect the relationship between the United States and its allies?

1950
NOBEL PEACE
PRIZE

Ralph Bunche

Ralph Bunche, an internationally acclaimed diplomat, always attributed the success he achieved in life to the advice that his beloved grandmother had given him years before. "Just slip into the other fellow's skin," she advised him, "and see how you would feel."

This saying was to remain a principle upon which Bunche ordered his life. First as a teacher, in later years as an advisor to President Franklin Roosevelt, and finally as undersecretary of the United Nations, Bunche was concerned with safeguarding the rights and feelings of others.

Born in Detroit in 1904, Bunche was a successful scholar in the field of government. After receiving a master's degree from Harvard University, he was invited to organize the new political science department at Howard University. Later he travelled through French West Africa, studying government systems. Between 1938 and 1940 he worked with eminent Swedish sociologist Gunnar Myrdal on a study of race relations in the United States. This work was published as *An American Dilemma* in 1944.

During World War II, Bunche served in the United States War Department as an analyst of African and Far Eastern affairs. At the conclusion of the war, he was sent by President Roosevelt to help plan the charter of the United Nations at the Dumbarton Oaks Conference. Bunche served the remainder of his life in this organization.

Bunche is best-known for his role as mediator in the Arab-Israeli conflict of 1948. For his efforts in obtaining an Arab-Israeli ceasefire, he was awarded the Nobel Peace Prize in 1950.

Bunche was promoted to the post of undersecretary in 1955. One of his chief tasks in this role was working on a UN program for peaceful uses of atomic energy. In 1956 he supervised the UN forces that were sent to Egypt during the Suez Canal crisis. He always looked for peaceful, rather than military, solutions to problems.

Bunche also championed the rights of his own people in their struggle for civil rights at home. In 1965 he joined Martin Luther King and thousands of other Americans on their freedom march from Selma to Montgomery, Alabama. On the steps of the state capital, Bunche spoke eloquently of the grievances of black Americans. His death in 1971 was mourned by citizens throughout the entire world.

The Israelis began their attack in the Sinai Peninsula in October 1956. Britain and France then joined in the invasion and landed troops near the northern end of the Suez Canal. In a few hours the Israeli army nearly destroyed Nasser's forces, and the British and French secured their positions.

The Eisenhower administration was angered by the Suez invasion. Fearing the total loss of western influence among the Arabs, the United States opposed the actions of its three allies. Both it and the Soviet Union supported a United Nations' resolution calling for an immediate truce. Britain and France vetoed the resolution and blocked Security Council action. The Soviet Union then warned that it would send troops to Egypt and launch atomic weapons against France and Britain if they did not leave the Suez area.

The United States also demanded that the British and French pull out of the area. On November 6 the British and French agreed to a cease-fire and withdrew their troops. The Israelis also withdrew. A United Nations Emergency Force arrived to patrol the borders between Israel and Egypt.

The Suez crisis led to a serious rift between the United States and its major allies. Both Britain and France were humiliated, and they blamed the United

One reason for the crisis in the Middle East is that the region held 75 percent of the world's oil supply.

MIDDLE EAST CRISES, 1945–1965

States for putting them in a dilemma. At the same time, the Soviets increased their prestige in the Arab world, and the pro-Soviet Nasser remained a powerful Arab leader.

The Eisenhower Doctrine. After the Suez crisis, the United States decided to extend its containment policy to the Middle East. In January 1957 the Eisenhower Doctrine was announced. It allowed the President to use armed force anywhere in the Middle East against "aggression from any country controlled by international communism."

In 1958 the Eisenhower Doctrine was put to a severe test when Nasser's Egypt united with Syria to form the United Arab Republic, and the pro-western monarchy in Iraq was overthrown. Lebanon and Jordan, two Arab states bordering Israel, feared similar revolutions in their territories. Each asked the West for aid. Eisenhower sent about 6000 sailors and marines to help Lebanon, while Britain sent paratroopers to protect Jordan.

Critics charged that the Eisenhower Doctrine placed too much pressure on Middle Eastern countries to join the Cold War and involved the United States in local conflicts not directly related to its interests. Further, the doctrine divided the Middle East. It was supported by the Middle Eastern members of the pro-western Baghdad Pact, a

regional defense alliance formed in 1955 by Britain, Turkey, Pakistan, Iran, and Iraq. But Nasser and his supporters saw the doctrine as another example of American imperialism.

New Directions

In the late 1950's and early 1960's, the "thaw" in the Cold War continued despite occasional setbacks. Although Khrushchev's power in the Soviet Union increased, he faced stiff opposition to his "peaceful coexistence" policy from Communist China. The Communist Chinese challenged the Soviet's leadership of the communist world and accused them of softness toward the West and of "selling out" the Third World.

Soviet and American Policy. The Soviets pursued a "zig-zag" course in foreign policy during this period. Although Khrushchev continued to seek closer contacts with capitalist countries, he sometimes followed a hard line with them to prevent a complete break with the Chinese. He tried to gain an advantage over the West by encouraging unrest in the trouble spots of the world. In the Third World, the Soviets backed **"wars of liberation,"** or revolutionary movements against western political and economic influence. In 1960 the Soviets aided pro-communist

The launching of Sputnik stimulated efforts in the United States to strengthen the science curriculum in public schools.

East Germans continued to try to escape despite the wall.

forces in a civil war in the Congo, a newly independent nation in the heart of Africa.

Meanwhile, the United States remained committed to the containment policy while increasing contacts with the Soviet Union. In September 1959, in an attempt to resolve the Cold War peacefully, Eisenhower met with Khrushchev at Camp David, the presidential retreat in the mountains of Maryland. No significant agreements were made, but the meeting was so friendly that observers spoke of the "Spirit of Camp David."

American-Soviet cordiality ended in May 1960 when the Soviets shot down an American U-2 spy plane. An angry Khrushchev broke off a scheduled summit conference with Eisenhower and other western leaders.

In 1961 Eisenhower was succeeded by John F. Kennedy, who wanted to have a dynamic foreign policy that would impress the Soviets with American strength and boost United States prestige abroad. Under Kennedy, the United States increased its military budget and built up its armed forces. At the same time, it also used peaceful means to extend American help and influence in the Third World. The Alliance for Progress, for example, aided economic development in Latin America, while the Peace Corps sent Americans to Third World countries as teachers, farmers, and technicians to promote economic development.

Military Strategy. In spite of the growth of American military power, most Americans feared that the United States was falling behind the Soviet Union. In the fall of 1957, the Soviets had launched the first artificial earth satellite, Sputnik I. The Americans did not launch theirs until January of the following year. Many Americans believed that this showed a Soviet lead over the United States in the development of rockets, and critics of the Eisenhower administration spoke of a "missile gap." However, United States intelligence reports later revealed a substantial American lead in nuclear weapons.

Each power had enough weapons to place them in a nuclear "balance of terror." Neither side could win a nuclear war without suffering an unacceptable amount of damage to itself. This fact acted as a **deterrent,** or check, and prevented one side from attacking the other.

Germany

During the late 1950's and early 1960's, Germany remained the most important "battleground" of the Cold War. The Soviets, alarmed at the large numbers of skilled East Germans escaping to the West through West Berlin, demanded that the western powers leave West Berlin. In a November 1958 speech, Khrushchev threatened to hand over to East Germany control of West Berlin's access routes if the West did not withdraw its troops. The United States and its allies, however, rejected the Soviet threat.

In 1959 the Soviets backed down temporarily, but presented their demand again at a June 1961 summit conference in Vienna, Austria. Khrushchev told President Kennedy that the West must move out of Berlin and insisted on an agreement by the end of the year. Kennedy rejected Khrushchev's demand. To emphasize the West's right to stay in West Berlin, the United States later sent more troops to the city.

In the summer of 1961, a large number of East Germans fled to the West. On August 13 the East German government, with Soviet backing, acted to stop the flow of refugees. It closed the border between East and West Berlin and built a wall of concrete blocks and barbed wire along it, splitting the city in two and stopping the flight of East Germans to the West. Although the wall became a symbol of communist repression, it had the effect of easing Cold War tensions. Khushchev was now willing to accept West Berlin, since it could no longer aid escapes that had threatened the stability of East Germany. Kennedy was able to tolerate the Berlin wall as long as West Berlin remained part of the West.

Latin America

After World War II, the United States committed itself to cooperation with Latin American nations. In September 1947 a regional defense pact was signed at Rio de Janeiro, Brazil. The following year, the Organization of American States (OAS) was founded to encourage closer ties among nations of the Western Hemisphere.

Since the beginning of the Cold War, the United States had largely neglected Latin America.[5] Lack of

[5] In 1950 Congress passed the Truman administration's Point Four program to provide economic assistance to Latin America and other developing areas. But the program had little effect.

Most of the Cuban refugees came to Miami, which is about 150 miles from Cuba.

industry and poor agricultural methods brought economic problems to the region. Corrupt governments controlled by the military and the wealthy classes did little to promote economic progress and improve living conditions. Radical Latin Americans accused the United States of supporting these governments, while conservative Latin Americans blamed the United States for not supplying enough economic aid.

In the 1950's the United States, concerned with stopping the spread of communism, directed its attention to Latin America once again. In 1954 the Central Intelligence Agency (CIA) helped to overthrow the leftist government of Jacobo Arbenz Guzman in Guatemala. In following years, in order to prevent communist takeovers, the United States continued to support unpopular conservative or military governments in Latin America.

Castro's Cuba. Anti-American feeling grew throughout Latin America and became a part of a growing revolutionary movement in Cuba. Beginning

in 1953, guerrilla forces led by a young Cuban lawyer named Fidel Castro conducted a war against the government of Fulgencio Batista. Batista, who had ruled Cuba since 1933 with the support of the United States, had refused to carry out reforms, and he had used an American-equipped army to keep order. In 1959 Castro overthrew Batista and established a revolutionary government.

The American people at first supported Castro and welcomed his promise of democratic reforms. But Castro soon revealed his dislike of the United States and its Latin American policies. He angered the American business community by seizing American property in Cuba and offended American respect for civil liberties by persecuting his opponents. Thousands of Cubans fled to the United States to escape the Castro regime. His government became a dictatorship and formed close ties with the Soviets. In February 1960 Cuba negotiated a trade agreement with the Soviet Union that enabled the Soviets to obtain Cuban sugar at low prices. The United States

CARIBBEAN CRISES, 1955–1965

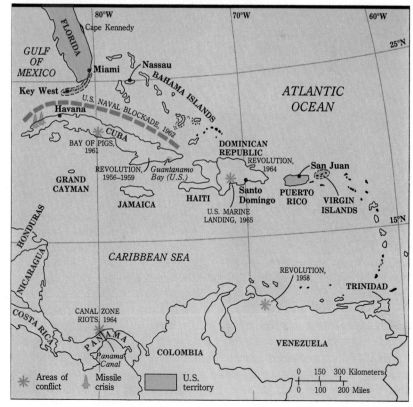

Using the map, discuss with students the changes in world alliances since World War II. Point out that there are more nonaligned nations today than there were after the war.

THE WORLD AND WESTERN ALLIANCES

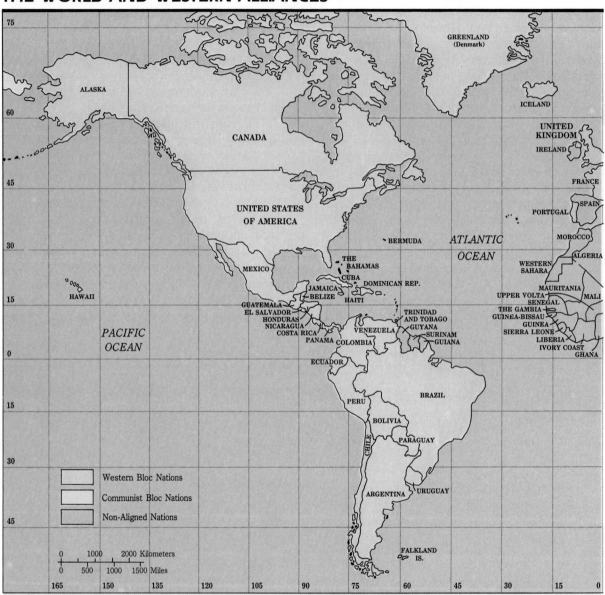

responded by banning the import of Cuban sugar to the United States. Khrushchev then promised Soviet protection to Cuba, claiming that the Monroe Doctrine had "outlived its time." By the end of 1960, Castro's government was openly communist and had become popular in many Latin American countries.

The United States began to look for a democratic substitute to Castro, one who would not endanger American interests. In January 1961 diplomatic relations with Cuba were ended. That same month, the CIA began to help Cuban exiles in the United States with a plan to invade Cuba and overthrow Castro. It started training 2000 Cuban exiles based in Central America in methods of guerrilla warfare.

When John Kennedy took office, he gave approval for the planned invasion of Cuba and provided the Cuban exiles with guns and ships. However, he was unwilling to risk direct American involvement and

Some historians believe that after the Bay of Pigs Kennedy relied less on experts and more on his own initiative. He decided what action to take in Laos, the Congo, Berlin, and South Vietnam.

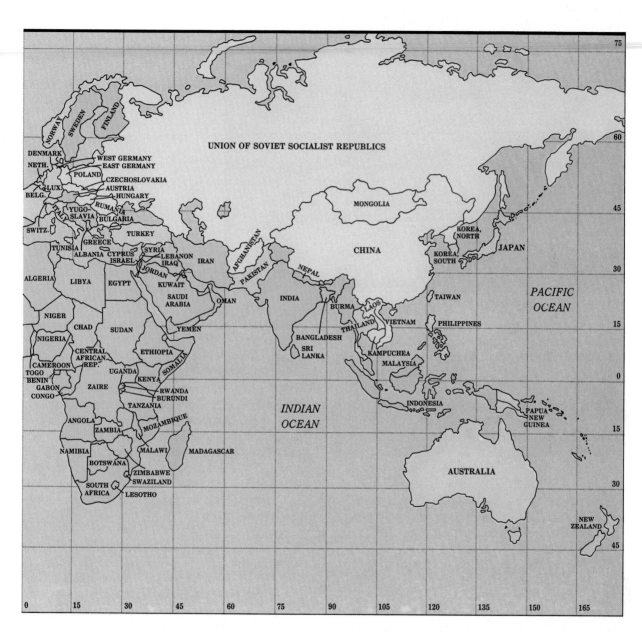

refrained from using United States troops and planes in the operation. On April 17, 1961, the exiles landed at the Bay of Pigs on Cuba's southern coast. They intended to set up a base on Cuban territory that would spark a national uprising against Castro. The local population, however, failed to give their support. Castro's air force controlled the skies and soon destroyed the exiles' base as well as their supply ships. Within a few days, the invaders surrendered.

The unsuccessful Bay of Pigs invasion strengthened Castro's control over Cuba. For the United States, it meant a serious loss of prestige, especially among Third World nations, many of which accused the United States of immoral conduct. Cuban-American relations sank to a new low, and Cuba drew even closer to the Soviet Union.

The Cuban Missile Crisis. The American setback in the Bay of Pigs invasion encouraged Khrushchev to

The Navy established a 2100-mile ring around Cuba, using 180 ships and 8 aircraft carriers.

Aerial photographs revealed the presence of Soviet missiles in Cuba. This photograph shows a medium-range ballistic missile base near San Cristobal. President Kennedy's firm handling of the crisis forced the Soviets to back down. How was the prestige of the United States affected by the crisis?

adopt a more aggressive stance in the Cold War. He decided to use Cuba to gain a military advantage for the Soviet Union over the United States. During the summer of 1962, he sent military advisors and supplies to Cuba.

Soon American intelligence reports showed that the Soviet Union was installing offensive missiles in Cuba. Kennedy ordered U-2 spy planes to photograph the missile sites. By mid-October, the administration had proof that missiles with a range of 1000 miles (1600 kilometers) were rapidly being completed. A Soviet nuclear threat now existed within 90 miles (144 kilometers) of the Florida coast and would soon endanger most cities in North and South America.

Kennedy realized that, for reasons of security and prestige, the missiles had to be removed from Cuba. But he faced the difficult decision of how to accomplish this goal without causing a war. The Pentagon favored an all-out invasion of Cuba to get rid of Castro and advised beginning it by carrying out an air strike. However, the Pentagon's position was opposed by Robert F. Kennedy, the President's brother and closest advisor. Such an operation, he said, could result in a third world war. Instead he proposed a naval blockade of Cuba, accompanied by a firm demand to the Soviets that the missiles be removed. A naval blockade would be less risky, would keep Soviet military goods out of Cuba, and would

force Khrushchev to make an immediate response to the demand.

After a week of meetings and much thought, the President decided on the blockade. On October 22 he announced his decision to the American people and the world on television. After explaining the situation, he declared that the United States Navy would stop and search all ships bound for Cuba. Those carrying offensive weapons would be made to turn back. He appealed to Khrushchev to remove the missiles and bases and warned that any missile launched from Cuba would result in a "full, retaliatory response upon the Soviet Union."

During the next few days, several Soviet ships on the high seas turned back to avoid a showdown, but work on the missile bases continued. Then, on October 26, Khrushchev sent a note stating that he would remove the missiles if Kennedy lifted the blockade and promised never to invade Cuba. He then sent a second letter in which he offered to remove the missiles only if the United States dismantled its missile bases in Turkey.

Kennedy was anxious to reach a settlement but did not want to damage American prestige by agreeing to such a deal. On his brother's advice, he ignored Khrushchev's second letter and responded favorably to his first one. Khrushchev accepted Kennedy's pledge and withdrew the missiles. Kennedy, in turn, lifted the blockade.

Installation of missile bases in Cuba would cut the warning time for an attack on the United States from 15 minutes to under 3 minutes.

Historians differ on why Kennedy was able to go to the brink and force Khrushchev to back down. Some claim that Kennedy succeeded because of United States superiority over the Soviet Union in nuclear weapons. Others believe that he succeeded because of Cuba's geographical closeness to the United States and its exposure to an American attack.

Kennedy's firmness and cool judgment in the missile crisis erased the shame of the Bay of Pigs and boosted United States prestige. The settlement of the crisis preserved a balance of power acceptable to both sides. The Soviet Union recognized the security interests of the United States in the Western Hemisphere, while the United States allowed the existence of a communist government in Cuba.

In the short run, the crisis led to a reduction of Cold War tensions. Both the United States and the Soviet Union had faced the prospect of nuclear war and were not willing to face it again. As a result, a new period of American-Soviet relations began. In 1963 a "hot line" telephone linked Washington and Moscow for the first time, so that leaders of both nations could instantly communicate with each other. In the same year, the United States, the Soviet Union, and other world powers signed a treaty banning the testing of nuclear weapons in the atmosphere.

The Dominican Crisis. The communist government in Cuba continued to challenge American interests in the Caribbean area. Cuban leaders vowed to spread communist revolutions throughout Latin America. The United States, in turn, promised to guard Latin American countries against communist takeovers. It developed a military strategy called **flexible response,** which allowed United States armed forces to move quickly and decisively to settle crises. This flexible response strategy required the buildup of conventional troops and weapons and the development of specially-trained guerrilla forces, such as the army's Green Berets.

The flexible response strategy was first used in the Dominican Republic, a country occupying half of the island of Hispaniola in the Caribbean Sea. Since 1930 the Dominican Republic had been ruled by dictator Rafael Trujillo. In 1961 Trujillo was shot and killed by his opponents, and his government was overthrown. The following year, Juan Bosch, a writer and opponent of Trujillo, was freely elected president. He promised to improve the economy and raise the living standards of the people.

The army and upper-class leaders ousted Bosch in September 1963, accusing him of supporting communism. They replaced the democratic system with a

A soldier from an international peace-keeping force of the Organization of American States distributes food and water to a crowd of Dominicans during the civil war. President Johnson sent American marines to the Dominican Republic in 1965 to protect American citizens. Why was Johnson's action criticized?

Discuss with students how the allies of United States in Latin America might have reacted to the Bay of Pigs, the Cuban Missile Crisis, and to American troops in the Dominican Republic.

military government. In the spring of 1965, a rebellion broke out. A group of young army officers wanted Bosch returned to power, and they turned against the older officers of the military, plunging the country into a civil war.

President Lyndon B. Johnson sent 400 marines to the Dominican Republic to protect Americans living there. Fearing a communist takeover, he then raised the number of American troops to 20,000. Johnson, however, did not consult the Organization of American States before sending the additional troops. This led to charges that the action was in violation of the OAS charter, which forbids the interference by one American country in the affairs of another. Many Latin Americans wondered whether the United States had returned to a "big stick" policy to block communism in the Western Hemisphere. To silence this criticism, Johnson persuaded other OAS members to send troops to the Dominican Republic.

In May 1965 a truce was finally arranged, and by the fall of 1966 all foreign troops had withdrawn. In June 1966 Joaquin Balaquer, a political moderate, was elected President of the Dominican Republic.

Since the Dominican crisis, historians have concluded that few Communists were actually involved in the uprising. However, Johnson was proud of American success in the crisis, and he believed it proved that the flexible response strategy was sound. Therefore he used it again in Southeast Asia. Others saw dangers in the way United States foreign policy was moving. In trying to stop communist expansion, they said, the United States was taking on the role of a "world policeman" and relying too much on military solutions. Critics began to point out the limits and strengths of growing American power overseas.

SECTION REVIEW

1. Identify the following: Nikita Khrushchev, Abdel Nasser, Eisenhower Doctrine, Peace Corps, Sputnik I, Fulgencio Batista, "hot line."
2. What was accomplished at Geneva in 1955?
3. Why did the United States fail to aid Hungary?
4. How did the Suez crisis increase the power of the Soviet Union in the Middle East?
5. What was the significance of the Berlin Wall?
6. How did Kennedy handle the Cuban missile crisis?

CHAPTER 28   REVIEW

SUMMARY

1. After World War II, growing differences between the United States and the Soviet Union led to a struggle for world influence known as the Cold War.
2. Under Presidents Truman and Eisenhower, the United States followed a foreign policy designed to contain the spread of communism.
3. The need to contain communism forced the United States to give up its isolationist stance and to involve itself in active military alliances in Europe, Asia, and Latin America.
4. During the late 1940's and 1950's, the Soviets tightened their hold over Eastern Europe and made gains in the Middle East, but the United States was largely successful in protecting Western Europe from the spreading threat of communism.
5. Japan, after a period of American military occupation, emerged as a strong ally of the United States.

6. When communist forces took over mainland China in 1949, the United States allied itself with the exiled Chinese government in Taiwan.
7. In the early 1950's, the United States successfully helped to defend South Korea against a communist takeover by North Korea.
8. In the 1960's and 1970's, the Cold War increasingly shifted to the developing nations of Asia, Africa, and South America.
9. The United States suffered a major setback when Cuba was taken over by a pro-Soviet communist dictatorship.
10. The United States lost prestige by supporting an unsuccessful invasion of Cuba but regained it by forcing the Soviets to back down from installing missile bases on the island.
11. The Kennedy administration developed a more aggressive foreign policy, designed to allow quick American intervention wherever communism threatened any part of the world.

VOCABULARY

bipolarism	containment	domino theory	Third World	deterrent
arms race	airlift	massive retaliation	nonaligned	flexible response
satellites	repatriation	summit conference	de-Stalinization	
iron curtain	limited warfare	peaceful coexistence	wars of liberation	

REVIEW QUESTIONS

1. What role did other countries play in the power conflict between the United States and the Soviet Union?

2. How did that role change between the 1940's and the 1960's?

3. How did the development of nuclear weapons affect the Cold War?

4. What role did the United Nations play in the Cold War?

5. What was the relationship between the United States and Taiwan?

6. How did Soviet policy change after Stalins' death?

7. What was the relationship of the United States with Israel?

8. What was American policy toward Latin America during the Cold War?

9. What attempts were made to reduce the tensions of the Cold War?

DISCUSSION

1. Should the United States take on the role of "world policeman"? Why or why not?

2. Is communism as much of a threat today as it was in the 1940's and 1950's? Why or why not?

3. Should the United States support dictatorships or unpopular governments in countries that are threatened by communism? Why or why not?

4. How can the threat of nuclear war be reduced?

USING MAPS

Refer to the maps on page 620–621 and answer the following questions:

1. What countries in Europe were nonaligned with any power?

2. What countries in the Western Hemisphere were not members of the OAS?

3. Which alliances did the United States join?

4. What countries were allied with the Soviet Union?

USING SKILLS

Refer to the discussion of George Kennan's article on containment, page 602. Which of the following ideas are assumed by Kennan's proposal for containment of communism?

1. The interests of the Soviet Union are in conflict with the interests of the United States.

2. Eventually the United States will have to go to war with the Soviet Union.

3. The United States can prevent the spread of communism without going to war.

4. The United States and the Soviet Union will always be enemies.

SUMMARY

1. After World War I, the United States pursued a foreign policy of non-involvement, while totalitarian governments rose to power in Europe and Asia.
2. When World War II began in 1939, the United States attempted to remain officially neutral, while at the same time giving material aid to the Allies.
3. After Japan attacked Pearl Harbor in 1941, the United States joined the Allies to defeat the Axis Powers.
4. World War II ended in 1945, after the atomic bomb was dropped on Japan.
5. After the war, the United States and the Soviet Union emerged as superpowers engaged in a struggle for world influence.
6. The Cold War between the United States and the Soviet Union led the United States to abandon isolationism and to adopt an active foreign policy that was designed to prevent the spread of communism.

REVIEW QUESTIONS

1. How did the rise of totalitarianism in the 1930's lead to World War II?
2. What role did the United States play in the defeat of the Axis Powers?
3. How did World War II affect the position of the United States in world affairs?
4. How successful was the United States in its attempt to prevent the spread of communism?

SUGGESTED ACTIVITIES

1. Develop a chart comparing the elements Woodrow Wilson's Fourteen Points and the Atlantic Charter.
2. Interview several people who experienced World War II and find out how the war affected their lives.
3. Research and report on recent attempts of Japanese-Americans to seek compensation for their treatment by the United States government during World War II.
4. Role-play a meeting between Truman and his top advisors on the proposed use of the atomic bomb. Research and present the views of military experts, scientists, and leading politicians.
5. Develop a time line indicating the major events of the Cold War from 1945 to 1960.

SUGGESTED READINGS

1. Goldman, Eric F. *The Crucial Decade & After: America 1945–1960*. New York: Random House, Inc., 1961. Paperback. Describes the issues facing Americans after World War II and the people who influenced the country's direction.
2. Hersey, John R. *Hiroshima*. New York: Bantam Books, 1968. Interviews with survivors of the atomic bomb give a compassionate account of the effects of modern warfare.
3. Lash, Joseph J. *Eleanor & Franklin*. New York: American Library, 1973. Paperback. Describes the relationship of the Roosevelts.
4. Michener, James A. *Bridges at Toko-Ri*. New York: Fawcett Book Group, 1978. Paperback. Story about a navy flier who carries out orders but does not understand why.
5. Tregaskis, Richard. *Guadalcanal Diary*. New York: Random House, Inc., 1955. A vivid story of World War II, describing the heroism and ordeals of combat soldiers.
6. Truman, Margaret. *Harry S. Truman*. New York: William Morrow & Co., Inc., 1973. A daughter's view of the man who lived in the White House during the turbulent years following World War II.

THE HISTORIAN'S CRAFT

A famous American historian once wrote that "each era writes the history of the past with reference to the conditions uppermost in its own time." This point helps to explain why historians interpret the past differently. It also suggests that historians from the same era, looking at the past from similar perspectives, frequently agree on a good deal of the history they write. This similarity of perspective brings about the phenomenon of "schools" of history—groups of scholars who hold the same basic assumptions.

There have been many different schools of American history. For example, historians writing during the Progressive Era, who were concerned about widening class distinctions in their own society, tended to describe much of American history in terms of tension between different social and economic classes. Simply put, American history was seen as the continuing struggle for control of government between people with wealth—especially business wealth—and the common people.

Another aspect of the phenomenon of schools is revisionism. For example, historians writing in the 1920's about the Civil War tended to reject the argument that the war was an inevitable conflict between two different societies or cultures. Influenced by the tragedy of World War I, many scholars felt that war was never justified. Therefore, they emphasized the failure of leaders, the failure of the democratic system, or the irrational behavior of politicians during the late 1850's as explanations for the war. Since they rejected the traditional view of the war as inevitable, they were called revisionists. That is, they *revised* the prevailing explanation of the war.

It is important that students of history be aware of the existence of historical schools. Awareness of this fact makes it easier to evaluate a historian's work. If you can identify the school to which a historian belongs, you gain insight into some of the assumptions underlying the work.

Recognizing a school of history from a historical quotation requires the student to determine the key point or points the historian makes in the passage. At the same time, the student must apply his or her own knowledge of historical schools and analyze their underlying assumptions. The following exercise will give you practice in recognizing schools of history. The subject of the exercise is the Cold War.

As with so many other topics in American history, Cold War interpretations have been revised. At least two major schools can be identified. The first school, labeled the traditional school, closely followed the official government explanation of the Cold War. The second school, called the revisionist school, questioned the arguments of the traditionalists. Some of the revisionists were no doubt influenced by the disenchantment with American foreign policy arising from the Vietnam War.

According to the traditional school, the end of World War II saw Americans looking forward to an era of peace. However, Soviet domination of Eastern Europe, aggression in the Middle East, and support for communist revolutions in Asia soon forced the United States to recognize a new threat to freedom. In reaction, the United States adopted the policy of containment. By 1947 the "Cold War" had developed. Although details varied, the traditionalists blamed the Cold War on the Soviets.

Revisionists, on the other hand, were more critical of America's role in bringing about the Cold War. Some argued that the Soviet Union was, in fact, weak after World War II, and American actions—like "saber-rattling" with the atomic bomb—led the Soviets to act in defense of their security. In short, revisionists said, the Soviets were reacting defensively to an American drive to establish economic and political influence around the world.

Following are several quotations from Cold War historians. Study the quotations in order to identify the schools to which the historians belong.

Historian A

In the next few weeks the Russians emphatically and crudely worked their will in Eastern Europe, above all in the test country of Poland. They were ignoring the Declaration on Liberated Europe, ignoring the Atlantic Charter, self-determination, human freedom and everything else the Americans considered essential for a stable peace. "We must clearly

627

recognize," Harriman wired Washington a few days before Roosevelt's death, "that the Soviet program is the establishment of totalitarianism, ending personal liberty and democracy as we know and respect it."

Historian B

. . . (t)he increasingly militarized holy war mounted by American leaders was grossly irrelevant to the situation and highly conducive to producing problems that were more dangerous than those the policy was supposed to resolve.

Historian C

Stalin's record in the early Cold War is less than that of a fairytale monster on the prowl . . . than that of a small, cold, very practical nationalist in a tight, dangerous situation. Stalin accepted the Cold War. He seems to have had little choice. . . . But that does not prove that he created it. The terms of that eerie battle were mainly set by the power that held the initiative and commanded the heights, and those powers were England in the rear and the United States far out in front.

Historian D

The Cold War could have been avoided only if the Soviet Union had not been possessed by convictions both of the infallibility of the communist word and of the inevitability of a communist world. These convictions transformed an impasse between national states into a religious war, a tragedy of possibility into one of necessity.

Historian E

Soviet Russia carried forward her revolutionary program, first in contiguous states, next in remoter regions, finally through fifth columns of communists all over the world. Russian power flowed irresistibly into the vacuums left by the collapse of German and Japanese authority in Europe and Asia. The USSR clenched its hold on the territorial occupations in Eastern Europe. Then it

intervened with the force of revolution, syphoned out of Soviet military might, to overturn the principles of real democracy and free and unfettered elections agreed to at Teheran and Yalta. One by one it installed Communist governments in the satellite states to the west and southwest and imposed upon them a structure of alliances and political and economic control in the form of "co-operation" and "collaboration" for cultural and economic purposes. . . .

Historian F

Nevertheless, in its aftermath of deception, Yalta was in a sense another Munich. It was Stalin who called the tune.

Historian G

The uniformly powerful West wanted—and believed . . . that it had to obtain—a guarantee against the spread of revolution and . . . a guarantee of economic and political access to all of Europe. The unevenly powerful Soviet Union wanted development capital without strings, heavy German machinery, and some reprieve from militant Wagnerism.

Historian H

I believe new evidence proves not only that the atomic bomb influenced diplomacy, but that it determined much of Mr. Truman's shift to a tough policy aimed at forcing Soviet acquiescence to American plans for Eastern and Central Europe.

Historian I

Ever since a Russian czar had married the daughter of the last Byzantine emperor four centuries earlier, the Russians had felt a sense of mission in Asia, as a result of which Imperial Russian control was extended from European Russia throughout north and central Asia. This expansionist urge, far from being reversed by the Bolshevik revolution, was merely reinforced by it. The chief practical difference was that the tactics of infiltration and propaganda were added to the standard *forms of nineteenth-century expansionism. Monolithic in power and ideology, with a fanatical historical sense of mission, the USSR hung over fragmentized Asia in 1947, as it does today, like a dark and heavy sky over a patchwork countryside.*

Historian J

Even where the United States had yet to develop all of its objectives in specific detail, it was imperative that it prevent any Great Power from totally dominating Eastern Europe or any other region of the world for that matter, because the United States considered all political and economic blocs or spheres of influence that it did not control as directly undermining its larger political, and especially economic, objectives for an integrated world capitalism and a political structure which was the prerequisite to its goals.

Historian K

The Russians understood the American intention and the risks of any covert aid to the Left, and they gave precious little of it during

and immediately after the war, when they discovered that even an obviously conservative policy failed to blunt the American belief that behind all the world's social and economic ills, somehow, and in some critical fashion, a Russian plot and device existed.

Historian L

How could the United States counter such a policy—a policy that was always pushing, seeking weak spots, attempting to fill power vacuums? Kennan's answer was that American policy would have to be one of "long-term, patient but firm and vigilant containment."

QUESTIONS

1. What is the basic assumption of the traditional school? Of the revisionist school?
2. Which historians reflect the views of the traditional school?
3. Which ones reflect the views of the revisionist school?
4. What key phrases in each quotation help you to identify the historian's school?

1946	1950–54	1957	1961	1963
Taft-Hartley	Era of	Sputnik	New	Assassination
Act	McCarthyism	Launch	Frontier	of JFK

1949	1954	1957	1962–73
Fair	*Brown*	Little	Vietnam
Deal	Decision	Rock	War

THE UNITED STATES IN A NEW ERA

Truman and Eisenhower

The Kennedy-Johnson Years

The Nixon-Ford Era

American Society in Transition

Carter and Reagan

1964	1965		1969	1972		1977	1979	1981
Civil	Great		Moon	ERA submitted		Panama	Camp David	New
Rights Act	Society		Landing	to Congress		Canal Treaties	Accords	Federalism

1964		1967		1971	1973–74		1979–80
24th		25th		26th	Watergate		Hostage
Amendment		Amendment		Amendment	Scandal		Crisis

1	Truman's First Term	**633**
2	Truman's Second Term	**637**
3	The Eisenhower Era	**640**
4	Life in the 1950's	**645**

TRUMAN AND EISENHOWER

The moving van is a symbol of more than our restlessness; it is a most conclusive possible evidence of our progress.

LOUIS KRONENBERGER

After World War II, the United States entered its greatest period of economic growth. More Americans than ever before enjoyed a high standard of living. People felt good about themselves and the country. However, the Cold War and rapid social change brought fears and uncertainties that sometimes dimmed their optimism.

In politics, the nation as a whole was moderately conservative and opposed to drastic changes in the status quo. It elected two Presidents during this period who represented the reassuring traditional values of small-town America. Democrat Harry S Truman, President from 1945 to 1953, came from Missouri and was known for his "plain speaking." Dwight D. Eisenhower, President from 1953 to 1961, was born in Texas and raised in Kansas. Eisenhower led the Allied forces in Europe during World War II and became a popular war hero. "Ike," as he was affectionately called, represented honesty, simplicity, and friendliness to many Americans.

1 Truman's First Term

Harry Truman became the 33rd President of the United States following the death of Franklin Roosevelt on April 12, 1945. Both Truman and the nation were unprepared for the sudden change in administrations. Truman had no previous experience in making important policy decisions. As a Senator, he had chaired a wartime Senate committee that investigated defense contracts and saved the federal government a great deal of money. However, he had little responsibility as Vice President. He was not included in foreign and military policy-making. The day after taking office, the new President told reporters:

> *Boys, if you ever pray, pray for me now. I don't know whether you fellows ever had a load of hay fall on you, but when they told me yesterday what happened, I felt like the moon, the stars, and all the planets had fallen on me. I've got the most terribly responsible job a man ever had.*

Truman assumed the Presidency at a difficult period in American history. World War II had to be won. Then, the United States needed a domestic policy to establish a peacetime economy. Truman immediately set out to assert leadership in domestic and foreign policies. He placed on his Oval Office desk a sign that read "The buck stops here." In other words, all important decisions affecting the country are the final responsibility of the President.

Return to Peace

Assuming office so suddenly, Truman had little time to prepare a program for returning the American economy to a peacetime basis. Instead, the new administration had to develop its policies gradually as specific problems emerged.

Social Welfare. After World War II the federal government cut military spending. Many Americans feared that this would lead to another depression. They looked to the Truman administration to prevent a return to high unemployment. Congress, with Truman's backing, passed the Employment Act of 1946, which required the federal government to promote economic growth that would create jobs. The act also set up a Council of Economic Advisors to assist the President in making economic policy. In signing the measure into law, Truman said that the act was "a commitment by the government to the people, a commitment to take any and all measures necessary for a healthy economy."

The federal government also provided assistance to soldiers returning home from the war. It put into effect the Readjustment Act of 1944 or, as it is

634 TRUMAN AND EISENHOWER

The biggest rise in consumer prices during the postwar period was 7.9 percent in 1951.

commonly called, the "GI Bill of Rights." This law helped war veterans to find jobs, housing, education, and medical care. Between 1945 and 1953 the federal government spent $13.5 billion dollars on education and job training for veterans.

Inflation. Instead of a depression, the United States enjoyed an economic boom in the first postwar years. People wanted to invest in business and buy scarce consumer goods, such as appliances and automobiles. Increased demand soon led to inflation.

Truman hoped to check the upward movement of wages and prices by a gradual removal of wartime government controls. Most Americans, however, wanted an end to these restrictions as soon as possible. Pressured by Congress and the public, the President ended most controls in 1946. As a result, prices jumped even higher. Since wages did not rise as rapidly as prices, the cost of living increased for many Americans.

Labor Troubles. When the cost of living rose, labor unions demanded wage boosts as well as **"fringe benefits"**—extra aids such as pensions and health insurance. When they were turned down, union leaders threatened to strike.

The most serious strike threats came from the United Mine Workers (UMW) and the railroad unions. In the spring of 1946, UMW President John L. Lewis ordered the closing of soft coal mines. This led to fuel shortages. At the same time, the railroad unions threatened a strike that would shut down the country's transportation system.

Truman was concerned about the effects of coal and rail strikes on the nation's economy. On May 21, 1946, he seized the coal mines. The miners were forced to accept a government-negotiated settlement and went back to work. A few days later, Truman warned that he would draft striking rail workers into the army and force them to run the trains. With this threat, the railroad union agreed to a settlement.

Agriculture. Truman also had problems with the nation's farmers. During the war, farmers had profited greatly from government price supports and the increased demand for food. At the war's end, however, they disliked the rigidity of government controls and wanted a freer market. In the fall of 1946, cattle farmers declared a meat strike and stopped sending beef to market. This action, along with rising demand, led to a meat shortage in the cities.

Political Effects. Many people began to blame the Truman administration for inflation, shortages, and strikes. Thinking that Truman was weak, Congress rejected or delayed legislation sponsored by the President. Also, many Democrats turned away from Truman and began to search for a new party leader. By the end of 1946, the administration had so many

Veterans faced many problems after their return to civilian life. Housing was one. Many families had no choice but to live in refurbished barracks or trailer parks because construction of new houses had virtually stopped during the war. What programs were started by the government to help returning veterans?

Presidents were often reluctant to support civil rights strongly, not for philosophical reasons, but for political ones.

enemies and faced so many problems that people jokingly said "to err is Truman."

Taft-Hartley Act

In the 1946 congressional elections, the Republicans gained control of both houses of Congress for the first time since 1928. Ohio Senator Robert A. Taft, the leading Republican in the new Eightieth Congress, was a strong supporter of business and agriculture. In the spring of 1947, he and Representative Fred A. Hartley, a conservative Republican from New Jersey, introduced a bill to limit the powers of labor unions.

The Taft-Hartley bill outlawed the closed shop, which banned the hiring of non-union workers. It also required unions to make their financial records public and made it illegal for unions to contribute to political campaigns. Employers were allowed to sue unions for broken contracts or for damages due to strikes.

In addition, the bill required a 60-day "cooling-off" period before workers could strike. The President was allowed to seek court injunctions to block any strikes that endangered the national economy. These injunctions would hold for 80 days. During this period a fact-finding committee could investigate and make recommendations for a settlement.

Truman vetoed the bill. Although he opposed the recent strikes, he also knew that Democrats needed the support of labor. Therefore he objected to any legislation that was strongly anti-labor. In his veto message, the President said that "this bill will go far toward weakening our trade [labor] movement. . . . It contains seeds of discord which would plague the nation for years to come."

Congress overrode Truman's veto, and the bill became law as the Taft-Hartley Act in June 1947. Labor leaders attacked the act as a "slave labor law." They claimed that its allowing of court injunctions would force workers to work against their will. Labor unions rallied to the support of the Democratic party and began to work to overturn the act.

Civil Rights

After World War II, civil rights became an important national issue for the first time since the late 1800's. Wartime changes were responsible for this development. Many black Americans who had left the rural South and moved to northern cities became strong backers of the Democratic party. Black males had also served in the armed forces, and some had acquired good educations and jobs. As a result of these changes, blacks were in a better position to demand their full rights as Americans.

The Truman administration recognized the importance of civil rights and began to take steps to end racial discrimination. In 1946 the President appointed a Commission on Civil Rights to determine ways to safeguard and improve the civil rights of all Americans. A year later the commission issued a report entitled *To Secure These Rights*. The report called for a Federal Employment Protection Commission to end discrimination in federal job-hiring practices. It also called for an end to lynching and the poll tax. The commission favored a strengthening of existing civil rights laws and better enforcement. Above all, it wanted an end to segregation in all areas of American life.

Truman publicly stated that blacks had a right to education, welfare, jobs, and the right to vote. At the Lincoln Memorial on June 29, 1947, he declared:

> We must keep moving forward with new concepts of civil rights. . . .
> The extension of civil rights today means not the protection of people against the government, but the protection of people by the government. . . .
> We must make the Federal government a friendly, vigilant defender of the rights and equalities of all Americans. . . .

Truman's civil rights stand was opposed by many people in the South. The Democratic party was soon split between northern liberals and southern moderates who supported civil rights and southern conservatives who favored segregation. As a result, Truman could not get Congress's support for his civil rights proposals.

Government Reorganization

One issue on which Truman and Congress agreed was the need to improve the administration of the federal government, which had greatly expanded since the New Deal. In 1947 Truman appointed a

The Department of Defense was the Department of War until 1947.

Discuss with students whether predictions by newscasters and pollsters can influence an election.

commission headed by former President Herbert Hoover to study ways of improving the efficiency of government. Out of this commission's work came plans to create new government departments and agencies.

In 1947 Congress passed the National Security Act. It unified the army, navy, marines, and air force under the Department of Defense. A Secretary of Defense headed the new department. The act also set up a permanent Joint Chiefs of Staff, made up of the heads of each of the armed forces, to coordinate military policy. A National Security Council was set up to help the President in handling international crises.

Another institution that the act established was the Central Intelligence Agency (CIA). The CIA aided American foreign policy by collecting and analyzing secret data about other countries. Many Americans feared that the CIA would be used to spy on American citizens. Truman, however, promised that the new agency would operate only in foreign lands and would not bring "police state methods" into American society.

The Election of 1948

Truman decided to seek another term in 1948. Voters, however, were deeply divided about Truman's candidacy. Although the nation's economy had improved, Truman was still blamed for many problems.

Democrats. Many moderate and liberal Democrats wanted to "dump" Truman, but they could not agree on a suitable substitute. Some wanted General Eisenhower. But when Eisenhower refused to run, they reluctantly agreed on Truman. Others in this group left party ranks altogether and formed a third party known as the Progressives. The Progressive party nominated Secretary of Commerce Henry A. Wallace as its presidential candidate. Wallace opposed Truman's foreign policy and called for closer ties between the United States and the Soviet Union.

On the other hand, many conservative southern Democrats were alarmed about Truman's support of civil rights for black Americans. These conservatives also left the Democratic party and founded the States' Rights, or "Dixiecrat" party, which nominated J. Strom Thurmond, governor of South Carolina, for President.

In spite of these setbacks, Truman was able to gain the Democratic presidential nomination. Senator Alben W. Barkley of Kentucky was nominated for Vice President.

Republicans. The Republicans, confident of victory, again chose Governor Thomas E. Dewey of New York as their nominee. A moderate, Dewey supported the New Deal but wanted the states to have more power in running social programs. Governor Earl Warren of California, another moderate, was nominated for Vice President.

The Campaign. In spite of Dewey's unimpressive performance as a campaigner, various polls predicted a Republican victory. But Truman believed that he and the Democrats could win. He conducted a strong campaign, traveling across the country by train. He stopped wherever people gathered to hear him. In his speeches, Truman joked with his listeners, but he also attacked what he called the "do-nothing, good-for-nothing" Eightieth Congress for rejecting his legislation.

On election day, experts still expected the Republicans to win. The voters, however, surprised the pollsters and news commentators. With the help of labor, farmers, and northern blacks, Truman was returned to office in one of the biggest political upsets in American history. Truman received 24 million popular votes, while Dewey got 22 million. In the Electoral College, Truman had 303 votes to Dewey's

President Truman displays the *Chicago Daily Tribune* that had wrongly projected Thomas Dewey as winner of the 1948 presidential election. What coalition helped Truman upset Dewey?

ELECTION OF 1948

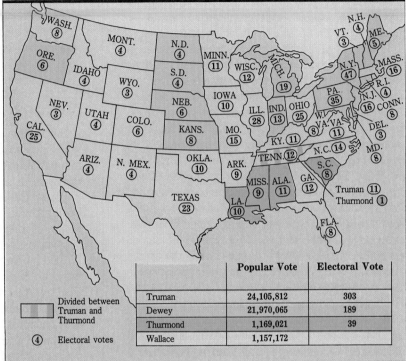

	Popular Vote	Electoral Vote
Truman	24,105,812	303
Dewey	21,970,065	189
Thurmond	1,169,021	39
Wallace	1,157,172	

Divided between Truman and Thurmond

④ Electoral votes

Truman ⑪
Thurmond ①

189. The Democrats also carried both houses of Congress and won important victories in state races.

SECTION REVIEW

1. Identify the following: Employment Act of 1946, GI Bill of Rights, Robert A. Taft, J. Strom Thurmond.
2. What caused inflation in the postwar years?
3. What were the provisions of the Taft-Hartley Act?
4. What effects did World War II have on black Americans?
5. Why was Truman expected to lose the election of 1948?

2 Truman's Second Term

As a result of the 1948 election, Truman expected his administration to make progress in carrying out its programs. He believed that most Americans had voted for him because they wanted the federal government to update and extend the reforms of the New Deal.

The Fair Deal

In January 1949 Truman promoted an extensive package of reforms that he called the "Fair Deal." These reforms, he hoped, would provide fair treatment to all Americans. In a message to Congress, he declared:

We have rejected the discredited theory that the fortunes of the nation shall be in the hands of a privileged few. Instead, we believe that our economic system shall rest on a democratic foundation and that wealth shall be created for the benefit of all. The recent election shows that the American people are in favor of this kind of society and want to go on improving it. . . .
Every segment of our population and every individual has a right to expect from this government a fair deal.

Truman called for civil rights legislation, federal aid to education, a low-cost housing program, and an end to the Taft-Hartley Act. He also supported higher

Note that the two-term limit was a precedent set by Washington and observed by every President until Franklin Roosevelt.

Chambers and another witness, Elizabeth Bentley, accused 37 government employees of aiding the Communists.

social security benefits and an extension of the program to 10 million more workers. Finally, he asked for a national health insurance plan, to be funded by taxes on employers and workers.

Truman's proposals, however, ran against a growing conservative mood in the country. Many people wanted to "hold the line" on the New Deal and were opposed to further social reforms. The new Congress, in particular, disliked federal controls, heavy government spending, and high taxes. A coalition of Republicans and southern Democrats blocked the passage of much of Truman's Fair Deal program. The Taft-Hartley Act remained in effect. Proposals for a national health insurance program and for federal aid to education were defeated. Civil rights laws also failed to pass, but Truman acted whenever he could without Congress. In July 1948 he signed executive orders ending discrimination in the armed forces and guaranteeing fair employment practices in the civil service system.

Congress did pass the National Housing Act of 1949, which provided for the construction of housing for low-income families. Otherwise, liberal and moderate Democrats generally had to be satisfied that the President was able to prevent a rollback of existing New Deal reforms.

Democratic Decline

By 1950 Truman's popularity had fallen once again. Defense spending for the Korean War led to higher taxes and inflation. In the 1950 congressional elections, the Democrats lost seats in both houses. Many of the defeated members of Congress had been Truman's supporters. In the new Congress the conservative coalition was stronger than ever.

One measure passed by Congress was the McCarran Immigration Act of 1952. It raised slightly the total number of immigrants allowed into the country. However, it kept the quota system that restricted immigration from areas outside of northern and western Europe.

Conservatives in Congress also wanted to reduce the powers of the executive branch. They hoped to keep a long-term Presidency such as Roosevelt's from happening again. In 1947 they succeeded in passing the Twenty-Second Amendment, making two terms the maximum to which a person could be

elected. The amendment also barred the election for more than one term of a person who had held the office of President for more than two years of a term to which someone else was elected. This amendment was ratified by the required 36 states in February 1951.

National Security

During the late 1940's and early 1950's, the Cold War influenced events within the United States. Many Americans became alarmed about the spread of communism in American society.

Spies. Reports of American citizens spying for the Soviet Union disturbed Congress and the public. Some of these cases of **espionage,** or spying, involved incidents in the 1930's. For instance, in 1948 Wittaker Chambers, who admitted to having been a member of the Communist party, accused Alger Hiss, a former high-ranking State Department official, of being a member of a prewar Soviet spy ring in Washington. In January 1950, Hiss was convicted by a jury for **perjury,** or lying while under oath. He was sentenced to five years in prison.

Other cases involved postwar incidents. In March 1949, Judith Coplon, a Justice Department employee, was arrested for passing documents to a Soviet spy. During the same period Julius Rosenberg, an engineer, and his wife Ethel were accused of giving

National attention in the late 1940's focused on charges of subversion in government and, in particular, on the trial of Alger Hiss. What was done to check subversive influence?

Note the similarity between the McCarran Act provision that suspected Communists could be held in camps and the action taken against Japanese-Americans during World War II. In either case the government did not have to prove disloyalty. Group affiliation was enough.

atomic secrets to the Soviets. They were eventually convicted of espionage and executed in June 1953.

Loyalty Program. In 1947 Truman issued an executive order to ensure that all government employees were loyal to the United States and were not working for the Soviet Union. The executive order provided for loyalty boards to examine the personal and political activities of federal employees. Department and agency heads were then expected to fire persons who were proven to be disloyal or who were thought to be security risks. The order also authorized the FBI to investigate the backgrounds of all persons entering government work. By December 1952, 6.6 million federal workers had been checked. No cases of spying were uncovered, although some people who were regarded as security risks had to resign from their jobs.

The loyalty program sparked controversy. Critics charged that the program was endangering free speech and other individual rights. On the other hand, Truman supporters claimed that a democracy had to take measures against a violent minority that threatened its freedoms.

Crackdown. Other moves were taken to check communist influence. In early 1949 the federal government brought legal action against top leaders of the American Communist party. In the fall of that year, a federal jury in New York convicted them for conspiring to teach the violent overthrow of the American government.[1] At the same time persons suspected of communist sympathies were removed from the entertainment industry, the leadership of labor unions, and the teaching staffs of universities.

McCarthy. In 1950 the anti-communist movement reached its peak and soon threatened to disrupt the nation. In February of that year, Senator Joseph R. McCarthy, a Republican from Wisconsin, charged that there were a large number of Communists in the State Department. He made pointed attacks on Owen Lattimore, a professor at The John Hopkins University and a former State Department advisor. McCarthy accused Lattimore of being the "top Russian spy in the State Department." The Wisconsin Senator held the Truman administration responsible and called for Secretary of State Dean Acheson to resign.

McCarthy's charges led to the appointment of a Senate investigating sub-committee under Maryland Senator Millard Tydings. After weeks of hearings, the Tydings sub-committee decided that McCarthy's statements were "a fraud and a hoax." McCarthy then accused Tydings of being a Communist.

By this time McCarthy's crusade had attracted national attention and won widespread support. McCarthy backers in Maryland were able to defeat Tydings in the fall congressional elections. After that happened, many political leaders became afraid to speak out against McCarthy.

Due to McCarthy's influence, Congress passed the McCarran Internal Security Act in September 1950. This law required the Communist party and all suspected "front" organizations to register with the Justice Department.[2] It also forbade aliens having communist ties to enter the country and allowed the **deportation,** or expulsion, of those already here. The act set up a Subversive Activities Control Board to watch communist activities in the United States. It permitted the federal government to hold suspected Communists in detention camps in the event of war. Truman vetoed the bill stating:

> *This would be a very dangerous course to take, not because we have any sympathy for Communist opinions, but because any governmental stifling of the free expression of opinion is a long step toward totalitarianism.*
>
> *There is no more fundamental axiom of American freedom than the famous statement: In a free country we punish men for the crimes they commit but never for the opinions they have.*

Congress, however, passed the bill over Truman's veto. Meanwhile, as public excitement mounted over national security, the actual communist threat decreased. The American Communist party was weakened by the Cold War and the revelations of Stalinist terror in Eastern Europe. It lost members, and its influence declined among workers and intellectuals.

---

[1] In 1951 the Supreme Court in *Dennis* v. *United States* backed the lower courts' conviction of the communist leaders. The Court ruled that the government did not have to wait until a plot was actually ready before acting against the conspirators. It could do so if their behavior was a "clear and probable" danger to the country.

[2] In 1965 the Supreme Court ruled that the registration provision of the McCarran Internal Security Act was unconstitutional.

The practice of choosing a vice-presidential candidate with a different background from the presidential candidate is known as "balancing the ticket."

The Election of 1952

On the eve of the 1952 presidential election, the Democrats faced many challenges. Republicans, led by McCarthy, attacked the Truman administration for "softness" toward communism. At the same time, Senate investigations turned up illegal financial dealings between top administration officials and business people. Although the accused or guilty left office, it was too late for the Democrats to regain public confidence.

Democrats. Truman decided not to seek a second full term in 1952. His choice for the Democratic presidential nomination was Governor Adlai E. Stevenson of Illinois. Stevenson at first refused to run. But he was persuaded to accept the nomination at the party's convention. To gain southern support, party delegates chose Senator John Sparkman of Alabama as Stevenson's running mate.

Republicans. The Republicans were confident of winning the election. General Eisenhower came home from his NATO assignment in Europe and sought the Republican presidential nomination. He received the support of Republicans who favored moderate New Deal policies and the NATO alliance. Eisenhower's chief opponent was Senator Robert Taft of Ohio. Taft had the backing of the isolationist and conservative wing of the party.

At the Republican convention, Eisenhower had enough support to capture the nomination on the first ballot. Senator Richard M. Nixon of California, known for his strong anti-communist views, became Eisenhower's running mate. During the campaign, Eisenhower remained aloof from political debate. He allowed Nixon to charge the Democrats with political corruption and weakness in foreign policy. Soon Nixon himself was accused of improperly receiving gifts from California business friends. Eisenhower considered asking Nixon to leave the ticket. But Nixon appeared on nationwide television to defend himself. He tearfully claimed that the only gift he had ever accepted was a small dog, a spaniel named Checkers, for his two small children. This famous Checkers speech won Nixon public support and saved his political career.

Election Results. Although Stevenson presented himself as a dignified and informed candidate, he could not match the personal charisma of Eisenhower. The Republicans won the election by a landslide. Eisenhower received almost 34 million popular votes, while Stevenson received 27.3 million. In the Electoral College, 442 votes went to Eisenhower, 89 to Stevenson. The Republicans also won a slim majority in both Houses of Congress.

SECTION REVIEW

1. Identify the following: Alger Hiss, Millard Tydings, Adlai E. Stevenson, Checkers.
2. What was Truman's Fair Deal program?
3. What was the purpose of the Twenty-Second Amendment to the Constitution?
4. Why did Senator McCarthy gain so much influence in the early 1950's?

3 The Eisenhower Era

The period of Eisenhower's Presidency was a time of relative peace and national unity. The Cold War eased, and the United States enjoyed a peak of postwar prosperity, without serious inflation or unemployment. Most Americans supported Eisenhower. They were attracted to his appealing fatherly image and regarded him as a symbol of hope and confidence.

Eisenhower's First Term

Eisenhower wanted to be known as a President who was above politics and who represented all Americans. Therefore, he did not try to be a strong and active President like Roosevelt or Truman. Eisenhower used the powers of his office to set broad policy guidelines. But he left the details to the White House staff and cabinet members. Eisenhower also stressed a peaceful working relationship with Congress and avoided open criticism of the Supreme Court.

Modern Republicanism. Eisenhower's approach to government was what he called "modern Republicanism." This meant backing the basic New Deal reforms while opposing more expansion of the federal government in social and economic affairs.

Above all Eisenhower supported a free-enterprise economy, in which business could operate with a minimum of government interference. He also

Some theorists believe that the great highway network furthered the decline of the larger cities. Easier travel encouraged car buying, resulting in pollution and congestion in the central zones.

In addition, the more affluent moved outside the city and commuted to work, a pattern that eroded the city's tax base.

wanted to halt the relentless growth of the federal government, and he suggested that the states take over many of its existing programs.

During his first term, Eisenhower set out to achieve these goals. He promised to reduce government spending, balance the federal budget, and cut taxes. However, new needs forced government spending to increase. The largest increases were for defense, social security, and veterans benefits. Eisenhower himself even reversed course and favored a limited growth of federal involvement in housing, medical care, and education. For example, in 1955 he signed into law a housing act that financed the building of 45,000 new homes over a four-year period.

Interested in creating favorable conditions for business growth, the Eisenhower administration

Dwight D. Eisenhower was the first Republican to be elected President in 20 years. As a war hero, he was popular with the electorate, winning by landslides in 1952 and 1956. How did his administration differ from his Democratic predecessors?

backed projects for improving water and highway transportation. With the cooperation of Canada, construction was started on the Saint Lawrence Seaway. By the time of its completion in 1959, the seaway had created an inland waterway connecting ports in the Great Lakes region with the Atlantic Ocean.

The administration also promoted the Federal Highway Aid Act of 1956. This law provided federal money for an interstate highway network linking the nation's major cities. At completion, the network would consist of 42,000 miles (67,200 kilometers) of highways. When Eisenhower left office in 1961, more than 7500 miles (12,000 kilometers) was already open to traffic. The Highway Act received strong support from car manufacturers. It furthered the postwar boom in automobile production and sales. As a result, the automobile became the chief means of transportation in the United States.

During his first term, Eisenhower also carried out the government reorganization begun under Truman. The Department of Health, Education, and Welfare was created in 1953.[3] Oveta Culp Hobby, commander of the Women's Army Corps during World War II, became the head of the department. She was the second woman in American history to hold a cabinet post.

Eisenhower and McCarthy. In 1953 Senator McCarthy began attacking the Eisenhower administration for allowing Communists in the government. He nearly blocked Eisenhower's appointment of Charles E. Bohlen as the nation's ambassador to the Soviet Union. McCarthy claimed that Bohlen was a security risk. A special Senate committee later cleared Bohlen. A year later, McCarthy charged that the United States Information Agency had communist books in its libraries in Europe. He threatened the agency's employees and had the books removed.

Meanwhile, Eisenhower refused to involve himself directly in the McCarthy controversy. Many of McCarthy's opponents criticized the President for keeping silent. Eisenhower, however, privately stated that he preferred to let McCarthy destroy himself. The administration responded to the threat of communism in its own way. It enforced a loyalty program in the federal government. In 1954, with

---

[3] What was the Department of Health, Education, and Welfare is now two departments—the Department of Education and the Department of Health and Human Services.

Censure does not remove a member of Congress from office. It often leads to the end of a politician's career, however.

When Senator Joseph McCarthy charged that Communists were shaping foreign policy, few challenged him. Yet by 1954, his support was fading and the Senate voted to censure him. Why?

Eisenhower's support, Congress passed the Communist Control Act. This law limited the legal rights of the American Communist party and made membership in it virtually illegal.

The McCarthy Hearings. By the spring of 1954, McCarthy's support began to decline. The Cold War was easing, and many Americans feared that McCarthy's obsession with national security was ruining the lives and careers of many innocent people.

At this time, McCarthy began a search for Communists in the United States Army. Army leaders, in turn, accused McCarthy of demanding special treatment for a congressional aide who had just been drafted. From April to June, a series of televised hearings were held in which McCarthy and army officials presented their cases. McCarthy's rude behavior and use of phony evidence in the hearings damaged his cause and led to his public disgrace. In December the Senate censured McCarthy.

The Election of 1956

During the mid-1950's the Republicans appeared to be in serious trouble. In 1954 they lost control of Congress. During the next two years Eisenhower was in poor health. There were doubts that he would run for a second term. However, the President's health improved, and he finally decided to run again. In the summer of 1956 Eisenhower and Nixon were renominated by the Republicans.

The Democrats again named Adlai Stevenson as their presidential candidate. The choice for Stevenson's running mate was left in the hands of the convention delegates. They chose Senator Estes Kefauver of Tennessee over a young rival, Senator John F. Kennedy of Massachusetts.

During the campaign Stevenson accused Eisenhower of being a "part-time" President and warned that "Ike" might not survive a second term. Eisenhower ignored the issue of his health. Instead, he pointed to the peace and prosperity that the nation had enjoyed since 1953.

Eisenhower's personal popularity led him to a decisive victory. He won 35.6 million popular votes to Stevenson's 26 million. Eisenhower had 457 electoral votes, while Stevenson had 74. But his success did not carry over to the Republican party as a whole. The Democrats had a slight majority in the Senate, 49 to 47, and a sizeable majority in the House, 232 to 199. Thus, Eisenhower became the first President in more than 100 years to take office without his party controlling either house of Congress.

Eisenhower's Second Term

The second Eisenhower term was less tranquil than the first. The United States faced many serious problems at home and abroad. In the fall of 1956 American foreign policy suffered major setbacks in the Suez and Hungarian crises. After the 1957 launch of Sputnik I, many Americans wondered whether the United States was losing its lead in science and technology to the Soviets. As a result, American schools shifted their emphasis from the humanities to the sciences. At the same time racial violence in various parts of the United States showed that real equality still had to be won for many of the nation's citizens.

Civil Rights

Beginning in the mid-1950's, race relations and civil rights dominated domestic events. For the first time, black Americans in large numbers began to organize and struggle for their rights.

The Brown Decision. Not wanting to create controversy, the Eisenhower administration and Congress refused to pass civil rights legislation. As a

Discuss with students the question of how the Supreme Court can reverse itself.

Allowing local courts to oversee integration guaranteed that the process in the South would move slowly.

result, civil rights groups turned to the courts for settlement of their grievances.

In 1953 Eisenhower appointed Governor Earl Warren of California as Chief Justice of the United States Supreme Court. Warren began to move the Court toward a more liberal interpretation of the Constitution in decisions on individual rights. Also in 1953 the NAACP brought a number of civil rights cases before the Court. Thurgood Marshall, the NAACP's leading lawyer, wanted the Court to strike down state laws that required racial segregation in public schools. He argued that black children were not getting the same quality of education as white children.

On May 17, 1954, the Court handed down a historic decision in *Brown* v. *Board of Education of Topeka*. It overturned the 1896 *Plessy* v. *Ferguson* decision that segregation was constitutional as long as equal facilities were provided for both races. The Court declared:

> *We conclude that in the field of public education, the doctrine of "separate but equal" has no place. Separate educational facilities are inherently unequal.*

A year later the Court called on school authorities to make plans for school **integration,** or bringing the races together. Local courts were given the responsibility of deciding whether the plans were suitable. The Court also ordered that integration was to be carried out as soon as possible.

The nation's black population welcomed the Court rulings. However, groups in the South opposing school integration denounced the Supreme Court. They began to form White Citizens' Councils, whose purpose was to block integration by using business boycotts, job dismissals, and other threats. In the spring of 1956, members of Congress from the South issued a manifesto declaring that they would use "all lawful means" to overturn the Brown decision. Some southern states began passing laws to prevent school integration. They even set up private schools for whites with state funds.

The Eisenhower administration found itself caught between the civil rights supporters and the southern resisters. Eisenhower himself had never been a strong backer of civil rights. He also believed that the federal government could do very little to improve race relations because laws could not change what was in people's hearts. However, he regarded the Brown decision as the law of the land and recognized that it was his duty as President to enforce the law.

Little Rock. In the fall of 1957 Eisenhower was forced to act firmly in support of civil rights. At that time, resistance to the Brown decision reached its peak in Little Rock, Arkansas. Arkansas Governor Orval Faubus opposed integration. He used his state's National Guard to prevent black students from enrolling in Little Rock's Central High School.

Eisenhower tried to persuade Faubus to enforce the law. Faubus agreed and withdrew the Guard. But the black students trying to enter the school soon faced crowds of hostile whites. At the urging of Attorney General Herbert Brownell, Eisenhower finally sent federal troops into Little Rock to enforce school integration. Order was restored, and the black students attended classes without major incident.

In spite of Little Rock, however, few places in the South during the late 1950's obeyed the Brown decision. A number of school districts even closed rather than accept integration.

Congressional Action. After the Court rulings, the other branches of the federal government began to act on behalf of civil rights. In the fall of 1957, Congress passed the first civil rights act since 1875. The leading defender of the measure on the floor of Congress was Lyndon B. Johnson of Texas, Senate Majority Leader and a civil rights moderate.

The new civil rights law called for the Justice Department to seek court injunctions to promote black voting rights. It appointed referees to ensure that blacks were not kept away from or cheated at the polls. Federal courts were also given power to hear any case brought by a person whose voting rights were violated.

The Civil Rights Act of 1957 did not meet the hopes of civil rights supporters. Eisenhower was cautious in enforcing it. In addition, the law had many "loopholes," and tougher legislation was needed. In 1960 another civil rights law was passed. It set heavy fines and prison terms for interfering with black voting.

Black leaders, such as Roy Wilkins of the NAACP and labor union leader A. Philip Randolph, wanted more legislation to further civil rights in areas besides education and voting. They hoped that federal officials would actively register black voters and end racial

The Montgomery bus boycott marked the beginning of direct action to end segregation.

Little Rock, Arkansas, was the scene of unrest when Governor Faubus used state troops to prevent blacks from enrolling at Central High. How did the Eisenhower administration respond?

discrimination in employment and housing. But neither Eisenhower nor a majority in Congress was willing to take these steps.

Montgomery Bus Boycott. During the mid-1950's black Americans began to act on their own to end racial discrimination. On December 3, 1955, the blacks of Montgomery, Alabama, began a boycott of the city's segregated bus system. A few days earlier, a 43-year-old seamstress named Rosa Parks had refused to give up her bus seat to a white man. She was arrested and fined for breaking a law that required segregation on city buses. The black community was outraged at the arrest. The following day, black leaders met and planned the boycott. Martin Luther King, Jr., a young Baptist minister, was chosen to lead it.

King was strongly influenced by the ideas of American reformer Henry David Thoreau and India's independence leader, Mohandas K. Gandhi. He asked the blacks of Montgomery to avoid violence and to practice civil disobedience. The black community supported King for an entire year by refusing to ride city buses. As a result, the bus company lost 65 percent of its usual income. Finally, in December 1956, the Supreme Court ruled that the Montgomery bus segregation law was unconstitutional. A few days later the boycott ended, and Montgomery integrated its buses.

Civil Rights Movement. Because of the bus boycott, Martin Luther King, Jr. became a nationally-known figure. He soon formed the Southern Christian Leadership Conference (SCLC) to press for civil rights through peaceful means. Other organizations joined in the effort. They included the Congress of Racial Equality (CORE) and the Student Non-Violent Coordinating Committee (SNCC).

During the winter of 1959 and 1960, civil rights groups held marches, demonstrations, and boycotts to end segregation in public places. They especially challenged the practice of not serving blacks at many southern lunch counters. In February 1960 four black students sat down at a segregated lunch counter in a local store in Greensboro, North Carolina. They refused to leave until they were served. Their action, known as a **"sit-in,"** spread rapidly throughout the South. It received the support of northern liberals and moderate southern whites.

By 1960 the crusade for civil rights had become a national movement. Practical results were slow in coming. Defenders of segregation often used violence against civil rights supporters. However, many Americans were now beginning to recognize the moral evil of racial discrimination. King wrote:

> *The law cannot change the heart—but it can restrain the heartless. It will take education and religion to change bad internal attitudes—but legislation and court orders can control their external aspects. Federal court decrees have, for example, altered transportation patterns and changed social mores—so that the habits, if not the hearts, of people are being altered every day by federal action. And these major social changes have a*

Discuss with students the reasons behind the National Defense Education Act.

cumulative force conditioning other segments of life.

End of the Eisenhower Era

During the late 1950's Eisenhower remained a popular President. However, his second term was less successful than his first. Critics often charged that Eisenhower was ignoring important national issues, like civil rights and the protection of natural resources. They also claimed that he was not assuming enough responsibility for the health of the nation's economy.

In 1957 and 1958 a major recession occurred. Unemployment rose to 7.7 percent of the work force, the highest rate since the end of the Great Depression. Eisenhower refused to support a large government spending program to create jobs. He believed that such a program would lead to inflation.

At the same time, the administration also faced a series of scandals. The most important scandal concerned the President's closest advisor, Sherman B. Adams. In the spring of 1958, congressional hearings revealed that Adams had received gifts from a wealthy New England industrialist who was being investigated by the government. Adams was forced to resign.

The scandals and the recession helped the Democrats to strengthen their control of Congress in the 1958 elections. But in spite of these difficulties, Eisenhower received praise for some of his efforts. In foreign policy, he sought to ease world tensions. At home, he supported government grants to aid the construction of more schools for the nation's growing school-age population. Eisenhower also backed the National Defense Education Act of 1958. This law provided government loans to college students for their education.

In 1959 two new states were added to the union. On January 3 Eisenhower issued a proclamation making Alaska the 49th state—the first new state since Arizona and New Mexico joined the Union in 1912. On August 21, Hawaii became the 50th state.

As Eisenhower's second term came to an end, he made it clear that, although he was famous as a man of war, he wanted to be remembered as a President of peace. In his January 1961 farewell address to the nation, he expressed his concern about the growth of the **"military-industrial complex,"** or the close involvement of government and industry in preparing for war:

> *The conjunction of an immense military establishment and a large arms industry is new in American experience. The total influence—economic, political, even spiritual—is felt in every city, every State house, every office of the federal government. We recognize the imperative need for this development. Yet we must not fail to comprehend its grave implications. Our toil, resources and livelihood are all involved; so is the very structure of our society.*

Eisenhower believed that the military-industrial complex had greatly contributed to "big government" and warned about its destructive effects on traditional American values. Indeed, American life was changing.

SECTION REVIEW

1. Identify the following: Saint Lawrence Seaway, Oveta Culp Hobby, Charles E. Bohlen, Thurgood Marshall, Orval Faubus, Martin Luther King, Jr.
2. What were the effects of the Highway Aid Act of 1956?
3. Why did Senator McCarthy's influence decline in the mid-1950's?
4. Why did Eisenhower send federal troops to Little Rock, Arkansas in 1957?
5. What problems did Eisenhower experience during his second term?

4 Life in the 1950's

During the 1950's observers began to refer to the United States as the world's first **affluent,** or wealthy, society. They pointed out that the American economy had gone beyond merely satisfying the basic needs of food, clothing, and shelter. It now produced an increasing volume and wide variety of "luxury" goods and services. These benefits were widely distributed among a large number of Americans.

The Economy

During the 1950's government, business, and labor grew in size, and all played important roles in

Hiram Fong

On March 12, 1959, Congress voted to admit the territory of Hawaii as a state. The people of Hawaii ratified the vote on June 27. A month later, they elected representatives to the United States Congress. One of the two Senators elected was Hiram L. Fong, a Republican who had served 14 years in the territorial legislature. Fong and his colleagues were sworn in as members of the Eighty-sixth Congress in August after Hawaii was officially proclaimed the 50th state. Fong served in the Senate until 1977.

As the first person of Chinese descent to hold a seat in the Senate, Fong hoped to promote better understanding between the United States and Asia. With this goal in mind, the Senator and his wife embarked on a tour of the Far East in October 1959. On this trip, Fong expressed his belief that Chinese people should be integrated into the various nations in which they lived. Only in this way, he believed, could they achieve complete success. He cited himself as an example of this process.

Senator Fong came from humble beginnings. His parents left China and emigrated to Hawaii, where they began life as indentured workers on a sugar plantation. Hiram, born in 1907, was one of 11 children and at an early age had to find work to help support the family. To make money, he sold newspapers, shined shoes, and delivered groceries.

Because of the continuing lack of money, Hiram had to postpone college. However, after working for three years, he enrolled at the University of Hawaii, from which he graduated with honors. With the aid of a scholarship, Hiram entered Harvard Law School. He received his degree in 1935 and returned to Hawaii, where he established the first multiracial law firm in Honolulu. The firm was so successful that Fong began to invest his money. Soon he was a millionaire. In 1970, because of his achievements, he received the Horatio Alger award.

promoting economic growth. In his 1952 book *American Capitalism,* economist John Kenneth Galbraith described each of these institutions as a **"countervailing power,"** or an influence that checked the ambitions of the others. As a result, he claimed, the economy was stable, yet flexible enough to grow.

Government. The federal government especially influenced economic performance in the 1950's. It helped to prevent a return to the massive unemployment of the Great Depression. Government spending aided industry, created jobs, and boosted the economy. Federal agencies financed the building of homes. As a result, more Americans were able to buy and own their own houses. At the same time, the federal government limited the power of business and labor. For example, government negotiators had an important influence in the making of wage settlements between employers and workers.

Business. Large corporations, which dominated the business world of the 1950's, also aided economic prosperity with their large financial resources. They spent heavily on research and developed new products. Companies also worked hard to produce more goods and cut costs. Many of them cooperated to end unfair price competition and to set fair standards for business conduct.

Companies also advertised more effectively to convince consumers to buy more products. In addition, private credit expanded, allowing shoppers to buy goods without having a large amount of savings in the bank.

Reasons for the postwar baby boom included the return of the soldiers, a healthy economy, and the desire to forget the war and return to normal family life.

Agriculture. The 1950's saw great changes in American agriculture. The number of small family farms continued to decline. Between 1949 and 1959 almost 1.2 million farm families left agriculture for other pursuits. Large business enterprises bought vast areas of available farm land. They used large sums of money to transform agriculture into a thriving business. New machines and new chemical fertilizers helped produce an abundance of food for American and foreign consumers. High government price supports guaranteed farmers a steady income that matched that of other producers in the economy.

Industrial Workers. Industrial workers also benefited from the prosperity of the 1950's. Their incomes rose and brought a higher standard of living. As a result, the social gulf between the middle classes and the working classes was significantly reduced.

Relations between business and labor also improved. Labor unions grew wealthier and larger; they became the equals of many corporations. By 1955, 25 percent of the nation's workers belonged to labor unions. In the same year, the American Federation of Labor (AFL) and the Congress of Industrial Organizations (CIO) merged into the AFL-CIO. The AFL-CIO had a combined membership of 16 million workers.

Federal legislation, however, checked organized labor's growth and influence. Also, union prestige was damaged by revelations of corruption among certain union leaders.[4] By 1960 labor unions were having difficulty attracting new recruits from a growing and changing work force.

New Workers. New technology in the 1950's transformed the nature of work and the type of jobs. Increasing **automation,** or the extensive use of machinery in place of human labor, boosted productivity and efficiency. Although some unemployment resulted, labor and money were released for other tasks. Now fewer Americans were **"blue-collar workers,"** or people who work in factories or on farms. More of them were **"white-collar workers,"** or people working in offices and performing services for others. Many of these new workers did not join labor unions.

---

[4] In 1959 Congress passed the Landrum-Griffin Act to end corruption and criminal activities in labor unions. The act ensured the fair election of all union officials. It also protected individual union members against illegal actions by their union leaders.

Criticism. Despite prosperity, observers saw weaknesses in the American economy. Many of them doubted that government, business, and labor could check each other's power and guarantee a just economic system. They pointed out that millions of Americans still lived in poverty and were not benefiting from the affluent society. Wealth was not fairly distributed. In 1960 the top 5 percent of families received 14.4 percent of the nation's income, while the lowest 20 percent received only 5.5 percent.

Some critics thought that the country's prosperity relied too heavily on defense spending. By the late 1950's, the Defense Department had become the greatest single customer of the nation's leading businesses. Many observers feared that this close alliance of government and industry would turn the United States into a society permanently geared for war.

Others claimed that American mass production was creating a lot of wasteful and unnecessary products. To keep the economy going, advertisers led Americans to buy things they did not really need. In *The Affluent Society* (1958) John K. Galbraith wrote that too much money was being spent on consumer goods and not enough on schools, hospitals, and scientific research. As a result, he and other critics said, the United States was becoming a materialistic society in danger of losing its moral fibre.

Population

After World War II the population of the United States significantly increased. In 1950 there were 151 million Americans; by 1960 this number increased to 179 million. The large jump was caused partly by a decline in the death rate due to better medical care. Another cause of population increase was the **"baby boom,"** or the postwar increase in the birth rate. Millions of new school-age children soon brought a growing need for more schools and universities. During the 1950's classrooms were often crowded, and teachers were in short supply.

At the same time, immigration to the United States decreased. As a result, the United States became a more uniform society. Since a greater number of Americans were native-born, there was less attachment to ancestral homelands. Instead, people stressed what all Americans had in common.

Critics charged that suburban living encouraged conformity. Residents were usually ethnically and economically similar.

There were 3 million television sets in the United States in 1950. Within a year 7 million more sets had been purchased.

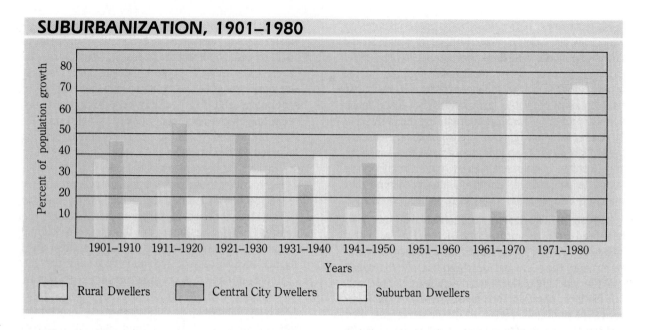

SUBURBANIZATION, 1901–1980

Percent of population growth

Years

☐ Rural Dwellers   ☐ Central City Dwellers   ☐ Suburban Dwellers

Women. In the 1950's women made up the majority of the American population. After World War II many of those who had been in the work force quit their jobs and returned home to concentrate on taking care of their families. Women were encouraged by the government and by advertising to be homemakers and not to pursue careers away from their families. They even made up a smaller proportion of college students than they had in the 1920's. Thus their impact on the job market declined.

Suburban Life. During the postwar years, a large number of Americans changed their place of residence. There was a mass movement of people from the farms and cities to the suburbs. By 1960 the suburban population nearly doubled and almost equalled that of the cities. Better incomes and government home loans were responsible for this shift in population. Also, many people viewed the suburbs as an escape. They wanted to avoid the crime, high taxes, and pollution of the cities and to find suitable surroundings for their children.

Suburban residents settled in large housing developments. These were made up of rows of almost identical houses. Shopping centers, schools, places of worship, parks, and recreation areas were built in the new suburban communities. Many suburban residents, however, continued to work in the cities. New highways were built to take them to

their jobs in the morning and bring them back home at night. More and more Americans became **commuters,** or people who travel back and forth regularly.

Leisure Time

The new technology and prosperity enabled many Americans to enjoy more leisure time. At the same time, the number of available leisure activities increased.

Television. Television was the primary source of entertainment. Developed in the 1930's, it went on the market in the late 1940's. In 1950, 3.2 million Americans owned television sets; in 1960, 50 million had them. By 1952 television broadcasting was controlled by three large networks and a number of advertising agencies.

The most popular of the early television programs were variety shows and comedies. Comedian Milton Berle attracted a huge nationwide audience with his variety show, "The Texaco Star Theater." Another famous situation-comedy show was "I Love Lucy," starring Lucille Ball. Other popular programs were quiz shows and soap operas.

Although some television programs were excellent, critics commented on the poor quality of much of the television fare. They claimed that television was not adequately informing viewers about serious

West Side Story was the first musical to focus on the problems of immigrants in a large city and use a modern, dissonant musical style.

issues. Edward R. Murrow, the leading television newscaster of the early 1950's, stated that "television in the main is being used to distract, delude, amuse, and insulate." However, television covered many special news events. Although not providing much "in-depth" analysis, it did much to arouse public interest in national and world affairs.

Movies. With the coming of television, movies declined in popularity as family entertainment. Rising costs and decreasing revenues ended the era of the Great Hollywood studios. Moviemakers tried to attract customers with three-dimensional projection, enlarged screens, and lavish productions. Finally, independent producers arose and made more sophisticated movies that appealed to adults. By 1960 the motion picture and television industries were working closely together. Film, whether on television or on the screen, was now viewed as an art form as well as a means of mass entertainment.

Sports. Spectator sports became increasingly popular in the postwar era. Attendance at baseball and football games soared. Games were shown on television, players' salaries increased, and professional athletics became a multimillion-dollar business. Sports figures, such as baseball's Willie Mays and Mickey Mantle and football's Johnny Unitas and Jim Brown, became national heroes.

Other Pastimes. Americans found a variety of ways to use their new leisure time. They were active as amateurs in sports, such as bowling, skiing, golf, fishing, and hunting.

People had longer vacations and were able to take trips. The age of mass air travel began, and many Americans went abroad for the first time. An even larger group traveled throughout the country by family car.

Americans also pursued many hobbies, such as "do-it-yourself" repair, auto maintenance, gardening, cooking, and antique-collecting. They often joined organizations that promoted their concerns.

Culture. With increased affluence, more Americans enjoyed cultural activities. The Broadway theater thrived and produced many musicals, such as *South Pacific, The King and I, My Fair Lady,* and *The Sound of Music.* In 1957 Leonard Bernstein, conductor of the New York Philharmonic Orchestra, helped create *West Side Story,* a popular musical drama about teenage gang life in New York City. *West Side Story's* theme of two young lovers was based on Shakespeare's play, *Romeo and Juliet.* Theater groups were active around the country. Art galleries and museums drew about 35 million viewers annually. There was also a growing interest in all forms of music. Concerts were well-attended, and record sales reached an all-time high.

Rock 'n Roll. During the 1950's young people began to develop their own culture. Rock 'n Roll became their favorite music. It grew out of jazz,

Baseball's color barrier was broken in 1947 when Jackie Robinson became a member of the Brooklyn Dodgers. A fast, exciting base runner and a good hitter, Robinson helped the Dodgers win six National League pennants and the World Series in 1955. What effect do you think Robinson's accomplishments had on blacks?

rhythm and blues, country-western music, and "pop" ballads. In 1956 Elvis Presley became the first big rock 'n roll star with "hits" such as "Heartbreak Hotel" and "Hound Dog." Although parents disapproved, his songs and style were popular among young people and were soon imitated by others.

Religion

Although largely a secular society, the United States experienced a revival of religion during the 1950's. Americans in larger numbers joined churches and felt the need to express some form of religious belief. In a 1954 survey, 56 percent of the men and 69 percent of the women claimed to be active participants in worship services. Books, songs, and movies on religious themes were popular.

Protestantism, Roman Catholicism, and Judaism were recognized as the three "American faiths," and there was now a growing tolerance among their members toward differences in religious beliefs. The most popular religious leaders were the Jewish rabbi, Joshua Loth Liebman; the Catholic priest, Monsignor Fulton J. Sheen; and the Protestant evangelist, Billy Graham. All three had large followings, wrote books, and made extensive use of radio or television.

Many observers, however, questioned the depth of this revival. Some recognized that religious faith for many Americans was a vital source of meaning in a troubled world. Others thought that many of the faithful lacked a real understanding of traditional religious beliefs. Consequently, these observers felt that religion in the 1950's was more a way of meeting personal or social needs than an expression of commitment to religious truth.

The Arts

The 1950's was a creative period in the arts. Writers, painters, and architects started new trends. For the first time, the United States became one of the leading cultural centers of the world.

Many of America's artistically-talented people celebrated the country's greatness in their works. Some, however, felt that prosperity had brought conformity, boredom, and apathy to American life. They often criticized social injustices and hoped for a brighter future. They also expressed despair and questioned survival in the nuclear age.

Literature.   Many American writers took a realistic, and sometimes brutal, view of life in their works. The first important novels of the period used World War II as their theme. Norman Mailer, in *The Naked and the Dead* (1948); James Jones, in *From Here to Eternity* (1951); and Herman Wouk, in *The Caine Mutiny* (1951) revealed the frustrations of individuals in the face of modern warfare.

Much American fiction after World War II dealt sympathetically with ordinary, downtrodden, or homely characters who were caught in tragic situations. Carson McCullers, one of the leading female writers of the late 1940's and 1950's, wrote about small-town life in the South. In novels such as *A Member of the Wedding* (1946) and *The Ballad of the Sad Cafe* (1951), she examined the lives of lonely people searching for love and understanding in an indifferent world. J.D. Salinger, in *Catcher In the Rye* (1951), described the problems of a confused adolescent growing up in New York City.

Minority groups contributed to the literature of the period. Jewish writers, such as Saul Bellow, Philip Roth, and Bernard Malamud, described Jewish life in the United States. Many of them dealt with the conflict between religious tradition and modern secular society. Blacks also became an important part of the literary scene and wrote about their experiences. Ralph Elison, in *Invisible Man* (1952), described a young black man's search for identity in a racist environment. James Baldwin, another black writer, wrote *Go Tell It on the Mountain* (1953), a novel about a poor black boy and his family in New York City's Harlem.

In the mid-1950's, a group of writers known as "The Beat Movement" emerged in cities such as New York, San Francisco, and New Orleans. Often called **"beatniks,"** they showed a strong dislike of American middle-class society. They rebelled against its attachment to affluence, family life, and success in business. The "beatniks" stressed individual freedom and adopted their own style of dress, speech, and music. The leading "beat" writers, such as the poets Allen Ginsberg and Lawrence Ferlinghetti and the writer Jack Kerouac, described violence, insanity, and other unpleasant situations in ways that often shocked middle-class readers.

Several important playwrights emerged in the United States during the late 1940's and the 1950's. In

A mass society is one in which individuals interact outside their own immediate environment, and contact with others is impersonal.

plays such as *The Glass Menagerie* (1945) and *A Streetcar Named Desire* (1947), Tennessee Williams wrote about confused people trying to face the harsh realities of their lives. Arthur Miller, another leading playwright, looked at conflict between the individual and society in works such as *Death of a Salesman* (1949) and *The Crucible* (1953).

Architecture and Art. After World War II American architecture consisted of a variety of styles. Tall, box-like buildings of steel and glass expressed the "international" style that had emerged during the 1920's. It became popular in the 1950's due to its relatively low cost and simple method of construction. However, other types of architecture developed that used traditional building materials such as brick, wood, and stone. Frank Lloyd Wright, one of the most noted architects of the period, built homes that were made to fit into a natural setting.

During the late 1940's and early 1950's, New York City became the world's leading center of modern art. There, a style of painting developed known as **abstract expressionism.** Painters such as Jackson Pollock and Willem de Kooning moved away from depicting recognizable subjects and began to portray torn-apart images, geometric forms, and swirling colors. They wanted to express their inner feelings directly rather than use the forms of the objective world. As a result, many of their paintings were difficult for the general public to understand and

accept. Other artists, however, continued to work in more traditional realistic styles. Andrew Wyeth, for example, was known for his paintings of rural American scenes.

Social Thinkers. During the 1950's leading social thinkers analyzed the complexity of modern mass society. They wrote about its effects on individual behavior. David Reisman, in *The Lonely Crowd* (1950), claimed that Americans conformed too easily to group opinions and were losing their individuality. William H. Whyte, Jr., in *The Organization Man* (1956), studied American business life. He concluded that typical executives adjusted every area of their lives to the expectations of their companies.

If it was true that America in the 1950's was a nation of conformists, that situation was soon to change. Beneath the surface, new forces were at work—forces that would erupt in the decade to come.

SECTION REVIEW

1. Identify the following: John K. Galbraith, Edward R. Murrow, Elvis Presley, James Baldwin, Tennessee Williams, Jackson Pollock.
2. How did the role of women change after World War II?
3. What criticisms were made of the American economy?
4. How did the American population change in the postwar years?

CHAPTER 29   REVIEW

SUMMARY

1. After World War II ended, the Truman administration developed policies to return the American economy to a peacetime basis.
2. Civil rights became an important national issue, but Truman could not get the support of Congress for civil rights legislation.
3. Truman was reelected in 1948 in one of the biggest upsets in political history.
4. During Truman's second term, he promoted a number of social and economic reforms, but had little success.

5. National security became a major issue during the late 1940's and 1950's, and Senator Joseph McCarthy undertook a crusade to check communist influence in the United States.
6. In 1952 General Dwight D. Eisenhower became President.
7. The Eisenhower administration opposed extending the role of the federal government in the economy, but, at the same time, it supported projects that would promote business growth.

8. By 1954 Senator McCarthy's extremism in the fight against communist influence began to lose support.

9. During Eisenhower's second term, the civil rights issue came to a head when the Supreme Court found segregation of public schools to be unconstitutional.

10. By 1960 the black civil rights movement was well underway.

11. Alaska and Hawaii became the 49th and 50th states.

12. During the Truman-Eisenhower years, the United States enjoyed an economic boom and was characterized as the world's first affluent society.

13. Prosperity and new forms of technology had a strong impact on American lifestyles and culture.

VOCABULARY

fringe benefits	integration	countervailing power	baby boom
espionage	sit-in	automation	commuter
perjury	military-industrial complex	blue-collar worker	beatniks
deportation	affluent	white-collar worker	abstract expressionism

REVIEW QUESTIONS

1. What problems were involved in returning the American economy to a peacetime basis?

2. How did labor unions fare during the Truman-Eisenhower years?

3. Why was Truman's Fair Deal program generally unsuccessful?

4. How was the federal government reorganized during the Truman-Eisenhower years?

5. What influence did the Cold War have on United States domestic affairs?

6. What were Eisenhower's goals as President of the United States?

7. What progress was made by the civil rights movement in the 1950's?

8. What major changes took place in American lifestyles?

DISCUSSION

1. How did Eisenhower's approach to the Presidency compare to Truman's?

2. What role do you think the federal government should take in trying to improve race relations? Why?

3. Does the danger of the "military-industrial complex" still exist today? Why or why not?

4. If you had been a member of Congress in 1950, would you have voted for or against the McCarran Internal Security Act? Why?

USING GRAPHS

Refer to the graph on page 648 and answer the following questions:

1. During what period did the suburbs show the highest percentage of population growth?

2. Has the decline in rural population been constant?

3. What has been the overall trend in suburban population?

4. When did the percentage of growth in suburbs begin to exceed the percentage of growth in cities? When did it begin to exceed the growth in rural areas?

USING SKILLS

Below are two arguments concerning the Supreme Court's decision in *Brown* v. *Topeka Board of Education*. Read the arguments and answer the questions that follow.

The first argument is part of the manifesto signed by 100 southern members of Congress declaring their opposition to the Court's decision:

> *In the case of* Plessy v. Ferguson, *in 1896, the Supreme Court expressly declared that under the Fourteenth Amendment no person was denied any of his rights if the states provided separate but equal public facilities. This decision has been followed in many other cases. . . .*
>
> *This interpretation, restated time and again, became a part of the life of the people of many of the states and confirmed their habits, customs, traditions and way of life. . . .*
>
> *Though there has been no constitutional amendment or act of Congress changing this established legal principle almost a century old, the Supreme Court of the United States, with no legal basis for such action, undertook to exercise their naked judicial power and substituted their personal political and social ideas for the established law of the land.*

The second argument is part of the official court decision, written by Chief Justice Earl Warren:

> *In the South, the movement toward free common schools, supported by general taxation, had not yet taken hold [when the Fourteenth Amendment was adopted in 1868]. Education of white children was largely in the hands of private groups. Education of Negroes was almost nonexistent, and practically all of the race were illiterate. In fact, any education of Negroes was forbidden by law in some states. Today, in contrast, many Negroes have achieved outstanding success in the arts and sciences as well as in the business and professional world. . . . Even in the North, the conditions of public education did not approximate those existing today. . . .*
>
> *In approaching this problem, we cannot turn the clock back to 1868 when the Amendment*

> *was adopted, or even to 1896 when* Plessy v. Ferguson *was written. We must consider public education in the light of its full development and its present place in American life throughout the Nation. Only in this way can it be determined if segregation in public schools deprives these plaintiffs of the equal protection of the laws. . . .*
>
> *To separate them [black children] from others of similar age and qualifications solely because of their race generates a feeling of inferiority as to their status in the community that may affect their hearts and minds in a way unlikely ever to be undone. The effect of this separation on their educational opportunities was well stated by a finding in the Kansas case by a court which nevertheless felt compelled to rule against the Negro plaintiffs:*
>
> *"Segregation of white and colored children in public schools has a detrimental effect upon the colored children. The impact is greater when it has the sanction of the law; for the policy of separating the races is usually interpreted as denoting the inferiority of the Negro group. A sense of inferiority affects the motivation of a child to learn. Segregation with the sanction of law, therefore, has a tendency to retard the educational and mental development of Negro children and to deprive them of some of the benefits they would receive in a racially integrated school system."*
>
> *Whatever may have been the extent of psychological knowledge at the time of* Plessy v. Ferguson, *this finding is amply supported by modern authority. Any language in* Plessy v. Ferguson *contrary to this finding is rejected.*

1. What is the chief legal argument made by the manifesto?

2. How does the Court decision relate to the Fourteenth Amendment?

3. On what grounds does the Court justify its overturning the previous decision in *Plessy* v. *Ferguson?*

1	The New Frontier	655
2	The Great Society	664
3	Foreign Affairs Under Johnson	669
4	Unrest in the Nation	673

THE KENNEDY-JOHNSON YEARS

The world is very different now. For man holds in his mortal hands the power to abolish all forms of human poverty and all forms of human life.

JOHN F. KENNEDY

The inauguration of John Fitzgerald Kennedy in 1961 heralded an era of progress—social, economic, and technological. Indeed, much progress was made under Kennedy and under his successor, Lyndon B. Johnson. As time passed, however, domestic strife increased. Oppressed minorities continued their struggle for equal rights, and much of the nation rose in protest over the conduct of foreign affairs. The decade that had dawned with such promise ended in bitterness.

1 The New Frontier

Although the Eisenhower years had been a time of both peace and general prosperity, the country faced certain challenges at the end of the 1950's. Poverty remained a problem that was especially evident in city slums, and race relations were tense. The U-2 incident and the Cuban revolution under Castro seemed to show that the United States was losing ground in the Cold War. Against this background, the nation prepared for another presidential election.

The Election of 1960

As Eisenhower prepared to leave office in 1960, both Republicans and Democrats turned their attention to the coming election. In July the Republicans selected Vice President Richard M. Nixon as their candidate. Nixon chose Henry Cabot Lodge, Jr. of Massachusetts, the United States ambassador to the United Nations, as his running mate. At the convention, Nixon pledged to continue both the foreign and domestic policies of the Eisenhower administration.

Meanwhile, the Democrats chose Senator John F. Kennedy of Massachusetts as their candidate for President. Kennedy named Senate majority leader Lyndon B. Johnson of Texas, runner-up in the race for the nomination, as his Vice President. In accepting the nomination, Kennedy challenged the American people to turn to a New Frontier:

> We stand today on the edge of a New Frontier—the frontier of the 1960's—a frontier of unknown opportunities and perils—the frontier of unfulfilled hopes and threats.
>
> Woodrow Wilson's New Freedom promised our nation a new political and economic framework. Franklin Roosevelt's New Deal promised security and succor to those in need. But the New Frontier of which I speak is not a set of promises—it is a set of challenges. It sums up, not what I intend to offer the American people, but what I intend to ask of them. It appeals to their pride, not their pocket-book—it holds out the promise of more sacrifice instead of more security.

For much of the campaign, polls showed Nixon in the lead. One reason for this was the fact that Kennedy was a Roman Catholic. No Catholic had ever been President, and many Americans feared that, if Kennedy won the election, the Pope would influence government policy. Kennedy tried to meet this issue in a direct manner, stating publicly his commitment to the separation of church and state. In a speech to a group of Protestant ministers in Houston, Texas, he said:

> I believe in an America where the separation of church and state is absolute—where no Catholic prelate would tell the President (should he be Catholic) how to act, and no Protestant minister would tell his parishioners for whom to vote—where no church or church school is granted any public funds or political preference—and where no man is denied public office merely because his religion differs from the President who might appoint him or the people who might elect him.

Through statements such as this, Kennedy was able to allay the fears of most non-Catholic voters. Nixon left the religious issue alone, and after a time, it seemed to become less important.

Late in the year, Kennedy moved ahead in the polls and maintained a narrow lead for the rest of the campaign. This was due partly to four nationally televised debates between the two candidates. During these debates, Kennedy stressed the need to reverse the downward trend of the nation's fortunes and promised to "get America moving again." Nixon, on the other hand, argued that the United States was stronger than ever—both at home and abroad—and pledged to consolidate the country's gains. The results of the debates were inconclusive, but Kennedy benefited from his good looks and poise during his television appearances. The debates also helped Kennedy to overcome the handicap of being less well-known than Nixon.

In November nearly 70 million voters turned out to choose between Kennedy and Nixon. For the first time, the people of Alaska and Hawaii took part in a presidential election. As expected, the results were extremely close. In the popular vote, Kennedy won by a narrow margin of 118,574. In the electoral vote, his margin was wider—303 to 217.

On January 20, the new President took office. In his inaugural address, Kennedy elaborated upon the theme of challenge presented during his presidential campaign:

> *Since this country was founded, each generation of Americans has been summoned to give testimony to its national loyalty. . . .*
>
> *Now the trumpet summons us again—not as a call to bear arms, though arms we need—not as a call to battle, though embattled we are—but a call to bear the burden of a long twilight struggle, year in and year out, 'rejoicing in hope, patient in tribulation'—a struggle against the common enemies of man: tyranny, poverty, disease and war itself. . . .*
>
> *And so, my fellow Americans: ask not what your country can do for you—ask what you can do for your country.*

The New President

John F. Kennedy, at 43 years of age, was the youngest man ever to be elected President, as well as the first Roman Catholic. Born into a wealthy Irish-American family, the young Kennedy studied at the London School of Economics and Political Science and Princeton University before graduating from Harvard University in 1940.

During his Harvard years, he spent a good deal of time in Europe, especially in England, where his father served as the American ambassador. Kennedy's experiences there led to his writing *Why England Slept* (1940), which dealt with England's policy toward Hitler prior to World War II.

Following graduation, Kennedy joined the United States Navy. After the United States entered the war, he was assigned active duty in the Pacific. In August 1943 the PT (patrol torpedo) boat that he commanded was sunk by the Japanese. Kennedy helped to rescue his crew and was awarded the Navy and Marine Corps Medals. He was considered a war hero, and the circumstances of the rescue were later recounted in Robert Donovan's book *PT 109*.

Kennedy's political career began in 1946 when he was elected to the House of Representatives from Massachusetts. He moved to the Senate after challenging Henry Cabot Lodge in the 1952 election.

With his marriage to Jacqueline Bouvier on September 12, 1953, he became somewhat of a celebrity. Kennedy gained added recognition for his

Presidential hopefuls John Kennedy (right) and Richard Nixon (left) met in a series of televised debates during the 1960 campaign. For the first time, presidential candidates discussed issues face to face. Did the debates affect the election?

Kennedy entered and won presidential primaries in seven states. The most important of these was West Virginia, which was basically Protestant.

A group of Kennedy's advisors, led by his brother Robert, were called the "Irish Mafia" by critics.

ELECTION OF 1960

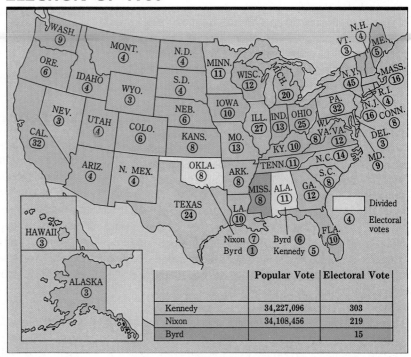

	Popular Vote	Electoral Vote
Kennedy	34,227,096	303
Nixon	34,108,456	219
Byrd		15

best-seller *Profiles in Courage,* which described difficult political decisions made by past United States Senators. This work won the Pulitzer Prize for biography in 1957.

In 1956 Kennedy tried and failed to win the Democratic nomination for Vice President. In 1958 he was reelected to the Senate and began campaigning formally for the 1960 Democratic presidential nomination. Kennedy employed his wealth, organizational skills, and charisma to achieve victory over Nixon.

The Kennedy Administration

To assist him in his role as President, Kennedy filled his administration with people of intellect and expertise. Some came from the world of business and finance. Others came from the academic world. Still others were experienced politicians. For the most part, these advisors were loyal to Kennedy, but they were also people of independent thought. Like Franklin Roosevelt, Kennedy favored controversy.

Kennedy's two principal advisors were Clark Clifford, a Washington lawyer who had been special counsel to President Truman, and Richard Neustadt,

a political scientist from Columbia University. Neustadt had also served in the Truman administration. Ted Sorensen, Kennedy's special counsel, was also close to the President. Other advisors were Arthur Schlesinger, Jr., a Harvard historian; Adolf Berle, who had served under Franklin D. Roosevelt; and Walter Heller, an economist from the University of Minnesota.

For his cabinet, Kennedy chose Dean Rusk, head of the Rockefeller Foundation, as Secretary of State. Robert McNamara, head of the Ford Motor Company, was named Secretary of Defense. As Secretary of the Treasury, Kennedy appointed New York financier Douglas Dillon, a Republican who had served in the Eisenhower administration. Finally, the President appointed his younger brother Robert Kennedy as Attorney General.

Other cabinet posts were filled by experienced politicians. They included Luther Hodges, governor of North Carolina, as Secretary of Commerce; Abraham Ribicoff, governor of Connecticut, as Secretary of Health, Education, and Welfare; and Representative Stewart Udall of Arizona as Secretary of the Interior.

Shepherd's flight was a suborbital one of 300 miles (480 kilometers).

In the 1960's, Kennedy urged that wages rise no higher than output. Thus, if the workers' hourly output increased 2 percent, employers could increase wages 2 percent.

Space

With his administration chosen, Kennedy began implementing his New Frontier. One of his chief interests was the space program. The United States was competing with the Soviet Union in missile development, and Kennedy felt it was America's destiny to conquer this newest of frontiers.

The space age had opened when the Soviet Union launched Sputnik, the first successful satellite, on October 4, 1957. On April 1, 1961, Russian cosmonaut Yuri Gagarin became the first person to orbit the earth. One month later, Alan Shepard, Jr., became the first American to make a space flight.

Shortly after Shepard's flight, Kennedy challenged the nation to a great undertaking. He delivered a message to Congress stating that the United States "should commit itself to achieving the goal, before the decade is out, of landing a man on the moon and returning him safely to earth."

This idea aroused a good deal of criticism. Many people felt that the money should be spent to solve problems on earth. Others doubted that the idea was feasible. Kennedy, however, was not deterred. The space program continued. On February 20, 1962, Lieutenant-Colonel John Glenn became the first American to orbit the earth. Meanwhile, the National Aeronautics and Space Administration (NASA), created in 1958, had begun the Apollo Project for the purpose of accomplishing a moonshot. One side effect of all this activity was that the space industry provided jobs for thousands of American workers.

The Economy

When the New Frontier began, the economy was in a recession. One of Kennedy's major tasks was to stimulate economic growth without causing too much inflation. To accomplish this, he used modern methods of economic control rather than the laissez-faire approach practiced by Eisenhower.

Kennedy had several problems. One was the power exerted over the economy by business and labor. For example, if labor got an increase in wages, business raised prices to make up for lost profits, causing inflation to spiral upward. To correct this problem, Kennedy established informal **wage-price guideposts**—voluntary guidelines for wages and prices.

He was primarily concerned with the steel industry. Because steel was so widely used in other industries, a rise in prices could affect the economy as a whole. In April 1962, Kennedy persuaded the steelworkers to agree to a moderate wage increase. This was done with the understanding that the steel companies would hold prices down. However, United States Steel and certain other major producers announced substantial price increases a few days later. Kennedy was angry and stated that this action was a "wholly unjustified and irresponsible defiance of our public interest."

In reaction, the President directed Secretary of Defense McNamara to announce that the government would not purchase steel from companies that had raised their prices. This forced the large steel companies to back down. Although Kennedy won this battle, the incident damaged his relationship with business. Thereafter, Kennedy used **"jawboning,"** or verbal persuasion, rather than the power of the government to hold down wages and prices.

Another problem Kennedy faced was the decline in business investment. He attempted to deal with this by liberalizing the tax deduction for **depreciation,** or the gradual wear and tear on machinery and equipment. Businesses could subtract a certain

The United States space program received a dramatic boost in 1962 when John Glenn became the first American astronaut to orbit the earth. Glenn circled the earth three times in less than five hours. What space aim did Kennedy propose?

The Trade Expansion Act allowed the President to cut tariffs up to 50 percent.

Have students consider the positive and negative aspects of technological progress.

amount for depreciation from their total taxable income each year. In 1962, at Kennedy's urging, Congress liberalized the tax guidelines. Congress also authorized an **investment tax credit** that lowered taxes for firms that invested in new equipment. Together, these measures resulted in an 11 percent tax cut for business.

Kennedy was also worried about mounting deficits in the country's **balance of payments** (the difference between total payments made to foreign countries and total payments received from foreign countries over a given period of time). Because the United States was spending more on imports than it was making on exports, money was leaving the country. This situation worsened with the creation in 1957 of the European Economic Community (EEC), often called the European Common Market.[1] This group of Western European countries had lowered tariffs on each other's products. As a result, American businesses could not compete on equal terms, and exports to these countries declined.

To remedy this situation, Congress passed the Trade Expansion Act on October 11, 1962. This act gave the President the authority to enter into reciprocal trade agreements with the EEC that would cut United States tariffs drastically in exchange for lower tariffs on American products. In practice, however, the administration found it difficult to arrange satisfactory agreements.

As a general measure to revive the economy, Kennedy proposed a general tax cut in 1963. The President believed—as did many economists—that, if the government reduced taxes, people would have more money to spend on consumer items. This would put money back into the economy and stimulate growth. Although Congress began debate on this measure, it was not passed until after Kennedy's successor took office.

Social Welfare

Kennedy then turned his attention to social welfare—to the problems of housing, poverty, and unemployment. At his urging, Congress passed the Area Redevelopment Act on May 1, 1961. This act was designed to reduce poverty in urban slums and in rural areas such as Appalachia, which stretched from Pennsylvania through West Virginia, Kentucky, and Tennessee into Alabama. Under this act, the federal government could give loans and grants, as well as technical assistance, to these areas.

On June 30 Congress passed the Housing Act of 1961, providing money for **urban renewal** (programs to restore city slums). The act also provided for long-term loans at low interest rates for the improvement of low-income and moderate-income housing.

Kennedy tried to do something about unemployment as well. In February 1961 the unemployment rate stood at 8.1 percent, or about 5.5 million people. Although this was due in part to automation, it was also due to changes in the American economy that called for new skills from workers. Therefore, in 1962, Congress passed the Manpower Development and Training Act, which focused on retraining jobless workers. A $900 million public works program was authorized to provide jobs for the retrained workers.

Civil Rights

Kennedy also favored civil rights legislation, but he proceeded carefully during his first year in office. He needed the support of Congress to get other parts of his program passed. Therefore, he tried to avoid antagonizing southern Democrats over civil rights.

Although he felt he could not ask Congress to pass legislation, Kennedy did support civil rights by using his presidential powers. For one thing, he filled several key government posts with blacks. Carl Rowan was named Ambassador to Finland, Robert Weaver became Home Finance Administrator, and Thurgood Marshall was chosen to serve on the United States Circuit Court.

In March 1961 Kennedy issued an executive order setting up a Committee on Equal Employment Opportunity. Vice President Lyndon B. Johnson, as head of this committee, managed to persuade major defense contractors to open their doors to blacks. Kennedy also tried to enforce the voting rights provisions of the 1957 and 1960 Civil Rights Acts and supported the Twenty-Fourth Amendment to the Constitution. This amendment, passed in August 1962, outlawed poll taxes. It was ratified in 1964.

---

[1] The original six members were Belgium, France, Italy, Luxembourg, the Netherlands, and West Germany. Ireland and Great Britain joined in 1973, and Greece in 1981.

After graduation, James Meredith was wounded by a sniper while on a one-man civil rights march in Mississippi.

The President's attempts to further the cause of civil rights were backed by Attorney General Robert Kennedy. Under his direction, the Department of Justice brought over 50 suits in 4 states where blacks had been denied the right to vote.

Robert Kennedy also brought his influence to bear when blacks were denied other rights. For example, in June 1962 James Meredith, a black, was denied admission to the all-white University of Mississippi at Oxford. A United States Circuit Court issued an injunction to force the University to accept Meredith, and this decision was upheld by the Supreme Court. However, Governor Ross Barnett, with the aid of the state police, prevented Meredith from registering. When President Kennedy sent federal marshalls to escort Meredith to campus, riots erupted. On the advice of his brother, the President placed the Mississippi National Guard under the control of the United States government and sent federal troops to help them settle the disturbance. In early October, after 2 people had been killed and 70 wounded, the riots ended. Meredith entered the university, but several hundred soldiers remained on campus to protect him until he received his degree.

A little over a month after the Meredith crisis, Kennedy took action to eliminate housing discrimination. During his campaign, Kennedy had promised to do something about this problem. Once in office,

James Meredith became the first black to attend classes at and to graduate from the University of Mississippi. What progress was made in other areas of civil rights in the early 1960's?

however, he had delayed action in the hope of gaining support in the 1962 elections. When this did not materialize, Kennedy decided to go ahead. On November 20, 1962, he issued an executive order outlawing racial discrimination in federally supported housing.

Despite progress in the area of civil rights, the Kennedy administration was not moving fast enough for most blacks. Tired of waiting for further action by the federal government, they stepped up their protest activities in the spring of 1963. Violence often erupted and was generally directed at the protesters.

Another confrontation between state and federal power took place in June 1963—this time in Alabama. Governor George Wallace tried to prevent desegregation of the University of Alabama at Tuscaloosa in much the same way Governor Barnett had tried to do so at the University of Mississippi. Kennedy, acting again with the advice of his brother, federalized the Alabama National Guard and ordered them to ensure the entry of blacks to the university. As a result, Wallace backed down.

By then, Kennedy had finally decided to take his fight for civil rights to Congress. He made his commitment to equality on nationwide television:

> *It ought to be possible for American students of any color to attend any public institution without having to be backed up by troops. It ought to be possible for American consumers of any color to receive equal service in places of public accommodation, such as hotels and restaurants and theaters and retail stores, without being forced to demonstrations in the streets, and it ought to be possible for American citizens of any color to register and to vote in a free election without interference or fear of reprisal. . . .*
>
> *In short, every American ought to have the right to be treated as he would wish to be treated, as one would wish his children to be treated.*
>
> *But this is not the case.*

On June 18, 1963, Kennedy proposed comprehensive civil rights legislation that would ban discrimination in employment, guarantee equal voting rights, and provide all Americans with equal access to public accommodations. Congress, however, failed to pass this civil rights package, and violence multiplied.

Federal District Judge Sarah T. Hughes administered the oath of office to Johnson.

Johnson was a protégé of Speaker of the House Sam Rayburn.

Kennedy's Assassination

Indeed it was an incident of violence that brought an end to the New Frontier. On November 22, 1963, Kennedy was in Dallas, Texas, on a political tour with his wife and Vice President Johnson. As his motorcade proceeded through the city, Kennedy and Governor John B. Connally of Texas were shot. Connally recovered, but Kennedy died a short while later at a Dallas hospital. The same afternoon, Lyndon B. Johnson was sworn in as President of the United States while returning to Washington aboard *Air Force 1* with Mrs. Kennedy and the assassinated President's body.

Shortly after the shooting, the police arrested Lee Harvey Oswald, a known Marxist, and charged him with the murder. Two days later, while being moved by the police, Oswald was shot and killed by Dallas nightclub owner Jack Ruby. In March Ruby was convicted of murder and sentenced to die.

Kennedy's assassination shocked the nation. Many people questioned whether Oswald had acted alone or was part of a conspiracy. This issue stirred up so much controversy that Johnson appointed a commission headed by Chief Justice Earl Warren to investigate the circumstances surrounding Kennedy's death. The Warren Commission's report came out in late September 1964. It concluded that Oswald was, in fact, Kennedy's only assassin and that there was no evidence of any conspiracy.[2]

SECTION REVIEW

1. Identify the following: Henry Cabot Lodge, Jr., Ted Sorensen, Robert McNamara, John Glenn, European Common Market, James Meredith, Warren Commission.

2. Why was religion an issue in the 1960 presidential election?

3. Why did Kennedy promote a space program for the United States?

4. What did Kennedy do to control the American economy?

5. What was Kennedy's position on civil rights?

---

[2] Critics have disputed the findings of the Warren Commission, and several investigations have been made. A 1978 House Committee, after months of study, reported that the Kennedy assassination was probably the result of a conspiracy. But this report was also criticized.

2 The Great Society

During his first five years in office, Johnson dedicated himself to achieving Kennedy's vision for America—to building what the new President called a Great Society, "where freedom from the wants of the body can help fulfill the needs of the spirit." Johnson used his political skills to push a variety of liberal measures through Congress. The ease with which he did this was not only due to the nation's grief for Kennedy, but also to Johnson's background.

Johnson's Background

The 55-year-old Texan who became the nation's 36th President had considerable political experience. After a brief stint as a teacher, Johnson obtained a job as secretary to a member of Congress and moved to Washington, D.C. Before long, young Johnson caught the eye of President Franklin D. Roosevelt, who appointed him Texas director of the National Youth Administration.

Johnson continued his political career in the House of Representatives, to which he was elected in 1937. In 1948 he won a seat in the Senate and in 1953 became minority leader. Within five years, the Democrats had achieved a majority in the Senate, and Johnson thus became majority leader. Johnson's legislative experience was of value when he sought to institute his Great Society.

The Warren Court

A spirit of liberalism and activism characterized the Great Society, as it had the New Frontier. This spirit was supported by actions of the Supreme Court. The Court had taken a liberal course since Earl Warren became Chief Justice in 1953. It continued to do so throughout the 1960's. During these years the Warren Court handed down rulings that liberalized politics at the state and local levels and protected the rights of accused criminals.

In the past, state legislators had kept themselves in office through their hold over legislative districts. They often refused to redraw districts as populations changed. Because of this, growing urban areas often had fewer representatives than rural areas with far fewer people.

The Supreme Court dealt with this issue in *Baker* v. *Carr* (1962) by ruling that federal courts had jurisdiction over **legislative apportionment**—the allocation of legislative seats. Up to this time, the Court had felt the question of malapportionment was political. Now, however, it said that malapportionment could violate the Fourteenth Amendment and should be handled through the courts. This and later decisions upheld the "one-person, one-vote" (equal representation) principle. According to this principle, every district should have close to the same number of people so that every person's vote will carry equal weight.

The Supreme Court also extended coverage of the Fourteenth Amendment to people facing criminal charges. In *Mapp* v. *Ohio* (1961) the Court said that evidence seized illegally by the police could not be used against the accused. In *Gideon* v. *Wainwright* (1963) the Court ruled that the state must give free legal counsel to indigent (poor) defendants accused of a **felony**—a crime for which punishment was death or imprisonment for more than one year. Finally, in *Miranda* v. *Arizona* (1966), the Court said that any statement a suspect made to the police while in custody could not be used as evidence unless the suspect had first been informed of certain rights. These included the right to remain silent, the right to consult an attorney, and the right to a court-appointed lawyer if needed.

Congress

Domestic legislation, like the Court rulings, showed an activist spirit. In 1964, under Johnson's leadership, Congress compiled a substantial legislative record. In February Congress passed the Tax Reduction Act, which cut personal and corporate income taxes by $11.5 billion. Thus there was more money for investment and consumer spending. The resulting increase in demand stimulated production and reduced unemployment. During the Johnson years, unemployment never rose above 4 percent, and the **gross national product** (GNP)—the total dollar value of all final goods and services produced in a country during one year—grew at a rate of 5 percent a year.

Congress then turned its attention to civil rights. After a long battle, civil rights forces in the Senate ended a southern **filibuster** (a way to block passage of a bill by making long speeches) to pass the Civil Rights Act of 1964. This act embodied the basic proposals Kennedy had set forth in 1963. It ensured equal access to public accommodations; gave the Attorney General power to bring suits to desegregate schools; prohibited discrimination in employment on the basis of race, color, religion, sex, or national origin; and strengthened guarantees of equal voting rights. The act also allowed the federal government to withhold funds from federally supported programs that discriminated against blacks.

Johnson, aided by Congress, also furthered government efforts to help the poor. In 1964 one-fifth of American families had incomes below the **poverty level**—an income below which a family lacks the means to meet its basic needs. In his State of the Union Address on January 8, Johnson called for a "War on Poverty."

The war was carried forward with the passage of the Economic Opportunity Act on August 30. This act authorized nearly $1 billion for ten different programs under the newly created Office of Economic Opportunity (OEO). A Job Corps provided training and work experience for those who had dropped out of school. The Upward Bound program helped bright slum children gain a college education. Operation Head-

Poverty was a major concern of the Johnson administration. Economic troubles had hit Appalachia especially hard. The President visited the multistate area to view conditions firsthand. What programs were started to fight poverty?

For 20 years the American Medical Association fought increased government assistance to those needing medical care.

start offered preschool training to children of poor families. Volunteers in Service to America (VISTA) served as a domestic Peace Corps. There were also Community Action Programs (CAP), which were intended to get people who lived in slums to take part in planning and running antipoverty programs.

The Election of 1964

The War on Poverty, as well as the rest of the Great Society, was the chief issue of the 1964 presidential campaign. In July the Republicans nominated Senator Barry M. Goldwater of Arizona for President. Goldwater chose Representative William E. Miller of New York as his running mate.

Goldwater's nomination was a triumph for the conservatives in the Republican party. The Senator favored states' rights and a limited role for the federal government in American life. For example, he wanted to abolish the graduated income tax and sell the TVA to private business. He also advocated the freedom not to associate with blacks, which implied that private individuals and businesses had a right to discriminate against blacks. Such extreme views drew criticism. Goldwater's reply to this criticism was, "Extremism in defense of liberty is no vice. Moderation in pursuit of justice is no virtue."

In August the Democrats nominated Lyndon B. Johnson as their candidate. Johnson's choice for Vice President was Senator Hubert H. Humphrey of Minnesota. During the campaign, Johnson and Humphrey portrayed themselves as moderates and pointed out the danger of Goldwater's views. Most of the voting public agreed.

In one of the biggest landslides in American history, Johnson was elected President. He had 43.1 million popular votes to Goldwater's 27.1 million and 486 out of 538 electoral votes. In addition, the Democrats increased their majorities in both houses of Congress. Thus Johnson would have congressional support to continue his Great Society.

Johnson's Second Term

By the time Congress adjourned in 1965, nearly all of Johnson's major proposals had been passed. Not since the New Deal had so much legislation been passed in a single session. Although Johnson's Great Society lost momentum after 1965, Congress still continued to pass some important legislation.

Education. In the field of education, Congress sought to provide federal aid at all levels. Earlier bills had often failed to pass because of arguments about aid to segregated schools and parochial schools (private schools operated by religious organizations). On April 11, 1965, however, Congress passed the Elementary and Secondary School Act, which granted $1.3 billion to school districts on the basis of the number of needy children, including those in private and parochial schools. On October 20 Congress passed the Higher Education Act, which provided government scholarship funds to college undergraduates.

Medical Care. One of the most important measures enacted during the 1965 congressional session was the Medicare Act, which was passed on July 30. This act provided medical care for people 65 years of age and over. Social security taxes were intended to pay most of the costs of the program. Medicare included a voluntary supplemental coverage, which allowed people covered by social security to buy low-cost health insurance to cover doctors' bills. The act also provided federal grants to the states to set up a Medicaid program to help needy people of all ages who were not covered by Medicare.

Civil Rights. Congress next turned its attention to civil rights. Despite previous laws, local officials in the South had continued to deny blacks the right to vote. Johnson addressed Congress on behalf of blacks, speaking about the Constitution and the words "All men are created equal":

> Those words are promised to every citizen that he shall share in the dignity of man. This dignity . . . rests on his right to be treated as a man equal in opportunity to all others.
>
> It says that he shall share in freedom. He shall choose his leaders, educate his children, provide for his family according to his ability and merits as a human being.
>
> To apply any other test, to deny a man his hopes because of his color or race or religion or place of birth is not only to do injustice, it is to deny America. . . .

Immigration

The United States has long been known as a nation of immigrants. Throughout its history, people from other countries came to its shores seeking a better way of life. These immigrants brought with them varied traditions, and the diversity helped shape America:

Yes, East and West, and North and South, the palm and the pine, the pole and the equator, the crescent and the cross. . . . Here shall they all unite to build the Republic of Man and the Kingdom of God. . . . What is the glory of Rome and Jerusalem where all nations and races come together to worship and look back, compared with the glory of America where all races and nations come to labor and look forward!

The earliest immigrants—English, Dutch, and Swedish settlers—arrived in America in the 1600's. A century later, there was an influx of German and Scotch-Irish settlers. Between 1840 and 1860, millions of Irish came to this country. A large number of Germans arrived during these years as well. In the late 1800's and early 1900's, an increasing number of people from southern and eastern Europe entered the United States. After reaching a peak around 1920, immigration slowed until the end of World War II. During the last thirty years, most immigrants have come from Asia and Latin America—particularly Mexico.

For a long time, the government placed no restrictions on immigrants. Americans were committed to helping those who were politically, socially, and economically oppressed. In addition, it was recognized that the nation needed people to help develop its resources. Indeed, immigrants helped the country to grow from a colonial outpost to a powerful nation.

Many Americans, however, resented the newcomers. As the labor force expanded, native-born workers lost jobs to immigrants, who were willing to work for lower wages. Ethnocentrism, or the feeling that one's own racial or cultural group is superior to others, also contributed to a movement to restrict immigration.

The rise of antiforeign sentiment led Congress to pass its first law to control immigration. This was the Chinese Exclusion Act of 1882, which barred Chinese laborers from entering the country. Next, a law was passed that excluded criminals, the poor, and the mentally ill. In 1907 the Gentlemen's Agreement prevented Japanese workers from coming to the United States. A 1917 act set up a literacy test for all adult immigrants. This act also prohibited immigration from most of Asia.

In 1921 Congress established a quota system that limited the number of immigrants from a country to 3 percent of the number of people from that country living in America in 1910. Several years later, a new quota law changed this to 2 percent of the number of people from a country living in America in 1890. This law favored immigrants from northern and western Europe.

After World War II, restrictions were eased to accommodate refugees from abroad. In 1952 the McCarran-Walter Act set up quotas for Asian countries. A 1965 amendment to this act changed the quota system. Overall ceilings were set for the Eastern and Western Hemispheres. Individual countries in the Eastern Hemisphere were limited to 20,000 persons annually, but no limits were set on countries in the Western Hemisphere.

Despite these limits, American immigration policy has always been tempered by humanitarianism. For example, an immigrant's spouse is allowed to join him or her regardless of existing quotas. Likewise, quotas have been lifted for refugees from political oppression, such as the recently-arrived Cubans and Indochinese. Even though unemployment has been high, the United States continues to admit many immigrants. The government has even been reluctant to crack down on illegal aliens. These patterns show the American commitment to remain a land of opportunity and a haven for the oppressed.

QUESTIONS

1. What was the first immigration law?
2. Why is the quota system sometimes ignored?

BLACKS REGISTERED TO VOTE IN THE SOUTH

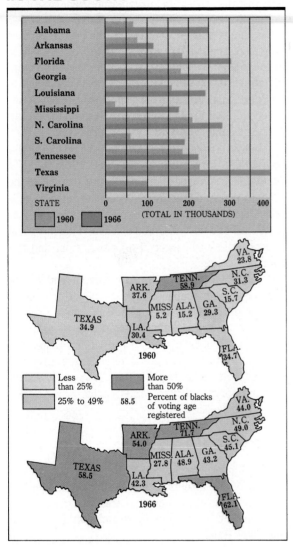

On August 6 Congress passed the Voting Rights Act of 1965. It provided that the federal government supervise registration where fewer than half of those eligible had registered or voted. By 1968 one million new black voters had registered.

On April 1, 1968, Congress passed another civil rights measure. This was the Open Housing Act, which barred discrimination in the sale or rental of housing. This act, however, did not include private homes sold by individual owners without the services of a real estate agent.

Housing. Efforts were also made to improve the quality of housing and to help the poor. On August 10, 1965, Congress passed the Omnibus Housing Act, which authorized the payment of rent supplements to low-income families.

Another measure, the Housing Act, provided funds for the construction of low-income and middle-income housing. The act also set up the Department of Housing and Urban Development (HUD) to run government programs. Johnson appointed Robert Weaver, the first black to serve in the cabinet, as head of the department.

One program administered by Weaver was the Model Cities program, set up under the Demonstration Cities and Metropolitan Area Redevelopment Act, passed by Congress in November 1966. This act provided selected cities with money for slum rehabilitation.

Immigration. Congress liberalized the immigration laws when it passed the Immigration Act of 1965 in October of that year. This act set annual quotas of 120,000 people from the Western Hemisphere and 170,000 from other parts of the world. Although there were no national quotas within the Western Hemisphere, elsewhere there was a maximum of 20,000 per nation. Nevertheless, the act did eliminate most of the discriminatory restrictions that had been operative since the 1920's.

Other Measures. Congress passed several other measures as well. In 1965 excise taxes on consumer items were lowered, the National Foundation of the Arts and Humanities was set up to give federal aid to the arts, and Congress took steps to address the growing problem of pollution. In 1966 Congress gave educational benefits to veterans and set federal safety standards for automobiles. In 1968 it granted federal money to improve local police forces.

SECTION REVIEW

1. Identify the following: *Baker* v. *Carr,* Operation Headstart, Barry M. Goldwater, Robert Weaver.
2. What decisions affecting the rights of accused criminals were made by the Supreme Court?
3. What were the provisions of the Civil Rights Act of 1964?
4. How did Johnson carry out his "war on poverty"?
5. What was the purpose of the Medicare program?

3 Foreign Affairs Under Johnson

One reason for the slowdown of the Great Society after 1965 was Johnson's increasing preoccupation with foreign affairs, including trouble with allies, the Middle East, and the war in Vietnam. In foreign affairs, Johnson had planned to continue Kennedy's policies. Before long, however, the President had embarked on his own course—one that aroused criticism around the world.

Trouble with Allies

During the 1960's the bipolarism that had developed after World War II was breaking down. In the East, Communist China and the Soviet Union were moving toward a major split. In the West, relations between anti-communist countries were strained.

Relations were especially strained between the United States and France, which was challenging America's position as leader of the free world. French President Charles DeGaulle wanted to form an alignment of nations headed by France that would offset the power of the United States and the Soviet Union. In January 1963 DeGaulle prevented Great Britain, which had close ties to the United States, from entering the European Common Market. DeGaulle also insisted that France develop a nuclear force of its own. This action jeopardized the unity of NATO. The greatest strain came in 1966, when DeGaulle pulled France out of NATO.

The Middle East

Johnson became concerned about the Middle East when war again broke out between Arabs and Israelis. Israel, Syria, and Egypt had been mobilizing for some time. When President Nasser of Egypt succeeded in getting the United Nations peace-keeping force to withdraw and then blocked the Gulf of Aqaba to Israeli ships, Israel decided to move. On June 5, 1967, the Israeli air force attacked airfields in Egypt, Jordan, Syria, and Iraq, destroying a large number of planes. At the same time, Israeli ground troops drove deep into these countries.

On the day that war broke out, the United States announced that it would maintain a neutral position in the conflict. At this point, Soviet Premier Aleksei N. Kosygin, using the Hot Line for the first time, made it clear that the Soviet Union would intervene only if the United States did. Neither intervened.

On June 8, Nasser appealed to the United Nations to arrange a **cease-fire,** or a temporary agreement to stop fighting. By June 10, when the cease-fire went into effect, Israel had taken Egypt's Sinai Peninsula to the Suez Canal, seized the Golan Heights from Syria, and occupied all Jordanian territory west of the Jordan River, including the Old City of Jerusalem.

The Six-Day War, as it was called, did not settle the Arab-Israeli conflict. In November 1967 the UN General Assembly passed a resolution that called for Israel to return all territories occupied since June 5. Arab states were to negotiate permanent boundaries for all nations in the Middle East. This proposal aroused little enthusiasm from either side, and the hostilities continued.

Both the Israelis and the Arabs needed additional equipment and supplies. The Soviet Union soon began to give military aid to the Arab states. Early in 1968, after France banned shipments of arms to Israel, the Israelis turned to the United States for help. After much debate, the United States agreed to sell them combat aircraft. This decision was based on a commitment to maintain Israel's military superiority in the Middle East.

Vietnam

Although problems with France and the Middle East called for attention, it was trouble in Vietnam that dominated the Johnson years. As time passed, the United States became more and more involved in Southeast Asia.

Background. The Geneva Accord of 1954, which ended the war in Indochina, had called for free elections to be held in Vietnam in 1956. Their purpose was to determine whether Vietnam would remain divided or be unified. The elections, however, were never held, and the country remained divided. Ho Chi Minh controlled the North and Ngo Dinh Diem, who had replaced Bao Dai, controlled the South.

In the late 1950's thousands of South Vietnamese Communists (Viet Cong) rebelled against Diem. In 1960 they set up their own government, the National Liberation Front. Before long, the Viet Cong

In May 1961 Kennedy sent 400 Special Forces soldiers and 100 advisors to South Vietnam.

Explain that the provocative nature of United States actions in the area was concealed during congressional hearings prior to the passage of the Tonkin Gulf Resolution.

controlled most of the countryside. In some areas they used harsh tactics to subdue the people. In other areas, such tactics were not necessary because the Viet Cong had the support of the people. This was due in part to the fact that Diem's regime was corrupt.

Despite this corruption, the United States was committed to Diem. There were two major reasons for this commitment. The first was the need to honor American obligations as a member of SEATO, which had promised to protect South Vietnam. The second was the desire to prevent the spread of communism.

Both Eisenhower and Kennedy had urged Diem to make reforms, but they had little success. Nevertheless, in May 1961, Kennedy sent military aid and advisors to counteract the help the Viet Cong were receiving from the Communists in North Vietnam.

Conditions in South Vietnam worsened in the spring of 1963. Diem, who was a Catholic, began widespread oppression of Buddhists, who were in a majority in South Vietnam. There were demonstrations against his regime. In fact, several Buddhists burned themselves to death in public places. Opposition to Diem's regime continued to mount. Finally, on November 1, 1963, a military **coup** (forcible overthrow of a government) occurred, and Diem was assassinated. The United States, which had become more concerned with Diem's autocratic ways, immediately recognized the new government.

The new government, however, fared little better than Diem's, and the change brought no real stability to the country. Several more coups took place. In February 1965 General Nguyen Van Thieu took control of the government. Thieu was later elected president of South Vietnam. Although his regime like Diem's was corrupt, the United States continued to uphold its commitment to South Vietnam.

Increasing Involvement. Under Johnson the United States became more involved in Vietnam. On February 1, 1964, Operation Plan 34A—a program of secret, hit-and-run military operations against North Vietnam—was begun. This program was carried out by the South Vietnamese under the direction of American personnel.

In late July the South Vietnamese on a 34A mission raided two North Vietnamese islands in the Gulf of Tonkin. While pursuing the raiders, North Vietnamese PT boats encountered the United States destroyer *Maddox*, which was on patrol in the Gulf, and fired upon it. The next day, two more 34A raids were staged against North Vietnam. On August 4 the North Vietnamese attacked both the *Maddox* and another destroyer, *Turner Joy*.

In response, Johnson ordered retaliatory air strikes against North Vietnam. He also submitted to Congress the Tonkin Gulf Resolution, authorizing the President to "take all necessary measures to repel any armed attack against forces of the United States and to prevent further aggression." This gave Johnson almost complete freedom of action to escalate the war. Congress, on August 7, passed the resolution almost unanimously.

Johnson still maintained that he did not intend to commit American troops to war in Asia. He said, "We are not about to send American boys nine or ten thousand miles away from home to do what Asian boys ought to be doing for themselves." Nevertheless, as Viet Cong attacks continued, the United States moved toward deeper involvement.

Escalation. A Viet Cong attack on Pleiku, in which eight American advisors were killed, triggered Johnson's decision to escalate the war. On February 13, 1965, he ordered sustained bombing of North Vietnam. The so-called Rolling Thunder campaign began on March 2. Less than a week later, the first United States combat troops landed in Vietnam. On April 1 Johnson decided to increase American forces in South Vietnam and to use combat troops for offensive action.

As American involvement in Vietnam grew, helicopters were relied on because they were effective at pinpointing enemy positions. What triggered the decision to escalate the war?

Shortly after Johnson made this decision, he gave a speech at The Johns Hopkins University. In it he explained why the United States was in Vietnam:

> We are there because we have a promise to keep. Since 1954 every American President has offered support to the people of South Vietnam. We have helped to build and we have helped to defend. Thus, over many years we have made a national pledge to help South Vietnam defend its independence. . . .
>
> We are also there to strengthen world order. Around the globe—from Berlin to Thailand—are people whose well-being rests on the belief that they can count on us if attacked. To leave Vietnam to its fate would shake the confidence of all these people in the value of American commitment. The result would be increased unrest and instability, or even war.
>
> We are also there because there are great stakes in the balance. Let no one think that retreat from Vietnam would bring an end to conflict. The battle would be renewed in one country and then another. The central lesson of our time is that the appetite of aggression is never satisfied. . . .

As the war escalated, North Vietnam increased its support of the Viet Cong. During the early stages of the war, Hanoi had provided the Viet Cong with supplies and a few soldiers. In 1965, however, the North Vietnamese government began sending regular troops south over the Ho Chi Minh Trail.

To meet the situation, General William C. Westmoreland, American commander at Saigon, asked for 200,000 additional troops and a United States commitment to a land war in Vietnam. On July 28, Johnson responded, "We will meet his needs."

By the end of 1965, there were 184,000 American troops in South Vietnam. By the end of 1968, the total had increased to over 500,000. "Search and destroy" missions became the typical land operation of the war. On these missions, American troops would move into an area, evacuate the civilians, and devastate it. This made it more difficult for the Viet Cong to hold. In the air, the United States began using B-52's to bomb targets in North Vietnam.

Opposition to the War. As United States involvement in the war increased, so did opposition to

it. Some Americans felt that the conflict in Vietnam was a civil war and should not involve the United States. Others were concerned that the cost of America's commitment to Vietnam, which was about $25 billion a year, was hurting domestic programs. All deplored the devastation of the countryside and the lives lost during the course of the war.

In 1965–1966, debate intensified in Congress between the "doves," who wanted to end the war, and the "hawks," who favored increased military efforts. This debate was publicized through a televised hearing of the Senate Foreign Relations Committee. J. William Fulbright, chairman of the committee and a leading "dove," used the hearing to criticize United States policy in Southeast Asia.

There were critics within Johnson's administration as well. One was Secretary of Defense Robert McNamara. In October 1966 he sent a memorandum to the President on Vietnam:

> The picture of the world's greatest superpower killing or seriously injuring 1,000 noncombatants a week, while trying to pound a tiny backward nation into submission on an issue whose merits are hotly disputed, is not a pretty one. It could conceivably produce a costly distortion in the American national consciousness and in the world image of the United States—especially if the damage to North Vietnam is complete enough to be successful.

Debate over the war led to protest demonstrations beginning with university "teach-ins" in the spring of 1965. In April 1967 massive antiwar parades were held in major cities, and in late October 200,000 people marched on the Pentagon.

Johnson's Retreat. Although all was not well at home, the government was receiving favorable reports on the progress of the war in Vietnam. On January 30, 1968, however, Viet Cong and North Vietnamese forces launched a major offensive throughout South Vietnam. This was unexpected, as a truce had been declared for Tet, or the Lunar New Year. After a difficult struggle, American and South Vietnamese troops finally stopped the Communists.

After the Tet offensive, Johnson recognized how little headway had been made against communism in Vietnam. The war of attrition (a process of wearing

WAR IN VIETNAM

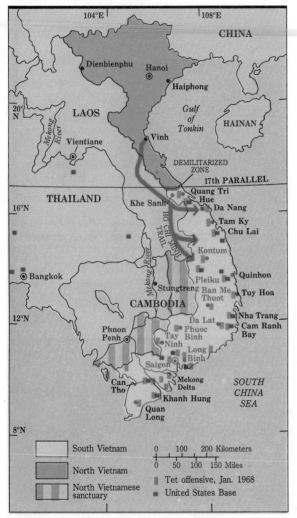

South Vietnam

North Vietnam

North Vietnamese sanctuary

0   100   200 Kilometers

0   50   100   150 Miles

Tet offensive, Jan. 1968

United States Base

down) waged by United States and South Vietnam had failed to counter successfully the guerrilla tactics used by the Viet Cong and North Vietnamese. Casualties had risen from 1130 in 1965 to 12,588 in 1968.

Therefore, when Westmoreland requested an additional 200,000 troops in February 1968, Johnson sent only 30,000. On March 31 Johnson suspended the bombing of North Vietnam above the Demilitarized Zone (DMZ)—a neutral piece of land separating North and South Vietnam. At the same time, the President called upon the leaders of North Vietnam to negotiate. They agreed, and in May preliminary peace talks began in Paris.

SECTION REVIEW

1. Identify the following: Six-Day War, Ngo Ninh Diem, Tonkin Gulf Resolution, William C. Westmoreland, DMZ.
2. What problems did the United States have with France?
3. Why did the United States agree to sell military aircraft to the Israelis?
4. How did Johnson justify American involvement in Vietnam?

4 Unrest in the Nation

While Johnson focused his attention on foreign affairs, a growing turmoil spread throughout the United States. The black civil rights movement inspired other groups who felt the government should do more to further the cause of equal rights. Youth rebelled against society in general and the Vietnam War in particular. Many of the disenchanted turned to violence, and it was in an atmosphere of domestic strife that the next presidential election took place.

The Struggle for Equality

During the 1960's a number of groups engaged in a struggle for equal rights. Not only blacks, but Hispanics, Indians, and women joined in the effort to end discrimination in American life. By the end of the decade, strides had been made, but much remained to be done.

Blacks. In the early 1960's blacks pursuing their civil rights followed a policy of nonviolence. They sought integration into American society on an equal basis with whites. The leading advocate of nonviolence was the Reverend Martin Luther King, Jr., head of the Southern Christian Leadership Conference (SCLC). King stated his views on violence:

> *The ultimate weakness of violence is that it is a descending spiral, begetting the very thing it seeks to destroy. Instead of diminishing evil, it multiplies it. Through violence, you may murder the liar, but you cannot murder the lie, nor establish the truth. Through violence you may murder the hater, but you do not murder hate. In fact, violence merely increases*

Note that King was influenced by Ghandi.

hate. So it goes. Returning violence for violence multiplies violence, adding deeper darkness to a night already devoid of stars. Darkness cannot drive out darkness; only light can do that; Hate cannot drive out hate; only love can do that.

The tactics used by King and his followers varied. In the South, sit-ins continued to be employed to integrate public places. Civil rights workers, refusing to be segregated on buses and trains, took "freedom rides" throughout the region. Protest marches occurred when voting rights were denied. In the North, where blacks were confined to ghettoes by **de facto segregation** (segregation that exists in fact but is not required by law), they staged rent strikes to protest poor housing. They also boycotted stores that discriminated against blacks in hiring.

Peaceful methods were used in Birmingham, Alabama, where King led a massive demonstration for equal rights in the spring of 1963. In August 200,000 people—both white and black—marched in Washington, D.C., for the same cause. The highlight of that event was a speech by King:

I have a dream that one day this nation will rise up and live out the true meaning of its creed: We hold these truths to be self-evident: that all men are created equal. I have a dream that one day even the state of Mississippi, a desert state sweltering with the heat in injustice and oppression, will be transformed into an oasis of freedom. I have a dream that my four little children will one day live in a nation where they will be judged not by the color of their skin but by the content of their character.

In support of his ideals, King led over 3000 people on a 54-mile march from Selma to Montgomery, Alabama, in March of 1965. But King's peaceful tactics were often met with violence. Mobs attacked freedom riders, police used electric cattle prods to break up crowds, and some civil rights workers were jailed.

More than 200,000 persons took part in the 1963 March on Washington (left) to push for civil rights. Adapting the philosophies of Thoreau and Gandhi, Martin Luther King (right) sought to bring change through nonviolent means. Why did some blacks turn to other means to effect change?

Have students debate which philosophy—nonviolence or black nationalism—was more effective in the struggle for civil rights.

After King's death, riots broke out in 100 cities across the land.

Despite gains made at the national, state, and local levels, progress in black civil rights was slow. It was especially slow in social and economic areas. Black unemployment, for example, was much higher than the national average. As a result, a growing number of blacks were becoming more radical by the mid-1960's. They demanded immediate action not only to gain political and legal rights, but to end discrimination in housing, education, and employment. Instead of King's philosophy of integration and nonviolence, radical groups began to put forward the theory of black nationalism and expressed their willingness to use violence to achieve their goals.

One of these groups was the Black Muslims, originally founded in 1930. Led by Elijah Muhammed, the Black Muslims preached complete separation from white society and advocated a program of self-defense. Their ideas—spread by Malcolm Little, a Black Muslim minister who became known as Malcolm X—received national attention in the early 1960's. By 1964, however, Malcolm X came to favor an integrated society instead of separatism. Therefore, he broke with the Black Muslims. Apparently as a result, he was shot and killed in February 1965.

By the late 1960's the Student Non-Violent Coordinating Committee (SNCC) and the Congress of Racial Equality (CORE), which had originally supported King's tactics, came to be more radical. In May 1966 Stokely Carmichael, head of the SNCC, advanced the idea of "black power." This was a philosophy of racial pride that said blacks should take control of all aspects of their lives—social, political, and economic. As expounded by the black nationalists, it meant separation from white society, by violent means if necessary. Although rejected by such groups as the NAACP, which saw it as a threat to law and order, the idea of black power had a great impact on the civil rights movement.

One of the most militant black-power groups was the Black Panthers. Founded in 1966 by Huey Newton, Bobby Seale, and Eldridge Cleaver, the Black Panthers urged blacks to arm themselves and confront white society in order to force whites to grant them equal rights. Cleaver's *Soul On Ice* (1967) served as a statement of Black Panther aims.

Influenced by the growing militancy and frustrated by their situation, blacks rioted in cities throughout the nation. In the summer of 1964, bloody riots took

Police make an arrest during a disturbance in Detroit. Riots erupted in many cities during the 1960's, reaching a peak in 1967 when disorders were reported in 114 cities in 32 states. What was the fundamental cause of the riots in the mid-1960's?

place in Harlem. One of the worst riots in the nation's history occurred in Watts, a Los Angeles ghetto, in August 1965. By the time the National Guard restored order, 28 blacks were dead, and damages reached $200 million. Riots occurred in Newark and Detroit during the summer of 1966. Violence intensified following the assassination of Martin Luther King, Jr., in Memphis, Tennessee, on April 4, 1968.[3]

In an attempt to do something about the problem of growing violence, Johnson appointed the National Advisory Commission on Civil Disorders. This commission, headed by Governor Otto Kerner of Illinois, studied the causes and consequences of the riots and released a report on February 29, 1968.

The report named "white racism" as the cause of the riots. It stated, "Our nation is moving toward two societies, one black, one white—separate and unequal." The report pointed out that, although some progress had been made, there was much more to be done. It concluded, "Only a commitment to national action—compassionate, massive, and sustained" could bring about equality for all.

Hispanics. During the 1960's Hispanics (people with a common Spanish heritage), like blacks, sought

---

[3] His killer was James Earl Ray, an escaped convict, who was sentenced to 99 years in prison for the crime. Although Ray pleaded guilty, some people doubted that he had acted alone. A House committee reported in 1978 that a conspiracy was likely, but nothing was proved.

SAN JUAN

PUERTO RICO

Luis Muñoz Marín

In 1964, Luis Muñoz Marín stepped down as governor of Puerto Rico after 16 years. The son of a diplomat who had helped Puerto Rico obtain its autonomy from Spain, Muñoz Marín had been the leading political power on the island for more than a generation.

Born in San Juan in 1898, he was raised in Washington, D.C. After studying law at Georgetown University, he served as secretary to the resident commissioner for Puerto Rico. During this period, Muñoz Marín wrote two books and contributed articles to various newspapers and magazines. Later he became editor of *La Revista de Indias,* a journal of Latin American culture published in New York City.

In 1926 Muñoz Marín returned to Puerto Rico, where he became the editor of *La Democracia,* a newspaper founded by his father. Muñoz Marín used his position as editor to urge complete independence for Puerto Rico and to call attention to economic problems on the island.

In 1932 Muñoz Marín was elected to the Puerto Rican Senate as a member of the Liberal party. In the Senate, he continued to call for independence and worked to secure money from the United States government to help the island's ailing economy.

In 1937, however, Liberal party leaders expelled Muñoz Marín from their ranks. They had modified their position on independence and felt his views were too extreme. In addition, large sugar growers, angered by his plan to break up their holdings, had threatened to cut off contributions if he remained in the party.

Muñoz Marín then founded his own party—the Partido Popular Democrático (Popular Democratic party). Its motto, "Bread, land, and liberty," was meant to appeal chiefly to landless Puerto Ricans called *jíbaros.* In 1940 the Popular Democratic party won control of the Senate and elected Muñoz Marín its president.

Gradually, Muñoz Marín changed his views and began working for Puerto Rico's economic progress under United States guidance rather than complete independence. In 1942 he organized Operation Bootstrap to attract mainland industry to Puerto Rico with generous tax incentives and cheap labor.

In 1948, when the United States gave Puerto Rico the right to elect its own governor, Muñoz Marín was overwhelmingly elected. He persuaded the United States to approve a commonwealth status for the island in 1952. When he died in 1980, he was mourned as a national hero.

equal rights. Hispanics included several different groups. The most numerous were Mexican-Americans. Among them were descendants of Mexicans who lived in the Southwest when the United States annexed the territory from Mexico in 1848. The rest came to the United States more recently. Most were migrant workers, many of whom came to the United States in search of work.

Many Puerto Ricans, who were American citizens, also emigrated to this country in search of jobs. Before World War II there were approximately 70,000 Puerto Ricans in the United States, mostly in New York City. By 1960 there were about 600,000 in New York and other large northeastern cities. These immigrants provided a source of cheap, unskilled labor for the nation's factories. In addition, during the 1960's over 200,000 Cubans arrived in the United States. Most of them settled in Florida. Many of these people had fled Cuba when Castro established his communist regime there.

All of these groups faced discrimination in education because they could not speak English, and few schools were equipped to handle foreign-language students. Hispanics faced discrimination in other areas as well. In large cities, they lived in slums, while as migrant workers they often lived in shacks. Most had to work for low pay in poor conditions, whether in the fields or in the factories.

In the early 1960's Mexican-American labor leader Cesar Chavez began efforts to organize migrant farm workers in California. These efforts culminated in the formation of the National Farm Workers Association, which later became the United Farm Workers. In 1965 grape pickers led by Chavez struck against California growers. The workers also called for a boycott of California wines. In 1970 an agreement was finally reached with the growers, and the strike came to an end.

Others besides Chavez actively worked to secure equal rights for Hispanics. Reies López Tijerina formed an organization to reopen the question of Spanish and Mexican land grants. José Ángel Gutier-

rez worked to end discrimination through the political process. Rodolfo Gonzales organized the Crusade for Justice. Gonzales was also active in the Chicano Movement, an effort of young, militant Mexican-Americans. They formed organizations such as the Brown Berets in Los Angeles. This organization and others like it stressed cultural pride and preached "Chicano power" along with self-defense.

Indians. Toward the end of the 1960's, Indians also began protesting their unequal status in American society. The government's changing policies had left many Indians embittered. For years, government policy had alternated between Americanizing the Indians and encouraging their separation from white society. The Dawes Act (1887) had been designed to break up tribal organization by allotting Indians individual pieces of land. The Indian Reorganization Act (1934), however, repealed the allotment policy and returned to tribal ownership Indian lands previously open to sale. Other parts of the act

Beginning in the 1960's minorities demanded a stronger voice in their own affairs. Mexican-American labor leader Cesar Chavez (left) organized migrant farm workers in an effort to improve their wages and living conditions. American Indians (right) pressed for economic and political equality and compensation for the loss of their land. What gains did these minorities make?

fostered tribal government and improved economic conditions for the Indians.

In the 1950's policy changed again when the government tried to "terminate" its responsibilities to the Indians. "Termination" meant turning responsibility over to the states. By the 1960's the federal government was once more trying to encourage a return to tribal ways. However, at that time almost one-half of the 850,000 Indians in the United States lived in cities.

In reaction to these shifts in government policy and to continuing discrimination, Indians began to organize. The first organization, the National Congress of American Indians (NCAI) was founded in 1940. It became increasingly active in the 1960's, when the Native Indian Youth Council and the Native American Movement joined in the battle for equal rights.

Later in the 1960's, some groups became more radical in character. One of these was the American Indian Movement (AIM), founded in Minnesota by Dennis Banks and Clyde Bellecourt. AIM favored violent tactics and engaged in a number of confrontations with the federal government. Not all Indians supported such tactics, however, and the Indian rights movement lost some of its force as a result.

Women. American women were also involved in the struggle for equality in the 1960's. Their struggle became known as the women's liberation movement. One of the chief objectives of this movement was to eliminate discrimination in employment. Women were often barred from jobs that were considered the province of males, and if a woman managed to get such a job, she generally received less pay.

One of the leaders in the fight for women's rights was Betty Friedan, whose book, *The Feminine Mystique,* was published in 1963. She supported **feminism,** the theory that women should have political, economic and social rights equal to those of men.

In 1966 Friedan founded the National Organization for Women (NOW). NOW and other groups worked for laws that would guarantee women equal pay for equal work as well as opportunity at all levels of employment. Another goal of women's groups was publicly financed day-care centers for the children of working mothers. The Civil Rights Act of 1964, which prohibited discrimination on the basis of sex as well as race, color, religion, and national origin, provided a legal basis from which to work. However, most

groups sought a constitutional amendment to further guarantee equal rights for women.

The Youth Protest

Unrest spread to young people as well. The 1960's was a period of political activism on college campuses. The New Frontier stimulated students to join the Peace Corps, Vista, and the civil rights movement. However, after President Kennedy's assassination and the escalation of American involvement in Vietnam, this activism took a new direction. Many young people came to view society as corrupt and saw the older generation as the instrument of that corruption. This led to conflict with the **"establishment,"** or the controlling groups in society, such as government and business.

The university was viewed as part of the establishment and, as such, drew increasing criticism from students. They wanted to play a greater part in running schools that had grown so large as to seem mere assembly lines of education. Students who were against the war in Vietnam objected to military training in the form of the Reserve Officers Training Corps (ROTC) on campus. They also objected to research financed by the Pentagon being carried on at universities.

Protest intensified as changes in the draft made students, who had been exempt, subject to military service. Many burned their draft cards or fled abroad to avoid the draft. When student demonstrations seemed to be getting out of control, university authorities called the police. During 1968–1969, about 4000 students were arrested.

Many students were part of a movement known as the New Left.[4] Members of this movement sought basic changes in American society. The New Left was a varied group. Within it there were those whose major goal was peace, and others who were primarily concerned with racial equality. Still others were involved in the fight for students' rights. Some were pacifists, while others, such as the Weatherman faction of the Students for a Democratic Society (SDS), were violent revolutionaries.

The establishment saw members of the New Left as dangerous, and New Left tactics—whether

---

[4] The "old left" of the 1930's had held Marxist views and supported the Soviet Union.

ELECTION OF 1968

State/Candidate		
WASH.	9	
MONT.	4	
N.D.	4	
MINN.	10	
N.H.	4	
VT.	3	
ME.	4	
ORE.	6	
IDAHO	4	
WYO.	3	
S.D.	4	
WISC.	12	
D.C.	3	
N.Y.	43	
MASS.	14	
NEV.	3	
UTAH	4	
COLO.	6	
NEB.	5	
IOWA	9	
ILL.	26	
IND.	13	
OHIO	26	
MICH	21	
PA.	29	
N.J.	17	
R.I.	4	
CONN.	8	
CAL.	40	
KANS.	7	
MO.	12	
KY.	9	
W.VA	7	
VA.	12	
DEL.	3	
ARIZ.	5	
N. MEX.	4	
OKLA.	8	
ARK.	6	
TENN.	11	
N.C.	13	
MD.	10	
TEXAS	25	
MISS.	7	
ALA.	10	
GA.	12	
S.C.	8	
LA.	10	
FLA.	14	
HAWAII	4	
ALASKA	3	

Divided between Nixon and Wallace

④ Electoral votes

Nixon ⑫
Wallace ①

	Popular Vote: 73,185,466	Electoral Vote: 538
Nixon	31,785,480	301
Humphrey	31,275,166	191
Wallace	9,906,473	46

peaceful or violent—were often met with force. There were even instances of police brutality. The government was determined to break up the movement. FBI agents infiltrated New Left groups, and the Department of Justice succeeded in sending many members of the movement to prison. Thus, the New Left lost most of its influence after 1968.

The Election of 1968

Amidst all this unrest, the election of 1968 was held. With the election at hand, opposition to Johnson within his own party consolidated. A leading critic of the war, Senator Eugene McCarthy of Minnesota, entered the race for the nomination and ran unexpectedly well in the New Hampshire primary. Shortly after this, Senator Robert F. Kennedy, who had criticized the United States involvement in Vietnam, became a candidate.

Because of the growing dissent over the war and the increasing opposition within his own party, Johnson announced that he had decided not to run for reelection. Once the President withdrew, Vice President Hubert H. Humphrey entered the race.

During the campaign, Robert Kennedy achieved a number of victories over his opponents. One of the most important of his victories took place in California. However, on June 5, 1968, the night of his victory in the California primary, Kennedy was shot.[5] He died the next day.

At the Democratic convention in Chicago in August, while violent clashes occurred in the streets between antiwar protesters and the police, Humphrey was nominated for President. He chose Senator Edmund S. Muskie of Maine as his running mate. Humphrey pledged to uphold Johnson's policies, but in time he disassociated himself from the administration's policy in Vietnam.

Meanwhile, Richard Nixon received the Republican nomination at Miami. By campaigning for Republicans in the 1966 elections, Nixon had accumulated a number of political favors that stood him in good stead at the convention. He named Governor Spiro T. Agnew of Maryland as his Vice President. Nixon promised to re-establish law and order and end the war in Vietnam.

---

[5] Kennedy was shot by Sirhan Sirhan, a Palestinian who opposed Kennedy's support of Israel.

The election was close. Nixon won by a slim margin in the popular vote, receiving 43.4 percent to Humphrey's 42.7 percent. George Wallace, a candidate of the American Independent Party, received 13.5 percent. The final electoral vote was 301 for Nixon, 191 for Humphrey, and 46 for Wallace. Although the Republicans had won the Presidency, the Democrats retained their hold on Congress. Thus, Nixon would be a **minority President,** or one who had a majority of the electoral votes but less than 50 percent of the popular votes. This fact was one indication how divided the country was when Nixon took office. It remained to be seen whether he could bring unity to the American people.

SECTION REVIEW

1. Identify the following: Malcolm X, Otto Kerner, Cesar Chavez, Brown Berets, Dennis Banks, Betty Friedan.
2. What tactics were advocated by Martin Luther King, Jr.?
3. What problems were faced by Hispanic Americans?
4. How did government policy toward the Indians fluctuate?
5. What were the goals of the women's liberation movement?
6. Why did many American youth rebel in the 1960's?

CHAPTER 30 REVIEW

SUMMARY

1. In 1960 John F. Kennedy became the first Catholic President of the United States.
2. Unlike Eisenhower, Kennedy was an activist President favoring an ambitious space program, government control of the economy, and broad social welfare and civil rights legislation.
3. On November 22, 1963, Kennedy was assassinated, and Vice President Lyndon B. Johnson became President.
4. Johnson, an experienced politician, pushed a variety of liberal measures through Congress, including legislation designed to help the poor and support civil rights.
5. During the 1960's the Supreme Court under Chief Justice Earl Warren pursued a liberal course.

6. Johnson was reelected President by a landslide in 1964.
7. Although Johnson continued to promote his domestic program during his second term, his attention was occupied by foreign affairs.
8. Under Johnson the United States became increasingly involved in the Vietnam War.
9. The 1960's was a time of political unrest, during which opposition to the war in Vietnam increased, minorities and women carried on a struggle for equal rights, and young people rebelled against society.
10. Growing dissent over the Vietnam War forced Johnson to de-escalate American involvement and to withdraw from the presidential election of 1968.

VOCABULARY

wage-price guideposts	urban renewal	filibuster	de facto segregation
"jawboning"	legislative apportionment	poverty level	feminism
depreciation	felony	cease-fire	establishment
investment tax credit	gross national product	coup	minority President
balance of payments			

REVIEW QUESTIONS

1. What factors affected the outcome of the 1960 presidential election?

2. What was the state of the American economy during the 1960's?

3. What was the New Frontier?
4. What steps were taken under Kennedy and Johnson to help the poor?
5. What progress was made by the civil rights movement?

6. Why did the United States become involved in Vietnam?
7. Was the Vietnam War controversial?
8. Why was the period of the 1960's a time of political turmoil?

DISCUSSION

1. Is religion still likely to be an issue in presidential elections, as it was in 1960? Why or why not?
2. Why do you think the attitude of the public is important in determining American foreign policy?

3. Are nonviolent techniques effective in achieving social change? Why or why not?
4. Do young people today have attitudes toward authority that are similar to those of youth in the 1960's? Why or why not?

USING MAPS

Refer to the maps on page 665 and answer the following questions:

1. Which southern state had the largest number of blacks registered to vote in 1960?
2. Which southern state had the least number of blacks registered to vote in 1960?

3. Which state showed the largest increase in black registration between 1960 and 1966?
4. Which states had more than 50 percent black registration in 1960? In 1966?
5. How can you account for the changes in black registration between 1960 and 1966?

USING SKILLS

During the 1960 election campaign, Reverend W. A. Criswell of Houston, Texas gave a sermon stating his objections to having a Catholic President. Below is an excerpt from that sermon. Read it and answer the questions that follow.

When the Roman Catholic hierarchy is able to seize political power in a nation, what happens? Here are a few examples: The Constitution of Argentina states: "To be eligible to the office of President or Vice-President of the Nation, a person must belong to the Roman Catholic Church." The Constitution of Paraguay states: "The President of the Republic must profess the Roman Catholic religion." The Constitution of Spain states: "To exercise the office of Chief of State or King or Regent, it shall be necessary to profess the Roman Catholic religion." In the South American nation of Colombia, during the past eight years, with a government dominated by the Roman Catholic Church, 49 Protestant churches have been destroyed, 34 Protestant churches have been confiscated, and

89 Protestant church leaders have been murdered. . . .

The Roman Church wins most of its victories with the weapons of time. If Kennedy wins, with strong emphasis on separation of church and state, then the door is open for another Roman Catholic later who gives the Pope his Ambassador, the church schools state support, and finally, recognition of one church above all others in America. Then religious liberty has also died in America as it has died in Spain, as it has died in Colombia, as it has died wherever the Roman Catholic Hierarchy has the ableness and power to shut it down and destroy it in death.

1. What is the main point of Reverend Criswell's argument?
2. What evidence does he offer to support his argument?
3. Is it valid to compare the United States with other countries? Why or why not?
4. Did any of Reverend Criswell's fears come to pass after Kennedy became President?

1	Nixon and Foreign Affairs	679
2	Domestic Affairs Under Nixon	684
3	The Presidency in Crisis	690
4	The Ford Administration	694

THE NIXON-FORD ERA

We have found ourselves rich in goods, but ragged in spirit; reaching with magnificent precision for the moon, but falling into raucous discord on earth.

RICHARD M. NIXON

On January 20, 1969, Richard Nixon became the 37th President of the United States. During his campaign, Nixon had promised to unify the country. He hoped to do this by pursuing conservative policies that appealed to a growing number of Americans who were tired of the rapid social change of the 1960's.

Although the Nixon administration at first brought a measure of stability to American life, it soon became clear that the turmoil of the 1960's had persisted into the 1970's. The war in Vietnam continued to plague the nation, and the struggle for equal rights continued. During Nixon's second term, scandal led to a crisis in the Presidency. Nixon's successor, Gerald R. Ford, faced the task of restoring the people's confidence in government.

1 Nixon and Foreign Affairs

When he took office, Richard Nixon was faced with a number of problems in foreign affairs. Aided by Henry Kissinger, his national security advisor, he tried to deal with problems such as the war in Vietnam, relations with communist powers, and trouble in the Middle East. Nixon understood that the international balance of power was changing and that many Americans were unhappy with the role of the United States in Vietnam. He tried to be realistic in his approach to foreign policy. For support he appealed to what he called the **"silent majority."** In Nixon's view, the silent majority was made up of middle-class Americans who stressed traditional values such as hard work, law and order, love of country, and material progress.

The War in Vietnam

One of the first problems Nixon faced was Vietnam. By the end of 1969, polls showed that most Americans felt the war in Vietnam had been a mistake. Nixon had campaigned on a "secret plan" for peace. In March 1969 he revealed his plan.

Vietnamization. Nixon's plan to achieve "peace with honor" was called Vietnamization. This was not a plan to end the war, but a plan for the gradual withdrawal of American troops from Vietnam. As American troops were withdrawn, the United States would step up efforts to train and equip South Vietnamese forces. In time these forces would take over total responsibility for the war. In keeping with his plan, Nixon announced in June that 25,000 American troops would leave Vietnam by the end of August.

Vietnamization was consistent with a new statement of American foreign policy made by the President in the summer of 1969. This was the Nixon Doctrine, which said that the United States would keep its treaty commitments, provide protection to allies under threat of nuclear attack, and furnish aid in other cases of aggression. The doctrine made clear, however, that the United States would not fight an ally's war.

Many Americans were not satisfied with the withdrawal of the first American troops and the Nixon Doctrine. More antiwar demonstrations took place. To rally support for his policy, Nixon gave a television speech on November 3, 1969, explaining his plan:

> *My fellow Americans . . . we really have only two choices open to us if we want to end this war.*
>
> *I can order an immediate, precipitate withdrawal of all Americans from Vietnam without regard to the effects of that action.*
>
> *Or we can persist in our search for a just peace through a negotiated settlement if possible, or through continued implementation of our plan for Vietnamization if necessary— a*

Vietnamization was implemented, and American troops in Vietnam reached a low of 60,000 by 1972.

There were 3500 bombing raids over Cambodia in 14 months. The extent of these raids was concealed from Congress.

Reacting against the anti-war demonstrations, members of the "silent majority" began to counter with demonstrations in favor of administration policy. The "hardhat" became a symbol of this movement. Who comprised the "silent majority"?

plan in which we will withdraw all of our forces from Vietnam in accordance with our program, as the South Vietnamese become strong enough to defend their own freedom.

I have chosen the second course.

It is not the easy way.

It is the right way.

It is a plan which will end the war and serve the cause of peace—not just in Vietnam but in the Pacific and in the world.

The speech was effective. Despite revelations of the American massacre of 450 unarmed civilians at the Vietnam village of My Lai on March 16, 1968, support for Nixon's policy grew.[1]

---

[1] Several officers and enlisted men were tried in military courts for war crimes as a result of this incident. One man, Lieutenant William Calley, Jr., was convicted of murder and sentenced to prison.

Cambodia and Laos. Nixon's hope was that ultimately the North Vietnamese would grow tired of the war and negotiate peace. To hasten that end, Nixon involved the United States in Cambodia and Laos. In March 1969 he secretly ordered the bombing of Cambodia because the Viet Cong and the North Vietnamese were using sanctuaries (safe places) there as springboards for offensives into South Vietnam. The bombing, however, merely caused the enemy to flee deeper into Cambodia.

The United States stepped up its involvement in Cambodia in 1970. In March of that year, Prince Norodom Sihanouk, Cambodia's ruler, was overthrown by Lon Nol. Under Prince Sihanouk, Cambodia had maintained a neutral position in Southeast Asia. Lon Nol, however, who was alarmed by the communist threat, appealed to Nixon for help.

On April 30, 1970, Nixon announced the invasion of Cambodia. This was to be an attack by the United States and South Vietnam on communist sanctuaries. Nixon justified the attack as follows:

A majority of the American people . . . are for the withdrawal of our forces from Vietnam. The action I have taken tonight is indispensable for the continuing success of that withdrawal program.

A majority of the American people want to end this war rather than to have it drag on interminably. The action I have taken tonight will serve that purpose.

A majority of the American people want to keep the casualties of our brave men in Vietnam at an absolute minimum. The action I take tonight is essential if we are to accomplish that goal.

We take this action not for the purpose of expanding the war into Cambodia but for the purpose of ending the war in Vietnam and winning the just peace we all desire.

On May 1 American and South Vietnamese troops struck into Cambodia. Although most of the Communists had pulled back in expectation of attack, supplies were seized. However, the Cambodian invasion spread the war into Cambodia.

In the United States, the Cambodian invasion sparked demonstrations on college campuses throughout the nation. Many demonstrations were

Ho Chi Minh died in 1969.

THE UNITED STATES IN A NEW ERA   **681**

Remind students that Nixon was a member of the House Un-American Activities Committee in the 1950's.

accompanied by violence. On May 4, 1970, the Ohio National Guard was sent in to quell a disturbance at Kent State University. Guards fired into a crowd of students, killing four. Shortly after that, at Jackson State College in Mississippi, two black students were killed by state police.

The killings angered many Americans, and protest against the Vietnam War increased. One demonstration drew more than 100,000 people to Washington, D.C. Antiwar forces also intensified their lobbying campaign. Finally, on December 31, 1970, Congress repealed the Tonkin Gulf Resolution. However, this action by Congress did not have much impact. Nixon did not consider the resolution necessary to justify American involvement in the war. Also, despite growing disillusionment with the war, Congress continued to approve appropriations to fund it.

Although many Americans were outraged by Nixon's policy, the silent majority supported him. Indeed, polls showed that 57 percent of the American people accepted his argument that Vietnamization would be helped more by offensive actions such as the Cambodian invasion. In other words, they believed that the war could be shortened by being widened.

The war was widened again in February 1971. At this time, South Vietnamese troops, with United States air support, marched into Laos to attack North Vietnamese supply bases along the Ho Chi Minh Trail. The South Vietnamese suffered heavy losses with little result. Although many people still approved of Nixon's policy, growing numbers of people were becoming concerned about the widening of the war.

The End of American Involvement. Up to this point, little progress had been made at the official peace talks in Paris. Secret negotiations had begun in August 1969 between Henry Kissinger and Le Duc Tho, a North Vietnamese leader. But the talks broke down in October 1971.

Meanwhile, in an effort to bolster crumbling South Vietnamese forces, Nixon in April 1972 ordered bombing of the North to begin again. Less than a month later, he announced that he had ordered the mining of Haiphong Harbor and a blockade of North Vietnam as well. United States troop withdrawals, however, continued.

In October a breakthrough occurred in secret negotiations, which had resumed between Kissinger and Le Duc Tho. The United States and Hanoi were close to agreement, and Kissinger announced that "peace was at hand." The news was premature, however. The final agreement was not reached until late January 1973, when the United States, South Vietnam, North Vietnam, and the Viet Cong's Provisional Revolutionary Government signed an "Agreement on Ending the War and Restoring Peace in Vietnam."

Under its terms, the North Vietnamese and Viet Cong would release all American prisoners of war. The United States would withdraw its remaining troops—about 23,500—from South Vietnam. There would be an end to foreign military activities in Laos and Cambodia. The Saigon regime would continue to receive aid and would remain under Nguyen Van Thieu until elections could be organized.

Relations With Communist Powers

Nixon had succeeded in pulling the United States out of Vietnam, but his major foreign policy achievements lay in improving relations with China and the Soviet Union. Many people were surprised that Nixon, a long-time opponent of communism, should take such action. Some conservatives did not approve. Nevertheless, by the time he became President, Nixon could see that the national interest was more important than ideology. He pursued a balance of power among nations rather than the division of the world into two power blocs. He felt he could achieve a "full generation of peace" through negotiation:

> After a period of confrontation, we are entering an era of negotiation.
> Let all nations know that during this Administration our lines of communication will be open.
> We seek an open world—open to ideas, open to the exchange of goods and people, a world in which no people, great or small, will live in angry isolation.
> We cannot expect to make everyone our friend, but we can try to make no one our enemy.

China. Nixon's first overtures were toward the People's Republic of China. Undoubtedly, the fact that China and the Soviet Union were feuding influenced the President's actions. If the United States could improve its relations with China, a former ally of the Soviet Union, the latter would be forced into a more cautious approach in foreign affairs.

In 1969 the administration lifted travel and trade restrictions on China and suspended patrol of the Taiwan Straits. At first the Chinese did not respond. Then, in the spring of 1971, the American ping pong team was invited to visit the People's Republic, and the embargo on United States' trade with Communist China was lifted. In July Kissinger met secretly with Premier Chou En-lai at Peking. Following this meeting, Nixon announced that he would visit China the next year "to seek normalization of relations between the two nations."

The thaw in relations between China and the United States was reflected in another Nixon move. The United States, which recognized the government of Taiwan as the sole representative of the Chinese people, had long opposed Communist China's attempts to join the UN. Nixon, however, modified this stand in favor of a two-China policy. In September 1971, the United States recommended that the People's Republic represent China in the Security Council and that Taiwan keep its representation in the General Assembly. However, the United Nations admitted the People's Republic and expelled Taiwan.

In February 1972 Nixon made the promised visit to China. During the course of this visit, Nixon and Chou En-lai issued an official statement in which they agreed to the need for closer relations between the two countries. The United States agreed that Taiwan was part of mainland China and as such its future would be decided by the Chinese. American military forces ultimately would be withdrawn from Taiwan. A year after this statement was made, the United States and China announced that they would set up liaison offices in each other's capital—a step toward full diplomatic relations.

The Soviet Union. Nixon was also interested in improving the United States' relations with the Soviet Union. He wanted to establish **détente,** or a relaxing of tensions between the two countries. One area of tension was arms control. In November 1969 Nixon and Soviet President Nikolai V. Podgorny signed the Nuclear Nonproliferation Treaty, which had been

As Cold War tensions eased in the early 1970's, friendlier relations developed between the United States and the Soviet Union. What agreements did the two nations reach?

approved by the Senate in March. This treaty prohibited the transfer of nuclear weapons to non-nuclear states.

About the same time, the United States and the Soviet Union held preliminary Strategic Arms Limitation Talks (SALT) at Helsinki, Finland. These were followed by full-scale SALT negotiations, which began in April 1970 at Vienna, Austria. In May 1972 Nixon went to Moscow to meet with Soviet Premier Leonid Brezhnev and to sign the SALT agreements.

Two agreements on arms control were signed at the first summit conference. One was a treaty that limited the number of antiballistic missile systems (ABMS)—defensive missile systems that intercept and destroy certain kinds of missiles—allowed each country. This treaty was ratified by the Senate in August. The other was a five-year executive agreement that limited the number of offensive weapons built to those under construction or already deployed (strategically placed).

Soviet agricultural production has often failed to meet the people's needs.

Other agreements were signed at the Moscow summit to establish closer ties between the two countries. Under the terms of these agreements, the United States and the Soviet Union promised to cooperate in fields such as medical research, environmental protection, and space. The two countries also agreed to develop commercial and economic relations. A major result of this meeting was the Soviet agreement to buy at least $750 million in American grain over the next three years.

In June 1973 Brezhnev visited Washington, D.C. During the visit, known as Summit II, it was agreed that both the United States and the Soviet Union would continue to work on arms control and avoid actions that might lead to nuclear war. Brezhnev and Nixon also signed agreements extending cooperation in the fields of science, culture, and commerce. The real significance of the visit, however, was that it indicated that the Nixon-Kissinger policy of détente was working. The commitment to détente was reinforced at a third summit meeting in the summer of 1974.

The Middle East

The strength of détente was tested in the Middle East, where Arab nations were still angry about Israeli occupation of territory gained during the Six Day War of June 1967. On October 6, 1973, Egypt

THE MIDDLE EAST, 1967–1974

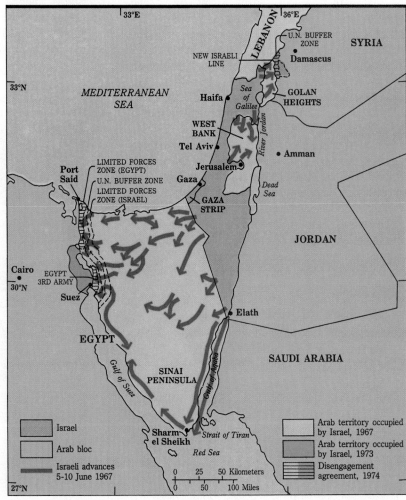

The Yom Kippur War demonstrated Israeli military vulnerability as well as the vulnerability of the West regarding oil.

and Syria launched a surprise attack against Israel. Because it was the eve of the Jewish holy day of Yom Kippur, the conflict that followed was known as the Yom Kippur War.

The Israelis, who at first were thrown back, appealed to the United States for aid. On October 15 the United States announced that it would send military equipment and supplies to Israel to offset the support the Arabs had received from the Soviet Union. This angered the Arabs, and 11 Middle Eastern nations declared an oil embargo against the United States. Meanwhile, the rearmed Israelis had launched a counteroffensive. They laid siege to the city of Suez and cut the supply lines of Egypt's Third Army, opening the way to Cairo.

To bring peace to the Middle East, the UN called for a cease-fire. Although sporadic fighting continued, the cease-fire was accepted by Egypt, Syria, and Israel in late October. At this point, however, the Soviet Union threatened to move troops into the Middle East to supervise the truce, and United States armed forces throughout the world were placed on alert as a precautionary measure. An international crisis was avoided when the Soviet Union agreed to the creation of a UN peace-keeping force to be sent to the Middle East.

For some time, Kissinger traveled back and forth between the Arab and Israeli capitals in the cause of peace. This was called **shuttle diplomacy.** Kissinger arranged cease-fire agreements between the warring countries and helped to set up Middle East peace talks at Geneva. Eventually, an uneasy peace was achieved, and the oil embargo was lifted. Nixon visited the Middle East, symbolizing changes in United States policy that would lead to a better understanding with Arab countries.

SECTION REVIEW

1. Identify the following: Henry Kissinger, Nixon Doctrine, Lon Nol, SALT.
2. What was Nixon's plan for "peace with honor" in Vietnam?
3. Why did the war in Vietnam spread to Cambodia and Laos?
4. Why were people surprised at Nixon's overtures toward Communist China?
5. How did the Yom Kippur War test the policy of détente?

2 Domestic Affairs Under Nixon

Nixon faced many problems at home as well as in foreign affairs. Here also the President tried to apply realism to politics. He was willing to change his conservative tactics when they proved ineffective. As a result, his domestic policy, like his foreign policy, was criticized for being inconsistent.

The Space Program

In the late 1960's, many Americans continued to be critical of the amount of money spent on the space program. But criticism was temporarily stilled when, six months after Nixon's inauguration, the United States landed a person on the moon. In July 1969 Commander Neil A. Armstrong, Colonel Edwin E. Aldrin, Jr., and Lieutenant Colonel Michael Collins took off in Apollo II. When they reached the moon,

One goal of space exploration was reached on July 20, 1969, when Neil Armstrong and Edwin Aldrin set foot on the moon. What other space projects were underway during this period?

Have students discuss what other steps Nixon could have taken to offset stagflation.

THE UNITED STATES IN A NEW ERA   **685**

In 1971 the balance of payments deficit reached a total of $29.6 billion.

Collins remained aboard the command spacecraft while Aldrin and Armstrong descended to the surface in a lunar module. Millions watched on television as Armstrong became the first human being to set foot on the surface of the moon. As he stepped out of the module, the astronaut said, "That's one small step for man, one giant leap for mankind."

By the end of 1972, the United States had made five more moon landings. Following the sixth successful landing, Project Apollo was concluded. The total cost had been $25 billion. Nonetheless, Nixon was able to get support for the Skylab program. Skylab was to be an orbiting laboratory designed to test the ability of human beings to live and work in outer space. Three successive missions were launched in 1973, at a cost of $2.6 billion.

The Economy

When Nixon took office, the economy was in poor shape. One of the biggest problems the country faced was inflation. Lyndon Johnson's attempt to fight the Vietnam War and expand domestic programs without increasing taxes had brought about an inflationary spiral that was truly alarming by the end of the 1960's.

Stagflation. To stop inflation, Nixon at first tried conservative techniques and called for a tight money policy. Interest rates were raised so that people would borrow less and spend less. Government spending was also cut. With less money in circulation, prices dropped. However, as demand slowed, businesses began to cut back and output fell. Although prices kept on rising, recession set in. The result was **stagflation,** or a combination of inflation and recession.

To meet the problem of stagflation, Nixon turned to other, less conservative methods. In August 1971 he announced his New Economic Policy, which called for a 90-day freeze on wages, prices, and rents. This was followed by a system of wage and price controls in November. In January 1973 Nixon relaxed controls, and prices climbed sharply. Therefore, in June a new freeze was imposed.

Nixon also took steps to end the recession by stimulating the economy. He proposed tax cuts for both businesses and individuals, hoping that when demand went up, production would rise and unemployment would fall. After making some revisions in the President's proposals, Congress enacted tax cuts in December 1971. Nixon also used deficit spending to fight recession.

These measures, however, failed to solve the problem of stagflation. Although the tax cuts and deficit spending helped to ease the recession, they added to inflation. On the other hand, while the controls slowed inflation for a time, they did little to help the economy grow or to lower unemployment.

Balance of Trade. The country's economic woes were compounded by a deficit in the balance of trade. A deficit in this balance meant that the country imported more goods than it exported. This, in turn, contributed to a deficit in the balance of payments—more money left the country than came in.

The trade deficit was due in part to inflation, which was increasing the cost of American exports to foreign buyers and weakening the dollar abroad. The dollar had been the principal currency in the international monetary system since the Bretton Woods Conference in 1944. The International Monetary Fund (IMF) established there set up a system of **fixed exchange rates**—a system under which the price of one country's currency is set according to that of another so that the rate does not change. Thereafter, all countries defined their currencies in terms of a given amount of gold. However, since a good deal of gold had come into the United States because of political unrest in Europe, countries defined their currencies in terms of dollars as well.

Over time the dollar grew weaker abroad. As the United States bought more imports, an increasing number of dollars went to other countries. Only a portion of these dollars flowed back into the United States as other countries bought American exports. At first foreign countries willingly held the dollars, since they had always been used as international currency. However, as the dollars began to accumulate, many countries became concerned that the United States could no longer honor its promise to redeem dollars with gold. Some sent their dollars back to the United States and demanded gold in return.

By the late 1960's, the United States had a problem due to the vast number of foreign-held dollars that the government could be asked to redeem. In August 1971 Nixon met the problem by informing foreign

Point out the fact that the debate over the role of the federal government has continued to the present.

Welfare costs rose from $2.1 billion in 1960 to almost $18 billion in 1972.

governments that the United States would no longer redeem dollars with gold.[2] This move was followed several months later by a formal **devaluation** (reduction in the exchange value of currency by lowering its gold equivalency) of the dollar.

Devaluation meant that the dollar would be worth less in relation to foreign currencies. It would take less foreign currency to buy American exports, and more American goods would be bought in foreign countries. On the other hand, it would take more American dollars to buy imports in the United States, and thus fewer imports would be bought. In theory, then, devaluation would improve the balance of trade. However, the trade deficit worsened in 1972. In February 1973 the dollar was again devalued.

The New Federalism

In addition to dealing with economic problems, Nixon sought to reduce the role of the federal government in American life. The President felt that the national government had grown cumbersome and inefficient and that too many people were dependent on it. In August 1969 he gave a speech in which he announced his "New Federalism"—a plan for turning over to state and local governments many of the responsibilities of the federal government:

> *After a third of a century of power flowing from the people and the states to Washington it is time for a new federalism in which power, funds and responsibility will flow from Washington to the states and to the people.*

To help state governments handle their new responsibilities, Nixon proposed **revenue-sharing.** That is, the federal government would give part of its revenue to state and local governments. The State and Local Fiscal Assistance Act, which was passed by Congress in October 1972, set up a program to distribute over $30 billion in federal tax revenues.

Welfare Reform

In the same speech, Nixon proposed a new approach to the way in which government cared for the poor. During the 1960's relief rolls had grown,

---

[2] The government had informed United States citizens that they could not redeem paper money for gold in 1932.

especially in the category of Aid to Families with Dependent Children (AFDC). Johnson's War on Poverty program had taught the poor how to apply for welfare. Unemployment, brought on by Nixon's conservative economic policies, swelled the rolls. In 1972 there were 14.9 million people receiving aid, putting a strain on the welfare system.

Nixon called for AFDC to be replaced with a Family Assistance Plan. Under this plan the federal government would pay a guaranteed minimum income of $1600 a year to every family of four on welfare with no outside income. This plan aroused a good deal of opposition. Many Democrats felt the benefits were too low. Conservative Republicans felt the measure was too liberal. As a result, the measure was never passed.

Law and Order

One of the issues upon which Nixon campaigned in 1968 was law and order—a major concern of conservative Americans. Just after he took office, Nixon appointed his law partner, John Mitchell, as Attorney General. With Mitchell leading the way, the President backed a series of law and order measures. These measures were passed by Congress in 1970. One provided for immunity from prosecution for criminals giving testimony, special grand juries to investigate organized crime, and limited disclosure of evidence obtained through electronic surveillance. Another provided for stiff law-enforcement measures such as no-knock search warrants. These allowed police to enter a person's home forcibly without knocking. Still another measure authorized $3.55 billion in federal aid to state and local law enforcement agencies.

In addition to backing these measures, Nixon made four conservative appointments of Justices to the Supreme Court. Nixon shared the belief of many Americans that the Court under Earl Warren had been too liberal—too conscientious in protecting the rights of those accused of crime at society's expense.

In 1969 Warren retired, and Nixon appointed Warren Burger, a conservative, as Chief Justice. Nixon's next two appointments, however, were turned down by the Senate. In May 1970 the Senate did confirm Harry A. Blackmun. Later, Lewis F.

Shirley Chisholm

Shirley Chisolm took an active part in the struggle for equal rights that continued during the Nixon-Ford years. Born on November 30, 1924, Chisolm was the daughter of poor immigrants. Her father, who had come to the United States from British Guiana (now Guyana), was an unskilled laborer in a factory. Her mother, who had emigrated from Barbados, was a seamstress and domestic worker. Chisolm's parents, however, wanted their children to receive an education and saved money for that purpose.

Chisolm completed high school in Brooklyn and in 1946 graduated with honors from Brooklyn College. After graduation, she taught nursery school and took courses at Columbia University, where she earned her Master of Arts degree. Later, Chisolm directed day-care centers in Brownsville, Texas, and New York City. She also served as an educational consultant to New York City's Bureau of Child Welfare.

Meanwhile, Chisolm had begun laying the foundations for a political career. A Democrat, she ran successfully for the New York State Assembly in 1964. While there, she helped get a bill passed that set up a program at state universities enabling black and Puerto Rican students to receive remedial training to make up for requirements they lacked.

In 1968, after four years in the State Assembly, Chisolm decided to run for the House of Representatives from New York's Twelfth Congressional District. Despite the fact that her opponent was a nationally recognized civil rights leader, she won the election.

When she took her seat in the House, Shirley Chisolm became the first black woman to serve in Congress. In her autobiography, *Unbought and Unbossed* (1970), she wrote, "I hope that my having made it, the hard way, can be some kind of inspiration, particularly to women."

Representative Chisolm was elected for a second term in 1970. In 1972 she ran against George McGovern for the Democratic nomination for President. She served in Congress for the next decade and continued to support equal rights for minorities and women. After serving in Congress, she then turned her talent to teaching on the college level.

Powell and William Rehnquist, two other conservative nominees, were approved.

The conservatism of the Burger Court was apparent in its attitude toward criminals. The Court held that, although statements obtained in violation of the *Miranda* v. *Arizona* decision (1966) could not be introduced as evidence, they could be used to discredit the accused's testimony. The Court also ruled that, while evidence illegally seized by the police could not be used against the accused in a trial, questions based on that evidence could be asked at a grand jury hearing. This narrowed the scope of the *Mapp* v. *Ohio* decision.

Equal Rights

As a conservative, Nixon had little interest in the problems of minorities and women. However, the struggle for equal rights that had gained strength under Kennedy and Johnson continued during the Nixon administration.

Blacks. A major concern of civil rights advocates was equality of education for blacks. Despite the decision in *Brown* v. *Topeka Board of Education*, dual systems in the South had changed little. Segregation remained the rule. Nixon, however, held a conservative view of integration:

Have students debate the issue of busing.

AIM's march on Washington, D.C., was called "The Trail of Broken Treaties."

I am convinced that while legal separation is totally wrong, forced integration is just as wrong.

I realize that this position will lead us to a situation in which blacks will continue to live for the most part in black neighborhoods and where there will be predominantly black schools and predominantly white schools in the metropolitan areas.

Part of the reason for Nixon's conservative attitude was that the Republicans wanted to win the support of white southerners. To further this cause, the administration worked to delay desegregation. In August 1969 arguments presented by the Department of Justice influenced a lower federal court's decision to delay desegregation in Mississippi schools. The Nixon administration also tried to delay desegregation through lawsuits and by cutting off funds.

Despite the administration's resistance, the Supreme Court in *Alexander* v. *Holmes Co.* (1969) ordered an immediate end to all school segregation. Further, in a unanimous decision, the Court endorsed busing students out of their neighborhoods to end school segregation.

Busing was a controversial issue. Some civil rights leaders and some parents favored the use of busing, but many parents did not want their children to go to school out of their neighborhoods. Nixon was one who opposed busing:

I believe that there may be some doubt as to the validity of the Brown philosophy. . . . But while there may be some doubt as to whether segregated education is inferior, there is no doubt whatever on another point—that education requiring excessive transportation for students is definitely inferior. I come down hard and unequivocally against busing for the purpose of racial balance.

Nevertheless, the courts continued to order busing as a means of ending segregation. A series of district and circuit court decisions, growing out of an NAACP suit against the Detroit public schools, ordered busing across urban-suburban school district lines. The Court of Appeals, which reviewed the case, argued as follows:

Big city school systems for blacks surrounded by suburban school systems for whites cannot represent equal protection under the law.

Civil rights under Nixon was slowed but did not stop. Once the courts made a decision, Nixon felt that he had to enforce it. After *Alexander* v. *Holmes Co.*, the Justice Department assigned more attorneys and agents to the South. Nixon also endorsed a bill to extend the life of the Civil Rights Commission and set racial quotas for all-white construction companies that received government contracts.

Indians. Like blacks, Indians continued to seek equal rights. Sometimes they dramatized their demands through militant action. In November 1969 a small group of Indians took over Alcatraz Island, a former federal prison in San Francisco Bay. They wanted the island as a cultural center. The incident ended in June 1971 when the Indians surrendered to United States marshals.

In the fall of 1972, members of the American Indian Movement (AIM) occupied the Bureau of Indian Affairs at Washington, D.C. They demanded the lands and rights guaranteed Indians under treaties with the United States. They surrendered the building after receiving assurances that the government would review their complaints.

The climax of Indian militancy came at Wounded Knee, South Dakota, the site of an army massacre of Indians in 1890. AIM members occupied the village from February through May 1973. They wanted reforms in tribal government because it was dominated by leaders who cooperated too closely with white interests. In the end, the Indians once again surrendered to United States marshals.

Meanwhile, the federal government again changed its policy. Instead of Americanization, Nixon called for "self-determination without termination" for Indians. This would give them the freedom to choose their own way of life. The federal government would not "terminate" its responsibilities to the Indians as it had tried to do after World War II. Instead, it would support them by providing aid for housing and vocational training and by protecting their land and resources. Congress failed to pass the laws needed to make self-determination effective. Nevertheless, the idea of termination was given up.

The Indians did make some progress. The federal government returned some of the lands that the

Indians felt had been taken from them illegally. In December 1970 Congress passed an act that authorized the return of 48,000 acres (19,200 hectares) of land of New Mexico to the Taos Pueblo Indians. This included Blue Lake, which they considered sacred. A year later, another act granted 40 million acres (16,007,680 hectares) of federal lands and $962.5 million to Alaskan Indians. Some 21,000 acres (5040 hectares) of land in Washington state were returned to the Yakima Indians by executive order in May 1972.

Women. Women, too, continued to press for their rights during Nixon's years in office. They made some gains. In 1972 Congress passed the Equal Employment Opportunity Act. This act gave the Equal Employment Opportunity Commission power to enforce the sex discrimination provisions of the 1964 Civil Rights Act through the courts.

In 1972 Congress also voted to submit an Equal Rights Amendment (ERA) to the states. This amendment stated:

> *Equality of rights under the law shall not be denied or abridged by the United States or by any state on account of sex.*

The ERA, however, encountered strong opposition. Most of those who opposed the amendment— men and women alike—feared that it would undermine family life as well as other traditional values.

The Energy Crisis

One of the country's most important concerns during the Nixon administration was the energy crisis. After World War II the use of energy in the United States had greatly increased. By this time the country was getting most of its energy from nonrenewable mineral resources, such as coal, gas, and oil. In the 1800's much of the energy produced in the United States had come from sustainable sources such as water power.

By the 1970's domestic reserves of mineral resources had declined. As demand continued to grow, the country began to rely more and more on imports. An increasing proportion of these imports came from the Middle East. Thus, when the Arab nations declared the oil embargo in October 1973, the United States was faced with an energy crisis. Long lines of cars at gas stations were a sign of the times.

President Nixon addressed the nation on the energy crisis:

> *Let us unite in committing the resources of this Nation to a major new endeavor, an endeavor that in this bicentennial era we can appropriately call "Project Independence." Let us set as our national goal, in the spirit of Apollo . . . that by the end of this decade we will have developed the potential to meet our own energy needs without depending on any foreign energy sources.*

The Equal Rights Amendment, proposing complete equality before the law for men and women, was passed by Congress in 1972. Opponents of the amendment stymied ratification by the states, however. What reason did the anti-ERA forces use to justify their opposition?

In 1972 the relative stability of the economy, Nixon's new policies toward communist powers, and Kissinger's announcement that "peace was at hand" in Vietnam combined to solidify Nixon's position.

When Arab states instituted the oil embargo in 1973, oil shipments to many pro-Israeli nations were stopped or reduced. The embargo cut off about 25 percent of the oil supply of the United States, resulting in a sharp rise in price and long lines of cars at the gas pumps. What steps were taken to lessen the impact of the embargo?

We have an energy crisis, but there is no crisis of the American spirit. Let us go forward, then, doing what needs to be done, proud of what we have accomplished together in the past, and confident of what we can accomplish together in the future.

To achieve the goal set forth in his address—that of making America self-sufficient in energy by 1980—Nixon recommended immediate conservation measures by individuals, business, and government. He also called for wiser use of mineral resources and development of alternate energy sources.

Various steps were taken, such as lowering speed limits to force gas conservation. Gas stations were closed on Sunday. On November 16, 1973, Nixon signed the Alaska Pipeline Act to ensure that the country would have access to Alaskan oil. In December Congress passed a measure that put the United States on daylight savings time for two years.

SECTION REVIEW

1. Identify the following: Neil A. Armstrong, Family Assistance Plan, John Mitchell, Warren Burger.
2. What was the purpose of the "New Federalism"?
3. How did Nixon promote law and order?
4. Why was busing for integration controversial?
5. What were the provisions of the Equal Rights Amendment?
6. What caused the energy crisis?

3 The Presidency in Crisis

During Nixon's first term, he was supported in most of his domestic and foreign policies by the "silent majority." As the election of 1972 drew near, he continued to enjoy solid support. However, events that occurred during the campaign eventually led to the President's undoing.

The Election of 1972

Nixon's challenger was the liberal Senator George McGovern of South Dakota, who was nominated by the Democrats in July. McGovern had strong support from minorities, women, and youth.[3] He named Senator Thomas Eagleton of Missouri as his running mate. Later, however, reporters discovered that Eagleton had received psychiatric treatment, and McGovern asked him to withdraw. R. Sargent Shriver of Maryland, former director of the Peace Corps and a Kennedy in-law, replaced Eagleton.

McGovern focused his campaign on the Vietnam War. The Democratic platform called for the immediate withdrawal of American troops from Vietnam. Other planks called for an end to the draft

[3] The Twenty-Sixth Amendment, lowering the voting age to 18, was ratified in 1971. Thus, young adults (age 18-20) would be voting in a presidential election for the first time.

and **amnesty** (a general pardon) for draft-resisters. McGovern also called for a guaranteed minimum income above the poverty level. The Republicans, who renominated Nixon and Agnew in August, supported Vietnamization and opposed amnesty. They also opposed busing to achieve racial balance in the schools.

In the campaign, Nixon had the advantage. The Democrats were badly divided. Many of them felt that McGovern was too liberal and failed to give him their full support. His credibility was tarnished by the Eagleton affair. He was seen by many Americans as representative of radical groups against which conservative Americans were reacting. The Republicans were quick to exploit this idea, calling McGovern the friend of "hippies, drug addicts, and welfare mothers." Furthermore, Kissinger's announcement just before the election that peace was "at hand" in Vietnam neutralized McGovern's strongest issue.

Nixon's position was made stronger when Alabama Governor George C. Wallace, who appealed to many of the same people as Nixon, was seriously wounded in an assassination attempt. Wallace, who had been considering running as a third-party candidate, withdrew from the presidential race. In November Nixon won a landslide victory over McGovern, receiving nearly 61 percent of the popular vote and 520 electoral votes. Of the 50 states, 49 went to Nixon, with only Massachusetts and the District of Columbia going to McGovern. Even the youth vote did not go substantially to McGovern. However, the Democrats retained control of Congress.

The Imperial Presidency

Nixon's term of office was called the "Imperial Presidency," especially after 1972. Because he faced a legislative branch dominated by Democrats and frequently had his initiatives blocked, Nixon began to expand the powers of his office to achieve what he wanted.

Congress began to feel that Nixon's expansion of presidential power was putting the system of checks and balances set up by the Constitution in danger. In the past, increases in executive power had been justified in cases of international crisis. However, members of Congress felt that in Vietnam Nixon had

ELECTION OF 1972

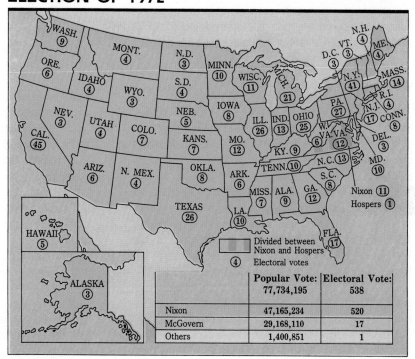

	Popular Vote: 77,734,195	Electoral Vote: 538
Nixon	47,165,234	520
McGovern	29,168,110	17
Others	1,400,851	1

virtually taken over the war-making powers given to the legislative branch by the Constitution.

Congress was also upset by Nixon's practice of **impoundment,** or the refusal to spend money allotted by Congress for various programs. Other Presidents had used this practice to save money. But Nixon impounded more money than his predecessors, and he used impoundment to set aside the will of Congress. In 1973–1974, federal courts found such actions to be against the law.

Congress also opposed Nixon's use of **executive privilege.** This is the principle that executive officials have a right to withhold information from Congress on the ground of national security. It also included the right to refuse to appear before a court.

Within the executive branch itself, Nixon concentrated power in the White House at the expense of the cabinet. He turned over cabinet responsibilities to his closest aides, H. R. Haldeman and John D. Ehrlichman. In fact, the Domestic Council under Ehrlichman controlled domestic policy, just as Kissinger's National Security Staff controlled foreign policy.

Congress took steps to curb the growth of presidential power. In 1973 it passed the War Powers Act. This act gave the President the authority to go to war in certain circumstances, but set a 60-day limit on the war unless Congress authorized it to continue. Nixon vetoed the act, but was overridden. In 1974 Congress passed an act which limited impoundment.

Watergate

Meanwhile, Nixon's credibility was strained to the breaking point over a scandal known as "Watergate." The scandal began with news stories about Nixon's reelection campaign and soon became a crisis involving the highest officials in the land.

The Beginnings. On June 17, 1972, just before the election, five men were arrested for breaking into the Democratic National Committee Headquarters. The break-in was discovered by the night guard at the Watergate building in Washington, D.C., where the Democratic headquarters was located. Shortly after the break-in, links were established between the burglars and White House Consultant E. Howard Hunt, Jr. Links were also established to G. Gordon Liddy, the counsel for the Committee to Reelect the President (CRP). This evidence seemed to show that the burglars had been working for CRP, or CREEP, as it became known. CRP's chairman, John Mitchell, who had left his post as Attorney General to head Nixon's campaign, denied this. The White House minimized the incident as a "third-rate burglary."

However, two *Washington Post* reporters, Robert Woodward and Carl Bernstein, refused to believe these denials and began digging into the story. They revealed that unethical and illegal means had been used by the Republicans to raise money for Nixon's campaign and to sabotage Democratic operations.

The burglary and other revelations had little impact on the election. However, in January 1973 the five burglars plus Hunt and Liddy—the Watergate Seven—went on trial. Judge John J. Sirica presided. Five of the defendants pleaded guilty, and two were convicted by a jury. When Sirica was passing sentence, he read aloud a letter from James W. McCord. McCord was one of the defendants and former chief of security for CRP. The letter said that the defendants were not the only ones involved in the break-in. It stated further that they had been pressured into pleading guilty, and that certain people had committed perjury during the course of the trial.

Investigation. Meanwhile, in early February the Senate had established a committee headed by Senator Sam Ervin of North Carolina to investigate corruption in the 1972 election. While this investigation was going on, John Dean, the President's counsel, and Jeb Stuart Magruder, CRP's deputy director, followed McCord's example and turned **state's evidence.** That is, they gave testimony against others involved in the break-in. On April 30 Nixon fired Dean and announced the resignations of Haldeman and Erlichman.

A month later, Nixon finally admitted that a cover-up had taken place, but he denied knowledge of it. Just before he made this statement, the Ervin Committee began televised hearings that brought the Watergate scandal to the public's eye. In June, testifying before the committee, Magruder confessed to committing perjury before the grand jury in the trial of the Watergate Seven. He also implicated Mitchell in planning the break-in.

At the end of the month, Dean testified that Nixon had known about the break-in since it happened and had offered **executive clemency** (a lessening of punishment by order of the President) to the

The plumbers also forged official documents in order to implicate John F. Kennedy in the assassination of Ngo Dinh Diem.

There was also some indication that Agnew had accepted bribes while he was Vice President.

defendants. Dean implicated Haldeman and Ehrlichman in the cover-up as well. He told the committee about a White House "Enemies List," containing names of opponents for potential harassment.

Dean also told the committee about the "plumbers." This was a special investigation unit that was intended to stop "leaks" by using electronic surveillance, mail interception, and other illegal practices—all in the name of national security.

This "plumbers" unit was set up after the affair of the so-called "Pentagon Papers," a series of articles published in the *New York Times* beginning in June 1971. Dr. Daniel Ellsberg, a Defense Department aide, had leaked a top-secret study of the Vietnam War to the *Times*. Ellsberg was charged with stealing government property and violating the Espionage Act. These charges were dropped in the midst of Watergate when the court learned that there had

been a wiretap placed on Ellsberg's telephone. The court had learned earlier that Hunt and Liddy, two of the "plumbers," had broken into the office of Ellsberg's former psychiatrist, hoping to find something they could use against Ellsberg.

Dean's testimony, although impressive, was open to question because of his involvement in the scandal. In July 1973, however, the committee was astonished to learn that Nixon had routinely tape-recorded all of his conversations in the White House. The Ervin Committee and Special Prosecutor Archibald Cox, who had been appointed in April by Attorney General Elliot Richardson, asked Nixon for the tapes. Nixon claimed executive privilege and refused to release them. Both the committee and Cox then served **subpoenas** (written legal orders) on the President.

Meanwhile, the administration suffered another blow. Vice President Agnew was forced to resign on October 10, 1973, after investigations revealed that he had accepted bribes as governor of Maryland. In exchange for his resignation and agreement not to contest a charge of income tax evasion, other charges were dropped. Agnew was fined $10,000 and put on probation. After Agnew left office, Nixon appointed House Minority leader Gerald R. Ford of Michigan as his new Vice President.[4]

The American public finally lost all faith in the administration when, within two weeks of Agnew's resignation, the "Saturday Night Massacre" occurred. After failing to respond to the subpoenas from the Ervin Committee and Cox, the President was ordered by Judge Sirica to turn the tapes over to him. Instead, Nixon offered written summaries of the tapes if Cox would agree not to seek any other tapes. When Cox turned down the offer, Nixon ordered him fired. However, neither Attorney General Richardson nor the deputy Attorney General would fire Cox, and both resigned. The acting Attorney General finally fired Cox. The firing and the resignations aroused a storm of public protest.

Under pressure from the public, Nixon finally turned over some of the tapes in question. However, there was an 18-minute gap on one on them that experts later determined had been erased.

The Watergate hearings led to criminal charges against several top White House aides and ultimately to the resignation of President Nixon. What effect did Watergate have on the nation?

[4] Ford was the first person to serve as Vice President under the Twenty-Fifth Amendment, which established procedures for replacing the President or Vice President should either be unable to handle the responsibilities of office.

The Final Outcome. Shortly after the "Saturday Night Massacre," 16 impeachment resolutions were introduced in the House of Representatives. These resolutions were turned over to the House Judiciary Committee, which was chaired by Representative Peter Rodino of New Jersey. Late in 1973 the committee began its investigation.

In March 1974, during the course of this investigation, the grand jury indicted John Mitchell, H. R. Haldeman, and John Erlichman for conspiracy, obstruction of justice, and perjury. All three were convicted and sentenced to prison. The grand jury report cited Nixon as a "co-conspirator." Judge Sirica gave the report to the Judiciary Committee. In April the committee subpoenaed additional tapes from the President, and he refused to turn them over. Instead, he released edited transcripts of the desired tapes. At the release, Nixon still claimed his innocence:

> If read with an open and a fair mind and read together with the record of the actions I took, these transcripts will show that what I have stated from the beginning to be the truth has been the truth: that I personally had no knowledge of the break-in before it occurred, that I had no knowledge of the coverup until I was informed of it by John Dean on March 21, that I never offered clemency for the defendants, and that after March 21 my actions were directed toward finding the facts and seeing that justice was done, fairly and according to the law.

It soon became clear that much was missing from the transcripts. In May Judge Sirica ordered Nixon to turn over 64 tapes to special Prosecutor Leon Jaworski, who had taken Cox's place. Again Nixon refused. He appealed his case to the Supreme Court, claiming executive privilege. The Court, however, ruled that Nixon had no right to withhold the tapes and directed him to turn them over.

At the end of July, after weeks of closed hearings, the House Judiciary Committee debated the question of impeachment over nationwide television. At the close of the debates, the committee voted three articles of impeachment against Nixon, charging him with obstruction of justice, abuse of presidential power, and defiance of the committee's subpoenas. Impeachment seemed probable.

A tape made public in August suggested that Nixon had known about the Watergate break-in all along and had even tried to use the CIA to block the FBI investigation of the incident. This tape, the so-called "smoking pistol," ended remaining doubts about Nixon's guilt. On August 9, 1974, certain that he would be removed from office, Nixon resigned. He was the first President to do so.

Americans greeted Nixon's resignation with relief as well as sadness. Despite the trauma of Watergate, the American system of constitutional government had worked and survived.

SECTION REVIEW

1. Identify the following: George McGovern, George C. Wallace, H. R. Haldeman, John Dean, "plumbers," "Saturday Night Massacre."
2. What factors contributed to Nixon's victory in 1972?
3. What was the initial cause of the Watergate scandal?
4. What was the evidence that Nixon was involved in the Watergate cover-up?
5. What charges did the House Judiciary Committee vote against Nixon?

4 The Ford Administration

After Nixon resigned, Gerald Ford became President. In accordance with the Twenty-Fifth Amendment, he named Governor Nelson Rockefeller of New York as Vice President. For the first time in American history, both the President and the Vice President were not elected but appointed.

Restoring Confidence

Watergate had shaken people's confidence in government. Ford's first goal was to restore that confidence:

> I believe that truth is the glue that holds governments together—not only our Government but civilization itself. That bond, though strained, is unbroken at home and abroad.
>
> In all my public and private acts as your President, I expect to follow my instincts of

openness and candor with full confidence that honesty is always the best policy in the end.

My fellow Americans, our long national nightmare is over. Our Constitution works. Our great Republic is a government of laws and not of men. Here, the people rule.

Ford's reputation for honesty and his sincere desire to put Watergate behind the nation brought the promise of stability to the American people. But one of his first acts destroyed much of this confidence.

Nixon's Pardon

In September 1974, after some consideration, Ford granted Nixon a full pardon for all federal crimes he committed while President. Thus, Nixon could not be prosecuted for his part in the cover-up. Ford hoped that the pardon would help heal the wounds of Watergate:

After years of bitter controversy and divisive national debate . . . I am compelled to conclude that many months and perhaps more years will have to pass before Richard Nixon could obtain a fair trial by jury in . . . the United States. . . .

During this long period of delay and potential litigation, ugly passions would again be aroused. And our people would again be

polarized in their opinions. And the credibility of our free institutions of government would again be challenged at home and abroad.

My conscience tells me clearly . . . that I cannot prolong the bad dreams that continue to reopen a chapter that is closed. My conscience tells me that only I, as President, have the constitutional power to firmly shut and seal this book. My conscience tells me that it is my duty, not merely to proclaim domestic tranquillity, but to use every means that I have to insure it.

The pardon aroused widespread criticism. Many Americans felt that Ford was using a double standard of justice. They believed that the former President should be punished along with those who had acted for him. Some people even accused Ford of striking a bargain with Nixon in advance—the promise of a pardon in exchange for his resignation.

Domestic Affairs

In another attempt to heal the divided nation, Ford offered amnesty to those who had illegally avoided military service in Vietnam. In order to receive amnesty, draft-resisters had to serve two years of alternative national service. Ford's plan was highly controversial. While many people approved, others thought it was too lenient.

Gerald Ford had been Vice President for nine months when he succeeded Richard Nixon as President. Ford's principal task was to bring the nation together after the Watergate scandal. What actions did Ford take to heal the nation's wounds?

Compare President Ford's actions in the Mayagüez incident to those of Richard Nixon had he been in a similar situation.

Meanwhile, one of the most pressing problems Ford faced was continued stagflation. Concentrating on inflation rather than recession, Ford vetoed spending bills and launched a campaign called Whip Inflation Now (WIN). This was a program of voluntary wage-price controls. Ford, like Nixon, did not favor such controls but was willing to use them if necessary. Inflation did drop temporarily, but unemployment remained high. To counter recession, deficit spending was increased.

Another problem was the energy shortage. Ford agreed with Nixon's goal of self-sufficiency and tried to achieve it through **deregulation,** or the relaxation of government controls on business. Theoretically, if price controls on gas and oil were removed, prices would rise, and people would use less fuel. Gas and oil companies would receive higher profits, which could be used in developing new forms of energy. Although Congress did not accept this idea, it did pass the Energy Policy and Conservation Act of 1975, which dealt with saving fuel and finding new forms of energy.

Foreign Affairs

In foreign affairs, Ford faced many of the same problems as Nixon and pursued basically the same policies. To ensure continuity in policy, the new President kept Kissinger as Secretary of State.

U.S. FOREIGN AID, 1946–1976

In Cambodia, Ford favored the continued support of the pro-western government. Lon Nol's forces, with United States support, held on until 1975 when the Khmer Rouge (the Cambodian Communists) began closing in. At this point, Ford urged Congress to provide over $200 million in aid to Cambodia. Congress, however, refused. On April 17, 1975, the Khmer Rouge took the capital, Phnom Penh, and gained total control of the country.

Ford also wanted to continue aid to South Vietnam. The South Vietnamese army was losing to the Communists, but Congress refused to send additional aid. On April 30, Saigon fell. The Provisional Revolutionary Government of South Vietnam took over. North and South Vietnam were reunited under the Communists.

Ford soon faced another crisis in Southeast Asia. This was the *Mayagüez* incident. In May 1975 the Khmer Rouge seized an unarmed American ship, the *Mayagüez*. Ford, without consulting Congress as provided by the War Powers Act, moved at once. He ordered air strikes and sent in the marines, who captured the ship and rescued the crew. Then he informed Congress of his actions. Most people praised the President's handling of the incident.

Elsewhere, Ford pursued Nixon's policy of détente with the Soviet Union. The two countries continued negotiations on nuclear arms control. Ford traveled to the Soviet Union, where he signed the Vladivostok Accord with Brezhnev in December 1974. This agreement helped lay the foundation for Salt II, a second round of talks on nuclear arms control.

In July 1975 détente was reinforced when Ford and leaders from 34 other countries met in Helsinki, Finland, to sign several sets of accords. These accords guaranteed more liberal relations between eastern and western countries, recognized the boundaries of Soviet-dominated Eastern European nations, and protected certain human rights.

Helsinki appeared to be a great stride forward, but questions grew about the Soviets' sincerity. Political oppression and restriction of Jewish immigration continued. In 1974 Senator Henry Jackson of Washington had proposed that a trade agreement then being negotiated between the United States and the Soviet Union not be approved until the Soviets relaxed their immigration restrictions. At first the Soviet Union seemed to accept the "Jackson

Ask students to determine whether Ford could have done anything to win the election of 1976.

Amendment." Within a few months, however, Moscow rejected the trade agreement, declaring that it would not allow the United States to interfere. This was a setback for détente.

Détente was further jeopardized by the fact that the Soviet Union was supporting communist revolutions throughout the world. By the end of his term, Ford was backing away from détente to the applause of the conservatives in his party. Later, the rift between the United States and the Soviet Union would grow even wider.

The Election of 1976

In 1976 Ford received his party's nomination for President. Senator Robert Dole of Kansas was nominated for Vice President. But Ford's prospects did not look particularly good. Although he had helped to restore confidence in government, Watergate was still fresh in the minds of the American people.

To oppose Ford, the Democrats selected the former governor of Georgia, Jimmy Carter, who was relatively unknown to the American public. Carter chose Senator Walter Mondale of Minnesota as his running mate. Carter promised to clean up the government and ran as much against the memory of Nixon and government corruption as against Ford. "I'll never lie to you," he told his audiences.

The campaign was capped by a series of nationally televised debates between Ford and Carter. Neither candidate distinguished himself, although Carter fared slightly better. As in the rest of the campaign, no clearly defined issues emerged.

In November Carter swept the South, with the exception of Virginia and won enough eastern and midwestern states to carry the day. The margin was slim, however. Carter received 40.8 million popular votes to Ford's 39.1 million. The electoral vote was 297 to 241. It remained to be seen whether Carter and the Democrats would bring much-needed stability to the nation.

SECTION REVIEW

1. Identify the following: Khmer Rouge, Mayagüez, "Jackson Amendment," Walter Mondale.
2. How did Ford justify his pardon of Nixon?
3. How did Ford try to deal with the energy crisis?
4. What was the progress of détente under Ford?

CHAPTER **31**   REVIEW

SUMMARY

1. As President, Richard Nixon was a conservative who was supported chiefly by middle-class Americans with traditional values.
2. Under Nixon American troops were gradually withdrawn from Vietnam.
3. Nixon's major accomplishment as President was establishing improved relations with both Communist China and the Soviet Union.
4. Nixon expanded the powers of his office to such a degree that his term was called the "Imperial Presidency."
5. In 1972 Nixon was reelected by a large margin.
6. During and after the election campaign, a scandal erupted over illegal and unethical methods used by people working under Nixon.
7. Meanwhile, Vice President Spiro T. Agnew was forced to resign after it was discovered that he had accepted bribes, and Gerald R. Ford was appointed to take his place.
8. Under threat of impeachment, Nixon resigned as President on August 9, 1974.
9. In 1976 Jimmy Carter was elected President.

VOCABULARY

"silent majority"	stagflation	revenue-sharing	executive privilege	subpoenas
détente	fixed exchange rates	amnesty	state's evidence	deregulation
shuttle diplomacy	devaluation	impoundment	executive clemency	

REVIEW QUESTIONS

1. How did Nixon achieve an end to United States involvement in Vietnam?
2. How did American relations with communist powers change under Nixon?
3. What was the condition of the American economy during the Nixon administration?
4. What progress did minorities and women make during the Nixon years?

5. What conflicts did the Democratically-controlled Congress have with Nixon?
6. How did the Watergate break-in nearly lead to Nixon's impeachment?
7. How did Ford attempt to restore confidence in government?
8. What policy was pursued by Ford in foreign affairs?

DISCUSSION

1. Was the United States right to pull out of Vietnam? Why or why not?
2. Was détente with the Soviet Union realistic or unrealistic? Why?

3. If you could have voted in 1972, would you have voted for Nixon or McGovern? Why?
4. Should Richard Nixon have been prosecuted for his role in Watergate? Why or why not?

USING GRAPHS

Refer to the graph on page 696 and answer the following questions:

1. How much money did the United States spend on military aid from 1946–1952?
2. During which periods did total foreign aid exceed $30 billion?

3. During which time period did the United States spend the largest amount of money on total foreign aid?
4. During which time period did the United States spend more money on military aid to foreign countries than on economic aid?

USING SKILLS

Read the following excerpt from John J. Sirica's book about Watergate and answer the questions that follow the excerpt:

The country should take great pride that this naked attempt to thwart the Constitution of the United States—to substitute the will of a few powerful men for the rule of law . . . was in the end defeated. . . . Yet I can never forget Senator Sam Ervin's observation that "they almost got away with it." I think it's worth asking, Why didn't they get away with it?

Everyone has a tendency to find heroes, to claim that individual acts of decency or bravery or devotion bring about great historical events. But I think the lesson of Watergate is quite the opposite. I firmly believe it was our system of

government and our system of law that ended that crisis and saved the very constitutional form of government that gave us that system and those laws.

Take the role of the press, for example. The two young reporters at the Washington Post, Carl Bernstein and Bob Woodward, became popular heroes. . . . They deserve the attention and the acclaim, of course. And so does the owner of the Post, Mrs. Katharine Graham. . . . But what is more important is that the Post is part of a free press, protected by the Constitution. Who emerged in the press to expose Watergate is less important than the fact that our system allows reporters the freedom to do so.

And consider the role of Congress. Sam Ervin, to my mind, represented in his conduct of the Watergate hearings the best traditions of American political leadership. But I believe that had there been no Sam Ervin from North Carolina, there would have been someone on Capitol Hill capable of and willing to lead the kind of fair-minded investigation Senator Ervin did manage. It is more important that we have an independent legislative branch than that a particular senator or group of senators be seen as heroes.

In the difficult days of 1974, as the Watergate crisis was reaching some sort of breaking point, many in Washington doubted that the often unruly politicians in the House of Representatives could manage an impeachment inquiry that would be seen as nonpartisan and fair. Peter Rodino and other members of the House Judiciary Committee did just that. . . . Peter Rodino deserves enormous credit for his role. But I think the fact that our Constitution gives Congress the remedy of impeachment to use against a chief executive who breaks the law is ultimately more important than any one legislator's role.

I feel the same way about the courts. It is more important that we had a totally independent judiciary than that I, or any other judge or group of judges, happened to be presiding over the case. . . .

It was the courts and the law that throughout this crisis could compel that the truth be told. Despite efforts in our executive branch to distort the truth, to fabricate a set of facts that looked innocent, the court system served to set the record straight. When the President and his aides lied about their own activities, it was our courts and our law that compelled them to produce the best evidence in the case—the presidential tapes—to test their versions of what happened. And when the most powerful men in our government tried to obstruct the law, to ignore it, to frustrate the process of justice, the law itself penalized them. The law and our faith in that law was too powerful for even those powerful men.

I don't mean to suggest that our system guarantees that misuses of power such as were engineered by the Nixon White House will always be found out, always be punished and cleaned up. There were, without doubt, some amazing accidents, some incidents of pure good fortune, that helped save us. Had Frank Wills, the night guard at the Watergate complex, not found the telltale tape on the door, the whole business might have gone undetected. The greatest accident of all, of course, was that Nixon had chosen to tape his conversations in the White House. Without this evidence, and of course without the court's power to compel that it be made public, I wonder whether the real truth of Watergate would ever have come out.

1. What is the main point made by Judge Sirica in this excerpt?

2. What details does he offer to support his main point?

3. What details, if any, contradict his main point?

1	The Counterculture	**701**
2	The Arts	**704**
3	Religion	**711**
4	The Media	**713**
5	A Changing World	**716**

AMERICAN SOCIETY IN TRANSITION

"The Times They Are A-Changin' "

Bob Dylan

Most Americans were not prepared for the social and cultural revolution that overtook them in the 1960's. For the first time in America's history, the young were in the majority. Many young people began to question the country's long-standing basic ethic of hard work, respectability, and competition for material success. Because there were so many youths, they and their opinions had an influence they had never had before.

By the 1970's things had calmed down. Middle Americans,[1] whom President Nixon called the "forgotten Americans," began to stand up and demand to be counted. They called for—and to a certain extent got—a return to the traditional system and its norms. Some of the changes effected in the 1960's, however, remained.

1 The Counterculture

Early in the 1960's, a **generation gap** developed between many older and younger Americans. The young condemned what they called the hypocrisy of the older generation, which meant anyone over the age of 30. The older generation, they said, was too materialistic, too obsessed with power and wealth, and too addicted to violence. Many young people rebelled against authority and discipline of any kind. These youths formed their own culture. In the words of one observer, their culture had as its central institutions "the high school and the mass media" and as its principal activities "consuming goods and enacting courtship rituals."

By the late 1960's, the generation gap had widened and spread, especially in the cities and on college campuses. The term **youth culture,** which referred to the way adolescents lived, no longer seemed

---

[1] The term "Middle America" was first used in June 1968 by newspaper columnist Joseph Kraft. To him, it meant "the great mass of some 40 million persons who have recently moved from just above the poverty line to just below the level of affluence."

comprehensive enough. It was replaced with the term **counterculture,** which covered everything about the young from their clothes and hair styles to their views on life, sex, and politics. Many older people also began to absorb countercultural values and act out countercultural lifestyles. The counterculture, basically a revolt against American affluence and technology, became a special feature of the 1960's. It put emphasis on the individual, and it made personal commitment and freedom to "do your own thing" its major goals.

Some adults, however, believed that the younger generation was creating its own "establishment," which was a mirror-image of the adult one they were rebelling against. Instead of the big houses and cars sought by their elders, the material goals of the young were motorcycles, electric guitars, and stereo systems. Some rock musicians were just as eager for power and wealth as any corporate executive. And some radical political groups were as well acquainted with violence as any member of the armed forces.

Hippies

At the core of the counterculture were the **hippies,**[2] young people characterized by their emphasis on universal love and their withdrawal from conventional society. The hippies also had other names—flower children, love children, gentle people, free people. But no matter what name they went by, they all professed to be anti-establishment, anti-capitalist, anti-military, and anti-violence. Their values centered on peace, love, brotherhood, and beauty of the spirit.

The hippie movement had its origins in the beat generation of the 1950's. Like the beatniks, the hippies rejected conformity and were interested in self-exploration, mysticism, and drugs. In the 1960's

---

[2] The word "hippie" was derived from "hipster," meaning one who is interested in the new and unconventional.

Have students consider why the hippie movement attracted more youths from the middle and upper classes than from the working classes.

they took "Make love, not war" as their slogan. Folk singer Arlo Guthrie spoke for them all:

> *We're finally gonna get to the point*
> *where there's no more bigotry or greed or war.*
> *Peace is on the way. . . . People are simply*
> *gonna learn that they can get more by*
> *going groovy than being greedy.*

Two of the largest congregations of hippies were in New York and in California. In New York the hippies lived in a section of New York City called the East Village. In California they took over a section of San Francisco called Haight-Ashbury near Golden Gate Park. By the mid-1960's more than 5000 hippies lived in Haight-Ashbury. Some got money from home or worked at casual labor. Others resorted to **panhandling** (begging from passers-by on the streets) or stealing. Still others opened boutiques, small retail shops, and sold handcrafted items to the tourists who flocked to stare at them.

Haight-Ashbury attracted young people from all over the country. It was one of the first places police and parents looked for runaway teenagers. In January 1967 the World's First Human Be-In—a celebration of countercultural values that drew more than 20,000 young people—was held in Haight-Ashbury. It was followed that summer by a series of "love-ins" both in Haight-Ashbury and the East Village.

The publicity given to the "Summer of Love" by the media brought thousands of disturbed young people to Haight-Ashbury and the East Village. This led to the downfall of the hippie movement, the ranks of which had already been thinned by drug poisoning, hepatitis, and diseases brought on by malnutrition and exposure. In Buena Vista Park in California, the summer—and the movement—was brought to a symbolic end with a funeral for "Hippie, devoted Son of Mass Media." But, although the hippie movement was over, many aspects of the hippie lifestyle continued and were taken up by other groups in American society.

At its peak, the hippie movement could boast of more than 300,000 followers. More than half of these were fairly mature young people from the middle class with a year or more of college behind them. Some had responsible jobs in the business or academic world. But, as time passed, more of them consisted of confused high-school-age runaways.

Although the hippies claimed to be dedicated to love of humankind, many Americans thought they were really dedicated to filth, irresponsibility, and drugs. Middle America, especially, found them and all they stood for degenerate and un-American. One midwestern newspaper stated that the hippies "took their tactics from Gandhi, their idealism from philosophy class, and their money from Daddy."

In 1969 several brutal murders took place that strengthened this negative attitude. Charles Manson, a 35-year-old ex-convict turned hippie, was arrested for the murders. Manson headed a hippie "family" of nine young women and five young men. Manson and three of the women were found guilty of murder.

In September 1975 the Manson family made the headlines again when family member Lynette Alice Fromme tried to assassinate President Ford. In December 1975 she was sentenced to a life term in prison for her crime.

Communal Societies

One of the outgrowths of the counterculture was a new interest in the **commune,** a community whose members share or own property jointly. The hippies saw the commune as another way to withdraw from established traditions and rules. During the 1960's and 1970's, communes of all kinds sprang up in different parts of the United States as some Americans tried to find more meaningful ways of living with nature and with one another.

One of the earliest communal societies of the period was the Diggers, headed by Emmett Grogan. During the 1967 "Summer of Love," the Diggers set up centers to distribute free lodging, food, and clothing to the thousands of young people who flocked to San Francisco. The Diggers obtained most of the things they distributed by going from one end of the city to the other asking for money, goods, and tools.

Another of the well-known communes of the 1960's was Hog Farm. It was made up of 30-to-50 artists, musicians, and film technicians led by Hugh Romney, an ex-coffeehouse comedian. At first the commune members lived in tents and shacks in the foothills near Los Angeles. Later they bought a half-dozen old schoolbuses, installed bunks in them, and painted them in bright colors. With their pet, a 400-pound (180-kilogram) pig named Pigasus, they spent their

Some commune members were married couples seeking an alternative to single-family living.

time traveling from one rock festival to another. Sometimes they set up free kitchens, gave first aid, and helped persons with drug-related problems.

One of the most successful communes, however, did not come into being until 1971. Called the Farm, it was started by Stephen Gaskin, an ex-marine and creative writing instructor at San Francisco State College. Unlike the members of most other communes, those of the Farm did not try to live solely off the land, their own handicrafts, or handouts from their neighbors. They grew sorghum, which they processed into molasses at a nearby mill. The Farm also had its own medical clinic on the premises. Some of the commune members attended medical school at the expense of the commune. In return, they agreed to come back after graduation and staff the clinic.

Although many Americans believed that the communes were just another form of rebellion, some psychologists saw them in a different light. They argued that the communes had saved the lives of many people who felt alienated from society for one reason or another. The communes gave these people a family and a reason to find a purposeful life.

Drugs

Another aspect of the counterculture was drugs. Many young people saw drugs as the means to truth and the road to pleasure. Using drugs was their way of expressing their new religion of love and freedom. This view was one of the greatest sources of tension between the older and young generations.

Not only the young, however, were attracted to the drug scene. Two of its biggest supporters were Timothy Leary and Richard Alpert, scientific researchers at Harvard University who were studying the effects of **hallucinogens,** drugs which induce altered perceptions. Their study centered chiefly on lysergic acid diethylamide (LSD).

Discovered by a Swiss chemist in 1938, LSD was introduced for experimental purposes in the United States in 1949. Taken in certain dosages, it could produce changes in emotion and in the perception of color, space, and time. The changes could go on in varying degrees for several hours. An enjoyable experience on the drug was known as a "good trip." A frightening loss of reality was known as a "bad trip."

In 1961 both Leary and Alpert were fired for using undergraduates in their experiments. This, however, did not stop them from experimenting with LSD and other psychedelic drugs. Before long, they were habitual users and were urging others to do the same.

In 1966 Leary and Alpert formed the League of Spiritual Discovery, a religious sect whose rites centered on the use of LSD and other drugs. The league's members were expected to use LSD once a

Rock music festivals were popular gathering spots for members of the counterculture. The views of the counterculture regarding life, politics, fashion, and music differed sharply from those held by most Americans. What values did the counterculture emphasize?

The use of drugs is not new. Opium was popular among upper-class Europeans in the 19th century. Heroin, cocaine, and marijuana were used in the United States from the start of the 20th century.

One reason that youth were influential was their number. By the mid-1960's half of the population was less than 27 years old.

week in "mind-expanding" experiments. Dressed in long white robes, Leary traveled all over the country preaching his message of "tune in, turn on, and drop out" and pledging to "change the spiritual level of the United States." However, he never gained a large personal following.

When research suggested that LSD caused genetic damage, its use began to decline. But by then it had put many young people in hospitals, strait jackets, jails, and graves. This, however, did not stop the use of other drugs. The most popular of these was marijuana, also known as "grass" and "pot." In 1960 only a few hundred thousand Americans admitted to having sampled marijuana. By 1970 the number had increased to 8 million. American youth argued that marijuana was less dangerous than alcohol. They also said that for adults to condemn the one while permitting the other was just another sign of their hypocrisy. Some research suggested that physical and mental damage might be caused by marijuana, but other research contradicted those findings, and usage continued to grow.

Harsher laws and campaigns designed to bring home the harmful effects of drugs failed to stop many Americans from experimenting with them. In the 1970's three "new" drugs began to cause concern. One was Quaaludes, a drug that had been synthesized in 1951 to treat malaria. Another was phencyclidine, or PCP. Known as "angel dust," it had been developed in the 1950's as a tranquilizer for animals. The third was cocaine, which had been developed 400 years earlier by the Inca Indians. It soon became the "in" drug of the 1970's, used by people of all ages. Like Quaaludes and PCP, it could kill.

Lasting Effects

By the end of the 1970's, much of the countercultural movement had dissipated. The baby boom generation grew older and became part of the over-30 age group that they had once distrusted. One former member of the counterculture, political activist Jerry Rubin, wrote about his generation "growing up."

> *I saw us move out of youth-oriented . . . consciousness to think of ourselves as parents, adults. . . . I want to be politically active again—but not at the expense of my happiness and health.*

Despite its transience and its excesses, the counterculture had some lasting effects on American society. It led many people of all generations to examine their beliefs and commitments. Some of the values of the counterculture, such as the emphasis on personal relationships and on spiritual rather than material progress, had a strong influence on the establishment culture. Some of the counterculture's goals, such as peace and saving the environment, became more acceptable to society in general. Unfortunately, some of the worst features of the counterculture—particularly the use of drugs—also spread to other parts of society.

SECTION REVIEW

1. Identify the following: Arlo Guthrie, Haight-Ashbury, Diggers.
2. Why did Middle Americans disapprove of hippies?
3. Why did drugs become a central part of the counterculture?
4. What harmful effects were caused by drugs?

2 The Arts

The cultural revolution of the 1960's could be seen in the arts as well as in the counterculture. In 1959 Allan Kaprow, an art historian at Rutgers University, staged what he called "Eighteen Happenings in Six Parts" at the Reuban Gallery in New York City. It was the first of many **happenings,** or improvized spectacles or performances. Most happenings involved human actors assisted by different artifacts and relying on technical effects. For the most part, they were mixtures of theater, dance, kinetic sculpture, and vaudeville. The important thing was not that the happenings were creative but rather that they were different, chic, and often outrageous. They reflected the change and turbulence of the times.

Happenings amused the public for only a few years before passing out of vogue. But they were an indication of the change that was taking place in American art, literature, theater, cinema, and music.

Pop Art

In 1960 an artist named Jasper Johns introduced a work entitled "Painted Bronze." It consisted of a

The Dada movement, abstract expressionism, and the collages of
Kurt Schwitters influenced the pop art movement.

casting of two Ballantine Ale cans with the labels
painted on them. One of the cans was open; the other
was closed. This type of work came to be known as
pop art, or art that adapts techniques of commercial
art and depicts objects of everyday life.

Other artists in the past had depicted recognizable
subject matter in their works, but not like these. Pop
artists used as their subjects soup cans, light bulbs,
soft drink bottles, comic strip characters, and movie
stars. They represented them in shining colors and in
exaggerated detail, often blowing them up to huge
sizes. For further impact, they sometimes tacked on
objects as appendages to their paintings.

In 1963 the Gallery of Modern Art in Washington,
D.C., organized a show displaying the works of a
dozen New York pop artists. The art critics were
quick to criticize and poke fun at the works. The critic
for *The Los Angeles Times* was kinder than most when
he stated that pop "is painting of a sort; it may even be
art, but it certainly is poor art." Some modern art
dealers and collectors, however, did not agree and
began to give pop art their support.

By 1965 pop art was being displayed in most of the
major galleries and museums, and the average
American was familiar with the movement. Of all the
pop artists, four stood out. One was Andy Warhol,
best known for his three-foot (90-centimeter)-tall
Campbell's soup can. A second was Roy Lichtenstein,
who created dot-studded, oversized, cartoon-style
paintings. A third was Claes Oldenburg, who sculpted
king-sized hamburgers and chocolate cream pies. A
fourth was James Rosequist, best known for his
massive murals that included such things as orange
mounds of spaghetti and pouty lips smeared with
bright red lipstick.

Philip Johnson, an art collector and one of the first
to buy pop art, explained it in this way:

> *What pop art has done for me is to make the
> world a pleasanter place to live in. . . . I look
> at things with an entirely different eye—at
> Coney Island, at billboards, at Coca Cola
> bottles. One of the duties of art is to make you
> look at the world with pleasure. Pop art is the
> only movement in this century that has tried to
> do it.*

Many others agreed with Johnson. The media liked
pop artists because they were colorful, outgoing, and

Though pop art has often been an object of ridicule, some critics
have defended it as a valid art form. In the 1960's, museums
began to feature the work of such pop artists as Andy Warhol.
Why did pop art become popular?

agreeable—all of which made them good copy.
Business liked pop art because it was easy to sell. The
jet set, the rich and famous people who traveled from
one fashionable place to another aboard jetliners and
whose activities were the constant focus of the
media, liked pop art because it was fashionable. The
young liked pop art because it was easy to
understand. The subjects were familiar and unde-
manding. Pop art was above all a product and symbol
of its time.

Literature

The changes taking place in American society in the
1960's and 1970's were also reflected in the literature
of the time. The stage was set in 1960 by Joseph

Rachel Carson

biologist with the Bureau of Fisheries. The Bureau later became part of the United States Fish and Wildlife Service.

Carson combined her scientific and literary talents by writing articles on marine life for a number of journals. She also wrote several books on the subject. *Under the Sea-wind* was published in 1941. Although praised by the critics, it sold only a few thousand copies. However, *The Sea Around Us* (1951) was an immediate best-seller. Carson's success enabled her to give up her position as editor of publications, which she had held since 1947, and become a full-time writer. In 1955 she produced her third book, *The Edge of the Sea.*

In Carson's last book, *Silent Spring* (1962), she dealt with the subject of environmental pollution, pointing out the damages caused to plant and animal life by pesticides. She warned that the continued uncontrolled use of pesticides would bring about a silent spring—a spring unrelieved by the sounds of nature. Although this work aroused a certain amount of criticism, it stimulated concern for the environment and increased demands for conservation.

Carson assumed leadership of the growing environmental movement. Partly as a result of her efforts, a number of states passed bills that limited the use of pesticides. The Department of Agriculture required that such products be registered and their contents labeled. In 1963 President Kennedy directed the Science Advisory Committee to investigate charges of irresponsible pesticide use. Shortly before her death in April 1964, Rachel Carson was named Conservationist of the Year.

Rachel L. Carson, author and scientist, was born on May 27, 1907, in Springdale, Pennsylvania. During her youth, she developed a love of both nature and literature that would shape her life. After graduation from high school, Carson entered the Pennsylvania College for Women with the intention of becoming a writer. Before long, however, she changed her major from English to zoology and received her Bachelor of Arts degree in 1929. Carson earned a Master of Arts degree from The John Hopkins University in 1932.

While doing her postgraduate work, Carson took a position on the zoological faculty at the University of Maryland. She remained there until 1936, when she accepted a job as an aquatic

---

Heller's *Catch-22,* an anti-war satire. The story line was set in World War II. But it was just as appropriate to the war going on in Indochina at the time—a war in which many Americans thought the real enemy was not the other side but someone supposedly on their own side.

Catch-22 was a major example of **black humor,** the treatment of tragic personal and social phenomena in a humorous, often absurd, manner. It attacked the very perceptions on which the entire Cold War was built and became an expression of dissatisfaction with the establishment and its way of doing things.

Protest and the need for change were recurring themes during the 1960's. In 1962 Rachel Carson's *Silent Spring* sent shock waves through much of the United States. In her book, Carson examined the disastrous effects that indiscriminate use of pesticides such as DDT were having on the environment. While many Americans did not believe Carson's thesis at first, much of what she said was proven to be true. Ultimately, her work led the federal government to severely restrict the use of DDT.

The following year, Betty Friedan's *The Feminine Mystique* wrought another kind of change. The work

Friedan placed part of the blame for the stereotype of the submissive woman on psychologist Sigmund Freud and anthropologist Margaret Mead, who argued that women were naturally suited for such a role.

argued that there was something "very wrong with the way American women are trying to live their lives today." Friedan charged that, instead of seeking their own individual identities, women were trying to live their lives through their husbands. The book kindled a fire in the minds of a great many women and stimulated the women's movement in general.

That same year, James Baldwin's *The Fire Next Time* was published. It consisted of two "letters"— "My Dungeon Shook: Letter to My Nephew on the One Hundredth Anniversary of the Emancipation" and "Down at the Cross: Letter from a Region of My Mind." Baldwin's message was a simple one—blacks were through being patient with the uncompromising attitude of whites.

Black militancy also prevailed in *The Autobiography of Malcolm X* (1965), written with the help of Alex Haley. One of the major autobiographies of the twentieth century, it appealed immediately to the militant blacks who had given up on Martin Luther King's brand of nonviolence. It stimulated general interest not only in black culture but also in Third World liberation movements. In 1966 a paperback version of the book appeared, and by 1970 it had sold more than 4 million copies. It is believed to have found greater readership among American blacks than any other book except the Bible.

Two other themes that permeated the literature of the 1960's and 1970's were violence and sex. Although both offended Middle America, only in small towns and cities was there any effective censorship. Among the best-selling books of this type were Mario Puzo's *The Godfather* and Philip Roth's *Portnoy's Complaint*. Both came out in 1969. The former revolved around Don Vito Corleone, a Mafia patriarch. The latter revolved around Alex Portnoy, a Jewish lawyer involved in liberal causes.

One of the most popular works of the 1970's was Alex Haley's *Roots*. The work, for which Haley won a Pulitzer Prize, was called a "symbolic history of a people." It was the slightly fictionalized story of Kunta Kinte, an ancestor of Haley's, and his journey from a privileged life in what is now Gambia to one of slavery in the United States. In 1977 the book formed the basis for an eight-part television series that drew more than 130 million viewers. Two years later, a seven-part sequel was televised. It drew an audience of 110 million.

The Theater

As in other areas of the arts, the theater was geared to the young and to the romantic. By the late 1960's there was no doubt that the values of the counterculture dominated the theater. This became most apparent in 1967 when a show called *Hair* opened in the New York Public Theater off Broadway. Inspired by the hippie culture, it was billed as the first tribal-love-rock musical and was meant to underscore the huge gap between the generations. Young people were entranced by the theme and the music. Older, more conservative people were shocked. The play was a success. Before long, it moved to Broadway, where it made a great deal of money and inspired a great many imitations.

Two years later, *Oh! Calcutta!* opened in New York. It was one of the most controversial musicals in history. A series of loosely woven skits, it featured nude performers. When it turned out to be a huge success, one critic acidly remarked that "the public chose this relatively painless way to join the avant-garde." It was so successful, in fact, that it opened the following year in London. Veteran performer Helen Hayes, however, voiced the opinion of many Americans when she stated, "We had nudity on the stage in my youth, you know, in the Ziegfeld Follies. But it was beautiful nudity. Now it's sort of grubby."

In 1977 both *Hair* and *Oh! Calcutta!* were revived on Broadway. Neither was as successful as it had been in the 1960's. What had seemed so shocking then no longer shocked at all.

The Movies

The movies, like the theater, were the domain of the young in the 1960's. Three-quarters of the American moviegoers were under 40 years of age. Half were under 24. For the most part, those who regularly went to the movies once a month or more were college students or recent graduates.

Early in the decade, Hollywood tried to compete with television by offering epics such as *Ben Hur*, *Spartacus*, and *Exodus*. The theory was that epics with casts of thousands were too expensive for television to produce. They also were too great in scope for the small screen of a television. The epics drew large audiences, but not ones large enough to

Although some movies continued to break box office records in the early 1970's, 80 percent of the new films lost money.

make the movies profitable. Consequently, movie-makers began to experiment. The result was a decade of diversity, vitality, and growth.

In 1964 the film to see was *Dr. Strangelove, or How I Learned to Stop Worrying and Love the Bomb,* a satire about a nuclear holocaust. It portrayed the lunacy of the world situation and the madness of scientists, politicians, and generals. Thought by many to be a masterpiece of black humor, it used technological effects more effectively than had been thought possible.

In 1964 the hero of the movies was James Bond, the creation of novelist Ian Fleming. Crowds flocked to see the British spy, played by Sean Connery, in action, romancing beautiful women and using incredible gadgets and weapons to escape from impossible situations. The Bond thrillers had everything—music, technology, sex, violence, and subtle humor. Before long, products associated with Bond were selling in 70 countries. They appealed to all ages and all groups and ranged from gold underwear to transistor radios that converted to toy rifles.

In 1967 two movies especially captured the era. One was *Bonnie and Clyde,* starring Faye Dunaway as Bonnie Parker and Warren Beatty as Clyde Barrow. Although the film was set in the 1930's, it exemplified the spirit of the 1960's. The film took liberties with historical fact, making two small-town gangsters into romantic, misunderstood heroes. This made it a subject of controversy. Some older people thought the film was immoral. Many younger people, however, saw something of themselves in Bonnie and Clyde. To them, the two gangsters were likable youth at odds with their environment and their times. The result of the controversy was financial success for the film.

The other movie of the year was *The Graduate,* a satire on the tyranny of America's social customs. In it, Dustin Hoffman portrayed a 21-year-old student who refused to conform. The film established Hoffman's career. At the same time, it helped Hollywood capture the 18-to-25-year-old market. According to one expert, *"The Graduate* became almost holy writ for many students who identified with the befuddled anti-hero's attempts to find himself."

A turning point for the movie industry came in 1969 due mostly to two films, *Easy Rider* and *Alice's Restaurant.* Both were low-budget, unpolished, personalized films by young filmmakers. Both dealt with the generation gap, were pro-youth, and attacked traditional values. Both were box-office smashes. Their success made it possible for other young filmmakers to show what they could do.

By the 1970's films had come to be thought of more as an art form than as simple entertainment. Movies had become America's favorite form of personal expression. Different films were made to appeal to different audiences, most of them young. Movies the whole family could go to see together were few and far between.

Comedy came into its own again in the 1970's via the talents of Mel Brooks and Woody Allen. Although both wrote, performed, and directed, the similarities ended there. In *Blazing Saddles* (1974), *Young Frankenstein* (1974), and *Silent Movie* (1976), Brooks used burlesque, wild puns and insults, and odd sounds to create zany, disorganized comedy. Allen, on the other hand, was lower-keyed and more sophisticated. *Bananas* (1971), *Play It Again, Sam* (1972), *Sleeper* (1974), and *Annie Hall* (1977) all held special appeal for the college audience.

Blacks also made their mark in the movies in the 1970's. Their achievements included *Super Fly* (1972), the first black-oriented film financed by blacks, and *Sounder* (1972), which most critics considered the best film of the year.

Of all the films of the decade, however, the one that proved to be the greatest hit was George Lucas' *Star Wars.* Released in 1977, it was a science-fiction tale peopled with comic-book characters, full of suspense and adventure, and rich in special effects. *Star Wars* appealed to people of all ages. It was a film the entire family could watch—and enjoy—together. Many Americans hoped it would set a new trend and make movies a family event once again.

Music

More than any of the other arts, music became the domain—and in some cases the obsession—of the young. What had been known as rock 'n roll in the 1950's became just plain "rock" and helped identify the young as a distinct force in society.

Until 1963 the music scene was dominated by **folk rock,** rock music characterized by poetic ballads of

The charleston of the 1920's and the twist of the 1960's were considered scandalous. Both dances involved minimal physical contact.

Singers Rudy Vallee, Frank Sinatra, and Elvis Presley also attracted enormous and devoted followings.

social protest and emotional despair. Two of the most popular singers of folk rock were Bob Dylan and Joan Baez. Dylan's style was intense, and his songs were bitter protests. One Dylan song, "Blowin' in the Wind," became an anthem of the civil rights movement.

The Twist. At the same time young Americans were listening to the ballads of the folk rockers, they were shocking the older generation with a new dance called the Twist. The Twist had been introduced in 1960 in Philadelphia by Chubby Checker, a black pop singer and recording artist.

To do the Twist, partners faced one another and moved their shoulders, hips, and arms to the beat of the music. Checker described it in this way:

> *The first position of the stance is like a boxer's. Then you move your hips like you're wiping yourself with a towel. Your body goes back and forth in one direction and your hands go in the other direction. From that point on, you ad-lib energetically.*

Promoted by disc jockeys such as Dick Clark, Clay Cole, and Murray the K, the Twist swept the country and then moved on to other nations. Many adults, however, viewed the dance as scandalous. For example, it was declared off limits in community centers in Tampa, Florida, and banned in Catholic schools and parishes in Buffalo, New York. The reaction in some foreign cities and countries was even more intense. The Twist was banned in Egypt, outlawed in Saigon, declared illegal in Beirut, and led to arrest in Indonesia. The Soviet Union called it "bourgeois decadence at its very worst."

Nevertheless, the Twist remained popular. In time it gave birth to other dances such as the Mashed Potato, the Jerk, the Swim, the Monkey, and the Watusi. It also led to the creation of **discotheques,** nightclubs featuring dancing to recorded music that has been amplified.

Beatlemania. In 1963 both the Twist and folk rock were pushed out of the limelight by four young performers from Liverpool, England—John Lennon, Paul McCartney, George Harrison, and Ringo Starr. As a singing group called the Beatles, they contributed more to the counterculture than any other group. Their first big hit song, "She Loves You," came out in 1963. When they appeared for the first

time on American television in February of the following year, 50,000 fans tried to get tickets to see them. The theater, however, could seat only 800. Beatlemania had begun.

At first, many older Americans believed that the Beatles were just another fad that would die out in a short time. There was no doubt, they said, that the Beatles, with their long hair and elegant style of dress called "mod," were showmen. But all their songs were about love, freedom, innocence, and happy living, and people would soon tire of that.

The Beatles proved the doubters wrong. Their recording "Can't Buy Me Love" set a new world's record by selling more than 3 million copies before it was even released. Their first movie, *A Hard Day's Night,* was not only a hit with the general public but won critical acclaim as well. The Beatles learned to play new instruments and developed a complex music that attracted serious inquiry. Further, they were

Young people have always been attuned to trends in fashion and music. Dance fads have ranged from the twist to disco (below). What are some new trends in music?

Have students analyze why rock has attracted listeners throughout the world, despite the variations in taste from culture to culture.

among the first to take advantage of new recording techniques that made it possible for several sound tracks to be played at the same time.

Beatlemania remained at a fever pitch for three years before starting to taper off. In the late 1960's, the group changed their lifestyles and their music, causing them to lose some of their followers. Those who remained, however, were more intense and loyal than ever. Even after the group broke up and each member went his separate way, Beatles music and movies remained popular. Of the four Beatles, Paul McCartney went on to achieve the greatest success in the music world. With his wife Linda, he formed a new group called Wings. By 1979 he had become one of the best-selling songwriters of all time.

Acid Rock. In 1966 a new musical genre emerged called **acid rock,** rock music characterized by the emotional intensity of electronic instruments. It first became popular at the San Francisco Tripps Festival, a multimedia happening that combined live rock bands, dancing, strobe lights and other technical gimmicks with the taking of LSD.

From this beginning emerged such groups as the Grateful Dead, the Jefferson Airplane, and Big Brother and the Holding Company. For years afterwards, rock and light shows attracted big audiences and helped launch countercultural music groups into the pop culture mainstream.

Woodstock and Altamont. As rock became less a movement and more a business, it lost some of its impact. Its popularity, however, continued to grow, and rock festivals became more prominent. Two of the most publicized festivals were Woodstock and Altamont, both of which took place in 1969.

Woodstock, a rock festival held in August in Bethel, New York, was an attempt by counterculture advocates to show to an America divided by the Vietnam War that love and cooperation were both desirable and possible. The festival was the idea of two 24-year-olds, Michael Land and John Roberts. They leased a 600-acre (240-hectare) dairy farm and got big-name rock stars such as Joan Baez, Janis Joplin, Jimi Hendrix, and the Jefferson Airplane to agree to perform. They flew in 50 doctors from New York City to take care of any medical problems that might arise. They also arranged for members of the Hog Farm commune to police the area. Land and Roberts counted on selling 50,000 tickets to the

event at $7 apiece. More than 300,000 people attended, most of whom did not bother to buy tickets.

Those who attended Woodstock thought that the festival was a huge success. The establishment, on the other hand, pointed to the large and unruly crowds, insufficient food and water supplies, and the people suffering from bad drug trips. Woodstock, they said, was a perfect example of the younger generation's lack of discipline.

That same month, the Altamont Festival was held in Livermore, California. It was to be a free concert, a gift to fans from the British rock group, the Rolling Stones, to climax their tour of the United States. Altamont, however, was far from a success. Fights broke out, and people were beaten. The members of Hell's Angels, a motorcycle gang that the Stones had hired to police the area, attacked some of the fans. *Rolling Stone* magazine called it the Altamont Death Festival because of the violence that resulted in four deaths and the "commercial cynicism" behind the festival in the first place.

New Trends. By the 1970's rock had become a big business with international appeal. Experimentation with electronic effects had made the music more sophisticated, and new groups and new variations had begun to appear.

In 1975 a new dance called the Hustle took hold. Said to have originated years before among the blacks and Puerto Ricans of New York City, it brought bodily contact back into dancing. Featured in the 1978 movie, *Saturday Night Fever,* it made a national pastime of **disco,** music punctuated by insistent rhythms said to approximate the beat of the human heart. Disco dancing became fashionable all over the country. Elegant clothes that enhanced the fixed dance steps and routines of the couples on the dance floor sold in huge quantities at all price ranges.

In 1976 more innovations came in the form of New Wave bands, which tried to recover the simplicity and raw energy of early rock. With the New Wave arrived the punk rockers. They wore their spiky dyed hair in bizarre styles; dressed in crude colors, black leather, and chains; painted their faces with startling color; and sang songs with lyrics that were earthy and deliberately shocking.

By the end of the decade, rock was stronger than ever before. The difference was in the number and variety of styles of the groups who performed it.

Discuss with students what followers of the eastern theologies found that they did not find in traditional western religions.

SECTION REVIEW

1. Identify the following: Allan Kapnow, Roy Lichtenstein, Joseph Heller, Alex Haley, Woodstock.
2. Why was pop art representative of the times?
3. How did movies such as *Easy Rider* affect the film-making industry?
4. Why did the Beatles have so much influence on the music world?

3 Religion

In the 1960's many young Americans began to express a new interest in religion, and college courses in the subject grew in number and diversity. For some, however, the traditional religions did not provide the answers they sought. They began to look toward eastern theologies, magic, mysticism, and the supernatural. As a result, American religious life became more diverse than it had been at any time since the 1800's. The established churches became more secular, and new sects based on the beliefs of the East began to appear and take hold.

The Hare Krishna

One such sect was the Hare Krishna, which was founded in New York City in 1965. Its founder was His Divine Grace A. C. Bhaktivedanta Srila Prabhupad, who established a temple in the East Village upon his arrival from India. His mystical teachings attracted many hippies.

Older Americans could not understand the sect's attraction for young people who had rebelled against authority. If anything, the Hare Krishna were more authoritative and rigid than the American establishment had ever been. The Hare Krishna regarded themselves as the most orthodox component of the Hindu religion.

Dressed in saffron-colored robes, disciples paid homage to the Hindu god Krishna by chanting "Hare Krishna" to the accompaniment of tinkling bells. A mystical sect, it distinguished itself from other such sects by forbidding smoking, drinking, drugs, gambling, and the eating of meat, fish, and eggs. Engaging in sex was prohibited for any purpose but procreation.

Despite its severe lifestyle, the Hare Krishna flourished. By the late 1970's their home in New York City had become a 14-story temple-hostel. In addition, the sect had about 30 temples in the United States and even more in various parts of Western Europe. In 1978 the sect opened a $2 million temple in Juhu, India. Hare Krishna membership had grown rapidly and was represented by some 10,000 full-time monks in various parts of the world.

Beginning in the 1960's, the nation experienced a rebirth in religious participation. Most Americans became involved in traditional religions. Others became members of religious sects based on Eastern thought, such as Hare Krishna. What other changes occurred in American religious life?

Point out that evangelical preachers with flamboyant styles and large followings were criticized by more traditional ministers in the mid-18th and early 19th centuries. Some television evangelists are criticized for similar reasons.

The Old-Time Religions

By the 1970's a reaction had set in, and a move to restore Christ and Christianity to America was well underway. **Evangelists,** those who enthusiastically preach and disseminate the Gospel, began to gather more and more followers. Such preachers as Oral Roberts, Rex Humbard, Billy Graham, and Jim Bakker spread their messages far and wide. In the late 1970's, there were more than 800 radio and television shows devoted to Christian doctrine. In the opinion of one well-known sociologist, the evangelicals had become "the most active and vital aspect of American religion today."

More and more Americans became Born Again Christians, bringing God and Christianity back into their lives. Their numbers included Black Panther leader Eldridge Cleaver, Watergate conspirator Charles W. Colson, and movie idol John Travolta. One Born Again Christian spoke for many when he told how he felt when he decided to "return to Christ."

I cannot describe it, except a serene feeling came over me. I felt like crying but I was very happy. I felt very much in tune with God, all filled with love, totally nonviolent, compassion for everyone. I begged forgiveness for hurting anyone, and I asked God to get into my life.

The Unification Church

The growth of Born Again Christianity did not mean an end to American interest in other sects. One such sect, which became the subject of much debate and controversy, was the Holy Spirit Association for the Unification of World Christianity. The Association's first church had been established in 1954 in Seoul, Korea, by Reverend Sun Myung Moon. In 1973 Reverend Moon toured the United States in the hope of bringing Americans into his church. He told his audiences that Jesus had revealed to him the "true meaning of the Bible's coded message." Reverend Moon then went on to share the revelation with his listeners.

In 1974 Reverend Moon held a mass meeting in New York City's Madison Square Garden. There he announced that "The time of the Second Coming of Christ is near, and America is the landing site!" Two years later, he held another rally in the Garden—the "Bicentennial God Bless America" festival. By this time he had built up a small but very devoted following in the United States and a worldwide following of millions.

By the end of the decade, Reverend Moon had acquired financial and other enterprises in various parts of the world and was said to be worth many millions of dollars. His assets in the United States alone, which included the $1.2 million Unification Church headquarters in New York City, land in California, and real estate in New York's Hudson's Valley, were estimated at more than $20 million. In addition, he was chairman of five Korean corporations that produced everything from rifles to ginseng tea. The corporations increased his wealth by anywhere from $15 to $30 million.

Although Reverend Moon's followers had complete faith in him, many of their families and relatives did not. In the United States and Japan, parents of some Moonies, as his followers were called, began to claim that their children had been brainwashed. They insisted that their children were being psychologically coerced into remaining with the Unification Church. When the youth refused to leave the Church, some parents took their claims to court. Others simply kidnapped their own children and sent them to centers like the Freedom of Thought Foundation in Tucson, Arizona, for "deprogramming"—a kind of brainwashing in reverse.

The People's Temple

Another sect, or cult, that came to prominence in the 1970's was the People's Temple. It was originally founded in Indianapolis, Indiana, in 1955 by James Warren Jones. In 1964 Jones, who by then was head of the Indiana Human Rights Commission and a dedicated champion of desegregation, became an ordained minister of the Disciples of Christ. In 1967 he moved to California and established the People's Temple cult in Los Angeles and San Francisco.

By the mid-1970's Jones was convinced that the CIA and other federal agencies in the United States were out to destroy him. He was just as sure that the United States was doomed to suffer a full-fledged war between the races. As a result, he bought a 900-acre (360-hectare) plot of land in Guyana. There he established a colony for his followers called Jonestown.

The mass suicide at Jonestown illustrates the power a cult leader can have over followers. Discuss whether the government has any right to investigate or regulate such cults.

In August 1977 *New West* magazine came out with an exposé of activities in the People's Temple. According to *New West,* members of the Temple had been beaten and threatened with death to get them to sign over their financial assets to the cult. In this way, millions of dollars in assets had been accumulated by Temple leaders.

Relations of the Jonestown colonists also claimed that Jones was abusing the rights of his followers. They charged that he considered any form of criticism as treason and would not allow anyone to leave the colony. In November 1978 Representative Leo J. Ryan of California headed a special group that went to Guyana to investigate. On November 17, three days after the group's arrival, Ryan, who had angered Jones by agreeing to take some colonists back to the United States, was gunned down with four others at a nearby airstrip.

Late that same night, Jones called together his followers. He told them that he had ordered the killings and that the Guyanese army was on its way to Jonestown. He urged the colonists not to be taken and to "die with dignity." The result was what came to be known as one of history's largest mass murders and suicides. More than 900 colonists, 180 of whom were children, died from drinking a mixture of Kool-Aid and cyanide prepared in barrels made from rusty oil drums. Jones was found at the suicide site with a bullet in his head. The Jonestown massacre, which received extensive coverage from the media, horrified the nation.

SECTION REVIEW

1. Identify the following: Oral Roberts, Sun Myung Moon, James Jones.
2. What lifestyle was practiced by members of the Hare Krishna?
3. How did evangelists use the media to spread Christian doctrine?
4. Why did many people object to the Unification Church?
5. Why did members of the People's Temple move to Guyana?

4 The Media

In 1964 Marshall McLuhan, a Canadian sociologist and the director of the Centre for Culture and Technology at Toronto University, released his book, *Understanding Media.* It became an immediate best-seller in the United States. In it, McLuhan put forth his theory that "the medium is the message." In other words, the key fact in history was not content or information but the way in which people got that content or information. He claimed that traditional intellectual and aesthetic standards had been changed

UTILIZATION OF MEDIA, 1950–1980

ITEM	UNIT	1950	1955	1960	1965	1970	1975	1980
Households with								
Radio sets	Percent	92.6	96.4	96.3	98.6	98.6	98.6	99.0
Average number of sets	Number	2.1	2.4	3.7	4.1	5.1	5.6	5.5
Television sets	Percent	9	65	87	93	95	97	98
Average number of sets	Number	1.01	1.03	1.13	1.22	1.39	1.54	1.67
Color set households	Millions	—	.05	.3	2.8	20.9	46.9	63.4
Average viewing per day	Hours	4.6	4.9	5.1	5.5	5.9	6.1	6.3
Cable television								
Systems	Number	70	400	640	1325	2490	3506	4225
Subscribers	Millions	.01	.15	.65	1.3	4.5	9.8	15.5
Daily newspaper circulation								
Number	Millions	53.8	56.1	58.9	60.4	62.1	60.7	62.2

or had been totally destroyed by the new mass media.

A great many Americans agreed with McLuhan. Many parents in particular were happy to blame the media rather than themselves for the changing attitudes of their children. However, the media could not be given full responsibility for all the changes taking place, although it could be called a contributor to them.

Television

In 1961 Newton Minnow, the new chairman of the Federal Communications Commission, strongly criticized the television industry. He told the communications executives who had gathered to hear him speak what they would find if they watched their television screens:

> *I can assure you that you will observe a vast wasteland. You will see a procession of game shows, violence, audience participation shows, formula comedies about totally unbelievable families, blood and thunder, mayhem, violence, sadism, murder, western badmen, western good men, private eyes, gangsters, more violence, and cartoons. And endlessly, commercials—many screaming, cajoling, and offending.*

He then went on to warn that there was "nothing permanent or sacred about a broadcast license." Minnow's warning led to some changes. But since the general viewing public seemed satisfied with what they were being offered, there was no major transformation of the industry.

Three years later, Marshall McLuhan made a totally different type of statement about television. In his view, television, along with other new forms of electronic communications, were "hatching one of the greatest revolutions ever to hit Western man." This time, there was general agreement. Some of the new shows on television not only reflected but also helped foster some of the changes taking place in American society at the time.

When McLuhan made his comment, one of the most popular shows on television was *That Was the Week That Was*, an irreverent weekly news summary. Two years later, the number one show was

Batman, a tongue-in-cheek presentation of the comic strip superhero. It led to the sale of more than 1000 different items from toy Batmobiles to Batmasks to Batman posters to Batman record albums. Americans were so crazy about the show that, when it was interrupted for special news bulletins on the fate of the *Gemini* spaceship and its astronauts, the television network was flooded with calls from angry viewers.

Batman was not the only hero to capture devoted fans in 1966. That same year, a science-fiction series called *Star Trek* was launched. It centered on the interstellar adventures of the crew of the spaceship *Enterprise*. The two leading characters were the strongwilled Captain Kirk, played by William Shatner, and the pointy-eared "Vulcan" Mr. Spock, played by Leonard Nimoy. Although only 78 episodes of the series were made before the show was cancelled, it had a lasting effect. Ardent fans who called themselves "Trekkies" kept the phenomenon of the series going.

By 1972 Star Trek books, magazines, model kits, posters, and other items related to the series had developed into a multimillion dollar industry. The following year, the networks began broadcasting reruns of the show. This led to annual Trekkie conventions all over the country. *Star Trek's* place in history was assured when the Smithsonian Institute acquired a copy of the show's pilot script and several of the props used in the show's filming.

In 1967 a comedy show called *Laugh-In* came into vogue. Hosted by Dan Rowan and Dick Martin, it featured a group of young comedians in stand-up comedy routines, blackout sketches, zany songs and dances, and other camera-oriented quick studies. The show made stars of such people as Lily Tomlin and Goldie Hawn. It also contributed new clichés, such as "Sock it to Me," to the American vocabulary.

Of all the new television series to air in the 1970's, three very different types of comedies attracted the most attention. One was *The Mary Tyler Moore Show*, which was about a single woman trying to build a career at a Minneapolis television station. It ran for seven years before Moore decided to end the series while it was still popular.

Another was *M*A*S*H*, the continuing saga of a medical unit in Korea during the Korean War. It ran even longer than *The Mary Tyler Moore Show*. It, too,

One reason that critics fear the power of the media is that the number of news outlets is shrinking, resulting in less coverage and fewer points of view. Only 185 cities have more than two newspapers. Two wire services, the three national television networks, and four national radio networks are the prime sources for our national and international news.

was brought to an end while still very high in the ratings.

The third comedy was *All in the Family,* created by producer Norman Lear. The pilot show, which aired in January 1971, was not very successful. But by the end of the year, the show had won four Emmies, including one for the best new show of the year, and was being viewed by 35 million people. By 1978 it had an audience of 50 million. The show, which centered on the trials and tribulations of a working-class New Yorker trying to cope with the changing society of the 1970's, was an unconventional comedy. It broke taboos by discussing topics not generally allowed on television. Further, it put common prejudices and bigotry up front for everyone to see. While some people were offended, that did not stop most of them from watching it.

The New Journalism

Newspapers, too, changed a great deal in the 1960's and 1970's. During the 1960's, 160 daily newspapers ceased to exist, and 176 new ones appeared. Some of these were part of the **underground press**—newspapers put out by members of the counterculture.

Established newspapers also changed. In 1963 Clay Felker, the editor of the Sunday supplement of the *New York World Journal Tribune,* began featuring a different style of reporting. Called New Journalism, it was highly personal and very expressionistic. Instead of merely stating basic facts, it incorporated some of the techniques previously used only in works of fiction. Language became more colorful. Stories became more dramatic. Reporters even began to make inferences and to editorialize. For many Americans, New Journalism made the daily news more alive and certainly more exciting.

A prime example of the power and impact of the media could be found in the coverage of the Patty Hearst case, which made headlines and inspired commentary in all forms of the media for a period of several years. The case involved the kidnapping of 19-year-old Patty Hearst, the granddaughter of William Randolph Hearst, the founder of the Hearst publishing empire, and the daughter of Randolph A. Hearst, the publisher of the *San Francisco Examiner.*

The Patty Hearst kidnapping became one of the major news stories of 1974. Hearst was seized by members of a revolutionary group, but within two months was aiding her captors. Later Hearst claimed she did so only under duress. What is significant about the news coverage of the Hearst story?

The crime was carried out by a violent revolutionary group known as the Symbionese Liberation Army (SLA).

The SLA demanded that Randolph Hearst distribute $230 million in free food to the poor in exchange for his daughter. Hearst began a food distribution program, but soon afterwards he received a taped message from her, saying that she was not satisfied with what was being done to obtain her release. Eventually, Patty Hearst announced that she no longer wanted her freedom and that she was joining the SLA. A few weeks later, she was identified as one of a group of armed robbers who had held up a San Francisco bank. Despite extensive efforts on the part

Psychologists note that people in captivity under extreme stress may come to admire and identify with their captors. This mental defense mechanism helps people cope with a situation in which they have no control.

of the authorities, she was not apprehended until September 18, 1975. Following a highly publicized trial in which she testified that she had not joined the SLA voluntarily, she was sentenced to 35 years in jail. In May 1978, after a series of appeals, her sentence was reduced to 7 years. In 1979 she was released under an executive clemency order signed by President Carter.

From the moment the kidnapping had taken place, the media had remained in the forefront, keeping the American people informed. Each incident was reported and discussed at length. Some of the reports, however, were highly sensationalized and not very objectively presented. The episode led many Americans to question the role and the authority of the media in America.

SECTION REVIEW

1. Identify the following: Marshall McLuhan, Trekkies, Norman Lear.
2. What is meant by the theory that "the medium is the message"?
3. What criticisms were made of television?
4. What was New Journalism?

5 A Changing World

The changes that took place in the United States during the 1960's and 1970's affected not just youth and the middle class but Americans of all ages, ethnic groups, and classes.

In the 1960's, for example, the physical condition of Americans in general became better. Real income went up and poverty declined, especially among blacks. Corporations grew and merged and grew some more. Universities expanded as never before, and the first black studies programs were launched. Older Americans found a new lifestyle as the first **retirement town,** a community tailored exclusively for those 50 years of age or older, was opened in Arizona. Unmarried Americans found a new way to improve their social lives as the first singles-only weekend was held at Grossinger's Hotel in the Catskill Mountains of New York and the first singles-only apartment complex opened in California. And, under the lead of a young lawyer named Ralph Nader, Americans began to band together to form

Sports journalists and announcers helped create sports' first golden era in the 1920's.

consumer groups to help protect their rights in the marketplace.

The Sports Arena

The decade of the 1960's also was a turning point in the history of athletics. This was due in great part to television. When the television networks offered the professional athletic leagues deals amounting to many millions of dollars for telecasting rights, they set off an unexpected series of events. Professional athletes began to make demands that previously would never have been considered. Salary became a big issue for athletes such as baseball's Johnny Bench and basketball's Wilt Chamberlain.

The network deals also stimulated a period of great expansion in professional sports. In 1960 there were

Sports are no longer dominated by men. Women athletes, such as golfer Nancy Lopez, have made their mark. On the amateur level, scholastic programs for women athletes are growing. What are other significant trends in sports?

Discuss with students whether the commercialization of sports has benefited sports or hurt them.

The laser is one of many devices that appeared in science fiction before becoming a reality.

Muhammad Ali is the first boxer to win the heavyweight title on four different occasions. His accomplishments in the ring, his lively personality, and the controversies surrounding him made Ali one of the best-known athletes of the 1960's. What accounted for the growing interest in athletes and sports during the 1960's?

16 major league baseball teams, and they drew 16.1 million people as fans. By 1969 the number of teams had risen to 24 and the number of fans to 27.2 million. The same was true in other sports. Between 1967 and 1969 the number of teams in the National Hockey League doubled. The National Football League expanded first to 16 teams and then, through a merger with the American Football League, to 24 teams.[3]

At the same time, an age of athletic entrepreneurship had gotten underway. It began in 1965 when the American Football League offered Joe Namath, a quarterback from the University of Alabama, $427,-000 to play for the New York Jets. The Jets hoped that Namath would make their games exciting enough to lure fans away from the National League's established New York Giants. Namath, who was known as "Broadway Joe," became an overnight celebrity, entertaining the fans both on and off the football field. He began endorsing products, doing spots in commercials, appearing on television shows, and performing in movies. Soon other professional athletes followed suit.

By the 1970's sports had become a bigger business than ever before. The competition was tough, and the various leagues found themselves bargaining for

[3]Today the NFL has 28 teams and baseball has 26 major league teams.

talent. As a result, even rookies could demand—and get—top dollar. Some players signed contracts for salaries far beyond the comprehension of the average American.

The Computer Age

With the 1960's came rapid progress in science and technology. The first big step was taken in 1960 when a scientist at the Hughes Aircraft Company in California built the first **laser**, an instrument that produces a highly concentrated beam of light. It could release concentrated electrical energy as laser light. By the 1970's, lasers were refined enough to be used in such diverse applications as industrial drilling, medical surgery, weather studies, and holography, a form of three-dimensional photography.

Computers, which had been developed in the 1950's, were greatly improved by the 1960's. The earlier computers had been large and cumbersome, with circuits controlled by bulky vacuum tubes. In the 1960's scientists invented transistors, which shrank the size of computers. Computers suddenly were in demand everywhere. Life insurance firms, for example, established a Medical Information Bureau that used computers to maintain files on 11 million insurance applicants. The more than 2000 investigating firms of the Associated Credit Bureaus used

Projects are underway to devise computers that understand ordinary speech and to improve computer memories and auxiliary storage equipment.

The computer was once the domain of science, business, and industry. Today many homes have one. What changes are taking place because of the computer?

computers to store and exchange information on more than 100 million persons who had applied for credit. Even finding a date for Saturday night could be achieved by computer. Hundreds of computerized dating agencies sprang up all over the country.

In the 1970's computers became even more sophisticated as their circuits were miniaturized in **micro chips**—tiny chips of silicon smaller than a postage stamp. Before long, the computer was in use everywhere from supermarket checkout counters to high school classrooms to doctors' offices. As computers enabled more and more industries and professions to automate, they began to threaten some jobs and create others. As a result, by the end of the decade, some Americans were beginning to view them and other advances in technology as mixed blessings.

SECTION REVIEW

1. Identify the following: Ralph Nader, Joe Namath, Wilt Chamberlain.
2. How did television affect sports?
3. What changes were made in computers between the 1950's and the 1970's?
4. What were some of the uses of computers?

CHAPTER **32**   REVIEW

SUMMARY

1. In the 1960's many young people rebelled against the values of the older generation and developed their own culture.
2. The youth culture, or counterculture, included positive elements, such as an emphasis on peace and love, and negative elements, such as drug use.
3. Some elements of the counterculture were gradually absorbed by other groups in American society.
4. The arts reflected the rapidly changing social and cultural values of the 1960's and 1970's.
5. A new interest in religion led to both a revival of Christianity and the establishment of new religious cults.
6. Developments in the media both contributed to and were affected by social and cultural changes.
7. Rapid advancements in science and technology brought the age of computers to American society.

VOCABULARY

generation gap	panhandling	pop art	discotheques	underground press
youth culture	commune	jet set	acid rock	retirement town
counterculture	hallucinogens	black humor	disco	laser
hippies	happenings	folk rock	evangelists	micro chips

REVIEW QUESTIONS

1. Why did young people have so much influence on American culture in the 1960's and 1970's?
2. How did countercultural values differ from establishment values?
3. How did American society react to the counterculture movement?
4. How did literature reflect the changes taking place in America?
5. What major developments took place in music in the 1960's and 1970's?
6. What changes took place in the world of sports?
7. What were some of the effects of computers?

DISCUSSION

1. Do young people today have the same attitudes toward the older generation as the youth of the 1960's? Why or why not?
2. Should any action be taken to restrict the actions of religious cults? Why or why not?
3. How much influence does the media have on the way people think and behave?
4. Why are changes in technology sometimes seen as a threat? Are such fears justified? Why or why not?

USING TABLES

Refer to the table on page 713 and answer the following questions:

1. How many households had color television in 1960? In 1975?
2. What trend is apparent in the number of hours per day spent viewing television?
3. How does the number of subscribers to cable television systems in 1970 compare to 1980?
4. What is indicated by the change in newspaper circulation between 1950 and 1980?
5. In general, which medium is used by the most people?

USING SKILLS

Study the following general statements about hippies and then decide which ones show evidence of emotional bias and which ones show an attempt to be objective:

1. "They took their tactics from Gandhi, their idealism from philosophy class, and their money from Daddy."
2. "I have no objection to any herd of semi-domesticated animals roaming the country, uttering their mating cries and scratching their pelts, as long as they avoid centers of civilization and congregate only in college auditoriums."
3. "Many of them are fools, and most of them will be sellouts but they're a better generation than we were."
4. "The media viewed them as harmless, even amusing, freaks—which was probably closest to the truth."

1	Domestic Affairs Under Carter	721
2	Carter's Foreign Policy	725
3	The Election of 1980	731
4	Reagan's Domestic Policy	733
5	Reagan's Foreign Policy	737
6	Staying the Course	743

CARTER AND REAGAN

Our government has no power except that granted it by the people. It is time to check and reverse the growth of government which shows signs of having grown beyond the consent of the governed.

RONALD REAGAN

During the late 1970's and early 1980's, Americans were uncertain about the future of their country. At home the economy suffered from high inflation, rising unemployment, and a continuing energy crisis. Abroad the United States faced the growing power of the Soviet Union and a Third World that increasingly acted independently of the two superpowers. Instability in the Third World, however, often helped the Soviet Union and worked against American interests. Because of this, the United States began to rebuild its military strength and to intervene in world "trouble spots."

Frustrated by developments in foreign affairs and disillusioned by the Watergate scandal, Americans looked for new national leaders who would be committed to traditional values and creative in solving difficult problems. In 1976 and 1980, voters elected Presidents who came from outside the established political circles in Washington, D.C.

1 Domestic Affairs Under Carter

Jimmy Carter was sworn in as the 39th President of the United States on January 20, 1977. He was the first President from the deep South since before the Civil War. In his inaugural address, Carter promised an open administration that would "restore the confidence of the American people in their own government."

An Informal Presidency

After the inaugural ceremony, Carter and his family walked up Pennsylvania Avenue from the Capitol to the White House instead of riding in the traditional limousine. This gesture symbolized Carter's desire to create a more informal Presidency. Carter wanted to be seen as a common person. For this reason, he wanted to be known officially as "Jimmy Carter" rather than "James Earl Carter, Jr." On trips throughout the country, he often attended public meetings and answered questions from ordinary citizens. He also visited people in their homes.

In the White House, Carter and his wife Rosalyn lived a relatively simple lifestyle.[1] Both of them came from close-knit southern families that stressed hard work, dedication, simplicity, and religion. Many of Carter's personal and political attitudes sprang from his Baptist faith. In his autobiography, *Why Not the Best?*, Carter emphasized the importance of religious ideals in national life.

In keeping with his religious beliefs, Carter was concerned about bringing thrift and morality back to government. He worked to reduce "red tape" at the White House and cut down on "frills" such as chauffeur service for his staff. Carter also issued guidelines to guard against political corruption and other forms of unethical conduct in his administration.

Efficient Government

One of Carter's goals was to provide more efficient government at less cost to taxpayers. In March 1977 he received authority from Congress to reorganize the executive branch of government over a three-year period. With this grant of power, Carter merged existing agencies and created new government departments. He set up the Department of Energy in 1977 and the Department of Education in 1979.

Welfare and Taxes. Carter also tried to reform federal government spending for social programs. His administration planned to lower welfare benefits for people with higher incomes, while raising those for

---

[1] Rosalyn Carter was an active First Lady. She participated in many of her husband's decisions and became involved in social causes. In February 1977 she appeared before a Senate committee to press for more federal programs for the mentally ill. Her Senate testimony was the first one given by a First Lady since Eleanor Roosevelt.

the truly needy. To obtain more money for social programs, the Carter administration wanted to simplify the payment of taxes. At the same time, it hoped to end certain tax breaks for business and close **"loopholes,"** or technicalities in the law that allowed people to avoid paying taxes. Congress, however, rejected Carter's welfare and tax reforms because of opposition from special interest groups. The fact that Congress failed to pass these reforms was a major setback for the President.

Civil Service Reform.   Carter also wanted to reform the federal civil service system. In the fall of 1978, with the President's backing, Congress passed the first civil service reform law since the Pendleton Act of 1883. The new legislation tightened promotion rules, linked pay raises to job performance, and ended automatic pay increases for certain employees. In signing the bill into law, Carter hailed the reform as a fulfillment of his campaign pledge to improve the federal bureaucracy and to make it more responsive to citizens' needs.

Supreme Court Decisions

During Carter's term of office, the Supreme Court made a number of landmark decisions in civil rights. Two important cases concerned **affirmative action**—programs that promote the employment or education of women or minority groups. Many such programs were begun in the late 1960's and early 1970's. Some were required by local, state, or federal law, while others were voluntary. All were intended to remedy the effects of past discrimination. But some people felt that giving special treatment to certain groups amounted to "reverse discrimination."

For example, the University of California turned down Allan Bakke, a white, when he applied to medical school. The university admitted that Bakke was better qualified than some minority students, but it had set a quota of 16 minorities out of every 100 students. Bakke sued.

In June 1977 the Supreme Court ruled in *University of California* v. *Bakke* that universities and colleges could not use specific quotas to achieve racial balance. However, institutions of higher learning could still give special consideration to minority groups in choosing among applicants for admission. On the other hand two years later, the Court stated in *Kaiser Aluminum and Chemical Corporation* v. *Weber* that employers and unions could establish voluntary programs, including the use of quotas, to aid minorities and women in employment.

Immigration

The increasing number of immigrants coming to the United States put new pressures on the Carter administration. In the spring of 1980, thousands of

The role of women in the work force has changed dramatically in this century. More women now work outside the home than ever before. Many women also work in fields that a few years ago were dominated by men. The affirmative action programs of the 1970's have helped women and members of minorities gain higher-paying jobs. What do affirmative action programs do?

refugees fled Cuba and arrived in Florida. Carter at first declared a policy of "open hearts and open arms" to the new arrivals. However, more Cubans came than he had expected. Cuban leader Fidel Castro also responded to Carter's generosity by opening his prisons and shipping many "undesirables" out of Cuba. Florida authorities soon complained that they could not handle the housing, employment, and medical needs of the refugees. Carter then imposed restrictions to reduce the flow of Cubans to a more manageable level.

At the same time, other refugees from the Caribbean island of Haiti—most of whom were black and French-speaking—tried to enter the United States. The Justice Department, however, blocked their admission. It claimed that the Haitians were not political refugees like the Cubans. The Haitians claimed that they were fleeing oppression as well as poverty. They demanded that American officials give them equal treatment. Black and civil rights groups pressured the government to grant refugee status and aid to the Haitians. The administration finally changed its policy and admitted the Haitians to the United States under the same terms that it had granted to the Cubans.

Energy

Carter believed that the energy crisis was America's most serious domestic problem. In the late 1970's, the United States, with 6 percent of the world's population, was using 30 percent of the world's energy. Foreigners complained about Americans using too much energy. At home, experts warned that the country had to reduce its use of oil if the world supply was to last. At the same time, the United States was still dependent on foreign oil, which hurt the American economy. Whenever OPEC nations raised their oil prices, inflation climbed in the United States.

Carter's Program. In April 1977 Carter presented a national energy program to Congress. The purpose of the program was to promote conservation and to move away from depending on oil to using coal and renewable energy sources. In his address, Carter stated:

Our program will emphasize conservation. The amount of energy wasted which could be saved

Although members of OPEC often squabbled among themselves, they did unite in the late 1970's to raise the price of oil several times. In 1977 President Carter presented a national energy program to Congress. What proposals did he make?

is greater than the total energy that we are importing from foreign countries. We will also stress development of our rich coal reserves in an environmentally sound way. We will emphasize research on solar energy, and other renewable energy sources, and we will maintain strict safeguards on necessary atomic energy production.

To encourage conservation, Carter wanted to put higher tariffs on imported oil. He also wanted a gradual lifting of federal controls on domestic oil prices. Both actions were intended to raise prices at gas stations and cause people to use less fuel.

Carter also called for a new cabinet-level Department of Energy to carry out the program. The progam included taxes for owners of cars that used a great deal of gasoline, a 5-cents per gallon tax on gas "at the pump," and tax credits to industries and individuals who conserved energy in their factories and homes. A tax penalty would also be placed on industries that relied too heavily on oil instead of on coal and other energy sources.

Opposition. Carter's energy program met with strong opposition from business, labor, and consumer groups. Energy producers charged that the program

The nuclear power industry has suffered severe setbacks because of public protests and rising costs.

Review the relationship between budget deficits and inflation.

stressed conservation to the neglect of energy production. They wanted a total lifting of government controls on domestic oil prices and rejected any government taxes or penalties that would interfere with their profits. The auto industry was against the tax on cars. It believed that such a tax would lead to a loss of car sales and add to unemployment.

Consumer groups criticized the gradual lifting of gasoline prices. They said that it would hurt both the poor and working people who had to depend on trucks or cars for their work. Many Americans believed that the energy crisis was a hoax. Some of them felt that energy producers were hoarding gasoline and creating shortages to raise their profits. Others blamed the federal government for poor management of the economy.

Congress also opposed many features of Carter's energy plan and rewrote much of it. At the end of 1977, Congress finally passed a bill that was acceptable to the President. The new energy law gave industry and individual citizens tax breaks for conserving energy, placed penalty taxes on "gas-guzzling" cars, and approved the creation of the Department of Energy.

Although energy legislation was finally passed, oil imports remained at a high level, and gasoline prices rose. However, people gradually began to use less gasoline and conserve energy.

Nuclear Power. During Carter's term of office, the public became increasingly concerned about the safety of nuclear power. In April 1979 a major accident occurred at the Three Mile Island nuclear power plant near Harrisburg, Pennsylvania. The plant's nuclear reactor released a small amount of radiation over a five-mile area. Uncertain of the danger, the governor of Pennsylvania ordered an immediate evacuation. Five days later, the crisis eased. At that time, nuclear officials announced that the reactor was stable and that radiation levels near Three Mile Island were safe.

However, the accident frightened many people and threatened the future growth of nuclear power in the United States. An anti-nuclear protest movement soon spread throughout the country. In the fall of 1979, 200,000 people marched in New York City against the use of nuclear power. President Carter, however, was unwilling to halt the nuclear energy program, which provided about 13 percent of the nation's energy needs. At the same time, supporters of nuclear power tried to reassure Americans that nuclear power with proper safeguards was no danger to people or the environment.

The Economy

During the Carter administration, the American economy continued to be troubled by inflation and unemployment. When Carter took office in 1977, a mild recession had caused an increase in unemployment. At the same time, severe winter weather and fuel shortages added to the economic slowdown. The President introduced a $31.2 billion program to create jobs, cut taxes, and increase production. However by the year's end, the economy had improved enough for the Carter administration to drop many features of the program.

Inflation. In 1978 inflation replaced unemployment as the country's chief economic problem. To fight inflation, Carter worked to reduce government spending and balance the budget. He also urged business to avoid big price increases and asked labor to hold down wage demands. Carter's calls for restraint, however, were not heeded by business and labor leaders. Some critics demanded that the President impose mandatory, or enforced, wage and price controls. But Carter regarded mandatory controls as unworkable.

The Carter administration also found it difficult to control government spending. It faced higher and higher budget deficits. State and local governments also had trouble controlling spending. As a result, inflation continued to rise.

Taxpayers' Revolt. In mid-1978 citizens began to act on their own to reduce government spending and stop inflation. At that time, California voters passed Proposition 13, a state constitutional amendment to reduce property taxes by 57 percent. The California tax issue attracted national attention. Soon a taxpayers' revolt swept the country. Laws curbing government spending were passed in many states. Also, 26 state legislatures called on Congress to pass a constitutional amendment that would bar the federal government from spending beyond its means.

"Supply-side" Economics. Meanwhile Republicans began to promote new ideas to cut government spending. They adopted a new economic theory

Carter had the Department of State issue annual reports on the status of human rights in every country that received foreign aid from the United States. Carter also spoke out against the apartheid policies of Rhodesia and South Africa.

UNEMPLOYMENT, 1941–1983

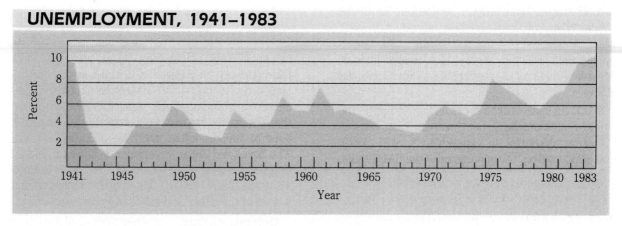

known as **"supply-side" economics.** The theory called for increasing the production (supply) of goods by means of tax cuts and other incentives to work, save, and invest.

This way of stimulating production was in contrast to "demand-side" policies used by the government since the New Deal. "Demand" policies sought the same goal of increased production through a different method—that of increased government spending. Supporters of the supply-side theory said that tax cuts would encourage people to invest in business. As a result, business would grow, provide jobs, and bring the government additional revenue in taxes. Economic growth, they claimed, would occur without inflation.

Influenced by supply-side theory, Senator William Roth of Delaware and Representative Jack Kemp of New York, both Republicans, introduced a bill in Congress. The Kemp-Roth bill called for a 33 percent cut in federal income taxes over a three-year period. It received strong backing from Ronald Reagan, the major spokesperson for conservative Republicanism. Through his newspaper column, radio broadcasts, and public appearances, Reagan convinced a large number of Republicans to support supply-side economics.

Congressional Elections.   Inflation became a major issue in the 1978 congressional elections. Reflecting a national trend against "big" government, voters in 13 states passed laws placing limits on state taxation and spending. The Republicans benefited from this trend. They picked up 3 Senate seats, 12 House seats, and 6 governorships. But the Democrats still held majorities in both Houses of Congress.

SECTION REVIEW

1. Identify the following: Three Mile Island, Proposition 13, Jack Kemp.
2. How did Carter reorganize the executive branch of government?
3. What important decision did the Supreme Court make in the area of civil rights?
4. Why were refugees from Haiti at first denied admission to the United States?
5. Why did Ronald Reagan call for tax cuts?

---

2 Carter's Foreign Policy

When Carter first took office, he stressed the importance of idealism and morality in American foreign policy. In his inaugural address, he stated:

> Our foreign policy shall be based on cooperation with our allies, worldwide respect for human rights, reduction in world armaments, and it must always reflect our moral values. I want our nation's actions to make you proud.

The Communist World

Carter hoped to continue détente with the Soviet Union. At the same time, he wanted to promote human rights in Soviet-bloc nations. In early 1977 he sent a letter to Andrei Sakharov, a leading Soviet **dissident,** or opponent of government policies. In his letter, Carter expressed support for Sakharov's stand on human rights issues. The President also defended other human rights activists in the Soviet Union. Many of them had been arrested or were being persecuted by Soviet authorities. The Soviet government reacted angrily to Carter's actions, regarding them as an interference in Soviet internal affairs.

SALT. In spite of differences on human rights, the United States and the Soviet Union continued talks on nuclear arms control. In a speech on April 25, 1979, Carter pointed out the importance of the SALT talks:

The issue is whether we will move ahead with strategic arms control or resume a relentless nuclear weapons competition. This is the choice we face—between an imperfect world with a SALT agreement, or an imperfect and more dangerous world without a SALT agreement.

In June 1979 President Carter and Soviet leader Leonid Brezhnev met in Vienna and signed the SALT II treaty. Both leaders hailed their agreement as a step that would reduce the threat of nuclear war.

Soviet Moves. The SALT II treaty had to be ratified by the Senate before it could go into effect. Many Senators, however, were against the treaty. They believed that it did not provide for effective **monitoring** (checking) of arms movements inside the Soviet Union. Thus they felt there was no way to be sure that the Soviets would abide by the terms of the treaty.

Above all, the anti-SALT Senators were concerned about a massive overall Soviet military buildup that had been going on since the mid-1960's. Military experts stated that the Warsaw Pact nations were improving the quality and quantity of their forces faster than the NATO allies. At the same time, the Soviets, according to some reports, seemed to be moving ahead of the United States in nuclear strength.

These fears were heightened by growing Soviet influence around the world. Most Soviet actions were carried out by their allies. In Africa, Cuban troops armed with Soviet weapons backed pro-communist governments in Angola and Ethiopia. The Carter administration wanted to respond to these developments. But since the mid-1970's, Congress had blocked American military aid for armed struggles in Africa. It feared the commitment of American troops and the possibility of another Vietnam.

The United States was also concerned about Soviet activities in Asia and Latin America. In the late 1970's, Soviet-supported Vietnam expanded its influence into neighboring Laos and Cambodia (Kampuchea). In August 1979 the Carter administration revealed that the Soviets had between 2000 and 3000 troops in Cuba. American concern arose that the troops were recent arrivals that might be used to support leftist guerrillas in Latin America. The Soviet and Cuban governments, however, stated that the forces were defensive and had been in Cuba since the early 1960's. The Carter administration later confirmed this, and the controversy soon ended.

Defense Buildup. To offset charges of American military weakness, Carter pledged to boost overall United States military spending. The most controversial weapons system proposed by the administration was the MX, or Mobile-Experimental missile. The MX was a 4-stage rocket equipped with 10 nuclear warheads, each of which could be fired at a separate target. To avoid Soviet detection, the MX missiles were to be based in underground trenches and moved from place to place by a system of tracks. Another weapons system was the cruise missile, a small, highly accurate rocket capable of flying close to the ground to avoid radar detection.

China. Because both the United States and China were concerned about growing Soviet power, they drew closer together. On January 1, 1979, full diplomatic relations were established by the United States and Chinese governments. In the spring of that year, Chinese leader Teng Hsiao-ping became the first Communist Chinese leader to visit the United States. In establishing ties with mainland China, the United States broke official diplomatic ties with the Nationalist government on Taiwan. However, it continued commercial and cultural links and supplied Taiwan with arms.

Israel and Egypt

The Carter administration continued American efforts to reach peace between Israel and the Arab nations. It tried to treat both sides equally. In early 1977, Carter expressed sympathy for a Palestinian "homeland" in the West Bank and Gaza Strip. However, he also affirmed America's support for the independence and security of Israel.

Ask students if they think the Camp David Accords have produced a lasting effect on the conflicts in the Middle East.

At the end of 1977, President Anwar Sadat of Egypt decided to seek peace with Israel. He needed peace to improve Egypt's economy and raise the living standards of its people. In November Sadat visited Israel and met with Israeli Prime Minister Menachem Begin. It was the first visit by an Arab leader to Israel.

Egypt and Israel soon began negotiations to end their differences. A deadlock, however, developed; and both countries called on the United States for help. President Carter then invited the Egyptian and Israeli leaders to a summit meeting at Camp David, the presidential retreat in Maryland. For 13 days, Carter isolated himself with Sadat and Begin. An agreement was finally reached and signed by the three leaders at the White House.

In the Camp David Accords, Sadat and Begin agreed to negotiate a peace treaty and establish diplomatic relations. Egypt would recognize Israel's right to exist. In return Israel would gradually withdraw from the Sinai peninsula and turn it back to the Egyptians. Finally the Egyptian and Israeli leaders pledged to start talks on Palestinian self-rule. After a difficult round of negotiations, both nations finally signed a peace treaty in Washington, D.C., on March 26, 1979. It was the first peace agreement between Israel and an Arab country.

The Camp David Accords were bitterly opposed by some of the other Arab states, such as Libya, Syria, Iraq, and Algeria. They attempted to disrupt Sadat's efforts to bring about peace between Israel and the Arab world. However, moderate Arab states, such as Jordan and Saudi Arabia, refused either to condemn or support Sadat. The United States worked to improve relations with these moderate states and to encourage them to join in Sadat's efforts.

Western Allies

The Carter administration also tried to strengthen the western alliance system. In the late 1970's, the world's industrial democracies faced similar problems of unemployment and inflation. From 1977 to 1980 Carter and other western leaders held economic summit meetings to coordinate their economic policies.

However, ties between the United States and its NATO allies were sometimes strained. Carter

Meetings at Camp David between Anwar Sadat, Jimmy Carter, and Menachem Begin led to a peace treaty and the establishment of normal relations between Egypt and Israel. What was the reaction of Arab nations to the treaty?

wanted prosperous Japan and West Germany to follow trade policies that would help the sluggish American economy. To protect their own economies, these countries refused Carter's advice. Also many of the western allies were against Carter's human rights policies. They claimed that his stand would only cause the Soviets to use harsher measures against dissidents. Meanwhile détente and arms control would be endangered.

In spite of differences, the western allies worked out a common defense policy to meet the Soviet military buildup. In December 1979 European NATO members agreed to install American-made, medium-range missiles in their territories by 1983. The new missiles were needed to match the growing number of similar weapons being installed by the Soviet Union in its territory.

At the same time, President Carter agreed to negotiate with the Soviets on the subject of medium-range missiles. If the Soviets removed their weapons, the United States would negotiate about plans to install medium-range missiles in Western Europe. The Soviets agreed to negotiate, but refused in advance to remove their medium-range missiles. Instead they protested the NATO missiles and began

Compare Carter's foreign policy to that of Woodrow Wilson. Note that Wilson also negotiated a new treaty on the Panama Canal, but failed to get it ratified (see p. 440).

U.S. Marines had helped put Somoza's father in power in 1933.

an intense diplomatic effort to convince Western Europe not to accept them.

Latin America

The Carter administration wanted to see right-wing military governments in Latin America give way to democratic governments. In 1977 it cut economic and military aid to Argentina, Brazil, Guatemala, Nicaragua, Chile, El Salvador, and Uruguay. At the same time, it supported human rights and assured Latin American countries that the United States would treat them as equals.

Panama Canal. Carter also acted to end Latin American bitterness over the Panama Canal. Over the years, American ownership of the canal and its control of the canal zone had caused much friction between the United States and Panama. For nearly two decades, the two countries had been negotiating to reach an agreement on the status of the canal. Finally, in the summer of 1977, an agreement was announced. President Carter and Panamanian leader Omar Torrijos then signed two Panama Canal treaties in Washington, D.C.

Under the terms of the treaties, American rule over the canal zone would continue until December 31, 1999. During this time, the United States would operate, control, and defend the canal. After 1999, Panama would have sovereignty over the zone and the canal. However, the United States was guaranteed the right to use the canal forever. Also, American troops would always have the right to defend the canal in time of war.

Many Americans were opposed to giving the canal to Panama. In the Senate, conservative Republicans tried to block ratification of the treaties. However, Democrats and moderate Republicans supported the treaties. After the treaties were ratified, Carter declared:

> The treaties mark the beginning of a new era in our relations not only with Panama but with all the rest of the world. They symbolize our determination to deal with the . . . small nations of the world on the basis of mutual respect and understanding.

Nicaragua. In 1979 the Carter administration became concerned about the spread of communism in

President Carter and President Torrijos sign the treaties giving Panama eventual control of the Panama Canal and Canal Zone. What did Carter hope to achieve?

Central America. Most of the countries of Central America were ruled by right-wing military governments. Leftist guerrillas backed by Cuba fought against these governments and received wide public support. As a result Carter found himself caught in a dilemma. He did not want to back oppressive right-wing governments. On the other hand, he did not want to support leftist movements that would open the door to communism.

The Carter administration faced its greatest challenge in Nicaragua. There, President Anastasio Somoza refused to allow democracy and freedom. Nicaraguan business groups, students, and peasants opposed Somoza's government. Many of them supported the Sandinista National Liberation Front (SNLF), a left-wing guerrilla organization. Nicaragua became divided by a fierce civil war between Somoza forces and the SNLF.

Carter's human rights policy weakened the long-standing ties between Somoza and the United States. Somoza was soon isolated at home and abroad. In 1977 the United States decided that Somoza had to

Have students discuss what courses of action were open to the United States a) before the Shah was admitted into the country for medical treatment and b) after the hostages were taken.

resign in order to stop a communist takeover by the Sandinistas. American officials tried to negotiate an agreement with the Sandinistas, while pressing for Somoza to quit. When the SNLF agreed not to support communism, Somoza left the country. The Sandinistas then formed a government. Once in power, they established close ties with Cuba and the Soviet Union.

Carter recognized the new Nicaraguan government but watched it closely. To prevent communist takeovers and the need for American military intervention, he increased economic aid to countries in Central America. He hoped that this aid would encourage the rise of moderate, democratic governments.

Iran

In the 1970's Iran was one of the strongest American allies in the Persian Gulf area, a region vital to western oil needs. Shah Mohammed Reza Pahlavi, Iran's ruler, used American aid to build up a powerful military force. He also tried to develop Iran's economy with western technology. When the Shah visited the United States in November 1977, Carter hailed Iran as "a strong, stable, and progressive" society.

At home, however, the Shah ruled as an absolute monarch. He refused to allow political freedoms and jailed his opponents. Many Iranians hated the Shah and the western influences he brought to Iran. They wanted to restore the religion of Islam to a central place in Iranian life. Religious leaders became prominent in the struggle against the Shah.

Revolution. The Carter administration urged the Shah to make reforms and respect human rights. During 1978 the Shah relaxed censorship, allowed greater freedoms to his opponents, and promised free elections. As a result, Iranians believed that the Shah's power was weakening. Demonstrations against his rule soon swept Iran.

By January 1979 the trouble in Iran had become an Islamic revolution. To stop the violence, the Shah finally ended his 37-year reign and went into exile overseas. Meanwhile, critics in the United States blamed the Carter administration for not recognizing how much the Iranians hated the Shah. The critics said that congressional reforms had weakened the

CIA's ability to gather information. They urged an increase in the agency's powers to prevent further setbacks to American interests abroad.

After the Shah left, Ayatollah Ruhollah Khomeini, the most powerful Iranian religious leader, returned to Iran from exile in France. He set up an Islamic republic and removed western influences from Iranian society. Khomeini attacked the United States for backing the Shah and vowed to carry his anti-American Islamic revolution throughout the Middle East.

The Hostage Crisis. In October 1979 the United States admitted the Shah into the country for medical treatment.[2] This action further inflamed Iranian hatred for the United States. On November 4 about 500 Iranian radicals seized the American Embassy in the Iranian capital of Teheran. They held 65 Americans as hostages. The Iranians later released 13 of the hostages. However, they refused to let the others go until the United States returned the Shah to Iran for trial.

The United States turned down the radicals' demands and ordered the Iranian government to release the hostages. Khomeini, however, backed the radicals. Carter then condemned Iran's holding of the hostages as "an act of terrorism outside the boundaries of international law."

The United States threatened to take military action against Iran if the hostages were harmed or put on trial. As a show of strength, it ordered a naval task force into the Indian Ocean near the Persian Gulf. To pressure Iran into releasing the hostages, Carter barred American imports of Iranian oil and seized Iranian deposits in American banks. He also engaged in secret diplomacy with Iranian moderates.

The Iranian seizure of the hostages was condemned by most of the world. The United States got the backing of the United Nations, the International Court of Justice, and the members of NATO. At home, American concern for the hostages led to the greatest outpouring of patriotism since World War II.

By the spring of 1980, Carter's efforts to free the hostages had not succeeded. As a result the President took firmer measures. On April 1 he broke diplomatic relations with Iran, banned all trade (with the exception of food and medicine), and took over

---

[2] The Shah eventually left the United States for Panama. Later he went to Egypt. He died of cancer in Egypt in May 1980.

billions of dollars of Iranian assets in American businesses.

Later in the month, Carter gave the "go-ahead" for a secret mission to go to Iran and rescue the hostages. Before the rescue could be made, a helicopter developed engine trouble in a landing area in the Iranian desert, and the mission was called off. As the Americans left, two planes collided in a take-off accident, killing eight and injuring several others. Americans were shocked and humiliated, and Carter was blamed for a lack of leadership. After the rescue mission failed, the United States again pursued secret diplomacy for the hostages' release.

Afghanistan

While the hostage crisis was going on in Iran, a new international crisis developed in the neighboring country of Afghanistan. In December 1979 Soviet troops invaded the country and set up a communist government loyal to Moscow. They began to fight Muslim guerrillas who opposed communist rule.

The United States and most of the non-communist world denounced the Soviet takeover in Afghanistan. On January 4 Carter said that the Soviet involvement in Afghanistan "was an extremely serious threat to peace. . . . A Soviet-occupied Afghanistan threatened Iran and Pakistan and was a stepping stone to possible control over much of the West's oil supplies" in the Persian Gulf area. Carter tried to convince Brezhnev to withdraw the troops. But the Soviets did not intend to leave until they had established a strong communist state.

The Carter administration then began taking a "hard line" toward the Soviet Union. In an address to Congress, Carter warned that the United States would use military force to protect the Persian Gulf. This Carter Doctrine promised American military aid to all of the countries bordering Afghanistan. To carry out this policy, Carter proposed the creation of a quick-strike military force that could intervene anywhere in the world at short notice. He also called for a draft registration of 18 to 20-year-old men. Finally, the President asked Congress to allow the CIA to increase its intelligence-gathering activities.

The administration followed up its announcement of the Carter Doctrine by taking other actions against the Soviet Union. It asked the Senate to delay passing

After 444 days in captivity, the American hostages in Iran were freed. The release was worked out in the last days of the Carter administration. What were the conditions of the release?

the SALT II treaty. It cancelled all shipments of American grain to the Soviet Union.[3] American firms were also forbidden to sell high technology, such as computers, to the Soviets. One of Carter's most controversial acts was his announcement that the United States would boycott the 1980 Summer Olympic Games in Moscow.

Hostage Settlement

In September 1980 Iran and its neighbor Iraq went to war over a border dispute. The conflict soon led to a break in the hostage crisis. Iran needed military supplies from the United States to fight Iraq. In November Iran laid down conditions for the release of the hostages. A month later, the United States and

---

[3] American farmers opposed the ban on grain shipments to the Soviet Union. Their protests led to removal of the ban in 1981.

Iran began negotiations through a third party, the North African nation of Algeria. After a few weeks of bargaining, an agreement was reached. In return for the release of the hostages, the United States agreed to end sanctions and return $14 billion in assets.

After signing the agreement, Iran released the 52 hostages, who were flown to an American air base in West Germany. Their freedom came only moments after Carter's term of office had ended. Carter was sent to Germany by the new President, Ronald Reagan, to greet the hostages.

SECTION REVIEW

1. Identify the following: Andrei Sakharov, Omar Torrijos, Anastasio Somoza, Ruhollah Khomeini.
2. How did Carter help Egypt and Israel to negotiate?
3. What were the terms of the new Panama Canal treaties?
4. What was the relationship between the United States and the Shah of Iran?
5. How did Carter attempt to free the hostages?

3 The Election of 1980

By July 1980 public opinion polls showed that only 21 percent of Americans approved of Carter's performance as President. It was the lowest score on record for any chief executive. A number of factors were responsible for the public's image of Carter as a weak leader. Many political observers pointed to conflicts within the administration on foreign policy and economic issues. Some noted the legislative conflicts between the President and Congress. Others stressed Carter's lack of support among Democratic party leaders. Also, Carter's high standard of ethics often worked against him. The President, some observers said, had led the people to expect too much. As a result, many were disappointed.

The 1980 Primaries

In late 1979 Carter announced that he would seek another term in 1980. However, his political problems dimmed chances for reelection. Because of this, the 1980 presidential campaign began as an open race. Many candidates entered the primaries, which had become increasingly important in determining party nominees.

Republicans. Ten Republicans entered the race for their party's presidential nomination. Among these were Ronald Reagan, former governor of California; George Bush, UN ambassador during the Nixon administration; and Representative John Anderson of Illinois.

After repeated primary victories, Ronald Reagan emerged as the front runner. Reagan's lead forced John Anderson to withdraw from the race. Anderson, known for his strong liberal views, then announced that he was running as an independent candidate. He chose Patrick J. Lucey, former Democratic governor of Wisconsin, as his running mate.

Democrats. Liberal Democrats who were dissatisfied with Carter put their hopes on Senator Edward Kennedy of Massachusetts. Kennedy entered the primaries against Carter. Carter won a majority of primaries and captured most state Democratic party caucuses. Kennedy, however, refused to give up and vowed to "stick it out" until the convention.

The 1980 Conventions

The Republican convention, meeting in Detroit, adopted a conservative platform calling for less government, lower taxes, and more defense spending. The platform also endorsed voluntary group prayer in public schools and opposed abortion, busing, and the Equal Rights Amendment. Reagan gained the Republican presidential nomination on the first ballot. He chose George Bush, who had won second place in the primaries, as his running mate.

The Democrats met in New York City. Their platform combined a commitment to social reform with calls for government aid for the unemployed. Carter's supporters were able to gain control of the convention, and Kennedy quit the race. Carter easily won the presidential nomination and received Kennedy's reluctant endorsement. Mondale was again chosen as the nominee for Vice President.

The Campaign

During the campaign Carter stressed the peace issue. He claimed that a Reagan victory would lead to

Reagan's emphasis on the economy was a winning issue because inflation had soared, causing a recession in the housing and automobile industries.

a "massive arms race with the Soviet Union that would threaten the peace of the world . . ." Reagan concentrated on the economy. Accusing Carter of "weak leadership" at home and abroad, he promised jobs, lower taxes, an expanded economy, and increased defense spending.

John Anderson traveled throughout the country, winning support among university students, intellectuals, and backers of liberal causes. He often found fault with both Carter and Reagan, particularly on nuclear weapons policy.

During most of the campaign, the polls pointed to a "toss up" between Carter and Reagan. However, two or three days before the election, Reagan began to pull ahead in most polls.

Election Results

On election day, Reagan defeated Jimmy Carter by a wide margin. Reagan won 43,200,000 popular votes to Carter's 34,900,000. Anderson received only 5,600,000 popular votes. In the electoral college, Reagan had 489 votes to Carter's 49. Anderson won no electoral votes. Reagan had solid support nationwide, while Carter carried only 6 states and the District of Columbia.

Reagan's victory reflected at least a temporary breakup of the traditional Democratic coalition of labor, ethnic, regional, and minority groups that had been forged by Franklin D. Roosevelt during the 1930's. Blue-collar workers, southerners, white ethnic groups, and the elderly broke with the Democratic party and voted for Reagan. Fundamentalist Christian groups such as the Moral Majority, a conservative political lobby headed by Reverend Jerry Falwell, also supported Reagan.

Some observers noted that Reagan's triumph was due to his own personal appeal as well as to growing public support for his conservative policies. Others, however, stated that Reagan's victory was based more on dissatisfaction with Jimmy Carter than on what was interpreted as solid backing for political conservatism.

The Republicans also captured the Senate in the 1980 elections, although the Democrats kept control of the House. In both houses of Congress, many long-standing liberal Democrats were replaced by young conservative Republicans.

ELECTION OF 1980

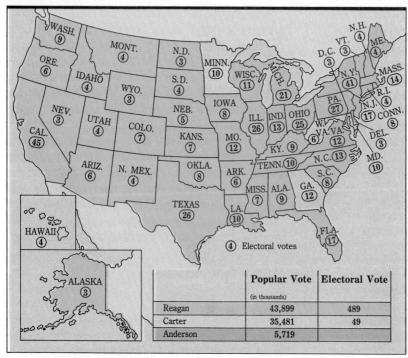

4 Electoral votes

	Popular Vote (in thousands)	Electoral Vote
Reagan	43,899	489
Carter	35,481	49
Anderson	5,719	

Have students research and report on the effects of deregulation on energy prices.

SECTION REVIEW

1. Identify the following: George Bush, John Anderson, Moral Majority.
2. Why did the presidential election of 1980 become an open race?
3. What was the Republican platform in 1980?
4. What did Reagan's victory indicate about the Democratic party?

4 Reagan's Domestic Policy

In his inaugural address, Reagan promised to reverse the course taken by the federal government since the New Deal. He said he would reduce the size of the federal government, cut taxes, and balance the budget. He called for less government regulation of business and a reduction in federal welfare programs. He also pledged to increase military spending and to follow a tough foreign policy.

Hostage Return

On Reagan's inauguration day, the American hostages were released from Iran, ending 444 days of captivity. Upon their return to the United States, they were met by President Reagan at a White House reception. In welcoming home the hostages, Reagan made the following remark:

Let terrorists be aware that when the rules of international law are violated, our policy will be one of swift and effective retribution.

However, Reagan stated that his administration would not be guided by a "spirit of revenge" toward Iran. It would accept the hostage deal worked out with Iran by Carter.

Reagan's Style

At 69 years of age, Ronald Reagan was the oldest person ever to become President. However, he was vigorous and had an outgoing personality. Reagan believed strongly in conservative political and economic policies. He had a relaxed, confident style of governing. He abandoned the tiring 12-hour schedule of earlier Presidents. Instead, he followed a 9-to-5 routine, with Wednesdays and weekends off for relaxation. He and his wife Nancy especially liked to spend time at their ranch in California.

The Reagans lived an elegant lifestyle in the White House. They held many lavish balls, concerts, and receptions. The presidential inauguration was one of the most expensive and colorful in the country's history. Many people criticized this display of White House pomp. Others, however, believed that it was needed to reflect the dignity of the office.

In his decision-making, Reagan relied on his cabinet members and close aides. He set major policy goals, while leaving the details and management of programs to others. Because of his experience as an actor, Reagan placed a high value on the communication of ideas. He spent more time than any other modern President writing and editing his own remarks for public presentation. His skill as a speaker and campaigner won him much popularity.

Limiting Government

Reagan acted quickly to limit the size of the federal government. His first act as President was to put a freeze on the hiring of federal employees. At the same time, he began to ease government controls on many business activities. He set up a task force headed by Vice President Bush to review federal regulations. Reagan won the support of big business for his efforts. For example, he allowed cutbacks in safety regulations to help auto manufacturers boost their falling profits. Also, rather than raise tariffs, he persuaded foreign competitors to reduce the amount of goods they sent the United States.

Energy and the Environment

Reagan also believed that less government regulation would ease the energy crisis. In 1981 he lifted all federal controls on the production and pricing of oil. Reagan called this move " a positive first step towards a balanced energy program . . . one designed to promote conservation and vigorous domestic production."

At the same time, the Reagan administration supported less government protection of natural resources. Beginning in 1981, Secretary of the Interior James Watt opened up more federal

The Environment

From the beginning, America's natural abundance complicated the basic dilemma confronting people everywhere in their relationship to the environment: how to *use* resources without *destroying* them. As long as there seemed to be an endless supply of resources, settlers in America had little incentive to practice conservation measures.

Moreover, the traditional western approach to life has always called for conquering nature. American Indians took an alternative approach, seeing human life as part of nature. But most white Americans paid little attention to this novel idea. Indeed, white settlers stripped much of the land of its forests and almost eradicated the beaver and the buffalo. White pioneers left debris beside every trail they traveled, much to the disgust of the Indians.

Significant concern for the environment first surfaced after the Civil War. Organized efforts were made to gather information so that intelligent policies could be established. The federal government sponsored several surveys of western lands during the 1860's and 1870's, including one by geologist and naturalist John Wesley Powell.

As settlement proceeded westward and people became more aware that resources were scarce, Congress acted. For example, the Timber Culture Act of 1878 encouraged homesteaders to plant trees, and the Forest Reserve Act of 1891 authorized the President to establish forest reserves on public lands.

Conservation received a big boost in the early 1900's when Theodore Roosevelt became President. He placed nearly 150 million acres of western lands off limits to buyers. At his urging, Congress created 5 National Parks and more than 50 wildlife refuges. Under Roosevelt, the foundations of a national conservation program were established.

Many conservation projects were begun during the Great Depression, mostly as a means of providing jobs for the unemployed. During the same period, the Dust Bowl tragedy demonstrated the need for soil conservation.

As time went on, scientists discovered more about the effects of pollutants on the environment, and people became more concerned with environmental health. By the 1960's, government officials faced mounting pressure from the public to control pollution. In response, Congress passed the National Environmental Policy Act of 1969, which required "environmental impact statements" for all planned construction projects. In October 1970 the Environmental Protection Agency (EPA) was established to set and enforce pollution control standards.

Recently environmental issues have become more controversial because environmental concerns have come into conflict with economic interests. For example, many people want to preserve America's scenic wilderness areas. But with traditional sources of vital minerals drying up, mining companies (and the people whose jobs are disappearing) want to take advantage of the vast expanse of federal lands.

Other problems reflect similar conflicts. Some parts of the country have been made uninhabitable by leaks from chemical dumps. But the cost of cleaning up is tremendous. In 1980 Congress created a $1.6 billion EPA "Superfund" to help clean up the worst of the hazardous waste sites. But use of the fund ran into legal and political snags. Meanwhile, as of 1983, there were an estimated 180,000 open sites and 50,000 underground dumps filled with chemicals. Increasingly, the words of a 1968 House Subcommittee on Science, Research, and Development ring ominously true:

> In certain ways, the environment may have Achilles' heels which can lead to unwanted changes very rapidly. There is very little room for mistakes in an over-populated and underfed world.

QUESTIONS

1. What did Roosevelt do for conservation?
2. Why have environmental issues become more controversial in recent years?

Discuss the concept of "trade-offs" between the economy and the environment.

During 1981 a number of attacks were made on other world leaders. On May 13 a Turkish terrorist shot and seriously wounded Pope John Paul II. On October 6 Egyptian President Sadat was assassinated.

wilderness lands for mining, oil drilling, and other forms of economic development. He also allowed private companies to search for oil and natural gas in government-owned coastal waters.

Watt's actions were opposed by people concerned about the environment. They felt that the opening of protected areas to resource development would destroy much of the nation's scenic beauty. Watt, on the other hand, believed that it was important to find more sources of energy so that the United States would be less dependent on foreign oil. He also felt that his policies would create new jobs.

The New Federalism

Reagan reintroduced an idea that Richard Nixon had proposed in 1969—a plan for a new relationship between the national government and the states. The plan, known as "the New Federalism," involved the transfer of many federal welfare programs to state and local authorities. In January 1982 Reagan urged states and cities to take over the Food Stamp program and Aid to Families with Dependent Children (AFDC). In return the federal government would take over the total responsibility for the cost of Medicaid. He also suggested turning over to the states more than 40 other federal programs.

Some state and city government officials, however, were critical of Reagan's "New Federalism." Many of them had financial problems and doubted if they could handle the added burden of more social services. Some claimed that it would lead to higher state and local taxes. Others felt that the "New Federalism" would eventually lead to reduced benefits for the poor, elderly, and disabled.

Attempted Assassination

On March 31, 1981, Reagan was shot in the chest outside a Washington, D.C. hotel. Three other

President Reagan survived an assassination attempt outside a Washington hotel. His press secretary, a police officer, and a secret service agent were also wounded. What changes in protecting the President were made as a result of the assassination attempt?

"EQUAL JUSTICE UNDER THE LAW"

Sandra Day O'Connor

Sandra Day O'Connor stands as a symbol of the improving status of women in the 1980's. O'Connor was born in El Paso, Texas, on March 26, 1930. She spent her early childhood on the family's 155,000-acre (62,000 hectares) ranch in southeastern Arizona. After graduating from high school at 16, she entered Stanford University. She received a Bachelor of Arts degree in 1950 and a law degree two years later.

While waiting for her husband to complete law school, O'Connor served as a county deputy attorney in San Mateó, California. In 1954 she and her husband went to Frankfurt, West Germany, where O'Connor worked as a civilian lawyer for the United States Army. After their stay in West Germany, the couple settled in Phoenix, Arizona. In 1959 O'Connor opened a law office there. She remained in private practice until 1965 when she became assistant attorney general for Arizona.

In 1969 O'Connor was appointed to complete the unexpired term of a Republican state senator. The following year, she was elected to the Arizona Senate in her own right. In 1972 she was reelected and chosen majority leader. O'Connor was the first woman in the entire country to hold that office. In 1974 she was elected to the Maricopa County Superior Court. She held that position until 1979 when she was appointed to the Arizona Court of Appeals.

In July 1981 Sandra Day O'Connor was appointed to the Supreme Court by President Ronald Reagan. She was the first woman to serve in such a position. Although some Americans protested Reagan's action, most approved his choice. During her first term as an associate justice, O'Connor participated in 84 cases. In 62 of them, she voted with the conservative justices. On issues such as equal rights, however, she demonstrated a more liberal view.

persons, including the President's press secretary, James Brady, were also struck by the bullets. The gunman was John Hinckley, Jr., a young man who apparently acted in the hope of winning the love of a certain movie actress. Hinckley was later found not guilty on the grounds that he was insane. This verdict sparked a nationwide debate on the insanity defense.

Reagan was taken to the hospital, where surgeons successfully removed the bullet. The President made a remarkable recovery. At later presidential appearances, the Secret Service took increased precautions to protect the President's life.

The Economy

The Reagan administration's chief concern was the economy. In 1981 administration officials developed a plan for economic recovery based in part on the principles of supply-side economics. This plan called for decreases in taxes and sharp cuts in federal spending. On February 18, 1981, Reagan presented the details of his plan to a joint session of Congress. He proposed a 30 percent reduction in income taxes over a three-year period. He also called for increased defense spending and sharp cuts in social programs.

Reagan's proposals received strong support from Republicans and conservative Democrats in Congress. However, liberal Democrats, led by House Speaker Thomas P. O'Neill, were against the Reagan plan, which was nicknamed **"Reaganomics."** They said that the rich would receive the most benefit from the proposed tax cuts and that the government would lose needed revenue. Also the tax cuts would encourage people to spend and increase inflation. The cuts in social programs, they believed, were too sharp and would cause hardships for the poor.

In 1983 Reagan appointed two other women to cabinet posts: Elizabeth Dole as Secretary of Transportation and Margaret Heckler as Secretary of Health and Human Services.

AMERICAN BUSINESS CYCLES, 1940–1983

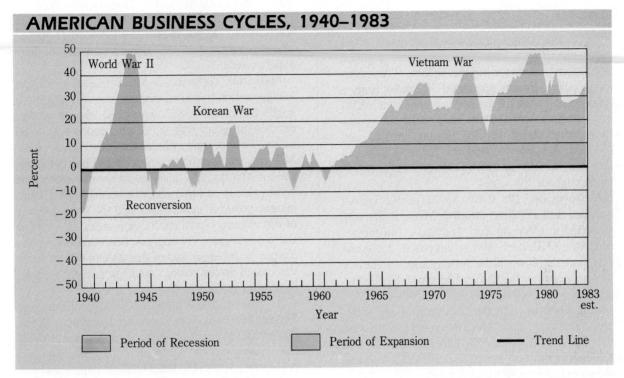

| Period of Recession | Period of Expansion | Trend Line |

Reagan made some compromises, but he was able to get most of what he wanted passed. Congress approved substantial cuts in social programs and a 25 percent reduction in income taxes spread over a three-year period. On August 13 Reagan signed the measures into law, saying that they marked an end to "excessive growth" in government spending and taxing.

The Reagan cuts in government spending affected nearly all of the federal government's social programs. The administration cut welfare payments and tightened the requirements for receiving them. People on the Food Stamp program were especially affected. Congress also lowered Medicaid payments to the states by three percent. Other changes were made that required the elderly and disabled to pay more for their medical care. Unemployment insurance benefits were cut from 39 to 26 weeks in most states. Funding for public service jobs under the Comprehensive Employment and Training Act (CETA) was also cut.

The Reagan administration counted on private groups and volunteer agencies to play a greater role in charities and social services. To provide jobs for minorities, Reagan called for **"free enterprise zones"** in inner cities. Tax breaks would be given to companies who located in these areas and hired local residents.

SECTION REVIEW

1. Identify the following: James Watt, John Hinckley, Jr., Thomas P. O'Neill.
2. Why was Secretary Watt's policy of opening up federal lands for development opposed by environmentalists?
3. Why was Reagan's "New Federalism" criticized by some state and city officials?
4. What groups were affected by Reagan's cuts on social programs?

5 Reagan's Foreign Policy

The Reagan administration also took a more conservative direction in foreign policy. It placed less importance on human rights, took a "hard line" toward countries opposed to American interests, and raised defense spending. Reagan's goal was to return the United States to the dominant position it had enjoyed in world affairs after World War II.

Reagan and the Soviets

The Reagan administration took a strong stand against the Soviet Union and its allies. Fighting communism became the major emphasis of American foreign policy. Reagan appointed Alexander Haig, a professional soldier and former commander of NATO forces, as Secretary of State. Haig spoke out against Soviet involvement in Afghanistan, Africa, and Indochina. He also accused the Soviet Union and other communist countries of aiding terrorist activities throughout the world.

On November 10, 1982, Soviet leader Leonid Brezhnev died of a heart attack in Moscow. He was succeeded in office by Yuri Andropov, the former head of the KGB, the Soviet secret police. It seemed likely that there would be little change in the icy relations between the Soviet Union and the United States.

Arms Control. At the beginning of his term, Reagan was reluctant to enter into arms control talks with the Soviet Union. He believed that it was important to build up American defenses before any new agreement could be negotiated.

Many people thought that Reagan was not concerned about the dangers of nuclear war. Pressure mounted for him to make some effort to negotiate arms control with the Soviets. In Western Europe and, to a lesser extent in the United States, demonstrations took place calling for a **nuclear freeze,** or a halt by both superpowers in the buildup of their nuclear arsenals. Finally, in the spring of 1981, the Reagan administration announced that the United States and the Soviet Union would hold negotiations on long-range or **strategic nuclear weapons.** They would also negotiate on medium-range missiles in Europe.

In November 1981, before the start of the medium-range missile negotiations, Reagan presented an arms reduction plan. He proposed that the Soviets remove all of their medium-range missiles aimed at Western Europe. In return, the United States would cancel its plan to give similar missiles to NATO forces in Europe. Although the Soviets turned down the proposal, the administration hoped it had shown its concern about preventing an arms race.

In June 1982 another set of negotiations on strategic weapons began between the United States and the Soviet Union. Reagan named the negotiations START (Strategic Arms Reduction Talks) rather than SALT. He hoped that the talks would lead to sharp reductions in the nuclear arsenals of both superpowers.

National Defense. Meanwhile the Reagan administration began to increase America's military might. In October 1981 it announced a 6-year national defense program that would cost more than $180 billion. The program included the construction of 100 MX missiles, the development of 100 B-1 bombers, the construction of a new Stealth bomber that would be invisible to enemy radar, the building of 6 Trident nuclear powered submarines, and the strengthening of the military communications system. In outlining the arms program to Congress, Secretary of Defense Caspar Weinberger stated that its aim was to make the United States strong enough to prevent a Soviet attack.

As part of the American defense buildup, the Reagan administration encouraged advances in the United States space program. In the spring of 1981, the space shuttle *Columbia,* the world's first reuseable space craft, lifted off from Cape Canaveral and successfully orbited the earth. After 36 orbits and 54 hours in space, *Columbia* landed in California. The crew of *Columbia* were John Young, a veteran of four space flights, and Robert Crippen, who was making his first trip as an astronaut. In the following months, several other successful missions were made by astronauts on *Columbia.*

Poland. The United States reacted strongly against Soviet actions in Eastern Europe. In the summer of 1980, the workers of Poland went on strike, demanding higher pay, economic reforms, and free labor unions. Communist leaders in Poland gave in to the workers' demands. Led by Lech Walesa, the workers then formed Solidarity, the first labor organization in the Soviet bloc that was not controlled by the government.

As Solidarity's support grew, the power of the Polish government and Communist party weakened. Poland moved slowly towards a freer society until the Polish government assumed special military powers in late 1981. The government used these powers to limit the freedoms of the Polish people and ban the activities of Solidarity.

Reagan reacted angrily to the actions of the Polish government. He ordered a set of sanctions against

President Reagan's plan to strengthen the nation's military defenses included revival of the B-1 (above), a long-range supersonic bomber. The proposed defense program also included development of the MX missile and the Stealth bomber. Why did the President feel a defense buildup was needed?

Poland. The sanctions included the cutting off of $25 million of credit to Poland, suspending the right of Polish National Airlines to land in the United States, and banning Polish fishing boats from United States coastal waters.

Reagan also suspected that the Soviet Union had played a part in the Polish government's actions. Because of this, he also placed sanctions on the Soviet Union. The President suspended the right of Aeroflot, the Soviet airline, to land in the United States. He also refused to renew several United States-Soviet agreements involving energy, space, science, and technology.

In December 1982 the Polish government released imprisoned Solidarity leaders and removed some of its restrictions on the Polish people. However the Reagan administration refused to lift sanctions against Poland until all of the rights of the Polish people were restored.

The Pipeline Controversy

Reagan wanted the United States and its allies to have a unified trade policy that would punish the Soviets for their actions in Poland and Afghanistan. This, however, was difficult to achieve. Western Europeans and many Americans still wanted to carry on trade with the Soviet Union.

In 1982 American and Western European companies began cooperating with the Soviet Union in the construction of a 3000-mile (4800-kilometers) pipeline. The purpose of the pipeline was to carry natural gas from Siberia in the Soviet Union to Western Europe.

Reagan, however, came out against involvement by American or Western European companies in the project. He feared that the pipeline would make America's European allies too dependent on the Soviets for their energy supplies. He also did not want the Soviets to profit financially from the sale of natural gas.

Western companies, however, ignored Reagan's objections and continued to take part in the project. Reagan then imposed a ban on the sale of American equipment to the Soviets for use in building the pipeline. He also threatened trade penalties against any American companies that violated the ban. Reagan's action angered Western European governments and nearly caused a split in the western alliance. To avoid this danger, Reagan finally lifted the ban in December 1982. In return the allies agreed to cooperate in restricting overall trade with the Soviets.

The Third World

In keeping with its stand against the Soviet Union, the Reagan administration showed little sympathy for left-wing countries in the Third World. In 1981 a summit meeting of both industrial and developing nations was held in Mexico. At this meeting, Reagan called on Third World countries to renounce socialism and create free enterprise economies.

At the same time, the administration established closer ties with right-wing governments in the Third World. It believed that these regimes were important partners with the United States in the global struggle against communism. For example, the administration set up more contacts with the white government in South Africa, a move that angered neighboring black nations. In addition, the administration annoyed Communist China by continuing unofficial ties and arms sales to Taiwan.

Central America. The Reagan administration also acted to stop the spread of communist or left-wing movements in Central America. In January 1981 Secretary of State Haig confirmed reports that Cuba and Nicaragua were aiding leftist guerrillas in El Salvador. The administration immediately stopped economic aid to Nicaragua and resumed arm sales to the military government of El Salvador.

Meanwhile, the Sandinista government in Nicaragua was receiving arms from Cuba and was beginning to build a strong military force. Because of this, the Reagan administration saw Nicaragua as a threat to the rest of Central America. It warned that the United States would support Nicaraguan exiles seeking to overthrow the Sandinista government. Mexico, Venezuela, and Colombia, however, spoke out against American intervention. They offered to sponsor peace talks between the United States and Nicaragua. Although deep suspicions remained, the United States and Nicaragua agreed to negotiate their differences.

The United States was also concerned about growing unrest in El Salvador. There, the military government tried to introduce land reforms. But these efforts were often hindered by the small upper class. As a result, many people turned against the government and backed the guerrillas. The government reacted by arresting its opponents and carrying out mass executions. Many Americans wanted all military and economic aid to El Salvador stopped until conditions improved. The Reagan administration, however, claimed that support for the military government was the only way to stop a communist takeover.

In July 1981 the military government of El Salvador, with American support, announced that it would hold free elections for a civilian government. Elections were held in March 1982, but the guerrillas refused to run candidates and urged people not to vote at all. The Reagan administration hoped for a victory by the moderates. Instead right-wing parties received a majority of votes and formed a coalition government. The new government moved to undo the land reform program. This action led to a renewal of the civil war and the possibility of a guerrilla victory.

The Lebanon War. In June 1982 war broke out in the Middle East when Israeli troops crossed into neighboring Lebanon. The purpose of the Israeli action was to destroy bases of the Palestine Liberation Organization (PLO). For months the PLO had used these bases in Lebanon to make strikes at Israeli settlements near the border.

The Israeli forces moved quickly through the southern part of Lebanon and reached the Lebanese capital of Beirut. They surrounded the western section of the city, where most of the PLO forces were located. The Israelis began air attacks against West Beirut, demanding that PLO forces surrender and leave the country.

The United States finally intervened in the crisis. President Reagan sent special envoy Philip Habib to

During the crisis, Secretary of State Haig publicly backed the Israeli move on Lebanon. Because of this and other disagreements with the Reagan administration, Haig resigned. He was succeeded by George Schultz, Secretary of the Treasury under Nixon.

the Middle East to work out a peace settlement. In late August Habib arranged a ceasefire and settlement between the Israelis and the PLO. Under the terms of the agreement, the PLO forces left West Beirut and went to various Arab countries. Their departure was supervised by a small peace-keeping force of French, Italian, and American troops. The peace-keeping force remained in Lebanon after the crisis to help the shaky Lebanese government maintain order.

After the end of the Lebanese crisis, Reagan announced a new peace proposal for the Middle East. He reaffirmed America's pledge to support and defend Israel. However he also suggested a plan to grant the Palestinians full control over their own affairs in association with Jordan. To achieve this goal, he called on Israel to halt the building of settlements in the West Bank and Gaza Strip. In making his proposal, Reagan hoped to reach a compromise between the Arab and Israeli positions.

LATIN AMERICA AND THE CARIBBEAN

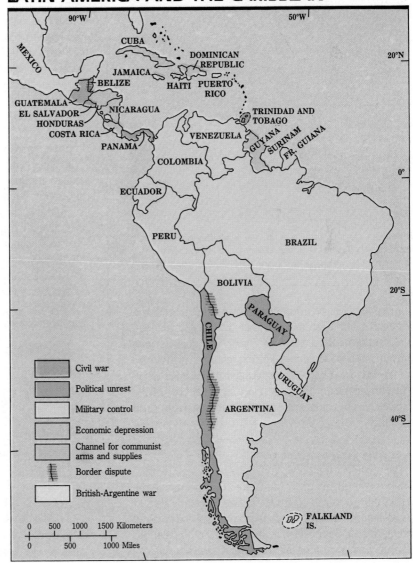

American marines took part in the peacekeeping mission in Lebanon during the ceasefire. Envoy Philip Habib mediated an agreement between the Israelis and the PLO. What was Reagan's peace proposal for the Middle East?

The Israeli government, however, rejected the Reagan plan. It announced that it was going ahead with settlements in the West Bank. This put a serious strain on United States-Israeli relations. However moderate Arab nations expressed initial interest in the Reagan plan. They saw it as a sign that the United States was becoming more understanding of the Arab position.

The Falklands War

In the spring of 1982, the United States found itself indirectly involved in a war between two allies. In April several thousand troops from Argentina invaded the British-held Falkland Islands in the South Atlantic. Britain had gained the islands from Argentine settlers in 1833. However Argentina still claimed to own the islands. Tensions between Britain and Argentina mounted in the early 1980's when rumors spread of possible major oil deposits near the Falklands.

The British government responded immediately to the Argentine invasion. Prime Minister Margaret Thatcher sent a naval task force to the Falklands. She threatened that British forces would retake the islands if the Argentines refused to withdraw.

The actions of both countries placed the United States in a dilemma. On the one hand, British military action could be interpreted as a violation of the Monroe Doctrine. On the other, Britain was America's closest ally. Britain also had the support of the majority of the people of the Falklands, most of whom were British settlers.

Faced with this dilemma, Secretary of State Haig tried for several weeks to reach a settlement between Britain and Argentina. When these negotiations collapsed, the Reagan administration announced that it would support Britain. Along with other members of NATO, the United States agreed to impose sanctions on Argentina.

In May serious fighting broke out between Britain and Argentina. Combining sea power with effective air cover, Britain landed troops in the Falklands and swiftly captured Argentine defensive positions. A month later, the Argentines surrendered, and the British regained control of the islands. The brief war, however, caused bitter feelings between Argentina and the United States. The Argentines, along with other Latin Americans who had sided with them, believed that the United States had failed to uphold the principles of the Monroe Doctrine.

SECTION REVIEW

1. Identify the following: Alexander Haig, Yuri Andropov, START, Lech Walesa, PLO, Philip Habib, Margaret Thatcher.
2. How did Reagan react to events on Poland?
3. Why did Reagan object to the construction of a pipeline from Western Europe to the Soviet Union?
4. What was Reagan's policy in El Salvador?
5. What was Reagan's proposal for peace in the Middle East?
6. Why did the Falklands War place the United States in a dilemma?

6 Staying the Course

By the middle of 1982, Reagan faced serious challenges to his economic program. Inflation had declined, but the economy had entered a serious recession. Unemployment increased to more than 10 percent, the highest since the Great Depression. At the same time, the poor, elderly, and disabled were affected by the Reagan cuts in social programs.

Reagan also had to postpone his goal of a balanced budget by 1984. In spite of cutbacks, government spending, especially for defense and unemployment insurance, had increased. At the same time, tax revenues had decreased. As a result the administration faced a record budget deficit of more than $100 billion.

Tax Increases

In the summer of 1982, Congress became concerned about growing budget deficits. Both Republican and Democratic members put pressure on Reagan to make changes in his economic program. The President, however, did not want to cut defense spending or abandon the promised cuts in income taxes passed the year before. To raise more government revenue, he instead proposed changes in the tax laws. These changes would provide the government with an additional $98.3 billion. The new legislation called for withholding taxes on interest, dividend payments, and money earned in tips by restaurant workers. It also increased excise taxes on cigarettes, telephone service, and air travel, and reduced certain tax breaks.

Reagan blamed the need for the tax increases on the budget deficit and the "big spending" policies of earlier administrations. He appealed for bipartisan support in Congress. However, conservative Republicans opposed any tax increases. They accused Reagan of abandoning the heart of his economic program. Reagan finally had to rely on liberal Democrats to get the bill passed by a slim margin.

At Mid-Term

As the 1982 congressional elections approached, Reagan's economic policy became the leading political issue. Democrats and some Republicans accused Reagan of supporting business and favoring the well-to-do at the expense of labor and the poor. These critics called for only moderate increases in defense spending and a halt to further cuts in social programs. They also demanded a government jobs program to help the unemployed. On October 13 the

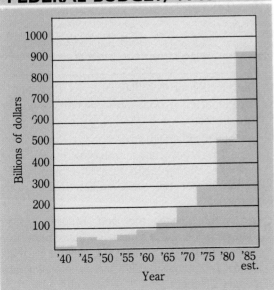

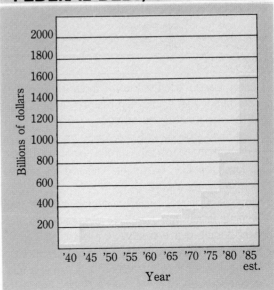

President answered his critics in a nationwide television address. He said that economic recovery would only come by "staying the course," or following through with his program. He stated that his administration was laying "the groundwork for a recovery that will mean more jobs and more opportunities for all our people."

The 1982 Elections. Political observers saw the congressional elections of 1982 as a test of public support for Reagan's economic program. They watched to see whether the groups that had backed Reagan in 1980 would vote Republican in 1982. The results of the election showed a setback for the administration. The Democrats picked up 26 seats in the House. They also won 7 governorships. The Republicans, however, kept control of the Senate.

The election showed that the Republicans had lost significant support among several groups that had voted for Reagan in 1980: blue-collar workers, white ethnics, southerners, and the elderly. Many of these voters returned to the Democratic party. More than one-half of the defeated Republican incumbents, or candidates up for reelection, ran in economically troubled areas and were strong backers of Reagan's program. On the other hand, many of the Republicans who were reelected were critical of Reagan's program.

In spite of setbacks, the Republicans had not experienced overwhelming losses in the election.

Analysts thought the vote showed that people wanted less drastic cuts in social programs and only moderate increases in defense spending. At the same time, they still showed support for the administration's overall goals of reducing federal spending and controlling inflation.

After the Election. The election results put pressure on Reagan to make changes in his program, and he expressed willingness to compromise with Congress on certain points. For example, in late December he signed into law a gasoline tax increase that was expected to bring in $5.5 billion a year. The measure provided that the tax (5 cents a gallon) be used to repair the nation's bridges, roads, and transportation systems. The repair program would create an estimated 320,000 jobs for the unemployed. However Reagan refused to compromise on the main points of his program: increased defense spending and income tax cuts.

SECTION REVIEW

1. What was the status of the American economy in mid-1982?
2. Why did Reagan fail to achieve his goal of a balanced budget?
3. What tax increases did Reagan propose?
4. What were the results of the congressional elections of 1982?

CHAPTER **33**   REVIEW

SUMMARY

1. Jimmy Carter tried to create an informal, ethical Presidency that would help restore people's trust in the American government.
2. Continued inflation and high levels of spending by government led to a widespread taxpayers' revolt.
3. In foreign policy, Carter emphasized the promotion of human rights.
4. One of Carter's main accomplishments was helping Israel and Egypt to negotiate the first Arab-Israeli peace treaty.
5. The major crisis of Carter's Presidency was the taking of American hostages by a group of Iranian revolutionaries.

6. The election of Ronald Reagan as President in 1980 reflected growing public support for conservative policies.
7. One of Reagan's chief goals was to reduce the size of the federal government by easing regulations on business, cutting social programs, and turning responsibilities for public welfare over to the states.
8. In foreign policy, the goal of the Reagan administration was to return the United States to a position of world dominance by taking a hard line against communism and increasing American military strength.

VOCABULARY

loopholes	supply-side economics	Reaganomics	strategic nuclear weapons
affirmative action	dissident	free enterprise zones	incumbent
	monitoring	nuclear freeze	

REVIEW QUESTIONS

1. How did Carter try to achieve more efficient government?
2. How did Carter attempt to deal with the energy crisis?
3. How did Carter's policy on human rights affect foreign affairs?
4. What were the major issues of the 1980 presidential election?

5. How did Reagan's style as President differ from Carter's?
6. What was Reagan's plan for the economic recovery of the United States?
7. How did American-Soviet relations progress under Reagan?
8. How did the congressional elections of 1982 affect Reagan's policies?

DISCUSSION

1. Should human rights be a major consideration in determining American foreign policy? Why or why not?
2. What is the difference between "liberal" and "conservative" political positions?

3. If you has been President during the hostage crisis, would you have handled it differently? If so, how?
4. What difficulties are involved in trying to achieve nuclear arms control?

USING GRAPHS

Refer to the graphs on page 743 and answer the following questions:

1. In what year was the federal budget the largest?
2. When did the largest increases in the national debt take place?

3. In what years did the federal budget decrease? In what years did the national debt decrease? Why did this occur?
4. In general, how does the national debt compare to the federal budget?

USING SKILLS

Study the following statements and determine which one of each pair would be *more* difficult to prove:

1. (a) In the late 1970's, the United States was using excessive amounts of energy.
   (b) In the late 1970's, the United States was using 30 percent of the world's energy.
2. (a) The United States has fallen behind in the nuclear arms race.
   (b) Many people are worried that the United States has fallen behind in the nuclear arms race.

3. (a) Unemployment in 1982 was over 10 percent of the work force.
   (b) Unemployment was the most serious economic problem in 1982.
4. (a) The decision of the Supreme Court in *University of California* v. *Bakke* was a landmark decision.
   (b) The decision of the Supreme Court in *University of California* v. *Bakke* was that college admissions programs could not use specific quotas to achieve racial balance.

SUMMARY

1. During the 1950's and 1960's, the United States enjoyed a period of unparalleled economic growth, creating the world's first affluent society.
2. The 1960's and 1970's were characterized by rapid social change, including strong movements for equal rights by women and minorities and a rebellion by young people.
3. The political stability of the 1950's was replaced in the 1960's and 1970's by political disillusionment resulting from American involvement in the Vietnam War, the Watergate scandal, and economic problems.
4. Despite shifts in the balance of world power, the Cold War dominated American foreign policy in the 1960's and 1970's.
5. In the 1980's Americans continued to face the communist challenge around the world as well as economic problems at home.

REVIEW QUESTIONS

1. What common problems were faced by the Presidents of the post-World War II period?
2. How has the Cold War influenced the attitudes and actions of Americans?
3. How has technology changed American lifestyles since World War II?
4. How has the position of the United States in the world changed since World War II?

SUGGESTED ACTIVITIES

1. Research the development of your community during the past three decades. Try to find information about the following topics: changes in size and composition of population; new roads, buildings, and institutions; changes in employment; changes in government; cultural developments.
2. Prepare a list of items you would put in a time capsule to be opened in 50 years. Write a letter to the people who would be opening the capsule, explaining the significance of the items.
3. Organize a bulletin board display comparing lifestyles of the early 1900's to lifestyles today.
4. Find out what American history textbooks were being used in your community in 1950 and in 1970. Compare them to your current textbook.
5. Role-play a congressional committee as it hears testimony on the status of labor unions in the 1950's and 1960's. Have class members represent union members, employers, and consumers.

SUGGESTED READINGS

1. Deloria, Jr., Vine. *Custer Died for Your Sins: An Indian Manifesto*. New York: Macmillan Publishing Co., 1974. The condition of Indians in the 1960's as related to the actions of whites throughout history.
2. Flexner, Eleanor. *Century of Struggle: The Woman's Rights Movement in the United States*. New York: Atheneum Publications, 1972. A balanced presentation of the woman's movement.
3. Haley, Alex. *Roots*. New York: Dell Publishing Co., Inc., 1977. Paperback. A history of the author's ancestors in Africa and as seven generations of Americans.
4. Herring, George C. *America's Longest War: The U.S. & Vietnam 1950–1975*. New York: John Wiley & Sons, Inc., 1980. Paperback. A portrait of the war, its challenges, and the decisions of five Presidents.
5. Magruder, Jeb. *An American Life: One Man's Road to Watergate*. New York: Atheneum Publications, 1974. Story of a strong ambition that led to corruption.
6. Meier, Matt S. and Feliciano Rivera. *The Chicanos: A History of Mexican-Americans*. New York: Hill & Wang, Inc., 1972. Paperback. Traces the history of Mexicans in America.

THE HISTORIAN'S CRAFT

In this activity you must combine all you have learned about the historian's craft to write a balanced, objective paper. The subject of the activity is the Panama Canal Treaty debate of 1977–1978. The information below reflects the views of both those who favored the treaties and those who opposed them.

Before you begin to read these documents, review Chapter 21, pages 429-33 on Theodore Roosevelt and the Panama Canal, and Chapter 33, page 728 on the 1977 treaties. Further background information is provided by the first document, an excerpt from Time. The questions at the end of the activity will help you to analyze the arguments for and against the 1977 treaties.

After reading the material, write a two- or three-page paper describing the debate. The first part of your paper should be an introduction, with some background information on the 1903 and 1977 treaties. The second part should discuss the various viewpoints. The third part should be a conclusion, summarizing your discussion. You may wish to express your own point of view on the 1977 treaties.

From "Ceding the Canal—Slowly," *Time*, August 22, 1977:

> The treaty is very much a compromise—neither a triumph nor a defeat for either side [the U.S. or Panama]. Not only does it settle a nagging quarrel with Panama, it also removes a major irritant in U.S. relations with Latin America, which regards American control of the canal as a humiliating relic of the colonial era. It also assured continued U.S. control over a long transitional period; there is to be no radical, overnight shift of authority. Said [chief Panamanian negotiator] Escobar: "Getting control of the Canal Zone and the canal is one of Panama's oldest national desires. To generation after generation of Panamanians, the canal has symbolized the country's national patrimony—in the hands of foreigners. We developed a kind of national

> religion over the canal." [U.S. negotiator] Linowitz told Time, "In the world as a whole, Panama is regarded as a colonial enclave. The treaty sets off a whole new relationship between the U.S. and Latin America. We can prove how a great nation can deal magnanimously with a small nation at a time when Third World and North-South relations are at stake."

> The treaty gives Panama full sovereignty over the canal—but slowly. Not until the year 2000 will the U.S. relinquish complete control of the 51-mile-long waterway. In the meantime, the U.S. will continue to operate the canal, as well as the 14 military bases in the zone. The bases will be phased out at U.S. discretion over the life of the treaty. Under the terms of a separate treaty to be signed later by all of the hemisphere's nations, the U.S. will guarantee the neutrality of the canal and its accessibility to all the world's shipping even after the year 2000. If the safety of the canal is threatened, the U.S. is free to intervene with military force. . . .

From Emmett B. Ford, Jr., "Conservative Support for Panama Treaty":

> I support it [the 1977 treaty] because it corrects a gross injustice which we perpetrated against Panama, Colombia, and indeed all of Latin America three quarters of a century ago. (Is the preception of injustice and inequality reserved only for liberals?)

> I support it because it slowly and subtly phases out an anachronistic colonial arrangement which has increasingly soured our relations not only with Panama, but with all of our neighbors to the south.

> I find that I can, in good conscience, support it because I am persuaded absolutely that our security interests in the canal are safeguarded. A Panama with which we have concluded a mutually satisfactory agreement is far less likely to create difficulties for us over the use of the canal than would a Panama

with a permanent 10-mile-wide strip of foreign occupation right through its middle. . . .

What [Ronald] Reagan . . . [said] about the canal during the election campaign last year has gradually become the rallying cry of the opposition: "We bought it, we paid for it, we built it. And we are going to keep it. . . ."

But there is a good deal of loose rhetoric in his position. Certainly there is more emotion than fact in his arguments.

To begin with the Canal Zone is not "ours" and never has been. Even in 1903, when we could have dictated any terms we wished to impose upon the newly created Panamanian state, we did not choose to acquire full and sovereign rights to the territory.

According to the treaty of that date, Panama granted to the United States, in perpetuity, "all the rights, power, and authority . . . which (it) would possess and exercise if (repeat, if) it were the sovereign" of the zone. Thus, as we confirmed in a subsequent agreement with the Republic of Panama, that country has always retained legal sovereignty over the Canal Zone, despite the fact that we exercise full control in perpetuity over it.

Similarly, we may have paid enormous sums as rent, construction costs, and bribes, but we have never "bought" the Canal Zone from anyone. . . .

. . . It is historically of enormous significance to the Panamanians that no Panamanian had anything to do with drawing up the document which rented out part of their country forever.

The 1903 treaty was negotiated in Washington between Phillippe Bunau-Varilla, a French businessman serving as Panama's envoy to the United States, and John Hay, the American secretary of state.

It was approved by the U.S. Senate before the arrival of the official Panamanian delegation and ratified later by the Panamanian provisional government under threat of the withdrawal of American military protection. A thoroughly sneaky and discreditable performance.

From M. Northrup Buechner, "Why We Must Keep the Canal":

How should the new treaties be opposed? The most damning evidence against the treaties is the arguments that are given in their favor. Those arguments fall into two general categories: the practical arguments and the moral arguments; or the arguments from fear and the arguments from guilt.

The Practical Arguments

The most extreme, and therefore the clearest, of the practical arguments holds that if the Senate rejects the new treaties, Panama will become "another Vietnam." In other words, we should give up the canal out of fear of a war with Panama or, even more disgraceful, out of fear of independent guerrillas. . . .

For example, it was argued explicitly before the Senate Foreign Relations Committee that the best way to retain access to the canal is to give it to Panama so they will be on our side if we should have to defend it. It is very revealing (and somewhat frightening) that this argument was taken at face value by all the news media, and its implications went completely unnoticed.

Militarily, observe the helplessness of the United States implied by so desperate a need for support, and from Panama of all places, as to justify giving away the canal.

Strategically, observe the absurdity of assuring access to the canal by placing all the complex, delicate machinery and equipment and controls for its operation in the hands of a potential enemy.

And finally, since attacks by Panama are the only current danger to the canal's security, observe the threat implied by raising the issue of, and hence doubts about, our access to the canal. The real meaning of that argument was that if we try to keep the canal, Panama will deprive us of its use, and therefore we had better give it to them. . . .

There is no way that Panama could become another Vietnam. . . . In this case . . . fighting of any kind can be avoided altogether. All that is necessary is a statement by the *president that an attack on any part of the Canal Zone would be considered an attack on the United States, and that any country supporting such an attack would be considered an enemy of the United States and treated accordingly.*

The practical argument also holds that surrender of the canal is essential for good diplomatic relations with the Latin American countries. But even if they were the great powers of this hemisphere, it would be obviously self-defeating to curry their favor by giving away our possessions. . . . [I]t is we who are the great power here, and if anyone should worry about good opinions, it is our southern neighbors who should worry about ours.

The Moral Arguments

But if the practical arguments are insulting the moral arguments are worse, much worse.

It is said we stole the canal and our presence in the area represents a colonialist affront to the sensitive feelings of the Latin American people. We should give up the canal, it is implied, out of guilt for these offenses.

The charge of colonialism, though repeated mindlessly by everyone, is a transparent fraud. A colony was a settlement of people, not an industrial engineering enterprise. A colony, by definition, was administered for the economic benefit of the mother country. The Panama Canal is not a colony, nor has the United States ever had a colony anywhere in the world.

But the vilest distortion in the whole debate is the charge we stole the canal. It is the exact opposite of the truth.

The opposite of theft is production. We did not steal the canal; we built it. The moral right of the United States to the canal is the right of any creator to what he has created. . . .

Not only did the United States pay the costs of constructing the canal, it was her citizens who figured out how to conquer the previously unconquerable obstacles and then directed the construction in an enormously heroic effort. The Panama Canal was the greatest

engineering feat in the history of many up to that time and we did it. . . .

Whatever shenanigans were involved in getting sovereignty over the Canal Zone, and no one's account makes them very serious, they are nothing next to the incredible achievement of the canal itself. Without us, the Canal Zone would be just so much empty deadly, malaria infested lakes and jungle—as would the rest of Panama. . . .

The canal is a hatred symbol all right, but not of a nonexistent American colonialism. What the canal really symbolizes, and what the value-haters want symbolically to wipe out by making us give it up, is the overflowing abundance of energy, efficacy, and pride of a free people.

To surrender the canal in the face of such a motive is unthinkable. It would mean accepting their view of our virtues as vices and our achievements as stains on our national character. It would mean sanctioning hatred of the United States as natural and right and deserving a positive response. To what portion of our wealth and achievements could we claim a right after that and on what grounds?

That is the most important reason for keeping the Panama Canal. If there were no other reason whatever, that would be sufficient to hold on to it for dear life.

QUESTIONS

1. Why does *Time* see the new treaty as a compromise?

2. What three reasons does Emmett Ford give for his support of the treaty?

3. What was Ronald Reagan's argument as quoted by Ford? How does Ford respond to Reagan's argument?

4. What is the principal reason for Buechner's opposition to the treaties?

5. Why does Buechner reject the idea that Panama might become another Vietnam?

6. How does he feel about the issue of good relations with Latin American nations?

7. What does Buechner say in response to the "moral" arguments for the treaty?

1	Foreign Policy	751
2	The Economy	752
3	Social Questions	753

CHALLENGES FOR THE FUTURE

Let us rediscover the old strengths of the American people and apply them to the problems of a new age.

WILLIAM M. AGEE

As Americans make their way through the 1980's, they are being forced to wrestle with a large number of diplomatic, economic, and social problems. Some problems are of relatively recent origin, while others were long in the making. All defy easy solutions.

1 Foreign Policy

American foreign policy in the 1980's, as in the past, must try to balance competing political, economic, social, and strategic goals—a most difficult task. The goals themselves are not controversial. Almost all Americans would support a policy that made it possible for the United States to enhance its international trade, ensure its national security, strengthen the western alliance, and promote human freedom and well-being around the world. Unfortunately, these goals often conflict with one another.

Relations with Allies

Countries in the western alliance often have goals of their own that are incompatible with those of the United States. Many Western Europeans, for example, feel more directly threatened by the Soviet Union simply because they are closer to it. As a result, they are more likely to "go along" with the Soviets than are Americans. This has led to controversies over the deployment of nuclear weapons on European soil, which many Europeans think might provoke a Soviet attack.

Trade

Similarly improving American trade may depend on what other countries are willing to do. A case in point is Japan, whose economic growth since World War II has been called a "modern miracle."

The United States imports enormous quantities of Japanese products. However, the reverse is not true. One reason for Japan's more limited importing is that the Japanese government subsidizes Japanese manufacturers, allowing them to undercut American prices. Another reason is that the Japanese government places tight restrictions on imports. Under pressure from the United States government, Japan has finally agreed to limit some of its exports to this country. However, many Americans still feel that trade relations with Japan are unfair.

A different problem arises in dealing with countries that have natural resources vital to the United States. Many of these resources must be imported from abroad. Among them are manganese, chromium, tin, bauxite, uranium, and diamonds.

It is clearly important for the United States to maintain good relationships with countries possessing these minerals. But many of them are Third World nations with politically repressive governments. Alliances with these countries do not fit with the American desire to support democratic, or at least non-oppressive, regimes. Choosing between humanitarian goals and economic goals is a painful and controversial part of modern foreign policy.

National Security

The need for national security sometimes poses a similar dilemma, because many of the countries in areas of strategic importance to us are undemocratic. But there are many other problems connected with national security needs. For example, should the technology to wage chemical and germ warfare be expanded when accidents or uncontrolled usage could cause worldwide chaos? Evidence that the Soviets used chemicals in Southeast Asia and Afghanistan rekindled this debate in the early 1980's. Is it necessary to match the Soviet Union's nuclear

Remind students that it was American money, through the Marshall Plan, that helped build new factories in Germany and Japan.

arsenal? Many Americans support a nuclear freeze, while others claim that any unilateral move in this direction is sheer folly.

While new weapons systems are becoming more and more sophisticated, recruiters for the armed services have periodically found themselves obliged to lower standards in order to meet enlistment quotas. This has led some people to predict that our military strength is less than it seems. Another problem is that weapons may become obsolete soon after they are deployed. With the cost of a single tank climbing above the $1 million mark, this problem cannot be ignored, especially in light of the nation's economic problems.

2   The Economy

The economic growth of the United States was built on such products as steel, rubber, chemicals, and machinery. But by now, many of the factories turning out these items are painfully old-fashioned. Their machines are outmoded and inefficient.

Meanwhile other industrial countries, such as West Germany and Japan, have enjoyed several competitive advantages. Since many of their old factories were destroyed in World War II, both countries now have factories that are far newer than those in the United States. Labor costs, especially in Japan, are lower. Thus a number of major United States

One reason economists feel that it is important that manufacturing remain the major part of the economy is that this is the central element in our balance of trade with other countries. Only a very limited number of services can be exported to help pay for imported goods.

manufacturers have been forced to close plants, lay off workers, and even go into bankruptcy.

Employment

At the same time, the impact of the post-World War II baby boom, the women's liberation movement, and a growing taste for material comforts have combined to bring more and more people into the job market. With jobs in heavy industry drying up, many workers have gone into the **service sector,** which includes banks, law firms, insurance companies, health care organizations, retail stores, and other establishments that serve the public.

Growth in the service sector has far outstripped growth in traditional blue-collar fields in recent years. This trend seems likely to continue. But many experts feel that a nation's economic well-being ultimately must rest on the production of goods. They see the answer to this nation's long-term economic problems in **reindustrialization**—a reorienting of manufacturing away from "smokestack industries" toward the production of high technology items.

Technology

The United States has always led the world in the development of new technology, including the field of electronics. Computers, which have revolutionized everything from industry to communications to

These University of Maryland students are learning to operate CRT's. The television-like screen enables the operator to see how to make corrections quickly and easily. As more and more jobs require computer use, additional computer training programs will be needed. What could limit the number of training programs?

Point out that the high demand for technologically-skilled people has helped create a shortage of teachers in these fields. With salaries in industry much higher than those in schools and colleges, schools are hard-pressed to fill vacancies in their staffs.

Note that the United States ranked only tenth in the world in longevity in the early 1980's.

entertainment, are constantly becoming more sophisticated and less expensive. As a result, the market for such products is expanding at a remarkable rate, with no end in sight. Other electronic devices promise to improve the quality of life in a myriad of ways.

3 Social Questions

Advances in technology, however, raise difficult questions even as they excite the imagination. There are problems regarding the control of high technology. For example, recent breakthroughs in gene-splicing could lead to the release of dangerous new organisms into the environment. The potential use of laser beams and orbiting satellites as weapons of war likewise presents a frightening prospect. Another problem is that high technology devices, such as computers and robots, may displace large numbers of workers. The fear of being replaced by a machine is an old one, but it is very real. Indeed, when *Time* chose the computer to receive its traditional "Man of the Year" award in 1982, few newspapers failed to comment on the meaning of this choice.

Job Training

There are also problems concerning job training. As the need for workers in high technology grows, should government money be spent to retrain workers? Are cutbacks in funds for higher education going to limit the number of skilled engineers, mathematicians, and scientists just when the country needs more of them? The United States already lags behind Japan and the Soviet Union in the proportion of students entering these vital fields.

As working knowledge of computers becomes more essential for the average American to function successfully, many people argue that schools need to expose children to these machines at an early age. But with public school districts throughout the nation facing severe financial strains, especially in poorer areas, computers are likely to be an extravagance.

Health Care

The cost of technology is yet another area of concern. For example, CAT scanners and kidney

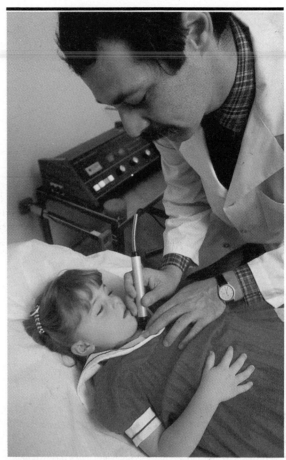

Modern machines and instruments such as the laser are invaluable in diagnosing, treating, and preventing disease. What benefits have Americans derived from these technological advances?

dialysis machines have helped save many lives. But the high cost of advanced medical technology has led to higher medical expenses for everyone and to cost-cutting measures in other areas of health care.

The high cost of health care has become a major subject of debate. What can be done to keep costs from rising further? Should ability to pay have anything to do with the kind of medical treatment an individual receives?

The Graying of America

Problems relating to health care are complicated by an important change in population known as "the graying of America." Life expectancy has increased dramatically—from 47 in 1900 to 73 in 1980. As a

Point out that for political reasons, it has become increasingly difficult for legislators to take a stand against proposals aiding senior citizens. Not only has the proportion of people over 65 increased substantially, but as a group, they are more likely than most to go to the polls on election day, and they have also become a very well organized and vocal political pressure group.

Today Americans live longer, more active lives. There are more than 25 million people who are 65 years old or older in the United States. For many who have retired, social security is the primary source of income. Why are some observers fearful that the system could bankrupt?

result, the proportion of Americans over the age of 65 has grown markedly. And senior citizens require significantly more medical treatment than any other age group.

The growth of the elder sector of the population has also put strains on the social security system. In 1945 the ratio of retirees to workers paying social security taxes was 1:42. By the early 1980's, the figure was close to 1:3, and the system was approaching bankruptcy in spite of increases in social security taxes.

In 1983 Congress passed a social security reform bill as an emergency measure. The bill moved ahead scheduled tax increases, delayed cost-of-living increases for those receiving payments, taxed some of the benefits of higher-income recipients, raised taxes for the self-employed, and included more workers in the social security system. President Reagan was pleased with the bill, saying, "A dark cloud has been lifted." However, the social security system still faces financial troubles in the future.

Equal Rights

Fixing the social security system is controversial because it involves a conflict between two groups: those who receive benefits and those who pay taxes. Many other social questions likewise involve balancing the rights of one group versus the rights of another. For example, affirmative action programs that help minorities and women may do so at the expense of white males.

The United States has done more than any other nation in history to provide equal rights for all. The most recent minority group to benefit from the American commitment to equal rights is persons with

By the early 1980's, the courts were moving beyond the idea of "equal pay for equal work" to promote "equal pay for equivalent work," an effort to counter society's tendency to automatically denigrate jobs in which women are predominant. The issue of whether "equality" necessarily means "sameness" has contin- ued to generate debate over the Equal Rights Amendment. In 1982 the amendment failed to receive ratification by the required two-thirds of the states, but it was reintroduced in Congress in 1983.

handicaps. Many people have become more aware of the problems faced by those with physical disabilities, and steps have been taken to reduce those problems. For example, public buildings are now required to have certain facilities, such as entrances for wheelchairs. Laws have been passed to prevent job discrimination against persons with handicaps. Attempts have also been made to help children with mental handicaps by **"mainstreaming,"** or integrating them into regular school programs.

Progress has also been made by other minorities. For example, college enrollments for blacks jumped four-fold between 1960 and 1980. During the same time, the number of black doctors doubled, and the number of black lawyers multiplied six-fold. Despite progress, however, the majority of blacks continue to suffer major disadvantages. Unemployment for blacks is about twice the national average.

Most problems for blacks and other minorities are related to the fact that they have lower incomes. One of the chief complaints of women, too, has been against economic discrimination. In general the incomes of working women are less than two-thirds that of working men. Women's rights advocates also point out that jobs in fields dominated by women pay less even when they require high levels of skill.

The Family

Women have focused on economic issues partly because poverty has increasingly become a women's issue. One reason for this is that women, who tend to live longer than men, make up a majority of the elderly poor. Another reason is the rise in the number of single-parent households, 90 percent of which are female-headed. These households tend to be signifi-

Urban areas have a greater incidence of single-parent households than do rural areas. In addition, a lower percentage of single-parent households exists among people of Spanish origin than among blacks or whites. How does the income of single-parent households compare with two-parent households?

SINGLE-PARENT HOUSEHOLDS

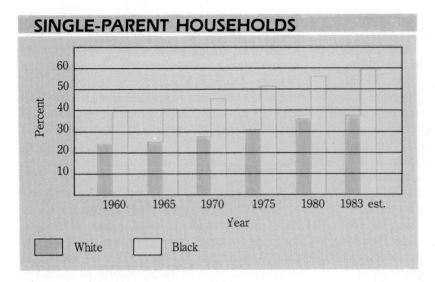

cantly poorer than two-parent households, and they place a special strain on children.

Although a majority of divorced men and women remarry, and many parents keep in touch with the children from previous marriages, society is just beginning to come to grips with the step-family phenomenon. The breakdown of the traditional family unit is disturbing to many Americans. To solve the problem, many people call for a return to traditional values, such as the sanctity of the family (including traditional roles for men and women).

Debating the Issues

Debate over social and political questions has been part of American life since the beginning of the nation's history. The nation's Founders struggled with such issues as the role of government in the life of the individual and the balance between freedom and order. The fact that people still openly debate these issues suggests that the American tradition remains strong—strong enough to meet the many challenges that lie ahead.

FOR FURTHER DISCUSSION

1. Why is foreign policy more complicated today than it was in the early 1800's or immediately after World War II?

2. Should the United States develop an extensive civil defense system to protect at least part of the population in case of nuclear war? Explain.

3. What is the major economic problem faced by the United States today? What are some alternative solutions? Is it necessary to increase the role of the federal government to solve economic problems? Why or why not?

4. How has the economy of your community, state, or region changed over the years? What changes do you expect in the future?

5. What should be done to ensure that all groups receive equal opportunity in American society? What conditions are necessary to create equal opportunity?

6. What are some of the major social issues of today? How do they represent the competing interests of different groups? How does the American system of government resolve such issues?

APPENDIX

Atlas and Historical Data

United States

The World

Climate

Land Use

Mineral Resources and Deposits

Industry and Manufacturing

The American People

The American Society

The American Economy

The Government Sector

The States of the Union

Presidents and Vice Presidents

Political Parties

Declaration of Independence
Constitution of the United States
Glossary
Index

PACIFIC OCEAN

45°

40°

35°

125°   120°   115°   50°   110°   105°   10

WASHINGTON

Victoria   Bellingham   Lethbridge   Regina

Seattle   Spokane   Great Falls   Minot

Tacoma   Puget S.   Columbia River   Flathead Lake

Olympia   Mt. Rainier 14,408   Walla Walla   **MONTANA**   Fort Peck Lake   **NORTH DAKOTA**

Portland   Pendleton   Lewiston   Missoula   Helena   Bismarck

Salem   **ROCKY**   Butte   Bozeman   Billings   Miles City   **SOUTH DAKOTA**

Eugene   **OREGON**   **IDAHO**   Yellowstone River

Medford   Burns   Boise   Nampa   Idaho Falls   Sheridan   BLACK HILLS   Rapid City   Pierre

Eureka   Winnemucca   Elko   Twin Falls   **WYOMING**   Casper   Scottsbluff   **NEBRASKA**

Reno   **NEVADA**   **GREAT**   Logan   Green River   Rawlins   Laramie   Cheyenne   North Platte

Sacramento   Carson City   **BASIN**   Great Salt Lake   Ogden   Rock Springs   Fort Collins   Greeley

San Francisco   Oakland   Stockton   Ely   Salt Lake City   **MOUNTAINS**   Denver

San Jose   **SIERRA NEVADA**   Tonopah   Provo   Price   Grand Junction   Mt. Elbert 14,431   **COLORADO**

Monterey   Mt. Whitney 14,495   **UTAH**   **WASATCH RANGE**   Colorado Springs

Santa Barbara   DEATH VALLEY -282   Cedar City   Las Vegas   **COLORADO**   Pueblo   Arkansas River

Los Angeles   Long Beach   San Bernardino   GRAND   Lake Powell   Durango   Trinidad

San Diego   Salton Sea -241   **ARIZONA**   **CANYON**   **PLATEAU**   Flagstaff   Winslow   Santa Fe   Las Vegas   Tucumcari   Amarillo

Tijuana   Prescott   Phoenix   Gila River   Albuquerque   Clovis   Lubbock

Yuma   **SONORAN DESERT**   **NEW MEXICO**   Roswell

Tucson   Silver City   Carlsbad   Midland   Odessa

Nogales   Douglas   El Paso   **TEXAS**

Ciudad Juárez   Agua Prieta

MEXICO   Rio Grande   Pecos River

125°   120°   115°   110°   105°   100°

ALASKA
Scale in miles and kilometers
758   One inch 420 miles
One centimeter 265 kilometers | 420 | | 265 | 530 |

U.S.S.R.   ARCTIC CIRCLE   Barrow   Pt. Barrow

Bering Strait   Nome   St. Lawrence Island   **BROOKS RANGE**   Fort Yukon   **RICHARDSON MTS**   Mackenzie

BERING SEA   Yukon River   Fairbanks   Dawson   Norman Wells

Mt. McKinley 20,320   **ALASKA RANGE**   Whitehorse

Anchorage

ALEUTIAN IS.   **GULF OF ALASKA**   Juneau

KODIAK I.   Sitka   Petersburg   Ketchikan

180°   170°   160°   150°   140°   130°

HAWAII
Scale in miles and kilometers
One inch 200 miles
One centimeter 125 kilometers | 200 | | 125 | 250 |

KAUAI   NIIHAU   OAHU   Honolulu   MOLOKAI   LANAI   MAUI   KAHOOLAWE   HAWAII   Hilo

PACIFIC OCEAN

160°   110°   100°

UNITED STATES

Lambert Conformal Conic Projection

One inch 200 miles
One centimeter 125 kilometers

⬡ National Capital
⬥ State Capital

■ 1,000,000 Population and Over
● 500,000 to 1,000,000 Population
○ Under 500,000 Population

ARCTIC OCEAN

ALASKA
(UNITED STATES)

ARC

ICELAND

C A N A D A

UNITED

IRELAND
London
KINGDO

NORTH

FRA

AMERICA

Ottawa

UNITED STATES

New York

PORTUGAL
SPAIN
Mad

Washington, D.C.

ATLANTIC

Los Angeles

MOROCCO

MEXICO

ALC

BAHAMAS

A

HAWAII
(U.S.)

CUBA
DOMINICAN
REPUBLIC

MAURITANIA

Mexico City

HAITI

SENEGAL
CAPE
VERDE GAMBIA

BELIZE
HONDURAS
GUATEMALA
EL SALVADOR

JAMAICA

MALI

GUINEA-BISSAU
GUINEA

VOLTA

NICARAGUA

TRINIDAD
AND
TOBAGO

Caracas

SIERRA LEONE

COSTA RICA

VENEZUELA

PANAMA

GUYANA

LIBERIA

Bogotá

SURINAME
FR. GUIANA

COLOMBIA

PACIFIC

EQUATOR

ECUADOR

EQUAT

SOUTH

OCEAN

BRAZIL

Lima

AMERICA

PERU

Brasilia

BOLIVIA

OCEAN

PARAGUAY

Santiago

URUGUAY

CHILE

Buenos Aires

ARGENTINA

INTERNATIONAL DATE LINE

PRIME MERIDIAN

THE WORLD

SCALE IN MILES AND KILOMETERS

One inch 1800 miles

One centimeter 1140 kilometers

1800

1140   2280

Mercator Projection

CLIMATE

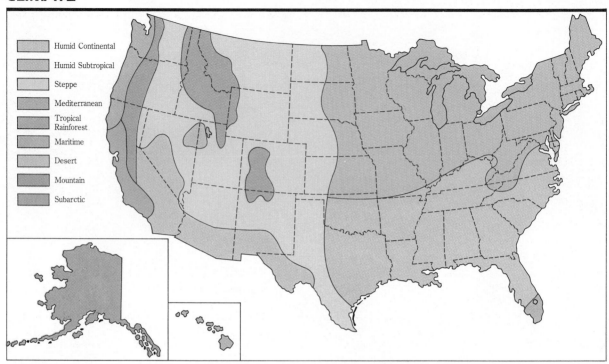

Humid Continental
Humid Subtropical
Steppe
Mediterranean
Tropical Rainforest
Maritime
Desert
Mountain
Subarctic

LAND USE

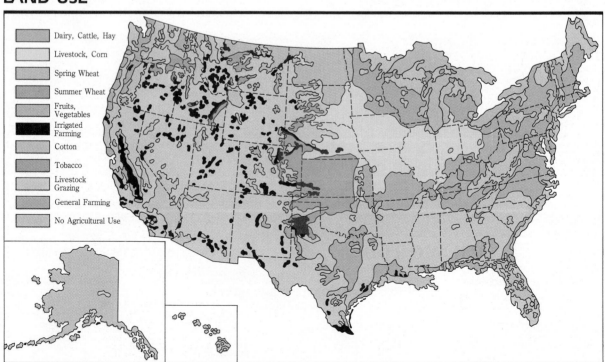

Dairy, Cattle, Hay
Livestock, Corn
Spring Wheat
Summer Wheat
Fruits, Vegetables
Irrigated Farming
Cotton
Tobacco
Livestock Grazing
General Farming
No Agricultural Use

MINERAL RESOURCES AND DEPOSITS

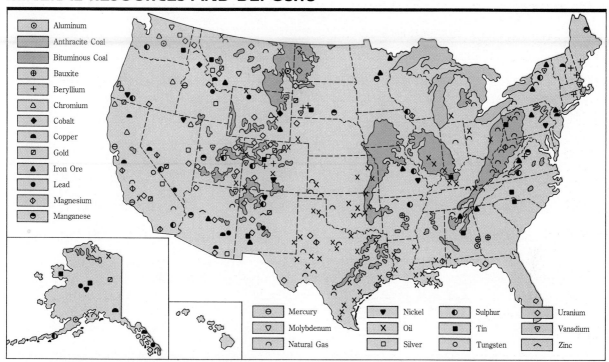

Aluminum
Anthracite Coal
Bituminous Coal
Bauxite
Beryllium
Chromium
Cobalt
Copper
Gold
Iron Ore
Lead
Magnesium
Manganese

Mercury
Molybdenum
Natural Gas
Nickel
Oil
Silver
Sulphur
Tin
Tungsten
Uranium
Vanadium
Zinc

INDUSTRY AND MANUFACTURING

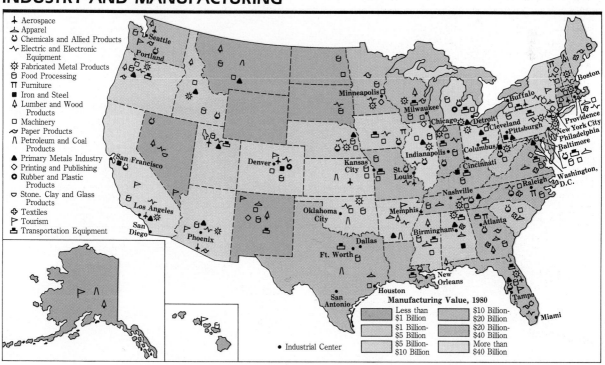

Aerospace
Apparel
Chemicals and Allied Products
Electric and Electronic Equipment
Fabricated Metal Products
Food Processing
Furniture
Iron and Steel
Lumber and Wood Products
Machinery
Paper Products
Petroleum and Coal Products
Primary Metals Industry
Printing and Publishing
Rubber and Plastic Products
Stone. Clay and Glass Products
Textiles
Tourism
Transportation Equipment

Manufacturing Value, 1980

Less than $1 Billion
$1 Billion–$5 Billion
$5 Billion–$10 Billion
$10 Billion–$20 Billion
$20 Billion–$40 Billion
More than $40 Billion

• Industrial Center

763

THE AMERICAN PEOPLE

POPULATION

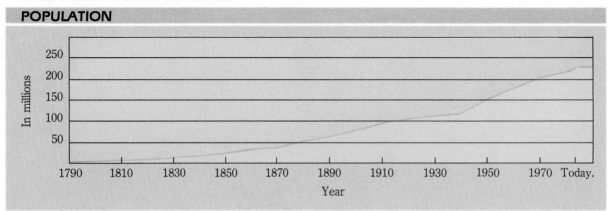

DISTRIBUTION BY AGE

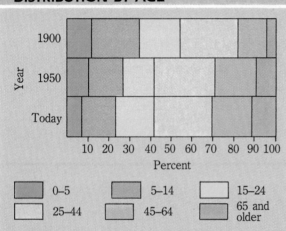

POPULATION BY RACE AND ORIGIN

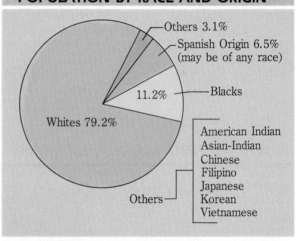

BIRTH AND DEATH RATE

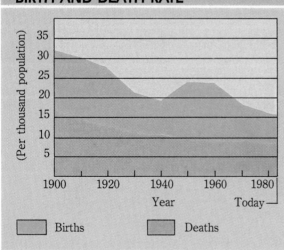

LIFE EXPECTANCY AT BIRTH

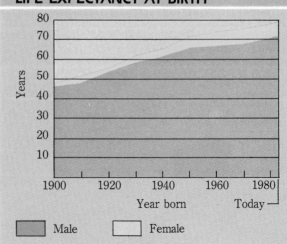

THE AMERICAN SOCIETY

EDUCATION

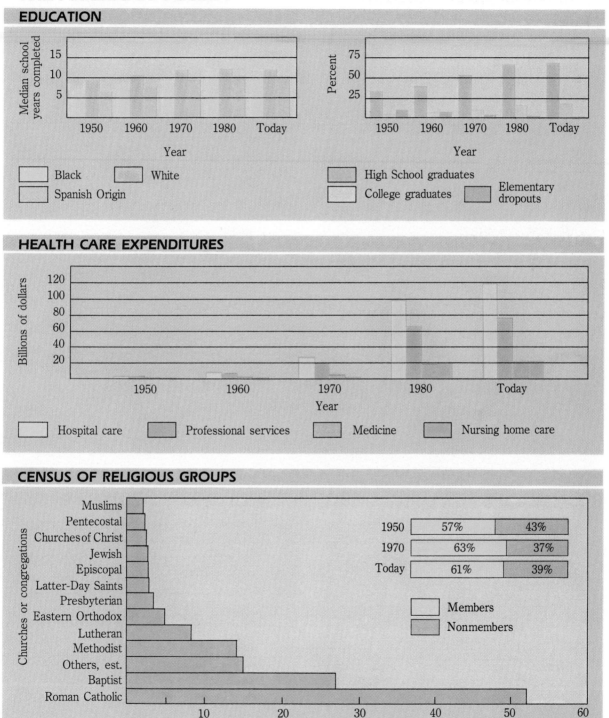

Black   White   High School graduates

Spanish Origin   College graduates   Elementary dropouts

HEALTH CARE EXPENDITURES

Hospital care   Professional services   Medicine   Nursing home care

CENSUS OF RELIGIOUS GROUPS

	Members	Nonmembers
1950	57%	43%
1970	63%	37%
Today	61%	39%

Members
Nonmembers

THE AMERICAN ECONOMY

GROSS NATIONAL PRODUCT

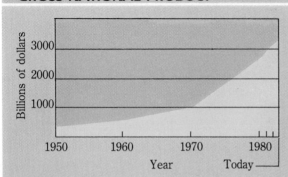

MEDIAN INCOME OF FAMILIES

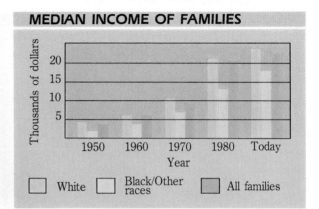

- ☐ White
- ☐ Black/Other races
- ☐ All families

AMERICA AT WORK

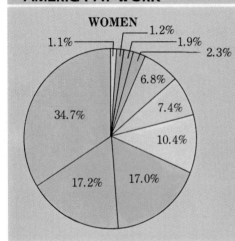

WOMEN
- 1.1%
- 1.2%
- 1.9%
- 2.3%
- 6.8%
- 7.4%
- 10.4%
- 34.7%
- 17.2%
- 17.0%

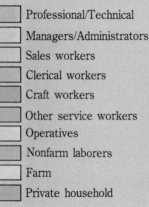

- ☐ Professional/Technical
- ☐ Managers/Administrators
- ☐ Sales workers
- ☐ Clerical workers
- ☐ Craft workers
- ☐ Other service workers
- ☐ Operatives
- ☐ Nonfarm laborers
- ☐ Farm
- ☐ Private household

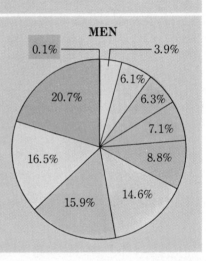

MEN
- 0.1%
- 3.9%
- 6.1%
- 6.3%
- 7.1%
- 8.8%
- 20.7%
- 16.5%
- 15.9%
- 14.6%

PURCHASING POWER OF THE DOLLAR

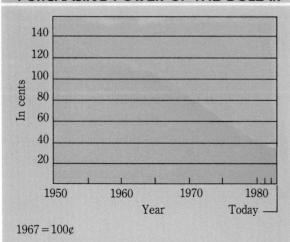

1967 = 100¢

CONSUMER AND WHOLESALE PRICES

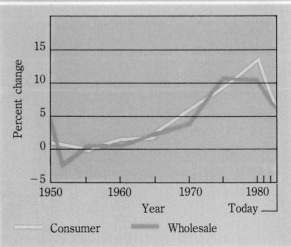

- Consumer
- Wholesale

THE GOVERNMENT SECTOR

PUBLIC EMPLOYEES

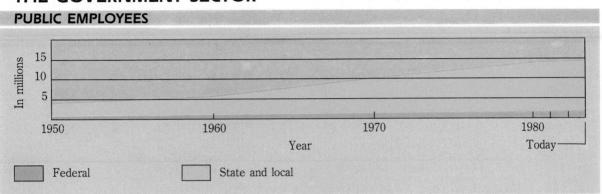

FEDERAL GOVERNMENT RECEIPTS AND EXPENDITURES

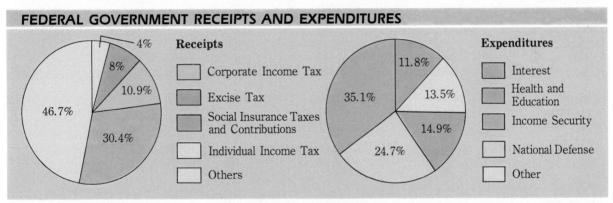

EXPENDITURES BY STATE AND LOCAL GOVERNMENT

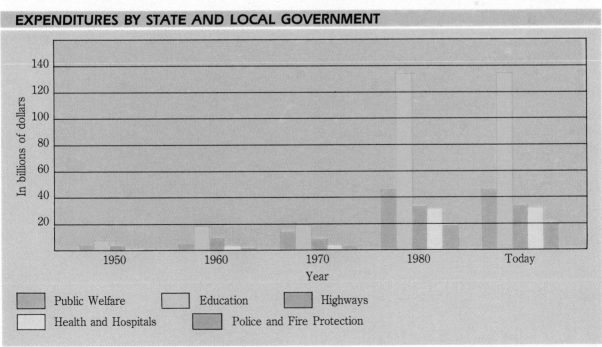

THE STATES OF THE UNION

STATE	CAPITAL	ENTERED UNION	POPULATION 1980	PCT. CHANGE FROM 1970	AREA IN SQ. MILES
Alabama	Montgomery	1819	3,890,061	+12.9	51,609
Alaska	Juneau	1959	400,481	+32.4	586,412
Arizona	Phoenix	1912	2,717,866	+53.1	113,909
Arkansas	Little Rock	1836	2,285,513	+18.8	53,104
California	Sacramento	1850	23,668,562	+18.5	158,693
Colorado	Denver	1876	2,888,834	+30.7	104,247
Connecticut	Hartford	1788	3,107,576	+2.5	5,009
Delaware	Dover	1787	595,225	+8.6	2,057
Florida	Tallahassee	1845	9,739,992	+43.4	58,560
Georgia	Atlanta	1788	5,464,265	+19.1	58,876
Hawaii	Honolulu	1959	965,000	+25.3	6,450
Idaho	Boise	1890	943,935	+32.4	83,557
Illinois	Springfield	1818	11,418,461	+2.8	56,400
Indiana	Indianapolis	1816	5,490,179	+5.7	36,291
Iowa	Des Moines	1846	2,913,387	+3.1	56,290
Kansas	Topeka	1861	2,363,208	+5.1	82,264
Kentucky	Frankfort	1792	3,661,433	+13.7	40,395
Louisiana	Baton Rouge	1812	4,203,972	+15.3	48,523
Maine	Augusta	1820	1,124,660	+15.2	33,215
Maryland	Annapolis	1788	4,216,446	+7.5	10,577
Massachusetts	Boston	1788	5,737,037	+0.8	8,257
Michigan	Lansing	1837	9,258,344	+4.2	58,216
Minnesota	St. Paul	1858	4,077,148	+7.1	84,068
Mississippi	Jackson	1817	2,520,638	+13.7	47,716
Missouri	Jefferson City	1821	4,917,444	+5.1	69,686
Montana	Helena	1889	786,690	+13.3	147,138
Nebraska	Lincoln	1867	1,570,006	+5.7	77,227
Nevada	Carson City	1864	799,184	+63.5	110,540
New Hampshire	Concord	1788	920,610	+24.8	9,304
New Jersey	Trenton	1787	7,364,158	+2.7	7,836
New Mexico	Sante Fe	1912	1,299,968	+27.8	121,666
New York	Albany	1788	17,557,288	−3.8	49,576
North Carolina	Raleigh	1789	5,874,429	+15.5	52,586
North Dakota	Bismarck	1889	652,695	+5.6	70,665
Ohio	Columbus	1803	10,797,419	+1.3	41,222
Oklahoma	Oklahoma City	1907	3,025,266	+18.2	69,919
Oregon	Salem	1859	2,632,663	+25.9	96,981
Pennsylvania	Harrisburg	1787	11,866,728	+0.6	45,333
Rhode Island	Providence	1790	947,154	−0.3	1,214
South Carolina	Columbia	1788	3,119,208	+20.4	31,055
South Dakota	Pierre	1889	690,178	+3.6	77,047
Tennessee	Nashville	1796	4,590,750	+16.9	42,244
Texas	Austin	1845	14,228,383	+27.1	267,339
Utah	Salt Lake City	1896	1,461,037	+37.9	84,916
Vermont	Montpelier	1791	511,456	+15.0	9,609
Virginia	Richmond	1788	5,346,279	+14.9	40,817
Washington	Olympia	1889	4,130,163	+21.0	68,192
West Virginia	Charleston	1863	1,949,644	+11.8	24,181
Wisconsin	Madison	1848	4,705,335	+6.5	56,153
Wyoming	Cheyenne	1890	470,816	+41.6	97,914
District of Columbia			637,651	−15.7	67

PRESIDENTS AND VICE PRESIDENTS

President	Born	Died	Term of Office	Party	State*	Vice-President
George Washington	1732	1799	1789–1797	Federalist	Va.	John Adams
John Adams	1735	1826	1797–1801	Federalist	Mass.	Thomas Jefferson
Thomas Jefferson	1743	1826	1801–1809	Republican	Va.	Aaron Burr George Clinton
James Madison	1751	1836	1809–1817	Republican	Va.	George Clinton Elbridge Gerry
James Monroe	1758	1831	1817–1825	Republican	Va.	Daniel D. Tompkins
John Quincy Adams	1767	1848	1825–1829	Republican	Mass.	John C. Calhoun
Andrew Jackson	1767	1845	1829–1837	Democratic	Tenn.	John C. Calhoun Martin Van Buren
Martin Van Buren	1782	1862	1837–1841	Democratic	N.Y.	Richard M. Johnson
William H. Harrison	1773	1841	1841	Whig	Ohio	John Tyler
John Tyler	1790	1862	1841–1845	Whig	Va.	
James K. Polk	1795	1849	1845–1849	Democratic	Tenn.	George M. Dallas
Zachary Taylor	1784	1850	1849–1850	Whig	La.	Millard Fillmore
Millard Fillmore	1800	1874	1850–1853	Whig	N.Y.	
Franklin Pierce	1804	1869	1853–1857	Democratic	N.H.	William R. King
James Buchanan	1791	1868	1857–1861	Democratic	Pa.	John C. Breckinridge
Abraham Lincoln	1809	1865	1861–1865	Republican	Ill.	Hannibal Hamlin Andrew Johnson
Andrew Johnson	1808	1875	1865–1869	Democratic	Tenn.	
Ulysses S. Grant	1822	1885	1869–1877	Republican	Ill.	Schuyler Colfax Henry Wilson
Rutherford B. Hayes	1822	1893	1877–1881	Republican	Ohio	William A. Wheeler
James A. Garfield	1831	1881	1881	Republican	Ohio	Chester A. Arthur
Chester A. Arthur	1830	1886	1881–1885	Republican	N.Y.	
Grover Cleveland	1837	1908	1885–1889	Democratic	N.Y.	Thomas A. Hendricks
Benjamin Harrison	1833	1901	1889–1893	Republican	Ind.	Levi P. Morton
Grover Cleveland	1837	1908	1893–1897	Democratic	N.Y.	Adlai E. Stevenson
William McKinley	1843	1901	1897–1901	Republican	Ohio	Garret A. Hobart Theodore Roosevelt
Theodore Roosevelt	1858	1919	1901–1909	Republican	N.Y.	Charles W. Fairbanks
William H. Taft	1857	1930	1909–1913	Republican	Ohio	James S. Sherman
Woodrow Wilson	1856	1924	1913–1921	Democratic	N.J.	Thomas R. Marshall
Warren G. Harding	1865	1923	1921–1923	Republican	Ohio	Calvin Coolidge
Calvin Coolidge	1872	1933	1923–1929	Republican	Mass.	Charles G. Dawes
Herbert Hoover	1874	1964	1929–1933	Republican	Cal.	Charles Curtis
Franklin D. Roosevelt	1882	1945	1933–1945	Democratic	N.Y.	John Garner Henry Wallace Harry Truman
Harry Truman	1884	1972	1945–1953	Democratic	Mo.	Alben Barkley
Dwight Eisenhower	1890	1969	1953–1961	Republican	N.Y.	Richard Nixon
John F. Kennedy	1917	1963	1961–1963	Democratic	Mass.	Lyndon Johnson
Lyndon Johnson	1908	1973	1963–1969	Democratic	Texas	Hubert Humphrey
Richard Nixon	1913		1969–1974	Republican	N.Y.	Spiro Agnew Gerald Ford
Gerald Ford	1913		1974–1977	Republican	Mich.	Nelson Rockefeller
Jimmy Carter	1924		1977–1981	Democratic	Ga.	Walter Mondale
Ronald Reagan	1911		1981–	Republican	Cal.	George Bush

*State of residence at election

AMERICAN POLITICAL PARTIES

POLITICAL PARTIES IN POWER

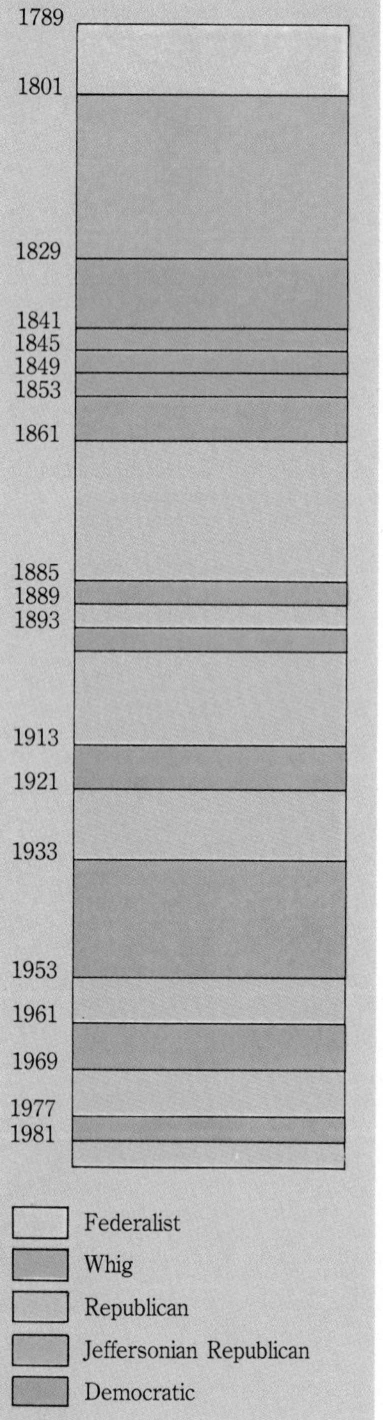

1789	
1801	
1829	
1841	
1845	
1849	
1853	
1861	
1885	
1889	
1893	
1913	
1921	
1933	
1953	
1961	
1969	
1977	
1981	

Legend:
- Federalist
- Whig
- Republican
- Jeffersonian Republican
- Democratic

THIRD PARTY MOVEMENTS

PARTY	STRONGEST SHOWING	ISSUE	STRENGTH
Anti-Masonic	1832	Against secret societies	Pa., Vt.
Liberty	1840–44	Anti-Slavery	North
Free Soil*	1848	Anti-Slavery	N.Y., Ohio
American (Know Nothing)*	1856	Anti-Immigrant	Northeast, South
Constitutional Union*	1860	Preservation of the Union	Ky., Tenn., Va.
Greenback	1876–80	"Cheap Money" 8-Hour Work Day	National
Prohibition	1884	Anti-Liquor	National
Union Labor	1888	Pro-Industrial Worker	Northeast
Populist*	1892	Free Coinage of Silver	South, West
Socialist	1900–20	Collective Ownership	National
Progressive (Bull Moose)*	1912	End High Tariffs, Women's Suffrage	Midwest, West
Farmer Labor	1924	Social Security, Farm-Labor Support	Iowa, Minn.
Progressive*	1924	Labor Reform	Midwest, West
Socialist	1928–48	Liberal Reforms	National
Communist	1932	Working Class Control	West, Northeast
Union	1936	Anti-New Deal	National
States' Rights (Dixiecrats)	1948	Pro-Segregation	South
Progressive	1948	Anti-Cold War	Cal., N.Y.
American Independent*	1968	States' Rights	South
American	1972	Law and Order	West
Libertarian	1980	Limited Government	National

*Received more than 10% of the popular votes cast.

DECLARATION OF INDEPENDENCE

When in the course of human events, it becomes necessary for one people to dissolve the political bands which have connected them with another, and to assume among the powers of the earth, the separate and equal station to which the laws of nature and of nature's God entitle them, a decent respect to the opinions of mankind requires that they should declare the causes which impel them to the separation.

We hold these truths to be self-evident, that all men are created equal, that they are endowed by their Creator with certain unalienable rights, that among these are life, liberty, and the pursuit of happiness. That to secure these rights, governments are instituted among men, deriving their just powers from the consent of the governed; that whenever any form of government becomes destructive of these ends, it is the right of the people to alter or to abolish it, and to institute new government, laying its foundation on such principles, and organizing its powers in such form, as to them shall seem most likely to effect their safety and happiness. Prudence, indeed, will dictate that governments long established should not be changed for light and transient causes; and accordingly all experience hath shown, that mankind are more disposed to suffer, while evils are sufferable, than to right themselves by abolishing the forms to which they are accustomed. But when a long train of abuses and usurpations, pursuing invariably the same object, evinces a design to reduce them under absolute despotism, it is their right, it is their duty, to throw off such government, and to provide new guards for their future security. Such has been the patient sufferance of these colonies; and such is now the necessity which constrains them to alter their former systems of government. The history of the present King of Great Britain is a history of repeated injuries and usurpations, all having in direct object the establishment of an absolute tyranny over these states. To prove this, let facts be submitted to a candid world.

He has refused his assent to laws, the most wholesome and necessary for the public good.

He has forbidden his governors to pass laws of immediate and pressing importance, unless suspended in their operation till his assent should be obtained; and when so suspended, he has utterly neglected to attend to them.

He has refused to pass other laws for the accommodation of large districts of people, unless those people would relinquish the right of representation in the legislature, a right inestimable to them and formidable to tyrants only.

He has called together legislative bodies at places unusual, uncomfortable, and distant from the depository of their public records, for the sole purpose of fatiguing them into compliance with his measures.

He has dissolved representative houses repeatedly, for opposing with manly firmness his invasions on the rights of the people.

He has refused for a long time, after such dissolutions, to cause others to be elected; whereby the legislative powers, incapable of annihilation, have returned to the people at large for their exercise; the state remaining in the meantime exposed to all the dangers of invasion from without and convulsions within.

He has endeavored to prevent the population of these states; for that purpose obstructing the laws for naturalization of foreigners, refusing to pass others to encourage their migrations hither, and raising the conditions of new appropriations of lands.

He has obstructed the administration of justice, by refusing his assent to laws for establishing judiciary powers.

He has made judges dependent on his will alone, for the tenure of their offices, and the amount and payment of their salaries.

He has erected a multitude of new offices, and sent hither swarms of officers to harass our people, and eat out their substance.

He has kept among us, in times of peace, standing armies without the consent of our legislatures.

He has affected to render the military independent of and superior to the civil power.

He has combined with others to subject us to a jurisdiction foreign to our constitution, and unacknowledged by our laws; giving his assent to their acts of pretended legislation:

For quartering large bodies of armed troops among us;

For protecting them, by a mock trial, from punishment for any murders which they should commit on the inhabitants of these states;

For cutting off our trade with all parts of the world;

For imposing taxes on us without our consent;

For depriving us, in many cases, of the benefits of trial by jury;

For transporting us beyond seas to be tried for pretended offenses;

For abolishing the free system of English laws in a neighboring province, establishing therein an arbitrary government, and enlarging its boundaries so as to render it at once an example and fit instrument for introducing the same absolute rule into these colonies;

For taking away our charters, abolishing our most valuable laws, and altering fundamentally the forms of our governments;

For suspending our own legislatures; and declaring themselves invested with power to legislate for us in all cases whatsoever.

He has abdicated government here, by declaring us out of his protection and waging war against us.

He has plundered our seas, ravaged our coasts, burned our towns, and destroyed the lives of our people.

He is at this time transporting large armies of foreign mercenaries to complete the works of death, desolation, and tyranny, already begun with circumstances of cruelty and perfidy scarcely paralleled in the most barbarous ages, and totally unworthy the head of a civilized nation.

He has constrained our fellow citizens taken captive on the high seas to bear arms against their country, to become the executioners of their friends and brethren, or to fall themselves by their hands.

He has excited domestic insurrections among us, and has endeavored to bring on the inhabitants of our frontiers, the merciless Indian savages, whose known rule of warfare is an undistinguished destruction of all ages, sexes, and conditions.

In every stage of these oppressions we have petitioned for redress in the most humble terms; our repeated petitions have been answered only by repeated injury. A prince, whose character is thus marked by every act which may define a tyrant, is unfit to be the ruler of a free people.

Nor have we been wanting in our attentions to our British brethren. We have warned them from time to time of attempts by their legislature to extend an unwarrantable jurisdiction over us. We have reminded them of the circumstances of our emigration and settlement here. We have appealed to their native justice and magnanimity, and we have conjured them by the ties of our common kindred to disavow these usurpations, which would inevitably interrupt our connections and correspondence. They too have been deaf to the voice of justice and consanguinity. We must, therefore, acquiesce in the necessity which denounces our separation, and hold them as we hold the rest of mankind, enemies in war, in peace friends.

We, therefore, the representatives of the United States of America, in General Congress, assembled, appealing to the Supreme Judge of the world for the rectitude of our intentions, do, in the name and by authority of the good people of these colonies, solemnly publish and declare, that these united colonies are, and of right ought to be, free and independent states; that they are absolved from all allegiance to the British Crown, and that all political connection between them and the State of Great Britain is and ought to be totally dissolved; and that as free and independent states, they have full power to levy war, conclude peace, contract alliances, establish commerce, and to do all other acts and things which independent states may of right do. And for the support of this declaration, with a firm reliance on the protection of Divine Providence, we mutually pledge to each other our lives, our fortunes, and our sacred honor.

John Hancock, **President**

NEW HAMPSHIRE
Josiah Bartlett
William Whipple
Matthew Thornton

MASSACHUSETTS
Samuel Adams
John Adams
Robert Treat Paine
Elbridge Gerry

DELAWARE
Caesar Rodney
George Read
Thomas M'Kean

RHODE ISLAND
Stephen Hopkins
William Ellery

PENNSYLVANIA
Robert Morris
Benjamin Rush
Benjamin Franklin
John Morton
George Clymer
James Smith
George Taylor
James Wilson
George Ross

VIRGINIA
George Wythe
Richard Henry Lee
Thomas Jefferson
Benjamin Harrison
Thomas Nelson, Jr.
Francis Lightfoot Lee
Carter Braxton

CONNECTICUT
Roger Sherman
Samuel Huntington
William Williams
Oliver Wolcott

MARYLAND
Samuel Chase
William Paca
Thomas Stone
Charles Carroll
* of Carrollton*

NEW JERSEY
Richard Stockton
John Witherspoon
Francis Hopkinson
John Hart
Abraham Clark

NEW YORK
William Floyd
Philip Livingston
Francis Lewis
Lewis Morris

NORTH CAROLINA
William Hooper
Joseph Hewes
John Penn

SOUTH CAROLINA
Edward Rutledge
Thomas Heyward, Jr.
Thomas Lynch, Jr.
Arthur Middleton

GEORGIA
Button Gwinnett
Lyman Hall
George Walton

CONSTITUTION OF THE UNITED STATES

PREAMBLE

We the People of the United States, in order to form a more perfect union, establish justice, insure domestic tranquility, provide for the common defense, promote the general welfare, and secure the blessings of liberty to ourselves and our posterity, do ordain and establish this CONSTITUTION for the United States of America.

The Preamble is an introduction that explains why the Constitution is necessary and lists the purposes and goals to be achieved.

Article 1   Legislative Branch

Section 1 Congress

All legislative powers herein granted shall be vested in a Congress of the United States, which shall consist of a Senate and House of Representatives.

In addition to establishing a bicameral legislature, Section 1 grants Congress the sole power to enact law at the national level. By custom, however, other branches do possess law-making powers.

Section 2 House of Representatives

1. The House of Representatives shall be composed of members chosen every second year by the people of the several states, and the electors in each state shall have the qualifications requisite for electors of the most numerous branch of the state legislature.

This paragraph sets the House term at two years and provides for the popular election of Representatives. The term "electors" is synonymous to voters here.

2. No person shall be a Representative who shall not have attained to the age of twenty-five years, and been seven years a citizen of the United States, and who shall not, when elected, be an inhabitant of that state in which he shall be chosen.

Paragraph 2 sets the constitutional qualifications which must be met to serve as a Representative. States are not restricted from setting others. Though it is not a qualification, tradition dictates that candidates legally reside in the district they run to represent.

3. Representatives and direct taxes shall be apportioned among the several states which may be included within this Union, according to their respective numbers, which shall be determined by adding to the whole number of free persons, including those bound to service for a term of years, and excluding Indians not taxed, three fifths of all other persons. The actual enumeration shall be made within three years after the first meeting of the Congress of the United States, and within every subsequent term of ten years, in such manner as they shall by law direct. The number of Representatives shall not exceed one for every thirty thousand, but each state shall have at least one Representative; and until such enumeration shall be made, the State of New Hampshire shall be entitled to choose three; Massachusetts, eight; Rhode Island and Providence Plantations, one; Connecticut, five; New York, six; New Jersey, four; Pennsylvania, eight; Delaware, one; Maryland, six; Virginia, ten; North Carolina, five; South Carolina, five; and Georgia, three.

In regard to income taxes, the direct tax requirement was voided by the Sixteenth Amendment. The 3/5 reference to slaves was cancelled by the Thirteenth and Fourteenth Amendments.

Since a state's representation in the House is based on its population, a census has been taken every 10 years, beginning with the first in 1790. The current size of the House—435 members—was set by law in 1929. Since then, there has been a reapportionment of seats based on population shifts rather than an addition of seats.

4. When vacancies happen in the representation from any state, the executive authority thereof shall issue writs of election to fill such vacancies.

A vacancy in the House is filled through a special election called by the state's governor.

5. The House of Representatives shall choose their Speaker and other officers; and shall have the sole power of impeachment.

Selecting House officers is strictly by party vote. In addition to the Speaker, House officers include the chaplain, clerk, sergeant of arms, doorkeeper, and postmaster. Only the Speaker is selected from among elected members of the House.

Only the House may impeach, or charge, federal officials with not carrying out their duties. Military officers are not subject to impeachment. Nor are members of Congress, since either house can expel its own members if it sees fit.

Section 3 Senate

1. The Senate of the United States shall be composed of two Senators from each state, chosen by the legislature thereof, for six years; and each Senator shall have one vote.

This paragraph establishes that each state will have two Senators and sets the senatorial term at six years. Selection of Senators by state legislatures was ended with the adoption of the Seventeenth Amendment.

2. Immediately after they shall be assembled in consequence of the first election, they shall be divided as equally as may be into three classes. The seats of the Senators of the first class shall be vacated at the expiration of the second year, of the second class at the expiration of the fourth year, of the third class at the expiration of the sixth year, so that one-third may be chosen every second year, and if vacancies happen by resignation, or otherwise, during the recess of the legislature of any state, the executive thereof may make temporary appointments until the next meeting of the legislature, which shall then fill such vacancies.

Paragraph 2 provides for one third of the membership of the Senate to be chosen every two years. A state's governor can fill a vacancy in that state's membership by temporary appointment until the next general election.

3. No person shall be a Senator who shall not have attained to the age of thirty years, and been nine years a citizen of the United States, and who shall not, when elected, be an inhabitant of that state for which he shall be chosen.

Like those for the House, the only constitutional requirements that must be met for membership in the Senate deal with age, citizenship, and residency.

4. The Vice President of the United States shall be President of the Senate, but shall have no vote, unless they be equally divided.

The Vice President is the presiding officer of the Senate. The Vice President may (but is not required to) vote only when there is a tie vote on a bill or issue.

5. The Senate shall choose their other officers, and also a President *pro tempore,* in the absence of the Vice President, or when he shall exercise the office of President of the United States.

In addition to the Vice President and the President *pro tempore,* Senate officers include a chaplain, clerk, sergeant of arms, doorkeeper, and postmaster. Like the House, these officers are not selected from among the membership.

6. The Senate shall have the sole power to try all impeachments. When sitting for that purpose, they shall be on oath or affirmation. When the President of the United States is tried, the Chief Justice shall preside; and no person shall be convicted without the concurrence of two thirds of the members present.

Only the Senate may try persons impeached by the House. The Senate sets the date for trial and provides the accused with the "articles of impeachment" (a copy of the formal charges). The accused has the same basic legal rights of any defendant on trial. Conviction requires a two-thirds vote of "guilty" by the members present.

Except in the case of the President, the presiding officer of the Senate presides over the trial. In the trial of a President, the Chief Justice presides.

7. Judgment in cases of impeachment shall not extend further than to removal from office, and disqualification to hold and enjoy any office of honor, trust, or profit under the United States; but the party convicted shall nevertheless be liable and subject to indictment, trial, judgment, and punishment, according to law.

Punishment is limited to removal from office and, if the Senate chooses, being barred from holding office in the future. But a person who has been impeached can still be tried in court for any crimes committed.

Section 4 Congressional Elections and Meetings

1. The times, places, and manner of holding elections for Senators and Representatives shall be prescribed in each state by the legislature thereof; but the Congress may at any time by law make or alter such regulations, except as to the places of choosing Senators.

Until 1842 Congress set no election regulations. That year it required members of the House to be elected from districts in states having more than one Representative. In 1845 it set the first Tuesday after the first Monday in November as the day for selecting presidential electors. In 1872 it set the same day in even-numbered years as the date for congressional elections. In 1913, following adoption of the Seventeenth Amendment, it extended the date to senatorial elections.

2. The Congress shall assemble at least once in every year, and such meeting shall be on the first Monday in December, unless they shall by law appoint a different day.

The opening date was changed to January 3 by the Twentieth Amendment. A new Congress begins on that date of each odd-numbered year and continues for two years regardless of the number of sessions held.

Section 5 Congressional Powers and Duties

1. Each house shall be the judge of the elections, returns, and qualifications of its own members, and a majority of each shall constitute a quorum to do business; but a smaller number may adjourn from day to day, and may be authorized to compel the attendance of absent members, in such manner, and under such penalties, as each house may provide.

Each house has the power to exclude, or to refuse to seat, a member elect. Until 1969, each house viewed its power to judge qualifications as the power to set informal standards beyond the specified constitutional qualifications of age, citizenship, and residency. In 1969 the U.S. Supreme Court in *Powell* v. *McCormack* limited Congress' power to judgment of constitutional qualifications only.

Technically to conduct business, 218 members must be present in the House and 51 in the Senate. The quorum rule is seldom enforced, however, in handling of routine matters.

2. Each house may determine the rules of its proceedings, punish its members for disorderly behavior, and, with the concurrence of two thirds, expel a member.

Each house sets its own rules. There are a few unique ones. Under the "seniority" rule, committee chairmanships go to the majority party member who has served the longest on the committee. Under "senatorial courtesy," the Senate will refuse to confirm a presidential appointment if a Senator from the appointee's state and of the same party as the President objects to the appointment.

In the House, debate is limited to one hour per member, unless that Representative has unanimous consent to speak longer. In the Senate, however, a member can hold the floor indefinitely by filibustering. Filibustering can be formally stopped, however, by a two-thirds vote of the members present to invoke cloture, a curtailment of "free" debate.

Though both houses can censure (rebuke) or expel members for misconduct, both have rarely been used.

3. Each house shall keep a journal of its proceedings, and from time to time publish the same, excepting such parts as may in their judgment require secrecy; and the yeas and nays of the members of either house on any question shall, at the desire of one fifth of those present, be entered on the journal.

In addition to the journals, a complete official record of everything said on the floor, as well as the roll call votes on all bills or issues, is available in the *Congressional Record* published daily by the Government Printing Office.

4. Neither house, during the session of Congress, shall, without the consent of the other, adjourn for more than three days, nor to any other place than that in which the two houses shall be sitting.

Neither house may recess for more than 3 days without consent of the other, nor may it conduct business in any place other than the Capitol.

Section 6 Privileges and Restrictions of Members

1. The Senators and Representatives shall receive a compensation for their services, to be ascertained by law, and paid out of the Treasury of the United States. They shall in all cases except treason, felony, and breach of the peace, be privileged from arrest during their attendance at the session of their respective houses, and in going to and returning from the same; and for any speech or debate in either house, they shall not be questioned in any other place.

To strengthen the federal government, the Framers set congressional salaries to be paid by the U.S. Treasury rather than by members' respective states. Originally, members were paid $6 per day. Annual salaries began in 1857, when members were paid $3000 per year. Today salaries are $79,125 for the Speaker, $65,000 for the President pro tem and floor leaders, and $60,663 for regular members. Members also receive numerous monetary benefits such as travel allowances, free postage ("franking" privilege), and a special tax exemption for maintaining a second home in Washington, D.C.

The "immunity" privilege is of little importance today. It was included as a safeguard against the British colonial practice of arresting legislators to keep them from performing their duties. More important is immunity from slander or libel for anything said on the floor of either house or published in official publications.

2. No Senator or Representative shall, during the time for which he was elected, be appointed to any civil office under the authority of the United States, which shall have been created, or the emoluments whereof shall have been increased, during such time; and no person holding any office under the United States shall be a member of either house during his continuance in office.

A person cannot serve as a member of Congress and hold another government office at the same time. A member of Congress also cannot hold any office established by Congress or receive any increased salary for an office that may have been approved during the time that member served in Congress.

Section 7 The Legislative Process

1. All bills for raising revenue shall originate in the House of Representatives; but the Senate may propose or concur with amendments as on other bills.

All money bills must begin in the House. Money bills include two types—tax bills for raising revenues and appropriation bills for spending funds.

2. Every bill which shall have passed the House of Representatives and the Senate shall, before it becomes a law, be presented to the President of the United States; if he approves, he shall sign it, but if not he shall return it, with his objections, to that house in which it shall have originated, who shall enter the objections at large on their journal, and proceed to reconsider it. If after such reconsideration two thirds of that house shall agree to pass the bill, it shall be sent, together with the objections, to the other house, by which it shall likewise be reconsidered, and if approved by two thirds of that house, it shall become a

law. But in all such cases the votes of both houses shall be determined by yeas and nays, and the names of the persons voting for and against the bill shall be entered on the journal of each house respectively. If any bill shall not be returned by the President within ten days (Sundays excepted) after it shall have been presented to him, the same shall be a law, in like manner as if he had signed it, unless the Congress by their adjournment prevent its return, in which case it shall not be a law.

Paragraph 2 of Section 7 outlines the basic requirements for enacting legislation. These are (1) bills must be approved in like form by both houses, (2) be submitted to the President for his signature, and (3) be approved (signed) by the President.

Vetoed bills must be returned to Congress with objections for reconsideration. They can be enacted into law by a two-thirds vote of both houses. Should the President fail to sign a submitted bill within 10 days, it automatically becomes law unless Congress has adjourned. If Congress has adjourned, then the bill fails to becomes law (pocket veto). Unlike some governors, the President cannot veto certain items. He must veto a bill in its entirety.

3. Every order, resolution, or vote to which the concurrence of the Senate and House of Representatives may be necessary (except on a question of adjournment) shall be presented to the President of the United States; and before the same shall take effect, shall be approved by him, or being disapproved by him, shall be repassed by two thirds of the Senate and House of Representatives, according to the rules and limitations prescribed in the case of a bill.

The Framers included this paragraph to prevent Congress from passing joint resolutions instead of bills to avoid the possibility of a presidential veto. A bill is a draft of a proposed law, whereas a resolution is a formal expression of opinion or intent on a matter.

Section 8 Legislative Powers

Most of Congress' legislative powers are found in this section. Its powers fall basically within seven categories—financial (Clauses 1, 2, and 5); commercial (Clauses 3 and 4); political (Clauses 4 and 14 and Article 5); judicial (Clauses 6, 9, and 10 and Article 3, Section 3); military (Clauses 1, 11, 12, 13, 15, and 16); territorial (Clause 17 and Article 4, Section 3); and general (Clause 18).

The Congress shall have power:

1. To lay and collect taxes, duties, imposts, and excises, to pay the debts and provide for the common defense and general welfare of the United States; but all duties, imposts, and excises shall be uniform throughout the United States;

Congress may tax only for public purposes, and it must exercise its power with respect to all other constitutional provisions. In addition it can levy a variety of taxes.

Taxes must be uniform—the same rate—throughout the country. That is, the federal excise on tires must be the same in Florida as it is in Illinois.

2. To borrow money on the credit of the United States;

When need arises, Congress can borrow funds. The most common means of borrowing is through the sale of bonds. There is no constitutional limit on the amount Congress can borrow, though Congress has placed a ceiling, which it periodically revises, on the amount the federal government can go into debt. This clause, extended by Clause 18, is the basis for Congress' power to create a national banking system.

3. To regulate commerce with foreign nations, and among the several states, and with the Indian tribes;

Congress has exclusive power to control foreign and interstate commerce. Like its taxing power, Congress' commerce power has expanded over time and today is quite broad. Congress can exercise control over not only the buying, selling, and transporting of goods, but also the means by which they are traded. And it can use its power to encourage, promote and protect, as well as to prohibit, restrain, and restrict.

The scope of Congress' power to regulate foreign commerce extends to approval of trade agreements, to levy and collect duties on imports, to prohibit harmful products from import and restrict essential goods from export, to control immigration, and to improve transportation and communication in all areas of trade by land, sea, or air.

4. To establish a uniform rule of naturalization, and uniform laws on the subject of bankruptcies throughout the United States;

Naturalization is the process by which immigrants become citizens. Uniform rules adopted by Congress, include being legally admitted to the United States; age, residency, and education requirements; and an oath of allegiance to the United States to renounce allegiance to any foreign power.

Bankruptcy is the process by which debtors are relieved of debt obligations when they cannot pay in full. Unlike naturalization, which is an exclusive power of Congress, bankruptcy is subject to both federal and state regulation.

5. To coin money, regulate the value thereof, and of foreign coin, and fix the standard of weights and measures;

Since the Washington administration, the federal government has issued coins in gold (until 1933), silver, and other metals. Paper currency was not made legal tender (money a creditor is required by law to accept as payment) until 1863. The U.S. monetary system is based on the decimal system, with dollars as the base unit. Congress adopted the English system of weights and measures as a national standard in 1838.

6. To provide for the punishment of counterfeiting the securities and current coin of the United States;

Counterfeiting is punishable by a fine up to $5000 and/or imprisonment up to 15 years.

7. To establish post offices and post roads;

Since colonial times, the postal service has been a government monopoly. Until 1970, it operated as an executive department. That year Congress established it as an independent agency, headed by an 11-member board of governors. Until 1970, Congress determined postal rates under its power to appropriate money for government operations. Today rates are set by an independent Postal Rate Commission and cannot be vetoed or altered by either Congress or the President.

8. To promote the progress of science and useful arts, by securing for limited times to authors and inventors the exclusive right to their respective writings and discoveries;

The works of authors are protected by copyrights which today extend for the life of an author plus 50 years. The works of inventors are protected by patents which vary in length of protection from 3½ to 17 years. Patents are obtainable on processes as well as products.

One other type of protection exists—trademarks, which can be a word, letter, symbol, sound, or device, or some combination of these, that signifies the origin or ownership of products. Registration of a trademark is for 20 years, but it can be renewed innumerous times.

9. To constitute tribunals inferior to the Supreme Court;

This clause gave Congress the power to create the federal court system under the Supreme Court.

10. To define and punish piracies and felonies committed on the high seas, and offenses against the law of nations;

Though piracy was a common practice in colonial times, cases today are quite rare. Congress does have the power, however, to protect American ships on the high seas as well as safeguarding individuals traveling on American ships.

11. To declare war, grant letters of marque and reprisal, and make rules concerning captures on land and water;

Only Congress can declare war. But the President can, as Commander in Chief, use the armed forces much as he chooses. Presidents have used the armed forces abroad without a declaration of war on well over 100 occasions. The power to commit troops to battle, however, was limited by the War Powers Act of 1973.

Letters of marque and reprisal, authorizing private parties to attack enemy vessels in time of war, have been forbidden under international law since 1856.

12. To raise and support armies, but no appropriation of money to that use shall be for a longer term than two years;

The restriction on funding was intended to ensure the army would always be subject to civilian control.

13. To provide and maintain a navy;

Rules and procedures for the Navy are similar to those for the other armed services.

14. To make rules for the government and regulation of the land and naval forces;

Under this provision, Congress has established the uniform Code of Military Justice.

15. To provide for calling forth the militia to execute the laws of the Union, suppress insurrections, and repel invasions;

Militia refers to the National Guard, the citizen soldiers of each state. During times of natural disaster or major domestic disturbances, it is used to enforce state or federal law. It is subject to the call of the governor, and it can be called into federal service by either Congress or the President.

16. To provide for organizing, arming, and disciplining the militia, and for governing such part of them as may be employed in the service of the United States, reserving to the states respectively the appointment of the officers, and the authority of training the militia according to the discipline prescribed by Congress;

When called into federal service, the National Guard is subject to the same rules and regulations that Congress has set for the armed services.

17. To exercise exclusive legislation in all cases whatsoever over such district (not exceeding ten miles square) as may, by cession of particular states, and the acceptance of Congress, become the seat of the government of the United States, and to exercise like authority over all places purchased by the consent of the legislature of the state in which the same shall be, for the erection of forts, magazines, arsenals, dock-yards, and other needful buildings;—and

In order to check state interference and to avoid interstate jealousy, the Framers provided for a national seat of government outside of any state—the District of Columbia.

18. To make all laws which shall be necessary and proper for carrying into execution the foregoing powers, and all other powers vested by this Constitution in the government of the United States, or in any department or officer thereof.

This provision is the basis of Congress' implied powers. Any implied power, however, must be related to an expressed power and must be constitutional in all other respects.

Section 9 Powers Forbidden the United States

1. The migration or importation of such persons as any of the states now existing shall think proper to admit, shall not be prohibited by the Congress prior to the year one thousand eight hundred and eight, but a tax or duty may be imposed on such importation, not exceeding ten dollars for each person.

Paragraph 1 contains the agreement the Framers reached regarding regulation of the slave trade in exchange for Congress' exclusive control over interstate commerce.

2. The privilege of the writ of habeas corpus shall not be suspended, unless when in cases of rebellion or invasion the public safety may require it.

A writ of habeas corpus is a court order to release or to bring an individual before the court to determine if that person should be charged with a crime. It is intended to prevent persons from being imprisoned for no reason. The writ may be suspended only during wartime. It was suspended twice—during the Civil War and during World War II in Hawaii. The Hawaiian suspension was later held unconstitutional in *Duncan* v. *Kahanomoku*.

3. No bill of attainder or ex post facto law shall be passed.

A bill of attainder is a law that is directed against an individual or group and provides punishment without a trial. An ex post facto law is one which prescribes punishment for an act committed before the law's enactment.

4. No capitation, or other direct, tax shall be laid, unless in proportion to the census or enumeration herein before directed to be taken.

A capitation tax is a direct tax imposed on individuals. The income tax, authorized by the Sixteenth Amendment, is the exception to this prohibition.

5. No tax or duty shall be laid on articles exported from any state.

The prohibiting of the taxing of exports was part of the Commerce and Slave Trade Compromise.

6. No preference shall be given by any regulation of commerce or revenue to the ports of one state over those of another; nor shall vessels bound to, or from, one state, be obliged to enter, clear, or pay duties in another.

This prohibition prevents Congress from favoring one state or region over another in the regulation of trade.

7. No money shall be drawn from the treasury, but in consequence of appropriations made by law; and a regular statement and account of the receipts and expenditures of all public money shall be published from time to time.

This paragraph ensures legislative control of the nation's purse strings. That is, the executive branch cannot spend money without authorization by Congress.

8. No title of nobility shall be granted by the United States: And no person holding any office of profit or trust under them, shall, without the consent of the Congress, accept of any present, emolument, office, or title, of any kind whatever, from any king, prince, or foreign state.

The prohibitions listed here were intended to prevent creation of a monarchy and the bribery of American officials by foreign powers. Acceptance of a title can be grounds for expatriation, or giving up citizenship.

Section 10 Powers Forbidden the States

1. No state shall enter into any treaty, alliance, or confederation; grant letters of marque and reprisal; coin money; emit bills of credit; make any thing but gold and silver coin a tender in payment of debts; pass any bill of attainder, ex post facto law, or law impairing the obligation of contracts, or grant any title of nobility.

The powers listed here belong solely to the federal government or are denied to both it and the states. The restrictions on the states were designed, in part, to prevent an overlapping in functions and authority with the federal government that could create conflict and chaos.

2. No state shall, without the consent of the Congress, lay any imposts or duties on imports or exports, except what may be absolutely necessary for executing its inspection laws; and the net produce of all duties and imposts, laid by any state on imports or exports, shall be for the use of the treasury of the United States; and all such laws shall be subject to the revision and control of the Congress.

If states were permitted to tax imports and exports, they could use their taxing power in a way to weaken or destroy Congress' power to control interstate and foreign commerce. Furthermore, the power to tax could result in conditions similar to those under the Articles of Confederation.

3. No state shall, without the consent of Congress, lay any duty of tonnage, keep troops, or ships of war in time of peace, enter into any agreement or compact with another state, or with a foreign power, or engage in war, unless actually invaded, or in such imminent danger as will not admit of delay.

There are exceptions to some of the prohibitions listed here. For example, states can maintain a militia. But a militia's use is limited to internal disorders that arise within a state unless the militia is called into federal service. States can enter into interstate compacts regarding problems that require joint or regional action. But interstate compacts require the approval of Congress.

Article 2 Executive Branch

Section 1 President and Vice President

1. The executive power shall be vested in a President of the United States of America. He shall hold his office during the term of four years, and, together with the Vice President, chosen for the same term, be elected, as follows:

Though the Constitution confers certain powers and duties on the President, growth of presidential power has come from two sources—(1) conferred by act of Congress, and (2) concluded by the President as the result of actions taken as chief administrator, chief executive, chief diplomat, or commander-in-chief. Inasmuch as the Presidency was established to provide an executive branch, it is logical for Congress to legislate in general terms and to leave to the President and the executive agencies discretionary power to execute (establish the details) its acts.

Until the Twenty-Second Amendment, there was no constitutional restriction on the number of terms a President could serve. Washington established the precedent of two terms which was not broken until Franklin D. Roosevelt was elected to a third term in 1940.

2. Each state shall appoint, in such manner as the legislature thereof may direct, a number of electors, equal to the whole number of senators and representatives to which the state may be entitled in the Congress; but no senator or representative, or person holding an office of trust or profit under the United States, shall be appointed an elector.

The number of presidential electors is determined by a state's representation (Senators and Representatives) in Congress. No member of Congress or federal officer may be an elector.

3. The electors shall meet in their respective states, and vote by ballot for two persons, of whom one at least shall not be an inhabitant of the same state with themselves. And they shall make a list of all the persons voted for, and of the number of votes for each; which list they shall sign and certify, and transmit sealed to the seat of the government of the United States, directed to the President of the Senate. The President of the Senate shall, in the presence of the Senate and House of Representatives, open all the certificates, and the votes shall then be counted. The person having the greatest number of votes shall be the President, if such number be a majority of the whole number of electors appointed; and if there be more than one who have such majority, and have an equal number of votes, then the House of Representatives shall immediately choose by ballot one of them for President; and if no person have a majority, then from the five highest on the list the said house shall in like manner choose the President. But in choosing the President, the votes shall be taken by states, the representation from each state having one vote; a quorum for this purpose shall consist of a member or members from two thirds of the states, and a majority of all the states shall be necessary to a choice. In every case, after the choice of the President, the person having the greatest number of votes of the electors shall be the Vice President. But if there should remain two or more who have equal votes, the Senate shall choose from them by ballot the Vice President.

Coupled with the previous paragraph, Paragraph 3 outlines the original method of selecting the President and Vice President. It has been replaced by the method outlined in the Twelfth Amendment. It should be noted, however, that there has been considerable change in the machinery created by the Framers. For example, the Framers did not envision the rise of political parties, the development of primaries and conventions, or the broadening of democracy whereby electors would be elected rather than chosen by state legislatures.

4. The Congress may determine the time of choosing the electors, and the day on which they shall give their votes; which day shall be the same throughout the United States.

Congress set the first Tuesday after the first Monday in November of every fourth year (leap year) as the general election date for selecting presidential electors in 1845.

5. No person except a natural-born citizen, or a citizen of the United States, at the time of the adoption of this Constitution, shall be eligible to the office of President; neither shall any person be eligible to that office who shall not have attained to the age of thirty-five years, and been fourteen years a resident within the United States.

This paragraph provides the only constitutional qualifications to be President. Similar to that for Representative and Senator, the age qualification must be met at the time the oath of office is taken, and not necessarily at the time of election. Though not expressly stated, the qualifications to be Vice President are the same.

Note that only Martin Van Buren of the first nine Presidents was a natural-born citizen, since the others were born prior to American independence. Nevertheless, they qualified for the Presidency having been American citizens at the time of the adoption of the Constitution.

6. In case of the removal of the President from office, or of his death, resignation, or inability to discharge the powers and duties of the said office, the same shall devolve on the Vice President, and the Congress may by law provide for the case of removal, death, resignation, or inability, both of the President and Vice President, declaring what officer shall then act as President, and such

officer shall act accordingly, until the disability be removed, or a President shall be elected.

Until the adoption of the Twenty-Fifth Amendment, which expressly provides for the Vice President to succeed to the Presidency, succession was based on a precedent set by John Tyler in 1841. This paragraph raises the question whether the Framers intended the Vice President to become President or to serve as Acting President since nothing in the Constitution requires the Vice President to take a new oath of office when the powers and the duties of the President devolve upon him.

In 1947 Congress provided for an official line of succession in cases when there is no Vice President to qualify.

7. The President shall, at stated times, receive for his services a compensation, which shall neither be increased nor diminished during the period for which he shall have been elected, and he shall not receive within that period any other emolument from the United States, or any of them.

Originally, the President's salary was $25,000 per year. It was raised by Congress to $50,000 per year in 1873, to $75,000 in 1909, and to $100,000 plus a $50,000 taxable expense account in 1949. The President's current salary of $200,000 plus a $50,000 taxable expense account per year was enacted in 1969. The President, like members of Congress, also receives numerous fringe benefits including a $40,000 nontaxable allowance for travel and entertainment, and living accommodations in two residences (the White House and Camp David).

8. Before he enter on the execution of his office, he shall take the following oath or affirmation:—"I do solemnly swear (or affirm) that I will faithfully execute the office of President of the United States, and will, to the best of my ability, preserve, protect, and defend the Constitution of the United States."

The oath of office is generally administered by the Chief Justice, but can be administered by any official authorized to administer oaths. All Presidents-elect except Washington have been sworn into office by the Chief Justice. Only Vice Presidents John Tyler, Calvin Coolidge, and Lyndon Johnson in succeeding to the office have been sworn in by someone else.

Section 2 Powers of the President

The President's powers can loosely be categorized under executive, legislative, diplomatic, military, and judicial.

1. The President shall be commander in chief of the army and navy of the United States, and of the militia of the several states, when called into the actual service of the United States; he may require the opinion, in writing, of the principal officer in each of the executive departments, upon any subject relating to the duties of their respective offices, and he shall have power to grant reprieves and pardons for offenses against the United States, except in cases of impeachment.

Though not an active field commander, all military personnel is subordinate to the President. This provision insures civilian control over the military. The President's military powers are not without limit; Congress has the power to raise and support the armed forces, while the President has the power to command, deploy, and use them as the need arises.

The provision that the President "may require the opinion . . ." is the constitutional base for the Cabinet.

Like his other powers, the President's judicial powers are limited. Presidential clemency is limited to those accused or convicted of federal crimes. A reprieve is a delay in carrying out a sentence. A pardon is a legal absolution of responsibility for a crime. The President can also commute (reduce) and parole (suspend the completion of) an imposed sentence.

2. He shall have power, by and with the advice and consent of the Senate, to make treaties, provided two thirds of the senators present concur; and he shall nominate, and by and with the advice and consent of the Senate, shall appoint ambassadors, other public ministers and consuls, judges of the Supreme Court, and all other officers of the United States, whose appointments are not herein otherwise provided for, and which shall be established by law; but the Congress may by law vest the appointment of such inferior officers, as they think proper, in the President alone, in the courts of law, or in the heads of departments.

The President is the chief architect of American foreign policy. He is responsible for the conduct of foreign relations, or dealings with other countries. Though requiring Senate approval, a treaty is ratified (signed upon approval) by the President. If it is not ratified or made public, an approved treaty is voided, and Congress cannot override the President's decision to kill it. In addition to treaties, the President can make executive agreements with other countries. Executive agreements do not require Senate approval.

Most federal positions today are filled under the rules and regulations of the civil service system. Most presidential appointees serve at the pleasure of the President. Removal of an official by the President is not subject to congressional approval. But the power can be restricted by conditions set in creating the office.

3. The President shall have power to fill up all vacancies that may happen during the recess of the Senate, by granting commissions which shall expire at the end of their next session.

Presidential appointments requiring Senate approval are made on a temporary basis if the Senate is in recess.

Section 3 Duties of the President

He shall from time to time give to the Congress information of the state of the Union, and recommend to their consideration such measures as he shall judge necessary and expedient; he may, on extraordinary occasions, convene both houses, or either of them, and in case of disagreement between them with respect to the time of adjournment, he may adjourn them to such time as he shall think proper; he shall receive ambassadors and other public ministers; he shall take care that the laws be faithfully executed, and shall commission all the officers of the United States.

Today the President is the chief designer of the nation's major legislative programs. Presidential recommendations are put forth in the State of the Union address, the federal budget, and special messages dealing with specific proposals.

The provision to "receive ambassadors . . ." is the constitutional basis of the President's power to extend and to withdraw diplomatic recognition of a foreign government.

All military commissions (appointments as officers in the armed forces) require presidential authorization and congressional approval.

Section 4 Impeachment

The President, Vice President and all civil officers of the United States, shall be removed from office on impeachment for, and conviction of, treason, bribery, or other high crimes and misdemeanors.

Presidential appointees can be removed by the impeachment process as well as by being asked to resign by the President.

Article 3   Judicial Branch

Section 1 United States Courts

The judicial power of the United States shall be vested in one Supreme Court, and in such inferior courts as the Congress may from time to time ordain and establish. The judges, both of the Supreme and inferior courts, shall hold their offices during good behavior, and shall, at stated times, receive for their services, a compensation, which shall not be diminished during their continuance in office.

Section 1 creates a national judiciary. Congress established the national court system in 1789. Today there are 11 judicial circuits, with a Court of Appeals in each, and 98 judicial districts. At least one district with a District Court is in every state. Other constitutional courts include (1) the Court of Claims, established in 1855; (2) the Customs Court, established in 1890; and (3) the Court of Customs and Patent Appeals, established in 1910.

Federal judges are appointed by the President with Senate approval and nearly all hold office during good behavior for life. Originally, judges' salaries were $3500 ($4000 for the Chief Justice). In 1983, Supreme Court Justices are paid $93,000 (the Chief Justice $96,800); Courts of Appeals judges $74,300; and District Court judges $70,300.

Section 2 Jurisdiction

1. The judicial power shall extend to all cases, in law and equity, arising under this Constitution, the laws of the United States, and treaties made, or which shall be made, under their authority;—to all cases affecting ambassadors, other public ministers, and consuls;—to all cases of admiralty and maritime jurisdiction;—to controversies to which the United States shall be a party;—to controversies between two or more states;—between a state and citizens of another state;—between citizens of different states;—between citizens of the same state claiming lands under grants of different states; and between a state, or the citizens thereof, and foreign states, citizens or subjects.

Jurisdiction is the right of a court to try a case. Federal courts have jurisdiction over a case because of its subject matter or the parties involved. Since the adoption of the Eleventh Amendment, however, a state cannot be sued in federal court by a resident of another state or a citizen of a foreign country.

The judicial power of the United States includes civil cases (private wrongs that arise under common law or equity) as well as criminal cases. Common law is the rules and principles that developed in England from decisions made on the basis of custom. Equity is a branch of law that provides legal remedy when strict application of common law results in an injustice.

2. In all cases affecting ambassadors, other public ministers and consuls, and those in which a state shall be party, the Supreme Court shall have original jurisdiction. In all other cases before mentioned, the Supreme Court shall have appellate jurisdiction, both as to law and fact, with such exceptions, and under such regulations as the Congress shall make.

The Supreme Court has both original and appellate jurisdiction. Original jurisdiction refers to cases to be tried for the first time. Appellate jurisdiction refers to cases to be reviewed after being tried in a lower court. The vast majority of cases the Supreme Court hears are on appeal. Its decisions are by majority opinion.

3. The trial of all crimes, except in cases of impeachment, shall be by jury; and such trial shall be held in the state where the said crimes shall have been committed; but when not committed within any state, the trial shall be at such place or places as the Congress may by law have directed.

All persons accused of committing a crime for which they can be tried in federal court are guaranteed the right of trial by jury in the state where the crime takes place. For crimes committed at sea, Congress has provided that the accused be tried by the District Court of the district where that person is surrendered into custody.

Section 3 Treason

1. Treason against the United States shall consist only in levying war against them, or in adhering to their enemies, giving them aid and comfort. No person shall be convicted of treason unless on the testimony of two witnesses to the same overt act, or on confession in open court.

Treason is the only crime specifically defined in the Constitution, and Congress cannot alter or amend the criteria for conviction. The charge can be levied against American citizens at home or abroad and resident aliens.

2. The Congress shall have power to declare the punishment of treason, but no attainder of treason shall work corruption of blood, or forfeiture except during the life of the person attained.

Congress has set the punishment for treason to be from a minimum of five years imprisonment and a $10,000 fine to a maximum of death. No person convicted of treason has ever been executed by the United States.

Article 4   Relations Among the States

Section 1 Official Acts

Full faith and credit shall be given in each state to the public acts, records, and judicial proceedings of every other state. And the Congress may by general laws prescribe the manner in which such acts, records, and proceedings shall be proved, and the effect thereof.

States must honor the laws, records, and court decisions of other states. Regarding judicial proceedings, there are two exceptions: (1) one state does not have to enforce another state's criminal code, and (2) one state does not have to recognize another state's grant of a divorce if legitimate residence was not established by the person obtaining the divorce.

Section 2 Privileges of Citizens

1. The citizens of each state shall be entitled to all privileges and immunities of citizens in the several states.

In other words, a resident of one state may not be discriminated against unreasonably by another state.

2. A person charged in any state with treason, felony, or other crime, who shall flee from justice, and be found in another state shall, on demand of the executive authority of the state from which he fled, be delivered up, to be removed to the state having jurisdiction of the crime.

The process of returning a fugitive to the state where a crime has been committed is known as extradition. Most requests are routinely processed, but the Constitution does not absolutely require that a fugitive be surrendered. A governor can refuse to honor the request for extradition if it will result in an injustice to the fugitive.

3. No person held to service or labor in one state, under the laws thereof, escaping into another, shall, in consequence of any law or regulation therein, be discharged from such service or labor, but shall be delivered up on claim of the party to whom such service or labor may be due.

This provision applied to fugitive slaves. It was cancelled by the Thirteenth Amendment.

Section 3 New States and Territories

1. New states may be admitted by the Congress into this Union; but no new state shall be formed or erected within the jurisdiction of any other state; nor any state be formed by the junction of two or more states, or parts of states, without the consent of the legislatures of the states concerned as well as of the Congress.

Only Congress can admit states to the Union. New states are admitted on the basis of equality with older states. The general process is outlined by the Northwest Ordinance of 1787.

Though a new state cannot be carved out of an existing state without its consent, there has been one unusual exception—West Virginia, which was admitted in 1863 after Virginia had seceded and Congress held that the 40 counties of western Virginia that remained loyal to the Union constituted a "legal" government.

2. The Congress shall have power to dispose of and make all needful rules and regulations respecting the territory or other property belonging to the United States; and nothing in this Constitution shall be so construed as to prejudice any claims of the United States, or of any particular state.

Congress has the power to control all property belonging to the United States. It can set up governments for territories, establish national parks and forests, authorize reclamation projects, and exercise eminent domain (taking of private property for public use through condemnation).

Section 4 Protection of the States

The United States shall guarantee to every state in this Union a republican form of government, and shall protect each of them against invasion; and on application of the legislature, or of the executive (when the legislature cannot be convened) against domestic violence.

Though the Constitution does not define "republican form of government," the Supreme Court has held it to mean one in which the people choose their own representatives to run the government and make the laws in accord with delegated power.

The federal government can use whatever means are necessary to prevent foreign invasion and to put down domestic violence.

Article 5   The Amendment Process

The Congress, whenever two thirds of both houses shall deem it necessary, shall propose amendments to this Constitution, or, on the application of the legislatures of two thirds of the several states, shall call a convention for proposing amendments, which, in either case, shall be valid to all intents and purposes, as part of this Constitution, when ratified by the legislatures of three fourths of the several states, or by conventions in three fourths thereof, as the one or the other mode of ratification may be proposed by the Congress; provided that no amendment which may be made prior to the year one thousand eight hundred and eight shall in any manner affect the first and fourth clauses in the ninth section of the first article; and that no state, without its consent, shall be deprived of its equal suffrage in the Senate.

There are four methods for amending the Constitution—two of proposal and two of ratification. To date, all amendments have been proposed by Congress, and only the Twenty-First has been ratified by convention instead of by state legislature.

Today there is one prohibition against change—that is, no state can be denied its equal representation in the Senate.

Article 6   General Provisions

1. All debts contracted and engagements entered into, before the adoption of this Constitution, shall be as valid against the United States under this Constitution, as under the Confederation.

This provision assured the nation's creditors that the new federal government would assume the existing financial obligations of the country.

2. This Constitution, and the laws of the United States which shall be made in pursuance thereof; and all treaties made, or which shall be made, under the authority of the United States, shall be the supreme law of the land; and the judges in every state shall be bound thereby, anything in the Constitution or laws of any state to the contrary notwithstanding.

This is known as the "supremacy clause" and guarantees that federal law will take priority over state law in cases of conflict. To be valid, however, any law must be constitutional.

3. The Senators and Representatives before mentioned, and the members of the several state legislatures, and all executive and judicial officers, both of the United States and of the several states, shall be bound by oath or affirmation to support this Constitution; but no religious test shall ever be required as a qualification to any office or public trust under the United States.

Almost all government officials must affirm or take an oath to uphold the Constitution. No religious qualification can be set as a requirement for holding public office.

Article 7   Ratification

The ratification of the conventions of nine states shall be sufficient for the establishment of this Constitution between the states so ratifying the same.

To become operable, nine states were required to ratify. Delaware was first and New Hampshire ninth, but not until Virginia (10th) and New York (11th) ratified, was the Constitution assured of going into effect.

Done in convention by the unanimous consent of the states present the seventeenth day of September in the year of our Lord one thousand seven hundred and eighty-seven, and of the independence of the United States of America the twelfth. In witness whereof we have hereunto subscribed our names.

George Washington, **President and Deputy from Virginia**

New Hampshire
John Langdon
Nicholas Gilman

Massachusetts
Nathaniel Gorham
Rufus King

Connecticut
William Samuel
*   Johnson*
Roger Sherman

New York
Alexander Hamilton

New Jersey
William Livingston
David Brearley
William Paterson
Jonathan Dayton

Pennsylvania
Benjamin Franklin
Thomas Mifflin
Robert Morris
George Clymer
Thomas Fitzsimons
Jared Ingersoll
James Wilson
Gouverneur Morris

Delaware
George Read
Gunning Bedford, Jr.
John Dickinson
Richard Bassett
Jacob Broom

Maryland
James M'Henry
Daniel of St. Thomas
*   Jenifer*
Daniel Carroll

Virginia
John Blair
James Madison, Jr.

North Carolina
William Blount
Richard Dobbs
*   Spaight*
Hugh Williamson

South Carolina
John Rutledge
Charles C. Pinckney
Charles Pinckney
Pierce Butler

Georgia
William Few
Abraham Baldwin

Attest: *William Jackson,* **Secretary**

Of the 55 delegates who attended the Constitutional Convention, only 38 signed the document. The 39th signature—that of John Dickinson—was written by George Read at Dickinson's request. Elbridge Gerry of Massachusetts and Edmund Randolph and George Mason of Virginia refused to sign. Thirteen delegates left the convention prior to its end. Rhode Island sent no delegates to the convention.

The Bill of Rights consists of the first ten amendments. They were proposed by Congress during its first session and were adopted in body in 1791. Originally, the prohibitions limited only the federal government. But many of the guarantees have been extended against state action by the "due process" clause of the Fourteenth Amendment.

Amendment 1 Freedoms of Expression

Congress shall make no law respecting an establishment of religion, or prohibiting the free exercise thereof; or abridging the freedom of speech, or of the press; or the right of the people peaceably to assemble, and to petition the government for a redress of grievances.

The First Amendment protects five basic civil liberties—freedom of religion, of speech, and of the press and the rights to assemble peacefully and to petition for redress of grievances. Like all civil rights, however, these liberties are not absolute; they must be exercised in a manner relative to the rights of others.

Under the guarantee of religious freedom, the government cannot establish an official religion or place restrictions on religious beliefs. Though the First Amendment does create a separation of church and state, it does not prohibit the government from expressing a friendly attitude toward religion. What the government may not do is support religion or religious activity officially.

Freedoms of speech and of the press guarantee to all individuals the right to express themselves freely, both orally and in writing, and to free and unrestricted discussion of public affairs. However, one can still be held accountable under the law for false and malicious use of words.

The rights to assemble and petition guarantee the means to protest, including the right to demonstrate. Public meetings and picketing must be peaceable, however. Ones that result in violence can lawfully be broken up.

Amendment 2 Right to Keep Arms

A well-regulated militia being necessary to the security of a free state, the right of the people to keep and bear arms shall not be infringed.

The right to keep and bear arms is not free from government restriction. The federal government and the states can and do regulate the possession and use of firearms, such as requiring the licensing of guns and prohibiting the carrying of concealed weapons.

Amendment 3 Quartering of Troops

No soldier shall, in time of peace, be quartered in any house, without the consent of the owner, nor in time of war, but in a manner to be prescribed by law.

Like the Second Amendment, this amendment was designed to prevent what had been common practice by the British during the colonial period. It is of little importance today, even though Congress could authorize the boarding of troops in private homes during wartime.

Amendment 4 Searches and Seizures

The right of the people to be secure in their persons, houses, papers, and effects, against unreasonable searches and seizures, shall not be violated, and no warrants shall issue, but upon probable cause, supported by oath or affirmation, and particularly describing the place to be searched, and the persons or things to be seized.

This amendment prohibits unreasonable searches and seizures. Similar to the Second and Third Amendments, it was designed to prevent actions similar to British colonial practices in the years preceding the American Revolution.

Searches and seizures authorized by court warrants are permissible. Also, the police do not need a warrant for a search and seizure if they are a witness to a crime or are in hot pursuit of a criminal. Nor do they need one to search a movable object, such as a car, since it could vanish while a warrant is sought.

To be proper, a warrant must be issued by a judge, there must be good reason for its use, and it must describe in specific terms the place to be searched and the person or thing to be seized. Evidence secured by an improper search and seizure is inadmissible in any court.

Amendment 5 Rights of the Accused

No person shall be held to answer for a capital, or otherwise infamous crime, unless on a presentment or indictment of a grand jury, except in cases arising in the land or naval forces, or in the militia, when in actual service in time of war or public danger; nor shall any person be subject for the same offense to be twice put in jeopardy of life or limb; nor shall be compelled in any criminal case to be a witness against himself, nor to be deprived of life, liberty, or property, without due process of law; nor shall private property be taken for public use, without just compensation.

The Fifth Amendment protects the legal rights of people in criminal proceedings. No person may be brought to trial for a felony without first being charged with a specific crime by either a presentment or indictment of a grand jury. A presentment is a formal accusation brought by a grand jury acting on its own knowledge against a person believed to have committed a crime. An indictment is a formal accusation by a grand jury against a person whom the district attorney has brought to the grand jury's attention and whom the jury thinks probably committed the crime. A grand jury's decision does not have to be unanimous.

No person may be tried for the same crime twice. But there are exceptions to the prohibition against double jeopardy. For example, if a person commits an act which violates both federal and state law, that person can be tried for that crime in both federal and state courts.

Persons may not be forced to give testimony against themselves. However, the prohibition against self-incrimination does not bar voluntarily testifying against one's self. The protection applies to any proceedings where testimony is legally required, including congressional hearings. The Supreme Court has held that evidence obtained by electronic eavesdropping (wiretaps) is not admissible in court since it violates the principle of self-incrimination.

Government cannot take private property for public use without payment of a fair market price.

Amendment 6 Criminal Proceedings

In all criminal prosecutions, the accused shall enjoy the right to a speedy and public trial, by an impartial jury of the state and district where in the crime shall have been committed, which district shall have been previously ascertained by law, and to be informed of the nature and cause of the accusation; to be confronted with the witnesses against him; to have compulsory process for obtaining witnesses in his favor, and to have the assistance of counsel for his defense.

The Sixth Amendment protects the procedural rights of people in criminal proceedings.

The right to a speedy and public trial was to prevent a person from languishing in jail or being tried by a secret tribunal. But a trial must not be so speedy as to prevent time for preparing an adequate defense nor so public that the trial is not fair.

The right to confront witnesses guarantees an accused the right to cross-examination. A witness can be compelled to testify by means of a subpoena, a writ ordering that person to appear in court. Failure to comply with a subpoena will result in being held in contempt of court.

Though a person can act as his or her own counsel, all persons accused of a crime are entitled to counsel. If a person cannot afford counsel, the government must provide one. The right to counsel includes questioning by police as well as during trial.

Amendment 7 Jury Trial in Civil Cases

In suits at common law, where the value in controversy shall exceed twenty dollars, the right of trial by jury shall be preserved, and no fact tried by a jury shall be otherwise re-examined in any court of the United States than according to the rules of common law.

This amendment deals with certain guarantees in civil law in federal courts. Civil suits involve disputes between individuals or groups. The government may or may not be a party in a civil suit. If the value in controversy exceeds $20 in a civil case, the right of trial by jury is guaranteed. Most states also guarantee jury trials in civil cases in which the controversy exceeds $200.

Amendment 8 Excessive Punishments

Excessive bail shall not be required, nor excessive fines imposed, nor cruel and unusual punishments inflicted.

Bail is security (money) put up to obtain the release of an accused from jail pending trial. Bail is set by the court at the time of arraignment. Failure to appear for trial is grounds for forfeiture of the bail to the government. Bail can be, and often is, denied for those accused of capital offenses such as murder.

For it to be unconstitutional, a punishment must be both cruel and unusual. Like bails and fines, a punishment must not be unreasonably severe in relation to the crime. Rarely have bails, fines, and punishments been contested as violating the Eighth Amendment, since most are imposed in accordance with what is prescribed by law. The Supreme Court has ruled that the death penalty has to be specified for specific crimes, that it cannot be left to the discretion of a judge or jury in determining sentence.

Amendment 9 Rights of the People

The enumeration in the Constitution of certain rights shall not be construed to deny or disparage others retained by the people.

The Constitution does not specifically list all the rights of the people. This amendment protects their unenumerated rights.

Amendment 10 Reserved Powers

The powers not delegated to the United States by the Constitution, nor prohibited by it to the states, are reserved to the states respectively, or to the people.

The Tenth Amendment safeguards the reserved powers of the states. But with the adoption of the Fourteenth Amendment, a state's reserved powers, particularly its police powers, are subject to closer scrutiny.

Amendment 11 Suits Against States

The judicial power of the United States shall not be construed to extend to any suit in law or equity, commenced or prosecuted against one of the United States by citizens of another state, or by citizens or subjects of any foreign state.

Adopted in 1798, the Eleventh Amendment changed a provision in Article 3, Section 2. It resulted from strong opposition to the Supreme Court's ruling in *Chisholm* v. *Georgia* in which the Court held that if a state could bring suit against citizens of another state, then certainly citizens of another state could bring suit against a state. The ruling was seen as weakening state sovereignty.

Under the Eleventh Amendment, foreign citizens or citizens of another state must sue a state in its courts in accordance with its law.

Amendment 12 Election of President and Vice President

The electors shall meet in their respective states and vote by ballot for President and Vice President, one of whom, at least, shall not be an inhabitant of the same state with themselves; they shall name in their ballots the person voted for as President, and in distinct ballots the person voted for as Vice President, and they shall make distinct lists of all persons voted for as President, and of all persons voted for as Vice President, and of the number of votes for each, which lists they shall sign and certify, and transmit sealed to the seat of the government of the United States, directed to the President of the Senate;—the President of the Senate shall, in the presence of the Senate and House of Representatives, open all the certificates and the votes shall then be counted;—the person having the greatest number of votes for President, shall be the President, if such number be a majority of the whole number of electors appointed; and if no person have such majority, then from the persons having the highest numbers not exceeding three on the list of those voted for as President, the House of Representatives shall choose immediately, by ballot, the President. But in choosing the President, the votes shall be taken by states, the representation from each state having one vote; a quorum for this purpose shall consist of a member or members from two thirds of the states, and a majority of all the states shall be necessary to a choice. And if the House of Representatives shall not choose a President whenever the right of choice shall devolve upon them, before the fourth day of March next following, then the Vice President shall act as President, as in the case of the death or other constitutional disability of the President. —The person having the greatest number of votes as Vice President, shall be the Vice President, if such number be a majority of the whole number of electors appointed, and if no person have a majority, then from the two highest numbers on the list, the Senate shall choose the Vice President; a quorum for the purpose shall consist of two thirds of the whole number of senators, and a majority of the whole number shall be necessary to a choice. But no person constitutionally ineligible to the office of President shall be eligible to that of Vice President of the United States.

Adopted in 1804, the Twelfth Amendment changed the procedure for electing the President and Vice President as outlined in Article 2, Section 1, Paragraph 3.

To prevent the recurrence of the election of 1800 whereby a candidate running for Vice President (Aaron Burr) could tie a candidate running for President (Thomas Jefferson) and thus force the election into the House of Representatives, the Twelfth Amendment specifies that the electors are to cast separate ballots for each office. Other changes include: (1) a candidate must receive a majority of the electoral votes cast rather than votes from a majority of the electors, (2) a reduction from five to the three highest candidates receiving votes among whom the House is to choose if no candidate receives a majority of the electoral votes, and (3) provision for the Senate to choose the Vice President from the two highest candidates if neither has received a majority of the electoral votes.

The electoral system has been subject to criticism for many years. For example, in any presidential election, it is possible for a candidate to capture fewer popular votes than an opponent and still win a majority of the electoral votes. In fact, both Hayes (in 1876) and Harrison (in 1888) did so. Then, too, electors are not legally bound to vote for the choice of the people in two-thirds of the states.

The Twelfth Amendment does place one restriction on electors. Though never tested, it prohibits electors from voting for two candidates (President and Vice President) from their home state.

Amendment 13 Slavery

Section 1. Neither slavery nor involuntary servitude, except as a punishment for crime whereof the party shall have been duly convicted, shall exist within the United States, or any place subject to their jurisdiction.

Section 2. Congress shall have power to enforce this article by appropriate legislation.

Adopted in 1865, the Thirteenth Amendment ended slavery in the United States. It also prohibits the binding of a person to perform a personal service due to debt. Not all involuntary servitude (forced labor) is prohibited, however. In addition to imprisonment for crime, the Supreme Court has held that the draft (selective service) is not a violation of the amendment.

This amendment is the first adopted to be divided into sections. It is also the first to contain specifically a provision granting Congress power to enforce it by appropriate legislation.

Amendment 14 Rights of Citizens

Section 1. All persons born or naturalized in the United States, and subject to the jurisdiction thereof, are citizens of the United States and of the state wherein they reside. No state shall make or enforce any law which shall abridge the privileges or immunities of citizens of the United States; nor shall any state deprive any person of life, liberty, or property, without due process of law, nor deny to any person within its jurisdiction the equal protection of the laws.

Section 2. Representatives shall be apportioned among the several states according to their respective numbers, counting the whole number of persons in each state, excluding Indians not taxed. But when the right to vote at any election for the choice of electors for President and Vice President of the United States, representatives in Congress, the executive or judicial officers of a state, or the members of the legislature thereof, is denied to any of the male inhabitants of such state, being twenty-one years of age, and citizens of the United States, or in any way abridged, except for participation in rebellion, or other crime, the basis of representation therein shall be reduced in the proportion which the number of such male citizens shall bear to the whole number of male citizens twenty-one years of age in such state.

Section 3. No person shall be a Senator or Representative in Congress, or elector of President or Vice President, or hold any office, civil or military, under the United States, or under any state, who, having previously taken an oath, as a member of Congress, or as an officer of the United States, or as a member of any state legislature, or as an executive or judicial officer of any state, to support the Constitution of the United States, shall have engaged in insurrection or rebellion against the same, or given aid or comfort to the enemies thereof. But Congress may by a vote of two thirds of each house, remove such disability.

Section 4. The validity of the public debt of the United States, authorized by law, including debts incurred for payment of pensions and bounties for services in suppressing insurrection or rebellion, shall not be questioned. But neither the United States nor any state shall assume or pay any debt or obligation incurred in aid of insurrection or rebellion against the United States, or any claim for the loss or emancipation of any slave; but all such debts, obligations and claims shall be held illegal and void.

Section 5. The Congress shall have power to enforce, by appropriate legislation, the provisions of this article.

Adopted in 1868, the Fourteenth Amendment is one of the most important. It is the basis for numerous Supreme Court decisions, particularly relating to civil rights.

Until its adoption, the Constitution contained no definition of citizen, despite the fact that "citizens" are mentioned in numerous provisions. In addition to defining citizenship and extending it to blacks, Section 1 prohibits states from denying privileges and immunities of citizenship to any citizen. The guarantee of due process was intended to prevent states from denying blacks their civil rights. The guarantee of equal protection of the laws prohibits states from making unreasonable distinctions between different groups of people in laws or executive actions.

Section 2 abolishes the three-fifths compromise as worded in Article 1, Section 2, Paragraph 3. In addition to an attempt to guarantee blacks the right to vote, it also provides the government with the power to reduce a state's representation in the House in proportion to that state's improper disfranchisement of qualified voters.

Section 3 was aimed at punishing the leaders of the Confederacy. By 1872, most were permitted to return to political life, and in 1898, amnesty was granted to all still living.

Like Section 3, Section 4 dealt with matters directly related to the Civil War. It validated the debt of the United States, prohibited assumption of any of the Confederate debt, and prohibited payment for any loss resulting from freeing of the slaves.

Amendment 15 Black Suffrage

Section 1. The right of citizens of the United States to vote shall not be denied or abridged by the United States or by any state on account of race, color, or previous conditions of servitude.

Section 2. The Congress shall have power to enforce this article by appropriate legislation.

Adopted in 1870, the Fifteenth Amendment replaced Amendment 14, Section 2 in guaranteeing blacks the right to vote. Yet, despite its prohibition against both the federal government and the states, blacks were disfranchised by many states following Reconstruction by such means as poll taxes, literacy tests, "grandfather clauses," and white primaries. Not until the 1960's did Congress take firm action to enforce the guarantee of the amendment and end voter discrimination.

Amendment 16 Income Tax

The Congress shall have power to lay and collect taxes on incomes, from whatever source derived, without apportionment among the several states, and without regard to any census or enumeration.

Adopted in 1913, the Sixteenth Amendment provided an exception to the restrictions placed on direct taxation by Article 1, Section 2, Paragraph 3, and Section 9, Paragraph 4. Like the Eleventh Amendment, it was adopted to reverse a Supreme Court ruling. Although there had been a temporary income tax during the Civil War, the tax's constitutionality was not tested until it was reinstated by the Wilson-Gorman Tariff Act of 1894. The Court held that it was unconstitutional since it was a direct tax imposed without apportionment or regard to enumeration in *Pollack* v. *Farmer Loan and Trust Company.*

Amendment 17 Election of Senators

Section 1. The Senate of the United States shall be composed of two senators from each state, elected by the people thereof, for six years; and each senator shall have one vote. The electors in each state shall have the qualifications requisite for electors of the most numerous branch of the state legislatures.

Section 2. When vacancies happen in the representation of any state in the Senate, the executive authority of such state shall issue writs of election to fill such vacancies: Provided, that the legislature of any state may empower the executive thereof to make temporary appointments until the people fill the vacancies by election as the legislature may direct.

Section 3. This amendment shall not be so construed as to affect the election or term of any senator chosen before it becomes valid as part of the Constitution.

Adopted in 1913, the Seventeenth Amendment provided for the direct election of Senators by the people and replaced their method of selection as outlined by Article 1, Section 3, Paragraphs 2 and 3.

The governor of a state can fill a vacancy by calling a special election or, if authorized by the state legislature, making a temporary appointment until the next general election.

Amendment 18 National Prohibition

Section 1. After one year from the ratification of this article the manufacture, sale, or transportation of intoxicating liquors within, the importation thereof into, or the exportation thereof from the United States and all territory subject to the jurisdiction thereof for beverage purposes is hereby prohibited.

Section 2. The Congress and the several states shall have concurrent power to enforce this article by appropriate legislation.

Section 3. This article shall be inoperative unless it shall have been ratified as an amendment to the Constitution by the legislatures of the several states, as provided in the Constitution, within seven years from the date of the submission hereof to the states by the Congress.

Adopted in 1919, the Eighteenth Amendment established national prohibition by barring the manufacture, sale, and transportation of alcoholic beverages throughout the United States.

Note the Eighteenth Amendment was the first to specify the method of ratifying and to set a time limit on ratification. It also was the first to provide for enforcement by both Congress and the states.

Amendment 19 Woman Suffrage

Section 1. The right of citizens of the United States to vote shall not be denied or abridged by the United States or by any state on account of sex.

Section 2. Congress shall have power to enforce this article by appropriate legislation.

Adopted in 1920, the Nineteenth Amendment established woman suffrage on a nationwide basis and indirectly established the right of women to hold public office. Prior to its adoption, some western states did allow women to vote. Wyoming (in 1890) was the first.

Amendment 20 Change of Terms, Sessions, and Inauguration

Section 1. The terms of the President and Vice President shall end at noon on the 20th day of January, and the terms of Senators and Representatives at noon on the 3rd day of January, of the years in which such terms would have ended if this article had not been ratified; and the terms of their successors shall then begin.

Section 2. The Congress shall assemble at least once in every year, and such meeting shall begin at noon on the 3rd day of January, unless they shall by law appoint a different day.

Section 3. If, at the time fixed for the beginning of the term of the President, the President-elect shall have died, the Vice President-elect shall become President. If a President shall not have been chosen before the time fixed for the beginning of his term, or if the President-elect shall have failed to qualify, then the Vice President-elect shall act as President until a President shall have qualified; and the Congress may by law provide for the case wherein neither a President-elect nor a Vice President-elect shall have qualified, declaring who shall then act as President, or the manner in which one who is to act shall be selected, and such person shall act accordingly until a President or Vice President shall have qualified.

Section 4. The Congress may by law provide for the case of the death of any of the persons from whom the House of Representatives may choose a President whenever the right of choice shall have devolved upon them, and for the case of the death of any of the persons from whom the Senate may choose a Vice President whenever the right of choice shall have devolved upon them.

Section 5. Sections 1 and 2 shall take effect on the 15th day of October following the ratification of this article.

Section 6. This article shall be inoperative unless it shall have been ratified as an amendment to the Constitution by the legislatures of three fourths of the several states within seven years from the date of its submission.

Adopted in 1933, the Twentieth Amendment changed the start of congressional terms (from March 4 to January 3) and presidential and vice presidential terms (from March 4 to January 20) following general elections.

It is known as the "lame duck" amendment because it shortened the time between the general election and the date newly-elected officials took office and eliminated "lame ducks" (defeated Representatives and Senators) from continuing to serve in Congress for four months during a new session (which began in December prior to the amendment's adoption).

The amendment also provides for presidential succession in case of death or disability of a President-elect.

Amendment 21 Repeal of National Prohibition

Section 1. The eighteenth article of amendment to the Constitution of the United States is hereby repealed.

Section 2. The transportation or importation into any state, territory, or possession of the United States for delivery or use therein of intoxicating liquors, in violation of the laws thereof, is hereby prohibited.

Section 3. This article shall be inoperative unless it shall have been ratified as an amendment to the Constitution by conventions in the several states, as provided in the Constitution, within seven years from the date of the submission hereof to the states by the Congress.

Adopted in 1933, the Twenty-First Amendment repealed national prohibition (the Eighteenth Amendment). It is the only amendment that has repealed a prior amendment. And it repealed national prohibition but not prohibition. States still maintain their power to prohibit the manufacture and sale of alcoholic beverages. Note also that the transportation of liquor into a "dry" state is a federal crime as well as a state crime. The Twenty-First Amendment is also the only amendment to date to be ratified by state conventions rather than by state legislatures.

Amendment 22 Presidential Tenure

Section 1. No person shall be elected to the office of the President more than twice, and no person who has held the office of President, or acted as President, for more than two years of a term to which some other person was elected President shall be elected to the office of the President more than once. But this article shall not apply to any person holding the office of President when this article was proposed by the Congress, and shall not prevent any person who may be holding the office of President, or acting as President, during the term within which this article becomes operative from holding the office of President or acting as President during the remainder of such term.

Section 2. This article shall be inoperative unless it shall have been ratified as an amendment to the Constitution by the legislatures of three fourths of the several states within seven years from the date of its submission to the states by the Congress.

Adopted in 1951, the Twenty-Second Amendment limited the number of terms a person can be elected as President to two. Thus, it formalized the two-term tradition established by Washington, which was broken by Franklin Roosevelt.

Notice that it is possible for a person to serve more than two terms, or 8 years. Lyndon Johnson, who assumed the Presidency following the assassination of John F. Kennedy, was eligible to run for reelection in 1968. Had he chosen to run and won, he could have served 9 years, 1 month, and 28 days. Note, too, the amendment was not applicable to Harry Truman, President at the time of the amendment's ratification.

Amendment 23 Presidential Electors for D.C.

Section 1. The District constituting the seat of government of the United States shall appoint in such manner as the Congress may direct:

A number of electors of President and Vice President equal to the whole number of Senators and Representatives in Congress to which the District would be entitled if it were a state, but in no event more than the least populous state; they shall be in addition to those appointed by the states, but they shall be considered, for the purposes of the election of President and Vice President, to be electors appointed by a state; and they shall meet in the district and perform such duties as provided by the twelfth article of amendment.

Section 2. The Congress shall have power to enforce this article by appropriate legislation.

Adopted in 1961, the Twenty-Third Amendment provides for the choosing of electors for the District of Columbia. Until its adoption, residents of the District were excluded from presidential elections. By the wording of the amendment, the District is limited to three electors, the same number as the least populous state. If the District were a state, it would be entitled to four electors based on its probable representation in Congress.

Amendment 24 Prohibition of Poll Tax

Section 1. The right of citizens of the United States to vote in any primary or other election for President or Vice President, for electors for President or Vice President, or for Senator or Representative in Congress, shall not be denied or abridged by the United States or any state by reason of failure to pay any poll tax or other tax.

Section 2. The congress shall have power to enforce this article by appropriate legislation.

Adopted in 1964, the Twenty-Fourth Amendment prohibits both the federal government and the states from denying a qualified voter the right to vote in federal elections for failure to pay any tax. The amendment did not prohibit states from imposing a poll tax as a voting qualification in state and local elections. However, the Supreme Court held the poll tax to be a denial of the "equal protection" clause of the Fourteenth Amendment and, therefore, unconstitutional in *Harper* v. *Virginia State Board of Elections* in 1966.

Amendment 25 Presidential Succession and Disability

Section 1. In case of the removal of the President from office or his death or resignation, the Vice President shall become President.

Section 2. Whenever there is a vacancy in the office of the Vice President, the President shall nominate a Vice President who shall take the office upon confirmation by a majority vote of both houses of Congress.

Section 3. Whenever the President transmits to the President pro tempore of the Senate and the Speaker of the House of Representatives his written declaration that he is unable to discharge the powers and duties of his office, and until he transmits to them a written declaration to the contrary, such powers and duties shall be discharged by the Vice President as Acting President.

Section 4. Whenever the Vice President and a majority of either the principal officers of the executive departments, or of such other body as Congress may by law provide, transmit to the President pro tempore of the Senate and the Speaker of the House of Representatives their written declaration that the President is unable to discharge the powers and duties of his office, the Vice President shall immediately assume the powers and duties of the office of Acting President.

Thereafter, when the President transmits to the President pro tempore of the Senate and the Speaker of the House of Representatives his written declaration that no inability exists, he shall resume the powers and duties of his office unless the Vice President and a majority of either principal officers of the executive departments, or of such other body as Congress may by law provide, transmit within four days to the President pro tempore of the Senate and the Speaker of the House of Representatives their written declaration that the President is unable to discharge the powers and duties of his office. Thereupon Congress shall decide the issue, assembling within 48 hours for that purpose if not in session. If the Congress, within 21 days after receipt of the latter written declaration, or, if Congress is not in session, within 21 days after Congress is required to assemble, determines by two-thirds vote of both houses that the President is unable to discharge the powers and duties of his office, the Vice President shall continue to discharge the same as Acting President; otherwise, the President shall resume the powers and duties of his office.

Adopted in 1967, the Twenty-Fifth Amendment clarifies Article 2, Section 1, Paragraph 6. Until its adoption, the assumption of the office of the President by the Vice President because of vacancy was based upon the precedent set by John Tyler following the death of William Henry Harrison in 1841. The Twenty-Fifth Amendment clearly states the Vice President assumes the office of President should it become vacant. Nine times in American history it has become vacant—four times because of natural deaths (Harrison in 1841, Taylor in 1850, Harding in 1923, and Franklin Roosevelt in 1945); four times because of assassinations (Lincoln in 1865, Garfield in 1881, McKinley in 1901, and Kennedy in 1963); and once because of resignation (Nixon in 1974).

The amendment also provides for the Vice President becoming acting President should the President become disabled.

In addition, the Twenty-Fifth Amendment provides for filling the office of the Vice President by presidential appointment and congressional approval should it become vacant. Eighteen times in American history there has been a vacancy—9 times because of assumption to the Presidency (Tyler in 1841, Fillmore in 1850, Andrew Johnson in 1865, Arthur in 1881, Theodore Roosevelt in 1901, Coolidge in 1923, Truman in 1945, Lyndon Johnson in 1963, and Ford in 1974); 7 times through death (Clinton in 1812, Gerry in 1814, King in 1853, Wilson in 1875, Hendricks in 1885, Hobart in 1899, and Sherman in 1912); and 2 times by resignation (Calhoun in 1832 and Agnew in 1973).

Gerald Ford is the first person to be appointed Vice President by a President, with Nelson Rockefeller being the second. Ford also became President following Nixon's resignation. Thus, he is the only person to hold both offices having never been elected to either.

Amendment 26 Eighteen-Year-Old Vote

Section 1. The right of citizens of the United States, who are eighteen years of age or older, to vote shall not be denied or abridged by the United States or by any state on account of age.

Section 2. The Congress shall have power to enforce this article by appropriate legislation.

Adopted in 1971, the Twenty-Sixth Amendment lowered the voting age to 18. Note, however, that the amendment does not prohibit any state from allowing citizens less than 18 to vote if it so chooses. Thus, the amendment does not, in fact, establish a minimum voting age.

GLOSSARY

A

abolition putting an end to slavery

absolutism the idea that total power should be vested in one or more rulers

abstinence refraining from all alcoholic drink

abstract expressionism style of painting featuring surreal objects, figures, or scenes in swirling colors

acquittal verdict of not guilty

administered markets markets in which control is exercised by corporation owners and managers

affirmative action programs designed to further employment and education of women and minorities

affluent wealthy

agricultural revolution period of increased farm productivity due to new techniques and machinery

airlift system of transporting supplies through the air to an otherwise inaccessible area

amendment formal change in the Constitution

Americanizing assimilation to white American culture

amnesty general pardon from legal penalties

amphibious carried out by coordinated land and sea action

anarchist one who advocates the overthrow of all government restraints in favor of complete freedom

annexation attachment of a country or territory

annuities yearly allowances granted by government

antebellum existing before the Civil War

appeasement offering concessions to aggressors to keep peace

apprentice one who receives food, clothing, shelter, and instruction in a trade in exchange for work

arbitration arrangement whereby two disputants agree to accept the decision of an impartial third party

armistice truce

arms race competition to improve and strengthen weapons and military forces

assimilation process of absorbing into a culture or society

assumption act of taking over or becoming responsible for

atomic bomb bomb whose destructive force results from the splitting of atoms

automation use of machinery to replace human workers

autonomy right of self-government

B

baby boom sharp increase in birth rate after World War II

balance of payments difference between total payments made to a foreign country and total payments received from a foreign country over a period of time

balance of trade difference in value between a country's imports and exports over a period of time

ballot stuffing filling ballot box with extra or illegal votes

bank note promissory note issued by a bank

barter direct exchange of goods or services

bears speculators who sell securities or commodities because they expect a price decline

bicameral made up of two houses (legislature)

big stick policy aggressive foreign policy used by Theodore Roosevelt involving the threat of force

bill of rights statement of the fundamental rights guaranteed to the people by a government

bills of exchange written orders to pay someone a certain sum of money

bimetallism policy of using two metals (gold and silver) to back paper money

bipartisan involving members of two political parties

bipolarism domination of world affairs by two powers

black humor treatment of the tragic in a humorous or absurd way

blacklist to circulate a list of persons to be boycotted or disapproved of in unions

black market illegal trade in goods

black power philosophy asserting that blacks should control their own lives

blank check freedom for any course of action

blitzkrieg attack carried out with great force and speed

blockade runners ships used to slip goods into and out of a blockaded port

blue-collar workers people who work in factories or on farms

bootleggers people who produce or sell something illegally

bounty extra payment

boycott buyers' strike

brain trust government advisors from the academic world who, often without official status, make policy

breadlines lines of people waiting for free food

broker-state government government in which the President acts as an intermediary between groups

brokers' loans money borrowed from banks by stock market agents

bull market condition of the stock market in which stock values are rising

bulls speculators who buy securities or commodities because they are optimistic that prices will rise

bunker fortified chamber below ground

bureaucracy system of administration characterized by specialization of functions and fixed rules

business cycle recurring changes in the level of business activity

buying on margin using a small down payment and borrowed funds to invest in the stock market

C

cabinet heads of executive departments and official advisors to the President

call loans loans that are payable on demand

capital investment money; also equipment used in production

capitalism economic system based on private property and free enterprise

capitalist person who invests money in business or believes in capitalism

carpetbaggers Northerners who moved South after the Civil War

cash and carry selling goods on a cash only basis

cash crop crop that can be exported for a profit

casualty member of the military lost through death, injury, capture, sickness, or through being missing in action

cattle barons cattle ranchers with vast holdings

caucus private meeting of members of a political party to choose candidates or decide course of action

cease-fire temporary suspension of fighting

censured officially reprimanded

cession formal surrender of territory or rights

charter colony colony governed in accordance with a royal charter without interference from the crown

checks and balances system used to maintain the balance of power in government by giving each branch a number of checks on the others

city-manager government city government in which an official is hired to direct administration of city business

civil disobedience refusal to obey (unjust) laws in order to call attention to their injustice

civil service rules covering government jobs

closed shop shop in which only union members are employed

cloture closing or limiting of debates in a legislative body by calling for a vote

collateral property used as security to guarantee loans

collective bargaining negotiation of workers, represented by union leaders, with employers

collectivization organizing economic production and distribution under control of the government

commerce raiders large, fast warships designed for use against commercial ships on the high seas

commission government city government in which voters elect a number of commissioners to administer city business

commonwealth political unit having local autonomy but voluntarily united with the United States

commune community whose members share or own property jointly

communism government in which the means of production are owned by the state

commuter one who travels from home in suburbs to work in the city

company town town, including houses, stores, and services, built and controlled by company

compulsory attendance laws laws that require children to attend school

concurrent powers powers shared by both the national and state governments; neither granted exclusively to the national government nor denied to the states

confederation league of independent states

conference committee committee appointed to resolve differences between House and Senate versions of a bill

conflict of interest conflict between personal interests and official responsibilities of a person in a position of trust

conscientious objector person who refuses to bear arms or serve in the military because of religious or moral principles

conscription forced military service

conservation saving of natural resources

consortium international business association

constituency citizens represented by a government official

constitution written statement of the principles of government

containment policy devised to prevent the spread of communism

contraband prohibited goods

convoy technique system by which merchant ships traveled in a pack surrounded by a small number of armed vessels

cooling-off treaties treaties that require parties to an international dispute to refrain from war while waiting for the report of an investigating committee (used by President Wilson)

cooperative enterprise in which workers manage their own production and sell their own goods

corporate saving investment in better equipment by a business or corporation

corporation legal entity with the same legal status as a person

corollary proposition that follows from one that has already been established

corrupt bargain bargain allegedly made between Henry Clay and John Quincy Adams concerning the election of 1824; the idea that Clay had helped Adams in return for a top post in Adams' administration

counterculture culture with values that are at odds with those of established society

countervailing power sufficient power to check the ambitions of another

counting coup practice of Plains Indians in which they tried to touch an enemy during battle and escape unharmed

cowhands workers who tend or drive cattle

craft union organization of workers in one line of work (same as trade union)

crop-lien system system under which tenant farmers buy supplies by pledging part of their crops as payments

creditors people to whom debts are owed

D

dark horse political candidate who is unknown or whose chances are not good for winning an election

de facto segregation segregation that exists in fact, but is not required by law

default failure to pay debt

deficit spending the practice of spending funds raised by borrowing

demagogue leader who gains power by false claims of being champion of the common people

demand willingness and ability to buy

deportation expulsion of an alien from a country

depreciated fallen in value

depreciation wear and tear on machinery, buildings, and equipment

depression period of slow economic activity accompanied by low prices and high unemployment

deregulation relaxation of restrictions on business

de-Stalinization effort to rid Soviet Union of policies associated with Joseph Stalin

détente relaxation of tensions between nations

deterrent something that serves as a restraint

devaluation reduction in exchange value of currency by lowering its gold equivalency

direct primary election to choose candidates for a general election or delegates to a nominating convention

direct representation form of representation in which representatives must live in the same towns or districts as the voters who elected them

direct tax tax that is paid directly to the government rather than being included in the price of goods

discrimination difference in treatment on a basis other than individual merit

disfranchisement loss of the right to vote

dissident one who is critical of government policies

diversified based on many different kinds

divine right theory holding that a ruler received authority directly from God

dollar diplomacy foreign policy of William Howard Taft involving the promotion of American business and banking interests throughout the world

dollar matching system in which the federal government contributed an amount equal to that contributed by the state for a specific purpose

domino theory theory that if one country in Southeast Asia becomes communist-controlled, neighboring countries will also become communistic

doves those who support an end to war

dry farming plowing deep furrows in the soil to allow water to reach the roots of crops

dual court system system in which the national courts exist independently from the state courts

due process of law legal procedures carried out in accordance with established rules

dugout shelter built into the earth on the Great Plains in the late 1800's

E

easy money policy course of action taken by Federal Reserve Board to increase money supply

elastic clause clause in Constitution stating that Congress has the power to make all laws that are "necessary and proper" (also called necessary and proper clause)

elect those chosen by God for entry to Heaven

elective system system that allows college students to choose some of their courses

emancipation setting free from bondage

embargo order that prohibits trade between nations

empresario person who obtains grants and brings in settlers to develop an area

enemy aliens people of Japanese, German, or Italian birth who lived in the United States during World War II and who were not naturalized

entrepreneur one who organizes, manages, and assumes the risks of a business enterprise

enumerated commodities certain colonial raw materials that could only be sold to England, according to England's Navigation Acts

espionage using spies to obtain information about plans and activities of a foreign country

establishment the political, economic, and social authority of a society

eugenics theory that holds that certain racial groups are superior because of inherited characteristics

evangelist one who preaches with emotion at special services

evolution theory that human life developed from lower forms of life by natural selection

ex post facto law law that prescribes the punishment for an act committed before the law against it was passed

excise tax domestic tax on the manufacture or sale of a product

executive agreement agreement between the President and a foreign power not requiring the approval of the Senate

executive clemency lessening of punishment by order of the President

executive privilege right of President to withhold information from Congress

expansionist person who supported expanding the land area of the United States

exposé revelation of scandal

expressed powers those powers explicitly granted to the national government in the Constitution

F

face value value printed on the face of money

factors of production resources necessary for economic production: land, labor, capital

factory system system in which the total process of manufacturing takes place at one location

fascism political philosophy that exalts nation and race and advocates government by dictatorship and totalitarianism

federal system system in which power is divided between a central government and a number of regional governments

felony crime for which punishment is greater than imprisonment for more than one year

feminism theory of political, economic, and social equality between men and women

filibuster delaying tactics used in the Senate to block passage of a bill

finance capitalism system in which corporations are owned by banks

financial panic sudden, widespread fear about the value of money

fixed exchange rate system under which the price of one country's currency is tied to that of another so the rate does not change

flexible response military strategy designed for quick and decisive action in time of crisis

folk rock music featuring social protest

foreclose take control of property

forty-niners name given to people who went to California during the 1849 gold rush

franchise right to vote; also, a contract to handle goods and services in a certain territory exclusively

free enterprise economic system in which there is private ownership and free competition

free enterprise zone zone in which industries and businesses are given government incentives to locate

free list list of items exempt from tariff

free market economy based on supply and demand

free trade trade without tariff barriers

freedmen freed slaves

freedom rides tactic used by Civil Rights advocates to protest segregation on buses and trains

fringe benefits advantages such as holidays, pensions, and insurance offered by an employer

fundamentalists persons who believe in a literal interpretation of the Bible

G

generation gap disparity in values and beliefs between youth and adults

genocide methodical destruction of a racial group

ghost town once-thriving town now almost totally deserted

gold rush movement of large numbers of people in search of gold

gold standard using gold to back paper money

graduate study course of study for those continuing education after college graduation

graduated income tax tax system in which people with higher incomes pay higher taxes

graft illegal gain

grandfather clause clause in constitutions of some southern states in the late 1800's that allowed persons to vote only if their ancestors had been eligible to vote on Jan. 1, 1867

greenbacks paper money

gross national product total value of final goods and services produced in a country in one year

guerrilla warfare method of warfare using irregular hit-and-run tactics

H

habeas corpus right to be brought before a judge as a protection against illegal imprisonment

hallucinogens substances that induce hallucinations

happenings improvised spectacles or performances

hard money gold and silver coins

hawks supporters of war

headright land grant given to encourage colonization

hierarchy of laws idea that some laws are superior to others

holding company company that buys controlling shares in other corporations

homestead tract of land acquired from public lands by living on and farming the tract

horizontal integration expanded ownership in one area of production in an industry

hyphenated Americans Americans tied by birth or ancestry to another country

I

impeach to charge a public official with a crime

imperialism policy or practice of extending the domination of one country over another

implied powers powers that may be reasonably implied from the expressed powers of the Constitution

impoundment refusal by the President to spend money allotted by Congress for various programs

impress to take by force for public service, as into the navy

incumbent present officeholder

indemnity payment for damages

indentured servant person, in colonial times, who contracted to work for a certain period of time, usually in exchange for passage to America

industrial capitalism system in which corporations are controlled by industrial owners

industrial union organization of all workers, skilled or unskilled, in one industry

inelastic currency condition in which a change in demand for money causes little change in supply

inherent powers those powers which are not specifically given to the federal government but which it possesses because it is a national government

initiative method by which citizens can propose new laws

injunction court order

integration ending the segregation of races or groups

interchangeable parts identical parts that can be quickly assembled to make a complete product

internal improvements program of road and bridge construction intended to aid the national economy

interstate commerce trade between two or more states

intrastate commerce   commerce that takes place within a state

investment tax credit   tax breaks for firms investing in new equipment

iron-clad   kind of battleship covered with thick iron plates, first used during the Civil War

iron curtain   political and ideological barrier separating free and communist Europe

ironclad oath   loyalty oath required of southerners by the Wade-Davis plan of reconstruction

irreconcilables   members of Congress opposed to America's joining the League of Nations

isolationism   policy of avoiding involvements with other nations

J

jawboning   persuasion through discussion

jazz   American musical form that combined the rhythms and scales of African music with the instrumentation and harmony of European music

Jim Crow laws   laws passed to segregate blacks and whites

jingoes   persons of extreme chauvinism or nationalism who believe in a warlike foreign policy

joint occupation   occupation of the same territory by people from two or more nations

joint resolution   resolution that is passed by both houses of a legislature and has the force of law when signed by the President or passed over a presidential veto

judicial review   power of the courts to determine the constitutionality of a law

K

kamikaze   member of Japanese air force assigned to make suicidal crash on a target

L

laissez-faire   doctrine that an economy should be run without government interference

land grant colleges   colleges established with the help of land grants from the federal government

laser   device that produces a highly-concentrated beam of light; used in scientific experiments, medicine, industry, and communications

legal tender   money that is legally valid for the payment of debts

legislative apportionment   distribution of legislative seats

lend-lease plan   policy of aiding an ally by lending war equipment

libel   publication of a false statement with intent to do harm

limited government   idea that government may exercise only those powers given to it by the people

limited warfare   warfare in which each side limits its military operations

literacy test   test of reading and ability to explain state constitution given to determine eligibility to vote

lobby   group that tries to influence government officials

lobbyists   individuals who represent the views of a certain group to public officials

lockout   closing of a factory to workers by management

long drive   cattle drive from southern Texas to Abilene in the late 1800's

loopholes   technicalities in the law that are used to evade a contract or obligation

loose construction   broad interpretation of the Constitution

Loyalists   colonists who remained loyal to England during the American Revolution

lyceums   mutual improvement societies that sponsor discussions and lectures, put together libraries, and promote better schools

M

mainstreaming   incorporating children with mental handicaps into regular school programs

mandate   people's authorization given to a representative

manifest destiny   belief in the destiny of the United States to stretch from ocean to ocean

manifesto   public declaration of intentions or views

margin requirement   minimum amount of money required to purchase securities

martial law   law administered by military forces

mass production   production in large quantities

massive retaliation   policy of all-out nuclear attack in case of provocation

melodramas   plays built upon exaggerated emotionalism

mercantilism   economic policy followed by European countries in the 1690's and 1700's that aimed to attain a favorable balance of trade, the development of agriculture and manufactured goods, and the establishment of foreign trading monopolies

mercenaries   soldiers who serve for pay in the army of a foreign country

micro chip   miniature electronic integrated circuit

midnight appointments   appointment of Federalists to judiciary offices by John Adams during his last days in office

militarism   policy of maintaining strong armed forces and being ready to use them

military-industrial complex   close involvement of government and industry in preparing for war

minority President   one who receives a majority of electoral votes, but less than a majority of the popular vote

minutemen   members of the colonial militia ready to take the field at a moment's notice

missionary diplomacy   foreign policy designed to help other countries

moderate   one who favors limited change

monitoring   observing or checking

monopoly   exclusive control of a trade or industry

moratorium   authorized period of delay

most favored nation   nation that is guaranteed tariff as low or lower than those granted to any other nation

muckrakers   writers who exposed social, economic, and political problems

mudslinging   use of insulting or abusive language, particularly against a political opponent

N

national debt   debt owed by the national government

national income   total amount of money earned by all the people of a nation

national planning   economic planning by the federal government

nationalist   one who believes in national independence or a strong national government

nativism   policy of favoring inhabitants as opposed to immigrants

natural laws   laws, according to Enlightenment philosophy, that govern the universe

natural rights   basic rights, according to Enlightenment philosophy, that people had before governments were formed

natural selection   process, according to the theory of evolution, by which species that best adapt to their environment are most likely to survive

naturalization   process by which foreign immigrants become citizens of the United States

necktie parties   lynchings

neutralize   to make ineffective

new immigrants   those who emigrated to America primarily from southern and eastern Europe in the late 1800's

new manifest destiny   idea that it was the fate of the United States to extend its boundaries beyond the seas

nomadic   wandering

nonaligned   not allied with one of the world superpowers

nonbelligerency   state in which a nation provides aid to one side during a war, but stops short of entering the conflict

nonimportation agreements   agreements signed by colonial merchants banning the importing of British goods

nuclear freeze   halt on nuclear arms buildup

nullify   to declare invalid

O

occupation   control of an area by foreign forces

old immigrants   those who emigrated to America, primarily from Great Britain, Germany, and northern Europe, in the early and mid-1800's

open market operations   bond market in which government securities are bought and sold

open range   unclaimed public grasslands

open shop   shop in which owners may hire anyone they wish

operetta   comic light opera

original jurisdiction   authority to hear cases the first time they go to court, or initial authority to interpret and apply the law

oversoul   Transcendentalist concept of the soul, of which everything is a part

P

pacifist   person opposed to war or violence as a means of settling a dispute

parity   formula intended to give farmers the purchasing power they had before World War I

parochial schools   private schools maintained by a religious organization

partisan   displaying strong support for a party, cause, faction, or person

patents   exclusive rights of inventors to the profits from their ideas

Patriots   colonists who supported the idea of American independence

patronage   power to make appointments to government jobs on a basis other than merit alone

peaceful coexistence   policy in which opposing nations attempt to settle differences through negotiation rather than through threats or war

peculiar institution   slavery

perjury   lying while under oath

personal liberty laws   laws to stop state and local officials from obeying the federal fugitive slave laws

pet banks   state banks into which President Jackson deposited governments funds after they had been removed from the Second Bank of the United States

photojournalism   journalism in which written copy is subordinate to photographs

pigeon-hole   to postpone indefinitely the consideration of a bill

placer method   method of mining gold using pick, shovel, and pan

plantation method   large-scale systematic production of profitable crops, requiring an abundant labor supply

platform   statement of political party principles

plurality   largest number of votes cast but less than one half of the total

pocket veto   process by which the President may stop legislation by not signing measure within ten days of congressional adjournment

pogrom   organized massacre, especially of Jews

police power   state's authority to protect the health, safety, morals, and welfare of its citizens

political bosses   politicians who dominate party organizations

political machine   party organization headed by a boss or a small group of politicians whose efforts are directed at keeping themselves in power

political party   group of people organized for the purpose of directing government policy

poll tax   tax to be paid at election time in order to be allowed to vote

pool agreement by rival companies to eliminate competition by dividing business

pop art art using commonplace objects for subject

popular sovereignty idea that ultimate political authority rests with the people; also, local determination of the slavery question (squatter sovereignty)

poverty level income below which a family cannot meet its basic needs

pragmatism philosophy calling for a practical approach to problems

precedent something that serves as an example in later situations

predestination doctrine that mortals enter Heaven through grace of God, rather than by faith and good works

preparedness military readiness for war

presidential primary state election to determine the delegates to a national convention that will nominate a party's candidate for President or to determine the candidate for whom a state's delegate must vote at the convention

price fixing secret agreements made by companies in the same industry to charge the same or similar prices

privateers armed private ships

prohibition law banning the manufacture, sale, and transportation of alcoholic beverages

proletarian literature literature that relies on pro-worker and anti-capitalist themes

promissory note written promise to pay a specified sum to the noteholder

propaganda ideas, facts, or rumors spread deliberately to help or hurt a cause

proprietary colony colony granted by the king of England, including the right to govern in accordance with English law

protection money money paid by owners of illegal businesses to prevent police raids

protective tariff taxes on imports high enough to protect American industry from foreign competitors

protectionist one who favors protective tariffs

protectorate relationship in which one country has authority over another

provisional government temporary government subject to change

proviso clause that imposes a condition

public domain public lands owned by the United States government

pump priming investing government funds into the economy in order to stimulate the flow of money

puppet regime government controlled by an outside power

Q

quarter to house or lodge

R

radical one who favors extreme and immediate change

range wars conflicts over land among cattle-raisers, sheepraisers, and farmers in the Old West

ratification formal approval (i.e., of a treaty)

rationing system of distributing scarce goods

reactionary one who is against change or favors a return to an old political or social system

Reaganomics economic plan of the Reagan administration stressing tax cuts, decreases in social services spending, and increases in defense spending

real wages wages with the inflation factor taken out

realism attempt in art and literature to show the world as it really is

rebate return of part of a payment

recall means to remove elected officials from office

receivership arrangement by which a receiver administers the property of another person

reclamation replacing natural resources

recognition acknowledgement of a nation's independence

Reconstruction process of readmitting the southern states to the Union after the Civil War

redemption restoration of white leadership in the South after Reconstruction

redemptioner person who contracted to work for a certain period of time to redeem unpaid passage to America during colonial times

rediscount rates interest rate for banks

referendum method by which citizens approve or disapprove the passing of a bill by the legislature

refugee one who flees to escape danger or persecution

reindustrialization shift of American manufacturing from traditional to high technology industries

repatriation return of prisoners of war to their homeland

republic government in which the power is held by citizens entitled to vote for direct representation

reservation area set aside by the government (as for Indians)

reservationists members of Congress who approved joining the League of Nations under certain conditions

reserve requirement amount of money a bank must have deposited in the Federal Reserve Bank

reserved powers those powers not granted to the national government and not denied to the states by the Constitution

residence requirement requirement that a person live in a place for a certain period of time in order to receive a privilege (e.g., citizenship, voting)

revelation special message from God

revenue-sharing federal program to return tax money to state and local government

revolution overthrow of an established government or political system

rider unrelated amendment to a bill

right of deposit right to unload cargoes

robber baron entrepreneur or capitalist who used ruthless or unethical business methods

roll-call vote vote taken in Congress in which each member's vote is recorded

romanticism movement in art and literature that valued imagination and emotion more than reason

royal colony colony governed directly by the Crown through appointed officials

S

sanction measure adopted by a nation or a group of nations to punish another nation that is violating international law

sanctity of contracts idea that contracts are legally binding and may not be changed by government action

satellites nations controlled by another more powerful nation

scalawags southern Unionists

scientific management application of study and research to make production more efficient

scorched-earth policy policy of widespread destruction (followed by Cubans in Spanish-American War)

secession act of withdrawing from the Union

sectionalism rivalry and conflict among regions of a country

securities documents showing ownership of stocks, bonds, or mortgages

securities exchanges places where stocks and bonds are bought and sold

sedition inciting resistance to lawful authority

segregation separation of one race or group from another

selective service military draft

separation of powers division of power between the different parts of a government

service sector part of the economy that produces services rather than goods

settlement houses neighborhood centers established in the late 1800's and early 1900's to offer services to the poor

sharecroppers tenant farmers who received a share of the value of the crops they grew in exchange for their labor

shuttle diplomacy negotiations carried out by a diplomat traveling back and forth between disputing nations

silent majority term used to describe Americans who support traditional values

sit-down strike work stoppage in which workers occupy their place of employment

sit-in act of occupying seats in a segregated establishment to protest discrimination

slave codes laws that defined slaves as property, with few if any legal rights

slums areas of substandard housing

soap operas daytime radio serials, often sponsored by soap companies

social contract idea that people make an original agreement to enter society and obey its laws in exchange for government protection of their natural rights

Social Darwinism theory that social progress is based on the human struggle for survival

social gospel view that the church should take an active role in improving society

social mobility ability to improve one's social class

socialism political and economic system in which the government controls the means of production

soft money paper currency

sovereignty right of self-government

speakeasies saloons established during prohibition where alcoholic beverages were served

specialization method of farming that concentrates on one or two cash crops

specie money in coin

speculators people who purchase something for the purpose of selling it later for a profit

sphere of influence areas under the indirect control of an outside power

spoils system system under which a new President can replace individuals in government positions to which they have been appointed by previous administrations

squatter one who settles land without a legal title

squatter sovereignty local determination of the slavery question; same as popular sovereignty

stagflation period of combined inflation and recession

standard time system by which the country is divided into zones, each of which goes by the sun time of its central meridian

standing committee regular committee of Congress that considers bills within a given subject area

state's evidence testimony given in court by accused persons against one or more of their alleged associates

status quo ante bellum conditions that existed before a war

steerage section of a ship for passengers who pay low fares

stock certificates of ownership in a company

strategic nuclear weapons nuclear missiles with long-range capability

strict construction narrow interpretation of the Constitution

subsidies government grants to aid an enterprise considered good for the public

submarine ship capable of operating under water

subpoenas written legal orders

subsistence minimum necessary to support life

subsistence farmers farmers who consume all they produce and sell very little

suffrage right to vote

suffragist person who believes in extending suffrage, especially to women

summit conference meeting of highest-level officials

supply-side economics theory that incentives to work, save, and invest will strengthen economy

suspension bridge bridge hanging from cables attached to towers

swastika symbol of the Nazi Party

swing form of jazz music that features a lively rhythm and improvisation by soloists

syncopation changing of the musical accent, usually by emphasizing the weak beat rather than the strong

T

tabloid half-size newspaper featuring condensed news and lurid photographs

tariff duties or taxes imposed on items of overseas trade

temperance control of drinking of alcoholic beverages; organized movement to outlaw intoxicants

tenant farmer farmer who rents land

tenements apartment houses that are crowded, unsafe, uncomfortable, and unsanitary

tenure of office length of time a person can stay in office

test case case in which the outcome is likely to serve as a precedent

theocracy government by officials who are regarded as divinely guided

third party significant new political party, in a two-party system, that has enough support to affect the outcome of an election

Third World developing nations of Asia, Africa, and Latin America

tight money policy course of action taken by Federal Reserve Board to take money out of circulation

tonnage duties duty on goods per ton transported, or duty based on cargo capacity of ships

total war war against civilians and property as well as the military forces of the opposing nation

totalitarian political regime that suppresses opposition and controls most aspects of people's lives

tract societies groups whose purpose is to publish religious tracts and pamphlets

trade union organization of skilled workers in one line of work (same as a craft union)

transcendentalism idea that humans can transcend or rise above reason

transit rights permission to cross another's land

trench warfare method of warfare used in World War I in which lines of opposing soldiers fired at each other from ditches

triangular trade colonial trade route in which ships traveled a triangular route from the colonies to Africa, to the West Indies, and back to the colonies

tribute protection money to another country

trust combination of corporations that reduces or eliminates competition in an industry

trustbusting forcing trusts to break up

two-party system political system in which two parties dominate

U

unalienable rights basic human rights that cannot be taken away

underemployment less than full-time work or work that does not utilize a person's skills

underground organization engaging in secret operations against occupation forces

underground press newspapers that are not considered part of the establishment

urban renewal program to rebuild slums

urbanization rise in the percentage of total population living in cities

utopias communities designed to achieve an ideal society

V

vagrancy laws laws that make it illegal to wander around without an established home or visible means of support

vaudeville stage shows featuring many different kinds of acts

vertical integration ownership of all levels of production within an industry

veto right of the President to reject legislation

vigilantism system whereby a citizens' group takes law into its own hands

voice vote vote taken in either house of Congress in which the members proclaim their decision aloud in chorus

W

wage-price guideposts guidelines drawn up by government to control level of wages and prices

war materiel weapons and equipment not expected to be used up or destroyed

ward person or group of persons under the protection of the government

war of liberation Soviet-backed revolutionary movement in Third World countries

white-collar workers people with office jobs

work ethic belief in the value of hard work

workmen's compensation payment to workers injured in on-the-job accidents

writ of mandamus written order issued by a superior court commanding the performance of a specified official act or duty

writ of assistance search warrant used by British customs officials in the colonies to enforce the laws against smuggling

Y

Yankee ingenuity American inventiveness

yellow dog contracts agreement in which the workers disavow union membership

yellow journalism newspaper reporting that emphasizes the sensational

yeoman farmers farmers with small holdings who cultivate their own land

youth culture lifestyle of adolescents

INDEX

A

AAA. See Agricultural Adjustment Act.
Aachen, Battle of, 590
ABC Powers, 443
ABMS. See Antiballistic missile systems.
Abolitionist movement, 219–221, 225, 235, 280; in Civil War, 256; and Frederick Douglas, 285; propaganda for, 236; and women, 217, 218. See John Brown, Liberty party.
Abstract expressionism, 651
Acheson, Dean, 607, 639
Act Concerning Aliens, 136
Act for the Punishment of Certain Crimes, 136
Act of Algeciras, 437
Act of Chapultepec, 580
Act of Havana, 564
Act Respecting Alien Enemies, 136
Adams, Abigail Smith, 91
Adams, John, 135, 136; and Declaration of Independence, 67; and first Congress, 119; and Judiciary Act of 1801, 146; lawyer, 60; minister to England and Holland, 133; as President, 133; as radical, 64; and Treaty of Paris, 72
Adams, John Quincy, 91, 151, 159; earliest photograph, 169; on Indians, 188; on Missouri Compromise, 164; as President, 167–169; as Secretary of State, 159
Adams, Samuel, 58, 60; at First Continental Congress, 61; and Philadelphia Convention, 90; as radical, 64; warned by Revere, 63
Adams, Sherman B., 645
Adamson Act (1916), 399
Adams-Onís Treaty, 159, 194
Addams, Jane, 378
Advertising, in late 1800's, 377; in the 1920's, 498
AFDC. See Aid to Families with Dependent Children.
Affirmative action, 722, 754
Affluence, 645–647
Afghanistan, 730, 738, 739, 751
AFL. See American Federation of Labor.
AFL-CIO, 647
Africa, 216, 396, 484, 560, 738; armed struggles in, 726; and Barbary states, 147; foreign aid to, 611; imperialism in, 411, 413, 414; influence on jazz, 496, 499; Italian aggression in, 555–556; returning slaves to, 219; rivalry between East and West in, 614, 618; and slave trade, 223; in WWI, 447; in WWII, 573, 574
Africans, 359; in colonial period, 45
Age of Big Business, 301
Age of Imperialism, 414
Age of Jackson, 167, 170–172, 174, 225; and education, 371; and romanticism, 210
Agnew, Spiro T., 675; resignation of, 693
Agricultural Adjustment Act, 517, 528, 530, 532; Second, 533
Agricultural Credit Banks, 511
Agriculture: in Antebellum South, 222–223, 225; in California, 193; after Civil War, 272, 356–357; in Civil War, 258, 260, 261, 262; in colonial period, 29, 42; corn in Plymouth Colony, 33; in Depression, 506, 508–509, 510, 517–518, 530; in 1920's, 499; on frontier, 185–187; inventions in, 210, 260; on Plains, 329–335; problems in, 86–97, 352; reform in 532–533; revolution in, 352; southern, after Reconstruction, 287, 311; tobacco, 30; and WWII, 585, 634; in 1950's, 647
Aguinaldo, Emilio, 419
Aid to Families with Dependent Children, 686, 735
AIM. See American Indian Movement.
Alabama, 156, 275, 358, 659; during Reconstruction, 280; enters Union, 162; secedes, 245
Alamo, Battle of, 191
Alaska, 488, 656; becomes state, 645; purchase of, 409–410
Alaskan Indians, 689
Alaska Pipeline Act, 690
Albania, 602; Italian invasion of, 561

Albany Congress, 54
Albany Plan of Union, 54
Alcohol abuse, 704
Alcott, Louisa May, 219
Alden, John, 63
Aldrich, Nelson, 395
Aldrich-Vreeland Act (of 1908), 394, 398
Aldrin, Edwin E. Jr., 684–685
Alexander v. *Holmes Co.,* (1969), 688
Algeciras Conference, 436–437
Alger, Horatio, 302
Algeria, 727, 731
Algonquin Indians, 24
Alien and Sedition Acts, 135, 136, 146; expiration of, 145
Allen, Ethan, 64
Allen, Fred, 537
Allen, Frederick Lewis, 512
Allen, Gracie, 537
Allen, William F., 298
Allen, Woody, 708
Alliance for Progress, 618
Allied Control Commission, 584
Allied Powers (Allies): and President Johnson, 666; relations with in future, 751; in WWI, 447, 449, 450, 453, 455, 458, 460–464, 466, 487–488, 548–550; in WWII, 573–576, 582–585, 588–596, 601
Allison, William B., 350
Alpert, Richard, 703
Altamont festival, 710
Amadas, Philip, 17
Ambrose, Stephen L., 604
Amendments, Constitutional: Bill of Rights, 104–105, 240; process, 114, 115; 1st, 48; 5th, 279; 12th, 108, 137; 13th, 257, 274, 276, 278, 285; 14th, 48, 278, 279, 280, 285, 307, 358, 662; 15th, 277, 280, 285; 16th, 395, 398; 17th, 105, 395; 18th, 484, 485; 19th, 112, 218, 277, 399; 21st, 485; 22nd, 116, 638; 24th, 659; 25th, 693, 694; 26th, 112, 690
America First Army, 463
America First Committee, 565, 566
American Antislavery Society, 220
American-Asiatic Association, 425
American Civil Liberties Union (ACLU), 486
American Colonization Society, 219
American Communist party, 522
American Federation of Labor (AFL), 317–318, 647; and blacks, 506; in Boston Police Strike, 477–478; during New Deal, 529; in Steelworkers Strike, 478
American Independent party, 676
American Indian Movement, 674, 688
American Liberty League, 522
American party, 238, 239
American Peace Society, 217
American Protective Association, 368
American Railway Union, 323
American Red Cross, 258
American Revolution. See Revolution, American.
"American System," 157–158
Amnesty: After Civil War, 271, 274; for Vietnam draft evaders, 691, 695
Anaconda Plan, 250, 252
Anarchists, 480; and labor movement, 320–321
Anderson, John, 731–732
Anderson, Maxwell, 539
Anderson, Maj. Robert, 246
Andropov, Yuri, 738
Andros, Sir Edmund, 361
Anglo-American Conference, 584, 588
Angola, 223
Annapolis Convention, 90
Anthony, Susan B., 218
Antiballistic Missile Systems, 682
Anti-Comintern Pact, 556
Anti-communist movement, 638–639
Antietam, Battle of, 256, 262
Antifederalists, 94–96, 121, 126
Anti-Masonic Party, 171, 178
Anti-Saloon League, 484
Antislavery movement. See Abolitionist movement.
Antitrust laws. See Trustbusting.
Antwerp, Belgium, 563; liberation of, 590
Anzio, Battle of, 591
Apache Indians, 23–24; resistance of, 337, 339–340
Apollo Project, 658

Apollo II, 684
Appalachia, 659
Appalachian Mountains: as boundary between whites and Indians, 56; as western border, 162
Appomattox Courthouse, Virginia, 265, 268, 271
Apportionment, legislative, 662
Apprentice system, 41
Arab nations: of 17th century, 414; and Lebanon War, 741; relations with under Nixon, 683–684; relations with under Carter, 726, 727; and war with Israel, 666
Arapaho Indians, 337
Arbitration, 316, 323, 350, 392
Architecture. See Art and Architecture.
Ardennes, Battle of, 591
Area Redevelopment Act, 659
Argentina, 443, 580, 728; and Falklands War, 742
Arizona, 200, 454, 585, 716; enters Union, 331
Arkansas, 509; enters Union, 235; in Civil War, 254; and Granger laws, 353; in Reconstruction, 280; return to Union, 272, 276; secession of, 249
"Arkies," 533
Armour, Philip, 302, 303, 305
Arms race, 599. See Nuclear weapons.
Armstrong, Louis, 496, 497, 537
Armstrong, Neil A., 684–685
Army, U.S., 134, 577, 623, 642; in California rebellion, 193; cut by Jefferson, 145; in demonstrations, 512; and exploration of West, 149; and Indian resistance, 337–340; in Japan, 606–607; in Korean War, 608–610; Medical Dept. of, 432–433; in Mexican War, 418, 419; in Revolution, 69–72; in Vietnam War, 667–669; in War of 1812, 153–155; in WWI, 455, 457, 458, 460–465; in WWII, 566, 582–585
Army of Northern Virginia, 256, 263, 265, 268
Army of the Potomac, 254–255, 262, 263, 264, 265
"Army of the West," 198
Arnold, Benedict, 64, 70
Arnold, Thurmond, 534
Art and Architecture: Ash Can School, 375–376; and bridges, 364; in colonial period, 49; in Depression, 538–539; in late 1800's, 375–376; in 1950's, 650–651; skyscrapers, 363; Spanish influence on, 21. See Painting.
Arthur, Chester A., 349–350
Articles of Confederation, 81–83, 92, 535; changes in, 82; executive branch in, 106, 107; and interpretation of laws, 108; and limited government, 100; plans to revise, 90; power of state governments under, 82; problems with, 83–86; ratification, 82–83
Artichoke Plan, 556
"Ash Can School," 375–376
Ashmun Institute, 216
Asia, 539, 559, 569, 646; balance of power in, 614; foreign aid to, 611; immigrants from, 366; Soviet activities in, 726; and Yalta Agreement, 592. See Southeast Asia.
Assimilation: of American Indians, 338, 340–341; of "old immigrants," 366, 368; and schools, 371
Assumption controversy (state debts), 123–124
Astaire, Fred, 538
Aswan High Dam, 615
"Atlanta Compromise," 358
Atlanta, Georgia, 483; capture of in Civil War, 266
Atlanta, Georgia, Battle of, 266, 267
Atlantic Charter, 566, 573
Atlantic Ocean, 198, 223, 429, 433, 641; Lindbergh crosses, 494; telegraph cables across, 205; in WWI, 458; in WWII, 566–567, 573
Atomic bomb, 578, 599; attempts to control, 601–602; development, 593–594; on Hiroshima and Nagasaki, 594; Soviet, 602
Atomic Energy Commission, 601
Auburn System, 214
Audubon, John James, 211, 212, 213
Austin, Moses, 190–191
Austin, Stephen, 191
Australia, and SEATO, 612; in WWII, 575, 576, 582
Austria, 466, 549, 613; German aggression in, 556; in Mexico, 409

Austria-Hungary, in WWI, 447, 460, 466, 548
Automation, 647, 659, 718
Automobile, 490–491, 498, 500
Automobile industry, 724; in Depression, 506; and Labor, 529; after WWII, 641
Axis powers, 569; defeat of in Africa, 583; defeats in E. Europe, 583–584, 587–591; and Latin America, 580; support for, 573; in WWII, 573–577. See Rome-Berlin Axis.
Aztecs, 20

B

Babcox, Orville, 345–346
Baby boom, 704, 752
Badoglio, Pietro, 584
Baer, George F., 392
Baez, Joan, 709, 710
Baghdad Pact, 617
Baily, Frederick. See Frederick Douglas.
Baja. See Lower California.
Baker, Newton, 458
Baker, Ray Stannard, 385
Baker v. *Carr* (1962), 661
Bakke, Allan, 722
Bakker, Jim, 712
Balanced budget, 536
Balance of power, 623, 681
Balance of powers: in Constitution, 100–101; and philosophy of James Madison, 101; in republic, 128
Balance of trade, 685–686; in colonial period, 43, 44
Balaguer, Joaquin, 624
Balboa, Vasco Nuñez de, 10
Baldwin, James, 650, 707
Balkans, 447, 591
Ball, Lucille, 648
Ballads, 21
Ballinger, Richard A., 396
Ballinger-Pinchot controversy, 396
Baltic states, 460, 558
Baltimore, Maryland, 123, 155; changes in population of, 363
Baltimore and Ohio (B&O) Railroad, 204; strike against, 320
Bankhead-Jones Farm Tenant Act, 533
Banking: during Depression, 515–516; and Hamilton, 535; international system, 611; and Panic of 1907, 394; reform under Wilson, 398. See Banking Act, Bank of the U.S., Pet Banks.
Banking Act of 1933, 516, 526–527
Bank of England, 504
Bank of the United States, 124–125, 145, 153
Banks, Dennis, 674
Bank War, the, 176–179
Banneker, Benjamin, 123
Bao Dai, 612
Barbary pirates, 85, 88, 147
Barbed wire, 330
Barkley, Alben W., 636
Barlow, Arthur, 17
"Barnburners," 233, 234, 236
Barnett, Gov. Ross, 660
Barrow, Clyde, 708
Barry, Leonora, 315, 316
Barter: in colonial period, 42; and whiskey, 126
Barton, Clara, 258
Baruch, Bernard M., 455, 599, 601
Baseball, 374, 492, 536; in the 1950's, 649; in the 60's and 70's, 716–717
Basie, "Count," 537
Basketball, 374, 536, 537; in the 1960's and 70's, 716–717
Basket Makers, 23
Bastogne, Battle of, 591
Battle of Britain, 564
Battle of France, 563
Battle of Seven Days, 255
Battle of the Bulge, 591
Battle of the Wilderness, 265–266
Bay of Pigs, invasion of Cuba, 621, 623
Batista, Fulgencio, 619
Bear Flag Republic. See Republic of California.
Beat generation, 701
Beatles, 709–710
Beatty, Warren, 708
Beauregard, Gen. Pierre G.T., 246; at Bull Run, 252
Beecher, Catherine, 216

Beecher, Henry Ward, 306, 384
Begin, Menachem, 727
Beiderbecke, Leon "Bix," 496
Belgium: and EEC, 659; invasion of, 562; and Locarno Pact, 556; liberation of, 590; and NATO, 606; war debt of, 548; in WWI, 447–449, 456, 460; in WWII, 590, 591
Bell, Alexander Graham, 297, 364
Bellecourt, Clyde, 674
Bell, John, 244
Bellamy, Edward, 377
Belleau Wood, Battle of, 461
Bellow, Saul, 650
Bench, Johnny, 716
Benny, Jack, 537
Benton, Thomas Hart, 539
B-1 bombers, 738
Bering Strait, 9
Bering, Vitus, 19
Berkeley, Lord John, 36
Berle, Adolf, 657
Berle, Milton, 648
Berlin, Germany, 591; divided, 592, 618; meeting about Samoa in, 412
Berlin airlift, 605
Berlin blockade, 605
Berlin Decree, 150
Berlin wall, 618
Bernstein, Carl, 692
Bernstein, Leonard, 649
Berry, Chuck, 497
Bessemer process, 296, 303
Beveridge, Albert J., 414
Bicycling, 374–375, 536
Biddle, Nicholas, 177, 178, 179
Big bands, 537, 538
Big Brother and the Holding Company, 710
Big business: and Kennedy, 658; during New Deal, 521, 522, 528, 536; and progressive reform, 384, 388, 392, 396; and Reagan, 736; regulation of, 306–308, 350, 397; rise of, 301–306; in 1950's, 645–647
Big stick policy, 434, 624
Bill of Rights, 104–105; and Alien and Sedition Acts, 136; desired, 95; developed, 120; and laissez-faire, 305; and James Madison, 101, 120
Bimetallism, 348
Bipolarism, era of, 599
Birney, James, 220
Bismarck Sea, Battle of, 582
Black, Hugo, 532
Black codes, 276, 278
Blackfoot Indians, 23
"Black Friday," 345
Black humor, 706, 708
Black Kettle, Chief, 337
Blacklist, 319
Blackmun, Harry A., 686
Black Muslims, 671
Black nationalism, 484, 671
Black Panthers, 671, 712
Black power, 671
Blacks, 239, 483; in Age of Jackson, 172; after WWII, 635; antebellum, 216, 222–223; in army, 257, 275; citizenship of, 278; civil rights of, 218, 219, 285, 643, 669–671; colleges, 216, 372; colonization of, 271; cowboys, 329, 331; and Democrats, 357; disfranchisement of, 357–358; films about, 708; in 1980's, 754; and Johnson, 662–665; and Kennedy, 659–660; in labor movement, 316, 318; literature about, 376; movement to cities, 313, 457, 585; and music, 497; and Nixon, 687–688; in Progressive Era, 394; in Reconstruction, 275, 280, 282–285; and Roosevelt, 529–531; schools, 283; struggle for equality, 669–671; suffrage, 263, 277, 280; and Truman, 636; as workers, 506; writers, 538, 650, 707. See Civil Rights Movement, Freedmen, Slavery.
Black studies programs, 716
"Black Thursday," 504
Blackwell, Elizabeth, 217, 218–219
Blaine, James G., 283, 348, 350
Bland-Allison Act, 350–351
Blockade runners, 253
Blue Lake, 689
Blues, 497
Blume, Peter, 539
Bly, Nellie, 373
Board of Indian Commissioners, 338
Bogotá, Colombia, 431

Bohemia. See Czechoslovakia.
Bohlen, Charles E., 641
Bolivia, 412
Bolsheviks, 479
Bonaparte, Napoleon. See Napoleon.
Bonus Bill of 1816, 158
Bonus Expeditionary Force, 511–512
Boone, Daniel, 333
Booth, Edwin, 375
Booth, John Wilkes, 273
Borah, William E., 467, 561, 562
Border ruffians, 239
Borglum, Gutzon, 495
Borglum, Lincoln, 495
Bosch, Juan, 623–624
Bosin, Blackbear, 336
Bosque, Redondo, 337
Boston, 34, 205, 213, 215, 220; in colonial period, 42; changes in population in, 363; in Revolution, 64–66; and Shays' Rebellion, 87
Boston Massacre, 59–60, 457, 477–478
Boston Police Force Strike, 477–478, 487
Boston Policemen's Union, 477–478
Boston Tea Party, 61
Bouvier, Jacqueline, 656
Bow, Clara, 494
Bowie, Jim, 191
Boxer Protocol, 426
Boxer Rebellion, 425–426, 427
Boxing, 374
Boycotts, 316, 670, 673
Bozeman Road, 337, 338
Braddock, General Edward, 54
Brady, James, 736
Bragg, General Braxton, 255–256, 263, 265
"brain trust," Roosevelt's, 521
Brandeis, Louis D., 521
Brazil, 10, 223, 443, 566, 728
Breckinridge, John C., 244
Breed's Hill, 65. See Battle of Bunker Hill.
Bretton Woods Conference, 591, 685
Brezhnev, Leonid, 682, 683, 696, 726, 738
Briand, Aristide, 499
Bribery, 346
Bricker, John W., 587
Bridger, James, 195
Bridges, 364
"Brinkmanship," 614
Bristow, George F., 211
British Empire, 220
British Guiana, 415. See Guyana.
Brook Farm, 213
Brooklyn College, 687
Brooks, Mel, 708
Brooks, Preston, 239
Brotherhood of Sleeping Car Porters, 506
Brown, Jim, 649
Brown, John, 239, 243, 244
Brown, Joseph E., 262
Brown, Moses, 161–162
Brown Berets, 673
Brownell, Herbert, 643
Brown v. *Board of Education of Topeka* (1954), 643, 687
Bryan-Chamorro Treaty, 440
Bryan, William Jennings, 355–356, 391, 394, 414, 451; Sec. of State, 439; Scopes Trial, 486
Bryant, William Cullen, 161
Buchanan, James: and Dred Scott decision, 240; and Ostend Manifesto, 237; as President, 239; and secession, 245
Buck, Pearl, 539
Buddhists, in Vietnam, 667
Buena Vista, Battle of, 199
Buffalo, 203, 332, 333; and Plains Indians, 335–337, 340
Bulganin, Nikolai, 613
Bulgaria, 558, 599, 600, 602; in WWI, 447, 466
Bull Moose Party, 397
Bull Run, 1st Battle of, 252; 2nd Battle of, 255
Bulwer, Henry Lytton, 429
Bunau-Varilla, Philippe, 431, 432
Bunche, Ralph, 615, 616
Bunker Hill, Battle of, 65
Bunyan, John, 385
Burchard, Reverend Samuel D., 350
Bureau of Corporations, 392
Bureau of Fisheries, 706
Bureau of Indian Affairs, 337; seizure of, 688
Bureau of Internal Revenue, 484

Bureau of Refugees, Freedmen, and Aban-doned Lands. See Freedmen's Bureau.
Burger, Warren, 686
Burger Court, 687
Burgess, John W., 411
Burgoyne, John, 65, 70
Burke-Wadsworth bill. See Selective Training and Service Act.
Burma, 574, 612
Burns, George, 537
Burnside, Maj. Gen. Ambrose E., 263
Burr, Aaron, 133; and duel with Hamilton, 149–150; and Essex Junto, 149; and western lands conspiracy, 150
Bush, George, 731, 733
Bush, Vannevar, 577
Busing: as campaign issue, 731; during Nixon era, 688
Butler Act, 486

C

Cable, George Washington, 376
Cabot, John, 15
Cabot, Sebastian, 15
Cabral, Pedro Alváres, 9–10
Cairo Declaration, 582
Caldwell, Erskine, 538, 539
Calhoun, John C., 74, 153, 157–159, 164, 168, 169, 225; and Compromise of 1850, 235; and nullification controversy, 173, 174
California, 185, 193–195, 198, 303, 376, 538, 716; Chinese immigrants in, 301; conquest of, 198–200; debate over, 234–235; gold rush in, 200, 327; hippies in, 702; immigrant workers in, 673; Mexican possession of, 193; migrants in, 533, 538; settlement of, 193; treatment of Japanese in, 428–429, 580; vote for women in, 388; Zoot Suit Riots in, 585
Calley, William, Jr., 680
Calvert, Cecelius, 35–36
Calvert, George, Lord Baltimore, 35
Cambodia, 610, 612, 680–681, 696
Camp David Accords, 727
Camp David summit, 618
Camp meeting revivals, 211–212
Canada, 484; before Revolution, 61, 66; border disputes, 156, 159; coveted, 151; French and Indian War, 55; French in, 12–14, 53, 55; Indian resistance in, 338, 340; NATO, 606; Saint Lawrence Seaway in, 641; Slaves in, 224; War of 1812, 155
Canal Zone. See Panama Canal.
Canals, 203, 204
Cannon, Joseph G., 395
Cape Kennedy, 738
Capitalism, 303, 319, 399, 522, 602
Capitalists, 328, 356
Capone, Al, 484
Capra, Frank, 538
Cardozo, Francis L., 282
Carmichael, Stokely, 671
Carnegie, Andrew, 260, 302–303, 305–306
Carpetbaggers, 282–283, 290
Carranza, Venustiano, 442–444
Caribbean Sea, 438, 484, 564, 623, 723; British troops in, 430; Spanish-American War in, 419–420
Carson, Kit, 337
Carson, Rachel, 706
Carter, James, Earl Jr. See Jimmy Carter.
Carter, Jimmy, 716; Presidency, 721–731
Carter, Rosalyn, 721
Carter Doctrine, 730
Carteret, Sir George, 36
Cartier, Jacques, 12
Cartoons, 538
Casablanca Conference, 582, 583
Cass, Senator Lewis, 234
Castro, Cipriano, 434
Castro, Fidel, 619, 621, 655, 672, 723
Catalogs, 373
Catherine of Aragon, 32
Catholic Church: and feudalism, 7–8; and Reformation, 8; and Spanish Civil War, 560
Catholics, 209, 483, 489; and Democratic party, 529; immigrants, 366–368, 529; in Maryland, 36; prejudice against, 208–209, 350
ttle barons, 330
ttle ranching, 328–330

Cavelier, Robert, 14
Cavell, Edith, 449
CCC. See Civilian Conservation Camps.
CDA. See Committee to Defend America by Aiding the Allies.
"Cease and desist orders," 398
Censorship, 707; of the press in WWI, 457, 459, 465
Central America, 237, 620, 728–729; Columbus in, 5; and Reagan, 740; and transoceanic canal, 429, 430
Central Intelligence Agency, 636, 712, 730; in Latin America, 619, 620; and Nixon, 694; in Iran, 729
Central Pacific Railroad, 298–301
Central Powers, 447, 448, 449, 450; After WWI, 548
Cervera y Topete, Pascual, 419
CETA. See Comprehensive Employment and Training Act.
Ceylon. See Sri Lanka.
Chafee, C. C., 240
Chamberlain, Neville, 556
Chamberlain, Wilt, 716
Chambers, Whittaker, 638
Chancellor, Richard, 15
Chancellorsville, Battle of, 263
Channing, William Ellery, 212
Chaplin, Charlie, 494
Charbonneau, Toussaint, 149
Charities, 509
Charles I, King of England, 33, 34
Charles II, King of England, 34, 36
Charleston, South Carolina, 164, 245; in colonial period, 42; 1860 Democratic convention in, 244
Charleston, Battle of, 71
Chase, Samuel, 146, 281
Chateau-Thierry, Battle of, 461, 464
Chattanooga, Battle of, 265
Chavez, Cesar, 673
Checker, Chubby, 709
Checks and balances, 105, 109–110; and Nixon, 691–692
Cherokee Indians, 26, 175
Chesapeake Bay, 90, 155, 156, 255
Cheves, Langdon, 153, 162
Chevington, Col. John, 337
Cheyenne, 337
Chiang Kai-Shek, 582, 607, 610, 612
Chiang Kai-Shek, Madam, 582
Chicago, 322–324, 373, 513, 538; Democratic conventions in, 513, 675; fire in, 377; Haymarket Riot, 320–321; Hull House, 378; industry in, 311; and Kansas-Nebraska Act, 238; meatpacking in, 385; population of, 363; symphony, 375
Chicamauga Creek, Battle of, 265
Chicano movement, 673
Chickasaw Indians, 337
Chief Joseph, 338, 340
Child labor, 311–312, 314, 316, 389, 390, 395, 399, 534
Children's Bureau, 395
Chile, 412, 443, 580, 728
China, 6, 193; Boxer Rebellion in, 425–426; civil war in, 607; conferences in, 591, 592; immigration from, 301, 317, 350; Japanese aggression in, 554, 555, 568; Nationalists, 612–613; Open Door policy in, 425–426, 487; railroads in, 437, 439; trade with, 205, 410, 413; WWI, 447, 458; WWII, 582
China, People's Republic of: and Korean War, 609; and Soviet Union, 617, 666; relations with under Nixon, 681–682; Carter, 726; Reagan, 740; and Vietnam, 610, 612
Chinese Exclusion Act, 317, 368
Chinese immigrants, 301, 317, 350
Chippewa, 155
Chiricahua Apache, 340
Chisholm, Shirley, 687
Chisholm Trail, 329
Choctaw Indians, 337
Chouart, Médard, 14
Christianity: and Indians, 9, 31–32; Born Again movement, 712; spread of, 414
Churchill, Winston, 564–567; 573–574; and Cold War, 599, 600, 601; conferences with, 591, 592, 594; meeting with FDR, 566–567; with Stalin, 574
Church of Jesus Christ of Latter-Day Saints. See Mormons.

CIA. See Central Intelligence Agency.
Cincinnati Red Stockings, 374
CIO. See Congress of Industrial Organizations.
Citizenship, 278, 371
City governments, and Progressive reform, 387
City-manager government, 387
Civil disobedience, 211, 644
Civilian Conservation Corps, 516
Civil liberties: during WWI, 457; Lincoln's restrictions of, 262
Civil Rights Act of 1866, 278, 279
Civil Rights Act of 1957, 643, 659
Civil Rights Act of 1960, 659
Civil Rights Act of 1964, 662, 674, 689
Civil rights movement, 359, 506, 530, 644–645, 669–674, 709; after WWI, 484; after WWII, 635, 637, 638; and Eisenhower, 642–645; and Johnson, 662, 663, 665; and Kennedy, 659–660; Reconstruction, 278, 283, 359. See Affirmative Action, Desegregation.
Civil Rights Commission, 688
Civil Service, reform in, 346–347, 348–349, 350, 395, 722
Civil Sevice Commission, 350
Civil War, 160, 174, 218, 242, 249–268, 272, 280, 285, 327, 350, 352, 417, 539; army in, 283, 285; economics of, 260–261, 347; home fronts in, 258–260; industrialization and, 302–303; in East, 254–256; in literature, 539; in West, 253–256; major battles, 252–256, 262–267; propaganda in, 459; strategies in, 250, 254; technology in, 578; veterans of, 350
Civil Works Administration, 516, 525
Clark, Dan Elbert, 187
Clark, Dick, 709
Clark, George Rogers, 71
Clark, William, 149
Class distinctions: in colonial period, 46–47; in education, 371; in housing, 369–370; in leisure, 373; in work, 372
Clay, Henry, 153, 157–158, 167–168, 174, 181, 193, 238; and Bank War, 179; and Compromise of 1850, 235; and election of 1832, 178, 181; and tariff, 176
Clayton, John M., 429
Clayton Antitrust Act, 398, 399
Clayton-Bulwer Treaty, 429–430
Cleaver, Eldridge, 671, 712
Clemenceau, Georges, 466
Clemens, Samuel L., 376–377
Cleveland, 458, 528
Cleveland, Grover, 350–351, 352, 363; and annexation of Hawaii, 415; and Cuba, 416; and Pullman Strike, 323–324
Clifford, Clark, 657
Clinton, Dewitt, 153
Clinton, George, 95, 107, 149–150
Clinton, Sir Henry, 65, 71
Clipper ships, 205
Closed shops, 320, 635
Coal, 295, 296, 303, 356, 357, 689, 723; industry prior to 1900, 313–314; in WWI, 455–456
Coalminers Strike (of 1919), 479
Cobb, Ty, 492
Cocaine, 704
Cochise, 337, 340
Coercive Acts. See Intolerable Acts.
Cohan, George M., 456, 459
Cohens v. Virginia (1821), 158
Cold Harbor, Battle of, 266
Cold War, 599–624, 638–642, 655, 706
Cole, Clay, 709
Cole, Thomas, 211, 212
Colfax, Schuyler, 345
Collective bargaining, 317
Collectivization, 550
Colleges and universities: antebellum growth of, 216; in late 1800's, 372; and women, 372
Collins, Michael, 684–685
Colombia, 740; and Panama, 430–432, 433, 440; and Peru, 547
Colonial period: culture during, 45–50; education during, 371; governments, 38–40, 81; population, 45–47; problems during, 29–30, 44; protests during, 57–62; religion, 212; slave trade, 223
Colonies: Dutch, 14–15; English, 17, 19; French, 12, 14; Spanish, 9, 11–12, 21; types of, 39
Colorado, 328–331; Dust Bowl in, 532; Indians in, 337; and women's vote, 385, 388

Colson, Charles W., 712
Columbus, Christopher, 5–6; 12, 21, 26
COMECON. See Council of Mutual Economic Assistance.
Commager, Henry Steele, 542–543
Commanche Indians, 23–24
Command of the Army Act, 280
Commerce. See Trade and commerce.
Commerce raiders, 253
Commission government, 387
Commission on Civil Rights, 635
Commission on Interracial Cooperation, 484
Committee for European Economic Cooperation, 604
Committee for Peace through Revision of the Neutrality Law, 564–565
Committee of Correspondence, 60
Committee on Equal Employment Opportunity, 659
Committee on Public Information, 457, 458, 459
Committee to Defend America by Aiding the Allies (CDA), 564–565
Committee to Reelect the President (CRP), 692
Common Market. See European Common Market.
Commonwealth v. *Hunt* (1842), 216
Communes, 702, 703
Communication: antebellum improvements in, 205; and Civil War, 249; improvements in prior to 1900, 297, 364; in WWI, 458; and the mass market, 301
Communications Act, 522
Communism, 479, 480, 539, 560, 602; in American society, 638–639; containment of, 604; in governments after WWII, 599–600; and Reagan, 738–740; in Third World, 619–624, 740–742
Communist Control Act, 642
Communist party, American, 638–639
Communist party, Russian, 550
Communists, 480, 522, 523, 562
Communists, Chinese, 607, 608
Community Action Programs, 663
Company towns, 312
Comprehensive Employment and Training Act, 737
Compromise of 1850, 174, 235–237
Compromise of 1877, 286, 349
Computers, 717–718, 752–753
Confederate States of America, 245, 246, 249, 250–256, 263–268, 275
Congress: and Constitution, 105–106, 115; first, 119–121
Connery, Sean, 708
Conscientious objectors, 457
Constitution, U.S., 160; amendment process, 114; Articles of Confederation, 92; and Bank of U.S., 124, 125, 136; completion of, 93; compromises in, 90–93; and courts, 146; distribution of powers in, 102–104; and Jefferson, 145–146; and Madison, 101; and national government, 173, 535; ratified, 94–96; and territories, 148. See Amendments.
Comstock Lode, 327
Concentration camps: American for Japanese-Americans, 580–581; German, 591
Concord, Battle of, 63–64
Concurrent powers, 103
Confederacy: after Civil War, 271–274; leaders, 271, 274–275
Confederation Congress, 82, 84, 85–89
Confederation of the U.S.: problems with, 122. See Articles of Confederation.
Congress of Industrial Organizations (CIO), 506, 529, 530, 647
Congress of Racial Equality, 644, 671
Conkling, Roscoe, 348–349
Connally, John B., 661
Connecticut, 35, 508; drafts constitution, 81; and interstate commerce, 86; ratifies Constitution, 94
Conquistadores, 11
"Conscience Whigs," 233, 234
Conscription. See Draft.
Conservation, 389; during energy crisis, 690; and Taft, 396; and T. Roosevelt, 393
Conspiracy: and Kennedy assassination, 661; and King assassination, 671

Constitutional Convention, 90–93; commercial compromises, 93; completing Constitution, 93; debates in, 107; delegates to, 90; question of representation, 90–92
Constitution Union party, 244
Consumer protection, 389, 534
Consumers' groups, 385, 716, 723
Containment policy, 602, 604, 618; in Asia, 610; in Indochina, 610, 612–613; in Middle East, 617
Continental Army, 64, 69–70
Continental Association, 62
Continental Congress, 122. See Confederation Congress.
Contract Labor Law, 317
Convention of 1800, 134
Convoy technique, 458
Conwell, Russell H., 306, 384
Cook, James, 413
Coolidge, Calvin: governor, 478; Presidency, 477, 488; and the stock market, 503; Vice Presidency, 487
"Cooling-off" treaties, 439
Cooper, James Fenimore, 161, 211
Coplon, Judith, 636
Copperheads. See Peace Democrats.
Coral Sea, Battle of the, 576, 588
CORE. See Congress of Racial Equality.
Cornell, Alonzo B., 349
Cornwallis, Lord Charles, 71, 72
Coronado, 21
Corporations, 206, 303; and consolidation, 304–305; growth of in 1960's and 1970's, 716; investigation of, 398
Corregidor, Battle of, 575
Corruption (in Politics), 345–347
Cortés, Hernando, 11, 20
Cotton, 242, 335, 499, 508; and Civil War, 249, 252, 261, 311; and Depression, 517; first mill, 162; in South, 162, 222, 224, 249; in WWI, 449
Cotton diplomacy, 250, 257
Cotton gin, 222
Coughlin, Father Charles E., 522–523, 524, 528
Council of Economic Advisors, 633
Council of Mutual Economic Assistance, 604–605
Counterculture, 701–704
Cove, Emile, 491
Covenant of the League of Nations. See League of Nations.
Cowboys, 21, 329–330, 333
Cowpens, S. C., Battle of, 72
Cox, Archibald, 693
Cox, James M., 487
Crane, Stephen, 377
Crawford, William, 167
Crazy Horse, 338
Crédit Mobilier, 345
Creek Indians, 22, 156, 170, 337
Creek War, 156
Creel, George, 457
Crime, 378. See Prostitution, Gang Warfare, Organized Crime.
Crippen, Robert, 738
Critical Period, 83–89
Croatoans, 17, 19
Crockett, Davy, 191
Cromwell, William Nelson, 431
Crop-lien system, 287, 356
Crosby, Bing, 537
Cruickshank, R., 170
Cruise missile, 726
Crusade for Justice, 673
Crusades, 6
Cuba, 564, 672; Bay of Pigs, 620–621; and big stick policy, 436; diseases in, 433; and Latin America, 728, 740; missile crisis, 621–623; Ostend Manifesto, 237; relations with, 547–548; revolutions in, 416–418, 547, 619, 655; Soviet troops in, 726; Spanish-American War, 419, 420, 430; transition to self-rule in, 421
Cumberland Road, 175
Cumming v. *County Board of Education* (1899), 358
Cunningham, Admiral Sir Andrew, 574
Currency. See Money.
Currency Act, 56
Currency reform, 315, 316
Currier and Ives, 161
Curtis, Edwin, 477–478

Custer, George Armstrong, 338, 340
CWA. See Civil Works Administration.
Czechoslovakia, 466, 548, 604, 606; German aggression in, 556–558, 561, 564; immigrants from, 367
Czolgosz, Leon, 391

D

da Gama, Vasco, 9
Daguerre, L. J. M., 169
Dakota Territory, 335, 338; Indian resistance in, 338, 339, 340
Daladier, Edward, 556
Dance: in the 1920's, 495–496; in the 1960's, 709; in the 1970's, 710
Dare, Virginia, 17
Darrow, Clarence: and Scopes trial, 486; and Leopold-Loeb trial, 493
Dartmouth College v. *Woodward* (1810), 158
Darwin, Charles, 305, 485, 486
Daugherty, Harry M., 488
Davie, Governor William, 134
Davis, Judge David, 315
Davis, Jefferson, 244, 245, 246; in Civil War, 249, 261–262, 266, 268
Davis, Stuart, 494
Davis, Henry Winter, 272
Dawes, Charles G., 548
Dawes, Henry L., 349
Dawes, William, 63
Dawes Act, 340–341, 350, 673
Dawes Plan, 548–549
Daylight savings time, 456, 690
D-Day, 590, 591
Dean, John, 692, 693
Debs, Eugene V., 323, 324, 397, 457
Decatur, Stephen, 160
de Champlain, Samuel, 14
Declaration and Resolves, 62
Declaration of Independence, 67, 68, 164
Declaration of Rights and Grievances, 58
Deficit spending, 521
Deforest, John W., 274
de Gardoqui, Don Diego, 84–85
DeGaulle, Charles, 666
Deists, 212
de Kooning, William, 651
Delaware, 244; in colonial period, 37; ratifies Constitution, 94; remains in Union, 251
Delaware, Lord, 30
del Cano, Juan Sebastián, 11
de León, Ponce, 10, 333
de Lesseps, Ferdinand, 430–431
de Lôme, Enrique Dupuy, 418
de Lôme letter, 417–418
Demarest, Henry, 377
Demilitarized zone, 669
Democracy: in colonial period, 50; Federalist fears of, 128–129; freedom of expression and, 135; Wilson and, 439
Democratic party, 113, 169, 181, 236, 238, 247; blacks in, 635; effect of Dred Scott decision upon, 241; first modern political party, 169; Jacksonians, 273; in Gilded Age, 347–349; during New Deal era, 529–530; opposition to Lincoln, 261; and political machines, 529; Progressives and, 383; Reconstruction and, 280, 286; Redeemers and, 284
Democratic People's Republic of Korea. See North Korea.
Democratic Republic of Vietnam. See North Vietnam.
Democratic Republicans. See Republican party, Jeffersonian.
Demonstration Cities and Metropolitan Area Redevelopment Act, 665
Dempsey, Jack, 492
Denmark, 410, 562
Dennis v. *U. S.*, 135, 639
Department of Agriculture, 517, 706
Department of Commerce and Labor, 392, 395
Declaration of Rights and Sentiments, 218
Declaration of the Causes and Necessities of Taking up Arms, 65
Declaratory Act, 58, 59
Department of Defense, 636, 647

Department of Education, 641, 721
Department of Energy, 721, 723, 724
Department of Health, Education, and Welfare, 641. See Department of Education, and Department of Health and Human Services.
Department of Health and Human Services, 641
Department of Housing and Urban Development, 665
Department of the Interior, 337, 393, 533
Department of Justice, 480, 639, 643, 660, 675, 688; and Haitian immigrants, 723
Department of Labor, 315, 395
Department stores, 373
Depression: after Revolutionary War, 85; of 1893, 323. See Great Depression.
Deprogramming, 712
Desegregation, 643, 688, 712
Desert Land Act, 331
de Soto, Hernando, 11
Détente, 682–683; under Carter, 725–727; under Ford, 696–697
Detention camps, 639; Spanish-run, in Cuba, 416–417. See Concentration Camps.
de Vaca, Alvar Nuñez Cabeza, 11, 21
Devaluation, 686
Dewey, George, 419
Dewey, John, 372, 383–384
Dewey, Thomas E., 587, 636
Dial, the, 217
Dias, Bartolomeu, 9
Diaz, Adolfo, 437
Diaz, Porfirio, 441
Dickinson, Charles, 171
Dickinson, John, 53, 64, 81
Didrikson, Mildred "Babe," 537
Dien Bien Phu, 610, 612
Diggers, 702
Dillon, Douglas, 657
Dime novels, 333
Dingley Tariff of 1894, 394
Dinwiddie, Gov. Robert, 53
Diplomacy: in Civil War, 257; in Cold War, 613
Directory, the, 134
Direct primary, 387, 389, 397
Discrimination: against blacks, 47, 506, 635, 671; and immigration quotas, 665; in armed forces and Civil Service, 638; on basis of religion, 47; sex, 689
Disney, Walt, 538
District of Columbia, 123; and Compromise of 1850, 235; and electors, 106
Divorce, in the 1920's, 496
Dix, Dorothea, 214
Dixiecrat party. See States' Rights party.
DMZ. See Demilitarized Zone.
Dodge, Grenville, 300–301
Dole, Robert, 697
Dole, Sanford B., 413–415
"Dollar Diplomacy," 437–438, 439, 442
Dominican crisis, 623–624
Dominican Republic, 411, 623–624; "big stick policy" in, 434–436; U.S. intervention in under Wilson, 440–441
Dominion of New England, 36
Domino theory, 610
Donovan, Robert, 656
Doolittle, Major General James H., 576
Dorsey, Tommy, 537
Dos Passos, John, 538
Doubleday, Abner, 374
Douglass, Frederick, 220, 257, 285
Douglas, Lewis W., 521
Douglas, Stephen, 241, 244; campaign tours, 180; and "popular sovereignty," 234; and Compromise of 1850, 235; and Kansas-Nebraska Act, 237, 238
Draft: in Civil War, 261–262; in Vietnam, 674, 690; in WWI, 455; in WWII, 564
Drago, Louis M., 434
Drago Doctrine, 434
Drake, Sir Francis, 16
Drew, Daniel, 346
Drugs, 701, 703–704
DuBois, William E. B., 223, 358–359
du Guast, Pierre, 14
Dulles, John Foster, 610, 612, 615; and brinkmanship, 614
Dumbarton Oaks Conference, 591
Dunaway, Faye, 708
Dust Bowl, 532–533, 538

Dutch East India Company, 14
Dutch East Indies. See Indonesia.
Dutch West India Company, 14
Dylan, Bob, 701, 709

E

Eagleton, Thomas, 690, 691
Eakins, Thomas, 375
Eastern Europe, 639
East Germany, 605
East India Company, 16; and Tea Act, 60
Eaton, John H., 174–175
Eaton Affair, 174–175
Eccles, Marrinu, 536
Economic Opportunity Act, 662
Economy: and Alexander Hamilton, 122–126; antebellum progress, 209; campaign issue, 1980, 732; under Carter, 724–725; in Civil War, 249; Civil War to 1900, 295; colonial period, 40–44; Depression, 506–507; 509–510; economic war with Britain, 151; entrepreneurs, 302; in the future, 752–753; in the 1950's, 645–647; Jefferson and laissez-faire, 127; under Kennedy, 658–659; laissez-faire, 305–307, 509; Mormons, 197; during New Deal, 521–522, 534–536; under Nixon, 685–686; prohibition, 485; under Reagan, 736–737, 743–744; stagflation, 685; post WWI, 477, 487; during WWII, 579–581, 586; post WWII, 633–634
Economy Act, 515
Ederle, Gertrude, 496
Education: and blacks, 276; changes in, 370–372; in colonial period, 49; federal aid to, 637, 638; financing, 371; and Freedmen's Bureau, 276; and philanthropy, 306; public, 370–371; pupils in, 370; reform in antebellum period, 215–216; and urbanization, 370; and women, 215–216. See Colleges and Universities, Desegregation.
Edward I, King of England, 38
Edwards, Jonathan, 47
EEC. See European Economic Community.
Eggleston, Edward, 376
Egypt, 223, 666, 709; WWII in, 574; and Suez crisis, 615–617; in Yom Kippur War, 684
Eight-hour day, 313, 314, 316, 321, 354, 399
Einstein, Albert, 578, 593
Eisenhower, Dwight David, 606, 655, 657, 658, 667; as general, 574, 582, 588, 590; as President, 610–618, 640–645
Eisenhower Doctrine, 617
El Alamein, Battle of, 574
Elastic Clause, 102–103; and national bank, 115
El Caney, Battle of, 419
Elections and Campaigns: 1796, 133; 1800, 136–137; 1804, 150; 1808, 151; 1816, 157; 1824, 167, 168; 1828, 167–169; 1832, 178; 1836, 181; 1840, 182, 220; 1844, 193, 195, 220; 1848, 233–234; 1852, 236, 238; 1854, 238; 1856, 239; 1860, 244–245, 271; 1864, 266–267; 1866, 280; 1868, 285; 1872, 285, 315, 346; 1876, 286; 1880, 349; 1884, 350; 1888, 351; 1890, 353; 1892, 351–352, 354; 1896, 352, 354–355; 1900, 391–397; 1904, 391, 397; 1908, 394, 395, 397; 1912, 396–397, 398, 439; 1916, 399–400, 452; 1918, 465; 1920, 487; 1928, 488–489; 1932, 513–514; 1936, 524, 528; 1940, 564–565; 1944, 587; 1948, 636–637; 1952, 640; 1956, 642; 1960, 655–656; 1964, 663; 1968, 675–676; 1972, 690–692; 1976, 697; 1980, 731–732; 1982, 744
Electoral College System, 81, 106, 107, 108, 114
Electric power, 296–297, 364–365; in 1920's, 490; in New Deal, 526
Electronics, 752. See Computers.
Elementary and Secondary School Act, 663
Elevators, electric, 363
El Gueltar, Battle of, 503
Eliot, Charles, 372
Elizabeth I of England, 16–17
Elkins Act, 393
Ellicott, Major Andrew, 123
Ellington, Duke, 496, 497
Ellis Island, New York, 367
Ellison, Ralph, 650
Ellsworth, Chief Justice Oliver, 134
Els, 364
Ellsberg, Dr. Daniel, 693
El Salvador, 728, 740

Emancipation Proclamation, 256–257, 261
Embargo Act, 151
Emergency Banking Relief Act, 515
Emergency Price Control Act, 519
Emergency Relief Appropriation Act, 525
Emerson, John, 240
Emerson, Ralph Waldo, 64, 160, 210, 211, 214
Employment: and automobile industry, 491; in depression, 510; discrimination in, 506; during WWII, 585, 586; in the future, 752; and women, 674, 752
Employment Act of 1946, 633
Empress Augusta Bay, Battle of, 582
"Enemies List," 693
Enemy aliens, 580
Energy crisis, 689–690, 723–724; and Reagan, 733, 735
Engel v. Vitale (1962), 48
England, 203, 285, 656; colonialism in New World, 15–17; defeat by Spanish Armada, 16–17; immigrants from, 313; Glorious Revolution in, 36; and slave trade, 223. See Great Britain.
English colonies, 29–38
Enlightenment, the, 99, 100, 210, 212, 305
Enola Gay, 594
Environment, 704, 706, 735
Equal Employment Opportunity Act, 689
Equal Employment Opportunity Commission, 689
Equal opportunity and schools, 371
Equal Rights Amendment, 689, 731
ERA. See Equal Rights Amendment.
Era of Good Feelings, 157
Ericsson, John, 253
Ericson, Leif, 5
Erie Canal, 203
Ehrlichman, John D., 692, 694
Ervin, Sam, 692
Escalators, 373
Eskimos, 22
Espionage, 638–639. See U-2 spy planes.
Espionage Act of 1917, 457, 693
Essex Junto, 149–150
Estonia, 460, 558
Ethiopia, Italian conquest of, 555–556, 559
Eugenics, 411
Europe, 210, 465, 480, 495, 539, 559, 587, 592, 614, 656; aid to, 603–605; balance of power in, 614; economy between World Wars, 548–550; economy after WWII, 603; foreign aid in, 611; foreign policy under Roosevelt, 436–437; nonintervention in, 437; 15th-century changes in, 5; immigration from, 207; influence on U.S. art, 375; influence on U.S. music, 375; Marshall Plan, 604; NATO, 606; Napoleon's war with, 150; Nazi, threat to, 565; Reformation, 8; relations with, future, 751; revolutions in, 479; Soviet hold on, 599–600; Soviet pipeline, 739–740; United States missiles in, 727–728; Warsaw Pact, 606; WWII in, 573–574, 583–585, 588–591
European Advisory Commission, 584
European Common Market, 659, 666
European Economic Community. See European Common Market.
European Recovery Program, 604
"Ever-normal granary," 533
Evolution, theory of, 305, 485–486
Executive branch: in early state constitutions, 81; increase in power under Nixon, 691–692
Executive privilege, 692–694
Expansionism, 443. See Manifest Destiny.
Export-Import Bank, 551
Expressed powers. See Powers of the national government

F

Fairbanks, Douglas, 494
Fair Deal, 637, 638
Fair Employment Practices Committee, 506
Fair Labor Standards Act, 534, 536
Falklands War, 742
Fall, Albert B., 488
Fallen Timbers, Battle of, 132
Falwell, Jerry, 732
Family Assistance Plan, 686
Far East, 411, 414, 422, 465, 554, 646; Cold War containment, 606–610, 612–613; foreign aid in,

611; missionary diplomacy in, 439–440; Open Door, 425–429, 434, 437, 439–440; stability in, 429; trade, 7, 430; WWII in, 568–570, 573, 576–577, 584, 592–594. See China.

Fisk, Jim, 345–346
Farm Credit Act, 517
Farmers: decline in family farm, 647; and Jefferson, 127; and New Deal, 526; and Truman, 636; and Whiskey Rebellion, 125–126; and Wilson, 399
Farm Security Administration, 533
Farming: in colonial period, 40–42; decline in population, 363. See Agriculture.
Farragut, Admiral David, 266
Farrell, Frank, 316
Farrell, James T., 538
Faure, Edgar, 613
Fascism, 560; in America, 522; in Italy, 551–552, 584; in Germany, 552–553
Faubus, Orval, 643
Faulkner, William, 495
FBI. See Federal Bureau of Investigation.
FCC. See Federal Communications Commission.
FDIC. See Federal Deposit Insurance Corporation.
Fed. See Federal Reserve Board.
Federal Bureau of Investigation, 639, 675; and Nixon, 694
Federal Communications Commission, 522, 714
Federal Deposit Insurance Corporation, 516
Federal Emergency Relief Administration, 516, 525
Federal Employment Protection Commission, 635
Federal Farm Loan Act (1916), 399
Federal Home Loan Bank Act, 511
Federal Highway Act of 1956, 641
Federal Republic of Germany. See West Germany.
Federal Reserve Act of 1913, 398
Federal Reserve Board, 398, 521–522, 526–527, 536
Federal Reserve notes, 398
Federal Reserve System, 398
Federal Securities Act, 516
Federal Theatre Project, 539
Federal Trade Commission, 516, 534
Federal Trade Commission Act, 398
Federalist, The, 95–96, 108–109
Federalists, 94–96, 119, 121, 124, 133, 134, 145, 151; split, 127; opinion of common people, 128–129; and newspaper war, 129; and French Revolution, 130; factionalism in, 133; and Alien and Sedition Acts, 136; during Jefferson's term, 145–146; in decline, 148–150; discredited, 156–157. See Essex Junto.
Felker, Clay, 715
Feminism, 674. See Women.
Fenno, John, 129
FERA. See Federal Emergency Relief Administration.
Ferdinand, Archduke Franz, 447, 448
Ferdinand, King of Spain, 5–6
Ferlinghetti, Lawrence, 650
Fetterman, William J., 337
Fetterman Massacre, 337
Feudalism, 6, 7
Field, Cyrus, 205
Filibustering, 112
Fillmore, Millard, 233; becomes President, 235; election of 1856, 239
Film. See Movies.
Fink, Mike, 195
Finland, 460, 550, 558, 659; invasion of by Stalin, 562
Finlay, Carlos, 433
Finley, James, 212
Finney, Charles, 213, 220
First Continental Congress, 61
First Sioux War, 337, 349
Fitzgerald, F. Scott, 495
Fitzhugh, George, 225
Five Nations. See Iroquois.
Flappers, 496, 498
Fleming, Ian, 708
Fletcher v. *Peck* (1810), 158
Flexible response strategy, 623–624
Florence, Italy, liberation of, 591
Florida, 171, 622; boundary set, 132; Cuban immigrants in, 672, 723; enters Union, 235;

Haitian immigrants in, 723; in Reconstruction, 280, 286; real estate speculation in, 499–500; Spanish-owned after Revolution, 73, 84
Florida, East, 152, 159
Florida, West, 147–148, 152
Foch, Ferdinand, 461
Folk rock, 708–709
Fong, Hiram L., 646
Food Administration, 456
Food and Drug Administration, 534
Food, Drug, and Cosmetic Act, 534
Food Stamp program, 737
Football, 374, 492, 536, 649
Foote, Andrew, 253
Foraker Act, 421
Forbes, Charles R., 488
Force Bill, 176
Ford, Gerald, 679, 693; attempted assassination, 702; debates with Carter, 697; Presidency, 694–697
Ford, Henry, 490–491; on Depression, 506; pacifism of, 452
Foreign aid, 611, 696; and Latin America, 618; and Marshall Plan, 603–605; and Truman Doctrine, 602–603; and Vietnam, 667–669
Foreign policy: Adams, 130–132; brinkmanship, 614; Carter, 725–731; China, 425–429, 437; CIA, 636; after Civil War, 409–411; Cold War, 599; containment, 602, 610, 612–613, 617; Eisenhower, 645; flexible response, 623–624; Ford, 696–697; in future, 751–752; in Hawaii, 413; imperialism, 411, 414, 421; isolationism, 411, 414, 606; Japan, 428–429; Johnson, 666–669; Kennedy, 618–623, 667; Monroe Doctrine, 159; new manifest destiny, 411–415; Nixon, 679–684, 692; Pierce, 237; Reagan, 733, 737–742; Taft, 437–439; Truman Doctrine, 602–603; T. Roosevelt, 434–437; Washington, 130–132; Wilson, 439–444; in WWI, 547–550; in WWII, 559–570
Formosa. See Taiwan.
Fort Duquesne, 53, 54. See Fort Pitt.
Fort Erie, 155
Fort Henry, 253
Fort Laramie, Wyoming, 336, 337, 338
Fort Leavenworth, Kansas, 198
Fort Lyons, 337
Fort McHenry, 155, 157
Fort Necessity, 54
Fort Niagara, 55, 56
Fort Oswego, 70
Fort Pitt, 54
Fort Stanwix, 70
Fort Sumter, 246, 248, 251
Fort Ticonderoga, 66, 70
Fort Wagner, Battle of, 257
"Forty-niners," 200, 234
Foster, Stephen, 212, 213
Four Acts. See Alien and Sedition Acts.
Fourteen Points, 465–466, 566–567
Framers of Constitution, 89–93, 99
France, 487, 499, 559, 729; in China, 437; and the Confederation, 85, 88; conferences, 592; foreign policy after WWII, 605, 606; and Haiti, 440; Louisiana Purchase, 147–148; and Maryland, 83; in Mexico, 409; in Morocco, 437; in Panama, 430–431; Reign of Terror, 130; Revolution, 130; and slave trade, 223; South, sympathy for, 249–250; Spain, war with, 132; Statue of Liberty, 367; war with Spain, 132; in WWI, 447, 448, 455, 458, 460–464, 465; in WWII, 556–558, 561, 562, 563, 564, 573, 574, 590, 591; XYZ Affair, 133–134
France, Battle of, 590
Francis Joseph I, of Austria, 409
Franco-American treaties of 1778, 134
Franco, Francisco, 560
Frankford am Main, Battle of, 591
Franklin, Aretha, 497
Frankfurter, Felix, 521
Franklin, Benjamin, 47, 456; Albany Plan of Union, 54; Declaration of Independence, 68; Philadelphia convention, 90, 93; Treaty of Paris, 72
Franklin, John Hope, 291
Fredendall, Lloyd R., 583
Fredericksburg, Battle of, 263
Freedmen, 356; Bureau of, 275, 278; economic role, 276; in Reconstruction, 271, 273, 275, 276, 283, 284; suffrage, 280
Freedmen's Bureau, 275–276, 278–279

"Freedom rides," 670
Freedom of religion. See Religious Freedom.
Freedom of speech and press, 50, 135, 136, 160, 262, 451, 486
Free enterprise system, 521; and trusts, 304
Freeport Doctrine, 241
Free soil issue, 233–239
Free Soil Party, 234, 236
Frémont, John C.: in election of 1856, 239; "the pathfinder," 193, 199
French, Daniel Chester, 375
French and Indian War, 53–55, 147
French Revolution of 1789, 130, 159
Freneau, Philip, 129
Freud, Sigmund, 496
Frick, Henry, 321
Friedan, Betty, 674, 706–707
Frobisher, Martin, 16
Fromme, Lynette Alice, 702
Frontier: expansion of to West Coast, 185; farmer, 186–187; life and role of women, 217; myth of, 195; and suffrage, 277; Turner thesis, 185
Frost, A. B., 353
FSA. See Farm Security Administration
Fuel Administration, 455–456
Fugitive Slave Law of 1793, 235
Fulbright, J. William, 668
Fuller, Alvan T., 480
Fuller, Margaret, 217
Fulton, Robert, 203
Fundamental Constitution of Carolina, 36
Fundamental Orders of Connecticut, 35
Fundamentalists, 485–486, 732
Fur traders, 12–14, 327

G

Gadsden, James, 200
Gagarin, Yuri, 658
Gage, General Thomas, 63, 65
Galbraith, John Kenneth, 646, 647
Gallatin, Albert, 146, 147
Galloway, Joseph, 61
Gambia, 707
Gandhi, Mohandas K., 644, 702
Gang warfare, 378
Gangsters, 484
Gannett, Samuel, 63
Garfield, James A., 349, 350
Garment industry, 372
Garment workers, 539
Garrison, William Lloyd, 220
Garvey, Marcus, 484
Gaskin, Stephen, 703
Gasoline, 689, 724; rationing in WWII, 580; tax on, 744
Gaspee, 60
Gates, General Horatio, 70, 71
Gaza Strip, 726, 741
Gazette of the United States, 129
Gemini, 714
General Amnesty Act (of 1872), 285
General Court, 34
Generation gap, 701, 708
Genêt, Edmond, 130
Geneva, Switzerland, 547; meeting to discuss disarmament, 613; meeting on Indochina, 612; Middle East peace talks in, 684
Geneva Accords, 612, 666
Geneva Disarmament Conference, 556
Genocide, 591
Gentlemen's Agreement, 429
Geography, urban, 364–365, 369–370
George, Henry, 377
Georgia: Civil War in, 260, 265–267; drafts constitution, 81; during Reconstruction, 280; Indian raids in, 132; literature about, 376; ratifies Constitution, 94; Revolutionary War in, 71–72; secedes, 245
George III, King of England, 60, 68
Georgetown University, 672
German Democratic Republic. See East Germany.
Germantown, Pa., Battle of, 70
Germany: 237, 443, 484, 561, 599; alliance with Italy, 556; alliance with Japan, 556; Axis, 569; Berlin Wall, 618; in China, 425, 426, 437; and Cold War, 605–606, 618; division of, 592; Europe, aggression in, 556–558; fascism in, 552–553; and Haiti, 440; immigration, 37, 45,

206, 207, 331, 365; in Morocco, 436–437; in Revolutionary War, 69; in Rome, 584; in Samoan Islands, 412–413; in WWI, 447, 448–453, 454, 460–464; post WWI, 465–466, 548–550; in WWII, 561–567, 573, 574, 590–591
Geronimo, 339, 340
Gerry, Elbridge, 134
Gershwin, George, 496
Gettysburg, Battle of, 263–264
Ghana, 359
Ghettos, 367, 369, 484, 499, 670
Ghost Dance Movement, 339–349
Ghost towns, 327
Gibbons v. *Ogden* **(1824),** 158–159
"G.I. Bill of Rights." See Readjustment Act of 1944.
Gideon v. *Wainwright* **(1963),** 662
Gilbert, Sir Humphrey, 17
Gilded Age, 345
Ginsberg, Allen, 650
Gladden, Washington, 384
Glass-Steagall Act. See Banking Act of 1933.
Glidden, Joseph F., 330
Glorious Revolution, 36
GNP. See Gross national product.
Godkin, E. F., 417
Goethals, George W., 432
Golan Heights, 666
Gold, 337, 338, 385, 386; "Black Friday," 345; and currency, 124; Depression, 514, 515; discovery of in California, 200, 234; in Latin America, 415; and Europe after WWI, 549, 559; and greenbacks, 348; and Indian removal, 175; and opening of West, 327–328, 333
Gold rush, 234, 327–328
Gold standard, 348, 351, 507, 516, 521, 549
Goldwater, Barry M., 663
Gompers, Samuel, 317, 321, 324, 355, 399
Gomulka, Vladyslaw, 614
Gonzales, Rodolfo, 673
Goodman, Benny, 590
Good Neighbor policy, 547–548
Goodyear, Charles, 206
Gorgas, William C., 432–433
"The Gospel of Wealth," 306
Gorges, Ferdinando, 35
Gould, Jay, 345–346
Graduated income tax. See Income Tax, graduated.
Graham, Billy, 649, 712
Grandfather clauses, 358
Grange, 335, 352–353
Grange, Red, 492
Granger era, 352. See Populism.
Granger laws, 352–353
Grant, Ulysses S., 253–254, 263–267; as President, 285, 345–347
Grateful Dead, 710
Great Awakening, 47, 212
Great Basin, 193, 195, 327
Great Britain, 130, 133, 145, 193, 282; and American freedom of the seas, 150–151; and Baghdad Pact, 617; Battle of, 590; and canal zone, 429–430; in China, 425, 426; and Chinese railroads, 437; in Civil War, 252; Conferences, 571; and EEC, 659, 666; and Falklands War, 742; and German aggression, 556–558; immigration from, 365; and Italian aggression, 556–558; and Locarno Pact, 556; in Mexico, mid-1800's, 409; and Monroe Doctrine, 415; in Morocco, 436–437; Oregon compromise, 194–195; Polish alliance, 558; and Samoan Islands, 412–413; sympathy for South, 249, 250; and stock market crash, 504; and Suez Crisis, 615–617; treaties with, 159; in UN, 596; U.S. aid to, WWII, 561, 563–567; and Vietnam, 612; War of 1812, 153, 155–156; in WWI, 447, 448–452, 461–464, 465; in WWII, 573, 588; post-WWII foreign policy, 602, 605, 606. See England.
Great Compromise, 91–92
Great Depression, 503, 505–518; 521–536; causes of, 506–507; relief in, 509–512; New Deal, 514–518
Great Plains, 327, 333; cattle ranching on, 328–330; Dust Bowl, 532; farming on, 331–334, 353; Indians of, 23–24, 335–341
Great Society, 661–665, 666
"Great White Fleet," 429
Greece, 447, 466, 558, 564, 601–603, 606, 659

Greeley, Horace, 256, 346–347
Green, General Nathaniel, 72
Greenback party, 349, 352
Greenbacks, 260, 347–348
Green Berets, 623
Greenland, in WWII, 566; Vikings reached, 5
Green Mountain Boys, 64
Grenville, George, 56
Grew, Joseph C., 554
Grey, Zane, 333
Grimké, Angelina, 217
Grimké, Sarah, 217
Grogan, Emmett, 702
Gropper, William, 539
Gross national product, 662
Grundy, Felix, 153
Guadalcanal, Battle of, 576–577
Guadalupe Hidalgo, Treaty of, 200
Guam, 420; Magellan in, 11; taken by Japanese, 574; transition to American rule, 421
Guatemala, 619, 728
Guyana, 687, 712–713
Guerrilla warfare, 620; in Afghanistan, 730; in American Revolution, 68; in Latin America, 728, 740; in Philippines, 422; in Vietnam, 669
Guilford Courthouse, N.C., Battle of, 721
Guinea Coast, and slave trade, 223
Gulf Coast, and cattle drives, 329
Guthrie, Arlo, 702
Gutierrez, José Ańgel, 673
Guzman, Jacobo Arbenz, 619

H

Habib, Philip, 740–742
Hagen, Walter, 492
Hague, The, Netherlands, 434
Haig, Alexander, 738, 740, 742
Haiti, 148, 547–548; immigrants from, 723; U.S. intervention in, 440
Haldeman, H. R., 692, 694
Hale, John, 236
Haley, Alex, 707
"Half Breeds," 349
Halleck, General Henry W., 255
Hamilton, Alexander, 137, 157, 535; at Annapolis Convention, 90; appointed Secretary of the Treasury, 121; and assumption controversy, 123–124; on the courts, 108–109; defends executive, 107; dies in duel, 149–150; and French Revolution, 130; and national debt, 122–123; at Philadelphia Convention, 90; *Report on Public Credit,* 122; supports Constitution, 95–96; and tariffs, 125; vs. Jefferson, 129; and Whiskey Rebellion, 125–126, 134
Hamilton, Andrew, 49, 50
Hancock, John, 58, 68, 95
Hancock, Winfield Scott, 349
Handicapped, 755
Hanson, Ole, 477, 479
Harding, Warren G., 487–488, 492
Hardwick, Thomas R., 479
Hardy, Oliver, 494
Harlan, Senator James, 186
Harlem, 495, 506, 650
Harlem Renaissance, 495
Harper's, 538
Harper's Ferry, Virginia, 243
Harriman, Averell, 600
Harris, Joel Chandler, 376
Harris, Sam, 456
Harrison, Benjamin, 351–352, 413, 414
Harrison, George, 709
Harrison, William Henry, 152, 155, 333, 351; and election of 1836, 181; and election of 1840, 182
Harte, Bret, 376
Hartford, Connecticut, 35
Hartford Convention, 156–157
Hartley, Fred A., 635
Harvard University, 291, 358, 372, 390, 417, 513, 521, 603, 656, 657, 703
Hat Act of 1732, 43
Hawkins, Sir John, 16
Hawaiian Islands, 237, 410, 429, 656; annexation, 415; economy of, 413; statehood, 645, 656; U.S. in, 413, 415; in WWII, 569–570
Hitler, Adolf, 552, 556–558, 561, 562, 564–566, 656; aids Franco's Nationalists, 560; assassination attempt on, 590; suicide of, 591
Hobby, Oveta Culp, 641

Hawley-Smoot Tariff, 510
Hawn, Goldie, 714
Hawthorne, Nathaniel, 211
Hay, John, 425–426; and canal zone rights, 430, 431, 432
Hay-Bunau-Varilla Treaty, 432
Hayes, Rutherford B., 286, 349
Hay–Herrán Treaty, 431
Haymarket Riot, 320–321, 350
Hayne, Robert Y., 173
Hay-Pauncefote Treaty, 430, 432
Headright system, 31
Health care, 753
Hearst, Patty, 715–716
Hearst, Randolf A., 715
Hearst, William Randolf, 377, 417, 715
Heller, Joseph, 706
Heller, Walter, 657
Helper, Hinton, 242
Helsinki, Finland, 696; SALT talks in, 682
Hemingway, Ernest, 495, 560
Hendrich, Anthony Philip, 211
Hendrix, Jimi, 497, 710
Henri, Robert, 375–376
Henry, Patrick, 57; and Anti-federalists, 95; refuses to attend Philadelphia Convention, 90
Henry, Prince of Portugal, 8
Henry VII, King of England, 15
Henry VIII, King of England, 15; and Church of England, 32
Hepburn Act, 393
Herbert, Victor, 375
Hermitage, The, 170
Herrán, Tomás, 431
Higher Education Act, 663
Hill, James J., 299, 391
Hindenburg, Paul von, 553
Hinkley, John, Jr., 736
Hippies, 701–702, 707
Hirohito, Emperor of Japan, 569
Hiroshima, 578, 594
Hispanic influence in America, 21
Hispanic civil rights movement, 669, 671–673
Hispaniola, 5
Hiss, Alger, 638
Historiography, 76–77, 140–141, 228–229, 290–291, 403–405, 471–473, 542–543, 627–629, 747–749
Ho Chi Minh, 610, 612, 666
Ho Chi Minh Trail, 668, 681
Hodges, Luther, 657
Hoffman, Dustin, 708
Hog Farm, 702, 710
Holland: commercial treaties with, 87; immigrants from, 365; in New World, 14–15; Puritan separatists in, 32; religious freedom in, 32; war with France, 130
Holmes, Oliver Wendell, Jr., 135, 384, 479
Holocaust, 591
Homestead Act of 1862, 260, 331
Homesteading, 331–335
Homestead Steel Strike, 321–322, 403
Honduras, foreign aid in, 611
Hood, John Bill, 266–267
Hooker, Gen. Joe, 263, 264
Hooker, Thomas, 35
Hoover, Herbert, 456, 488–489, 636; and black vote, 530; and Great Depression, 505, 507, 509–513; and inflation in Europe, 549; Presidency, 490, 498–514
"Hoovervilles," 511
Hopkins, Harry, 525
Hopper, Edward, 494
Horsecars, 364
Hostage crisis, 729–731, 733
"Hot line," 623, 666
House Judiciary Committee and Nixon, 694
House of Representatives, 133, 137; and assumption controversy, 123; and Bill of Rights, 120; and bills, 110, 112; in Constitution, 92, 94, 105–106, 114; in first Congress, 119; power to impeach federal judges, 146
House of Burgesses, 31
House of Commons, 38, 58, 128
House of Lords, 38, 39, 128
Housing Act (1955), 641
Housing Act (1961), 659
Housing: and Kennedy, 659; discrimination in, 660, 665; inadequacy of, 670; in late 19th century, 369; and New Deal, 533–534

Houston, Sam, 191, 192
Howard University, 372
Howe, Admiral Richard, 69
Howe, Elias, 206
Howe, Gen. Sir William, 65, 66, 69, 70
Howells, William Dean, 377
HUD: See Department of Housing and Urban Development.
Hudson, Henry, 14
Hudson River, 70, 155, 203
Hudson Valley school of landscape painting, 161
Huerta, Victoriano, 441–444
Hughes, Charles Evans, 388, 400, 452, 531
Hughes, Langston, 495
Hull, Cordell, 547, 561, 569, 584, 585
Hull, Isaac, 160
Hull, William, 155
Human rights, 696; and Carter's foreign policy, 725, 727–729; and foreign aid, 611; and Reagan, 737; and the Shah of Iran, 729
Humbard, Rex, 712
Humphrey, Hubert H., 663, 675
Humphreys, Benjamin G., 275
"Hundred Days," 521
Hungary, 466, 599; crisis in, 614–615, 642; immigrants from, 366
Hunt, E. Howard, Jr., 692, 693
Hunt, W., 210
Hutchinson, Anne, 34
Hutchinson, Lieutenant Governor Thomas, 58, 61
Hydrogen bombs, 613

I

ICC. See Interstate Commerce Commission.
Iceland: and NATO, 606; in WWII, 566, 567
Ickes, Harold, 530, 586
Idaho, 495; enters Union, 331; and Indians, 338; vote for women in, 385, 388
Illinois, 171, 220, 240, 307, 509; enters Union, 162; Granger laws, 353; Mormons in, 196
IMF. See International Monetary Fund.
Immigration, 203, 207, 365–368; and anarchists, 321; Chinese, 301; before Civil War, 207; Cuban, 723; German, 206; Japanese, 429, 439; Haitian, 723; hyphenated Americans, 457–458, 467; opposition to, 478–479, 480, 483; and political machines, 346; and schools, 371; restrictions on, 481–482; in 1950's, 647; in 1960's, 664–665
Immigration Act of 1965, 665
Impeachment: in Constitution, 109; of Johnson, 281; of Nixon, 694
Imperialism: American, 412–415, 421; European, 411, 414
Implied powers, 102-103
Impoundment, 692
Impressment, 150, 151
Impressment Act, 262
Inca Indians, 20, 22, 704
Income Tax, 354, 456, 535; during Civil War, 260, 395; federal, 395; graduated, 398; reduced, 662, 737
Indentured servants, 41. See Labor.
Independent Treasury Act, 182
India, 612; and the Hare Krishnas, 711; Portuguese trade in, 9–10
Indiana, 171, 213; enters Union, 162; literature about, 376
Indian Removal Act of 1830, 176
Indian Reorganization Act (1934), 673
Indian Rights Movement, 340–341
Indians: attitudes towards land, 188; Articles of Confederation, affairs under, 82; buffalo, dependence on, 335–336; in Civil War, 337; conversion attempts, 9, 21; and cowboys, 329; Croatoans, 17, 19; and Dawes Act, 340–341, 350; discovered by Columbus, 19; diversity, 19; equal rights movements, 669, 673–674, 688; in Florida (Spanish), 132; in French and Indian War, 53–54; and French colonies, 12, 14; geographic groupings, 22–26; and horses, 335; influence on colonial culture, 45; influence on language, 49, 131; influence on pioneers, 185, 186, 187; and Jackson, 170–171, 172; Jamestown, attack on, 32; medicine, 259; and mountain men, 195; Northwest, 194; and

Pilgrims, 33; policy toward, 188–190, 336, 673–674; removal of, 189–190; resistance, 151–152, 335–341; and slavery, 223; and Spanish colonies, 11, 12; and Spanish missionaries, 9; territory, loss of, 156; threat to, by settlements, 35; and tobacco, 30; trade with, 189; treaties with, 132; treaty cessions, 189, 190; in Virginia, 31–32
Individualism: and counter-culture, 701; and cowboys, 330; and Depression, 513; and Emerson, 210; and the frontier, 185; and problems with organizing workers, 319; and Thoreau, 210–211; and the West, 330, 333
Indochina, 610, 612, 666, 738
Indonesia, 574, 579, 709
Industrial Revolution, 535; in England, 161; in the North, 161–162; in 1920's, 490
Industrialization, 203, 345; changes in, 207–208; and Civil War, 302; and education, 216; and factories, 205–206; growth of, 295; and progressives, 384; and production, 301; and railroads, 204, 297; and technology, 206; and textiles, 206; and urbanization, 363
Industrial unions, 317
Industrial Workers of the World (IWW), 399
Industry: in Civil War, 258, 260, 261; in Colonial Period, 44; in Depression, 518; government ownership of, 397; and Hamilton's plan, 125; after Reconstruction, 287; after Revolution, 85; safety in, 390
Inflation, 124, 721, 724–725, 727, 736
Initiative, 387
Insurgents (Republicans), 395, 396, 397
Integration. See Desegregation.
Inter-American Conference of 1933, 547
Interchangeable parts, 162, 206
Interlocking directorates, 398
Internal improvements, 244; and American System, 157–158; and antebellum sectionalism, 164, 233; and West, 162, 163. See Canals and Roads.
Internal Revenue Service, 659
International Bank for Reconstruction and Development, 591
International banking system, 685–686
International Court of Justice, 729
International Monetary Fund, 591, 685
Interstate Commerce, 158–159, 307–308, 393; and Confederation, 86; and Constitution, 102
Interstate Commerce Act, 308, 350, 393, 535
Interstate Commerce Commission, 308, 393, 395
Intolerable Acts, 61
Intolerance: anti-foreign sentiment, 209; against blacks after Reconstruction, 284–285; and colonial immigrants, 45; against Irish immigrants, 208; against Japanese immigrants in Calif., 428; and the Ku Klux Klan, 483–484; against Mormons, 196–197; against non-Puritans, 34; and problems with labor movement, 319; against Puritans in England, 33; against Quakers, 37; and racial violence, 671; in reconstructed South, 331
Intrastate Commerce, 527
Iowa, 485; in Civil War, 258; enters Union, 235; Granger Laws, 353
Iran, 585, 601, 615; hostage deal with, 733; Islamic revolution and hostage crisis, 729–731
Iraq, 615, 617, 666, 727; war with Iran, 730
Ireland, 315; and EEC, 659; immigrants from, 207–209, 366; in WWI, 450, 467; neutrality in WWII, 573
Iron Act of 1750, 44
Ironclad oaths, 272
Ironclad ships, 252–253, 412, 578
"Iron Curtain," 600–601
Iroquois Indians, 24, 54
Irreconcilables, 467
Irving, Washington, 161
Isabella, Queen of Spain, 5–6
Islamic revolution (Iran), 729
Isolationism, 414, 421; after WWI, 547; and George Washington, 130, 132; and NATO, 606; and WWII, 559–561, 566
Israel, 615–617, 675; army of, 616; conflict with Arabs, 615; during Carter term, 726–727; during Nixon era, 683–684; Six-Day War, 666
Isthmus of Panama, 234; crossed by Balboa, 10
Italy, 396, 487, 559; aggression in Africa, 555–556; aggression in Albania, 561; aggression

with Germany and Japan, 556; Axis power, 569; in China, 425; and EEC, 659; and fascism, 551–552; immigrants from, 366, 369, 478–479, 480; invasion of, 584; in Morocco, 436–437; in WWI, 447, 465, 466; in WWII, 561, 563, 564, 566, 570, 573, 584; WWII debts, 549
Ivan the Terrible, Tsar of Russia, 15
Iwo Jima, Battle of, 592–593

J

Jackson, Andrew, 155, 156, 333; California policy of, 193; campaign tactics, 180; duel with Dickinson, 171; election of 1824, 169; and frontier democracy, 186; and Indian removal policy, 175–176; and nullification controversy, 174; popularity of, 170–171; Presidency, 169–179; and Seminole Campaign, 159, 171, 175; and Texas policy, 191, 192
Jackson, Battle of, 264
Jackson, Helen Hunt, 340
Jackson, Henry, 696–697
Jackson, Rachel, 169
Jackson, Thomas J. "Stonewall," 252, 255, 263
"Jackson Amendment," 697
Jackson State University, 681
Jacksonian Democrats, 273
Jamaica, 10
James, Duke of York, 36
James, William, 383
James I, King of England, 29
James II, King of England, 36
Jamestown, 29–32
Japan, 487, 561, 591, 712, 727; alliance with Germany, 556; alliance with Italy, 556; Axis power, 569; and China, 437, 555; expansionism, 428; issues in 1980's, 751, 752, 753; and Korea, 607–608; and Manchuria, 437, 554; relations with, 428–429, 439–440; and Russo-Japanese War, 425; and Sino-Japanese War, 425; and Soviet Union, 551; and spheres of influence, 425, 437; totalitarianism, rise of, 554; trade with, 205; WWI, 447; post-WWI, 548; WWII, 568–570, 573, 574–577, 582, 591–595
Japanese-Americans: in California, 428–429; during WWII, 580–581
Jaworski, Leon, 694
Jay, John, 72, 84–85; Chief Justice of Supreme Court, 121; and The Federalist, 95; negotiates Jay Treaty, 131–132
Jay Treaty, 130–132, 133
Jazz, 496, 497, 649
Jefferson, Thomas, 90, 123, 134, 136, 535; and Declaration of Independence, 67, 68; and Deists, 212; and economics, 127, 305; and education, 371; and farmer, 188; and Federalists, 129; and frontier democracy, 186; and Genêt, 130; and Hamilton, 123–124, 128, 129; and industrialization, 127; as President, 136–137, 145–148, 150, 151; and religious freedom, 48; and Republican party, 127; as Secretary of State, 121, 130; Vice Presidency, 133; and Whiskey Rebellion, 126
Jefferson Airplane, 710
Jefferson Day Dinner, 174
Jenyns, Soame, 58
Jet set, 705
Jewett, Sarah Orne, 376
Jews, 483, 522, 523; and Holocaust, 591; and Israel, 615; immigrants, 313, 366–368, 696–697; in colonial period, 45; treatment of under Hitler, 552, 553; writers in 1950's, 650
"Jim Crow" Laws, 358; Black response to, 358–359
Job Corps, 662
John, King of England, 38
Johns, Jasper, 704
Johnson, Andrew, 409; impeachment, 281, 347; Reconstruction, 273–276, 278–279
Johnson, Hiram, 388
Johnson, James Weldon, 495
Johnson, Lyndon, 685; and Civil Rights, 643, 687; and Dominican Crisis, 624; foreign affairs, 666–669; Presidency, 661–675; Vice President, 655, 659
Johnson, Philip, 705
Johnson, Richard, 153
Johnson, Tom M., 387
Johnston, Gen. Albert Sidney, 253, 254
Johnston, Gen. Joe, 265–266, 268

Joint-stock companies, 29–35
Joliet, Louis, 14
Jolson, Al, 494
Jones, Bobby, 492
Jones, James, 650
Jones, James Warren, 712–713
Jones, Samuel H. ("Golden Rule"), 387
Jones Act of 1916, 422
Jonestown, Guyana, 713
Joplin, Janis, 710
Joplin, Scott, 375, 497
Jordan, 617, 666, 727, 741
Juaréz, Benito, 409
Judicial review, 109–110
Judiciary: colonial, 39, 40; function of under Constitution, 108–109; in early state constitutions, 81. See Supreme Court.
Judiciary Act of 1789, 120–121
Judiciary Act of 1801: Jefferson opposes, 146; repealed, 146; signed, 146

K

Kaiser Aluminum and Chemical Company v. *Weber* (1979), 722
Kamikazes, 592
Kansas, 332, 352, 353; and Dust Bowl, 532; enters Union, 331; Kansas-Nebraska Act, 237–238; Lecompton constitution, 242; violence in, 239
Kansas-Nebraska Act, 237–239, 242
Kaprow, Allan, 704
Karlsevni, Thorfinn, 5
Kasserine Pass, Battle of, 583
Katsura, Taro, 428
Kearney, Stephen W., 198
Keating-Owen Act, 399
Keaton, Buster, 494
Kefauver, Estes, 642
Kelley, Oliver, 335
Kellogg-Briand Pact of 1922, 499, 548
Kelly, William, 296
Kemp-Roth bill, 725
Kennan, George, 602
Kennedy, Edward, 731
Kennedy, Jacqueline, 661
Kennedy, John F., 599, 667, 674, 706; and Berlin crisis, 618; and civil rights, 687; Cuban crisis, 620–623; debates on television, 656; election, 655–656; foreign policy of, 618; Presidency, 506, 656–661
Kennedy, Robert: Attorney General, 657, 660; and Cuban missile crisis, 622–623; election of 1968, 675
Kent State University, killings at, 681
Kentucky, 155, 167, 175, 185, 244, 295, 333, 486, 509, 659; and Civil War, 251, 253, 254, 255–256
Kentucky Resolution, 135, 136, 173
Keppler, Joseph, 368
Kerner, Otto, 671
Kerouac, Jack, 650
Key, Francis Scott, 155, 157
Keynes, John Maynard, 536
KGB, 738
Khmer Rouge, 696
Khomeini, Ayatollah Ruhollah, 729
Khrushchev, Nikita S., 613, 614, 617, 618; Berlin crisis, 618; Cuban missile crisis, 620–623
Kiev, Battle of, 583
King, Dr. Martin Luther, Jr., 506, 644–645, 669–671, 707
King, Rufus, 157
King Philip. See Metacomet.
King's Mountain, Battle of, 72
Kino, Fr. Eusebio Francisco, 9
Kipling, Rudyard, 411
Kirby-Smith, Gen. Edmund, 268
Kissinger, Henry, 679; and China, 682; and Ford, 696; Middle East diplomacy, 679, 684; Vietnam peace talks, 687, 691
"Kitchen Cabinet," 172
Knights of Labor, 315, 316–317, 321
Knights of the White Camelia, 284
"Know-Nothing party," 209, 238
Knox, Henry, 66; appointed Secretary of War, 121
Knox, Philander C., 437, 438, 440
Knox-Castrillo Treaty, 437
Koch, Robert, 259

Konoye, Prince Fumimaro, 569
Korea, 582, 592; Japanese control over, 427, 428; Korean War, 608–610; post-WWII civil war in, 607–608
Korean War, 608–610; effect on economy, 638
Korematsu v. *the United States* (1944), 581
Kostov, Battle of, 574
Kosygin, Aleksei N., 666
Kraft, Joseph, 701
Ku Klux Klan, 284, 291, 483–484
Kurusu, Saburo, 569
Kuwait, 615

L

Labor, 523, 732, 752; attitudes toward, 318–319; blacks, 239, 506; and Carter, 723, 724; in Civil War, 260, 261; Clayton Act, 399; in colonial times, 40–41, 46; conditions of, 207, 208, 312–314; displacement of, 208; and education, 216; in election of 1896, 356; factor of production, 295; and freedmen, 276; growth of, 311–312; and immigration, 207, 295, 368; and Indians, 12; and Kennedy, 658; movement, 319–320, 321, 506, 518; and New Deal, 529–530, 534; in 1950's, 645–647; Populist support, 364; problems with before 1920, 318–320; protection of, 397; reform of, 216; rise of, 311; and T. Roosevelt, 392; scarcity of, 206; slave vs. free, 257; Truman support for, 636; unions and progressives, 383; in utopian communities, 313, 314; post-WWI, 477–479; during WWII, 580, 586; post-WWII, 634, 635. See Unions.
Ladd, William, 217
Lafayette, Marquis de, 69, 72, 160
Laffite, Jean, 155
La Follette, Robert M., 387, 389, 397
La Follette Seaman's Act (1915), 399
Laissez-faire economics, 305, 306, 521, 535, 658; and Great Depression, 509–510; and the Progressives, 383; and the Supreme Court, 307
Land, 244, 393, 396, 735; attitudes toward, 188; cattle and public domain, 330; after Civil War, 276; as factor of production, 295; Indian, 189, 336, 337, 688–689; ownership of, 31, 34, 46; policies in West, 331, 333; railroad giveaways, 300; post-Revolution, 86, 87, 88; sectionalism, 233; settlement of, 185–187; speculation in, 331
Land, Michael, 710
Land-grant colleges, 372
Landon, Alfred M., 528
Land Ordinance of 1785, 89
Landrum-Griffin Act, 647
Lane, Lunsford, 220
Lanman, James B., 188
Laos, 610, 612, 680–681
Laser, 717, 753
Latin America, 412, 415, 465, 480, 587; Alliance for Progress, 618; anti-American feeling in, 619, 621; and Falklands War, 742; foreign aid in, 611; and Good Neighbor Policy, 547–548; Nazi sympathy in, 573; Organization of American States, 618; policies under Carter, 728–729; policies under Roosevelt, 434–437; policies under Taft, 437–439; policies under Wilson, 440–441; revolution in, 416, 623, 726; rivalry between East and West in, 614; WWII solidarity, 580
Lattimore, Owen, 639
Latvia, 460, 558
Laurel, Stan, 494
League of Nations, 465–468, 547, 551, 585, 596; German withdrawal from, 556; Japanese withdrawal from, 555; violations of covenant of, 555–556
Lear, Norman, 715
Leary, Timothy, 703–704
Lease, Mary Ellen, 353, 354
Lebanon, 617
Lecompton Constitution, 242
Le Duc Tho, 681
Lee, Ann, 214
Lee, Henry, 126
Lee, Richard Henry, 67, 119
Lee, Robert E., 255–256, 263–266, 268
Leeuwenhoek, Anton van, 259
Legislative process, 110–112
Legislatures: British colonial, 39; in early state constitutions, 81

Lemke, William M., 528
Lend-Lease Act, 566
Lenin, Nikolai, 479, 550
Leningrad, Battle of, 574
Lennon, John, 709
Leopold, Nathan, Jr., 493
Leopold-Loeb trial, 493
Levin, Meyer, 539
Levine, Jack, 539
Lewis, John L., 479, 529–530, 634
Lewis, Meriwether, 149
Lewis, Sinclair, 494, 538
Lexington, Battle of, 62–63, 578
Leyte Gulf, Battle of, 588
Liberalism, 661
Liberal Republican party, 285, 346–348
Liberia, 219
Liberty bonds, 456, 458
Liberty party, 220, 234
Lichtenstein, Roy, 705
Liddy, G. Gordon, 692, 693
Liebman, Rabbi Joshua, 649
Liliuokalani, Queen of Hawaii, 413
Lima Declaration, 548
Limitation of powers: in colonial America, 39; in Constitution, 103–104; in England, 38. See Bill of Rights.
Limited government, concept of, 99–100
Limited warfare, 610
Lincoln, Abraham, 244, 262, 280, 409; assassination of, 273; beginning of Civil War, 249; debates with Douglas, 241–243; inaugural address of, 246; leadership of, 249, 261–262; opposition to, 261; plan for reconstruction, 271–273; position on Union and slavery, 241, 256–257; and presidential powers, 107
Lincoln, Gen. Benjamin, 87
Lincoln-Douglas debates, 241–242, 244
Lincoln University, 216
Lindbergh, Charles A., 493–494, 565
Line of demarcation, 10
Lippman, Walter, 384, 547
Lister, Joseph, 259
Literacy test, 357, 358
Lithuania, 460
Little, Malcolm. See Malcolm X.
Little Big Horn, Battle of, 338, 340
Little Rock, Arkansas, 643
Livingston, Belle, 484
Livingston, Robert, 67, 147–148
Lloyd, Harold, 494
Lobbyists, 110, 346
"Local-color writers," 376
Local governments: British colonial, 40; in Depression relief, 509
Locarno Pact, 556
Locke, Alain, 495
Locke, John, 68, 99–100, 305
Lockouts, 319
Lodge, Henry Cabot, 438–439, 465, 467, 655, 656
Lodge Corollary, 439
Loeb, Richard, 493
London Company, 29
Long, Crawford, 259
Long, Huey P., 523–524, 528
Long drive, 329
Longfellow, Henry Wadsworth, 211
Longhorns, 329
Long Island, 69
Longworth, Alice Roosevelt, 565
Lon Nol, 680, 696
Los Angeles, 12; changes in population of, 363; riots in, 585
"Lost Battalion," 463
Lost generation, 494–495, 560
Louisiana, 358, 509, 523; Civil War in, 264, 268; enters Union, 162; Granger Laws in, 353; literature about, 376; in Reconstruction period, 272, 276, 280, 286
Louisiana Purchase, 147–148, 159, 190
Louisiana Territory, 149, 164, 237, 241
Lovejoy, Elijah, 220
Lovell v. *Griffin* (1938), 48
l'Overture, Toussaint, 148
Lowell, Frances, 206
Lowell, Mass., 206
Lower California (Baja), 438
Lowndes, William, 153

Loyalists: compensation for, 73, 84; support for British, 66, 68, 71
Loyalists (in Spanish Civil War), 560
Loyal Publication Societies, 459
Loyalty oaths (Reconstruction), 271, 272, 274
Loyalty program, 639, 641
LSD, 703–704, 710
Lucas, Eliza, 42
Lucas, George, 708
Lucey, Patrick, 731
Ludlow Resolution, 568
Lumber, 356, 357
Lumpkin, Gran Grace, 539
Lundy, Benjamin, 219
Lusitania, 450
Luxembourg: and EEC, 659; invasion of, 562; liberation, 590; and NATO, 606; and WWII, 590, 591
Lyceums, 211
Lynchings, 330, 483, 484, 635
Lyon, Mary, 216
Lyon, Matthew, 135

MC

McAdoo, William G., 456
MacArthur, Douglas, 512; and Japan, 606–607; and Korean War, 608–610; and WWII, 573, 574, 575, 582, 588
McCarran Immigration Act of 1952, 638
McCarran Internal Security Act, 639
McCarthy, Senator Joseph R., 639, 640, 675; censured by Senate, 642; and Eisenhower, 641–642
McCarthy Hearings, 642
McCartney, Linda, 710
McCartney, Paul, 709, 710
McClellan, George B., 254–256, 262
McClure's Magazine, 377; and muckrakers, 385, 386
McCord, James W., 692
McCoy, Joseph, 329
McCullers, Carson, 650
McCulloch v. *Maryland* (1819), 158, 177
Mcdonough, Capt. Thomas, 155
McDowell, Gen. Irvin, 252
McGovern, George, 687, 690–691
McKay, Claude, 495
McKay, Donald, 205
McKinley, William, 391; and annexation of Hawaii, 415; and canal zone, 430; and Cuba, 416; and de Lôme letter, 418; and free-silver issue, 354–356; and Guam, 421; and Philippines, 420–421, 422
McKinley Tariff of 1890, 361, 413, 416
McLuhan, Marshall, 713–714
McNamara, Robert, 657, 658, 668
McNary-Haugen bill, 488
McPherson, Aimee Semple, 491

M

Machine politics, 356, 357, 529; and reformers, 379–380
Macon's Bill Number Two, 151
Macune, C. W., 353
Madero, Francesco, 441
Madison, James, 90, 101, 107, 122, 123, 136, 155; and Bill of Rights, 120; elected President, 151; and *The Federalist,* 95; and first Congress, 119; as Jefferson's Secretary of State, 146; opposes Bank of the United States, 124; and relations with Britain, 151; supports Constitution, 95; vetoes bill for internal improvements, 158; and Virginia Plan, 90; and War of 1812, 153–157
Magazines: in late 1800's, 377; in 1930's, 538
Magellan, Ferdinand, 10–11
Maginot Line, 562
Magna Charta, 38
Magruder, Jeb Stuart, 692
Mahan, Alfred Thayer, 411–412
Mailer, Norman, 650
Maine, 35, 163–164
Maine, 418
Mainstreaming, 754
Makin, Battle of, 582
Malamud, Bernard, 650
Malaya. See Malaysia.
Malaysia, 612

Malcolm X, 671, 707
Maltz, Albert, 539
Manchuria, 425, 426, 427, 554, 592, 610; Japan and Russia in, 437, 554, 555, 568
Manhattan Island: purchased by Dutch, 14–15; in Revolutionary War, 69
Manhattan Project, 594
Manifest Destiny, 194, 198, 200, 237, 333. See New Manifest Destiny.
Manila, Philippine Islands, 574, 575, 612; in Spanish-American War, 419, 420
Mann, Horace, 215–216
Mann-Elkins Act of 1910, 395
Mannheim, Battle of, 591
Manpower Development and Training Act, 659
Manson, Charles, 702
Mantle, Mickey, 649
Manufacturing. See Industry.
Mao Tse Tung, 607
Mapp v. *Ohio* (1961), 662, 687
Marbury, William, 146
Marbury v. *Madison* (1803), 146, 158
Marconi, Guglielmo, 297
Marijuana, 704
Marín, Luis Muñoz, 672
Marines, U.S.: in Haiti, 440, 547; in WWI, 457, 461; in WWII, 576–577, 582
Marinettes, 457
Maritime Territory, 551
Marne River, Battle of, 461
Marquette, Fr. Jacques, 14
Married Women's Property Act of 1848, 218
Marsh, Reginald, 539
Marshall, George, 603, 607
Marshall, James, 200
Marshall, John: important rulings of, 146, 158–159, 176; in travel, 134
Marshall, Thurgood, 643, 659
Marshall Islands, 582
Marshall Plan, 603–605
Martin, Dick, 714
Martin, Luther, 93
Martineau, Harriet, 210
Martin v. *Hunter's Lessee* (1816), 158
Marx, Karl, 479
Marx Brothers, 538
Marxists, 553
Maryland, 35–36, 123, 244, 285, 618; in Civil War, 255, 256, 263; ratifies Constitution, 95
Mason, George, 95
Mason, John, 35
Mason, John Y., 237
Massachusetts: in Civil War, 257; drafts constitution, 81; early government, 34; first public schools, 49; Plymouth colony, 33; Puritan migration, 33; ratifies Constitution, 94; reform of mental hospitals, 215; Shays' Rebellion, 87; slave trade, 223
Mass media: and counterculture, 701, 702; during 1960's and 1970's, 713–715; and pop art, 705; use of in WWI, 458
Mass production, 499, 647; and magazines, 377
Mathis, Johnny, 497
Maximilian affair, 409
Mayagüez, 696
Mayas, 19–20
Mayflower, 32
Mayflower Compact, 32, 33
Mays, Henry T., 442, 443
Mays, Willie, 649
Maysville Road Bill veto, 175
Meade, Gen. George G., 264, 265
Meat Inspection Act of 1906, 393
Meat-packing industry, 385, 393; and Armour, 303; and meat shipping, 296
Media. See Mass media.
Medicaid, 663, 735, 737
Medical Information Bureau, 717
Medicare Act, 663
Medicine, 259. See Health Care.
Medicine Lodge, 337
Mellon, Andrew, 487, 509
Melville, Herman, 211
Memphis, Battle of, 254
Mencken, H. L., 494–495
Mental hospitals: antebellum reform, 214–215
Mercantilism, 42–44
Meredith, James, 660
Merit System, 395

Merrimac, 252–253
Merritt, Wesley, 419
Metacomet, 35
Meuse-Argonne, Battle of, 463, 464–465
Mexican-Americans, 672–673; as cowboys, 329; migration to California during WWII, 585
Mexican War, 197–200, 233, 250, 256; battles and campaigns, 198–199; debts from, 200; disputes leading to, 197–198; opposition to, 217; peace treaty, 200
Mexico, 480, 740; and California, 193; Cortés in, 11; French in, after Civil War, 409; independence, 197; and Texas, 190–191
Michigan, 275, 333, 515; enters Union, 235
Middle America, 701, 702, 707
Middle East: American-Soviet rivalry, 601, 602, 603; and Carter, 726–727; and Crusades, 6; Cold War, 615–617; and energy crisis, 689; Islamic revolution, 729; and Johnson, 666; and Nixon, 683–684; and Reagan, 740–742; in WWI, 447. See Arab nations, Israel, Oil.
"Middle Passage," 223
Midway, Battle of, 576
Migrant workers, 532, 672–673
Milan Decree, 150
Miles, Nelson A., 419, 421
Military-Industrial Complex, 645, 647
Miller, Arthur, 651
Miller, Glenn, 537
Miller, John C., 120
Miller, William E., 663
Mills, Roger, 361
Mines: safety in, 395; in West, 327–328; work conditions in, 313
Minimum wage laws, 397; for women, 389
Minnesota, 295, 333, 674; enters Union, 244; Granger laws in, 353
Minnesota territory, 240, 299
Minnow, Newton, 714
Minorities: and Eleanor Roosevelt, 587; during Progressive Era, 394; during WWI, 457. See Civil rights.
Minuit, Peter, 14–15
Minutemen, 63, 578
Miranda v. *Arizona* (1966), 662, 687
Missionaries, 413; and Northwest Indians, 194; Spanish, 9; and women's education, 216
"Missionary Diplomacy," 439, 440
Missions, Spanish: architectural style, 21; at San Diego, 9
Mississippi, 681; after Civil War, 275, 276, 278; during Civil War, 256, 263, 264; enters Union, 62; in Reconstruction, 280; secedes from Union, 245
Mississippi River, 175–176; in Civil War, 253, 264; discovered, 21; and exploration, 149; French exploration of, 14; navigation rights, 131; problems with Spain, 84, 126; treaty with Spain concerning, 132; and westward expansion, 189, 190
Mississippi Valley, 193, 194
Mississippi v. *Williams* (1898), 358
Missouri, 167, 171, 196, 239, 240, 244, 509; in Civil War, 251, 254; enters Union, 163–164; in literature, 377
Missouri Compromise, 163–164, 222, 233; found unconstitutional, 241; repeal of, 237–238
Missouri River, 149, 196, 301
Mitchell, Charles E., 504
Mitchell, John, 392, 686, 692, 694
Mitchell, Margaret, 539
Mitchell, Maria, 219
Mobile Bay, Battle of, 266
Mobile Doctrine, 442
Mobile-Experimental missile. See MX missile.
Model Cities program, 665
Modern art, 651
"Modern Republicanism," 640
Molasses Act of 1733, 44
Molotov, Vyacheslav, 584, 600
Monarchies, 7
Mondale, Walter, 697, 731
Money, 158, 177; in Civil War, 260–261; in colonial period, 42; under Constitution, 102; and economy under Nixon, 685–686; and election of 1832, 178; Gilded Age issue, 347–348; hard vs. soft, 177–178, 182; Indian, 189; New Deal regulation, 522, 527, 530, 533, 536; in Panic of 1907; reform under Wilson, 398; after WWI, 487
"Money Trust," 394, 398

Monopolies, 304, 305, 322, 377, 507, 534; and progressive reform, 384
Monroe, James, 131, 168; administration of, 171; American minister to France, 131; elected President, 157; and Louisiana Purchase, 148; plans for Indians, 189; supports Jackson, 159
Monroe Doctrine, 159, 168, 434, 438, 454, 466, 467, 620; after Civil War, 409, 415; and Falklands War, 742; extension to Greenland, 566; Lodge Corollary, 439; Roosevelt Corollary, 434, 438; transformed in multinational agreement, 548
Montana: enters Union, 331; gold in, 337; lands, 396; and vote for women, 396
Montcalm, Marquis de, 55
Monterey, Battle of, 198, 199
Montesquieu, 100
Montezuma II, 20
Montgomery, Bernard L., 583
Montgomery bus boycott, 644
Monticello, 147
Moody, Paul, 206
Moon, Reverend Sun Myung, 712
Moonies, 712
Moore, Albert Burton, 290–291
Moral majority, 732
Morgan, Helen, 484
Morgan, John Pierpont, 260, 303, 351, 391, 479
Morrill Tariff Act of 1862, 260, 372
Morison, Samuel Eliot, 90
Mormons, 196–197
Moroccan Crisis, 436–437
Morocco, 95; foreign powers in, 436–437; French Morocco, 582; Spanish Morocco, 559–560
Morris, Governeur, 130
Morris, Robert, 88
Morse, Samuel F., 205
Morton, William, 259
Moscow, Battle of, 574
Moscow Conference (1942), 574
Moscow, Russia, 550, 605, 682–683; conference in, 591; hotline to, 623; meeting of Allied leaders, 584; Olympics in, 730; in WWI, 591
Mott, Lucretia, 217–218
Mountain men, 195, 333
Mountbatten, Lord Louis, 584
Mount Vernon, 89
Movies, 333; beginnings, 494, 498; in Depression, 537–538; in the 1950's, 649; in the 1960's and 1970's, 707–708
Muckrakers, 385–386
Mudslinging, 349
Mugwumps, 348–349, 350, 351
Muhammed, Elijah, 671
Muir, John, 393
Munich, Germany, 537
Munich Pact, 556–557, 558
Municipal Leagues, 380
Munn* v. *Illinois (1877), 307
Murdock* v. *Pennsylvania (1943), 48
Murrow, Edward R., 649
Music: in late 1800's, 375; in the 1960's and 1970's, 708–710. See Jazz.
Muskhogean Indians, 24–26
Muskie, Edmund, 675
Mussolini, Benito, 551–552, 563, 584; accord with Hitler, 556; aids France, 560; in Albania, 561; captured, 591; in Ethiopia, 555–556
MX missile, 726, 738
My Lai massacre, 680

N

NAACP. See National Association for the Advancement of Colored People.
Nader, Ralph, 716
Nagasaki, 594, 595
Naismith, Dr. James, 374
Namath, Joe, 717
Napoleon I, 134, 155; defeated by Britain, 155; Louisiana Purchase, 147–148; War in Europe and American freedom of the seas, 150–151
Napoleon III, Emperor of France, 409
Napoleonic Wars, 150–151, 159
Narragansett Indians, 34
NASA. See National Aeronautics and Space Administration.
Nashville, Battle of, 267
Nasser, Abdel Gamal, 615, 617, 666

Nast, Thomas, 348
Natchez Indians, 26
National Advisory Commission on Civil Disorders, 671
National Aeronautics and Space Administration, 658
National American Woman Suffrage Association, 218
National Association for the Advancement of Colored People (NAACP), 359, 484, 530, 688; Supreme Court suits, 643
National Colored Farmer's Alliance, 353
National Congress of American Indians, 674
National debt: after Revolution, 122; in Critical Period, 88; Jefferson's commitment to reduce, 146
National Defense Education Act of 1958, 645
National Farmer's Alliance and Industrial Union. See Southern Alliance.
National Farmer's Alliance of the Northwest. See Northern Alliance.
National Farm Workers Association, 673
National Guard: in demonstrations, 643, 660, 671; in strikes, 529; in WWI, 445; in WWII, 563
National Health Insurance, 638
National Housing Act. See Wagner-Steagall Act.
National Housing Act of 1949, 638
National Industrial Recovery Act, 518, 526, 527, 529
Nationalism: after War of 1812, 157–160; before Civil War, 174; flowering of, 160
Nationalist China, 607, 608, 726. See Taiwan.
National Labor Reform Party, 315
National Labor Relations Act. See Wagner Act.
National Labor Relations Board, 526, 529
National Labor Union, 315
National Liberation Front, 666
National Monetary Commission, 394, 398
National Organization for Women, 674
National Origins Act, 482
National Progressive Republican League, 397
National Prohibition Enforcement Act, 484
National Reclamation Act, 393
National Republican Party, 169, 180; and election of 1832, 178, 181; founded, 169
National Security Act, 636
National Security Council, 636
National Socialist German Worker's Party. See Nazi party.
National Union for Social Justice, 523
National War Labor Board, 580
National Youth Administration, 525, 530, 661
Nation-states, 7
Native American Movement, 674
Native Indian Youth Council, 674
NATO. See North Atlantic Treaty Organization.
Natural gas, 735; and Soviet pipeline, 739–740
Naturalization, 136, 145; residence requirement reduced to 5 years, 145
Naturalization act, 136
Natural resources, 645, 751; as factor of production, 295; and Reagan, 733, 735
Navaho Indians, 221; resistance in Southwest, 337, 339
Naval Act of 1890, 412
Naval Expansion Act of 1938, 561
Naval War College at Newport, Rhode Island, 411–412
Navigation Acts, 43, 84
Navy, U.S., 513; after Civil War, 412, 413; in Civil War, 252–253; Cuban blockade, 622; "great white fleet," 429; in Korean War, 608; in Mexican War, 198; in Spanish-American War, 418, 419–420; in War of 1812, 153–155; women in, 457; in WWI, 455, 458, 460; in WWII, 563, 566, 567
Navy Department, 134, 563; and administration of Guam, 421
Nazi party, 552, 558, 564, 615; and Holocaust, 591; at Nuremburg, 594
NCAI. See National Congress of American Indians.
Nebraska, 516; enters Union, 331; and Farmers' Alliances, 353; and Kansas-Nebraska Act, 237–238
Nelson, Donald M., 579
Neustadt, Richard, 657

Neutrality, 130, 132, 133–134, 150–151; and Monroe Doctrine, 159; in WWI, 447, 448–453; in WWII, 559–567. See Isolationism.
Neutrality Act of 1939, 562, 566, 567
Neutrality Acts of 1935 & 1936, 559, 560, 561
Nevada: enters Union, 331; Indian resistance, 339; and silver, 327, 328
New Amsterdam, 15
New Deal, 515–518, 521, 524–527, 529, 564, 587, 637, 638, 640, 655, 663, 733; critics of, 522–524, 528; impact on American culture, 536–539; Supreme Court attack on, 527–528
New England, 149, 151, 239; literature about, 376; public schools, 215; textile industry, 206
New England colonies, 29–38, 41–42
"New Federalism," 686, 735
Newfoundland, 566; claimed by England, 17; fishing rights in, 73
New Freedom, 397, 521, 535, 655
New Frontier, 655–661, 674
New Hampshire, 86, 158, 171, 675; drafts constitution, 81; migration to, 35; as royal colony, 35; ratifies Constitution, 95
New Jersey, 86, 167, 295, 304; ratifies Constitution, 94; in Revolution, 70
New Jersey Plan, 91
New journalism, 715
Newlands Act of 1902. See National Reclamation Act.
New left, 674–675
New manifest destiny, 411–415
New Mexico, 185, 234, 454, 585, 689; and compromise of 1850, 235; conquest of, 198–200; and Dust Bowl, 532; enters Union, 331
New Nationalism, 397, 521, 535
New Orleans, 84, 126, 147–148, 155–156, 157, 170, 650; in Civil War, 268; and jazz, 496, 497; race riots in during Reconstruction, 279; right of deposit, 132
New Orleans, Battle of, 254
Newspapers: abolitionist, 219–220, 230, 285; black, 359; censorship of, 457, 459, 465; in colonial period, 50; and counterculture, 701, 702; ethnic, 367; and freedom of press, 135; and labor movement, 317; and progressive reform, 386; and Scopes trial, 486; in "war" between Federalists and Republicans, 135, 136; and war propaganda, 459; in WWI, 450; in WWII, 562; and Watergate, 692; in 1800's, 377; in 1920's, 493–494; in 1950's, 649; in 1960's and 1970's, 715–716. See Yellow journalism.
Newton, Huey, 671
Newton, Sir Isaac, 99
New York, 36, 86, 214, 285, 303, 490; drafts constitution, 81; ratifies Constitution, 95
New York City: and arts in 1960's and 1970's, 704; changes in population of, 363; in colonial period, 42; commercial center, 203; hippies in, 702; housing in, 369–370; nation's first capital, 119; political machines in, 346, 399; Puerto Ricans in, 672; in Revolution, 69–70; stock market crash, 504; symphony, 375
New York Stock Exchange, 503
New York Times: and Atlantic Charter, 567; and Homestead steel strike, 322; and Pentagon Papers, 693; and stock market crash, 504
Nez Percé Indians, 23, 338–339, 340
Niagara Movement, 359
Nicaragua, 728–729, 740; as possible canal route, 429–431; U.S. intervention in, 437–438, 440
Nichols, Red, 496
Nimitz, Admiral Chester W., 582, 587, 595
Nimoy, Leonard, 714
NIRA. See National Industrial Recovery Act.
Nisei, 581
Nixon, Richard M., 640, 642, 701, 735; "Checkers" speech, 640; and economy, 685–686; election of 1960, 655, 656, 657; election of 1968, 675–676; and foreign affairs, 679–684; pardon of, 695; resignation, 694; and space program, 684–685; and television debates, 180; Watergate, 692–694
Nixon Doctrine, 679
NLRB. See National Labor Relations Board.
Nobel Prize, 378; in literature to Ernest Hemingway, 560; in peace to Frank B. Kellog, 499; in peace to T. Roosevelt, 428
Nomura, Admiral Kichisaburo, 569
Non-Importation agreements, 58–59

Non-Intercourse Act, 151
Nootkas Indians, 22
Normandy, invasion of, 588–590
Norris, George W., 395, 455, 516
North, 173, 242; and abolition, 220; and assumption of state debts, 123; black education in, 216; and Civil War, 260, 263–264; Industrial Revolution, 161–162; politics before Civil War, 233–235; race problems after WWI, 483–484; railroads, 204; slavery, 163–164; tariff, 119
North Atlantic Treaty, 606
North Atlantic Treaty Organization, 606, 640, 726, 729, 738, 742; allies, 727; and France, 666; and U.S. nuclear power, 606
North Carolina, 119, 170, 244, 260, 291; in Civil War, 267, 268; enters Union, 120; ratifies Constitution, 96; in Reconstruction, 280; secedes, 249
North Dakota, 331, 333, 528, 559
North, Lord Frederick, 60
Northern Alliance, 353
Northern Securities Company v. United States (1902), 392
North Korea, 608–610
North Vietnam, 612; bombing of, 668–669; in Vietnam War, 666–669
North Vietnamese, 680–681
Northwest Indians: Treaty of Greenville, 156; under Tecumseh, 151
Northwest Ordinance, 88–90, 189
Northwest Passage, 12, 14; and Dutch exploration, 14; and English exploration, 16
Northwest Territory: British fail to evacuate, 84; and Indians, 132; and Northwest Ordinance, 89; and slavery, 219
Norway, invasion of, 562
NOW. See National Organization for Women.
Noyes, John Humphrey, 214
NRA. See National Recovery Administration.
Nuclear Nonproliferation Treaty, 682
Nuclear power, 724
Nuclear war, 708, 738
Nuclear weapons, 601, 606, 613, 618, 622, 623, 666; control of, 623, 682, 683, 696, 726, 727, 738; controversies, 751. See Atomic bomb, SALT, START.
Nullification controversy, 173–174, 222
Nullification Crisis of 1832, 176
Nuremberg trials, 594
NWLB. See National War Labor Board.
NYA. See National Youth Administration.
Nye, Gerald P., 559

O

OAS. See Organization of American States.
Oberlin College, 216
OCD. See Office of Civil Defense.
OEO. See Office of Economic Opportunity.
Office of Civil Defense, 580
Office of Economic Opportunity, 662
Office of Price Administration, 579–580
Office of Scientific Research and Development, 577–579
Oglethorpe, James, 37
Ohio, 167, 216, 295, 509; admitted as state, 147; Mormons in, 196
Oil embargo, 684, 689
O'Keefe, Georgia, 494
"Okies," 533
Okinawa, Battle of, 592–593
Oklahoma: and Dust Bowl, 532, 538; reservations, 339
Oldenburg, Claes, 705
Old Guard Republicans, 395, 396, 397
"Old Ironsides," 155
Olive Branch Petition, 64–65
Oliver, Andrew, 58
Olmstead, Frederick Law, 375
Olney Corollary, 415
Olney, Richard, 415
Olympics: 1932, 536–537; 1936, 537; 1980, boycott of, 730
Omnibus Housing Act, 665
O'Neale, Peggy, 174
Oneida Community, 214
O'Neill, Eugene, 456, 494
O'Neill, Thomas P., 736
Ontario, 299
OPA. See Office of Price Administration.

OPEC, 723
Opechancanough, 32
Open Door: in Cuba, 425–429, 487, 555; in Morocco, 436; in Manchuria, 437
Open Housing Act, 665
Open Market Committee, 527
Open shops, 320
"Open Skies" agreement, 613
Opera, 375
Operation Bootstrap, 672
Operation Headstart, 662–663
Operation Husky, 584
Operation Overlord, 588–590
Operation Torch, 574
Operetta, 375
Oppenheimer, J. Robert, 594
Orders in Council, 150
Oregon, 159, 185, 195, 338; annexation of, 198; border, 233; conflicting claims, 194–195; enters Union, 244; and migrants, 533; and women in labor force, 389
"Oregon fever," 194
Oregon Territory, 159, 195
Organization of American States, 618, 624
Organized crime, 686; rise of, 484; and WWII rationing, 580
Orr, James L., 275
OSRD. See Office of Scientific Research and Development.
Ostend Manifesto, 237, 239
Ostrogorski, Moisei, 347
Oswald, Lee Harvey, 661
Owen, Chandler, 506
Owen, Robert, 213
Owens, Jesse, 537

P

Pacific Ocean, 147, 149, 198, 412, 433, 609; discovered, 10–11; possessions in, 487; Spanish-American War in, 419; territorial rights in, 429–430; in WWII, 569–570, 574–577, 582, 588, 591–593, 656
Pacific Railway Acts, 299–300
Pacifists: in WWI, 452; in WWII, 562. See Conscientious objectors.
Pahlavi, Shah Mohammed Reza, 729
Paine, Thomas, 67, 212
Paiute Indians, 339
Painting: Ash Can School, 375–376; Currier and Ives, 161; de Kooning, William, 651; Eakins, Thomas, 375; Hopper, Edward, 494; Hudson Valley School, 161; Lichtenstein, Roy, 705; modern art, 651; O'Keefe, Georgia, 494; Pop Art, 704–705; realism in, 375–376
Pakenham, Sir Edward, 155
Pakistan, 730; and SEATO, 612
Palestine, 615
Palestine Liberation Organization, 740–741
Palestinian Arabs, 615; homeland for, 726; refugees, 675
Palmer, A. Mitchell, 479, 480
Palmer raids, 480
Pan-Africanism, 359
Panama, 727; and canal, 107, 429–433; digging rights, 429–431; end of intervention in, 548; environment of, 421, 432–433; revolt in, 431–432; railroad across, 205
Panama Canal, 429–433, 438, 569; building of, 432–433; crisis concerning, 430–433, 440; and diseases, 432–433; neutrality of, 429, 432; treaties under Carter, 728
Panama Canal Commission, 433
Pan-American Union, 564
Panay, 568
Panic of 1819, 162–163, 177
Panic of 1837, 181, 216
Panic of 1907, 393–394, 398
Paris, France, 458, 494, 495, 560, 604, 606; peace conferences, 465–466, 669, 681; in WWI, 458–461; in WWII, 564, 590
Parker, Alton B., 391
Parker, Bonnie, 708
Parks, Rosa, 644
Parliament, English, 38; and colonies, 57–62; and rebellion, 65, 68
Parrington, Vernon Louis, 352
Pasteur, Louis, 259
Patents, 210, 296
Paterson, William, 91

Patman, Wright, 511
Patriotism: and schools, 371; and songs, 160
Patrons of Husbandry. See Grange.
Pattison, Robert, 322
Patton, Gen. George S., 583
Payne, Sereno, 395
Payne-Aldrich Tariff, 395, 398
PCP, 704
Peace Corps, 618, 674, 690
Peace Democrats, 261, 280
Peaceful coexistence, 613; opposition from China, 617. See Détente.
Peace of Paris, 466
Pea Ridge, Battle of, 254
Pearl Harbor, 413, 569–570, 586, 594; attack on, 459; effects of attack, 573
Peck, John Mason, 186
Pemberton, Gen. John C., 264
Pendleton Act of 1883, 350, 722
Penn, William, 37
Pennsylvania, 167, 214, 659; in Civil War, 263–264; and coal strike in 1902, 392; during Depression, 508; and factory inspection, 315; founded and settled, 37; in French and Indian War, 53–54; and labor unrest, 321–322; ratifies Constitution, 94; in Revolutionary War, 70; and Whiskey Rebellion, 126
Pennsylvania Railroad, 302–303; strike against, 320
Pennsylvania System, 214
Pentagon, 674; and Cuban missile crisis, 622; march on, 668
"Pentagon Papers," 693
People's party. See Populist party.
People's Republic of China. See China.
Pequot Indians, 35
Perkins, Frances, 526
Permanent Court of Arbitration, 434
Perry, Capt. Oliver Hazard, 155
Perry, Commodore Matthew, 205
Perryville, Battle of, 256
Pershing, Gen. John J., 458, 461; in Mexico, 444
Persian Empire, 414
Persian Gulf, 729, 730
Personal liberty laws, 236
Peru, 11, 412, 547
Pétain, Henri-Philippe, 564
Pet banks, 179
Peters, Andrew, 478
Philadelphia, 304, 320, 373, 528, 709; capital of Confederation, 84; first medical school in, 259; as nation's capital, 123; in Revolutionary War, 70; site of Constitutional Convention, 90; site of First Continental Congress, 61; symphony, 375
Philippine Government Act, 422
Philippine Islands, 569; acquisition of, 420–421; conflicts regarding, 425, 428, 429, 439; Japanese siege of, 574–575; Magellan in, 11; militia, 569; resistance to American rule in, 422; and SEATO, 612; in Spanish-American War, 419; Taft as civil governor of, 394; WWII in, 588
Philippine Sea, Battle of, 588
Phillips, David Graham, 385
Phillips, Wendell, 279
Phnom Penh, Cambodia, 696
Photography, 376
Photojournalism, 538
Pickering, John, 146
Pickett's Charge, 264
Pickford, Mary, 494
Pierce, Charles, 383
Pierce, Franklin, 236; foreign policy, 237; and violence in Kansas, 239
Pike, Zebulon, 149
Pilgrims, 32–33
Pinchot, Gifford, 396
Pinckney, Charles Cotesworth, 134, 136, 151
Pinckney, Thomas, 132, 133. See Treaty of San Lorenzo.
Pingree, Hazen S., 387
Pinkerton Private Detective Agency, 322
Pioneers, 185–187
Pitcairn, Maj. John, 63
Pitt, William, 54
Pittsburgh, Pennsylvania, 302, 303, 304, 320, 492; as industrial center, 311; symphony, 375
Pizarro, Francisco, 11, 20
Placer method, 328
Plantations, 222–223, 224; early, in Virginia, 31; liability during Civil War, 261; slave system, 42

Platt Amendment, 421, 436; annulled, 547
Pleiku, Battle of, 667
Plessy v. *Ferguson* **(1896),** 358, 643
PLO. See Palestine Liberation Organization.
"Plumbers," 693
Plunkitt, George Washington, 379
Plymouth Colony, 32–33
Pocahontas, 31–32
Pocket veto, 112
Podgorny, Nikolai V., 682
Poe, Edgar Allen, 211
Pogroms, 367
Point Four program, 618
Poland, 592, 599, 600, 604; crisis in, 614; German aggression in, 557–558, 561; immigrants from, 366, 367, 368; and Reagan, 738–739; and Solidarity, 738–739; in WWI, 460, 466; in WWII, 583
Political bosses, 346
Political campaigns, 180
Political cartoons, 54, 348, 457
Political parties: formation of, 119, 127–129; Washington warns against, 132. See names of specific parties.
Polk, James K., 233; elected President, 193; and California policy, 193; and manifest destiny, 198; and war with Mexico, 198
Polo, Marco, 6, 7
Pollock, Jackson, 651
Poll tax, 357, 635, 659
Pollution, 665, 706
Pontiac's Rebellion, 56, 189
Pope, Maj. General John, 255
Popular sovereignty, 32, 35, 68, 99–100, 234, 238, 239, 241, 242
Population: antebellum, 209; and urbanization, 363; in 1950's, 647–648
Populism: failure of in South, 357; philosophy of, 352–356; and Progressive Era, 382
Populist party, 352, 353–356, 357, 383
Portugal, 487; empire, 9–10; explorations, 8–9; neutrality in WWII, 573; and slave trade, 223
Post Office Department, 120, 205
Potsdam Conference, 594, 599
Poverty, 655, 659; in 1960's and 1970's, 716. See Slums.
Powderly, Terence, 316
Powell, Lewis F., 686–687
Powhatan, 31, 32
POW's. See Prisoners of War.
Pragmatism, philosophy of, 383–384
Prayer in public schools, 73
Presidency, 106, 107, 108, 115, 116
President's Committee on Unemployment Relief, 509
Presley, Elvis, 497, 649
Prester, John, 8
Prevost, Sir George, 155
Price, Leontyne, 497
Price-fixing, 398
Princeton, Battle of, 70
Princip, Gavrilo, 447
Printing press money, 261
Prisoners of War, in Vietnam, 681
Prisons, antebellum reform, 214
Proclamation of Neutrality, 130
Proclamation of 1763, 56, 189
Progressive party, 389. See Bull Moose party.
Progressive party (1948), 636
Progressivism, 383–400, 516
Prohibition, 484–485, 489, 498; repeal of, 485
Project Apollo, 685
Proletarian literature, 539
Propaganda, anti-British, 150; antislavery, 236; and Compromise of 1850, 235; northern, 243; promotional literature about West, 331; and WWI, 448–449, 457–459
Prophet, the, 152
Proposition 13, 724
Proprietary colonies, 35–38
Prostitution, in late 1800's, 378
Protection money, 380
Protective tariff, 119
Protestant Churches: in Progressive Era, 384–385; Great Awakening, 47; and Social Darwinism, 306; and Reformation, 8, 32; splintering in, 209; in 1950's, 649
Protestant ethic, 701
Prussia: commercial treaties with, 87; East, 558
Public domain, 88
Public health nursing, 378

Public Utilities Holding Company Act, 527
Public Works Administration, 518
Pueblo Indians, 23
Puerto Ricans, 672, 687
Puerto Rico, 672; claimed by Spain, 10; in Spanish-American War, 420; transition to America rule, 421
Pulaski, Count Casimir, 69
Pulitzer, Joseph, 377, 417, 493
Pulitzer Prize, 417; to Haley, 707; to Hemingway, 560; to Kennedy, 657
Pullman, George M., 260, 322–324
Pullman Company, 297, 324
Pure Food and Drug Act, 393, 534
Puritans, 30, 33, 34; and freedom of religion, 48; influence weakened, 212; and schools, 371
Puritan work ethic, 34, 306
Puzo, Mario, 707
PWA. See Public Works Administration.

Q

Quakers: founded Pennsylvania, 37; protest against slavery, 146, 218
Quaaludes, 704
Quartering Act, 56
Quebec, 584; first permanent French colony in New World, 14; in French and Indian War, 55
Quebec Act, 61
Quincy, Josiah, 60
Quotas: and affirmative action, 688, 722; and immigration, 481–482, 638, 665

R

RA. See Resettlement Administration.
Race Riots. See Riots and Demonstrations.
Racism, See Intolerance.
Radar, 579
Radical Reconstruction, 278–283
Radical Republicans, 261, 271, 274. See Radical Reconstruction.
Radio, 333, 522–523, 537; early, 492, 493; influence on political campaigns, 180; invention of, 297; and war propaganda, 459
Radisson, Pierre, 14
Ragtime, 375
Railroads: 203–204, 272, 535; in cattle marketing, 329; in Civil War, 249, 266; financing of, 299–300; influence on campaigns, 180; land companies, 331; "monied" interest, 352; in Panama, 205; in Reconstruction, 283; regulation of, 307–308, 350, 352, 354, 388, 389, 391–392, 393; safety of, 297–298; segregation, 388; specialized cars, 297; steel rails, 296; strikes in, 320, 323; time and gauge standardized, 298; trade and industry, 204; transcontinental, 237, 298–301; in West, 331
Railway Strike of 1877, 320
Raleigh, Sir Walter, 5, 17
Randolf, Asa Philip, 506, 643
Randolf, Edmund, 121, 124
Range wars, 330
Rationing, 579–580
Rauschenbush, Walter, 384–385
Ray, James Earl, 671
REA. See Rural Electrification Administration.
Readjustment Act of 1944, 633–634
Reagan, Nancy, 733
Reagan, Ronald, 535, 725, 730; Presidency, 733–744
Reaganomics, 736
Realism: in art, 375–376; in literature, 376–377
Recall election, 387
Reclamation Service, 393
Reconstruction, 483; under Johnson, 273–276, 278; Lincoln's plan, 271–274; Radical, 278–283, 291
Reconstruction Finance Corporation (RFC), 510–511, 514, 536
Recreation: in late 1800's, 373–375; in the 1920's, 491–495; in Depression, 536–537; in the 1950's, 649
Red Cloud, Chief, 337, 340
Red Cloud's War. See First Sioux War.
Red Cross, 457
Redemptioners, 41
Red Scare, 479–480
Reed, Walter, 433

Referendum, 387
Reform, 203, 345, abolition, 219–221; in civil service, 346–347; in education, 215–216; in labor, 216; literature of protest, 377; mental hospitals, 214–215; New Deal, 524–528; peace, 216–217; of prisons, 214; in Progressive Era, 383–389, 397–399; and T. Roosevelt, 391–394; social, 373; under Taft, 395–396; temperance movement, 215; urban, 377–380; under Wilson, 398–399; women's rights, 218–219
Reformation. See Protestant Reformation.
Rehnquist, William, 687
Reichstag, 553
Reisman, David, 651
Relief and Construction Act, 511
Religion: in colonial period, 12, 32, 33–34, 47; radical communities, 214; revivals, 211–212; in 1100's and 1200's, 6, 7, 8; in 1950's, 649; in 1960's and 1970's, 711–713. See Deists, Great Awakening, Second Great Awakening, Puritans.
Religious freedom, 48; in colonial period, 33, 36, 37, 47; and Mormons, 195–197
Renaissance, 7
Representative government, 31, 32, 33, 35, 36, 38, 39. See Popular Sovereignty.
Republican party, 113, 347; blacks in, 530; and conservation, 391; Dred Scott, effect of, 241; and election of 1896, 354–356; and farmers revolt, 357; formation of, 238–239; in Gilded Age, 347–349; and Lincoln, 271; modern, 640; in Progressive Era, 383, 385–387; and Radical Reconstruction, 280, 284, 285; in Spanish Civil War, 560
Republican party (Jeffersonian), 134, 136; elections in, 133, 188; established, 127; and French Revolution, 130; and Jay Treaty, 131; and newspaper war, 129; opinion of, 128; policies, 157; Presidency, 145; War of 1812, 153
Republic of California, 193–194
Republic of Hawaii, 415
Republic of Korea. See South Korea.
Republic of West Florida, 152
Reservations, Indian, 337, 338
Reservationists, 467
Reserve Officers Training Corps, 674
Resettlement Administration, 526, 532
Revels, Senator H. R., 282
Revenue-sharing, 686
Revere, Paul, 49, 63, 457
Revolution, American, 185; causes of, 55–62; debt from, 122, 160; finance of, 69; forces, balance of, 68–69; foreign officers in, 70–72; negotiations, 72, 73; in the North, 68, 71; propaganda, 67, 459; French aid, 448; in the South, 71–72; technology in, 578; in the West, 71
RFC. See Reconstruction Finance Corporation.
Rhode Island, 119; drafts constitution, 81; joins Union, 120; and Philadelphia convention, 90; ratifies Constitution, 96; religious freedom in, 34–35, self-government, 35; and slave trade, 223
Ribicoff, Abraham, 657
Rice, George, 304
Richardson, Elliot, 693
Richmond, Battle of, 255
Rickenbacker, Eddie, 565
Ridgway, Gen. Matthew, 610
Riis, Jacob, 367, 376, 377
Rio de Janeiro Conference (1942), 580
Riots and Demonstrations: anti-nuclear, 724; and civil rights, 670–671; and Indians, 688; Little Rock, Ark., 643; racial, 484, 585; and Reconstruction, 279; and Vietnam War, 668, 674, 675, 681
Ripley, George, 213
Roads: in Civil War, 249; first National Road, 158; improvements in antebellum, 203; paving of and urbanization, 364, 365
Roanoke, 17–18
"Robber barons," 305
Roberts, John, 710
Roberts, Oral, 712
Roberts, Owen, 528, 531
Robinson, Edgar E., 542
Robinson, Joseph T., 532
Rock, 649, 708–709, 710
Rockefeller, John D., 260; 303–305, 385
Rockefeller, Nelson, 694
Rockne, Knute, 492

Rocky Mountains, 149, 159, 185, 190, 193, 195, 197, 327, 333
Rodeo, 21
Rodino, Peter, 694
Rogers, Ginger, 538
Rogers, Will, 491, 516
Rolfe, John, 31, 32
Rolling Stones, 710
Roman Catholicism. See Catholics.
Roman Empire, 414, 551, 556
Romanticism, 210–212, 213
Romberg, Sigmund, 375
Rome-Berlin Axis, 556
Rome, Italy, 223, 551, 556; liberation of, 591
Rommel, Field Marshall Erwin, 574, 583
Romney, Hugh, 702
Roosevelt, Eleanor, 530, 587, 721
Roosevelt, Franklin D., 456, 489, 506, 587, 633, 655, 657, 661, 732; advisors of, 521–522; and the bomb, 593–594; and Churchill, 582; and Cold War, 599, 600; and conferences, 585, 591, 592; critics of, 522–524; "fireside chats," 459; and Good Neighbor policy, 547–548; and international organization, 585; Presidency, 514–518, 521; radio, use of, 180, 515–516; terms elected, 116; and WWII, 559, 561, 562–567, 568–570, 593–594
Roosevelt, Theodore, 387, 395, 425, 452, 456–513, 521, 534, 535, 565, 587; and "big stick," 434–436; and Bull Moose party, 397; and Indians, 343; and Japan, 428–429; and Morocco, 436–437; and muckrakers, 385; Nobel Peace Prize, 428; and Panama, 429–432; Presidency, 107; and reforms, 390–394; and Russo-Japanese War, 427–428; and Spanish-American War, 418–419
Roosevelt Corollary, 434
Root, Elihu, 429
Root-Takahira Agreement, 429
Rosenberg, Julius and Ethel, 638–639
Rosequist, James, 705
ROTC. See Reserve Officers Training Corps.
Roth, Philip, 650, 707
Roth, William, 725
"Rough Riders," 391, 418, 419
Rowan, Carl, 659
Rowan, Dan, 714
Rubin, Jerry, 704
Ruby, Jack, 661
Rumania, 447, 460, 466, 558, 564, 599
Rural Electrification Administration, 526
Rusk, Dean, 657
Russell, Charles E., 385
Russia: 150; and Alaska, 409; and China, 425, 426, 437; immigrants from, 366, 367; and Manchuria, 437; and Oregon, 194; revolution in, 454, 460; Russo-Japanese War, 426–428; WWI, 447, 460, 464, 465, 466
Russo-Japanese War, 554
Rutgers University, 374, 704
Ruth, "Babe," 492
Ryan, Cornelius, 588
Ryan, Leo J., 713

S

Sacajawea, 149
Sacco, Nicola, 480
Sadat, Anwar, 727
Saigon, South Vietnam, 668, 681, 709; fall of, 696
St. Clair, Gen. Arthur, 132
St. Lawrence River: exploration of, 12; and French and Indian War, 54
St. Leger, Col. Barry, 70
St. Lô, 590
Saint-Mihiel, Battle of, 463, 464–465
Sakharov, Andrei, 725
Salinger, J.D. 650
Salisbury, Lord, 415
SALT talks. See Strategic Arms Limitation Talks.
SALT II, 696, 726, 730
Sam, Vibrun Guillaume, 440
Sampson, Deborah, 63
Sampson, William T., 419
Sand Creek Massacre, 337
Sandinista National Liberation Front, 728, 740
Sanford, John F.A., 240

San Francisco, 205, 320, 417, 429, 495, 592, 595, 596, 650, 712; and hippie culture, 702; and Japanese persecution, 428–429; in Mexican War, 199; and transcontinental railroads, 301
Sanger, Margaret, 496
San Juan Hill, Battle of, 419
San Salvador, 5
Santa Anna, Gen. Antonio Lopez de, 191–192, 200
Santa Clara County v. *Southern Pacific Railroad* (1886), 307
Saratoga, Battle of, 71
Sargent, John Singer, 375
Satellites, artificial, 618
Satellites, Soviet, 600
"Saturday Night Massacre," 693, 694
Saudi Arabia, 615, 727
Savannah, Georgia, Battle of, 71
Savo Island, Battle of, 577
Scalawags, 282–283
Scandinavia, 452; immigrants from, 331, 365; in WWII, 573
Schechter v. *The United States* (1935), 527
Schenck, Christopher, 135
Schenck, v. *United States* (1919), 135
Schlesinger, Arthur, Jr., 657
Schools: colonial, 49, 50; desegregation, 688; enrollment, 370; financing of, 371; function of, 311; in Northwest territory, 88; parochial, 663; prayer in, 48; public, 283, 371, 372; segregation in, 358, 663; tax support of, 371; and WPA, 525. See Colleges, Universities, Education, Busing.
Science Advisory Committee, 706
SCLC. See Southern Christian Leadership Conference.
Scopes, John Thomas, 486
Scotland, 302; immigrants from, 313
Scott, Dred, 240, 241
Scott, Thomas A., 302
Scott v. *Sanford* (1857), 240
Scott, Gen. Winfield, 199, 236, 250
SDS. See Students for a Democratic Society.
Seale, Bobby, 671
SEATO, See Southeast Asia Treaty Organization, 612, 667
SEC. See Securities and Exchange Commission.
Second Bank of the United States, 157, 158; and 1819 depression, 162; and Jackson, 176–179
Second Continental Congress, 64, 67, 68, 70; and new state governments, 81
Second Great Awakening, 196, 211–212, 215, 225; and abolitionist movement, 219
Second Sioux War, 338
Secession: idea of, 173, 237, 244; and Lincoln, 245–246; of the South, 245
Secret ballot, 354
Sectionalism, 161–164, 174, 233–235, 242, 244
Securities and Exchange Commission, 521
Securities Exchange Act, 521
Security Council, UN, 608
Sedition Act (1918), 457, 480
Sedition Act. See Alien and Sedition Acts.
Segregation, 358; black codes, 276, 278; ending of, 635; in government under Wilson, 399; and schools 371, 372. See "Jim Crow" laws.
Selassie, Haile, 556
Selective Service Act, 455
Selective Training and Service Act, 564
Seminole Indians, 159, 171, 337
Senate: and Bill of Rights, 120; and bills, 110, 112; in first Congress, 119; and Constitution, 105–106, 114; proposed, 92, 94; sectional balance in, 163–164
Senate Foreign Relations Committee, 605, 668
Senate Munitions Investigation Committee, 559
Separation of church and state, 34, 47, 48
Separation of powers, 100
Separatists. See Puritans.
Serbia, 447, 460, 466
Serra, Fr. Junipero, 9
Settlement houses, 377–379, 385, 485
Sevastopol, Battle of, 574
Seven Years' War. See French and Indian War.
Sevier, John, 188
Seward, William H., 235, 236, 409–411
Sewell, Arthur, 355
SHAEF. See Supreme Headquarters of the Allied Expeditionary Forces.

Shafter, Gen. William, 419
Shah of Iran. See Pahlavi, Mohammed Reza.
Shakers, 214
SHAPE. See Supreme Headquarters, Allied Powers, Europe.
Sharecroppers, 286, 287, 311, 532
Share Our Wealth Plan, 524
Shatner, William, 714
Shawnee Indians, 151–152
Shaw, Artie, 537
Shawnee Indians, 188
Sheen, Monsignor Fulton J., 649
Sheffield, Lord, 84
Shenandoah Valley, 263, 267; Battle of, 255
Shepard, Alan, Jr., 658
Sheridan, General Philip, 267
Sherman Antitrust Act of 1890, 308, 319–320; 324, 391
Sherman, Roger, 67, 90, 91
Sherman Silver Purchase Act of 1890, 351
Sherman, William T., 249, 265–268
Sherman Act. See Sherman Antitrust Act.
Shiloh, Battle of, 254
Shipbuilding, 41
Shipyard workers' strike, 477
Sholes, Christopher, 296
Shoshone Indians, 149
Shriver, R. Sargent, 690
Shuttle diplomacy, 684
Siberia, 554, 739; migration of Indians across, 19
Sicily: immigrants from, 366; in WWII, 584
Siegfried Line, 562
Sihanouk, Prince Norodom, 680
Silent majority, 679, 690
Silver: as campaign issue, 354–355; and currency, 124, 350–351; and West, 327–328, 333
Sims, William S., 458
Sinai Peninsula, 616, 666, 727
Sinclair, Upton, 385, 386
Single-parent households, 755
Sino-Japanese War, 425
Sioux, 23–24; Hunkpapa, 340; Resistance in Southwest, 337, 338, 339
Sirhan, Sirhan, 675
Sirica, Judge John J., 692, 693, 694
Sit-ins, 644, 670
Sitting Bull, 338
Six-Day War, 666, 683
Six Nations, 54
Skylab, 685
Skyscrapers, 363
SLA. See Symbionese Liberation Army.
Slater, Samuel, 161
Slaughterhouse cases (1873), 358
Slavery, 172, 203, 222–225, 244, 280; and abolition, 272, 280; and B. Banneker, 123; and Britain, 131; and Brown, John, 243; in Civil War, 257, 261; codes, 223; in colonies, 41, 42, 45; and compromise, 92–93; in Confederacy, 245; and Dred Scott, 240–241; education of slaves, 216; and Emancipation Proclamation; 256–257; expansion of, 238; fear of, 243; in Haiti, 148; and Indians 35; and sectionalism, 163–164; and social class, 46–47; in South Carolina, 164; and Thirteenth Amendment, 257, 278; in territories, 89, 163, 233–234; trade, 16, 219; and Nat Turner, 224. See Abolition, Emancipation, Kansas-Nebraska Act, Underground Railroad.
Slavs, 447; as immigrants 367
Slidell, John, 198
Sloat, Commodore John D., 198
Slums, 369, 377–378, 390, 391, 530, 655, 659, 662–663, 665
Smith, Alfred E., 489–490
Smith, Bessie, 497
Smith, Francis, 63
Smith, Reverend Gerald L.K., 524, 528
Smith, Jesse, 488
Smith, Capt. John, 30–31, 40
Smith-Connally Anti-Strike Act, 586
Smith-Hughes Act, 399
Smith, Jedadiah, 195
Smith, Joseph, 196–197
Smith-Lever Act, 399
SNCC. See Student Non-Violent Coordinating Committee.
SNLF. See Sandinista National Liberation Front.
Soap operas, 537, 648
Social contract theory, 99, 100

Social Darwinism, 305–306; and progressives, 383; and new manifest destiny, 411
Social Democrats, 553
"Social gospel," 385
Socialism, 319
Socialist party, 397, 457
Social Security, 526, 531, 638, 663, 754
Social Security Act of 1935, 526, 531
Society of Friends. See Quakers.
Soil Conservation and Domestic Allotment Act, 532, 538
Solar energy, 723
Solidarity, 738
Somoza, Anastasio, 728
Sonar, 579
Sons of Liberty, 57, 58, 61
Sorensen, Ted, 657
Soulé, Pierre, 237
Sousa, John Philip, 375, 376
South, 151, 173, 177, 220, 239; and abolition, 220–221; antebellum society, 222–223; antislavery movement in, 219; after Civil War, 356–359; and debts from Revolutionary War, 123; economy of in Civil War, 260; and election of 1824, 167; and railroads, 204; rebuilding of, 328; Reconstruction, 286–287; and Republican party (Jeffersonian), 127; and sectional politics, 233–235; and slavery, 163–164, 222–225; and tariffs, 119; and War of 1812, 152–153; After WWI, 483–484
South Africa, 740
South Carolina, 221, 282, 291; after Civil War, 275–276; in Civil War, 267; constitution, drafting of 81; Constitution, ratification of, 95; secession of, 245; and slavery, 93; and states' rights, 172–173, 176; and Reconstruction, 280, 283, 286
South Carolina Act of 1737, 188
South Dakota: enters Union, 331; and Indian resistance, 134
Southeast Asia, 680, 751; flexible response strategy in, 624; Ford's policy in, 696; Johnson's policy in, 666
Southeast Asia Treaty Organization, 612
Southern Alliance, 353
Southern Christian Leadership Conference, 644, 669–670
Southern Manchurian Railroad, 427, 437
South Korea, 608–610
South Vietnam, 680–681; fall of, 696; foreign aid to, 611; U.S. involvement in, 666–669
Soviet Union, 573, 591, 592, 594, 641, 709, 732; and Afghanistan, 730; agreements with, 592; aid to, 566, 567; and China, 666; and Cold War, 599–602; COMECON, 604–605; and conferences, 591; containment, 602, 603; and Cuba, 619–623; and Depression, 539; and détente under Carter, 725–726; and détente under Ford, 682–683, 696–697; and espionage, 638–639; and Germany, 556, 557–558; and Hitler, 558; and Indochina, 610, 612; issues, 1980's, 751, 753; Jewish immigration from, 696; and Korea, 607–608; and Latin America, 729; Leningrad, seige of, 583; pipeline controversy, 739–740; and policies under Nixon, 682–683; and policies under Reagan, 738–740; and space, 658; and Suez, 616, 617; trade with Europe, 739–740; and UN, 596; Warsaw Pact, 606; and WWII, 556–558, 573–574, 591, 592, 594, 595
Space program: under Kennedy, 658; under Nixon, 684–685; under Reagan, 738
Spain: and cattle, 329; Civil War in, 559–560; and England, 16; and exploration, 10–12, 21; and Florida, 73, 159; and France, 130; horses, 335; issues with, 84; and Louisiana, 147; and Mexico, 409; and Morocco, 436; and Napoleonic Wars, 159; and New Orleans, 126; Spanish-American War, 418–420; and WWII, 573; Treaty of San Lorenzo, 132
Spanish-American War, 385, 391, 414, 418, 425, 433; acquisitions of U.S., 420–421; army in, 418; navy in, 419; and propaganda, 459; treaty, 420
Spanish Armada, 16–17
Spanish Civil War, 559–560
Sparkman, John, 640
Specie. See Money.
Specie Circular, 179, 181, 182
Speculators: and continental notes, 122–123, 127; and "monied interest," 352; and real

estate, 499, 500; and Specie Circular, 179, 181; and western lands, 82
Spencer, Herbert, 305
Spheres of influence, 425, 426
Spies, August, 320–321
Spoils System: and Cleveland, 351; and Jackson, 171–172; reform in, 348, 350
Sports: in the 1800's, 374–375; in the 1920's, 492; in the 1950's, 649; in the 1960's and 1970's, 716–717
Spotsylvania Courthouse, Battle of, 266
Sputnik, 618, 642, 658
"Square Deal," 391
Squatter sovereignty. See Popular sovereignty.
Stagflation, 685, 696
Stalin, Joseph, 550–551, 562, 566, 605, 610, 613, 639; conferences with, 591; de-Stalinization, 614; and Spanish Civil War, 560; and WWII, 574, 582, 585
Stalingrad, Battles at, 574, 583
Stamp Act, 56
Stamp Act Congress, 58
Standard Oil Company, 303–304, 395, 425, 568
Standard Oil Trust, 304, 377
Standard time, 298
Standish, Miles, 63
Stanford, Leland, 299
Stanton, Edwin M., 261, 281
Stanton, Elizabeth Cady, 217–218
Stanton, Henry, 218
Staple Act, 44
Starr, Ellen, 378
Starr, Ringo, 709
"Star Spangled Banner," 155, 157, 459
START. See Strategic Arms Reduction Talks.
State and Local Fiscal Assistance Act, 686
State Department, 562; Communists in, 638–639; established, 120, 129; in WWII, 562, 569
States' Rights ("Dixiecrat") party, 636
Statue of Liberty, 367
Steamboats, 195, 203
Steel industry, 295, 372, 658, 752; Bessemer process in, 296; in skyscraping, 363
Steelworkers Strike of 1919, 478–479
Steffens, Lincoln, 385, 401
Steiglitz, Alfred, 376
Steinbeck, John 538
Stella, Joseph, 494
Stephens, Alexander, 245, 275
Stephenson, David C., 484
Stevens, John L., 413, 415
Stevens, Thaddeus, 261, 271, 279, 280, 285
Stephens, Uriah, 316
Stevenson, Adlai E., 640, 642
Stimson Doctrine, 555
Stock market, crash in, 500, 503, 505–507; in the 1920's, 499, 500, 503–505
Stone's Creek, Battle of, 263
Story, Joseph, 169
Stowe, Harriet Beecher, 236, 237
Strategic Arms Limitation Talks, 682; under Carter, 726–727
Strategic Arms Reduction Talks, 738
Streetcars, 365
Strikes; antebellum, 216; early, 316, 317; and government, 350; post-WWII, 477–479. See Railroad Strike, Haymarket Riot, Homestead Strike, Pullman Strike.
Strong, Josiah, 384
Student Non-violent Coordinating Committee, 644, 671
Student for a Democratic Society, 674
Submarines, 578; in WWI, 450–452, 453, 454, 458, 460, 487; in WWII, 566, 567
Suburbs, development of, 369; in the 1950's, 648
Subversive Activities Control Board, 639
Subways, 364
Suez Crisis, 615–617, 642
Suffolk Resolves, 61
Suffrage. See Voting Rights and Voting Qualification.
Sugar, 222, 223, 224, 308; Cuban, 548, 619, 620; Hawaiian, 413; rationing in WWII, 580
Sugar Act, 56
Sullivan, Louis, 376
Summer, William Graham, 305, 414
Sumner, Charles, 239, 261, 271, 279
Summit conferences, 618
Summit II, 683
Supply-side economics, 724–725, 736

Supreme Court, 135, 173, 581; and communism, 639; cases in, 240; in Carter administration, 122; and civil rights, 643, 644, 660, 688, 722; and Constitution, 108–109, 115; Judiciary Act of 1789, 120–121; and judicial review, 146; and Marshall, 158–159; and New Deal, 527–528, 531–532; and Nixon, 694; and Washington, 212; and Warren, 661–662
Supreme Headquarters of the Allied Expeditionary Forces, 588
Supreme Headquarters, Allied Powers, Europe, 606
Supremes, the, 497
Sussex crisis, 451, 453
Sutter, John, 200
Sweatshops, 314, 390
Sweden, 87, 573
Swing, 537. See Jazz.
Switzerland, 550, 591; neutrality in WWII, 573
Sylvis, William, 315
Symbionese Liberation Army, 715
Syria, 617, 666

T

Taft, Robert, 606, 635, 640
Taft, William Howard, 394–397; foreign policy, 434, 437–439; and Japan, 425; and Mexico, 441; in Philippines, 422
Taft-Hartley Act, 635, 637–638
Taft-Katsura Agreement, 428
Taiwan, 425, 607, 608, 610, 740; relations with, 682, 726; tensions with China, 612–613
Takahira, Kogoro, 429
Talleyrand, 134
Tallmadge Amendment, 163
Tallmadge, James, 163
Taney, Roger, 240–241
Taos Pueblo Indians, 689
Tappan, Arthur and Lewis, 220
Tarawa, Battle of, 582
Tarbell, Ida M., 385, 386
Tariff, 162, 164, 172, 535; and Clay, 157, 185; in colonial period, 56, 59, 60; and EEC, 659; and favored nation status, 131; and finance of government, 119–120; issues of, 162, 163, 164, 347, 350; and oil, 723; in Progressive Era, 394, 395, 398; and protectionism, 125; and sectionalism, 233; Tariff of 1789, 119; Tariff of 1792, 125; Tariff of 1816, 158
Tariff of 1816, 158
"Tariff of Abominations." See Tariff of 1828.
Tariff of 1828, 172, 173
Tariff of 1832, 176
Tatanka Iyotake. See Sitting Bull.
Taxpayers' revolt, 724–725
Tax Reduction Act, 662
Tax system: reform in New Deal, 527; under Reagan, 743
Taylor, Frederick Winslow, 490
Taylor, Zachary, 198–199; 233–235, 333
Tea Act, 60, 61. See Boston Tea Party.
Teapot Dome Affair, 488
Technology: advances in, antebellum, 206; in late 1800's, 373; and warfare, 751
Tecumseh, 151–152, 155, 188
Telegraph, 205, 297
Telephone, 297, 364; use in 1920's, 490
Television: debates, Ford-Carter, 697; debates, Kennedy-Nixon, 656; influence of, 716–717; and propaganda, 459; in the 1950's, 648–649; in the 1960's and 70's, 714–715
Teller Amendment, 418, 421
Thatcher, Margaret, 742
Temperance, 315, 316; antebellum, 215
Temporary National Economic Committee, 534
Tenements, 369, 379
Tennessee, 155, 170, 185, 186, 188, 244, 284, 486, 509, 657; in Civil War, 253, 254, 255, 256, 263, 265, 266, 267, 273; return to Union, 272; secession of, 249
Tennessee River, 253
Tennessee Valley Authority, 516–517
Tenochtitlán, 20
Tenskwatawa. See the Prophet.
Tenure of Office Act, 280–281
Texas: 159, 185, 335, 454, 585, 661; and cattle, 329; Dust Bowl, 532; and Grangers, 353; and Mexico, 197; and Reconstruction, 280; return to

Union, 274; secession of, 245; settlement of, 190–191; statehood of, 193, 235; War for Independence, 191–192
Thames, Battle of the, 152, 155
Thanksgiving, 33
Third parties, 113, 524, 528, 676; Populists, 353–355
Third World: 621, 623, 721; aid to, 611; issues on, 751; liberation movement in, 707; and Peace Corps, 618; relations with, 740–742; rivalry in, 614; and Soviets, 617–618
Thomas, George, 189, 267
Thomas, Jesse, 163
Thoreau, Henry David, 210–211, 333, 644
Three-fifths Compromise, 92–93, 219
Three Mile Island, 724
Thurmond, J. Strom, 636
Ticonderoga, Battle of, 64
Tijerina, Reies López, 673
Tilden, Bill, 492
Tilden, Samuel J., 286
Tillman, Benjamin R., 284
Timber Culture Act, 331
Tippecanoe, Battle of, 152, 182
TNEC. See Temporary National Economic Committee.
Tobacco, 356; in colonial period, 42; farming of, 30–31; industry of, 313; in Maryland, 36; in South, 222–223, 224; in Virginia, 30
Tojo, Gen. Hideki, 569, 588
Tokyo, Japan, 428, 429; bombing of, 576
Toleration Act, 36
Tomlin, Lily, 714
Tonkin Gulf Resolution, 667; repealed, 681
Tonnage duties, 119–120
Torgeau, Battle of, 591
Torrijos, Omar, 728
Town meetings, 40
Townsend, Dr. Francis E., 523, 524, 528
Townshend, Charles, 59
Townshend Acts, 59–60
Trade: balance of, 685–686; and Bank of United States, 124; in California, 193; and Central America, 438; centers of, 405; and China, 425; colonial period, 42, 84, 86; pre-Depression, 507; and England, 15; foreign, importance of, 412–414; exploration, influence on, 6, 7; exports, 30, 88, 204–205; interstate, 203–204, 307–308; in the 1980's, 751; in Massachusetts colony, 33; and national government, 93; and Oregon, 195; policies under Reagan, 739; and railroads, 204; and roads, national, 147; routes, 43; and Russia, 15; and slaves, 223; and South America, 159; and tariff, 125; treaties, commercial, 87; with the West, 126, 194; in WWI, 449–450
Trade Expansion Act, 659
"Trail of Tears," 175, 176
Transcendentalism, 210–211
Trans-Mississippi West, 327–341
Transportation: Civil War and, 261; improvements in prior to 1900, 295, 364, 365; and mass market, 30. See Roads, Railroads, Shipping.
Travis, William B., 191
Travolta, John, 712
Treaty of Brest-Litovsk, 460
Treaty of Paris (1898), 420
Treasury, U.S., 120, 129, 345, 562
Treaty of 1818, 159
Treaty of Ft. Jackson, 156
Treaty of Ghent, 156, 157
Treaty of Greenville, 156
Treaty of Paris (1783), 72–73; and Confederation, 83
Treaty of Portsmouth, 427–428
Treaty of San Lorenzo, 132
Treaty of Tordesillas, 10
Treaty of Versailles, 466, 467–468, 548, 552; violation of, 556
Trenton, Battle of, 70
Triangular trade, 42, 44
"Trickle down" theory, 511
Tripartite Agreement. See Triple Alliance.
Triple Alliance, 447, 569. See Axis Powers.
Triple Entente, 447
Tripoli, Battle of, 583
Trolley, electric, 364
Trujillo, Rafael, 623
Truman, Harry S., 587, 606, 657; and Berlin airlift, 605; and bomb, 594; and Cold War, 600, 601; and containment, 602; and Far East, 606,

607; and Indochina, 610; and Israel, 615; and Korea, 608–610; and Latin America, 618; and Marshall Plan, 603–605; and NATO, 605–606; Presidency, 506, 633–640
Truman Doctrine, 602–603
Trustbusting, 388, 389, 507, 535; and T. Roosevelt, 391–392
Trusts, 304; and the progressives, 383, 384; and Wilson, 398–399
Truth, Sojourner, 220
Tsushina Strait, Battle of, 427
Tunio, Battle of, 583
Tunney, Gene, 492
Turkey, 601, 602–603, 622; joins NATO, 606; in WWI, 447, 466
Turner, Frederick Jackson, 185
Turner, Nat, 224
TVA. See Tennessee Valley Authority.
Twain, Mark, 345
Tweed, "Boss" William M., 346, 350
Tweed Ring, 346
Tydings, Millard, 639
Tyler, John, 182; and annexation of Texas, 193; and California, 193; Presidency, 182
Typewriter, 296, 311

U

U-boats. See Submarines.
Udall, Stewart, 657
UMW. See United Mine Workers.
Uncle Tom's Cabin, 236, 237
Underground press, 715
Underground Railroad, 220
Underwood-Simmons Act, 398
Unemployment: in Allied countries, 727; black, 530, 671; in Carter administration, 724; in Depression, 505, 507–508, 510, 511, 516–517; insurance, 513, 526, 737, 743; in Johnson administration, 662; in Kennedy administration, 659; in Nixon administration, 685–686; in Reagan administration, 743, 774; relief for, in New Deal, 524–525, 526; in 1920's, 487
Union of Soviet Socialist Republics. See Soviet Union.
Union Pacific Railroad, 298–301, 345
Unions, 311; antebellum, 216; and eight-hour day, 536; in New Deal, 529–530; prior to 1920, 314–318. See Organized labor.
Unitas, Johnny, 649
United Arab Republic, 617
United Automobile Workers, 529
United Farm Workers, 673
United Mine Workers of America, 392, 479, 529, 530, 634
United Nations, 587, 592, 599, 601, 602, 606; Charter of, 591, 595–596; and hostage crisis, 729; Human Rights Commission, 587; and Israel, 615; and Korean War, 608–609, 610; peacekeeping force in Middle East, 666, 684, 741; Security Council, 601, 608, 616; structure of, 595–596; and Suez Crisis, 616; and two Chinas, 682; and Yom Kippur War, 684
United Nations Declaration, 573
United States Housing Authority, 533–534
United States Civil Service Commission, 391
United States Employment Service, 456
United States Fish and Wildlife Service, 706
United States Forestry Service, 396
United States Information Agency, 641
United States Railroad Administration, 456
United States Steel, 303, 338, 394, 507, 529, 658
United States v. Butler (1936), 528
United States v. E.C. Knight (1895), 308, 391
Universal Declaration of Human Rights, 587
Universal Negro Improvement Association, 484
Universalism, 212
University of California v. Bakke (1978), 722
Urban renewal, 659
Urbanization, 363–365; and problems in late 1800's, 377–378
Uruguay, 547, 728
USHA. See United States Housing Authority.
Utah, 185; enters Union, 331; vote for women in, 385, 388
Utah, Territory of, 195, 196, 197; and Compromise of 1850, 235

Utilities: in Depression, 510, 517; regulation of under New Deal, 527
Utopian Communities, 213–214
U-2 spy planes, 618, 622; incident, 655

V

Valentino, Rudolf, 494
Vallee, Rudy, 493, 537
Valley Forge, 70
Van Buren, Martin, 172, 179, 233; and Eaton Affair, 174; in election of 1836, 181; and ten-hour day; Texas policy of, 193; and Treasury, 182; Vice Presidency, 178
Vance, Zebulon B., 262
Vandenburg, Arthur H., 605–606
Vanderbilt, Commodore, 346
Vanderbilt, Cornelius, 299
Van Devanter, William, 531, 532
Vans Murray, William, 134
Vanzetti, Bartolomeo, 480
Vaudeville, 375, 494, 537
V-E day. See Victory in Europe Day.
Venezuela, 415, 740; "big stick policy" in, 434
Vera Cruz, Battle of, 199
Vermont, 171
Versailles, France, 466, 548
Versailles Treaty. See Treaty of Versailles.
Vesey, Denmark, 164
Veterans: educational benefits for, 665; of WWI, 477, 511–512, 515, of WWII, 663–664
Veterans' Bureau, 488
Vichy France, 564
Vicksburg, Battle of, 263, 264–265
Victor Emmanuel II, King of Italy, 584
Victory bonds, 456
Victory in Europe Day, 591
Victory gardens, 456
Viet Cong, 666–669, 680, 681
Viet Cong's Provisional Revolutionary Government, 681
Viet Minh, 610, 612
Vietnam, 610, 612, 666–669; involvement in Laos and Cambodia, 726
Vietnamization, 679–681, 691
Vietnam War, 710; as campaign issue, 675–676, 690–692; during Nixon's term, 679–681; and economy, 685; and "Pentagon Papers," 693; protests over, 669, 674–675, 681
Vigilantism, in western mining towns, 327–328
Vikings, 5
Villa, Francisco (Pancho), 444
Vincennes, 71
Vinson Naval Act. See Naval Expansion Act of 1938.
Virgin Islands, 410
Virginia, 224, 244, 265, 303, 509; in Civil War, 254–255, 256, 267–268; colonized by English, 29–32; early government, 31; opposition to assumption plan, 123–124; opposition to protective tariff, 125; in Radical Reconstruction, 280; ratifies Constitution, 95
Virginia Plan, 90–91
Virginia Resolution, 57, 135, 136, 173
Virtual representation, 58
VISTA. See Volunteers in Service to America.
Vladivostok Accord, 696
Volunteers in Service to America, 663, 674
Volstead Act. See National Prohibition Enforcement Act.
von Steuben, Baron Friedrich, 69, 70
Voting rights: blacks, 172, 276, 357–358, 663, 665, 670, 689; in colonial period, 38; and Constitution, 112; to 18-year-olds, 112, 277, 690; grandfather clauses, 358; and Jacksonian democracy, 171; and literacy test, 357; and poll tax, 357; universal white male suffrage, 112, 216; for women, 173, 218, 277. See Amendments.
Voting Rights Act of 1965, 665

W

WAACS. See Women's Auxiliary Army Corps.
Wabash, St. Louis and Pacific Railway v. Illinois (1886), 307
Wade, Benjamin F., 272
Wade-Davis Bill, 272, 274
Wadsworth, William H, 272

Wage and price controls, 685, 724; under Ford, 696; under Nixon, 685
Wages: during Depression, 507; before 1900, 312, 313
Wagner Act, 526 529, 531
Wagner-Steagall Act, 533
Wainwright, Gen. Jonathan M., 575
Wake Island, 609; taken by Japanese, 574
Wald, Lillian, 378
Walesa, Lech, 738
Walker, David, 220
Wallace, Gov. George, 660, 676, 691
Wallace, Henry, 605, 636
Waller, Fats, 497
Waltham system, 205–206
War Department, 120, 563
War Industries Board, 455
War Manpower Commission, 586
War of 1812, 160, 169, 170, 174; American manufacturing, 162; British offensive, 155–156; financial problems, 153; peace movements after, 217; peace treaty, 156; propaganda in, 459
"War on Poverty," 662, 663, 686
War Policies Board, 456
War Powers Act, 692; and Ford, 696
War Production Board, 579
War Revenue Act, 456
Ward, John W., 171
Ward, Samuel, 220
Warhol, Andy, 705
Warmouth, Henry C., 283
Warner, Charles Dudley, 377
Warren, Earl, 636, 661; Chief Justice, 643, 661–662; and investigation of Kennedy Assassination, 661; and Japanese-Americans, 580
Warren Commission, 661
Warren Court, 686
Warsaw Pact, 606, 614, 726
Washington: enters Union, 331; and migrants, 533; return of land to Indians in, 689; women's vote in, 388
Washington, Booker T., 358, 359; at White House, 394
Washington, George, 123, 133, 160; and Bank of United States, 124–125; cabinet, 121; as Continental Army commander, 64, 66, 126, 134; death of, 136; on education, 371; election of, 119, 129; Farewell Address, 132–133, 371; foreign policy, 122, 130–132; in French and Indian War, 53–54; Indian policy, 132; at Philadelphia Convention, 90, 95; as President, 116, 122, 126, 129
Washington Conference for the Limitation of Armaments, 487
Washington, D.C., 157, 168, 169, 350, 398, 429, 573, 584, 591, 661; attacked by British, 155, 156; Brezhnev in, 683; in Civil War, 252, 255; hot line to, 623; marches in, 506, 511–512, 670; protests in, 681, 688
Washington Post, 692
Washington, Treaties of 1922, 548
Watergate scandal, 692–694
Watson, Tom, 354, 355, 357
Watt, James, 733, 735
Watts, Andre, 497
Watts riot, 671
WAVES. See Women Appointed for Voluntary Emergency Service.
Wayne, General Anthony, 132
Wealth Tax Act, 527
Weaver, James B., 349, 352, 354
Weaver, Robert, 659, 665
Webster, Daniel, 153, 174, 181, 238; and California policy, 193; and Compromise of 1850, 235; and sovereignty of Union, 173
Webster, Noah, 81, 161
Webster-Ashburton Treaty, 194–195
Wedemeyer, Albert, 607
Weinberger, Caspar, 738
Welfare capitalism, 319
Welfare system: under Carter, 721–722; under Reagan, 735, 737; reform of, 686
West, the, 151, 158, 167, 173, 177, 242; Civil War in, 253–254, 263; expansionism in, 160; exploration of, 149; free land, 260; frontier, 185–187; and individualism, 330; literature, 330; myth of, 333; and railroads, 203–204, 300; and religious revivals, 211–212; sectional politics, 233–235; sectionalism, 162; settlement of, 56,

200; and transportation, 203–204; and War of 1812, 151, 153, 156. See Trans-Mississippi West.
West Bank, 726
West Berlin, 605, 618
West Germany, 727, 731; and EEC, 659; formed, 605; industry, 752
West Indies: in Age of Exploration, 17; in colonial times, 37; English raids in, 17; and French, 55; and Jay Treaty, 131; and slave trade, 46
Western Hemisphere, 618, 624; communism in, 624; defense of, 429; and immigration, 665; and Monroe Doctrine, 159; Nazi threat to, 564, 565, 566, 567, 573
Western lands: conflicts over in ratifying Articles of Confederation, 82; sale of, 186
Western Union, 297
Westinghouse, George, 297, 298
Westmoreland, General William C., 668, 669
West Virginia, 295, 659; formed, 249
Weyler, Valeriano, 416
Whig party, 179, 181, 233, 244, 271, 284, 347, 356; and Compromise of 1850, 235; demise of, 238
Whip Inflation Now program, 696
"Whiskey Ring," 346
Whiskey tax, 125–126; repealed, 146
Whistler, James McNeill, 375
White, Hugh Lawson, 181
White, John, 17
White, Walter, 495
White, William Allen, 480, 564
White Citizens' Councils, 643
White House, 170; burned by British, 155, 156
White supremacy, 284, 285, 411, 483
Whitefield, George, 47
Whiteman, Paul, 496
Whitman, Marcus and Narcissa, 194
Whitman, Walt, 211
Whitney, Eli, 162, 206
Whittlesey, Charles, 463
Whyte, William H., 651
Wilhelm, Kaiser, 437
Wilkins, Roy, 643
Willard, Emma Hart, 216
William and Mary, King and Queen of England, 36
Williams, Roger, 34, 48
Williams, Tennessee, 651
Willkie, Wendell L., 564
Willoughby, Sir Hugh, 15
Wills, Helen, 492
Wilmot, David, 233
Wilmot Proviso, 233–234, 236
Wilson, James, 86
Wilson, William B., 399
Wilson, Woodrow, 397–400, 513, 521, 534, 535, 548, 585, 655; foreign policy, 439–443; and immigration, 481; League of Nations, 465–468; peace negotiations, 465–466; and railroads, 388; and WWI, 448, 450, 451–452, 463, 465–468
Wilson-Gorman Tariff, 416
WIN. See Whip Inflation Now program.
Windham, Thomas, 15
Wings, 710
Winthrop, John, 33
Winthrop, Robert C., 198
Wirt, William, 178
Wisconsin, 333; enters Union, 235; Granger laws in, 353; progressive reform in, 387–389
Wister, Owen, 333
WMC. See War Manpower Commission.
"Wobblies." See Industrial Workers of the World.
Wolfe, General James, 55
Women: and affirmative action, 722; and Age of Jackson, 172; in American Revolution, 63, 76–77; in cabinet, 526; in Civil War, 258, 260; and education, 215, 372; first black in Congress, 687; and KKK, 483; in labor, 311, 312, 315, 316, 318, 389; liberation movement, 667, 674, 752; literature in 1960's, 706–707; in mining towns, 327; and Nixon administration, 689; pioneers, 332; rights, 217–219, 587, 754, 755; suffrage, 173, 277, 385, 387–388, 397, 399; and Wilson administration, 399; in WWI, 457; in WWII, 585–586; in 1800's, 372–373; in 1920's, 496; in 1950's, 648
Women's Army Corps, 641
Women's Auxiliary Army Corps, 585

Women's Christian Temperance Union, 484
Women's Loyal National League, 218
Women's Trade Union League, 312
Wood, Grant, 494, 539
Wood, Leonard, 418, 421
Wood, Gen. Robert E., 565
Woodstock festival, 710
Woodward, Robert, 692
Woolens Act of 1679, 44
Worcester v. *Georgia* (1832), 176
Workers' party, 479
Workingmen's parties, 216
Workmen's Compensation laws, 389, 397
Works Progress Administration, 525, 530, 536
World Antislavery Convention, 217, 218
World Peace movement, 378; conference on, 434; and Wilson, 439
World Series, 374
World War Adjusted Compensation Act, 488
World War I, 447, 480, 506, 508, 516, 517, 535; American neutrality in, 447–453; causes of, 447; and causes of WWII, 547–550; civil liberties in, 457; debts, 487–488; declaring war, 454–455; economy, 449–452, 457; effect on immigration, 480–481; effects of, 496, 499; and freedom of the press, 135; homefront, 452–453, 455–458; and imperialism, 414; industry, 455–457; medicine in, 259; peace treaty, 465–466; and prohibition, 484; propaganda, 457–458, 459; reparations, 510, 548–550; shipping rights, 449–452; technology in, 578; weapons in, 460. See Army, Navy, Draft, Pacifism, Preparedness, Submarine warfare.
World War II, in Africa, 582, 583; American neutrality in, 559–567; blitzkrieg, 562–563; and economy, 579–581; effects of, 595–596, 599; events leading to, 547-558; in Europe, 573, 583; in Far East, 573, 574, 582; homefront, 585–586; and imperialism, 414; in literature, 650, 706; in Mediterranean, 573–574; in Pacific, 574–577, 582; and propaganda, 459; rationing, 579–580; technology, 577–579, 589
Wouk, Herman, 650
Wounded Knee, Battle of, 339–340
Wounded Knee, S.D., occupation of by Indians, 688
WPA. See Works Progress Administration.
WPB. See War Production Board.
Wright, Frank Lloyd, 376, 651
Wright, Jonathan J., 282–283
Wright, Richard, 538
Writ of habeas corpus, 251–252
Wyeth, Andrew, 651
Wyoming: cattle raising in, 329; enters Union, 331; Indians in, 338; lands in, 396; women's suffrage in, 277, 385 388

Y

Yakima Indians, 689
Yalta Agreement, 592
Yalta conference, 592, 595, 599
Yalu River, 609, 610
Yamamoto, Admiral Isorokee, 582
Yellow dog contracts, 319
Yellow journalism, 377; and Spanish-American War, 417–418, 493
Yeomanettes, 457
YMCA, 374, 457
Yom Kippur War, 684
Yorktown, Battle of, 72
Yorktown, siege of, 72
Young, Brigham, 196, 197
Young, James S., 228
Young, John, 738
Young, Owen D., 549
Young Plan, 549
Yugoslavia, 466, 548, 602
"XYZ Affair," 134

Z

Zaharias, George, 537
Zelaya, José, 437
Zenger, John Peter, 49, 50, 135
Ziegfield Follies, 494
Zimmerman note, 454
"Zoot Suit Riots," 585